FOUNDED IN 1947

Publisher **JACK DOZIER**
jdozier@waterwayguide.com

Associate Publisher **CRAIG DOZIER**
cdozier@waterwayguide.com

Operations Manager **TED STEHLE**
tstehle@waterwayguide.com

Production Manager/Editor **JANI PARKER**
jparker@waterwayguide.com

Graphic Production Artist **CAROLYN AUGUST**
carolyn@waterwayguide.com

Advertising Sales Manager and Acount Executive **MIKE KUCERA**
mkucera@waterwayguide.com

Marketing & Sales Associate **SANDY HICKEY**
sandy@waterwayguide.com

Product Sales Manager **HEATHER SADEG**
heather@waterwayguide.com

Online News Editor **MIKE AHART**
mahart@waterwayguide.com

Web Master **MIKE SCHWEFLER**

Accounts Manager **ARTHUR CROWTHER**
accounts@waterwayguide.com

Administrative Assistant **MARGIE MOORE**

Properties Manager **ROBERT MATALIK**

EDITORIAL, CORPORATE & ACCOUNTING OFFICES

Waterway Guide/Skipper Bob Publications
Dozier Media Group, LLC
Send Correspondence to:
P.O. Box 1125
Deltaville, VA 23043
804-776-8999

CONTRIBUTORS

Ken Bloomfield • Chris Caldwell
Bill Donovan • Henry (Hank) Evans
Doug Freeman • Pascal Gademer
Bob Gascoine • Keith Gray
Ted Guy • Jim Healy • Bill Hezlep
K.L. Hughes • Tom Jones
Rick Kennedy • Diane & Michael Marotta
Jane Minty• Quinn Sale
Larry & Ruth Smithers • Fred Wehner

ADVERTISING SALES

GENERAL ADVERTISING INQUIRIES
MIKE KUCERA
mkucera@waterwayguide.com

BOOK SALES:
www.WaterwayGuide.com
800-233-3359

CRUISING EDITORS

BAHAMAS EDITION
KATHI BARRINGTON
ALAN & SUSANN SYME
ROBERT WILSON

SOUTHERN EDITION
JAY CORZINE
BUD & ELAINE LLOYD

ATLANTIC ICW EDITION
BUD & ELAINE LLOYD
KENNETH & AMY BRASWELL

CHESAPEAKE BAY EDITION
TOM HALE
VICKI LATHOM

NORTHERN EDITION
BARBARA MCGOWAN
CAROL PIERINI

GREAT LAKE EDITION
BOB & CAROL KUNATH
WALLY MORAN
TED & AUDREY STEHLE

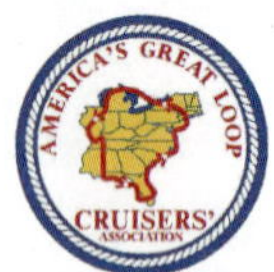

Proud Sponsor of AGLCA

On the cover: An aerial view of St. Michaels, MD (Waterway Guide Photography); Racing on the Rappahannock River in Virginia (photo courtesy of Mike Kucera); Skyline in Baltimore, MD.

Waterway Guide is published annually in six regional editions—Bahamas, Southern, Atlantic Intracoastal Waterway, Chesapeake Bay, Northern and Great Lakes—by Dozier Media Group, LLC © 2013. All rights reserved. Reproduction in whole or part or use of any data compilation without written permission from the publisher is prohibited. The title Waterway Guide is a registered trademark. Library of Congress Catalog Number: 543653. ISBN Number: 978-0-9833005-7-1 for the Chesapeake Bay Waterway Guide 2013 Edition. Purchase and use of Waterway Guide constitutes acceptance of the restrictions set forth herein.

Price per copy: $39.95. When ordering by mail or telephone, add shipping and handling charges. Direct all orders to: Waterway Guide, P.O. Box 1125, Deltaville, VA 23043; or call 800-233-3359, fax 804-776-6111.

To provide the most complete and accurate information, all facilities have been contacted within the past year. Although facility operators supplied this data, we cannot guarantee accuracy or assume responsibility for errors. Entrance and dockside soundings tend to fluctuate. Always approach marinas carefully. Reference numbers on spotting charts indicate marina locations. Aerial photos are for general overview only and are not to be used for navigation.

Member of National Marine Manufacturers Association – Printed In U.S.A.

Representing Quality Marinas Throughout Chesapeake Bay

Premium Slips to Lease or Own

Quality Boat & Yacht Service

1819 Bay Ridge Ave., Suite 400, Annapolis, MD 21403

COASTAL PROPERTIES MANAGEMENT, INC.

Management · Sale · Purchase

Consulting · Design · Evaluation

410.269.0933

cpm@erols.com

www.coastal-properties.com

THE GANGPLANK MARINA

202.554.5000 – WASHINGTON, DC

309 Slip Marina in the Protected Washington Channel
30/50/100 Amp • Laundry • Showers • Cable TV
Pump-Out • In-Water Service/Repair • Parking

THE CRESCENT MARINA AT FELL'S POINT

443.510.9341 – BALTIMORE, MD

52 Slips in the historic Fell's Point district of Baltimore's Inner Harbor • 30/50 Amp • Pump-Out
Gated Docks & Parking • Within easy walking distance to art galleries, retail shops, bars, restaurants, cultural and historical locations

PINEY NARROWS YACHT HAVEN

410.643.6600 – KENT ISLAND, MARYLAND

Covered & Open Slips To Own, Lease or Visit up to 67'
Gas & Diesel Year Round • Pump-Out • Pool
Card Key Entry • 30/50 Amp • Wet Winter Storage
Private Heads & Showers • Cable TV

NATIONAL HARBOR

301.749.1582 – NATIONAL HARBOR, MARYLAND

Yearly & Transient Floating Slips to 120'
Located on the Potomac River in MD at the Wilson Bridge • Laundry • Heads/Showers • Restaurants
Retail Shops • Special Events • Cable TV
Gas/Diesel • Pump-Out • WI-FI

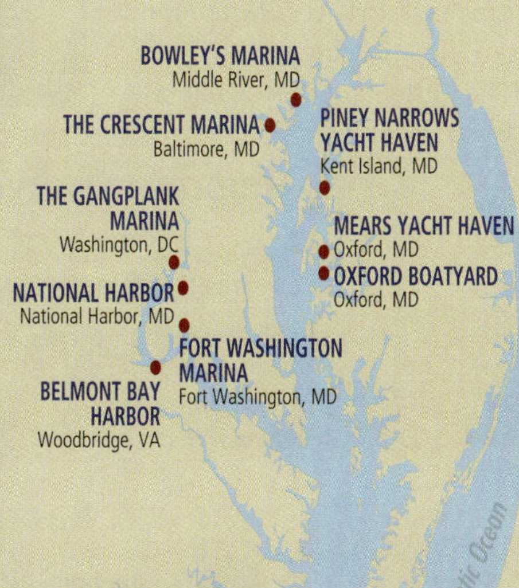

MEARS YACHT HAVEN

410.226.5450 – OXFORD, MARYLAND

Yearly & Transient Slips To 140' • 110V/220V
Cable TV • Pool • Party Patio • Picnic Area
Gas/Diesel • Pump-Out • Lounge • Yacht Club Atmosphere • Complimentary WI-FI
VHF Channels 09 & 16

FORT WASHINGTON MARINA

301.292.7700 – FORT WASHINGTON, MARYLAND

300 Slips on the Potomac River • 50/30 Amp
Pump-Out • Gas/Diesel • Heads & Showers
Laundry • Restaurant • 35 Ton Lift
Do-It-Yourself Service Yard • Land Storage

OXFORD BOATYARD

410.226.5101 – OXFORD, MARYLAND

Deep Water Slips To 120'• 75 Ton Travel Lift
Full Service • Awlgrip/Imron • Temperature Controlled Paint Shed • Pump-Out • Mechanical • Carpentry
Electronic Services • Established 1866

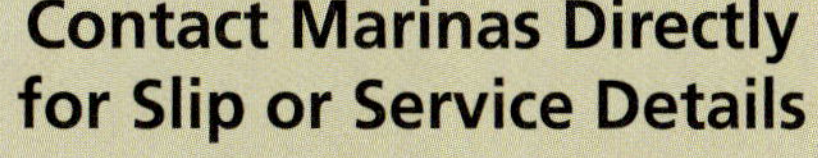

BELMONT BAY HARBOR

703.490.5088 – WOODBRIDGE, VIRGINIA

155 Slip Marina on the Occoquan River • Golf Course
Floating Docks • Fuel • Ice • Pump-Out • Heads
Showers • Laundry • Brokerage • New Boat Sales
Ample Parking • WI-FI

Coastal Properties marinas participate in clean marina programs

RIVERWALK LANDING

757.890.3370 – YORKTOWN, VIRGINIA

York River in Historic Yorktown, VA • New Floating Docks to Accommodate Boats from 20' to 400' feet
Restaurants • Retail Shops • Ice
Pump-Out • Heads/Showers • Ample Parking

Navigating Your Guide

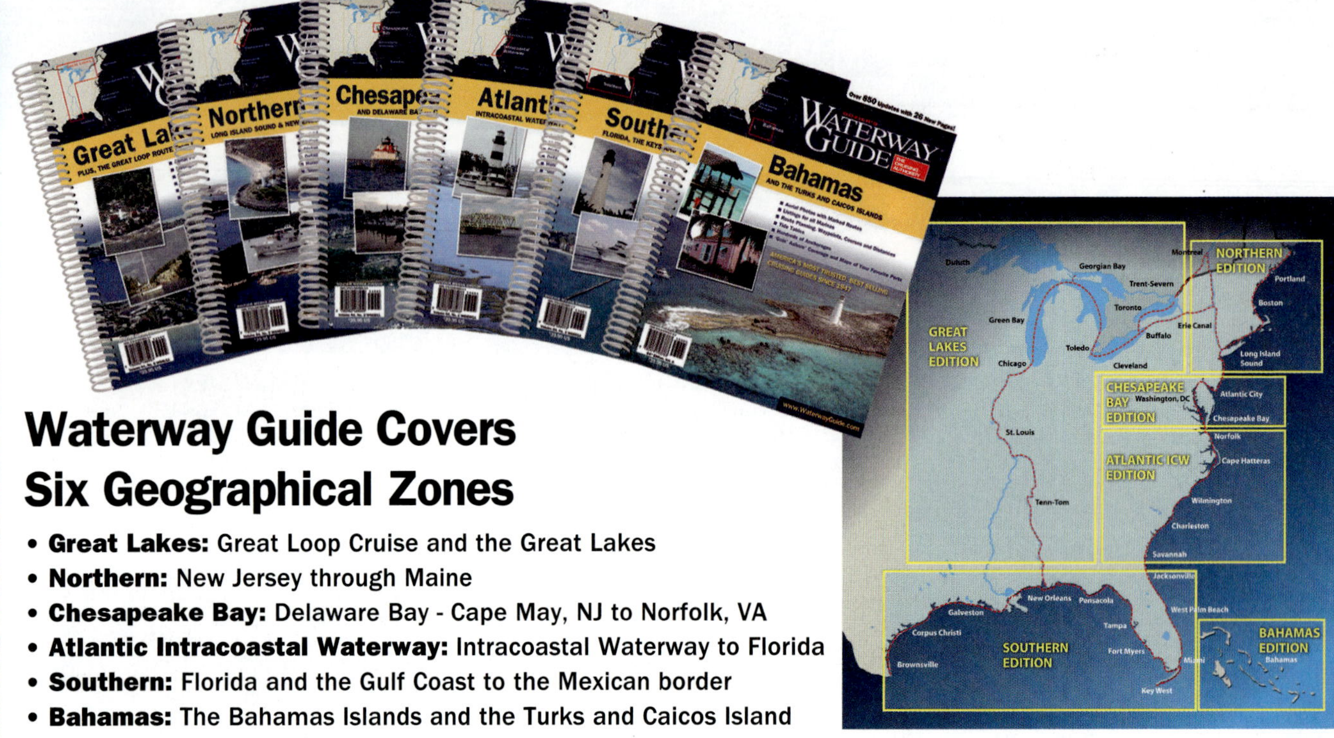

Waterway Guide Covers Six Geographical Zones

- **Great Lakes:** Great Loop Cruise and the Great Lakes
- **Northern:** New Jersey through Maine
- **Chesapeake Bay:** Delaware Bay - Cape May, NJ to Norfolk, VA
- **Atlantic Intracoastal Waterway:** Intracoastal Waterway to Florida
- **Southern:** Florida and the Gulf Coast to the Mexican border
- **Bahamas:** The Bahamas Islands and the Turks and Caicos Island

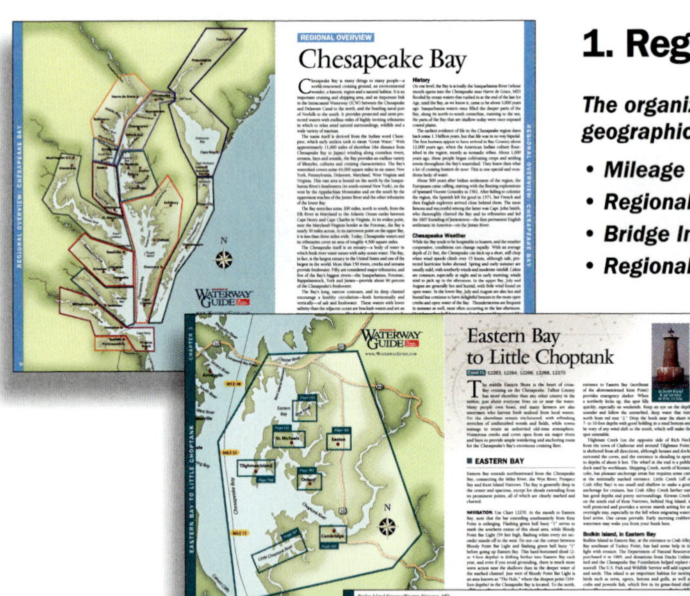

1. Regional Overview

The organization of the guide begins with large geographical regions. Information includes:

- ***Mileage Tables***
- ***Regional Maps***
- ***Bridge Information***
- ***Regional History***

2. Section Contents

Sections focus on smaller areas of geographical coverage within the regions. Sections feature:

- ***Color-coding for Easy Reference***
- ***Detailed, Smaller-scale Maps***
- ***A List of Chapters Within Each Section***

3. Chapters

Chapters focus on even smaller coverage areas within the sections. Chapter information includes:

- ***Aerial Photos With Marked Routes***
- ***Navigational Reports***
- ***Dockage and Anchorage Information***
- ***Goin' Ashore Features for Towns Along the Way***

Marina Listings and Locator Charts

The Chesapeake Bay Waterway Guide covers hundreds of marinas with the following information:

- ***Clearly Labeled Charts***
- ***Marina Locator Arrows***
- ***Marina Amenities***
- ***Phone Numbers***
- ***Internet and Wireless Internet Capabilities***
- ***Fuel, Services and Supplies***
- ***GPS Coordinates and Bold Type for Advertising Sponsors***

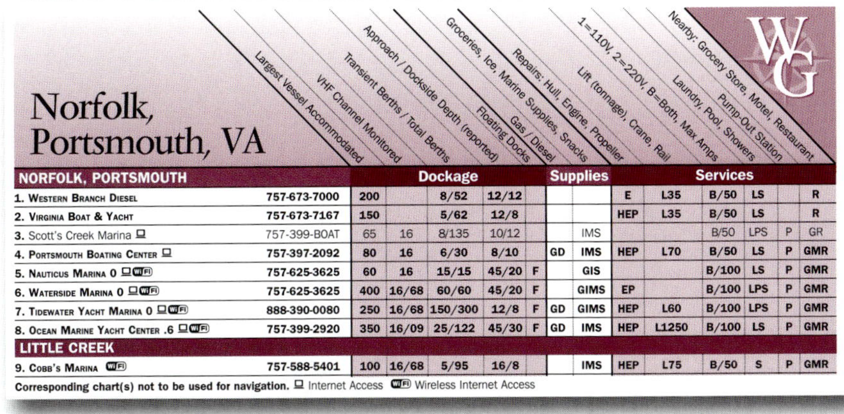

Norfolk, Portsmouth, VA

NORFOLK, PORTSMOUTH		Largest Vessel Accommodated	VHF Channel Monitored	Transient Berths / Total Berths	Approach / Dockside Depth (reported)	Floating Docks	Gas / Diesel	Groceries, Ice, Marine Supplies, Snacks	Repairs: Hull, Engine, Propeller	Lift (tonnage), Crane, Rail	1=110V, 2=220V, B=Both, Max Amps	Laundry, Pool, Showers	Pump-Out Station	Nearby: Grocery Store, Motel, Restaurant
		Dockage					**Supplies**		**Services**					
1. **Western Branch Diesel**	**757-673-7000**	200		8/52	12/12				E	L35	B/50	LS		R
2. **Virginia Boat & Yacht**	**757-673-7167**	150		5/62	12/8				HEP	L35	B/50	LS		R
3. Scott's Creek Marina (Internet)	757-399-BOAT	65	16	8/135	10/12			IMS			B/50	LPS	P	GR
4. **Portsmouth Boating Center** (Internet)	**757-397-2092**	80	16	6/30	8/10		GD	IMS	HEP	L70	B/50	LS	P	GMR
5. **Nauticus Marina 0** (Internet, WiFi)	**757-625-3625**	60	16	15/15	45/20	F		GIS			B/100	LS	P	GMR
6. **Waterside Marina 0** (Internet, WiFi)	**757-625-3625**	400	16/68	60/60	45/20	F		GIMS	EP		B/100	LPS	P	GMR
7. **Tidewater Yacht Marina 0** (Internet, WiFi)	**888-390-0080**	250	16/68	150/300	12/8	F	GD	GIMS	HEP	L60	B/100	LPS	P	GMR
8. **Ocean Marine Yacht Center .6** (Internet, WiFi)	**757-399-2920**	350	16/09	25/122	45/30	F	GD	IMS	HEP	L1250	B/100	LS	P	GMR
LITTLE CREEK														
9. **Cobb's Marina** (WiFi)	**757-588-5401**	100	16/68	5/95	16/8			IMS	HEP	L75	B/50	S	P	GMR

Corresponding chart(s) not to be used for navigation. Internet Access   WiFi Wireless Internet Access

Marina and Contact Information (advertising sponsors are bolded)   ***Dockage***   ***Supplies***   ***Services***

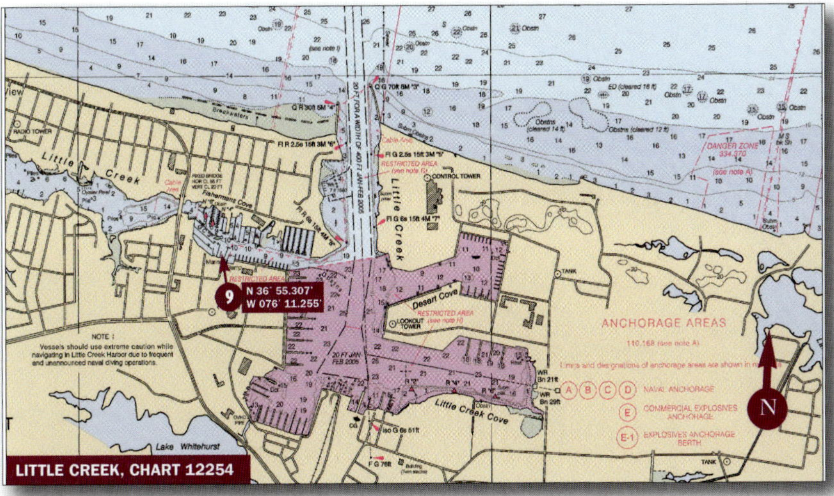

Clearly labeled marina locator charts help tie it all together.

Skipper's Handbook

A whole section with useful boating references.

Skipper's Handbook
A Guide to Cruising Essentials
Coast Guard
SKIPPER'S HANDBOOK

Bridges and Distances

Tables give you opening times and mileage between points.

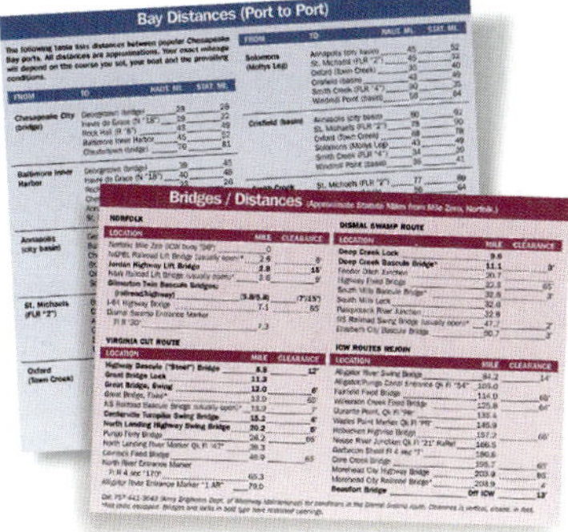

Goin' Ashore

Quick-read features on ports and towns you'll visit along the way.

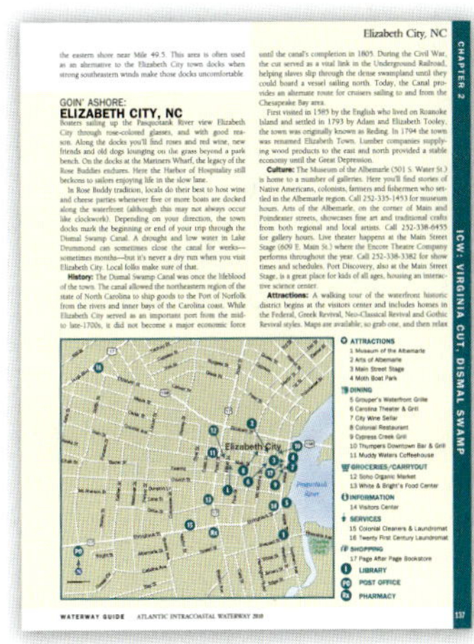

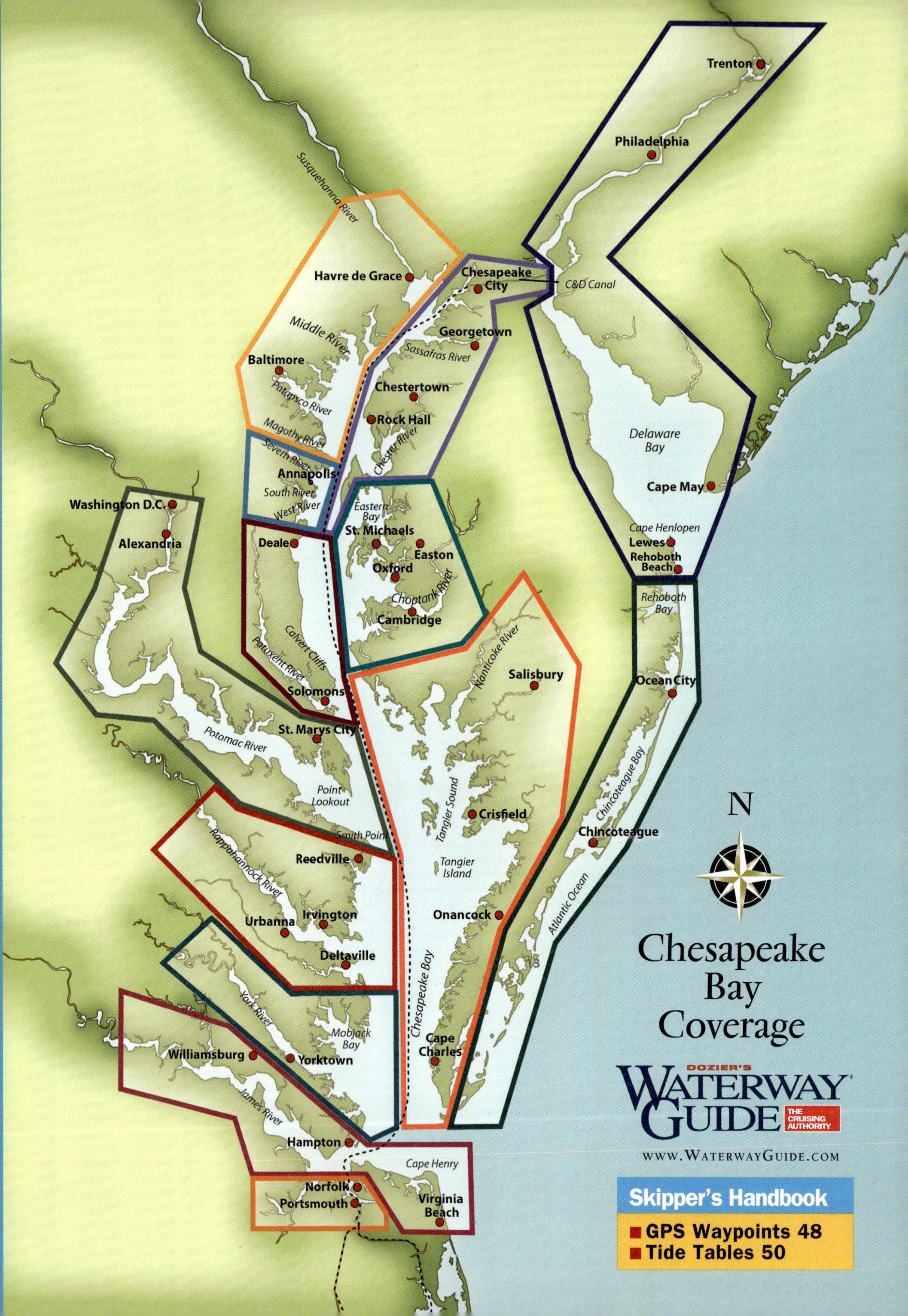

Chesapeake Bay Coverage

Trenton
Philadelphia
Susquehanna River
Havre de Grace
Chesapeake City
C&D Canal
Middle River
Georgetown
Sassafras River
Baltimore
Patapsco River
Chestertown
Rock Hall
Magothy River
Chester River
Severn River
Annapolis
South River
West River
Delaware Bay
Cape May
Washington D.C.
Alexandria
Eastern Bay
St. Michaels
Easton
Oxford
Deale
Cape Henlopen
Lewes
Rehoboth Beach
Choptank River
Cambridge
Rehoboth Bay
Calvert Cliffs
Patuxent River
Nanticoke River
Salisbury
Solomons
Ocean City
St. Marys City
Potomac River
Point Lookout
Chincoteague Bay
Smith Point
Tangier Sound
Crisfield
Chincoteague
Reedville
Rappahannock River
Tangier Island
Atlantic Ocean
Irvington
Urbanna
Onancock
Deltaville
York River
Chesapeake Bay
Mobjack Bay
Williamsburg
Yorktown
Cape Charles
James River
Hampton
Cape Henry
Norfolk
Portsmouth
Virginia Beach
N

DOZIER'S WATERWAY GUIDE
THE CRUISING AUTHORITY
www.WaterwayGuide.com

Skipper's Handbook

Contents

VOLUME 66, NO. 2

The waters of the Delaware Bay are considered by many boaters to be rough, tedious and inhospitable, but this area has another face—a remote and lonely mystique with great appeal for adventurous mariners who enjoy exploring.

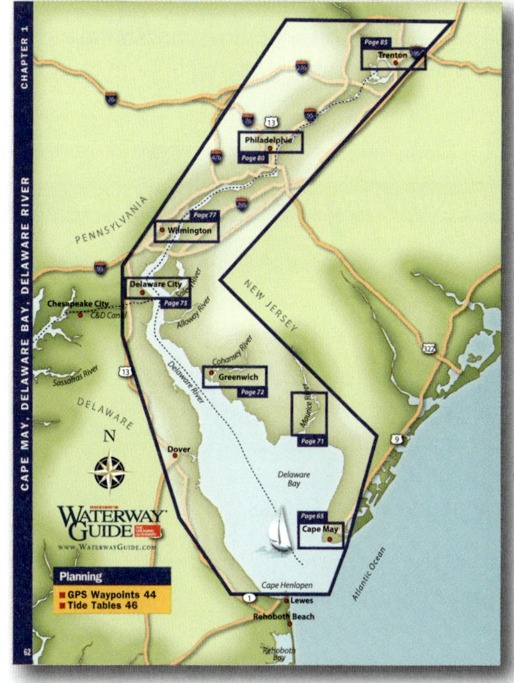

Chesapeake Bay

C&D Canal to Kent Island

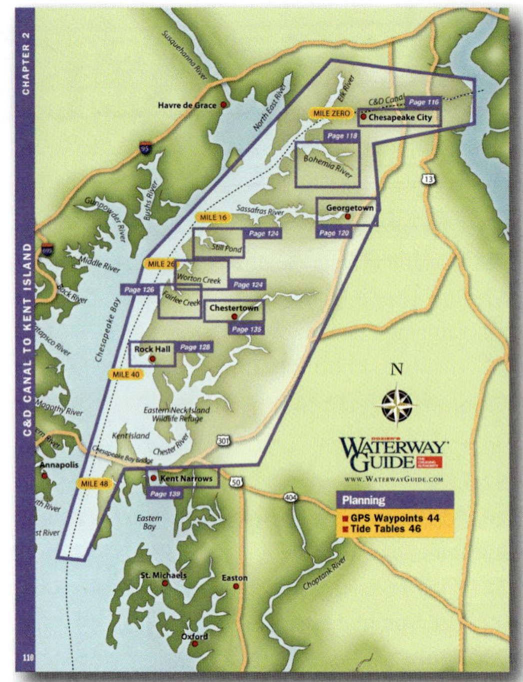

This somewhat sparsely populated northern section of the Eastern Shore presents the first real taste of Chesapeake country after transiting the C&D Canal. You would be wise to savor it. After all, who could complain about the beautiful shorelines, the abundance of jellyfish-free swimming holes or the soft and forgiving bottom predominant hereabouts?

Eastern Bay to Little Choptank

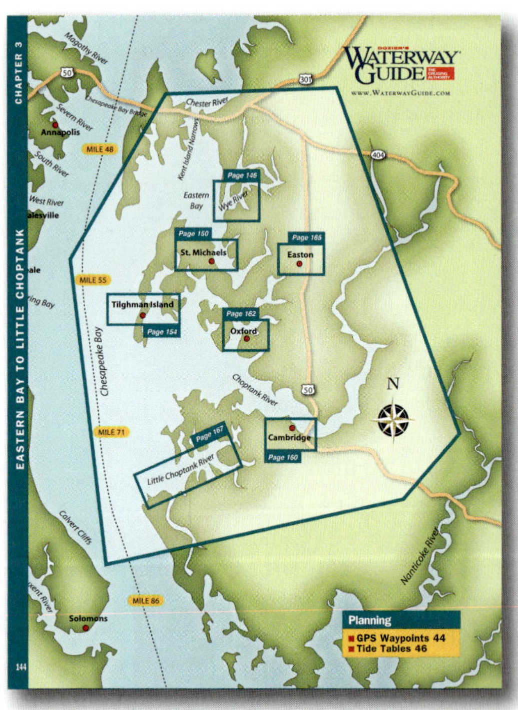

The middle Eastern Shore is the heart of cross-Bay cruising. Talbot County has more shoreline than any other county in the nation—just about everyone lives on or near the water. Many people own boats, and many farmers are also watermen who harvest fresh seafood from local waters. Yet the shorelines remain uncluttered, with refreshing stretches of undisturbed woods and fields, while towns manage to retain an unhurried old-time atmosphere.

Little Choptank to Cape Charles

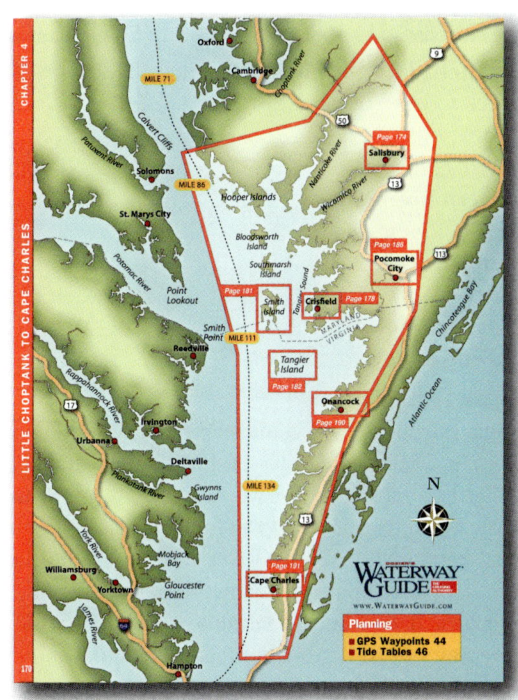

The broad expanses of water as you cruise south along the lower Eastern Shore are often shallow, with wide marshes and flat shorelines. Working the soil and water is still the way of life here, where there has been far less change over the years than on any other part of the Bay. Change is coming, though, with retirees moving into towns like Onancock, VA and Cape Charles, VA, and increased traffic across the Chesapeake Bay Bridge-Tunnel at the mouth of the Bay.

Maryland's Western Shore/Potomac

North East River to Magothy River

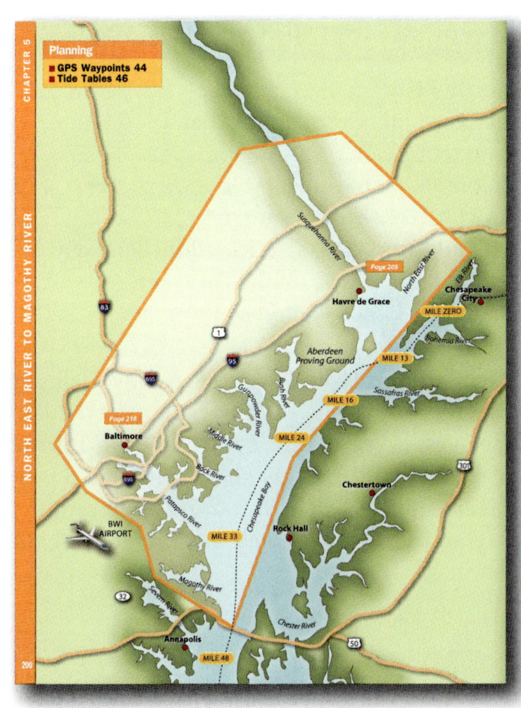

The northern part of Maryland's Western Shore represents one of the most remarkable cruising grounds on the Chesapeake. For starters, you have the mighty Susquehanna River, the Bay's mother tributary, and the pleasant town of Havre de Grace, with excellent boating facilities and transportation connections. As you go down the Bay, you pass miles of vacant waterfront land whose development is unlikely, thanks to frequent military explosions at Aberdeen Proving Ground.

Contents

Severn River to Rhode/West Rivers

This portion of Maryland's Western Shore is probably the busiest on the entire Chesapeake Bay. Besides Annapolis, there are cruising grounds like the high-banked Severn River, whose Round Bay area and assorted creeks enclose some of the finest anchorages anywhere. Not far south is the ever-bustling South River, a haven for both powerboaters and sailors. There is also the serene splendor of the Rhode and West rivers and the pleasantly laid-back boating town of Galesville, the birthplace of one of the Bay's most famous indigenous racing sailboat, the Chesapeake 20.

Herring Bay to Patuxent River

An interesting vista of fossil-filled cliffs—tall, rugged and interrupted only by dredged basins—characterizes Maryland's Western Shore between the West River and the Patuxent River. Herring Bay, in fact, is the only natural harbor on this shore for some 35 miles before the Patuxent River below Cove Point. Eight miles south of West River, Herring Bay and Rockhold Creek provide good shelter and have a variety of marinas.

Potomac River

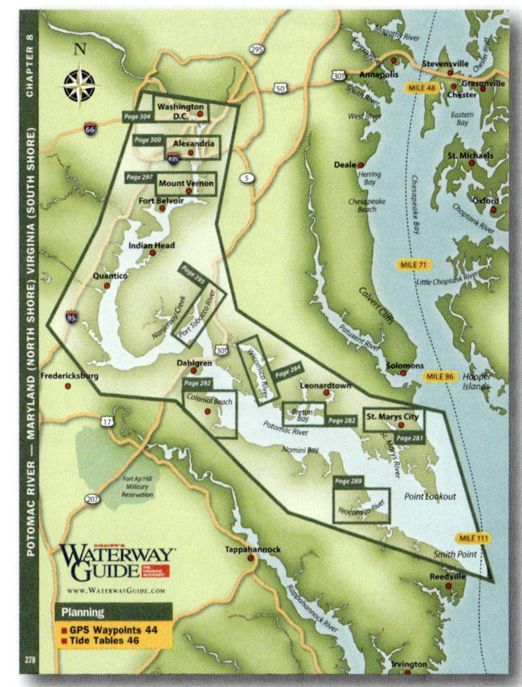

One of the nation's most historic rivers and one of its most productive, the Potomac is second only to the Susquehanna in the amount of freshwater it contributes to the Chesapeake Bay.

Virginia's Western Shore

Smith Point to Deltaville

Scenic Tidewater Virginia occupies Chesapeake Bay's lower Western Shore. The Bay and its many tributaries here are dotted with crab-pot floats—the area is still an active fishing ground for crabs and oysters. These bustling Virginia rivers are busy with recreational craft, along with traditional commercial fishing boats.

Deltaville to Hampton Roads

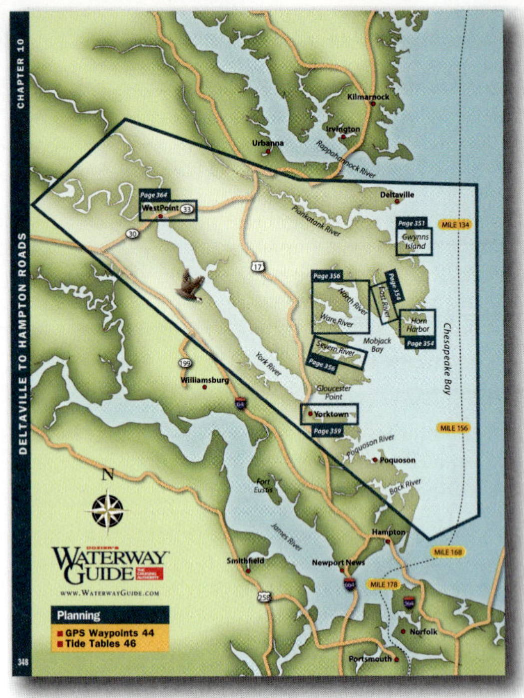

This stretch of Tidewater Virginia is brimming with attractive anchorages and ports of call, particularly for cruisers with a serious bent toward the historical.

Hampton Roads/James River/Cape Henry

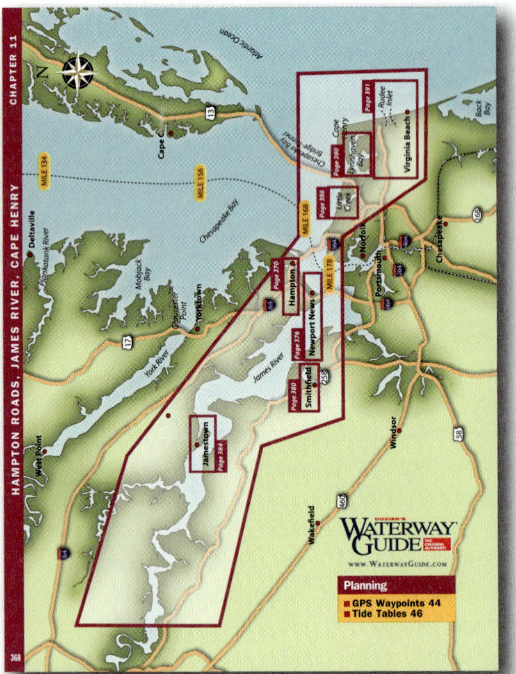

Hampton Roads, site of the famous *Monitor* and *Merrimac* naval battle of 1862, continues today as one of the world's greatest natural harbors. Hampton Roads is also home to the world's largest naval base, a shipbuilder and several great commercial ports.

Norfolk, Elizabeth River

Strategically situated at Mile Zero, the "official" beginning of the Atlantic Intracoastal Waterway, Norfolk, VA, offers nearly every kind of marine service and equipment and is an especially good fitting-out place in preparation for the cruise south or north. Norfolk is also an exciting place to visit, with its rejuvenated waterfront filled with shops, restaurants, hotels, museums and historic sites.

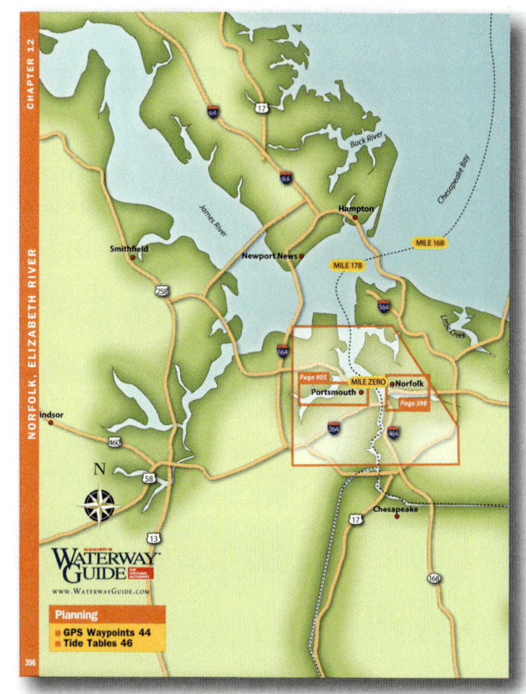

Delmarva Coast

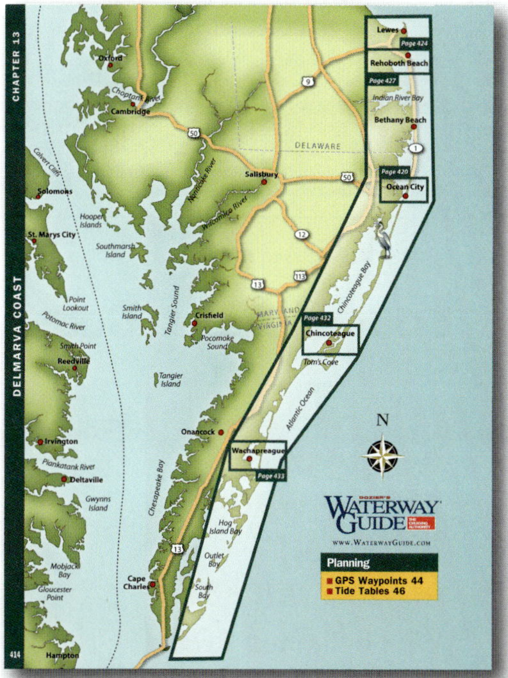

Cruising the Delmarva (Delaware, Maryland, Virginia) coast presents an alternative if you choose to run offshore or behind the Atlantic barrier islands—rather than transiting the Chesapeake Bay. Of course, prudence dictates that you must have a thorough understanding of yourself, your boat, your charts and your crew's abilities before running offshore.

TABLE OF CONTENTS

Boating Lifestyle Doing Just Fine

Looking back three years ago, while writing my publisher's letter, it was difficult to find much positive news to talk about. The economy was falling off a cliff as banks failed, credit dried up, housing prices tumbled and consumer optimism turned to pessimism. Some talked about the demise of boating and the boating lifestyle as we know it. But we all know such extreme talk is usually unfounded, and three years later this has proved to be the case as evidenced by the uptick in boating activity and boat sales.

While the economy overall has made only minimal strides, and there is still no clear-cut path to long-term improvement, consumers, especially cruising boaters, have decided that they no longer wish to keep their plans on hold. "Let's get on with our lives" is a theme we often hear, in spite of the unknowns ahead. We have seen a significant increase in reservations, slip rentals and activities at our marinas this season, and we are getting similar reports from many of our sponsor marinas. At *Waterway Guide* and *Skipper Bob* sales are up again and sponsors are committing to their participation earlier than ever, a good leading indicator of their business expectations for the coming year. On top of that boat sales—both new and used—are rebounding significantly as people take advantage of lower prices and artificially low interest rates.

This renewed enthusiasm is emblematic of the mind set of serious boaters: Come hell and high water, we will find a way to enjoy our passion for being on the water. Some may adjust by taking shorter cruises, others may run at slower speeds to conserve fuel, but the important point is that the boating lifestyle is doing just fine, thank you. It's one area of our lives where we can still enjoy relative freedom from everyday stress and, to a lesser degree, from government interference.

Speaking of government, we are more than a bit concerned about the relentless spread of regulations written to favor small non-boating groups, or written because of the actions of a very few "thorn in the side" boaters, at the expense of the larger boating community. A fact often overlooked is that boaters, especially serious cruisers, are the best stewards of our waterways. Be on the lookout for excessive government regulations and policies that restrict your boating freedoms. Anchoring restrictions enacted by numerous jurisdictions are a prime example. In many cases enforcing existing laws, especially overboard discharge laws, would have dealt with the real issues at hand. As cruisers we encourage you to take an active role in protecting your rights to use America's waterways. Follow news of pending restrictive regulations on www.waterwayguide.com and other boating advocacy sites, such as BoatUS, and voice your opinion. It's our future, and it's up to us to protect it.

There are many instances where our collective voices have favorably changed the outcome of ill-conceived proposals. And we do have friends in government who are looking after us, as shown by many recent dredging projects and funding for waterfront access. All this plays into the bigger picture of keeping the boating lifestyle dream alive. It's a wonderful activity for adults and children alike, and we are fortunate to have some of the finest cruising grounds and marine facilities in the world.

On behalf of all the staff at Waterway Guide, I would like to thank everyone who has stopped in to visit us at our new headquarters in Deltaville, Virginia. This was certainly the right move for us as we gained access to a wide pool of experienced talent in a business-friendly community of active regional, national and international boaters. We welcome your input, both in person and online.

See you on the water,

Jack Dozier,
Publisher

Cruising Editors

Kathi Barrington

Kathi Barrington

Kathi Barringon helped her husband, Mike Robertson, build their Rodriguez Passagemaker 41 trimaran, MINX, which they launched in 1984, the day after her 30th birthday. A month later they sailed out of Toronto Harbour and headed south, with their German Shepherd Dog, Suntan. Twenty eight years later, they have cruised extensively in the Bahamas, the Windward and Leeward Islands, coastal Venezuela, Bonaire, Bermuda and the eastern seaboard. Today they are mostly weekend sailors, cruising the Caicos Cays, with occasional overnights to the Turks Islands. MINX races in the Annual Fools' Regatta and usually wins! They built a home in Long Bay Hills, Providenciales, in the Turks & Caicos Islands, which they share with three dogs and three cats–all of them rescued animals. (Kathi is a volunteer with the local SPCA).

Kathi has written for *Cruising World, Multihulls Magazine,* and *Times of the Islands Magazine*. Currently she is with *Discover Turks & Caicos Magazine*, which she has edited for the past six years. She also produces a detailed annual road map of Providenciales. On weekends and during slow times, she is either sailing with Mike and friends on MINX or riding at Provo Ponies, which is minutes from their home.

Kenneth and Amy Braswell

Kenneth and Amy Braswell

Kenneth and Amy Braswell are WATERWAY GUIDE'S cruising editors for the Albemarle and Pamlico Sounds for the ICW 2012 Guide. Ken and Amy spent weekends growing up on the Pamlico River at their parents respective cottages in view of Indian Island. Marriage led to a succession of sailboats they still own today: a Minisail 14, ComPac 16 (Emanuel Wynn), SunCat 19 (Miss Claire), ComPac 23 (John Newbern) and ComPac 27 (Tryumph II). They enjoy sailing with their Airedale, Kirby, on the Pamlico to Ocracoke, Oriental, Washington and Bath.

This Fall the Tryumph II will return to the Albemarle Sound in the wake of her namesake, a blockage runner captained by Amy's great-grandfather. When not cruising, Ken is a Plant Manager for a food company while Amy manages a family farm. Ken serves as the Treasurer of the River Rat Yacht Club and Amy serves on the Cruising Committee. Both are involved in Pirates on the Pungo, an annual fundraiser for the Pungo District Hospital in Belhaven.

Jay Corzine

Jay Corzine

Jay began boating on the Great Lakes with his parents aboard a trailerable wood lapstrake cruiser, visiting a number of ports and anchorages. Moving to Fort Lauderdale in the early 60s only led to more fun on the water and larger explorations including the Keys and Lake Okeechobee. Finally, by moving to Texas during the late 1970s, he realized a dream by purchasing his first sailing vessel and sailing Galveston Bay and the Texas coast. Now, with Buffy, his wife of 20 years, also an avid cruiser, they concentrate solely on the Texas coast, making their home in Rockport on Aransas Bay. "We did the cruising thing by spending three years on the east coast and the Bahamas, ranging as far north as Bar Harbor, Maine and as far south as Georgetown, Exuma Islands. It provided a giant step for us in both experience and confidence."

Upon getting his Captain's license in 1997, he became a delivery skipper and tangled with a number of contrary vessels. "Sailboat deliveries usually entail fix and repair in foreign ports before they are able to go to sea. Otherwise, the owners would take them home." The year 2000 found him employed by the currents owners of Bluewater Books and Charts in Fort Lauderdale, Florida, where he became manager of the chart department and specialized in both paper and electronic charts for cruising yachtsmen and Megayacht owners.

In 2009, he self-published the "Guide to Cruising Texas Southern and Central Coast: Brazos Santiago to Galveston Bay" and wrote several articles for Telltales Magazine in Kemah, Texas. His fledgling writing career now includes contributions to WATERWAY GUIDE for the Texas portion of the Southern edition.

Tom Hale

Tom Hale and Cristina Sison

Tom Hale and Cristina Sison are cruising editors for the Chesapeake Bay from Smith Point to the York River on the western shore, and from the Little Choptank to Cape Charles on the Eastern Shore. Tom grew up in his father's boatyard on Martha's Vineyard. He found his way to the Chesapeake in the mid-1980s. Cristina grew up in the Philippines and came to the U.S. in 1982. After more than 20 years sailing and cruising out of Annapolis, they moved aboard *Tadhana*, their 2009 37-foot Mariner Seville Pilothouse. Tom and Cristina recently relocated from Deltaville to Deale, MD, where Tom works for Zimmerman Marine. They continue to cruise extensively in the middle and southern Chesapeake Bay.

Tadhana is more likely to be found swinging on her anchor than in a marina. Not content to visit only the usual anchorages, they have sought out and found many unique anchorages off the beaten path. The southern Bay has quite a number of completely deserted white sand beaches; Tom and Cristina have found many of them and are looking for more.

Although still in the work-a-day world, Tom and Cristina are looking forward to the day that they can take off and utilize the rest of the Dozier's Waterway Guides.

Bob and Carol Kunath

Bob and Carol Kunath

Bob and Carol Kunath have owned about a dozen sail and powerboats over the past 40 years. They've ranged from small-lake open boats to those equipped for offshore shark and tuna fishing, to sail and powerboats on Lake Michigan, where they have been cruising for the past 15 years. During those years they have cruised extensively throughout Lake Michigan and the North Channel of Lake Huron. Both are past commodores of the Bay Shore Yacht Club in Illinois and members of the Waukegan, IL, Sail and Power Squadron, where Bob has served as an officer and instructor. He has also contributed to the U.S. Power Squadron national magazine, *Ensign*, and holds a U.S. Coast Guard Master's license.

During 2005, Bob and Carol completed a two-year cruise of the Great Loop in their Pacific Seacraft 38T trawler, *Sans Souci,* logging 9,000 miles on the Loop and many of its side trips. Recently they have resumed cruising all of Lake Michigan, but have plans to expand that area, perhaps back into the rivers of the Midwest or canals of Canada. Bob has also been a seminar presenter at Passagemaker Trawler Fests over the past four years, sharing his knowledge of Lake Michigan. For 2012, Bob and Carol cover Lake Michigan for Waterway Guide, including Green Bay and Door County.

Vicki Lathom

Vicki Lathom

Vicki has been a writer and sailor for 40 years. She retired as director of public information for Montgomery County, MD, in 1996 and went to work for Maryland Governor William Donald Schaefer as his speechwriter. Vicki is currently a freelance travel writer and photographer as well as a writing instructor for the University of Maryland.

Bud and Elaine Lloyd

Elaine and Bud Lloyd

Bud and Elaine Lloyd, are the cruising editors for South Florida, the Keys and Okeechobee Waterway. After being long-time sailors (they had several sailboats over the years), the Lloyds decided that in order to do the type of cruising they dreamed of they needed a trawler. *Diamond Girl* is a 36-foot 1990 Nova/Heritage East Sundeck. From their home port of Long Beach, California, they cruised all over southern California and parts of Mexico extensively for over 30 years. After retiring from the printing business in 2005, they decided that it was time to get serious about fulfilling a life-long dream of cruising the Chesapeake Bay and ICW. So in December 2005, they put *Diamond Girl* on a ship and sent her to Ft. Lauderdale, Florida. They have now been cruising on the East Coast for almost 5 years and have found the experience even more rewarding than they ever imagined. They have made several trips up and down the ICW, have spent the summers cruising on the Chesapeake Bay, and have made numerous crossings of the Okeechobee Waterway. Bud and Elaine are full-time liveaboard cruisers and can't wait to see what awaits them over the next horizon. Now the Waterway Guide has given them the opportunity to write about what they enjoy most…cruising!

Barbara and Patrick McGowan

Barbara and Patrick McGowan with Kona

Barbara and Patrick McGowan are cruising editors for Waterway Guide's Northern edition from Cape Cod through Maine. Barbara embraced sailing as a junior racer in the Sandy Hook area of NJ, starting in Turnabouts and Bluejays, and gradually working her way up to J24's. Her marketing/graphic design career took her to Marblehead MA, where the dream continued meeting and marrying Patrick in 2006.

An avid power boater since age 14, Pat became a sailor in 2001 after an epiphany on a sunset cruise in Annapolis Harbor. He purchased Kismet V, a 28' O'Day exactly one month to the day later. Ten years past and now retired from corporate America as a division sales manager, he pursues his passion for exploring and photographing his favorite haunts in New England waters.

In October 2011, the McGowans moved aboard Pegasus, a Beneteau Oceanis 381. They have been cruising nonstop ever since with Kona, their cockapoo. Their shakedown cruise on the ICW took them from New York City to Charleston where they spent the winter in "Velcro Harbor" (planning only a two-week stay, hence the nickname). Summers will find Barbara and Pat discovering new points of interest along the New England coast, using the Jubilee Yacht Club in Beverly, MA as their home base.

Wally Moran

Wally Moran

Wally Moran has been boating on the North Channel and Georgian Bay since the late 1970s, and has never tired of spending his summers there. "There's always something new to discover up here," he claims. Wally spends his winters cruising south from his northern paradise to the Bahamas, Cuba and the U.S. east coast. When he's not sailing, he writes for SAIL Magazine, and has produced several videos for The Sailing Channel, including "Forbidding, Forbidden Cuba" and "Sailing South, the First Timer's Guide to the ICW."

Carol Pierini

Carol Pierini has been boating since her childhood on Barnegat Bay, New Jersey. While the sizes of her boats have changed over the years, her love of cruising the waters of the mid-Atlantic coast remains constant. Carol and her husband, Jim Woller, make their home on Raritan Bay in Perth Amboy, New Jersey where they sail a Bristol 35.5, *Mimi*, from the Chesapeake Bay through New England. Carol has been a writer since an early age and has published extensively in the health care area. While her career as a medical writer continues, her love of the eastern waters of the United States has drawn her more and more into maritime writing about the area.

Carol Pierini

Audrey and Ted Stehle

Audrey and Ted Stehle are Waterway Guide's cruising editors for the inland rivers and the Tenn-Tom Waterway, from Chicago to Mobile Bay, for the Great Lakes 2012 Guide.

They began boating as sailors in the early 1970s on the Chesapeake Bay and then switched to power after retirement. In addition to extensive cruising of Chesapeake Bay and its tributaries, they have traveled the ICW to Florida many times, completed the Great Loop, cruised the Ohio, Tennessee and Cumberland rivers and made six trips on the Tenn-Tom Waterway. Their Californian 45 is presently on Chesapeake Bay, but plans call for returning it to Kentucky Lake to resume cruising the Cumberland and Tennessee rivers. When not cruising, the Stehles reside in Cincinnati, OH, to be near their children and grandchildren and engage in volunteer work.

Audrey and Ted Stehle

Alan and Susann Syme

Alan and Susann began boating in earnest in 1974 on Big Rideau Lake, Ontario Canada. They loved boating, beaching, and swimming with the family on their 15 foot run-about, but wake, wind and waves were often uncomfortable on such a small boat. Six incrementally larger boats later, they are very comfortable aboard *Kaos,* their 46 foot, 1988 Sea Ranger Trawler. They have cruised some 30,000 miles since purchasing her in 2003. Cruises include, Houston to Chattanooga, spending several summers on the Tennessee and Tombigbee systems, the Great Loop almost twice, the Down East Loop, and most recently, a seven month cruise from Florida to the British Virgin Islands with stops at all of the magnificent Island nations in between.

Alan and Susann are active members of the AGLCA (America's Great Loop Cruisers Association) and serve on the Advisory Council. Moreover, they have presented at several AGLCA Rendezvous' speaking about their cruising lifestyle including their extensive travel in the Bahamas.

Alan and Susann Syme

Robert Wilson

Robert Wilson has been cruising in the Bahamas from his homeport in Brunswick, GA, for the past nine years. He and his wife, Carolyn, began sailing on Lake Lanier, just north of Atlanta, GA, shortly after they met 25 years ago. Robert is a former employee benefits consultant and is a Past Commodore of the Royal Marsh Harbour Yacht Club in Abaco. Together they have written extensively about their sailing adventures throughout the Bahamas on their 38-foot Island Packet, *Gypsy Common.* Their current boat, *Sea Island Girl*, is a North Pacific 42 pilothouse trawler, which they cruised in the Pacific Northwest along the coast of British Columbia, before shipping the boat to Florida to continue cruising throughout the Bahamas aboard their new trawler.

Robert Wilson

When not cruising, the Wilsons reside in Atlanta, GA, where Carolyn teaches pre-school, and Robert continues consulting and writing. Robert is Waterway Guide's cruising editor for the northern Bahamas. ■

Things to Know Before You Go

There are many reasons we go cruising, but they can all be summed up in one word—adventure. The thought of casting off the dock lines with a fully provisioned boat and a reasonably blank calendar is intoxicating indeed. Exploring the waters of Chesapeake Bay can take a lifetime. Let's get started!

For Chesapeake Bay boaters, the ultimate experience is the long-range cruise—the one that continues through several seasons.

The Time Factor

A trip on Chesapeake Bay can last a week, a month or as long as you choose. It all depends on how fast you go, which route you choose and how long you decide to linger along the way.

If you plan to keep moving under power almost every day—stopping each evening to enjoy the amenities of a marina or anchorage—the following running times are fairly typical. In about two weeks (barring weather or mechanical delays), you can explore much of the upper Bay. Many Bay cruisers take longer, however, stopping along the way to explore towns and take in the sights. It is smart to allow time along the way for sightseeing, resting, waiting out bad weather or making repairs to the boat. Of course, the boat's features and the skipper's temperament will determine whether the pace is fast or slow. Sailboats averaging 5 to 8 knots can cover the same number of miles on a given day as a powerboat that cruises at 20 to 25 knots. The only difference is that the sailboat's crew will have a much longer day underway.

Those who are eager to reach southern waters can cruise the length of Chesapeake Bay in two days or less, while others who want to poke around in the Bay's scores of harbors, creeks and coves can spend months without seeing everything. You are here now. Slow down and enjoy it! Most cruisers find that their time on the Bay is the highlight of their trip north and south.

Dinghies at dock ready for departure.
WATERWAY GUIDE PHOTOGRAPHY

First-Aid Basics

A deep cut from a filet knife is normally not a big deal at home where medical help is close at hand, but on the Bay (where you may be a long way from help), you will need to be able to patch yourself up until you can get to an emergency clinic or hospital emergency room. Adequate first-aid kits are essential, along with a medical manual that you can understand quickly; the standard reference is "Advanced First-Aid Afloat" by Dr. Peter F. Eastman. Good first-aid kits can be found at most marine supply stores and better pharmacies or drug stores.

Cruisers who take medication should make sure their current prescription has plenty of refills available so supplies can be topped off along the way. Additionally, make sure crew members are aware of any medication you are on in case you become injured and unable to answer questions regarding your health.

All safety equipment—harnesses, life preservers, jack lines, medical kit, etc.—should be in good working condition, within easy reach and ready at a moment's notice. All aboard, both crew and guests, should know where to find the emergency equipment. In addition to having the proper first-aid gear aboard, all aboard should be versed in basic "first responder" procedures including CPR and making a "May-Day" call on the VHF radio.

Check out our Goin' Ashore sections of this Guide; they provide contact information for local hospitals and emergency clinics. Most importantly, if someone's life is in imminent danger, make a "May-Day" call on VHF Channel 16. This is the best way to get quick help. Making a 911 call on your cell phone is also an option, but not one you should count on because of variable coverage in the Bay by cellular providers.

A Note on Clean Marinas

The next time you pull into your favorite Chesapeake Bay facility, you might want to look around for some indication of it being a designated Clean Marina. Many states around the country— including those covered in this edition of Waterway Guide— have launched programs in recent years aimed at making marina owners and boaters more aware of how their activities affect the environment. In order for one's marina to be designated a "Clean Marina," the facility's owner has to take a series of steps prescribed by that state's respective program, anything from making sure tarps are laid down when boat bottoms are worked on, to providing pump-out facilities. (The steps were derived from an Environmental Protection Agency document presented to states across America.)

The underlying principle behind these voluntary, incentive-based programs is this: If the waters we cruise are not clean, then we will cruise elsewhere and the marine businesses in the polluted areas will suffer. The programs represent a nice coupling of economics and environmental management that is catching on with marina owners and boaters alike. So if you see the Clean Marina designation at your favorite facility, rest assured they are doing the right thing for the environment.

Considerations for Sailors

Sailors sometimes worry about travel on the Bay, but unless your mast is higher than 65 feet, or your keel draws more than 7 feet, the trip is easy. A Bay passage allows for evening rest stops instead of pushing along overnight offshore. The truth of the matter is that more sailboats than powerboats can sometimes be seen transiting the Bay.

Sailors obviously cannot pace motorboats on plane, but they do have the option of using occasional fair winds to enjoy the quieter ride and save some fuel, often simply by unrolling the jib. There may be some good-natured ribbing when a sailboat pulls up to the fuel dock and tops off with five gallons instead of 500.

THINGS YOU WILL NEED

To minimize time spent waiting for spare parts—which can be considerable in some areas Waterway Guide recommends that cruising mariners take along certain equipment.

Spare Parts

For the engine, bring spare seals for the raw-water pump and an extra water-pump impeller, along with V-belts, points and plugs for gas engines (injectors for diesel engines), a fuel pump and strainer, a distributor cap, fuses, lube oil and filter cartridges. Also, carry a list of service centers for your type of equipment and bring the engine manual and the parts list.

Other things to bring: spare deck cap keys, a head-repair kit, fresh water pump repair kit, spare hose clamps, lengths of hose and an extra container of fuel. (Keep in mind that if you want to anchor out fueling up during the day when there are no crowds at the fuel docks is a good idea.)

Carry a good tool kit with varying sizes of flat- and Phillips-head screwdrivers, socket wrenches (metric and standard), pliers, etc. Remember that all the spare parts in the world are fairly useless without a proper bag of tools aboard to install them with.

For Docking and Anchoring

Your docking equipment should include a minimum of four bow and stern lines made of good, stretchy nylon (each at least two-thirds the length of your boat) and two spring lines (at least 1.5 times the length of your boat) with oversized eyes to fit over pilings. If you have extra dock lines, consider bringing them along with your shore power cord and a shore power adapter or two.

For anchoring, the average 30-foot boat needs 150 to 200 feet of 7/16- to 1/2-inch nylon line with no less than 15 feet of 5/16-inch chain shackled to a 20- to 30-pound plow-type or Bruce anchor—or a 15-pound Danforth-type anchor. Storm anchors and a lunch hook are also recommended. Larger yachts should use 7/8-inch nylon and heavier chain. While one anchor will get you along, most veteran cruisers carry both a plow and fluke-type anchor to use in varying bottom conditions. Ground tackle is always the subject of debate and every skipper has their own ideas of how much chain versus rode and the type of anchor.

Consult a good reference like *Chapman's Piloting* or West Marine's "West Advisor" articles (available online) if you are unsure about proper anchoring techniques and make sure that you master them before setting off down the ICW.

Tenders and Dinghies

A dinghy is needed if you plan to anchor out, gunkhole or carry an anchor to deeper water to kedge off a shoal. Inflatable dinghies are popular, but they require an outboard motor to get them around easily. On the other hand, rowing a hard dinghy is excellent exercise. Check registration laws where you plan to spend any length of time, as certain states (including Florida) have become very strict in enforcing dinghy registration.

Always chain and lock your dinghy when you leave it unattended, even if it is tied off to your boat, as more than one cruiser has woken to a missing dinghy while at anchor on the waterways. Outboard engines should always be padlocked to the transom of your dinghy or on a stern rail, as they are often targets of thieves.

Keeping Comfortable

Another consideration when equipping your boat for a cruise is temperature control inside the cabin. Many powerboats—particularly trawlers—are equipped with an air-conditioner for those hot, steamy nights. Others can get away with fans and wind scoops. When considering heating options for your boat, select something that is not going to suck your batteries dead—and, even more important, something that is safe. Many reliable and safe marine propane and diesel heaters are available nowadays for those cruising late into the fall season. If you plan to spend a lot of time in the northern part of the Bay, a built-in diesel heater may fit the bill.

Since the weather can turn chilly or even downright cold in the northern Bay any time in winter, some Bay cruisers choose to have full cockpit enclosures to guard the crew from the elements.

Battling the Sun and Bugs

Cruisers in an open cockpit need the protection of a dodger, awning, or bimini top, not to mention sunscreen and a hat. In fact, many hard-core cruisers have an enclosure that surrounds the entire cockpit. Whatever method, take measures to make sure you are not out in the elements all day without protection if you can avoid it.

You will want a good quality sunscreen on board with you if you have any intention of enjoying the topside portion of your boat. Bug screens for hatches, ports and companionways are a must, as you will want to have the boat open for adequate cross ventilation in warm weather.

Glare off the water can be a major contributor to fatigue. Consider purchasing a quality pair of sunglasses and make sure they are polarized, as this feature removes annoying reflected light from your view. They also help prevent long-term damage to your eyes and vision.

Navigating Essentials

Charts for coastal piloting belong at the helm station, not in the cabin, so a clipboard or spray-proof plastic case comes in handy. Many waterway veterans like to use the spiral bound chart "kits" that feature small-scale charts laid out in order according to the route. Since the local conditions change constantly, use only the latest charts, and keep them updated with the U.S. Coast Guard's *Local Notices to Mariners*, which are available online at www.navcen.uscg.gov/lnm. For planning, many charts and nautical publications (Coast Pilots, light lists, tide tables) can be downloaded free of charge via the Internet. See the Skipper's Handbook section for more detail on how to access this valuable information with your computer.

Many cruisers are now equipping themselves with the latest GPS chartplotters and computer-driven electronic gizmos, and while convenient, they are not a requirement for cruising the ICW. Radar is a wonderful aid, not only to "see" markers and other vessels but also to track local storms; many boats have it. Single-Sideband (SSB) and amateur (ham) radio are excellent for long-range communications, but you can get by without either one on the Bay. You will not want to cruise the Bay without a depth sounder; this item is essential.

You should learn how to operate all of your navigation electronics inside and out before you rely on them for navigation. A dense fogbank is no place to figure out how your navigation equipment works. As always, you should have paper charts available as backup in case your electronic unit malfunctions.

A VHF marine radio is the cruiser's lifeline to the Coast Guard, marinas and other boats and is also necessary for contacting bridges. Mount yours at the helm or keep a handheld unit nearby. Many manufacturers now offer a RAM (remote access microphone) option, which allows the skipper to use the hand unit and control the radio from the helm.

Most cruisers carry cell phones, but you cannot count on coverage everywhere, as these systems are optimized for land users. See the "VHF Radio" section of the Skipper's Handbook located at the front of the book for more detail on VHF radio operation and regulations.

Have a compass adjuster swing (calibrate) your steering compass before departure so you can run courses with confidence. Also carry a good hand-bearing compass or binoculars with a built-in compass for getting bearings to fixed marks or points ashore.

The Money Issue

Everyone is concerned about money, but when you are a long-range cruiser, the issue becomes a bit more complicated. Luckily, cruisers today can get by with much less cash than in the past. Almost all banks have ATMs. Many grocery stores and drugstores (and even fast food restaurants) accept ATM and Visa or MasterCard check cards. Remember that most banks will honor the cash advance feature of Visa cards and the MasterCard. In addition, American Express offices will accept a cardholder's personal check in payment for Travelers Checks and will also dispense cash to cardholders.

Most marinas, especially the large ones, accept major credit cards and oil company credit cards for dockage, fuel and marine supplies. Most restaurants, motels and grocery stores will also accept major credit cards. Credit card statements also serve as excellent records of expenses while traveling.

A majority of banks now offer online banking services that allow you to pay your bills remotely via the Internet. With online banking, you can pay bills, set up new payees, transfer funds, check your balances, and much more. You can also set up recurring payments on an "auto-pay" system that pays your bills automatically every month or when your payee sends your bank an "e-bill."

Do be careful where you conduct your online banking sessions. Many public marina computers "remember" passwords and forms (handy for a thief looking to steal your identity or your money), and many marina Internet WiFi (wireless) connections are not totally secure. It is best to use your own computer that is hooked up to a terrestrial network with your own secure firewall running.

Boating Education

The most important thing to know before you go is how to operate your boat safely. Operating a boat safely is like operating an automobile safely. Both activities require knowledge, skill and safety awareness. Mastery of these factors leads to a more enjoyable boating experience for everyone on board, and it begins with education.

An effective boating education program begins with an orientation in the equipment involved—the boat, its means of propulsion (sails or engines), instrumentation, and those items that will keep you and any passengers on board safe while underway. The program should include a study of the "rules of the road" which you, as operator, should follow at all times. (Unfortunately, many boaters do not follow the rules because they have never taken a course in boating.) The best programs include hands-on training aboard a vessel while underway.

A good beginners' course is one approved by the State or National Association of State Boating Law Administrators (NASBLA). Such a test is mandatory in some states. A good reference book is *Chapman's Piloting & Seamanship* published by Hearst Marine Books and is available in most bookstores and libraries. "An educated boater is a safe boater," stated Tom Danti, Dean of Instruction at the Chapman School of Seamanship. "Such a boater will be alert and prepared to act effectively should an emergency arise and, in all other respects, make the boating experience an enjoyable one for all on board."

Please note: Each state has its own boater safety regulations. Those with more stringent regulations generally allow exemptions for non-residents who are visiting for a limited (e.g., 45 or 90 days) amount of time. To see state-by-state requirements, visit www.boatus.org/onlinecourse/default.asp.

Float Plan

Give your float plan to someone who will keep it handy until you telephone to report your safe arrival. You should set a "fail safe" time. If he or she has not heard from you by then, a call should be made to the U.S. Coast Guard to report that you are overdue.

Waterway Guide Online

Waterway Guide has made so many recent updates to our website (www.waterwayguide.com) that it is hard to know where to begin. We have added Marina Close-ups so you can look ahead to plan your next marina stop with one of our sponsors. Our Waterway Planner can help you plan your trip and locate marinas, bridges/locks and anchorages. The Discussion Board lets you post information about areas through which you are traveling or get information from those traveling ahead of you. These website upgrades strongly focus on reader interaction.

Waterway Guide continues to provide other helpful services on our website: "Navigation Updates" offers the most up-to-date information on such items as Waterway conditions, changing bridge schedules and hazards to navigation; and "Cruising News" reports events, marina updates, fuel prices and general information about the waterways.

Skipper's Handbook

Photo courtesy: U.S. Coast Guard.

Coast Guard

The U.S. Coast Guard is on duty 24 hours a day, 7 days a week to aid recreational boaters and commercial vessels alike. They have search and rescue capabilities and may provide lookout, communication or patrol functions to assist vessels in distress.

Fifth Coast Guard District (Includes coastal waters and tributaries from Toms River, NJ, to the North Carolina/South Carolina border.)

District Office .... Federal Building, 431 Crawford St., Portsmouth, VA 23704, 757-398-6000, www.uscg.mil/d5.

Pennsylvania (Sector Delaware Bay)

Station Philadelphia, PA.. 215-271-4915

Delaware (Sector Delaware Bay)

Station Roosevelt Inlet (Lewes), DE

Call Station Indian River Inlet... 302-227-2440

New Jersey (Sector Delaware Bay)

Station Fortescue, NJ.. 856-447-4422

Station Cape May, NJ.. 609-898-6995

Chesapeake Bay

Station Still Pond, MD, (seasonal)

On the north side of the entrance to Still Pond Creek 410-778-2201

Station Curtis Bay, MD, At the Curtis Bay Coast Guard Base at Curtis Creek Cove... 410-576-2625

Station Annapolis, MD, On the west side of Fishing Creek, about one mile west-northwest of Thomas Point................. 410-267-8108

Station Oxford, MD, Near Bachelors Point....................... 410-226-0580

Station Crisfield, MD, On the southwest side of Somers Cove Marina, next to the state dock 410-968-0323

Station Washington, D.C.

In the Pentagon Lagoon off the Potomac........................... 202-767-1194

Station St. Inigoes, MD

On the west side of entrance to Mulls Cove 301-872-4345

Delmarva Coast (Sector Delaware Bay/Baltimore)

Station Indian River Inlet, DE

On the north shore inside the inlet..................................... 302-227-2440

Station Ocean City, MD

On the north shore inside the inlet..................................... 410-289-7559

Station Chincoteague, VA, On the east side of the Chincoteague Channel just south of the Route 175 bridge....................... 757-336-2874

Station Wachapreague, VA

On the south end of Cedar Island 757-787-9526

Hampton Roads (Sector Hampton Roads)

Station Portsmouth, VA

On the west side of the entrance to Craney Island Creek..... 757-483-8526

Station Little Creek, VA, About a mile south of the entrance to Little Creek, 4.5 miles west of Lynnhaven Inlet.......................... 757-464-9371

Station Milford Haven, Hudgins, VA

Adjacent to the Gwynns Island Bridge................................. 804-725-2125

Station Cape Charles City, VA

Located on Cape Charles Harbor 757-331-2000

Additional Resources

U.S. Coast Guard www.uscg.mil

SKIPPER'S HANDBOOK

Customs

Operators of small pleasure vessels arriving in the United States from a foreign port are required to report their arrival to Customs and Border Patrol (CBP) immediately. CBP has designated specific reporting locations within the Field Offices that are staffed during boating season for pleasure boats to report their arrival and be inspected by CBP. If you are clearing back in to the U.S. anywhere from the Sebastian Inlet south down the east coast of Florida, including Ft. Pierce, Palm Beach, Ft. Lauderdale, and Miami and on through the Keys to Key West and as far north on the west coast as Ft. Myers, the master of the boat must call in to the CBP (1-800-432-1216 or 800-451-0393) so as to be directed to the nearest Port of Entry to satisfy the face-to-face requirement, or to the nearest designated reporting location for inspection. Only the captain may disembark to make this call; all others must await clearance onboard. (To avoid all this, see "Small Vessel Reporting System" below.) Numbers for clearing in at other locations are provided below.

You may be required to rent a car or take a cab to the nearest airport or federal office several miles away for the inspection. These offices are often closed on weekends. If your arrival is after working hours, you are required to stay on board and clear in the next morning. You must clear in within 24 hours of your arrival. Everyone on board, regardless of nationality, has to report in person. U.S. nationals must take their passports or passport cards. All non-U.S. nationals should take their passports with valid visas and a Green Card, if held. Take your boat papers, either U.S. documentation or state registration with state decal number. You will need to show:

- Registered name of vessel and the declared home port
- Your FCC call sign
- Your hull identification number
- LOA, LWL, beam and draft

Additionally, have a list of firearms and ammunition on board and your U.S. Customs decal number, if required. U.S. Customs decals are required for any boat over 30 feet long. For information regarding CBP Decal, visit www.cbp.gov. Decals are not required for non-U.S. boats and one-time entries from the Bahamas or elsewhere. Decals must be renewed annually. To eliminate potential problems or questions regarding any items of value that you have on board, obtain a U.S. Customs Form 4457, Certificate of Registration for Personal Effects Taken Abroad, before you depart for the islands. You will need to visit a U.S. Customs Office and bring the items with you. There is no fee for obtaining this form.

Designated Ports of Entry

NEW JERSEY
205 Jefferson Street
Perth Amboy, NJ 08861
973-368-6100

DELAWARE
908 New Churchman's Road, Suite C
New Castle, DE 19720
302-326-0600

MARYLAND
40 South Gay Street
Baltimore, MD 21202
410-962-2666

WASHINGTON, D.C. (DULLES)
22685 Holiday Park Drive, Suite 15
Sterling, VA 20598
703-318-5900

VIRGINIA
101 E. Main Street
Norfolk, VA 23510
757-533-4200

NORTH CAROLINA
534H 35th Street
Morehead City, NC 28557
252-726-5845

721 Medical Center Drive
Suite 200
Wilmington, NC 28401
910-772- 5900

Small Vessel Reporting System

Small Vessel Reporting System (SVRS) is a voluntary effort that enables boaters to report their arrival from foreign waters to CBP quickly and easily. It is available to U.S. Citizens or Lawful Permanent Residents of the U.S., as well as Canadian citizens and permanent residents of Canada who are nationals of a Visa Waiver Program country. Current Local Boater Option (LBO) participants, Trusted Traveler Program members and current holders of an I-68 must apply for enrollment in SVRS online to participate but do not need to schedule an interview with a CBP officer. All others need to:

1. Complete an application at: cbp.gov/SVRS.
2. Schedule an interview online with a CBP officer.
3. Receive a boating registration number and password by email.
4. File a float plan.

Float plans consist of biographical information of all persons intending on traveling, vessel registration information and itinerary information. Once a float plan is entered and activated, SVRS will issue a float plan number. Upon return to the United States, the SVRS participant should contact an SVRS dedicated telephone line manned by a CBP Officer or an automated attendant. Who will ask a series of questions reflecting those on a Customs Declaration (CBP Form 6059B) and provide the participant with their arrival number. (The CBP reserves the right to hold an in-person inspection if needed.) The system is currently available around the Southeast in Florida, Puerto Rico and the United States Virgin Islands. It is also deployed at the U.S./Canada border.

Advance Notice of Arrival

With limited exceptions, the Coast Guard Advance Notice of Arrival (ANOA) regulations apply to US and foreign vessels bound for or departing from ports or places in the United States. The requirement does not apply to US recreational vessels, but does apply to foreign recreational vessels.

There are various methods for submitting an NOA, but the preferred method is electronically via the web site at the National Vessel Movement Center (NVMC). This is referred to as an electronic Notice of Arrival (eNOA). If the vessel is on a voyage of 96 hours or more, the NOA must be received by the NVMC at least 96

Customs, cont'd.

hours before the vessel enters a port or place in the United States. If the voyage is of less than 96 hours, the NOA must be received by the NVMC before the vessel departs for the US port or place, but at least 24 hours before entering the US port or place. To access the eNOA, go to the NVMC website at https://enoad.nvmc.uscg.gov/. The form can be completed and sent to the NVMC from that link. The NVMC can also be contacted at 800-708-9823 or 304-264-2502.

eNOA and Day Trips

The Coast Guard understands that due to Florida's close proximity to the Bahamas, recreational boaters frequently visit foreign ports spontaneously or for short durations of time. If your voyage time is 96 hours or more, you must submit an NOA at least 96 hours before entering the U.S. port or place of destination. However, if your voyage time is less than 96 hours, you must submit an NOA before departure, but at least 24 hours before entering the U.S. port or place of destination. It is also recommended that recreational boaters emphasize in their eNOA that they will be following the reported trip itinerary, weather permitting. In the event that weather conditions prevent boaters from adhering to their proposed schedule, they should notify the appropriate authority within the time limits specified above. Consequently, all boaters must notify the appropriate authority of any modifications to their itinerary within the time limits specified in the previous section. Changes to the estimated time of arrival that are less than 6 hours do not need to be reported. If they are greater than 6 hours, you must email your itinerary changes to the NVMC at sana@nvmc.uscg.gov.

For boats outward bound for the Bahamas and the Turks and Caicos, it is a good idea to check (before leaving the U.S.) with the nearest office of the Bureau of Customs and Border Protection at your intended port of return to find out exactly what they will require from you as you clear in.

Note: If you feel you have been treated unjustly by a CBP officer, call 1-877-246-8253 or email Joint.Intake@dhs.gov.

Port Security

Since September 11, 2001, the U.S. Coast Guard and other law enforcers have increased their presence at ports, near military vessels and throughout the length of the Intracoastal Waterway. The Coast Guard—a division of the U.S. Department of Homeland Security—requires that all recreational boaters make themselves aware of local security zones, permanent and temporary, before leaving the dock. Cruise ships, military vessels and tankers carrying hazardous materials constitute temporary security zones, and, furthermore, the rules apply whether they are dockside or under way.

Any violation of the security zones is punishable by civil penalties of up to $27,500 per violation, while criminal penalties call for imprisonment for up to six years and fines reaching $250,000. Ignorance of the security zones is no excuse. Having said that, because the regulators could not foresee every eventuality when mandating an 100-yard no-enter zone around moving vessels, law-abiding boaters sometimes find themselves unable to comply with the letter of the law, without hitting a jetty, for example. In such cases, common sense and good communication should prevail.

Homeland Security officials are always considering measures to better protect maritime targets. Federal agencies are seriously considering a national scheme to license all boaters as well as mandating the onboard installation of expensive identification transponders called AIS or automatic identification systems. It should be no surprise that boaters have responded negatively, ridiculing the proposal as an expensive, invasive and ineffective burden.

Government officials view the recreational boating community as an ally. We can do our part—and perhaps stave off draconian licensing and surveillance measures—by becoming familiar with a Coast Guard program called America's Waterway Watch. Think of it as a neighborhood watch program for the waterways.

It is not the intent of America's Waterway Watch to spread paranoia or to encourage spying on one another, and it is not a surveillance program. Instead, it is a simple deterrent to potential terrorist activity. The purpose of the program is to allow boaters and others who spend time along the water to help the authorities counter crime and terrorism.

To report suspicious behavior, call the National Response Center at 877-249-2824. For immediate danger to life or property, call 911, or call the Coast Guard on Marine VHF-FM Channel 16. To learn more about the program, visit www.americaswaterwaywatch.org.

At the end of this section are listed the ports and places that require a little forethought and vigilance on your part. Following the steps in the action plan below will help ensure a trouble-free journey and keep you and your crew out of the headlines.

Prepare:

- Before you leave, check the current charts for the area in which you will be traveling and identify any security areas. Security zones are highlighted and outlined in magenta with special notes regarding the specific regulations pertaining to that area.
- Check the latest *Local Notice to Mariners* (available online at www.navcen.uscg and posted at some marinas) and identify any potential security areas that may not be shown on the chart.
- Listen to VHF Channel 16 for any Sécurité alerts from the Coast Guard (departing cruise ships, Naval vessels, fuel tankers, etc.) for the area you will be cruising prior to departure.
- Talk to other boaters in your anchorage or marina about the areas where you will be traveling. They will most likely have tips and suggestions on any potential security zones or special areas they may have encountered on their way.

Stay Alert While Underway:

- Mind the outlined magenta security areas noted on your charts.
- Look for vessels with blue or red warning lights in port areas and, if approached, listen carefully and strictly obey all instructions given to you.

■ Keep your VHF radio switched to Channel 16 and keep your ears tuned for bulletins, updates and possible requests for communication with you.

■ Avoid commercial port operation areas, especially those that involve military, cruise-line or petroleum facilities. Observe and avoid other restricted areas near power plants, national monuments, etc.

■ If you need to pass within 100 yards of a U.S. Naval vessel for safe passage, you must contact the U.S. Naval vessel or the Coast Guard escort vessel on VHF Channel 16.

■ If government security or the U.S. Coast Guard hails you, do exactly what they say, regardless of whether or not you feel their instructions have merit.

Sensitive Chesapeake Bay Port Areas

■ **Annapolis, MD –** U.S. Naval Academy boating activity in and around the Academy on the Severn River. Keep clear of Academy training vessels.

■ **Washington, DC –** Heavy security in the area of the Washington Channel, upstream on the Anacostia River and north on the Potomac River toward Memorial Bridge. Boats anchoring in the Washington Channel must notify Metropolitan Marine Police: 202-727-4582.

■ **Baltimore, MD –** Large shipping area, with cruise ship and commercial shipping traffic. Keep a lookout for cruise ships or freight vessels under Coast Guard escort on the Patapsco River and on the Chesapeake Bay approach.

Sensitive Northern Port Areas

■ **Delaware Bay** – Area with heavy commercial freight traffic. Keep clear and give plenty of room to freighters, tankers, vessels under tugboat assist and other large craft.

Additional Resources

Department of Homeland Security: www.dhs.gov

U.S. Coast Guard: www.uscg.mil

Local Notice to Mariners: www.navcen.uscg.gov/lnm

America's Waterway Watch: www.americaswaterwaywatch.org.

Rules of the Road

It is all about courtesy. Much like a busy highway, our waterways can become a melee of confusion when people don't follow the rules of the road. But unlike Interstate 95 and its byways, the U.S. waterways aren't fitted with eight-sided stop signs or the familiar yellow, green and red traffic lights. You will need to rely on your own knowledge to safely co-exist with fellow boaters and avoid collisions.

Most heated waterway encounters can be avoided by simply slowing down, letting the other boat go first and biting your tongue, regardless of whether you think they are right or wrong. Pressing your agenda or taking out your frustrations with the last bridge tender you encountered normally leads to unpleasantness. When in doubt, stand down and get out of the other guy's way. The effect on your timetable will be minimal.

Anyone planning to cruise our waterways should make themselves familiar with the rules of the road. *Chapman Piloting: Seamanship and Small Boat Handling* and *The Annapolis Book of Seamanship* are both excellent on-the-water references with plentiful information on navigation rules. For those with a penchant for the exact regulatory language, the Coast Guard publication *Navigation Rules: International-Inland* covers both international and U.S. inland rules. (Boats over 39.4 feet are required to carry a copy of the U.S. Inland Rules at all times.) These rules are also available online here: www.navcen.uscg.gov. Click on NavRules on the top menu.

The following is a list of common situations you will likely encounter on the waterways. Make yourself familiar with them, and if you ever have a question as to which of you has the right-of-way, let the other vessel go first.

Passing or being passed:

■ If you intend to pass a slower vessel, try to hail them on your VHF radio to let them know you are coming.

■ In close quarters, BOTH vessels should slow down. Slowing down normally allows the faster vessel to pass quickly without throwing a large wake onto the slower boat.

■ Slower boats being passed have the right-of-way and passing vessels must take all actions necessary to keep clear of these slower vessels.

At opening bridges:

■ During an opening, boats traveling with the current go first and generally have the right-of-way.

■ Boats constrained by their draft, size or maneuverability (e.g., dredges, tugs and barges) also take priority.

■ Standard rules of the road apply while circling or waiting for a bridge opening.

Tugs, freighters, dredges and naval vessels:

■ These vessels are usually constrained by draft or their inability to maneuver nimbly. For this reason, you will almost always need to give them the right-of-way, and keep out of their path.

■ You must keep at least 100 yards away from any Navy vessel. If you cannot safely navigate without coming closer than this, you must notify the ship of your intentions over VHF (Channel 16).

■ Keep a close watch for freighters, tugs with tows and other large vessels while offshore or in crowded ports. They often come up very quickly, despite their large size.

■ It is always a good practice to radio larger vessels (VHF Channel 13 or 16) to notify them of your location and your intentions. The skippers of these boats are generally appreciative of efforts to communicate with them. This is especially true with dredge boats on the Intracoastal Waterway (ICW).

In a crossing situation:

■ When two vessels under power are crossing and a risk of collision exists, the vessel that has the other on her starboard side must keep clear and avoid crossing ahead of the other vessel.

■ When a vessel under sail and a vessel under power are crossing, the boat under power is usually burdened and must keep clear. The same exceptions apply as per head-on meetings.

■ On the Great Lakes and western rivers (Mississippi River system), a power-driven vessel crossing a river shall keep clear of a power-driven vessel ascending or descending the river.

Power vessels meeting one another or meeting vessels under sail:

■ When two vessels under power (sailboats or powerboats) meet "head-to-head," both are obliged to alter course to starboard.

■ Generally, when a vessel under power meets a vessel under sail (i.e., not using any mechanical power), the powered vessel must alter course accordingly.

■ Exceptions are: Vessels not under command, vessels restricted in ability to maneuver, vessels engaged in commercial fishing or those under International Rules, such as a vessel constrained by draft.

Two sailboats meeting under sail:

■ When each has the wind on a different side, the boat with the wind on the port side must keep clear of the boat with the wind on the starboard side.

■ When both have the wind on the same side, the vessel closest to the wind (windward) will keep clear of the leeward boat.

■ A vessel with wind to port that sees a vessel to windward but cannot determine whether the windward vessel has wind to port or starboard will assume that windward vessel is on starboard tack and keep clear.

Resources

The Coast Guard publication "Navigation Rules – International-Inland" is available at most well-stocked marine stores, including West Marine (www.westmarine.com) and Bluewater Books and Charts (www.bluewaterweb.com). These establishments normally stock the aforementioned Chapman's and Annapolis Seamanship books also.

(Photo courtesty of U.S. Coast Guard.)

Bridge Basics

Depending on where you cruise, you may be dependent on bridge openings; a particular bridge's schedule can often decide where you tie up for the evening or when you wake up and get underway the next day.

Because many bridges restrict their openings during morning and evening rush hours, to minimize inconvenience to vehicular traffic, you may need to plan an early start or late stop to avoid getting stuck waiting for a bridge opening. Take a few minutes before setting out to learn whether bridge schedules have changed; changes are posted in the Coast Guard's *Local Notice to Mariners* reports, which can be found online at www.navcen.uscg.gov.

The easiest way to hail a bridge is via VHF radio. Bridges in most states use VHF Channel 13, while bridges in Florida, Georgia and South Carolina monitor VHF Channel 09. Keep in mind that bridge tenders are just like the rest of us; everyone has their good and bad days. The best way to thwart any potential grumpiness is to follow the opening procedures to the letter and act with professionalism. This will almost always ensure a timely opening.

Bridge Procedures:

■ First, decide if it is necessary to have the drawbridge opened. You will need to know your boat's clearance height above the waterline before you start down the ICW. Drawbridges have "Clearance Gauges" to show the closed vertical clearance with changing water levels, but a bascule bridge typically has 3 to 5 feet more clearance than what is indicated on the gauge at the center of its arch at mean low tide. Bridge clearances are also shown on NOAA charts.

■ Contact the bridge tender well in advance (even if you can't see the bridge around the bend) by VHF radio or phone. Alternatively, you can sound one long and one short horn blast to request an opening. Tugs with tows and U.S. government vessels may go through bridges at any time, usually signaling with five short blasts. A restricted bridge may open in an emergency with the same signal. Keep in mind bridge tenders will *not* know your intentions unless you tell them.

■ If two or more vessels are in sight of one another, the bridge tender may elect to delay opening the bridge until all boats can go through together.

■ Approach at slow speed and be prepared to wait, as the bridge cannot open until the traffic gates are closed. Many ICW bridges are more than 40 years old and the aged machinery functions slowly.

■ Once the bridge is open, proceed at no-wake speed. Keep a safe distance between you and other craft, as currents and turbulence around bridge supports can be tricky.

■ There is technically no legal right-of-way (except on the Mississippi and some other inland rivers), but boats running with the current should always be given the right-of-way out of courtesy. As always, if you are not sure, let the other boat go first.

■ When making the same opening as a commercial craft, it is a good idea to contact the vessel's captain (usually on VHF Channel 13), ascertain his intentions and state yours to avoid any misunderstanding in tight quarters.

■ After passing through the bridge, maintain a no-wake speed until you are well clear and then resume normal speed.

Bridge Types

Swing Bridges:

Swing bridges have an opening section that pivots horizontally on a central hub, allowing boats to pass on one side or the other when it is open.

Lift Bridges:

Lift bridges normally have two towers on each end of the opening section that are equipped with cables that lift the road or railway vertically into the air.

Pontoon Bridges:

A pontoon bridge consists of an opening section that must be floated out of the way with a cable to allow boats to pass.

Bascule Bridges:

This is the most common type of opening bridge you will encounter. The opening section of a bascule bridge has one or two leaves that tilt vertically on a hinge like doors being opened skyward.

VHF Communications

Skippers traveling the U.S. inland waterways use their VHF radios almost every day to contact other vessels and bridge tenders, make reservations at marinas, arrange to pass other vessels safely and conduct other business. Waterway Guide has put together the following information to help remove any confusion as to what frequency should be dialed in to call bridges, marinas, commercial ships or your friend anchored down the creek.

Channel Usage Tips

- VHF Channel 16 (156.8 MHz) is by far the most important frequency on the VHF-FM band. It is also the most abused. Channel 16 is the international distress, safety and calling frequency.

- FCC regulations require boaters to maintain a watch on either Channel 09 or 16 whenever the radio is turned on and not being used to communicate on another channel. Since the Coast Guard does not have the capability of announcing an urgent marine information broadcast or weather warning on Channel 09, it recommends that boaters normally keep tuned to and use Channel 16, but no conversations of any length should take place there; its primary function is for emergencies only.

- The Coast Guard's main working channel is 22A, and both emergency and non-emergency calls generally are switched to it in order to keep 16 clear. Calling the Coast Guard for a radio check on Channel 16 is prohibited.

- The radio-equipped bridges covered in this edition use Channel 13, except for South Carolina, Georgia, and Florida, which use VHF Channel 09.

- Recreational craft typically communicate on Channels 68, 69, 71, 72 or 78A. Whenever possible, avoid calling on Channel 16 altogether by prearranging initial contact directly on one of these channels. No transmissions should last longer than three minutes.

- The Bridge-to-Bridge Radio Telephone Act requires many commercial vessels, including dredges and tugboats, to monitor Channel 13. Channel 13 is also the frequency most used by bridges in several states.

- Warning: The Coast Guard announces urgent marine information broadcasts and storm warnings on Channel 9 in the First Coast Guard District only (waters off the coast of northern New Jersey, New York, and New England). For that reason, we strongly urge boaters to use Channel 9 in these waters. Use of Channel 9 in other waters is optional, and we recommend boaters keep tuned to and use Channel 16 in those waters unless otherwise notified by the Coast Guard.

Note: The Coast Guard has asked the FCC to eliminate provisions for using Channel 09 as an alternative calling frequency to Channel 16 when it eliminates watch-keeping on Channel 16 by compulsory-equipped vessels.

VHF Channel 16— In Case of Emergency

MAYDAY—The distress signal MAYDAY is used to indicate that a vessel is threatened by grave and imminent danger and requests immediate assistance.

PAN PAN—The urgency signal PAN PAN is used when the safety of the ship or person is in jeopardy.

SÉCURITÉ—The safety signal SÉCURITÉ is used for messages about the safety of navigation or important weather warnings.

Distress Calls

VHF Channel 16 is the distress call frequency. The codeword "Mayday" is the international alert signal of a life-threatening situation at sea. After a Mayday message is broadcast, Channel 16 must be kept free of all traffic, other than those directly involved in the rescue situation, until the rescue has been completed. If you hear a Mayday message and no one else is responding, it is your duty to step in to answer the call, relay it to the nearest rescue organization and get to the scene to help.

Remember, a Mayday distress call can only be used when life is threatened. If you have run on the rocks but no one is going to lose their life, that is not a Mayday situation.

How to Make a Distress Call

Hello All Ships. MAYDAY! MAYDAY! MAYDAY!

This is [give your Vessel name and callsign].

Our position is [read it off the GPS, or give it as something like "two miles southwest of Royal Island." Your rescuers must be able to find you!].

We are [then say what's happening: on fire? have hit a reef and are sinking?].

We have [say how many people are on board].

At this time we are [say what you're doing about the crisis: abandoning ship?]

For identification we are [say what your boat is: type, length, color, so that your rescuers can identify you at a distance more easily].

We have [say what safety equipment you have: flares? smoke? ocean dye markers? EPIRB?]

We will keep watch on Channel 16 as long as we can.

VHF Channels

09—Used for radio checks and hailing other stations (boats, shoreside operations). Also used to communicate with drawbridges in Florida.

13—Used to contact and communicate with commercial vessels, military ships and drawbridges. Bridges in several states monitor 13.

16—Emergency use only. May be used to hail other vessels, but once contact is made, conversation should be immediately switched to a working (68, 69, 71, 72, 78A) channel.

22—Used for U.S. Coast Guard safety, navigation and Sécurité communications.

68, 69, 71, 72, 78A—Used primarily for recreational ship-to-ship and ship-to-shore communications.

Resources

U.S. Coast Guard VHF Channel Listing: www.navcen.uscg.gov. Click on VHS Channels & Freqs.

FCC VHF Channel Listing: *www.wireless.fcc.gov/services.* Click on Maritime Mobile.

SKIPPER'S HANDBOOK

Hurricanes

With visions of hurricanes Irene, Isabel and Katrina still fresh in the country's collective minds, more folks are tuned into turbulent tropical weather than ever. Hurricanes can create vast swaths of devastation but ample preparation can help increase your boat's chances of surviving the storm.

While all coastal areas of the country are vulnerable to the effects of a hurricane (especially from June through November), the Gulf Coast, Southern and Mid-Atlantic states typically have been the hardest hit. But northern locales aren't immune; several destructive hurricanes and tropical storms have dealt a blow to areas in New England over the last 100 years, including Hurricane Irene in 2011.

Hurricane Conditions

■ According to the National Weather Service, a mature hurricane may be 10 miles high with a great spiral several hundred miles in diameter. Winds are often well above the 74 mph required to classify as hurricane strength—especially in gusts.

■ Hurricane damage is produced by four elements: tidal surge, wind, wave action and rain. Tidal surge is an increase in ocean depth prior to the storm. This effect, amplified in coastal areas, may cause tidal heights in excess of 15 to 20 feet above normal. Additionally, hurricanes can produce a significant negative tidal effect as water rushes out of the waterways after a storm.

■ The most damaging element of a hurricane for boaters is usually wave action. The wind speed, water depth and the amount of open water determine the amount of wave action created. Storm surges can transform narrow bodies of water into larger, deeper waters capable of generating extreme wave action.

■ Rainfall varies; hurricanes can generate anywhere from 5 to 20 inches or more of rain. If your boat is in a slip, you have three options: Leave it where it is (if it is in a safe place); move it to a refuge area; or haul it and put it on a trailer or cradle.

■ The National Weather Service reports that wind gusts can exceed reported sustained winds by 25 to 50 percent. So, for example, a storm with winds of 150 mph might have gusts of more than 200 mph.

■ Some marinas require mandatory evacuations during hurricane alerts. Check your lease agreement, and talk to your dockmaster if you are uncertain. After Hurricane Andrew, Florida's legislature passed a law prohibiting marinas from evicting boats during hurricane watches and warnings. Boaters may also be held liable for any damage that their boat inflicts to marina piers or property; check locally for details.

■ Rivers, canals, coves and other areas away from large stretches of open water are best selected as refuges. Your dockmaster or fellow mariners can make suggestions. Consult your insurance agent if you have questions about coverage.

■ Many insurance agencies have restricted or cancelled policies for boats that travel or are berthed in certain hurricane-prone areas. Review your policy and check your coverage, as many insurance companies will not cover boats in hurricane-prone areas during the June through November hurricane season. Riders for this type of coverage are notoriously expensive.

Storm Intensity

Saffir-Simpson Categories

- **Category 1** . . . . . . 74–95 mph
- **Category 2** . . . . . 96–110 mph
- **Category 3** . . . . 111–130 mph
- **Category 4** . . . . 131–155 mph
- **Category 5** . . . . 155+ mph

Preparing Your Boat

■ Have a hurricane plan made up ahead of time to maximize what you can get done in amount of time you will have to prepare (no more than 12 hours in some cases). You won't want to be deciding how to tie up the boat or where to anchor when a hurricane is barreling down on you. Make these decisions in advance.

■ Buy hurricane gear in advance (even if there is no imminent storm). When word of a hurricane spreads, local ship stores run out of storm supplies (anchors and line, especially) very quickly.

■ Strip every last thing that isn't bolted down off the deck of the boat (canvas, sails, antennas, bimini tops, dodgers, dinghies, dinghy motors, cushions, unneeded control lines on sailboats—everything), as this will help reduce windage and damage to your boat. Remove electronics and valuables and move them ashore.

■ Any potentially leaky ports or hatches should be taped up. Dorades (cowls) should be removed and sealed with their deck caps.

■ Make sure all systems on board are in tip-top shape. Fuel and water tanks should be filled, bilge pumps should be in top operating condition and batteries should be fully charged.

■ You will need many lengths of line to secure the boat; make certain it is good stretchy nylon (not Dacron). It is not unusual to string 600 to 800 feet of dock line on a 40-foot-long boat in preparation for a hurricane.

■ If you can, double up your lines (two for each cleat), as lines can and will break during the storm. Have fenders and fender boards out and make sure all of your lines are protected from chafe.

cont'd

Special Notice

There was a particularly busy hurricane and tropical storm season in 2012, with extensive flooding and wind damage experienced along the Gulf and East Coasts. All of the marinas and businesses listed in this guide were open at press time (summer 2012); however, it is always a good idea to call ahead to ensure facilities are operational prior to your arrival.

Hurricanes, cont'd.

■ If you are anchored out, use multiple large anchors; there is no such thing as an anchor that is too big. If you can, tie to trees with a good root system, such as mangroves or live oaks. Mangroves are particularly good because their canopy can have a cushioning effect. Be sure mooring lines include ample scope to compensate for tides 10 to 20 feet above normal. Keep in mind that many municipalities close public mooring fields in advance of the storm.

■ Lastly, do not stay aboard to weather out the storm. Many people have been seriously injured (or worse) trying to save their boats during a hurricane. Take photos of the condition in which you left your boat and take your insurance binder with you.

Returning Safely After the Storm

■ Before hitting the road, make sure the roads back to your boat are open and safe for travel. Beware of dangling wires, weakened docks, bulkheads, bridges and other structures.

■ Check your boat thoroughly before attempting to move it. If returning to your home slip, watch the waters for debris and obstructions. Navigate carefully because markers may be misplaced or missing. If your boat is sunk, arrange for engine repairs before floating it, but only if it is not impeding traffic. Otherwise, you will need to remove it immediately.

■ Contact your insurance company right away if you need to make a claim.

Resources

NOAA Hurricane Resource Center
www.hurricanes.noaa.gov

National Hurricane Center:
www.nhc.noaa.gov

BoatU.S. Hurricane Resource Page:
www.boatus.com/hurricanes

Waterway Guide Navigation Updates:
www.waterwayguide.com

VHF-FM Broadcasts/NOAA Weather Radio VHF Frequencies

WX1	162.550 MHz
WX2	162.400 MHz
WX3	162.475 MHz
WX4	162.425 MHz
WX5	162.450 MHz
WX6	162.500 MHz
WX7	162.525 MHz

Weather

While large portions of the U.S. inland waterways are protected from harsh weather, skippers should always check the latest forecasts before casting off their lines or weighing anchor (especially if hopping offshore).

Staying out of bad weather is relatively easy if you plan ahead. The National Weather Service (NWS) provides mariners with continuous broadcasts of weather warnings, forecasts, radar reports and buoy reports over VHF-FM and Single Side Band (SSB) radio. Reception range for VHF radios is usually up to 40 miles from the antenna site, although Florida stations are frequently picked up in the near Bahamas. There are almost no areas on the U.S. coast where a good quality, fixed-mount VHF cannot pick up one or more coastal VHF broadcasts. Also, there is no substitute for simply looking at the sky, and either stay put or seek shelter if you don't like what you see.

SSB Offshore Weather

SSB reports are broadcast from station NMN Chesapeake, VA and from station NMG, New Orleans, LA. The broadcasts are not continuous, so refer to the latest schedules and frequency lists (see below) to catch them. SSB reports provide the best source of voice offshore weather information. Two major broadcasts alternate throughout the day. The High Seas Forecast provides information for mariners well offshore, including those crossing the North Atlantic Ocean. Coastal cruisers will be more interested in the Offshore Forecast, which includes information on waters more than 50 miles from shore. The forecast is divided into various regions.

On the Web:

■ **NOAA National Weather Service:** www.nws.noaa.gov. This site provides coastal and offshore forecasts for the continental U.S. and nearby waters, including Puerto Rico and the U.S. Virgin Islands, weather maps, station reports and marine warnings.

■ **NOAA Marine Weather Radio:** www.weather.gov/om/marine. Provides coverage areas and frequencies for VHF weather radio products in all 50 states.

■ **National Hurricane Center:** www.nhc.noaa.gov. Tropical warnings, advisories and predictions are available here. There is also access to historical data relating to hurricanes and tropical weather. Weatherfax schedules are available online.

■ **National Data Buoy Center:** http://seaboard.ndbc.noaa.gov. This site provides near-real-time weather data from buoys and light stations.

Weather Frequencies

UTC	CHESAPEAKE, VA NMN FREQUENCIES (kHz)	NEW ORLEANS, LA NMG FREQUENCIES (kHz)
0330 (Offshore)	4426.0, 6501.0, 8764.0	4316.0, 8502.0, 12788.0
0515 (High Seas)	4426.0, 6501.0, 8764.0	4316.0, 8502.0, 12788.0
0930 (Offshore)	4426.0, 6501.0, 8764.0	4316.0, 8502.0, 12788.0
1115 (High Seas)	6501.0, 8764.0, 13089.0	4316.0, 8502.0, 12788.0
1530 (Offshore)	6501.0, 8764.0, 13089.0	4316.0, 8502.0, 12788.0
1715 (High Seas)	8764.0, 13089.0, 17314.0	4316.0, 8502.0, 12788.0
2130 (Offshore)	6501.0, 8764.0, 13089.0	4316.0, 8502.0, 12788.0
2315 (High Seas)	6501.0, 8764.0, 13089.0	4316.0, 8502.0, 12788.0

(UTC, or Coordinated Universal Time, is equivalent to Greenwich Mean Time)

Hurricane Tracker

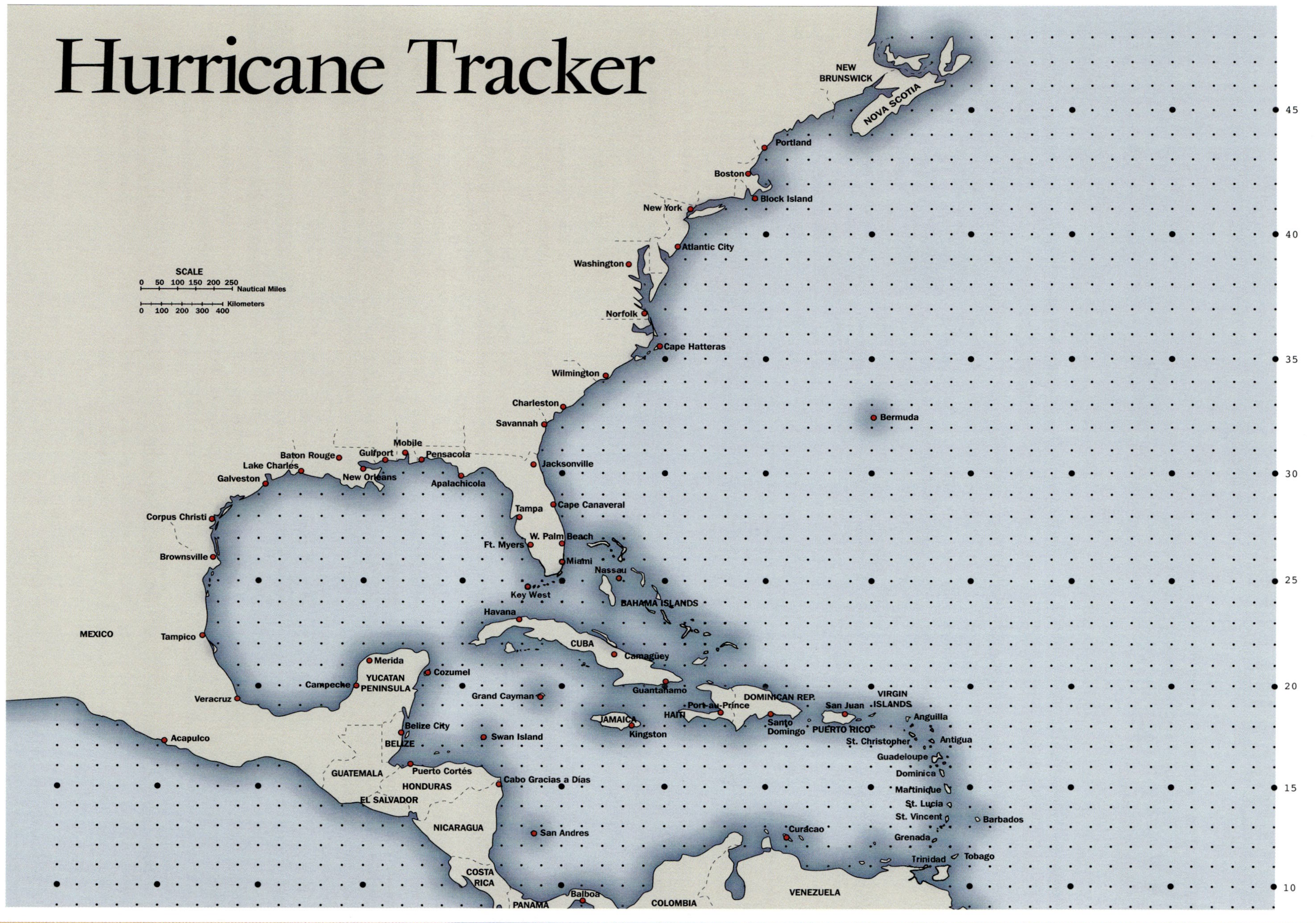

Lightning

Water and metal are excellent conductors of electricity, making boating in a thunderstorm a risky prospect. Add that to the fact that 33 percent of all lightning strikes in the U.S. are from Florida and 29 percent are from the Chesapeake Bay, and it's a forgone conclusion that staying in port during a storm is the best course of action.

The best advice if you are out on the water and skies are threatening is get back to land and seek safe shelter, but that's not always practical for cruisers who live aboard or are not near land.

Reading the Skies

Thunderstorms occur when air masses of different temperatures meet over inland or coastal waters. An example of this would be when air with a high humidity that is warm near the ground rises and meets cooler air, which condenses and creates water droplets. This releases energy, which charges the atmosphere and creates lightning. This is why thunderstorms are a daily occurrence between March and October near southern waterways.

A tell-tale sign of a thunderstorm is cumulonimbus clouds: those tall clouds with an anvil-shaped (flat) top. Thunderstorms can also precede even a minor cold front. Keep in mind that thunderstorms generally move in an easterly direction so if you see a storm to the south or southeast of you, start preparing!

Don't Wait Until It's Too Late

Almost all lightning will occur within 10 miles of its parent thunderstorm, but it can strike much farther than that. Further, the current from a single flash will easily travel for long distances. Because of this, if you see lightning or hear thunder, you CAN get struck! The ability to see lightning will depend on the time of day, weather conditions and obstructions, but on a clear night it is possible to see a strike more than 10 miles away. Thunder can also be heard for about 10 miles, provided there is no background noise, such as traffic, wind or rain.

If you see lightning, you can determine the distance from you by timing how long it takes for you to hear the thunder. Every five seconds of time equals one mile of distance. If it takes 20 seconds to hear thunder after you see lighting, then the storm is 4 miles away. This is the time to drop anchor and "hunker down."

Safety Tips

Lightning tends to strike the tallest object and boats on the open water fit this profile to a tee. The lightning will try to take the most direct path to the water, which is usually down the mast on a sailboat or the VHF antenna on a power boat. However, both sailboats and power boats with cabins, especially those with lightning protection systems properly installed, are relatively safe, provided you keep a few things in mind.

- Before the storm strikes, lower, remove or tie down all antennas, fishing rods and flag poles.
- Stay down below and in the center of the cabin. Avoid keel-stepped masts and chain plates (sailboats) and large metal appliances, such as microwaves or TVs. Remove any metal jewelry.
- Disconnect the power and antenna leads to all electronics, including radios. Do not use the VHF radio unless absolutely necessary.
- If you are stuck on deck, stay away from metal railings, the wheel, the mast and stays (sailboats) or other metal fittings. Do not stand between the mast and stays as lightning can "side-flash" from one to the other.
- Stay out of the water. Don't fish or dangle your feet overboard. Salt water conducts electricity, which means that it can easily travel through the water toward you.
- Don't think your rubber-soled deck shoes will save you; while rubber is an electric insulator, it's only effective to a certain point. The average lightning bolt carries about 30,000 amps of charge, has 100 million volts of electric potential and is about 50,000°F.

Don't Rush Back Out

Because electrical charges can linger in clouds after a thunderstorm has passed, experts agree that you should wait at least 30 minutes after a storm before resuming activities.

If You Get Hit By Lightning

A lightning strike to a vessel can be catastrophic. If you do get hit:

- **Check people first. Many individuals struck by lightning or exposed to excessive electrical current can be saved with prompt and proper cardiopulmonary resuscitation (CPR). Contrary to popular belief, there is no danger in touching persons after they have been struck by lightning.**
- **Check the bilge as strikes can rupture through-hull fittings and punch holes in hulls. Props and rudders are natural exit points on power boats.**
- **Check electronics and the compasses. Typically everything in the path of the lightning is destroyed on the way down to the water, including instruments, computers and stereos.**
- **Consider a short haul to check the bottom thoroughly. The challenge with lightning strikes is that they sometimes leave hard to find traces of damage that may only be seen when the boat is out of the water.**

Resources

Seaworthy, the BoatUS Marine Insurance & Damage Avoidance Report
www.boatus.com/seaworthy

NOAA National Severe Storms Laboratory
www.nssl.noaa.gov

Going Aground

"Either you have gone aground or you lie," say the old salts, meaning that sooner or later every boat touches bottom. Of late, cruisers transiting the Intracoastal Waterway (ICW) have found this to be particularly true because of chronically insufficient government funds for dredging.

That said, most of the ICW is lined with soft, forgiving mud (save for some coastal inlet and river areas that are typically sand), so going aground may be an inconvenience, but it is rarely dangerous, let alone life-threatening. Still, it is wise to have a plan of action and basic familiarity with the tried-and-true techniques for getting unstuck from the muck, whether traveling on the ICW or the upper reaches of the Chesapeake Bay. (It gets more complicated in areas with rocky bottoms, such as some areas in the Great Lakes.)

To avoid trouble, a prudent mariner will invest a few minutes in research before leaving the dock. For the latest updates on dredging and shoaling, visit www.waterwayguide.com and click on the "Navigation Updates" and "Cruising News" sections. These pages are updated daily with the latest shoaling and dredging updates, which are fed to our main office by Waterway Guide's intrepid cruising editors and cruisers like yourself.

What to do First

■ Throttle back immediately and put the engine into neutral. If under sail, douse and properly stow all sails to avoid being blown farther onto the shoal.

■ Assess the situation. Look back from where you came (it had to be deep enough or you wouldn't be here) and in all other directions for landmarks that might tell you exactly where you are.

■ Determine next the direction to deeper water so you can plan your escape. A quick glance at the GPS and a chart often reveals where you have gone wrong and where the deepest water is relative to your location.

■ When all else fails, it is not a bad idea to sound around the boat with your boat hook (or a fishing rod in a pinch) to determine on which side of the boat is the deeper water. Some skippers carry a portable depth sounder that can work from the dinghy during occasions like this.

■ Determine the state of the tide, especially if you are in an area with a wide range. If it is dropping, you must work fast. If it is rising, you will have some help getting the boat off.

How to Break Free

■ In less severe situations, you may be able to simply back off the bar, but begin gently to avoid damaging the propeller(s).

■ If the tide is low and rising, it may be best to simply set an anchor on the deep side and wait to be floated free. If it is falling, and you have a deep-keel boat, be sure that the hull will lie to the shallower side of the shoal so the incoming tide does not fill the cockpit.

■ Sailboats usually come off after turning the bow toward deep water and heeling over to reduce the draft. Placing crewmembers out on the rail works too. Leading a halyard to the dinghy and pulling gently can also provide tremendous leverage for heeling the boat.

■ Keeping wakes to a minimum is common courtesy on the ICW, but a boat aground can actually benefit from the rising motion of a good wake to free itself from the bottom. One commonly used technique is to radio a passing powerboater and actually request a wake. As the waves lift the boat aground, the helmsman should apply throttle and turn toward deeper water. (Passing powerboats should never create wake without a request for assistance from the vessel aground.)

■ A powered dinghy can also be used to tow a boat off a shoal. If you know where the deep water is, you can tie a line off to the bow and pivot the boat into deeper water.

■ Kedging, or pulling off with an anchor, is the next logical step. Use the dinghy to carry an anchor (or float it on a life jacket and push it ahead of you while wading and, of course, wearing one yourself) as far into deep water as possible. Then use a winch, windlass or your own muscle to pull the boat into deeper water. You may need to repeat the process a few times, resetting the anchor in progressively deeper water until the boat is free of the bottom.

■ The U.S. Coast Guard long ago ceased towing recreational vessels, but if you are aground and in imminent danger (e.g., aground in a dangerous inlet and taking on water), you may make an emergency request for assistance. Simple groundings in calm weather with no immediate danger do not warrant a call to the Coast Guard.

■ If you need outside help from a commercial towboat or Good Samaritan be sure both of you understand in advance exactly what you plan to do. Fasten the towline to a secure cleat at the bow and stand well clear of the end when it comes taut, as it can snap with deadly force.

Resources

Waterway Guide (Navigation Updates): www.waterwayguide.com
Atlantic Intracoastal Waterway Assn.: www.atlintracoastal.org
TowBoatU.S.: www.boatus.com/towing
Sea Tow: www.seatow.com

Insurance Matters

Boat insurance provides physical damage coverage to repair your boat if it is accidentally damaged or destroyed by a covered peril such as collision, fire, theft, vandalism, windstorm or lightning. The coverage is broad, and provides insurance for the boat, including its machinery, fittings and auxiliary equipment, outboard motors, boat trailer, permanently attached equipment (e.g., anchors)—up to an agreed value—and personal property. It also covers: damage caused to someone else's property; medical payments, for injuries to the boat owner and other passengers; bodily injury, for injuries caused to another person; and guest passenger liability, for any legal expenses incurred by someone using the boat with the owner's permission.

"Insurers assess the size, type and value of the boat, and the waterways in which it will be navigated, when determining how much you will pay for insurance coverage," said Loretta Worters, vice president with the Insurance Information Institute (I.I.I.).

A boat insurance policy can provide physical damage coverage on an Actual Cash Value or an Agreed Amount Value basis. Both types of boat insurance policies offer important coverage, but with significant differences.

■ **Actual Cash Value** policies pay for replacement costs less depreciation at the time of the loss. In the event of a total loss, used boat pricing guides and other resources are used to determine the approximate market value of the vessel. Partial losses are settled by taking the total cost of the repair less a percentage for depreciation.

■ **Agreed Amount Value** basis policies mean that you and your insurer have agreed on the value of your vessel and in the event of a total loss you will be paid that amount. Agreed Amount Value policies also replace old items for new in the event of a partial loss, without any deduction for depreciation.

According to the I.I.I., typical boat insurance policies include deductibles of $250 for property damage, $500 for theft and $1000 for medical payments. Higher limits may be available. Additional coverage can be purchased for trailers and other accessories. Most companies offering boat insurance have liability limits that start at $15,000 and can be increased to $300,000. Boat owners may also consider purchasing an umbrella liability policy which will provide additional protection for their boat, home and car. Boaters should also inquire about special equipment kept on the boat, such as fishing gear, to make sure it is covered and verify that towing coverage is included in the policy.

Boat owners should also ask about discounts for the following:

- Diesel-powered craft, which are less hazardous than gasoline-powered boats as they are less likely to explode
- Coast Guard approved fire extinguishers
- Ship-to-shore radios
- Two years of claims-free experience
- Multiple policies with the same insurer, such as an auto, homeowners or umbrella policy
- Completion of safety education courses

Source: Insurance Information Institute: www.iii.org

Ditch Bag Checklist

Rescue Items

- Functioning, registered EPIRB
- Handheld VHF radio (waterproof or in sealed pouch, with extra batteries)
- Sea anchor, drogue and line
- Manual inflation pump
- Selection of flares (parachute and handheld) and smoke signals
- Strobe light (may be present in inflatable PFD)
- Flashlight & batteries (headlamp is ideal)
- Whistle (may be present in inflatable PFD)
- Signal mirror
- Handheld GPS or compass (for position)
- Small pair of binoculars (to confirm a boat or plane spotting before using flares)

Survival Items

- Sponges and bailer (with handle)
- Patch kit for inflatable dinghy or life raft (or emergency clamps)
- Water (individually sealed or in collapsible containers)—at least 2 gallons per person
- Emergency food rations and can opener (if needed)
- Power Bars
- Prescription medications
- Seasickness medications/remedies
- First aid kit
- Multipurpose tool or sailor's knife
- Waterproof matches

Other Items

- Solar blanket
- Heavy-duty coated gloves
- Duct tape
- Sewing kit
- Simple fishing gear (line, jigs, hooks)
- Polypropylene line
- Waterproof sunscreen and zinc oxide
- Bug repellent
- Ziploc bags (gallon size)
- Paper and pen in Ziploc bag
- Spare prescription glasses and sunglasses (polarized to reduce glare)
- Laminated copies of passports or License
- Cash ($50 in small bills)
- Copy of the yacht's papers (including insurance)

Getting Mail and Paying Bills

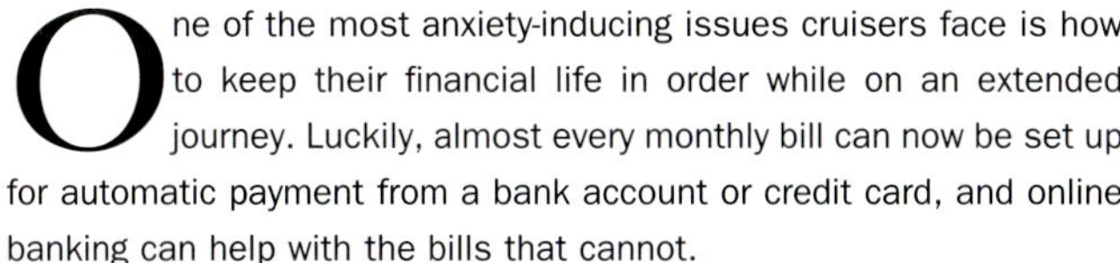

One of the most anxiety-inducing issues cruisers face is how to keep their financial life in order while on an extended journey. Luckily, almost every monthly bill can now be set up for automatic payment from a bank account or credit card, and online banking can help with the bills that cannot.

"Paperless Billing" can significantly lighten your mail load, and mail services can batch and send your mail wherever you are, when you need it. Some mail services automatically scan each envelope for you to see in your online account...You decide whether to shred, recycle, store, forward, or open and scan the contents for you to view online.

Options for Mail

General Delivery: If you have someone collecting the mail for you at home, and you plan to be often on the move.

■ Bundles of your mail can be sent by the person collecting your mail to different post offices ahead of your arrival as you move from place to place. The receiving post office will generally hold these for up to 30 days.

■ The mail should be addressed as follows:

JOHN DOE
BOAT NAME
GENERAL DELIVERY
ANYTOWN ST 12345-9999

"Hold for Arrival" should be printed on both sides.

■ In medium to large cities with multiple ZIP Codes, you'll want to make sure senders use the ZIP Code for the area's main Post Office. The ZIP+4 extension 9999 indicates general delivery. To find the main Post Office in an area, speak to any Post Office associate or call 1-800-ASK-USPS (1-800-275-8777).

■ Once you're settled, forward your mail to your new address. Just complete and turn in a change of address form or change your address online.

Temporary Mail Forwarding: Best if you are actively cruising from place to place and are using a third-party mail forwarding service. You may designate any date range up to 6 months, but you may extend it for up to another 6 months.

■ Each piece of mail is sent individually by the USPS, but magazines, periodicals, catalogs and junk mail will not be forwarded.

■ Use the third-party mail forwarding company that best suits your needs and budget.

Permanent Mail Forwarding: Best if you have slipped your land ties completely and plan to cruise indefinitely.

■ Change your permanent address to the address of your mail forwarding service.

Hold Mail: Best if you're taking a short journey (3 to 30 days) and do not expect any urgent mail.

■ You can have your mail held at your home post office and retrieve it when you return.

Premium USPS Forwarding Service: An option only if you plan to stay in one place (2 weeks to 1 year) and need frequent delivery of all mail.

■ Once a week, all of your mail is bundled in Priority Mail packaging and sent to you at a single specified temporary address.

■ Premium Forwarding includes all mail including magazines, catalogs and, yes, junk mail.

■ Mail can be sent to a general delivery address (as long as that post office accepts general delivery mail, of course).

■ There is an enrollment fee and a nominal charge for each weekly Priority Mail shipment.

■ Once you pick a temporary forwarding address, it cannot be changed unless you cancel and re-enroll.

Paying Bills

■ Set up auto-pay on as many recurring accounts that you can, including your credit cards. Remember, you can always review the bills online before the auto-payment is made, and the payment is usually debited just before the due date.

■ Set up online banking with your bank, so you can pay your other bills online. You can also set up automatic recurring payments.

■ Many companies will take credit card numbers over the phone for payment.

■ Some mail forwarding companies also offer bill-paying services.

Resources

United States Postal Service: www.usps.com
St. Brendan's Isle: www.boatmail.net
NATOMail: www.natomail.com
Earth Class Mail: www.earthclassmail.com
Mailbox Forwarding: www.mailboxforwarding.com
U.S. Global Mail: www.usglobalmail.com

Mail Drops

All U.S. post offices receive and hold mail for transients for as long as 30 days. This is only a partial listing. See Goin' Ashore sections for specific Post Office locations.

State	Address	ZIP Code
New Jersey		
Trenton	20 S. Montgomery St.	08608
Pennsylvania		
*Philadelphia	1500 John F. Kennedy Blvd., Ste. C31	19102
Delaware		
Rehoboth Beach	179 Rehoboth Ave.	19971
Lewes	116 Front St.	19958
Maryland		
Annapolis	3 Church Circle	21401
Baltimore	111 N. Calvert St.	21202
Cambridge	301 High St.	21613
Crisfield	400 W. Main St.	21817
Galesville	948 Galesville Road	20765
Havre de Grace	301 N. Juniata St.	21078
Ocean City	7101 Coastal Highway	21842
Oxford	101 Wilson St.	21654
Solomons	13946 Solomons Island Road	20688
St. Michaels	303 S. Talbot St.	21663
District of Columbia		
*Washington	800 K St. NW	20001
Virginia		
*Alexandria	1100 Wythe St.	22314
*Chesapeake	1425 Battlefield Blvd. N.	23320
Chincoteague	4144 Main St.	23336
Deltaville	17283 General Puller Highway	23043
*Hampton	89 Lincoln St.	23669
Irvington	4473 Irvington Rd.	22480
*Norfolk	126 Atlantic St.	23514
Onancock	35 Market St.	23417
Portsmouth	431 Crawford St., Floor 1	23704
Reedville	284 Morris Ave.	22539
Urbanna	251 Virginia St.	23175
Yorktown	126 Ballard St.	23690

* Post office not within walking distance of the waterfront.

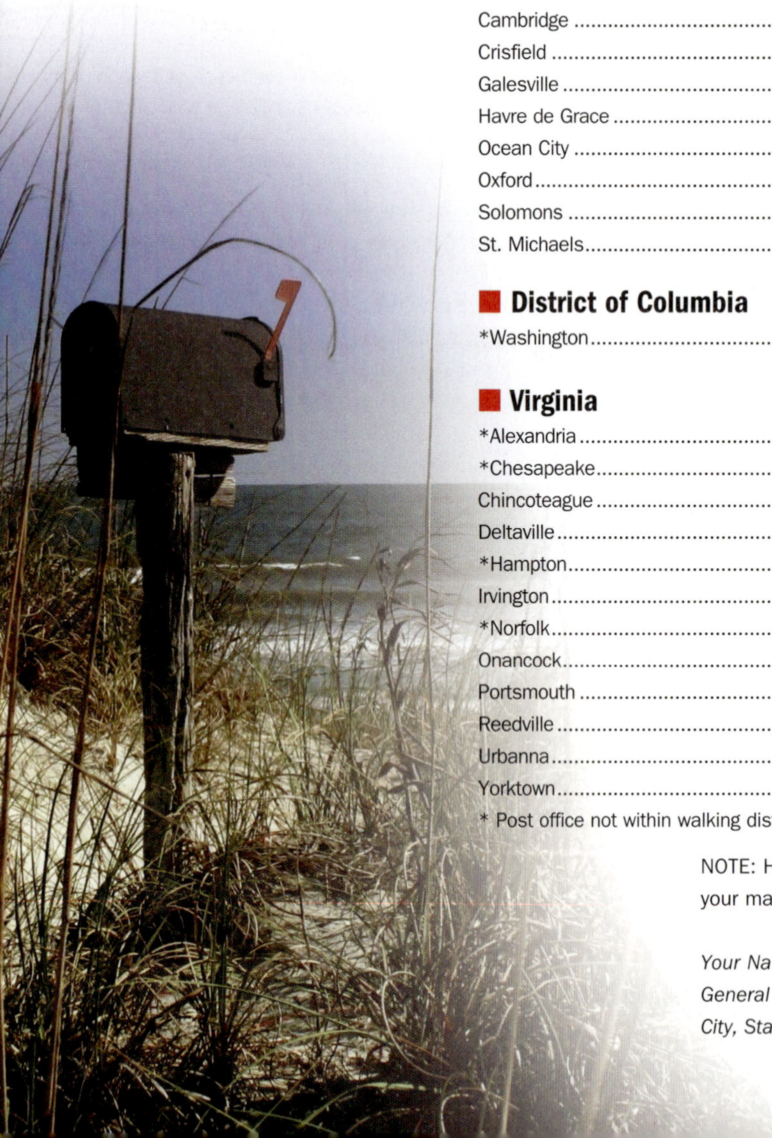

NOTE: Have your mail forwarder address your mail as shown:

Your Name, Boat Name
General Delivery
City, State, Zip Code

Vessel Registration/Fees

A Coast Guard boarding can be unnerving, but if you are responsible and prepared, it will be a piece of cake. First, have your boat in order. This includes having your vessel documentation, registration and insurance documents on hand, as well as your passport. Organize this in a binder and keep it in the nav station so you don't have to fumble around looking for documents and paperwork.

As you travel from state to state, remember that boating laws will change with the state lines, as described below. And did you know 46 states now have some form of mandatory education requirement to operate a boat? The details vary from state to state, but it's important to know that not all states accept out-of-state boater education certification for visitors afloat. In most cases, however, a boater education certificate, issued by your home state and bearing the NASBLA seal, will satisfy the requirements of the state you're visiting, either in your own boat or when operating a friend's boat there.

The bottom line in vessel registration and education is: Know before you go. Make sure you display a valid registration sticker from your home state and follow your host state's regulations. Some specifics are provided here, but visit the individual web sites listed below for additional information and updates.

New Jersey

Registration Grace Period (Days): 180 days
Boat Sales & Use Tax Rate: 7%
Credit For Tax Paid In Another State: Yes
State Decal Required For Documented Vessel: Yes
Boat Titles Issued: Yes
Boater License: All persons who wish to operate a power vessel must possess a Boating Safety Certificate (regardless of age). Out-of-state residents in New Jersey for less than 90 days with a certificate issued by their home state or country; OR written proof of completion of a substantially similar course to the NJ-approved course will satisfy the education requirements.
Boating Registration Website: www.state.nj.us/mvc/Vehicle/VehicleBoats.htm
State Tax Department Website: www.state.nj.us/treasury/taxation
For Registration Questions: (609) 292-6500

Delaware

Registration Grace Period (Days): 60 days
Boat Sales & Use Tax Rate: 0%
Credit For Tax Paid In Another State: No
State Decal Required For Documented Vessel: No
Boat Titles Issued: No
Boater License: All operators born on or after January 1, 1978, must have completed a boating course approved by the Delaware Department of Natural Resources and Enforcement Control.
Notes: There is a Gross Receipts Tax that will increase the cost of vessels purchased from dealers.
Boating Registration Website: www.dnrec.delaware.gov/fw/Boating/Pages/Delaware_Boating_Registration.aspx
State Tax Department Website: www.state.de.us/revenue
For Registration Questions: (302) 739-9916

Washington, D.C.

Registration Grace Period (Days): 50 days
Boat Sales & Use Tax Rate: 6%
Credit For Tax Paid In Another State: No
State Decal Required For Documented Vessel: No
Boat Titles Issued: Yes
Boater License: No one under the age of 18 may operate a vessel 16 feet in length or more unless they have completed an approved boating safety course, or are under the supervision of someone 18 years of age or older who has completed a boating safety course.
Boating Registration Website: mpdc.dc.gov/mpdc/cwp
State Tax Department Website: cfo.dc.gov/otr/site/default.asp
For Registration Questions: (202) 727-4582

Maryland

Registration Grace Period (Days): 90 days
Boat Sales & Use Tax Rate: 5%
Credit For Tax Paid In Another State: Yes
State Decal Required For Documented Vessel: Yes
Boat Titles Issued: Yes
Boater License: Any person born on, or after July 1, 1972, must have in their possession a certificate of boating safety education while operating a numbered or documented vessel on Maryland waters. A certificate of boating safety education is not required if a person is visiting the State for 90 days or less in a vessel from a foreign country.
Notes: Excise tax is used to fund Waterway Improvement Fund
Boating Registration Website: www.dnr.state.md.us/boating/registration/index.asp
State Tax Department Website: www.comp.state.md.us/default.asp
For Registration Questions: (877) 620-8367

Virginia

Registration Grace Period (Days): 90 days
Boat Sales & Use Tax Rate: 2%
Credit For Tax Paid In Another State: Yes
State Decal Required For Documented Vessel: No
Boat Titles Issued: Yes
Boat License: By 2016, all boaters in the state of Virginia will be required to complete a boating safety course under a "phase-in plan." Visitors using the water of Virginia for a period of 90 days or less must prove their boat is registered in another state as the "state of principal use" and meet any applicable boating safety education requirements for the state of residency.
Notes: $2,000 Maximum Sales Tax; State decal for documented vessels is available upon request.
Boating Registration Website: www.dgif.virginia.gov/boating/registration/
State Tax Department Website: www.tax.virginia.gov/
For Registration Questions: (877) 898-2628

North Carolina

Registration Grace Period (Days): 90 days
Boat Sales & Use Tax Rate: 3%
Credit For Tax Paid In Another State: Yes
State Decal Required For Documented Vessel: No
Boat Titles Issued: Yes
Boater License: Every person under the age of 26 must complete a NASBLA-approved boating education course before operating any vessel propelled by a motor of 10 HP or greater in the state of North Carolina. Those who possess a U.S. Coast Guard operator's license, temporary operator's certificate, renter's or lease agreement, or are a resident of another state or country operating on the waters of North Carolina for less than 90 days are exempt from the education requirement if under the age of 26.
Notes: Maximum tax due is $1,500
For Registration Questions: 800-628-3773
Boating Registration Website: www.ncwildlife.org/License/Vessels_Registration_Titling_Info.htm
State Tax Department Website: www.dor.state.nc.us/

Sources: *Boat US/Government Affairs:* www.boatus.com/gov/StateTaxRegistration.asp
Boat US Foundation Online Learning Center: www.boatus.org/onlinecourse/default.asp

Onboard Waste and No Discharge Zones

Up until the late 1980s, many boaters simply discharged their untreated sewage overboard into the water. After a revision to the Clean Water Act was passed in 1987, the discharge of untreated sewage into U.S. waters within the three-mile limit was prohibited. Shortly thereafter, pump-out stations became a regular feature at marinas and fuel docks throughout the Intracoastal Waterway (ICW).

Simply stated, if you have a marine head installed on your vessel and are operating in coastal waters within the U.S. three-mile limit (basically all of the waters covered in the Guide you are now holding), you need to have a holding tank, and you will obviously need to arrange to have that tank pumped out from time to time.

Government regulation aside, properly disposing of your waste is good environmental stewardship. While your overboard contribution to the ICW may seem small in the grand scheme of things, similar attitudes among fellow boaters can quickly produce unsavory conditions in anchorages and small creeks. The widespread availability of holding tank gear and shoreside pump-out facilities leaves few excuses for not doing the right thing.

No Discharge Zones

■ No Discharge means exactly what the name suggests. No waste, even waste treated by an onboard Type I marine sanitation device (MSD), may be discharged overboard. All waste must be collected in a holding tank and pumped out at an appropriate facility.

■ Keep in mind that there are some areas that forbid overboard discharge of any waste, including gray water from showers or sinks. Familiarize yourself with local regulations before entering new areas to ensure you don't get hit with a fine.

The Law

■ If you have a marine head onboard and are operating on coastal waters within the U.S. three-mile limit (basically all of the waters covered in this Guide), you need to have an approved holding tank or Type 1 MSD.

■ All valves connected to your holding tank or marine head that lead to the outside (both Y-valves AND seacocks) must be wire-tied, padlocked or absent of the valve handle and in the closed position. Simply having them closed without the (non-releasable) wire ties will not save you from a fine if you are boarded.

■ You may discharge waste overboard from a Type 1 MSD in all areas except those designated as No-Discharge Zones. A Type I MSD treats waste by reducing bacteria and visible solids to an acceptable level before discharge overboard.

■ While small and inconvenient for most cruisers, "Port-A-Potties" meet all the requirements for a Type III MSD, as the holding tank is incorporated into the toilet itself.

Pump-Out Station and Holding Tank Basics

■ Many marinas are equipped with pump-out facilities, normally located at the marina's fuel dock. Check the included marina listing tables throughout this Guide for the availability of pump-out services at each facility. Most marinas charge a fee for the service.

■ Several municipalities and local governments have purchased and staffed pump-out boats that are equipped to visit boats on request, especially those at anchor. Radio the local harbormaster to see if this service is available in the area you are visiting. There is normally a small fee involved.

■ You will want to keep an eye out on your holding tank level while you are cruising, especially if you are getting ready to enter an area where you many not have access to proper pump-out services for a few days. Plan a fuel stop or marina stay to top off the fuel and water tanks and empty the other tank before you set out into the wild.

Marine Sanitation Devices

■ **Type I MSD:** Treats sewage before discharging it into the water using maceration. The treated discharge must not show any visible floating solids and must meet specified standards for bacteria content. Raritan's Electro Scan and Groco's Thermopure systems are examples of Type I MSDs. Not permitted in No Discharge Zones.

■ **Type II MSD:** Type II MSDs provide a higher level of waste treatment than Type I units and are larger as a result. They emply biological treatment and disinfection. These units are usually found on larger vessels due to their higher power requirements. Not permitted in No-Discharge Zones.

■ **Type III MSD:** Regular holding tanks store sewage until the holding tank can either be pumped out to an onshore facility or at sea beyond the U.S. boundary waters (three miles offshore).

Resources

BoatU.S. Guide to Overboard Discharge: www.boatus.com/foundation/guide/environment_7.html

EPA Listing of No-Discharge Zones: water.epa.gov/polwaste/vwd/vsdnozone.cfm

SKIPPER'S HANDBOOK

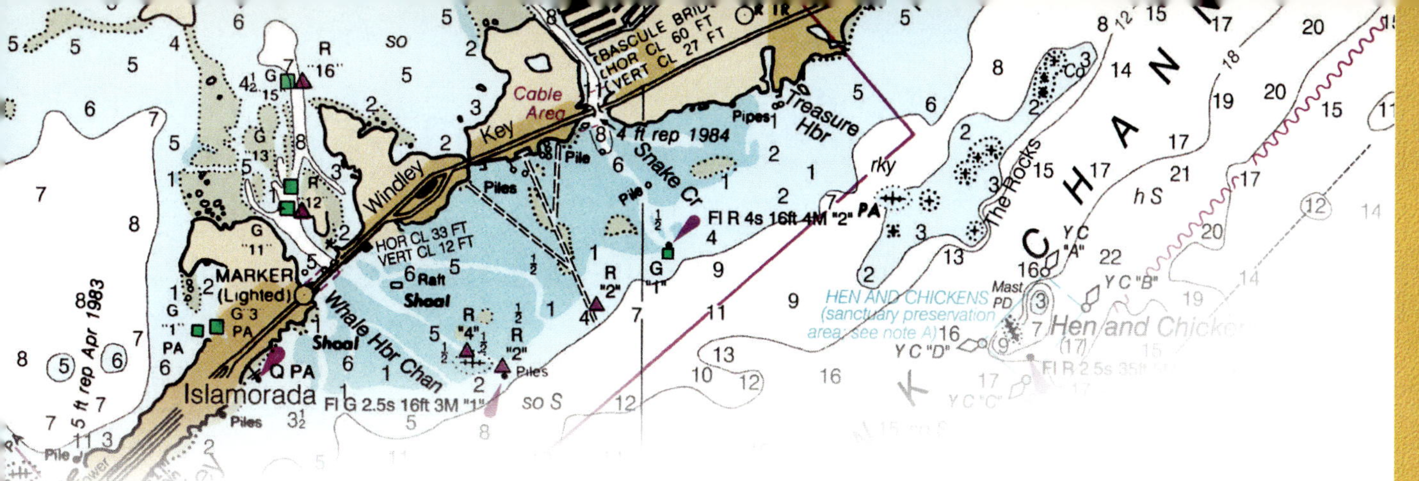

Charts and Publications

Charts are a must-have for any passage on U.S. inland waterways. Charts are a two-dimensional picture of your boating reality—shorelines, channels, aids to navigation and hazards. Even in an age of electronic chartplotters, most experts agree that paper charts have value and should be carried as a back up. ICW charts incorporate an extremely helpful feature, a magenta line that traces the Waterway's path. Some cruisers call it "The Magenta Highway."

The Internet Age

With widespread availability of the Internet, most all of the publications you will need are available for download from the government in Adobe Portable Document File (PDF) format free of charge. While this is handy, keep in mind that the electronic versions are mainly for reference and planning purposes, as they are not readily accessible while you are at the helm underway.

Once you download them, Coast Pilots and Light Lists can be printed, but since each edition weighs in at about 350-plus pages, they are best viewed online. If you think you will be accessing one of these volumes frequently, buy the bound version from your chart agent.

Most of NOAA's chart catalog is now available for viewing online. Since you can't print these charts, they are best used for planning and reference purposes. Many cruisers hop on their laptops the evening before their next departure and use these online charts to plan out the following day's travel, since they are essentially up-to-date at the moment you view them.

NOAA Charts

■ For the ICW, you will primarily use harbor and small-craft charts. Small craft charts are the small, folded strip charts that cover the ICW portion of the coast. Harbor charts, as the name suggests, cover smaller Waterways and ports. For other cruising areas, you will want chart kits.

■ NOAA Charts are updated and printed by the government on regular schedules—normally every one to two years. (Each new printing is called an edition.)

■ Third-party companies often reproduce NOAA charts into book/chart kit form. Many veteran ICW cruisers use these, as they have all the charts laid out in page order, which means you don't have to wrestle with large folded charts at the helm. Keep in mind that even the latest versions of these charts need to be updated with the *Local Notice to Mariners* to be timely and accurate.

■ Changes to the charts between printings are published in the U.S. Coast Guard *Local Notice to Mariners,* which is available exclusively online at www.navcen.uscg.gov . (Click on LNMs on the menu bar.)

■ A disadvantage of printed NOAA Charts is that the version on the shelf at your local store may be a year old or more. For the sake of accuracy, it is necessary to check back through the *Local Notice to Mariners* and note any corrections, especially for shoal-prone areas.

■ NOAA's complete chart catalog is also available for viewing as a planning or reference tool online at www.nauticalcharts.noaa.gov/index.html.

■ Even if you have electronic charts on board, you should always have a spare set of paper charts as a backup. Electronics can and do fail. What's more, electronic viewing is limited by the size of the display screen, whereas a paper chart spread over a table is still the best way to realize "the big picture."

Print-on-Demand Charts

■ Print-on-Demand charts are printed directly by the chart agent at the time you purchase the chart. The charts are the ultimate in accuracy, as they are corrected with the *Local Notice to Mariners* on a weekly basis.

■ Print-on-Demand charts are water resistant and include two versions with useful information in the margins, including tide tables, emergency numbers, frequencies, rules of the road, etc. There are two versions: One version is for recreational boaters and one for professionals.

■ Print-on-Demand charts are available through various retailers, including Bluewater Books and Charts and West Marine.

cont'd

Charts and Publications, cont'd.

Local Notice to Mariners

■ Each week, the U.S. Coast Guard publishes corrections, urgent bulletins and updates in the *Local Notice to Mariners.* One example of this is the removal or addition of a navigational mark. Serious boaters will pencil changes such as these directly on the charts as they are announced.

■ *Local Notices to Mariners* are available online at www.navcen.uscg.gov. (Click on LNMs on the menu bar.)

Light Lists

■ Light Lists provide thorough information (location, characteristics, etc.) on aids to navigation such as buoys, lights, fog signals, daybeacons, radio beacons and RACONS.

■ Light Lists can now be downloaded in PDF format free of charge from the U.S. Coast Guard by visiting the Web site at www.navcen.uscg.gov. Look for Nav Pubs and Documents then Current Light Lists.

■ Alternatively, you can order or purchase bound copies of Coast Pilots from your chart agent.

Coast Pilots

■ The U.S. Coast Pilot is a series of nine books providing navigational data to supplement the National Ocean Service (NOS) charts. Subjects include navigation regulations, outstanding landmarks, channel and anchorage peculiarities, dangers, weather, ice, routes, pilotage and port facilities.

■ Coast Pilots can be downloaded free of charge from NOAA by visiting http://nauticalcharts.noaa.gov/nsd/cpdownload.htm.

■ You can order Coast Pilots from your chart agent if a bound copy is more convenient for your use.

Tides and Currents

■ Tide tables give predicted heights of high and low water for every day in the year for many important harbors. They also provide correction figures for many other locations.

■ Tidal current tables include daily predictions for the times of slack water, the times and velocities of maximum flood and ebb currents for a number of waterways, and data enabling the navigator to calculate predictions for other areas.

■ Tide tables and tidal current tables are no longer published by NOS; several private publishers print them now and many chart agents carry them.

■ Additionally, tide and tidal current tables are available for viewing online at http://tidesandcurrents.noaa.gov.

Launch Ramps

Lists of public launch ramps operated by government agencies, both state and local, can be obtained for the states covered in this guide by visiting the web sites noted below.

■ **New Jersey Department of Environmental Protection**
P.O. Box 420
Trenton, NJ 08625-0420
609-292-2965
www.state.nj.us/dep/fgw/pdf/boat_ramp_guide.pdf

■ **Delaware Division of Fish & Wildlife**
89 Kings Highway
Dover, DE 19901
302-739-9910
www.dnrec.delaware.gov/fw/Fisheries/Pages/TidalWaterFishingAndBoatAccessAreas.aspx

■ **Maryland Department of Natural Resources**
580 Taylor Avenue, E-4
Annapolis, MD 21401
410-260-8778
www.dnr.state.md.us/boating/boatramps.asp

■ **Virginia Department of Game and Inland Fisheries**
4010 West Broad Street, P.O. Box 11104
Richmond, Virginia 23230
804-367-1000
www.dgif.virginia.gov/boating/access

■ **North Carolina Wildlife Resource Commission**
1701 Mail Service Center, Raleigh, NC 27699-1701
(919) 707-0010
www.ncwildlife.org/Boating/WheretoBoat.aspx

www.BoatUS.com/FloatPlan

1. Phone Numbers

Coast Guard:______________________________

Marine Police:______________________________

BoatUS 24 Hour Dispatch: 800-391-4869

2. Owner/Skipper Information

Owner/Skipper (Filing Report):______________________________

Phone:______________________________Age:________

Address:______________________________

Marina (Home Port):____________________Phone:____________

Auto Parked At:______________________________

Model/color:____________________Lic. #____________

Trailer Lic. #______________

3. Description of the Boat

Boat Name:____________________Hailing Port:____________

Type:____________________Model Year:____________

Make:__________Length:________Beam:________Draft:________

Color, Hull:_______Cabin:_____Deck:______Trim:______Dodger:_____

Other Colors:____________________# of Masts:__________

Distinguishing Features:______________________________

Registration No:____________________Sail No:____________

Engine(s) Type:________Horsepower:________Cruising Speed:________

Fuel Capacity, Gallons:________________Cruising Range:__________

Electronics/Safety Equipment Aboard

VHF Radio:_________Cell Phone:__________CB:_______SSB:_______

Frequency Monitored:______________________________

Depth Sounder:___________Radar:____________GPS:___________

Raft:____________ Dinghy: ____________ EPIRB: ____________

4. Trip Details

Additional Persons Aboard, Total:____________

Name:______________________________Age:_______

Address:______________________________Phone:____________

Boating Experience:______________________________

Name:______________________________Age:_______

Address:______________________________Phone:____________

Boating Experience:______________________________

Name:______________________________Age:_______

Address:______________________________Phone:____________

Boating Experience:______________________________

Name:______________________________Age:_______

Address:______________________________Phone:____________

Boating Experience:______________________________

Name:______________________________Age:_______

Address:______________________________Phone:____________

Boating Experience:______________________________

Departure Date/Time:__________ Return No Later Than:____________

Depart From:______________________________

Destination: ______________________________

____________________ETA:__________No Later Than:________

Phone:______________________________

Anticipated Stopover Ports:______________________________

____________________ETA:__________No Later Than:________

Phone:______________________________

____________________ETA:__________No Later Than:________

Phone:______________________________

____________________ETA:__________No Later Than:________

Phone:______________________________

____________________ETA:__________No Later Than:________

Phone:______________________________

____________________ETA:__________No Later Than:________

Phone:______________________________

Plan Filed With:______________________________

Name:______________________________Phone:____________

Get in the habit of filing a Float Plan. It can assure quicker rescue in the event of a breakdown, stranding or weather delay. Fill out the permanent data in Sections 1, 2, and 3. If you file a Float Plan with someone not at your home, such as a harbormaster or boating friend, be sure to notify them as soon as you return. Don't burden friends or authorities with unnecessary worry and responsibility if you are safe.

Chesapeake Bay Mileage

This distance chart was designed expressly for cruising the Chesapeake Bay where few ports lie directly on the main channel, and distances from the Bay to a selected port must be reckoned carefully. On the chart's skeletal outline, therefore, the heavy backbone represents the main Chesapeake Bay channel—from Chesapeake City on the C&D Canal (Mile Zero) to the Norfolk-Portsmouth area (Mile 190). The narrower branch lines signify distances from the main channel to some of the Bay's more popular boating locales.

Skipper's Handbook

- **GPS Waypoints 48**
- **Tide Tables 50**

Distance Table

Chesapeake City (Mile Zero) To Main Bay Tributaries

Location	Mile
Chesapeake City	**0**
Susquehanna/Northeast River	13
Sassafras River	16
Pooles Island	**24**
Worton Creek	26
Patapsco River	**33**
Rock Hall Harbor	40
Chester River	42
Severn River	**48**
Bay Bridge	49
South River	54
Eastern Bay	**55**
Rhode & West rivers	56
Herring Bay	64
Choptank River	**71**
Patuxent River	**86**
Potomac River	**111**
Smith Point Lighthouse	**115**
Great Wicomico River	**121**
Rappahannock River	**134**
Deltaville	137
Piankatank River	138
Wolf Trap Light	**145**
York River	**156**
Hampton Roads/Thimble Shoal	**168**
Elizabeth River	**178**

Main Chesapeake Bay Channel
Distances (approx.) in nautical miles from Main Bay Channel to various ports

SCALE 10 20 30 40 50

Chesapeake Bay Distances

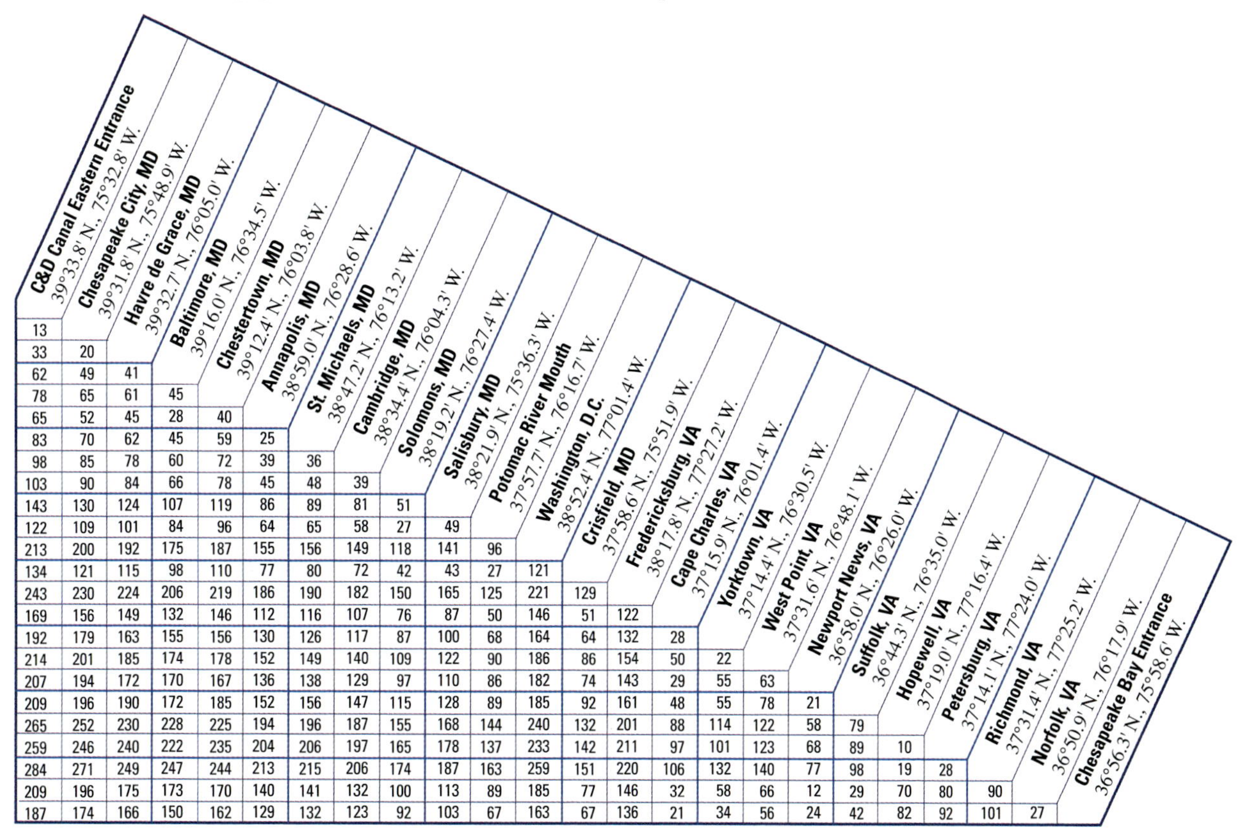

C&D Canal Eastern Entrance 39°33.8' N., 75°32.8' W.	Chesapeake City, MD 39°31.8' N., 75°48.9' W.	Havre de Grace, MD 39°32.7' N., 76°05.0' W.	Baltimore, MD 39°16.0' N., 76°34.5' W.	Chestertown, MD 39°12.4' N., 76°03.8' W.	Annapolis, MD 38°59.0' N., 76°28.6' W.	St. Michaels, MD 38°47.2' N., 76°13.2' W.	Cambridge, MD 38°34.4' N., 76°04.3' W.	Solomons, MD 38°19.2' N., 76°27.4' W.	Salisbury, MD 38°21.9' N., 75°36.3' W.	Potomac River Mouth 37°57.7' N., 76°16.7' W.	Washington, D.C. 38°52.4' N., 77°01.4' W.	Crisfield, MD 37°58.6' N., 75°51.9' W.	Fredericksburg, VA 38°17.8' N., 77°27.2' W.	Cape Charles, VA 37°15.9' N., 76°01.4' W.	Yorktown, VA 37°14.4' N., 76°30.5' W.	West Point, VA 37°31.6' N., 76°48.1' W.	Newport News, VA 36°58.0' N., 76°26.0' W.	Suffolk, VA 36°44.3' N., 76°35.0' W.	Hopewell, VA 37°19.0' N., 77°16.4' W.	Petersburg, VA 37°14.1' N., 77°24.0' W.	Richmond, VA 37°31.4' N., 77°25.2' W.	Norfolk, VA 36°50.9' N., 76°17.9' W.	Chesapeake Bay Entrance 36°56.3' N., 75°58.6' W.
13																							
33	20																						
62	49	41																					
78	65	61	45																				
65	52	45	28	40																			
83	70	62	45	59	25																		
98	85	78	60	72	39	36																	
103	90	84	66	78	45	48	39																
143	130	124	107	119	86	89	81	51															
122	109	101	84	96	64	65	58	27	49														
213	200	192	175	187	155	156	149	118	141	96													
134	121	115	98	110	77	80	72	42	43	27	121												
243	230	224	206	219	186	190	182	150	165	125	221	129											
169	156	149	132	146	112	116	107	76	87	50	146	51	122										
192	179	163	155	156	130	126	117	87	100	68	164	64	132	28									
214	201	185	174	178	152	149	140	109	122	90	186	86	154	50	22								
207	194	172	170	167	136	138	129	97	110	86	182	74	143	29	55	63							
209	196	190	172	185	152	156	147	115	128	89	185	92	161	48	55	78	21						
265	252	230	228	225	194	196	187	155	168	144	240	132	201	88	114	122	58	79					
259	246	240	222	235	204	206	197	165	178	137	233	142	211	97	101	123	68	89	10				
284	271	249	247	244	213	215	206	174	187	163	259	151	220	106	132	140	77	98	19	28			
209	196	175	173	170	140	141	132	100	113	89	185	77	146	32	58	66	12	29	70	80	90		
187	174	166	150	162	129	132	123	92	103	67	163	67	136	21	34	56	24	42	82	92	101	27	

DISTANCES ARE APPROXIMATE; FOR PLANNING PURPOSES ONLY.

Skipper's Notes

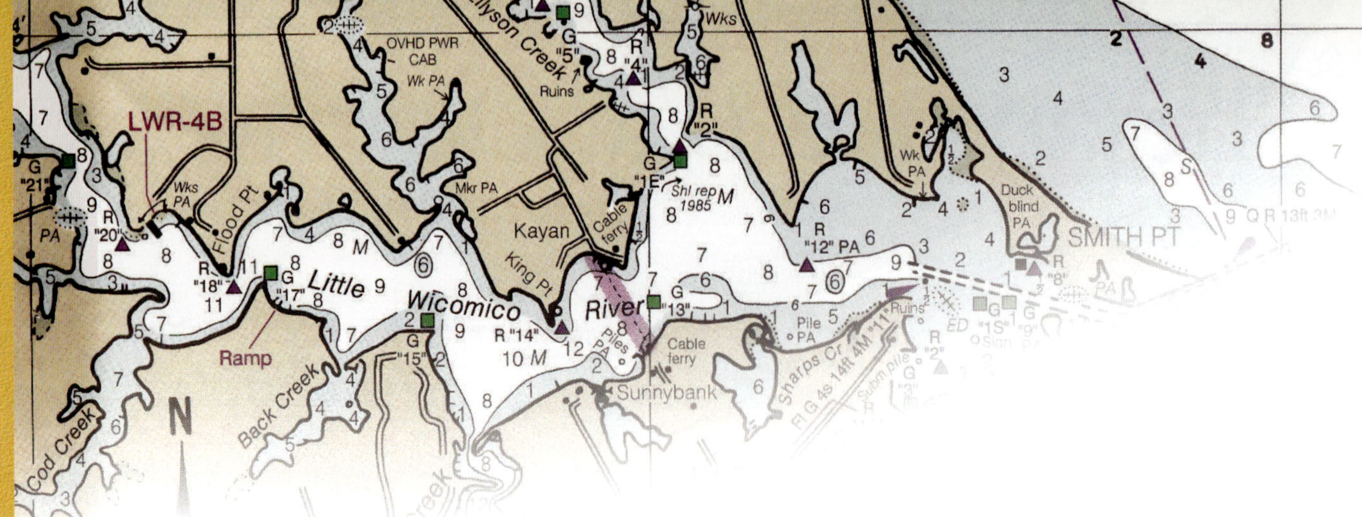

GPS Waypoints

The following list provides selected waypoints for the waters covered in this book. The latitude/longitude readings are taken from government light lists and must be checked against the appropriate chart and light list for accuracy. Some waypoints listed here are lighthouses and should not be approached too closely, as they may be on land, in shallow water or on top of a reef. Many buoys must be approached with caution, as they are often located near shallows or obstructions.

The positions of every aid to navigation should be updated using the Coast Guard's *Local Notices to Mariners,* which are now exclusively available via the Internet.

On May 2, 2000, the Selective Availability (SA) degradation of GPS signals was turned off. With SA turned on, users could expect GPS positions to fall within 100 meters of a correct position 95 percent of the time. Now, with the SA degradation turned off, users should obtain positions accurate to within 20 meters or less.

The U.S. Coast Guard will continue to provide Differential GPS (DGPS) correction signals for those who need positions accurate to within 10 meters or less. Most GPS units require the addition of a separate receiver to obtain DGPS broadcasts.

Delaware Bay to C&D Canal

LOCATION	LAT.	LON.
Entrance Channel Lighted Buoy 6	N 38° 47.550′	W 075° 01.800′
Elbow of Cross Ledge Light	N 39° 10.933′	W 075° 16.100′
Ship John Shoal Light	N 39° 18.317′	W 075° 22.600′
Junction Lighted Bell Buoy CD	N 39° 33.867′	W 075° 33.300′

C&D Canal to Kent Island

LOCATION	LAT.	LON.
Bohemia River Light 2	N 39° 28.533′	W 075° 53.183′
Elk River Lighted Buoy 1ER	N 39° 23.850′	W 076° 03.283′
Sassafras River Lighted Buoy 2	N 39° 22.683′	W 075° 59.650′
Still Pond Creek Entrance Light 2S	N 39° 20.117′	W 076° 08.233′
Worton Point Light	N 39° 19.100′	W 076° 11.183′
Fairlee Creek Light 2F	N 39° 16.250′	W 076° 12.517′
Rock Hall Harbor Entrance Buoy 1	N 39° 07.717′	W 076° 15.100′
Kent Island Narrows Approach Light 1K	N 38° 57.233′	W 076° 14.600′

Eastern Bay to Little Choptank

LOCATION	LAT.	LON.
St. Michaels Harbor Entrance Light 2	N 38° 47.350′	W 076° 12.983′
Knapps Narrows E. Channel Appr. Light 1	N 38° 41.400′	W 076° 18.717′
Knapps Narrows West Channel Light 1	N 38° 43.283′	W 076° 20.767′
Sharps Island Light	N 38° 38.333′	W 076° 22.650′
Choptank River Entrance Buoy 4	N 38° 34.467′	W 076° 22.417′
Tred Avon River Light 1	N 38° 39.900′	W 076° 11.317′
Town Creek Light 2	N 38° 41.917′	W 076° 10.083′
Little Choptank River Light 13	N 38° 33.000′	W 076° 13.100′

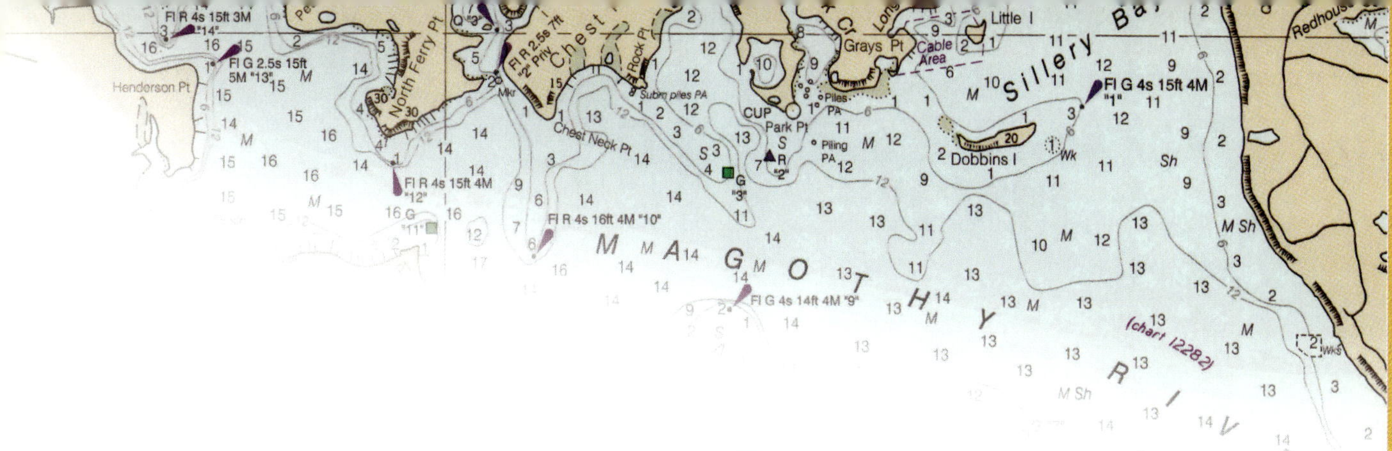

Hooper Island to Cape Charles

LOCATION	LAT.	LON.
Approach Lighted Bell Buoy 1	N 38° 12.283′	W 076° 09.333′
Hooper Strait Light	N 38° 13.600′	W 076° 04.500′
Big Thorofare Channel Light 1	N 37° 58.400′	W 075° 58.783′
Old Plantation Flats Light	N 37° 13.733′	W 076° 02.817′
Cape Charles Light	N 37° 07.383′	W 075° 54.383′

Annapolis to West River

LOCATION	LAT.	LON.
Greenbury Point Shoal Light	N 38° 58.100′	W 076° 27.250′
Horn Point Light HP	N 38° 58.417′	W 076° 28.150′
Eastport Harbor Entrance Light 1E	N 38° 57.950′	W 076° 28.150′
Lake Ogleton Entrance Light 1L	N 38° 57.133′	W 076° 27.467′
Thomas Point Shoal Light	N 38° 53.933′	W 076° 26.150′
South River Entrance Buoy 2	N 38° 53.733′	W 076° 27.867′
West River, Saunders Pt. Shoal Jct. Light	N 38° 53.033′	W 076° 28.617′

Herring Bay to Point Lookout

LOCATION	LAT.	LON.
Herring Bay Entrance Light 1	N 38° 44.417′	W 076° 30.850′
Chesapeake Beach Light 1	N 38° 41.517′	W 076° 31.267′
Flag Harbor Light 1	N 38° 27.833′	W 076° 28.283′
Cove Point Light	N 38° 23.183′	W 076° 22.900′
Drum Point Light 4	N 38° 19.133′	W 076° 25.250′
St. Jerome Creek Light 1 SJ	N 38° 06.917′	W 076° 20.150′
Point Lookout Light	N 38° 01.500′	W 076° 19.407′

North East River to Magothy River

LOCATION	LAT.	LON.
North East River Lighted Buoy 2	N 39° 29.200′	W 075° 59.933′
Susquehanna Rvr. Jct. Lighted Buoy A	N 39° 26.517′	W 076° 02.083′
Middle River Approach Lighted Buoy 1	N 39° 16.267′	W 076° 20.017′
Back River Buoy 2	N 39° 16.300′	W 076° 22.300′
Baltimore Light	N 39° 03.550′	W 076° 23.667′
Brewerton Channel Lighted Buoy 2BE	N 39° 08.917′	W 076° 19.983′
Craighill Channel Ent. Lighted Buoy 1C	N 39° 01.383′	W 076° 22.683′
Sevenfoot Knoll Light	N 39° 09.317′	W 076° 24.550′
Magothy River Entrance Light 2	N 39° 03.367′	W 076° 25.783′

Smith Point to Stingray Point

LOCATION	LAT.	LON.
Smith Point Light	N 37° 52.800′	W 076° 11.017′
Great Wicomico River Light	N 37° 48.200′	W 076° 15.983′
Windmill Point Light	N 37° 35.817′	W 076° 14.167′
Stingray Point Light	N 37° 33.683′	W 076° 16.367′

Wolf Trap to Hampton Roads

LOCATION	LAT.	LON.
Wolf Trap Light	N 37° 23.433′	W 076° 11.367′
York Spit Light	N 37° 12.583′	W 076° 15.250′
Thimble Shoal Light	N 37° 00.867′	W 076° 14.383′
Old Point Comfort Light	N 37° 00.100′	W 076° 18.383

Atlantic City, New Jersey, 2012

Times and Heights of High and Low Waters

September

Day	Time (h m)	Height (ft)	Height (cm)	Day	Time (h m)	Height (ft)	Height (cm)
1 Sa	02:27 AM 08:36 AM 02:45 PM 08:53 PM	-0.1 4.7 0.0 5.0	-3 143 0 152	16 Su	01:50 AM 08:03 AM 02:11 PM 08:18 PM	-0.1 5.0 -0.2 5.0	-3 152 -6 152
2 Su	03:06 AM 09:16 AM 03:29 PM 09:32 PM	0.0 4.7 0.2 4.7	0 143 6 143	17 M	02:31 AM 08:46 AM 02:59 PM 09:02 PM	-0.3 5.3 -0.2 4.9	-9 162 -6 149
3 M	03:44 AM 09:55 AM 04:12 PM 10:12 PM	0.1 4.7 0.4 4.4	3 143 12 134	18 Tu	03:14 AM 09:31 AM 03:50 PM 09:49 PM	-0.3 5.4 -0.2 4.7	-9 165 -6 143
4 Tu	04:21 AM 10:33 AM 04:56 PM 10:51 PM	0.3 4.6 0.6 4.1	9 140 18 125	19 W	04:00 AM 10:20 AM 04:43 PM 10:39 PM	-0.2 5.4 0.0 4.5	-6 165 0 137
5 W	04:58 AM 11:13 AM 05:41 PM 11:33 PM	0.6 4.4 0.8 3.8	18 134 24 116	20 Th	04:50 AM 11:13 AM 05:41 PM 11:35 PM	0.0 5.3 0.2 4.2	0 162 6 128
6 Th	05:36 AM 11:56 AM 06:30 PM	0.8 4.3 1.1	24 131 34	21 F	05:45 AM 12:12 PM 06:44 PM	0.2 5.1 0.4	6 155 12
7 F	12:20 AM 06:19 AM 12:45 PM 07:25 PM	3.5 1.0 4.2 1.2	107 30 128 37	22 Sa	12:40 AM 06:48 AM 01:19 PM 07:51 PM	3.9 0.4 4.9 0.5	119 12 149 15
8 Sa	01:14 AM 07:08 AM 01:41 PM 08:25 PM	3.3 1.1 4.1 1.3	101 34 125 40	23 Su	01:53 AM 07:58 AM 02:29 PM 08:59 PM	3.8 0.6 4.8 0.5	116 18 146 15
9 Su	02:16 AM 08:05 AM 02:42 PM 09:25 PM	3.2 1.2 4.1 1.3	98 37 125 40	24 M	03:08 AM 09:08 AM 03:38 PM 10:03 PM	3.8 0.6 4.8 0.4	116 18 146 12
10 M	03:20 AM 09:06 AM 03:42 PM 10:19 PM	3.3 1.1 4.2 1.1	101 34 128 34	25 Tu	04:16 AM 10:15 AM 04:40 PM 11:00 PM	4.0 0.5 4.8 0.3	122 15 146 9
11 Tu	04:18 AM 10:05 AM 04:36 PM 11:07 PM	3.4 1.0 4.4 0.9	104 30 134 27	26 W	05:15 AM 11:15 AM 05:35 PM 11:51 PM	4.2 0.4 4.9 0.2	128 12 149 6
12 W	05:10 AM 10:59 AM 05:25 PM 11:50 PM	3.7 0.8 4.6 0.6	113 24 140 18	27 Th	06:05 AM 12:09 PM 06:23 PM	4.4 0.2 4.9	134 6 149
13 Th	05:56 AM 11:49 AM 06:10 PM	4.0 0.5 4.8	122 15 146	28 F	12:36 AM 06:50 AM 12:57 PM 07:07 PM	0.1 4.7 0.1 4.8	3 143 3 146
14 F	12:30 AM 06:39 AM 12:37 PM 06:53 PM	0.3 4.4 0.2 4.9	9 134 6 149	29 Sa	01:17 AM 07:31 AM 01:42 PM 07:47 PM	0.0 4.8 0.1 4.7	0 146 3 143
15 Sa	01:10 AM 07:21 AM 01:24 PM 07:35 PM	0.1 4.7 0.0 5.0	3 143 0 152	30 Su	01:55 AM 08:09 AM 02:25 PM 08:26 PM	0.1 4.9 0.1 4.6	3 149 3 140

October

Day	Time (h m)	Height (ft)	Height (cm)	Day	Time (h m)	Height (ft)	Height (cm)
1 M	02:32 AM 08:45 AM 03:05 PM 09:04 PM	0.2 4.9 0.2 4.4	6 149 6 134	16 Tu	02:02 AM 08:22 AM 02:44 PM 08:43 PM	-0.4 5.6 -0.5 4.7	-12 171 -15 143
2 Tu	03:07 AM 09:21 AM 03:46 PM 09:42 PM	0.3 4.8 0.4 4.2	9 146 12 128	17 W	02:49 AM 09:11 AM 03:36 PM 09:33 PM	-0.4 5.7 -0.4 4.6	-12 174 -12 140
3 W	03:41 AM 09:57 AM 04:26 PM 10:20 PM	0.5 4.7 0.6 3.9	15 143 18 119	18 Th	03:39 AM 10:02 AM 04:31 PM 10:28 PM	-0.3 5.6 -0.3 4.3	-9 171 -9 131
4 Th	04:16 AM 10:34 AM 05:09 PM 11:00 PM	0.7 4.6 0.8 3.7	21 140 24 113	19 F	04:32 AM 10:57 AM 05:29 PM 11:27 PM	-0.1 5.4 -0.1 4.1	-3 165 -3 125
5 F	04:53 AM 11:14 AM 05:54 PM 11:45 PM	0.9 4.4 1.0 3.5	27 134 30 107	20 Sa	05:31 AM 11:57 AM 06:31 PM	0.1 5.2 0.1	3 158 3
6 Sa	05:35 AM 12:00 PM 06:45 PM	1.0 4.2 1.1	30 128 34	21 Su	12:33 AM 06:36 AM 01:02 PM 07:35 PM	3.9 0.4 4.9 0.3	119 12 149 9
7 Su	12:37 AM 06:24 AM 12:52 PM 07:40 PM	3.3 1.2 4.1 1.2	101 37 125 37	22 M	01:45 AM 07:46 AM 02:11 PM 08:39 PM	3.8 0.6 4.6 0.3	116 18 140 9
8 M	01:37 AM 07:22 AM 01:51 PM 08:37 PM	3.2 1.2 4.1 1.1	98 37 125 34	23 Tu	02:56 AM 08:56 AM 03:17 PM 09:40 PM	3.9 0.6 4.5 0.3	119 18 137 9
9 Tu	02:40 AM 08:26 AM 02:52 PM 09:31 PM	3.3 1.2 4.1 1.0	101 37 125 30	24 W	04:01 AM 10:02 AM 04:18 PM 10:34 PM	4.0 0.6 4.4 0.3	122 18 134 9
10 W	03:39 AM 09:28 AM 03:50 PM 10:19 PM	3.5 1.0 4.2 0.7	107 30 128 21	25 Th	04:56 AM 11:01 AM 05:11 PM 11:23 PM	4.2 0.5 4.4 0.2	128 15 134 6
11 Th	04:32 AM 10:27 AM 04:43 PM 11:05 PM	3.9 0.7 4.4 0.5	119 21 134 15	26 F	05:44 AM 11:53 AM 05:59 PM	4.5 0.3 4.3	137 9 131
12 F	05:20 AM 11:21 AM 05:33 PM 11:49 PM	4.3 0.4 4.6 0.2	131 12 140 6	27 Sa	12:06 AM 06:27 AM 12:40 PM 06:42 PM	0.1 4.6 0.2 4.3	3 140 6 131
13 Sa	06:06 AM 12:12 PM 06:20 PM	4.7 0.1 4.7	143 3 143	28 Su	12:46 AM 07:05 AM 01:23 PM 07:22 PM	0.1 4.8 0.2 4.2	3 146 6 128
14 Su	12:32 AM 06:51 AM 01:03 PM 07:07 PM	-0.1 5.1 -0.2 4.8	-3 155 -6 146	29 M	01:23 AM 07:41 AM 02:04 PM 08:00 PM	0.2 4.8 0.2 4.1	6 146 6 125
15 M	01:16 AM 07:36 AM 01:53 PM 07:54 PM	-0.3 5.4 -0.4 4.8	-9 165 -12 146	30 Tu	01:59 AM 08:17 AM 02:44 PM 08:38 PM	0.2 4.8 0.2 4.0	6 146 6 122
				31 W	02:33 AM 08:52 AM 03:23 PM 09:16 PM	0.3 4.8 0.3 3.8	9 146 9 116

November

Day	Time (h m)	Height (ft)	Height (cm)	Day	Time (h m)	Height (ft)	Height (cm)
1 Th	03:08 AM 09:27 AM 04:02 PM 09:54 PM	0.4 4.7 0.4 3.7	12 143 12 113	16 F	02:22 AM 08:47 AM 03:17 PM 09:16 PM	-0.6 5.6 -0.6 4.2	-18 171 -18 128
2 F	03:43 AM 10:04 AM 04:41 PM 10:34 PM	0.6 4.6 0.6 3.5	18 140 18 107	17 Sa	03:18 AM 09:42 AM 04:14 PM 10:16 PM	-0.3 5.4 -0.4 4.0	-9 165 -12 122
3 Sa	04:20 AM 10:42 AM 05:23 PM 11:16 PM	0.7 4.4 0.7 3.3	21 134 21 101	18 Su	04:17 AM 10:40 AM 05:12 PM 11:19 PM	-0.1 5.0 -0.2 3.9	-3 152 -6 119
4 Su	04:01 AM 10:23 AM 05:08 PM 11:04 PM	0.8 4.3 0.8 3.2	24 131 24 98	19 M	05:21 AM 11:41 AM 06:11 PM	0.2 4.7 0.0	6 143 0
5 M	04:48 AM 11:09 AM 05:56 PM 11:58 PM	1.0 4.1 0.8 3.2	30 125 24 98	20 Tu	12:26 AM 06:28 AM 12:44 PM 07:10 PM	3.8 0.4 4.4 0.1	116 12 134 3
6 Tu	05:44 AM 12:02 PM 06:47 PM	1.0 4.0 0.8	30 122 24	21 W	01:32 AM 07:35 AM 01:47 PM 08:08 PM	3.8 0.5 4.1 0.2	116 15 125 6
7 W	12:57 AM 06:47 AM 01:01 PM 07:39 PM	3.3 1.0 4.0 0.7	101 30 122 21	22 Th	02:34 AM 08:40 AM 02:47 PM 09:01 PM	3.9 0.5 3.9 0.2	119 15 119 6
8 Th	01:57 AM 07:52 AM 02:01 PM 08:31 PM	3.6 0.9 4.0 0.5	110 27 122 15	23 F	03:29 AM 09:39 AM 03:41 PM 09:49 PM	4.1 0.5 3.8 0.2	125 15 116 6
9 F	02:52 AM 08:55 AM 03:00 PM 09:21 PM	3.9 0.6 4.1 0.2	119 18 125 6	24 Sa	04:17 AM 10:32 AM 04:30 PM 10:33 PM	4.2 0.4 3.7 0.2	128 12 113 6
10 Sa	03:45 AM 09:54 AM 03:56 PM 10:10 PM	4.4 0.3 4.2 -0.1	134 9 128 -3	25 Su	05:00 AM 11:20 AM 05:15 PM 11:14 PM	4.4 0.3 3.7 0.1	134 9 113 3
11 Su	04:35 AM 10:50 AM 04:50 PM 10:59 PM	4.8 -0.1 4.3 -0.4	146 -3 131 -12	26 M	05:39 AM 12:03 PM 05:57 PM 11:52 PM	4.5 0.2 3.7 0.1	137 6 113 3
12 M	05:24 AM 11:44 AM 05:42 PM 11:48 PM	5.2 -0.4 4.4 -0.6	158 -12 134 -18	27 Tu	06:16 AM 12:44 PM 06:37 PM	4.6 0.1 3.6	140 3 110
13 Tu	06:13 AM 12:36 PM 06:34 PM	5.6 -0.6 4.4	171 -18 134	28 W	12:29 AM 06:52 AM 01:23 PM 07:16 PM	0.1 4.7 0.1 3.6	3 143 3 110
14 W	12:38 AM 07:03 AM 01:29 PM 07:27 PM	-0.7 5.7 -0.7 4.4	-21 174 -21 134	29 Th	01:05 AM 07:29 AM 02:02 PM 07:54 PM	0.2 4.7 0.1 3.5	6 143 3 107
15 Th	01:29 AM 07:54 AM 02:23 PM 08:20 PM	-0.7 5.8 -0.7 4.3	-21 177 -21 131	30 F	01:41 AM 08:04 AM 02:39 PM 08:32 PM	0.2 4.6 0.2 3.4	6 140 6 104

December

Day	Time (h m)	Height (ft)	Height (cm)	Day	Time (h m)	Height (ft)	Height (cm)
1 Sa	02:17 AM 08:40 AM 03:17 PM 09:11 PM	0.3 4.5 0.2 3.3	9 137 6 101	16 Su	03:04 AM 09:25 AM 03:53 PM 09:58 PM	-0.6 5.2 -0.7 4.0	-18 158 -21 122
2 Su	02:55 AM 09:16 AM 03:54 PM 09:51 PM	0.4 4.4 0.3 3.3	12 134 9 101	17 M	04:01 AM 10:18 AM 04:46 PM 10:56 PM	-0.3 4.8 -0.5 3.9	-9 146 -15 119
3 M	03:35 AM 09:54 AM 04:33 PM 10:34 PM	0.5 4.2 0.4 3.2	15 128 12 98	18 Tu	05:00 AM 11:13 AM 05:40 PM 11:55 PM	-0.1 4.4 -0.3 3.8	-3 134 -9 116
4 Tu	04:21 AM 10:35 AM 05:15 PM 11:21 PM	0.6 4.1 0.4 3.3	18 125 12 101	19 W	06:02 AM 12:10 PM 06:33 PM	0.2 4.0 -0.1	6 122 -3
5 W	05:13 AM 11:21 AM 06:01 PM	0.7 3.9 0.3	21 119 9	20 Th	12:56 AM 07:05 AM 01:08 PM 07:27 PM	3.7 0.4 3.7 0.1	113 12 113 3
6 Th	12:15 AM 06:14 AM 12:15 PM 06:51 PM	3.4 0.7 3.8 0.2	104 21 116 6	21 F	01:55 AM 08:09 AM 02:07 PM 08:20 PM	3.7 0.5 3.4 0.2	113 15 104 6
7 F	01:14 AM 07:19 AM 01:16 PM 07:45 PM	3.6 0.6 3.7 0.1	110 18 113 3	22 Sa	02:52 AM 09:10 AM 03:05 PM 09:10 PM	3.8 0.5 3.2 0.2	116 15 98 6
8 Sa	02:13 AM 08:26 AM 02:20 PM 08:41 PM	4.0 0.4 3.7 -0.1	122 12 113 -3	23 Su	03:43 AM 10:06 AM 03:58 PM 09:57 PM	3.9 0.4 3.2 0.2	119 12 98 6
9 Su	03:12 AM 09:30 AM 03:24 PM 09:37 PM	4.4 0.1 3.7 -0.3	134 3 113 -9	24 M	04:29 AM 10:56 AM 04:47 PM 10:41 PM	4.1 0.3 3.2 0.2	125 9 98 6
10 M	04:08 AM 10:30 AM 04:25 PM 10:32 PM	4.8 -0.2 3.8 -0.5	146 -6 116 -15	25 Tu	05:12 AM 11:41 AM 05:32 PM 11:23 PM	4.2 0.2 3.2 0.1	128 6 98 3
11 Tu	05:03 AM 11:27 AM 05:23 PM 11:26 PM	5.2 -0.5 4.0 -0.7	158 -15 122 -21	26 W	05:52 AM 12:22 PM 06:14 PM	4.3 0.1 3.3	131 3 101
12 W	05:56 AM 12:22 PM 06:19 PM	5.4 -0.8 4.1	165 -24 125	27 Th	12:03 AM 06:30 AM 01:02 PM 06:54 PM	0.0 4.4 0.0 3.3	0 134 0 101
13 Th	12:20 AM 06:48 AM 01:16 PM 07:14 PM	-0.9 5.6 -0.9 4.1	-27 171 -27 125	28 F	12:41 AM 07:08 AM 01:39 PM 07:33 PM	0.0 4.5 -0.1 3.4	0 137 -3 104
14 F	01:14 AM 07:40 AM 02:08 PM 08:08 PM	-0.9 5.6 -0.9 4.1	-27 171 -27 125	29 Sa	01:19 AM 07:44 AM 02:15 PM 08:11 PM	0.0 4.5 -0.1 3.4	0 137 -3 104
15 Sa	02:09 AM 08:32 AM 03:01 PM 09:03 PM	-0.8 5.5 -0.9 4.1	-24 168 -27 125	30 Su	01:57 AM 08:19 AM 02:50 PM 08:48 PM	0.0 4.5 -0.1 3.4	0 137 -3 104
				31 M	02:35 AM 08:53 AM 03:25 PM 09:26 PM	0.0 4.4 -0.1 3.4	0 134 -3 104

Heights are referred to mean lower water which is the chart datum of sounding. All times are local. Daylight Saving Time has been used when needed.

Atlantic City, New Jersey, 2013

Times and Heights of High and Low Waters

January

Day	Time (h m)	Height (ft)	Height (cm)	Day	Time (h m)	Height (ft)	Height (cm)
1 Tu	03:15 AM 09:28 AM 04:00 PM 10:04 PM	0.1 4.2 -0.1 3.4	3 128 -3 104	16 W	04:36 AM 10:42 AM 05:04 PM 11:19 PM	-0.2 4.2 -0.4 3.8	-6 128 -12 116
2 W	04:00 AM 10:07 AM 04:39 PM 10:48 PM	0.2 4.1 -0.1 3.5	6 125 -3 107	17 Th	05:31 AM 11:33 AM 05:53 PM	0.1 3.8 -0.1	3 116 -3
3 Th	04:50 AM 10:51 AM 05:23 PM 11:39 PM	0.3 3.9 -0.1 3.6	9 119 -3 110	18 F	12:12 AM 06:29 AM 12:26 PM 06:43 PM	3.7 0.4 3.4 0.1	113 12 104 3
4 F	05:48 AM 11:42 AM 06:14 PM	0.3 3.7 -0.1	9 113 -3	19 Sa	01:09 AM 07:31 AM 01:24 PM 07:35 PM	3.6 0.5 3.1 0.3	110 15 94 9
5 Sa	12:37 AM 06:53 AM 12:43 PM 07:11 PM	3.8 0.3 3.5 -0.1	116 9 107 -3	20 Su	02:06 AM 08:33 AM 02:23 PM 08:28 PM	3.6 0.6 3.0 0.4	110 18 91 12
6 Su	01:41 AM 08:02 AM 01:52 PM 08:12 PM	4.0 0.2 3.4 -0.2	122 6 104 -6	21 M	03:02 AM 09:32 AM 03:22 PM 09:20 PM	3.6 0.6 2.9 0.3	110 18 88 9
7 M	02:46 AM 09:10 AM 03:03 PM 09:14 PM	4.3 0.0 3.4 -0.4	131 0 104 -12	22 Tu	03:55 AM 10:25 AM 04:15 PM 10:09 PM	3.8 0.4 3.0 0.3	116 12 91 9
8 Tu	03:49 AM 10:14 AM 04:10 PM 10:16 PM	4.6 -0.3 3.5 -0.6	140 -9 107 -18	23 W	04:42 AM 11:12 AM 05:04 PM 10:55 PM	3.9 0.3 3.1 0.1	119 9 94 3
9 W	04:48 AM 11:14 AM 05:12 PM 11:14 PM	4.9 -0.6 3.7 -0.8	149 -18 113 -24	24 Th	05:26 AM 11:55 AM 05:48 PM 11:38 PM	4.1 0.1 3.2 0.0	125 3 98 0
10 Th	05:44 AM 12:09 PM 06:09 PM	5.2 -0.8 3.9	158 -24 119	25 F	06:06 AM 12:33 PM 06:29 PM	4.3 0.0 3.4	131 0 104
11 F	12:10 AM 06:37 AM 01:02 PM 07:03 PM	-0.9 5.4 -1.0 4.1	-27 165 -30 125	26 Sa	12:19 AM 06:44 AM 01:10 PM 07:08 PM	-0.1 4.4 -0.2 3.5	-3 134 -6 107
12 Sa	01:04 AM 07:28 AM 01:52 PM 07:55 PM	-1.0 5.4 -1.1 4.2	-30 165 -34 128	27 Su	12:58 AM 07:20 AM 01:45 PM 07:46 PM	-0.2 4.5 -0.3 3.6	-6 137 -9 110
13 Su	01:57 AM 08:17 AM 02:41 PM 08:46 PM	-1.0 5.2 -1.0 4.2	-30 158 -30 128	28 M	01:37 AM 07:55 AM 02:19 PM 08:22 PM	-0.3 4.5 -0.3 3.7	-9 137 -9 113
14 M	02:50 AM 09:06 AM 03:29 PM 09:36 PM	-0.8 5.0 -0.9 4.1	-24 152 -27 125	29 Tu	02:17 AM 08:30 AM 02:53 PM 08:59 PM	-0.3 4.4 -0.4 3.8	-9 134 -12 116
15 Tu	03:42 AM 09:54 AM 04:16 PM 10:27 PM	-0.5 4.6 -0.7 4.0	-15 140 -21 122	30 W	02:58 AM 09:06 AM 03:29 PM 09:38 PM	-0.2 4.3 -0.4 3.9	-6 131 -12 119
				31 Th	03:43 AM 09:45 AM 04:09 PM 10:21 PM	-0.1 4.1 -0.3 3.9	-3 125 -9 119

February

Day	Time (h m)	Height (ft)	Height (cm)	Day	Time (h m)	Height (ft)	Height (cm)
1 F	04:33 AM 10:29 AM 04:53 PM 11:11 PM	0.0 3.9 -0.3 4.0	0 119 -9 122	16 Sa	05:50 AM 11:43 AM 05:53 PM	0.4 3.3 0.3	12 101 9
2 Sa	05:29 AM 11:20 AM 05:44 PM	0.1 3.6 -0.2	3 110 -6	17 Su	12:15 AM 06:47 AM 12:38 PM 06:44 PM	3.6 0.6 3.0 0.5	110 18 91 15
3 Su	12:09 AM 06:34 AM 12:22 PM 06:44 PM	4.0 0.2 3.4 -0.1	122 6 104 -3	18 M	01:12 AM 07:49 AM 01:39 PM 07:39 PM	3.5 0.7 2.9 0.6	107 21 88 18
4 M	01:16 AM 07:44 AM 01:34 PM 07:50 PM	4.1 0.2 3.3 -0.1	125 6 101 -3	19 Tu	02:13 AM 08:51 AM 02:42 PM 08:37 PM	3.5 0.7 2.8 0.6	107 21 85 18
5 Tu	02:26 AM 08:55 AM 02:50 PM 08:59 PM	4.3 0.0 3.3 -0.2	131 0 101 -6	20 W	03:13 AM 09:47 AM 03:41 PM 09:33 PM	3.6 0.6 2.9 0.5	110 18 88 15
6 W	03:34 AM 10:00 AM 04:01 PM 10:04 PM	4.5 -0.2 3.4 -0.4	137 -6 104 -12	21 Th	04:06 AM 10:37 AM 04:33 PM 10:24 PM	3.8 0.5 3.1 0.3	116 15 94 9
7 Th	04:36 AM 11:00 AM 05:03 PM 11:04 PM	4.8 -0.5 3.7 -0.6	146 -15 113 -18	22 F	04:53 AM 11:20 AM 05:19 PM 11:10 PM	4.0 0.3 3.3 0.1	122 9 101 3
8 F	05:32 AM 11:54 AM 05:59 PM	5.0 -0.7 4.0	152 -21 122	23 Sa	05:36 AM 11:59 AM 06:01 PM 11:54 PM	4.2 0.1 3.6 -0.1	128 3 110 -3
9 Sa	12:00 AM 06:24 AM 12:44 PM 06:50 PM	-0.8 5.1 -0.9 4.2	-24 155 -27 128	24 Su	06:15 AM 12:35 PM 06:40 PM	4.4 -0.1 3.8	134 -3 116
10 Su	12:53 AM 07:12 AM 01:31 PM 07:38 PM	-0.9 5.1 -1.0 4.3	-27 155 -30 131	25 M	12:35 AM 06:53 AM 01:10 PM 07:17 PM	-0.3 4.5 -0.3 4.0	-9 137 -9 122
11 M	01:43 AM 07:58 AM 02:16 PM 08:24 PM	-0.9 5.0 -0.9 4.4	-27 152 -27 134	26 Tu	01:17 AM 07:30 AM 01:46 PM 07:55 PM	-0.4 4.5 -0.4 4.2	-12 137 -12 128
12 Tu	02:32 AM 08:43 AM 03:00 PM 09:08 PM	-0.8 4.8 -0.8 4.3	-24 146 -24 131	27 W	01:59 AM 08:07 AM 02:22 PM 08:33 PM	-0.4 4.4 -0.5 4.4	-12 134 -15 134
13 W	03:20 AM 09:26 AM 03:42 PM 09:53 PM	-0.5 4.4 -0.5 4.2	-15 134 -15 128	28 Th	02:42 AM 08:46 AM 03:01 PM 09:14 PM	-0.4 4.3 -0.5 4.5	-12 131 -15 137
14 Th	04:08 AM 10:10 AM 04:25 PM 10:37 PM	-0.2 4.1 -0.3 4.0	-6 125 -9 122				
15 F	04:57 AM 10:55 AM 05:08 PM 11:24 PM	0.1 3.7 0.0 3.8	3 113 0 116				

March

Day	Time (h m)	Height (ft)	Height (cm)	Day	Time (h m)	Height (ft)	Height (cm)
1 F	03:29 AM 09:28 AM 03:43 PM 09:59 PM	-0.4 4.1 -0.4 4.5	-12 125 -12 137	16 Sa	05:25 AM 11:21 AM 05:24 PM 11:39 PM	0.2 3.6 0.3 4.0	6 110 9 122
2 Sa	04:20 AM 10:14 AM 04:30 PM 10:50 PM	-0.2 3.9 -0.3 4.4	-6 119 -9 134	17 Su	06:13 AM 12:06 PM 06:06 PM	0.4 3.3 0.5	12 101 15
3 Su	05:17 AM 11:08 AM 05:24 PM 11:50 PM	0.0 3.6 -0.1 4.3	0 110 -3 131	18 M	12:25 AM 07:05 AM 12:57 PM 06:54 PM	3.8 0.7 3.1 0.7	116 21 94 21
4 M	06:21 AM 12:13 PM 06:28 PM	0.1 3.4 0.0	3 104 0	19 Tu	01:18 AM 08:02 AM 01:56 PM 07:50 PM	3.7 0.8 2.9 0.8	113 24 88 24
5 Tu	12:58 AM 07:31 AM 01:28 PM 07:38 PM	4.3 0.2 3.3 0.1	131 6 101 3	20 W	02:19 AM 09:03 AM 03:01 PM 08:51 PM	3.6 0.9 2.9 0.9	110 27 88 27
6 W	02:11 AM 08:40 AM 02:45 PM 08:49 PM	4.3 0.1 3.4 0.0	131 3 104 0	21 Th	03:22 AM 10:00 AM 04:02 PM 09:52 PM	3.6 0.8 3.0 0.7	110 24 91 21
7 Th	03:20 AM 09:45 AM 03:54 PM 09:55 PM	4.5 -0.1 3.6 -0.2	137 -3 110 -6	22 F	04:21 AM 10:51 AM 04:56 PM 10:48 PM	3.8 0.6 3.3 0.6	116 18 101 18
8 F	04:22 AM 10:43 AM 04:53 PM 10:55 PM	4.6 -0.3 3.9 -0.4	140 -9 119 -12	23 Sa	05:12 AM 11:35 AM 05:43 PM 11:39 PM	3.9 0.4 3.6 0.3	119 12 110 9
9 Sa	05:18 AM 11:34 AM 05:46 PM 11:50 PM	4.8 -0.5 4.2 -0.5	146 -15 128 -15	24 Su	05:58 AM 12:16 PM 06:26 PM	4.1 0.2 3.9	125 6 119
10 Su	07:07 AM 01:22 PM 07:33 PM	4.8 -0.6 4.4	146 -18 134	25 M	12:26 AM 06:41 AM 12:54 PM 07:07 PM	0.0 4.3 -0.1 4.3	0 131 -3 131
11 M	01:40 AM 07:53 AM 02:06 PM 08:17 PM	-0.6 4.8 -0.7 4.6	-18 146 -21 140	26 Tu	01:11 AM 07:22 AM 01:33 PM 07:47 PM	-0.2 4.4 -0.3 4.6	-6 134 -9 140
12 Tu	02:28 AM 08:37 AM 02:48 PM 08:59 PM	-0.6 4.7 -0.6 4.6	-18 143 -18 140	27 W	01:55 AM 08:03 AM 02:12 PM 08:27 PM	-0.4 4.5 -0.4 4.8	-12 137 -12 146
13 W	03:13 AM 09:18 AM 03:28 PM 09:39 PM	-0.5 4.5 -0.5 4.6	-15 137 -15 140	28 Th	02:41 AM 08:44 AM 02:53 PM 09:09 PM	-0.5 4.5 -0.5 5.0	-15 137 -15 152
14 Th	03:57 AM 09:59 AM 04:07 PM 10:18 PM	-0.4 4.2 -0.3 4.4	-12 128 -9 134	29 F	03:27 AM 09:28 AM 03:36 PM 09:54 PM	-0.6 4.4 -0.5 5.0	-18 134 -15 152
15 F	04:41 AM 10:39 AM 04:45 PM 10:57 PM	-0.1 3.9 0.0 4.2	-3 119 0 128	30 Sa	04:17 AM 10:14 AM 04:22 PM 10:42 PM	-0.5 4.2 -0.4 5.0	-15 128 -12 152
				31 Su	05:10 AM 11:05 AM 05:14 PM 11:36 PM	-0.3 4.0 -0.2 4.8	-9 122 -6 146

April

Day	Time (h m)	Height (ft)	Height (cm)	Day	Time (h m)	Height (ft)	Height (cm)
1 M	06:07 AM 12:04 PM 06:12 PM	-0.1 3.7 0.0	-3 113 0	16 Tu	06:27 AM 12:23 PM 06:12 PM	0.7 3.2 0.8	21 98 24
2 Tu	12:37 AM 07:11 AM 01:11 PM 07:18 PM	4.7 0.0 3.6 0.2	143 0 110 6	17 W	12:32 AM 07:18 AM 01:18 PM 07:05 PM	3.9 0.8 3.1 1.0	119 24 94 30
3 W	01:45 AM 08:17 AM 02:25 PM 08:29 PM	4.5 0.1 3.5 0.3	137 3 107 9	18 Th	01:27 AM 08:12 AM 02:18 PM 08:06 PM	3.8 0.9 3.1 1.0	116 27 94 30
4 Th	02:56 AM 09:23 AM 03:38 PM 09:40 PM	4.4 0.1 3.7 0.2	134 3 113 6	19 F	02:27 AM 09:05 AM 03:18 PM 09:09 PM	3.7 0.8 3.3 0.9	113 24 101 27
5 F	04:04 AM 10:25 AM 04:43 PM 10:46 PM	4.4 0.0 3.9 0.1	134 0 119 3	20 Sa	03:27 AM 09:56 AM 04:13 PM 10:09 PM	3.8 0.7 3.5 0.7	116 21 107 21
6 Sa	05:05 AM 11:20 AM 05:39 PM 11:44 PM	4.4 -0.1 4.2 -0.1	134 -3 128 -3	21 Su	04:22 AM 10:43 AM 05:02 PM 11:04 PM	3.9 0.4 3.9 0.4	119 12 119 12
7 Su	05:59 AM 12:10 PM 06:28 PM	4.5 -0.2 4.4	137 -6 134	22 M	05:14 AM 11:28 AM 05:48 PM 11:56 PM	4.0 0.2 4.3 0.1	122 6 131 3
8 M	12:37 AM 06:47 AM 12:55 PM 07:12 PM	-0.2 4.5 -0.3 4.6	-6 137 -9 140	23 Tu	06:02 AM 12:12 PM 06:33 PM	4.2 -0.1 4.7	128 -3 143
9 Tu	01:25 AM 07:32 AM 01:38 PM 07:53 PM	-0.3 4.5 -0.3 4.7	-9 137 -9 143	24 W	12:45 AM 06:49 AM 12:56 PM 07:17 PM	-0.2 4.3 -0.3 5.0	-6 131 -9 152
10 W	02:10 AM 08:13 AM 02:17 PM 08:32 PM	-0.3 4.4 -0.3 4.8	-9 134 -9 146	25 Th	01:34 AM 07:36 AM 01:40 PM 08:02 PM	-0.4 4.4 -0.5 5.3	-12 134 -15 162
11 Th	02:53 AM 08:53 AM 02:55 PM 09:09 PM	-0.3 4.2 -0.1 4.7	-9 128 -3 143	26 F	02:23 AM 08:23 AM 02:26 PM 08:48 PM	-0.6 4.4 -0.5 5.4	-18 134 -15 165
12 F	03:35 AM 09:33 AM 03:32 PM 09:46 PM	-0.1 4.0 0.0 4.6	-3 122 0 140	27 Sa	03:13 AM 09:12 AM 03:15 PM 09:37 PM	-0.6 4.3 -0.5 5.5	-18 131 -15 168
13 Sa	04:16 AM 10:12 AM 04:09 PM 10:23 PM	0.0 3.8 0.3 4.5	0 116 9 137	28 Su	04:05 AM 10:04 AM 04:06 PM 10:28 PM	-0.6 4.2 -0.4 5.4	-18 128 -12 165
14 Su	04:57 AM 10:52 AM 04:46 PM 11:02 PM	0.3 3.6 0.5 4.3	9 110 15 131	29 M	04:59 AM 10:59 AM 05:02 PM 11:24 PM	-0.5 4.1 -0.2 5.1	-15 125 -6 155
15 M	05:41 AM 11:35 AM 05:26 PM 11:44 PM	0.5 3.4 0.7 4.1	15 104 21 125	30 Tu	05:57 AM 12:00 PM 06:03 PM	-0.3 3.9 0.1	-9 119 3

May

Day	Time (h m)	Height (ft)	Height (cm)	Day	Time (h m)	Height (ft)	Height (cm)
1 W	12:24 AM 06:57 AM 01:06 PM 07:09 PM	4.9 -0.1 3.8 0.3	149 -3 116 9	16 Th	06:37 AM 12:42 PM 06:28 PM	0.7 3.3 0.9	21 101 27
2 Th	01:29 AM 08:00 AM 02:16 PM 08:18 PM	4.6 0.0 3.8 0.4	140 0 116 12	17 F	12:41 AM 07:23 AM 01:35 PM 07:25 PM	4.0 0.7 3.3 1.0	122 21 101 30
3 F	02:36 AM 09:01 AM 03:23 PM 09:27 PM	4.4 0.0 4.0 0.4	134 0 122 12	18 Sa	01:34 AM 08:11 AM 02:31 PM 08:27 PM	3.8 0.6 3.5 0.9	116 18 107 27
4 Sa	03:41 AM 09:59 AM 04:24 PM 10:31 PM	4.3 0.0 4.1 0.3	131 0 125 9	19 Su	02:31 AM 09:01 AM 03:26 PM 09:29 PM	3.8 0.5 3.8 0.8	116 15 116 24
5 Su	04:41 AM 10:53 AM 05:18 PM 11:29 PM	4.2 0.0 4.4 0.2	128 0 134 6	20 M	03:30 AM 09:52 AM 04:19 PM 10:29 PM	3.8 0.4 4.1 0.5	116 12 125 15
6 M	05:35 AM 11:41 AM 06:06 PM	4.1 0.0 4.5	125 0 137	21 Tu	04:28 AM 10:42 AM 05:11 PM 11:26 PM	3.9 0.1 4.6 0.2	119 3 140 6
7 Tu	12:20 AM 06:23 AM 12:26 PM 06:49 PM	0.1 4.1 0.0 4.7	3 125 0 143	22 W	05:24 AM 11:32 AM 06:00 PM	4.0 -0.1 5.0	122 -3 152
8 W	01:08 AM 07:07 AM 01:07 PM 07:28 PM	0.0 4.1 0.0 4.8	0 125 0 146	23 Th	12:21 AM 06:19 AM 12:23 PM 06:50 PM	-0.1 4.1 -0.3 5.3	-3 125 -9 162
9 Th	01:52 AM 07:49 AM 01:46 PM 08:06 PM	0.0 4.0 0.0 4.8	0 122 0 146	24 F	01:14 AM 07:12 AM 01:13 PM 07:40 PM	-0.4 4.2 -0.5 5.6	-12 128 -15 171
10 F	02:33 AM 08:29 AM 02:24 PM 08:42 PM	0.0 3.9 0.1 4.8	0 119 3 146	25 Sa	02:06 AM 08:05 AM 02:05 PM 08:30 PM	-0.6 4.3 -0.6 5.7	-18 131 -18 174
11 Sa	03:13 AM 09:09 AM 03:01 PM 09:19 PM	0.0 3.8 0.3 4.7	0 116 9 143	26 Su	02:59 AM 08:58 AM 02:58 PM 09:22 PM	-0.7 4.3 -0.5 5.7	-21 131 -15 174
12 Su	03:53 AM 09:48 AM 03:37 PM 09:55 PM	0.1 3.7 0.4 4.6	3 113 12 140	27 M	03:52 AM 09:53 AM 03:53 PM 10:15 PM	-0.7 4.3 -0.4 5.6	-21 131 -12 171
13 M	04:33 AM 10:28 AM 04:15 PM 10:33 PM	0.3 3.5 0.5 4.4	9 107 15 134	28 Tu	04:46 AM 10:50 AM 04:50 PM 11:11 PM	-0.6 4.2 -0.2 5.3	-18 128 -6 162
14 Tu	05:12 AM 11:09 AM 04:54 PM 11:12 PM	0.4 3.4 0.7 4.3	12 104 21 131	29 W	05:41 AM 11:50 AM 05:51 PM	-0.5 4.1 0.0	-15 125 0
15 W	05:54 AM 11:54 AM 05:38 PM 11:54 PM	0.6 3.3 0.8 4.1	18 101 24 125	30 Th	12:09 AM 06:38 AM 12:52 PM 06:55 PM	5.0 -0.3 4.1 0.2	152 -9 125 6
				31 F	01:09 AM 07:36 AM 01:56 PM 08:01 PM	4.6 -0.1 4.1 0.4	140 -3 125 12

June

Day	Time (h m)	Height (ft)	Height (cm)	Day	Time (h m)	Height (ft)	Height (cm)
1 Sa	02:11 AM 08:33 AM 02:59 PM 09:07 PM	4.3 0.0 4.1 0.5	131 0 125 15	16 Su	12:50 AM 07:24 AM 01:46 PM 07:51 PM	3.9 0.4 3.8 0.9	119 12 116 27
2 Su	03:13 AM 09:28 AM 03:58 PM 10:10 PM	4.1 0.1 4.3 0.5	125 3 131 15	17 M	01:44 AM 08:13 AM 02:42 PM 08:55 PM	3.8 0.4 4.0 0.7	116 12 122 21
3 M	04:12 AM 10:21 AM 04:51 PM 11:08 PM	3.9 0.2 4.4 0.4	119 6 134 12	18 Tu	02:45 AM 09:07 AM 03:40 PM 09:59 PM	3.7 0.2 4.4 0.5	113 6 134 15
4 Tu	05:07 AM 11:09 AM 05:39 PM	3.8 0.2 4.5	116 6 137	19 W	03:49 AM 10:04 AM 04:37 PM 11:00 PM	3.8 0.1 4.7 0.2	116 3 143 6
5 W	12:00 AM 05:56 AM 11:54 AM 06:23 PM	0.4 3.7 0.2 4.6	12 113 6 140	20 Th	04:53 AM 11:00 AM 05:34 PM 11:59 PM	3.8 -0.1 5.1 -0.1	116 -3 155 -3
6 Th	12:47 AM 06:42 AM 12:37 PM 07:03 PM	0.3 3.7 0.2 4.7	9 113 6 143	21 F	05:54 AM 11:57 AM 06:28 PM	4.0 -0.3 5.4	122 -9 165
7 F	01:31 AM 07:25 AM 01:17 PM 07:41 PM	0.2 3.7 0.3 4.8	6 113 9 146	22 Sa	12:56 AM 06:52 AM 12:53 PM 07:22 PM	-0.4 4.1 -0.5 5.7	-12 125 -15 174
8 Sa	02:12 AM 08:06 AM 01:56 PM 08:18 PM	0.2 3.7 0.3 4.8	6 113 9 146	23 Su	01:50 AM 07:49 AM 01:48 PM 08:15 PM	-0.6 4.3 -0.6 5.8	-18 131 -18 177
9 Su	02:52 AM 08:46 AM 02:34 PM 08:55 PM	0.2 3.7 0.3 4.7	6 113 9 143	24 M	02:43 AM 08:44 AM 02:44 PM 09:08 PM	-0.7 4.4 -0.6 5.8	-21 134 -18 177
10 M	03:30 AM 09:25 AM 03:11 PM 09:32 PM	0.2 3.6 0.4 4.7	6 110 12 143	25 Tu	03:35 AM 09:39 AM 03:40 PM 10:00 PM	-0.8 4.4 -0.5 5.6	-24 134 -15 171
11 Tu	04:08 AM 10:05 AM 03:49 PM 10:08 PM	0.3 3.6 0.5 4.6	9 110 15 140	26 W	04:28 AM 10:34 AM 04:36 PM 10:53 PM	-0.7 4.4 -0.3 5.3	-21 134 -9 162
12 W	04:44 AM 10:44 AM 04:28 PM 10:44 PM	0.3 3.5 0.6 4.4	9 107 18 134	27 Th	05:20 AM 11:31 AM 05:35 PM 11:47 PM	-0.6 4.4 -0.1 4.9	-18 134 -3 149
13 Th	05:21 AM 11:25 AM 05:10 PM 11:22 PM	0.4 3.5 0.7 4.2	12 107 21 128	28 F	06:12 AM 12:29 PM 06:35 PM	-0.4 4.3 0.2	-12 131 6
14 F	05:59 AM 12:07 PM 05:57 PM	0.5 3.5 0.8	15 107 24	29 Sa	12:43 AM 07:06 AM 01:28 PM 07:38 PM	4.5 -0.1 4.3 0.5	137 -3 131 15
15 Sa	12:03 AM 06:39 AM 12:54 PM 06:51 PM	4.1 0.5 3.6 0.9	125 15 110 27	30 Su	01:41 AM 07:59 AM 02:27 PM 08:41 PM	4.1 0.1 4.2 0.6	125 3 128 18

Heights are referred to mean lower water which is the chart datum of sounding. All times are local. Daylight Saving Time has been used when needed.

Atlantic City, New Jersey, 2013

Times and Heights of High and Low Waters

July

Day	Time (h m)	Height (ft)	Height (cm)	Day	Time (h m)	Height (ft)	Height (cm)
1 M	02:40 AM 08:53 AM 03:25 PM 09:44 PM	3.8 0.3 4.2 0.7	116 9 128 21	16 Tu	01:10 AM 07:36 AM 02:06 PM 08:27 PM	3.8 0.3 4.3 0.7	116 9 131 21
2 Tu	03:39 AM 09:45 AM 04:19 PM 10:42 PM	3.6 0.4 4.3 0.7	110 12 131 21	17 W	02:12 AM 08:34 AM 03:09 PM 09:35 PM	3.7 0.3 4.6 0.6	113 9 140 18
3 W	04:35 AM 10:35 AM 05:09 PM 11:36 PM	3.5 0.5 4.4 0.6	107 15 134 18	18 Th	03:22 AM 09:36 AM 04:12 PM 10:40 PM	3.7 0.1 4.9 0.3	113 3 149 9
4 Th	05:28 AM 11:23 AM 05:55 PM	3.5 0.5 4.5	107 15 137	19 F	04:32 AM 10:39 AM 05:13 PM 11:41 PM	3.8 0.0 5.2 0.0	116 0 158 0
5 F	12:24 AM 06:16 AM 12:07 PM 06:37 PM	0.5 3.5 0.4 4.6	15 107 12 140	20 Sa	05:37 AM 11:40 AM 06:12 PM	4.0 -0.2 5.5	122 -6 168
6 Sa	01:08 AM 07:00 AM 12:50 PM 07:17 PM	0.4 3.6 0.4 4.7	12 110 12 143	21 Su	12:39 AM 06:38 AM 12:39 PM 07:07 PM	-0.3 4.2 -0.4 5.7	-9 128 -12 174
7 Su	01:49 AM 07:42 AM 01:30 PM 07:55 PM	0.3 3.6 0.4 4.8	9 110 12 146	22 M	01:33 AM 07:34 AM 01:35 PM 08:00 PM	-0.5 4.4 -0.5 5.8	-15 134 -15 177
8 M	02:27 AM 08:22 AM 02:09 PM 08:32 PM	0.3 3.7 0.4 4.8	9 113 12 146	23 Tu	02:24 AM 08:29 AM 02:31 PM 08:51 PM	-0.7 4.6 -0.6 5.7	-21 140 -18 174
9 Tu	03:04 AM 09:01 AM 02:48 PM 09:08 PM	0.2 3.7 0.4 4.7	6 113 12 143	24 W	03:15 AM 09:21 AM 03:25 PM 09:41 PM	-0.7 4.7 -0.5 5.5	-21 143 -15 168
10 W	03:39 AM 09:39 AM 03:26 PM 09:43 PM	0.2 3.8 0.4 4.6	6 116 12 140	25 Th	04:04 AM 10:13 AM 04:19 PM 10:31 PM	-0.6 4.7 -0.3 5.2	-18 143 -9 158
11 Th	04:13 AM 10:16 AM 04:05 PM 10:17 PM	0.2 3.8 0.5 4.5	6 116 15 137	26 F	04:52 AM 11:05 AM 05:14 PM 11:21 PM	-0.5 4.7 0.0 4.8	-15 143 0 146
12 F	04:46 AM 10:54 AM 04:46 PM 10:52 PM	0.3 3.8 0.6 4.4	9 116 18 134	27 Sa	05:41 AM 11:57 AM 06:10 PM	-0.2 4.5 0.3	-6 137 9
13 Sa	05:22 AM 11:33 AM 05:32 PM 11:31 PM	0.3 3.9 0.7 4.2	9 119 21 128	28 Su	12:13 AM 06:30 AM 12:51 PM 07:09 PM	4.4 0.1 4.4 0.6	134 3 134 18
14 Su	06:00 AM 12:17 PM 06:23 PM	0.3 4.0 0.7	9 122 21	29 M	01:07 AM 07:21 AM 01:47 PM 08:10 PM	4.0 0.3 4.3 0.8	122 9 131 24
15 M	12:16 AM 06:45 AM 01:08 PM 07:22 PM	4.0 0.3 4.1 0.8	122 9 125 24	30 Tu	02:04 AM 08:13 AM 02:45 PM 09:12 PM	3.7 0.6 4.2 0.9	113 18 128 27
				31 W	03:04 AM 09:07 AM 03:42 PM 10:12 PM	3.5 0.7 4.2 0.9	107 21 128 27

August

Day	Time (h m)	Height (ft)	Height (cm)	Day	Time (h m)	Height (ft)	Height (cm)
1 Th	04:03 AM 10:00 AM 04:35 PM 11:07 PM	3.4 0.8 4.3 0.9	104 24 131 27	16 F	03:08 AM 09:19 AM 03:55 PM 10:24 PM	3.7 0.3 4.9 0.4	113 9 149 12
2 F	04:58 AM 10:51 AM 05:24 PM 11:56 PM	3.4 0.7 4.4 0.7	104 21 134 21	17 Sa	04:21 AM 10:26 AM 04:59 PM 11:25 PM	3.8 0.2 5.2 0.1	116 6 158 3
3 Sa	05:48 AM 11:39 AM 06:09 PM	3.5 0.7 4.5	107 21 137	18 Su	05:27 AM 11:29 AM 05:58 PM	4.1 -0.1 5.4	125 -3 165
4 Su	12:39 AM 06:33 AM 12:23 PM 06:50 PM	0.6 3.6 0.5 4.7	18 110 15 143	19 M	12:21 AM 06:26 AM 12:28 PM 06:52 PM	-0.2 4.4 -0.3 5.6	-6 134 -9 171
5 M	01:19 AM 07:15 AM 01:05 PM 07:29 PM	0.5 3.8 0.4 4.8	15 116 12 146	20 Tu	01:13 AM 07:20 AM 01:24 PM 07:43 PM	-0.4 4.7 -0.4 5.6	-12 143 -12 171
6 Tu	01:56 AM 07:55 AM 01:45 PM 08:06 PM	0.3 3.9 0.4 4.8	9 119 12 146	21 W	02:02 AM 08:11 AM 02:17 PM 08:32 PM	-0.5 4.9 -0.5 5.5	-15 149 -15 168
7 W	02:31 AM 08:33 AM 02:24 PM 08:41 PM	0.3 4.0 0.3 4.8	9 122 9 146	22 Th	02:49 AM 08:59 AM 03:08 PM 09:19 PM	-0.5 5.0 -0.4 5.3	-15 152 -12 162
8 Th	03:04 AM 09:09 AM 03:03 PM 09:16 PM	0.2 4.1 0.3 4.7	6 125 9 143	23 F	03:35 AM 09:47 AM 03:59 PM 10:06 PM	-0.4 5.0 -0.2 5.0	-12 152 -6 152
9 F	03:37 AM 09:45 AM 03:43 PM 09:50 PM	0.2 4.2 0.4 4.6	6 128 12 140	24 Sa	04:20 AM 10:34 AM 04:50 PM 10:52 PM	-0.2 4.9 0.1 4.7	-6 149 3 143
10 Sa	04:11 AM 10:22 AM 04:25 PM 10:26 PM	0.2 4.3 0.4 4.4	6 131 12 134	25 Su	05:05 AM 11:21 AM 05:42 PM 11:40 PM	0.0 4.7 0.4 4.3	0 143 12 131
11 Su	04:47 AM 11:01 AM 05:11 PM 11:06 PM	0.2 4.4 0.5 4.2	6 134 15 128	26 M	05:51 AM 12:10 PM 06:36 PM	0.4 4.5 0.7	12 137 21
12 M	05:27 AM 11:46 AM 06:03 PM 11:52 PM	0.3 4.4 0.6 4.0	9 134 18 122	27 Tu	12:31 AM 06:39 AM 01:02 PM 07:34 PM	3.9 0.6 4.3 0.9	119 18 131 27
13 Tu	06:14 AM 12:38 PM 07:02 PM	0.3 4.5 0.7	9 137 21	28 W	01:27 AM 07:31 AM 01:59 PM 08:35 PM	3.6 0.9 4.2 1.1	110 27 128 34
14 W	12:47 AM 07:08 AM 01:39 PM 08:09 PM	3.8 0.4 4.6 0.7	116 12 140 21	29 Th	02:27 AM 08:26 AM 02:59 PM 09:36 PM	3.4 1.0 4.1 1.1	104 30 125 34
15 Th	01:54 AM 08:11 AM 02:47 PM 09:18 PM	3.7 0.4 4.7 0.6	113 12 143 18	30 F	03:29 AM 09:24 AM 03:56 PM 10:32 PM	3.4 1.1 4.2 1.1	104 34 128 34
				31 Sa	04:27 AM 10:18 AM 04:49 PM 11:21 PM	3.4 1.0 4.3 0.9	104 30 131 27

September

Day	Time (h m)	Height (ft)	Height (cm)	Day	Time (h m)	Height (ft)	Height (cm)
1 Su	05:18 AM 11:09 AM 05:36 PM	3.6 0.8 4.5	110 24 137	16 M	05:19 AM 11:21 AM 05:43 PM	4.3 0.1 5.2	131 3 158
2 M	12:04 AM 06:03 AM 11:55 AM 06:19 PM	0.7 3.8 0.7 4.6	21 116 21 140	17 Tu	12:02 AM 06:14 AM 12:19 PM 06:36 PM	-0.1 4.7 -0.1 5.3	-3 143 -3 162
3 Tu	12:43 AM 06:45 AM 12:39 PM 06:58 PM	0.6 4.0 0.5 4.7	18 122 15 143	18 W	12:51 AM 07:04 AM 01:12 PM 07:25 PM	-0.3 4.9 -0.2 5.3	-9 149 -6 162
4 W	01:18 AM 07:24 AM 01:20 PM 07:36 PM	0.4 4.3 0.4 4.8	12 131 12 146	19 Th	01:37 AM 07:51 AM 02:02 PM 08:11 PM	-0.4 5.1 -0.3 5.2	-12 155 -9 158
5 Th	01:53 AM 08:01 AM 02:00 PM 08:12 PM	0.3 4.5 0.3 4.8	9 137 9 146	20 F	02:22 AM 08:35 AM 02:50 PM 08:56 PM	-0.3 5.2 -0.2 5.0	-9 158 -6 152
6 F	02:27 AM 08:38 AM 02:41 PM 08:48 PM	0.2 4.6 0.2 4.7	6 140 6 143	21 Sa	03:04 AM 09:18 AM 03:38 PM 09:39 PM	-0.2 5.2 -0.1 4.7	-6 158 -3 143
7 Sa	03:01 AM 09:14 AM 03:22 PM 09:24 PM	0.1 4.7 0.2 4.6	3 143 6 140	22 Su	03:46 AM 10:01 AM 04:25 PM 10:23 PM	0.0 5.0 0.2 4.4	0 152 6 134
8 Su	03:37 AM 09:52 AM 04:06 PM 10:03 PM	0.1 4.8 0.3 4.5	3 146 9 137	23 M	04:28 AM 10:43 AM 05:13 PM 11:08 PM	0.3 4.8 0.5 4.1	9 146 15 125
9 M	04:16 AM 10:34 AM 04:54 PM 10:47 PM	0.2 4.9 0.4 4.2	6 149 12 128	24 Tu	05:11 AM 11:28 AM 06:03 PM 11:56 PM	0.6 4.6 0.7 3.8	18 140 21 116
10 Tu	05:00 AM 11:22 AM 05:48 PM 11:37 PM	0.3 4.8 0.5 4.0	9 146 15 122	25 W	05:56 AM 12:16 PM 06:57 PM	0.9 4.4 1.0	27 134 30
11 W	05:51 AM 12:17 PM 06:49 PM	0.4 4.8 0.6	12 146 18	26 Th	12:49 AM 06:46 AM 01:10 PM 07:55 PM	3.5 1.1 4.2 1.1	107 34 128 34
12 Th	12:37 AM 06:51 AM 01:21 PM 07:56 PM	3.8 0.5 4.8 0.6	116 15 146 18	27 F	01:49 AM 07:43 AM 02:10 PM 08:54 PM	3.4 1.2 4.1 1.2	104 37 125 37
13 F	01:49 AM 07:59 AM 02:32 PM 09:04 PM	3.7 0.6 4.8 0.6	113 18 146 18	28 Sa	02:52 AM 08:43 AM 03:10 PM 09:49 PM	3.3 1.2 4.1 1.1	101 37 125 34
14 Sa	03:05 AM 09:11 AM 03:42 PM 10:09 PM	3.8 0.5 4.9 0.4	116 15 149 12	29 Su	03:51 AM 09:41 AM 04:06 PM 10:37 PM	3.5 1.1 4.2 1.0	107 34 128 30
15 Su	04:16 AM 10:19 AM 04:46 PM 11:08 PM	4.0 0.3 5.1 0.1	122 9 155 3	30 M	04:43 AM 10:35 AM 04:56 PM 11:20 PM	3.7 1.0 4.3 0.8	113 30 131 24

October

Day	Time (h m)	Height (ft)	Height (cm)	Day	Time (h m)	Height (ft)	Height (cm)
1 Tu	05:29 AM 11:24 AM 05:41 PM 11:59 PM	3.9 0.8 4.4 0.6	119 24 134 18	16 W	05:59 AM 12:08 PM 06:18 PM	4.8 0.0 4.8	146 0 146
2 W	06:11 AM 12:10 PM 06:22 PM	4.2 0.5 4.5	128 15 137	17 Th	12:27 AM 06:46 AM 12:59 PM 07:05 PM	-0.2 5.0 -0.1 4.8	-6 152 -3 146
3 Th	12:36 AM 06:50 AM 12:53 PM 07:02 PM	0.4 4.5 0.3 4.6	12 137 9 140	18 F	01:11 AM 07:30 AM 01:47 PM 07:49 PM	-0.2 5.1 -0.2 4.7	-6 155 -6 143
4 F	01:12 AM 07:28 AM 01:36 PM 07:41 PM	0.2 4.8 0.1 4.6	6 146 3 140	19 Sa	01:53 AM 08:11 AM 02:32 PM 08:32 PM	-0.2 5.2 -0.1 4.5	-6 158 -3 137
5 Sa	01:49 AM 08:06 AM 02:19 PM 08:20 PM	0.0 5.0 0.0 4.6	0 152 0 140	20 Su	02:34 AM 08:51 AM 03:17 PM 09:14 PM	0.0 5.1 0.0 4.3	0 155 0 131
6 Su	02:27 AM 08:46 AM 03:03 PM 09:01 PM	0.0 5.2 0.0 4.5	0 158 0 137	21 M	03:14 AM 09:30 AM 04:00 PM 09:55 PM	0.1 5.0 0.2 4.1	3 152 6 125
7 M	03:08 AM 09:28 AM 03:50 PM 09:45 PM	0.0 5.3 0.0 4.4	0 162 0 134	22 Tu	03:53 AM 10:09 AM 04:45 PM 10:38 PM	0.4 4.8 0.4 3.8	12 146 12 116
8 Tu	03:52 AM 10:14 AM 04:41 PM 10:34 PM	0.0 5.2 0.1 4.2	0 158 3 128	23 W	04:33 AM 10:50 AM 05:30 PM 11:23 PM	0.6 4.6 0.6 3.6	18 140 18 110
9 W	04:41 AM 11:05 AM 05:37 PM 11:30 PM	0.2 5.1 0.2 4.0	6 155 6 122	24 Th	05:15 AM 11:35 AM 06:19 PM	0.8 4.3 0.8	24 131 24
10 Th	05:37 AM 12:03 PM 06:38 PM	0.3 5.0 0.4	9 152 12	25 F	12:14 AM 06:03 AM 12:24 PM 07:11 PM	3.4 1.0 4.1 1.0	104 30 125 30
11 F	12:34 AM 06:41 AM 01:08 PM 07:43 PM	3.8 0.5 4.8 0.4	116 15 146 12	26 Sa	01:10 AM 06:57 AM 01:18 PM 08:05 PM	3.3 1.2 4.0 1.0	101 37 122 30
12 Sa	01:47 AM 07:52 AM 02:18 PM 08:49 PM	3.8 0.6 4.7 0.4	116 18 143 12	27 Su	02:10 AM 07:57 AM 02:17 PM 08:57 PM	3.3 1.2 3.9 1.0	101 37 119 30
13 Su	03:01 AM 09:04 AM 03:27 PM 09:51 PM	3.9 0.5 4.7 0.2	119 15 143 6	28 M	03:09 AM 08:58 AM 03:14 PM 09:45 PM	3.4 1.1 3.9 0.8	104 34 119 24
14 M	04:08 AM 10:11 AM 04:30 PM 10:48 PM	4.2 0.4 4.8 0.1	128 12 146 3	29 Tu	04:02 AM 09:56 AM 04:08 PM 10:30 PM	3.7 1.0 4.0 0.6	113 30 122 18
15 Tu	05:07 AM 11:12 AM 05:26 PM 11:39 PM	4.5 0.2 4.8 -0.1	137 6 146 -3	30 W	04:49 AM 10:49 AM 04:57 PM 11:11 PM	4.0 0.7 4.1 0.4	122 21 125 12
				31 Th	05:33 AM 11:38 AM 05:43 PM 11:52 PM	4.3 0.5 4.2 0.2	131 15 128 6

November

Day	Time (h m)	Height (ft)	Height (cm)	Day	Time (h m)	Height (ft)	Height (cm)
1 F	06:15 AM 12:25 PM 06:27 PM	4.7 0.2 4.3	143 6 131	16 Sa	06:09 AM 12:31 PM 06:28 PM	4.9 -0.1 4.1	149 -3 125
2 Sa	12:33 AM 06:56 AM 01:12 PM 07:11 PM	0.0 5.0 -0.1 4.3	0 152 -3 131	17 Su	12:27 AM 06:48 AM 01:14 PM 07:10 PM	-0.1 4.9 -0.1 4.0	-3 149 -3 122
3 Su	01:15 AM 06:39 AM 12:59 PM 06:56 PM	-0.2 5.3 -0.3 4.4	-6 162 -9 134	18 M	01:06 AM 07:26 AM 01:57 PM 07:50 PM	0.0 4.9 0.0 3.8	0 149 0 116
4 M	12:59 AM 07:22 AM 01:46 PM 07:43 PM	-0.3 5.4 -0.4 4.3	-9 165 -12 131	19 Tu	01:45 AM 08:04 AM 02:38 PM 08:31 PM	0.1 4.8 0.1 3.7	3 146 3 113
5 Tu	01:45 AM 08:09 AM 02:36 PM 08:32 PM	-0.3 5.5 -0.4 4.2	-9 168 -12 128	20 W	02:23 AM 08:42 AM 03:18 PM 09:12 PM	0.3 4.7 0.2 3.5	9 143 6 107
6 W	02:34 AM 08:58 AM 03:29 PM 09:25 PM	-0.3 5.4 -0.3 4.1	-9 165 -9 125	21 Th	03:01 AM 09:20 AM 04:00 PM 09:54 PM	0.4 4.5 0.4 3.4	12 137 12 104
7 Th	03:28 AM 09:52 AM 04:25 PM 10:24 PM	-0.1 5.3 -0.2 3.9	-3 162 -6 119	22 F	03:41 AM 10:00 AM 04:42 PM 10:40 PM	0.6 4.3 0.5 3.3	18 131 15 101
8 F	04:27 AM 10:50 AM 05:24 PM 11:29 PM	0.1 5.0 -0.1 3.9	3 152 -3 119	23 Sa	04:25 AM 10:42 AM 05:26 PM 11:29 PM	0.8 4.1 0.6 3.2	24 125 18 98
9 Sa	05:32 AM 11:54 AM 06:26 PM	0.3 4.8 0.0	9 146 0	24 Su	05:14 AM 11:29 AM 06:11 PM	0.9 3.9 0.7	27 119 21
10 Su	12:39 AM 06:42 AM 01:01 PM 07:28 PM	3.9 0.4 4.5 0.1	119 12 137 3	25 M	12:22 AM 06:10 AM 12:20 PM 06:59 PM	3.2 1.0 3.7 0.6	98 30 113 18
11 M	01:49 AM 07:53 AM 02:08 PM 08:28 PM	4.0 0.4 4.4 0.0	122 12 134 0	26 Tu	01:18 AM 07:11 AM 01:16 PM 07:47 PM	3.4 1.0 3.6 0.6	104 30 110 18
12 Tu	02:53 AM 08:59 AM 03:10 PM 09:23 PM	4.2 0.3 4.3 0.0	128 9 131 0	27 W	02:13 AM 08:12 AM 02:13 PM 08:35 PM	3.6 0.8 3.6 0.4	110 24 110 12
13 W	03:50 AM 10:00 AM 04:06 PM 10:14 PM	4.4 0.2 4.2 -0.1	134 6 128 -3	28 Th	03:04 AM 09:11 AM 03:09 PM 09:23 PM	3.9 0.6 3.6 0.2	119 18 110 6
14 Th	04:41 AM 10:55 AM 04:58 PM 11:01 PM	4.7 0.1 4.2 -0.2	143 3 128 -6	29 F	03:53 AM 10:06 AM 04:03 PM 10:11 PM	4.3 0.3 3.7 -0.1	131 9 113 -3
15 F	05:27 AM 11:45 AM 05:44 PM 11:45 PM	4.8 -0.1 4.1 -0.2	146 -3 125 -6	30 Sa	04:41 AM 10:59 AM 04:55 PM 10:59 PM	4.7 0.0 3.9 -0.3	143 0 119 -9

December

Day	Time (h m)	Height (ft)	Height (cm)	Day	Time (h m)	Height (ft)	Height (cm)
1 Su	05:28 AM 11:50 AM 05:46 PM 11:47 PM	5.0 -0.3 4.0 -0.5	152 -9 122 -15	16 M	12:02 AM 06:27 AM 12:56 PM 06:50 PM	-0.1 4.6 -0.1 3.5	-3 140 -3 107
2 M	06:15 AM 12:40 PM 06:36 PM	5.3 -0.5 4.1	162 -15 125	17 Tu	12:42 AM 07:05 AM 01:37 PM 07:30 PM	-0.1 4.6 -0.1 3.5	-3 140 -3 107
3 Tu	12:37 AM 07:04 AM 01:31 PM 07:27 PM	-0.6 5.5 -0.7 4.1	-18 168 -21 125	18 W	01:21 AM 07:42 AM 02:15 PM 08:09 PM	0.0 4.6 -0.1 3.5	0 140 -3 107
4 W	01:28 AM 07:54 AM 02:22 PM 08:20 PM	-0.7 5.5 -0.8 4.1	-21 168 -24 125	19 Th	01:58 AM 08:18 AM 02:53 PM 08:48 PM	0.0 4.5 0.0 3.4	0 137 0 104
5 Th	02:21 AM 08:45 AM 03:15 PM 09:15 PM	-0.6 5.4 -0.7 4.1	-18 165 -21 125	20 F	02:36 AM 08:54 AM 03:29 PM 09:27 PM	0.1 4.4 0.1 3.3	3 134 3 101
6 F	03:17 AM 09:39 AM 04:09 PM 10:13 PM	-0.5 5.2 -0.6 4.0	-15 158 -18 122	21 Sa	03:14 AM 09:30 AM 04:06 PM 10:07 PM	0.3 4.2 0.1 3.3	9 128 3 101
7 Sa	04:16 AM 10:35 AM 05:05 PM 11:15 PM	-0.3 4.9 -0.5 3.9	-9 149 -15 119	22 Su	03:54 AM 10:07 AM 04:42 PM 10:48 PM	0.4 4.0 0.2 3.3	12 122 6 101
8 Su	05:20 AM 11:35 AM 06:03 PM	0.0 4.6 -0.4	0 140 -12	23 M	04:39 AM 10:46 AM 05:20 PM 11:34 PM	0.5 3.8 0.3 3.3	15 116 9 101
9 M	12:21 AM 06:27 AM 12:38 PM 07:01 PM	3.9 0.1 4.2 -0.2	119 3 128 -6	24 Tu	05:29 AM 11:30 AM 06:03 PM	0.6 3.6 0.3	18 110 9
10 Tu	01:26 AM 07:35 AM 01:42 PM 07:59 PM	4.0 0.3 4.0 -0.2	122 9 122 -6	25 W	12:24 AM 06:26 AM 12:20 PM 06:50 PM	3.4 0.7 3.4 0.3	104 21 104 9
11 W	02:30 AM 08:41 AM 02:45 PM 08:55 PM	4.1 0.3 3.8 -0.1	125 9 116 -3	26 Th	01:19 AM 07:29 AM 01:19 PM 07:43 PM	3.6 0.6 3.3 0.2	110 18 101 6
12 Th	03:27 AM 09:43 AM 03:43 PM 09:47 PM	4.2 0.2 3.6 -0.1	128 6 110 -3	27 F	02:17 AM 08:34 AM 02:23 PM 08:39 PM	3.8 0.5 3.3 0.0	116 15 101 0
13 F	04:19 AM 10:38 AM 04:36 PM 10:35 PM	4.4 0.1 3.6 -0.1	134 3 110 -3	28 Sa	03:15 AM 09:36 AM 03:27 PM 09:35 PM	4.2 0.2 3.4 -0.2	128 6 104 -6
14 Sa	05:06 AM 11:28 AM 05:24 PM 11:20 PM	4.5 0.0 3.6 -0.1	137 0 110 -3	29 Su	04:10 AM 10:34 AM 04:27 PM 10:31 PM	4.5 -0.1 3.5 -0.5	137 -3 107 -15
15 Su	05:48 AM 12:14 PM 06:08 PM	4.6 -0.1 3.6	140 -3 110	30 M	05:04 AM 11:30 AM 05:25 PM 11:27 PM	4.9 -0.5 3.7 -0.7	149 -15 113 -21
				31 Tu	05:57 AM 12:23 PM 06:20 PM	5.2 -0.8 3.9	158 -24 119

Heights are referred to mean lower water which is the chart datum of sounding. All times are local. Daylight Saving Time has been used when needed.

Philadelphia, Pennsylvania, 2012

Times and Heights of High and Low Waters

September

Day	Time (h m)	Height (ft)	Height (cm)
1 Sa	02:24 AM	7.2	219
	09:21 AM	0.3	9
	02:51 PM	6.8	207
	09:38 PM	0.5	15
2 Su	03:09 AM	7.0	213
	10:04 AM	0.4	12
	03:35 PM	6.8	207
	10:24 PM	0.6	18
3 M	03:54 AM	6.8	207
	10:45 AM	0.5	15
	04:19 PM	6.8	207
	11:09 PM	0.7	21
4 Tu	04:39 AM	6.6	201
	11:24 AM	0.6	18
	05:02 PM	6.8	207
	11:54 PM	0.8	24
5 W	05:25 AM	6.4	195
	12:04 PM	0.7	21
	05:47 PM	6.7	204
6 Th	12:39 AM	0.9	27
	06:13 AM	6.2	189
	12:44 PM	0.7	21
	06:34 PM	6.7	204
7 F	01:26 AM	0.9	27
	07:03 AM	6.1	186
	01:27 PM	0.7	21
	07:24 PM	6.6	201
8 Sa	02:15 AM	1.0	30
	07:55 AM	5.9	180
	02:14 PM	0.8	24
	08:16 PM	6.6	201
9 Su	03:07 AM	1.0	30
	08:49 AM	5.9	180
	03:06 PM	0.8	24
	09:10 PM	6.6	201
10 M	04:01 AM	1.0	30
	09:44 AM	5.9	180
	04:01 PM	0.8	24
	10:04 PM	6.7	204
11 Tu	04:55 AM	0.9	27
	10:36 AM	6.0	183
	04:57 PM	0.7	21
	10:56 PM	6.8	207
12 W	05:48 AM	0.8	24
	11:27 AM	6.2	189
	05:53 PM	0.7	21
	11:46 PM	7.0	213
13 Th	06:38 AM	0.7	21
	12:15 PM	6.4	195
	06:47 PM	0.6	18
14 F	12:33 AM	7.1	216
	07:27 AM	0.6	18
	01:00 PM	6.6	201
	07:39 PM	0.5	15
15 Sa	01:18 AM	7.2	219
	08:13 AM	0.5	15
	01:44 PM	6.9	210
	08:30 PM	0.5	15
16 Su	02:02 AM	7.2	219
	08:59 AM	0.4	12
	02:26 PM	7.1	216
	09:21 PM	0.5	15
17 M	02:46 AM	7.1	216
	09:44 AM	0.4	12
	03:10 PM	7.2	219
	10:11 PM	0.5	15
18 Tu	03:32 AM	7.0	213
	10:30 AM	0.4	12
	03:55 PM	7.3	223
	11:03 PM	0.6	18
19 W	04:21 AM	6.8	207
	11:18 AM	0.4	12
	04:44 PM	7.3	223
	11:56 PM	0.6	18
20 Th	05:14 AM	6.6	201
	12:08 PM	0.5	15
	05:38 PM	7.3	223
21 F	12:51 AM	0.7	21
	06:11 AM	6.4	195
	01:01 PM	0.5	15
	06:36 PM	7.2	219
22 Sa	01:48 AM	0.8	24
	07:12 AM	6.2	189
	01:57 PM	0.6	18
	07:38 PM	7.0	213
23 Su	02:47 AM	0.8	24
	08:15 AM	6.1	186
	02:56 PM	0.7	21
	08:41 PM	7.0	213
24 M	03:46 AM	0.8	24
	09:17 AM	6.2	189
	03:57 PM	0.7	21
	09:44 PM	7.0	213
25 Tu	04:44 AM	0.7	21
	10:18 AM	6.3	192
	04:57 PM	0.6	18
	10:43 PM	7.0	213
26 W	05:40 AM	0.5	15
	11:15 AM	6.5	198
	05:54 PM	0.5	15
	11:39 PM	7.1	216
27 Th	06:33 AM	0.4	12
	12:08 PM	6.8	207
	06:49 PM	0.4	12
28 F	12:29 AM	7.1	216
	07:22 AM	0.3	9
	12:57 PM	6.9	210
	07:41 PM	0.4	12
29 Sa	01:17 AM	7.1	216
	08:08 AM	0.4	12
	01:43 PM	7.0	213
	08:29 PM	0.4	12
30 Su	02:02 AM	7.0	213
	08:51 AM	0.5	15
	02:26 PM	7.1	216
	09:15 PM	0.5	15

October

Day	Time (h m)	Height (ft)	Height (cm)
1 M	02:45 AM	6.9	210
	09:32 AM	0.6	18
	03:07 PM	7.1	216
	10:00 PM	0.6	18
2 Tu	03:28 AM	6.7	204
	10:11 AM	0.7	21
	03:48 PM	7.0	213
	10:43 PM	0.7	21
3 W	04:11 AM	6.5	198
	10:50 AM	0.8	24
	04:29 PM	6.9	210
	11:25 PM	0.8	24
4 Th	04:55 AM	6.3	192
	11:27 AM	0.8	24
	05:11 PM	6.8	207
5 F	12:09 AM	0.9	27
	05:41 AM	6.1	186
	12:06 PM	0.8	24
	05:54 PM	6.7	204
6 Sa	12:53 AM	1.0	30
	06:28 AM	6.0	183
	12:47 PM	0.8	24
	06:42 PM	6.7	204
7 Su	01:40 AM	1.0	30
	07:19 AM	5.9	180
	01:34 PM	0.8	24
	07:33 PM	6.6	201
8 M	02:30 AM	1.0	30
	08:11 AM	5.9	180
	02:26 PM	0.8	24
	08:27 PM	6.6	201
9 Tu	03:22 AM	1.0	30
	09:05 AM	5.9	180
	03:24 PM	0.8	24
	09:23 PM	6.6	201
10 W	04:16 AM	0.9	27
	09:59 AM	6.1	186
	04:23 PM	0.8	24
	10:17 PM	6.7	204
11 Th	05:09 AM	0.8	24
	10:50 AM	6.3	192
	05:22 PM	0.7	21
	11:09 PM	6.8	207
12 F	06:01 AM	0.7	21
	11:39 AM	6.6	201
	06:19 PM	0.6	18
	11:59 PM	6.9	210
13 Sa	06:51 AM	0.5	15
	12:27 PM	6.9	210
	07:15 PM	0.5	15
14 Su	12:48 AM	7.0	213
	07:40 AM	0.4	12
	01:13 PM	7.2	219
	08:08 PM	0.4	12
15 M	01:35 AM	7.0	213
	08:29 AM	0.4	12
	01:58 PM	7.4	226
	09:01 PM	0.4	12
16 Tu	02:23 AM	6.9	210
	09:17 AM	0.3	9
	02:45 PM	7.5	229
	09:54 PM	0.4	12
17 W	03:12 AM	6.8	207
	10:06 AM	0.3	9
	03:33 PM	7.6	232
	10:47 PM	0.4	12
18 Th	04:03 AM	6.6	201
	10:56 AM	0.4	12
	04:24 PM	7.5	229
	11:40 PM	0.5	15
19 F	04:58 AM	6.4	195
	11:48 AM	0.4	12
	05:20 PM	7.3	223
20 Sa	12:34 AM	0.5	15
	05:56 AM	6.3	192
	12:43 PM	0.5	15
	06:19 PM	7.1	216
21 Su	01:30 AM	0.6	18
	06:56 AM	6.1	186
	01:39 PM	0.5	15
	07:20 PM	6.9	210
22 M	02:26 AM	0.6	18
	07:58 AM	6.1	186
	02:38 PM	0.6	18
	08:23 PM	6.8	207
23 Tu	03:22 AM	0.5	15
	09:00 AM	6.2	189
	03:37 PM	0.5	15
	09:24 PM	6.7	204
24 W	04:18 AM	0.4	12
	09:59 AM	6.4	195
	04:36 PM	0.5	15
	10:22 PM	6.7	204
25 Th	05:12 AM	0.3	9
	10:55 AM	6.6	201
	05:33 PM	0.4	12
	11:16 PM	6.7	204
26 F	06:03 AM	0.2	6
	11:46 AM	6.8	207
	06:27 PM	0.3	9
27 Sa	12:06 AM	6.7	204
	06:52 AM	0.2	6
	12:34 PM	6.9	210
	07:18 PM	0.3	9
28 Su	12:53 AM	6.7	204
	07:37 AM	0.2	6
	01:18 PM	7.0	213
	08:06 PM	0.3	9
29 M	01:38 AM	6.6	201
	08:20 AM	0.3	9
	02:00 PM	7.0	213
	08:52 PM	0.3	9
30 Tu	02:22 AM	6.5	198
	09:01 AM	0.5	15
	02:40 PM	7.0	213
	09:35 PM	0.4	12
31 W	03:04 AM	6.3	192
	09:40 AM	0.6	18
	03:20 PM	6.9	210
	10:18 PM	0.5	15

November

Day	Time (h m)	Height (ft)	Height (cm)
1 Th	03:46 AM	6.1	186
	10:18 AM	0.7	21
	03:59 PM	6.8	207
	10:59 PM	0.6	18
2 F	04:28 AM	6.0	183
	10:56 AM	0.7	21
	04:38 PM	6.7	204
	11:41 PM	0.7	21
3 Sa	05:11 AM	5.8	177
	11:34 AM	0.6	18
	05:19 PM	6.6	201
4 Su	12:23 AM	0.7	21
	04:55 AM	5.7	174
	11:15 AM	0.6	18
	05:02 PM	6.5	198
5 M	12:07 AM	0.7	21
	05:42 AM	5.7	174
	12:00 PM	0.6	18
	05:50 PM	6.5	198
6 Tu	12:54 AM	0.7	21
	06:32 AM	5.7	174
	12:52 PM	0.6	18
	06:43 PM	6.4	195
7 W	01:44 AM	0.6	18
	07:25 AM	5.8	177
	01:50 PM	0.6	18
	07:40 PM	6.4	195
8 Th	02:36 AM	0.6	18
	08:19 AM	6.0	183
	02:51 PM	0.6	18
	08:37 PM	6.4	195
9 F	03:30 AM	0.5	15
	09:12 AM	6.3	192
	03:53 PM	0.5	15
	09:33 PM	6.4	195
10 Sa	04:24 AM	0.4	12
	10:04 AM	6.6	201
	04:53 PM	0.4	12
	10:27 PM	6.5	198
11 Su	05:17 AM	0.2	6
	10:54 AM	6.9	210
	05:52 PM	0.3	9
	11:19 PM	6.5	198
12 M	06:09 AM	0.1	3
	11:44 AM	7.2	219
	06:48 PM	0.2	6
13 Tu	12:10 AM	6.5	198
	07:01 AM	0.1	3
	12:33 PM	7.3	223
	07:42 PM	0.1	3
14 W	01:01 AM	6.4	195
	07:52 AM	0.0	0
	01:23 PM	7.4	226
	08:36 PM	0.1	3
15 Th	01:53 AM	6.3	192
	08:44 AM	0.0	0
	02:14 PM	7.4	226
	09:29 PM	0.1	3
16 F	02:46 AM	6.2	189
	09:36 AM	0.0	0
	03:07 PM	7.2	219
	10:22 PM	0.1	3
17 Sa	03:41 AM	6.1	186
	10:29 AM	0.0	0
	04:02 PM	7.0	213
	11:15 PM	0.1	3
18 Su	04:38 AM	6.0	183
	11:23 AM	0.1	3
	05:00 PM	6.8	207
19 M	12:08 AM	0.1	3
	05:37 AM	5.9	180
	12:19 PM	0.1	3
	05:59 PM	6.6	201
20 Tu	01:01 AM	0.0	0
	06:37 AM	5.9	180
	01:15 PM	0.2	6
	06:59 PM	6.4	195
21 W	01:54 AM	0.0	0
	07:36 AM	6.0	183
	02:13 PM	0.2	6
	07:57 PM	6.2	189
22 Th	02:47 AM	0.0	0
	08:33 AM	6.1	186
	03:11 PM	0.2	6
	08:54 PM	6.1	186
23 F	03:39 AM	-0.1	-3
	09:27 AM	6.3	192
	04:07 PM	0.1	3
	09:48 PM	6.1	186
24 Sa	04:30 AM	-0.1	-3
	10:19 AM	6.4	195
	05:01 PM	0.0	0
	10:39 PM	6.1	186
25 Su	05:19 AM	-0.1	-3
	11:07 AM	6.6	201
	05:52 PM	-0.1	-3
	11:28 PM	6.0	183
26 M	06:05 AM	-0.1	-3
	11:52 AM	6.6	201
	06:41 PM	-0.1	-3
27 Tu	12:14 AM	6.0	183
	06:49 AM	0.0	0
	12:34 PM	6.6	201
	07:27 PM	0.0	0
28 W	12:58 AM	5.9	180
	07:30 AM	0.1	3
	01:15 PM	6.6	201
	08:10 PM	0.0	0
29 Th	01:40 AM	5.7	174
	08:11 AM	0.2	6
	01:55 PM	6.5	198
	08:53 PM	0.1	3
30 F	02:22 AM	5.6	171
	08:50 AM	0.2	6
	02:33 PM	6.4	195
	09:34 PM	0.2	6

December

Day	Time (h m)	Height (ft)	Height (cm)
1 Sa	03:02 AM	5.5	168
	09:29 AM	0.2	6
	03:11 PM	6.3	192
	10:14 PM	0.2	6
2 Su	03:43 AM	5.4	165
	10:08 AM	0.2	6
	03:49 PM	6.3	192
	10:55 PM	0.2	6
3 M	04:24 AM	5.4	165
	10:50 AM	0.1	3
	04:29 PM	6.2	189
	11:37 PM	0.1	3
4 Tu	05:07 AM	5.4	165
	11:35 AM	0.1	3
	05:12 PM	6.1	186
5 W	12:20 AM	0.1	3
	05:53 AM	5.5	168
	12:25 PM	0.1	3
	06:03 PM	6.0	183
6 Th	01:07 AM	0.0	0
	06:44 AM	5.6	171
	01:22 PM	0.2	6
	07:00 PM	5.9	180
7 F	01:59 AM	0.0	0
	07:39 AM	5.8	177
	02:24 PM	0.2	6
	08:00 PM	5.8	177
8 Sa	02:53 AM	0.0	0
	08:35 AM	6.0	183
	03:27 PM	0.2	6
	09:00 PM	5.8	177
9 Su	03:50 AM	-0.1	-3
	09:30 AM	6.3	192
	04:30 PM	0.1	3
	09:58 PM	5.8	177
10 M	04:46 AM	-0.2	-6
	10:25 AM	6.5	198
	05:30 PM	0.0	0
	10:54 PM	5.8	177
11 Tu	05:43 AM	-0.3	-9
	11:19 AM	6.8	207
	06:28 PM	-0.2	-6
	11:49 PM	5.8	177
12 W	06:38 AM	-0.4	-12
	12:12 PM	6.9	210
	07:24 PM	-0.3	-9
13 Th	12:42 AM	5.8	177
	07:31 AM	-0.4	-12
	01:04 PM	7.0	213
	08:18 PM	-0.4	-12
14 F	01:35 AM	5.8	177
	08:25 AM	-0.5	-15
	01:57 PM	6.9	210
	09:10 PM	-0.4	-12
15 Sa	02:29 AM	5.8	177
	09:17 AM	-0.5	-15
	02:50 PM	6.8	207
	10:01 PM	-0.5	-15
16 Su	03:23 AM	5.7	174
	10:10 AM	-0.5	-15
	03:44 PM	6.6	201
	10:52 PM	-0.5	-15
17 M	04:18 AM	5.7	174
	11:03 AM	-0.4	-12
	04:39 PM	6.3	192
	11:42 PM	-0.5	-15
18 Tu	05:13 AM	5.7	174
	11:56 AM	-0.4	-12
	05:34 PM	6.1	186
19 W	12:31 AM	-0.5	-15
	06:09 AM	5.7	174
	12:50 PM	-0.3	-9
	06:30 PM	5.8	177
20 Th	01:21 AM	-0.5	-15
	07:05 AM	5.7	174
	01:45 PM	-0.2	-6
	07:26 PM	5.7	174
21 F	02:12 AM	-0.4	-12
	08:00 AM	5.7	174
	02:41 PM	-0.2	-6
	08:22 PM	5.5	168
22 Sa	03:03 AM	-0.4	-12
	08:54 AM	5.8	177
	03:37 PM	-0.2	-6
	09:17 PM	5.4	165
23 Su	03:53 AM	-0.4	-12
	09:46 AM	5.9	180
	04:31 PM	-0.3	-9
	10:09 PM	5.4	165
24 M	04:43 AM	-0.4	-12
	10:36 AM	6.0	183
	05:23 PM	-0.4	-12
	11:00 PM	5.4	165
25 Tu	05:31 AM	-0.4	-12
	11:23 AM	6.1	186
	06:13 PM	-0.4	-12
	11:47 PM	5.4	165
26 W	06:17 AM	-0.4	-12
	12:08 PM	6.1	186
	06:59 PM	-0.4	-12
27 Th	12:33 AM	5.3	162
	07:01 AM	-0.4	-12
	12:51 PM	6.1	186
	07:44 PM	-0.4	-12
28 F	01:16 AM	5.3	162
	07:44 AM	-0.3	-9
	01:31 PM	6.1	186
	08:27 PM	-0.3	-9
29 Sa	01:57 AM	5.2	158
	08:25 AM	-0.3	-9
	02:10 PM	6.0	183
	09:08 PM	-0.3	-9
30 Su	02:37 AM	5.2	158
	09:06 AM	-0.3	-9
	02:47 PM	6.0	183
	09:48 PM	-0.3	-9
31 M	03:15 AM	5.2	158
	09:47 AM	-0.3	-9
	03:24 PM	5.9	180
	10:28 PM	-0.3	-9

Heights are referred to mean lower water which is the chart datum of sounding. All times are local. Daylight Saving Time has been used when needed.

Philadelphia, Pennsylvania, 2013

Times and Heights of High and Low Waters

January

Day	Time (h m)	Height (ft)	Height (cm)
1 Tu	03:52 AM 10:30 AM 04:00 PM 11:08 PM	5.2 -0.3 5.8 -0.3	158 -9 177 -9
2 W	04:32 AM 11:15 AM 04:42 PM 11:51 PM	5.3 -0.3 5.8 -0.4	162 -9 177 -12
3 Th	05:16 AM 12:06 PM 05:31 PM	5.4 -0.2 5.6	165 -6 171
4 F	12:38 AM 06:07 AM 01:02 PM 06:29 PM	-0.4 5.5 -0.2 5.5	-12 168 -6 168
5 Sa	01:29 AM 07:04 AM 02:04 PM 07:32 PM	-0.4 5.6 -0.1 5.3	-12 171 -3 162
6 Su	02:25 AM 08:04 AM 03:08 PM 08:35 PM	-0.4 5.7 -0.1 5.3	-12 174 -3 162
7 M	03:25 AM 09:05 AM 04:12 PM 09:37 PM	-0.4 5.9 -0.2 5.3	-12 180 -6 162
8 Tu	04:25 AM 10:04 AM 05:13 PM 10:36 PM	-0.4 6.1 -0.3 5.3	-12 186 -9 162
9 W	05:24 AM 11:02 AM 06:12 PM 11:33 PM	-0.6 6.3 -0.5 5.4	-18 192 -15 165
10 Th	06:21 AM 11:57 AM 07:07 PM	-0.7 6.5 -0.6	-21 198 -18
11 F	12:27 AM 07:16 AM 12:51 PM 08:00 PM	5.5 -0.8 6.6 -0.8	168 -24 201 -24
12 Sa	01:21 AM 08:09 AM 01:43 PM 08:50 PM	5.6 -0.9 6.5 -0.9	171 -27 198 -27
13 Su	02:13 AM 09:01 AM 02:34 PM 09:39 PM	5.7 -0.9 6.4 -0.9	174 -27 195 -27
14 M	03:04 AM 09:51 AM 03:25 PM 10:27 PM	5.7 -0.9 6.3 -0.9	174 -27 192 -27
15 Tu	03:55 AM 10:42 AM 04:16 PM 11:13 PM	5.7 -0.8 6.1 -0.8	174 -24 186 -24
16 W	04:46 AM 11:32 AM 05:07 PM 11:59 PM	5.7 -0.7 5.9 -0.8	174 -21 180 -24
17 Th	05:38 AM 12:22 PM 06:00 PM	5.7 -0.6 5.6	174 -18 171
18 F	12:46 AM 06:30 AM 01:14 PM 06:53 PM	-0.7 5.6 -0.5 5.4	-21 171 -15 165
19 Sa	01:34 AM 07:22 AM 02:07 PM 07:48 PM	-0.6 5.6 -0.4 5.3	-18 171 -12 162
20 Su	02:23 AM 08:16 AM 03:01 PM 08:42 PM	-0.6 5.6 -0.4 5.2	-18 171 -12 158
21 M	03:14 AM 09:09 AM 03:56 PM 09:35 PM	-0.5 5.6 -0.4 5.2	-15 171 -12 158
22 Tu	04:05 AM 10:01 AM 04:49 PM 10:27 PM	-0.5 5.7 -0.4 5.2	-15 174 -12 158
23 W	04:55 AM 10:50 AM 05:40 PM 11:17 PM	-0.5 5.8 -0.4 5.2	-15 177 -12 158
24 Th	05:44 AM 11:38 AM 06:28 PM	-0.5 5.8 -0.5	-15 177 -15
25 F	12:03 AM 06:31 AM 12:22 PM 07:14 PM	5.2 -0.5 5.9 -0.5	158 -15 180 -15
26 Sa	12:47 AM 07:17 AM 01:04 PM 07:57 PM	5.2 -0.5 5.9 -0.4	158 -15 180 -12
27 Su	01:29 AM 08:01 AM 01:44 PM 08:39 PM	5.2 -0.5 5.9 -0.4	158 -15 180 -12
28 M	02:08 AM 08:45 AM 02:22 PM 09:20 PM	5.3 -0.5 5.8 -0.4	162 -15 177 -12
29 Tu	02:47 AM 09:29 AM 03:00 PM 10:01 PM	5.3 -0.5 5.8 -0.4	162 -15 177 -12
30 W	03:24 AM 10:13 AM 03:39 PM 10:42 PM	5.4 -0.5 5.8 -0.5	165 -15 177 -15
31 Th	04:04 AM 11:00 AM 04:22 PM 11:25 PM	5.5 -0.4 5.7 -0.5	168 -12 174 -15

February

Day	Time (h m)	Height (ft)	Height (cm)
1 F	04:47 AM 11:51 AM 05:12 PM	5.7 -0.4 5.5	174 -12 168
2 Sa	12:12 AM 05:38 AM 12:47 PM 06:09 PM	-0.5 5.7 -0.3 5.4	-15 174 -9 165
3 Su	01:04 AM 06:36 AM 01:47 PM 07:12 PM	-0.4 5.8 -0.2 5.2	-12 177 -6 158
4 M	02:02 AM 07:39 AM 02:50 PM 08:16 PM	-0.4 5.8 -0.1 5.1	-12 177 -3 155
5 Tu	03:03 AM 08:42 AM 03:53 PM 09:18 PM	-0.3 5.9 -0.1 5.2	-9 180 -3 158
6 W	04:05 AM 09:45 AM 04:54 PM 10:19 PM	-0.4 6.0 -0.3 5.3	-12 183 -9 162
7 Th	05:05 AM 10:44 AM 05:52 PM 11:16 PM	-0.5 6.2 -0.4 5.5	-15 189 -12 168
8 F	06:03 AM 11:41 AM 06:46 PM	-0.7 6.3 -0.6	-21 192 -18
9 Sa	12:11 AM 06:58 AM 12:34 PM 07:37 PM	5.7 -0.8 6.4 -0.7	174 -24 195 -21
10 Su	01:02 AM 07:50 AM 01:25 PM 08:26 PM	5.9 -0.9 6.4 -0.8	180 -27 195 -24
11 M	01:52 AM 08:41 AM 02:14 PM 09:13 PM	6.0 -0.9 6.4 -0.7	183 -27 195 -21
12 Tu	02:40 AM 09:30 AM 03:02 PM 09:57 PM	6.0 -0.8 6.2 -0.7	183 -24 189 -21
13 W	03:27 AM 10:18 AM 03:50 PM 10:41 PM	6.0 -0.7 6.0 -0.6	183 -21 183 -18
14 Th	04:14 AM 11:05 AM 04:38 PM 11:24 PM	6.0 -0.6 5.9 -0.5	183 -18 180 -15
15 F	05:02 AM 11:52 AM 05:28 PM	5.9 -0.5 5.7	180 -15 174
16 Sa	12:08 AM 05:51 AM 12:41 PM 06:19 PM	-0.4 5.8 -0.3 5.5	-12 177 -9 168
17 Su	12:53 AM 06:42 AM 01:32 PM 07:13 PM	-0.3 5.7 -0.2 5.3	-9 174 -6 162
18 M	01:41 AM 07:35 AM 02:24 PM 08:07 PM	-0.2 5.7 -0.1 5.2	-6 174 -3 158
19 Tu	02:32 AM 08:29 AM 03:18 PM 09:01 PM	-0.1 5.7 -0.1 5.2	-3 174 -3 158
20 W	03:25 AM 09:23 AM 04:12 PM 09:54 PM	-0.1 5.7 -0.1 5.3	-3 174 -3 162
21 Th	04:18 AM 10:15 AM 05:04 PM 10:45 PM	-0.1 5.8 -0.1 5.4	-3 177 -3 165
22 F	05:11 AM 11:05 AM 05:54 PM 11:32 PM	-0.2 5.9 -0.1 5.5	-6 180 -3 168
23 Sa	06:01 AM 11:52 AM 06:41 PM	-0.3 6.0 -0.2	-9 183 -6
24 Su	12:17 AM 06:50 AM 12:35 PM 07:26 PM	5.6 -0.3 6.0 -0.2	171 -9 183 -6
25 M	12:59 AM 07:37 AM 01:17 PM 08:09 PM	5.7 -0.3 6.1 -0.2	174 -9 186 -6
26 Tu	01:40 AM 08:24 AM 01:57 PM 08:52 PM	5.9 -0.3 6.1 -0.2	180 -9 186 -6
27 W	02:18 AM 09:10 AM 02:38 PM 09:34 PM	6.0 -0.3 6.0 -0.2	183 -9 183 -6
28 Th	02:57 AM 09:58 AM 03:20 PM 10:17 PM	6.1 -0.3 6.0 -0.2	186 -9 183 -6

March

Day	Time (h m)	Height (ft)	Height (cm)
1 F	03:39 AM 10:47 AM 04:07 PM 11:03 PM	6.2 -0.2 5.9 -0.2	189 -6 180 -6
2 Sa	04:25 AM 11:38 AM 04:58 PM 11:52 PM	6.3 -0.1 5.7 -0.1	192 -3 174 -3
3 Su	05:17 AM 12:33 PM 05:56 PM	6.3 0.0 5.6	192 0 171
4 M	12:46 AM 06:17 AM 01:32 PM 06:57 PM	0.0 6.2 0.1 5.5	0 189 3 168
5 Tu	01:44 AM 07:20 AM 02:33 PM 08:01 PM	0.0 6.2 0.1 5.5	0 189 3 168
6 W	02:45 AM 08:25 AM 03:34 PM 09:03 PM	0.0 6.2 0.1 5.6	0 189 3 171
7 Th	03:47 AM 09:28 AM 04:33 PM 10:03 PM	0.0 6.3 0.0 5.8	0 192 0 177
8 F	04:48 AM 10:28 AM 05:30 PM 11:00 PM	-0.1 6.4 -0.2 6.0	-3 195 -6 183
9 Sa	05:45 AM 11:24 AM 06:23 PM 11:53 PM	-0.3 6.5 -0.3 6.3	-9 198 -9 192
10 Su	07:40 AM 01:16 PM 08:12 PM	-0.4 6.6 -0.3	-12 201 -9
11 M	01:43 AM 08:31 AM 02:05 PM 08:59 PM	6.5 -0.5 6.6 -0.3	198 -15 201 -9
12 Tu	02:29 AM 09:20 AM 02:51 PM 09:44 PM	6.6 -0.4 6.5 -0.2	201 -12 198 -6
13 W	03:14 AM 10:07 AM 03:37 PM 10:27 PM	6.6 -0.4 6.4 -0.1	201 -12 195 -3
14 Th	03:58 AM 10:53 AM 04:23 PM 11:08 PM	6.6 -0.3 6.2 0.0	201 -9 189 0
15 F	04:42 AM 11:38 AM 05:09 PM 11:49 PM	6.5 -0.1 6.1 0.1	198 -3 186 3
16 Sa	05:27 AM 12:23 PM 05:57 PM	6.4 0.0 5.9	195 0 180
17 Su	12:30 AM 06:13 AM 01:08 PM 06:46 PM	0.2 6.3 0.1 5.8	6 192 3 177
18 M	01:13 AM 07:02 AM 01:56 PM 07:38 PM	0.3 6.2 0.2 5.7	9 189 6 174
19 Tu	01:59 AM 07:54 AM 02:46 PM 08:31 PM	0.4 6.1 0.3 5.6	12 186 9 171
20 W	02:50 AM 08:48 AM 03:38 PM 09:25 PM	0.4 6.0 0.4 5.6	12 183 12 171
21 Th	03:44 AM 09:43 AM 04:32 PM 10:18 PM	0.4 6.0 0.4 5.7	12 183 12 174
22 F	04:41 AM 10:37 AM 05:25 PM 11:09 PM	0.4 6.1 0.4 5.9	12 186 12 180
23 Sa	05:36 AM 11:28 AM 06:16 PM 11:58 PM	0.4 6.2 0.4 6.1	12 189 12 186
24 Su	06:31 AM 12:17 PM 07:05 PM	0.3 6.3 0.3	9 192 9
25 M	12:44 AM 07:23 AM 01:03 PM 07:52 PM	6.3 0.2 6.3 0.3	192 6 192 9
26 Tu	01:27 AM 08:13 AM 01:48 PM 08:37 PM	6.5 0.1 6.4 0.3	198 3 195 9
27 W	02:09 AM 09:03 AM 02:31 PM 09:22 PM	6.7 0.1 6.4 0.3	204 3 195 9
28 Th	02:50 AM 09:52 AM 03:16 PM 10:08 PM	6.8 0.1 6.4 0.3	207 3 195 9
29 F	03:32 AM 10:42 AM 04:02 PM 10:54 PM	7.0 0.1 6.3 0.3	213 3 192 9
30 Sa	04:17 AM 11:32 AM 04:52 PM 11:43 PM	7.0 0.1 6.2 0.3	213 3 189 9
31 Su	05:07 AM 12:25 PM 05:46 PM	7.0 0.2 6.1	213 6 186

April

Day	Time (h m)	Height (ft)	Height (cm)
1 M	12:34 AM 06:02 AM 01:19 PM 06:44 PM	0.4 6.9 0.3 6.0	12 210 9 183
2 Tu	01:29 AM 07:02 AM 02:16 PM 07:45 PM	0.4 6.8 0.3 6.0	12 207 9 183
3 W	02:28 AM 08:05 AM 03:14 PM 08:47 PM	0.5 6.7 0.4 6.0	15 204 12 183
4 Th	03:28 AM 09:09 AM 04:13 PM 09:48 PM	0.5 6.6 0.3 6.2	15 201 9 189
5 F	04:29 AM 10:11 AM 05:10 PM 10:47 PM	0.4 6.6 0.3 6.4	12 201 9 195
6 Sa	05:29 AM 11:09 AM 06:04 PM 11:42 PM	0.3 6.7 0.2 6.7	9 204 6 204
7 Su	06:26 AM 12:04 PM 06:56 PM	0.2 6.7 0.1	6 204 3
8 M	12:33 AM 07:20 AM 12:54 PM 07:45 PM	6.9 0.1 6.7 0.1	210 3 204 3
9 Tu	01:21 AM 08:11 AM 01:42 PM 08:30 PM	7.1 0.0 6.7 0.2	216 0 204 6
10 W	02:05 AM 08:59 AM 02:28 PM 09:14 PM	7.2 0.1 6.7 0.3	219 3 204 9
11 Th	02:48 AM 09:44 AM 03:13 PM 09:55 PM	7.2 0.1 6.5 0.5	219 3 198 15
12 F	03:30 AM 10:28 AM 03:57 PM 10:36 PM	7.1 0.2 6.4 0.6	216 6 195 18
13 Sa	04:11 AM 11:12 AM 04:41 PM 11:15 PM	7.0 0.4 6.3 0.7	213 12 192 21
14 Su	04:53 AM 11:54 AM 05:27 PM 11:54 PM	6.9 0.5 6.2 0.8	210 15 189 24
15 M	05:37 AM 12:37 PM 06:14 PM	6.8 0.5 6.1	207 15 186
16 Tu	12:35 AM 06:23 AM 01:22 PM 07:03 PM	0.8 6.7 0.6 6.0	24 204 18 183
17 W	01:20 AM 07:12 AM 02:09 PM 07:55 PM	0.8 6.5 0.7 6.0	24 198 21 183
18 Th	02:10 AM 08:05 AM 02:58 PM 08:47 PM	0.9 6.4 0.7 6.0	27 195 21 183
19 F	03:05 AM 09:00 AM 03:50 PM 09:39 PM	0.9 6.4 0.7 6.2	27 195 21 189
20 Sa	04:03 AM 09:55 AM 04:43 PM 10:31 PM	0.9 6.4 0.7 6.4	27 195 21 195
21 Su	05:02 AM 10:48 AM 05:36 PM 11:20 PM	0.8 6.4 0.7 6.6	24 195 21 201
22 M	06:00 AM 11:40 AM 06:27 PM	0.7 6.5 0.7	21 198 21
23 Tu	12:08 AM 06:55 AM 12:29 PM 07:17 PM	6.9 0.6 6.6 0.6	210 18 201 18
24 W	12:53 AM 07:49 AM 01:17 PM 08:05 PM	7.1 0.5 6.6 0.6	216 15 201 18
25 Th	01:38 AM 08:41 AM 02:05 PM 08:54 PM	7.4 0.4 6.6 0.6	226 12 201 18
26 F	02:23 AM 09:33 AM 02:54 PM 09:43 PM	7.5 0.4 6.6 0.6	229 12 201 18
27 Sa	03:09 AM 10:25 AM 03:44 PM 10:33 PM	7.6 0.4 6.5 0.6	232 12 198 18
28 Su	03:59 AM 11:17 AM 04:37 PM 11:24 PM	7.6 0.3 6.5 0.6	232 9 198 18
29 M	04:51 AM 12:09 PM 05:32 PM	7.5 0.4 6.4	229 12 195
30 Tu	12:18 AM 05:48 AM 01:03 PM 06:31 PM	0.6 7.3 0.4 6.4	18 223 12 195

May

Day	Time (h m)	Height (ft)	Height (cm)
1 W	01:13 AM 06:48 AM 01:57 PM 07:31 PM	0.7 7.2 0.4 6.4	21 219 12 195
2 Th	02:11 AM 07:49 AM 02:52 PM 08:31 PM	0.7 7.0 0.4 6.5	21 213 12 198
3 F	03:10 AM 08:50 AM 03:48 PM 09:30 PM	0.7 6.9 0.4 6.7	21 210 12 204
4 Sa	04:09 AM 09:50 AM 04:43 PM 10:27 PM	0.6 6.8 0.3 6.9	18 207 9 210
5 Su	05:08 AM 10:47 AM 05:36 PM 11:20 PM	0.6 6.8 0.3 7.1	18 207 9 216
6 M	06:04 AM 11:40 AM 06:26 PM	0.5 6.8 0.3	15 207 9
7 Tu	12:10 AM 06:58 AM 12:31 PM 07:15 PM	7.3 0.4 6.7 0.4	223 12 204 12
8 W	12:56 AM 07:48 AM 01:18 PM 08:00 PM	7.4 0.3 6.7 0.5	226 9 204 15
9 Th	01:40 AM 08:35 AM 02:04 PM 08:43 PM	7.5 0.4 6.6 0.7	229 12 201 21
10 F	02:22 AM 09:20 AM 02:48 PM 09:25 PM	7.4 0.4 6.5 0.8	226 12 198 24
11 Sa	03:03 AM 10:04 AM 03:32 PM 10:05 PM	7.3 0.5 6.4 1.0	223 15 195 30
12 Su	03:43 AM 10:46 AM 04:15 PM 10:44 PM	7.2 0.6 6.3 1.0	219 18 192 30
13 M	04:23 AM 11:27 AM 04:59 PM 11:23 PM	7.1 0.7 6.2 1.0	216 21 189 30
14 Tu	05:04 AM 12:08 PM 05:43 PM	7.0 0.7 6.1	213 21 186
15 W	12:03 AM 05:47 AM 12:50 PM 06:29 PM	1.0 6.9 0.7 6.1	30 210 21 186
16 Th	12:46 AM 06:33 AM 01:33 PM 07:18 PM	1.0 6.8 0.7 6.2	30 207 21 189
17 F	01:35 AM 07:22 AM 02:20 PM 08:08 PM	1.0 6.6 0.7 6.3	30 201 21 192
18 Sa	02:29 AM 08:16 AM 03:09 PM 08:59 PM	1.0 6.5 0.7 6.4	30 198 21 195
19 Su	03:28 AM 09:12 AM 04:01 PM 09:51 PM	1.1 6.5 0.7 6.6	34 198 21 201
20 M	04:29 AM 10:08 AM 04:55 PM 10:42 PM	1.0 6.5 0.7 6.9	30 198 21 210
21 Tu	05:30 AM 11:03 AM 05:49 PM 11:32 PM	1.0 6.5 0.7 7.2	30 198 21 219
22 W	06:29 AM 11:56 AM 06:43 PM	0.8 6.5 0.7	24 198 21
23 Th	12:21 AM 07:26 AM 12:49 PM 07:35 PM	7.5 0.7 6.5 0.7	229 21 198 21
24 F	01:10 AM 08:20 AM 01:40 PM 08:28 PM	7.7 0.6 6.5 0.6	235 18 198 18
25 Sa	01:59 AM 09:14 AM 02:32 PM 09:20 PM	7.8 0.5 6.5 0.6	238 15 198 18
26 Su	02:49 AM 10:07 AM 03:25 PM 10:13 PM	7.8 0.4 6.5 0.6	238 12 198 18
27 M	03:42 AM 10:59 AM 04:20 PM 11:06 PM	7.8 0.3 6.5 0.6	238 9 198 18
28 Tu	04:36 AM 11:51 AM 05:16 PM	7.6 0.2 6.5	232 6 198
29 W	12:00 AM 05:32 AM 12:43 PM 06:14 PM	0.6 7.5 0.2 6.6	18 229 6 201
30 Th	12:55 AM 06:30 AM 01:35 PM 07:12 PM	0.6 7.2 0.2 6.6	18 219 6 201
31 F	01:51 AM 07:29 AM 02:27 PM 08:10 PM	0.6 7.0 0.2 6.8	18 213 6 207

June

Day	Time (h m)	Height (ft)	Height (cm)
1 Sa	02:48 AM 08:27 AM 03:20 PM 09:07 PM	0.6 6.8 0.2 6.9	18 207 6 210
2 Su	03:46 AM 09:25 AM 04:12 PM 10:02 PM	0.6 6.7 0.2 7.1	18 204 6 216
3 M	04:43 AM 10:21 AM 05:04 PM 10:54 PM	0.6 6.6 0.3 7.2	18 201 9 219
4 Tu	05:39 AM 11:14 AM 05:54 PM 11:43 PM	0.5 6.5 0.3 7.3	15 198 9 223
5 W	06:32 AM 12:05 PM 06:43 PM	0.4 6.5 0.4	12 198 12
6 Th	12:30 AM 07:23 AM 12:53 PM 07:29 PM	7.4 0.4 6.5 0.6	226 12 198 18
7 F	01:14 AM 08:10 AM 01:39 PM 08:13 PM	7.4 0.4 6.4 0.7	226 12 195 21
8 Sa	01:57 AM 08:55 AM 02:24 PM 08:55 PM	7.3 0.5 6.3 0.8	223 15 192 24
9 Su	02:38 AM 09:38 AM 03:07 PM 09:36 PM	7.2 0.5 6.2 0.9	219 15 189 27
10 M	03:17 AM 10:20 AM 03:49 PM 10:16 PM	7.1 0.6 6.1 1.0	216 18 186 30
11 Tu	03:56 AM 11:00 AM 04:31 PM 10:56 PM	7.0 0.6 6.1 1.0	213 18 186 30
12 W	04:35 AM 11:40 AM 05:13 PM 11:36 PM	6.9 0.6 6.1 0.9	210 18 186 27
13 Th	05:15 AM 12:19 PM 05:55 PM	6.8 0.6 6.1	207 18 186
14 F	12:19 AM 05:56 AM 01:00 PM 06:40 PM	0.9 6.7 0.6 6.2	27 204 18 189
15 Sa	01:07 AM 06:42 AM 01:43 PM 07:27 PM	0.9 6.6 0.5 6.3	27 201 15 192
16 Su	02:00 AM 07:34 AM 02:31 PM 08:18 PM	0.9 6.5 0.5 6.5	27 198 15 198
17 M	02:59 AM 08:32 AM 03:22 PM 09:11 PM	1.0 6.4 0.5 6.7	30 195 15 204
18 Tu	04:01 AM 09:31 AM 04:18 PM 10:05 PM	1.0 6.3 0.6 7.0	30 192 18 213
19 W	05:04 AM 10:30 AM 05:15 PM 10:59 PM	0.9 6.2 0.6 7.2	27 189 18 219
20 Th	06:05 AM 11:28 AM 06:13 PM 11:53 PM	0.8 6.2 0.6 7.5	24 189 18 229
21 F	07:04 AM 12:23 PM 07:10 PM	0.7 6.3 0.5	21 192 15
22 Sa	12:46 AM 08:00 AM 01:18 PM 08:05 PM	7.6 0.5 6.3 0.5	232 15 192 15
23 Su	01:39 AM 08:54 AM 02:12 PM 09:00 PM	7.8 0.3 6.4 0.4	238 9 195 12
24 M	02:31 AM 09:47 AM 03:06 PM 09:54 PM	7.8 0.2 6.5 0.4	238 6 198 12
25 Tu	03:25 AM 10:38 AM 04:01 PM 10:47 PM	7.7 0.1 6.5 0.4	235 3 198 12
26 W	04:18 AM 11:29 AM 04:56 PM 11:41 PM	7.5 0.0 6.6 0.4	229 0 201 12
27 Th	05:13 AM 12:19 PM 05:52 PM	7.3 0.0 6.6	223 0 201
28 F	12:34 AM 06:08 AM 01:08 PM 06:47 PM	0.4 7.1 0.0 6.7	12 216 0 204
29 Sa	01:29 AM 07:04 AM 01:58 PM 07:43 PM	0.4 6.8 0.0 6.8	12 207 0 207
30 Su	02:24 AM 08:00 AM 02:48 PM 08:37 PM	0.5 6.6 0.1 6.8	15 201 3 207

Heights are referred to mean lower water which is the chart datum of sounding. All times are local. Daylight Saving Time has been used when needed.

Philadelphia, Pennsylvania, 2013

Times and Heights of High and Low Waters

July

Day	Time (h m)	Height (ft)	Height (cm)
1 M	03:19 AM 08:56 AM 03:39 PM 09:31 PM	0.5 6.4 0.1 6.9	15 195 3 210
2 Tu	04:15 AM 09:51 AM 04:30 PM 10:24 PM	0.5 6.3 0.2 7.0	15 192 6 213
3 W	05:10 AM 10:45 AM 05:20 PM 11:14 PM	0.5 6.2 0.3 7.1	15 189 9 216
4 Th	06:04 AM 11:37 AM 06:10 PM	0.4 6.2 0.4	12 189 12
5 F	12:02 AM 06:54 AM 12:26 PM 06:57 PM	7.1 0.4 6.2 0.5	216 12 189 15
6 Sa	12:48 AM 07:42 AM 01:13 PM 07:43 PM	7.1 0.4 6.2 0.5	216 12 189 15
7 Su	01:31 AM 08:28 AM 01:58 PM 08:27 PM	7.1 0.4 6.1 0.6	216 12 186 18
8 M	02:13 AM 09:11 AM 02:41 PM 09:09 PM	7.1 0.4 6.1 0.7	216 12 186 21
9 Tu	02:53 AM 09:52 AM 03:23 PM 09:51 PM	7.0 0.5 6.0 0.8	213 15 183 24
10 W	03:31 AM 10:32 AM 04:03 PM 10:32 PM	6.9 0.5 6.0 0.8	210 15 183 24
11 Th	04:09 AM 11:11 AM 04:42 PM 11:14 PM	6.8 0.5 6.1 0.8	207 15 186 24
12 F	04:46 AM 11:50 AM 05:21 PM 11:57 PM	6.7 0.4 6.1 0.8	204 12 186 24
13 Sa	05:24 AM 12:29 PM 06:02 PM	6.6 0.4 6.3	201 12 192
14 Su	12:45 AM 06:08 AM 01:11 PM 06:48 PM	0.8 6.5 0.4 6.4	24 198 12 195
15 M	01:37 AM 07:00 AM 01:58 PM 07:39 PM	0.8 6.4 0.4 6.6	24 195 12 201
16 Tu	02:35 AM 07:59 AM 02:50 PM 08:35 PM	0.9 6.2 0.4 6.7	27 189 12 204
17 W	03:38 AM 09:02 AM 03:48 PM 09:34 PM	0.9 6.1 0.5 6.9	27 186 15 210
18 Th	04:41 AM 10:04 AM 04:49 PM 10:33 PM	0.9 6.0 0.5 7.1	27 183 15 216
19 F	05:43 AM 11:04 AM 05:49 PM 11:30 PM	0.8 6.1 0.5 7.3	24 186 15 223
20 Sa	06:43 AM 12:03 PM 06:49 PM	0.6 6.2 0.4	18 189 12
21 Su	12:26 AM 07:40 AM 12:59 PM 07:46 PM	7.5 0.4 6.3 0.3	229 12 192 9
22 M	01:21 AM 08:33 AM 01:53 PM 08:41 PM	7.6 0.2 6.4 0.2	232 6 195 6
23 Tu	02:14 AM 09:25 AM 02:47 PM 09:35 PM	7.6 0.1 6.5 0.2	232 3 198 6
24 W	03:06 AM 10:15 AM 03:40 PM 10:27 PM	7.5 0.0 6.6 0.2	229 0 201 6
25 Th	03:58 AM 11:03 AM 04:32 PM 11:19 PM	7.4 -0.1 6.7 0.2	226 -3 204 6
26 F	04:50 AM 11:51 AM 05:25 PM	7.2 -0.1 6.7	219 -3 204
27 Sa	12:11 AM 05:43 AM 12:38 PM 06:17 PM	0.3 6.9 0.0 6.8	9 210 0 207
28 Su	01:03 AM 06:36 AM 01:26 PM 07:10 PM	0.4 6.7 0.1 6.8	12 204 3 207
29 M	01:56 AM 07:30 AM 02:14 PM 08:03 PM	0.5 6.4 0.1 6.8	15 195 3 207
30 Tu	02:49 AM 08:25 AM 03:03 PM 08:57 PM	0.5 6.2 0.2 6.8	15 189 6 207
31 W	03:44 AM 09:20 AM 03:53 PM 09:50 PM	0.6 6.1 0.3 6.8	18 186 9 207

August

Day	Time (h m)	Height (ft)	Height (cm)
1 Th	04:38 AM 10:15 AM 04:45 PM 10:42 PM	0.6 6.1 0.4 6.9	18 186 12 210
2 F	05:31 AM 11:07 AM 05:35 PM 11:32 PM	0.5 6.1 0.4 6.9	15 186 12 210
3 Sa	06:23 AM 11:58 AM 06:25 PM	0.5 6.1 0.5	15 186 15
4 Su	12:20 AM 07:11 AM 12:46 PM 07:13 PM	7.0 0.4 6.1 0.5	213 12 186 15
5 M	01:05 AM 07:57 AM 01:31 PM 07:59 PM	7.0 0.4 6.2 0.5	213 12 189 15
6 Tu	01:47 AM 08:40 AM 02:14 PM 08:43 PM	7.0 0.4 6.2 0.6	213 12 189 18
7 W	02:27 AM 09:22 AM 02:54 PM 09:27 PM	6.9 0.5 6.2 0.6	210 15 189 18
8 Th	03:06 AM 10:02 AM 03:33 PM 10:10 PM	6.9 0.5 6.2 0.7	210 15 189 21
9 F	03:43 AM 10:41 AM 04:10 PM 10:53 PM	6.8 0.5 6.3 0.7	207 15 192 21
10 Sa	04:20 AM 11:21 AM 04:48 PM 11:39 PM	6.7 0.4 6.4 0.7	204 12 195 21
11 Su	04:59 AM 12:01 PM 05:28 PM	6.6 0.4 6.6	201 12 201
12 M	12:27 AM 05:43 AM 12:44 PM 06:13 PM	0.8 6.4 0.4 6.7	24 195 12 204
13 Tu	01:20 AM 06:36 AM 01:32 PM 07:07 PM	0.9 6.3 0.4 6.8	27 192 12 207
14 W	02:18 AM 07:37 AM 02:27 PM 08:07 PM	0.9 6.1 0.5 6.8	27 186 15 207
15 Th	03:19 AM 08:41 AM 03:27 PM 09:10 PM	1.0 6.0 0.6 6.9	30 183 18 210
16 F	04:22 AM 09:45 AM 04:29 PM 10:12 PM	0.9 6.0 0.6 7.1	27 183 18 216
17 Sa	05:24 AM 10:46 AM 05:31 PM 11:12 PM	0.8 6.1 0.5 7.3	24 186 15 223
18 Su	06:22 AM 11:45 AM 06:31 PM	0.6 6.3 0.4	18 192 12
19 M	12:10 AM 07:18 AM 12:41 PM 07:28 PM	7.4 0.4 6.5 0.3	226 12 198 9
20 Tu	01:04 AM 08:11 AM 01:35 PM 08:23 PM	7.5 0.2 6.7 0.2	229 6 204 6
21 W	01:56 AM 09:01 AM 02:26 PM 09:16 PM	7.5 0.1 6.9 0.2	229 3 210 6
22 Th	02:47 AM 09:49 AM 03:16 PM 10:07 PM	7.4 0.1 7.0 0.2	226 3 213 6
23 F	03:36 AM 10:35 AM 04:05 PM 10:57 PM	7.3 0.1 7.0 0.3	223 3 213 9
24 Sa	04:25 AM 11:21 AM 04:54 PM 11:46 PM	7.1 0.2 7.0 0.4	216 6 213 12
25 Su	05:15 AM 12:06 PM 05:44 PM	6.8 0.3 6.9	207 9 210
26 M	12:36 AM 06:06 AM 12:51 PM 06:34 PM	0.5 6.6 0.4 6.8	15 201 12 207
27 Tu	01:26 AM 06:59 AM 01:37 PM 07:26 PM	0.6 6.4 0.5 6.8	18 195 15 207
28 W	02:17 AM 07:53 AM 02:25 PM 08:19 PM	0.7 6.2 0.5 6.7	21 189 15 204
29 Th	03:09 AM 08:47 AM 03:15 PM 09:13 PM	0.8 6.1 0.6 6.7	24 186 18 204
30 F	04:03 AM 09:42 AM 04:07 PM 10:07 PM	0.8 6.1 0.6 6.8	24 186 18 207
31 Sa	04:56 AM 10:36 AM 05:00 PM 10:59 PM	0.7 6.1 0.6 6.8	21 186 18 207

September

Day	Time (h m)	Height (ft)	Height (cm)
1 Su	05:47 AM 11:27 AM 05:52 PM 11:48 PM	0.7 6.2 0.6 6.9	21 189 18 210
2 M	06:36 AM 12:15 PM 06:42 PM	0.6 6.3 0.6	18 192 18
3 Tu	12:35 AM 07:23 AM 01:01 PM 07:30 PM	7.0 0.5 6.4 0.6	213 15 195 18
4 W	01:18 AM 08:07 AM 01:44 PM 08:17 PM	7.0 0.5 6.5 0.6	213 15 198 18
5 Th	01:59 AM 08:50 AM 02:24 PM 09:03 PM	7.0 0.5 6.6 0.6	213 15 201 18
6 F	02:39 AM 09:31 AM 03:02 PM 09:49 PM	6.9 0.6 6.7 0.7	210 18 204 21
7 Sa	03:18 AM 10:12 AM 03:39 PM 10:35 PM	6.8 0.6 6.8 0.7	207 18 207 21
8 Su	03:57 AM 10:53 AM 04:18 PM 11:22 PM	6.7 0.6 6.9 0.8	204 18 210 24
9 M	04:39 AM 11:36 AM 04:59 PM	6.6 0.6 7.0	201 18 213
10 Tu	12:12 AM 05:26 AM 12:22 PM 05:47 PM	0.9 6.4 0.6 7.0	27 195 18 213
11 W	01:06 AM 06:21 AM 01:13 PM 06:44 PM	0.9 6.3 0.6 7.0	27 192 18 213
12 Th	02:03 AM 07:22 AM 02:10 PM 07:47 PM	1.0 6.1 0.7 7.0	30 186 21 213
13 F	03:03 AM 08:26 AM 03:11 PM 08:52 PM	1.0 6.1 0.7 7.0	30 186 21 213
14 Sa	04:04 AM 09:30 AM 04:13 PM 09:56 PM	0.9 6.1 0.7 7.1	27 186 21 216
15 Su	05:03 AM 10:31 AM 05:15 PM 10:56 PM	0.8 6.3 0.6 7.2	24 192 18 219
16 M	06:01 AM 11:30 AM 06:14 PM 11:53 PM	0.6 6.6 0.5 7.3	18 201 15 223
17 Tu	06:55 AM 12:24 PM 07:11 PM	0.4 6.8 0.3	12 207 9
18 W	12:47 AM 07:46 AM 01:16 PM 08:05 PM	7.4 0.3 7.1 0.3	226 9 216 9
19 Th	01:37 AM 08:35 AM 02:05 PM 08:56 PM	7.4 0.2 7.2 0.3	226 6 219 9
20 F	02:26 AM 09:21 AM 02:52 PM 09:46 PM	7.3 0.2 7.3 0.3	223 6 223 9
21 Sa	03:13 AM 10:06 AM 03:38 PM 10:34 PM	7.1 0.3 7.3 0.4	216 9 223 12
22 Su	04:00 AM 10:50 AM 04:23 PM 11:21 PM	6.9 0.5 7.2 0.6	210 15 219 18
23 M	04:47 AM 11:32 AM 05:10 PM	6.7 0.6 7.1	204 18 216
24 Tu	12:08 AM 05:36 AM 12:15 PM 05:57 PM	0.7 6.5 0.7 6.9	21 198 21 210
25 W	12:55 AM 06:27 AM 12:59 PM 06:47 PM	0.8 6.3 0.7 6.8	24 192 21 207
26 Th	01:43 AM 07:19 AM 01:46 PM 07:40 PM	0.9 6.2 0.8 6.7	27 189 24 204
27 F	02:33 AM 08:13 AM 02:35 PM 08:34 PM	0.9 6.1 0.8 6.7	27 186 24 204
28 Sa	03:24 AM 09:07 AM 03:28 PM 09:28 PM	0.9 6.1 0.8 6.7	27 186 24 204
29 Su	04:17 AM 10:01 AM 04:23 PM 10:22 PM	0.9 6.1 0.8 6.7	27 186 24 204
30 M	05:08 AM 10:52 AM 05:17 PM 11:13 PM	0.8 6.3 0.8 6.8	24 192 24 207

October

Day	Time (h m)	Height (ft)	Height (cm)
1 Tu	05:58 AM 11:42 AM 06:10 PM	0.7 6.5 0.7	21 198 21
2 W	12:01 AM 06:46 AM 12:28 PM 07:01 PM	6.9 0.6 6.6 0.6	210 18 201 18
3 Th	12:46 AM 07:32 AM 01:11 PM 07:51 PM	6.9 0.6 6.8 0.6	210 18 207 18
4 F	01:29 AM 08:16 AM 01:52 PM 08:40 PM	6.9 0.6 7.0 0.6	210 18 213 18
5 Sa	02:11 AM 09:00 AM 02:31 PM 09:28 PM	6.8 0.6 7.1 0.6	207 18 216 18
6 Su	02:53 AM 09:43 AM 03:11 PM 10:16 PM	6.7 0.6 7.2 0.7	204 18 219 21
7 M	03:35 AM 10:28 AM 03:52 PM 11:06 PM	6.6 0.6 7.2 0.7	201 18 219 21
8 Tu	04:21 AM 11:15 AM 04:38 PM 11:58 PM	6.5 0.6 7.2 0.8	198 18 219 24
9 W	05:12 AM 12:04 PM 05:30 PM	6.3 0.6 7.2	192 18 219
10 Th	12:51 AM 06:08 AM 12:58 PM 06:29 PM	0.8 6.2 0.7 7.1	24 189 21 216
11 F	01:47 AM 07:09 AM 01:55 PM 07:32 PM	0.8 6.1 0.7 7.0	24 186 21 213
12 Sa	02:45 AM 08:12 AM 02:56 PM 08:37 PM	0.8 6.1 0.7 6.9	24 186 21 210
13 Su	03:43 AM 09:15 AM 03:57 PM 09:39 PM	0.7 6.2 0.6 6.9	21 189 18 210
14 M	04:41 AM 10:16 AM 04:58 PM 10:39 PM	0.6 6.5 0.5 7.0	18 198 15 213
15 Tu	05:37 AM 11:13 AM 05:57 PM 11:35 PM	0.4 6.7 0.4 7.1	12 204 12 216
16 W	06:30 AM 12:06 PM 06:53 PM	0.2 7.0 0.3	6 213 9
17 Th	12:28 AM 07:20 AM 12:56 PM 07:46 PM	7.1 0.2 7.2 0.2	216 6 219 6
18 F	01:17 AM 08:08 AM 01:43 PM 08:36 PM	7.1 0.2 7.3 0.2	216 6 223 6
19 Sa	02:04 AM 08:53 AM 02:27 PM 09:24 PM	7.0 0.3 7.3 0.3	213 9 223 9
20 Su	02:50 AM 09:37 AM 03:11 PM 10:10 PM	6.8 0.4 7.2 0.4	207 12 219 12
21 M	03:35 AM 10:19 AM 03:54 PM 10:55 PM	6.6 0.5 7.1 0.5	201 15 216 15
22 Tu	04:20 AM 11:00 AM 04:38 PM 11:39 PM	6.4 0.6 7.0 0.6	195 18 213 18
23 W	05:07 AM 11:41 AM 05:23 PM	6.2 0.7 6.8	189 21 207
24 Th	12:24 AM 05:55 AM 12:23 PM 06:10 PM	0.7 6.1 0.7 6.7	21 186 21 204
25 F	01:09 AM 06:45 AM 01:07 PM 07:00 PM	0.8 6.0 0.7 6.6	24 183 21 201
26 Sa	01:55 AM 07:36 AM 01:56 PM 07:53 PM	0.8 5.9 0.7 6.5	24 180 21 198
27 Su	02:44 AM 08:29 AM 02:48 PM 08:47 PM	0.8 5.9 0.7 6.4	24 180 21 195
28 M	03:35 AM 09:22 AM 03:44 PM 09:41 PM	0.7 6.0 0.7 6.4	21 183 21 195
29 Tu	04:26 AM 10:14 AM 04:41 PM 10:33 PM	0.6 6.2 0.7 6.4	18 189 21 195
30 W	05:17 AM 11:04 AM 05:38 PM 11:24 PM	0.6 6.4 0.6 6.5	18 195 18 198
31 Th	06:07 AM 11:51 AM 06:32 PM	0.5 6.6 0.5	15 201 15

November

Day	Time (h m)	Height (ft)	Height (cm)
1 F	12:12 AM 06:55 AM 12:36 PM 07:25 PM	6.5 0.4 6.8 0.5	198 12 207 15
2 Sa	12:58 AM 07:43 AM 01:19 PM 08:17 PM	6.5 0.4 7.0 0.4	198 12 213 12
3 Su	01:43 AM 07:30 AM 01:02 PM 08:08 PM	6.5 0.3 7.2 0.4	198 9 219 12
4 M	01:29 AM 08:17 AM 01:46 PM 08:58 PM	6.4 0.3 7.2 0.4	195 9 219 12
5 Tu	02:15 AM 09:06 AM 02:32 PM 09:50 PM	6.3 0.3 7.3 0.4	192 9 223 12
6 W	03:05 AM 09:56 AM 03:22 PM 10:42 PM	6.2 0.3 7.2 0.4	189 9 219 12
7 Th	03:58 AM 10:48 AM 04:17 PM 11:35 PM	6.1 0.3 7.1 0.4	186 9 216 12
8 F	04:55 AM 11:43 AM 05:16 PM	6.0 0.3 6.9	183 9 210
9 Sa	12:29 AM 05:55 AM 12:40 PM 06:17 PM	0.3 6.0 0.3 6.7	9 183 9 204
10 Su	01:24 AM 06:57 AM 01:39 PM 07:19 PM	0.3 6.0 0.3 6.6	9 183 9 201
11 M	02:20 AM 07:58 AM 02:39 PM 08:21 PM	0.2 6.2 0.3 6.5	6 189 9 198
12 Tu	03:16 AM 08:57 AM 03:39 PM 09:19 PM	0.1 6.4 0.2 6.5	3 195 6 198
13 W	04:10 AM 09:53 AM 04:37 PM 10:15 PM	0.0 6.6 0.1 6.5	0 201 3 198
14 Th	05:03 AM 10:45 AM 05:33 PM 11:07 PM	-0.1 6.8 0.0 6.5	-3 207 0 198
15 F	05:53 AM 11:34 AM 06:25 PM 11:55 PM	-0.1 6.9 -0.1 6.5	-3 210 -3 198
16 Sa	06:40 AM 12:20 PM 07:14 PM	-0.1 7.0 -0.1	-3 213 -3
17 Su	12:42 AM 07:25 AM 01:04 PM 08:01 PM	6.4 0.0 7.0 0.0	195 0 213 0
18 M	01:27 AM 08:08 AM 01:46 PM 08:46 PM	6.2 0.1 6.9 0.1	189 3 210 3
19 Tu	02:11 AM 08:49 AM 02:28 PM 09:29 PM	6.1 0.3 6.8 0.2	186 9 207 6
20 W	02:55 AM 09:30 AM 03:09 PM 10:11 PM	5.9 0.3 6.6 0.3	180 9 201 9
21 Th	03:39 AM 10:10 AM 03:52 PM 10:53 PM	5.8 0.4 6.5 0.3	177 12 198 9
22 F	04:24 AM 10:50 AM 04:35 PM 11:35 PM	5.7 0.4 6.3 0.3	174 12 192 9
23 Sa	05:10 AM 11:32 AM 05:22 PM	5.6 0.3 6.2	171 9 189
24 Su	12:18 AM 05:58 AM 12:19 PM 06:11 PM	0.3 5.6 0.3 6.1	9 171 9 186
25 M	01:03 AM 06:48 AM 01:10 PM 07:03 PM	0.3 5.6 0.4 6.0	9 171 12 183
26 Tu	01:51 AM 07:40 AM 02:06 PM 07:58 PM	0.2 5.7 0.4 5.9	6 174 12 180
27 W	02:42 AM 08:31 AM 03:05 PM 08:52 PM	0.2 5.8 0.4 5.8	6 177 12 177
28 Th	03:34 AM 09:23 AM 04:05 PM 09:45 PM	0.2 6.0 0.3 5.8	6 183 9 177
29 F	04:27 AM 10:13 AM 05:03 PM 10:37 PM	0.1 6.3 0.2 5.9	3 192 6 180
30 Sa	05:20 AM 11:01 AM 06:00 PM 11:27 PM	0.0 6.5 0.1 5.9	0 198 3 180

December

Day	Time (h m)	Height (ft)	Height (cm)
1 Su	06:11 AM 11:49 AM 06:54 PM	-0.1 6.8 0.0	-3 207 0
2 M	12:17 AM 07:03 AM 12:37 PM 07:47 PM	5.9 -0.1 6.9 -0.1	180 -3 210 -3
3 Tu	01:06 AM 07:54 AM 01:25 PM 08:40 PM	5.9 -0.2 7.0 -0.1	180 -6 213 -3
4 W	01:57 AM 08:46 AM 02:15 PM 09:31 PM	5.9 -0.2 7.0 -0.2	180 -6 213 -6
5 Th	02:49 AM 09:38 AM 03:08 PM 10:23 PM	5.8 -0.3 6.9 -0.3	177 -9 210 -9
6 F	03:43 AM 10:31 AM 04:03 PM 11:15 PM	5.8 -0.3 6.7 -0.3	177 -9 204 -9
7 Sa	04:39 AM 11:26 AM 05:00 PM	5.8 -0.3 6.5	177 -9 198
8 Su	12:07 AM 05:37 AM 12:22 PM 05:59 PM	-0.4 5.8 -0.3 6.3	-12 177 -9 192
9 M	01:00 AM 06:36 AM 01:20 PM 06:59 PM	-0.4 5.8 -0.2 6.1	-12 177 -6 186
10 Tu	01:53 AM 07:35 AM 02:18 PM 07:58 PM	-0.4 5.9 -0.2 6.0	-12 180 -6 183
11 W	02:47 AM 08:33 AM 03:17 PM 08:55 PM	-0.5 6.1 -0.3 5.9	-15 186 -9 180
12 Th	03:41 AM 09:29 AM 04:14 PM 09:51 PM	-0.5 6.2 -0.3 5.8	-15 189 -9 177
13 F	04:33 AM 10:21 AM 05:09 PM 10:43 PM	-0.5 6.3 -0.4 5.8	-15 192 -12 177
14 Sa	05:24 AM 11:10 AM 06:02 PM 11:33 PM	-0.5 6.4 -0.4 5.8	-15 195 -12 177
15 Su	06:12 AM 11:57 AM 06:51 PM	-0.4 6.4 -0.4	-12 195 -12
16 M	12:20 AM 06:57 AM 12:41 PM 07:37 PM	5.7 -0.4 6.4 -0.4	174 -12 195 -12
17 Tu	01:05 AM 07:41 AM 01:23 PM 08:21 PM	5.7 -0.3 6.4 -0.3	174 -9 195 -9
18 W	01:48 AM 08:22 AM 02:04 PM 09:03 PM	5.6 -0.2 6.3 -0.2	171 -6 192 -6
19 Th	02:31 AM 09:03 AM 02:44 PM 09:44 PM	5.4 -0.1 6.2 -0.2	165 -3 189 -6
20 F	03:12 AM 09:42 AM 03:24 PM 10:23 PM	5.4 -0.1 6.0 -0.2	165 -3 183 -6
21 Sa	03:54 AM 10:22 AM 04:04 PM 11:02 PM	5.3 -0.1 5.9 -0.2	162 -3 180 -6
22 Su	04:36 AM 11:03 AM 04:46 PM 11:42 PM	5.3 -0.2 5.8 -0.2	162 -6 177 -6
23 M	05:19 AM 11:47 AM 05:31 PM	5.3 -0.2 5.7	162 -6 174
24 Tu	12:23 AM 06:05 AM 12:36 PM 06:20 PM	-0.3 5.3 -0.1 5.5	-9 162 -3 168
25 W	01:08 AM 06:53 AM 01:32 PM 07:14 PM	-0.3 5.4 0.0 5.4	-9 165 0 165
26 Th	01:58 AM 07:46 AM 02:32 PM 08:11 PM	-0.3 5.5 0.0 5.3	-9 168 0 162
27 F	02:52 AM 08:40 AM 03:35 PM 09:08 PM	-0.3 5.7 0.0 5.3	-9 174 0 162
28 Sa	03:50 AM 09:35 AM 04:36 PM 10:05 PM	-0.3 5.9 0.0 5.3	-9 180 0 162
29 Su	04:47 AM 10:29 AM 05:36 PM 11:00 PM	-0.3 6.2 -0.2 5.4	-9 189 -6 165
30 M	05:44 AM 11:22 AM 06:32 PM 11:53 PM	-0.4 6.4 -0.3 5.4	-12 195 -9 165
31 Tu	06:40 AM 12:15 PM 07:27 PM	-0.6 6.6 -0.5	-18 201 -15

Heights are referred to mean lower water which is the chart datum of sounding. All times are local. Daylight Saving Time has been used when needed.

Reedy Point, Delaware, 2012

Times and Heights of High and Low Waters

September

Day	Time (h m)	Height (ft)	Height (cm)
1 Sa	06:49 AM 12:23 PM 07:04 PM	0.1 6.0 0.2	3 183 6
2 Su	12:41 AM 07:29 AM 01:05 PM 07:49 PM	6.2 0.2 6.0 0.4	189 6 183 12
3 M	01:23 AM 08:08 AM 01:46 PM 08:32 PM	6.0 0.3 6.0 0.5	183 9 183 15
4 Tu	02:05 AM 08:45 AM 02:27 PM 09:15 PM	5.8 0.5 5.9 0.7	177 15 180 21
5 W	02:48 AM 09:21 AM 03:08 PM 09:59 PM	5.6 0.6 5.8 0.8	171 18 177 24
6 Th	03:34 AM 09:58 AM 03:52 PM 10:46 PM	5.4 0.7 5.8 1.0	165 21 177 30
7 F	04:23 AM 10:39 AM 04:40 PM 11:36 PM	5.2 0.8 5.7 1.0	158 24 174 30
8 Sa	05:16 AM 11:26 AM 05:33 PM	5.1 0.8 5.7	155 24 174
9 Su	12:30 AM 06:12 AM 12:20 PM 06:30 PM	1.1 5.0 0.8 5.7	34 152 24 174
10 M	01:25 AM 07:08 AM 01:17 PM 07:27 PM	1.0 5.1 0.8 5.8	30 155 24 177
11 Tu	02:20 AM 08:03 AM 02:16 PM 08:20 PM	0.9 5.2 0.7 5.9	27 158 21 180
12 W	03:13 AM 08:54 AM 03:13 PM 09:10 PM	0.7 5.3 0.6 6.0	21 162 18 183
13 Th	04:03 AM 09:41 AM 04:07 PM 09:57 PM	0.5 5.5 0.4 6.2	15 168 12 189
14 F	04:50 AM 10:26 AM 05:00 PM 10:42 PM	0.3 5.8 0.3 6.3	9 177 9 192
15 Sa	05:36 AM 11:08 AM 05:50 PM 11:25 PM	0.2 6.0 0.2 6.3	6 183 6 192
16 Su	06:20 AM 11:50 AM 06:41 PM	0.1 6.2 0.1	3 189 3
17 M	12:09 AM 07:04 AM 12:32 PM 07:31 PM	6.3 0.1 6.4 0.1	192 3 195 3
18 Tu	12:54 AM 07:48 AM 01:17 PM 08:23 PM	6.2 0.1 6.4 0.2	189 3 195 6
19 W	01:41 AM 08:35 AM 02:04 PM 09:17 PM	6.0 0.1 6.4 0.3	183 3 195 9
20 Th	02:33 AM 09:25 AM 02:57 PM 10:14 PM	5.8 0.2 6.3 0.5	177 6 192 15
21 F	03:30 AM 10:19 AM 03:56 PM 11:13 PM	5.6 0.3 6.2 0.6	171 9 189 18
22 Sa	04:33 AM 11:18 AM 05:01 PM	5.4 0.4 6.1	165 12 186
23 Su	12:14 AM 05:40 AM 12:20 PM 06:09 PM	0.6 5.3 0.5 6.0	18 162 15 183
24 M	01:15 AM 06:47 AM 01:23 PM 07:16 PM	0.6 5.3 0.5 6.0	18 162 15 183
25 Tu	02:14 AM 07:50 AM 02:24 PM 08:17 PM	0.4 5.4 0.4 6.1	12 165 12 186
26 W	03:10 AM 08:48 AM 03:23 PM 09:13 PM	0.3 5.6 0.3 6.1	9 171 9 186
27 Th	04:02 AM 09:41 AM 04:17 PM 10:04 PM	0.1 5.9 0.2 6.2	3 180 6 189
28 F	04:51 AM 10:30 AM 05:08 PM 10:50 PM	0.0 6.0 0.1 6.2	0 183 3 189
29 Sa	05:35 AM 11:15 AM 05:56 PM 11:34 PM	0.0 6.1 0.1 6.1	0 186 3 186
30 Su	06:17 AM 11:57 AM 06:41 PM	0.1 6.1 0.2	3 186 6

October

Day	Time (h m)	Height (ft)	Height (cm)
1 M	12:16 AM 06:56 AM 12:37 PM 07:24 PM	6.0 0.2 6.1 0.3	183 6 186 9
2 Tu	12:57 AM 07:33 AM 01:15 PM 08:06 PM	5.8 0.4 6.0 0.5	177 12 183 15
3 W	01:37 AM 08:07 AM 01:51 PM 08:47 PM	5.6 0.5 5.9 0.6	171 15 180 18
4 Th	02:18 AM 08:41 AM 02:28 PM 09:28 PM	5.4 0.6 5.9 0.8	165 18 180 24
5 F	02:59 AM 09:15 AM 03:06 PM 10:12 PM	5.2 0.7 5.8 0.9	158 21 177 27
6 Sa	03:44 AM 09:55 AM 03:50 PM 10:59 PM	5.1 0.8 5.7 1.0	155 24 174 30
7 Su	04:33 AM 10:42 AM 04:40 PM 11:50 PM	5.0 0.8 5.6 1.0	152 24 171 30
8 M	05:28 AM 11:37 AM 05:38 PM	5.0 0.8 5.6	152 24 171
9 Tu	12:44 AM 06:25 AM 12:38 PM 06:38 PM	0.9 5.0 0.8 5.7	27 152 24 174
10 W	01:38 AM 07:20 AM 01:40 PM 07:36 PM	0.8 5.2 0.7 5.7	24 158 21 174
11 Th	02:32 AM 08:14 AM 02:41 PM 08:31 PM	0.6 5.4 0.5 5.9	18 165 15 180
12 F	03:23 AM 09:04 AM 03:39 PM 09:22 PM	0.4 5.7 0.3 6.0	12 174 9 183
13 Sa	04:13 AM 09:51 AM 04:35 PM 10:11 PM	0.2 6.0 0.2 6.0	6 183 6 183
14 Su	05:01 AM 10:37 AM 05:29 PM 10:59 PM	0.0 6.2 0.0 6.1	0 189 0 186
15 M	05:48 AM 11:23 AM 06:22 PM 11:47 PM	-0.1 6.4 -0.1 6.0	-3 195 -3 183
16 Tu	06:36 AM 12:09 PM 07:15 PM	-0.1 6.6 -0.1	-3 201 -3
17 W	12:36 AM 07:24 AM 12:57 PM 08:09 PM	5.9 -0.1 6.6 0.0	180 -3 201 0
18 Th	01:26 AM 08:14 AM 01:47 PM 09:03 PM	5.8 0.0 6.5 0.1	177 0 198 3
19 F	02:20 AM 09:07 AM 02:42 PM 09:59 PM	5.6 0.1 6.3 0.2	171 3 192 6
20 Sa	03:18 AM 10:04 AM 03:42 PM 10:57 PM	5.4 0.2 6.1 0.3	165 6 186 9
21 Su	04:21 AM 11:03 AM 04:46 PM 11:54 PM	5.2 0.3 5.9 0.3	158 9 180 9
22 M	05:26 AM 12:04 PM 05:52 PM	5.2 0.4 5.8	158 12 177
23 Tu	12:52 AM 06:30 AM 01:05 PM 06:56 PM	0.3 5.3 0.4 5.8	9 162 12 177
24 W	01:48 AM 07:31 AM 02:04 PM 07:56 PM	0.2 5.5 0.3 5.8	6 168 9 177
25 Th	02:42 AM 08:28 AM 03:02 PM 08:50 PM	0.1 5.7 0.2 5.8	3 174 6 177
26 F	03:32 AM 09:19 AM 03:55 PM 09:40 PM	0.0 5.9 0.1 5.8	0 180 3 177
27 Sa	04:19 AM 10:07 AM 04:46 PM 10:27 PM	0.0 6.0 0.0 5.8	0 183 0 177
28 Su	05:03 AM 10:50 AM 05:33 PM 11:11 PM	0.0 6.1 0.0 5.7	0 186 0 174
29 M	05:44 AM 11:31 AM 06:18 PM 11:52 PM	0.1 6.1 0.1 5.6	3 186 3 171
30 Tu	06:23 AM 12:10 PM 07:00 PM	0.2 6.0 0.2	6 183 6
31 W	12:33 AM 07:00 AM 12:46 PM 07:41 PM	5.4 0.3 5.9 0.3	165 9 180 9

November

Day	Time (h m)	Height (ft)	Height (cm)
1 Th	01:12 AM 07:34 AM 01:21 PM 08:21 PM	5.3 0.4 5.8 0.4	162 12 177 12
2 F	01:50 AM 08:08 AM 01:54 PM 09:01 PM	5.1 0.5 5.8 0.5	155 15 177 15
3 Sa	02:29 AM 08:42 AM 02:29 PM 09:42 PM	5.0 0.5 5.7 0.6	152 15 174 18
4 Su	02:09 AM 08:20 AM 02:07 PM 09:25 PM	4.9 0.5 5.7 0.7	149 15 174 21
5 M	02:52 AM 09:06 AM 02:53 PM 10:12 PM	4.9 0.6 5.6 0.6	149 18 171 18
6 Tu	03:42 AM 10:00 AM 03:47 PM 11:02 PM	4.9 0.6 5.5 0.6	149 18 168 18
7 W	04:38 AM 11:01 AM 04:48 PM 11:55 PM	5.0 0.6 5.5 0.5	152 18 168 15
8 Th	05:35 AM 12:05 PM 05:51 PM	5.1 0.5 5.5	155 15 168
9 F	12:49 AM 06:31 AM 01:10 PM 06:51 PM	0.3 5.4 0.4 5.5	9 165 12 168
10 Sa	01:42 AM 07:26 AM 02:12 PM 07:48 PM	0.2 5.7 0.2 5.6	6 174 6 171
11 Su	02:36 AM 08:18 AM 03:12 PM 08:43 PM	0.0 6.0 0.0 5.6	0 183 0 171
12 M	03:28 AM 09:09 AM 04:10 PM 09:35 PM	-0.2 6.2 -0.2 5.7	-6 189 -6 174
13 Tu	04:20 AM 09:59 AM 05:05 PM 10:27 PM	-0.3 6.4 -0.3 5.6	-9 195 -9 171
14 W	05:11 AM 10:49 AM 06:00 PM 11:19 PM	-0.3 6.5 -0.3 5.6	-9 198 -9 171
15 Th	06:04 AM 11:40 AM 06:54 PM	-0.4 6.5 -0.3	-12 198 -9
16 F	12:12 AM 06:56 AM 12:33 PM 07:47 PM	5.4 -0.3 6.3 -0.3	165 -9 192 -9
17 Sa	01:06 AM 07:51 AM 01:28 PM 08:41 PM	5.3 -0.2 6.2 -0.2	162 -6 189 -6
18 Su	02:04 AM 08:47 AM 02:26 PM 09:35 PM	5.2 -0.1 5.9 -0.1	158 -3 180 -3
19 M	03:04 AM 09:44 AM 03:27 PM 10:29 PM	5.1 0.0 5.7 -0.1	155 0 174 -3
20 Tu	04:05 AM 10:42 AM 04:29 PM 11:23 PM	5.1 0.1 5.5 0.0	155 3 168 0
21 W	05:07 AM 11:41 AM 05:30 PM	5.2 0.2 5.4	158 6 165
22 Th	12:16 AM 06:05 AM 12:39 PM 06:28 PM	-0.1 5.3 0.1 5.4	-3 162 3 165
23 F	01:08 AM 07:00 AM 01:36 PM 07:22 PM	-0.1 5.5 0.1 5.4	-3 168 3 165
24 Sa	01:58 AM 07:52 AM 02:29 PM 08:13 PM	-0.1 5.6 0.0 5.4	-3 171 0 165
25 Su	02:45 AM 08:39 AM 03:20 PM 09:00 PM	-0.1 5.8 -0.1 5.3	-3 177 -3 162
26 M	03:30 AM 09:24 AM 04:08 PM 09:46 PM	-0.1 5.8 -0.1 5.3	-3 177 -3 162
27 Tu	04:12 AM 10:06 AM 04:53 PM 10:29 PM	-0.1 5.8 -0.1 5.2	-3 177 -3 158
28 W	04:52 AM 10:45 AM 05:36 PM 11:09 PM	0.0 5.8 -0.1 5.1	0 177 -3 155
29 Th	05:31 AM 11:21 AM 06:17 PM 11:48 PM	0.1 5.7 0.0 5.0	3 174 0 152
30 F	06:08 AM 11:56 AM 06:57 PM	0.1 5.7 0.1	3 174 3

December

Day	Time (h m)	Height (ft)	Height (cm)
1 Sa	12:25 AM 06:43 AM 12:28 PM 07:36 PM	4.8 0.2 5.6 0.2	146 6 171 6
2 Su	01:01 AM 07:19 AM 01:01 PM 08:14 PM	4.8 0.2 5.6 0.2	146 6 171 6
3 M	01:37 AM 07:57 AM 01:37 PM 08:54 PM	4.8 0.2 5.6 0.3	146 6 171 9
4 Tu	02:16 AM 08:40 AM 02:19 PM 09:35 PM	4.8 0.2 5.5 0.2	146 6 168 6
5 W	03:01 AM 09:31 AM 03:09 PM 10:21 PM	4.9 0.3 5.4 0.2	149 9 165 6
6 Th	03:53 AM 10:30 AM 04:07 PM 11:12 PM	5.0 0.3 5.3 0.1	152 9 162 3
7 F	04:51 AM 11:36 AM 05:11 PM	5.1 0.3 5.2	155 9 158
8 Sa	12:07 AM 05:51 AM 12:43 PM 06:16 PM	0.0 5.3 0.2 5.2	0 162 6 158
9 Su	01:04 AM 06:51 AM 01:49 PM 07:19 PM	-0.1 5.6 0.1 5.2	-3 171 3 158
10 M	02:03 AM 07:49 AM 02:52 PM 08:18 PM	-0.2 5.8 -0.1 5.2	-6 177 -3 158
11 Tu	03:00 AM 08:45 AM 03:52 PM 09:15 PM	-0.4 6.0 -0.3 5.2	-12 183 -9 158
12 W	03:57 AM 09:39 AM 04:49 PM 10:10 PM	-0.5 6.2 -0.5 5.2	-15 189 -15 158
13 Th	04:52 AM 10:33 AM 05:44 PM 11:03 PM	-0.6 6.2 -0.6 5.2	-18 189 -18 158
14 F	05:46 AM 11:26 AM 06:37 PM 11:57 PM	-0.6 6.2 -0.6 5.2	-18 189 -18 158
15 Sa	06:40 AM 12:18 PM 07:28 PM	-0.6 6.1 -0.6	-18 186 -18
16 Su	12:50 AM 07:33 AM 01:12 PM 08:19 PM	5.2 -0.5 5.9 -0.5	158 -15 180 -15
17 M	01:45 AM 08:27 AM 02:06 PM 09:09 PM	5.1 -0.4 5.7 -0.4	155 -12 174 -12
18 Tu	02:41 AM 09:21 AM 03:02 PM 09:59 PM	5.1 -0.2 5.5 -0.3	155 -6 168 -9
19 W	03:37 AM 10:16 AM 04:00 PM 10:49 PM	5.1 -0.1 5.3 -0.2	155 -3 162 -6
20 Th	04:35 AM 11:12 AM 04:57 PM 11:39 PM	5.1 0.0 5.1 -0.2	155 0 155 -6
21 F	05:32 AM 12:09 PM 05:54 PM	5.1 0.0 5.0	155 0 152
22 Sa	12:29 AM 06:26 AM 01:04 PM 06:49 PM	-0.1 5.2 0.0 4.9	-3 158 0 149
23 Su	01:19 AM 07:19 AM 01:59 PM 07:42 PM	-0.1 5.3 0.0 4.9	-3 162 0 149
24 M	02:07 AM 08:09 AM 02:51 PM 08:32 PM	-0.1 5.4 -0.1 4.9	-3 165 -3 149
25 Tu	02:55 AM 08:56 AM 03:40 PM 09:19 PM	-0.2 5.5 -0.2 4.9	-6 168 -6 149
26 W	03:40 AM 09:39 AM 04:27 PM 10:04 PM	-0.2 5.5 -0.2 4.9	-6 168 -6 149
27 Th	04:23 AM 10:20 AM 05:11 PM 10:45 PM	-0.2 5.5 -0.2 4.8	-6 168 -6 146
28 F	05:05 AM 10:58 AM 05:52 PM 11:24 PM	-0.2 5.5 -0.2 4.8	-6 168 -6 146
29 Sa	05:45 AM 11:33 AM 06:32 PM	-0.2 5.5 -0.2	-6 168 -6
30 Su	12:00 AM 06:23 AM 12:06 PM 07:10 PM	4.8 -0.2 5.5 -0.1	146 -6 168 -3
31 M	12:35 AM 07:01 AM 12:39 PM 07:47 PM	4.8 -0.1 5.5 -0.1	146 -3 168 -3

Heights are referred to mean lower water which is the chart datum of sounding. All times are local. Daylight Saving Time has been used when needed.

Reedy Point, Delaware, 2013

Times and Heights of High and Low Waters

January

Day	Time (h m)	Height (ft)	Height (cm)
1 Tu	01:06 AM 07:39 AM 01:11 PM 08:24 PM	4.8 -0.1 5.5 0.0	146 -3 168 0
2 W	01:43 AM 08:22 AM 01:52 PM 09:03 PM	4.9 0.0 5.4 -0.1	149 0 165 -3
3 Th	02:25 AM 09:11 AM 02:41 PM 09:47 PM	5.0 0.0 5.3 -0.1	152 0 162 -3
4 F	03:16 AM 10:10 AM 03:38 PM 10:38 PM	5.1 0.1 5.1 -0.1	155 3 155 -3
5 Sa	04:15 AM 11:17 AM 04:43 PM 11:36 PM	5.1 0.2 5.0 -0.1	155 6 152 -3
6 Su	05:19 AM 12:26 PM 05:52 PM	5.2 0.1 4.8	158 3 146
7 M	12:39 AM 06:25 AM 01:33 PM 06:59 PM	-0.2 5.4 0.0 4.8	-6 165 0 146
8 Tu	01:43 AM 07:29 AM 02:37 PM 08:02 PM	-0.3 5.6 -0.2 4.9	-9 171 -6 149
9 W	02:44 AM 08:29 AM 03:37 PM 09:01 PM	-0.4 5.8 -0.4 5.0	-12 177 -12 152
10 Th	03:43 AM 09:27 AM 04:34 PM 09:57 PM	-0.6 5.9 -0.6 5.1	-18 180 -18 155
11 F	04:40 AM 10:21 AM 05:27 PM 10:51 PM	-0.8 6.0 -0.8 5.2	-24 183 -24 158
12 Sa	05:33 AM 11:14 AM 06:18 PM 11:42 PM	-0.8 6.1 -0.8 5.3	-24 186 -24 162
13 Su	06:25 AM 12:04 PM 07:06 PM	-0.8 6.0 -0.8	-24 183 -24
14 M	12:33 AM 07:16 AM 12:54 PM 07:53 PM	5.3 -0.8 5.8 -0.7	162 -24 177 -21
15 Tu	01:23 AM 08:06 AM 01:44 PM 08:39 PM	5.3 -0.6 5.6 -0.6	162 -18 171 -18
16 W	02:14 AM 08:56 AM 02:35 PM 09:25 PM	5.2 -0.4 5.4 -0.4	158 -12 165 -12
17 Th	03:05 AM 09:47 AM 03:27 PM 10:11 PM	5.2 -0.2 5.2 -0.3	158 -6 158 -9
18 F	03:57 AM 10:39 AM 04:22 PM 10:58 PM	5.1 -0.1 5.0 -0.2	155 -3 152 -6
19 Sa	04:51 AM 11:33 AM 05:17 PM 11:47 PM	5.1 0.0 4.9 -0.1	155 0 149 -3
20 Su	05:46 AM 12:27 PM 06:13 PM	5.1 0.1 4.8	155 3 146
21 M	12:37 AM 06:40 AM 01:22 PM 07:07 PM	0.0 5.1 0.1 4.8	0 155 3 146
22 Tu	01:28 AM 07:33 AM 02:16 PM 07:59 PM	0.0 5.2 0.0 4.8	0 158 0 146
23 W	02:18 AM 08:22 AM 03:07 PM 08:48 PM	-0.1 5.3 -0.1 4.8	-3 162 -3 146
24 Th	03:07 AM 09:09 AM 03:55 PM 09:34 PM	-0.2 5.4 -0.1 4.9	-6 165 -3 149
25 F	03:54 AM 09:52 AM 04:40 PM 10:17 PM	-0.2 5.4 -0.2 4.9	-6 165 -6 149
26 Sa	04:39 AM 10:31 AM 05:23 PM 10:56 PM	-0.3 5.5 -0.2 4.9	-9 168 -6 149
27 Su	05:22 AM 11:08 AM 06:04 PM 11:32 PM	-0.3 5.5 -0.2 4.9	-9 168 -6 149
28 M	06:04 AM 11:42 AM 06:42 PM	-0.3 5.5 -0.2	-9 168 -6
29 Tu	12:06 AM 06:45 AM 12:17 PM 07:20 PM	5.0 -0.3 5.5 -0.2	152 -9 168 -6
30 W	12:40 AM 07:27 AM 12:54 PM 07:58 PM	5.1 -0.2 5.5 -0.2	155 -6 168 -6
31 Th	01:17 AM 08:12 AM 01:35 PM 08:37 PM	5.2 -0.2 5.4 -0.2	158 -6 165 -6

February

Day	Time (h m)	Height (ft)	Height (cm)
1 F	02:00 AM 09:02 AM 02:23 PM 09:21 PM	5.3 -0.1 5.2 -0.1	162 -3 158 -3
2 Sa	02:50 AM 09:59 AM 03:20 PM 10:13 PM	5.4 0.1 5.1 -0.1	165 3 155 -3
3 Su	03:48 AM 11:04 AM 04:25 PM 11:14 PM	5.3 0.2 4.9 0.0	162 6 149 0
4 M	04:55 AM 12:11 PM 05:34 PM	5.3 0.2 4.8	162 6 146
5 Tu	12:20 AM 06:04 AM 01:17 PM 06:43 PM	-0.1 5.4 0.1 4.8	-3 165 3 146
6 W	01:25 AM 07:12 AM 02:20 PM 07:47 PM	-0.2 5.5 -0.1 4.9	-6 168 -3 149
7 Th	02:28 AM 08:15 AM 03:19 PM 08:46 PM	-0.3 5.7 -0.3 5.1	-9 174 -9 155
8 F	03:28 AM 09:13 AM 04:14 PM 09:42 PM	-0.5 5.8 -0.5 5.3	-15 177 -15 162
9 Sa	04:24 AM 10:07 AM 05:06 PM 10:34 PM	-0.7 5.9 -0.7 5.4	-21 180 -21 165
10 Su	05:17 AM 10:57 AM 05:54 PM 11:23 PM	-0.8 6.0 -0.7 5.5	-24 183 -21 168
11 M	06:07 AM 11:45 AM 06:40 PM	-0.8 5.9 -0.7	-24 180 -21
12 Tu	12:10 AM 06:55 AM 12:32 PM 07:23 PM	5.6 -0.7 5.8 -0.6	171 -21 177 -18
13 W	12:56 AM 07:42 AM 01:18 PM 08:05 PM	5.6 -0.5 5.6 -0.4	171 -15 171 -12
14 Th	01:41 AM 08:29 AM 02:05 PM 08:47 PM	5.5 -0.3 5.4 -0.2	168 -9 165 -6
15 F	02:27 AM 09:15 AM 02:53 PM 09:29 PM	5.4 -0.1 5.2 0.0	165 -3 158 0
16 Sa	03:15 AM 10:04 AM 03:45 PM 10:13 PM	5.3 0.1 5.0 0.1	162 3 152 3
17 Su	04:06 AM 10:55 AM 04:39 PM 11:00 PM	5.2 0.2 4.8 0.2	158 6 146 6
18 M	05:01 AM 11:48 AM 05:35 PM 11:51 PM	5.1 0.3 4.8 0.3	155 9 146 9
19 Tu	05:57 AM 12:43 PM 06:30 PM	5.1 0.3 4.8	155 9 146
20 W	12:45 AM 06:52 AM 01:38 PM 07:24 PM	0.3 5.1 0.3 4.8	9 155 9 146
21 Th	01:40 AM 07:45 AM 02:30 PM 08:15 PM	0.2 5.2 0.2 4.9	6 158 6 149
22 F	02:33 AM 08:35 AM 03:20 PM 09:03 PM	0.1 5.3 0.1 5.0	3 162 3 152
23 Sa	03:24 AM 09:20 AM 04:07 PM 09:46 PM	-0.1 5.4 0.0 5.1	-3 165 0 155
24 Su	04:13 AM 10:02 AM 04:51 PM 10:26 PM	-0.2 5.5 -0.1 5.2	-6 168 -3 158
25 M	04:59 AM 10:41 AM 05:33 PM 11:03 PM	-0.2 5.6 -0.1 5.4	-6 171 -3 165
26 Tu	05:45 AM 11:19 AM 06:13 PM 11:39 PM	-0.3 5.6 -0.2 5.5	-9 171 -6 168
27 W	06:29 AM 11:57 AM 06:53 PM	-0.3 5.6 -0.1	-9 171 -3
28 Th	12:16 AM 07:15 AM 12:37 PM 07:33 PM	5.6 -0.2 5.5 -0.1	171 -6 168 -3

March

Day	Time (h m)	Height (ft)	Height (cm)
1 F	12:55 AM 08:03 AM 01:22 PM 08:15 PM	5.7 -0.2 5.4 -0.1	174 -6 165 -3
2 Sa	01:40 AM 08:55 AM 02:12 PM 09:03 PM	5.8 0.0 5.3 0.0	177 0 162 0
3 Su	02:31 AM 09:52 AM 03:10 PM 09:59 PM	5.7 0.1 5.1 0.1	174 3 155 3
4 M	03:31 AM 10:53 AM 04:15 PM 11:01 PM	5.6 0.2 5.0 0.2	171 6 152 6
5 Tu	04:39 AM 11:57 AM 05:23 PM	5.5 0.2 4.9	168 6 149
6 W	12:06 AM 05:50 AM 01:00 PM 06:30 PM	0.2 5.5 0.2 5.0	6 168 6 152
7 Th	01:11 AM 06:57 AM 02:01 PM 07:34 PM	0.1 5.6 0.0 5.2	3 171 0 158
8 F	02:14 AM 08:00 AM 02:58 PM 08:32 PM	-0.1 5.7 -0.2 5.4	-3 174 -6 165
9 Sa	03:12 AM 08:57 AM 03:51 PM 09:25 PM	-0.3 5.8 -0.4 5.6	-9 177 -12 171
10 Su	05:07 AM 10:49 AM 05:41 PM 11:15 PM	-0.5 5.9 -0.4 5.8	-15 180 -12 177
11 M	05:59 AM 11:38 AM 06:27 PM	-0.5 5.9 -0.4	-15 180 -12
12 Tu	12:01 AM 06:47 AM 12:24 PM 07:10 PM	5.9 -0.5 5.9 -0.3	180 -15 180 -9
13 W	12:45 AM 07:33 AM 01:08 PM 07:51 PM	5.9 -0.4 5.8 -0.2	180 -12 177 -6
14 Th	01:27 AM 08:18 AM 01:51 PM 08:30 PM	5.9 -0.3 5.6 0.0	180 -9 171 0
15 F	02:08 AM 09:01 AM 02:35 PM 09:08 PM	5.8 -0.1 5.4 0.2	177 -3 165 6
16 Sa	02:50 AM 09:44 AM 03:21 PM 09:47 PM	5.7 0.1 5.2 0.3	174 3 158 9
17 Su	03:33 AM 10:29 AM 04:09 PM 10:27 PM	5.5 0.3 5.1 0.5	168 9 155 15
18 M	04:20 AM 11:17 AM 05:00 PM 11:13 PM	5.4 0.4 5.0 0.6	165 12 152 18
19 Tu	05:11 AM 12:08 PM 05:55 PM	5.3 0.5 4.9	162 15 149
20 W	12:05 AM 06:08 AM 01:01 PM 06:51 PM	0.6 5.2 0.6 4.9	18 158 18 149
21 Th	01:02 AM 07:06 AM 01:56 PM 07:45 PM	0.6 5.2 0.6 5.0	18 158 18 152
22 F	02:00 AM 08:02 AM 02:49 PM 08:37 PM	0.5 5.3 0.5 5.1	15 162 15 155
23 Sa	02:58 AM 08:54 AM 03:41 PM 09:26 PM	0.4 5.4 0.3 5.3	12 165 9 162
24 Su	03:53 AM 09:43 AM 04:29 PM 10:11 PM	0.2 5.5 0.2 5.5	6 168 6 168
25 M	04:45 AM 10:29 AM 05:15 PM 10:53 PM	0.1 5.6 0.1 5.7	3 171 3 174
26 Tu	05:35 AM 11:12 AM 05:59 PM 11:33 PM	-0.1 5.7 0.0 5.9	-3 174 0 180
27 W	06:24 AM 11:54 AM 06:43 PM	-0.2 5.7 0.0	-6 174 0
28 Th	12:12 AM 07:13 AM 12:37 PM 07:26 PM	6.1 -0.2 5.7 0.0	186 -6 174 0
29 F	12:53 AM 08:02 AM 01:22 PM 08:10 PM	6.2 -0.2 5.6 0.0	189 -6 171 0
30 Sa	01:37 AM 08:52 AM 02:10 PM 08:58 PM	6.2 -0.1 5.5 0.1	189 -3 168 3
31 Su	02:25 AM 09:46 AM 03:03 PM 09:50 PM	6.2 0.0 5.4 0.2	189 0 165 6

April

Day	Time (h m)	Height (ft)	Height (cm)
1 M	03:19 AM 10:42 AM 04:02 PM 10:47 PM	6.1 0.1 5.3 0.3	186 3 162 9
2 Tu	04:20 AM 11:40 AM 05:07 PM 11:49 PM	5.9 0.2 5.2 0.4	180 6 158 12
3 W	05:28 AM 12:41 PM 06:13 PM	5.8 0.2 5.2	177 6 158
4 Th	12:53 AM 06:36 AM 01:40 PM 07:18 PM	0.3 5.7 0.2 5.4	9 174 6 165
5 F	01:56 AM 07:42 AM 02:38 PM 08:18 PM	0.3 5.7 0.1 5.6	9 174 3 171
6 Sa	02:57 AM 08:42 AM 03:33 PM 09:14 PM	0.1 5.8 -0.1 5.8	3 177 -3 177
7 Su	03:55 AM 09:38 AM 04:24 PM 10:06 PM	-0.1 5.8 -0.1 6.0	-3 177 -3 183
8 M	04:48 AM 10:28 AM 05:12 PM 10:53 PM	-0.2 5.9 -0.2 6.2	-6 180 -6 189
9 Tu	05:39 AM 11:16 AM 05:57 PM 11:38 PM	-0.2 5.9 -0.1 6.2	-6 180 -3 189
10 W	06:26 AM 12:01 PM 06:39 PM	-0.2 5.8 0.0	-6 177 0
11 Th	12:19 AM 07:11 AM 12:44 PM 07:18 PM	6.2 -0.1 5.7 0.2	189 -3 174 6
12 F	12:59 AM 07:53 AM 01:26 PM 07:56 PM	6.1 0.0 5.6 0.4	186 0 171 12
13 Sa	01:37 AM 08:35 AM 02:07 PM 08:32 PM	6.0 0.2 5.4 0.5	183 6 165 15
14 Su	02:15 AM 09:16 AM 02:50 PM 09:07 PM	5.9 0.3 5.3 0.6	180 9 162 18
15 M	02:53 AM 09:57 AM 03:35 PM 09:46 PM	5.8 0.5 5.2 0.7	177 15 158 21
16 Tu	03:35 AM 10:41 AM 04:22 PM 10:29 PM	5.7 0.6 5.1 0.8	174 18 155 24
17 W	04:21 AM 11:28 AM 05:14 PM 11:21 PM	5.6 0.7 5.0 0.8	171 21 152 24
18 Th	05:15 AM 12:18 PM 06:08 PM	5.5 0.7 5.1	168 21 155
19 F	12:19 AM 06:13 AM 01:11 PM 07:02 PM	0.8 5.4 0.7 5.2	24 165 21 158
20 Sa	01:20 AM 07:12 AM 02:04 PM 07:55 PM	0.8 5.4 0.6 5.4	24 165 18 165
21 Su	02:21 AM 08:09 AM 02:57 PM 08:45 PM	0.7 5.5 0.5 5.6	21 168 15 171
22 M	03:20 AM 09:02 AM 03:47 PM 09:32 PM	0.5 5.5 0.4 5.9	15 168 12 180
23 Tu	04:17 AM 09:53 AM 04:37 PM 10:18 PM	0.3 5.6 0.3 6.1	9 171 9 186
24 W	05:11 AM 10:41 AM 05:25 PM 11:02 PM	0.1 5.7 0.2 6.4	3 174 6 195
25 Th	06:04 AM 11:29 AM 06:13 PM 11:47 PM	0.0 5.7 0.1 6.5	0 174 3 198
26 F	06:56 AM 12:17 PM 07:01 PM	-0.1 5.7 0.1	-3 174 3
27 Sa	12:33 AM 07:47 AM 01:06 PM 07:51 PM	6.6 -0.1 5.6 0.1	201 -3 171 3
28 Su	01:21 AM 08:40 AM 01:58 PM 08:42 PM	6.6 -0.1 5.6 0.2	201 -3 171 6
29 M	02:13 AM 09:33 AM 02:54 PM 09:37 PM	6.5 -0.1 5.5 0.3	198 -3 168 9
30 Tu	03:09 AM 10:28 AM 03:53 PM 10:35 PM	6.3 0.0 5.4 0.4	192 0 165 12

May

Day	Time (h m)	Height (ft)	Height (cm)
1 W	04:10 AM 11:24 AM 04:56 PM 11:35 PM	6.1 0.1 5.4 0.4	186 3 165 12
2 Th	05:14 AM 12:20 PM 05:59 PM	5.9 0.1 5.5	180 3 168
3 F	12:36 AM 06:19 AM 01:16 PM 07:01 PM	0.4 5.8 0.1 5.7	12 177 3 174
4 Sa	01:37 AM 07:22 AM 02:11 PM 07:59 PM	0.4 5.8 0.1 5.9	12 177 3 180
5 Su	02:37 AM 08:20 AM 03:04 PM 08:53 PM	0.3 5.8 0.0 6.1	9 177 0 186
6 M	03:33 AM 09:14 AM 03:54 PM 09:43 PM	0.1 5.8 0.0 6.3	3 177 0 192
7 Tu	04:26 AM 10:04 AM 04:41 PM 10:29 PM	0.1 5.8 0.1 6.4	3 177 3 195
8 W	05:16 AM 10:52 AM 05:25 PM 11:13 PM	0.0 5.7 0.2 6.4	0 174 6 195
9 Th	06:03 AM 11:36 AM 06:07 PM 11:53 PM	0.0 5.6 0.3 6.3	0 171 9 192
10 F	06:47 AM 12:19 PM 06:46 PM	0.1 5.5 0.4	3 168 12
11 Sa	12:32 AM 07:29 AM 01:01 PM 07:24 PM	6.2 0.2 5.4 0.6	189 6 165 18
12 Su	01:09 AM 08:10 AM 01:41 PM 07:59 PM	6.1 0.3 5.3 0.7	186 9 162 21
13 M	01:44 AM 08:49 AM 02:22 PM 08:35 PM	6.1 0.4 5.2 0.8	186 12 158 24
14 Tu	02:19 AM 09:28 AM 03:02 PM 09:12 PM	6.0 0.5 5.2 0.8	183 15 158 24
15 W	02:56 AM 10:08 AM 03:45 PM 09:54 PM	5.9 0.6 5.2 0.8	180 18 158 24
16 Th	03:37 AM 10:50 AM 04:31 PM 10:43 PM	5.8 0.6 5.2 0.9	177 18 158 27
17 F	04:25 AM 11:36 AM 05:21 PM 11:40 PM	5.7 0.6 5.3 0.9	174 18 162 27
18 Sa	05:21 AM 12:25 PM 06:15 PM	5.6 0.6 5.4	171 18 165
19 Su	12:42 AM 06:22 AM 01:17 PM 07:09 PM	0.9 5.5 0.5 5.6	27 168 15 171
20 M	01:46 AM 07:23 AM 02:11 PM 08:02 PM	0.8 5.5 0.5 5.9	24 168 15 180
21 Tu	02:49 AM 08:22 AM 03:05 PM 08:54 PM	0.6 5.5 0.4 6.1	18 168 12 186
22 W	03:50 AM 09:18 AM 03:59 PM 09:45 PM	0.4 5.5 0.3 6.4	12 168 9 195
23 Th	04:48 AM 10:12 AM 04:53 PM 10:35 PM	0.2 5.6 0.2 6.6	6 171 6 201
24 F	05:44 AM 11:05 AM 05:46 PM 11:24 PM	0.1 5.6 0.1 6.7	3 171 3 204
25 Sa	06:38 AM 11:58 AM 06:39 PM	-0.1 5.6 0.1	-3 171 3
26 Su	12:15 AM 07:32 AM 12:51 PM 07:33 PM	6.8 -0.2 5.6 0.1	207 -6 171 3
27 M	01:07 AM 08:24 AM 01:45 PM 08:27 PM	6.7 -0.2 5.6 0.1	204 -6 171 3
28 Tu	02:00 AM 09:17 AM 02:41 PM 09:22 PM	6.6 -0.2 5.6 0.2	201 -6 171 6
29 W	02:57 AM 10:09 AM 03:39 PM 10:19 PM	6.4 -0.1 5.6 0.3	195 -3 171 9
30 Th	03:55 AM 11:02 AM 04:39 PM 11:17 PM	6.2 -0.1 5.7 0.4	189 -3 174 12
31 F	04:56 AM 11:55 AM 05:39 PM	6.0 0.0 5.8	183 0 177

June

Day	Time (h m)	Height (ft)	Height (cm)
1 Sa	12:16 AM 05:57 AM 12:47 PM 06:38 PM	0.4 5.8 0.0 5.9	12 177 0 180
2 Su	01:14 AM 06:57 AM 01:40 PM 07:34 PM	0.4 5.7 0.1 6.0	12 174 3 183
3 M	02:12 AM 07:53 AM 02:31 PM 08:27 PM	0.4 5.7 0.1 6.2	12 174 3 189
4 Tu	03:08 AM 08:47 AM 03:20 PM 09:16 PM	0.3 5.6 0.1 6.3	9 171 3 192
5 W	04:01 AM 09:38 AM 04:08 PM 10:03 PM	0.2 5.6 0.2 6.3	6 171 6 192
6 Th	04:51 AM 10:26 AM 04:53 PM 10:47 PM	0.2 5.5 0.3 6.3	6 168 9 192
7 F	05:38 AM 11:12 AM 05:36 PM 11:28 PM	0.2 5.5 0.4 6.3	6 168 12 192
8 Sa	06:23 AM 11:55 AM 06:17 PM	0.2 5.4 0.5	6 165 15
9 Su	12:07 AM 07:05 AM 12:36 PM 06:55 PM	6.2 0.3 5.3 0.6	189 9 162 18
10 M	12:43 AM 07:45 AM 01:16 PM 07:33 PM	6.2 0.3 5.3 0.7	189 9 162 21
11 Tu	01:18 AM 08:23 AM 01:54 PM 08:09 PM	6.1 0.4 5.2 0.7	186 12 158 21
12 W	01:51 AM 09:01 AM 02:31 PM 08:46 PM	6.0 0.5 5.2 0.8	183 15 158 24
13 Th	02:24 AM 09:38 AM 03:09 PM 09:27 PM	6.0 0.5 5.3 0.8	183 15 162 24
14 F	03:02 AM 10:15 AM 03:50 PM 10:13 PM	5.9 0.5 5.3 0.8	180 15 162 24
15 Sa	03:46 AM 10:56 AM 04:35 PM 11:07 PM	5.8 0.5 5.5 0.9	177 15 168 27
16 Su	04:38 AM 11:41 AM 05:27 PM	5.7 0.5 5.6	174 15 171
17 M	12:09 AM 05:38 AM 12:31 PM 06:24 PM	0.9 5.6 0.4 5.8	27 171 12 177
18 Tu	01:15 AM 06:42 AM 01:28 PM 07:22 PM	0.8 5.4 0.4 6.0	24 165 12 183
19 W	02:22 AM 07:47 AM 02:27 PM 08:20 PM	0.7 5.4 0.3 6.2	21 165 9 189
20 Th	03:26 AM 08:49 AM 03:27 PM 09:17 PM	0.5 5.4 0.3 6.5	15 165 9 198
21 F	04:27 AM 09:48 AM 04:27 PM 10:12 PM	0.3 5.4 0.2 6.6	9 165 6 201
22 Sa	05:25 AM 10:45 AM 05:25 PM 11:06 PM	0.1 5.5 0.1 6.8	3 168 3 207
23 Su	06:20 AM 11:40 AM 06:21 PM 11:59 PM	-0.1 5.6 0.0 6.8	-3 171 0 207
24 M	07:13 AM 12:34 PM 07:16 PM	-0.2 5.7 0.0	-6 174 0
25 Tu	12:52 AM 08:05 AM 01:28 PM 08:10 PM	6.8 -0.3 5.7 0.0	207 -9 174 0
26 W	01:46 AM 08:56 AM 02:23 PM 09:05 PM	6.6 -0.3 5.7 0.1	201 -9 174 3
27 Th	02:40 AM 09:45 AM 03:19 PM 09:59 PM	6.4 -0.3 5.8 0.2	195 -9 177 6
28 F	03:35 AM 10:35 AM 04:15 PM 10:55 PM	6.2 -0.2 5.8 0.3	189 -6 177 9
29 Sa	04:32 AM 11:25 AM 05:12 PM 11:51 PM	6.0 -0.1 5.9 0.4	183 -3 180 12
30 Su	05:30 AM 12:15 PM 06:08 PM	5.8 0.0 5.9	177 0 180

Heights are referred to mean lower water which is the chart datum of sounding. All times are local. Daylight Saving Time has been used when needed.

Reedy Point, Delaware, 2013

Times and Heights of High and Low Waters

July

Day	Time (h m)	Height (ft)	Height (cm)
1 M	12:47 AM	0.5	15
	06:27 AM	5.6	171
	01:05 PM	0.1	3
	07:03 PM	6.0	183
2 Tu	01:44 AM	0.5	15
	07:23 AM	5.5	168
	01:55 PM	0.2	6
	07:56 PM	6.1	186
3 W	02:39 AM	0.5	15
	08:18 AM	5.5	168
	02:45 PM	0.3	9
	08:47 PM	6.2	189
4 Th	03:32 AM	0.4	12
	09:10 AM	5.4	165
	03:34 PM	0.3	9
	09:35 PM	6.2	189
5 F	04:23 AM	0.3	9
	09:59 AM	5.4	165
	04:20 PM	0.4	12
	10:20 PM	6.3	192
6 Sa	05:10 AM	0.3	9
	10:46 AM	5.4	165
	05:05 PM	0.4	12
	11:03 PM	6.2	189
7 Su	05:55 AM	0.3	9
	11:30 AM	5.4	165
	05:48 PM	0.5	15
	11:43 PM	6.2	189
8 M	06:38 AM	0.3	9
	12:11 PM	5.3	162
	06:30 PM	0.5	15
9 Tu	12:19 AM	6.1	186
	07:18 AM	0.3	9
	12:50 PM	5.3	162
	07:09 PM	0.6	18
10 W	12:53 AM	6.1	186
	07:56 AM	0.4	12
	01:26 PM	5.3	162
	07:48 PM	0.6	18
11 Th	01:26 AM	6.0	183
	08:32 AM	0.4	12
	02:00 PM	5.3	162
	08:26 PM	0.7	21
12 F	01:58 AM	6.0	183
	09:07 AM	0.4	12
	02:34 PM	5.4	165
	09:07 PM	0.7	21
13 Sa	02:34 AM	6.0	183
	09:43 AM	0.4	12
	03:11 PM	5.6	171
	09:52 PM	0.8	24
14 Su	03:16 AM	5.9	180
	10:20 AM	0.4	12
	03:55 PM	5.7	174
	10:44 PM	0.8	24
15 M	04:07 AM	5.7	174
	11:04 AM	0.4	12
	04:47 PM	5.8	177
	11:46 PM	0.9	27
16 Tu	05:06 AM	5.5	168
	11:55 AM	0.4	12
	05:46 PM	6.0	183
17 W	12:53 AM	0.9	27
	06:13 AM	5.4	165
	12:55 PM	0.4	12
	06:50 PM	6.1	186
18 Th	02:00 AM	0.8	24
	07:21 AM	5.3	162
	02:00 PM	0.4	12
	07:53 PM	6.3	192
19 F	03:06 AM	0.6	18
	08:27 AM	5.3	162
	03:05 PM	0.3	9
	08:55 PM	6.4	195
20 Sa	04:08 AM	0.4	12
	09:28 AM	5.4	165
	04:08 PM	0.2	6
	09:54 PM	6.6	201
21 Su	05:06 AM	0.1	3
	10:27 AM	5.5	168
	05:07 PM	0.0	0
	10:50 PM	6.7	204
22 M	06:00 AM	-0.1	-3
	11:23 AM	5.7	174
	06:04 PM	-0.1	-3
	11:44 PM	6.8	207
23 Tu	06:52 AM	-0.2	-6
	12:16 PM	5.8	177
	06:59 PM	-0.1	-3
24 W	12:36 AM	6.7	204
	07:42 AM	-0.3	-9
	01:09 PM	5.9	180
	07:52 PM	-0.1	-3
25 Th	01:28 AM	6.6	201
	08:30 AM	-0.3	-9
	02:01 PM	6.0	183
	08:44 PM	0.0	0
26 F	02:19 AM	6.4	195
	09:17 AM	-0.2	-6
	02:52 PM	6.0	183
	09:37 PM	0.2	6
27 Sa	03:10 AM	6.1	186
	10:04 AM	-0.1	-3
	03:45 PM	6.0	183
	10:29 PM	0.4	12
28 Su	04:04 AM	5.9	180
	10:51 AM	0.1	3
	04:38 PM	5.9	180
	11:22 PM	0.5	15
29 M	04:58 AM	5.7	174
	11:38 AM	0.2	6
	05:32 PM	5.9	180
30 Tu	12:16 AM	0.6	18
	05:55 AM	5.5	168
	12:27 PM	0.4	12
	06:27 PM	5.9	180
31 W	01:11 AM	0.7	21
	06:51 AM	5.4	165
	01:17 PM	0.5	15
	07:22 PM	6.0	183

August

Day	Time (h m)	Height (ft)	Height (cm)
1 Th	02:06 AM	0.7	21
	07:46 AM	5.3	162
	02:08 PM	0.5	15
	08:14 PM	6.0	183
2 F	03:00 AM	0.6	18
	08:40 AM	5.4	165
	02:58 PM	0.5	15
	09:05 PM	6.1	186
3 Sa	03:51 AM	0.5	15
	09:30 AM	5.4	165
	03:48 PM	0.5	15
	09:52 PM	6.2	189
4 Su	04:39 AM	0.4	12
	10:18 AM	5.4	165
	04:35 PM	0.4	12
	10:36 PM	6.2	189
5 M	05:24 AM	0.4	12
	11:02 AM	5.5	168
	05:21 PM	0.4	12
	11:16 PM	6.2	189
6 Tu	06:07 AM	0.3	9
	11:43 AM	5.5	168
	06:05 PM	0.4	12
	11:54 PM	6.2	189
7 W	06:47 AM	0.3	9
	12:21 PM	5.5	168
	06:47 PM	0.5	15
8 Th	12:28 AM	6.1	186
	07:25 AM	0.3	9
	12:56 PM	5.5	168
	07:28 PM	0.5	15
9 F	01:01 AM	6.1	186
	08:02 AM	0.4	12
	01:28 PM	5.6	171
	08:09 PM	0.6	18
10 Sa	01:35 AM	6.0	183
	08:37 AM	0.4	12
	02:02 PM	5.8	177
	08:51 PM	0.7	21
11 Su	02:12 AM	5.9	180
	09:13 AM	0.4	12
	02:39 PM	5.9	180
	09:37 PM	0.7	21
12 M	02:54 AM	5.8	177
	09:51 AM	0.4	12
	03:24 PM	6.0	183
	10:31 PM	0.8	24
13 Tu	03:45 AM	5.7	174
	10:37 AM	0.4	12
	04:17 PM	6.0	183
	11:32 PM	0.9	27
14 W	04:46 AM	5.5	168
	11:33 AM	0.5	15
	05:19 PM	6.1	186
15 Th	12:38 AM	0.9	27
	05:54 AM	5.3	162
	12:37 PM	0.5	15
	06:27 PM	6.1	186
16 F	01:44 AM	0.8	24
	07:04 AM	5.3	162
	01:45 PM	0.5	15
	07:35 PM	6.2	189
17 Sa	02:48 AM	0.6	18
	08:11 AM	5.3	162
	02:51 PM	0.4	12
	08:40 PM	6.4	195
18 Su	03:49 AM	0.4	12
	09:13 AM	5.5	168
	03:53 PM	0.2	6
	09:39 PM	6.5	198
19 M	04:45 AM	0.1	3
	10:11 AM	5.7	174
	04:52 PM	0.0	0
	10:35 PM	6.6	201
20 Tu	05:38 AM	-0.1	-3
	11:06 AM	5.9	180
	05:48 PM	-0.1	-3
	11:28 PM	6.7	204
21 W	06:28 AM	-0.2	-6
	11:57 AM	6.1	186
	06:41 PM	-0.1	-3
22 Th	12:18 AM	6.6	201
	07:16 AM	-0.2	-6
	12:47 PM	6.2	189
	07:32 PM	-0.1	-3
23 F	01:06 AM	6.5	198
	08:02 AM	-0.2	-6
	01:35 PM	6.2	189
	08:22 PM	0.1	3
24 Sa	01:54 AM	6.3	192
	08:46 AM	0.0	0
	02:22 PM	6.1	186
	09:11 PM	0.3	9
25 Su	02:43 AM	6.0	183
	09:30 AM	0.2	6
	03:10 PM	6.0	183
	10:01 PM	0.5	15
26 M	03:33 AM	5.8	177
	10:13 AM	0.3	9
	04:00 PM	5.9	180
	10:51 PM	0.6	18
27 Tu	04:25 AM	5.6	171
	10:59 AM	0.5	15
	04:52 PM	5.9	180
	11:42 PM	0.8	24
28 W	05:20 AM	5.4	165
	11:46 AM	0.6	18
	05:47 PM	5.8	177
29 Th	12:36 AM	0.9	27
	06:16 AM	5.3	162
	12:36 PM	0.7	21
	06:43 PM	5.8	177
30 F	01:30 AM	0.9	27
	07:13 AM	5.3	162
	01:29 PM	0.7	21
	07:37 PM	5.9	180
31 Sa	02:23 AM	0.8	24
	08:07 AM	5.3	162
	02:22 PM	0.7	21
	08:30 PM	5.9	180

September

Day	Time (h m)	Height (ft)	Height (cm)
1 Su	03:15 AM	0.7	21
	08:59 AM	5.4	165
	03:14 PM	0.6	18
	09:19 PM	6.0	183
2 M	04:03 AM	0.5	15
	09:47 AM	5.5	168
	04:05 PM	0.5	15
	10:05 PM	6.1	186
3 Tu	04:49 AM	0.4	12
	10:31 AM	5.6	171
	04:53 PM	0.4	12
	10:46 PM	6.1	186
4 W	05:33 AM	0.3	9
	11:12 AM	5.7	174
	05:39 PM	0.4	12
	11:25 PM	6.1	186
5 Th	06:14 AM	0.3	9
	11:49 AM	5.8	177
	06:24 PM	0.4	12
6 F	12:02 AM	6.1	186
	06:53 AM	0.3	9
	12:24 PM	5.9	180
	07:08 PM	0.4	12
7 Sa	12:37 AM	6.0	183
	07:31 AM	0.3	9
	12:58 PM	6.0	183
	07:52 PM	0.5	15
8 Su	01:13 AM	6.0	183
	08:08 AM	0.4	12
	01:34 PM	6.1	186
	08:38 PM	0.6	18
9 M	01:53 AM	5.9	180
	08:47 AM	0.4	12
	02:14 PM	6.2	189
	09:27 PM	0.7	21
10 Tu	02:39 AM	5.7	174
	09:31 AM	0.4	12
	03:01 PM	6.2	189
	10:22 PM	0.8	24
11 W	03:32 AM	5.5	168
	10:22 AM	0.5	15
	03:57 PM	6.1	186
	11:22 PM	0.8	24
12 Th	04:34 AM	5.4	165
	11:22 AM	0.6	18
	05:02 PM	6.1	186
13 F	12:25 AM	0.8	24
	05:44 AM	5.2	158
	12:28 PM	0.6	18
	06:13 PM	6.1	186
14 Sa	01:29 AM	0.7	21
	06:53 AM	5.3	162
	01:34 PM	0.5	15
	07:22 PM	6.1	186
15 Su	02:30 AM	0.5	15
	07:59 AM	5.4	165
	02:39 PM	0.4	12
	08:26 PM	6.2	189
16 M	03:28 AM	0.3	9
	09:00 AM	5.7	174
	03:40 PM	0.2	6
	09:25 PM	6.4	195
17 Tu	04:23 AM	0.1	3
	09:56 AM	5.9	180
	04:37 PM	0.0	0
	10:19 PM	6.5	198
18 W	05:14 AM	-0.1	-3
	10:48 AM	6.2	189
	05:31 PM	-0.1	-3
	11:10 PM	6.5	198
19 Th	06:02 AM	-0.2	-6
	11:36 AM	6.3	192
	06:23 PM	-0.1	-3
	11:57 PM	6.4	195
20 F	06:48 AM	-0.1	-3
	12:23 PM	6.3	192
	07:12 PM	0.0	0
21 Sa	12:44 AM	6.2	189
	07:31 AM	0.0	0
	01:07 PM	6.3	192
	07:59 PM	0.1	3
22 Su	01:29 AM	6.0	183
	08:13 AM	0.2	6
	01:51 PM	6.2	189
	08:45 PM	0.3	9
23 M	02:15 AM	5.8	177
	08:54 AM	0.4	12
	02:35 PM	6.1	186
	09:31 PM	0.5	15
24 Tu	03:02 AM	5.6	171
	09:35 AM	0.5	15
	03:21 PM	5.9	180
	10:18 PM	0.7	21
25 W	03:51 AM	5.4	165
	10:17 AM	0.7	21
	04:10 PM	5.8	177
	11:07 PM	0.8	24
26 Th	04:44 AM	5.2	158
	11:03 AM	0.8	24
	05:03 PM	5.7	174
	11:58 PM	0.9	27
27 F	05:39 AM	5.2	158
	11:53 AM	0.8	24
	05:59 PM	5.7	174
28 Sa	12:50 AM	0.9	27
	06:35 AM	5.2	158
	12:47 PM	0.8	24
	06:55 PM	5.7	174
29 Su	01:42 AM	0.8	24
	07:30 AM	5.2	158
	01:43 PM	0.7	21
	07:50 PM	5.7	174
30 M	02:34 AM	0.7	21
	08:22 AM	5.4	165
	02:39 PM	0.6	18
	08:41 PM	5.8	177

October

Day	Time (h m)	Height (ft)	Height (cm)
1 Tu	03:23 AM	0.6	18
	09:11 AM	5.5	168
	03:32 PM	0.5	15
	09:28 PM	5.9	180
2 W	04:10 AM	0.4	12
	09:56 AM	5.7	174
	04:24 PM	0.4	12
	10:12 PM	5.9	180
3 Th	04:55 AM	0.3	9
	10:37 AM	5.9	180
	05:13 PM	0.3	9
	10:54 PM	6.0	183
4 F	05:38 AM	0.2	6
	11:16 AM	6.0	183
	06:01 PM	0.2	6
	11:34 PM	5.9	180
5 Sa	06:20 AM	0.2	6
	11:53 AM	6.1	186
	06:48 PM	0.2	6
6 Su	12:13 AM	5.9	180
	07:01 AM	0.2	6
	12:31 PM	6.3	192
	07:36 PM	0.3	9
7 M	12:54 AM	5.8	177
	07:43 AM	0.2	6
	01:11 PM	6.3	192
	08:25 PM	0.3	9
8 Tu	01:38 AM	5.7	174
	08:27 AM	0.3	9
	01:56 PM	6.3	192
	09:17 PM	0.4	12
9 W	02:28 AM	5.5	168
	09:17 AM	0.4	12
	02:47 PM	6.2	189
	10:12 PM	0.5	15
10 Th	03:24 AM	5.4	165
	10:13 AM	0.4	12
	03:45 PM	6.1	186
	11:11 PM	0.6	18
11 F	04:27 AM	5.2	158
	11:14 AM	0.5	15
	04:51 PM	6.0	183
12 Sa	12:11 AM	0.5	15
	05:35 AM	5.2	158
	12:18 PM	0.5	15
	06:01 PM	5.9	180
13 Su	01:11 AM	0.4	12
	06:42 AM	5.3	162
	01:22 PM	0.4	12
	07:08 PM	5.9	180
14 M	02:09 AM	0.3	9
	07:46 AM	5.5	168
	02:25 PM	0.2	6
	08:11 PM	6.0	183
15 Tu	03:05 AM	0.1	3
	08:44 AM	5.8	177
	03:24 PM	0.1	3
	09:08 PM	6.1	186
16 W	03:58 AM	-0.1	-3
	09:38 AM	6.0	183
	04:20 PM	-0.1	-3
	10:01 PM	6.1	186
17 Th	04:48 AM	-0.2	-6
	10:28 AM	6.2	189
	05:13 PM	-0.2	-6
	10:50 PM	6.1	186
18 F	05:34 AM	-0.2	-6
	11:15 AM	6.3	192
	06:03 PM	-0.2	-6
	11:36 PM	6.0	183
19 Sa	06:18 AM	-0.1	-3
	11:59 AM	6.3	192
	06:50 PM	-0.1	-3
20 Su	12:21 AM	5.9	180
	07:00 AM	0.0	0
	12:41 PM	6.2	189
	07:36 PM	0.1	3
21 M	01:04 AM	5.7	174
	07:40 AM	0.2	6
	01:22 PM	6.1	186
	08:20 PM	0.3	9
22 Tu	01:48 AM	5.5	168
	08:19 AM	0.4	12
	02:02 PM	6.0	183
	09:03 PM	0.4	12
23 W	02:32 AM	5.3	162
	08:57 AM	0.5	15
	02:44 PM	5.8	177
	09:46 PM	0.6	18
24 Th	03:18 AM	5.2	158
	09:37 AM	0.6	18
	03:28 PM	5.7	174
	10:31 PM	0.7	21
25 F	04:06 AM	5.0	152
	10:20 AM	0.7	21
	04:16 PM	5.6	171
	11:18 PM	0.7	21
26 Sa	04:58 AM	5.0	152
	11:10 AM	0.7	21
	05:10 PM	5.5	168
27 Su	12:07 AM	0.7	21
	05:53 AM	5.0	152
	12:05 PM	0.7	21
	06:06 PM	5.4	165
28 M	12:58 AM	0.7	21
	06:47 AM	5.1	155
	01:03 PM	0.7	21
	07:03 PM	5.4	165
29 Tu	01:49 AM	0.6	18
	07:40 AM	5.2	158
	02:01 PM	0.6	18
	07:57 PM	5.5	168
30 W	02:39 AM	0.4	12
	08:30 AM	5.4	165
	02:58 PM	0.4	12
	08:47 PM	5.5	168
31 Th	03:28 AM	0.3	9
	09:16 AM	5.7	174
	03:53 PM	0.3	9
	09:35 PM	5.6	171

November

Day	Time (h m)	Height (ft)	Height (cm)
1 F	04:16 AM	0.1	3
	10:00 AM	5.9	180
	04:47 PM	0.1	3
	10:21 PM	5.6	171
2 Sa	05:02 AM	0.0	0
	10:43 AM	6.1	186
	05:38 PM	0.0	0
	11:06 PM	5.6	171
3 Su	04:48 AM	0.0	0
	10:25 AM	6.2	189
	05:29 PM	0.0	0
	10:51 PM	5.6	171
4 M	05:34 AM	-0.1	-3
	11:08 AM	6.3	192
	06:20 PM	0.0	0
	11:37 PM	5.5	168
5 Tu	06:22 AM	-0.1	-3
	11:54 AM	6.4	195
	07:12 PM	0.0	0
6 W	12:25 AM	5.4	165
	07:12 AM	0.0	0
	12:43 PM	6.3	192
	08:04 PM	0.0	0
7 Th	01:18 AM	5.3	162
	08:05 AM	0.0	0
	01:36 PM	6.2	189
	08:59 PM	0.1	3
8 F	02:15 AM	5.2	158
	09:02 AM	0.1	3
	02:36 PM	6.0	183
	09:54 PM	0.1	3
9 Sa	03:17 AM	5.1	155
	10:02 AM	0.2	6
	03:40 PM	5.8	177
	10:51 PM	0.1	3
10 Su	04:22 AM	5.2	158
	11:04 AM	0.2	6
	04:46 PM	5.7	174
	11:48 PM	0.0	0
11 M	05:27 AM	5.3	162
	12:06 PM	0.1	3
	05:51 PM	5.7	174
12 Tu	12:44 AM	-0.1	-3
	06:28 AM	5.5	168
	01:07 PM	0.0	0
	06:52 PM	5.7	174
13 W	01:38 AM	-0.2	-6
	07:25 AM	5.7	174
	02:06 PM	-0.1	-3
	07:48 PM	5.7	174
14 Th	02:30 AM	-0.3	-9
	08:18 AM	5.9	180
	03:01 PM	-0.2	-6
	08:40 PM	5.7	174
15 F	03:19 AM	-0.3	-9
	09:07 AM	6.0	183
	03:53 PM	-0.3	-9
	09:28 PM	5.6	171
16 Sa	04:06 AM	-0.3	-9
	09:53 AM	6.1	186
	04:42 PM	-0.3	-9
	10:15 PM	5.6	171
17 Su	04:50 AM	-0.2	-6
	10:36 AM	6.1	186
	05:28 PM	-0.2	-6
	10:59 PM	5.4	165
18 M	05:31 AM	-0.1	-3
	11:16 AM	6.0	183
	06:12 PM	-0.1	-3
	11:41 PM	5.3	162
19 Tu	06:10 AM	0.1	3
	11:56 AM	5.9	180
	06:54 PM	0.1	3
20 W	12:23 AM	5.2	158
	06:48 AM	0.2	6
	12:34 PM	5.8	177
	07:35 PM	0.2	6
21 Th	01:04 AM	5.0	152
	07:25 AM	0.3	9
	01:12 PM	5.6	171
	08:15 PM	0.3	9
22 F	01:46 AM	4.9	149
	08:02 AM	0.4	12
	01:51 PM	5.5	168
	08:55 PM	0.4	12
23 Sa	02:29 AM	4.8	146
	08:42 AM	0.4	12
	02:33 PM	5.4	165
	09:37 PM	0.4	12
24 Su	03:15 AM	4.8	146
	09:29 AM	0.4	12
	03:20 PM	5.3	162
	10:22 PM	0.4	12
25 M	04:04 AM	4.8	146
	10:22 AM	0.5	15
	04:13 PM	5.2	158
	11:09 PM	0.4	12
26 Tu	04:57 AM	4.9	149
	11:21 AM	0.5	15
	05:10 PM	5.2	158
	11:59 PM	0.3	9
27 W	05:50 AM	5.1	155
	12:22 PM	0.4	12
	06:08 PM	5.1	155
28 Th	12:51 AM	0.2	6
	06:43 AM	5.3	162
	01:24 PM	0.3	9
	07:04 PM	5.1	155
29 F	01:44 AM	0.1	3
	07:34 AM	5.5	168
	02:24 PM	0.2	6
	07:58 PM	5.2	158
30 Sa	02:37 AM	-0.1	-3
	08:24 AM	5.7	174
	03:21 PM	0.0	0
	08:50 PM	5.2	158

December

Day	Time (h m)	Height (ft)	Height (cm)
1 Su	03:29 AM	-0.2	-6
	09:13 AM	6.0	183
	04:17 PM	-0.2	-6
	09:40 PM	5.2	158
2 M	04:21 AM	-0.3	-9
	10:01 AM	6.1	186
	05:11 PM	-0.3	-9
	10:30 PM	5.3	162
3 Tu	05:12 AM	-0.4	-12
	10:50 AM	6.2	189
	06:03 PM	-0.4	-12
	11:21 PM	5.3	162
4 W	06:04 AM	-0.4	-12
	11:40 AM	6.2	189
	06:56 PM	-0.4	-12
5 Th	12:12 AM	5.2	158
	06:58 AM	-0.4	-12
	12:32 PM	6.2	189
	07:48 PM	-0.4	-12
6 F	01:06 AM	5.2	158
	07:52 AM	-0.4	-12
	01:26 PM	6.0	183
	08:40 PM	-0.4	-12
7 Sa	02:02 AM	5.2	158
	08:48 AM	-0.3	-9
	02:24 PM	5.8	177
	09:33 PM	-0.4	-12
8 Su	03:02 AM	5.1	155
	09:46 AM	-0.2	-6
	03:25 PM	5.6	171
	10:27 PM	-0.4	-12
9 M	04:03 AM	5.2	158
	10:46 AM	-0.2	-6
	04:27 PM	5.4	165
	11:21 PM	-0.4	-12
10 Tu	05:05 AM	5.3	162
	11:46 AM	-0.1	-3
	05:28 PM	5.3	162
11 W	12:15 AM	-0.4	-12
	06:05 AM	5.4	165
	12:45 PM	-0.1	-3
	06:28 PM	5.3	162
12 Th	01:08 AM	-0.4	-12
	07:01 AM	5.5	168
	01:43 PM	-0.2	-6
	07:24 PM	5.2	158
13 F	02:00 AM	-0.4	-12
	07:54 AM	5.6	171
	02:39 PM	-0.3	-9
	08:16 PM	5.2	158
14 Sa	02:50 AM	-0.4	-12
	08:44 AM	5.7	174
	03:31 PM	-0.3	-9
	09:06 PM	5.2	158
15 Su	03:37 AM	-0.4	-12
	09:30 AM	5.8	177
	04:19 PM	-0.4	-12
	09:53 PM	5.2	158
16 M	04:22 AM	-0.3	-9
	10:13 AM	5.8	177
	05:05 PM	-0.3	-9
	10:37 PM	5.1	155
17 Tu	05:04 AM	-0.2	-6
	10:54 AM	5.7	174
	05:48 PM	-0.3	-9
	11:19 PM	5.0	152
18 W	05:44 AM	-0.2	-6
	11:33 AM	5.6	171
	06:29 PM	-0.2	-6
	11:59 PM	4.9	149
19 Th	06:22 AM	-0.1	-3
	12:09 PM	5.5	168
	07:08 PM	-0.1	-3
20 F	12:37 AM	4.8	146
	06:58 AM	0.0	0
	12:44 PM	5.5	168
	07:45 PM	0.0	0
21 Sa	01:15 AM	4.8	146
	07:35 AM	0.0	0
	01:19 PM	5.4	165
	08:21 PM	0.1	3
22 Su	01:52 AM	4.8	146
	08:12 AM	0.1	3
	01:55 PM	5.3	162
	08:58 PM	0.1	3
23 M	02:30 AM	4.8	146
	08:55 AM	0.1	3
	02:36 PM	5.2	158
	09:36 PM	0.1	3
24 Tu	03:12 AM	4.8	146
	09:44 AM	0.2	6
	03:23 PM	5.1	155
	10:19 PM	0.1	3
25 W	04:01 AM	4.9	149
	10:40 AM	0.3	9
	04:18 PM	5.0	152
	11:08 PM	0.0	0
26 Th	04:55 AM	5.0	152
	11:44 AM	0.3	9
	05:20 PM	4.9	149
27 F	12:02 AM	0.0	0
	05:54 AM	5.2	158
	12:51 PM	0.2	6
	06:23 PM	4.8	146
28 Sa	01:02 AM	-0.1	-3
	06:53 AM	5.4	165
	01:56 PM	0.1	3
	07:24 PM	4.8	146
29 Su	02:02 AM	-0.2	-6
	07:51 AM	5.6	171
	02:58 PM	-0.1	-3
	08:22 PM	4.9	149
30 M	03:01 AM	-0.4	-12
	08:46 AM	5.8	177
	03:56 PM	-0.3	-9
	09:18 PM	5.0	152
31 Tu	03:59 AM	-0.5	-15
	09:41 AM	6.0	183
	04:52 PM	-0.5	-15
	10:12 PM	5.1	155

Heights are referred to mean lower water which is the chart datum of sounding. All times are local. Daylight Saving Time has been used when needed.

Baltimore, Maryland, 2012

Times and Heights of High and Low Waters

September

Day	Time (h m)	Height (ft)	Height (cm)
1 Sa	01:47 AM 07:44 AM 02:24 PM 08:11 PM	0.5 1.8 0.4 1.7	15 55 12 52
2 Su	02:38 AM 08:21 AM 02:54 PM 08:57 PM	0.5 1.7 0.4 1.8	15 52 12 55
3 M	03:27 AM 08:58 AM 03:22 PM 09:41 PM	0.6 1.6 0.4 1.8	18 49 12 55
4 Tu	04:18 AM 09:35 AM 03:51 PM 10:26 PM	0.7 1.5 0.4 1.8	21 46 12 55
5 W	05:10 AM 10:13 AM 04:22 PM 11:11 PM	0.8 1.4 0.4 1.8	24 43 12 55
6 Th	06:07 AM 10:54 AM 04:58 PM 11:57 PM	0.9 1.4 0.4 1.8	27 43 12 55
7 F	07:06 AM 11:40 AM 05:41 PM	0.9 1.3 0.4	27 40 12
8 Sa	12:46 AM 08:07 AM 12:33 PM 06:31 PM	1.8 0.9 1.2 0.5	55 27 37 15
9 Su	01:38 AM 09:05 AM 01:32 PM 07:28 PM	1.7 0.9 1.2 0.5	52 27 37 15
10 M	02:32 AM 09:57 AM 02:33 PM 08:31 PM	1.7 0.8 1.2 0.6	52 24 37 18
11 Tu	03:25 AM 10:42 AM 03:34 PM 09:34 PM	1.7 0.7 1.3 0.6	52 21 40 18
12 W	04:14 AM 11:22 AM 04:29 PM 10:34 PM	1.8 0.7 1.4 0.6	55 21 43 18
13 Th	05:00 AM 11:59 AM 05:21 PM 11:31 PM	1.8 0.6 1.4 0.5	55 18 43 15
14 F	05:43 AM 12:33 PM 06:09 PM	1.8 0.5 1.6	55 15 49
15 Sa	12:27 AM 06:25 AM 01:07 PM 06:56 PM	0.5 1.8 0.4 1.7	15 55 12 52
16 Su	01:21 AM 07:06 AM 01:40 PM 07:42 PM	0.5 1.7 0.4 1.8	15 52 12 55
17 M	02:17 AM 07:49 AM 02:15 PM 08:29 PM	0.5 1.7 0.3 1.9	15 52 9 58
18 Tu	03:14 AM 08:33 AM 02:52 PM 09:18 PM	0.6 1.6 0.2 2.0	18 49 6 61
19 W	04:15 AM 09:20 AM 03:33 PM 10:10 PM	0.6 1.5 0.2 2.1	18 46 6 64
20 Th	05:18 AM 10:11 AM 04:19 PM 11:04 PM	0.6 1.4 0.2 2.1	18 43 6 64
21 F	06:24 AM 11:06 AM 05:12 PM	0.7 1.4 0.3	21 43 9
22 Sa	12:03 AM 07:30 AM 12:07 PM 06:15 PM	2.0 0.7 1.3 0.3	61 21 40 9
23 Su	01:07 AM 08:34 AM 01:12 PM 07:26 PM	2.0 0.7 1.3 0.4	61 21 40 12
24 M	02:13 AM 09:34 AM 02:21 PM 08:42 PM	1.9 0.6 1.3 0.4	58 18 40 12
25 Tu	03:18 AM 10:27 AM 03:28 PM 09:54 PM	1.8 0.6 1.4 0.4	55 18 43 12
26 W	04:18 AM 11:15 AM 04:30 PM 10:59 PM	1.8 0.5 1.5 0.4	55 15 46 12
27 Th	05:10 AM 11:58 AM 05:28 PM 11:58 PM	1.8 0.5 1.6 0.4	55 15 49 12
28 F	05:55 AM 12:36 PM 06:19 PM	1.7 0.4 1.7	52 12 52
29 Sa	12:53 AM 06:36 AM 01:09 PM 07:07 PM	0.5 1.6 0.4 1.7	15 49 12 52
30 Su	01:43 AM 07:13 AM 01:39 PM 07:51 PM	0.5 1.6 0.4 1.8	15 49 12 55

October

Day	Time (h m)	Height (ft)	Height (cm)
1 M	02:31 AM 07:50 AM 02:06 PM 08:32 PM	0.6 1.5 0.3 1.8	18 46 9 55
2 Tu	03:18 AM 08:26 AM 02:33 PM 09:12 PM	0.6 1.4 0.3 1.8	18 43 9 55
3 W	04:04 AM 09:03 AM 03:03 PM 09:51 PM	0.7 1.4 0.3 1.8	21 43 9 55
4 Th	04:50 AM 09:42 AM 03:37 PM 10:30 PM	0.7 1.3 0.3 1.8	21 40 9 55
5 F	05:38 AM 10:25 AM 04:17 PM 11:12 PM	0.7 1.3 0.4 1.7	21 40 12 52
6 Sa	06:28 AM 11:12 AM 05:02 PM 11:57 PM	0.8 1.2 0.4 1.7	24 37 12 52
7 Su	07:20 AM 12:04 PM 05:54 PM	0.8 1.2 0.5	24 37 15
8 M	12:47 AM 08:12 AM 01:02 PM 06:54 PM	1.7 0.7 1.2 0.5	52 21 37 15
9 Tu	01:39 AM 09:00 AM 02:02 PM 08:00 PM	1.6 0.7 1.2 0.5	49 21 37 15
10 W	02:32 AM 09:45 AM 03:01 PM 09:08 PM	1.6 0.6 1.3 0.5	49 18 40 15
11 Th	03:24 AM 10:25 AM 03:57 PM 10:14 PM	1.6 0.5 1.4 0.5	49 15 43 15
12 F	04:14 AM 11:03 AM 04:50 PM 11:17 PM	1.6 0.4 1.5 0.5	49 12 46 15
13 Sa	05:01 AM 11:40 AM 05:41 PM	1.6 0.3 1.7	49 9 52
14 Su	12:17 AM 05:48 AM 12:16 PM 06:29 PM	0.5 1.5 0.2 1.8	15 46 6 55
15 M	01:16 AM 06:34 AM 12:54 PM 07:18 PM	0.5 1.5 0.2 1.9	15 46 6 58
16 Tu	02:14 AM 07:22 AM 01:34 PM 08:07 PM	0.4 1.4 0.1 2.0	12 43 3 61
17 W	03:12 AM 08:10 AM 02:17 PM 08:58 PM	0.4 1.4 0.1 2.1	12 43 3 64
18 Th	04:10 AM 09:02 AM 03:05 PM 09:50 PM	0.4 1.3 0.1 2.0	12 40 3 61
19 F	05:09 AM 09:56 AM 03:59 PM 10:46 PM	0.5 1.3 0.1 2.0	15 40 3 61
20 Sa	06:09 AM 10:55 AM 04:59 PM 11:45 PM	0.5 1.2 0.2 1.9	15 37 6 58
21 Su	07:09 AM 11:57 AM 06:08 PM	0.5 1.2 0.3	15 37 9
22 M	12:48 AM 08:07 AM 01:04 PM 07:23 PM	1.8 0.5 1.3 0.3	55 15 40 9
23 Tu	01:51 AM 09:02 AM 02:12 PM 08:39 PM	1.7 0.4 1.3 0.4	52 12 40 12
24 W	02:52 AM 09:52 AM 03:18 PM 09:51 PM	1.6 0.4 1.4 0.4	49 12 43 12
25 Th	03:48 AM 10:38 AM 04:20 PM 10:56 PM	1.5 0.3 1.5 0.4	46 9 46 12
26 F	04:37 AM 11:18 AM 05:16 PM 11:55 PM	1.4 0.3 1.5 0.4	43 9 46 12
27 Sa	05:21 AM 11:53 AM 06:06 PM	1.4 0.2 1.6	43 6 49
28 Su	12:48 AM 06:02 AM 12:25 PM 06:50 PM	0.4 1.3 0.2 1.7	12 40 6 52
29 M	01:38 AM 06:41 AM 12:54 PM 07:31 PM	0.5 1.2 0.2 1.7	15 37 6 52
30 Tu	02:24 AM 07:19 AM 01:23 PM 08:08 PM	0.5 1.2 0.2 1.7	15 37 6 52
31 W	03:08 AM 07:57 AM 01:53 PM 08:44 PM	0.5 1.1 0.2 1.7	15 34 6 52

November

Day	Time (h m)	Height (ft)	Height (cm)
1 Th	03:49 AM 08:37 AM 02:27 PM 09:20 PM	0.5 1.1 0.2 1.7	15 34 6 52
2 F	04:29 AM 09:18 AM 03:05 PM 09:57 PM	0.5 1.1 0.2 1.6	15 34 6 49
3 Sa	05:10 AM 10:01 AM 03:46 PM 10:36 PM	0.5 1.1 0.2 1.6	15 34 6 49
4 Su	04:52 AM 09:47 AM 03:32 PM 10:18 PM	0.5 1.0 0.3 1.5	15 30 9 46
5 M	05:36 AM 10:38 AM 04:24 PM 11:04 PM	0.5 1.0 0.3 1.5	15 30 9 46
6 Tu	06:21 AM 11:32 AM 05:23 PM 11:53 PM	0.4 1.1 0.4 1.5	12 34 12 46
7 W	07:05 AM 12:30 PM 06:31 PM	0.4 1.1 0.4	12 34 12
8 Th	12:44 AM 07:47 AM 01:28 PM 07:44 PM	1.4 0.3 1.2 0.4	43 9 37 12
9 F	01:36 AM 08:28 AM 02:26 PM 08:56 PM	1.4 0.2 1.3 0.4	43 6 40 12
10 Sa	02:29 AM 09:08 AM 03:21 PM 10:05 PM	1.3 0.1 1.5 0.4	40 3 46 12
11 Su	03:21 AM 09:49 AM 04:14 PM 11:10 PM	1.2 0.0 1.6 0.3	37 0 49 9
12 M	04:13 AM 10:31 AM 05:06 PM	1.2 -0.1 1.8	37 -3 55
13 Tu	12:10 AM 05:05 AM 11:16 AM 05:57 PM	0.3 1.1 -0.1 1.9	9 34 -3 58
14 W	01:08 AM 05:57 AM 12:03 PM 06:49 PM	0.2 1.1 -0.2 1.9	6 34 -6 58
15 Th	02:03 AM 06:51 AM 12:54 PM 07:41 PM	0.2 1.1 -0.2 1.9	6 34 -6 58
16 F	02:57 AM 07:45 AM 01:48 PM 08:35 PM	0.2 1.1 -0.2 1.8	6 34 -6 55
17 Sa	03:51 AM 08:42 AM 02:47 PM 09:30 PM	0.2 1.1 -0.1 1.7	6 34 -3 52
18 Su	04:46 AM 09:41 AM 03:51 PM 10:26 PM	0.2 1.1 0.0 1.6	6 34 0 49
19 M	05:40 AM 10:43 AM 05:00 PM 11:24 PM	0.2 1.1 0.1 1.5	6 34 3 46
20 Tu	06:32 AM 11:49 AM 06:13 PM	0.2 1.1 0.2	6 34 6
21 W	12:20 AM 07:23 AM 12:56 PM 07:27 PM	1.4 0.1 1.1 0.2	43 3 34 6
22 Th	01:15 AM 08:10 AM 02:02 PM 08:39 PM	1.2 0.1 1.2 0.3	37 3 37 9
23 F	02:07 AM 08:53 AM 03:04 PM 09:46 PM	1.2 0.0 1.3 0.3	37 0 40 9
24 Sa	02:56 AM 09:32 AM 03:59 PM 10:46 PM	1.1 0.0 1.4 0.3	34 0 43 9
25 Su	03:42 AM 10:08 AM 04:48 PM 11:40 PM	1.0 0.0 1.4 0.3	30 0 43 9
26 M	04:26 AM 10:42 AM 05:31 PM	0.9 -0.1 1.5	27 -3 46
27 Tu	12:28 AM 05:09 AM 11:15 AM 06:10 PM	0.3 0.9 -0.1 1.5	9 27 -3 46
28 W	01:11 AM 05:52 AM 11:50 AM 06:46 PM	0.3 0.9 -0.1 1.5	9 27 -3 46
29 Th	01:51 AM 06:33 AM 12:26 PM 07:21 PM	0.3 0.8 -0.1 1.4	9 24 -3 43
30 F	02:28 AM 07:14 AM 01:03 PM 07:55 PM	0.2 0.8 -0.1 1.4	6 24 -3 43

December

Day	Time (h m)	Height (ft)	Height (cm)
1 Sa	03:04 AM 07:56 AM 01:43 PM 08:30 PM	0.2 0.8 0.0 1.4	6 24 0 43
2 Su	03:40 AM 08:38 AM 02:25 PM 09:07 PM	0.2 0.8 0.0 1.4	6 24 0 43
3 M	04:17 AM 09:23 AM 03:10 PM 09:46 PM	0.2 0.8 0.0 1.3	6 24 0 40
4 Tu	04:54 AM 10:11 AM 04:01 PM 10:29 PM	0.1 0.9 0.1 1.3	3 27 3 40
5 W	05:33 AM 11:03 AM 04:59 PM 11:14 PM	0.1 0.9 0.1 1.2	3 27 3 37
6 Th	06:12 AM 11:59 AM 06:08 PM	0.0 1.0 0.2	0 30 6
7 F	12:03 AM 06:53 AM 12:57 PM 07:26 PM	1.1 -0.1 1.1 0.2	34 -3 34 6
8 Sa	12:55 AM 07:35 AM 01:55 PM 08:44 PM	1.0 -0.1 1.2 0.2	30 -3 37 6
9 Su	01:50 AM 08:20 AM 02:54 PM 09:56 PM	1.0 -0.2 1.4 0.2	30 -6 43 6
10 M	02:46 AM 09:07 AM 03:50 PM 11:02 PM	0.9 -0.3 1.5 0.1	27 -9 46 3
11 Tu	03:44 AM 09:58 AM 04:46 PM	0.8 -0.4 1.6	24 -12 49
12 W	12:01 AM 04:41 AM 10:51 AM 05:41 PM	0.0 0.8 -0.4 1.6	0 24 -12 49
13 Th	12:55 AM 05:37 AM 11:45 AM 06:34 PM	0.0 0.8 -0.4 1.6	0 24 -12 49
14 F	01:47 AM 06:33 AM 12:42 PM 07:28 PM	0.0 0.8 -0.4 1.6	0 24 -12 49
15 Sa	02:37 AM 07:29 AM 01:40 PM 08:20 PM	0.0 0.9 -0.4 1.5	0 27 -12 46
16 Su	03:26 AM 08:25 AM 02:39 PM 09:12 PM	-0.1 0.9 -0.3 1.4	-3 27 -9 43
17 M	04:15 AM 09:23 AM 03:40 PM 10:03 PM	-0.1 0.9 -0.2 1.3	-3 27 -6 40
18 Tu	05:03 AM 10:23 AM 04:45 PM 10:53 PM	-0.1 0.9 -0.1 1.2	-3 27 -3 37
19 W	05:50 AM 11:26 AM 05:55 PM 11:43 PM	-0.1 0.9 0.0 1.0	-3 27 0 30
20 Th	06:36 AM 12:30 PM 07:07 PM	-0.1 1.0 0.1	-3 30 3
21 F	12:32 AM 07:20 AM 01:36 PM 08:20 PM	0.9 -0.2 1.0 0.1	27 -6 30 3
22 Sa	01:22 AM 08:02 AM 02:38 PM 09:28 PM	0.8 -0.2 1.1 0.2	24 -6 34 6
23 Su	02:12 AM 08:43 AM 03:35 PM 10:28 PM	0.7 -0.2 1.1 0.1	21 -6 34 3
24 M	03:03 AM 09:24 AM 04:25 PM 11:21 PM	0.7 -0.3 1.2 0.1	21 -9 37 3
25 Tu	03:53 AM 10:05 AM 05:09 PM	0.6 -0.3 1.2	18 -9 37
26 W	12:07 AM 04:41 AM 10:46 AM 05:49 PM	0.1 0.6 -0.3 1.2	3 18 -9 37
27 Th	12:48 AM 05:26 AM 11:27 AM 06:25 PM	0.1 0.6 -0.3 1.2	3 18 -9 37
28 F	01:25 AM 06:10 AM 12:08 PM 06:59 PM	0.0 0.6 -0.3 1.2	0 18 -9 37
29 Sa	01:59 AM 06:52 AM 12:48 PM 07:32 PM	0.0 0.7 -0.3 1.2	0 21 -9 37
30 Su	02:32 AM 07:33 AM 01:29 PM 08:06 PM	0.0 0.7 -0.2 1.2	0 21 -6 37
31 M	03:05 AM 08:14 AM 02:11 PM 08:41 PM	-0.1 0.7 -0.2 1.2	-3 21 -6 37

Heights are referred to mean lower water which is the chart datum of sounding. All times are local. Daylight Saving Time has been used when needed.

Baltimore, Maryland, 2013

Times and Heights of High and Low Waters

January

Day	Time (h m)	Height (ft)	Height (cm)
1 Tu	03:38 AM	-0.1	-3
	08:57 AM	0.7	21
	02:56 PM	-0.2	-6
	09:19 PM	1.1	34
2 W	04:12 AM	-0.1	-3
	09:43 AM	0.8	24
	03:46 PM	-0.1	-3
	10:00 PM	1.1	34
3 Th	04:48 AM	-0.2	-6
	10:34 AM	0.8	24
	04:45 PM	0.0	0
	10:45 PM	1.0	30
4 F	05:27 AM	-0.2	-6
	11:28 AM	0.9	27
	05:55 PM	0.0	0
	11:34 PM	0.9	27
5 Sa	06:09 AM	-0.3	-9
	12:26 PM	1.0	30
	07:13 PM	0.1	3
6 Su	12:27 AM	0.8	24
	06:56 AM	-0.4	-12
	01:27 PM	1.1	34
	08:32 PM	0.0	0
7 M	01:25 AM	0.7	21
	07:48 AM	-0.4	-12
	02:30 PM	1.2	37
	09:44 PM	0.0	0
8 Tu	02:25 AM	0.7	21
	08:45 AM	-0.5	-15
	03:31 PM	1.3	40
	10:47 PM	0.0	0
9 W	03:26 AM	0.7	21
	09:44 AM	-0.5	-15
	04:31 PM	1.4	43
	11:44 PM	-0.1	-3
10 Th	04:27 AM	0.7	21
	10:43 AM	-0.5	-15
	05:28 PM	1.4	43
11 F	12:35 AM	-0.1	-3
	05:24 AM	0.7	21
	11:42 AM	-0.6	-18
	06:22 PM	1.4	43
12 Sa	01:24 AM	-0.2	-6
	06:20 AM	0.8	24
	12:40 PM	-0.6	-18
	07:14 PM	1.3	40
13 Su	02:10 AM	-0.2	-6
	07:15 AM	0.8	24
	01:36 PM	-0.5	-15
	08:03 PM	1.3	40
14 M	02:55 AM	-0.2	-6
	08:09 AM	0.9	27
	02:32 PM	-0.4	-12
	08:50 PM	1.2	37
15 Tu	03:38 AM	-0.2	-6
	09:04 AM	0.9	27
	03:29 PM	-0.3	-9
	09:35 PM	1.1	34
16 W	04:21 AM	-0.3	-9
	09:59 AM	0.9	27
	04:28 PM	-0.2	-6
	10:20 PM	1.0	30
17 Th	05:02 AM	-0.3	-9
	10:56 AM	0.9	27
	05:31 PM	-0.1	-3
	11:05 PM	0.9	27
18 F	05:44 AM	-0.3	-9
	11:56 AM	0.9	27
	06:38 PM	0.0	0
	11:51 PM	0.8	24
19 Sa	06:26 AM	-0.3	-9
	12:57 PM	0.9	27
	07:48 PM	0.1	3
20 Su	12:40 AM	0.7	21
	07:11 AM	-0.3	-9
	01:59 PM	0.9	27
	08:54 PM	0.1	3
21 M	01:33 AM	0.6	18
	07:58 AM	-0.3	-9
	02:58 PM	1.0	30
	09:54 PM	0.1	3
22 Tu	02:27 AM	0.6	18
	08:47 AM	-0.3	-9
	03:52 PM	1.0	30
	10:46 PM	0.1	3
23 W	03:20 AM	0.6	18
	09:36 AM	-0.3	-9
	04:39 PM	1.0	30
	11:30 PM	0.1	3
24 Th	04:12 AM	0.6	18
	10:24 AM	-0.3	-9
	05:21 PM	1.0	30
25 F	12:10 AM	0.0	0
	04:59 AM	0.6	18
	11:09 AM	-0.3	-9
	05:58 PM	1.1	34
26 Sa	12:46 AM	0.0	0
	05:44 AM	0.7	21
	11:53 AM	-0.3	-9
	06:32 PM	1.1	34
27 Su	01:20 AM	-0.1	-3
	06:26 AM	0.7	21
	12:36 PM	-0.3	-9
	07:06 PM	1.1	34
28 M	01:52 AM	-0.1	-3
	07:07 AM	0.7	21
	01:18 PM	-0.3	-9
	07:40 PM	1.1	34
29 Tu	02:24 AM	-0.1	-3
	07:48 AM	0.8	24
	02:02 PM	-0.3	-9
	08:16 PM	1.1	34
30 W	02:56 AM	-0.2	-6
	08:31 AM	0.8	24
	02:50 PM	-0.2	-6
	08:55 PM	1.0	30
31 Th	03:29 AM	-0.2	-6
	09:17 AM	0.9	27
	03:42 PM	-0.2	-6
	09:36 PM	1.0	30

February

Day	Time (h m)	Height (ft)	Height (cm)
1 F	04:05 AM	-0.3	-9
	10:07 AM	1.0	30
	04:43 PM	-0.1	-3
	10:21 PM	0.9	27
2 Sa	04:45 AM	-0.3	-9
	11:01 AM	1.1	34
	05:52 PM	0.0	0
	11:11 PM	0.8	24
3 Su	05:31 AM	-0.3	-9
	12:00 PM	1.1	34
	07:06 PM	0.0	0
4 M	12:07 AM	0.7	21
	06:25 AM	-0.4	-12
	01:03 PM	1.2	37
	08:20 PM	0.0	0
5 Tu	01:07 AM	0.7	21
	07:27 AM	-0.4	-12
	02:09 PM	1.2	37
	09:28 PM	0.0	0
6 W	02:11 AM	0.7	21
	08:33 AM	-0.4	-12
	03:15 PM	1.2	37
	10:27 PM	0.0	0
7 Th	03:14 AM	0.7	21
	09:39 AM	-0.4	-12
	04:18 PM	1.2	37
	11:21 PM	-0.1	-3
8 F	04:14 AM	0.8	24
	10:42 AM	-0.5	-15
	05:16 PM	1.3	40
9 Sa	12:09 AM	-0.1	-3
	05:11 AM	0.9	27
	11:42 AM	-0.5	-15
	06:08 PM	1.2	37
10 Su	12:55 AM	-0.1	-3
	06:06 AM	0.9	27
	12:38 PM	-0.5	-15
	06:56 PM	1.2	37
11 M	01:37 AM	-0.2	-6
	06:58 AM	1.0	30
	01:31 PM	-0.4	-12
	07:41 PM	1.2	37
12 Tu	02:17 AM	-0.2	-6
	07:49 AM	1.0	30
	02:23 PM	-0.3	-9
	08:23 PM	1.1	34
13 W	02:54 AM	-0.2	-6
	08:39 AM	1.1	34
	03:15 PM	-0.2	-6
	09:04 PM	1.0	30
14 Th	03:31 AM	-0.2	-6
	09:29 AM	1.1	34
	04:09 PM	-0.1	-3
	09:46 PM	0.9	27
15 F	04:07 AM	-0.2	-6
	10:20 AM	1.0	30
	05:05 PM	0.0	0
	10:28 PM	0.8	24
16 Sa	04:45 AM	-0.2	-6
	11:12 AM	1.0	30
	06:05 PM	0.1	3
	11:14 PM	0.8	24
17 Su	05:28 AM	-0.2	-6
	12:08 PM	1.0	30
	07:08 PM	0.2	6
18 M	12:03 AM	0.7	21
	06:17 AM	-0.2	-6
	01:06 PM	1.0	30
	08:11 PM	0.2	6
19 Tu	12:57 AM	0.7	21
	07:12 AM	-0.1	-3
	02:07 PM	1.0	30
	09:08 PM	0.2	6
20 W	01:53 AM	0.7	21
	08:10 AM	-0.1	-3
	03:05 PM	1.0	30
	09:59 PM	0.2	6
21 Th	02:49 AM	0.7	21
	09:08 AM	-0.1	-3
	03:57 PM	1.0	30
	10:43 PM	0.1	3
22 F	03:43 AM	0.8	24
	10:02 AM	-0.2	-6
	04:42 PM	1.0	30
	11:23 PM	0.1	3
23 Sa	04:32 AM	0.8	24
	10:52 AM	-0.2	-6
	05:22 PM	1.1	34
	11:59 PM	0.1	3
24 Su	05:17 AM	0.9	27
	11:39 AM	-0.2	-6
	05:59 PM	1.1	34
25 M	12:33 AM	0.0	0
	05:59 AM	0.9	27
	12:25 PM	-0.2	-6
	06:35 PM	1.1	34
26 Tu	01:05 AM	0.0	0
	06:41 AM	1.0	30
	01:11 PM	-0.2	-6
	07:12 PM	1.1	34
27 W	01:37 AM	-0.1	-3
	07:23 AM	1.1	34
	01:59 PM	-0.2	-6
	07:50 PM	1.1	34
28 Th	02:11 AM	-0.1	-3
	08:07 AM	1.2	37
	02:49 PM	-0.1	-3
	08:31 PM	1.0	30

March

Day	Time (h m)	Height (ft)	Height (cm)
1 F	02:46 AM	-0.2	-6
	08:53 AM	1.3	40
	03:44 PM	-0.1	-3
	09:16 PM	1.0	30
2 Sa	03:26 AM	-0.2	-6
	09:43 AM	1.3	40
	04:44 PM	0.0	0
	10:04 PM	0.9	27
3 Su	04:11 AM	-0.2	-6
	10:38 AM	1.3	40
	05:49 PM	0.1	3
	10:57 PM	0.9	27
4 M	05:05 AM	-0.2	-6
	11:37 AM	1.3	40
	06:57 PM	0.1	3
	11:56 PM	0.9	27
5 Tu	06:09 AM	-0.2	-6
	12:43 PM	1.3	40
	08:04 PM	0.1	3
6 W	12:59 AM	0.9	27
	07:20 AM	-0.2	-6
	01:51 PM	1.3	40
	09:05 PM	0.1	3
7 Th	02:03 AM	0.9	27
	08:33 AM	-0.2	-6
	03:00 PM	1.3	40
	10:01 PM	0.1	3
8 F	03:06 AM	1.0	30
	09:42 AM	-0.2	-6
	04:03 PM	1.3	40
	10:52 PM	0.1	3
9 Sa	04:05 AM	1.1	34
	10:45 AM	-0.2	-6
	04:59 PM	1.3	40
	11:37 PM	0.0	0
10 Su	06:00 AM	1.2	37
	12:42 PM	-0.2	-6
	06:48 PM	1.2	37
11 M	01:19 AM	0.0	0
	06:52 AM	1.3	40
	01:36 PM	-0.2	-6
	07:33 PM	1.2	37
12 Tu	01:57 AM	0.0	0
	07:41 AM	1.3	40
	02:26 PM	-0.2	-6
	08:14 PM	1.2	37
13 W	02:32 AM	0.0	0
	08:27 AM	1.3	40
	03:15 PM	-0.1	-3
	08:54 PM	1.1	34
14 Th	03:05 AM	0.0	0
	09:12 AM	1.4	43
	04:03 PM	0.0	0
	09:34 PM	1.0	30
15 F	03:38 AM	0.0	0
	09:57 AM	1.3	40
	04:51 PM	0.1	3
	10:14 PM	1.0	30
16 Sa	04:13 AM	0.0	0
	10:41 AM	1.3	40
	05:40 PM	0.2	6
	10:57 PM	0.9	27
17 Su	04:52 AM	0.0	0
	11:27 AM	1.3	40
	06:31 PM	0.3	9
	11:42 PM	0.9	27
18 M	05:37 AM	0.1	3
	12:16 PM	1.2	37
	07:24 PM	0.3	9
19 Tu	12:32 AM	0.9	27
	06:30 AM	0.1	3
	01:09 PM	1.2	37
	08:18 PM	0.3	9
20 W	01:26 AM	0.9	27
	07:31 AM	0.1	3
	02:07 PM	1.1	34
	09:11 PM	0.4	12
21 Th	02:22 AM	0.9	27
	08:35 AM	0.2	6
	03:05 PM	1.1	34
	10:01 PM	0.3	9
22 F	03:18 AM	1.0	30
	09:39 AM	0.2	6
	04:01 PM	1.1	34
	10:45 PM	0.3	9
23 Sa	04:12 AM	1.1	34
	10:38 AM	0.1	3
	04:50 PM	1.1	34
	11:26 PM	0.3	9
24 Su	05:01 AM	1.1	34
	11:33 AM	0.1	3
	05:35 PM	1.2	37
25 M	12:03 AM	0.2	6
	05:47 AM	1.2	37
	12:25 PM	0.1	3
	06:18 PM	1.2	37
26 Tu	12:39 AM	0.2	6
	06:31 AM	1.3	40
	01:15 PM	0.1	3
	06:59 PM	1.2	37
27 W	01:14 AM	0.1	3
	07:14 AM	1.5	46
	02:05 PM	0.0	0
	07:41 PM	1.2	37
28 Th	01:49 AM	0.1	3
	07:58 AM	1.6	49
	02:56 PM	0.0	0
	08:24 PM	1.1	34
29 F	02:27 AM	0.0	0
	08:44 AM	1.6	49
	03:49 PM	0.1	3
	09:10 PM	1.1	34
30 Sa	03:08 AM	0.0	0
	09:32 AM	1.7	52
	04:44 PM	0.1	3
	09:59 PM	1.1	34
31 Su	03:54 AM	0.0	0
	10:23 AM	1.7	52
	05:41 PM	0.1	3
	10:52 PM	1.1	34

April

Day	Time (h m)	Height (ft)	Height (cm)
1 M	04:48 AM	0.0	0
	11:18 AM	1.6	49
	06:41 PM	0.2	6
	11:49 PM	1.1	34
2 Tu	05:51 AM	0.1	3
	12:19 PM	1.5	46
	07:41 PM	0.2	6
3 W	12:50 AM	1.1	34
	07:03 AM	0.1	3
	01:24 PM	1.5	46
	08:41 PM	0.2	6
4 Th	01:53 AM	1.2	37
	08:20 AM	0.1	3
	02:33 PM	1.4	43
	09:37 PM	0.3	9
5 F	02:57 AM	1.2	37
	09:35 AM	0.1	3
	03:39 PM	1.3	40
	10:29 PM	0.2	6
6 Sa	03:59 AM	1.3	40
	10:44 AM	0.1	3
	04:40 PM	1.3	40
	11:17 PM	0.2	6
7 Su	04:56 AM	1.4	43
	11:45 AM	0.1	3
	05:33 PM	1.3	40
	11:59 PM	0.2	6
8 M	05:49 AM	1.5	46
	12:42 PM	0.1	3
	06:20 PM	1.3	40
9 Tu	12:38 AM	0.2	6
	06:38 AM	1.6	49
	01:34 PM	0.1	3
	07:04 PM	1.2	37
10 W	01:13 AM	0.2	6
	07:23 AM	1.6	49
	02:22 PM	0.1	3
	07:45 PM	1.2	37
11 Th	01:45 AM	0.2	6
	08:05 AM	1.7	52
	03:08 PM	0.2	6
	08:25 PM	1.1	34
12 F	02:17 AM	0.2	6
	08:46 AM	1.6	49
	03:52 PM	0.3	9
	09:05 PM	1.1	34
13 Sa	02:50 AM	0.2	6
	09:25 AM	1.6	49
	04:34 PM	0.3	9
	09:46 PM	1.1	34
14 Su	03:27 AM	0.2	6
	10:05 AM	1.6	49
	05:15 PM	0.4	12
	10:30 PM	1.1	34
15 M	04:08 AM	0.3	9
	10:46 AM	1.5	46
	05:57 PM	0.4	12
	11:16 PM	1.1	34
16 Tu	04:56 AM	0.3	9
	11:30 AM	1.4	43
	06:41 PM	0.4	12
17 W	12:05 AM	1.1	34
	05:51 AM	0.4	12
	12:17 PM	1.4	43
	07:27 PM	0.5	15
18 Th	12:57 AM	1.1	34
	06:53 AM	0.4	12
	01:09 PM	1.3	40
	08:14 PM	0.5	15
19 F	01:52 AM	1.2	37
	08:00 AM	0.5	15
	02:04 PM	1.3	40
	09:00 PM	0.4	12
20 Sa	02:46 AM	1.3	40
	09:08 AM	0.4	12
	02:59 PM	1.3	40
	09:44 PM	0.4	12
21 Su	03:39 AM	1.4	43
	10:13 AM	0.4	12
	03:53 PM	1.3	40
	10:25 PM	0.4	12
22 M	04:29 AM	1.5	46
	11:14 AM	0.4	12
	04:44 PM	1.2	37
	11:05 PM	0.3	9
23 Tu	05:16 AM	1.6	49
	12:11 PM	0.3	9
	05:33 PM	1.2	37
	11:43 PM	0.2	6
24 W	06:02 AM	1.7	52
	01:06 PM	0.3	9
	06:22 PM	1.2	37
25 Th	12:23 AM	0.2	6
	06:48 AM	1.8	55
	01:59 PM	0.2	6
	07:10 PM	1.2	37
26 F	01:05 AM	0.2	6
	07:35 AM	1.9	58
	02:51 PM	0.2	6
	08:00 PM	1.2	37
27 Sa	01:50 AM	0.1	3
	08:23 AM	2.0	61
	03:44 PM	0.2	6
	08:51 PM	1.2	37
28 Su	02:39 AM	0.2	6
	09:13 AM	2.0	61
	04:36 PM	0.2	6
	09:44 PM	1.2	37
29 M	03:34 AM	0.2	6
	10:06 AM	1.9	58
	05:30 PM	0.3	9
	10:41 PM	1.2	37
30 Tu	04:35 AM	0.2	6
	11:02 AM	1.8	55
	06:24 PM	0.3	9
	11:40 PM	1.3	40

May

Day	Time (h m)	Height (ft)	Height (cm)
1 W	05:45 AM	0.3	9
	12:02 PM	1.7	52
	07:19 PM	0.3	9
2 Th	12:42 AM	1.4	43
	07:01 AM	0.4	12
	01:04 PM	1.6	49
	08:12 PM	0.3	9
3 F	01:46 AM	1.4	43
	08:19 AM	0.4	12
	02:08 PM	1.5	46
	09:04 PM	0.3	9
4 Sa	02:49 AM	1.5	46
	09:33 AM	0.4	12
	03:09 PM	1.4	43
	09:53 PM	0.3	9
5 Su	03:50 AM	1.6	49
	10:41 AM	0.4	12
	04:07 PM	1.3	40
	10:37 PM	0.3	9
6 M	04:46 AM	1.7	52
	11:43 AM	0.4	12
	04:59 PM	1.3	40
	11:18 PM	0.3	9
7 Tu	05:37 AM	1.8	55
	12:38 PM	0.4	12
	05:47 PM	1.2	37
	11:54 PM	0.3	9
8 W	06:23 AM	1.8	55
	01:29 PM	0.4	12
	06:32 PM	1.2	37
9 Th	12:29 AM	0.3	9
	07:05 AM	1.9	58
	02:16 PM	0.4	12
	07:15 PM	1.2	37
10 F	01:02 AM	0.3	9
	07:44 AM	1.9	58
	02:58 PM	0.4	12
	07:57 PM	1.2	37
11 Sa	01:36 AM	0.3	9
	08:21 AM	1.8	55
	03:38 PM	0.4	12
	08:39 PM	1.2	37
12 Su	02:12 AM	0.4	12
	08:57 AM	1.8	55
	04:15 PM	0.4	12
	09:22 PM	1.2	37
13 M	02:52 AM	0.4	12
	09:33 AM	1.7	52
	04:50 PM	0.5	15
	10:05 PM	1.2	37
14 Tu	03:36 AM	0.5	15
	10:11 AM	1.7	52
	05:26 PM	0.5	15
	10:51 PM	1.2	37
15 W	04:24 AM	0.5	15
	10:51 AM	1.6	49
	06:03 PM	0.5	15
	11:38 PM	1.3	40
16 Th	05:18 AM	0.6	18
	11:35 AM	1.6	49
	06:42 PM	0.5	15
17 F	12:28 AM	1.3	40
	06:18 AM	0.6	18
	12:22 PM	1.5	46
	07:22 PM	0.5	15
18 Sa	01:20 AM	1.4	43
	07:26 AM	0.6	18
	01:12 PM	1.4	43
	08:03 PM	0.4	12
19 Su	02:13 AM	1.5	46
	08:38 AM	0.7	21
	02:05 PM	1.4	43
	08:45 PM	0.4	12
20 M	03:05 AM	1.6	49
	09:49 AM	0.6	18
	03:00 PM	1.3	40
	09:27 PM	0.3	9
21 Tu	03:56 AM	1.7	52
	10:56 AM	0.6	18
	03:56 PM	1.3	40
	10:10 PM	0.3	9
22 W	04:46 AM	1.9	58
	11:58 AM	0.5	15
	04:52 PM	1.2	37
	10:54 PM	0.2	6
23 Th	05:36 AM	2.0	61
	12:55 PM	0.4	12
	05:47 PM	1.2	37
	11:41 PM	0.2	6
24 F	06:25 AM	2.1	64
	01:49 PM	0.4	12
	06:42 PM	1.2	37
25 Sa	12:31 AM	0.2	6
	07:15 AM	2.1	64
	02:41 PM	0.3	9
	07:37 PM	1.2	37
26 Su	01:24 AM	0.2	6
	08:06 AM	2.1	64
	03:31 PM	0.3	9
	08:33 PM	1.3	40
27 M	02:21 AM	0.2	6
	08:58 AM	2.1	64
	04:21 PM	0.3	9
	09:29 PM	1.3	40
28 Tu	03:22 AM	0.3	9
	09:51 AM	2.0	61
	05:10 PM	0.3	9
	10:27 PM	1.4	43
29 W	04:28 AM	0.4	12
	10:46 AM	1.9	58
	06:00 PM	0.3	9
	11:27 PM	1.5	46
30 Th	05:38 AM	0.4	12
	11:42 AM	1.7	52
	06:49 PM	0.3	9
31 F	12:29 AM	1.5	46
	06:54 AM	0.5	15
	12:39 PM	1.6	49
	07:38 PM	0.3	9

June

Day	Time (h m)	Height (ft)	Height (cm)
1 Sa	01:32 AM	1.6	49
	08:10 AM	0.5	15
	01:36 PM	1.5	46
	08:26 PM	0.3	9
2 Su	02:35 AM	1.7	52
	09:24 AM	0.6	18
	02:32 PM	1.4	43
	09:11 PM	0.3	9
3 M	03:35 AM	1.8	55
	10:33 AM	0.6	18
	03:28 PM	1.3	40
	09:54 PM	0.3	9
4 Tu	04:30 AM	1.8	55
	11:35 AM	0.5	15
	04:21 PM	1.2	37
	10:34 PM	0.3	9
5 W	05:20 AM	1.9	58
	12:30 PM	0.5	15
	05:12 PM	1.2	37
	11:12 PM	0.3	9
6 Th	06:05 AM	1.9	58
	01:19 PM	0.5	15
	06:01 PM	1.1	34
	11:49 PM	0.3	9
7 F	06:45 AM	1.9	58
	02:03 PM	0.5	15
	06:47 PM	1.1	34
8 Sa	12:27 AM	0.4	12
	07:23 AM	1.9	58
	02:42 PM	0.5	15
	07:32 PM	1.2	37
9 Su	01:06 AM	0.4	12
	07:58 AM	1.9	58
	03:17 PM	0.5	15
	08:16 PM	1.2	37
10 M	01:47 AM	0.4	12
	08:32 AM	1.8	55
	03:50 PM	0.5	15
	08:58 PM	1.2	37
11 Tu	02:29 AM	0.5	15
	09:07 AM	1.8	55
	04:21 PM	0.5	15
	09:41 PM	1.3	40
12 W	03:13 AM	0.5	15
	09:42 AM	1.8	55
	04:53 PM	0.5	15
	10:25 PM	1.3	40
13 Th	04:00 AM	0.6	18
	10:20 AM	1.7	52
	05:26 PM	0.4	12
	11:10 PM	1.3	40
14 F	04:52 AM	0.6	18
	10:59 AM	1.6	49
	06:00 PM	0.4	12
	11:57 PM	1.4	43
15 Sa	05:51 AM	0.7	21
	11:43 AM	1.6	49
	06:36 PM	0.4	12
16 Su	12:47 AM	1.5	46
	06:59 AM	0.7	21
	12:30 PM	1.5	46
	07:13 PM	0.3	9
17 M	01:39 AM	1.6	49
	08:14 AM	0.7	21
	01:22 PM	1.4	43
	07:54 PM	0.3	9
18 Tu	02:32 AM	1.7	52
	09:31 AM	0.7	21
	02:18 PM	1.3	40
	08:38 PM	0.3	9
19 W	03:25 AM	1.9	58
	10:41 AM	0.7	21
	03:17 PM	1.2	37
	09:26 PM	0.2	6
20 Th	04:19 AM	2.0	61
	11:45 AM	0.6	18
	04:18 PM	1.2	37
	10:18 PM	0.2	6
21 F	05:13 AM	2.1	64
	12:42 PM	0.5	15
	05:19 PM	1.2	37
	11:13 PM	0.2	6
22 Sa	06:06 AM	2.2	67
	01:34 PM	0.4	12
	06:19 PM	1.2	37
23 Su	12:11 AM	0.2	6
	06:59 AM	2.2	67
	02:23 PM	0.4	12
	07:17 PM	1.3	40
24 M	01:11 AM	0.2	6
	07:51 AM	2.2	67
	03:10 PM	0.3	9
	08:15 PM	1.4	43
25 Tu	02:12 AM	0.2	6
	08:43 AM	2.1	64
	03:57 PM	0.3	9
	09:12 PM	1.4	43
26 W	03:15 AM	0.3	9
	09:35 AM	2.0	61
	04:43 PM	0.3	9
	10:10 PM	1.5	46
27 Th	04:20 AM	0.4	12
	10:26 AM	1.9	58
	05:28 PM	0.3	9
	11:09 PM	1.6	49
28 F	05:28 AM	0.5	15
	11:17 AM	1.7	52
	06:13 PM	0.3	9
29 Sa	12:09 AM	1.6	49
	06:40 AM	0.6	18
	12:08 PM	1.6	49
	06:58 PM	0.3	9
30 Su	01:11 AM	1.7	52
	07:55 AM	0.7	21
	12:59 PM	1.4	43
	07:42 PM	0.3	9

Heights are referred to mean lower water which is the chart datum of sounding. All times are local. Daylight Saving Time has been used when needed.

Baltimore, Maryland, 2013

Times and Heights of High and Low Waters

July

Day	Time (h m)	Height (ft)	Height (cm)
1 M	02:13 AM 09:08 AM 01:53 PM 08:25 PM	1.8 0.7 1.3 0.3	55 21 40 9
2 Tu	03:13 AM 10:17 AM 02:48 PM 09:08 PM	1.8 0.7 1.2 0.3	55 21 37 9
3 W	04:08 AM 11:19 AM 03:44 PM 09:52 PM	1.9 0.7 1.2 0.3	58 21 37 9
4 Th	04:58 AM 12:13 PM 04:39 PM 10:35 PM	1.9 0.6 1.1 0.4	58 18 34 12
5 F	05:43 AM 12:59 PM 05:31 PM 11:19 PM	1.9 0.6 1.1 0.4	58 18 34 12
6 Sa	06:24 AM 01:39 PM 06:21 PM	1.9 0.6 1.2	58 18 37
7 Su	12:03 AM 07:01 AM 02:15 PM 07:07 PM	0.4 1.9 0.5 1.2	12 58 15 37
8 M	12:47 AM 07:35 AM 02:47 PM 07:51 PM	0.4 1.9 0.5 1.2	12 58 15 37
9 Tu	01:30 AM 08:08 AM 03:17 PM 08:34 PM	0.5 1.8 0.5 1.3	15 55 15 40
10 W	02:13 AM 08:41 AM 03:47 PM 09:15 PM	0.5 1.8 0.5 1.3	15 55 15 40
11 Th	02:56 AM 09:15 AM 04:16 PM 09:57 PM	0.6 1.8 0.4 1.4	18 55 12 43
12 F	03:43 AM 09:51 AM 04:46 PM 10:40 PM	0.6 1.7 0.4 1.5	18 52 12 46
13 Sa	04:34 AM 10:29 AM 05:17 PM 11:25 PM	0.7 1.7 0.4 1.5	21 52 12 46
14 Su	05:33 AM 11:11 AM 05:51 PM	0.7 1.6 0.3	21 49 9
15 M	12:14 AM 06:42 AM 11:57 AM 06:29 PM	1.6 0.8 1.5 0.3	49 24 46 9
16 Tu	01:06 AM 07:59 AM 12:49 PM 07:12 PM	1.8 0.8 1.4 0.3	55 24 43 9
17 W	02:01 AM 09:16 AM 01:48 PM 08:01 PM	1.9 0.8 1.3 0.2	58 24 40 6
18 Th	02:58 AM 10:26 AM 02:51 PM 08:56 PM	2.0 0.7 1.2 0.2	61 21 37 6
19 F	03:56 AM 11:27 AM 03:56 PM 09:57 PM	2.0 0.6 1.2 0.2	61 18 37 6
20 Sa	04:54 AM 12:22 PM 05:00 PM 11:00 PM	2.1 0.5 1.2 0.2	64 15 37 6
21 Su	05:50 AM 01:12 PM 06:01 PM	2.1 0.5 1.3	64 15 40
22 M	12:04 AM 06:45 AM 01:58 PM 07:00 PM	0.2 2.1 0.4 1.4	6 64 12 43
23 Tu	01:06 AM 07:36 AM 02:43 PM 07:57 PM	0.2 2.1 0.4 1.5	6 64 12 46
24 W	02:07 AM 08:26 AM 03:26 PM 08:53 PM	0.3 2.0 0.3 1.6	9 61 9 49
25 Th	03:08 AM 09:14 AM 04:08 PM 09:49 PM	0.4 1.9 0.3 1.7	12 58 9 52
26 F	04:10 AM 10:01 AM 04:49 PM 10:45 PM	0.5 1.8 0.3 1.7	15 55 9 52
27 Sa	05:14 AM 10:47 AM 05:30 PM 11:43 PM	0.6 1.7 0.3 1.7	18 52 9 52
28 Su	06:22 AM 11:33 AM 06:10 PM	0.7 1.5 0.3	21 46 9
29 M	12:41 AM 07:34 AM 12:22 PM 06:52 PM	1.8 0.7 1.4 0.3	55 21 43 9
30 Tu	01:41 AM 08:46 AM 01:14 PM 07:36 PM	1.8 0.8 1.3 0.3	55 24 40 9
31 W	02:40 AM 09:53 AM 02:10 PM 08:24 PM	1.8 0.8 1.2 0.4	55 24 37 12

August

Day	Time (h m)	Height (ft)	Height (cm)
1 Th	03:37 AM 10:52 AM 03:09 PM 09:14 PM	1.8 0.8 1.2 0.4	55 24 37 12
2 F	04:29 AM 11:43 AM 04:08 PM 10:06 PM	1.8 0.7 1.2 0.4	55 21 37 12
3 Sa	05:16 AM 12:26 PM 05:04 PM 10:57 PM	1.8 0.7 1.2 0.5	55 21 37 15
4 Su	05:57 AM 01:03 PM 05:55 PM 11:46 PM	1.8 0.6 1.3 0.5	55 18 40 15
5 M	06:34 AM 01:37 PM 06:42 PM	1.8 0.6 1.3	55 18 40
6 Tu	12:32 AM 07:08 AM 02:08 PM 07:25 PM	0.5 1.8 0.5 1.4	15 55 15 43
7 W	01:17 AM 07:41 AM 02:37 PM 08:06 PM	0.5 1.8 0.5 1.4	15 55 15 43
8 Th	02:01 AM 08:13 AM 03:05 PM 08:46 PM	0.6 1.8 0.5 1.5	18 55 15 46
9 F	02:46 AM 08:47 AM 03:34 PM 09:27 PM	0.6 1.8 0.4 1.6	18 55 12 49
10 Sa	03:33 AM 09:23 AM 04:03 PM 10:09 PM	0.7 1.7 0.4 1.6	21 52 12 49
11 Su	04:26 AM 10:02 AM 04:35 PM 10:54 PM	0.7 1.6 0.3 1.7	21 49 9 52
12 M	05:27 AM 10:45 AM 05:10 PM 11:43 PM	0.8 1.5 0.3 1.8	24 46 9 55
13 Tu	06:36 AM 11:33 AM 05:51 PM	0.8 1.4 0.3	24 43 9
14 W	12:36 AM 07:50 AM 12:28 PM 06:40 PM	1.9 0.8 1.3 0.3	58 24 40 9
15 Th	01:34 AM 09:02 AM 01:30 PM 07:37 PM	2.0 0.8 1.3 0.3	61 24 40 9
16 F	02:35 AM 10:07 AM 02:35 PM 08:42 PM	2.0 0.7 1.3 0.3	61 21 40 9
17 Sa	03:37 AM 11:05 AM 03:42 PM 09:51 PM	2.0 0.6 1.3 0.3	61 18 40 9
18 Su	04:38 AM 11:57 AM 04:47 PM 10:59 PM	2.0 0.6 1.4 0.3	61 18 43 9
19 M	05:36 AM 12:44 PM 05:48 PM	2.0 0.5 1.5	61 15 46
20 Tu	12:04 AM 06:29 AM 01:28 PM 06:45 PM	0.3 2.0 0.4 1.6	9 61 12 49
21 W	01:05 AM 07:18 AM 02:10 PM 07:40 PM	0.3 2.0 0.4 1.7	9 61 12 52
22 Th	02:04 AM 08:04 AM 02:49 PM 08:34 PM	0.4 1.9 0.4 1.8	12 58 12 55
23 F	03:02 AM 08:48 AM 03:27 PM 09:26 PM	0.5 1.8 0.3 1.8	15 55 9 55
24 Sa	04:00 AM 09:32 AM 04:04 PM 10:18 PM	0.6 1.7 0.3 1.8	18 52 9 55
25 Su	04:59 AM 10:15 AM 04:41 PM 11:11 PM	0.7 1.6 0.3 1.8	21 49 9 55
26 M	06:02 AM 11:00 AM 05:19 PM	0.7 1.5 0.4	21 46 12
27 Tu	12:04 AM 07:08 AM 11:47 AM 06:01 PM	1.8 0.8 1.4 0.4	55 24 43 12
28 W	12:59 AM 08:14 AM 12:39 PM 06:48 PM	1.8 0.8 1.3 0.4	55 24 40 12
29 Th	01:57 AM 09:17 AM 01:37 PM 07:41 PM	1.8 0.8 1.2 0.5	55 24 37 15
30 F	02:54 AM 10:12 AM 02:37 PM 08:40 PM	1.8 0.8 1.2 0.5	55 24 37 15
31 Sa	03:48 AM 10:59 AM 03:38 PM 09:39 PM	1.8 0.8 1.3 0.5	55 24 40 15

September

Day	Time (h m)	Height (ft)	Height (cm)
1 Su	04:37 AM 11:40 AM 04:35 PM 10:35 PM	1.8 0.7 1.3 0.5	55 21 40 15
2 M	05:19 AM 12:16 PM 05:27 PM 11:28 PM	1.8 0.7 1.4 0.6	55 21 43 18
3 Tu	05:58 AM 12:49 PM 06:14 PM	1.8 0.6 1.4	55 18 43
4 W	12:17 AM 06:33 AM 01:20 PM 06:57 PM	0.6 1.8 0.5 1.5	18 55 15 46
5 Th	01:04 AM 07:07 AM 01:49 PM 07:37 PM	0.6 1.8 0.5 1.6	18 55 15 49
6 F	01:51 AM 07:42 AM 02:18 PM 08:17 PM	0.6 1.7 0.4 1.7	18 52 12 52
7 Sa	02:39 AM 08:18 AM 02:48 PM 08:57 PM	0.6 1.7 0.4 1.8	18 52 12 55
8 Su	03:30 AM 08:57 AM 03:20 PM 09:40 PM	0.7 1.6 0.3 1.9	21 49 9 58
9 M	04:25 AM 09:39 AM 03:55 PM 10:26 PM	0.7 1.5 0.3 1.9	21 46 9 58
10 Tu	05:25 AM 10:26 AM 04:35 PM 11:17 PM	0.7 1.4 0.3 2.0	21 43 9 61
11 W	06:31 AM 11:18 AM 05:23 PM	0.7 1.4 0.3	21 43 9
12 Th	12:12 AM 07:38 AM 12:16 PM 06:20 PM	2.0 0.7 1.3 0.3	61 21 40 9
13 F	01:12 AM 08:44 AM 01:20 PM 07:28 PM	2.0 0.7 1.3 0.4	61 21 40 12
14 Sa	02:16 AM 09:44 AM 02:28 PM 08:42 PM	2.0 0.7 1.3 0.4	61 21 40 12
15 Su	03:21 AM 10:38 AM 03:34 PM 09:55 PM	1.9 0.6 1.4 0.4	58 18 43 12
16 M	04:22 AM 11:27 AM 04:38 PM 11:03 PM	1.9 0.5 1.5 0.4	58 15 46 12
17 Tu	05:18 AM 12:12 PM 05:37 PM	1.9 0.5 1.6	58 15 49
18 W	12:07 AM 06:08 AM 12:54 PM 06:32 PM	0.4 1.8 0.4 1.7	12 55 12 52
19 Th	01:05 AM 06:54 AM 01:32 PM 07:25 PM	0.4 1.8 0.4 1.8	12 55 12 55
20 F	02:02 AM 07:38 AM 02:09 PM 08:14 PM	0.5 1.7 0.3 1.9	15 52 9 58
21 Sa	02:56 AM 08:20 AM 02:43 PM 09:02 PM	0.5 1.6 0.3 1.9	15 49 9 58
22 Su	03:50 AM 09:02 AM 03:17 PM 09:49 PM	0.6 1.5 0.3 1.9	18 46 9 58
23 M	04:44 AM 09:44 AM 03:52 PM 10:36 PM	0.7 1.4 0.3 1.9	21 43 9 58
24 Tu	05:40 AM 10:28 AM 04:30 PM 11:24 PM	0.7 1.4 0.4 1.8	21 43 12 55
25 W	06:36 AM 11:16 AM 05:13 PM	0.8 1.3 0.4	24 40 12
26 Th	12:14 AM 07:34 AM 12:08 PM 06:04 PM	1.8 0.8 1.3 0.5	55 24 40 15
27 F	01:07 AM 08:29 AM 01:05 PM 07:02 PM	1.7 0.8 1.2 0.5	52 24 37 15
28 Sa	02:01 AM 09:20 AM 02:06 PM 08:05 PM	1.7 0.8 1.2 0.6	52 24 37 18
29 Su	02:55 AM 10:05 AM 03:07 PM 09:10 PM	1.6 0.7 1.3 0.6	49 21 40 18
30 M	03:45 AM 10:45 AM 04:04 PM 10:11 PM	1.6 0.7 1.3 0.6	49 21 40 18

October

Day	Time (h m)	Height (ft)	Height (cm)
1 Tu	04:30 AM 11:21 AM 04:56 PM 11:07 PM	1.6 0.6 1.4 0.6	49 18 43 18
2 W	05:11 AM 11:55 AM 05:43 PM	1.6 0.5 1.5	49 15 46
3 Th	12:00 AM 05:50 AM 12:27 PM 06:26 PM	0.6 1.6 0.4 1.6	18 49 12 49
4 F	12:52 AM 06:29 AM 12:58 PM 07:07 PM	0.6 1.6 0.4 1.7	18 49 12 52
5 Sa	01:43 AM 07:08 AM 01:30 PM 07:48 PM	0.6 1.5 0.3 1.8	18 46 9 55
6 Su	02:34 AM 07:49 AM 02:04 PM 08:30 PM	0.6 1.5 0.3 1.9	18 46 9 58
7 M	03:27 AM 08:33 AM 02:41 PM 09:15 PM	0.6 1.4 0.2 2.0	18 43 6 61
8 Tu	04:22 AM 09:20 AM 03:23 PM 10:03 PM	0.6 1.4 0.2 2.0	18 43 6 61
9 W	05:20 AM 10:11 AM 04:11 PM 10:56 PM	0.6 1.3 0.2 2.0	18 40 6 61
10 Th	06:20 AM 11:07 AM 05:07 PM 11:53 PM	0.6 1.3 0.3 1.9	18 40 9 58
11 F	07:21 AM 12:08 PM 06:13 PM	0.6 1.3 0.3	18 40 9
12 Sa	12:55 AM 08:20 AM 01:14 PM 07:28 PM	1.9 0.5 1.3 0.4	58 15 40 12
13 Su	01:58 AM 09:16 AM 02:22 PM 08:45 PM	1.8 0.5 1.4 0.4	55 15 43 12
14 M	03:01 AM 10:07 AM 03:28 PM 09:59 PM	1.7 0.4 1.4 0.4	52 12 43 12
15 Tu	04:00 AM 10:54 AM 04:31 PM 11:06 PM	1.7 0.4 1.6 0.4	52 12 49 12
16 W	04:53 AM 11:38 AM 05:28 PM	1.6 0.3 1.7	49 9 52
17 Th	12:08 AM 05:42 AM 12:17 PM 06:21 PM	0.4 1.6 0.2 1.7	12 49 6 52
18 F	01:05 AM 06:27 AM 12:54 PM 07:10 PM	0.4 1.5 0.2 1.8	12 46 6 55
19 Sa	01:59 AM 07:10 AM 01:28 PM 07:55 PM	0.4 1.4 0.2 1.8	12 43 6 55
20 Su	02:50 AM 07:52 AM 02:01 PM 08:39 PM	0.5 1.3 0.2 1.8	15 40 6 55
21 M	03:39 AM 08:33 AM 02:35 PM 09:21 PM	0.5 1.3 0.2 1.8	15 40 6 55
22 Tu	04:27 AM 09:16 AM 03:11 PM 10:03 PM	0.5 1.2 0.2 1.8	15 37 6 55
23 W	05:14 AM 10:00 AM 03:50 PM 10:46 PM	0.6 1.2 0.3 1.7	18 37 9 52
24 Th	06:01 AM 10:47 AM 04:35 PM 11:30 PM	0.6 1.1 0.3 1.6	18 34 9 49
25 F	06:47 AM 11:38 AM 05:26 PM	0.6 1.1 0.4	18 34 12
26 Sa	12:17 AM 07:34 AM 12:33 PM 06:24 PM	1.6 0.6 1.1 0.4	49 18 34 12
27 Su	01:07 AM 08:20 AM 01:32 PM 07:28 PM	1.5 0.6 1.1 0.5	46 18 34 15
28 M	01:56 AM 09:03 AM 02:31 PM 08:35 PM	1.5 0.5 1.2 0.5	46 15 37 15
29 Tu	02:46 AM 09:44 AM 03:28 PM 09:42 PM	1.4 0.4 1.3 0.5	43 12 40 15
30 W	03:33 AM 10:21 AM 04:21 PM 10:44 PM	1.4 0.3 1.4 0.5	43 9 43 15
31 Th	04:20 AM 10:58 AM 05:08 PM 11:43 PM	1.4 0.3 1.5 0.5	43 9 46 15

November

Day	Time (h m)	Height (ft)	Height (cm)
1 F	05:05 AM 11:33 AM 05:53 PM	1.3 0.2 1.6	40 6 49
2 Sa	12:40 AM 05:50 AM 12:10 PM 06:37 PM	0.4 1.3 0.1 1.7	12 40 3 52
3 Su	01:34 AM 05:36 AM 11:48 AM 06:22 PM	0.4 1.2 0.0 1.8	12 37 0 55
4 M	01:27 AM 06:23 AM 12:28 PM 07:07 PM	0.4 1.2 0.0 1.9	12 37 0 58
5 Tu	02:19 AM 07:12 AM 01:13 PM 07:55 PM	0.3 1.1 0.0 1.9	9 34 0 58
6 W	03:12 AM 08:04 AM 02:03 PM 08:46 PM	0.3 1.1 0.0 1.9	9 34 0 58
7 Th	04:06 AM 08:58 AM 02:58 PM 09:40 PM	0.3 1.1 0.0 1.8	9 34 0 55
8 F	05:01 AM 09:57 AM 04:01 PM 10:37 PM	0.3 1.1 0.1 1.7	9 34 3 52
9 Sa	05:57 AM 11:00 AM 05:12 PM 11:36 PM	0.3 1.1 0.2 1.6	9 34 6 49
10 Su	06:51 AM 12:06 PM 06:28 PM	0.3 1.2 0.2	9 37 6
11 M	12:37 AM 07:44 AM 01:13 PM 07:45 PM	1.5 0.2 1.3 0.3	46 6 40 9
12 Tu	01:36 AM 08:33 AM 02:20 PM 08:58 PM	1.4 0.1 1.3 0.3	43 3 40 9
13 W	02:31 AM 09:19 AM 03:22 PM 10:05 PM	1.3 0.1 1.4 0.3	40 3 43 9
14 Th	03:24 AM 10:01 AM 04:18 PM 11:06 PM	1.2 0.0 1.5 0.3	37 0 46 9
15 F	04:13 AM 10:41 AM 05:09 PM	1.2 0.0 1.6	37 0 49
16 Sa	12:02 AM 04:59 AM 11:18 AM 05:55 PM	0.3 1.1 0.0 1.6	9 34 0 49
17 Su	12:53 AM 05:43 AM 11:53 AM 06:37 PM	0.3 1.0 0.0 1.6	9 30 0 49
18 M	01:41 AM 06:26 AM 12:27 PM 07:17 PM	0.3 1.0 0.0 1.6	9 30 0 49
19 Tu	02:24 AM 07:08 AM 01:03 PM 07:56 PM	0.3 1.0 0.0 1.6	9 30 0 49
20 W	03:05 AM 07:51 AM 01:41 PM 08:34 PM	0.3 0.9 0.0 1.5	9 27 0 46
21 Th	03:44 AM 08:34 AM 02:22 PM 09:13 PM	0.3 0.9 0.1 1.5	9 27 3 46
22 F	04:22 AM 09:20 AM 03:06 PM 09:53 PM	0.3 0.9 0.1 1.4	9 27 3 43
23 Sa	05:01 AM 10:08 AM 03:54 PM 10:34 PM	0.3 0.9 0.2 1.3	9 27 6 40
24 Su	05:40 AM 11:00 AM 04:49 PM 11:17 PM	0.3 0.9 0.2 1.3	9 27 6 40
25 M	06:21 AM 11:55 AM 05:50 PM	0.2 1.0 0.3	6 30 9
26 Tu	12:03 AM 07:01 AM 12:52 PM 06:59 PM	1.2 0.2 1.0 0.3	37 6 30 9
27 W	12:50 AM 07:42 AM 01:48 PM 08:11 PM	1.2 0.1 1.1 0.3	37 3 34 9
28 Th	01:40 AM 08:22 AM 02:41 PM 09:21 PM	1.1 0.0 1.2 0.3	34 0 37 9
29 F	02:31 AM 09:03 AM 03:32 PM 10:26 PM	1.0 -0.1 1.3 0.3	30 -3 40 9
30 Sa	03:23 AM 09:45 AM 04:22 PM 11:26 PM	1.0 -0.1 1.5 0.2	30 -3 46 6

December

Day	Time (h m)	Height (ft)	Height (cm)
1 Su	04:15 AM 10:28 AM 05:10 PM	0.9 -0.2 1.6	27 -6 49
2 M	12:21 AM 05:07 AM 11:15 AM 05:59 PM	0.2 0.9 -0.3 1.6	6 27 -9 49
3 Tu	01:13 AM 06:00 AM 12:04 PM 06:49 PM	0.1 0.9 -0.3 1.7	3 27 -9 52
4 W	02:04 AM 06:53 AM 12:57 PM 07:40 PM	0.1 0.9 -0.3 1.7	3 27 -9 52
5 Th	02:54 AM 07:48 AM 01:53 PM 08:32 PM	0.0 0.9 -0.3 1.6	0 27 -9 49
6 F	03:44 AM 08:44 AM 02:53 PM 09:25 PM	0.0 0.9 -0.2 1.5	0 27 -6 46
7 Sa	04:35 AM 09:44 AM 03:58 PM 10:19 PM	0.0 1.0 -0.1 1.4	0 30 -3 43
8 Su	05:26 AM 10:46 AM 05:08 PM 11:14 PM	0.0 1.0 -0.1 1.3	0 30 -3 40
9 M	06:16 AM 11:52 AM 06:22 PM	-0.1 1.1 0.0	-3 34 0
10 Tu	12:09 AM 07:06 AM 12:59 PM 07:38 PM	1.2 -0.1 1.1 0.1	37 -3 34 3
11 W	01:04 AM 07:55 AM 02:05 PM 08:51 PM	1.1 -0.2 1.2 0.1	34 -6 37 3
12 Th	01:59 AM 08:41 AM 03:08 PM 09:58 PM	0.9 -0.2 1.2 0.1	27 -6 37 3
13 F	02:52 AM 09:25 AM 04:04 PM 10:59 PM	0.9 -0.2 1.3 0.1	27 -6 40 3
14 Sa	03:43 AM 10:07 AM 04:55 PM 11:53 PM	0.8 -0.3 1.3 0.1	24 -9 40 3
15 Su	04:32 AM 10:47 AM 05:40 PM	0.8 -0.3 1.4	24 -9 43
16 M	12:40 AM 05:19 AM 11:26 AM 06:21 PM	0.1 0.7 -0.3 1.3	3 21 -9 40
17 Tu	01:23 AM 06:03 AM 12:04 PM 06:59 PM	0.1 0.7 -0.3 1.3	3 21 -9 40
18 W	02:02 AM 06:46 AM 12:43 PM 07:35 PM	0.1 0.7 -0.2 1.3	3 21 -6 40
19 Th	02:37 AM 07:28 AM 01:22 PM 08:10 PM	0.1 0.7 -0.2 1.2	3 21 -6 37
20 F	03:10 AM 08:10 AM 02:02 PM 08:44 PM	0.1 0.7 -0.2 1.2	3 21 -6 37
21 Sa	03:43 AM 08:53 AM 02:44 PM 09:20 PM	0.0 0.7 -0.1 1.2	0 21 -3 37
22 Su	04:16 AM 09:38 AM 03:30 PM 09:57 PM	0.0 0.8 -0.1 1.1	0 24 -3 34
23 M	04:50 AM 10:26 AM 04:20 PM 10:36 PM	0.0 0.8 0.0 1.1	0 24 0 34
24 Tu	05:26 AM 11:16 AM 05:19 PM 11:18 PM	-0.1 0.8 0.1 1.0	-3 24 3 30
25 W	06:04 AM 12:09 PM 06:28 PM	-0.2 0.9 0.1	-6 27 3
26 Th	12:05 AM 06:45 AM 01:05 PM 07:44 PM	0.9 -0.2 1.0 0.2	27 -6 30 6
27 F	12:56 AM 07:28 AM 02:01 PM 08:59 PM	0.8 -0.3 1.1 0.1	24 -9 34 3
28 Sa	01:51 AM 08:16 AM 02:57 PM 10:07 PM	0.7 -0.3 1.2 0.1	21 -9 37 3
29 Su	02:48 AM 09:06 AM 03:53 PM 11:07 PM	0.7 -0.4 1.3 0.0	21 -12 40 0
30 M	03:46 AM 10:00 AM 04:47 PM	0.7 -0.5 1.4	21 -15 43
31 Tu	12:02 AM 04:44 AM 10:55 AM 05:41 PM	0.0 0.7 -0.5 1.4	0 21 -15 43

Heights are referred to mean lower water which is the chart datum of sounding. All times are local. Daylight Saving Time has been used when needed.

Hampton Roads (Sewells Point), Virginia, 2012

Times and Heights of High and Low Waters

September

Day	Time (h m)	Height (ft)	Height (cm)	Day	Time (h m)	Height (ft)	Height (cm)
1 Sa	04:05 AM 10:16 AM 04:31 PM 10:39 PM	0.0 3.0 0.1 2.9	0 91 3 88	16 Su	03:34 AM 09:46 AM 04:03 PM 10:06 PM	0.0 3.2 0.0 3.0	0 98 0 91
2 Su	04:44 AM 10:57 AM 05:14 PM 11:18 PM	0.1 3.0 0.2 2.8	3 91 6 85	17 M	04:17 AM 10:32 AM 04:51 PM 10:52 PM	-0.1 3.4 0.0 3.0	-3 104 0 91
3 M	05:22 AM 11:36 AM 05:56 PM 11:56 PM	0.1 3.0 0.3 2.7	3 91 9 82	18 Tu	05:01 AM 11:19 AM 05:41 PM 11:39 PM	-0.1 3.4 0.0 2.9	-3 104 0 88
4 Tu	06:00 AM 12:16 PM 06:38 PM	0.2 2.9 0.4	6 88 12	19 W	05:47 AM 12:09 PM 06:34 PM	0.0 3.4 0.1	0 104 3
5 W	12:34 AM 06:38 AM 12:56 PM 07:22 PM	2.5 0.3 2.8 0.6	76 9 85 18	20 Th	12:29 AM 06:38 AM 01:04 PM 07:30 PM	2.8 0.0 3.3 0.2	85 0 101 6
6 Th	01:14 AM 07:19 AM 01:39 PM 08:09 PM	2.4 0.5 2.7 0.7	73 15 82 21	21 F	01:24 AM 07:33 AM 02:03 PM 08:31 PM	2.7 0.2 3.2 0.4	82 6 98 12
7 F	01:58 AM 08:04 AM 02:28 PM 09:01 PM	2.3 0.6 2.6 0.8	70 18 79 24	22 Sa	02:25 AM 08:35 AM 03:08 PM 09:35 PM	2.6 0.3 3.1 0.4	79 9 94 12
8 Sa	02:48 AM 08:55 AM 03:22 PM 09:58 PM	2.2 0.6 2.5 0.8	67 18 76 24	23 Su	03:32 AM 09:43 AM 04:16 PM 10:41 PM	2.5 0.4 3.0 0.4	76 12 91 12
9 Su	03:45 AM 09:51 AM 04:21 PM 10:56 PM	2.2 0.7 2.5 0.8	67 21 76 24	24 M	04:42 AM 10:53 AM 05:23 PM 11:42 PM	2.5 0.4 2.9 0.4	76 12 88 12
10 M	04:47 AM 10:52 AM 05:20 PM 11:52 PM	2.2 0.7 2.6 0.7	67 21 79 21	25 Tu	05:49 AM 12:00 PM 06:24 PM	2.6 0.4 2.9	79 12 88
11 Tu	05:46 AM 11:51 AM 06:16 PM	2.3 0.6 2.7	70 18 82	26 W	12:38 AM 06:49 AM 01:00 PM 07:19 PM	0.3 2.8 0.3 3.0	9 85 9 91
12 W	12:42 AM 06:41 AM 12:47 PM 07:06 PM	0.6 2.5 0.5 2.8	18 76 15 85	27 Th	01:28 AM 07:41 AM 01:54 PM 08:08 PM	0.2 2.9 0.2 3.0	6 88 6 91
13 Th	01:28 AM 07:30 AM 01:39 PM 07:53 PM	0.4 2.7 0.4 2.9	12 82 12 88	28 F	02:13 AM 08:28 AM 02:42 PM 08:52 PM	0.2 3.0 0.2 2.9	6 91 6 88
14 F	02:11 AM 08:17 AM 02:28 PM 08:38 PM	0.3 2.9 0.2 3.0	9 88 6 91	29 Sa	02:54 AM 09:10 AM 03:27 PM 09:32 PM	0.1 3.1 0.2 2.9	3 94 6 88
15 Sa	02:53 AM 09:02 AM 03:15 PM 09:22 PM	0.1 3.1 0.1 3.0	3 94 3 91	30 Su	03:33 AM 09:49 AM 04:08 PM 10:10 PM	0.1 3.1 0.2 2.8	3 94 6 85

October

Day	Time (h m)	Height (ft)	Height (cm)	Day	Time (h m)	Height (ft)	Height (cm)
1 M	04:11 AM 10:27 AM 04:48 PM 10:47 PM	0.2 3.1 0.3 2.7	6 94 9 82	16 Tu	03:49 AM 10:10 AM 04:34 PM 10:31 PM	-0.2 3.5 -0.1 2.9	-6 107 -3 88
2 Tu	04:47 AM 11:04 AM 05:27 PM 11:23 PM	0.2 3.0 0.4 2.6	6 91 12 79	17 W	04:37 AM 11:00 AM 05:25 PM 11:21 PM	-0.2 3.5 -0.1 2.9	-6 107 -3 88
3 W	05:24 AM 11:41 AM 06:07 PM	0.3 3.0 0.5	9 91 15	18 Th	05:28 AM 11:53 AM 06:19 PM	-0.1 3.5 0.0	-3 107 0
4 Th	12:00 AM 06:02 AM 12:20 PM 06:48 PM	2.5 0.4 2.9 0.6	76 12 88 18	19 F	12:15 AM 06:22 AM 12:49 PM 07:15 PM	2.8 0.0 3.3 0.1	85 0 101 3
5 F	12:39 AM 06:41 AM 01:00 PM 07:32 PM	2.4 0.5 2.7 0.7	73 15 82 21	20 Sa	01:12 AM 07:20 AM 01:48 PM 08:15 PM	2.7 0.1 3.1 0.2	82 3 94 6
6 Sa	01:21 AM 07:25 AM 01:46 PM 08:21 PM	2.3 0.6 2.6 0.8	70 18 79 24	21 Su	02:14 AM 08:24 AM 02:52 PM 09:17 PM	2.6 0.2 3.0 0.3	79 6 91 9
7 Su	02:10 AM 08:15 AM 02:36 PM 09:14 PM	2.2 0.7 2.6 0.8	67 21 79 24	22 M	03:21 AM 09:32 AM 03:58 PM 10:18 PM	2.5 0.3 2.8 0.3	76 9 85 9
8 M	03:05 AM 09:11 AM 03:33 PM 10:09 PM	2.2 0.7 2.5 0.8	67 21 76 24	23 Tu	04:29 AM 10:41 AM 05:03 PM 11:17 PM	2.6 0.4 2.8 0.3	79 12 85 9
9 Tu	04:06 AM 10:13 AM 04:33 PM 11:04 PM	2.3 0.7 2.5 0.7	70 21 76 21	24 W	05:33 AM 11:47 AM 06:02 PM	2.7 0.4 2.7	82 12 82
10 W	05:06 AM 11:15 AM 05:31 PM 11:56 PM	2.4 0.6 2.6 0.5	73 18 79 15	25 Th	12:11 AM 06:30 AM 12:45 PM 06:55 PM	0.3 2.8 0.3 2.7	9 85 9 82
11 Th	06:02 AM 12:15 PM 06:25 PM	2.6 0.5 2.7	79 15 82	26 F	12:59 AM 07:20 AM 01:37 PM 07:43 PM	0.2 2.9 0.3 2.7	6 88 9 82
12 F	12:44 AM 06:55 AM 01:10 PM 07:17 PM	0.4 2.8 0.3 2.8	12 85 9 85	27 Sa	01:43 AM 08:05 AM 02:24 PM 08:26 PM	0.2 2.9 0.2 2.6	6 88 6 79
13 Sa	01:31 AM 07:44 AM 02:02 PM 08:06 PM	0.2 3.1 0.1 2.9	6 94 3 88	28 Su	02:24 AM 08:46 AM 03:06 PM 09:06 PM	0.1 3.0 0.2 2.6	3 91 6 79
14 Su	02:16 AM 08:33 AM 02:53 PM 08:54 PM	0.0 3.3 0.0 2.9	0 101 0 88	29 M	03:03 AM 09:24 AM 03:46 PM 09:43 PM	0.1 3.0 0.2 2.6	3 91 6 79
15 M	03:02 AM 09:21 AM 03:43 PM 09:42 PM	-0.1 3.4 -0.1 3.0	-3 104 -3 91	30 Tu	03:41 AM 10:01 AM 04:25 PM 10:20 PM	0.1 3.0 0.2 2.5	3 91 6 76
				31 W	04:17 AM 10:37 AM 05:03 PM 10:56 PM	0.2 2.9 0.3 2.4	6 88 9 73

November

Day	Time (h m)	Height (ft)	Height (cm)	Day	Time (h m)	Height (ft)	Height (cm)
1 Th	04:54 AM 11:14 AM 05:41 PM 11:33 PM	0.2 2.9 0.4 2.4	6 88 12 73	16 F	04:12 AM 10:38 AM 05:03 PM 11:00 PM	-0.3 3.3 -0.2 2.7	-9 101 -6 82
2 F	05:32 AM 11:50 AM 06:20 PM	0.3 2.8 0.4	9 85 12	17 Sa	05:07 AM 11:33 AM 05:57 PM 11:58 PM	-0.2 3.2 -0.1 2.6	-6 98 -3 79
3 Sa	12:11 AM 06:11 AM 12:29 PM 07:01 PM	2.3 0.4 2.7 0.5	70 12 82 15	18 Su	06:06 AM 12:31 PM 06:53 PM	-0.1 3.0 0.0	-3 91 0
4 Su	12:52 AM 05:54 AM 12:11 PM 06:45 PM	2.2 0.5 2.6 0.5	67 15 79 15	19 M	12:58 AM 07:08 AM 01:30 PM 07:50 PM	2.5 0.1 2.8 0.0	76 3 85 0
5 M	12:38 AM 06:41 AM 12:57 PM 07:32 PM	2.2 0.5 2.5 0.5	67 15 76 15	20 Tu	02:01 AM 08:14 AM 02:31 PM 08:47 PM	2.5 0.2 2.6 0.1	76 6 79 3
6 Tu	01:30 AM 07:36 AM 01:49 PM 08:23 PM	2.2 0.6 2.4 0.5	67 18 73 15	21 W	03:05 AM 09:20 AM 03:33 PM 09:43 PM	2.5 0.3 2.4 0.1	76 9 73 3
7 W	02:26 AM 08:36 AM 02:46 PM 09:16 PM	2.3 0.6 2.4 0.4	70 18 73 12	22 Th	04:06 AM 10:24 AM 04:31 PM 10:36 PM	2.5 0.3 2.3 0.1	76 9 70 3
8 Th	03:26 AM 09:40 AM 03:46 PM 10:09 PM	2.4 0.5 2.4 0.3	73 15 73 9	23 F	05:03 AM 11:22 AM 05:25 PM 11:25 PM	2.6 0.3 2.3 0.1	79 9 70 3
9 F	04:24 AM 10:43 AM 04:45 PM 11:01 PM	2.6 0.4 2.5 0.1	79 12 76 3	24 Sa	05:53 AM 12:15 PM 06:13 PM	2.6 0.2 2.3	79 6 70
10 Sa	05:20 AM 11:42 AM 05:41 PM 11:53 PM	2.8 0.2 2.5 0.0	85 6 76 0	25 Su	12:11 AM 06:39 AM 01:01 PM 06:58 PM	0.1 2.7 0.2 2.3	3 82 6 70
11 Su	06:15 AM 12:38 PM 06:36 PM	3.0 0.0 2.6	91 0 79	26 M	12:54 AM 07:21 AM 01:44 PM 07:39 PM	0.0 2.7 0.1 2.3	0 82 3 70
12 M	12:44 AM 07:08 AM 01:32 PM 07:29 PM	-0.2 3.3 -0.1 2.7	-6 101 -3 82	27 Tu	01:35 AM 08:01 AM 02:25 PM 08:18 PM	0.0 2.8 0.1 2.3	0 85 3 70
13 Tu	01:35 AM 08:00 AM 02:25 PM 08:21 PM	-0.3 3.4 -0.2 2.7	-9 104 -6 82	28 W	02:14 AM 08:39 AM 03:03 PM 08:56 PM	0.0 2.8 0.1 2.3	0 85 3 70
14 W	02:26 AM 08:52 AM 03:17 PM 09:13 PM	-0.4 3.5 -0.3 2.7	-12 107 -9 82	29 Th	02:53 AM 09:15 AM 03:41 PM 09:33 PM	0.0 2.7 0.1 2.2	0 82 3 67
15 Th	03:18 AM 09:45 AM 04:10 PM 10:06 PM	-0.4 3.4 -0.3 2.7	-12 104 -9 82	30 F	03:31 AM 09:51 AM 04:19 PM 10:10 PM	0.0 2.7 0.1 2.2	0 82 3 67

December

Day	Time (h m)	Height (ft)	Height (cm)	Day	Time (h m)	Height (ft)	Height (cm)
1 Sa	04:09 AM 10:27 AM 04:56 PM 10:48 PM	0.1 2.6 0.1 2.2	3 79 3 67	16 Su	04:53 AM 11:15 AM 05:35 PM 11:39 PM	-0.4 3.0 -0.4 2.5	-12 91 -12 76
2 Su	04:48 AM 11:04 AM 05:34 PM 11:28 PM	0.2 2.6 0.2 2.2	6 79 6 67	17 M	05:49 AM 12:08 PM 06:26 PM	-0.3 2.8 -0.3	-9 85 -9
3 M	05:29 AM 11:42 AM 06:13 PM	0.2 2.5 0.2	6 76 6	18 Tu	12:34 AM 06:47 AM 01:01 PM 07:17 PM	2.5 -0.1 2.5 -0.2	76 -3 76 -6
4 Tu	12:10 AM 06:14 AM 12:25 PM 06:55 PM	2.2 0.3 2.4 0.2	67 9 73 6	19 W	01:31 AM 07:47 AM 01:56 PM 08:09 PM	2.4 0.0 2.3 -0.1	73 0 70 -3
5 W	12:58 AM 07:06 AM 01:12 PM 07:41 PM	2.2 0.3 2.3 0.2	67 9 70 6	20 Th	02:30 AM 08:48 AM 02:53 PM 09:01 PM	2.3 0.2 2.1 0.0	70 6 64 0
6 Th	01:51 AM 08:04 AM 02:06 PM 08:32 PM	2.3 0.3 2.2 0.1	70 9 67 3	21 F	03:29 AM 09:51 AM 03:50 PM 09:54 PM	2.3 0.2 2.0 0.0	70 6 61 0
7 F	02:48 AM 09:07 AM 03:05 PM 09:26 PM	2.4 0.3 2.2 0.0	73 9 67 0	22 Sa	04:27 AM 10:50 AM 04:46 PM 10:46 PM	2.3 0.2 1.9 0.1	70 6 58 3
8 Sa	03:49 AM 10:13 AM 04:08 PM 10:23 PM	2.5 0.2 2.2 -0.1	76 6 67 -3	23 Su	05:21 AM 11:45 AM 05:38 PM 11:36 PM	2.4 0.2 1.9 0.0	73 6 58 0
9 Su	04:50 AM 11:16 AM 05:10 PM 11:21 PM	2.7 0.0 2.2 -0.2	82 0 67 -6	24 M	06:11 AM 12:35 PM 06:27 PM	2.4 0.2 1.9	73 6 58
10 M	05:50 AM 12:17 PM 06:10 PM	2.9 -0.1 2.3	88 -3 70	25 Tu	12:23 AM 06:56 AM 01:20 PM 07:11 PM	0.0 2.5 0.1 2.0	0 76 3 61
11 Tu	12:18 AM 06:47 AM 01:14 PM 07:07 PM	-0.4 3.1 -0.3 2.4	-12 94 -9 73	26 W	01:08 AM 07:38 AM 02:02 PM 07:53 PM	-0.1 2.5 0.0 2.0	-3 76 0 61
12 W	01:14 AM 07:43 AM 02:09 PM 08:03 PM	-0.5 3.2 -0.4 2.5	-15 98 -12 76	27 Th	01:50 AM 08:18 AM 02:41 PM 08:33 PM	-0.1 2.6 0.0 2.1	-3 79 0 64
13 Th	02:09 AM 08:38 AM 03:02 PM 08:57 PM	-0.6 3.3 -0.5 2.6	-18 101 -15 79	28 F	02:31 AM 08:55 AM 03:19 PM 09:12 PM	-0.1 2.6 -0.1 2.1	-3 79 -3 64
14 F	03:04 AM 09:31 AM 03:53 PM 09:51 PM	-0.6 3.2 -0.5 2.6	-18 98 -15 79	29 Sa	03:10 AM 09:31 AM 03:55 PM 09:49 PM	-0.1 2.6 -0.1 2.1	-3 79 -3 64
15 Sa	03:58 AM 10:23 AM 04:44 PM 10:45 PM	-0.5 3.1 -0.5 2.6	-15 94 -15 79	30 Su	03:49 AM 10:06 AM 04:31 PM 10:26 PM	-0.1 2.5 -0.1 2.2	-3 76 -3 67
				31 M	04:28 AM 10:41 AM 05:06 PM 11:04 PM	-0.1 2.5 -0.1 2.2	-3 76 -3 67

Heights are referred to mean lower water which is the chart datum of sounding. All times are local. Daylight Saving Time has been used when needed.

Hampton Roads (Sewells Point), Virginia, 2013

Times and Heights of High and Low Waters

January

Day	Time (h m)	Height (ft)	Height (cm)
1 Tu	05:09 AM 11:18 AM 05:43 PM 11:45 PM	-0.1 2.4 -0.1 2.2	-3 73 -3 67
2 W	05:53 AM 11:59 AM 06:23 PM	0.0 2.3 -0.1	0 70 -3
3 Th	12:30 AM 06:42 AM 12:44 PM 07:07 PM	2.3 0.0 2.2 -0.1	70 0 67 -3
4 F	01:21 AM 07:38 AM 01:36 PM 07:58 PM	2.3 0.1 2.2 -0.1	70 3 67 -3
5 Sa	02:18 AM 08:41 AM 02:35 PM 08:54 PM	2.4 0.1 2.1 -0.2	73 3 64 -6
6 Su	03:21 AM 09:48 AM 03:40 PM 09:56 PM	2.5 0.0 2.0 -0.2	76 0 61 -6
7 M	04:27 AM 10:55 AM 04:47 PM 10:59 PM	2.6 0.0 2.1 -0.3	79 0 64 -9
8 Tu	05:32 AM 11:59 AM 05:52 PM	2.7 -0.2 2.2	82 -6 67
9 W	12:01 AM 06:34 AM 12:58 PM 06:53 PM	-0.4 2.9 -0.3 2.3	-12 88 -9 70
10 Th	01:01 AM 07:31 AM 01:54 PM 07:51 PM	-0.6 3.0 -0.5 2.4	-18 91 -15 73
11 F	01:58 AM 08:25 AM 02:45 PM 08:45 PM	-0.6 3.1 -0.6 2.5	-18 94 -18 76
12 Sa	02:53 AM 09:17 AM 03:35 PM 09:37 PM	-0.7 3.1 -0.6 2.6	-21 94 -18 79
13 Su	03:46 AM 10:06 AM 04:22 PM 10:27 PM	-0.6 3.0 -0.6 2.6	-18 91 -18 79
14 M	04:38 AM 10:55 AM 05:09 PM 11:17 PM	-0.5 2.8 -0.5 2.6	-15 85 -15 79
15 Tu	05:29 AM 11:42 AM 05:55 PM	-0.4 2.6 -0.4	-12 79 -12
16 W	12:06 AM 06:21 AM 12:29 PM 06:41 PM	2.5 -0.2 2.4 -0.3	76 -6 73 -9
17 Th	12:56 AM 07:14 AM 01:18 PM 07:28 PM	2.4 0.0 2.2 -0.2	73 0 67 -6
18 F	01:49 AM 08:09 AM 02:09 PM 08:17 PM	2.3 0.1 2.0 0.0	70 3 61 0
19 Sa	02:44 AM 09:08 AM 03:03 PM 09:10 PM	2.2 0.3 1.9 0.0	67 9 58 0
20 Su	03:42 AM 10:08 AM 04:00 PM 10:04 PM	2.2 0.3 1.8 0.1	67 9 55 3
21 M	04:41 AM 11:07 AM 04:57 PM 10:59 PM	2.2 0.3 1.8 0.1	67 9 55 3
22 Tu	05:36 AM 12:00 PM 05:51 PM 11:52 PM	2.2 0.3 1.8 0.0	67 9 55 0
23 W	06:27 AM 12:49 PM 06:41 PM	2.3 0.2 1.9	70 6 58
24 Th	12:41 AM 07:12 AM 01:33 PM 07:26 PM	0.0 2.4 0.1 2.0	0 73 3 61
25 F	01:26 AM 07:52 AM 02:13 PM 08:08 PM	-0.1 2.5 0.0 2.1	-3 76 0 64
26 Sa	02:09 AM 08:31 AM 02:51 PM 08:47 PM	-0.2 2.5 -0.1 2.2	-6 76 -3 67
27 Su	02:50 AM 09:07 AM 03:27 PM 09:25 PM	-0.2 2.6 -0.2 2.3	-6 79 -6 70
28 M	03:29 AM 09:43 AM 04:02 PM 10:03 PM	-0.2 2.6 -0.2 2.3	-6 79 -6 70
29 Tu	04:10 AM 10:19 AM 04:38 PM 10:41 PM	-0.2 2.5 -0.3 2.4	-6 76 -9 73
30 W	04:51 AM 10:57 AM 05:15 PM 11:22 PM	-0.2 2.5 -0.3 2.5	-6 76 -9 76
31 Th	05:35 AM 11:38 AM 05:55 PM	-0.2 2.4 -0.3	-6 73 -9

February

Day	Time (h m)	Height (ft)	Height (cm)
1 F	12:07 AM 06:24 AM 12:23 PM 06:40 PM	2.5 -0.1 2.3 -0.2	76 -3 70 -6
2 Sa	12:58 AM 07:19 AM 01:14 PM 07:31 PM	2.5 0.0 2.2 -0.2	76 0 67 -6
3 Su	01:55 AM 08:21 AM 02:13 PM 08:30 PM	2.5 0.0 2.1 -0.2	76 0 64 -6
4 M	03:00 AM 09:28 AM 03:20 PM 09:35 PM	2.5 0.1 2.0 -0.2	76 3 61 -6
5 Tu	04:09 AM 10:37 AM 04:30 PM 10:43 PM	2.6 0.0 2.1 -0.2	79 0 64 -6
6 W	05:18 AM 11:42 AM 05:38 PM 11:49 PM	2.7 -0.1 2.2 -0.3	82 -3 67 -9
7 Th	06:21 AM 12:42 PM 06:40 PM	2.8 -0.2 2.3	85 -6 70
8 F	12:51 AM 07:19 AM 01:36 PM 07:37 PM	-0.4 2.9 -0.4 2.5	-12 88 -12 76
9 Sa	01:48 AM 08:11 AM 02:25 PM 08:30 PM	-0.5 2.9 -0.5 2.6	-15 88 -15 79
10 Su	02:41 AM 09:00 AM 03:12 PM 09:18 PM	-0.6 2.9 -0.5 2.7	-18 88 -15 82
11 M	03:31 AM 09:46 AM 03:56 PM 10:05 PM	-0.5 2.9 -0.5 2.7	-15 88 -15 82
12 Tu	04:19 AM 10:31 AM 04:39 PM 10:50 PM	-0.5 2.7 -0.4 2.7	-15 82 -12 82
13 W	05:05 AM 11:13 AM 05:21 PM 11:34 PM	-0.3 2.6 -0.3 2.6	-9 79 -9 79
14 Th	05:51 AM 11:56 AM 06:03 PM	-0.2 2.4 -0.2	-6 73 -6
15 F	12:18 AM 06:38 AM 12:38 PM 06:46 PM	2.5 0.0 2.2 -0.1	76 0 67 -3
16 Sa	01:04 AM 07:28 AM 01:24 PM 07:32 PM	2.4 0.2 2.0 0.1	73 6 61 3
17 Su	01:55 AM 08:21 AM 02:14 PM 08:22 PM	2.2 0.4 1.9 0.2	67 12 58 6
18 M	02:51 AM 09:20 AM 03:10 PM 09:19 PM	2.2 0.4 1.8 0.3	67 12 55 9
19 Tu	03:52 AM 10:21 AM 04:11 PM 10:18 PM	2.1 0.5 1.8 0.3	64 15 55 9
20 W	04:53 AM 11:18 AM 05:11 PM 11:16 PM	2.2 0.4 1.9 0.2	67 12 58 6
21 Th	05:49 AM 12:10 PM 06:05 PM	2.2 0.3 2.0	67 9 61
22 F	12:10 AM 06:38 AM 12:56 PM 06:54 PM	0.1 2.3 0.2 2.1	3 70 6 64
23 Sa	12:59 AM 07:21 AM 01:38 PM 07:37 PM	0.0 2.5 0.1 2.3	0 76 3 70
24 Su	01:44 AM 08:01 AM 02:17 PM 08:18 PM	-0.1 2.5 -0.1 2.4	-3 76 -3 73
25 M	02:27 AM 08:40 AM 02:54 PM 08:58 PM	-0.2 2.6 -0.2 2.6	-6 79 -6 79
26 Tu	03:09 AM 09:18 AM 03:31 PM 09:37 PM	-0.2 2.6 -0.2 2.7	-6 79 -6 82
27 W	03:51 AM 09:57 AM 04:09 PM 10:18 PM	-0.3 2.6 -0.3 2.8	-9 79 -9 85
28 Th	04:34 AM 10:37 AM 04:49 PM 11:01 PM	-0.3 2.6 -0.3 2.8	-9 79 -9 85

March

Day	Time (h m)	Height (ft)	Height (cm)
1 F	05:20 AM 11:20 AM 05:32 PM 11:48 PM	-0.2 2.5 -0.2 2.8	-6 76 -6 85
2 Sa	06:10 AM 12:07 PM 06:19 PM	-0.1 2.4 -0.2	-3 73 -6
3 Su	12:40 AM 07:05 AM 01:00 PM 07:13 PM	2.8 0.0 2.3 -0.1	85 0 70 -3
4 M	01:39 AM 08:06 AM 02:00 PM 08:15 PM	2.7 0.1 2.2 0.0	82 3 67 0
5 Tu	02:45 AM 09:13 AM 03:08 PM 09:23 PM	2.6 0.1 2.2 0.0	79 3 67 0
6 W	03:56 AM 10:20 AM 04:19 PM 10:33 PM	2.6 0.1 2.2 0.0	79 3 67 0
7 Th	05:05 AM 11:24 AM 05:27 PM 11:40 PM	2.7 0.0 2.4 -0.1	82 0 73 -3
8 F	06:08 AM 12:22 PM 06:28 PM	2.7 -0.1 2.5	82 -3 76
9 Sa	12:41 AM 07:04 AM 01:14 PM 07:22 PM	-0.2 2.8 -0.2 2.7	-6 85 -6 82
10 Su	01:36 AM 08:54 AM 03:02 PM 09:12 PM	-0.3 2.8 -0.3 2.8	-9 85 -9 85
11 M	03:27 AM 09:40 AM 03:46 PM 09:57 PM	-0.3 2.8 -0.3 2.9	-9 85 -9 88
12 Tu	04:14 AM 10:24 AM 04:27 PM 10:40 PM	-0.3 2.8 -0.3 2.9	-9 85 -9 88
13 W	04:58 AM 11:05 AM 05:08 PM 11:21 PM	-0.3 2.7 -0.2 2.9	-9 82 -6 88
14 Th	05:40 AM 11:44 AM 05:47 PM	-0.2 2.6 -0.1	-6 79 -3
15 F	12:01 AM 06:22 AM 12:23 PM 06:26 PM	2.8 0.0 2.4 0.0	85 0 73 0
16 Sa	12:41 AM 07:05 AM 01:02 PM 07:07 PM	2.6 0.2 2.3 0.1	79 6 70 3
17 Su	01:23 AM 07:49 AM 01:44 PM 07:50 PM	2.5 0.3 2.1 0.2	76 9 64 6
18 M	02:09 AM 08:38 AM 02:31 PM 08:39 PM	2.4 0.5 2.0 0.4	73 15 61 12
19 Tu	03:01 AM 09:32 AM 03:24 PM 09:34 PM	2.3 0.6 2.0 0.4	70 18 61 12
20 W	04:00 AM 10:30 AM 04:24 PM 10:35 PM	2.2 0.6 2.0 0.5	67 18 61 15
21 Th	05:01 AM 11:28 AM 05:26 PM 11:36 PM	2.2 0.5 2.0 0.4	67 15 61 12
22 F	06:01 AM 12:22 PM 06:23 PM	2.3 0.4 2.2	70 12 67
23 Sa	12:34 AM 06:54 AM 01:11 PM 07:15 PM	0.3 2.4 0.3 2.3	9 73 9 70
24 Su	01:27 AM 07:42 AM 01:55 PM 08:01 PM	0.2 2.5 0.2 2.5	6 76 6 76
25 M	02:15 AM 08:26 AM 02:37 PM 08:46 PM	0.0 2.6 0.0 2.7	0 79 0 82
26 Tu	03:01 AM 09:09 AM 03:18 PM 09:29 PM	-0.1 2.7 -0.1 2.9	-3 82 -3 88
27 W	03:47 AM 09:52 AM 03:59 PM 10:12 PM	-0.2 2.7 -0.2 3.0	-6 82 -6 91
28 Th	04:32 AM 10:34 AM 04:41 PM 10:56 PM	-0.2 2.7 -0.2 3.1	-6 82 -6 94
29 F	05:18 AM 11:19 AM 05:26 PM 11:43 PM	-0.3 2.7 -0.2 3.1	-9 82 -6 94
30 Sa	06:07 AM 12:05 PM 06:13 PM	-0.2 2.6 -0.2	-6 79 -6
31 Su	12:33 AM 06:58 AM 12:56 PM 07:04 PM	3.1 -0.1 2.5 -0.1	94 -3 76 -3

April

Day	Time (h m)	Height (ft)	Height (cm)
1 M	01:28 AM 07:54 AM 01:51 PM 08:02 PM	3.0 0.0 2.5 0.0	91 0 76 0
2 Tu	02:28 AM 08:54 AM 02:53 PM 09:06 PM	2.8 0.1 2.4 0.1	85 3 73 3
3 W	03:33 AM 09:58 AM 04:00 PM 10:15 PM	2.7 0.2 2.4 0.1	82 6 73 3
4 Th	04:42 AM 11:02 AM 05:09 PM 11:25 PM	2.7 0.2 2.4 0.1	82 6 73 3
5 F	05:49 AM 12:02 PM 06:14 PM	2.7 0.1 2.6	82 3 79
6 Sa	12:31 AM 06:49 AM 12:58 PM 07:12 PM	0.1 2.7 0.0 2.7	3 82 0 82
7 Su	01:30 AM 07:44 AM 01:48 PM 08:04 PM	0.0 2.7 0.0 2.8	0 82 0 85
8 M	02:22 AM 08:33 AM 02:34 PM 08:51 PM	-0.1 2.7 -0.1 2.9	-3 82 -3 88
9 Tu	03:10 AM 09:18 AM 03:17 PM 09:34 PM	-0.1 2.7 -0.1 3.0	-3 82 -3 91
10 W	03:54 AM 09:59 AM 03:58 PM 10:14 PM	-0.1 2.7 -0.1 3.0	-3 82 -3 91
11 Th	04:36 AM 10:38 AM 04:37 PM 10:53 PM	-0.1 2.6 0.0 2.9	-3 79 0 88
12 F	05:16 AM 11:16 AM 05:15 PM 11:31 PM	0.0 2.5 0.0 2.8	0 76 0 85
13 Sa	05:56 AM 11:54 AM 05:54 PM	0.1 2.4 0.1	3 73 3
14 Su	12:09 AM 06:36 AM 12:32 PM 06:33 PM	2.7 0.2 2.3 0.2	82 6 70 6
15 M	12:49 AM 07:17 AM 01:12 PM 07:16 PM	2.6 0.4 2.2 0.3	79 12 67 9
16 Tu	01:31 AM 08:01 AM 01:56 PM 08:02 PM	2.5 0.5 2.2 0.4	76 15 67 12
17 W	02:18 AM 08:49 AM 02:46 PM 08:55 PM	2.4 0.5 2.1 0.5	73 15 64 15
18 Th	03:10 AM 09:42 AM 03:42 PM 09:53 PM	2.3 0.6 2.1 0.5	70 18 64 15
19 F	04:07 AM 10:36 AM 04:40 PM 10:55 PM	2.3 0.5 2.2 0.5	70 15 67 15
20 Sa	05:06 AM 11:29 AM 05:38 PM 11:55 PM	2.3 0.4 2.3 0.4	70 12 70 12
21 Su	06:04 AM 12:20 PM 06:32 PM	2.3 0.3 2.5	70 9 76
22 M	12:51 AM 06:57 AM 01:09 PM 07:23 PM	0.3 2.4 0.2 2.7	9 73 6 82
23 Tu	01:44 AM 07:48 AM 01:56 PM 08:12 PM	0.1 2.5 0.0 2.9	3 76 0 88
24 W	02:35 AM 08:36 AM 02:42 PM 09:00 PM	-0.1 2.6 -0.1 3.1	-3 79 -3 94
25 Th	03:24 AM 09:24 AM 03:29 PM 09:48 PM	-0.2 2.7 -0.2 3.2	-6 82 -6 98
26 F	04:13 AM 10:12 AM 04:17 PM 10:37 PM	-0.3 2.7 -0.3 3.3	-9 82 -9 101
27 Sa	05:03 AM 11:01 AM 05:06 PM 11:28 PM	-0.3 2.7 -0.3 3.3	-9 82 -9 101
28 Su	05:54 AM 11:52 AM 05:58 PM	-0.2 2.7 -0.2	-6 82 -6
29 M	12:21 AM 06:46 AM 12:46 PM 06:53 PM	3.2 -0.2 2.6 -0.1	98 -6 79 -3
30 Tu	01:16 AM 07:41 AM 01:43 PM 07:53 PM	3.1 -0.1 2.6 0.0	94 -3 79 0

May

Day	Time (h m)	Height (ft)	Height (cm)
1 W	02:16 AM 08:39 AM 02:45 PM 08:57 PM	2.9 0.0 2.6 0.1	88 0 79 3
2 Th	03:19 AM 09:38 AM 03:49 PM 10:05 PM	2.8 0.1 2.6 0.2	85 3 79 6
3 F	04:23 AM 10:38 AM 04:54 PM 11:12 PM	2.6 0.1 2.6 0.2	79 3 79 6
4 Sa	05:26 AM 11:35 AM 05:55 PM	2.6 0.1 2.7	79 3 82
5 Su	12:15 AM 06:25 AM 12:28 PM 06:51 PM	0.2 2.5 0.1 2.8	6 76 3 85
6 M	01:13 AM 07:19 AM 01:18 PM 07:41 PM	0.1 2.5 0.1 2.8	3 76 3 85
7 Tu	02:04 AM 08:07 AM 02:04 PM 08:27 PM	0.1 2.5 0.0 2.9	3 76 0 88
8 W	02:50 AM 08:52 AM 02:47 PM 09:09 PM	0.0 2.5 0.0 2.9	0 76 0 88
9 Th	03:33 AM 09:33 AM 03:28 PM 09:49 PM	0.0 2.5 0.0 2.9	0 76 0 88
10 F	04:14 AM 10:12 AM 04:08 PM 10:28 PM	0.0 2.4 0.1 2.9	0 73 3 88
11 Sa	04:53 AM 10:50 AM 04:47 PM 11:05 PM	0.1 2.4 0.1 2.8	3 73 3 85
12 Su	05:32 AM 11:28 AM 05:26 PM 11:42 PM	0.1 2.4 0.2 2.7	3 73 6 82
13 M	06:10 AM 12:06 PM 06:05 PM	0.2 2.3 0.3	6 70 9
14 Tu	12:20 AM 06:49 AM 12:45 PM 06:47 PM	2.6 0.3 2.3 0.3	79 9 70 9
15 W	12:59 AM 07:29 AM 01:27 PM 07:31 PM	2.5 0.3 2.2 0.4	76 9 67 12
16 Th	01:42 AM 08:12 AM 02:13 PM 08:21 PM	2.4 0.4 2.2 0.5	73 12 67 15
17 F	02:28 AM 08:58 AM 03:04 PM 09:15 PM	2.3 0.4 2.3 0.5	70 12 70 15
18 Sa	03:20 AM 09:47 AM 03:58 PM 10:15 PM	2.3 0.4 2.3 0.5	70 12 70 15
19 Su	04:16 AM 10:38 AM 04:55 PM 11:16 PM	2.3 0.3 2.5 0.4	70 9 76 12
20 M	05:15 AM 11:31 AM 05:51 PM	2.3 0.2 2.6	70 6 79
21 Tu	12:16 AM 06:13 AM 12:24 PM 06:47 PM	0.2 2.3 0.1 2.8	6 70 3 85
22 W	01:13 AM 07:10 AM 01:17 PM 07:41 PM	0.1 2.4 0.0 3.0	3 73 0 91
23 Th	02:08 AM 08:05 AM 02:10 PM 08:34 PM	-0.1 2.5 -0.2 3.2	-3 76 -6 98
24 F	03:02 AM 08:59 AM 03:03 PM 09:27 PM	-0.2 2.6 -0.3 3.3	-6 79 -9 101
25 Sa	03:54 AM 09:52 AM 03:56 PM 10:20 PM	-0.3 2.7 -0.3 3.4	-9 82 -9 104
26 Su	04:46 AM 10:45 AM 04:49 PM 11:13 PM	-0.3 2.7 -0.3 3.3	-9 82 -9 101
27 M	05:38 AM 11:39 AM 05:45 PM	-0.3 2.7 -0.3	-9 82 -9
28 Tu	12:07 AM 06:31 AM 12:34 PM 06:42 PM	3.2 -0.3 2.7 -0.2	98 -9 82 -6
29 W	01:02 AM 07:24 AM 01:31 PM 07:42 PM	3.1 -0.2 2.7 -0.1	94 -6 82 -3
30 Th	01:59 AM 08:18 AM 02:30 PM 08:44 PM	2.9 -0.1 2.7 0.1	88 -3 82 3
31 F	02:58 AM 09:13 AM 03:31 PM 09:48 PM	2.7 -0.1 2.6 0.2	82 -3 79 6

June

Day	Time (h m)	Height (ft)	Height (cm)
1 Sa	03:58 AM 10:08 AM 04:32 PM 10:52 PM	2.5 0.0 2.6 0.2	76 0 79 6
2 Su	04:58 AM 11:03 AM 05:30 PM 11:53 PM	2.4 0.1 2.7 0.2	73 3 82 6
3 M	05:55 AM 11:55 AM 06:25 PM	2.3 0.1 2.7	70 3 82
4 Tu	12:50 AM 06:49 AM 12:46 PM 07:16 PM	0.2 2.3 0.1 2.7	6 70 3 82
5 W	01:41 AM 07:39 AM 01:33 PM 08:02 PM	0.2 2.3 0.1 2.8	6 70 3 85
6 Th	02:28 AM 08:24 AM 02:18 PM 08:45 PM	0.1 2.3 0.1 2.8	3 70 3 85
7 F	03:11 AM 09:07 AM 03:00 PM 09:26 PM	0.1 2.3 0.1 2.8	3 70 3 85
8 Sa	03:51 AM 09:47 AM 03:42 PM 10:04 PM	0.1 2.3 0.1 2.8	3 70 3 85
9 Su	04:30 AM 10:26 AM 04:22 PM 10:42 PM	0.1 2.3 0.1 2.7	3 70 3 82
10 M	05:08 AM 11:04 AM 05:01 PM 11:18 PM	0.1 2.3 0.2 2.7	3 70 6 82
11 Tu	05:45 AM 11:42 AM 05:41 PM 11:54 PM	0.1 2.3 0.2 2.6	3 70 6 79
12 W	06:22 AM 12:20 PM 06:22 PM	0.2 2.3 0.3	6 70 9
13 Th	12:31 AM 06:59 AM 01:00 PM 07:04 PM	2.5 0.2 2.3 0.3	76 6 70 9
14 F	01:10 AM 07:37 AM 01:43 PM 07:51 PM	2.4 0.2 2.3 0.4	73 6 70 12
15 Sa	01:53 AM 08:19 AM 02:29 PM 08:43 PM	2.4 0.2 2.4 0.4	73 6 73 12
16 Su	02:41 AM 09:04 AM 03:21 PM 09:40 PM	2.3 0.2 2.5 0.4	70 6 76 12
17 M	03:35 AM 09:55 AM 04:17 PM 10:42 PM	2.2 0.2 2.6 0.3	67 6 79 9
18 Tu	04:34 AM 10:50 AM 05:16 PM 11:45 PM	2.2 0.1 2.7 0.2	67 3 82 6
19 W	05:36 AM 11:47 AM 06:16 PM	2.3 0.0 2.9	70 0 88
20 Th	12:46 AM 06:38 AM 12:46 PM 07:16 PM	0.1 2.3 -0.1 3.1	3 70 -3 94
21 F	01:45 AM 07:39 AM 01:44 PM 08:13 PM	-0.1 2.4 -0.2 3.2	-3 73 -6 98
22 Sa	02:41 AM 08:37 AM 02:42 PM 09:09 PM	-0.2 2.5 -0.3 3.3	-6 76 -9 101
23 Su	03:36 AM 09:33 AM 03:39 PM 10:04 PM	-0.3 2.7 -0.4 3.3	-9 82 -12 101
24 M	04:28 AM 10:28 AM 04:35 PM 10:58 PM	-0.4 2.7 -0.4 3.3	-12 82 -12 101
25 Tu	05:19 AM 11:23 AM 05:31 PM 11:51 PM	-0.4 2.8 -0.3 3.2	-12 85 -9 98
26 W	06:10 AM 12:17 PM 06:27 PM	-0.4 2.8 -0.2	-12 85 -6
27 Th	12:44 AM 07:01 AM 01:12 PM 07:25 PM	3.0 -0.3 2.8 -0.1	91 -9 85 -3
28 F	01:37 AM 07:51 AM 02:08 PM 08:24 PM	2.8 -0.2 2.8 0.0	85 -6 85 0
29 Sa	02:31 AM 08:43 AM 03:04 PM 09:24 PM	2.6 -0.1 2.7 0.2	79 -3 82 6
30 Su	03:27 AM 09:35 AM 04:02 PM 10:25 PM	2.4 0.0 2.7 0.3	73 0 82 9

Heights are referred to mean lower water which is the chart datum of sounding. All times are local. Daylight Saving Time has been used when needed.

Hampton Roads (Sewells Point), Virginia, 2013

Times and Heights of High and Low Waters

July

Day	Time (h m)	Height (ft)	Height (cm)
1 M	04:24 AM 10:27 AM 04:59 PM 11:25 PM	2.3 0.1 2.6 0.3	70 3 79 9
2 Tu	05:21 AM 11:20 AM 05:55 PM	2.2 0.2 2.6	67 6 79
3 W	12:22 AM 06:16 AM 12:12 PM 06:47 PM	0.3 2.1 0.2 2.6	9 64 6 79
4 Th	01:14 AM 07:07 AM 01:02 PM 07:36 PM	0.3 2.1 0.2 2.7	9 64 6 82
5 F	02:01 AM 07:55 AM 01:50 PM 08:20 PM	0.3 2.2 0.2 2.7	9 67 6 82
6 Sa	02:45 AM 08:40 AM 02:35 PM 09:02 PM	0.2 2.2 0.2 2.7	6 67 6 82
7 Su	03:26 AM 09:21 AM 03:18 PM 09:41 PM	0.2 2.3 0.1 2.7	6 70 3 82
8 M	04:05 AM 10:01 AM 03:59 PM 10:18 PM	0.1 2.3 0.1 2.7	3 70 3 82
9 Tu	04:42 AM 10:40 AM 04:39 PM 10:54 PM	0.1 2.4 0.2 2.7	3 73 6 82
10 W	05:17 AM 11:17 AM 05:18 PM 11:29 PM	0.1 2.4 0.2 2.6	3 73 6 79
11 Th	05:52 AM 11:54 AM 05:58 PM	0.1 2.4 0.2	3 73 6
12 F	12:04 AM 06:27 AM 12:32 PM 06:40 PM	2.6 0.1 2.5 0.3	79 3 76 9
13 Sa	12:42 AM 07:04 AM 01:13 PM 07:25 PM	2.5 0.1 2.5 0.3	76 3 76 9
14 Su	01:24 AM 07:44 AM 01:59 PM 08:16 PM	2.4 0.1 2.6 0.3	73 3 79 9
15 M	02:10 AM 08:29 AM 02:50 PM 09:13 PM	2.4 0.1 2.6 0.3	73 3 79 9
16 Tu	03:04 AM 09:20 AM 03:47 PM 10:15 PM	2.3 0.1 2.7 0.3	70 3 82 9
17 W	04:04 AM 10:18 AM 04:49 PM 11:20 PM	2.3 0.1 2.8 0.3	70 3 85 9
18 Th	05:09 AM 11:20 AM 05:54 PM	2.3 0.0 2.9	70 0 88
19 F	12:24 AM 06:15 AM 12:24 PM 06:57 PM	0.2 2.3 -0.1 3.1	6 70 -3 94
20 Sa	01:25 AM 07:19 AM 01:27 PM 07:57 PM	0.0 2.5 -0.2 3.2	0 76 -6 98
21 Su	02:22 AM 08:19 AM 02:27 PM 08:54 PM	-0.1 2.6 -0.3 3.3	-3 79 -9 101
22 M	03:16 AM 09:16 AM 03:25 PM 09:48 PM	-0.3 2.8 -0.3 3.3	-9 85 -9 101
23 Tu	04:07 AM 10:11 AM 04:20 PM 10:40 PM	-0.4 2.9 -0.3 3.3	-12 88 -9 101
24 W	04:56 AM 11:04 AM 05:15 PM 11:30 PM	-0.4 3.0 -0.3 3.1	-12 91 -9 94
25 Th	05:44 AM 11:55 AM 06:08 PM	-0.3 3.0 -0.2	-9 91 -6
26 F	12:20 AM 06:32 AM 12:46 PM 07:02 PM	3.0 -0.3 2.9 0.0	91 -9 88 0
27 Sa	01:09 AM 07:19 AM 01:38 PM 07:57 PM	2.8 -0.1 2.9 0.1	85 -3 88 3
28 Su	02:00 AM 08:07 AM 02:31 PM 08:53 PM	2.6 0.0 2.8 0.3	79 0 85 9
29 M	02:52 AM 08:57 AM 03:26 PM 09:51 PM	2.4 0.2 2.7 0.4	73 6 82 12
30 Tu	03:46 AM 09:49 AM 04:23 PM 10:50 PM	2.2 0.3 2.6 0.5	67 9 79 15
31 W	04:43 AM 10:43 AM 05:20 PM 11:48 PM	2.1 0.3 2.6 0.5	64 9 79 15

August

Day	Time (h m)	Height (ft)	Height (cm)
1 Th	05:40 AM 11:38 AM 06:15 PM	2.1 0.4 2.6	64 12 79
2 F	12:42 AM 06:34 AM 12:32 PM 07:06 PM	0.5 2.1 0.4 2.6	15 64 12 79
3 Sa	01:31 AM 07:25 AM 01:22 PM 07:53 PM	0.4 2.2 0.3 2.7	12 67 9 82
4 Su	02:15 AM 08:11 AM 02:09 PM 08:35 PM	0.4 2.3 0.3 2.7	12 70 9 82
5 M	02:56 AM 08:54 AM 02:53 PM 09:14 PM	0.3 2.4 0.2 2.8	9 73 6 85
6 Tu	03:34 AM 09:34 AM 03:35 PM 09:51 PM	0.2 2.5 0.2 2.8	6 76 6 85
7 W	04:10 AM 10:12 AM 04:16 PM 10:27 PM	0.2 2.6 0.2 2.8	6 79 6 85
8 Th	04:45 AM 10:49 AM 04:55 PM 11:02 PM	0.1 2.7 0.2 2.8	3 82 6 85
9 F	05:20 AM 11:26 AM 05:36 PM 11:38 PM	0.1 2.7 0.2 2.7	3 82 6 82
10 Sa	05:55 AM 12:04 PM 06:18 PM	0.1 2.8 0.3	3 85 9
11 Su	12:17 AM 06:32 AM 12:46 PM 07:04 PM	2.6 0.1 2.8 0.3	79 3 85 9
12 M	12:59 AM 07:14 AM 01:33 PM 07:55 PM	2.5 0.2 2.8 0.4	76 6 85 12
13 Tu	01:47 AM 08:01 AM 02:26 PM 08:52 PM	2.5 0.2 2.9 0.4	76 6 88 12
14 W	02:42 AM 08:56 AM 03:26 PM 09:56 PM	2.4 0.2 2.9 0.4	73 6 88 12
15 Th	03:44 AM 09:58 AM 04:31 PM 11:02 PM	2.4 0.2 2.9 0.4	73 6 88 12
16 F	04:52 AM 11:04 AM 05:38 PM	2.4 0.2 3.0	73 6 91
17 Sa	12:07 AM 06:01 AM 12:11 PM 06:43 PM	0.3 2.5 0.1 3.1	9 76 3 94
18 Su	01:07 AM 07:05 AM 01:16 PM 07:43 PM	0.1 2.6 0.0 3.2	3 79 0 98
19 M	02:03 AM 08:05 AM 02:16 PM 08:38 PM	0.0 2.8 -0.1 3.3	0 85 -3 101
20 Tu	02:54 AM 09:00 AM 03:12 PM 09:30 PM	-0.1 3.0 -0.2 3.3	-3 91 -6 101
21 W	03:43 AM 09:52 AM 04:05 PM 10:19 PM	-0.2 3.1 -0.2 3.2	-6 94 -6 98
22 Th	04:30 AM 10:41 AM 04:56 PM 11:06 PM	-0.2 3.2 -0.1 3.1	-6 98 -3 94
23 F	05:15 AM 11:29 AM 05:46 PM 11:52 PM	-0.2 3.2 0.0 3.0	-6 98 0 91
24 Sa	05:59 AM 12:16 PM 06:36 PM	-0.1 3.1 0.1	-3 94 3
25 Su	12:38 AM 06:44 AM 01:04 PM 07:26 PM	2.8 0.1 3.0 0.3	85 3 91 9
26 M	01:25 AM 07:29 AM 01:53 PM 08:18 PM	2.6 0.2 2.8 0.5	79 6 85 15
27 Tu	02:13 AM 08:17 AM 02:44 PM 09:12 PM	2.4 0.4 2.7 0.6	73 12 82 18
28 W	03:05 AM 09:09 AM 03:41 PM 10:10 PM	2.3 0.5 2.6 0.7	70 15 79 21
29 Th	04:02 AM 10:05 AM 04:40 PM 11:09 PM	2.2 0.6 2.6 0.7	67 18 79 21
30 F	05:01 AM 11:03 AM 05:38 PM	2.2 0.6 2.6	67 18 79
31 Sa	12:04 AM 05:59 AM 12:00 PM 06:31 PM	0.7 2.2 0.6 2.6	21 67 18 79

September

Day	Time (h m)	Height (ft)	Height (cm)
1 Su	12:54 AM 06:51 AM 12:53 PM 07:19 PM	0.6 2.3 0.5 2.7	18 70 15 82
2 M	01:38 AM 07:39 AM 01:42 PM 08:02 PM	0.5 2.5 0.4 2.8	15 76 12 85
3 Tu	02:19 AM 08:22 AM 02:27 PM 08:42 PM	0.4 2.6 0.4 2.8	12 79 12 85
4 W	02:58 AM 09:02 AM 03:10 PM 09:20 PM	0.3 2.8 0.3 2.9	9 85 9 88
5 Th	03:34 AM 09:41 AM 03:51 PM 09:57 PM	0.2 2.9 0.2 2.9	6 88 6 88
6 F	04:10 AM 10:19 AM 04:32 PM 10:35 PM	0.2 3.0 0.2 2.9	6 91 6 88
7 Sa	04:46 AM 10:58 AM 05:14 PM 11:13 PM	0.1 3.0 0.2 2.8	3 91 6 85
8 Su	05:24 AM 11:39 AM 05:58 PM 11:54 PM	0.1 3.1 0.2 2.7	3 94 6 82
9 M	06:05 AM 12:23 PM 06:46 PM	0.2 3.1 0.3	6 94 9
10 Tu	12:39 AM 06:50 AM 01:12 PM 07:39 PM	2.7 0.2 3.1 0.4	82 6 94 12
11 W	01:30 AM 07:41 AM 02:08 PM 08:37 PM	2.6 0.3 3.0 0.4	79 9 91 12
12 Th	02:28 AM 08:40 AM 03:11 PM 09:41 PM	2.5 0.3 3.0 0.5	76 9 91 15
13 F	03:34 AM 09:46 AM 04:18 PM 10:47 PM	2.5 0.3 3.0 0.4	76 9 91 12
14 Sa	04:43 AM 10:56 AM 05:26 PM 11:50 PM	2.5 0.3 3.0 0.3	76 9 91 9
15 Su	05:52 AM 12:04 PM 06:30 PM	2.7 0.2 3.1	82 6 94
16 M	12:48 AM 06:54 AM 01:07 PM 07:28 PM	0.2 2.8 0.1 3.1	6 85 3 94
17 Tu	01:41 AM 07:51 AM 02:05 PM 08:21 PM	0.1 3.0 0.0 3.2	3 91 0 98
18 W	02:31 AM 08:43 AM 02:59 PM 09:10 PM	0.0 3.2 0.0 3.2	0 98 0 98
19 Th	03:17 AM 09:31 AM 03:48 PM 09:56 PM	-0.1 3.3 0.0 3.1	-3 101 0 94
20 F	04:01 AM 10:17 AM 04:36 PM 10:41 PM	-0.1 3.3 0.0 3.0	-3 101 0 91
21 Sa	04:44 AM 11:01 AM 05:22 PM 11:24 PM	0.0 3.3 0.1 2.9	0 101 3 88
22 Su	05:26 AM 11:45 AM 06:07 PM	0.1 3.2 0.3	3 98 9
23 M	12:06 AM 06:08 AM 12:28 PM 06:53 PM	2.7 0.2 3.0 0.4	82 6 91 12
24 Tu	12:49 AM 06:51 AM 01:13 PM 07:41 PM	2.6 0.4 2.9 0.6	79 12 88 18
25 W	01:34 AM 07:37 AM 02:02 PM 08:32 PM	2.4 0.5 2.7 0.7	73 15 82 21
26 Th	02:24 AM 08:28 AM 02:55 PM 09:27 PM	2.3 0.6 2.6 0.8	70 18 79 24
27 F	03:19 AM 09:24 AM 03:52 PM 10:23 PM	2.2 0.7 2.5 0.8	67 21 76 24
28 Sa	04:19 AM 10:24 AM 04:51 PM 11:19 PM	2.2 0.7 2.5 0.8	67 21 76 24
29 Su	05:19 AM 11:24 AM 05:47 PM	2.3 0.7 2.6	70 21 79
30 M	12:09 AM 06:13 AM 12:20 PM 06:37 PM	0.7 2.4 0.6 2.6	21 73 18 79

October

Day	Time (h m)	Height (ft)	Height (cm)
1 Tu	12:55 AM 07:02 AM 01:11 PM 07:23 PM	0.5 2.6 0.5 2.7	15 79 15 82
2 W	01:37 AM 07:46 AM 01:58 PM 08:05 PM	0.4 2.8 0.4 2.8	12 85 12 85
3 Th	02:17 AM 08:28 AM 02:42 PM 08:46 PM	0.3 2.9 0.3 2.8	9 88 9 85
4 F	02:56 AM 09:09 AM 03:26 PM 09:27 PM	0.2 3.1 0.2 2.9	6 94 6 88
5 Sa	03:35 AM 09:50 AM 04:09 PM 10:08 PM	0.1 3.2 0.1 2.9	3 98 3 88
6 Su	04:15 AM 10:32 AM 04:54 PM 10:50 PM	0.1 3.3 0.1 2.8	3 101 3 85
7 M	04:57 AM 11:17 AM 05:41 PM 11:35 PM	0.1 3.3 0.1 2.8	3 101 3 85
8 Tu	05:42 AM 12:05 PM 06:31 PM	0.1 3.3 0.2	3 101 6
9 W	12:24 AM 06:32 AM 12:57 PM 07:25 PM	2.7 0.1 3.2 0.3	82 3 98 9
10 Th	01:19 AM 07:28 AM 01:55 PM 08:24 PM	2.6 0.2 3.1 0.3	79 6 94 9
11 F	02:20 AM 08:30 AM 02:59 PM 09:27 PM	2.6 0.3 3.0 0.4	79 9 91 12
12 Sa	03:27 AM 09:39 AM 04:06 PM 10:30 PM	2.6 0.4 2.9 0.3	79 12 88 9
13 Su	04:36 AM 10:50 AM 05:12 PM 11:30 PM	2.6 0.3 2.9 0.3	79 9 88 9
14 M	05:42 AM 11:57 AM 06:14 PM	2.8 0.3 2.9	85 9 88
15 Tu	12:27 AM 06:42 AM 12:58 PM 07:11 PM	0.2 2.9 0.2 2.9	6 88 6 88
16 W	01:18 AM 07:36 AM 01:54 PM 08:02 PM	0.1 3.1 0.1 2.9	3 94 3 88
17 Th	02:06 AM 08:25 AM 02:44 PM 08:49 PM	0.0 3.2 0.0 2.9	0 98 0 88
18 F	02:51 AM 09:10 AM 03:31 PM 09:33 PM	0.0 3.3 0.0 2.9	0 101 0 88
19 Sa	03:33 AM 09:54 AM 04:16 PM 10:15 PM	0.0 3.3 0.1 2.8	0 101 3 85
20 Su	04:15 AM 10:35 AM 04:58 PM 10:56 PM	0.0 3.2 0.2 2.7	0 98 6 82
21 M	04:55 AM 11:15 AM 05:40 PM 11:36 PM	0.1 3.1 0.3 2.6	3 94 9 79
22 Tu	05:35 AM 11:56 AM 06:23 PM	0.2 3.0 0.4	6 91 12
23 W	12:16 AM 06:17 AM 12:38 PM 07:07 PM	2.5 0.3 2.8 0.5	76 9 85 15
24 Th	12:59 AM 07:01 AM 01:21 PM 07:53 PM	2.3 0.5 2.7 0.6	70 15 82 18
25 F	01:46 AM 07:49 AM 02:09 PM 08:42 PM	2.3 0.6 2.5 0.7	70 18 76 21
26 Sa	02:38 AM 08:43 AM 03:01 PM 09:34 PM	2.2 0.7 2.4 0.7	67 21 73 21
27 Su	03:35 AM 09:42 AM 03:57 PM 10:27 PM	2.2 0.7 2.4 0.6	67 21 73 18
28 M	04:33 AM 10:42 AM 04:54 PM 11:18 PM	2.3 0.7 2.4 0.6	70 21 73 18
29 Tu	05:29 AM 11:40 AM 05:48 PM	2.4 0.6 2.4	73 18 73
30 W	12:06 AM 06:20 AM 12:35 PM 06:38 PM	0.4 2.6 0.5 2.5	12 79 15 76
31 Th	12:52 AM 07:08 AM 01:25 PM 07:26 PM	0.3 2.8 0.3 2.6	9 85 9 79

November

Day	Time (h m)	Height (ft)	Height (cm)
1 F	01:36 AM 07:54 AM 02:14 PM 08:12 PM	0.2 3.0 0.2 2.6	6 91 6 79
2 Sa	02:19 AM 08:39 AM 03:01 PM 08:57 PM	0.0 3.1 0.0 2.7	0 94 0 82
3 Su	02:04 AM 08:24 AM 02:48 PM 08:43 PM	-0.1 3.3 0.0 2.7	-3 101 0 82
4 M	02:49 AM 09:11 AM 03:36 PM 09:31 PM	-0.1 3.3 -0.1 2.7	-3 101 -3 82
5 Tu	03:36 AM 09:59 AM 04:25 PM 10:20 PM	-0.2 3.3 -0.1 2.7	-6 101 -3 82
6 W	04:26 AM 10:50 AM 05:17 PM 11:12 PM	-0.1 3.3 -0.1 2.6	-3 101 -3 79
7 Th	05:19 AM 11:44 AM 06:11 PM	-0.1 3.2 0.0	-3 98 0
8 F	12:09 AM 06:18 AM 12:42 PM 07:08 PM	2.6 0.0 3.0 0.1	79 0 91 3
9 Sa	01:10 AM 07:22 AM 01:44 PM 08:08 PM	2.6 0.1 2.9 0.1	79 3 88 3
10 Su	02:16 AM 08:30 AM 02:49 PM 09:08 PM	2.6 0.2 2.7 0.1	79 6 82 3
11 M	03:23 AM 09:39 AM 03:53 PM 10:06 PM	2.6 0.2 2.6 0.1	79 6 79 3
12 Tu	04:26 AM 10:45 AM 04:54 PM 11:01 PM	2.7 0.2 2.6 0.0	82 6 79 0
13 W	05:25 AM 11:45 AM 05:50 PM 11:53 PM	2.8 0.1 2.6 0.0	85 3 79 0
14 Th	06:18 AM 12:39 PM 06:41 PM	2.9 0.1 2.6	88 3 79
15 F	12:41 AM 07:06 AM 01:28 PM 07:27 PM	-0.1 3.0 0.0 2.5	-3 91 0 76
16 Sa	01:25 AM 07:51 AM 02:13 PM 08:11 PM	-0.1 3.0 0.0 2.5	-3 91 0 76
17 Su	02:08 AM 08:32 AM 02:56 PM 08:51 PM	-0.1 3.0 0.0 2.5	-3 91 0 76
18 M	02:49 AM 09:12 AM 03:36 PM 09:31 PM	0.0 3.0 0.1 2.4	0 91 3 73
19 Tu	03:28 AM 09:51 AM 04:16 PM 10:09 PM	0.0 2.9 0.1 2.4	0 88 3 73
20 W	04:08 AM 10:29 AM 04:56 PM 10:49 PM	0.1 2.8 0.2 2.3	3 85 6 70
21 Th	04:48 AM 11:07 AM 05:35 PM 11:29 PM	0.2 2.7 0.3 2.2	6 82 9 67
22 F	05:30 AM 11:47 AM 06:16 PM	0.3 2.5 0.3	9 76 9
23 Sa	12:12 AM 06:15 AM 12:28 PM 06:59 PM	2.2 0.4 2.4 0.4	67 12 73 12
24 Su	12:58 AM 07:04 AM 01:14 PM 07:45 PM	2.1 0.5 2.3 0.4	64 15 70 12
25 M	01:49 AM 07:58 AM 02:04 PM 08:33 PM	2.1 0.5 2.2 0.4	64 15 67 12
26 Tu	02:44 AM 08:57 AM 02:58 PM 09:23 PM	2.2 0.5 2.2 0.3	67 15 67 9
27 W	03:40 AM 09:57 AM 03:55 PM 10:15 PM	2.3 0.4 2.2 0.2	70 12 67 6
28 Th	04:35 AM 10:56 AM 04:52 PM 11:06 PM	2.5 0.3 2.2 0.1	76 9 67 3
29 F	05:29 AM 11:52 AM 05:46 PM 11:56 PM	2.6 0.2 2.3 -0.1	79 6 70 -3
30 Sa	06:21 AM 12:46 PM 06:39 PM	2.8 0.0 2.4	85 0 73

December

Day	Time (h m)	Height (ft)	Height (cm)
1 Su	12:47 AM 07:12 AM 01:38 PM 07:31 PM	-0.2 3.0 -0.1 2.4	-6 91 -3 73
2 M	01:37 AM 08:03 AM 02:28 PM 08:22 PM	-0.3 3.2 -0.3 2.5	-9 98 -9 76
3 Tu	02:28 AM 08:54 AM 03:19 PM 09:14 PM	-0.4 3.2 -0.4 2.6	-12 98 -12 79
4 W	03:19 AM 09:45 AM 04:09 PM 10:06 PM	-0.5 3.2 -0.4 2.6	-15 98 -12 79
5 Th	04:13 AM 10:37 AM 05:01 PM 11:00 PM	-0.4 3.2 -0.4 2.6	-12 98 -12 79
6 F	05:08 AM 11:31 AM 05:53 PM 11:56 PM	-0.3 3.0 -0.3 2.6	-9 91 -9 79
7 Sa	06:07 AM 12:26 PM 06:47 PM	-0.2 2.9 -0.3	-6 88 -9
8 Su	12:56 AM 07:09 AM 01:25 PM 07:43 PM	2.5 -0.1 2.7 -0.2	76 -3 82 -6
9 M	01:58 AM 08:14 AM 02:25 PM 08:40 PM	2.5 0.0 2.5 -0.1	76 0 76 -3
10 Tu	03:01 AM 09:20 AM 03:27 PM 09:37 PM	2.5 0.1 2.3 -0.1	76 3 70 -3
11 W	04:04 AM 10:25 AM 04:28 PM 10:32 PM	2.5 0.1 2.2 -0.1	76 3 67 -3
12 Th	05:03 AM 11:26 AM 05:25 PM 11:25 PM	2.6 0.1 2.2 -0.1	79 3 67 -3
13 F	05:58 AM 12:21 PM 06:17 PM	2.6 0.0 2.2	79 0 67
14 Sa	12:15 AM 06:47 AM 01:10 PM 07:05 PM	-0.1 2.7 0.0 2.2	-3 82 0 67
15 Su	01:02 AM 07:32 AM 01:54 PM 07:49 PM	-0.1 2.7 0.0 2.2	-3 82 0 67
16 M	01:45 AM 08:13 AM 02:36 PM 08:30 PM	-0.2 2.7 -0.1 2.2	-6 82 -3 67
17 Tu	02:27 AM 08:52 AM 03:15 PM 09:09 PM	-0.2 2.7 -0.1 2.2	-6 82 -3 67
18 W	03:07 AM 09:30 AM 03:53 PM 09:47 PM	-0.1 2.7 -0.1 2.2	-3 82 -3 67
19 Th	03:46 AM 10:06 AM 04:30 PM 10:24 PM	-0.1 2.6 0.0 2.2	-3 79 0 67
20 F	04:25 AM 10:41 AM 05:06 PM 11:02 PM	0.0 2.5 0.0 2.1	0 76 0 64
21 Sa	05:04 AM 11:17 AM 05:42 PM 11:41 PM	0.1 2.4 0.0 2.1	3 73 0 64
22 Su	05:45 AM 11:53 AM 06:20 PM	0.1 2.3 0.1	3 70 3
23 M	12:22 AM 06:29 AM 12:33 PM 07:00 PM	2.1 0.2 2.2 0.1	64 6 67 3
24 Tu	01:07 AM 07:18 AM 01:18 PM 07:44 PM	2.1 0.3 2.1 0.1	64 9 64 3
25 W	01:57 AM 08:14 AM 02:09 PM 08:32 PM	2.2 0.3 2.0 0.1	67 9 61 3
26 Th	02:53 AM 09:15 AM 03:07 PM 09:26 PM	2.2 0.3 2.0 0.0	67 9 61 0
27 F	03:52 AM 10:18 AM 04:08 PM 10:24 PM	2.4 0.2 2.0 -0.1	73 6 61 -3
28 Sa	04:53 AM 11:21 AM 05:10 PM 11:22 PM	2.5 0.1 2.1 -0.2	76 3 64 -6
29 Su	05:53 AM 12:20 PM 06:11 PM	2.7 -0.1 2.2	82 -3 67
30 M	12:20 AM 06:50 AM 01:16 PM 07:09 PM	-0.4 2.9 -0.3 2.3	-12 88 -9 70
31 Tu	01:16 AM 07:45 AM 02:09 PM 08:04 PM	-0.5 3.0 -0.4 2.4	-15 91 -12 73

Heights are referred to mean lower water which is the chart datum of sounding. All times are local. Daylight Saving Time has been used when needed.

Page 89
Trenton
195
276
76
76
13
95
Philadelphia
Page 83
476
295
PENNSYLVANIA
Page 83
Wilmington
95
Delaware City
Salem River
Page 80
Chesapeake City
C&D Canal
Alloway River
NEW JERSEY
Cohansey River
322
Greenwich
Page 78
Delaware River
Sassafras River
13
DELAWARE
Maurice River
Page 77
9
N
Dover
Delaware Bay
Page 71
Cape May
Atlantic Ocean
Cape Henlopen
1
Lewes
Rehoboth Beach
Rehoboth Bay

DOZIER'S WATERWAY GUIDE
THE CRUISING AUTHORITY
WWW.WATERWAYGUIDE.COM

Skipper's Handbook
- GPS Waypoints 48
- Tide Tables 50

Cape May, Delaware Bay, Delaware River

CHARTS 12277, 12304, 12311, 12312, 12313, 12314

The waters of Delaware Bay are considered by many boaters to be rough, tedious and inhospitable, but this area has another face—a remote and lonely mystique with great appeal for adventurous mariners who enjoy exploring.

A boat must be able to proceed on her own to a safe harbor some distance away along stretches of coastlines belonging to both Delaware and New Jersey, no matter what weather and sea conditions are present. The entire 50-mile-long stretch from Cape May, NJ to where the C&D Canal joins Delaware Bay is notorious for building up short, choppy seas quickly and creating rougher weather than local reports may indicate. You might get a heavy blow anywhere along this stretch, even when the forecast is calling for moderate winds.

The skills of the navigator are likely to be tested here also, especially if one is accustomed to the line-of-sight navigation called for on the Intracoastal Waterway (ICW) farther south, or in the upper sections of Chesapeake Bay. Buoys might be out of sight, even in clear weather, so running an accurate compass or GPS course is a necessity. Big ships might rumble by at full speed, more mindful of their draft than they are of you.

The facilities here are adequate; in fact, some are the best on the coast. From the C&D Canal to Sandy Hook and the entrance to New York Harbor lie some of the most underrated bodies of water on the East Coast.

Delaware Bay

Delaware Bay is a passage of more than 50 miles from the C&D Canal to the Atlantic Ocean that is studded with shallow waters, sand flats and sandbars outside of the shipping channels. The tide tends to ebb for 7 hours and flood for 5. Prevailing winds are usually from the west in the fall, causing a rough ride for the mariner running the length of the bay from the C&D Canal to Cape May. In the summer, the winds prevail from the south with afternoon sea breezes often building to 15 to 25 knots. As a result of prevailing winds, seas can often build beyond the average 2-foot chop. Few cruisers transiting the Bay are aware of the rivers off of each shore, all sufficiently interesting and secure enough to rate as prime cruising grounds. However, cautious entry is advised as local entry marks are relocated frequently to show the deepest water.

On the New Jersey side of the Delaware Bay are two rivers: The Cohansey, entered through a winding but fairly well-marked channel, is charming and makes a good halfway stopover between the C&D Canal and the Cape May Canal; and the Maurice River, requiring more diligence, as markers are moved frequently and not charted, houses a picturesque oyster fishery and offers uncrowded cruising on its upper reaches. Westward, on the Delaware side of the bay, the Mispillion River, Murderkill River and within Port Mahon, the Leipsic and Smyrna rivers are seldom traveled. While they are picturesque, they are only receptive to shoal-draft boats.

Photos courtesy of Delaware Tourism

LOBSTER HOUSE

(609) 884-8296

Fisherman's Wharf | Cape May, NJ 08204
Exit No. 0 Garden State Parkway

Cocktails • Luncheons • Dinners

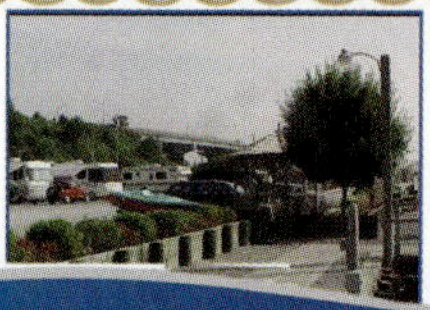

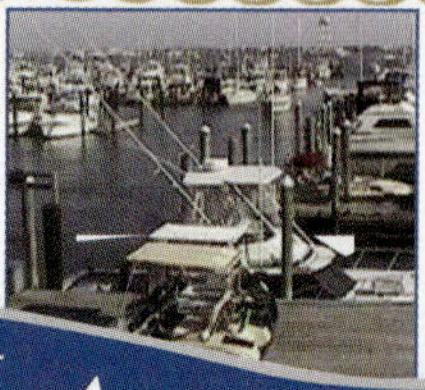

SINCE UTSCH'S MARINA 1951

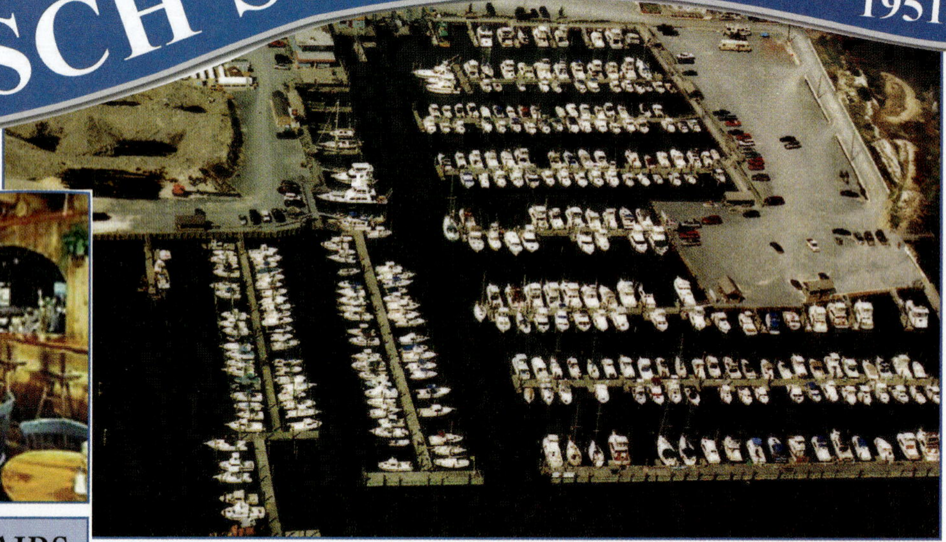

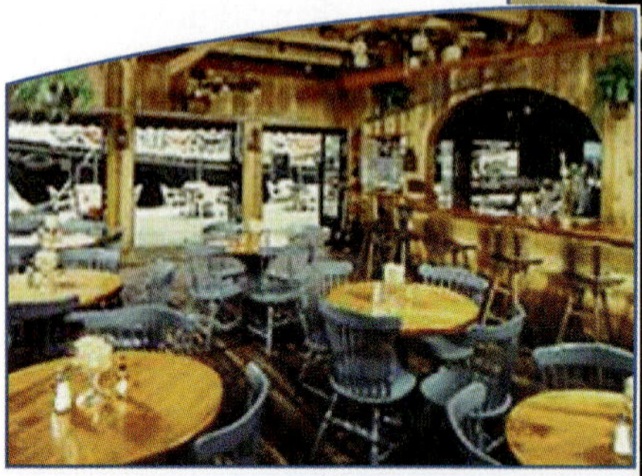

SERVICE AND REPAIRS:

- Wireless Internet Access
- 2 Travelifts for hauling your powerboat or sailboat more efficiently: 35 Ton Open End Lift, 25 Ton Open End Lift
- Propeller and Hull Repairs
- Standing inventory of over 150 propellers (both new and used)
- Winter Storage Available
- Marine Store (and we mean starters, alternators, manifolds, risers, etc.)
- Picnic Tables & Barbeque Area
- New Deluxe Tile Showers & Restrooms
- Transient Slips Available
- Space Provided for Dinghies
- 5 ft. Water at Low Tide
- Brokerage on All Types of Boats
- Cable TV
- Laundry / Light Groceries
- Tackle Shop
- Engine Franchises:

HONDA MARINE
Crusader ENGINES
MarinePower
P.C.M.

COMPLETE MARINE FACILITIES

Located in Cape May Harbor on the south side of the Cape May Canal is a 300 slip, family owned and operated marina, nestled next to the world famous Lobster House Restaurant and The Schooner America.

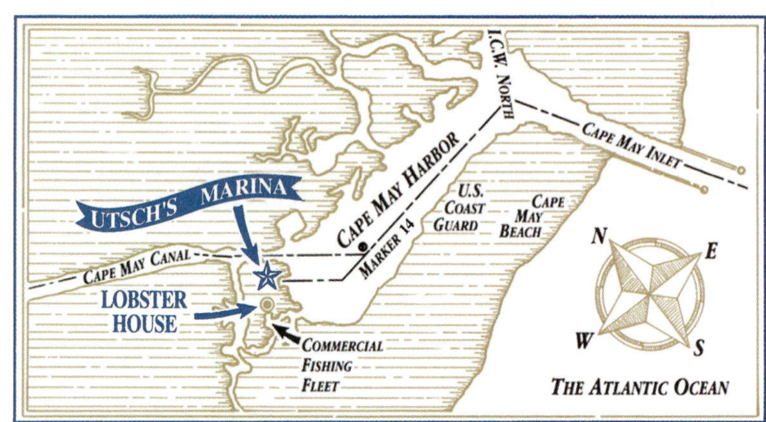

LOCATED BETWEEN CANAL AND SCHELLENGER'S LANDING

(609) 884-2051 www.capemayharbor.com

WE MONITOR CHANNEL 16 VHF

Discounts Available for Volume Fuel Purchases

We Love Sailboats!

WWW.CAPEMAYHARBOR

UTSCH'S MARINA (609) 884-2051

Cape May Harbor, NJ

CAPE MAY		Largest Vessel Accommodated	VHF Channel Monitored	Transient Berths / Total Berths	Approach / Dockside Depth (reported)	Floating Docks	Gas / Diesel	Groceries, Ice, Marine Supplies, Snacks	Repairs: Hull, Engine, Propeller	Lift (tonnage), Crane, Rail	Min/Max Amps	Laundry, Pool, Showers, Courtesy Car	Pump-Out Station	Nearby: Grocery Store, Motel, Restaurant
		Dockage					Supplies		Services					
1. Corinthian Yacht Club of Cape May 113.5	609-884-8000	50	-	3/	6/6	F	-	-	-	-	30/30	S	-	R
2. Miss Chris Marina 114.5	609-884-3351	80	16	2/13	8/6	F	GD	IS	-	-	30/50	-	P	GMR
3. South Jersey Marina 114	**609-884-2400**	**140**	**16/09**	**25/70**	**10/10**	**F**	**GD**	**IMS**	**HEP**	**L**	**30/100**	**LS**	**P**	**GMR**
4. Roseman's Boat Yard 114.5	609-884-3370	60	-	1/20	4/11	F	GD	IMS	HEP	L75	30/50	-	P	GMR
5. Cape May Marine 114.5	609-884-0262	70	-	10/210	10/10	F	GD	IM	HEP	L70	30/50	PS	-	GR
6. Utsch's Marina 114	**609-884-2051**	**75**	**16/09**	**25/350**	**8/7**	**F**	**GD**	**GIMS**	**HEP**	**L35**	**30/50**	**LS**	**P**	**GMR**
7. Canyon Club Resort Marina 114	**609-884-0199**	**125**	**16/09**	**40/260**	**10/6**	**F**	**GD**	**IMS**	**HEP**	**L80**	**30/100**	**LPS**	**P**	**GMR**
8. Bree-Zee-Lee Yacht Basin 112.8	609-884-4849	46	-	10/1100	4/6	F	GD	IM	HEP	L35	30/30	LS	-	MR
9. Hinch Marina 112.5	609-884-7289	33	16/68	10/116	10/5	F	-	IMS	-	L	30/50	S	P	R
10. Harbor View Marina 113	609-884-0808	50	16/66	20/200	7/20	F	GD	IMS	-	L	30/30	S	P	R

Corresponding chart(s) not to be used for navigation. Internet Access, Wireless Internet Access, Waterway Guide Cruising Club Partner

See www.WaterwayGuide.com for current rates, fuel prices, web site addresses, and other up-to-the-minute information.

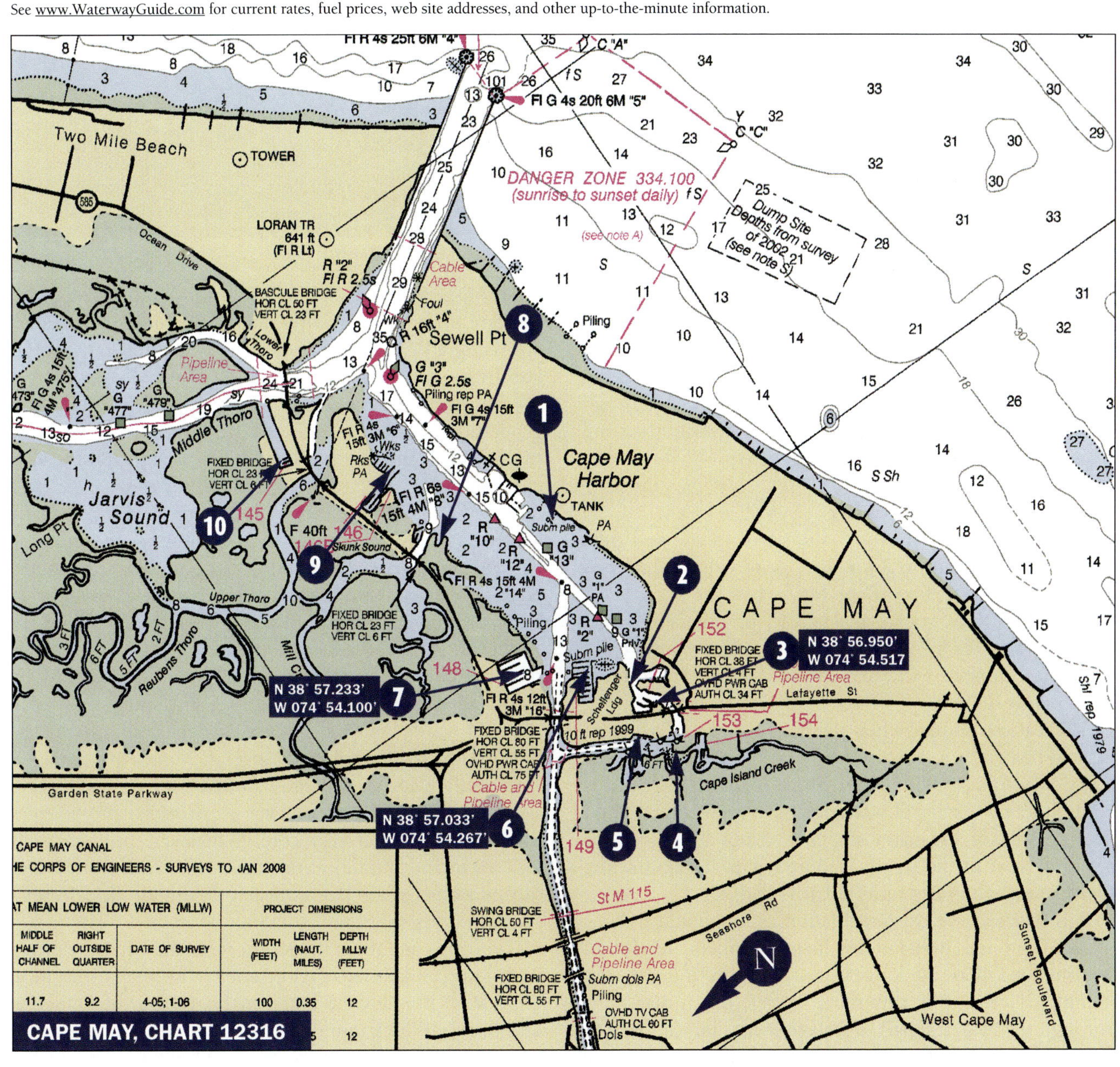

Looking southwest over Cape May Harbor. (Not to be used for navigation.) WATERWAY GUIDE PHOTOGRAPHY.

As with all marinas and anchorages surrounded by marshlands, screens are a must. Greenhead flies appear during the day from the end of June until the beginning of September, unless the wind is coming off the ocean. These cousins to the horsefly have been known to bite through clothing and leave large, painful whelps. Mosquitoes are troublesome for about an hour after sunset.

Running Delaware Bay

Tidal rise and fall is in the 5- to 7-foot range, and tidal currents can run up to 3 knots. A good rule of thumb is to head northward from Cape May when the tide is low, and head south from Chesapeake City on the C&D Canal at high water. This scheduling is especially important for sailboats equipped with auxiliary engines having limited horsepower.

The easiest course when visibility is good for recreational boaters is a rhumb line (across the flats) from the Cape May Canal to Ship John Shoal Lighthouse. On this route, there is plenty of water for most recreational craft; you are out of the main shipping channel and will be traveling east of the riprap of Brandywine Shoal and the abandoned lighthouse ruins at Cross Ledge.

Part of Delaware Bay's reputation as tough and tedious stems from the decision by many skippers, fearful of obstructions that no longer exist, to run the big-ship channel. Not only is this route longer, but it also runs through the roughest part of Delaware Bay and can lead to close encounters with huge commercial vessels.

The Delaware Bay oyster industry once marked the trap areas on the bay with stakes. Currently, oystermen are using PVC pipes, which bear watching, but are far less threatening than wood stakes. Many of the charted "obstructions" are mounds of oyster shells dumped a generation ago that are no longer dangerous. However, at the height of the flood or ebb, if you are outside the ship channel, watch for crab-trap marker floats, which have a tendency to submerge; the dark-colored ones are especially hard to spot. It is not advisable to run outside the shipping lane at night or when visibility is poor. For recreational boaters, it is best to run the ship channel from buoy to buoy, leaving the channel clear for commercial traffic.

Fog on the bay tends to burn off during the morning. It is most frequent in December, January and February, and tends to come in with easterly winds and go out with westerly winds. During the late fall, dense fog might last through the late morning for several consecutive days.

In the late spring and early summer, advection fogs are common. These occur whenever warm, moist air overrides waters that are still very cold. Whenever the forecast is for "warm and humid" at this time of year, advection fogs can be expected on Delaware Bay or any of New Jersey's coastal waters.

If you are caught out in a storm at the mouth of Delaware Bay, you can take emergency shelter in a small basin at Cape May, Brandywine Light, in the Harbor of Refuge at Lewes, DE or duck into Roosevelt Inlet, the entrance to the Lewes and Rehoboth Canal on the Delaware side.

CAPE MAY, NJ

The Cape May inlet is a safe, all-weather entrance from the Atlantic Ocean into Cape May Harbor at the southern terminus of the New Jersey ICW (Mile 114). The well-protected harbor makes it a popular layover for skippers waiting out bad weather before heading north along the New Jersey coast, or those headed to the Delaware Bay or the C&D Canal farther north.

Cape May is reputed to be "the nation's oldest seashore resort." That heritage dates from at least 1812, peaking architecturally in the late 19th century. The entire town has been proclaimed a National Historic Landmark. Cape May likely has the largest collection of Victorian period houses in the country. Small gingerbread cottages nestle beside grand showpieces, all preserved and restored, many tastefully pressed into commercial service. Curlicue porches and steeply peaked, lovingly rebuilt dormers adorn many houses within walking distance of the western harbor's marine facilities. Cape May's beaches are legendary, its dunes still nearly pristine and the harbor is a secure storm anchorage.

NAVIGATION: Use Charts 12304, 12214, 12316 and 12317. **Use Atlantic City tide tables. For Cape May Harbor high tide, add 33 minutes; for low tide, add 19 minutes.** Approaching Cape May Inlet from either the New Jersey ICW or the Atlantic Ocean, your landmark is a charted 641-foot tall LORAN tower, which is located on the east side of the inlet. Topped by a flashing red light, the tower is nearly four times the height of the 165-foot tall Cape May Lighthouse at the southwestern tip of the cape. One of the safest and best-marked inlets on the East Coast, Cape May Inlet is deep and visibly protected by substantial rock jetties on either side.

Cape May Lighthouse. *New Jersey Division of Travel and Tourism*

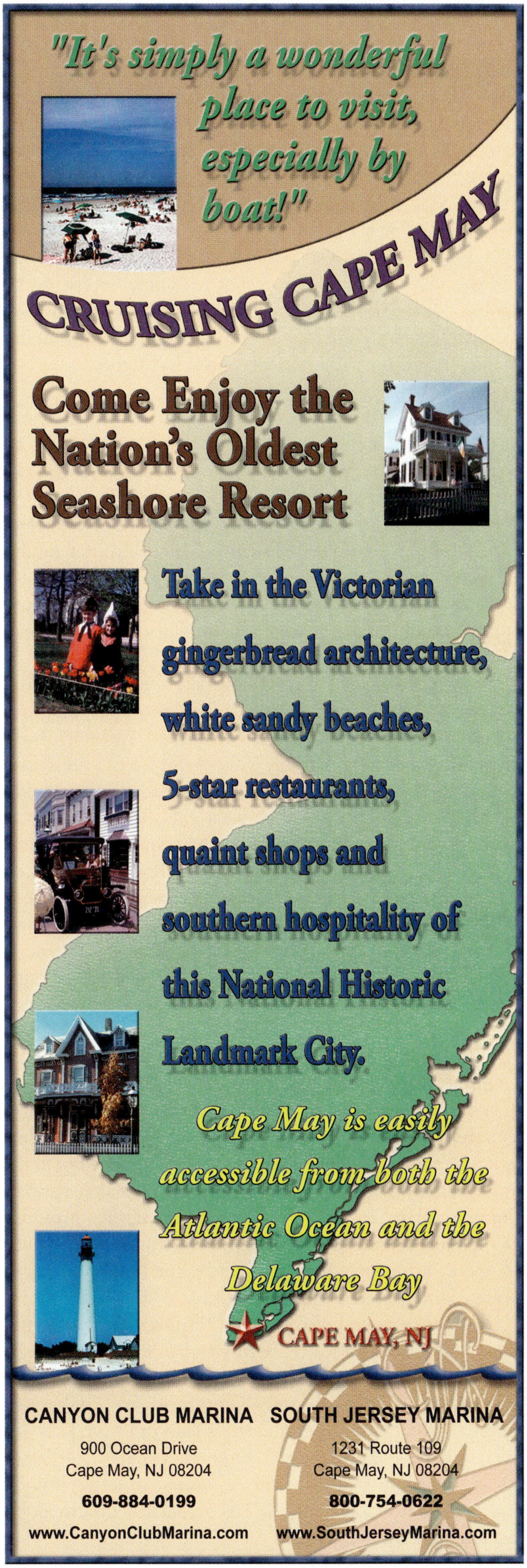

Entering Cape May Harbor is easy from every approach—from Delaware Bay through the jettied entrance to Cape May Canal, from the NJICW itself on the north, or through Cape May Inlet on the east. Ebb tides run east, both in the canal and in the inlet. NOAA Chart 12316 will be helpful in sorting out the buoys and depths for all three approaches.

Cape May Inlet is extremely busy at all times, and you can expect to meet every type of vessel at every speed imaginable. The inlet is also popular with the fishing crowd, and the mouth is often congested with small recreational fishing boats. The commercial fishing fleet generally has its outriggers extended while traversing the inlet, making them very beamy. The outriggers are not lighted and can be very difficult to see in poor light.

During the peak travel season when the weather and tide turn favorable, you can expect an armada of yachts to pour out of Cape May Harbor in both directions to take advantage of an opportunity for a smooth passage. On the other hand, it is also not uncommon to see yachts, even high-powered ones, return to Cape May after taking a pounding from the elements at work in both Delaware Bay and the Atlantic Ocean. Any attempt to challenge the opposition of both wind and tide along the axis of the bay is not recommended.

Dockage: Cape May has many large, accommodating marinas. They all have transient slips available. The first facility you will encounter is Corinthian Yacht Club on the south side of the harbor, west of the Coast Guard station. This is very popular with sailors and fill up quickly during the heavily traveled seasons. Miss Chris Marina is next and sells fuel as well as offering transient slips.

Deep-draft vessels up to 140 feet can be accommodated at South Jersey Marina, with its 10-foot approach and dockside depths. The marina has a new bulkhead and a spacious deck for its customers, rebuilt docks and a pump-out station. Situated on Cape Island Creek, South Jersey Marina is reached by a straight-ahead course into the creek between green daybeacon "1" and red daybeacon "2" (instead of turning to starboard toward Cape May Canal at flashing red "12"). The Marina lies just beyond the commercial dock and the highly visible Lobster House restaurant. Turning room is at a premium here, but there is plenty of depth, and the marina's staffers skillfully maneuver large craft into position to match various skippers' plans for time and tide. The marina provides in-slip fueling and has a very clean restroom and shower complex. Roseman's Boat Yard and Cape May Marina are nearby with fuel and transient slips.

Near the west end of Cape May Harbor, adjacent to the Cape May Canal entrance, both Utsch's Marina (immediately west of the canal entrance) and Canyon Club Resort Marina (just east of the canal entrance) are full-service facilities that can accommodate deep-draft vessels on approach and at berth. Utsch's offers transients water, electricity and cable TV, an on-site restaurant, Internet lounge and marine store. Utsch's also has a courtesy dinghy dock available for those anchored out.

Canyon Club Resort Marina's avenue-like docks are canopied by hundreds of outriggers, extending from the hulls of sport fishing boats dedicated to searching offshore canyons. There is usually ample transient space on floating cement docks that are accessible to the canal inlet with in-slip fueling. There is also a large in-ground pool in a well-landscaped setting, coin-operated laundry facilities, a convenient snack bar that serves breakfast (early) and lunch, a large repair shop and a ship's store with basic supplies.

The turn north from the channel into Harbor View Marina and Bree-Zee-Lee Yacht Basin should be made just after flashing green "7," adjacent to the Coast Guard's northernmost docks; head toward the middle entrance of the sea wall and then cruise adjacent to the wall to the westernmost entrance toward the fuel docks. Bree-Zee-Lee Yacht Basin and Hinch Marina may have transient space. Harbor View Marina, directly across from the Coast Guard Station, offers a deepwater fuel dock and transient slips (7-foot approach depth at mean low water).

Anchorage: Though marina slips are usually available, even during the peak of fall migration, all bets are off during Cape May's frequent fishing tournaments. Fortunately, considerable anchorage space is available along the south side of the harbor, both east and west of the U.S. Coast Guard station. West of the Coast Guard station, outside (or even in) the mooring field, there should be ample space for relatively shallow-draft vessels in 5- to 10-foot depths at mean low water. Deeper-draft boats typically anchor in front of the Coast Guard facility and to the east while awaiting favorable weather and tide to push on. Anchorage depths in this location, between the buoyed channel and the shore, range from 6 to 16 feet; holding is good in thick mud. (Be aware when anchoring here that you may experience early-morning Coast Guard reveilles and cadence calls as new recruits go through their paces at the base).

When the anchorage is crowded, particularly during the passage of cold fronts during fall and spring, two anchors may well be advisable. No launch service is available, but it is a relatively short dinghy ride to marine facilities and restaurants to the west.

GOIN' ASHORE: CAPE MAY, NJ

Picture-postcard-pretty, Cape May, NJ boasts one of the greatest concentrations of Victorian architecture in the nation. Walking Jackson Avenue is a feast for the eyes, as one after another, meticulously restored homes and inns assert their individuality in a language of paint, landscaping and seasonal flowers. Competing for your attention are cafés, boutiques and galleries featuring works by local artists. Horse and buggy tours complete this idealized 19th-century picture.

Lined almost entirely by marinas and restaurants, the harbor is a favorite layover for cruisers en route to or from the Delaware Bay. The harbor is an easy place to relax with friends, watch the boats pass by and enjoy fresh seafood at your waterfront table.

Those with bicycles on board will want to take a leisurely five-mile long ride to Cape May Point State Park and visit its stately lighthouse, originally built in 1821. If your visit happens to be during September or October, bring the ship's binoculars because the bird watching is nothing less than superb.

History: A Dutch captain, Cornelius Jacobsen Mey, explored the area and named the peninsula Cape Mey in 1620. The spelling was later changed to Cape May. By 1761, Cape May had become the first seashore resort in America.

The most distinctive feature about Cape May is its Victorian heritage, carefully retained in several hundred beautifully manicured houses throughout the city. The Victorian Era occurred from 1837 to 1901, when Queen Victoria ruled over England. The impact of her reign was felt throughout the world and in Cape May, which was then considered to be among the top vacation resorts in the United States.

Many Victorian structures, adorned with carved bargeboards, ornate verandas and crowned dormers, have been restored. Most of the homes, hotels, shops and other buildings were constructed in the late 1800s at the prime of the Victorian Era. Today, small gingerbread houses stand beside magnificent Victorian showplaces. Cape May was officially designated a National Historic Landmark city in 1976.

Points of Interest: Historic tours (walking or riding) are available throughout the Historic District. Bike tours are also available, and bikes can be rented at most marinas. The horse and buggy tours can be arranged at a location within the Historic District. There are many museums and historic sites as well that are accessible through walking tours. The Cape May beach is pristine and large and a major attraction in this area. Deep-sea fishing charters are abundant in the harbor and readily accessible.

Cape May is alive with theatrical activity. The three theater companies are Cape May Stage (609-884-1341 or www.capemaystage.com) at the Robert Shackleton Playhouse (405 Lafayette St.), East Lynne Theater Company (609-884-5898 or www.eastlynnetheater.org) at the First Presbyterian Church (500 Hughes St.), and Elaine's Dinner Theater (609-884-4358 or www.elainesdinnertheater.com) at 513 Lafayette St. Call ahead for reservations for any of these year-round venues.

The Cape May-Lewes Ferry (800-643-3779) makes it possible to for fun day trip across the Delaware Bay to Lewes, DE and walk along the Rehoboth-Lewes Canal, or spend some time at the Cape Henlopen beach. The trip takes about an hour and a half and can be done by car or on foot if you park In the ferry lot and take a shuttle bus. Each ferry can carry 1,000 passengers but holds only 100 cars, so reservations are recommended if you are driving (www.capemaylewesferry.com).

If you are a golfer, you may be interested in the Avalon Golf Club at 1510 Route Nine (609-465-4653).

Special Events: Not to be missed is the Jersey Fresh Farmers' Market, which is held from 3:00 p.m. to 7:30 pm, every Tuesday, June through August in West Cape May Borough Hall. For this and other food events, check www.westcapemaytoday.com. The annual Victorian Fair at the Physick Estate takes place in June, and the July 4th fireworks display is on at the beach where viewing is possible along the mile-long boardwalk. See www.capemay.com or www.capemaytimes.com for a complete listing of events.

Shopping: Shopping is abundant in Cape May, from the small boutiques and antique shops throughout the Historic District and along the beachfront. If you are looking for seafood to cook on board, stop at the Lobster House Fish Market (609-884-3064) in front of the restaurant on Fisherman's Wharf in the harbor and take home a ready-made clam bake to prepare in your own galley.

Dining: As with any resort, hours can vary depending on the season, so you should check beforehand. There is no shortage of good restaurants in Cape May, beginning in the harbor at The Lobster House on Fisherman's Wharf (609-884-8296) has been serving seafarers, tourists and locals for many years. They offer dockage for diners. Also close to the harbor, Lucky Bones Backwater Grille (1200 Route 109, 609-884-2663) is a casual restaurant created by the former Pelican Club family. The food is made from scratch; the atmosphere is warm and fun.

Copper Fish (416 Broadway, 609-898-1555) is a chic restaurant in the historic part of town and features bold, innovative cooking with a steak and seafood focus. Another Cape May tradition for over 30 years is the Mad Batter Restaurant (609-884-5970), at 19 Jackson Street, open seven days a week. The Oyster Bay Steak & Seafood Restaurant (609-884-2111, 615 Lafayette Street) opens at 5 pm for dinner and has a great menu with especially great desserts.

If you are looking for ocean-view dining, try Martini Beach (609-884-1925) at 429 Beach Avenue, Thursdays through Mondays or the romantic Peter Shield's Inn & Restaurant (609-884-9090), also on Beach Avenue (1301), serving dinner nightly starting at 5:30 p.m. and lunch during the summer. The contemporary Pier House (609-898-0300), at 1327 Beach Avenue, serves breakfast and dinner daily and lunch on weekends.

Aleathea's (609-884-5555), inside the Victorian four-story Inn of Cape May built In on Ocean Street, serves breakfast, lunch and dinner daily. Many Cape May restaurants are BYOB, making them a windfall for the conscientious diner.

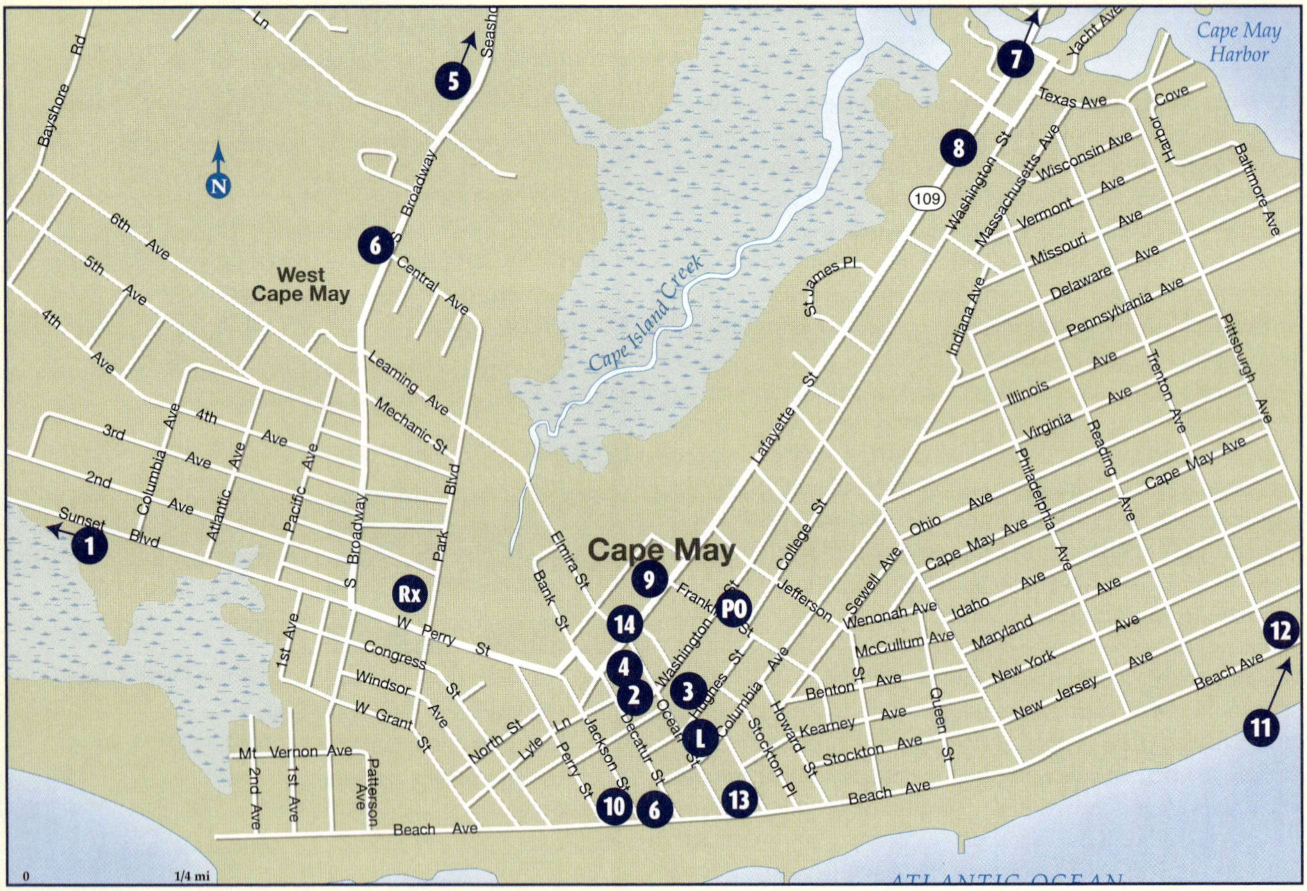

Reference the marina listing tables to see all the marinas in the area.

POINTS OF INTEREST

1 Cape May Point State Park & Lighthouse
2 Cape May Stage/Robert Shackleton Playhouse
3 East Lynne Theater Co.
4 Elaine's Dinner Theater
5 Cape May - Lewes Ferry
6 Farmers' Market at West Cape May Borough Hall

SHOPPING

7 Lobster House Fish Market

DINING

7 Lobster House Fish Market
8 Copper Fish Restaurant
9 The Oyster Bay Steak and Seafood Restaurant
10 Martini Beach
11 Peter Shield's Inn & Rest.
12 The Pier House
13 Aleathea's

INFORMATION

14 Welcome Center

LIBRARY

POST OFFICE

PHARMACY

ADDITIONAL RESOURCES

- CAPE MAY: **www.capemay.com**
- CAPE MAY CHAMBER OF COMMERCE: **www.capemaychamber.com**

NEARBY MEDICAL FACILITIES

Cape Urgent Care: 900 Route 109, Cape May, NJ 08204, 609-884-4357

Cape Regional Medical Center: 2 Stone Harbor Blvd., Cape May Court House, NJ 02810, 609-463-2000

CAPE MAY CANAL

The jettied entrance to Delaware Bay from Cape May Canal is about two miles north of Cape May Point. Keep a sharp eye out for the Cape May-Lewes ferries that use the western entrance of the Cape May Canal to reach their terminals about a half-mile from the breakwaters. They take up nearly the entire channel. A portion of the Cape May Canal is lined with homes and should be treated as a No-Wake Zone.

NAVIGATION: Use Chart 12316. Try to plan your transit of the Cape May Canal during daylight hours, as it is a very dark passage at night. There is plenty of water in the 100- to 150-foot-wide Cape May Canal channel (controlling depth is usually 6 feet), but shoals can build up rapidly outside the channel. Shoaling has been reported south of the ferry crossing in the canal.

The canal is crossed by two fixed bridges (clearance 55 feet) and a low (4-foot closed vertical clearance) railroad bridge. The tourist trains are in operation, and the railroad bridge is in use seven days a week from mid-June through Labor Day, from 10:00 a.m. until 7:30 p.m. Train service in the spring and fall is limited to weekends. The bridge will close to boat traffic, usually for less than 20 minutes when a train is passing; there is no published schedule available. Mariners are advised to plan their trips through the canal with this contingency in mind.

Mariners might think that a boat could pass on either side of the Cape May Railroad Swing Bridge, and, in fact, a boat heading east at twilight might decide to keep to the right upon seeing oncoming traffic, but beware: This passage (south of the swing span) is crossed by several electrical cables 8 to 15 feet over the water. A small striped board hanging from these cables could easily be missed. In addition, two submerged dolphins to the southwest of the span in the south channel make passage doubly hazardous.

Dockage: No dockage exists along the 3.5-mile length of the Cape May Canal.

Cape May Canal to Egg Island Flats

This run (about 15 nautical miles) is either the easiest or the longest and loneliest, depending on wind and tide.

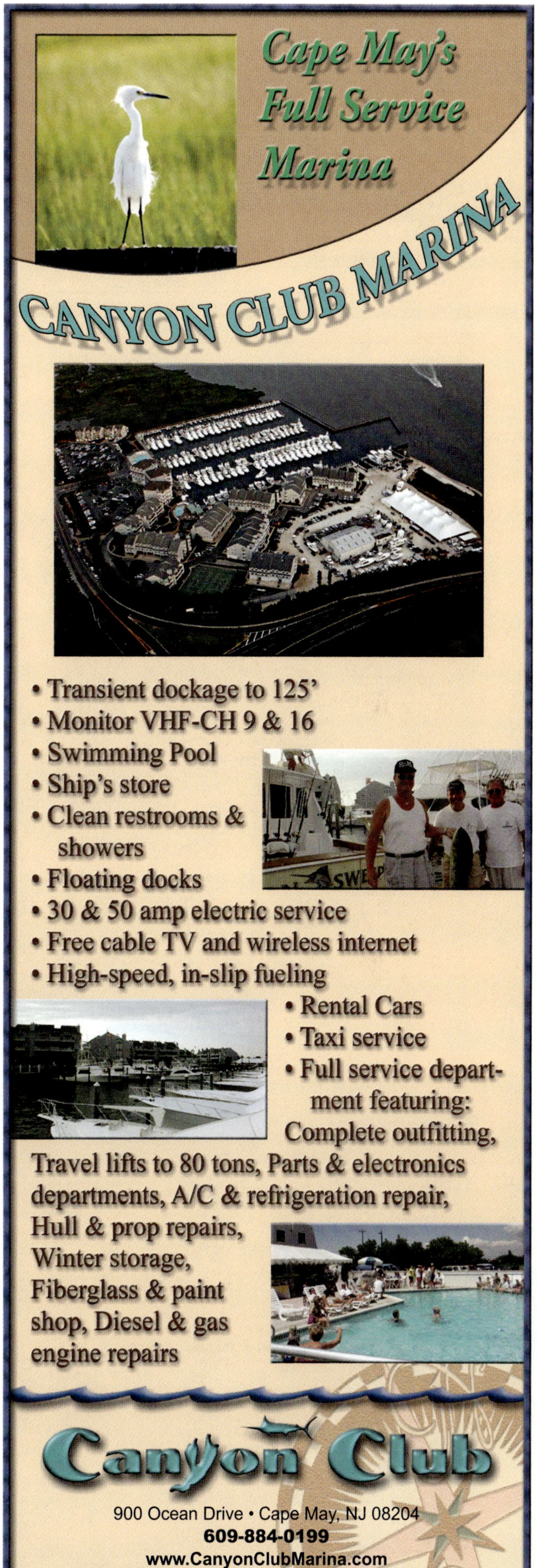

Maurice River to Cohansey River, NJ

MAURICE RIVER TO COHANSEY RIVER		Largest Vessel Accommodated	VHF Channel Monitored	Transient Berths / Total Berths	Approach / Dockside Depth (reported)	Floating Docks	Gas / Diesel	Groceries, Ice, Marine Supplies, Snacks	Repairs: Hull, Engine, Propeller	Lift (tonnage), Crane, Rail	Min/Max Amps	Laundry, Pool, Showers, Courtesy Car	Pump-Out Station	Nearby: Grocery Store, Motel, Restaurant
		Dockage					Supplies		Services					
1. Greenwich Marina & Boat Works 🖳	856-451-7777	100	16	24/150	15/30	F	GD	GIMS	HEP	L100	30/50	LS	P	GR
2. Hancock Harbor Marina 🖳	856-455-2610	110	16/68	10/250	40/25	F	GD	IM	HP	L50	30/50	LSC	-	GR
3. Sundog Marina	856-447-3992	36	16	10/60	5/5	F	G	GIMS	HEP	C5	30/30	S	P	R
4. Port Norris Marina	856-785-1205	31	10	/200	-	-	GD	IM	-	-	30/30	S	-	GR
5. Yank Marine Services	856-785-0100	150	-	-	15/8	F	-	MS	HEP	L200	30/30	S	-	-

Corresponding chart(s) not to be used for navigation. 🖳 Internet Access Wireless Internet Access Waterway Guide Cruising Club Partner

See www.WaterwayGuide.com for current rates, fuel prices, web site addresses, and other up-to-the-minute information.

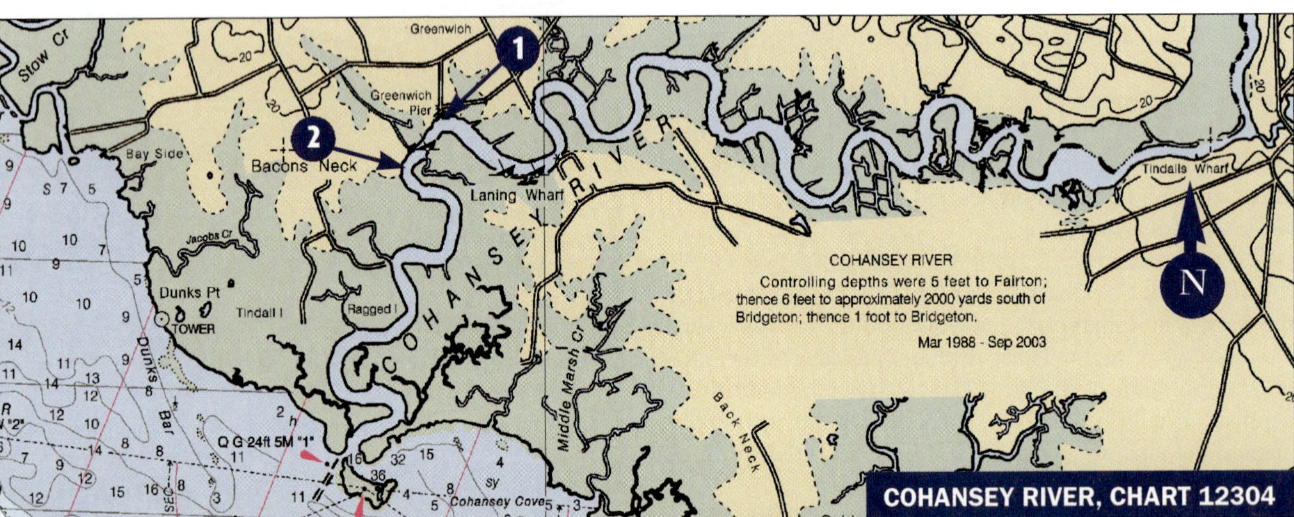

COHANSEY RIVER, CHART 12304

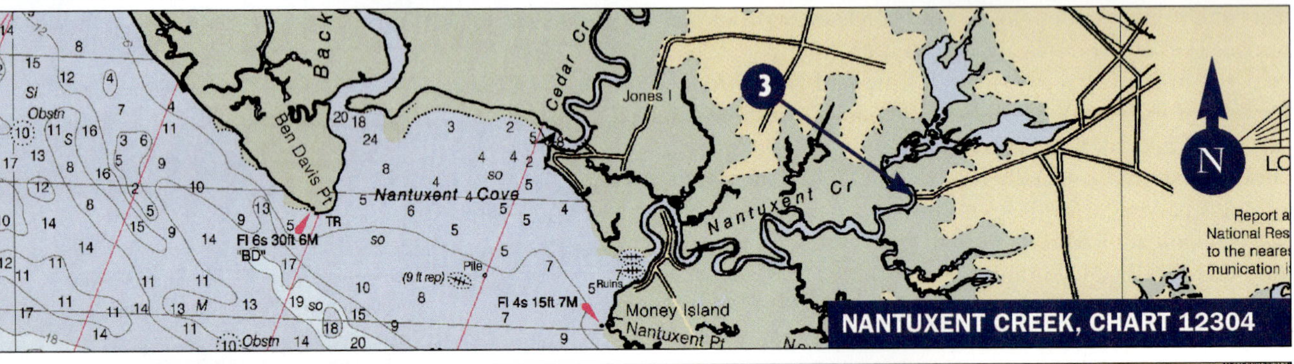

NANTUXENT CREEK, CHART 12304

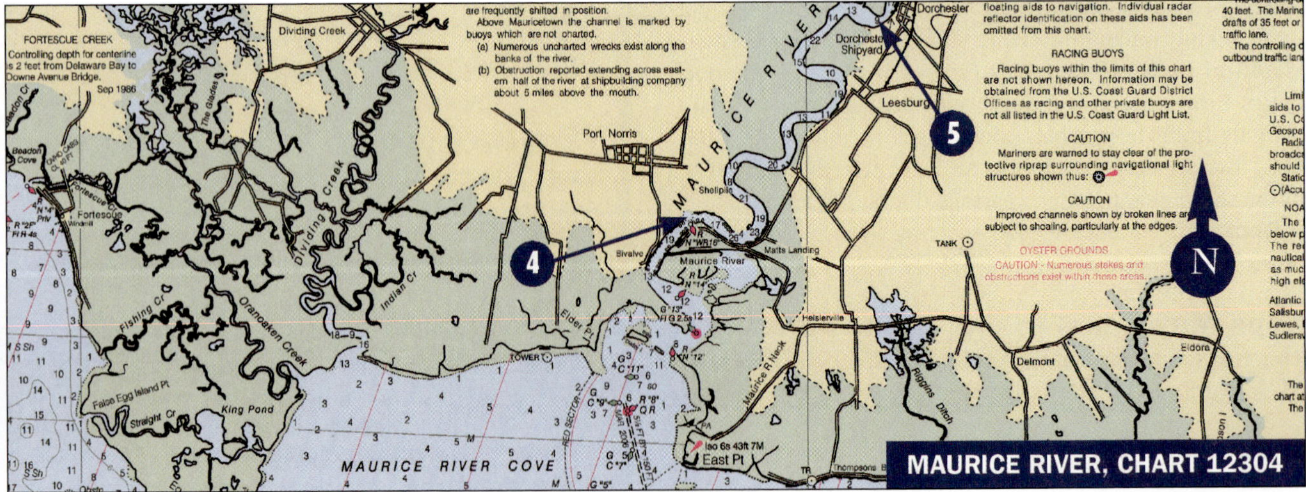

MAURICE RIVER, CHART 12304

NAVIGATION: Use Chart 12304. The light off Egg Island Point is 27 feet tall and flashes a white light every 4 seconds. The creeks in this area are not recommended for cruising vessels, as most are impassable. Note that PVC pipes with radar reflectors mark the corners of oyster grounds. The pipes are painted black and are difficult to see at night. Any gill nets must be lighted with flags or orange floats. If you are going down-bay with the ebb, crosscurrents might set you to the northeast. This side set will help ensure that you do not overshoot the Cape May Canal entrance, but often the big stacks at Cape May will be way off to starboard. If you are going up-bay and seas are bad, head more northward toward the light of Maurice River Cove. The Egg Island flats will make it a little easier run through the chop.

Maurice River

Just east of Egg Island Point is the Maurice River (pronounced "Morris"), an oyster packing and boatbuilding center, which carries deep water and a well-marked channel.

NAVIGATION: Use Chart 12304. Controlling low-water depths are about 5 feet across the bar at the mouth, 7 feet to Mauricetown and 5 feet to Millville. The red-roofed East Point Lighthouse, on the east side of the entrance to the Maurice River, is a daytime landmark that can be seen far down Delaware Bay.

During strong northwest winds, depths in the channel can be less than 3 feet. A sandbar has built up southwest of East Point to red nun buoy "2." After passing between quick flashing red buoy "8" and green can buoy "9," the channel doglegs to the right, passing south and then east of Fowler Island at the entrance to the Maurice River. The small, charted island and piles southeast of Fowler Island no longer exist, nor do the previously charted range markers north of Elder Point. Shoals now extend from Fowler Island to the northwest, thus cutting off the old channel.

The Delaware Bay oyster fleet makes its harbor here on the Maurice River, especially at Bivalve, as the name might suggest. The homes and buildings of Mauricetown are adorned with lacy ironwork decorations that could have come only from the French West Indies. A fixed bridge at Mauricetown stops any boat needing more than a 25-foot clearance, but the Maurice River itself is navigable several more miles to Millville, which has a municipal dock. The channel to Millville is not shown on Chart 12304, but is well buoyed and used constantly by grain boats and other small freighters.

Dockage: Both Port Norris Marina and Yank Marine Services are here. Port Norris sells fuel and Yank Marine is a full-service boat yard with a 200-ton lift.

Anchorage: You can anchor behind the island in the mouth of the Maurice River or in almost any bend away from the channel. However, old stakes and dolphins, some broken off with the stubs submerged at high water, extend into the river and must be watched for, whether you are anchoring or running. It is best to run up on a rising tide. Tidal range is 5 to 6 feet.

Nantuxent Cove

Between the Maurice River and Cohansey Rivers lies Nantuxent Cove. The northern approach brings you to Back Creek, which has deep water at the entrance. Across the Cove at Nantuxant Point is Nantuxant Creek. Call Sundog Marina for directions for getting inside and for depths. (The marina reports 5-foot approach/dockside depth.) Sundog sells fuel and has transient slips.

Egg Island Point to Ship John Shoal Light

The passage is straightforward, but if the weather pipes up, a few storm havens are available on the New Jersey shore. The best of these havens is an anchorage at Back Creek, inside Ben Davis Point. Back Creek has an easy entrance and is navigable two miles upstream.

Cohansey River

Two nautical miles north of Ship John Shoal Light is the mouth of the Cohansey River, one of New Jersey's prettiest, with an 18th-century village on its banks not far upstream.

NAVIGATION: Use Chart 12304. The better of two entrances is a dredged cut to the north, where a 42-foot tower on the island at the entrance is easy to spot from miles away. The other entrance is from Cohansey Cove to the east. Boats headed down Delaware Bay should leave red nun buoy "2" at the end of Dunks Bar well to port before turning into the cut approach to the Cohansey River. Dunks Bar Shoal is slowly moving farther out into Delaware Bay.

The cut is easy to enter and navigate in daylight, and the Cohansey River itself has plenty of water. Controlling depths are 10 feet as far as Greenwich. You can anchor in 36-foot depths in the crook at the natural mouth of the river, behind the island made by the cut, but currents run hard at the peak of the ebb and flood. You will need extra scope for your anchor, and the holding here is less than perfect. Many boaters anchor upstream after the first bend in the Cohansey River, which provides better protection in a blow. Coming upriver from the south, give the southern end of the island a good berth. Riprap from a light, destroyed in 1878, still remains. Also keep an eye out for fish trap markers in this area.

The Cohansey River winds its way east through largely uninhabited Jersey lowlands, offering what is likely to be the most unspoiled marshland cruise left in the state. The historic town of Greenwich (settled seven years before Philadelphia) stands on the left bank, three miles upriver.

Dockage: On approach, you will first notice Hancock's Harbor, a marina with extensive dockage paralleling the Cohansey River to port. From a berth here, you can enjoy much-praised home cooking at the Bait Box Restaurant and take on gas or diesel fuel, water and ice. Just ahead are the docks of the Greenwich Marina and Boat Works. VHF radios aren't much monitored here, and a 5- to 6-knot current at full flood or ebb can make docking assistance a near necessity except at slack water. With inexpensive dockage, this area may be the bargain of northern waters cruising. However, vacant space may be in short supply, since these facilities are quite popular with local boaters.

Cohansey River, NJ

Anchorage: If you continue on the river around several bends, you can find good spots for overnight. The river is not wide, but deep and with enough swinging room to accommodate the anchoring of several "boats in a row." Like any marshy area, you will find it a little buggy, but the natural and somewhat primitive environment makes it worth it.

GOIN' ASHORE: GREENWICH, NJ

Down Jersey is the area of southern New Jersey that refers to life along the Delaware Bay Shore of New Jersey. It has a flavor all its own, and no place represents it better than Greenwich on the Cohansey River, where natural, maritime, agricultural and cultural histories converge.

Greenwich's charm has a human face; its culture is the culture of local crabbers, fishermen, boat builders, oystermen, decoy carvers and others whose skills and way of life have been passed down through generations. Although Greenwich may be tiny and lack large hotels, fancy restaurants or big-box shopping, it is one of the most beautiful places in New Jersey.

History: Located within five miles of Delaware Bay, Greenwich was originally planned as a manor town by John Fenwick, who had previously established Salem. He died before the town was settled, but his plan was followed, and by 1690, a small port community was established on the Cohansey River.

The first settlers included Quakers, Baptists, Presbyterians and Episcopalians—a religious mixture quite unusual for a time when religion was the central part of most communities and religious tolerance was uncommon. Greenwich was recognized as an important location and quickly became a thriving port. By 1701, it was one of only three official ports of entry for New Jersey.

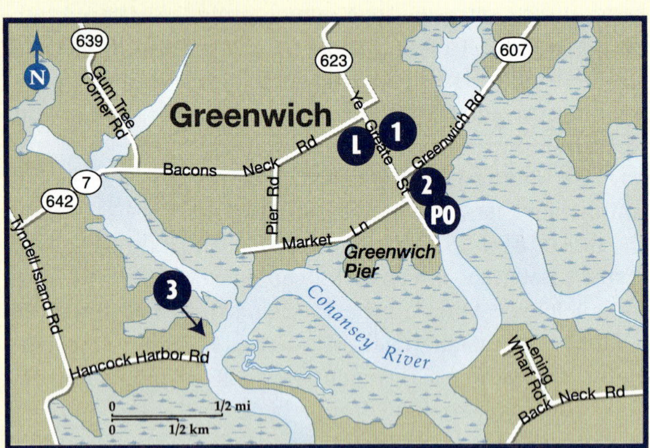

Reference the marina listing tables to see all the marinas in the area.

POINTS OF INTEREST
1 The Gibbon House/ Tea Burners Monument

SHOPPING
2 Greenwich Country Store

DINING
3 Bait Box Restaurant

PO POST OFFICE

L LIBRARY

A notable historic event in Greenwich was the "Tea Burning at Greenwich," where the merchants and townspeople were appalled by the same British taxation efforts that angered colonials in Boston, New York and Annapolis. A ship, Greyhound, bound for Philadelphia, put into Greenwich and the captain of the ship hid the tea shipment in a home there. The Greenwich locals broke into the cellar, stole the tea and burned it. Greenwich continued to thrive as an important port of entry during the Revolution, but gradually other towns began to emerge as more important sites.

Greenwich today exists as a small, quiet and quaint bayside town steeped in history, Victorian houses and museums.

Points of Interest: The Gibbon House at 960 Ye Greate Street is furnished with products of 18th- and 19th-century artisans. At the same site is the Tea Burners Monument.

Shopping: Most shopping can be found in Bridgeton, about six miles away. The Greenwich Country Store is a deli with a small grocery selection, located at 1016 Ye Greate Street (856-453-3622).

Dining: There is one restaurant in Greenwich, the Bait Box Restaurant at Hancock Harbor Marina—a bit of a hike at 30 Hancock Harbor Road (856-455-2610), which is open during the summer (be sure to check the hours before visiting). Additional restaurants are located in Bridgeton. (This is also, by the way, the location of the closest golf course: Cohanzick Country Club at 149 Bridgeton Fairton Road, 856-455-2127.)

ADDITIONAL RESOURCES

- GREENWICH TOWNSHIP: www.greenwichtwp.com
- NEW JERSEY PINES AND DOWN JERSEY: www.njpinelandsanddownjersey.com

NEARBY MEDICAL FACILITIES
Bridgeton Health Center, 333 Irving Ave., Bridgeton, NJ 08032, 609-451-6600

Ship John Shoal Light to Reedy Island Dike

This leg of the journey is about 13 nautical miles and can be covered either in the ship channel or the off-channel flats (passing Arnold Point Shoal to the northeast). Your decision will depend on the draft of your vessel, the state of the tide and the weather at the time of your passage.

The tide runs stronger in the deeper main channel, and seas tend to be steeper on the flats. While buoys are more frequent in the channel, the north shore is well marked, and lights and points of reference are easy to spot.

Heading up Delaware Bay, the same decision must be made at the Ben Davis Point Shoal. In either case, the choice is not irrevocable, and you can swing from one to another at will.

Storm shelters on the New Jersey side include Mad Horse Creek (about six miles south of Artificial Island) and Stow Creek, just south of Arnold Point. The long shelving bar south and west of the mouth of Mad Horse Creek, shown on the chart, is typical of north shore shoals, hooking out and down-bay like a submerged finger.

Avoid Cedar Creek, 1.5 miles east of Back Creek, as it is only navigable at high tide. Crab pots are thick throughout the area. Money Island, behind Nantuxent Point, has 5-foot depths over the bar, with the passage marked by stakes, but the village has little except safety to offer cruisers.

Fortescue, east and north of Cross Ledge Light, is also a safe harbor in this area; however, transient berths are scarce. It offers several marinas with restaurants within walking distance. The town and harbor are geared to commercial fishing and party boats and, in season, it can get congested with fishing party boats. A tricky dogleg is immediately inside the entrance, but from early May to early October, a Coast Guard search-and-rescue team operates from Fortescue Inlet and will lead you in if necessary. (If emergency assistance is needed during winter months, contact Coast Guard Group Cape May on VHF Channel 16.) Depths at the entrance range from 4 to 5 feet at low water. Inside, the channel is well marked.

Sailboats take note: A power cable (40-foot vertical clearance) crosses Fortescue Creek a quarter-mile from the entrance.

Reedy Island Dike to Salem River

NAVIGATION: Use Chart 12311. It is a six-nautical-mile journey from Reedy Island Dike to the C&D Canal. The tidal set is upriver or downriver, with no side set in this area. Alloway Creek, 3.5 miles south of the Salem River, should be avoided because of the sandbars across the mouth of its unmarked channel.

Danger Spots: This area has many hazards, including the Reedy Island Dike itself, which submerges and is not visible at high tide. A series of flashing lights is set on the jetty, with a line of white-and-orange warning buoys alongside. The southernmost warning buoy is on the Delaware side of the dike. Coming north, do not be misled, as many have been in the past, by the lights of Port Penn. Be sure to watch for the charted and lighted wreck east of the channel, about two miles north of Artificial Island.

Just north of the arbitrary Delaware Bay/Delaware River boundary between Liston Point and Hope Creek is a useful landmark on the New Jersey side. The domes of the nuclear power plants on Artificial Island dominate the landscape for miles around, and the vapor cloud coming from the cooling tower can be seen even farther.

Only two of these reactor domes are charted; the third dome, built in the late 1980s, has still not found its way onto the chart. Restrictions may apply to waters near the nuclear plant, so stand clear and check with authorities if in doubt. Security regulations forbid recreational vessels within 500 yards of the power plant. To the northwest of Artificial Island, between the channel and the island, is a commercial anchorage area. If visibility is poor or if a sea or swift tide is running, avoid shortcutting through this area. Large steel mooring buoys can be nearly submerged by the tidal chop and easily missed.

Anchorage: One place to stop is behind the Reedy Island Dike. Leave the river at green can buoy "3R" and head west for green daybeacon "1" and quick flashing red light "2." (Depths are at least 20 feet.) These two markers lead through the dike to a patch of deep water behind the island and dike that is used as an anchorage by local fishermen. Depths hold all the way to the southwest shore of the island.

Salem River

Opposite the entrance to the eastern end of the C&D Canal is New Jersey's Salem River, and a few miles upstream is the town of Salem. The town has a village square and a council oak, under which Dutch and Swedish colonists made treaties with the Native Americans in the 18th century.

NAVIGATION: Use Chart 12311. From the deep water of Delaware Bay, access to the Salem River is via a channel from the south through Salem Cove. Pay strict attention to the marker buoys of this channel. Spoils from the channel's dredging are deposited outside the channel markers, along with piles of rocks, below the surface but at shoal depth. Be especially vigilant between flashing red lights "6" and "8" where there was 3 to 4 feet of shoaling in Spring 2011. Any shortcut here could result in severe damage. The depth of the channel is reportedly 13 feet, but enter on a rising tide to be sure. (There is a 5-foot tidal range.) When entering the Salem River, keep a watchful eye on the ranges. Lighted buoys have now replaced the unlighted ones all the way from Delaware Bay to the Salem River marinas.

Currents run swiftly in the Salem River, especially at the fixed bridge (13-foot vertical clearance) crossing about two miles upriver. The Salem Port Authority dredges the channel to depths that are suitable for grain barges and a small container ship.

Note that power cables cross the Salem River before you enter the cut-off channel. Although they are charted at 59 feet, reports indicate a clearance of 50 feet. Skippers of large sailboats should keep a sharp eye aloft.

The Southwest Shore

We will now work our way south down the Delaware side of Delaware Bay toward Cape Henlopen, the southern boundary of Delaware Bay at its mouth. Coverage up the Delaware River continues later in this section, and for those traveling west on the C&D Canal, see the next section in this Guide, "C&D Canal to Kent Island." The southwestern shoreline of Delaware Bay resembles the desolate sections found along the bay's north shore. The low tidal marshes that make up this shore provide few landmarks.

NAVIGATION: Use Chart 12304. The small streams off Delaware Bay are narrow, winding and little used except by local fishermen and occasional barges. A few of these streams, with entrance jetties or buoys, give access to storm refuges and fuel. They are best entered (with caution) on a rising tide; observe local traffic.

Typical of these southwest shore streams is the Murderkill River at Bowers Beach, DE, near the midpoint between Cape Henlopen and the C&D Canal. The entrance channel is marked by a flashing green light, two pairs of buoys and range markers. An entrance bar shoals to 30 to 36 inches at low tide, despite frequent dredging.

Avoid nighttime navigation along the southwest shore of the bay. Fish and oyster stakes abound, and most navigational buoys are unlit.

Anchorage: Just inside the mouth of the Murderkill River on the western bank is a public dock, with groceries only a short walk away. This dock is exposed in an easterly blow. No other transient amenities are available, and those who wish to anchor farther upstream should note the cables 50 feet above the river's surface.

North to the Delaware River

Our coverage will now continue north at the C&D Canal where we will continue our coverage north along the Delaware River toward the exciting historical sights of Wilmington, DE and Philadelphia, PA, the birthplace of American independence and a first-class cruising destination. The journey continues up to Trenton, NJ.

■ NORTH ON THE DELAWARE RIVER

Refuge often missed by boaters in a hurry is Delaware City, two miles north of the eastern entrance to the C&D Canal. Fort Delaware, the famous Civil War prison now converted to a museum, stands nearby on Pea Patch Island, and the trip makes a fascinating excursion. A ferry carries visitors from the Delaware side at the Fort Delaware State Park dock in Delaware City.

NAVIGATION: Use Charts 12277, 12311, 12312 and 12314. **Use Reedy Point tide tables. For Delaware City high tide, add 3 minutes; for low tide add 8 minutes.** To reach Delaware City, use Bulkhead Shoal Channel and turn west at flashing green "1" at the Delaware City Branch Channel off the C&D Canal. Be careful not to stray out of Bulkhead Shoal Channel toward Pea Patch Island, a spoil area that is bare at low tide.

Access to Pea Patch Island (and the historic sites, detailed below) is limited to ferries; recreational craft may not land on the island. Note that the buoys on the Delaware River are numbered according to the range for the channel and usually use the first letter of the range. For example, the Marcus Hook Range has buoys "2M" through "9M." Above the Schuylkill River, they are numbered consecutively, beginning with flashing red buoy "44." The range lights, bright and easily seen even during daylight, are also helpful in fog and heavy haze.

The Delaware City Branch Channel reportedly has 12-foot depths up to the 6-foot fixed vertical clearance bridge at Delaware City. When entering from Delaware Bay, the Fort Delaware State Park building and floating dock are immediately to your right. This dock is not for public use but for the ferry service to Pea Patch Island. Just beyond the state park dock is a public dock where boats can tie up during the day, but overnight docking is prohibited. The depths next to this dock become very shallow at low tide (as low as 1 or 2 feet), so use this dock only in a dinghy or a shoal-draft vessel at high tide. Take particular care when maneuvering in the channel, as it is narrow, and the current can exceed 3 knots.

Anchorage: An anchorage is available to the southeast of the Delaware City Branch Channel entrance. It is exposed to the heavy wave action from passing ships and northwest to south winds. From the anchorage, it is a short dinghy ride into the public dock.

GOIN' ASHORE:

DELAWARE CITY, DE

Though often overlooked due to its location two miles north of the C&D Canal, Delaware City is a waterfront gem, especially for Civil War enthusiasts and architecture buffs, who will find themselves in the midst of more than 200 structures from the 19th and early 20th centuries. The city has much to offer anyone who enjoys hiking, bird watching, cycling, kayaking and the like. For that, a short ride on the Three Forts Ferry will take you to the Delaware Estuary marshes, Fort Delaware and Pea Patch Island.

History: The Newbold family from New Jersey originally purchased the tract of land known today as Delaware City in 1801. Their plans for the city included expectations that it would grow to be as important a commercial port as Philadelphia. Its location, at the original eastern terminus of the Chesapeake and Delaware Canal, did cause it to become an operating base and a way station for many shipping-related activities.

During the mid-to-late 1800s, a peach boom made Delaware City famous for peaches nationwide and created the famous Italianate "peach house buildings" that can be seen today on a walk throughout the Historic District.

When the C&D Canal opened in 1829, Delaware City was the site of the lock at the eastern terminus of the canal. Teams of mules and horses towed freight, passenger barges, schooners and sloops through the canal delivering cargo of practically every useful item between the Chesapeake and Delaware bays.

Loss of water in the locks was a constant problem, and eventually the canal was modernized and the locks removed, except the one in Delaware City. The new C&D Canal reopened in 1927, with the eastern terminus now two miles south of Delaware City.

Reference the marina listing tables to see all the marinas in the area.

POINTS OF INTEREST
1 Fort Delaware State Park
2 Diving Bell

SHOPPING
3 Crabby Dick's
4 The Imaginary Place Gift Shop
5 Delaware City Liquors

DINING
3 Crabby Dick's
6 Ice Cream Parlor
7 Olde Canal Inn
8 Kathy's Crab House

L LIBRARY

PO POST OFFICE

Of historic importance to Delaware City is Fort Delaware on Pea Patch Island. Pierre L'Enfant recognized the strategic significance of Pea Patch Island in 1819 when he recommended that a fort be built on the island to defend the cities of Philadelphia and New York. Several forts have been located on Pea Patch Island since that time.

In 1859, two years before the Civil War, wooden barracks were built on the perimeter to house the Confederate prisoners of war. A total of 32,000 prisoners passed through Fort Delaware; the last prisoner was released in 1866.

Fort Delaware State Park, located on the southern end of Pea Patch Island, is one of Delaware's first state parks, created in 1951. The northern end of the island is a bird sanctuary, recently recognized by the Audubon Society as a bird sanctuary of "continental significance."

Points of Interest: Clinton Street boasts antiques and gift shops, and Battery Park, on the Delaware River at the foot of Clinton Street, is a great spot for photographers, offering a picturesque view of Pea Patch Island, the New Jersey shoreline and a broad expanse of the river. The historic Diving Bell and the restored stonewalled lock from the original C&D Canal are also located here.

Fort Delaware State Park (302-834-7941) is open to the public on Saturdays and holidays from the last weekend in April through the last weekend in September. Access is by ferry and regular service is provided at to Pea Patch Island from 11:00 a.m. to 6:00 p.m. Call or go on line (www.destateparks.com) to make reservations. Pea Patch Island is also the site of a 90-acre nesting ground for 9 different species of birds. It is believed to be the largest heron rookery in the northeastern United States. More than 7,000 pairs of wading birds, including herons, egrets and ibis, have been observed here.

There are two nearby golf courses (although transportation will be needed). White Clay Creek Country Club is at 777 Delaware Park Blvd. in Wilmington (302-994-6700) and Back Creek Golf Course is in Middletown at 101 Back Creek Drive (302-378-6499).

Shopping: The main street, Clinton is lined with shops. Visit the fun Crabby Dick's, 30 Clinton Street (302-832-5100) for food, gifts, hats, t-shirts and many other sundries, as well as The Imaginary Place Gift Shop (60 Clinton Street, 302-834-5000), a specialty and antiques store. Delaware City Liquors is at 76 Clinton.

Dining: The water front Crabby Dick's is also a full-fledged restaurant (302-832-5100) that is open daily and famous for its Sunday brunch. The Ice Cream Parlor can be found on Clinton Street, as can the Olde Canal Inn (302-832-5100), a historic country inn built in 1826 on the Delaware River opposite Ft. Delaware. There you will find fine dining as well as a casual tavern and waterfront deck. There are beautiful views and a number of historic sites are adjacent to the inn. Kathy's Crab House (302-834-2279) is located south on Canal St.

ADDITIONAL RESOURCES

- **DELAWARE CITY: www.delawarecity.info**
- **DELAWARE STATE PARKS: www.dnrec.state.de.us/parks**

NEARBY MEDICAL FACILITIES

Bayhealth Medical Center, 209 E Main St., Middletown, DE 302-378-1199, www.bayhealth.org

Christiana Care Health System, 13 Reads Way, Ste. 203 New Castle, DE, 302-327-3959, www.christianacare.org

Essington, PA

ESSINGTON, PA		Largest Vessel Accommodated	VHF Channel Monitored	Transient Berths / Total Berths	Approach / Dockside Depth (reported)	Floating Docks	Gas / Diesel	Groceries, Ice, Marine Supplies, Snacks	Repairs: Hull, Engine, Propeller	Lift (tonnage), Crane, Rail	Min/Max Amps	Laundry, Pool, Showers, Courtesy Car	Pump-Out Station	Nearby: Grocery Store, Motel, Restaurant
		Dockage					Supplies		Services					
1. Corinthian Yacht Club of Philadelphia	610-521-4705	100	RECIPROCAL PRIVILEGES			-	-	-	-	-	30/30	PS	-	R
2. Anchorage Marina	610-521-0660	60	-	15/200	15/15	F	G	I	E	-	30/50	LS	P	MR

Corresponding chart(s) not to be used for navigation. Internet Access Wireless Internet Access Waterway Guide Cruising Club Partner

See www.WaterwayGuide.com for current rates, fuel prices, web site addresses, and other up-to-the-minute information.

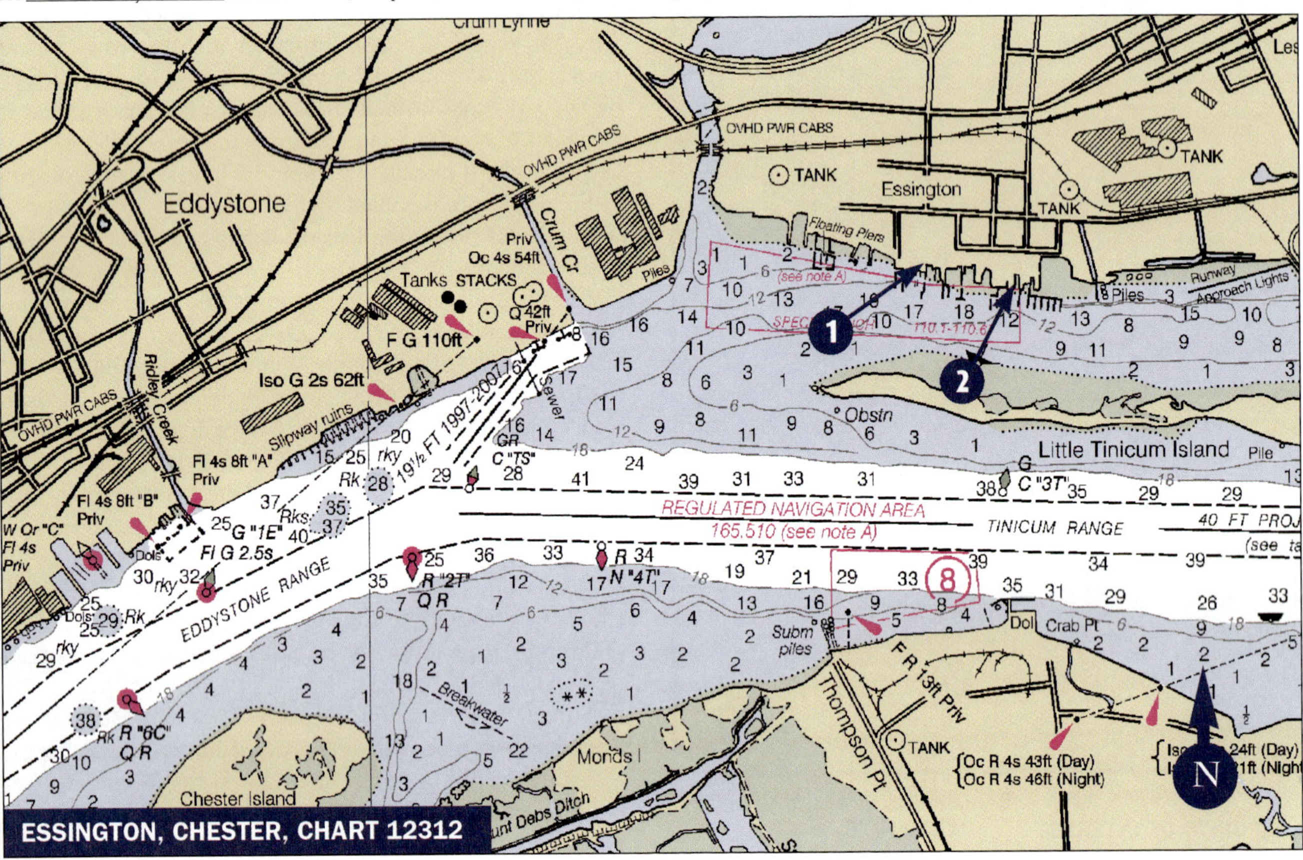

Pea Patch Island and Environs

Above Pea Patch Island, the Delaware River begins to turn industrial. Chemical plants, shipyards and refineries line the shores, while tugboats, tows, freighters and tankers are in the channel. In this area, recreational boat amenities are few, and those located on the Delaware River are not always well protected.

Opposite Pea Patch Island, on the eastern shore, stands Fort Mott State Park, with its abandoned fortifications. The dock is used for the ferry, which originates in Delaware City and stops at Pea Patch Island and Fort Mott from April until September. It cannot be used by recreational craft, but dinghies may still land on the sandy beach. Be careful of the old granite groins extending out into the water across the beach. Double-check your chart so you do not anchor in the underwater cable area between the mainland and Pea Patch Island. Mariners should not leave their anchored boats unattended. Tides, strong currents and large wakes from passing oceangoing ships make it vital that you properly secure your dinghy. Fort Mott may best be visited by car.

This historic area belongs to the state of New Jersey. Volunteers have restored the interesting fort, which stood in poor condition for years. A miniature version of the Washington Monument (shown on Chart 12311), which was near Finns Point, commemorates Confederate soldiers who died at Fort Delaware. Finns Point National Cemetery is only a short distance from Fort Mott. The U.S. government erected the 85-foot monument in 1910, featuring the names of 2,436 soldiers who died while imprisoned at Fort Delaware. A smaller monument for 135 Union soldiers was erected in 1879 and covered by a Grecian-columned cupola in 1935.

NAVIGATION: Use Charts 12311 and 12312. Above Pea Patch Island is Bulkhead Shoal. It is approximately three miles long and well marked with lights and daybeacons; but stay clear because parts of it are submerged at high tide.

The Delaware River is wide in this area, where currents run more than 3 knots on the ebb or flood, and strong winds can make the water rough. The Delaware River might have the worst collection of flotsam and jetsam anywhere, especially after a heavy rain. Everything from tree limbs and huge planks to refrigerators might be completely or partially submerged, so watch the surface carefully.

The Delaware River Memorial Bridge (175-foot fixed vertical clearance at center) crosses the Delaware River between Newcastle and Wilmington. On the New Jersey side is the huge DuPont chemical plant. Above the bridge, you can take the main channel by Wilmington and the Christina River, or leave the Cherry Island Flats to the west (port). Proceed past the marked auxiliary channel and return to the main channel before the Marcus Hook Bar.

Wilmington

This is a commercial area, but a short distance up the Christina River, providing protection from the currents on the Delaware River, you will find Up The Creek Marina and Restaurant, which can accommodate vessels up to 40 feet. While the approach depth is reported at 17 feet, the mean low water dockside depth is 6 feet. Upriver, beyond the second bridge (a swing bridge with a 6-foot closed vertical clearance), the Christina River's freight terminals give way to smaller industries and a hodgepodge of dilapidated docks. In this area, congested local traffic, deep water and poor holding ground make anchoring almost impossible. Fort Christina and the "rocks," which mark the original landing place of the Dutch-Swedish expedition of 1638, lie just beyond the second bridge. Here, you can see both an original sculpture by Carl Milles and an 18th-century log cabin.

NAVIGATION: Use Chart 12312. Upon reaching Marcus Hook (the Delaware-Pennsylvania border), be careful around the huge tankers loading fuel. Monitor VHF Channels 13 and 16 and stay clear as the ships maneuver in and out of the docks.

Marcus Hook

At the lower end of the Sun Oil Refinery on the western shore is the Delaware-Pennsylvania state line. The entire opposite side of the Delaware River and Delaware Bay is in New Jersey. You might see tankers in the anchorage area on the New Jersey side or docked at the refineries along the Pennsylvania side.

Chester, PA

This is the home of Scott Paper Company, and you can't miss its white water tower designed and painted to look like a roll of bathroom tissue. Helicopters are usually parked or hovering at the river shore near the Boeing aircraft plant. Pennsylvania Shipbuilding is also located here and might have a large commercial oceangoing vessel in dry dock.

NAVIGATION: Use Chart 12312. After crossing beneath the Commodore Barry Bridge in Chester (190-foot fixed vertical clearance), heading north, beware of the sandbar (Excelsior Bar) encroaching the channel on its southern edge off of Chester Island. Stay within the channel and run buoy to buoy through this area.

Essington, Little Tinicum Island

Essington is located six miles into Pennsylvania, north of Marcus Hook and Chester.

Dockage: You will find marinas, clubs and an anchorage sheltered from the ship channel behind Little Tinicum Island on the southern end. The private Corinthian Yacht Club of Philadelphia is here and offers reciprocal privileges to other yacht clubs. Call for details. Anchorage Marina sells gas and has transient slips on floating docks.

Anchorage: Enter from the southern end of Little Tinicum Island, because the area between Little Tinicum Island and the mainland is shoal and unmarked. The first building you will see is the Corinthian Yacht Club, but there are no slips here because the water is too shallow.

Drop the hook midway between the seaplane base and Little Tinicum Island in 15-foot depths with good holding in sand. Allow for 2-knot currents and a 6-foot tidal range. Buoy the anchor; reportedly, the bottom is littered with engine blocks once used as moorings. Note that this anchorage lies directly in the path of the main runway for Philadelphia International Airport. Stay near the western end of the island and show an anchor light at night.

North to Philadelphia

NAVIGATION: Use Chart 12312. **Use Philadelphia tide tables. Heading north, leave Little Tinicum Island to port, following the ship channel markers.** As you pass Little Tinicum Island, you will see the former Philadelphia Navy Yard, closed since 1995. This yard is now a state-of-the-art shipbuilding facility operated by Norwegian shipbuilder Kvaerner on the upper bank at the mouth of the Schuylkill River. The yard remains publicly owned, as Kvaerner signed a 99-year lease in 1998. Shipbuilding ended at the Philadelphia Navy Yard after World War II, but the yard is still being used for repairs and maintenance.

Be aware that a passenger ferry crosses between the Philadelphia Navy Yard and New Jersey. Past Little Tinicum Island, on the New Jersey side, are oil refineries and another part of the DuPont de Nemours Company. The Philadelphia International Airport occupies almost all of the Pennsylvania side as far as the Schuylkill River, where it has seemingly constant take-offs and landings.

Philadelphia

The city of Philadelphia, located about 35 miles above the Delaware River entrance of the C&D Canal, is an exciting and easy port for cruising boats to reach. The city offers something for everyone, particularly history buffs. The Philadelphia waterfront is an excellent central location for visiting Center City Philadelphia and the historic area. Also

Philadelphia, PA
Camden, NJ

PHILADELPHIA AREA		Largest Vessel Accommodated	VHF Channel Monitored	Transient Berths / Total Berths	Approach / Dockside Depth (reported)	Floating Docks	Gas / Diesel	Groceries, Ice, Marine Supplies, Snacks	Repairs: Hull, Engine, Propeller	Lift (tonnage), Crane, Rail	Min/Max Amps	Laundry, Pool, Showers, Courtesy Car	Pump-Out Station	Nearby: Grocery Store, Motel, Restaurant
		Dockage					Supplies		Services					
1. Philadelphia Marine Center	215-931-1000	130	16	65/338	30/10	F	GD	IMS	-	-	30/100	LS	P	GR
2. The Piers Marina (WiFi)	215-351-4101	70	-	6/110	35/5	F	-	I	-	-	30/50	LS	-	GMR
3. Penns Landing (Internet Access) (WiFi)	215-928-8803	165	16	/38	12/10	F	-	-	-	-	30/100	-	-	GMR
4. Wiggins Park Marina	856-541-7222	50	16/68	50/50	25/12	-	-	I	-	-	30/30	-	-	GMR

Corresponding chart(s) not to be used for navigation. Internet Access · Wireless Internet Access · Waterway Guide Cruising Club Partner

See www.WaterwayGuide.com for current rates, fuel prices, web site addresses, and other up-to-the-minute information.

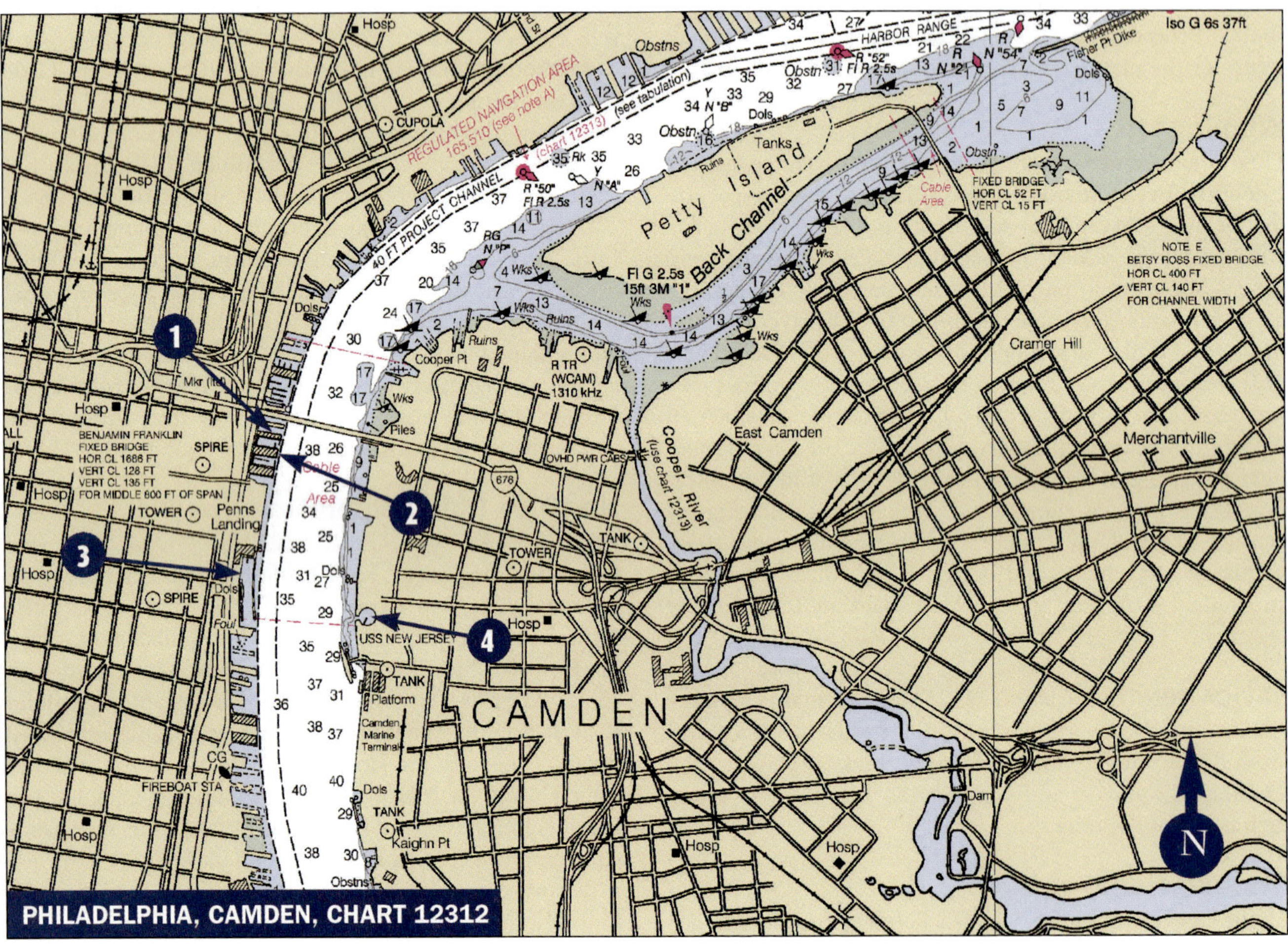

PHILADELPHIA, CAMDEN, CHART 12312

within easy walking distance is Society Hill, with a wide choice of shopping, sightseeing and dining opportunities.

Dockage: Several marinas in the Philadelphia area provide easy access to historic Philadelphia and the Camden Aquarium. As you travel upriver, the first marina on the Pennsylvania side is the municipal marina, Penn's Landing, which is easily identified by the outstanding collection of historic ships within the breakwater. The basin, 12 miles upriver from Essington and about three-quarters of a mile above the Walt Whitman Bridge (150-foot fixed vertical clearance at center), is just two blocks from the center of the Philadelphia Historic District.

Penn's Landing offers a number of floating historic attractions: the 344-foot *Olympia*, Admiral Dewey's flagship in the 1898 Battle of Manila Bay and one of the country's first steel warships; the 311-foot submarine *Becuna*; the magnificent barkentine, *Gazela*, of Philadelphia; the 101-foot *Jupiter*, a 147-ton charcoal iron tug dating back to 1902; and the Barnegat Lightship.

Between Penn's Landing and the Ben Franklin Bridge (135-foot fixed vertical clearance) is The Piers Marina, created by building a continuous breakwater across the openings of three old commercial piers. Entrance to the marina is after two right-angle turns through the breakwater. The marina has some transient slips on floating docks. A deli and restaurant are next door, and a motel is across the street.

Just above the Benjamin Franklin Bridge at Delaware Avenue and Vine Street is the Philadelphia Marine Center. Here, you will find everything: provisioning, sightseeing by horse-drawn carriage, car rentals, interpreters for foreign mariners and the customary cruiser amenities. The center operates a video scan of both basins and the Delaware River, and controls traffic lights at the exits of each basin. Red indicates river traffic; do not exit. On green, boats may exit, but they must head downstream before heading upriver.

Across the Delaware River from Penn's Landing, in Camden, NJ, is the Wiggins Park-Camden County Marina. Floating slips line the circumference of the circular-shaped marina, which offers water, electricity, 24-hour security and a picnic area. This attractive marina has hourly rates for those who would like to visit the battleship USS New Jersey and the Camden Aquarium, each just a short walk across the rolling lawns from the marina. The RiverLink Ferry System connects Penn's Landing and Camden, NJ, with boats leaving every hour on the hour (Penn's) or half hour (from Camden) during the season.

GOIN' ASHORE:
PHILADELPHIA, PA

From the moment you step off your vessel at Penn's Landing, the 10-block waterfront area where William Penn, Philadelphia's founder, first touched ground, you will feel a sense of awe. That feeling is not limited to first-timers visiting this "birthplace of democracy." There is actually much too much to see and do, even during a three-day layover. Most obvious must-sees are the Penn's Landing waterfront area, the Franklin Institute Science Museum, the Philadelphia Zoo and the Independence Seaport Museum. Some of these are outside of comfortable walking distance, but there is a metro station on Market St. for access to all the sites.

Just strolling the cobblestone streets of Philadelphia is enriching, full of big-city excitement and all within a square mile of the waterfront. Philadelphia is a family cruising destination of the best kind, made easier by the city's many pass programs, such as Philadelphia City Pass, that helps visitors hit the hot spots with just a single ticket. (See details at www.citypass.com/philadelphia.)

History: In 1681, as part of a repayment of a debt, Charles II of England granted William Penn a charter for what would become the Pennsylvania colony. Shortly after receiving the charter, Penn said he would lay out "a large Towne or City in the most convenient place upon the Delaware River for health and navigation."

Penn wanted the city to live peacefully in the area, without a fortress or walls, so he bought the land from the Lenape. The legend is that Penn made a treaty of friendship with Lenape chief Tammany under an elm tree at Shackamaxon, in what is now the city's Kensington section. Penn envisioned a city where all people, regardless of religion, could worship freely and live together. Having been a Quaker, Penn had experienced religious persecution. By 1682, the area of modern Philadelphia was inhabited by about 50 Europeans, mostly subsistence farmers.

Located on the banks of the Delaware River, Penn's Landing is just a few short blocks from Philadelphia's Historic District. Visitors strolling along the river can see many varieties of ships, old and new. *Photo courtesy of Edward Savaria, Jr.*

Extending northwest from City Hall, the Benjamin Franklin Parkway is lined with glorious fountains, flags from countries from around the world and a vast array of museums and libraries, all ending at the Philadelphia Museum of Art and the famous "Rocky" steps. *Photo courtesy of Edward Savaria, Jr.*

Penn also planned that the city's streets would be set up in a grid, with the idea that the city would be more like the rural towns of England than its crowded cities. The homes would be spread far apart and surrounded by gardens and orchards. The city would grant the first purchasers, the landowners who first bought land in the colony, land along the river for their homes. The city, which he named Philadelphia (philos, "love" or "friendship," and adelphos, "brother"), would have a commercial center for a market, state house and other key buildings.

"Philadelphia Freedom" (Elton John) and "Streets of Philadelphia" (Bruce Springsteen) were tributes to the city, and of course, who could forget Rocky Balboa's (from the movie "Rocky") victory sequences up the steps of the Museum of Art? Now, in a case of life imitating "art," tourists visiting the museum may pose with a bronze statue of the hero.

Points of Interest: Philadelphia's attractions, like those of any major city, are too numerous to all be mentioned. Two of the most popular outdoor venues are Penn's Landing on the Delaware River with the World Sculpture Garden, celebrating the quincentennial (600 years) of Columbus' arrival in America; and The Great Plaza, an amphitheater overlooking the Delaware River that contains a historical account of Philadelphia's waterfront history. An obvious attraction is Independence National Historic Park, where one can see the Liberty Bell and Independence Hall. Stop by the Visitors Center there for brochures and information. A walking tour of the numerous historic churches throughout the city is also a pleasant diversion.

The Independence Seaport Museum (211 South Christopher Columbus Blvd., 215-413-8655), which celebrates Philadelphia's maritime history, is located in a waterfront educational and cultural center on the Delaware River. Other popular museums (located farther out) are the Franklin Institute Science Museum (222 North 20th St., 215-448-1200), which focuses on science education; and The Academy of Natural Sciences, the oldest natural science research institution in the U.S. (founded in 1812). Philadelphia also has an amazing assortment of small, single-interest museums, such as the Edgar Allan Poe National Historical Site (7 Spring Garden St., 215-597-8780), the Mummers Museum (1100 South 2nd Street, 215-336-3050), the Insectarium (8046 Frankford Ave., 215-335-9500), and the Please Touch Museum (4231 Avenue of the Republic, 215-581-3181). All of these require transportation; the Betsy Ross Museum (239 Arch St., 215-629-4026), however, is located in the historic district.

Philadelphia boasts a wealth of art, culture and performing arts companies. There are numerous art galleries and museums; The Philadelphia Museum of Art (26th Street and Benjamin Franklin Pkwy. (215-763-8100) and the National Constitution Center (525 Arch St., 215-409-6600), with a live performance of "Freedom Rising", are two of the locations that deserve to be on your must-see list.

If you prefer to visit with nature, the Adventures Aquarium, featuring nearly 200,000 square feet of sea life and wildlife, is located nearby in Camden, NJ. (Round trip waterfront transportation is available at a nominal cost. Call 856-365-3300 for more information.) The Philadelphia Zoo (3400

INFORMATION
1 Visitors Center

POINTS OF INTEREST
2 Liberty Bell/Independence Hall
3 Independence Seaport Museum
4 Franklin Institute Science Museum
5 Academy of Nat. Sciences
6 Betsy Ross Museum
7 Philadelphia Museum of Art
8 National Constitution Center

SHOPPING
9 Italian Market

DINING
10 DiNardo's Famous Crabs
11 Q BBQ & Tequila
12 Marmont Steakhouse & Bar
13 City Tavern
14 Chart House Restaurant

PO POST OFFICE

RX PHARMACY

M METRO

Reference the marina listing tables to see all the marinas in the area.

West Girard Ave., 215-243-1100) is a 42-acre Victorian garden with more than 1300 animals, many of them rare and endangered.

For a different kind of nature visit, check out Golf Philly at www.golfphilly.com or play a round at Cobbs Creek Golf Club at 7200 Lansdowne Ave. (215-877-8707).

Special Events: One of the most famous annual events is the Mummers Parade on New Year's Day. (See www.phillymummers.com.) Troupes of actors spend many months preparing elaborate costumes and moveable scenery and practicing moves specific to them. They compete in four categories: comics, fancies, string bands, and fancy brigades.

Shopping: Philadelphia offers endless shopping (with no tax on clothes) that can mostly be found within the compact downtown places, most of which are within a short walk or cab ride from the Pennsylvania Convention Center and any downtown hotel. Center City contains many famous stores as well as boutiques. If your shopping likes tend toward cookery, visit the 9th Street Italian Market in South Philadelphia, open every day except Monday from 9:00 a.m. Here, you will find everything, including cheese, fresh fish, flowers, coffee, spices, pasta, baked goods and much more.

Dining: The following is a list of some of the eateries that are convenient to the waterfront. There are many more selections in the city center or on the Schuylkill River side of the city. DiNardo's Famous Crabs (312 Race St., 215-925-5115) has been serving up the blue crustaceans for 35 years. Q BBQ & Tequila serves barbecue in North Carolina, Memphis or Kansas City style sauces (207 Chestnut St., 215-625-8605). Marmont Steakhouse and Bar is Olde City's only steakhouse (222 Market St., 215-923-1100), serving steaks, salads and homemade desserts. City Tavern's menu is a reflection of 18th century cooking and recipes (138 S 2nd St., 215-413-1443). It is a unique experience to eat in a tavern that has been in operation since the First Continental Congress. The Chart House chain of restaurants also has a representative on the water at Penn's Landing along with several other restaurants (555 S. Columbus Blvd., 215-625-8383). For a unique and elegant experience, the Moshulu, a 294-foot sailing vessel launched in 1904, is permanently docked as a restaurant and bar at Penn's Landing on the Delaware River.

ADDITIONAL RESOURCES

- **OFFICIAL PHILADELPHIA VISITOR SITE: www.visitphilly.com**
- **CENTER CITY PHILADELPHIA: www.centercityphila.org**
- **CITY PASS: www.citypass.com**
- **PHILADELPHIA CHAMBER OF COMMERCE: www.greaterphilachamber.com**

NEARBY MEDICAL FACILITIES

Thomas Jefferson University Hospital, 111 S. 11th St., Philadelphia, PA 19107, 215-955-6000
www.jeffersonhospital.org

Pennsylvania Hospital, 800 Spruce St., Philadelphia, PA 19107, 215-829-3000, www.pennhealth.com

Dredge Harbor, NJ

DREDGE HARBOR, NJ		Largest Vessel Accommodated	VHF Channel Monitored	Transient Berths / Total Berths	Approach / Dockside Depth (reported)	Floating Docks	Gas / Diesel	Groceries, Ice, Marine Supplies, Snacks	Repairs: Hull, Engine, Propeller	Lift (tonnage), Crane, Rail	Min/Max Amps	Laundry, Pool, Showers, Courtesy Car	Pump-Out Station	Nearby: Grocery Store, Motel, Restaurant
		Dockage					Supplies		Services					
1. Riverside Marina and Yacht Sales (Wireless Internet Access)	856-461-1077	90	-	12/400	6/10	F	GD	M	HEP	L40	30/50	S	P	GR
2. G. Winter's Sailing Center Marina	856-461-3555	55	-	10/400	5/6	F	GD	M	HEP	L100, R	30/30	S	P	GMR
3. Clarks Landing Marina (Internet Access)	856-461-2700	50	69	6/300	6/6	F	-	IMS	E	L	30/50	PS	P	R
4. Dredge Harbor Boat Center, LLC	856-461-1194	55	-	/250	4/3	F	GD	IMS	HEP	L25	50/50	PS	P	GR

Corresponding chart(s) not to be used for navigation. Internet Access · Wireless Internet Access · Waterway Guide Cruising Club Partner

See www.WaterwayGuide.com for current rates, fuel prices, web site addresses, and other up-to-the-minute information.

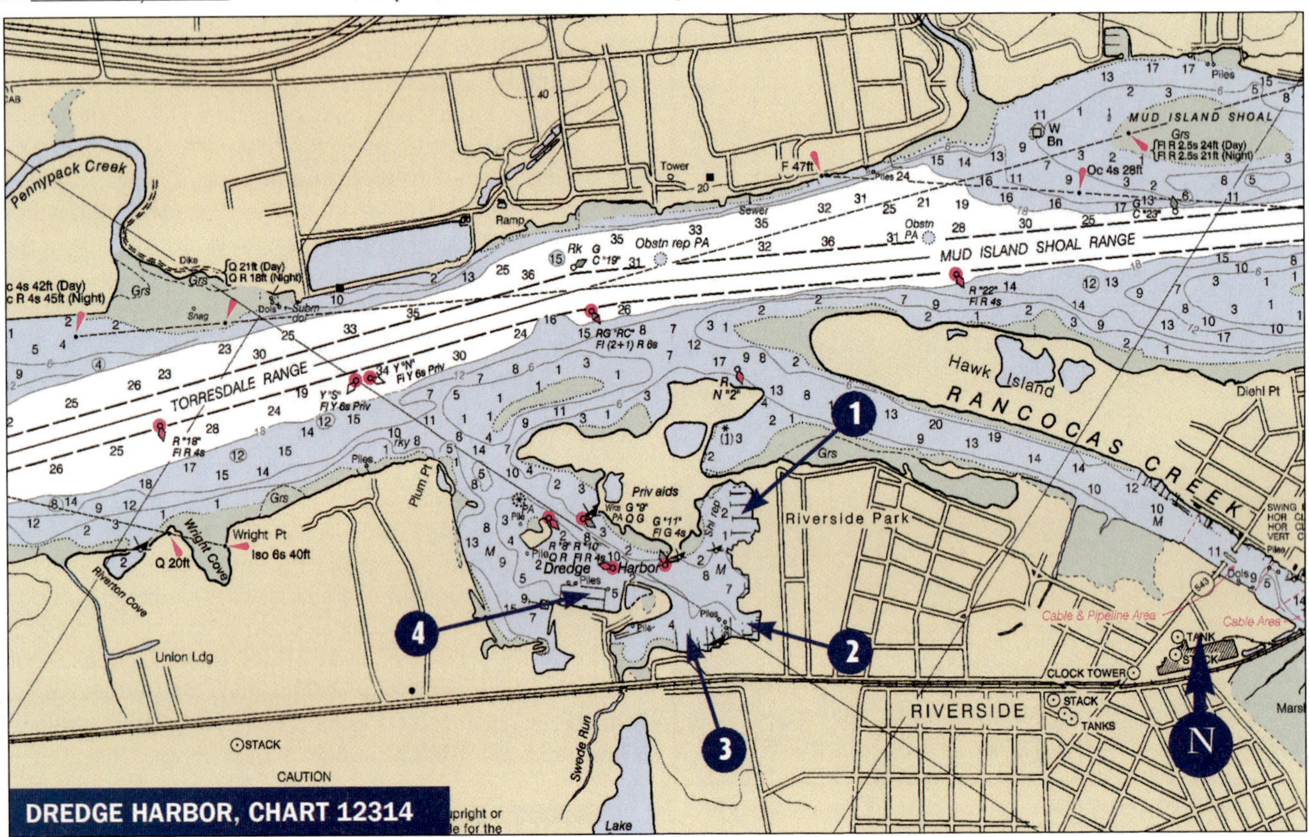

DREDGE HARBOR, CHART 12314

Above Philadelphia

NAVIGATION: Use Charts 12312 and 12314. When leaving Philadelphia, you pass under the Tacony Palmyra Bascule Bridge (50-foot closed vertical clearance). If your boat's height requires the bridge to open, the Coast Guard requests that you plan your passage to avoid the morning and evening rush hours.

Above Philadelphia, the Delaware River seems less industrial for a few miles. You will see homes and more frequent recreational boat amenities, most of them with moorings and launch services.

Dockage: Dredge Harbor, on the New Jersey side of the Delaware River about eight miles above the Benjamin Franklin Bridge, has several marinas and a large selection of small-craft services and facilities: fuel, supplies, haul-out, repairs, marine hardware, canvas work and more. The entrance is adequate if you stay in the channel. Dockage here provides a refuge from the noise and congestion of air traffic, and public transportation to Philadelphia is quick and easy. Marinas include Riverside Marina and Yacht Sales, G. Winter's Sailing Center Marina, Clarks Landing Marina and Dredge Harbor Boat Center. All have some transient space and offer boat repairs. Fuel is available as well. If you plan to stop overnight, it is a good idea to make advance reservations.

Anchorage: Slightly north of Philadelphia, anchorage is available behind Petty Island on the New Jersey side. No service is provided for going ashore here, and shoaling has been reported. Stay in mid-channel and anchor off Pine Point Park.

A good place to drop the hook is just inside Rancocas Creek, upriver from Philadelphia and Dredge Harbor on the New Jersey side. Be aware of the current and do not anchor in the channel. Another anchorage possibility is available by crossing the Delaware River to Poquessing Creek (west of Mud Island Shoal). Drop the hook in 10-foot depths. Both of these anchorages are favorites of local boaters seeking quiet evenings amid rural surroundings. A third anchorage, Neshaminy Creek, holds 7- to 8-foot depths and is located on the New Jersey side in Croydon.

Upriver to Trenton

The Delaware River is navigable 30 miles upriver from Penn's Landing in Philadelphia to Trenton, New Jersey's capital. Hospitable ports of call can be found at Burlington, about seven miles beyond Dredge Harbor, and for shoal-draft boats, the yacht club at Bordentown is eight miles farther up and four miles short of Trenton. The yacht club has reciprocal club privileges, but even powerboats need half tide or better to get in. The upper Delaware River, once serene most of the way from Philadelphia to Trenton, is now nearly as industrial as the lower river.

NAVIGATION: Use Chart 12314. The trip up the Delaware River can be an arduous one, with 8-foot tides and currents up to 2 knots. In the upper parts of the Delaware River's navigable waters, freshets (a rise or overflowing of a stream caused by heavy rains or melted snow) can raise river levels considerably, so bridgeboards and abutments to the bridges should be checked for actual clearance before committing to a passage. During March and April, freshets can cause the river to rise to 10 to 20 feet above mean low water at Trenton, and heavy summer rainstorms can cause a 9-foot rise.

Burlington, one of New Jersey's oldest towns, rivaled New York and Boston as a seaport in the 1740s and was the home of James Fenimore Cooper and 1812 naval hero, James Lawrence. Their houses stand side by side on South High Street and are open to the public.

About six miles above Burlington, you can visit Pennsbury Manor, a reconstruction of William Penn's riverside estate. Anchor off the estate, and take the dinghy in. Just viewing the little barge that he was rowed to and from Philadelphia in is worth the trip.

Anchorage: Farther up, about nine miles below Trenton, is a cove at Florence Bend known variously as Warner Cove, Tullytown Cove or PPI Cove (from letters on a nearby chimney). It is a popular local anchorage protected from traffic. Local knowledge claims 6 feet at the entrance and from 16 to 18 feet inside, but take your time and sound your way in.

At Bordentown, you are at the Delaware River end of the old Delaware and Raritan Canal. Until 1932, it provided an inland passage to the Raritan River and New York Bay.

Trenton

NAVIGATION: Use Chart 12314. Watch carefully for rocks about a quarter to a half-mile beyond the Trenton Marine Center. These rocks are not visible at high tide and have surprised many unsuspecting transients and locals. Trenton Marine Center is a storage and parts facility.

C&D Canal

Our coverage now continues west along the C&D Canal towards one of the world's great cruising grounds: the Chesapeake Bay. If you are cruising through the Bay to points beyond, see "Passing Through the Bay" in Chapter 2. ■

Waterway Guide advertising sponsors play a vital role in bringing you the most trusted and well-respected cruising guide in the country. Without our advertising sponsors, we simply couldn't produce the top-notch publication now resting in your hands. Next time you stop in for a peaceful night's rest, let them know where you found them—Waterway Guide, The Cruising Authority.

Waterway Guide is always open to your observations from the helm. Email your comments on any navigation information in the Guide to: editor@waterwayguide.com.

The Delaware River Bridge, AKA Trenton Makes Bridge. *Photo courtesy Mercer Regional Chamber of Commerce.*

Trenton
Philadelphia
Susquehanna River
Havre de Grace
Chesapeake City
C&D Canal
Middle River
Georgetown
Sassafras River
Baltimore
Patapsco River
Chestertown
Rock Hall
Magothy River
Severn River
Chester River
Annapolis
South River
West River
Delaware Bay
Cape May
Washington D.C.
Eastern Bay
St. Michaels
Easton
Alexandria
Deale
Oxford
Cape Henlopen
Lewes
Rehoboth Beach
Rehoboth Bay
Choptank River
Cambridge
Calvert Cliffs
Patuxent River
Nanticoke River
Salisbury
Solomons
Ocean City
St. Marys City
Potomac River
Point Lookout
Smith Point
Tangier Sound
Crisfield
Chincoteague Bay
Chincoteague
Reedville
Tangier Island
Rappahannock River
Irvington
Urbanna
Onancock
Atlantic Ocean
Deltaville
York River
Mobjack Bay
Chesapeake Bay
Cape Charles
Williamsburg
Yorktown
James River
Hampton
Cape Henry
Norfolk
Portsmouth
Virginia Beach
N
DOZIER'S WATERWAY GUIDE
THE CRUISING AUTHORITY
www.WaterwayGuide.com
Skipper's Handbook
GPS Waypoints 48
Tide Tables 50

Chesapeake Bay

Chesapeake Bay is many things to many people—a world-renowned cruising ground, an environmental wonder, a historic region and a natural habitat. It is an important cruising and shipping area, and an important link in the Intracoastal Waterway (ICW) between the Chesapeake and Delaware Canal to the north, and the bustling naval port of Norfolk to the south. It provides protected and semi-protected waters with endless miles of highly inviting tributaries in which to relax amid natural surroundings, wildlife and a wide variety of marinas.

The name itself is derived from the Indian word Chesepioc, which early settlers took to mean "Great Water." With approximately 11,000 miles of shoreline (the distance from Chesapeake Bay to Japan) winding along countless rivers, streams, bays and sounds, the Bay provides an endless variety of lifestyles, cultures and cruising characteristics. The Bay's watershed covers some 64,000 square miles in six states: New York, Pennsylvania, Delaware, Maryland, West Virginia and Virginia. This vast area is bound on the north by the Susquehanna River's headwaters (in south-central New York), on the west by the Appalachian Mountains and on the south by the uppermost reaches of the James River and the other tributaries of the lower Bay.

The Bay stretches some 200 miles, north to south, from the Elk River in Maryland to the Atlantic Ocean outlet between Cape Henry and Cape Charles in Virginia. At its widest point, near the Maryland-Virginia border at the Potomac, the Bay is nearly 30 miles across. At its narrowest point on the upper Bay, it is less than three miles wide. Today, Chesapeake waters and its tributaries cover an area of roughly 4,500 square miles.

The Chesapeake itself is an estuary—a body of water in which fresh river water mixes with salty ocean water. The Bay, in fact, is the largest estuary in the United States and one of the largest in the world. More than 150 rivers, creeks and streams provide freshwater. Fifty are considered major tributaries, and five of the Bay's biggest rivers—the Susquehanna, Potomac, Rappahannock, York and James—provide about 90 percent of the Chesapeake's freshwater.

The Bay's long, narrow contours, and its deep channel encourage a healthy circulation—both horizontally and vertically—of salt and freshwater. These waters with lower salinity than the adjacent ocean are brackish waters and are an immense natural resource. The level of salinity varies greatly on the Bay. At its juncture with the Atlantic Ocean, salinity levels match the ocean salinity 3.5 percent; in the extreme northern Bay, the water is fresh and salinity levels are less than 0.3 percent. Aquatic life in the Chesapeake takes full advantage of the unique conditions brought about by this brackish interplay, particularly the blue crab, which relies on a salt-water-freshwater circulation pattern in order to thrive.

History

On one level, the Bay is actually the Susquehanna River (whose mouth opens into the Chesapeake near Havre de Grace, MD) flooded by ocean waters that rushed in at the end of the last Ice Age, until the Bay, as we know it, came to be about 3,000 years ago. Susquehanna waters once filled the deeper parts of the Bay, along its north-to-south centerline, running to the sea; the parts of the Bay that are shallow today were once exposed coastal plains.

The earliest evidence of life in the Chesapeake region dates back some 1.3 billion years, but that life was in no way bipedal. The first humans appear to have arrived in Bay Country about 12,000 years ago, when the American Indian culture flourished in the region, mostly as nomadic tribes. About 1,000 years ago, these people began cultivating crops and settling towns throughout the Bay's watershed. They knew then what a lot of cruising boaters do now: This is one special and wondrous body of water.

About 500 years after Indian settlement of the region, the Europeans came calling, starting with the fleeting explorations of Spaniard Vicente Gonzalez in 1561. After failing to colonize the region, the Spanish left for good in 1571, but French and then English explorers arrived close behind them. The most famous and successful among the latter was Capt. John Smith, who thoroughly charted the Bay and its tributaries and led the 1607 founding of Jamestown—the first permanent English settlement in America—on the James River.

Chesapeake Weather

While the Bay tends to be hospitable to boaters, and the weather cooperative, conditions can change rapidly. With an average depth of 21 feet, the Chesapeake can kick up a short, stiff chop when wind speeds climb over 15 knots, although safe, protected hurricane holes abound. Spring and early summer are usually mild, with southerly winds and moderate rainfall. Calms are common, especially at night and in early morning; winds tend to pick up in the afternoon. In the upper Bay, July and August are generally hot and humid, with little wind found on open water. In the lower Bay, July and August are also hot and humid but continue to have delightful breezes in the more open creeks and open water of the Bay. Thunderstorms are frequent in summer as well, most often occurring in the late afternoon. Most last only a half-hour or so, but they can blow up quickly and line squalls moving across the Bay sometimes accompany them. Line squalls portend bursts of weather; sailors should drop all canvas and wait for the squall to pass.

Fall cruising lasts into November, with moderate temperatures, clear air, steady breezes, fewer boats and lovely fall foliage. The occurrence of hurricanes on the Bay during the fall months is rare, although the effects of hurricanes churning to the southeast are rather common. Again, hurricane holes are also common on the Chesapeake. During the autumn and winter months, northerlies occur with regularity and usually last a few days. Normally, they come from the northwest, swing to the northeast and, after a period of calm, southwest winds follow. Cruising the Bay is more challenging between December and February, as long stretches of below freezing temperatures are not uncommon. Most folks "winterize" or haul their boats out for the winter.

Navigating the Bay

Other than weather, the Bay can provide another challenge: shallow water. Generally depths are more than adequate for cruising boats. The Bay is well marked, and avoiding shoals is normally only a matter of following your chart and following this Guide. However, shoals can shift unpredictably following storms, and this problem is especially acute in dredged channels exposed to long wind fetch, as well as side creeks and coves otherwise suitable for anchorage. In many exposed channels, dredging simply does not keep up with shoaling. Charted soundings may or may not accurately reflect bottom conditions. For all passages off the major channels (where the charted water is blue), boaters should proceed with special caution in accordance with their boat's draft. One rule of thumb for avoiding shoals is to stay off points of land, as these points usually continue into the water. On rivers, the deepest water is generally found on the outside of bends where currents tend to scour the bottom.

On a positive note, the bottom in the Chesapeake is soft, usually sand, mud or a mixture of the two. The hardest bottom you are likely to encounter is hard-packed sand. Rocks are almost nonexistent. Also, currents are minimal compared to other areas of the coast, averaging less than a knot. The strongest currents usually occur in the upper rivers, as do the greatest tidal ranges, which can exceed three feet. On the Bay itself, the tidal range averages about 18 inches on the lower Bay and increases to about 30 inches on the upper reaches.

To Run Fast or to Gunkhole

Fast boats can run the entire Bay, from north to south, with perhaps one overnight stop. Some even manage this 200-mile journey in a single run, but why would you? Chesapeake Bay is a world-renowned cruising destination. We see "Loopers" doing the Bay in a few days, and opining "This area is so lovely, we cannot wait to come back and spend some time here." Snowbirds often rush through headed south or north, always wishing they had more time here. The typical cruiser with a little time on their hands, however, should take advantage of the Chesapeake's opportunities for exploration. You are here now! Explore, investigate and enjoy the Bay. If time permits, boaters lucky enough to cruise the region should savor the Bay's numerous port towns, winding tributaries and broad rivers. You can often draw a 25-mile radius around wherever you are and find a hundred anchorages.

Running at Night

Running the Bay at night is not difficult under good weather conditions, since aids to navigation tend to be well lighted, and fish traps no longer present the widespread hazard they did back in the days when herring runs were big and profitable. (You will want to keep an eye out for crab pot floats while traveling under power, however; many parts of the Bay are peppered with thousands of them). The main shipping channel is fairly far away from the Bay's tributary entrances, so exercise special caution when entering rivers and creeks at night. Also, if running the Bay at night, watch for floating debris and reduce speed. The Bay is a major area for commercial shipping traffic, too, so special attention to large, fast cruising ships and tugs is a must.

Charts You Will Need

Running the Chesapeake proper is a fairly straightforward proposition, navigationally speaking. Staying toward the middle of the Bay, parallel to the major shipping channels, helps avoid any shoaling. But, of course, watch for the normal navigational markers and any obstructions they denote.

That said, all boaters should travel with a good set of up-to-date charts (or a chartbook), and pay special attention to them. If you are running up or down the middle of the Bay, you will want to have some overview NOAA charts onboard. Chart numbers that cover individual cruising grounds on the Bay appear at the beginning of the "Navigation" sections in this book where they apply, with the current editions listed.

NOAA Charts, Coast Pilots, Light Lists and *Local Notice to Mariners* are all available to view online or as complimentary downloads. See our Skipper's Handbook section in the front of this book for links to these helpful documents, publications and web sites.

The Delmarva Coast: An Alternative to the Chesapeake Run

Heading north or south on the Atlantic Ocean along the Delaware, Maryland and Virginia coasts represents an alternative run to the Chesapeake between the Chesapeake and Delaware (C&D) Canal and Norfolk. Weather, your boat's speed and draft, and your own schedule and interests will determine whether you choose to run outside along the Delmarva (Delaware/Maryland/Virginia) coast.

Bypassed by most boaters, the Delmarva coast is nonetheless an intriguing cruising ground. This stretch balances lovely resort towns to the north—such as Lewes, DE and Ocean City, MD—with the wild coastline to the south. Also, Delmarva's inlets, such as the one at Ocean City, harbor world-class sportfishing fleets that rove the Atlantic Coast for trophy fish like blue marlin and tuna.

Besides this outside run, Delmarva features the ultimate in shallow-draft cruising behind its barrier islands. The bays, cuts and rivers along this inside stretch are relatively wild and rarely explored by cruisers, primarily because depths are so shallow. The inside channel wends through marshes and dunes that also happen to be prime birding territory. Waterway Guide covers the Delmarva Coast in the chapter "Delmarva Coast: An Alternative to the Chesapeake Run." ■

Bay Distances (North to South)

The following table gives distances between points along the main channel down the Chesapeake Bay. Distances, both statute and nautical, are approximate and should be used for planning purposes only. Chesapeake City serves as Mile Zero for the Chesapeake in this table.

LOCATION	NAUT.	STAT.	CUM STAT.
Chesapeake City (bridge)	0	0	0
Turkey Point	10.5	12	12
Sassafras River	6	7	19
Worton Point	7	8	27
Brewerton Ch. (bell "2 BE")	11.5	13	40
Bay Bridge	9.5	11	51
Thomas Point Light	6	7	58
Herring Bay (gong "83A")	9	10.5	68.5
Choptank River (bell "78A")	12	13.5	82
Cove Point Light	10.5	12	94
Cedar Point (buoy "1PR")	5	6	100
Point No Point Light	10.5	12	112
Point Lookout Light	6	7	119
Smith Point Light	10.5	12	131
Great Wicomico (bell "62")	6	7	138
Rappahannock (nun "2R")	13	15	153
Wolf Trap Light	9.5	11	164
New Point Comfort Light	5.5	6.5	170.5
York Channel	8	9	179.5
Back River	5	5.5	185
Old Point Comfort Light	7	8	193
Norfolk/ICW Mile Zero	10.5	12	205
Rudee Inlet	28.5	33	238

Chesapeake Bridges: Radio Equipped

All bridges monitor VHF Channels 13 and 16.
The Spa Creek Bridge also monitors Channel 68.

EASTERN SHORE

WATERWAY	LOCATION	CALL LETTER
Sassafras River	Georgetown, MD	KYU 699
Kent Island Narrows	Kent Island, MD	KXE 254
Knapps Narrows	Tilghman Island, MD	KZA 868
Cambridge Creek	Cambridge, MD	KZA 695
Fishing Creek (U.S. 335)	Honga, MD	KYU 695
Wicomico R. N. Prong	Salisbury, MD	KZA 869

WESTERN SHORE

WATERWAY	LOCATION	CALL LETTER
Spa Creek	Annapolis, MD	KZA 871
Stony Creek	Riviera Beach, MD	KAJ 667
York River	Yorktown, VA	HPS 168
James River	Newport News, VA	KQ7 169
James River	Hopewell, VA	KQ7 167
Pamunkey River	West Point, VA	KQ7 168

Bay Distances (Port to Port)

The following table lists distances between popular Chesapeake Bay ports. All distances are approximate and should be used for planning purposes only. Your exact mileage will depend on the course you set, your boat and the prevailing conditions.

FROM	TO	NAUT. MI.	STAT. MI.
Chesapeake City (bridge)	Georgetown (bridge)	23	26
	Havre de Grace (N "18")	19	22
	Rock Hall (R "8")	43	49
	Baltimore Inner Harbor	45	52
	Chestertown (bridge)	70	81
Baltimore Inner Harbor	Georgetown (bridge)	39	45
	Havre de Grace (N "18")	40	46
	Rock Hall (R "8")	23	26
	Chestertown (bridge)	42	48
	Annapolis (city basin)	27	31
	St. Michaels (FLR "2")	45	52
Annapolis (city basin)	Georgetown (bridge)	44	51
	Baltimore Inner Harbor	27	31
	Chestertown (bridge)	35	40
	St. Michaels (FLR "2")	25	29
	Oxford (Town Creek)	32	37
	Solomons (Mollys Leg)	45	52
St. Michaels (FLR "2")	Baltimore Inner Harbor	45	52
	Chestertown (bridge)	30	35
	Annapolis (city basin)	25	29
	Oxford (Town Creek)	30	35
	Solomons (Mollys Leg)	45	52
	Crisfield (basin)	78	90
Oxford (Town Creek)	Baltimore Inner Harbor	52	60
	Chestertown (bridge)	49	56
	Annapolis (city basin)	32	37
	St. Michaels (FLR "2")	30	35
	Solomons (Mollys Leg)	35	40
	Crisfield (basin)	68	78
Solomons (Mollys Leg)	Annapolis (city basin)	45	52
	St. Michaels (FLR "2")	45	52
	Oxford (Town Creek)	35	40
	Crisfield (basin)	43	49
	Smith Creek (FLR "4")	30	35
	Windmill Point (basin)	56	64
Crisfield (basin)	Annapolis (city basin)	80	92
	St. Michaels (FLR "2")	78	90
	Oxford (Town Creek)	68	78
	Solomons (Mollys Leg)	43	49
	Smith Creek (FLR "4")	34	39
	Windmill Point (basin)	36	41
Smith Creek (FLR "4")	St. Michaels (FLR "2")	77	89
	Oxford (Town Creek)	56	64
	Solomons (Mollys Leg)	30	35
	Crisfield (basin)	34	39
	Windmill Point (basin)	42	48
	Deltaville (Jackson Creek)	44	51
Windmill Point (basin)	St. Michaels (FLR "2")	91	105
	Solomons (Mollys Leg)	56	64
	Crisfield (basin)	36	41
	Smith Creek (FLR "4")	42	48
	Deltaville (Jackson Creek)	7	8
	Mobjack Bay (R "6")	28	32
Deltaville (Jackson Creek)	St. Michaels (FLR "2")	93	107
	Solomons (Mollys Leg)	57	66
	Crisfield (basin)	37	43
	Smith Creek (FLR "4")	44	51
	Mobjack Bay (R "6")	25	29
	Norfolk (Sewells Pt.)	45	52
Norfolk (Sewells Point)	Mobjack Bay (R "6")	29	33
	Deltaville (Jackson Creek)	44	51
	Windmill Point (basin)	47	54
	Crisfield (basin)	71	82
	Cape Charles (basin)	28	32
	Onancock	63	72

The Chesapeake Bay

NAVIGATION TIPS

One of the many joys of Chesapeake Bay cruising is that it is relatively forgiving for many of the types of navigational errors that could be very serious elsewhere. As an example, most of the bottom is either soft mud or sand, and the few rocky areas that do exist are well charted. Usually, if you go aground, it is merely a matter of backing or kedging off, or perhaps waiting for the tide. This makes exploration of gunkholes much less risky. But complacency can ruin any good cruise and is never a good idea on or near the water.

Keep track of where you are, noting landmarks or buoys as you pass them by. Not only will this be of general help in normal navigation, it will be important if visibility becomes obscured in rain or fog, and may be critical if you suddenly find that you need assistance. Aids to navigation are occasionally changed in the Bay, both in characteristic and location. Also, with the large areas of heavy population, it is not unusual for the shoreline and structures or landmarks thereon to change significantly over time.

Shipping on the Bay

Many vessels use the Bay, so knowledge of, and adherence to, the Rules of the Road are important. Many of the other vessels are huge freighters, tankers or tugs with barges. They have very limited maneuverability, require a lot of room to stop or change course (if they can), and even a close passing can be dangerous because of prop wash and suction.

The larger ships do not always stay in the main deep-water channels. If it is safe to do so in your area of navigation, it may be wise to avoid those channels. Note, however, that you are more likely to run into crab pots or pound nets if you are not in marked channel areas.

Tugs will often have a barge in tow, sometimes attached with a long cable. Failure to recognize this and passing astern of a tug with a barge behind would likely be a fatal mistake. Be especially watchful of this when cruising at night. There are barges that are not adequately lit to be easily seen by a craft low in the water. If your boat is not equipped with AIS (Automatic Identification System) you can monitor ship traffic in real time at www.marinetraffic.com/ais if you can receive a WiFi or a cell phone signal.

NASA Image

Satellite image of the upper Chesapeake Bay. Photo courtesy of NOAA.

There are a few commercial fishing vessels that trawl long nets in the Bay. Probably the ones that you will most often encounter are the menhaden boats. At this time, menhaden seiners are not allowed to fish in Maryland waters, but if you are coming up to the northern Bay through Virginia waters, you should watch for them. Many of these are stationed in Reedville, just below the Potomac River on the western shore, but they range far and wide.

A plane will often be seen above spotting the fish, and when a school is found, these boats will swoop in. When they reach the school, they will launch smaller "purse boats" to spread out a huge net around the school and then encircle the school, ultimately closing the net around it so that they can be brought on board. These and other commercial fishermen can understandably become upset if the school that can make their day's pay gets away because a recreational boater decides to insist on some notion of right-of-way and forces them to head off.

Fish Traps

Along the shores of the Chesapeake and particularly in Virginia's waters, you may see long rows of stakes driven into the bottom with nets spread between. These are "pound nets." At one end there will be a circular arrangement of stakes. As fish swim along the bottom, they encounter the line of net, and then head instinctively for deeper water. It is at the deeper end of the net that you will find the stakes that support the circular nets where the fish are trapped.

These nets can be both a hazard and a help. Often they are not lit at night, and if you sail or motor into them, you will probably become seriously snagged in the netting or possibly holed by a stake. They are not supposed to be in the marked channels. The watermen who fish these nets will probably be more upset than you will be if you run one down because their repair involves a great deal of expense, time and hard labor. Some do use lights, but the markings are unreliable and varied. In other words, if you see one, do not pass between the stakes, as there will probably be heavy netting just below the surface. And if you are out at night, stay in water over 30 feet deep, and when nearer to shore stick carefully to the marked channels. One good thing about these, from the navigator's viewpoint, is that you will generally be able to assume that the deeper water is at the end with the circular stakes. These pounds are only fished for one season and then are abandoned. However, the stakes will remain, gradually falling into the bay for several years, so keep your eyes open for the unused pounds as well.

In other areas, such as on the Sassafras River, you will see floats coming out in a line perpendicular to the shore. These usually support netting called "fykes." These are used to catch catfish and other varieties of fish. The principle of these is somewhat similar to pound nets, and it is important not to run between the floats, as you will, in all probability, snag a net.

In Virginia waters you may see gill nets. These are nets strung between two floats. The nets catch fish by the gills as they swim through, and they are set out both commercially and by individuals for private consumption. They may be deep enough for your boat to pass over or shallow enough to ensnare you. It is wise to avoid passing between gill net floats. Often they are similar in appearance to some crab pot floats, but they are supposed to have stakes attached to them, at least several feet tall, with flags or other warning symbols.

Crab Pots

One of the most common navigational hazards on the Bay are the thousands and thousands of crab pot floats. In the spring when the water is cool, the pots are set in shallower water. As the water warms the pots are moved to deeper water, but are rarely set in waters over 25 to 30 feet deep. They are not found in the deep channels. A crab pot is a square trap made of wire similar to thick chicken wire with a bait section full of fish (as bait) and a funnel for the crab to enter. Once the crab enters the cage, it is unable to escape. The trap has a long line connected to a float to enable the crabber to find it and pull it up. The floats are various-colored buoys, usually with sticks through the middle. The colors identify the individual waterman. Be aware that the colors can range from bright white to blue or black, which blend into the water and are hard to see.

Watermen tend these pots, usually once a day, pulling them up, emptying and then rebaiting them. Once the pot is empty and rebaited, the waterman drops the trap over the side. Since the crabber's boat normally remains running slowly during the operation to avoid delays, an individual crabber's pots will often be in a line. But with the great number of crabbers in the Bay, sometime the pots are so numerous that you could almost step from float to float. Keep a sharp watch for these. If you snag a line, you can damage your prop or cutless bearing, and if you snag them on your underbody while sailing, you will probably have to dive down to free them.

There are also clam lines and oyster lines delineating where those operations are not allowed. Small floating white buoys with the words "Crab Line" or "Clam Line" written on the sides usually mark these "lines" and are hard to read until you are very close. They are subject to change for various reasons, including political reasons, and are not noted on charts.

Aids to Navigation

It is not unusual to see that the aids to navigation are changed from what has been charted on the Chesapeake Bay, as it is an area of high-use navigation. The Bay is patrolled and checked often, and there has been a general revamping of the aids to navigation in the area.

You may see many private aids to navigation on the Bay and its side creeks. Some of these are quite elaborate, carefully maintained, regulated and reliable. Others are no more than stakes in the mud or small Styrofoam floats put out by area homeowners. Particularly in Virginia waters you may enter a creek and see a myriad of white PVC stakes that appear to have no rhyme or reason to their placement. These stakes mark individual oyster leases and have little or no relationship to the water depth as a general rule you can run between them at will. Long-established private aids are sometimes noted on the charts (usually labeled "Priv or priv aids"" on the chart itself), but this does not ensure that the entity responsible for their maintenance is still there and doing their job. Consequently, as conditions change, these private markers sometimes are not changed. Sometimes a new stake will be pushed into the mud with the old one still remaining, and private floats can drag off station. Reliance upon private aids should be observed with great caution, as they can be quite misleading.

When you encounter a privately maintained aid to navigation, look first to see if it makes sense with regard to what the chart and your observations show. If local boats are in the area, see if they are following them. Look also to see if they appear to be fresh. A new stick in the mud or a clean white Styrofoam float is more likely to be in place than an obviously old one. If possible, ask somebody about the floats; most people in the Bay will be helpful and friendly. Never take private markers for granted and proceed with care.

Shoaling

There are some areas where the shifting of shoals is much more likely than others. Almost any time you are entering a creek or river mouth with a channel through shallows that are exposed to a long fetch, you should expect shoaling and proceed with the assumption that things have changed since the last chartings. Whenever there is sand or mud to wash around and whenever there are waves to do it, it will happen. An excellent example of this is the northern side of Kent Island Narrows off the Chester River, which must be dredged frequently.

Wrecks and Obstructions

The Chesapeake Bay has been subjected to the march of "civilization" since the Europeans first began their encroachments in the 17th century. Since then, boats have been sinking, piers have been built, then crumbled with age, and pilings have been driven and disappeared with the ages. Despite it all, this is still one of the finest places to cruise, but remnants of our incursions remain throughout the waters, as the charts constantly remind us.

You may see the wreck symbol up in an otherwise perfect cove. Often this means generations ago a boat was left there to die on the shore. Check along the marsh to see if this is not the case. The problem is that where they occur, the creek or cove is narrow, and the symbol covers the entire cove or channel when actually the "wreck" is just a few old ribs up in the marsh on the shore or in about a foot of water.

There are some areas where there has been a great deal of industrial waterfront use and development over the years, and you should be especially careful to avoid these symbols in these areas. A prime example is some of the areas in Baltimore (not the Inner Harbor) as noted in Chapter 5: "North East River to Magothy River" in this guide.

Power Lines, Above and Below

Because of the abundance of civilization around the shores, there are power lines throughout the Bay. Some are stretched overhead; some are laid or buried along the bottom. In either case, tangling with one can be fatal. Not only can it ensnare your anchor or entangle your mast, it can allow huge voltages of electricity to shoot throughout the boat, causing electrocution and usually fire.

The charts generally denote cable areas. In these areas, there is usually a sign on the shore at each end of an underwater cable so that you can know where it is. However, we have noticed places where there were no signs, or they were obscured. The best rule to follow is to never put the anchor down without first checking the chart (latest updated NOS chart) and then the shore to be sure you are safe. You will be checking the chart anyway to learn the contours of the bottom and to see if there is any information as to type of bottom. If there are signs, anchor well away from any line between them. If there is a designated underwater cable area and you cannot find signs, anchor outside of that area unless you have a certain local knowledge that nothing is there. Always assume that you might drag in a blow and give yourself enough room to do so without snagging a cable.

Overhead power lines are also a serious danger. We are all accustomed to seeing power and telephone poles and accustomed to proceeding under them as we travel ashore. If you are in a sailboat or any boat with high protrusions such as outriggers, you should never take clearance for granted. First, look up (sometimes a difficult habit to get into) to see if there are wires, and then check the charts for clearance. Wires often sag for various reasons, and even a close passing could allow current to jump to the metal bits of your boat.

Overhead lines are not only a threat crossing rivers and streams. Always remember to look up as well as around when you have a mast or other tall protrusion.

Bridges

Fortunately, there are not as many bridges to deal with in Chesapeake Bay cruising as there are in other areas, like the Intracoastal Waterway. When you do encounter one that must be opened for your passages, the sound signal is one long and one short blast on your horn. Most bridges stand by on VHF Channel 13, and that is the best way to communicate with them. You will then know whether they can respond, and they can advise you of any problems.

The vertical clearance of each bridge should be posted on a sign on that bridge. It is also noted on the charts, but these do not always reflect recent changes. We have attempted to note these as of our last visit or as charted, but be aware that they may be different.

Bridges often have schedules and restrictions, but these can change. Restrictions of schedules are usually posted on a sign on the bridge, but often the signs are obscured by weathering or have writing that is too small to read until you are too close for safety. Check ahead, or call on VHF Channel 13.

Duck Blinds

Duck blinds are essentially small platforms or shacks on pilings out in the water or along the shore. These pilings are often slender pine trunks, and the sheds that are perched upon them may be partially camouflaged with branches and reeds fastened about the walls.

They are built to hide the hunter who sits inside with shotgun in hand over looking a raft of decoys set in front of the blind by the hunters. They dot the shoreline and are sometimes noted on charts but are rather unreliable for navigational purposes. They are usually put up in a flimsy fashion, with no thought in mind for navigation, and they are maintained only if hunters want to hunt the current location, as opposed to somewhere else, next year. Some are solidly built, but this is not the rule.

Therefore, whenever you see reference to one, treat it with great skepticism. When you do see a duck blind or the obvious remnants of one, you can be fairly certain that it is in shallow water. Hunters usually build them on shoals extending off the shore (often off points) just before the water deepens. Therefore, if there is no other clue, this might be helpful in determining where the shoal ends. Do not anchor near one in hunting season (usually late fall and winter) if the decoys have been set. Shooting starts with first light.

River Navigation and Exploring

Among the many pleasures of Chesapeake Bay are rivers and creeks that seem to wind forever into countryside of fields and woods. The main rivers are well marked, but small tributaries are often not marked, or, if so, only with an occasional aid to navigation to show a particularly troublesome shoal. Landmarks for the underwater configurations are obscure at best. Therefore, to enjoy this aspect of Bay cruising, it is helpful to learn a few of the tricks of river navigation. These will not be applicable to all situations, and none are foolproof, but they should be helpful.

As you head up or down a river, try to envision what the water is and has been doing to the bottom over the years as it flows along. This can help you to guess where the deepest part may be. For example, if you see a point of land ahead and a cove opposite, you may assume that there is a shoal extending off that point, that the water as it passes around that point has been deflected some away from it and probably cut the deeper channel around the point into the curve of the cove on the opposite side. You will also know, however, that as it was deflected and cut the channel into the opposite bank, it perhaps toppled some trees into the river. You would not want to pass too close to the shores of that cove opposite the point.

If the river intersects a side stream, look for a bar off the entrance. This is particularly the case when the side stream has a significant flow of current.

If the river widens significantly, slow down and assume that it may shallow significantly. Narrow banks often mean deeper channels because the water has to cut deep to get through, but if the water's passage is very wide, it may be just spreading out with no really deep channel. Often, when you approach these spots, there are no natural clues as to where the channel is, but local people usually will have placed stakes to mark the deepest water. If there are pound nets, you can generally assume that the circled stakes are toward the deeper water, and if there are crab pot floats and you cannot see the pots, you will generally know that there is at least enough water to cover them and tend them (generally around four feet). Often a string of crab pots close to a shore will mark an area of deeper water, so you will not want to pass inshore of the line, but, again, there is no guarantee.

Always watch the surface of the water for signs of what is going on below. For example, a very shallow area may appear flat and motionless as compared to a deeper area. An upwelling of water may indicate an obstruction or shoal down below. Eddies in the current could mean the same thing or simply a change in the channel bed far below.

Any time that you are far upstream, and especially if the shores around or above are wooded, beware of stumps, not only along the shore, but also floating along or stuck to the bottom of the channel. Sometimes a large tree will fall in, start downstream and stick on the bottom, leaving only some swirls in the surface or perhaps a snag sticking up to mark its presence. If you see a snag, always assume that it is connected to something else below the surface. If you see any changes in the surface movement, assume that something is causing it.

Any time you see stakes in the water, try to figure out what they mean. They may just be marking oyster beds or something else that has no relevance to navigation. They may, however, be marking shoals or obstructions. Generally, if they are close to the shore, pass outside of them; if they are in the middle, approach cautiously.

Anchor Lights

Because of the heavy amount of commercial and pleasure traffic, you should be operating with the proper lighting configuration. It is always important to show an anchor light, which by convention and law must meet two-mile visibility requirements. There are many deserted creeks and coves where you would never expect to see anyone, until suddenly, around 4:00 a.m., a workboat, with a sleepy waterman, heads out from a little slip up in the woods. Even in so-called "designated anchorages," if someone can't see you and hits you, there may be substantial civil liability.

CHESAPEAKE BAY WEATHER

Bermuda Highs

A primary consideration for any cruise is weather. The "dog days" of summer (usually early to mid-July through mid-September) often bring many periods of flat calm winds, very hot, humid and hazy days and nights, punctuated by violent thunderstorms with winds and lightning. Often during the summer months, dense high-pressure systems will settle off the eastern seaboard between the east coast and Bermuda. These can affect the weather for weeks, causing extreme heat and humidity, stagnant air with little or no wind and haze. These are known as "Bermuda Highs."

Deserted beach at Fort Story on the Chesapeake Bay.

Fog and Haze

Fortunately, fog is not very common, although at times it can be a very serious problem, usually in the fall. Most often, it will be associated with warm moist air over colder water. Fog is usually predicted over VHF weather radio, and visibility can quickly become totally obscured. Pay attention to the weather and listen to the VHF. Fortunately, it seldom occurs on the crisp fall days for which the Bay is so well known and on which most people like to travel.

Dense haze can not only make it difficult to sight approaching thunderstorms, but also obliterate the shoreline and aids to navigation until you are quite close. This makes navigation tricky, causing many people without radar and GPS to become lost. This sort of haze can sometimes occur on hot muggy days, particularly when there has been a dense high-pressure system dominating the weather. These conditions can, even on a sunny day, cause you to be totally out of sight of land, even in areas where the shore seems very close on very clear days. This is especially dangerous when approaching bridges, markers and buoys, and other boats.

Thunderstorms

Chesapeake Bay thunderstorms should be taken very seriously. They come up rapidly, usually from the southwest, west or northwest and can contain damaging hail and deadly cloud-to-ground lightning, with strong winds. The storm and winds seldom last long, but they can be quite serious. Remember, if you can hear thunder, you can get hit by lightening!

Because of the sudden nature of the wind shifts and the fact that the wind may go from dead still to over 70 miles per hour very suddenly, most experienced sailors take down all their sails and motor into the approaching storm if they are caught out. A knockdown could easily occur in these conditions, even with fully reefed sail.

The weather stations on VHF radio usually issue watches and warnings, and the Coast Guard will also issue weather bulletins on VHF Channel 16 when these storms are approaching. However, you should always keep a weather eye. Hot, humid conditions are most likely to produce these monster storms, particularly if a cold front is approaching. Usually the sky to the west will begin to gray, sometimes becoming dull blue or copper in color. High towering cumulus clouds should always be watched. Often, on the days when the storms are most likely to occur, there is so much haze in the air that you can't see the changes in the sky. In these conditions, it is particularly important to listen for thunder, observe the sky closely and check the weather stations. If such a storm threatens, seek a safe anchorage or marina and prepare for strong gusty winds.

Tornadoes and waterspouts are rare occurrences in the Bay area, but they may be associated with severe violent thunderstorms and the systems that produce these storms. Any time that there is a violent thunderstorm watch, and any time you observe the conditions that create these storms, be also on a lookout for twisters. If you see one, report it to the Coast Guard, not only to alert others, but also to alert them to your position and situation. If you have not had the time to get in and are still on the water, take evasive action.

We are all familiar with cold fronts; we know that they can bring sudden shifts of very strong wind and preceding thunderstorms. Usually, we relax after they have blown through, knowing that there will probably be at least several days of cool, comfortable, stable weather. Enjoy these post-frontal days, but do not automatically assume that no violent weather can occur, and heed any sky and cloud warnings.

Hurricanes

Hurricanes are of concern on Chesapeake Bay, as is true of other areas. Storms have swept up the Bay in full fury, leaving incredible destruction. Numerous landmarks around the Bay were either formed or demolished by these storms. Fortunately, the Bay is usually spared the bad ones. Many times, as they move up the East Coast, they seem to become diverted by the shallows of Cape Hatteras, spending the bulk of their energy there, before visiting the Bay with milder remnants, often in the form of a tropical storm. Don't become complacent, because we never know what these storms are going to do until they do it.

Chesapeake Bay is full of very good "hurricane holes." The criteria for a good hole will vary with the type of storm you are expecting, the type of boat you have, your draft and whether you plan to tie up or anchor.

You will want a landlocked area because of the customarily reversing winds as the storm passes over. It helps to have high land around you; the higher the better. It is also important to get as far from the ocean as possible. There are many deep and long rivers with innumerable coves running up into the western shore of Maryland and Virginia.

Storm surge can be a serious problem, particularly if you have chosen to tie up. In the upper Bay, you are more likely to get a tremendously high tide rather than the wave-like surge often experienced along the coast. The height of the tide will depend on the wind direction and strength, and other factors such as whether the storm is coinciding with a full or new moon. VHF weather radio will issue regular hurricane bulletins, giving late-developing information on this and other concerns. During Isabel in 2003, the storm surge was six to eight feet above normal in the lower Bay.

The ideal hurricane hole will vary with different boats. The recommended holes are usually the first to fill up and therefore are often dangerous with overcrowding. All it takes is a few protruding docks to ruin an otherwise good spot. If you are expecting a blow, look at the charts, and read our descriptions of the area to help you decide what is good for your situation and time. Do not wait for the storm to begin before you find your spot! Start looking and settling at least a day or two before the expected hurricane landfall. Preparing for a hurricane takes a lot of work and time.

In choosing your spot, check the type of bottom. We have found that thick mud, preferably mud and gray clay, holds anchors the best. Mud and sand is our next favorite. It is usually better to put out two anchors because the winds will shift 180 degrees if the storm passes directly overhead. Many people will place two anchors against the first expected direction (usually easterly or some quadrant thereof because that will generally be the direction of the strongest wind). Then they place a third to hold after the wind shift with the storm passage. There are many areas where you can tie off to the trees on land, and this is what many people do.

Observe piers, pilings or other structures on the shore that could cause damage if you drag. Anchor in a place where if you drag in the time of maximum wind, you will drag into a forgiving bank rather than a bunch of broken pilings, for example.

Once you are secured to the bottom or shore, remove or tightly tie down everything that is on your deck that could come loose. If you have a leak around a window or port that you haven't gotten around to fixing, cover it with duct tape. If you don't, the driving rain will find it.

As you settle to wait for the verdict, you may want to help others coming into the anchorage, if they need and want it. No matter how well you have prepared, if your neighbor does a poor job and drags into you or your lines, you may be no better off than they.

In the fall and winter, the Bay is visited by the occasional nor'easter, a storm that travels to the northeast from the south with a precipitation pattern similar to a tropical storm. It can include heavy snow in the winter months.

Weather Reports

For 24-hour weather that will include special alerts and sometimes tide information, turn to the weather stations on your VHF radio. In the Bay, the working weather frequencies are found on Channels 1, 2 and 3 depending on where you are. Some cruisers rely on Smart phones or computers for instant weather information, but you cannot count on coverage everywhere, as these systems are optimized for land users.

Nothing beats knowledgeable observation with your eyes and instincts, and the use of a barometer. We would strongly suggest having a quality, working barometer and learning how to use it.

Best Times to Cruise

Some people feel that the best times to cruise the Bay are spring and fall. Cruising is great from early May to mid-June, and from mid-September to early November. A spectacular bonus in the late fall will be the turning of the leaves, and in the crisp, cold mornings, the geese will fly in formation overhead, calling for you to follow them south. Winds will often be easterly, particularly with the afternoon onshore sea breezes on the lower Bay. Cold fronts usually bring a day or so of preceding southwesterlies, then northwesterlies, sometimes clocking around to the northeast after the frontal passage. The north-south fetch in the Bay is quite long, and the seas can get very rough with these winds.

FLYING INSECTS AND OTHER HAZARDS

Insects

With summer weather, there will be more problems from mosquitoes, although boats anchored a hundred yards away from the shore are often free of these pests. Nevertheless, for those seeking the quiet anchorages close in amongst tree- and marsh-lined shores for which the Bay is so well-known, some preparation is in order.

Mosquitoes are only a concern in the warm months. The best way to handle them is to have screens on your hatches and portholes. Nothing can take the place of these. As a rule, the farther you are from marsh or marsh shoreline, and the more breeze you have, the fewer the mosquitoes. Close wooded or marshy coves in the hot season will always bring these pests. They will be the worst just as light is waning. You should also have a repellent spray aboard, particularly if you don't want to spend a beautiful evening cowering below behind screens.

Gnats and "no-see-ums" are also encountered mostly in the early evening on quiet, warm nights where there is marsh and woods around. Usually bug spray and normal screening will help.

Flies can be a problem anywhere, even far out in the Bay. Some even bite. Again, screens are the ultimate answer.

Stinging Nettles (Jellyfish)

Many consider stinging nettles to be the greatest nemeses of the Bay. Without going into the wealth of scientific detail that is available, suffice it to say they almost all sting, and they are seldom, if ever, found in the far upper Bay or rivers where there is fresh water. They usually abound around late-June until mid- to late-August, depending on rainfall and temperatures. Some "jellyfish" have long red or white tentacles, while "moon jellies" are round and white with short tentacles. Moon jellies have a clover pattern on their tops and, although they sting, it is very mild compared to its long-tentacled cousins.

In certain times and places, you will see nettles everywhere. An interesting and useful site that predicts the occurrence of sea nettles is chesapeakebay.noaa.gov/forecasting-sea-nettles. They can be so numerous that they can clog up the water intake of small diesel engines like those in generators. They will also quickly clog up water-cooled air-conditioners. Therefore, it is a good idea to install a long and wide strainer on the hull outside the water intake if you plan to run a generator or air-conditioning. If you wish to swim, there are nets hung from round floats that you can tie to your stern, forming a small but protected pool. (Pool loungers made of net with inflatable sides offer some protection as well.) Another way to enjoy the refreshing water is to sit in the water at the edge of a sandy beach. You'll be able watch for and guard against nettles.

Oyster Shells and Other Sharp Objects

Whenever you are swimming or wading, take care where you put your feet until you know what is there. The Bay is famous for its oysters, but these can have sharp edges that make dirty cuts subject to serious infection if you step on them. Usually they are in a "bed" and can be in water that is wading depth. Beware also of other sharp objects around populated areas. A thoughtless person could throw a bottle overboard that would lie in wait for years until someone stepped on it.

SEA CONDITIONS

Although normally placid, the Chesapeake Bay can be very rough, uncomfortable and even dangerous during the right conditions when the wind is from a long fetch. Much of the Bay is relatively shallow, and, therefore, the seas develop a notoriously short, steep chop that can be merciless. If the wind is off the land, as it often is, the opportunities for brisk, but comfortable sails are endless. But beware the northerlies and southerlies that can build seas from either direction with the vast fetch from which to work.

Areas of strong and/or conflicting current can make the worst waves. These are often found off broad points of land (Wolftrap Light in the lower Bay is a good example) and off the mouths of large rivers (such as the Patuxent or Chester). One of the worst areas is the large body of open water off the Potomac in the lower Bay.

One of the great things about the Bay is that if it ever gets too rough, there are almost always places to duck in and wait it out, either at anchor or at a nice marina.

CURRENTS AND TIDES

Compared to many other cruising areas, the Chesapeake Bay is mild-mannered in these categories. Tides range from around one to two feet, and currents are seldom more than one to two knots. But there can be significant departures from the norm relating to wind and weather, moon phase and location. As a general rule, the northwest winds that arrive with a high pressure area will drive the water from the Bay, and it is common to see the water depths one to two feet below the charted depths. On the other hand, the easterly winds that accompany low pressure systems will generally cause the tides to run a foot or more above normal tidal range.

Phases of the moon affect both the heights of the tide and, therefore, the strength of the currents. A full or new moon will bring the greatest extremes between highs and lows. Since there is more water moving during these times, there will be more current. The "rule of two" says that two-thirds of the water movement occurs during the middle two hours of the tidal cycle.

A base high and low tide for much of the southeast north Atlantic is that of Hampton Roads at the lower end of the

Bay. Tides for the upper Bay, however, are reported for Baltimore Harbor. Tides for different locations are given in hours and minutes before or after low and high tides there. Differences can be considerable, particularly as you move up the tributaries.

The time of high and low time doesn't correspond with the time of zero current. As a general guide, for most of the main stem of the Bay the tide floods for five hours and ebbs for seven because it is still essentially a river. The current flow will stop and change at different times in relation to the tide peaks, and this will vary with the wind and moon. The "Tidal Current Tables, Atlantic Coast of North America" will give the norms expected, but don't rely on this completely. Predicting when the current will reverse flow while going up or down the Bay or a long river, such as the Chester, can be important to a slow-moving sail or motorboat. It may be of interest to navigators that the crest of high tide is always moving up the bay at about 15 miles an hour. At any given time there are two high tide crests and one low tide trough (or one crest and two troughs) rolling northward up the bay. A north bound vessel capable of maintaining 6 knots through the water, departing harbor at the end of ebb tide can carry a fair tide north up the bay for 8 hours or longer. But if you leave headed north just after high tide, you will be fighting the southbound ebb for a long time.

There are some areas in the upper Bay where winds have more effects than in others. Kent Narrows immediately comes to mind. A strong northerly can make it seem as though the tide is not coming in. Areas such as the Sassafras River and the Elk River are two good examples. Obviously, a strong southerly for several days can pile the water up in these areas, causing tides to be higher than normal.

Tidal current tables and time differences for locations around the Bay are included in your Waterway Guide.

ANCHORING

Without getting into the eternal debate as to which anchor is best, it is wise to have both plow or CQR- and Danforth-type working anchors in the Bay. One or the other almost always works, providing you use the proper length and weight of chain.

The weight of the chain will help to set any type of anchor, causing the pull to be more parallel to the bottom rather than vertical, which will tend to pull the anchor out of the bottom rather than dig it in. A lot of heavy chain is important in areas where the mud is very soft. Some bottoms are so soft that nothing will work, but long chain will sometimes save the day with this type of bottom.

Sand can also be good for holding but not always. Some sand is too hard even for a Danforth-type to easily dig in, although often this type will work in hard sand when a plow won't.

Grass is seldom good. Worse, it can be very misleading. An anchor may bite hard at first, but in a blow, the roots will often give, a few at a time, until suddenly the last ones break, and you are sailing downwind with a clump of weeds. Fortunately, there is not much grass in most Chesapeake anchorages. Bottom mixtures are common. Shell and mud is found in many areas. Shells can occasionally catch on the points of the anchor, making it impossible to set. However, many small or broken shells evenly mixed in mud can make good holding. Sand and mud is generally a good mixture as well, but very heavy concentrates of sand may require a Danforth-type anchor.

There are several ways to find what may be down there when you can't see. One way is to dig up some bottom with your anchor and check. No one wants to do this on purpose, although it is what often happens when you drag on the first try. If you don't want to do this, first look at the charts. They sometimes give cryptic clues such all "stk" (sticky) or "hrd" (hard). (NOAA charts have abbreviation guides that may indicate a different code than that actually used.) This occasionally helps but take it as very general advice.

Also, look along the shore for clues. Often, for example, shells on the bank will indicate shell below. If the banks are marsh held in mud, with a fair current to keep the bottom free from mush, there may be good mud below. Quiet coves surrounded by beautiful forest often hold slime bottoms caused from years of siltation and decay with little cleansing current. The Chesapeake Bay has many such areas. Sandy beaches ashore with a gently sloping bottom indicated on the chart often means sand out where you wish to anchor.

Time spent in properly anchoring could save you from a miserable night, property damage and/or personal injury. Remember that the wind and weather can change. For example, if you are expecting a front or thunder squalls, be sure that your anchor is set from the direction of the anticipated strong wind, unless you are already experiencing strong winds from another direction. Also, anticipate where you will swing when the wind shifts. If it is into a bank, or into another boat or over their anchor rode (or your own centerboard), reposition yourself.

If your anchor does hold after backing, don't stop there, particularly if you expect any weather. Continue backing down with slowly increasing power on the engine until you are sure. This is done by taking a bearing with an object on shore to ensure you are not dragging. If your boat jerks a little when the line tightens and the stern swings around straight behind, you are probably in for the night. Once you dig in, you can relax, enjoy the evening, and hope that your neighbor upwind has done the same.

PROVISIONING FOR A CRUISE

Planning a cruise usually includes a great deal of provisioning, but one of the features of the Bay is that if you prefer not to do much provisioning, you can take advantage of the many special restaurants, festivals and shopping opportunities that abound ashore. Unless you plan to avoid civilization as much as possible, you should go ashore and sample restaurants here and there. You can plan your cruise so that you can find some sort of market or restaurant every evening, if that is what you want. What you bring and how much you bring will depend on your preferences and the type of boat and storage you have. If you do not have refrigeration, you will find ice in almost all of the marinas and markets.

CLOTHING AND SUN PROTECTION

In the summer season, you should be safe with light clothing, but in the fall or spring, the temperatures can range from very warm to very cold, and you should be prepared. Swimwear may be all you need for much of the cruise, even if you don't go into the water. Sunglasses and clothing to protect you from the sun are very important, as is foul weather gear. Most restaurants around the Bay expect boating clientele and understand that fine clothing and cruising do not always mix well. You will find excellent restaurants that are quite happy to have you without jackets and ties (but do remember to bring shirts and shoes).

FISHING

Whether it is trolling, bottom fishing or crabbing, the Chesapeake Bay has bountiful fishing. Both Maryland and Virginia require fishing licenses, but they can be easily obtained from many fishing centers and marinas on the shore. Fishing laws and rules change from year to year depending on depletion of the species and other factors. When you get your license, you can obtain a set of the up-to-date rules. If you plan to do any fishing, you can pick up information on the current rules from most marinas or fishing shops.

You can bottom fish with gear ranging from a line on a spool to elaborate casting equipment. Many pleasant hours can be spent just fishing off the bottom with bloodworms or crab parts on a hook. Spot, striped bass, perch, sea trout, cobia, flounder (along the bottom) and catfish will be some of your rewards.

Bluefish run in the spring and make great trolling game. They fight hard and, if you find a school in a feeding frenzy, they may give you an exciting time. These fish have a stronger taste than some others, but most love them.

There are numerous good fishing publications relevant to the Chesapeake. Most marinas and boating stores up and down the Bay will have other fishing information, much of it free.

CRABBING

Crabbing is, and long has been, the classical pastime of the Bay, as well as a major part of its seafood industry. It is the blue crab we are talking about, callinectes sapidus ("beautiful swimmer"). They exist up and down the East Coast, in the Bahamas and in many other places, but a true believer will tell you that there is nothing that can compare to the Chesapeake Bay blue crab. When you visit the lower Bay, you will surely not want to miss the Crisfield Crab Derby, held in September, where there are many events to celebrate this crustacean, including parades, crab races and crab-picking contests with a high purse and much honor. Anyone cruising the Bay should read and have along the book "Beautiful Swimmers" written by William W. Warner and published by Little, Brown and Co. This is a beautiful book about the blue crab and also the Bay itself.

You can tell a female from a male by the apron on the underside. A male has a pointed arrow-like apron, while the female's is rounded. An adult male is usually called a "jimmy," an adult female is called a "sook," and a young female is called a "sally." When the sook is ready to release her fertilized eggs, you will see an orange or orange-brown spongy mass of the eggs protruding from the underside of the apron. Some people then call her a "sponge crab." It is currently illegal to possess sponge crabs in Maryland.

How to Catch Crabs

If you are going on a cruise, you should certainly be prepared to do a little crabbing. All it takes is a string with a weight, a crab net and a chicken neck (or some other piece of meat). Tie the meat onto one end of the string and hang it overboard, letting it come to rest on or just above the bottom. When a crab comes calling, you will feel the string begin to tug and sometimes stream out as the crab tries to swim away with its feast. Begin to gently pull the string in when you feel the tug. If you jerk or pull too fast, the crab will know that something is wrong and swim off. When he gets near the surface, you will be able to see him hanging onto the meat.

This will be the time that you will be glad you left your net nearby because, without disturbing the crab that is happily munching below, you must get the net and dip under him. Dipping him up is not as easy as it seems. You can't just splash the net into the water and hope to be fast enough. Instead, you must slip the net silently into the water, moving it slowly up behind the crab. When you think you are close enough (but not too close because it will scare him), swoop the net in under him and pull him up.

If you think that's fun, more is to come, for now it can get really sporting. It obviously doesn't do much good to stand there with a crab in a net. You have to get him into the bucket so that you can go back for more. Some crabs will oblige nicely, but others will fight you. You may be able to turn your net upside down over the bucket, and he will drop in. But more likely, he will hang on for dear life while you to shake the net. He may eventually drop free, but never over the bucket! You might even think of reaching into the tangled mess of crab and net and pulling him out by the backfin, but beware...A mad blue crab is a creature to be reckoned with. If he isn't already holding onto a piece of your flesh with agonizing tenacity, he will back into a

Crab pots drying in the sun. Photo courtesy of Jani Parker.

corner when you drop him and raise his claws before his face with a clicking and clattering, leaving no doubt of his intentions should he get the slightest chance!

How to Cook Crabs

Once you have corralled the critters without getting wounded, you will want to cook them. When you have enough crabs (called a "mess"), put them still alive in a large pot, pour in a can of beer, sprinkle very liberally with Old Bay Seasoning, and steam. They may get a bit lively when you begin to cook. Sometimes it is best to put a weighted top on to prevent them from climbing out and escaping into the galley. It does sound unkind to cook them alive, but that is the way it is done and is an assurance of freshness. Never cook a dead crab and then eat it; they should all be alive when you steam them until their shells are red (about 20 minutes). Let them cool, spread some newspaper, and start picking!

Crab picking is one of the Bay's finest arts, but fewer people seem to know how as each year goes by. You can tell when a person isn't experienced by the amount of shell mixed in with the meat. Here's how to do it correctly: When the crabs are cool enough, pick one up and lift its apron (described above). Put your thumb under the top shell to lift off that top shell from the back edge toward the face. The shell and apron should come off in one piece. Then use your fingers to clean out the "dead man's fingers" (the gills). The "mustard" is the yucky yellowish stuff and white sacs that are found in the depression underneath the top shell in the middle. To some this is delightful, while others claim it is not to be eaten. The gills, under the shell on each side, are long, grayish-white, slender and pointed. On the western shore of the Bay, crabs are eaten by smashing them with a crab mallet, whereas on the eastern shore, they are picked skillfully using a knife. You can generally tell which side of the Bay a person is from by the method they use to attack a pile of steaming crabs. In either case, break off the legs at their joint with the crab body and set aside. Break the crab in half by holding a side in each hand. Next, either using your fingers or a small knife, break or cut into the shell, and remove the white meat from each compartment. The biggest compartment contains backfin meat, the choice cut of the crab. (Serious crab pickers use a knife to do this.) The large claws can be opened with a knife or a mallet. You can eat the crabmeat while you are picking them or save it to make into crab cakes, soup or dip. If you get good at it and can get the claw meat out in one piece still attached to the small pincer of the claws, you can use these as crab finger hors d'oeuvres dipped in cocktail sauce. To see some top-notch crab picking, visit the Crisfield Crab Derby on Labor Day weekend. There you can watch some of the world's best professional crab pickers compete for serious prizes.

Crab Pots

Many people also cruise with a crab pot aboard. If you don't mind the clutter (and mess sometimes), these are great to have if you intend to stay anchored for a day or so in one spot. Sometimes, just leaving them in overnight will bring enough for a feast. Just bait them up with meat and drop them overboard. While just about any meat (preferably not overly fresh) will do, professional crabbers use fish (menhaden are popular) and eels. Most fishing shops will carry crab bait of one type or the other.

Trot Lines

In the upper waters of the Bay, you will often see one or two people in a boat slowly working down a line, pulling it aboard carefully, and netting, hopefully, crab after crab. This is called "trot lining." The line has numerous pieces of bait tied on. The crabber works from one end to the other, and then over again. It is important not to cut between a trot liner and his floats. If you jiggle his line, all the crabs may drop off. This method of crabbing is particularly popular on the Eastern Shore and throughout Maryland creeks and rivers where potting is not permitted.

Soft Shell Crabs

Now comes the part about the best crabs of all—soft-shell crabs. Periodically throughout the crab's life, it must shed its hard shell in order to grow. A crab will usually pick a quiet, safe place to shed. Often this will be in the grassy shallows, sometimes on the side of a piling, perhaps in your marina under your slip. Then begins a laborious shedding process where the crab slowly "busts" out, splitting at first along the backside, and then working free a little at a time.

The whole process takes hours, during which the crab is very vulnerable, not only to natural prey, but also to people. "Peelers" are considered excellent fishing bait and that is what the crab is during the time when he still wears his old shell with the soft one in place underneath. Experienced hands can tell, by looking, whether the crab has a new shell. It is also during this time that enterprising souls like to capture the crab and put it into a shedding float or pen, but more on that later.

Eventually, the crab completely sheds its old shell, at which point it is totally exhausted and almost immobile for a few hours while the shell hardens. Right after a crab comes out is the best time to eat them. This is, in the opinion of many people, the Bay's finest delicacy. You can find crabs peeling at just about any time during the summer, but periods of full and new moon seem to be the best. Once the soft crab is captured, if it is immediately killed and cleaned, his shell will, of course, remain soft. You can also chill them in a refrigerator or icebox, and they will remain alive for days, with very little hardening. As they harden, they are called "paper shells" and are less desirable.

If you want to watch the entire process, visit one of the commercial shedding pens scattered around the Bay. One of these is at Cantler's Restaurant in Annapolis, MD on Mill Creek, off Whitehall Bay. Another is Queen Anne's Marina on the west side of Kent Island, across the Bay from (east of) Thomas Point Light. Here, the operators collect the crabs before they begin to shed and put them into a series of boxes, floats or "pens" where they very carefully maintain an even and easy flow of natural Bay water. They then watch the crabs continuously, moving them from pen to pen according to the stage of their shedding. This is because crabs are cannibalistic and will sometimes attack weaker crabs during the process.

The shedding business requires hard work and constant attention to be sure that the new softies are removed from the hard pen before they are eaten and before they begin to harden. If there is someone around who has the time to point out the different stages and explain the process, it will be well worth the visit.

Soft shell crabs should be cleaned while they are alive for freshness. To clean the crab, cut off the apron and the face (not the top shell) with a sharp knife. Then, lift the top shell on each side and cut out the gills. Next, insert the knife into the hole left by the face and cut out the organs. When you have removed all of the organs, you are ready to cook. The top shell is left on.

To cook a soft-shell crab, simply melt butter in a frying pan and season with just salt and pepper. Now fry on both sides until golden brown.

OYSTERS

The Chesapeake oyster has been eaten both as a staple and as a delicacy for thousands of years. Along with blue crab, it is probably one of the most well-known examples of Bay seafood. In recent times, the population has suffered seriously from excessive human consumption and an oyster disease called MSX, which doesn't hurt people but ruins the oysters.

The amount of oysters harvested from the Chesapeake is now only a small fraction (one percent) of what it was during its heyday a generation or two ago. Oysters are taken by tonging (said with a hard "g") and dredging (pronounced "drudging"). Tonging is done by watermen in their low-sided boats in the shallows. They have long-handled, two-sided rakes or tonging tools, and you will see them working the handles and moving the apparatus up and down before pulling it up.

In most areas, this operation is now done by machinery, which requires much less strength and covers much more territory over a day's time. This equipment is called the "patent tong" because it was patented by an enterprising blacksmith from the Solomons Island, MD area. One of the most fascinating of the Bay's traditions was the dredging done by the skipjack fleet. Great dredges were pulled over the oyster beds by these beautiful white vessels while under full sail.

You will see oysters growing in the shallows all around the Bay. They like to adhere to hard surfaces, especially other oyster shells. They cannot survive on a soft, silty bottom because they suffocate in the mud. Many areas where you find oysters are now posted by authorities who fear pollution, and it is forbidden to take those oysters. In Virginia, many oyster beds are "owned" and considered private. At press time, the Maryland Government was partnering with various organizations to revitalize the oyster industry.

Like crabs, oysters must be alive and tightly closed just before being eaten. Open oysters should be tapped lightly; a live oyster will tightly close up its shell. Oysters are pried open at the hinge with a sharp knife with a twist to the blade until it pops. Slide the knife upward and cut the muscle holding the shell closed. This is called shucking. The oyster can then be slurped raw, straight from the shell or roasted, steamed, or served in any number of ways.

One of the festivals celebrating the arrival of the season is the Urbanna Oyster Festival on the Rappahannock River. It is always held on the first weekend in November, when the season traditionally starts in Virginia, based on lore that the waters get colder later down there because it is farther south. (Oyster are typically only taken in months that have an "r" in them.) There is always an oyster buy boat or two on display. In years past, you could see these buy boats, loaded to the gunnels with shells, steaming up and down the Bay. Don't miss the oyster shucking contest where you will see professionals and novices compete for prizes.

CLAMS

There are hard and soft shell clams in the Bay. The soft shells are long with a shell that you can easily break with long siphons for pulling in water. They are usually taken with hand tongs, rakes or hydraulic equipment. Many people favor them, but some prefer the hard shell clams because they tend to have less silt inside. These are usually taken with hand tongs or rakes or "patent tongs." The hard-shelled clams are generally referred to as "littlenicks," cherrystones or chowder clams, depending on size. The chowders can be large and rather tough but are still good for chowder or soup.

You will see people tonging and dredging for clams in a manner similar to oystering, but with slightly different equipment. A favorite weekend pastime for many is to go out in the shallows where clams are known to be living, walk around towing your boat or a basket in an inner tube behind you, feeling for them with your toes, and then eating them raw or steamed on the beach in the evening. Again, if you do this, be sure that this is not in a posted or private area. Some prefer to cook or steam clams rather than eat them raw because they feel that it helps to kill any bacteria that may be present.

CHESAPEAKE BAY SEAFOOD

The Bay has been a huge supplier of seafood since its earliest civilization. Far before that, the Native Americans used the Bay as a major source of food. There are oyster shell mounds scattered about the shores that have been dated back thousands of years. When a stingray, on what is now Stingray Point in the lower Bay, stung Capt. John Smith, he was actually spearing fish in the shallows with his sword. While visiting Herring Bay in the upper regions, he found the fish to be so plentiful that he tried to catch them with a frying pan.

In recent years, our consumption of Bay seafood and various ecological problems, some caused by man and others by natural processes, have depleted the resources. Oysters and rockfish have been felt to be dangerously under-populated, and severe restrictions on the taking of them have been enforced.

Thomas Point Lighthouse.

You will still see commercial vessels fishing, clamming, oystering and crabbing wherever you go on the Bay. Also, scattered liberally on the shores will be retail and wholesale seafood houses where you can buy the catch fresh. Both Maryland and Virginia actively attempt to regulate the seafood industry, trying to balance the needs of nature with those of civilization, sometimes with obvious success and sometimes not.

CHESAPEAKE BAY BOATS

The Chesapeake Bay is noted for many unique boats that have served its citizens over the generations, and for the seamen who build and work from them. Many of the ancient boats are still around today, not only in the museums, but also on the water, in use. Your cruise will be much more meaningful when you recognize them out on the water, and you should seek them out and absorb their lines and traditions in the many places they may be found.

One of the best places to begin learning is at The Chesapeake Bay Maritime Museum in St. Michaels, or any of the multitude of maritime museums scattered around the Bay, where authentic examples of most of them will be found either on land or in the water. The Calvert Marine Museum in Solomons Island, MD is another excellent place to learn about Bay craft.

There are many good resource books available. These include "Chesapeake Bay Sailing Craft" and "This Was the Chesapeake" both written by Robert H. Burgess and published by Tidewater Publishers, and "Steam Packets on the Chesapeake" by Alexander Crosby Brown, also published by Tidewater Publishers. Don't be surprised to see tall sets of sails on the horizon, as though the past were sailing over the curve of the earth to meet you.

Log Canoes

One example of boats unique to the Bay is the log canoe; some of the craft (many over a hundred years old) are still raced on the Miles River. These are actually built by fastening together several logs, and are beautiful and graceful, if not a bit tender, under sail. Log canoe races are frequently held off the entrance to St. Michaels, MD, up and down the Miles River. The Miles River Yacht Club in Long Haul Creek is famous for sponsoring many of these races. Anchor off the side during a windy race, and enjoy the show. The Chesapeake Bay Maritime Museum will usually know when they are going to race.

Skipjacks and Other Work Boats

Skipjacks are large, broad-beamed sailing craft with clipper bows and graceful sterns that were used for dredging for oysters under sail. You can tour preserved boats at museums around the Bay. There are also the Bugeyes, Pungies, Rams and many other types of sailing vessels developed to serve a specific use, usually for the seafood industry, but sometimes for cargo.

Baltimore Clippers

Among the more well-known Bay craft are the fast and famous schooners called the Baltimore Clippers. These were developed in the years prior to the War of 1812 and were used with great success for privateering during that war. President James Madison offered letters of Marque and Reprisal to many of the clipper captains, giving them an opportunity to show off their ships to the benefit of their own pocketbooks and the detriment of the British. They were slender and quite fast, sinking and capturing many British ships. These vessels gained the admiration of the British to the extent that they sent a delegation over after the war to attempt to learn how they were built. Needless to say, they did not find willing teachers. One of the most well known of these ships is the *Pride of Baltimore II*, operated as a public trust for educational purposes and to serve as an ambassador. Often you will find her at the Baltimore Inner Harbor city docks; sometimes she is open to the public. The original *Pride of Baltimore* was lost in a sudden and severe white squall at sea some years ago. A mast stands in memory to the vessel and her crew on the banks of the Inner Harbor.

Chesapeake Bay Deadrise

The proud, but humble, Chesapeake Bay deadrise is seen every day in many forms throughout the Bay tonging for oysters, dredging for crabs or tending nets. They may be anywhere from 16 to 18 feet, to over 100 feet long.

Today, the smaller ones, with small pilothouses forward, are used for crab potting, tonging and pound netting. The term "deadrise" refers to the form and manner of construction of her bow and underbody. Its lines are distinct, beautiful, graceful and very seaworthy.

The Chespaeake Bay buyboat F.D. Crockett after restoration.
Photo courtesy of the Deltaville Maritime Museum.

There are various forms that the deadrise may take. The stern, in particular, varies considerably, depending mostly upon where the boat was built. Most of the round stern workboats are "Deltaville built." The fame of the boat has spread far beyond the Bay. Some of these are even seen in the Bahamas, serving as fishing and freight craft, despite their aging timbers.

CHESAPEAKE WATERMAN

Although many may say that they are a dying breed, you will see watermen everywhere on the Bay, tonging for oysters, tending nets, running trot lines (a method of crabbing found mostly on the upper eastern shore), setting and pulling crab pots, raking for clams and just going and coming in general. The Chesapeake is one of the major seafood producing waters of the world. These people work hard, it is their living, and we should respect that as we cruise and perhaps find a crab pot or pound net in our way.

There are several books available about the watermen. One of these is entitled "Working the Chesapeake" by Mark E. Jacoby, a University of Maryland publication. You should be sure to buy and savor the book "The Watermen of the Chesapeake Bay" by John H. Whitehead, III. Its photographs and quotes from the Bay's watermen say it all.

Their work is incredibly difficult. In the hottest, most humid days of summer, they are out on the water bending over lines to pull in pots or nets. Their nets are usually full of stinging nettles, and the wind blows the strands into their faces and eyes.

In the bitter cold, they are out tonging or "drudging" for oysters. Their names are usually family names of mothers or wives, or the *Three Sons* or the *Five Daughters* or personal statements like *Island Pride*. It has been noted that the Maryland boats, particularly on the eastern shore and Smith island are named with a woman's name and an abbreviated letter. *Glenda C*, *Claudine S*, *Matty J* and *Myrtle M* are typical. In Virginia waters particularly on Tangier Island you will see the names are two female names: *Glenda Cristina*, *Claudine Sue*, *Mattie Joan* or *Myrtle Marie*.

CRUISE ITINERARIES FOR THE CHESAPEAKE BAY

To suggest a one-, two- or three-week cruise of the Chesapeake Bay is like suggesting that you attend a very fine banquet, the finest in the land, and then lightly sample only a few of the courses. The best that you can hope to do in such a short time is to hit a few of the many high spots, and whet your appetite for more. But it will be the finest sampling you have ever had. If you have already enjoyed some Bay cruising, you may prefer to pick one of the areas, and spend time delving deeply into the various pleasures that it offers.

However, if you are just beginning to explore this area, you may find the following cruise suggestions helpful. They were written with the thought of providing an overview of the many different types of areas and cruising experiences possible. You may then, in later cruises, want to concentrate on favorite areas, patterning each cruise to your preferences at the time. Never let this or any other guides limit your choices or exploration. After all, one of the great features of the Bay is that it is easy enough and user friendly enough for you to quickly become your own expert on the places that you enjoy most.

We have often met frustrated and disappointed cruisers because they missed parts of some suggested itinerary. That is not what cruising is about. Do what you can comfortably, and have fun. Therefore, we will give general suggestions with latitude as to length of stay and nearby explorations. If any point is to be made here, it is to try all of the places at one time or another. Each is special in its own way. Have a general idea of what you want to do with your time. The foldout chart inside the back cover of this book will help.

The destinations in these cruises are intended to be within an easy day's reach for most sailboats or slow powerboats. If you are in a powerboat, you will have more time to relax when you arrive, or you may want to explore an extra creek, cove or village. We have also "stuffed" the calendar with these cruises to give some options. For example, you may wish to emphasize marinas and restaurants instead of quiet gunkholes, or your boat may be fast enough to get to more places in less time.

While approximate mileages will be given, this can be somewhat misleading. For example, a trip from the Patuxent to the Choptank in a northeaster could take many hours longer than the same trip in a calm or with favoring

Passing Through the Chesapeake Bay

Chesapeake Bay is narrow relative to its length and since it curves a bit, there is no favored side. Heading south, initially your course favors the eastern shore until the Little Choptank, but then the course favors the western shore to Norfolk. It comes down to two factors:

1. How fast you are going.

2. What you require at each stop.

Starting from the north end, you will be traveling along the eastern shore. While the Sasafrass River eight miles or so from the canal is lovely, there are no convenient anchorages and marinas and supplies are nine miles upriver. There are good anchorages and marinas in Fairlee Creek mile 18 and Worton Creek mile 20. Baltimore, of course, has everything, but it is about 20 miles off the route. Middle River has lots of facilities as well, but it is 10 miles off course. If you are well supplied and making time, stay on the eastern shore.

The next port with marinas, anchorages and supplies is Rock Hall. Again, you will be a few miles off the route. Next is Annapolis. From here to Solomons the eastern shore harbors are well up rivers and far from the bay proper, so as great as they are to visit, if you are in a hurry to transit the Bay, the only relatively convenient anchorages are Tilghman Island (if your draft permits), and the little Choptank, with Hudson Creek and Slaughter Creek just a couple of miles off the main stem. There are no other anchorages or ports of refuge until you get to Solomons. While it is six to seven miles off the bay, Solomons has everything—anchorages, marinas, restaurants, repairs and groceries.

From Solomons, it is over 20 miles to the mouth of the Potomac. From there, you must go up river seven miles to get to a marina or restaurant. If you are trying to make time from Solomons headed south, in reality your next harbor is Reedville, about 40 miles, which has anchorages, marinas and restaurants. From Reedville it is 20 miles to Deltaville (the Rappahannock side). From Deltaville you are about 40 miles from Hampton and Hampton is 12 to14 miles from mile "0."

Chesapeake Bay is a world-renowned cruising ground. Stay as long as you can; you are here now, so enjoy it. But if you are merely trying for a quick transit, answer the two questions above, and we'll give you a route you will enjoy.

winds. Also, your draft may allow you to take many shortcuts. For example, if you are in Eastern Bay and wish to go to the Chester River, a draft of only 4 feet should allow you to pass through Kent Narrows. Check the latest as to shoaling. This saves you a day's trip up the Bay, under the Bay Bridges, around Love Point and into the Chester River. This will be required if your draft won't allow you to pass through the northern entrance to the Narrows.

NORTHERN BAY CRUISES

We must assume a starting point. You may be coming through the C&D Canal, up from the south or beginning from any of the creeks around the shores of the northern Bay. Since the middle of the northern Bay is usually within one day's journey from either end, and because there are many charter boat businesses in this area, we will assume the Annapolis, Rock Hall or Kent Island Narrows areas as a beginning point. You will see that we suggest the Chesapeake Bay Maritime Museum of St. Michaels as an early destination for all cruises. This is because you can learn much about the Bay and its culture here, thus making the rest of your cruise more meaningful. The Calvert Marine Museum at Solomons, MD also offers a similar experience and many fine displays, although it is not as large.

You will also note that we suggest that each cruise end with Baltimore's Inner Harbor. This is because this is such an excellent place to celebrate your cruise with a "grand finale." If, you wish to spend your last nights in seclusion, visit the Inner Harbor earlier, and pick one of the quieter spots mentioned for your last night.

A THREE-WEEK CRUISE OF THE UPPER BAY

Within the first day or two of any cruise, we would recommend that you visit the Chesapeake Bay Maritime Museum at St. Michaels, MD on the Miles River, which empties into broad Eastern Bay. Although there is enough within this museum to consume several days, within one very full day, you will be able to get a very interesting and helpful education about the Bay, its history, traditions, boats, people, problems and beauty. This will make the rest of your cruise much more meaningful and give a very helpful perspective to all that you see and experience. The town of St. Michaels, with its history and shopping, is one of the most popular boating destinations on the Bay.

Since most will be starting their cruise from some area of civilization and probably looking forward to quiet nights and anchorages, we hesitate to suggest this busy village as a first stop. The village is quaint and pretty, and there are many quiet rivers nearby for a retreat after you have visited the museum or just before. One of the most idyllic gunkholes of the entire Bay will be found only one or two hours away for most boats, in the Wye East River in Dividing Creek. St. Michaels to Dividing Creek is approximately eight nautical miles. This is a tree-surrounded cove on an island, most of which is park, thus protected from encroachments of civilization. Here, you can get your first taste of how nice Chesapeake gunkholing can be.

From the Miles River and Eastern Bay, you would probably enjoy a nice cruise heading down to the Choptank River. In Dun Cove on Harris Creek, you will find a very pleasant anchorage with fields, trees and marsh around. Dividing Creek to Dun Cove is approximately 37 nautical miles around (to the west of Poplar Island). If you can go through the Poplar Island Narrows and through Knapps Narrows, the distance will only be approximately 22 nautical miles.

From here, you could spend months going up the Tred Avon and the Choptank rivers. The village of Oxford and the interesting and inviting town of Cambridge both offer marinas, restaurants and other civilization opportunities. Far up the Choptank, Denton is scarce on marina facilities, but long on pleasant Maryland Eastern Shore small-town hospitality.

After a day or so enjoying the Choptank River, a visit to Little Choptank will take you even farther from areas of dense civilization. Try anchoring behind Casson Point in Hudson Creek off the Little Choptank. Dun Cove to Casson Point is approximately 17.5 nautical miles. There is a nice but small beach, and an opportunity to explore the next day any of other creeks of the River that you find interesting in this Guide.

From the Little Choptank, crossing the Chesapeake Bay to the Patuxent River offers the interesting village of Solomons Island with nice restaurants, shopping, extensive marina facilities and many quiet pretty creeks just up the river, above the bridge. Casson Point to St. Leonard Creek is approximately 30 nautical miles.

Annapolis harbor. Waterway Guide Photography.

Leaving the Patuxent, head back north up the Western Shore of the Bay. As you pass north up the Western Shore, you should take note of the Herring Bay area. Solomons to Herring Bay is approximately 36 nautical miles. Herrington Harbor South has excellent resort facilities, a restaurant and good repair shops. This is a great marina to visit at any time, but it is often a very convenient spot to duck in if weather changes as you transit this long fetch. This is also a great spot to meet members of your family who are jealous because they are not along. They can stay in the cottages a few minutes walk from your pier. They will have a nice beach and pool, and day sails in the Bay are easy from this location.

Consider trying next an anchorage, again in a seemingly remote area, in the Rhode River, among the islands. Herring Bay to Rhode River is approximately 21 nautical miles. Don't visit this anchorage on weekends unless you love a crowd. If you have a shallow-draft boat, you can get well up into Sellman Creek for near-wilderness surroundings. After this, a very short trip up the West River to the quaint village of Galesville will offer several nice restaurants that you can visit from anchor or marina, and a great country store with take-out food.

If you are ready for some high civilization, you may wish to bypass the West River this trip and head on to Annapolis, the undisputed boating capital of the Chesapeake. Rhode River to Annapolis is approximately 16 nautical miles. Spa Creek, Back Creek and the surrounding areas have an immense number of boating shops, both repair and retail. This is one of the best places to shop around for anticipated boat projects, improvements, new additions or even new boats. There are also a very large number of excellent restaurants within walking distance of the water, and sightseeing and shopping in the historic area of Annapolis should not be missed.

From Annapolis, take the long trip up beyond the Chesapeake Bay bridges, and explore the very northernmost areas. We would first begin this area by a side trip up the Chester River. Anchor overnight in one of its many perfect creeks, such as those found on the Corsica River or Langford Creek. Annapolis to Chester River in the vicinity of the Corsica and Langford Creek is approximately 28 nautical miles. This classic Chesapeake river takes you into the very heart of the Eastern Shore countryside. If you have the speed and/or time, travel upstream to enjoy river cruising, with the rich reward of Chestertown at the end of the run. Chestertown from the Corsica-Langford area is approximately 12 nautical miles. You will need a lay day at Chestertown to enjoy what it has to offer; walks through historical tree-shaded streets, fine shopping, dining and historical tours.

Chestertown to Rock Hall is approximately 29 nautical miles. Rock Hall is another place to stop for some good restaurants, good marinas and a beautiful and protected anchorage in nearby Swan Creek. This is another place to shop and visit very special small Chesapeake village dedicated to the Bay and those who love it. If you are not ready yet for even this much civilization, there are many creeks on the Eastern Shore for your next anchorages, including Worton and Still Pond Creeks. Rock Hall to Still Pond is approximately 20 nautical miles. In each of these, you can find lonely and pretty spots, with a smattering here and there of some civilization. Note that you will only want to visit Still Pond in settled easterly weather unless your draft (no more than 5 feet) will allow you to go up into the creek itself.

After gunkholing in one or more of the above creeks, cross back over the Bay, heading up to its far northwestern corner and visit Havre de Grace. Still Pond to Havre de Grace is approximately 17 nautical miles. Anchor or dock, and then arrange a trip up the Susquehanna River with its towering cliffs and upstream rapids. It would be worthwhile to charter a small fishing skiff with a guide to take you up into this area. You will get a true feeling of the nature of the river that is known as the Mother of the Bay.

Crossing back again to the Eastern Shore, plan to spend a day or two in the beautiful Sassafras River with its many pristine anchorages and good swimming. Havre de Grace to Sassafras River is approximately 15 nautical miles. Georgetown is upstream and offers marinas and restaurants.

You may wish to end your cruise of the upper Bay with a "grande finale" by visiting the Inner Harbor of Baltimore. Sassafras River to Inner Harbor is approximately 40 nautical miles. Consider stopping in Stony Creek to shorten the trip and allow your arrival in the morning to get the most for your dollar in the harbor. Sassafras to Stony Creek is approximately 30 nautical miles. If you have overindulged yourself with anchorages among woods, marsh and field, you can here overindulge yourself with the very finest that high civilization has to offer.

This includes museums, restaurants, historical sites, shopping and a constant carnival of cultural, ethnic and maritime shows, both in the amphitheater and on the water.

A TWO-WEEK CRUISE

It seems that most fellow cruisers that we encounter on the Bay are either out for a weekend or a two-week cruise. After spending around two days getting to and experiencing the Chesapeake Bay Maritime Museum at St. Michaels, head down to Casson Point on the Little Choptank River for a peaceful first evening away from civilization in a beautiful anchorage.

Then run up one of the creeks in this river. St. Michaels to Casson Point is approximately 36 nautical miles. A choice anchorage is Beckwith Creek just upstream from Cherry Island. Casson Point to Beckwith Creek is approximately three nautical miles. This will be another nearly all-natural anchorage. From here, a trip across the Chesapeake to Herring Bay and Herrington Harbor South, with its excellent marina and restaurant, may be in order. Beckwith Creek to Herrington Harbor is approximately 28 nautical miles. After Herring Bay, an easy few hours will bring you to another perfectly beautiful anchorage in Harness Creek in South River.

Herrington Harbor to Harness Creek is approximately 17 nautical miles. You may want to stay here for more than a day, but not on the weekend when it is very crowded. If you are here on a weekend and the crowd is bad in the first most popular anchorage just inside the entrance, go up the creek to the second spot mentioned off the park docks around the point. This is usually less busy.

From the South River, it is a short run around Thomas Point into the Severn. Harness Creek to the first Severn River Bridge is approximately 13 nautical miles.

Don't stop in Annapolis yet. Proceed up the Severn and pick any of the beautiful creeks to anchor there among tall wooded hills with nice homes interspersed among the trees. Then head back down the Severn, and stop at Annapolis, planning to arrive early to get the most from the town.

After Annapolis, head up the Bay to the Corsica River on the Chester, and spend a night at anchor. Annapolis to the Corsica River is approximately 21 nautical miles.

After the Chester, try the long trip up to Still Pond. The Corsica to Still Pond is approximately 34 nautical miles. If the weather is settled, and you are not expecting any westerlies, the anchorage outside in the Bay will be beautiful. If you wish, proceed into the narrow cut, past the Coast Guard station, and anchor inside this beautiful creek. We wouldn't recommend going in here with more than 5 feet of draft. Probably a day here will be enough, and you will be ready to move on to the Sassafras.

In the Sassafras are many prime anchorages. Still Pond to the Sassafras is approximately 10 nautical miles. If you want civilization, go up to Georgetown where there are several good marinas and restaurants. You can also moor or anchor here, and then walk around and dine out.

After the Sassafras, head on over to Havre de Grace for the unique delights of this special town where the Susquehanna, the Mother of the Bay, meets her daughter. The Sassafras River to Havre de Grace is approximately 15 nautical miles. It would be nice to rent a small boat with a guide to go upriver to the rapids, but unless you want to skip other stops, it may be best to save this for next year when you take your three-week cruise.

From Havre de Grace, it is a long trip down to the Patapsco River, but usually an easy one, unless the winds happen to be blowing from the wrong direction (southerly). Watch the shoals, stay in the deep water and out of the firing ranges at Aberdeen Proving Grounds. The trip may be too long for you to comfortably get all the way up to Baltimore's Inner Harbor and settled down. If so, anchor in one of the creeks at the entrance to the Patapsco. We prefer Rock Creek. Havre de Grace to Rock Creek is approximately 42 nautical miles.

The next day, head for Baltimore's Inner Harbor, bright and early. Rock Creek to Inner Harbor is approximately 11 nautical miles. If you get there early enough, there may still be time for a special morning coffee at one of the coffee shops.

A ONE-WEEK CRUISE

After a visit to the Chesapeake Bay Maritime Museum in St. Michaels, MD, head across the Bay into the Rhode River for a beautiful anchorage among the islands there. The distance from St. Michaels to the Rhode River is approximately 22 nautical miles. From the Rhode River, sail up to Annapolis for restaurants, shopping and sightseeing ashore. The distance between the Rhode River and Annapolis is approximately 12 nautical miles. Once you have taken in Annapolis, head up the Bay to anchor in Sillery Bay on the Magothy River, about 15 nautical miles away. If you desire more protection than Sillery Bay, go into the nearby cove on the north end of Gibson Island. Then, either sail across the Bay up to Worton Creek for a beautiful anchorage, or sail directly for the final destination—the Inner Harbor of Baltimore. Sillery Bay to Worton Creek is approximately 23 nautical miles. Worton Creek to the Inner Harbor is approximately 28 nautical miles, and Sillery Bay to the Inner Harbor is approximately 22 nautical miles.

SOUTHERN BAY CRUISING

The geography of the Bay changes significantly from the Potomac River south to the Norfolk area. This Virginia portion of the Bay is considerably wider, up to 24 miles in some places, and distances between ports are generally greater. The Potomac and Rappahannock rivers are wider themselves than some areas of the upper Bay. Weather will be more of a factor as seas have a chance to build, and the time required to move from port to port will require additional planning, with alternative destinations as a backup.

The attraction for southern Bay cruisers is that, outside of the immediate Norfolk area, crowds are almost nonexistent, prices are lower, and the pace is slower. "Laid Back" is the norm, especially in people's attitudes. Best to leave any aggressive tendencies behind when you cruise here.

The lower portions of the Potomac, Rappahannock and York rivers offer some of the most unspoiled cruising grounds on the entire East Coast. Here, you will find an almost limitless supply of creeks and anchorages, often lined with woods or farms, dotted with waterfront towns offering amenities for cruisers, including marinas, restaurants, shopping and museums. There are many long white sand beaches with not another soul upon them. The Rappahannock River area especially has developed into a cruising destination centered around the town of Deltaville, VA.

Farther south, in Hampton Roads, you suddenly enter city life and everything that that implies. Yet each of the cities that make up this metropolis on the water (Hampton, Portsmouth, Norfolk and Virginia Beach) has managed to retain or create attractive enclaves specifically catering to the lifestyle and needs of boaters.

Planning a cruise on the southern Bay is limited only by your timetable and preferences. Line up any number of towns, anchorages, marinas and city sites, and be flexible. With a fixed itinerary, you may be disappointed, but by adjusting to the southern Bay attitude, you will be rewarded with a unique and wonderful experience. Happy cruising! ■

Chesapeake Eastern Shore

C&D CANAL TO KENT ISLAND | EASTERN BAY TO LITTLE CHOPTANK | LITTLE CHOPTANK TO CAPE CHARLES

Waterway Guide Photography.

Chesapeake Eastern Shore

C&D CANAL TO KENT ISLAND · EASTERN BAY TO LITTLE CHOPTANK · LITTLE CHOPTANK TO CAPE CHARLES

Susquehanna River
Havre de Grace
95
North East River
Elk River
C&D Canal
MILE ZERO
Chesapeake City
Page 115
Page 121
Bohemia River
13
Bushs River
Gunpowder River
Sassafras River
Georgetown
Page 123
MILE 16
Page 126
Still Pond
695
Middle River
MILE 26
Worton Creek
Page 127
Back River
Page 127
Fairlee Creek
Chestertown
Page 136
Chesapeake Bay
atapsco River
Rock Hall
Page 130
MILE 40
N
Magothy River
Eastern Neck Island Wildlife Refuge
Kent Island
301
Chester River
ern River
Chesapeake Bay Bridge
Annapolis
Kent Narrows
MILE 48
50
Page 140
404
DOZIER'S WATERWAY GUIDE
THE CRUISING AUTHORITY
WWW.WATERWAYGUIDE.COM
uth River
Eastern Bay
st River
Choptank River
St. Michaels
Easton
Oxford

C&D Canal to Kent Island

CHARTS 12272, 12273, 12274, 12277, 12278

This somewhat sparsely populated northern section of the Eastern Shore presents the first real taste of Chesapeake country after transiting the Chesapeake and Delaware (C&D) Canal. You would be wise to savor it. After all, who could complain about the beautiful shorelines, the abundance of jellyfish-free swimming holes or the soft and forgiving bottom? Practically limitless opportunities abound for gunkholing—up rivers like the Bohemia and Chester—or at the great yachting centers, such as the ones at Georgetown, on the Sassafras River, and Rock Hall and Kent Narrows, not far south. Given the more famous cruising grounds farther south on the Bay, such as the waters around St. Michaels, it is easy to cruise right past this captivating area, but we wouldn't recommend it.

C&D CANAL

A vital link in the Intracoastal Waterway (ICW) system, the C&D provides for a safe, timesaving passage between Delaware Bay and the Chesapeake Bay. The 12-mile-long, sea level cut has no locks and no toll, inviting a great deal of commercial shipping traffic. The canal is not particularly scenic but provides pleasant stretches of woods and fields.

Dutch mapmaker Augustine Hermann first proposed the canal in 1661, and it won Benjamin Franklin's support in 1788. It finally opening in 1829 at a cost of $2.5 million, with four locks and six-mule teams to pull towboats through. The canal reduced, by nearly 300 miles, the water routes between Philadelphia and Baltimore. Ruins of one of the original locks remain at Delaware City, DE, which lies at the eastern end of the C&D Canal.

The C&D Canal today is administered by the U.S. Army Corps of Engineers, measuring out at 450 feet wide with a controlling depth of 35 feet. The maximum allowable length of a self-propelled vessel transiting the canal is 886 feet.

Cargo ships and military vessels from all over the world pass through the canal. Ships of this size—among the largest—require powerful bow-thrusters to keep them on course in the C&D's close quarters, and a pilot is normally on board to guide most large ships, through. Huge surges roll well ahead and astern of these behemoths, even when the ships are not speeding along, and the troughs left behind can send large and small yachts wallowing. For the most comfortable passing maneuvers, slow down and, if possible, head into wakes at an angle.

More than 15 million tons of cargo passes through the C&D Canal each year and, in one month, roughly 175 ships, 400 tugs, 480 barges and a stream of recreational craft transit the canal. For all the congestion, however, daytime passage is remarkably easy. Apart from dredging equipment (dredging is frequently ongoing in some part of the canal) and ship traffic, the only potential hazard is occasional debris carried in from Delaware Bay.

NAVIGATION: Use Chart 12277. **Use Reedy Point tide tables. For Chesapeake City high tide, subtract 45 minutes; for low tide, subtract 1 hour 12 minutes.**

The C&D Canal's buoy system is based on the perspective of vessels entering from seaward up Delaware Bay (i.e., even-numbered red lights and buoys are on the north side, and odd-numbered green lights and buoys are on the south side). At Chesapeake City, MD, the buoy-numbering system reverses, and down Back Creek toward the Chesapeake Bay, odd-numbered green lights and buoys are on the north side, and even-numbered red lights and buoys are on the south side. (In this scenario, Chesapeake City is the symbolic "home port" facilitating the "red right returning" rule.)

A dispatcher at Chesapeake City controls ship traffic by using red and green flashing lights at Reedy Point (at the canal's eastern entrance off Delaware Bay) and Town Point (at the Chesapeake Bay end). If the lights are flashing red at Reedy Point or Town Point Wharf, you may call the dispatcher on VHF Channel 13 to ask whether small boats may pass through. (The dispatcher uses remote cameras mounted along the canal's banks, and monitors VHF Channel 13. So, by monitoring Channel 13, you will also hear about traffic approaching from ahead or astern.) Avoid calling the dispatcher unless absolutely necessary.

Confine radio contact with the dispatcher to information concerning passage through the canal, and keep it brief. If you should experience engine failure, however, do call the dispatcher, who will promptly send a towboat. Six bridges and an overhead gas pipeline cross the canal. One is the Conrail Lift Bridge with a 45-foot closed vertical clearance (usually open); the others are fixed high-level spans with a minimum vertical clearance of 132 feet.

There is no speed limit on the C&D, but mind right-of-way rules and use common sense: Give a wide berth to big, hard-to-maneuver craft. Federal regulations declare, "No vessel in the waterway shall be raced or crowded alongside

Looking west into the C&D Canal's jettied east entrance at Reedy Point. (Not to be used for navigation.) Waterway Guide Photography.

another vessel. Vessels of all types, including recreational craft, are required to travel … at a safe speed throughout the canal and its approaches to avoid damage by suction or wave wash to vessels, landings, riprap protection, or other boats, or injury to persons." Waterskiing, sailing, anchoring and jet skiing are prohibited on the C&D. Sailboats may motorsail, but passage under sail alone is prohibited.

Transiting the canal at night is no problem, except perhaps for the first-timer. Ensure that you are awake and alert in this rock-lined passage. Shore illumination, flashing canal signals and the lights of passing vessels can merge into a muddle of lights and make a night passage less than pleasant. The difficult part is sorting out the entrance markers at each end. Pay close attention to your charts and, at the Chesapeake end in particular, carefully follow the markers through the many doglegs.

Also, note that you cannot follow Delaware City Branch Channel from Delaware Bay southwest to the channel's junction with the C&D Canal because a low, fixed bridge (6-foot vertical clearance) crosses it halfway through. You must go back out Bulkhead Shoal Channel and turn around Reedy Point to enter the canal. In good weather, anchor on either side of Bulkhead Shoal Channel to wait for a favorable current. Once tied up at Delaware City or another nearby port (see below), you are free to explore northern Delaware.

Tidal Ranges: Under normal conditions, Chesapeake City has a tidal range of about 3 feet; the Summit Bridge (near Summit North Marina), about 4 feet; St. Georges Bridge, about 4.5 to 5 feet; and Reedy Point, about 6 feet. The tidal range increases as you move from the Chesapeake toward Delaware Bay. Currents can run 2 knots or faster, so check the appropriate tidal current tables and plan for a favorable tide if possible. The flood sets easterly and the ebb westerly. On the Delaware Bay side, pay close attention to the effects of the current when entering or exiting the canal. The full force of the current will push the boat sideways as you travel between the jetties at Reedy Point.

Dockage: If you approach the C&D from Delaware Bay in late afternoon and want to avoid running the canal at night, dockage is available at Delaware City Marina, two miles north of the eastern (Reedy Point) entrance to the canal. From Delaware Bay, head up Bulkhead Shoal Channel, and then turn to port at flashing green "1" at the mouth of Delaware City Branch Channel. Depths are 7 feet at the entrance, with 6-foot depths down the long, narrow channel. Delaware City Marina works with the Coast Guard 24 hours a day and is convenient to Delaware City. A tour boat runs from Delaware City to Pea Patch Island for those who wish to visit historic Fort Delaware.

On the north side of the canal, approximately 2.5 miles west of the St. Georges West Bridge (142-foot fixed vertical clearance, a quarter-mile past the Conrail Lift Bridge), a privately marked channel leads just under a half-mile directly to Summit North Marina, with transient dockage at floating docks and the Firehouse Dockside Restaurant.

Looking east over the C&D Canal and Chesapeake City. (Not to be used for navigation.) Waterway Guide Photography.

This location offers the protection of a hurricane hole and the mature-forest peace and quiet of Delaware's Lums Pond State Park. Summit North owns its own dredge, but entrance depths can change frequently. Call ahead for the latest information before heading into the marina.

You can also go ashore on the south side of the C&D Canal at Chesapeake City, where the town offers complimentary 24-hour dockage at the well-maintained town dock by the park. The floating face dock can accommodate four or five medium-size boats, with rafting permitted (with room for no more than two vessels rafted together). There are also floating docks for boats 30 feet and smaller, including dinghies. The Chesapeake Inn, Restaurant and Marina, located inside the basin, also has slips at its floating docks (reservations recommended). The basin was dredged a few years ago and is currently 6 to 8 feet deep, with shallower water at the entrance. Here, you are out of the current, wakes and wash from passing traffic and close to the beautifully restored historic district of Chesapeake City (versus the town's more suburban-style quarter, overlooking the C&D's northern side). However, be aware there is no fuel available here.

Anchorage: Off the C&D's southern shore at Chesapeake City is Anchorage Basin, a location that is frequently dredged and is protected, but a fairly tight little spot to drop the hook. It pays to get there early. While tidal current tables report the current at the entrance at 2 knots, old hands know that the current across the entrance to the Anchorage Basin can be substantially greater, which can make entering an interesting experience. If you choose to try, stay away from the center because it is the shallowest part of the entrance channel. And remember not to block access to the slips at the Chesapeake Inn. Depths inside the basin entrance range from 6 to 8 feet.

GOIN' ASHORE: CHESAPEAKE CITY, MD

In Chesapeake City, it is all about waiting for the "Big One," which will probably be a freighter or tanker passing by about three times each day. From almost anywhere in town, you may glimpse the mighty tankers, led by tugs, chugging along the Chesapeake and Delaware (C&D) Canal. They clear the 140-foot high Chesapeake City Bridge with awe-inspiring ease.

The canal, a 14-mile shortcut between the Delaware River and the Chesapeake Bay, bisects the town into north and south sides. Head for the Victorian south side, a tiny jewel box that grew into Chesapeake City once the shovels hit the dirt in the early 19th century for canal construction. In more recent years, the sleepy burg has been discovered by folks in search of charm who browse its shops and enjoy its restaurants.

History: Dutch mapmaker Augustine Herrman first suggested building a canal across the top of the Delmarva Peninsula in the 17th century. By the 1760s, surveyors were scouting routes. Construction of the current canal began in 1824, and it opened in 1829. The route cuts 300 miles off the maritime route from Baltimore to Philadelphia. Originally, the canal was 10 feet deep, 66 feet wide at the waterline and 36 feet at the channel bottom, featuring several locks. In

C&D Canal, Elk River, Bohemia River, MD

C&D CANAL & ELK RIVER		Largest Vessel Accommodated	VHF Channel Monitored	Transient Berths / Total Berths	Approach / Dockside Depth (reported)	Floating Docks	Gas / Diesel	Groceries, Ice, Marine Supplies, Snacks	Repairs: Hull, Engine, Propeller	Lift (tonnage), Crane, Rail	Min/Max Amps	Laundry, Pool, Showers, Courtesy Car	Pump-Out Station	Nearby: Grocery Store, Motel, Restaurant
		Dockage					Supplies		Services					
1. Delaware City Marina (Internet Access, WiFi)	302-834-4172	65	16/09	10/100	7/7	F	GD	GIMS	HEP	L35, C7	30/50	LSC	P	GMR
2. Summit North Marina (Internet Access, WiFi)	302-836-1800	60	16	50/400	12/12	F	GD	IMS	HEP	L50, C15	30/100	LPS	P	GMR
3. Chesapeake Inn Restaurant & Marina (WiFi)	410-885-2040	120	16	45/60	6/7	F	-	IMS	-	-	30/50	S	-	GR
4. Town of Chesapeake City Docks (Internet Access, WiFi)	410-885-5298	-	13	6/10	20/8	F	-	GIS	-	-	30/30	LC	-	GR
5. Harbour North Marina (Internet Access, WiFi)	410-885-5656	50	16/09	5/150	3/3	-	G	IMS	HEP	L20	30/50	SC	P	R
6. Locust Point Marina (Internet Access, WiFi)	410-392-4994	40	-	/92	5/	-	-	MS	HEP	-	30/30	PS	P	R
BOHEMIA RIVER														
7. Bohemia Bay Yacht Harbour (Internet Access, WiFi)	410-885-2601	65	16/09	10/300	5/5	-	GD	IMS	HEP	L50	30/50	LPS	P	-
8. Aquamarina Bohemia Vista	410-885-2056	50	16	/153	6/6	F	-	IMS	HEP	L50, C	30/30	LPS	P	-
9. Two Rivers Yacht Basin	410-885-2257	43	16	2/150	3.5/3.5	F	G	IMS	HE	L25	30/30	PS	P	-
10. Long Point Marina Inc.	410-275-8181	40	-	/140	4/3.5	-	G	IMS	HEP	L25	30/30	LS	P	-
11. Aquamarina Hack's Point (Internet Access, WiFi)	410-275-2555	50	-	10/82	9/	F	-	IMS	HEP	L40	30/30	S	P	-
12. Bohemia Anchorage Inc.	410-275-8148	55	-	/65	6/12	F	-	I	HEP	L15	30/30	S	P	G

Corresponding chart(s) not to be used for navigation. Internet Access · WiFi Wireless Internet Access · Waterway Guide Cruising Club Partner

See www.WaterwayGuide.com for current rates, fuel prices, web site addresses, and other up-to-the-minute information.

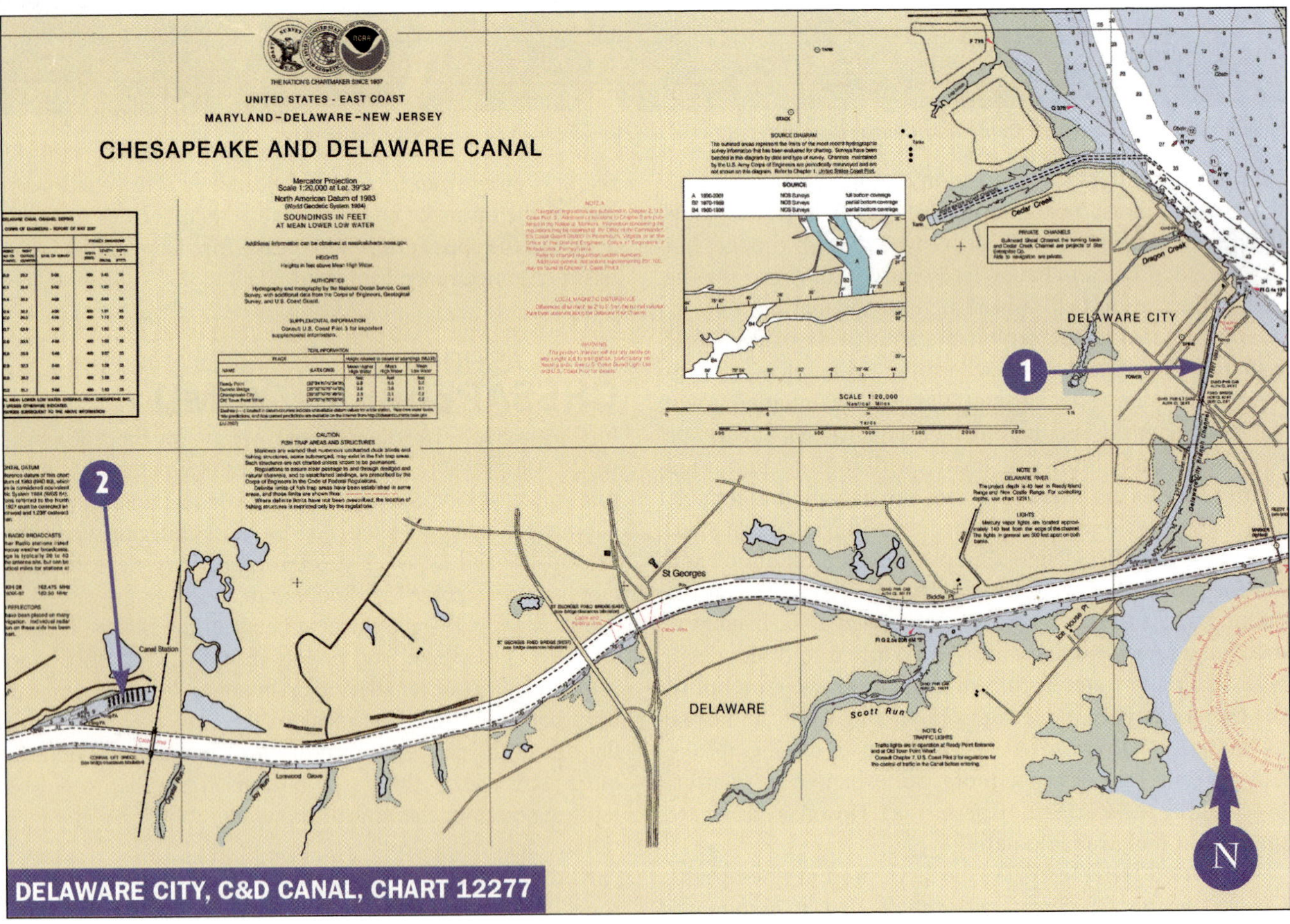

DELAWARE CITY, C&D CANAL, CHART 12277

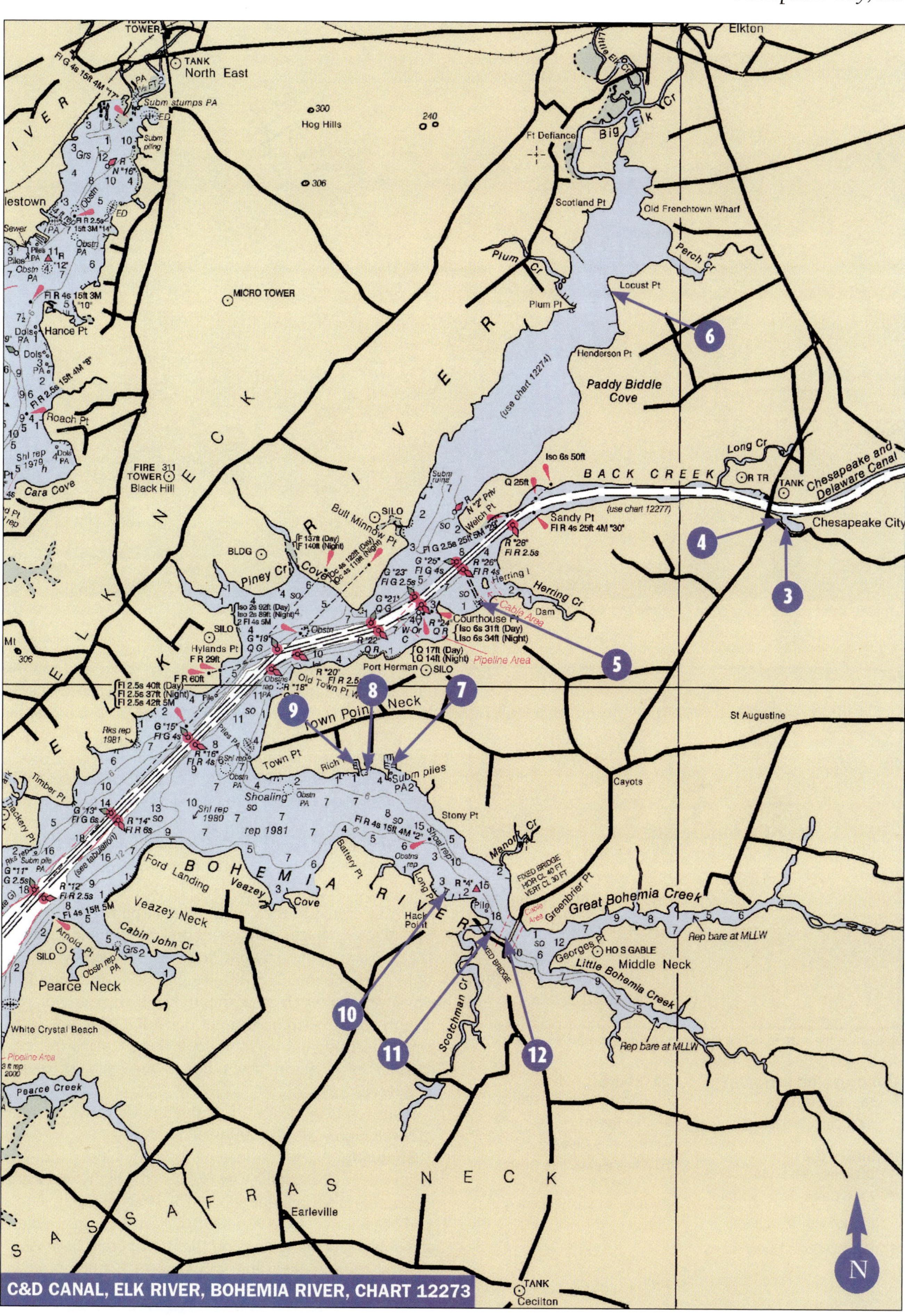
Elkton
North East
Hog Hills
Big Elk Cr
Little Elk Cr
Ft Defiance
Scotland Pt
Old Frenchtown Wharf
Perch Cr
Plum Cr
Plum Pt
Locust Pt
Henderson Pt
Paddy Biddle Cove
MICRO TOWER
Hance Pt
Roach Pt
Cara Cove
FIRE TOWER
Black Hill
E L K N E C K
E L K R I V E R
BACK CREEK
Long Cr
Chesapeake and Delaware Canal
Chesapeake City
Sandy Pt
Welch Pt
Bull Minnow Pt
Piney Cr
Cove
Herring I
Herring Cr
Courthouse Pt
Cable Area
Pipeline Area
Hylands Pt
Port Herman
Old Town Pt Wharf
Town Point Neck
Town Pt
Rich
Subm piles
St Augustine
Cayots
Timber Pt
Shoaling
Stony Pt
Manor Cr
B O H E M I A R I V E R
Ford Landing
Veazey Cove
Veazey Neck
Battery Pt
Long Pt
Hack Point
FIXED BRIDGE
Greenbrier Pt
Great Bohemia Creek
Rep bare at MLLW
Georges Pt
Middle Neck
Little Bohemia Creek
Cabin John Cr
Arnold Pt
Pearce Neck
Scotchman Cr
White Crystal Beach
Pearce Creek
S A S S A F R A S N E C K
Earleville
Cecilton
N
C&D CANAL, ELK RIVER, BOHEMIA RIVER, CHART 12273

Chesapeake City, MD

Looking west over Chesapeake City and the C&D Canal. (Not to be used for navigation.) Waterway Guide Photography.

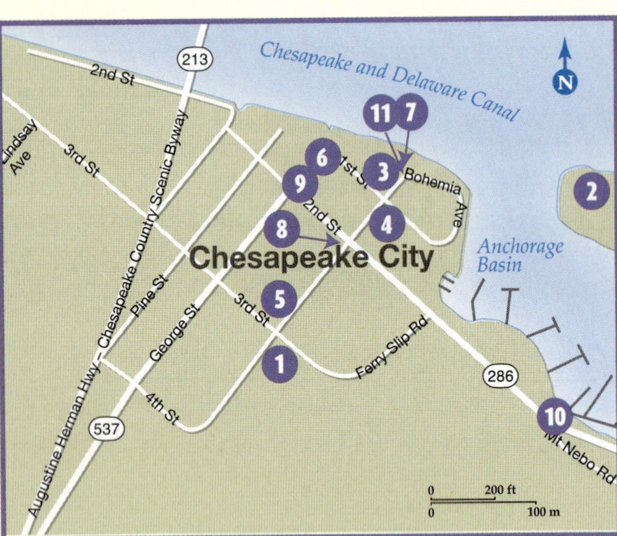

Reference the marina listing tables to see all the marinas in the area.

POINTS OF INTEREST
1 The Blue Max Inn
2 C&D Canal Museum

SHOPPING
3 Dragonfly Gift Shop
4 Back Creek General Store
5 Black Swan Antiques
6 Vulcan's Rest Fibers

DINING
7 Bayard House Restaurant
8 Tap Room
9 Bohemia Cafe
10 Chesapeake Inn, Restaurant & Marina
11 Kilby's Canal Creamery

1927, the U.S. government bought the canal, and renovations included the removal of locks. Several expansions later, the canal is now 450 feet wide and 35 feet deep. Chesapeake City grew up around the canal, and many mid-19th century buildings left over from the early days still stand.

As an interesting aside, author Jack Hunter wrote the "The Blue Max" here. The house he once occupied is now The Blue Max Inn.

Points of Interest: Plan to visit the free C&D Canal Museum (815 Bethel Rd., 410-885-5622; open M-F 8:00 a.m. to 4:00 p.m. and Saturdays, 10:00 a.m. to 3:00 p.m.), which is located in the canal's original pump house at the edge of town, replete with waterwheel and pumping engines. The best part of the museum, which is operated by the U.S. Army Corps of Engineers, may be the television screen upon which you can watch canal ship traffic. If you can, ride your bike there, and then head up or down the canal-side levees for an up-close-and-personal look. Bigger plans for more trails are in the works; stay tuned to www.nap.usace.army.mil/sb/c&d.thm.

Brantwood Golf Club is just three miles away, on Route 213 in Elkton. Call 410-398-8848 for details.

Shopping: A few blocks long by a few blocks wide, the south side of Chesapeake City offers a little of this and a little of that, especially antique shops. The Dragonfly Gift Shop at 19 Bohemia Ave. (410-885-9470) has stained glass, pottery and ship-watching rockers on the front porch. Back Creek General Store, circa 1861, stocks Vera Bradley products and gifts at 100 Bohemia Ave. (410-885-5377). Black Swan

Antiques has inhabited the corner of 3rd St. and Bohemia Ave. for years (410-885-5888). And Vulcan's Rest Fibers, a fiber artist heaven, brings you classes in such subjects as basket weaving, spinning and needlework, gatherings and gear from its 106 George St. location (410-885-2890).

Dining: Tops on any list has to be The Bayard House Restaurant (11 Bohemia Ave., 410-885-5040) with its award-winning Maryland crab soup. It was built in the 1780s and has a traditional Eastern Shore cuisine with a European flair.. The building is touted as Chesapeake City's oldest and sits along the canal. Crab-lovers might consider the Tap Room Crab House (2nd and Bohemia, 410-885-9873), and the Bohemia Café (401 Second St., 410-885-3066) is a favorite with locals and visitors alike and is open seven days a week, including for breakfast. The waterfront Chesapeake Inn, Restaurant & Marina (605 Second St., 410-885-2040), offers dockage as well as fine and casual dining. For dessert, try Kilby's Canal Creamery (9 Bohemia Ave., 410-885-3030) for ice cream made with dairy from Maryland Farms.

ADDITIONAL RESOURCES

- CHESAPEAKE CITY TOURISM: www.chesapeakecity.com
- CECIL COUNTY GOVERNMENT: www.seececil.org

NEARBY MEDICAL FACILITIES
Union Hospital in Elkton, 106 Bow St., Elkton, MD 21921, 410-398-4000 (7 miles)
www.uhcc.com/Directions

NEARBY AIRPORT
Cecil County Airport, 1737 Old Field Pt. Rd., Elkton, MD, 410-398-0234 (10 miles)

ELK RIVER

At its western end, the C&D Canal merges with Back Creek, which flows into the Elk River, about eight miles from Chesapeake Bay proper. The scenery here is among the most spectacular on the Eastern Shore. The Elk River separates high ground to the west from rolling farmland to the east. During the American Revolution, Continental and British ships used the Elk River to take troops to and from Head of Elk, where they began marching to Philadelphia.

NAVIGATION: Use Chart 12274. The Elk River intersects Back Creek east of the C&D Canal at Welch Point just north of flashing green buoy "25." If you wish to explore above Welch Point, get local knowledge, and check depths carefully. Tidal range on the Elk River is about 2 feet.

Dockage: Several marinas in the Plum Point, Locust Point and Henderson Point areas provide fuel and amenities. Harbor North Marina, at the mouth of Herring Creek, may have transient space but has three foot approach depths. Farther north, Locust Point Marina may have space as well and has five foot approach depths.

Anchorage: If you have a shoal-draft vessel and keep an eye on the depth sounder, you can anchor on the Elk River north of Welch Point. Anchor clear of the channel in 5- to 7-foot depths over a mud bottom.

Jacobs Nose Cove, off the Elk

The Coast Guard has designated this little bight on the west side of the mouth of the Elk River (north of flashing green buoy "9") a special anchorage area. (Vessels up to 65 feet are not required to show an anchor light.) It is open to the south and east with 5- to 6-foot depths. Also keep in mind that it is open to wakes from passing vessels, some of which are large, ocean-going freighters heading to or from the C&D Canal. If yours is a deep-draft vessel, and you need an anchorage south of the C&D, look in the Sassafras River rather than trying the anchorages between Welch Point and the mouth of the Sassafras.

BOHEMIA RIVER

The Bohemia River joins the Elk River about four miles below Back Creek. Wide and pleasant, it offers an opportunity for those with shallower drafts to cruise off the main shipping channel, which is often crowded with heavy traffic. A pretty river, the Bohemia offers the first taste of typical Chesapeake Bay scenery: Tree-lined heights, (magnificent in autumn), border fertile croplands that give way to gently rolling green shores, where beautiful modern homes and extensive farm estates overlook waters that were once the highways of the Colonial era. Big looping bights often shelter marine services and protected anchorages. Also, don't forget to enjoy jellyfish-free swimming in the freshwater Bohemia. (The Bay's resident stinging nettles prefer the more saline environment usually found farther south).

NAVIGATION: Use Chart 12274. The lower part of the Bohemia River has several charted shoals but reliably carries 7-foot depths throughout much of its length. Sailing vessels regularly cruise here, as evidenced by its sizable moored fleet. Favor the south side of the Bohemia's entrance (closer to Ford Landing and then Veazey Cove), as it carries 7-foot depths. (There is a shoal off Town Point on the northern side of the entrance.) Upriver, past flashing red "2" off of Long Point, the channel deepens but is rather narrow, with shoals on either side. Be sure to honor the red daymark "4" at Old Hack Point. (The general rule on the Bay and its tributaries is stay to midstream and give points of land a wide berth.) A fixed bridge (State Route 213) with a 30-foot vertical clearance is about 4 miles upstream, barring many sailboats from traveling farther upstream to Great and Little Bohemia creeks. There is a popular beach at the north end of the bridge.

Dockage: Hospitable yacht yards and marinas are on both banks of the Bohemia. On the north shore are Bohemia Bay Yacht Harbor, Aquamarina Bohemia Vista and Two Rivers Yacht Basin. All have transient slips and pump-out service. On the southern shore, near the Route 213 Bridge, are Long Point Marine, Aquamarina Hack's Point and Bohemia Anchorage Inc. Dining options are limited to Hack's Point General Store (410-275-2597), which has a coffee bar and deli. Otherwise, the closest restaurants are in Chesapeake City.

Anchorage: In calm weather, you can anchor in 7-foot depths near the mouth of the Bohemia River, but when the wind opposes the tide, it is an uncomfortable spot. If you can manage the depths, good anchoring can be found in the small cove that contains Manor Creek and Bohemia Manor. The south side of the Bohemia's mouth, just off the large, charted dock west of Veasey Cove, carries 9-foot depths. This anchorage is easy to find at night with radar—the dock serves as an excellent radar target. The south side of the river from here to Veazey Cove is often used by boats heading to or from the C&D as an excellent rest stop or to await the favorable current in the Canal.

The nice little tributaries of Great and Little Bohemia Creeks offer great protection from practically all quarters. The creeks both provide decent depths, but their channels are unmarked, so watch the depth sounder and proceed slowly before dropping the hook.

Cabin John Creek and Rogues Harbor, South of the Bohemia River

Anchorage: Just below the Bohemia River are Cabin John Creek and Rogues Harbor, the last two anchorages before the Sassafras River about six miles to the south. Popular on weekends and holidays, Cabin John Creek is east of Elk River flashing red buoy "12" and rather exposed to the northwest, although vessels with 4.5 feet of draft or less can proceed three-quarters of a mile upstream for almost complete protection, except from the west-northwest. The other anchorage, Rogues Harbor (directly across the Elk, west of Elk River flashing green buoy "11"), is protected from north to west. Boats drawing as much as 5 feet use both anchorages. With its high, wooded banks, Rogues Harbor is especially attractive but be aware that it is wide open to wash from ships transiting the Elk River Channel to or from the C&D Canal.

SASSAFRAS RIVER

One of the loveliest rivers on the Eastern Shore, the Sassafras has a fine yachting center, Georgetown, about eight miles above the river's broad entrance. The Sassafras has a deep, well-marked channel, high and attractive banks and plenty of anchorages with easy access.

The areas along both shores of the river mouth are justly popular anchorages for C&D Canal runners during the peak ICW traffic seasons (spring and fall). Water skiers and windsurfers use the waters of the Sassafras extensively.

NAVIGATION: Use Chart 12274. **Use Baltimore tide tables. For high tide at Betterton (Sassafras River), add 2 hours 35 minutes; for low tide, add 2 hours 15 minutes.** The mouth of the Sassafras River meets the Chesapeake Bay at Chesapeake Bay flashing red buoy "50," about 1.5 miles south of Grove Point. From here, mid-river depths range from 13 to 20 feet all the way east to Sassafras River flashing red buoy "2," about 4 miles in from the entrance.

Anchorage: There are several fine anchorages up the Sassafras River, located on both sides of the river. The Ordinary Point anchorage (Sassafras River flashing green buoy "5"), off the river's northern shore across from Turner Creek, is easy to locate on the chart but gets crowded on summer weekends. The Turner Creek anchorage is over a cable area and can be crowded and disappointing to boaters looking for a quiet, pastoral setting. When entering Turner Creek, stay close to the western shore to avoid the long sandbar extending out from the point. Turner Creek green can "1" marks this shoal.

Back Creek, off the Sassafras

Once you have set the hook on Back Creek, you can dinghy ashore to visit Mount Harmon Plantation, which is located across from Knight Island between Foreman and McGill creeks. Open from May through October, this fully restored 18th-century tobacco plantation, owned by the Friends of Mount Harmon (410-275-8819), offers tours Thursday through Sunday from 10:00 a.m. to 3:00 p.m. The plantation has no dinghy dock, although small boats may land on the beach to the right of the Tobacco Prize House (a historic pressing and storage house for tobacco waiting to be shipped), which is on the plantation's waterfront. The dock to the left is on private property. Walk about half a mile across the lawn to the manor house. You can also visit Mount Harmon from the area's marinas.

NAVIGATION: Use Chart 12274. The entrance to Back Creek—off the Sassafras' northern shore—is opposite red nun buoy "8." Favor the north side of Back Creek for the first half mile, then clear Knight Island and head southeast, feeling your way in as you go. Watch the depth sounder closely when entering Back Creek, as depths vary greatly and do not follow any "intuitive" pattern.

Anchorage: You can anchor near Back Creek on the Sassafras-proper, off the entrance to Back Creek or in Back Creek itself. Inside the creek, anchor close to the southeastern shore past the isthmus connecting Knight Island to the mainland, where depths are at least 6 feet.

Freeman and Woodland Creeks, off the Sassafras

Both of these little creeks are on the south side of the Sassafras just west of Georgetown. Boats drawing up to 6 feet may anchor in the mouth of Freeman Creek, but explore upstream only by dinghy because depths change rapidly. Woodland Creek, about a half-mile east of flashing red "10," has fairly good protection. If you draw less than

Georgetown, Sassafras River, MD

SASSAFRAS RIVER		Largest Vessel Accommodated	VHF Channel Monitored	Transient Berths / Total Berths	Approach / Dockside Depth (reported)	Floating Docks	Gas / Diesel	Groceries, Ice, Marine Supplies, Snacks	Repairs: Hull, Engine, Propeller	Lift (tonnage), Crane, Rail	Min/Max Amps	Laundry, Pool, Showers, Courtesy Car	Pump-Out Station	Nearby: Grocery Store, Motel, Restaurant
		Dockage					Supplies		Services					
1. Gregg Neck Boat Yard	410-648-5360	60	-	6/80	10/10	F	-	IM	HEP	L50, C	30/30	S	P	-
2. Georgetown Yacht Basin 🖳 WiFi	**410-648-5112**	**200**	**71/09**	**100/300**	**30/20**	**F**	**GD**	**GIMS**	**HEP**	**L110, C30**	**30/100**	**LPS**	**P**	**GMR**
3. Granary Marina 🖳 WiFi	410-648-5112	125	09/71	10/150	13/10	F	GD	IMS	HEP	L100, C15	30/100	LPS	P	GMR
4. Skipjack Cove Yachting Resort 🖳 WiFi	410-275-2122	120	16	40/368	17/8	-	GD	GIMS	HEP	L70	30/100	LPS	P	GMR
5. Duffy Creek Marina 🖳	410-275-2141	65	-	10/108	6/6	F	GD	IMS	HEP	L35	30/50	LPS	P	GR
6. Sailing Associates Inc. 🖳 WiFi	410-275-8171	60	16/68	10/80	15/12	F	-	IS	HEP	L	30/50	PS	P	GMR
7. Sassafras Harbor Marina 🖳 WiFi	410-275-1144	120	16/71	15/200	15/12	F	-	IMS	HEP	L70	30/100	LPS	P	GR

Corresponding chart(s) not to be used for navigation. 🖳 Internet Access WiFi Wireless Internet Access Waterway Guide Cruising Club Partner

See www.WaterwayGuide.com for current rates, fuel prices, web site addresses, and other up-to-the-minute information.

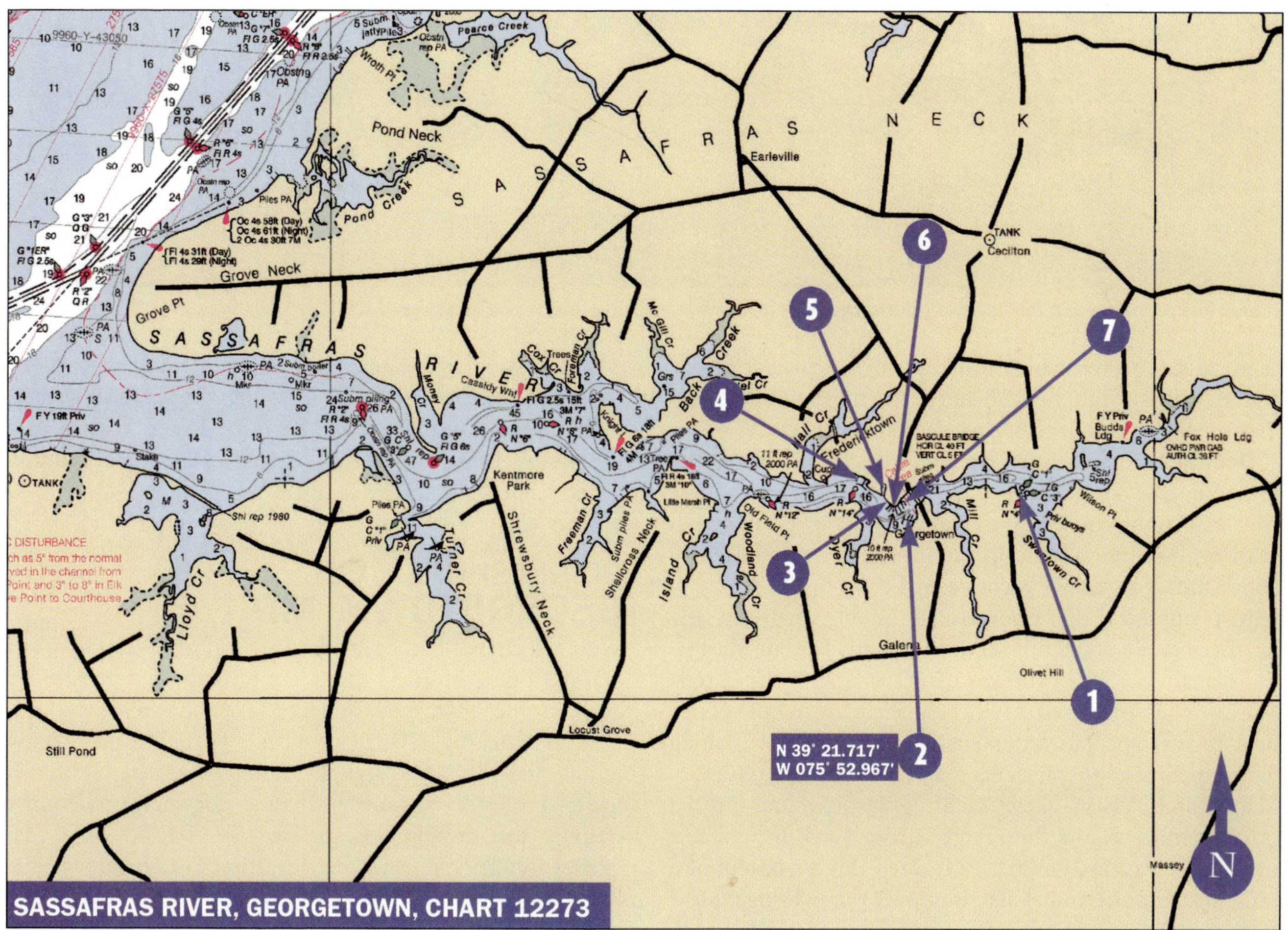

SASSAFRAS RIVER, GEORGETOWN, CHART 12273

4 feet, you can feel your way inside. You can anchor here with this draft on the north, or off the east side of Daffodil Island, but do not try to go around the island except by dinghy. Just inside Old Field Point is a fine little swimming hole.

Georgetown, on the Sassafras

The state Route 213 Bridge (bascule) at Georgetown has a closed vertical clearance of 5 feet and monitors VHF Channel 13 (or you can use the horn signal—one long blast followed by one short blast). The bridge opens on demand 24 hours daily from April 1 to October 31. From November 1 to March 31, the bridge opens on demand between the hours of 8:00 a.m. and midnight only. Past the bridge, the channel winds unmarked for another four miles before reaching a low fixed bridge. Unless you are headed for the additional marine facilities located beyond the drawbridge in Galena (depths range from 14 to 16 feet up to the Gregg Neck Boatyard in Galena, and then shallow quickly), make this passage by dinghy. The bottom beyond

A view over Georgetown looking west down the Sassafras River. (Not to be used for navigation.) Waterway Guide Photography.

the bridge, covered with decaying leaves, makes for poor anchor holding, but it is a sheltered, pretty spot. Locals say that the Sassafras above Swantown Creek has silted.

Dockage: The Georgetown Yacht Basin, just below the bridge on the south shore, is a full-service repair yard as well as a transient facility. (The Kitty Knight House, an 18th-century inn, restaurant and tavern, is located directly above the Georgetown Yacht Basin.)

Just opposite the Georgetown Yacht Basin on the northern shore is the full-service Sassafras Harbor Marina. Farther to the west (downstream) is the Duffy Creek Marina, which offers all services (specializing in full-service boat repair) and has an extensive parts inventory, along with amenities for transients. Sailing Associates, Granary Marina and Skipjack Cove Yachting Resort round out the other marinas below the bridge. Gregg Neck Boatyard, a unique and relaxed marina, is located three-quarters of a mile upstream from the state Route 213 drawbridge. Most of the marinas at Georgetown have moorings and launch services in addition to transient slips and several sell fuel.

Anchorage: The water at Georgetown is usually crowded with moorings, making it easier to rent a mooring than to anchor here. There is plenty of room to anchor west of Old Field Point and Woodland Creek, but passing vessels kick up wakes, so drop the hook as far away from the channel as possible. The tiny village of Galena, about a mile and a half down the road (south) from the state Route 213 Bridge, has groceries. This road has little or no shade, which is something to consider on hot days.

If you want to be near the restaurants and marinas of Georgetown, look for a spot among the sizable moored fleet opposite Skipjack Cove Yachting Resort (east of red nun buoy "14"). Depths run from 9 to 19 feet and holding is good.

GOIN' ASHORE: GEORGETOWN, MD

With a sheltered harbor along the Sassafras River and seven marinas doing business there, Georgetown is a magnet for boaters. Once there, you can rent a bike and explore the area, or head to nearby Galena (1.5 miles), where there are plenty of antiques shops and unique gift shops. Galena is known for its profusion of pink and white dogwoods and, more recently, the addition of cherry trees.

History: The most historic attraction in Georgetown, the Kitty Knight House (14028 Augustine Herman Hwy., 410-648-5200), operates as an inn and restaurant. Local lore and legend says that Kitty Knight saved a few homes as the British, advancing up the Sassafras, set fire to the town in 1813. Refusing to leave a sick neighbor in one of the houses, Kitty Knight beat out flames with a broom and famously asserted, "If you burn this house, you burn me with it." An 1855 newspaper article says that the British commander was so moved by her actions that he ordered his troops back to the barges, leaving a church and four houses standing. One of the houses later became her home and eventually, an inn. A plaque near the front door reads "In honor of Mistress Kitty

Knight, revolutionary Belle and Beauty, a friend of General George Washington."

Galena is named for the type of silver discovered in a mine near the town in 1813. The mine closed soon after, to keep it from British troops ravaging the area during the War of 1812.

Points of Interest: George Washington slept in Georgetown, and the town has the marker to prove it. The marker, at the intersection of Route 213 and Queen Street, near the post office, notes that the town was a base for Continental supplies from 1775 to 1783, and Washington stopped there "en route to points north and south." In Galena, shopping is the draw.

Special Events: Galena hosts an annual Dogwood Festival each May. The event features a road race, a parade, an 1812 militia re-enactment, a baby contest, line dancing and Eastern Shore food.

Shopping: If it is antiques you are after, Galena provides many options. Firehouse Antiques Center (410-648-5639), Galena Antiques Center (410-708-0247), and a few others, are all on North Main Street. Otwell's Market grocery store is less than two miles away at 120 E. Cross St. and will provide transportation (410-648-5111).

Dining: Located atop the banks of the Sassafras River, the Kitty Knight House Restaurant offers a spectacular sunset view of Georgetown Harbor and innovative cuisine (410-648-5200). It is also the site of an Inn with 11 guest rooms. Some of the best eats in Galena are served up at the Galena Fire Hall, where all-you-can-eat breakfasts and dinners are held a few times a month as fundraisers for the volunteer fire company.

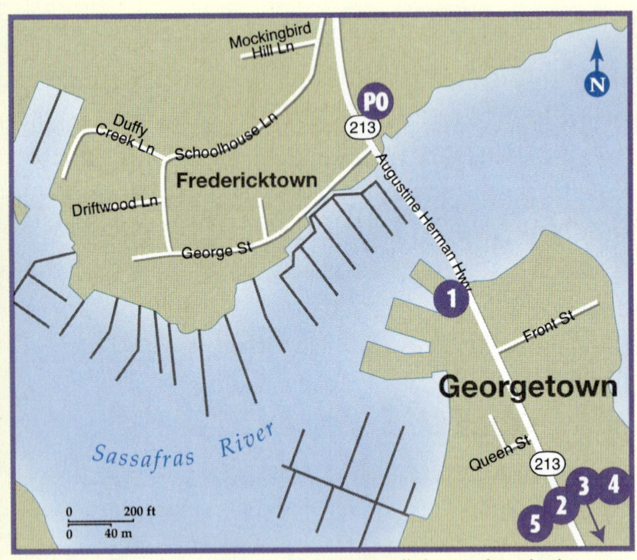

Reference the marina listing tables to see all the marinas in the area.

POINTS OF INTEREST
1 Kitty Knight House

SHOPPING
2 Firehouse Antiques Center (in Galena)
3 Galena Antiques Center
4 Otwell's Market (in Galena)

DINING
1 Kitty Knight House
5 Galena Fire Hall

POST OFFICE

ADDITIONAL RESOURCES

- KENT COUNTY, MD, www.kentcounty.com
- GALENA, MD: www.galenamd.com

NEARBY MEDICAL FACILITIES
Union Hospital in Elkton, 106 Bow St., Elkton, MD 21921, 410-398-4000 (7 miles) www.uhcc.com/Directions

Cecilton Family Practice: 251 S Bohemia Ave., Cecilton, MD 21913, 410-275-8157 (3 miles)

Chester River Hospital Center, 100 Brown St., Chestertown, MD 21620, 410-778-3300 (17 miles) www.chesterriverhealth.org

NEARBY AIRPORT
Cecil County Airport, 1737 Old Field Pt. Road, Elkton, MD, 410-398-0234 (10 miles)

Betterton, off the Sassafras

Betterton, off the south side of the Sassafras River's mouth, is enjoying a revival in tourism and popularity. For the first half of the 20th century, this was the site of one of the Chesapeake Bay's most beloved beach resorts. Vacationers came here in droves—usually by ferryboat from Baltimore—to enjoy Betterton's amenities, which included guesthouses, arcades, dance halls and beer gardens. But when the ferries stopped running in the 1950s, Betterton declined nearly into extinction.

While it might not be the full-fledged resort it once was, Betterton is still worth a short visit for other reasons. Besides a public fishing pier at which boats can load and unload in about 12 feet of water (keep your visit brief). Betterton also boasts county-owned transient slips (no hookups) with 5 feet of water. Dockage here is free, but there is a one-night-per-visit limit. Note that Betterton is not well protected, particularly from the north but does offer some protection from the south. Those who stop off at Betterton can also enjoy the five-acre waterfront park, with its large beach and some 700 feet of public waterfront. Here, you will find a bathhouse, public restrooms, a lighted boardwalk and a picnic pavilion.

STILL POND

This small bay, about two and a half nautical miles south of Howell Point is really two anchorages under one name. Still Pond Creek and the mouth of Churn Creek combine to provide excellent good weather anchoring options. There are no marine facilities here, though. To approach, take a bearing from red buoy "44" in the ship channel if approaching from the north, or Red "42" if from the south, towards flashing red light "2S" west of the old Coast Guard station. Approaching "2S", Churn Creek is to your south, forming a small bay that provides a popular anchorage in good weather or southerly winds. Locals refer to this as "Outside" Still Pond. Nine-foot depths continue deep into the cove near the bar across the actual Churn Creek entrance. For a more secure anchorage in northerly or west winds, moderate draft vessels can continue from "2S" into Still Pond Creek. The channel is well marked but extremely narrow after green "7". Staying close to the beach and the trees, and with careful attention to the markers, you will find depths of about 5 feet in spots. Watch for a strong current at the mouth of the creek. Vessels drawing more than 4 feet will likely find the entrance channel quite challenging except on a spring high tide. Once inside, you will find about a dozen permanent moorings and plenty of room to anchor with depths typically 8 feet. Both Still Pond Creek and Churn Creek are good for dinghy exploration and the banks of both are sparsely developed and quiet.

WORTON CREEK

Although it looks insignificant on the chart, Worton Creek rates high on almost all counts. It is convenient to the Bay's main shipping channel, the approach is unobstructed (except possibly by crab pots), and it provides attractive, protected anchorages and excellent land-based facilities. Worton Creek can provide protection in seriously bad weather and is the first such spot traveling south from the C&D Canal.

NAVIGATION: Use Chart 12278. The Creek's well-marked entrance is usually good for 8-foot depths to Green Point Marina but requires some attention because it is narrow and steep sided. On approaching the entrance, a shoal off Handy's Point builds out northeastward and is longer than it appears. Inside the creek, you are protected from almost any kind of weather. In periods of strong north winds, depths past The Wharf at Handy's Point marina may struggle to exceed 6 feet.

The approach to Worton Creek is straightforward, but if entering in bad weather, or at night, take a bearing from Chesapeake Bay quick flashing red buoy "36" in the main shipping channel to quick flashing red buoy "2" at the entrance to the creek to avoid the hazards, and then follow the green daybeacons "3" and "5" in from there. From green "5", turn to port and head for the bulkhead at Green Point Landing Marina. Follow close to the docks into the creek, where several small green buoys show the channel to Worton Creek Marina.

Dockage: There are 6- to 8-foot depths into all three marinas on the creek. The first two marinas (Green Point Landing and The Wharf at Handys Point) are just inside Handys Point on the east side of Worton Creek, while Worton Creek Marina, with its Harbor House Restaurant, is farther up Worton Creek at Buck Neck Landing. Green Point and Wharton Creek both sell gas and diesel.

Anchorage: In good weather, many boats anchor near Worton Creek's entrance, north of quick flashing red buoy "2" (in 9 feet of water), but be sure to avoid this area in strong west and northwest winds. On hot summer nights, this is a good spot to catch any light southerly breezes while providing a front row seat for boat and ship traffic on the Bay and a beach to stretch your legs. You can also anchor farther up the creek beyond the first two marinas, but before reaching Worton Creek Marina. Simply turn to starboard about midway to the mouth of Mill Creek and drop your hook anywhere. Depths of 5 feet carry quite close in to the western shore of the creek here. Mill Creek provides an excellent spot for kayaking, with resident bald eagles in addition to the usual ospreys and other wildlife. Or take your dinghy on up Worton Creek past the marina for an Eastern Shore surprise in the form of a private, local marina tucked up in the head of the creek.

Button Beach, South of Worton Creek

Just south of Worton Creek and Handys Point, the Bay's shoreline curves in a big half-moon, creating a crescent-shaped beach. Locally known as Button Beach, this is a popular place to swim and picnic, and good depths run almost up to the shore. Most boats run close in to drop the hook while houseboats, outboard-powered boats and other shoal-draft craft put their bows directly on the bank.

FAIRLEE CREEK

Fairlee Creek is like Worton Creek: Close to the Bay's main shipping channel with quite an attractive and sizeable anchorage. The beach just inside the creek's mouth is a popular spot for cruisers, particularly shoal-drafters, who often nudge their noses right against the sand. The entrance may be a little unnerving, since the channel almost looks like it's on the beach and traffic is heavy on weekends, but Fairlee Creek's pastoral scenery will more than repay you for the rigors of the entrance. Some consider St. Paul's Church, near the hamlet of Fairlee, to be the nation's oldest continuously used Episcopal Church. The congregation was established in 1650, and the building was erected in 1713.

NAVIGATION: Use Chart 12278. The entrance marker to Fairlee Creek has changed from a floating red to a fixed marker, flashing red "2F." The entrance is a somewhat difficult, narrow dogleg with a noticeable tidal current. A series of red and green buoys will lead you from "2F" along the beach to a sharp turn to starboard at the actual entrance. Follow the markers carefully, favoring the beach side of the channel. Currents can have some force, so be bold as you go through the narrow entrance, using enough forward speed to avoid being set onto the channel's shallow edges. Watch closely on your approach for boat traffic, swimmers and fisherman in and around the entrance.

Dockage: Great Oak Landing Marina, the only marina on Fairlee Creek, reports entrance depths of 7 feet at mean low water (lower on moon tides or with the wind blowing it

Worton Creek, Fairlee Creek, Tolchester, MD

		Largest Vessel Accommodated	VHF Channel Monitored	Transient Berths / Total Berths	Approach / Dockside Depth (reported)	Floating Docks	Gas / Diesel	Groceries, Ice, Marine Supplies, Snacks	Repairs: Hull, Engine, Propeller	Lift (tonnage), Crane, Rail	Min/Max Amps	Laundry, Pool, Showers, Courtesy Car	Pump-Out Station	Nearby: Grocery Store, Motel, Restaurant
		Dockage					Supplies		Services					
WORTON CREEK														
1. Green Point Landing (WiFi)	410-778-1615	55	16/79	4/57	12/10	-	GD	IMS	HEP	L15	30/30	S	P	-
2. The Wharf at Handy's Point	410-778-4363	60	16	/68	9/9	-	-	IS	HE	L35	50/50	LS	-	G
3. Worton Creek Marina	410-778-3282	80	16/09	25/110	6/6	-	GD	GIMS	HEP	L70	30/50	LPS	P	GR
FAIRLEE CREEK														
4. Great Oak Landing (Internet Access) (WiFi)	410-778-5007	80	09	50/350	7/6	-	GD	GIMS	HEP	L50	30/50	LPS	P	GMR
TOLCHESTER BEACH														
5. Tolchester Marina (WiFi)	**410-778-1400**	**60**	**16**	**20/263**	**6/6**	**-**	**GD**	**IMS**	**HEP**	**L50, C**	**30/50**	**LPS**	**P**	**MR**

Corresponding chart(s) not to be used for navigation. (Internet Access icon) Internet Access (WiFi icon) Wireless Internet Access (Club icon) Waterway Guide Cruising Club Partner

See www.WaterwayGuide.com for current rates, fuel prices, web site addresses, and other up-to-the-minute information.

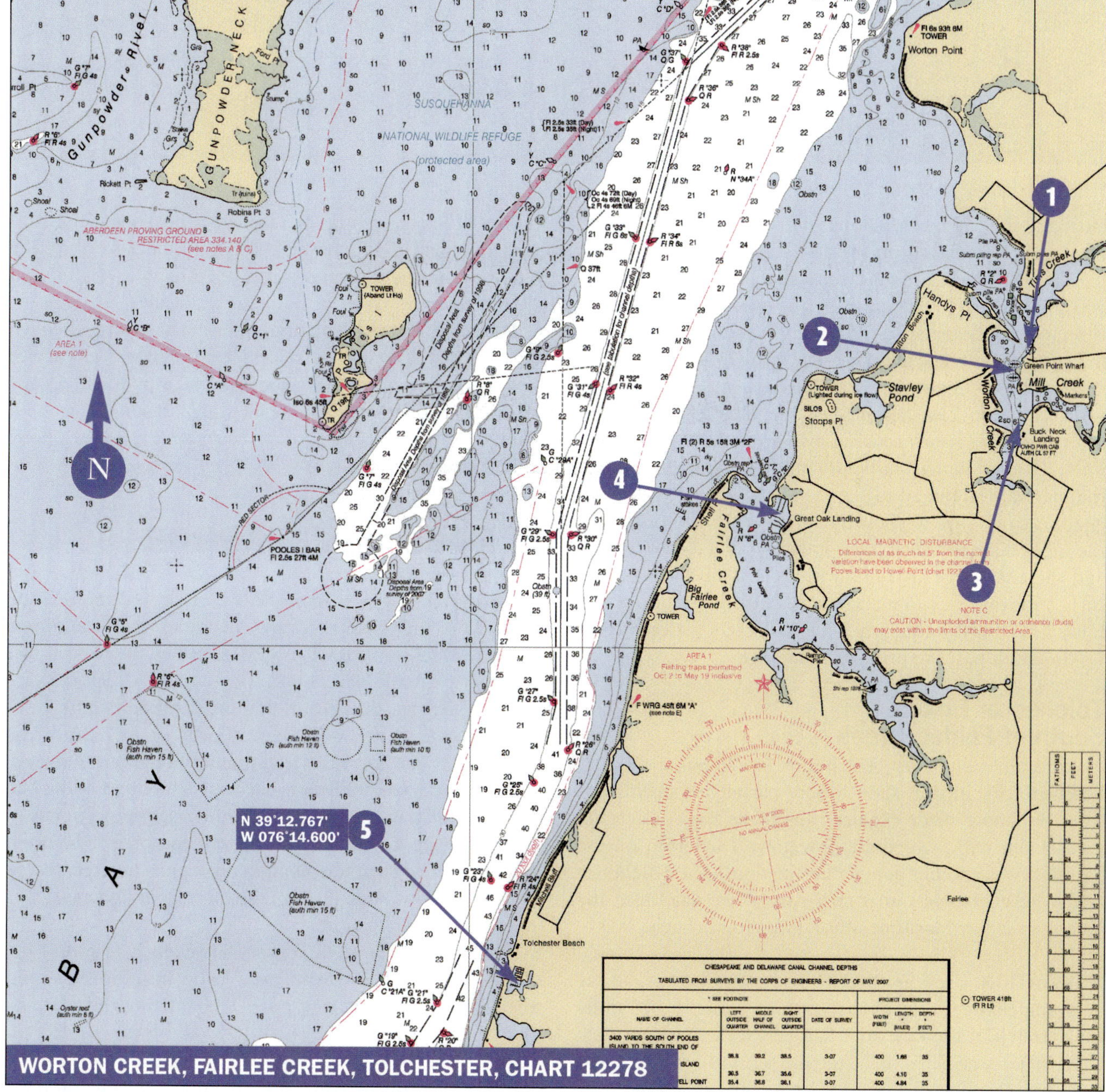

Looking north over Fairlee Creek and Great Oak, MD. (Not to be used for navigation.) Waterway Guide Photography.

out), and the channel width has narrowed to 50 to 75 feet. The marina is located on the east shore of Fairlee Creek, to port just inside the entrance. Jellyfish Joel's (410-778-5007), a popular weekend gathering spot for area boaters, is on a small beach at the marina. On summer weekends, the party goes on late and loud; if you are looking for peace and quiet, this might be a deal breaker.

Anchorage: The beaches at the creek's mouth are favorite fishing spots, so keep a sharp lookout for fishing lines. The anchorage starts just inside the creek, opposite the marina. Depths average 6 to 8 feet and the holding is good. Also be sure to show an anchor light if you stay for the night. Fairlee Creek is a popular weekend destination, and the anchorage area fills with dozens of boats. Arrive early and leave late to avoid the rush through the narrow inlet. There will frequently be water skiers active further up the creek past the primary anchorage.

Tolchester Beach, South of Fairlee Creek

A convenient stopover, Tolchester Beach was a popular beach resort in the days when passenger steamships from Baltimore made regular runs to its large hotel and amusement park, which are now gone. (Betterton on the Sassafras was another popular destination.) The Tolchester Beach Resort bandstand is now part of the display at the Chesapeake Bay Maritime Museum in St. Michaels, MD.

NAVIGATION: Use Chart 12278. The main Chesapeake Bay shipping channel runs almost onshore along the 10-mile-long stretch of the Bay from Fairlee Creek south to Rock Hall, MD. Large ships make the passage at high speed and leave considerable wake. The stretch is broken midway by the little community of Tolchester Beach and the strategically located Tolchester Marina, 30 miles south of the C&D Canal and 25 miles north of Annapolis, directly off the Bay with no rivers or points to navigate.

Dockage: Popular Tolchester Marina has a large dredged basin with quick direct access to the Bay, full-service repairs (engine repairs are a specialty), a pool and a cozy restaurant (open during the boating season). The pool bar overlooks the beach and gives an amazing view of any ships transiting the Bay.

ROCK HALL HARBOR

NAVIGATION: Use Chart 12272. **Use Baltimore tide tables. For high tide at Swan Creek, subtract 8 minutes; for low tide, subtract 9 minutes.** When heading down the Bay for Rock Hall, Gratitude or Swan Creek, beware of the extensive shoals building out west and south from Swan Point. Those who draw 4 feet or less can cross Swan Point Bar and run directly in although some deeper drafts with local knowledge can also do it. Follow the Brewerton Channel range until you near the front range light, then head almost due east to pass north around the 30-foot lighted structure about a mile and a quarter west of Deadman Point, then pick up the buoys and lights for your destination and head in.

The far more prudent course, however, is to round the three-mile-long bar's green can "1" off Eastern Neck, and then follow the deep, well-buoyed channel to the complex of harbors at Rock Hall, Gratitude and Swan Creek. Go slowly, and stick to the marked channel, as the water is shallow east and west of the channel. Do not cut short

Looking east into the entrance to Rock Hall Harbor. (Not to be used for navigation.) Waterway Guide Photography.

green can "5," which is located about three-quarters of a mile north-northwest of the Rock Hall Harbor breakwater, if you are bypassing the main harbor. Also, keep an eye out for stakes and shoals when turning into Rock Hall Harbor. The harbor's center entrance channel does have some underwater bumps, but presents no other problems, particularly for shoal-drafters who follow the channel markers closely. Cruisers have reported a shoal encroaching into the channel from flashing green "5," so it is best to favor the red (east) side. Be sure to follow the marked channel around the perimeter of the basin, as the center of the harbor is shoal.

Dockage: Rock Hall Harbor has a unique configuration that requires sailboats to go around the outside of a square-shaped channel and avoid the shallow middle. The center is used for anchoring by boats with shallow drafts.

A number of good marinas lie in the harbor. The Sailing Emporium sells diesel and has transient space, as well as some groceries. North Point Marina has gas and diesel, as does Rock Hall Landing Marina, which is the closest to downtown Rock Hall. Rock Hall Marine Railway is nearby with a 25-ton lift. Waterman's Crab House, just east along the waterfront, is a popular place to tie up and enjoy traditionally prepared Maryland blue crabs.

Gratitude, Swan Creek, The Haven, North of Rock Hall

This is a favorite area for Bay sailors, with a good anchorage and an extensive collection of marinas and shore side amenities. There are several good restaurants around the Haven, and the town is just a moderate walk away, or you can ride the Trolley from your marina.

NAVIGATION: Use Chart 12278. The channel into Swan Creek is clearly marked starting with flashing red "6" at Gratitude Marina. The channel depths will generally range upwards from 7 feet at MLW. From green can "11" to "15," favor the starboard side of the channel, near the mooring field. Depths continue to decline as you move your way upstream toward The Haven, but adhering to the well-placed daybeacons should keep you out of the mud and in 6-foot depths. The channel hugs the southwest side of the creek along the marinas.

Dockage: Moonlight Bay Marina & Inn, a bed and breakfast offering transient slips, and Gratitude Marina (with a distinctive bulkhead) face west toward the Chesapeake Bay at Gratitude, on the approach to Swan Creek. The channel continuing into Swan Creek and The Haven is well marked by daybeacons and carries 6-foot depths at mean low water, leading to a wealth of additional marina choices.

The first of these are full-service Swan Creek Marina and Swan Creek Boatyard, which are nestled in a protected cove behind a large mooring field to starboard on entry. (Swan Creek Boatyard is on the east side of the cove while the marina is to the west; both are run by the same owner.) Next up to starboard is Osprey Point Marina, with a pool, inn and restaurant. Just beyond Osprey Point, Haven Harbour Marina offers transient slips and does repair work. Spring Cove Marina is located north of Haven Harbour Marina and east of green daybeacon "3," but it must be approached from the south at green "7" and may be difficult for vessels drawing more than 5 feet.

Anchorage: The primary anchorage in Swan Creek is north of The Haven where the creek proper turns north. Take a wide turn around Swan Creek green "15" and head

Rock Hall, MD

Rock Hall, MD		Largest Vessel Accommodated	VHF Channel Monitored	Transient Berths / Total Berths	Approach / Dockside Depth (reported)	Floating Docks	Gas / Diesel	Groceries, Ice, Marine Supplies, Snacks	Repairs: Hull, Engine, Propeller	Lift (tonnage), Crane, Rail	Min/Max Amps	Laundry, Pool, Showers, Courtesy Car	Pump-Out Station	Nearby: Grocery Store, Motel, Restaurant
		Dockage					Supplies		Services					
ROCK HALL														
1. The Sailing Emporium (Internet Access, Wireless Internet Access)	410-778-1342	120	16/09	20/165	8/8	-	D	GIMS	HEP	L35, C15	30/50	LPS	P	GMR
2. Waterman's Crab House	410-639-2261	75	-	25/25	7/6	F	-	IS	-	-	30/50	-	-	GMR
3. Rock Hall Landing Marina (Internet Access, Wireless Internet Access, Waterway Guide Cruising Club Partner)	410-639-2224	80	16	15/75	8/8	F	GD	I	-	-	30/50	PS	P	GMR
4. Rock Hall Marine Railway	410-639-2263	50	-	/25	5/5	-	-	M	H	L25, R	30/30	S	-	GMR
5. North Point Marina Rock Hall (Internet Access, Wireless Internet Access)	410-639-2907	100	16/72	10/140	9/8	-	GD	IMS	-	-	30/50	LPS	P	GMR
GRATITUDE/SWAN CREEK														
6. Gratitude Marina (Wireless Internet Access)	410-639-7011	50	16	10/80	7/5	-	GD	IM	HEP	L35	30/50	SC	P	GMR
7. Moonlight Bay Marina/Inn	410-639-2660	42	-	20/50	4/7	-	-	I	-	L5	30/30	S	-	GMR
8. Swan Creek Marina (Wireless Internet Access)	410-639-7813	60	16/69	10/107	7/7	-	-	I	HEP	L40	30/50	S	P	GMR
9. Osprey Point (Internet Access, Wireless Internet Access)	410-639-2194	60	16/69	/160	6/6	F	-	IS	H	L35	30/50	LPS	P	GMR
10. Haven Harbour Marina, LLC (Internet Access, Wireless Internet Access)	410-778-6697	60	16/68	30/217	6/6	-	GD	GIMS	HEP	L50,C15	30/50	LPS	P	GMR
11. Spring Cove Marina (Internet Access, Wireless Internet Access)	410-639-2110	45	-	-	6/6	-	-	I	-	-	30/30	PS	P	GMR

Corresponding chart(s) not to be used for navigation. Internet Access · Wireless Internet Access · Waterway Guide Cruising Club Partner

See www.WaterwayGuide.com for current rates, fuel prices, web site addresses, and other up-to-the-minute information.

up the middle of the creek. The anchorage extends about 500 yards upstream, but don't stray too close to the banks where it shoals up rapidly. Holding is generally good in about 6 to 7 feet of water, and the protection is excellent from seas, although a good breeze from the north and west will be felt over the low marsh land in those directions. On weekends, Swan Creek is extremely popular, so it's best to show up early.

GOIN' ASHORE: **ROCK HALL, MD**

Rock Hall has a knack for making the far-away feel close by. Looking west over an expanse of the Chesapeake Bay, this laid-back fishing village is blessed with breathtaking sunsets. And once the sun has disappeared, the miles-away lights of Baltimore are visible in the distance across the harbor.

People who make the trip from Baltimore are often surprised that a way of life that seems to be from bygone years is so near at hand. The pace is slower than the one most of us know, and it is comforting to realize that way of life is not so far away after all.

The main area of town, with most of the non-marine businesses, is centered around Main Street between where it intersects with Chesapeake Avenue and where it crosses Rock Hall Avenue, about six country blocks from the waterfront. From the town dock area, walk or ride your bike along Bayside Avenue in an easterly direction, then turn right at Hawthorne and follow the waterfront until Hawthorne intersects with Chesapeake Avenue. Turn left, and follow this street in an easterly direction until it intersects with Main Street. A left turn onto Main Street will bring you into the main business area of town. Most of these businesses will be less than a mile away.

History: Rock Hall Crossroads, as the town originally was known, was officially established in 1707, but some believe that it was settled years before that. Main Street was part of Kent County's first road, created in 1675. Before it evolved into a fishing village, it was a thriving port for tobacco ships.

A ferry that ran between the Eastern Shore and Annapolis stopped here, and George Washington, James Madison and Thomas Jefferson passed through as they traveled to the Continental Congress in Philadelphia.

Points of Interest: The Waterman's Museum is located at Haven Harbour and is open seven days a week from 10:00 a.m. to 4:00 p.m. and by appointment). The key is available at the Ditty Bag Store in the main building of the marina. In addition to exhibits on oystering, crabbing and fishing, there is a reproduction, one-room shanty shack. These shanties, mounted on flat-bottomed boats and moored on the frozen bay, gave watermen winter shelter.

Occupying two rooms in the Municipal Building, the Rock Hall Museum (open weekends 11:00 a.m. to 3:00 p.m. and by appointment) chronicles the town's traditional way of life, with exhibits on decoy carving, watermen and boats and ships.

Tolchester Beach Revisited on Main Street (open weekends from 11:00 a.m. to 3:00 p.m. and by appointment) is a museum about an amusement park "as seen through the mists of years," as the web site describes it. After opening in 1877 with a merry-go-round and a hand organ pulled by a goat, the park grew into the most popular beach resort in the Bay. It operated for 85 years.

The town is flat, and its roads unclogged, making biking a popular choice. Bicycles can be rented at Rock Hall Landing Marina and at Swan Haven Bed & Breakfast. If you're not in the mood for that much exercise, the new tram service makes continuous loops around Rock Hall to various businesses and points of interest.

Fishing here is a lure (pun intended), and licenses are available either at River Rock Outdoor Store (6274 Rock Hall Ave., 410-778-2561) or West Marine (21386 Rock Hall Ave.,

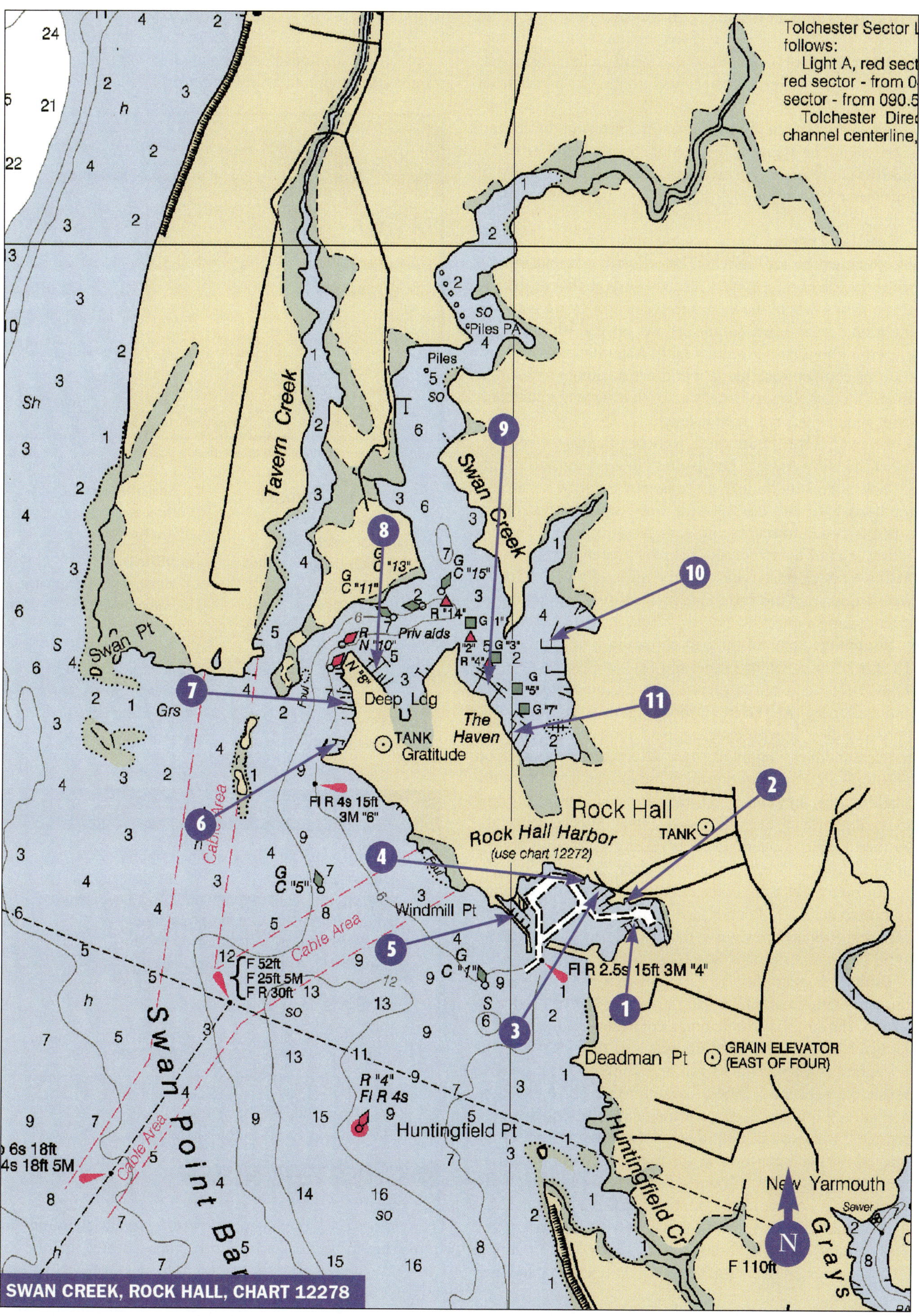

SWAN CREEK, ROCK HALL, CHART 12278

410-639-9959). Many charter fishing boats operate out of the harbor. You can also rent a kayak at Chester River Kayaks on Main Street (410-708-6547). A small swimming beach, known locally as Ferry Park, is just around the corner from the harbor.

For entertainment of a different sort, check out the concert schedule at The Mainstay (5753 Main Street, 410-639-9133) a 120-seat venue that has hosted an impressive array of musicians. Visit www.mainstayrockhall.org for a complete schedule.

Special Events: Fireworks are always held on July 3, accompanied by very moving, broadcasted patriotic music, which can be heard for miles. Boaters often anchor in the Bay at the jetties, where the view and the acoustics are grand. A traditional small-town parade follows on the 4th, only this one runs about an hour and a half! Waterman's Day in July features competitions like a workboat docking contest and an anchor toss contest. Usually a dozen or so watermen compete, while others raft up and watch.

A newer event, Pirates and Wenches Fantasy Weekend, is held in early August. Locals dress in costume and events include a treasure hunt. But the largest event by far is September's FallFest, a street and waterfront festival. Main Street is closed to traffic, and artisans set up shop. There is music around every corner—jazz here, steel drums there. At the Kids Corner, tykes can try milking a goat. On the waterfront, tour the boats or enter an oyster-shucking or crab-picking contest.

Shopping: Some of the best shopping is at the marinas. The Cat's Paw at Sailing Emporium (21144 Green Lane, 410-778-1342) has a bit of everything—clothing, housewares and stationery. At Haven Harbour, there is The Ditty Bag (410-778-6697), with clothes, toys, books and even some nautical antiques. Smilin Jake's Casual Apparel on Main Street (410-639-7280) is "where the Chesapeake Bay meets the islands." Also on Main Street, the purple storefront is home to the Rock Hall Gallery (410-639-2494). Also known as the Reuben Rodney Gallery, it offers furniture, jewelry, pottery and paintings by some of the more than 150 artists living in Kent County. Bayside Foods, offering a full line of groceries, is located at 21309 Rock Hall Ave. In addition to the West Marine mentioned previously, there is a Village Ace Hardware at 5811 Chesapeake Villa Road.

Dining: A great place to get crabs as well as a satisfying burger is Waterman's Crab House, on the harbor (410-639-2261). Harbor Shack is another colorful restaurant that is located waterfront on the northwest side of the harbor. The restaurant is known for its fish and chips and features live music on weekends (20895 Bayside Ave., 410-639-9996). For fine dining and a seasonal menu with dishes like pan-roasted Tasmanian salmon, there is the Inn at Osprey Point, located on the waterfront at the marina (20786 Rock Hall Ave., 410-639-2663). About a block from the Bay, Swan Point Inn is known for its prime rib (20658 Wilkins Ave., 410-639-2500). Downtown, you will find the Kitchen at Rock Hall, serving breakfast through dinner with outdoor seating (5757 Main St., 410-639-2700) and Java Rock, a coffee shop with lots of pastries and different types of java (21309 Sharp St., 410-639-9909). And for dessert, don't miss Durding's Store, an old-fashioned soda fountain serving ice cream and numerous fountain treats (Main Street, 410-778-7957).

Reference the marina listing tables to see all the marinas in the area.

POINTS OF INTEREST

1 The Waterman's Museum
2 The Rock Hall Museum
3 Tolchester Beach Revisited
4 Bicycle Rentals
5 River Rock Outdoor Store
6 Chester River Kayak Rental
7 The Mainstay

SHOPPING

8 The Cat's Paw
9 The Ditty Bag
10 Rock Hall Gallery
11 Smilin Jake's
12 Bayside Foods
13 Ace Hardware

DINING

14 Waterman's Crab House
15 Harbor Shack
16 Inn at Osprey Point
17 Swan Point Inn
18 Kitchen at Rock Hall
19 Java Rock
20 Durding's Store

LIBRARY

ADDITIONAL RESOURCES

- ROCK HALL, MD: www.rockhallmd.com, 410-639-7611
- ROCK HALL VISITORS CENTER: 5718 South Main St., Rock Hall, MD 21661, 410-639-7066

NEARBY MEDICAL FACILITIES

Townsend Memorial Medical Clinic: 5585 S Main St., Rock Hall, MD 21661, 410-639-2240 (1 mile)

Chestertown River Hospital Center, 100 Brown St., Chestertown, MD 21620, 401-778-3300 (16 miles)

CHESTER RIVER

The longest of the deep, navigable rivers winding far into the upper Eastern Shore, the Chester is one of the Bay's great tributaries. Rich in history and scenic charm, but comparatively free of waterborne tourists, it provides delightful, peaceful cruising 28 miles upstream to Chestertown, a jewel of a lovely small town. All the way up the Chester, you can find numerous anchorages with the aid of a chart and depth sounder. The river is well marked and easy to run, studded with small coves, interesting creeks and scenic views.

NAVIGATION: Use Chart 12272. About five nautical miles south of Rock Hall, you can head directly into the mouth of the Chester River, running south around Eastern Neck Island, now the Eastern Neck National Wildlife Refuge. Established in 1962 to preserve the 2,285-acre island for migratory waterfowl, it is also a home to the endangered Delmarva fox squirrel, a "jumbo" variant of the feisty tree-loving rodents common to many urban areas in the United States. As you gently curve around to the northeast, Kent Island will be off your starboard side.

If you are approaching the Chester from the south and going around Love Point, stay to port of the small buoys marking clamming limits, as the water is shoal beyond these markers. The river channel entrance is north and then east of Love Point Light, a 35-foot skeleton tower (the remnant of a screwpile lighthouse like the one at Thomas Point, farther south) with a red-and-white diamond-shaped daymark (flashing white light every six seconds). Stay clear of the tall range markers to the west of the light; they are for ships heading south from the channel to Baltimore. Crab pots are also quite prevalent here, so keep a sharp lookout for them.

Dockage: A red-and-white striped water tower (marked "TR" on the NOAA chart), painted to look like a lighthouse, stands on Kent Island, southwest of flashing red buoy "6." It is just beyond the entrance to the Castle Harbor Marina complex (described in more detail in the Kent Island Narrows section).

From here, the northern entrance to Kent Island Narrows is within sight. Any recent chart edition correctly shows the new channel into Kent Island Narrows from the Chester River. This entrance is from the northwest, not from the north, where the channel had been for more than 50 years. Fixed quick flashing green "1KN" and quick flashing red "2KN" are the first marks. From this point, go between the next set of markers (flashing green "3" and flashing red "4"), green can "3A," and then quick flashing green "5" and quick flashing red "6." At this point, turn to starboard, proceed past flashing red "8" and green daybeacon "9" and follow the well-marked channel as you work your way into Kent Narrows (but read the navigation details in "Kent Island Narrows" later in this chapter first).

Continuing on toward the northeast, the Chester River is well marked, with a plethora of creeks and coves, many sporting top-notch marine services. Some of these facilities cater to local boats; others welcome cruisers seeking a short stay.

Queenstown Creek, off the Chester

A few miles upstream from Kent Island Narrows you find Queenstown Creek, off the Chester's eastern shore. Its entrance channel is sometimes hard to spot, especially at night, as all the channel markers are unlighted. Once you have located red nun buoy "2Q" in the Chester River, it is a straight run southeast past green can "3" and green can "5" into the creek. Use the charted elevated tank as your marker, and keep an eye on the depth sounder as you enter.

The entrance is narrow and quite shoal on either side of the channel; and the shoals move with storms, so seek local knowledge. Recently, 5-foot draft vessels have had difficulty entering, and due to changing government priorities, there will not likely be any promise no dredging soon. Unlike the soft mud of most of the Bay, the bottom here is hard sand, and a grounding may require commercial help or a long wait for high tide.

Inside the entrance, the creek has depths of 8 feet, but the shoal at Blakeford Point extends south a good distance. You will find 7-foot depths and snug anchorage just past Salthouse Cove once inside Queenstown Creek. The town dock is on the shallower southern branch, Little Queenstown Creek on the chart; it is best to anchor elsewhere and dinghy in. Many beautifully preserved period houses are nearby, and it is about a mile to a large outlet shopping center with major clothing chain stores and a sizable gourmet shop. There is a golf course across the creek from town.

Reed Creek and the Corsica River, off the Chester

As you cruise upstream on the Chester, you will pass popular Reed Creek and the Corsica River off the Chester's eastern shore. Much intrigue has always surrounded the big estate overlooking the southeast entrance to the Corsica River. It once belonged to John J. Raskob, builder of the Empire State Building and millionaire chairman of the Democratic Party but was more recently owned by the government of the former Soviet Union and used by members of its embassy as a vacation retreat.

NAVIGATION: Use Chart 12272. If you take it carefully and run a slightly curving course to the entrance (to avoid the first shoal to port and the subsequent one to starboard), you will find 6-foot depths into Reed Creek. It can be a nail-biter, but locals do it all the time; try to follow one of them in. Reed Creek is a popular, but rarely crowded anchorage set amid pastoral fields and sparse waterfront housing. Red nun buoy "2," off Gordon Point inside the creek's entrance, is now the only marker to help you find your way in, but a charted duck blind shows the other side of the channel (if it has not been leveled by a storm just before you get there).

The Corsica River provides good anchorages. One of them lies to starboard, just past red nun "2" and Town Point at the river's entrance. Another anchorage lies farther upriver, north of daybeacon "4," at the mouth of Emory Creek. This area is spectacular in the fall. Banks lined by multicolored trees as waterfowl fly overhead by the thousands or land on the water for the night are signs of the

Chester River, MD

CHESTER RIVER		Largest Vessel Accommodated	VHF Channel Monitored	Transient Berths / Total Berths	Approach / Dockside Depth (reported)	Floating Docks	Gas / Diesel	Groceries, Ice, Marine Supplies, Snacks	Repairs: Hull, Engine, Propeller	Lift (tonnage), Crane, Rail	Min/Max Amps	Laundry, Pool, Showers, Courtesy Car	Pump-Out Station	Nearby: Grocery Store, Motel, Restaurant
		Dockage					Supplies		Services					
1. Lankford Bay Marina 🖳 WiFi	410-778-1414	50	16/71	15/106	7/7	-	GD	IMS	HEP	L40	30/50	LPS	P	-
2. Long Cove Marina	410-778-6777	65	16	19/104	9/6	-	GD	IMS	HEP	L75, C	50/50	S	P	-
3. Kennersley Point Marina WiFi	410-758-2394	55	-	-	4/5	-	-	IMS	HE	L25	50/50	LPS	P	G
4. Rolph's Wharf Marina 🖳	410-778-6389	45	16	5/40	22/7	-	GD	IMS	HEP	L25	30/50	LPS	P	MR
5. Chestertown Marina 🖳	410-778-3616	100	16	48/60	8/6	-	GD	IMS	E	L25	30/50	LS	P	GMR

Corresponding chart(s) not to be used for navigation. 🖳 Internet Access WiFi Wireless Internet Access Waterway Guide Cruising Club Partner

See www.WaterwayGuide.com for current rates, fuel prices, web site addresses, and other up-to-the-minute information.

seasonal change. The Corsica is deep up to Fort Point, but only small boats can use the dredged 2.5- to 3-foot-deep channel to the Centreville town dock, less than a mile away, with its historic district and shopping.

Grays Inn Creek, off the Chester

Several large creeks line the western bank of the Chester north and east of its mouth. Grays Inn Creek features outstanding examples of Eastern Shore private estates.

NAVIGATION: Use Chart 12272. The creek is wide, but the entrance is narrow. Proceed from green can "1" toward the small dock at the end of Spring Point. From there, head over to mid-channel to anchor in depths of 10 to 12 feet over a soft mud bottom. If you are seeking more protection and a quiet night, continue in 8- to 10-foot depths up the creek, favoring the middle of the channel. As you approach Skinners Neck, the creek branches east and west. Either branch provides excellent holding in a residential neighborhood of modest homes.

Langford Creek and Comegys Bight, off the Chester

The entrance to Langford Creek, off the Chester's northwestern shore, is clearly marked. There is a comfortable and secluded anchorage on the eastern side of Cacaway Island at the fork where the creek divides into an eastern and western branch. Do not go ashore on this private island without permission, and do not try to circumnavigate it; the north end extends almost to the river's bank. Note the unmarked shoal extending off Cacaway Island's southwestern shore. On weekends, Cacaway Island is a popular anchorage, and the nearby marinas have all the standard amenities. Continue up the east or west fork of Langford Creek for sheltered, less crowded water.

Back on the Chester River, upstream from the entrance to the Corsica River, is Comegys (pronounced "come-a-jis") Bight, an indentation between Cliffs and Deep points. The Bight provides good shelter from northwest winds and is also an excellent place to drop the hook if you are looking for breezy relief in the high heat of summer, when the Chesapeake's prevailing winds are from the south and southeast. The Bight's shoreline is bursting with trees that tend to obscure the houses nestled in their shade, making this a pleasant rural spot to anchor.

From Comegys Bight, the Chester River snakes its way nine miles up to Chestertown. You will steam pass rolling farmland, neat houses and forested hills. (If, however, you are moving against the current, you will move much slower.) The one navigable creek on this stretch is Southeast Creek, above nun "32." This shallow creek is home to Kennersley Point Marina.

Dockage: Long Cove Marina, which sells fuel and has a 75-ton lift, is behind Long Point, on the north side of Long Cove. Lankford Bay Marina is a full-service facility located just past Drum Point off beautiful Langford Creek. (The marina actually lies at the mouth of Davis Creek where it meets Langford Creek.) In addition to full-service repairs and haul-out, the marina welcomes transients. Kennersley Point Marina has a privately marked channel through shallow Southeast Creek with 4- to 5-foot depths. Farther north, Rolphs Wharf Marina is right on the Chester with deep water and a seasonal beach bar. When you dock at any of these upriver places, check the direction of the tidal current. The ebb, especially, can run rather swiftly.

Anchorage: Beyond Cacaway Island, the river branches east and west. Both branches provide countless possibilities for anchoring in relatively secluded areas, surrounded by farm fields and country homes. Navigable water continues more than two miles up either branch.

Chestertown, on the Chester

Navigation: Use chart 12272. **Use Baltimore tide tables. For Chestertown high tide, add 47 minutes; for low tide, add 34 minutes.**

The historic little city of Chestertown, while well up the Chester River, is worth taking time to explore. Contact the Kent County Tourism Office (410-778-0416) for boating-oriented pamphlets on different parts of the county. (Kent County is between the south side of the Sassafras River and the north side of the Chester.) If *Sultana*, a replica of an 18th-century revenue cutter, is at the town dock, be sure to take a close look. A group of dedicated folks built

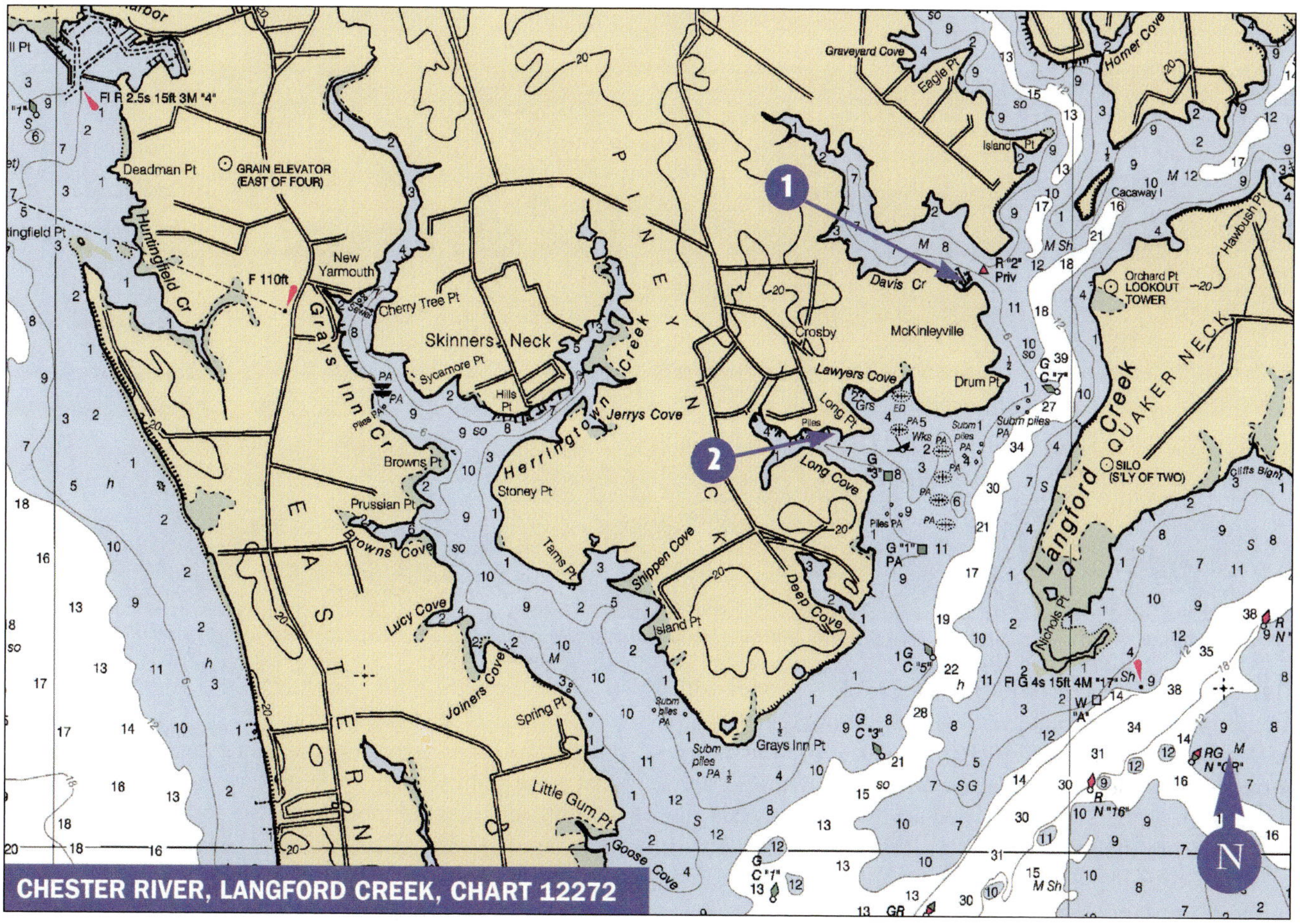

CHESTER RIVER, LANGFORD CREEK, CHART 12272

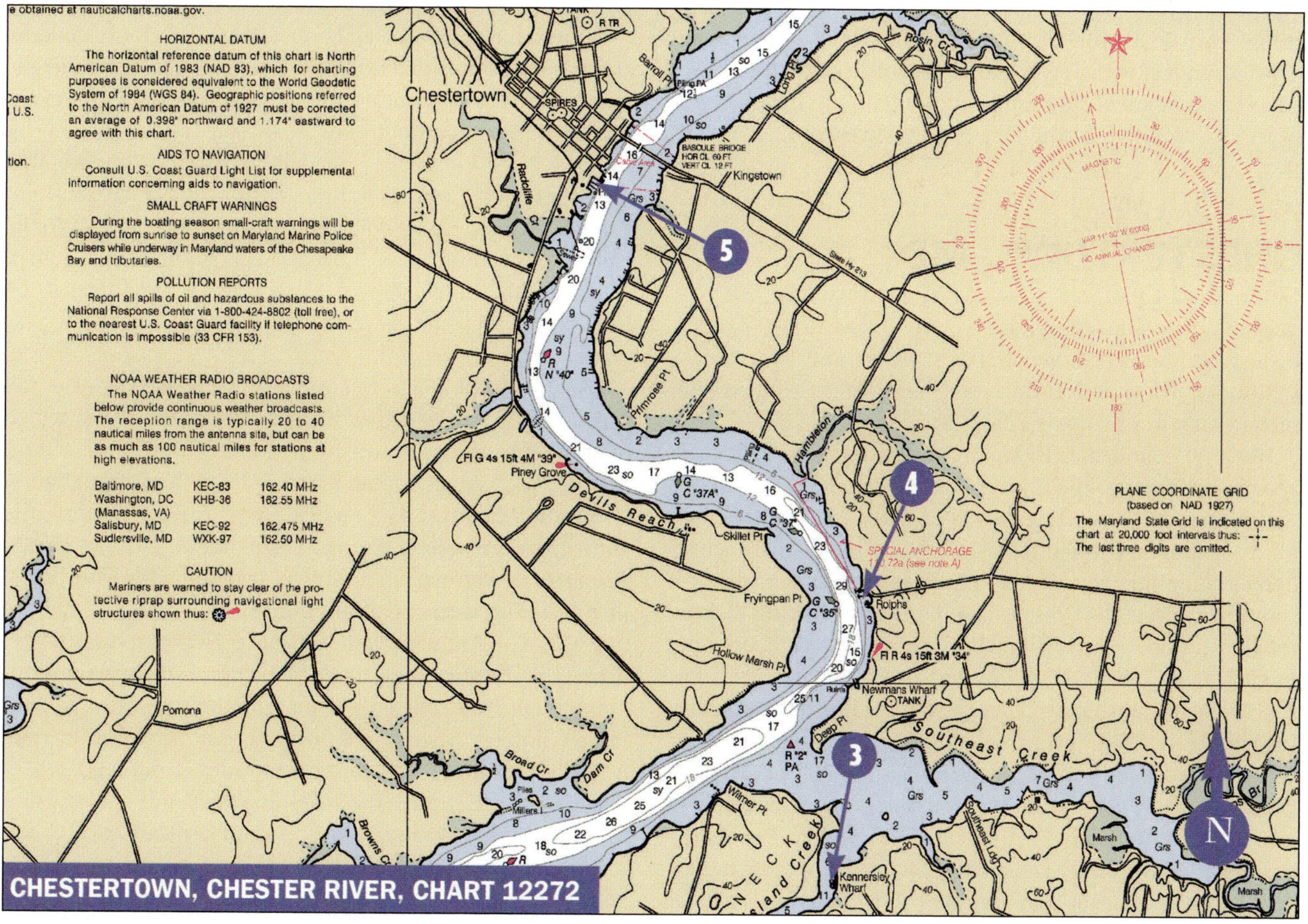

e obtained at nauticalcharts.noaa.gov.

HORIZONTAL DATUM

The horizontal reference datum of this chart is North American Datum of 1983 (NAD 83), which for charting purposes is considered equivalent to the World Geodetic System of 1984 (WGS 84). Geographic positions referred to the North American Datum of 1927 must be corrected an average of 0.398" northward and 1.174" eastward to agree with this chart.

AIDS TO NAVIGATION

Consult U.S. Coast Guard Light List for supplemental information concerning aids to navigation.

SMALL CRAFT WARNINGS

During the boating season small-craft warnings will be displayed from sunrise to sunset on Maryland Marine Police Cruisers while underway in Maryland waters of the Chesapeake Bay and tributaries.

POLLUTION REPORTS

Report all spills of oil and hazardous substances to the National Response Center via 1-800-424-8802 (toll free), or to the nearest U.S. Coast Guard facility if telephone communication is impossible (33 CFR 153).

NOAA WEATHER RADIO BROADCASTS

The NOAA Weather Radio stations listed below provide continuous weather broadcasts. The reception range is typically 20 to 40 nautical miles from the antenna site, but can be as much as 100 nautical miles for stations at high elevations.

Baltimore, MD	KEC-83	162.40 MHz
Washington, DC (Manassas, VA)	KHB-36	162.55 MHz
Salisbury, MD	KEC-92	162.475 MHz
Sudlersville, MD	WXK-97	162.50 MHz

CAUTION

Mariners are warned to stay clear of the protective riprap surrounding navigational light structures shown thus:

PLANE COORDINATE GRID (based on NAD 1927)

The Maryland State Grid is indicated on this chart at 20,000 foot intervals thus: The last three digits are omitted.

CHESTERTOWN, CHESTER RIVER, CHART 12272

Looking southwest over the Chester River and the approach to Chestertown. (Not to be used for navigation.) Waterway Guide Photography.

this beautiful little reproduction of a 1768 schooner with traditional methods right in the middle of town in 1997.

Dockage: Conveniently located close to downtown attractions, Chestertown Marina offers transient dockage. The town purchased the marina in 2012 with plans to refurbish and expand the docks. A three-block stroll down High Street will take you past restaurants, pubs, shops and a library, and into the center of the historical town.

Anchorage: You can anchor off the town before the bridge in 6 to 13 feet of water, being careful to avoid the charted underwater power cable just south of the marinas. Be aware that anchoring can be difficult due to the current. A public landing is at the foot of High Street.

GOIN' ASHORE: CHESTERTOWN, MD

Chestertown's past as a Colonial port is very much in evidence today. The consolidated, dense downtown exudes history. In fact, the town features one of the largest collections of 18th- and 19th-century structures in Maryland, second only to Annapolis, MD.

History: Founded in 1706, Chestertown was, by 1790, the geographic center of population in the United States. After it was named one of six Royal Ports of Entry in Maryland, the influx of money allowed merchants to build large, attractive homes along the river. Money was made in tobacco, then in shipping grain to the West Indies and in shipbuilding. Before the Revolution, trade with the West Indies was hampered by English taxes, resulting in Chestertown's own Tea Party in 1774, when a small cargo of tea was tossed into the Chester River. The event is reenacted annually at the end of May, during a weekend-long celebration. In 1782, Washington College—the 10th oldest liberal arts college in the country—was founded here.

Points of Interest: Perched on the banks of the Chester River, the town has a beautiful park, Fountain Park, which provides the setting for many activities. You can walk the town, which is set out in a grid pattern, in relatively short order, but that is assuming you don't stop anywhere. And what is the point of visiting Chestertown without meandering its brick sidewalks, admiring its architecture and browsing in the many shops and galleries? Banks, the library and the post office are also just a short walk from the waterfront. The Kent County Visitors Center on the corner of Cross Street and Route 213 is a good place to start (410-778-9737).

Tickets for two-hour sails aboard the schooner *Sultana* are available for various dates throughout the season at the Sultana Project on South Cross Street. Self-guided tours are available (Tues. through Sat. in season) at the circa-1784 Geddes Piper House, a Philadelphia-style townhouse that serves as headquarters for the Historical Society of Kent County, which has a collection of maritime and Colonial clothing, furniture and housewares. Another self-guided walking tour, which starts at the Visitors Center, goes to 24 historic sites around town. There also are three Civil War markers in Chestertown.

For those of you less interested in the past than your golf score, there's Chester River Yacht and Country Club, which offers golf, just two miles from the downtown waterfront. Visit www.crycc.org or call 410-778-1369 for information.

Special Events: The largest event in Kent County, the annual Tea Party reenactment on Memorial Day, draws 25,000 people to downtown Chestertown. Beginning the Saturday of Memorial Day weekend and running through August, there is free music in Fountain Park starting at 7:00 p.m. From April through December, a Farmer's Market on Saturday mornings at Fountain Park sells only items from Kent County, such as breads, flowers, pastries and plants. The Artisans Market right next door features local crafts on Saturdays from 9:00 a.m. to 1:00 p.m. In October, the Chestertown Wildlife Show and Sale features fine crafters, mostly wildlife decoy carvers and painters. On the first Saturday in October, historic homes can be toured during Tea Time House Tours. During Downrigging

Weekend in early November, tall ships and other traditional sailing vessels make their way to Chestertown to celebrate the close of the *Sultana's* sailing season. Artists open their studios to the public this week.

Shopping: Antiques shops, bookstores and art galleries are plentiful. Among the many you will find as you stroll the downtown are The Compleat Bookseller (301 High St., 410-778-1480) and Book Plate (112 S. Cross St., 410-778-4167), for current and collectible books. Twigs & Teacups (111 S. Cross #1, 410-778-1708) has ceramics, wind chimes and other gifts, and the Carla Massoni Gallery at 203 High Street (410-778-7330) offers stunning and varied artwork.

Dining: Fish Whistle (98 Cannon St., 410-778-3566) serves a wide variety of dishes on the waterfront. For dinner, try The Front Room Restaurant at the Imperial Hotel (410-778-5000) known for its Friday night specials. Dinner is also served at the Blue Heron Café at 236 Cannon St. (410-778-0188). Lunch locales include the coffee shop Play It Again Sam (108 S Cross St., 410-778-2688) and New York Kosher Style Deli (323 High St., 410-810-0900). For a drink, the White Swan Tavern (231 High St., 410-778-2300).

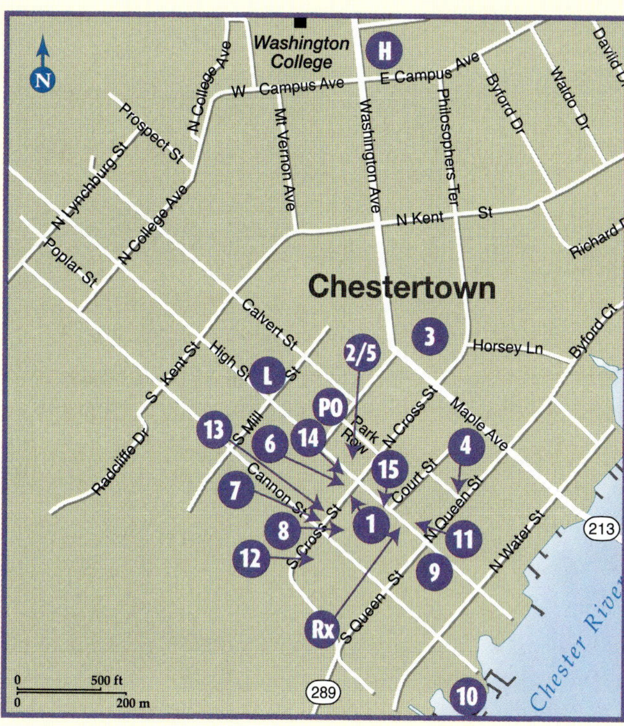

Reference the marina listing tables to see all the marinas in the area.

INFORMATION
1 Visitors Center

POINTS OF INTEREST
2 Fountain Park
3 Schooner Sultana Project
4 Geddes Piper House

SHOPPING
5 Farmers/Artisian Market
6 The Compleat Bookseller
7 Book Plate
8 Twigs & Teacups
9 Carla Massoni Gallery

DINING
10 Fish Whistle
11 Front Room, The Imperial Hotel
12 Blue Heron Café
13 Play It Again Sam
14 NY Kosher Style Deli
15 White Swan Tavern

L **LIBRARY**
Rx **PHARMACY**
PO **POST OFFICE**
H **HOSPITAL**

ADDITIONAL RESOURCES

■ **KENT COUNTY OFFICE OF TOURISM:**
www.chestertown.com

NEARBY MEDICAL FACILITIES
Chester River Hospital Center: 100 Brown St., Chestertown, MD 21620, 410-778-3300
www.chesterriverhealth.org (1 mile)

NEARBY AIRPORTS
Easton Airport: 29137 Newnam Road, Easton, MD 21601, 410-770-8055 (33 miles)

Chester River, Beyond Chestertown

The bridge at Chestertown (12-foot closed vertical clearance) opens on signal between 6:00 a.m. and 6:00 p.m., April 1 through September 30. It opens on signal with 6 hours' notice at all other times and during the rest of the year (410-778-1451). After passing through the channel at this bridge, you can explore the lovely upper reaches of the Chester, with shores untouched by development, and decent depths continuing for a good way upriver.

Anchorage: Downstream, at green can "37" a special anchorage, where vessels 65 feet and under need not show an anchor light, is along the eastern shore of the Chester River just north of Rolphs Wharf Marina. Upstream of red nun "42", the area beyond Possum Point is for dinghy exploration only. The buoys shown on the chart, beginning with "42", may not be reliable guides, as they are private.

KENT ISLAND

William Claiborne established a trading post called Kent Fort here in 1631; it was the first settlement within what later became Maryland. Kent Island is strategically located, with the Kent Island Narrows separating the Chester River to the north from the cruising grounds of Eastern Bay and the Miles River to the south. Boats with drafts up to 6 feet (and mast heights of 65 feet or less) routinely transit the Narrows, although shoaling near the northern entrance is a perpetual problem.

The fixed Kent Narrows Bridge (65-foot vertical clearance) carries U.S. 50 and U.S. Route 301 traffic across the narrowest part of the Chesapeake Bay to the western side of Kent Island. This highway access has transformed the area into a bedroom community for people working in Annapolis, Washington, D.C. and Baltimore.

A northeast view over the Chester River and Historic Chestertown. (Not to be used for navigation.) Waterway Guide Photography.

For cruisers, the island's south shore is teeming with creeks and anchorages (covered in the next chapter, "Eastern Bay to Little Choptank"), while its west shore is relatively featureless. However, there are some great little marina harbors along the island's west shore, and they are very convenient for boaters making the ICW run down the Chesapeake.

NAVIGATION: Use Chart 12270. **Use Baltimore tide tables. For high tide at Kent Island Narrows, subtract 1 hour 40 minutes; for low tide, subtract 1 hour 28 minutes.** There is no harbor of refuge on Kent Island's western shore, heading south from Love Point to the Kent Narrows Bridge, so as you cruise this stretch, give the shore a wider berth than a glance at the chart might indicate. Big clam rigs work here, and the spoils of their dredging tend to create humps in what is otherwise deep water. Note: If you want to visually check your speed while cruising along Kent Island's west shore, use the measured nautical mile south of Matapeake, marked by shore ranges and white-and-orange nun buoys.

Dockage: Three harbors south of the Kent Narrows Bridge have well-marked entrances. Bay Bridge Marina, a 230-slip powerboat-oriented complex with full services, yacht sales and a restaurant, is in the northernmost harbor just south of the Kent Narrows Bridge. They sell all fuels and have floating docks and a pool. Several more dining options are nearby, a general aviation airport adjoins the marina, and shopping centers are only a mile away. Farther south, you will find the well-marked entrances to Kentmorr Marina and, south of that, Queen Anne Marina (on Price Creek). These facilities offer everything from repairs and restaurants to charter boats and an airstrip. (Bay Bridge Airport is three miles away in Stevensville, 410-643-4364, and Baltimore-Washington International is 40 miles, www.bwiairport.com.) Close to the main channel, they make good stopovers for the through-traveler, but call ahead to find out the condition of the channel entrances to all three marinas; they may be quite shallow. Clarks Landing Marina Center is located just inside Crab Alley Creek (east side), off Crab Alley Bay.

KENT ISLAND NARROWS

Kent Island Narrows has become much more than a strip of water connecting the Chester River to Eastern Bay. It is a full-blown, legitimate destination for cruisers of all kinds, bursting with marinas, restaurants, hotels and more. The go-boat set gravitates toward the bars with bikini contests and homesick-looking palm trees, but you will find traditional seafood, steak and family-style restaurants nearby, too. On summer weekends, land-yachters and day-trippers add to the bustling scene. An outstanding paved bike/hike/skate trail extends from here through forests and fields across the island to a beachfront park on the Bay, adding to the activity.

For boating-oriented pamphlets or other tourism information on the Kent Island Narrows area, contact the Queen Anne's County Office of Tourism at 888-400-7787, which also operates an excellent visitor center at the Narrows with exhibits depicting the lives of watermen; look for the skipjack onshore. Since Queen Anne's County is in the center of Maryland's Eastern Shore and extends east to Delaware, the visitors center has information about the entire region.

NAVIGATION: Use Chart 12270. The northern entrance to the Narrows is from the Chester River. When entering from this direction, pass between quick flashing green "1KN" and quick flashing red "2KN," and follow the

RIVIERA INNOVATION CONTINUES

5000 Sport Yacht w/Zeus

4400 Sport Yacht w/IPS

3600 Sport Yacht w/IPS

5800 Sport Yacht w/IPS

The Riviera Sport Yacht.
A boat concept so good it became a collection.

Riviera began the creation of an entirely new type of leisure boat.

We sensed a need for a vessel that would embody the solid dignity of our Flybridge series with the sensual flair of new century design trends and lifestyle needs. The first toe in the water was the 3600 Sport Yacht.

Such was its startling success, we set to work creating a 4700; then a 4400.

All three boats have attracted awards the way they have buyers. The 3600 won Cruiser of the Year from Modern Boating Magazine; then Best Motor Yacht under 40 feet from Christophle Asia Boating Magazine Awards.

Hard on its heels, the 4700 took out Overall Cruiser of the Year, both with Modern Boating and separately, with AMIF, who also bestowed the Australian Manufactured Boat of the Year Award.

Then the hat trick: the newly-released 4400 took the Australian Manufactured Boat of The Year trophy; as well as Cruiser of the Year (over 10 metres).

No doubt some of these accolades also recognize the cutting edge Volvo IPS and Cummins Zeus pod-drive systems and their advantages in efficiency, maneuverability and space-savings.

Each share the core benefit of an uninterrupted space from the generous cockpit through opening glass door and window, to a galley placed centre-stage with a deep lounge area opposite, continuing up to an almost luxury-car-like helm control station, behind the wrap-around windshield.

The sliding side windows and large lift-up awning window and standard electronic sunroof places you in a totally fresh, open living space.

No clears, no canvas; these hardtop vessels are turnkey lock-up. Provisions stowed, boat fuelled, jump on board and you're away.

The only hesitation can be, which size to choose?

WE BUILD INTEGRITY

Ned L. Dozier, II · Mobile: 443-995-0732 · ned@theyachtgroup.com

Kent Island Shore, MD

KENT ISLAND SHORE		Largest Vessel Accommodated	VHF Channel Monitored	Transient Berths / Total Berths	Approach / Dockside Depth (reported)	Floating Docks	Gas / Diesel	Groceries, Ice, Marine Supplies, Snacks	Repairs: Hull, Engine, Propeller	Lift (tonnage), Crane, Rail	Min/Max Amps	Laundry, Pool, Showers, Courtesy Car	Pump-Out Station	Nearby: Grocery Store, Motel, Restaurant
		Dockage					Supplies		Services					
1. Clarks Landing Marine Center - Chester	410-604-4300	60	-	/75	12/8	-	G	IMS	HEP	L25	30/30	S	P	-
2. Bay Bridge Marina	**410-643-3162**	**130**	**68**	**50/230**	**6/8**	**F**	**GD**	**IM**	**HEP**	**L70**	**30/100**	**LPS**	**P**	**GR**
3. Kentmorr Marina	410-643-0029	60	-	5/100	5/	-	GD	I	HEP	L35	30/50	S	P	R
4. Queen Anne Marina	410-643-2021	50	16	2/110	5/5	F	GD	GIMS	-	L30	30/50	-	P	GR

Corresponding chart(s) not to be used for navigation. Internet Access Wireless Internet Access Waterway Guide Cruising Club Partner

See www.WaterwayGuide.com for current rates, fuel prices, web site addresses, and other up-to-the-minute information.

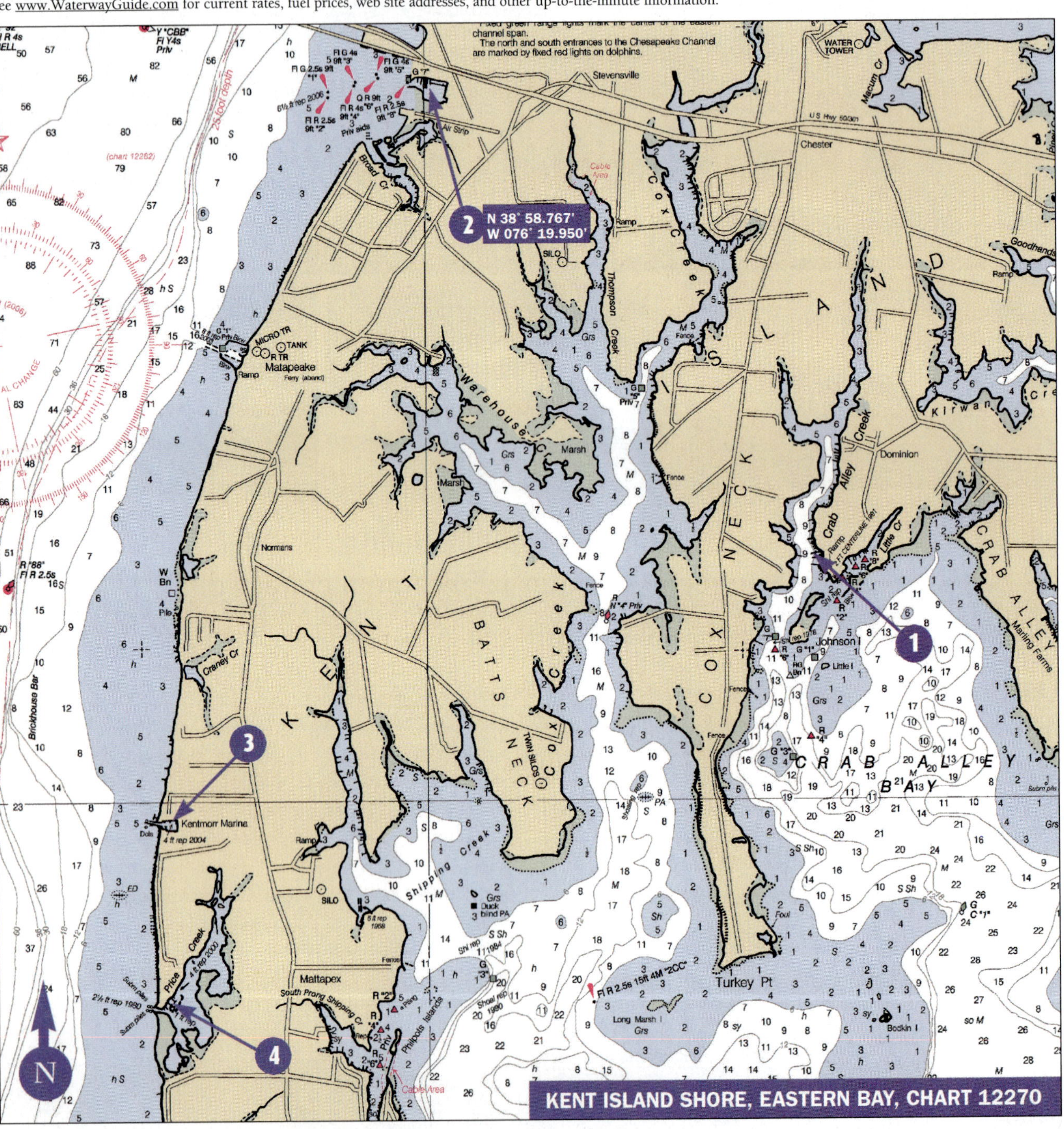

KENT ISLAND SHORE, EASTERN BAY, CHART 12270

Magothy River

Sandy Point

Chesapeake Bay

BAY BRIDGE MARINA

Chesapeake Bay Bridges

U.S. Route 50/301

From Kent Island, looking northwest over Chesapeake Bay. (Not to be used for navigation.) Waterway Guide Photography.

Kent Island Narrows, MD

KENT ISLAND NARROWS		Largest Vessel Accommodated	VHF Channel Monitored	Transient Berths / Total Berths	Approach / Dockside Depth (reported)	Floating Docks	Gas / Diesel	Groceries, Ice, Marine Supplies, Snacks	Repairs: Hull, Engine, Propeller	Lift (tonnage), Crane, Rail	Min/Max Amps	Laundry, Pool, Showers, Courtesy Car	Pump-Out Station	Nearby: Grocery Store, Motel, Restaurant
		Dockage					Supplies		Services					
1. Castle Harbor Marina (WiFi)	410-643-5599	55	16/09	/347	/6	-	GD	GIMS	-	-	30/50	LPS	P	R
2. Piney Narrows Yacht Haven (Internet)	**410-643-6600**	**67**	**16/09**	**15/278**	**7/7**	**-**	**GD**	**IS**	**HEP**	**L60**	**30/50**	**LPS**	**P**	**GMR**
3. Kent Narrows Yacht Yard	410-643-4400	58	-	-	8/8	-	-	M	HEP	L60	-	-	-	-
4. Mears Point Marina (Internet) (WiFi)	410-827-8888	80	09	20/540	6/6	-	GD	IMS	HEP	L50	30/50	LPS	P	MR
5. Lippincott Marine	410-827-9300	75	-	10/200	7/7	-	-	IM	HEP	L25	30/50	LPS	P	MR
6. Wells Cove Marina (Internet) (WiFi)	410-827-3869	100	-	90/100	7/5.5	F	-	-	-	-	30/50	LPS	P	MR
7. Kent Island Yacht Club (WiFi)	410-643-4101	60	-	10/70	6/10	-	-	IS	-	-	30/30	LPS	-	-
8. Anglers Restaurant & Marina	410-827-6717	42	-	5/60	15/10	-	-	IMS	-	-	30/30	-	-	MR

Corresponding chart(s) not to be used for navigation. Internet Access (WiFi) Wireless Internet Access Waterway Guide Cruising Club Partner

See www.WaterwayGuide.com for current rates, fuel prices, web site addresses, and other up-to-the-minute information.

well-marked channel. The project depth is 7 feet at mean low water, with a 75-foot-wide channel, and the channel was dredged in 2008. But in the late summer of 2012, the channel had shoaled significantly from the west. From G "1KN" to G "3" the starboard side of the channel headed into the Narrows shallows quickly. The best water is virtually on the line between G "1KN" and G "3." Pass "3" very closely (ten feet is about right), then stay close to the green side all the way to G "5." After that, the channel was more open and the center will work. Allow for strong currents all through the Narrows, but especially near the bridges. Flood current is northward from Prospect Bay toward the Chester, and it typically runs 1 to 2 knots, but may be faster. The mean tidal range is about 1.5 feet.

Shoaling is much less prevalent than it was with the old channel configuration, but as our 2011 experience shows, it can still change quickly, especially near the first and second sets of daybeacons in the Chester River. Call one of the local marinas for the latest information, as depths may be up to 8 feet after maintenance dredging, or less than 5 feet after a series of storms. You may find temporary buoys between the daybeacons that show the moving shoal edges. The channel markers are "red right returning" from both the Chester River (north) entrance and the Prospect Bay (south) entrance—similar to the buoy systems on Knapps Narrows and the C&D Canal.

The Kent Narrows fixed bridge (65-foot vertical clearance) carries through-traffic on busy U.S. 50/U.S. Route 301, but the old bascule bridge (18-foot closed vertical clearance) remains for local traffic. It opens on signal every half-hour from 6:00 a.m. to 9:00 p.m. from May 1 through November 1. During the remainder of the year, the bridge opens on demand at any time, from 6:00 a.m. to 6:00 p.m. Use one long blast followed by one short blast, or call the tender on VHF Channel 13. While waiting for the bridge to open, remember the current, and be especially careful to stay within the deepwater area. A vessel traveling with the current has the right-of-way over one going against the current.

Some skippers have found a small lump at low tide, about 100 feet north of the fixed bridge, right in the middle of the channel. Finally, take it easy in splitting the last pair of red and green markers of the south channel because a shoal occasionally forms there. Beyond them, you are in the clear and into Prospect Bay, thence Eastern Bay and the Miles River.

Dockage: Castle Harbor Marina complex is just before the red-and-white striped water tower (marked "TR" on the NOAA chart) that is southwest of flashing red buoy "6. This 350-slip marina offers fuel and supplies as well as transient slips. Once inside The Narrows, the shore is dotted on both sides with restaurants, entertainment, fuel docks and marine-related businesses. The marinas and yards above and below the bridge handle an impressive number of boats, resident and transient, power and sail, large and small. You will find the full range of boat services here. Piney Narrows Yacht Haven is located on the north side of the Kent Narrows Bridge in a sheltered and protected basin near Kent Narrows Yacht Yard. Both have 60-ton lifts. Mears Point Marina is farther south and east, in another sheltered basin. South of the Kent Narrows Bridge are Anglers Restaurant & Marina (with limited transient space) and Kent Island Yacht Club. Next is Wells Cove Marina with 5.5 dockside depth at floating docks. Located in nearby Marshy Creek is Lippincott Marine, which offers transient dockage and has 7-foot approach and dockside depths.

Anchorage: There is a quiet and amazingly secluded anchorage just west of the southern entrance to Kent Island Narrows from Prospect Bay, in Kirwan Creek to the northwest of Hog Island. The entrance carries 6-foot depths, not the 8-foot depths shown on the charts. Sound your way in carefully; there are no sudden shoals if you stay in the middle of the open water. The Kent Island Yacht Club uses this area for outrigger launching and for annual hydroplane powerboat races, so keep a sharp lookout.

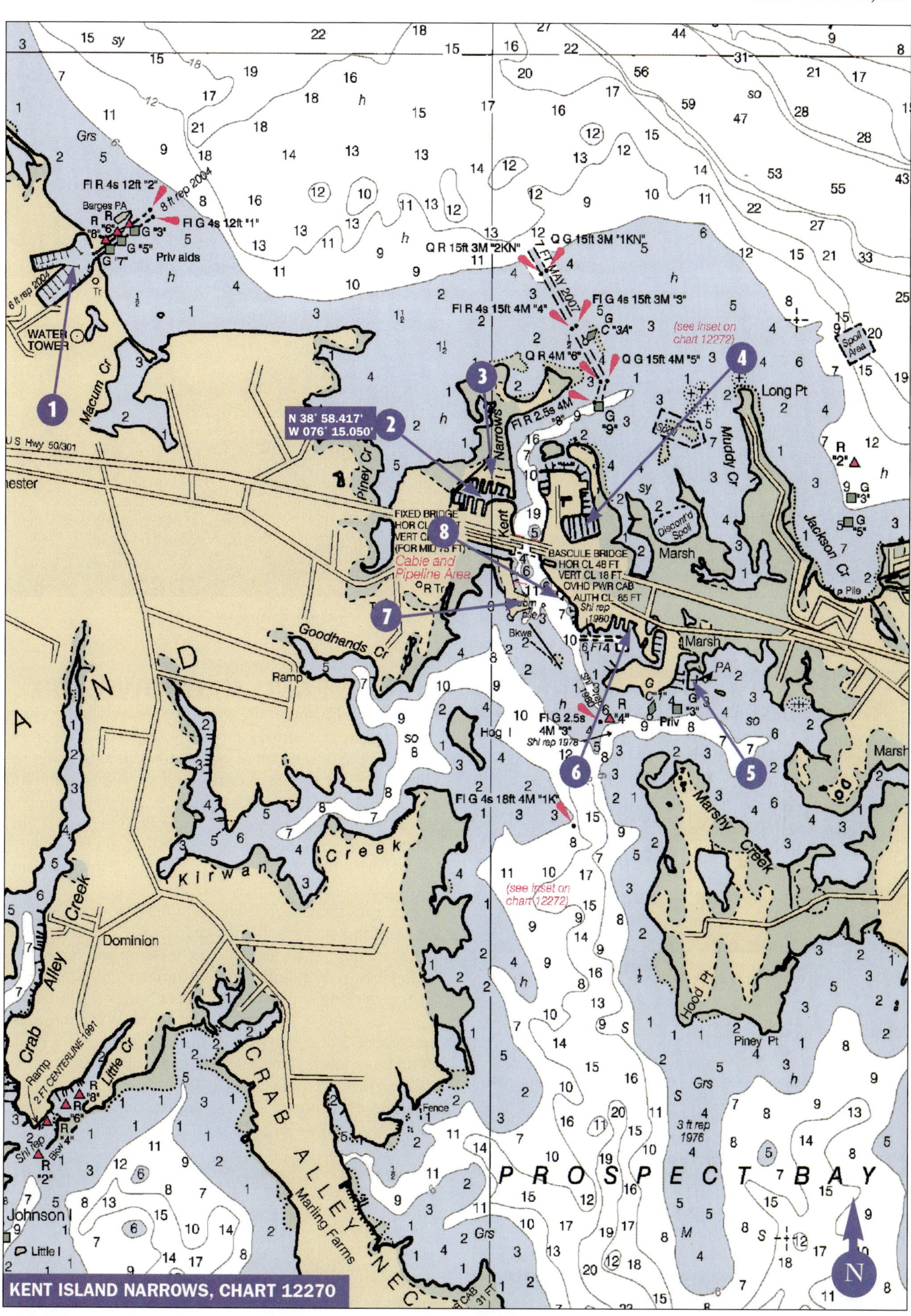
N 38° 58.417'
W 076° 15.050'
FIXED BRIDGE
BASCULE BRIDGE
HOR CL 48 FT
VERT CL 18 FT
OVHD PWR CAB
AUTH CL 65 FT
Cable and Pipeline Area
(see inset on chart 12272)
Long Pt
Muddy Cr
Jackson Cr
Marsh
Goodhands Cr
Kirwan Creek
Crab Alley Creek
Dominion
Little Cr
Johnson I
Little I
Marshy Creek
Hood Pt
Piney Pt
Hog I
PROSPECT BAY
CRAB ALLEY NECK
Marling Farms
WATER TOWER
Macum Cr
Piney Cr
Kent Narrows
US Hwy 50/301
KENT ISLAND NARROWS, CHART 12270

A northern view over Kent Island Narrows and the Chester River. (Not to be used for navigation.) Waterway Guide Photography.

GOIN' ASHORE:
KENT ISLAND NARROWS, MD

Kent Island Narrows, the waterway located along Kent Island's eastern shore is especially popular with power boaters. With a wide range of good restaurants lining the waterway and a couple of dock bar hot spots on the north and south sides (along with dockage for patrons and/or nearby marinas) the appeal here is simple: The place is fun.

History: Kent Island's first European settlers claimed it for Virginia back in 1631, when one William Clairborne came north to establish a trading post. He and his settlers soon tangled with the Calverts, who held the charter to establish the Maryland land grant, and, in 1638, the Calverts moved in. Like much of the Bay area, Kent Island was farmed up until fairly recent times, and watermen fished the Bay. Oyster-shucking houses lined the Kent Narrows. The Chesapeake Bay Bridge, formally known as the William Preston Lane Junior Bridge, was opened in 1952. Today, Kent Island has more or less become a suburb of Annapolis and, for that matter, Washington, D.C.

Points of Interest: The Chesapeake Exploration Center (425 Piney Narrows Rd., 410-604-2100) at Kent Narrows is a good place to get oriented about the area, and it also provides an interactive exhibit called "Our Chesapeake Legacy." This is also where you can link up with the Cross Island Trail, a 6.5-mile east-to-west trail across the island, a nice way to get around if you have a bike.

The Chesapeake Bay Environmental Center in nearby Grasonville offers 510 acres for hiking or mountain biking and has canoes and kayaks for rent during warm weather, marked water trails to enjoy during the latter and an exhibit area that includes two red-tail hawks and three species of owls that were rehabbed but cannot be released back into the wild (600 Discovery Lane, 410-827-6694).

Special Events: TieFest, held every year in February, is an opportunity for novices to create fishing flies or learn to cast a fly line. Call the Kent Island Yacht Club for more information (410-643-4101). Kent Island Day, held mid-May in Stevensville, celebrates the island's founding with a parade down Main Street, historic exhibits, vendors, costumes, activities for kids and crafts.. Thunder on the Narrows, the first weekend in August, is a major high-speed boat race (kentnarrowsracing.com). The Taste of Kent Narrows in mid-October celebrates hometown culinary chops (tasteofkentnarrows.org).

Shopping: From Kent Narrows, head west to Stevensville, a charming village with a few antiques shops including Stevensville Antiques (105 Market Court, 410-643-9533), a multi-dealer stop, and Lowery Turner Antiques (307 State St., 410-643-6250). Or, from the Narrows, taxi east to the nearby Prime outlets at Queenstown (441 Outlet Center Dr., 410-827-8699).

Dining: There are three very distinct and unique restaurants in a row on Kent Narrows Way N.: Annie's Paramount Steak and Seafood House offers fine dining (410-827-7103); reservations are recommended. Red Eye's has live music on a covered dock stage and an "active scene" as well as a casual menu (410-827-EYES). Harris' Crab House & Seafood Restaurant is a family-oriented restaurant specializing in seafood (410-827-9500). They have some transient slips reserved for diners, as does Fisherman's Inn, which has been a landmark since the 1930s at the Narrows (3116 Main St., 410-827-8807). They also have a more casual Crab Deck Restaurant (410-827-6666) and a Seafood Market (410-827-7323) for takeout. The Narrows Restaurant has casual fine dining and great water views (3023 Kent Narrows Way S., 410-827-8113). The Jetty Restaurant and Dock Bar (201 Wells Cove Rd., 410-827-49504959) is next to The Bridges Restaurant (321 Wells Cove Rd., 410-827-0282). They both offer enjoyable waterfront dining with seating inside or outside. The Bridges may have transient space for diners. ■

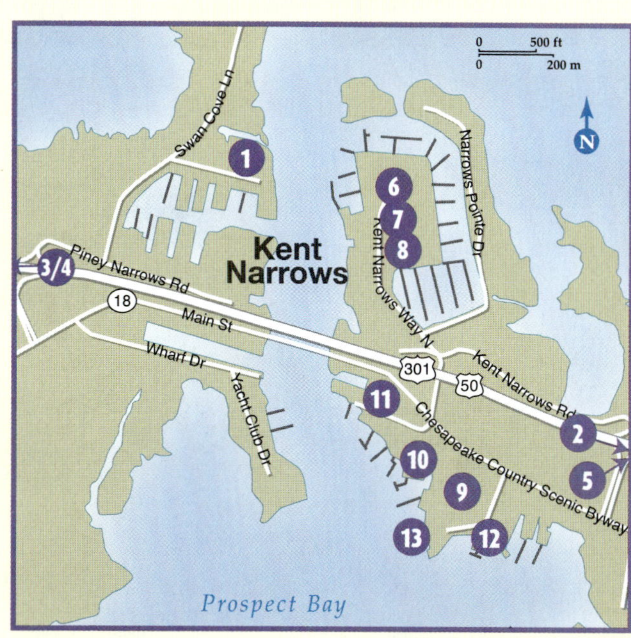

Reference the marina listing tables to see all the marinas in the area.

INFORMATION

1 The Chesapeake Exploration Center

POINTS OF INTEREST

2 Chesapeake Bay Environmental Center

SHOPPING

3 Stevensville Antiques
4 Lowry Turner Antiques
5 Prime Outlets at Queenstown

DINING

6 Annie's Paramount Steak and Seafood House
7 Red Eye's Dock Bar
8 Harris Crab House and Seafood Restaurant
9 Fisherman's Inn
10 Fisherman's Inn Crab Deck
11 The Narrows Restaurant
12 Jetty Restaurant and Dockbar
13 The Bridges Restaurant

ADDITIONAL RESOURCES

■ **DISCOVER QUEEN ANNE'S COUNTY:**
www.discoverqueenannes.com

NEARBY MEDICAL FACILITIES
Anne Arundel Medical Center, 2001 Medical Parkway, Annapolis, MD 21401, 443-481-4000 (18 miles)

NEARBY AIRPORT:
Baltimore-Washington International Thurgood Marshall Airport: www.bwiairport.com (40 miles)

Bay Bridge Airport, 202 Airport Road, Stevensville, MD 21666, 410-643-4364 (3 miles)

Skipper's Handbook

- GPS Waypoints 48
- Tide Tables 50

Eastern Bay to Little Choptank

CHARTS 12263, 12264, 12266, 12268, 12270

The middle Eastern Shore is the heart of cross-Bay cruising on the Chesapeake. Talbot County has more shoreline than any other county in the nation; just about everyone lives on or near the water. Many people own boats, and many farmers are also watermen who harvest fresh seafood from local waters. Yet the shorelines remain uncluttered, with refreshing stretches of undisturbed woods and fields, while towns manage to retain an unhurried old-time atmosphere. Numerous creeks and coves open from six major rivers and bays to provide ample wandering and anchoring room for the Chesapeake's Bay's enormous cruising fleet.

EASTERN BAY

Eastern Bay extends northeastward from the Chesapeake Bay, connecting the Miles River, the Wye River, Prospect Bay and Kent Island Narrows. The Bay is generally deep in the center and spacious, except for shoals extending from its prominent points, all of which are clearly marked and charted.

NAVIGATION: Use Chart 12270. At the mouth to Eastern Bay, note that the bar extending southeasterly from Kent Point is enlarging. Flashing green bell buoy "1" serves to mark the southern extent of this shoal area, while Bloody Point Bar Light (54 feet high, flashing white every six seconds) stands off to the west. Do not cut the corner between Bloody Point Bar Light and flashing green bell buoy "1" before going up Eastern Bay. This hard-bottomed shoal (2- to 4-foot depths) is drifting farther into Eastern Bay each year, and even if you avoid grounding, there is much more wave action near the shallows than in the deeper water of the marked channel. Just west of Bloody Point Bar Light is an area known as "The Hole," where the deepest point (164-foot depths) in the Chesapeake Bay is located. To the north, off Eastern Bay, are Cox Creek, Crab Alley Bay and Prospect Bay, all offering anchorage possibilities according to your boat's draft and the crew's inclination to explore. Crab Alley Bay also offers a number of small marinas and boatyards. Most of these are actually on Little Creek, east of Johnson Island at the entrance to Crab Alley Creek.

Anchorage: Outside of its peaceful tributaries, Eastern Bay is large, often long on wind (a blessing or a curse, depending on its force and your intended direction) and short on anchorages. In winds from the west through northeast, the half-moon-shaped cove southwest of Long Point at the entrance to Eastern Bay (northeast of the aforementioned Kent Point) provides emergency shelter. When a northerly kicks up, this spot fills quickly, especially on weekends. Keep an eye on the depth sounder and follow the unmarked, deep water that runs north from red nun "2." Drop the hook near the shore in 7- to 10-foot depths with good holding in a mud bottom and be wary of any wind shift to the south, which will make the spot untenable.

Waterway Guide Photography.

BLOODY POINT
N 38°50.033'
W 076°23.500'

Tilghman Creek (on the opposite side of Rich Neck from the town of Claiborne and around Tilghman Point) is sheltered from all directions, although houses and docks surround the coves, and the entrance is shoaling in spots to depths of about 6 feet. The wharf at the end is a public dock used by workboats. Shipping Creek, north of Romancoke, has pleasant anchorage areas but requires some care at the minimally marked entrance. Little Creek (off of Crab Alley Bay) is too small and shallow to make a good anchorage for cruisers, but Crab Alley Creek farther east has good depths and pretty surroundings. Kirwan Creek, on the south end of Kent Narrows, behind Hog Island, is well protected and provides a serene marsh setting for an overnight stay, especially in the fall when migrating waterfowl arrive. One caveat prevails: Early morning crabbers watermen may wake you from your bunk here.

Bodkin Island, in Eastern Bay

Bodkin Island in Eastern Bay, at the entrance to Crab Alley Bay southeast of Turkey Point, has had some help in its fight with erosion. The Department of Natural Resources purchased it in 1995, and donations from Ducks Unlimited and the Chesapeake Bay Foundation helped replace a seawall. The U.S. Fish and Wildlife Service will add topsoil and seeds. This island is an important habitat for nesting birds such as terns, egrets, herons and gulls, as well as crabs and juvenile fish, which live in its grass-lined shallows. The area is an excellent spot to cast a well-placed fly or lure for striped bass.

WYE RIVER

The Wye River is famous for its larger-than-average Maryland blue crabs and idyllic cruising grounds, with pretty coves and a surprisingly deep main stem. Historic Wye Island, once a Colonial plantation, is slowly developing with large estate homes, whose owners take care to preserve the island's natural beauty.

Although development has come to the Wye, it takes a more civilized form here than in places closer to the Baltimore/Washington corridor. Attractive houses line the shoreline in a variety of sizes, from modest to palatial, each with at least one dock and a boat. The folks who live here value their surroundings, so disturbances from raucous events ashore are rare. We urge you to adopt the mood of the place; get out the binoculars to enjoy the bird life and the stars.

If you need a marina, this is not the place to go. Drop the hook almost anywhere but show an anchor light. Since the entrance is easy and the shoals are few, local skippers often come in after dark.

NAVIGATION: Use Chart 12270. Heading southeast from flashing red buoy "4" near Tilghman Point, avoid the well-marked and charted shoal (formerly an island) southwest of the Wye River mouth at Bennett Point. To enter the Wye River, follow a marked passage either north or south of the shoal; deeper water is to the south. Skippers with local knowledge will take a direct route across the shoal between red daybeacon "2" and green daybeacon "3," and as long as you have a draft of 5 feet or less this route will be fine. If your draft is more than 5 feet, we suggest you follow the buoyed deep-water passage two miles south between flashing green buoy "11" and red nun "10" to enter the Wye from the south. Be sure to honor green can "1" on your passage north to the Wye River mouth once clear of the aforementioned buoys.

Beyond Bruffs Island, the river splits into two branches around large Wye Island: Wye River proper (locally called the "Front Wye") and Wye East River ("Back Wye"). (See below.) Deep, winding Wye Narrows connects these two branches at the north end of Wye Island, but a fixed 10-foot vertical clearance bridge and an overhead power line with a 32-foot vertical clearance stop all but the smallest vessels from circumnavigating the island.

Anchorage: Proceeding up the main stem of the Wye River proper, you can pull off the channel almost anywhere to anchor in pretty surroundings with water depths of 8 feet or better. There is an attractive circular anchorage behind Drum Point, and, while it is not as large as the Wye East's Shaw Bay, it has entirely natural shores. Choice spots are Grapevine Cove, an enclosed hurricane hole that might be warm and buggy in midsummer, and Bigwood Cove, farther south. Work your way into Grapevine Cove carefully (7- to 8-foot depths), as there is an unmarked 2-foot-deep shoal on the southern side of the entrance. Bigwood Cove carries 8- to 11-foot depths, if you favor the south side upon entry. (Note the charted 5-foot hump mid-river due west of the cove.)

WYE EAST RIVER

The Wye East River, beyond Shaw Bay, has nice houses spaced along both shores, with some natural areas, farms and cornfields visible in between. Particularly handsome homes line both sides of the Wye East River near its entrance.

This river is an immensely popular destination for Chesapeake Bay cruisers, and the natural beauty onshore hereabouts is quite stunning, as the Wye River Natural Resource Management Area (WRNRMA) protects the bulk of the island's acreage. The WRNRMA features hiking paths and nature trails, all maintained by the Maryland Department of Natural Resources.

Shaw Bay, off the Wye East

Anchorage: Just east of Bruffs Island, Shaw Bay, surrounded by lovely houses, is a large and popular anchorage. The holding ground is excellent in firm mud, and beachcombing along the sandy rim of the cove is a popular pastime. Many visitors also enjoy the swimming here. This is one of the busiest anchorages on the Wye River.

Lloyd, Dividing and Granary Creeks

Anchorage: Lloyd Creek, off the south shore of the Wye East just beyond Shaw Bay, offers a large anchorage, especially desirable on a still summer night when you wish to catch a cool breeze. But beware if a northerly kicks up, because the anchorage is open to the northwest.

A mile and a half beyond Lloyd Creek, Dividing Creek opens to the north. Large-scale charts indicate shoals extending toward the river from points at the mouth of Dividing Creek. It is best to enter mid-channel on a due-north magnetic heading. This anchorage is popular with local cruisers and may be crowded on weekends. Deep water continues past the Colonial estate at Wye Heights, all the way to the marine facilities at Wye Landing. Several creeks and coves present opportunities for gunkholing and anchoring along the way.

Off the northern shore of the Wye East River past Dividing Creek, Granary Creek has good protection, and although it is rather narrow, it carries good (8- to 10- foot) depths. Dividing Creek is much wider, also has good depths (8 to 10 feet) and the holding is good. There is a landing area with access to picnic tables and a path leading inland, but there is no development in this area.

MILES RIVER

The Miles River is one of the Eastern Shore's busiest waterways when warm weather rolls around. The crown jewel of this storied river is undeniably St. Michaels, but the Miles has much more to offer in the way of excellent anchorages in its many creeks and gunkholes. But again, it is difficult to talk about the Miles River without mentioning St. Michaels first.

A northern look over St. Michaels and the Miles River. (Not to be used for navigation.) Waterway Guide Photography.

St. Michaels, on the Miles River

Getting to St. Michaels is an annual pilgrimage for many Chesapeake cruisers. The town, which lies directly on the shore of the scenic Miles River, hosts a number of important regattas and cruising events each year. It also boasts two excellent harbors, several seafood restaurants and a good deal of Chesapeake-flavored history.

NAVIGATION: Use Chart 12270. **Use Baltimore tide tables. For high tide at St. Michaels (Miles River), subtract 2 hours 14 minutes; for low tide, subtract 1 hour 58 minutes.** The channel into St. Michaels is well buoyed, but the large number of boats, both anchored and docked, may make it look confusing to the first-timer. Straight ahead, the restored 1879 Hooper Strait Lighthouse on the grounds of the Chesapeake Bay Maritime Museum (CBMM) is an important landmark, separating the two harbors at St. Michaels. The northern harbor, Fogg Cove, is home to stately The Inn at Perry Cabin, condominiums and the CBMM, each with docks; otherwise, it is mainly an anchorage area. The southern harbor is the St. Michaels harbor proper, with two marinas, the local boatyard and the popular Crab Claw Restaurant.

Dockage: The red-roofed Chesapeake Maritime Museum has dockage for transients and can accommodate vessels up to 200 feet. Nearby Higgins Yacht Yard on the inner harbor is the last full-service boatyard in St. Michaels. It has haul-out and repair capabilities, plus limited transient dockage. To port on entry and south of the Chesapeake Bay Maritime Museum is St. Michaels Marina, with substantial transient dockage capacity, a pool and patio area, a marine store, a fuel dock and three restaurants on site, all adjacent to town. Make sure that you call for reservations at least a day ahead of your arrival, as this is a very popular spot during the summer season.

Across a narrow arm of water is St. Michaels Harbour Inn Marina & Spa with a resort-like setting and facilities for transients, including a spa, restaurant and 52-slip marina.

The Inn at Perry Cabin north of St. Michaels on Long Haul Creek provides dockage for its guests.

Anchorage: Both harbors now have small red-and- green buoys defining the channels through the maze of anchored boats. You may anchor to either side of these buoys but take care not to swing into the channel on a wind shift; marine police write tickets for boats that do. The St. Michaels harbor proper is not very large for the number of boats that crowd it in summer, especially on weekends, and they often anchor very close to one another. Fogg Cove, while a little farther from village attractions (other than the CBMM), is probably a safer place to set the hook. On very crowded days, many boats anchor in the Miles River just beyond green daybeacon "3" in 17 to 18 feet of water, taking care to not block the entrance to the harbor.

A water taxi service runs during the season and monitors VHF Channel 71 or answers by phone at 410-924-2198. Note the 6-mph speed limit when transiting the harbor.

An alternate anchorage on the south side of St. Michaels is reached from the Choptank River, the next river south of the Miles River. From the Choptank, enter Broad Creek to the north, then proceed to San Domingo Creek. You can walk into St. Michaels from the dinghy landing at the head

St. Michaels, MD

MILES RIVER		Largest Vessel Accommodated	VHF Channel Monitored	Transient Berths / Total Berths	Approach / Dockside Depth (reported)	Floating Docks	Gas / Diesel	Groceries, Ice, Marine Supplies, Snacks	Repairs: Hull, Engine, Propeller	Lift (tonnage), Crane, Rail	Min/Max Amps	Laundry, Pool, Showers, Courtesy Car	Pump-Out Station	Nearby: Grocery Store, Motel, Restaurant
		Dockage						Supplies	Services					
1. Miles River Yacht Club	410-745-9511	55	68	15/68	9/6	-	-	I	-	-	30/50	LPS	P	R
2. Inn at Perry Cabin (WiFi)	410-745-2200	100	-	3/3	8/6	-	-	Dockage	for guests	-	30/30	PS	-	MR
3. Chesapeake Bay Maritime Museum (Internet) (WiFi)	410-745-2916	200	16/09	20/20	8/6	-	-	I	-	-	30/50	S	P	G
4. Higgins Yacht Yard (WiFi)	410-745-9303	70	16	20/30	8/8	-	-	IM	HEP	L30, C	30/50	S	P	GMR
5. St. Michaels Marina (Internet) (WiFi)	**410-745-2400**	**220**	**16**	**54/54**	**12/9**	**-**	**GD**	**GIMS**	**-**	**-**	**30/100**	**LPS**	**P**	**GMR**
6. St. Michaels Harbour Inn Marina & Spa (WiFi)	**410-745-9001**	**230**	**16**	**52/52**	**10/8**	**-**	**-**	**IMS**	**-**	**-**	**30/100**	**LPS**	**P**	**GMR**

Corresponding chart(s) not to be used for navigation. Internet Access, WiFi Wireless Internet Access, Waterway Guide Cruising Club Partner

See www.WaterwayGuide.com for current rates, fuel prices, web site addresses, and other up-to-the-minute information.

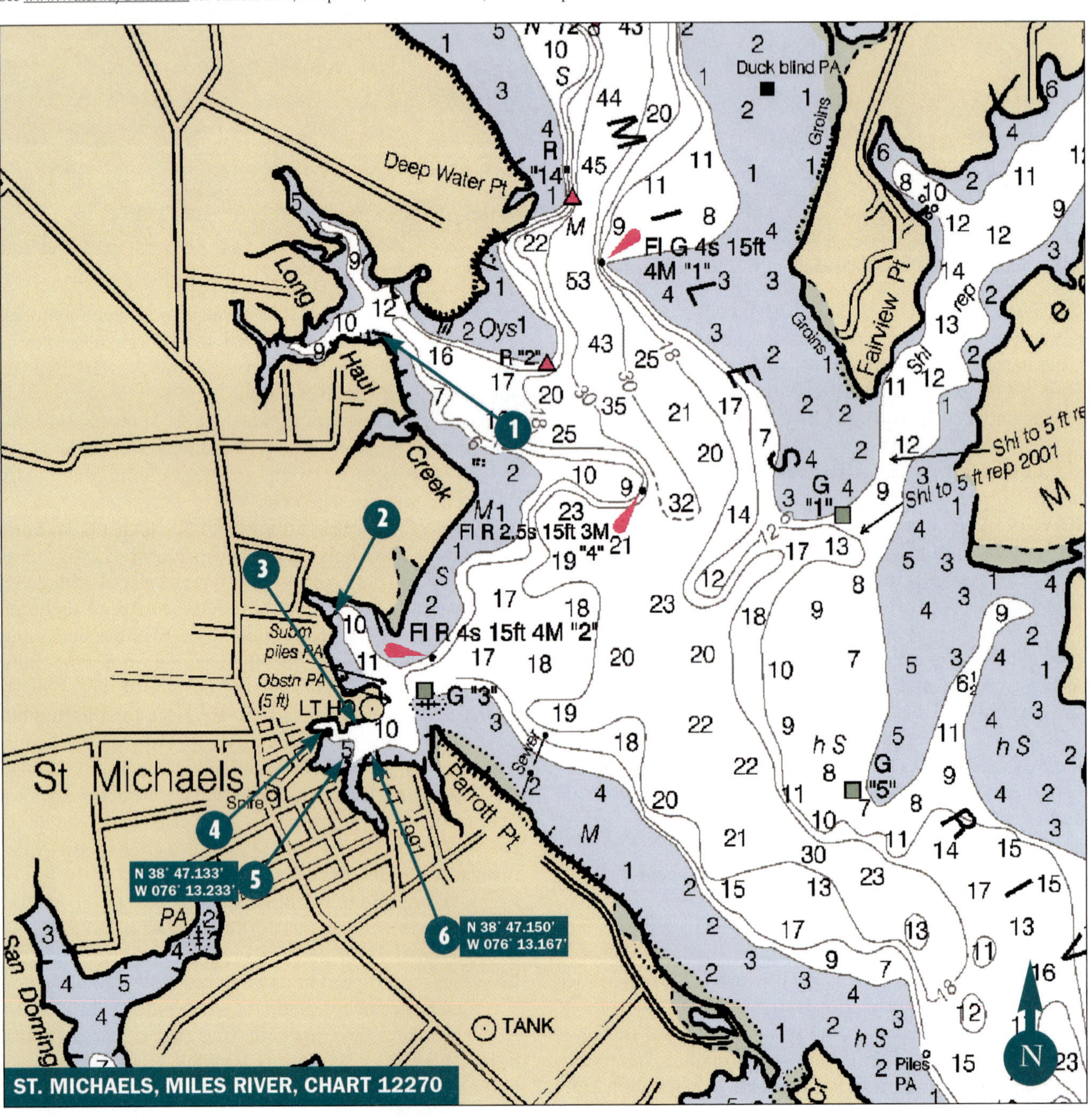

ST. MICHAELS, MILES RIVER, CHART 12270

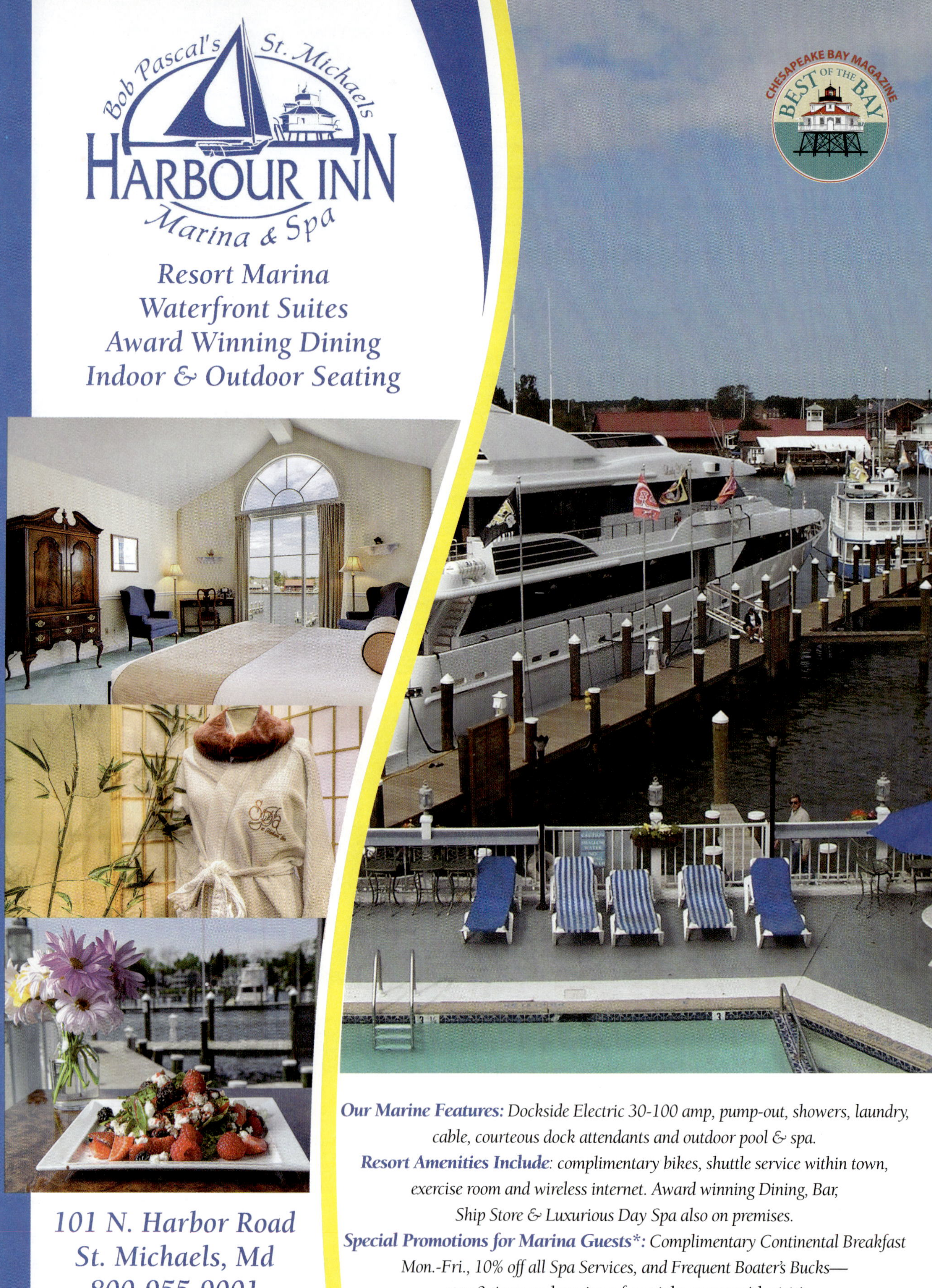
Bob Pascal's St. Michaels
HARBOUR INN
Marina & Spa
Resort Marina
Waterfront Suites
Award Winning Dining
Indoor & Outdoor Seating
CHESAPEAKE BAY MAGAZINE
BEST OF THE BAY
Our Marine Features: Dockside Electric 30-100 amp, pump-out, showers, laundry, cable, courteous dock attendants and outdoor pool & spa.
Resort Amenities Include: complimentary bikes, shuttle service within town, exercise room and wireless internet. Award winning Dining, Bar, Ship Store & Luxurious Day Spa also on premises.
Special Promotions for Marina Guests*: Complimentary Continental Breakfast Mon.-Fri., 10% off all Spa Services, and Frequent Boater's Bucks— stay 3 times and receive a free night on your 4th visit!
*Terms & conditions apply, current promotions, subject to change, call for details.
101 N. Harbor Road
St. Michaels, Md
800-955-9001
www.harbourinn.com

of San Domingo Creek, conveniently located at the foot of Chew Street, off Talbot Street, the town's main thoroughfare. The holding is good in mud with 7 to 10 feet of water. As you explore this anchorage be aware that if you venture too far in, the water gets skinny very quickly.

GOIN' ASHORE: **ST. MICHAELS, MD**

Once a waterman's enclave, St. Michaels has taken its transformation to tourist Mecca in a decidedly upscale direction of late. But the town hasn't lost its quaint flavor. Spas and a winery have joined an evolving array of restaurants and inns in historic homes, on the water or serving chic cuisine.

History: Located on the Miles River (once known as the St. Michaels River), the town is named for the Archangel St. Michael after the Christ Episcopal Church of St. Michael the Archangel parish, founded in the area about 1677. A British factor (a word once used instead of "agent") named James Braddock purchased and subdivided a land grant in 1778 that developed into the town just after the Revolutionary War.

At the heart of the town stands St. Mary's Square, a picturesque spot where one of two cannons commemorates one of St. Michaels signature moments, when it famously became known as "the town that fooled the British" during the War of 1812. As the story goes, the British began shelling the little town on August 10, 1813. Residents boosted lanterns into the tops of trees in order to fool the Redcoats into shooting too high.

Evidence of the evening remains at a private Mulberry Street residence called the Cannonball House. A Mrs. Merchant was carrying her baby downstairs as a cannonball tumbled down the same steps after bursting through her roof.

The port town, an early shipbuilding center where the swift Baltimore Clippers were built, went on to be a packing house center for seafood and tomatoes (a fine Eastern Shore staple come summer), as well as home to many a waterman. Log canoes, once American Indian transport and now working boats, are famously raced here.

Points of Interest: The 9-building, 18-acre Chesapeake Bay Maritime Museum (213 N. Talbot St., 410-745-2916) provides the premiere collection of Bay boats (including a working boatyard) as well as a detailed look into the region's maritime life. A busy calendar offers lectures and events, and folks traveling with kids should not miss the interactive oyster boat exhibit. The museum is located on the harbor, and cruisers can arrange temporary dockage there (www.cbmm.org).

St. Michael's Winery is a fun place worth visiting. Located at 609 So. Talbot St., 410-745-0808, the winery has tastings most afternoons. Or, if you prefer golfing, Harbourtowne Golf Resort & Conference Center on Route 33 is three miles away (410-745-9066 or 800-446-9066), and The Easton Club is 12 miles away (410-822-9800 or 800-277-9800).

Pick up a copy of the St. Michaels Walking Tour at the small visitor center on Talbot Street and take time to visit St. Mary's Square, replete with its small museum and two nearby cannons, including a replica of one that is said to have been used during the War of 1812.

Shopping: St. Michaels is a stand-out for provisioning on the Eastern Shore. An Acme Supermarket is in the heart of downtown (114 Talbot Street, 410-745-9819) and is great for long-term provisioning. A combined meat market, produce, delicatessen and liquor store called Village Shoppe sits close by (501 Talbot Street, 410-745-9300). A short walk along Talbot Street also takes you past the post office, several ATMs and a variety of restaurants, pubs and shops. Among the mainstays are Keepers of St. Michaels (300 Talbot Street, 410-745-6388), which sells outdoorsy-style clothes "for fine country living." Two blocks down at 100 North Talbot St. is Chesapeake Bay Outfitters (410-745-3107), which has footwear, sportswear, and resort wear. For jewelry and gifts, try Bliss (100-A South Talbot, 410-745-5533), and for your four-legged crew members, check out Flying Fred's gifts for pets (202 North Talbot St., 410-745-9601).

Dining: St. Michaels is full of good restaurants. Probably best known among boaters is the Crab Claw on the harbor which has been serving seafood and hard crabs since the 1960s (304 Mil Burns St., 41-745-2900). Sometimes there's space to tie up if you are eating. Bistro St. Michaels is a chic little French restaurant in a Victorian house with a garden patio (403 S. Talbot St., 410-745-9111).

The Inn at Perry Cabin is where you go if you think you deserve a reward. It's located on the water on an extension of the harbor (410-745-3737).

Then there is Carpenter Street Saloon (aka "C Street") for the best breakfast and where you might still catch an authentic waterman in white boots, or a game of pool and live music on weekends (113 S. Talbot St., 410-745-5111). Named after a little joint called Foxy's in Jost Van Dyke in the British Virgin Islands, Foxy's Harbor Grille is where the boaters hang out for the burgers and casual fare on a waterfront dock (125 Mulberry St., 410-745-4340); Characters Café, right downtown, serves casual burgers, seafood, chicken and beef (200 S. Talbot St., 410-745-2606); and be sure to try Ava's Pizzeria and Wine Bar (409 S. Talbot St., 410-745-3081).

At Town Dock Restaurant enjoy expansive views of St. Michaels Harbor (125 Mulberry St., 410-745-5577). For your caffeine fix, try Blue Crab Coffee Co., located in the former Freedom's Friends Lodge (102 Fremont St., 410-745-4155). Other waterfront restaurants include: St Michaels Harbour Lights, which is right on the harbor and has rooms and a spa, and St. Michaels Crab and Steak House, 305 Mulberry St.

Annual Events: The St. Michaels Food and Wine Festival has grown into an expansive event held at the maritime museum, replete with distinguished chefs from Washington and New York giving cooking demonstrations, as well as abundant tastings of various goodies (www.stmichaelsfoodandwinefestival.com). Numerous events take place at the Chesapeake Bay Maritime Museum, but two favorites are the Antique & Classic Boat Festival each June and the Mid-Atlantic Small Craft Festival in October. Visit www.cbmm.org for more information.

Reference the marina listing tables to see all the marinas in the area.

INFORMATION
1 Information Center

POINTS OF INTEREST
2 Chesapeake Bay Maritime Museum
3 St. Mary's Square
4 St. Michaels Winery

SHOPPING
5 Acme Supermarket
6 Village Shoppe
7 Keepers of St. Michaels
8 Chesapeake Bay Outfitters
9 Bliss
10 Flying Fred's

DINING
11 Crab Claw Restaurant
12 The Inn at Perry Cabin
13 Carpenter Street Saloon
14 Foxy's Harbor Grille
15 Characters Café
16 Ava's Pizzeria & Wine Bar
17 Town Dock Restaurant
18 Blue Crab Coffee Co.
19 St. Michaels Harbor Lights
20 St. Michaels Crab and Steakhouse

L LIBRARY

PO POST OFFICE

ADDITIONAL RESOURCES

- ST. MICHAELS, MD: www.stmichaelsmd.org
- TOUR TALBOT: www.tourtalbot.org
- ST. MICHAELS HARBOR SHUTTLE: 410-924-2198, operates mid-April to mid-October

NEARBY MEDICAL FACILITIES
Easton Memorial Hospital: 219 S. Washington St., Easton, MD 21601, 410-822-1000 (8 miles)

NEARBY AIRPORT
Easton Airport: Easton, MD (13 miles)
www.talbotcountymd.gov/index.php?page=Airport

Long Haul and Leeds Creeks, off the Miles

Anchorage: For a quieter resting place than St. Michaels, there are several anchorages near town and farther upstream on the Miles. Long Haul Creek opens to the west below Deep Water Point, before you reach St. Michaels itself. Long Haul Creek is home to the Miles River Yacht Club, sponsor of many of the log canoe races and local sailboat races, so anchorage space is limited. With any luck, your visit will coincide with a log canoe race. Made from trees hollowed out by fire more than a century ago, American Indians and then the British once used these indigenous canoes to ply the waters in and around the Bay. The British added sails to make the craft move more swiftly, and today towering masts and oversized canvas make these vessels fly through the water, as crews hike out on wooden planks to avoid capsizing. Leeds Creek—off the Miles' east shore—has some lovely spots to stay, as well as intriguing stories about the pink castle, with its watchtower gates and secret passages. The grounds are private, but there is a nice anchorage. Leeds Creek has a tricky and shoaling entrance, but channel depths are 9 feet-plus. After passing green marker "1" bear slightly to starboard, and you will notice short green and red markers. These were placed there by the locals, and it is recommended you pass between them. The shoals will still be seen on your depthsounder, but you should have about 7 feet at mid-tide. This is a very scenic creek and a convenient for visiting St. Michaels when it's crowded.

Hunting Creek, off the Miles

About 2.5 miles past St. Michaels, the Miles River makes an elbow turn around Long Point. Continuing up the Miles, the contemporary houses along both shores give way to some impressive manor homes.

Anchorage: You will find fewer coves and natural areas on the Miles than on the Wye River, but you can anchor almost anywhere off the channel and be well protected from wind and sea. On the far side of Long Point, a pair of privately maintained channel markers guides you into Hunting Creek for pleasant anchorage anywhere along its banks.

POPLAR ISLAND NARROWS

NAVIGATION: Use Chart 12270. Poplar Island Narrows is a three-mile-long strait south of Eastern Bay between the Eastern Shore mainland and Poplar Island, more than a mile offshore. It is well marked and has depths of 6 feet or more most of the way, with some shoaling at its southern end. Tidal currents may set you off course and into the shallows anywhere along this route.

Dockage: Lowes Wharf Marina Inn reports 5-foot depths at mean low water. The marina is located in the Poplar Island Narrows area, at Lowes Wharf inside Ferry Cove, opposite Poplar Island (two nautical miles east of the island itself). The beach restaurant and bar is a popular spot for weekend boaters.

Anchorage: Although it may look tempting from the chart, this area is not suitable as an overnight anchorage.

Poplar Island, in Poplar Island Narrows

Westerly winds and waves have been wearing away Poplar Island's shores—foot by foot, tree by tree—for years. Poplar, Coaches and Jefferson islands once comprised 1,100 acres for a community of three hundred people. By the 1990s, only 10 acres of Poplar Island remained and in 1997, Maryland and the federal government began rebuilding the island using dredge material from ship channels into Baltimore. By 2012, Poplar had grown to 1,140 acres with a heavy bulkhead, and by 2027 the project is projected to be finished. The Poplar Island project is drawing widespread interest as a positive use for dredge spoil. Besides providing habitat for nesting and roosting birds, the project is significantly alleviating the silting problem in Knapps Narrows to the south, which was filling in from the eroding island.

KNAPPS NARROWS

From Poplar Island Narrows, or from the open Bay, Knapps Narrows provides a shortcut into the Choptank River across the northern end of Tilghman Island. The short, artificial cut provides an alternative to the route south around the island and its exposed Black Walnut Point.

NAVIGATION: Use Chart 12266. Regular dredging at both ends of Knapps Narrows usually returns 7- to 12-foot depths at low water, but currents can quickly wash silt into the channel and change it. The deepest part of the channel is narrow, so follow the markers precisely. The project depth is 7 feet, and the mean tidal range here is 1.3 fee.

Most vessels of reasonable draft should have no difficulty in passing through Knapps Narrows, but it is not a bad idea to call the Knapp's Narrows bridge tender on VHF Channel 13 (or 410-886-2588) or the Coast Guard at Still Pond (410-778-2201) or Taylors Island (410-397-3103) for the latest conditions. You can also contact one of the marinas located along Knapps Narrows, or simply follow a local boat through. Stay to starboard as you proceed east.

When entering Knapps Narrows from the west (Bay), especially on a typical hazy summer day, do not stray too far north and confuse the entrance marker with the marker about a mile northwest at the lower entrance to Poplar Island Narrows. The channel is well marked, and you can check for drift by sighting markers ahead and astern, once inside. If approaching from the east (Choptank River), make sure to distinguish the channel markers leading to Knapps Narrows from those heading into Dogwood Harbor. From a distance they can be confusing. After leaving flashing red "2" to starboard, head slightly east of north to pick up flashing green "3" at the Narrows entrance. Red "4" on the western side the channel is deep, but very narrow right as you passes the daymarker. As you turn at that mark, the deep water channel is only 30- to 40-feet wide. Try to time it so that you are not passing another boat at this point in the channel; however, when there is heavy traffic, you may have trouble avoiding this.

Clam dredges, other workboats and recreational craft are always coming and going through this busy Waterway, and in summer, the Knapps Narrows Bridge (12-foot closed vertical clearance, opens on request 24 hours daily) is open as often as closed. Fortunately, the bridge tenders at Knapps Narrows are excellent, so you may travel this waterway for years and never have to touch your horn. Give vessels running with the current the right-of-way in passing through the bridge. Dock with caution at any of the facilities with slips directly perpendicular to the current flow. Tilghman Island is the home of many of the remaining skipjacks (the last sail-powered fishing vessels in the United States) that work the Bay, and you may see them tied up alongside the channel and in Dogwood Harbor.

Note that the buoy system reverses at the bridge. After you pass through, you are heading seaward going in either direction, and the numbers descend in order (e.g., "red-right-returning" going to and from the Narrows).

Dockage: Knapps Narrows Marina and Inn has a large yard and offers repairs, dockage, rental rooms and the Bay Hundred Restaurant; there is a 500-foot floating dock for transients and restaurant patrons. The Inn at Knapps Narrows, a 20-room hotel, is also located nearby on the Knapps Narrows Marina property. Fairbanks Bait & Tackle, which sells diesel and gas is across from the marina.

Tilghman Island Marina is located in the small basin just to the right (south side) as you enter Knapps Narrows from the Chesapeake (not to be confused with the Tilghman Island Inn, which overlooks the Narrows just west of the bridge and also has some transient slips). On the south side of the bridge is Severn Marine Services and Tilghman on Chesapeake Marina, which may have transient space.

Dogwood Harbor, at Tilghman Island

Dogwood Harbor is south of Knapps Narrows, on the east side of Tilghman Island. The Tilghman-on-Chesapeake Marina and Yacht Club, built on the site of an old oyster house and shell mound, lies just south of the marked entrance channel to this harbor.

Dockage: Inside Dogwood Harbor, Harrison's Chesapeake House is a marina and inn popular with power boaters and fishermen. Tilghman on Chesapeake Marina is here as well with transient space on floating docks
Anchorage: A shallow, temporary day anchorage where the chart shows "Dogwood Harbor" to the outside of the basin is the only anchorage available here.

Poplar I. Narrows, Knapps Narrows, Tilghman Island, MD

POPLAR ISLAND NARROWS/KNAPPS NARROWS		Largest Vessel Accommodated	VHF Channel Monitored	Transient Berths / Total Berths	Approach / Dockside Depth (reported)	Floating Docks	Gas / Diesel	Groceries, Ice, Marine Supplies, Snacks	Repairs: Hull, Engine, Propeller	Lift (tonnage), Crane, Rail	Min/Max Amps	Laundry, Pool, Showers, Courtesy Car	Pump-Out Station	Nearby: Grocery Store, Motel, Restaurant
		Dockage					Supplies		Services					
1. Lowes Wharf Marina Inn (Internet Access) (Wireless Internet Access)	410-745-6684	60	16	6/22	5/4.5	-	GD	IMS	-	-	30/30	LS	P	MR
2. Knapp's Narrows Marina and Inn (Internet Access) (Wireless Internet Access)	**800-322-5181**	**100**	**16/71**	**25/130**	**8/7**	**F**	**GD**	**I**	**HEP**	**L35**	**30/50**	**LPS**	**P**	**GMR**
3. Severn Marine Services	410-886-2159	57	-	4/48	8/6	-	-	M	HEP	L30, C5	30/30	S	P	GMR
4. Tilghman on Chesapeake Marina (Wireless Internet Access)	410-886-2389	70	16/71	8/55	8/6	F	-	I	-	-	30/50	LPS	P	GMR
5. The Tilghman Island Inn (Internet Access)	410-886-2141	36	16	9/21	10/3	-	-	I	-	-	50/50	PS	-	GMR
6. Tilghman Island Marina (Internet Access) (Wireless Internet Access)	410-886-2500	125	16/72	25/41	10/10	-	-	GIMS	E	-	30/50	PS	P	GMR
7. Fairbanks Bait & Tackle	410-886-9807	-	-	-	-	-	GD	GIS	-	-	30/30	-	-	-

Corresponding chart(s) not to be used for navigation. Internet Access; Wireless Internet Access; Waterway Guide Cruising Club Partner

See www.WaterwayGuide.com for current rates, fuel prices, web site addresses, and other up-to-the-minute information.

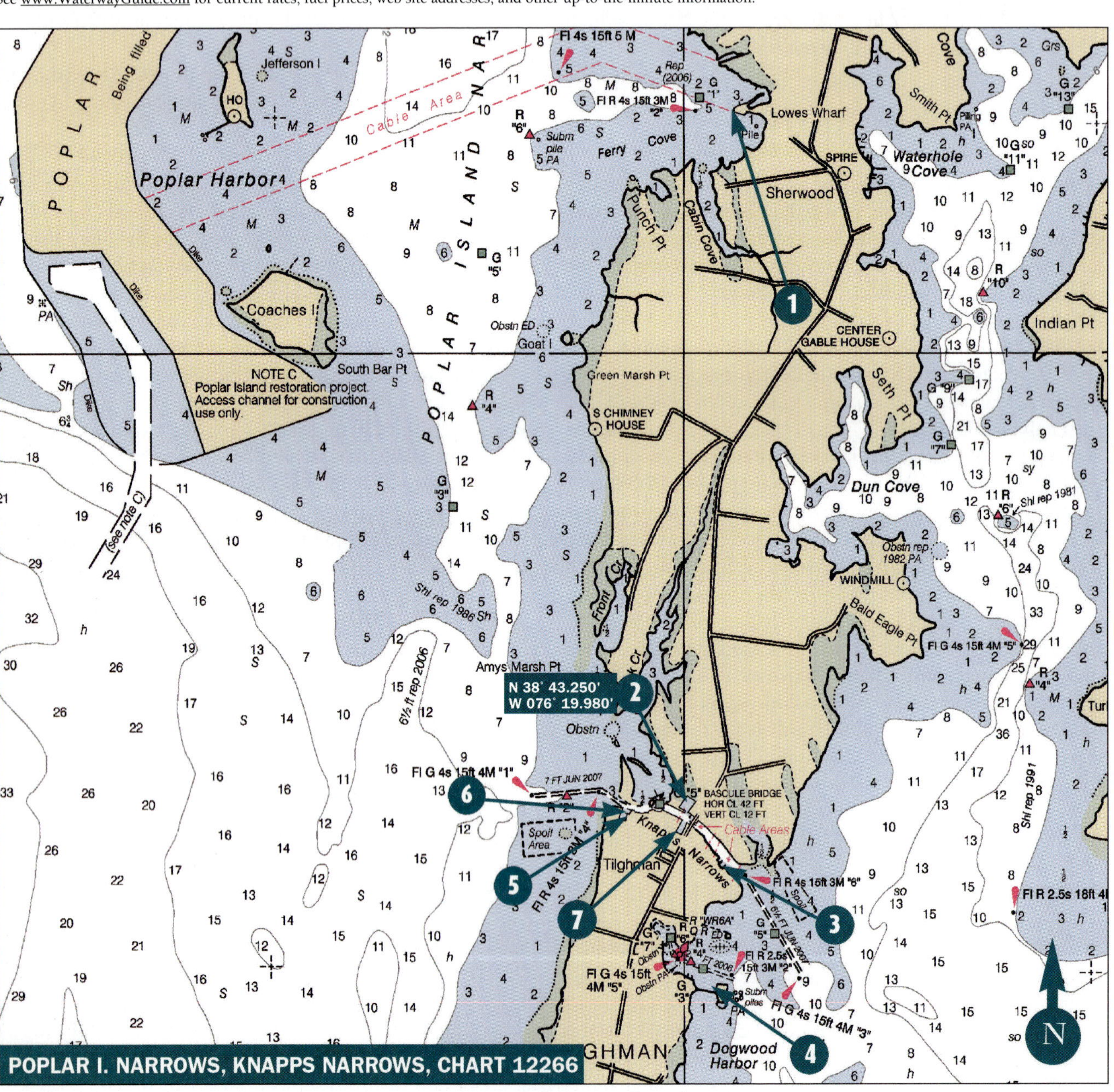

POPLAR I. NARROWS, KNAPPS NARROWS, CHART 12266

Looking east over Knapps Narrows. (Not to be used for navigation.) Waterway Guide Photography.

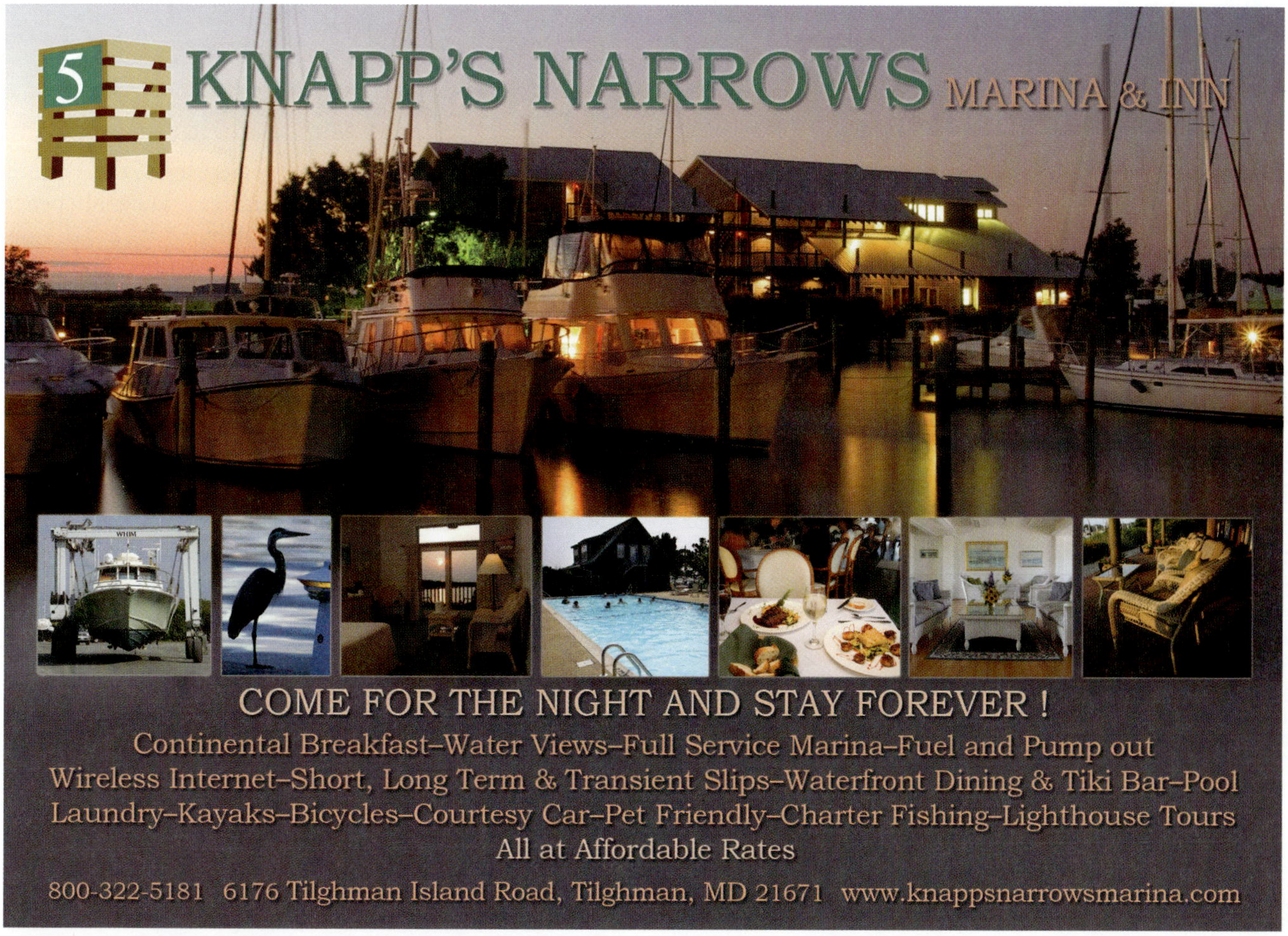

GOIN' ASHORE:
TILGHMAN ISLAND, MD

A drawbridge at Knapps Narrows guards the entry to Tilghman Island, whether you are entering by road or via the narrows on your boat. Workboats cluster at the harbor there in what is known as the "tonger's basin," while farther on up the island, you will see the skipjacks at the island's Dogwood Harbor. Tilghman retains the feel of the waterman's village it has been for generations, even though some gentrification has arrived. Today, you can find a skipjack to take you out on the water and see how oyster dredging is done.

History: The island, which was first called "Great Choptank Island," passed into the Tilghman family and earned its name. Oystermen looking for access to the water began moving here, and a waterman's way of life, still visible today, was established. Seafood packing plants came into importance during the 20th century.

Points of Interest: Dogwood Harbor is known as the home of the skipjacks (although you will also find them much farther south at Deale Island, north of Crisfield). The famous *Rebecca T. Ruark*, a National Historic Landmark, is docked here. The boat was built in 1886, and Capt. Wade Murphy stays at the helm. For information, call 410-886-2121 or see www.skipjack.org.

Chesapeake Light Tours (410-886-2215) operates from Tilghman, taking visitors up and down the Bay for an up-close look at Chesapeake lighthouses. See www.chesapeake-lights.com for more information.

Tilghman Island Marina (410-886-2500) rents waverunners, canoes, bicycles and mopeds at 6140 Mariners Court. You can also poke your way through Tilghman's watery "back roads" via the Tilghman Island Water Trail map.

Special Events: In late June, head for the Tilghman Island Seafood Festival (all things crab) sponsored by the island's volunteer fire department. And if you miss that, mark your calendar for mid-October and the VFW-sponsored Tilghman Island Day to sample oysters, crabs and clams alongside authentic watermen activities, such as boat docking contests.

Shopping: Find T-shirts and snacks at Fairbanks Bait & Tackle or books at Crawfords Nautical Books (aka the Book Bank). You can also swing over to Harrison's Chesapeake House to browse their gift shop, called Island Treasures.

Dining: Bay Hundred Restaurant (6176 Tilghman Island Road, 410-866-2126) is located right by Knapps Narrows Marina and offers outdoor seating on the Narrows. They have dockage for those who eat there. The Tilghman Island Inn (21384 Coopertown Road, 410-886-2141) has an outside dining deck and bar with sunset views (closed on Wednesday). Lowes Wharf Bayside Grill & Tiki Bar (21651 Lowes Wharf Road, 410-745-6684) offers dining by the beach north of Tilghman in Sherwood. Harrison's Chesapeake House (21551 Chesapeake House Drive, 410-886-2121) has a restaurant and inn, where fishermen have schooled up for decades. Their buffet draws a crowd on weekends. Also on the Island: Two-If-By-Sea restaurant (BYOB) and catering (5776 Tilghman Island Road, 410-886-2447) is convenient to Dogwood Harbor and Tilghman-On-Chesapeake Marina, and Tilghman Island Country Store (5949 Tilghman Island Road, 410-886-2777) at mid-island has some groceries, a deli counter, sandwiches and a selection of wines.

Reference the marina listing tables to see all the marinas in the area.

POINTS OF INTEREST
1 *Rebecca T. Ruark*
2 Chesapeake Light Tours
3 Tilghman Island Marina Rentals

SHOPPING
4 Fairbanks Bait & Tackle
5 Crawfords Nautical Books
6 Island Treasures

DINING
7 Bay Hundred Restaurant
8 Tilghman Island Inn
9 Lowes Wharf
10 Harrison's Chesapeake House
11 Two-If-By-Sea
12 Tilghman Island Country Store

POST OFFICE

CHOPTANK RIVER

The Choptank River is a major waterway of the Eastern Shore. Rich in scenery and historic interest, James Michener set his classic novel "Chesapeake" here.

You will notice a good number of watermen plying the Choptank River in their low-freeboard boats with hardtop shelters over the long working cockpits. Choptank tributaries, such as La Trappe Creek, are absolutely first-rate anchorages.

NAVIGATION: Use Chart 12266. Sharps Island Light, a 54-foot-high leaning brown tower on a cylindrical pier, is the beacon at the mouth of the Choptank River.

The light once stood upright, but massive ice floes (rare on the Chesapeake Bay) during the severe 1977 winter damaged it. Well-marked channels north and south lead through shoal areas, which were formerly Sharps Island. At about 900 acres in 1800s, Sharps was even home to a resort hotel, but it has eroded and submerged through the years and, by 1900, had shrunk to 94 acres, completely disappearing In the 1940s. What remains is about 9 to 12 feet of water around the tilting lighthouse

The conspicuous Choptank River Light (35-foot flashing white every four seconds) is actually about 6 miles

Looking northeast over Cambridge and the Choptank River. (Not to be used for navigation.) Waterway Guide Photography.

upstream, at the confluence of the Choptank and Tred Avon rivers.

Anchorage: Two major creeks open from the north side of the Choptank River just past the entrance. Harris Creek (to the north) is first—and the narrower of the two—although it is well marked and has several good anchorages. Dun Cove is especially popular with cruising groups. Broad Creek (also to the north) has several arms with good water depths that can provide enough anchorages for an entire vacation. As mentioned in the Miles River section, you can walk into St. Michaels from the dinghy landing (actually a waterman's dock and seawall) at the head of San Domingo Creek located at the foot of Chew Street. Watch your depth in this area as it gets very shallow near the dock and seawall.

La Trappe Creek, off the Choptank

Lined with beautiful historic homes (some previously occupied by late Maryland governors) and lush scenery, La Trappe Creek splits off from the Choptank River just south of Martin Point at flashing green "1."

Dockage: The first cove to port after red daybeacon "2" has a sand spit protruding about one-third of the way into the entrance from Martin Point. At the very back of the creek is Oxford Yacht Agency at Dickerson Harbor, which has transient slips and does some boat repair. The approach and dockside depths here, however, are reported at 4 and 4.5 feet, respectively.

Anchorage: Once clear of the protruding sandbar at the first cove, you can anchor in 7 to 8 feet of water, and explore lovely, quiet coves by dinghy and observe plenty of wildlife. Good anchorages are scattered farther up the creek, as well; just stay in the middle to avoid the numerous extending shoals. This is an area of true beauty, so be sure to enjoy it.

Island and Cabin Creeks, off the Choptank

NAVIGATION: Use Chart 12263. Due east of the Choptank River Light, just south of the Tred Avon River, 15-foot-high flashing green "1" marks the entrance to the popular anchorage at Island Creek. The 5-foot-deep (or less) entrance bar sets its controlling depth, although there is much more water inside.

A fixed highway bridge with a 50-foot vertical clearance at Cambridge limits passage farther up the Choptank for boats that have a lot of air draft. If you can clear the bridge, pass through the adjacent swing bridge (18-foot vertical clearance closed), then cruise upstream on this deep tributary past what was once important tobacco country, and explore some of the many side creeks.

Dockage: Gateway Marina & Ship's Store is located on the north shore at the foot of the U.S. 50 Bridge across the Choptank River from Cambridge and offers transient dockage. You will need to watch the depths, as they are reportedly 4.5-feet at dockside. The Suicide Bridge Restaurant, seven miles above Cambridge at Suicide Bridge on Cabin Creek, is a popular stop. Dock for dinner, and

Cambridge, Choptank River, MD

		Largest Vessel Accommodated	VHF Channel Monitored	Transient Berths / Total Berths	Approach / Dockside Depth (reported)	Floating Docks	Gas / Diesel	Groceries, Ice, Marine Supplies, Snacks	Repairs: Hull, Engine, Propeller	Lift (tonnage), Crane, Rail	Min/Max Amps	Laundry, Pool, Showers, Courtesy Car	Pump-Out Station	Nearby: Grocery Store, Motel, Restaurant
		Dockage					Supplies		Services					
CHOPTANK RIVER														
1. Oxford Yacht Agency at Dickerson Harbor	410-822-8556	60	-	12/50	4.5/4.5	-	-	-	HEP	L70	30/30	S	-	-
CAMBRIDGE														
2. Gateway Marina & Ship's Store	410-476-3304	50	16/68	6/112	4/4.5	-	GD	IMS	HEP	L55, C5	30/50	S	P	GMR
3. Cambridge Municipal Yacht Basin (WiFi)	410-228-4031	180	16/06	20/196	9.5/8	F	GD	I	-	-	30/50	LS	P	GMR
4. Yacht Maintenance Co. Inc.	410-228-8878	120	16	5/35	16/14	-	-	M	HEP	L60,C25,R250	30/200+	-	P	MR
5. Generation III Marina LLC	410-228-2520	120	16	5/50	12/10	-	-	-	HEP	L50	30/50	-	P	GMR
6. Mid-Shore Electronics	410-228-7335	100	10	/10	12/6	-	-	-	-	-	30/50	-	-	-
7. Hyatt Reg. C. Bay Golf Resort, Spa & Marina (WiFi)	410-901-1234	150	09/72	150/150	10/7	F	GD	GIMS	-	-	30/50	LPS	P	GMR

Corresponding chart(s) not to be used for navigation. Internet Access (WiFi) Wireless Internet Access Waterway Guide Cruising Club Partner

See www.WaterwayGuide.com for current rates, fuel prices, web site addresses, and other up-to-the-minute information.

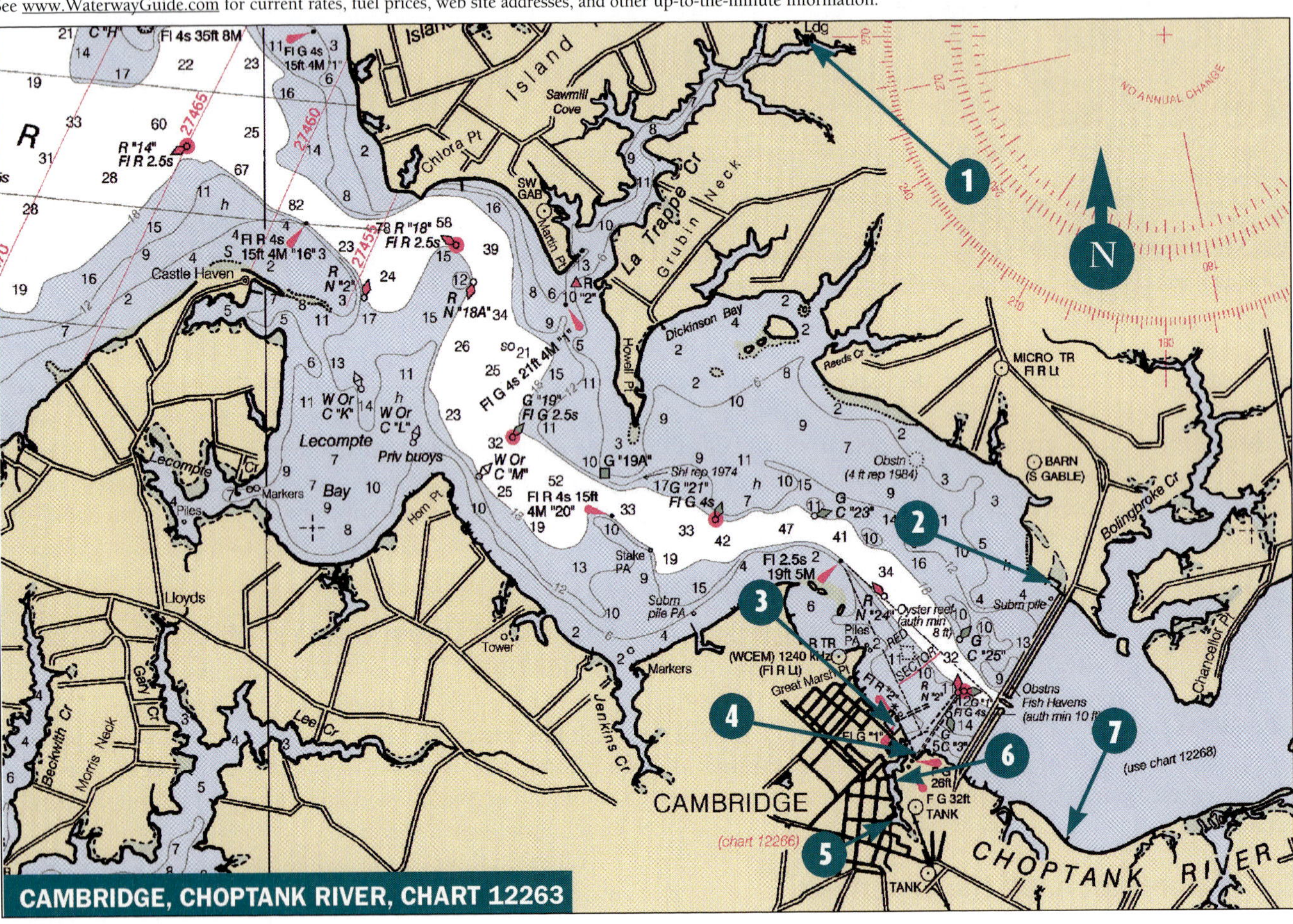

CAMBRIDGE, CHOPTANK RIVER, CHART 12263

check out the accurate replica of a paddlewheel steamboat. Reported depths at the entrance to Cabin Creek and the docks are around 4 feet.

Cambridge, on the Choptank

Cambridge is still a commercial harbor—Maryland's second largest by tonnage, eclipsed only by Baltimore—and tugboats pushing large barges need all the room they can get to maneuver. When approaching the town going up river, stay on the green side of the channel and notice three temporary white buoys on your starboard side. These are marking a shoal that is encroaching into the well-marked channel. Cambridge Creek, well-buoyed from the Choptank River channel, is the commercial harbor for the town, but developers have converted much of its banks into parkland and new high-rise condominiums, altering the charm of the creek. The Choptank River Lighthouse will welcome boaters to the Cambridge waterfront at the expanded municipal marina next to Long Wharf after its dedication ceremony planned for September 2012 (based on information at press time in summer 2012).

NAVIGATION: Use Charts 12263 and 12266. **Use Baltimore tide tables. For high tide at Cambridge (Choptank River), subtract 2 hours 42 minutes; for low tide, subtract 2 hours 28 minutes.** The Maryland Avenue Drawbridge over Cambridge Creek opens on signal daily except from 8:00 p.m. to 6:00 a.m., and from 12 noon to 1:00 p.m., Monday through Friday. The bridge tender monitors VHF Channels 13 and 16 (410-228-8311).

Dockage: Several boatyards are located up Cambridge Creek, above and below the Maryland Avenue Drawbridge. Many visiting boats dock in the large basin (depths of 4 to 7 feet) off the Choptank proper, just west of Cambridge Creek. Here, the Cambridge Yacht Club occupies the starboard side closer to the river, and its dockmaster's office is right at the entrance. The Cambridge Municipal Yacht Basin, whose dockmaster is located at the far end, fills the remainder of the basin. The Cambridge Municipal Yacht Basin reports that the entrance channel depth is 8 feet. A pretty waterfront park, only a block or two from historic High Street, lies at the basin's far end, next to the marina. Downtown shops require a longer walk.

A full-service boatyard, the Yacht Maintenance Company, is on the east bank of Cambridge Creek near the mouth. Mid-Shore Electronics is here and may have transient space in a pinch. They have electrical hookup but no other cruiser amenities. The J. M. Clayton Company, the only crab-picking house on Cambridge Creek, is next door. Generation III Marina is at the creek's far end past the Department of Natural Resources dock and a large cemetery.

Dockage is also available at the new Hyatt Regency Chesapeake Bay Resort, off the Choptank River about a half-mile east-southeast of the U.S. Route 50/Choptank River Bridge (50-foot fixed vertical clearance). This massive upscale complex has transformed the image of the little town, turning it into a nationally advertised tourist destination.

Anchorage: Boats anchor on Cambridge Creek, by Snappers Waterfront Café, just off the Dorchester County Building. It is a good idea to stay well off mid-channel, as the creek can get busy at times, and commercial vessels need plenty of maneuvering room. Depths are charted at 7 to 13 feet with good holding in mud. There is also a seawall that is available for overnight stays (no electric or water).

GOIN' ASHORE: **CAMBRIDGE, MD**

Times are changing in Cambridge, a pretty town that is hearing hammers pound as its downtown is being revitalized. The city's Main Street program has been helping to pave the way, as more historic buildings are renovated and new businesses move in. Once, luxury resorts might have seemed out of place in an old port town where some folks still enjoy trapping muskrat in their spare time. The tipping point may have occurred in 2002, when the Hyatt Regency Chesapeake Bay Golf Resort, Spa and Marina opened at the edge of town and immediately cranked up the local luxury factor. And the city does sit in a beautiful spot on the wide-open Choptank River.

History: Early Cambridge, a tobacco port, was shaped by its location along the Choptank. Traders and planters arrived as the region was settled by Europeans, although the Nanticoke and Choptank Indians had been here long before. As time went on, seafood packing became a prominent industry, as did oystering. Post-Civil War, Cambridge was a port for vegetables and grains. South of Cambridge is the birthplace of Harriet Tubman, who escaped from slavery and became an important Underground Railroad conductor. Trappers, farmers and fishermen continue to dominate life in surrounding Dorchester County, much of which remains rural.

It is noteworthy that Annie Oakley retired here with her husband after she left Buffalo Bill's Wild West Show. This is also literary lion John Barth's hometown.

Points of Interest: The Richardson Maritime Museum at 401 High St. (410-221-1871) is named for legendary local boat builder "Mr. Jim" Richardson, who died in 1991. Stop by his namesake museum, quartered in a former bank, to check out the exhibit of boat builder's tools, a ships' model exhibit and other elements of Cambridge's waterside life. The Dorchester Center for the Arts moved in 2008 to the redeveloped, historic Nathan Building. The 17,000-square-foot

Tred Avon/Choptank R. Pump-outs

Cambridge Marine	Choptank R.	410.228.4820
Cambridge Municipal Yacht Basin	Choptank R.	410.228.4031
Campbell's Bachelor Pt.	Tred Avon	410.226.5592
Campbell's Boatyard at Jack's Point	Tred Avon R./Town Cr.	410.226.5105
Campbell's Town Cr. Boatyard	Tred Avon R./Town Cr.	410.226.0213
Chapel Cove Marina	Chapel Cove/Slaughter Cr.	410.228.1320
Choptank Marina	Choptank R.	410.479.1695
Easton Point Marina	Tred Avon	410.822.1201
Gateway Marina	Choptank R.	410.476.3304
Generation III Marina	Choptank R./Cambridge Cr.	410.228.2520
Harrison's Sport Fishing Center	Choptank R.	410.886.2121
Hinckley Yacht Services	Tred Avon/Town Cr.	410.226.5115
Hyatt R. Marsh Marina	Choptank R.	410.901.1234
JM Clayton Co.	Choptank R./Cambridge Cr.	410.228.1661
Knapps Narrows Marina	Knapps Narrows	410.886.2159
Lowes Wharf Marina	Chesapeake Bay/Ferry Cove	410.745.6684
Madison Bay Marina	Choptank R./Madison Bay	410.228.4111
Mears Yacht Haven	Tred Avon/Choptank R.	410.226.5450
Old Harfordtown Maritime Center	Choptank R.	410.437.6975
Oxford Boat Yard	Tred Avon	410.226.5101
Suicide Bridge Restaurant & Marina	Choptank R./Cabin Cr.	410.943.4689
Taylors Island Family Campground and Marina	Chesapeake Bay Side of Taylors Island	410.397.3275
Taylors Island Marina	Little Choptank/Slaughter Cr.	410.397.3454
Tilghman Island Inn	Knapp Narrows	410.886.2141
Tilghman Island Marina	Knapp Narrows	410.886.2979
Tilghman on the Chesapeake	Choptank R./Dogwood Harbor	410.886.2389
Town of Secretary Marina	Choptank R./ Warwick R.	410.943.3113
Yacht Maintenance Co. Inc.	Choptank R./Cambridge Cr.	410.228.8878

space houses classrooms, galleries, a gift shop, performing arts spaces and a reception area. The center is at 321 High St. (410-228-7782), or visit www.dorchesterartscenter.org.

Blackwater National Wildlife Refuge is located 12 miles south of Cambridge in the wilds of Dorchester, and offers more than 27,000 acres of different habitat with plenty of options to enjoy nature. The birdwatching is great here at the home of the Atlantic coast's largest bald eagle population and the endangered Delmarva fox squirrel. The refuge is located at 2145 Key Wallace Drive. For more information, call 410-228-2677.

Special Events: Check out the Nanticoke Jamboree in June. Also in the spring, at Spocott Windmill Day, you can see the windmill south of town operate, and check out the collection of little structures there, such as a one-room Victorian schoolhouse; for information, call 410-476-5058. The Taste of Cambridge Crab Cookoff is in July, and the Peach Festival for Eastern Shore peaches, and the Seafood Feast-I-Val are both in August. The area is famous for its schooners, and an annual rendezvous is held in October.

Shopping: Aside from the galleries and gift shop in the Arts Center, more galleries are moving in along Race and Poplar streets. Look for Main Street Gallery (450 Race St., 410-228-0200413 Muir St.), which operates as something of a clearing house for local artists, while Joie de Vivre Gallery, at 410 Race St. (410-228-7000) offers jewelry, sculpture, paintings, and designer clothing. Dragonfly Boutique at 406 Race St. (410-228-6825) also sells women's designer clothing and accessories as does Crabi Gras on the same street with everything from food to Christmas tree ornaments to a selection of Eastern Shore boots (432 Race St., 410-228-0108). A Few of My Favorite Things at 414 Race St. (410-221-1960) has a wide selection of wine, cheese and chocolate delights.

If you need to provision the galley, Simmons Center Market is located at 600 Race St. Call 410-228-4313 for store hours. This is not a full "supermarket," but you can certainly get basic provisions here. For more shopping options, visit www.cambridgemainstreet.com.

Dining: Bistro Poplar is under the guidance of Cambridge-raised chef Ian Campbell (535 Poplar St., 410-228-4884). Bistro recently won the "Best of" category in a local magazine, which also included Leaky Pete's Oyster and Wine Bar at 404 Race Street (410-228-2245), and The High Spot at 305 High Street (410-228-7420), which is called the "best gastropub." Canvasback Restaurant and Irish Pub is located at 420 Race St. (410-220-5177). Snappers Waterfront Café has the views and casual fare as well as very active "happy hours" (112 Commerce St., 410-228-0112). They also provide slips for diners. Jimmy & Sook's Raw Bar and Grill (421 Race Street, 443-225-4115) offers a taste of the Eastern Shore using authentic recipes. The beautiful new Hyatt Regency Chesapeake Resort, Spa and Marina offers everything, including a full service restaurant, the Water's Edge Grill or enjoy an elegant happy hour in Michener's Library, named after the author of the epic novel "Chesapeake."

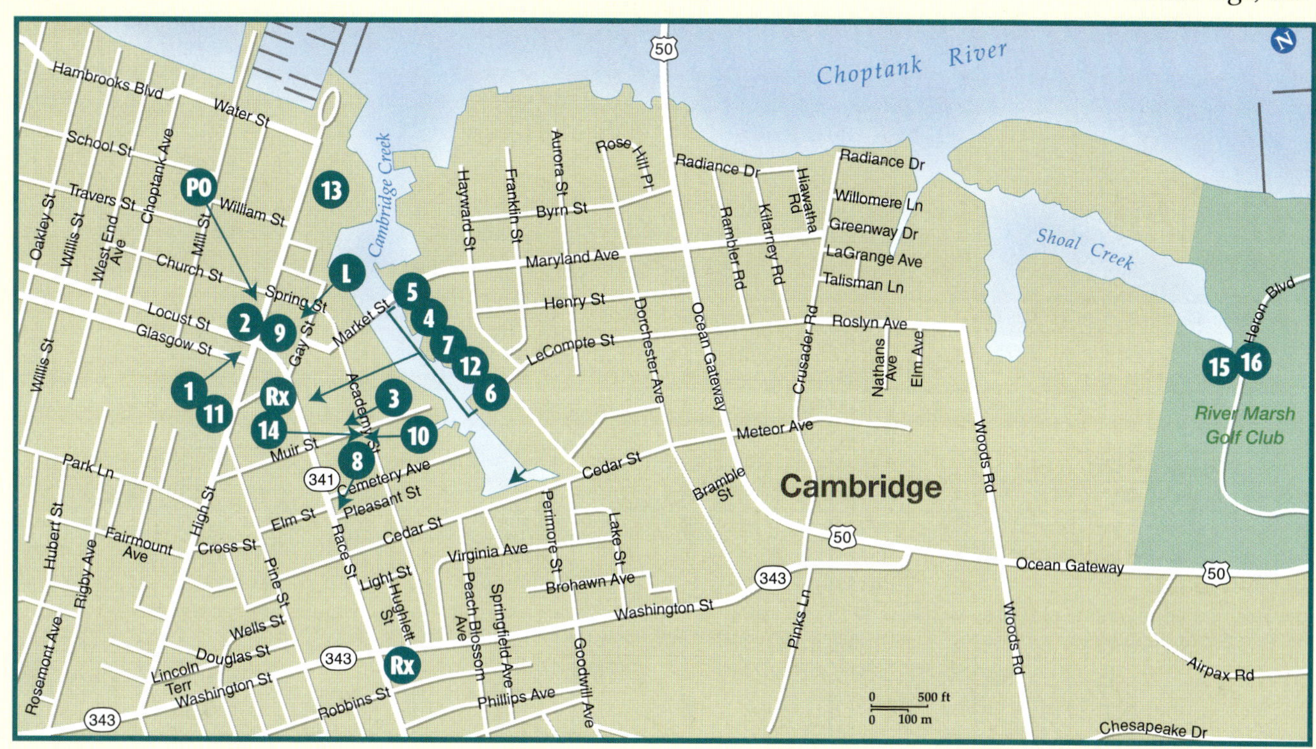

Reference the marina listing tables to see all the marinas in the area.

POINTS OF INTEREST

1 Richardson Maritime Museum
2 Dorchester Center for the Arts

SHOPPING

3 Main Street Gallery
4 Joie de Vivre Gallery
5 Dragonfly Boutique
6 Crabi Gras
7 A Few of My Favorite Things
8 Simmons Center Market

DINING

9 Bistro Poplar
10 Leaky Pete's Oyster & Wine Bar
11 The High Spot
12 Canvasback Restaurant and Pub
13 Snappers Waterfront Café
14 Jimmy & Sook's
15 The Waters Edge Grill
16 Micheners Library

L LIBRARY

Rx PHARMACY

PO POST OFFICE

OXFORD/TRED AVON RIVER

A major port during the 17th and 18th centuries, Oxford was an important boatbuilding and tobacco-shipping center. Its early glory faded with the American Revolution, and except for a brief resurgence in oyster packing around the turn of the 20th century, the village has retained a unique civility. That civility is its charm, the quality that endears Oxford to its legion of waterborne devotees.

Along with St. Michaels as a favorite cruising destination of the Eastern Shore, Oxford's harbor pulsates with activity. Every marine service is available at Oxford's marinas and boatyards, and the small anchorage is thick with boats on summer weekends. Boating activity continues here well into the fall.

NAVIGATION: Use Chart 12266. **Use Baltimore tide tables. For Oxford high tide, subtract 3 hours 1 minute; for low tide, subtract 2 hours 50 minutes.** Oxford lies about two miles up the Tred Avon River from its intersection with the Choptank. Be sure to honor 15-foot-tall flashing green "1" southeast of Benoni Point as you turn into the Tred Avon River, as it marks the end of a shoal extending one-third of the way across the river's entrance. The upriver course, past the Oxford-Bellevue ferry dock, follows Oxford's residential waterfront along Morris Street, then turns to starboard at quick flashing red "2" and follows the beach known as The Strand to the buoyed channel for Town Creek.

Dockage: On entering the protection of Town Creek, you will see two major marine facilities to starboard. The first, Mears Yacht Haven, has transient slips, a swimming pool, a fuel dock and you can rent a bike to ride around town. Next door, Oxford Boatyard is a full-service facility that boasts a 75-ton Travelift, a 10-ton crane and is just the place for that major refit you have been planning.

Cutts and Case, with ample facilities, also accepts transient guests. Their amenities include observation of the beautiful wooden boat renovations they undertake on site. Just beyond, still farther along Town Creek, Hinckley Yacht Services (formerly Crockett Brothers Boatyard) has transient space plus a 50-ton lift and does boat repair. At the head of Town Creek, Oxford Yacht Agency offers transient dockage. Campbell's operates three facilities in Oxford. Two are located on Town Creek. Campbell's

Oxford, MD

OXFORD	Phone	Largest Vessel Accommodated	VHF Channel Monitored	Transient Berths / Total Berths	Approach / Dockside Depth (reported)	Floating Docks	Gas / Diesel	Groceries, Ice, Marine Supplies, Snacks	Repairs: Hull, Engine, Propeller	Lift (tonnage), Crane, Rail	Min/Max Amps	Laundry, Pool, Showers, Courtesy Car	Pump-Out Station	Nearby: Grocery Store, Motel, Restaurant
		Dockage					Supplies		Services					
1. Campbell's Bachelor Pt. Yacht Co.	**410-226-5592**	**100**	**16**	**6/80**	**12/12**	**-**	**-**	**IMS**	**HEP**	**L70, C35**	**30/100**	**LPS**	**P**	**GMR**
2. Masthead Restaurant at Pier Street Marina	410-226-5171	60	-	20/62	5/5	-	-	I	-		30/50	S	-	GMR
3. Hinckley Yacht Services Oxford	**410-226-5113**	**60**	**78**	**30/66**	**7/6**	**F**	**-**	**IM**	**HEP**	**L50, C3**	**30/50**	**LPS**	**P**	**GMR**
4. Cutts & Case Inc.	410-226-5416	75	-	2/40	8/6	-	-	-	HEP	C, R	30/30	S	-	GMR
5. Tred Avon Yacht Club	410-226-5269	100	-	/6	12/8	F	-	GIMS	-	-	30/50	-	-	GMR
6. Mears Yacht Haven	**410-226-5450**	**150**	**16/09**	**35/95**	**10/8**	**-**	**GD**	**IMS**	**-**	**-**	**30/50**	**LPS**	**P**	**GMR**
7. Oxford Boatyard	**410-226-5101**	**105**	**16/71**	**22/65**	**11/10**	**-**	**-**	**I**	**HEP**	**L75, C10**	**30/50**	**L**	**P**	**GR**
8. Campbell's Boatyard @ Jack's Point	**410-226-5105**	**50**	**16**	**/56**	**9/7**	**-**	**GD**	**IMS**	**HEP**	**L20, C35**	**30/50**	**S**	**P**	**GMR**
9. Campbell's Town Creek Boatyard	**410-226-0213**	**50**	**16**	**4/48**	**6/6**	**-**	**-**	**IM**	**HEP**	**C35**	**30/50**	**LS**	**P**	**GMR**
10. Oxford Yacht Agency	410-226-5454	60	-	4/20	7/6	-	-	-	HEP	L70	50/50	LS	-	GMR

Corresponding chart(s) not to be used for navigation. Internet Access Wireless Internet Access Waterway Guide Cruising Club Partner

See www.WaterwayGuide.com for current rates, fuel prices, web site addresses, and other up-to-the-minute information.

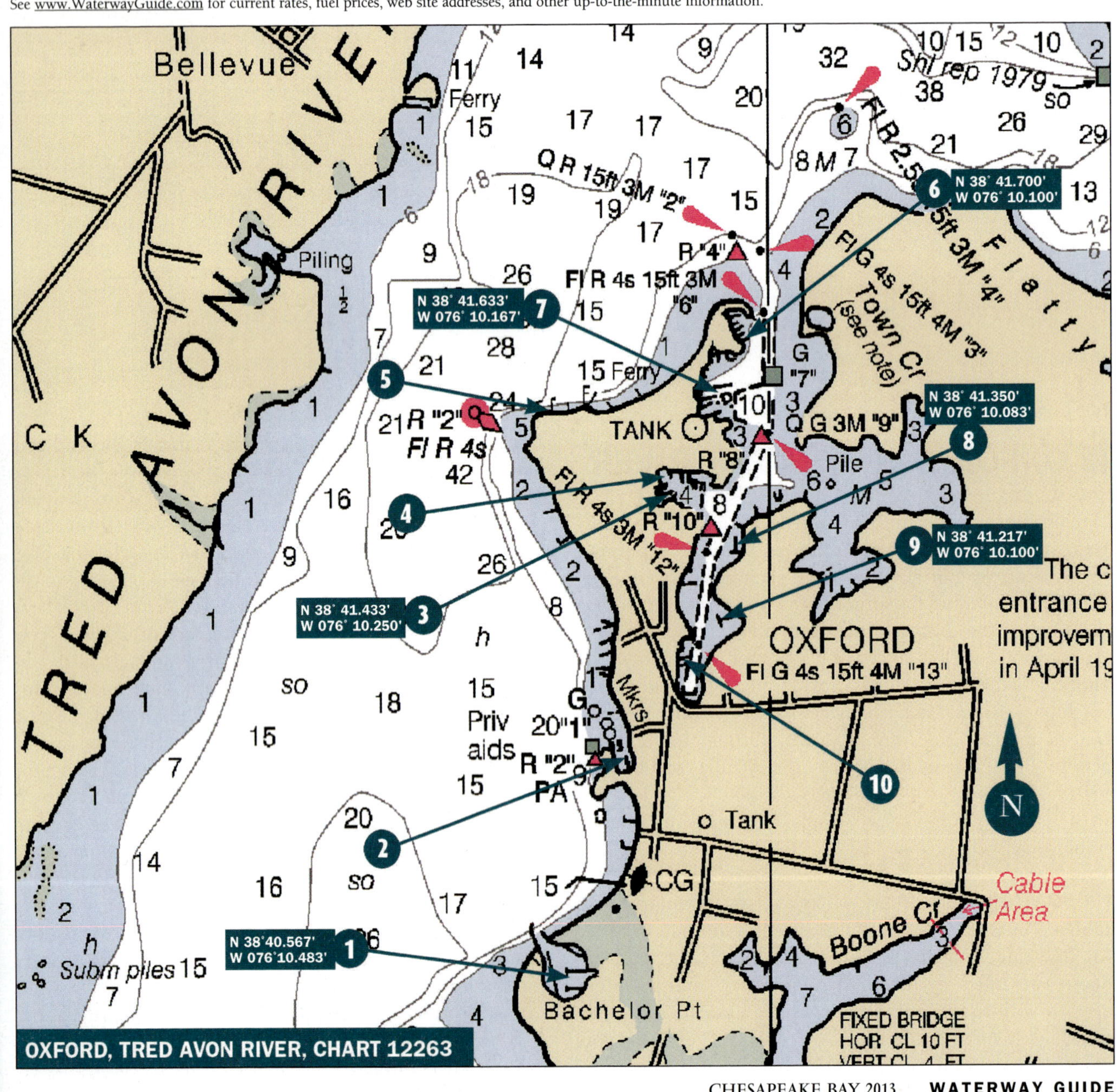

Looking north over Bachelor Point, Oxford and Town Creek. (Not to be used for navigation.) Waterway Guide Photography.

Boatyard at Jack's Point and Campbell's Town Creek Boatyard both accept transient guests, and the Jack's Point facility has gas and diesel fuel available. The other is the Bachelor Point facility, which you encounter on your way into Oxford via the Tred Avon River. Here, inside a protected basin just inside Bachelor Point, you will find a 75-ton Travelift, transient facilities and an extensive repair yard. Farther north is Masthead Restaurant at Pier Street Marina, with transient slips. Immediately after flashing red "2" is Tred Avon Yacht Club, which has transient space on floating docks.

Anchorage: After entering Town Creek, watch for shallow spots to the left of quick flashing green "9." A sandbar extends off the land toward the "Y" dock (about a third of the way across), though some spots between quick flashing green "9" and the "Y" dock still carry 6-foot depths at mean low water. Many skippers anchor outside the creek entrance, off The Strand on the Tred Avon River, and land their dinghies on the beach, just west of the ferry dock. This anchorage can be lively and filled with boats during the summer. Schooners restaurant has a dinghy landing to accommodate its restaurant patrons who choose to anchor on either side of the marked channel.

GOIN' ASHORE: **OXFORD, MD**

The term "picture perfect" risks overuse when it comes to describing Eastern Shore villages, but if there is one town that has earned that description, it is Oxford. "Picket fence picture perfect" wouldn't be an exaggeration, either.

This historic port made an early mark during the Revolutionary War, then spent a century or so settling into the slow life of its fellow Talbot County towns made up of shipbuilding, sailmaking, farming and the oystering and crabbing lives of watermen. Then came the second-home owners and tourists. Boaters love the place, too. Cutts and Case Shipyard, the famous boat builders with their patented planking method, is located here. The Strand, a beach running alongside the Tred Avon River right in town, adds to the charm, especially when you spot the Oxford-Bellevue Ferry picking up or discharging its passengers at the intersection of North Morris Street, as it has for more or less 300 years.

History: Back in 1683, Maryland's General Assembly proclaimed this little peninsula settlement a port of entry—the Eastern Shore's first—and the town of Oxford was laid out. Then came the ocean-going vessels, the wealthy interest in Chesapeake tobacco from abroad and a flourishing social era. One wealthy patron by the name of Robert Morris had a house built here in 1710, a part of which went on to be incorporated into the town's well-known Robert Morris Inn. His son, Robert Morris Jr., is remembered as "the Financier of the Revolution." The tobacco trade went into decline as the new country was born, and the next century saw oystering and tomato processing dominate the local economy. James Michener put the Robert Morris Inn on the map when he famously enjoyed their crab cakes while working on his book "Chesapeake."

George Washington chose an Oxford native as his attaché, and Tench Tilghman went on to greet history as the trusted aide who delivered news of the American triumph at Yorktown to Philadelphia, where the Continental Congress was meeting. His grave is located in the Oxford Cemetery just outside town on Route 33.

Points of Interest: Oxford is a great town for walking and bike riding. A good place to start is the Oxford Museum (410-226-0191), a small seasonal museum housed in a former grocery and confectionary store at 100 S. Morris St. that tells the tales of days gone by in this pretty little village. Changing exhibits, such as a recent one on early plantation life on the Oxford Neck, illuminate the area's life. Be sure to visit the Robert Morris Inn, and the nearby circa-1683 Oxford-Bellevue Ferry, which took a decades-long break after the Revolutionary War, and is thought to be the country's oldest privately operating ferry. See www.oxfordbellevueferry.com for a schedule. Take your bike when you catch the ferry at The Strand and North Morris Street, and head into St. Michaels, a seven-mile ride, after you get to tiny Bellevue. (See St, Michael's Goin' Ashore for more information.) Or, bike out highway 333, past Latitude 38 Bistro and continue for eight miles to Easton. (See Easton Goin' Ashore for more information.)

Before leaving town, swing by Cutts & Case Shipyard (306 Tilghman St., 410-226-5416). Their collection of wooden boats on display in the main building is worth a peak.

Speaking of leaving town…you will have to do so to find a golf course. The closest one is 8 miles away in Easton (Talbot Country Club, 410-822-0490).

Special Events: The Tred Avon Players put on a new show at the former school house-now-Oxford Community Center (200 Oxford Rd.,410-226-0061) every quarter (www.tredavonplayers.org). Oxford Day at the end of April celebrates the town with a 10-K run, a parade, kids' activities and sometimes reenactments ranging from pirate characters to Civil War soldiers. Oxford Invitational Fine Arts Fair takes place Memorial Day Weekend at the Oxford Community Center, which also houses a farmers' market on Wednesday evenings.

Shopping: Michener's literary heirs might be interested in the bookstore Mystery Loves Company. It is the Oxford outpost of a mystery bookstore based in Baltimore's Fell's Point. It is located in the old bank building at 202 S. Morris St. (410-226-0010). The Oxford Convenience Market (203 S. Morris St., 866-407-7129) carries limited grocery and deli items.

Dining: The Masthead at Pier Street Marina (410-226-5171) and Schooners Landing (410-226-0160) both provide a relaxed hangout on the water. Schooners has slips for diners. A more upscale meal can be had at Pope's Tavern at the Oxford Inn (410-226-5220) and at Latitude 38 Bistro & Spirits (410-226-5303). For fine dining be sure to visit the Robert Morris Inn and Tavern (314 N. Morris St., 410-226-5111). The tavern, called Salters, serves breakfast, lunch and dinner on the patio In the warm months or beside a fireplace in the winter months.

Reference the marina listing tables to see all the marinas in the area.

POINTS OF INTEREST

1 Oxford Museum
2 Robert Morris Inn
3 Oxford-Bellevue Ferry
4 Cutts & Case
5 Oxford Community Center

SHOPPING

6 Mystery Loves Company
7 Oxford Convenience Market

DINING

2 Robert Morris Tavern, Salters
7 Oxford Convenience Market
8 Masthead at Pier Street
9 Schooner's Landing
10 Pope's Tavern (Oxford Inn)
11 Latitude 38 Bistro & Spirits

ADDITIONAL RESOURCES

■ PORT OF OXFORD: www.portofoxford.com

NEARBY MEDICAL FACILITIES

Easton Memorial Hospital: 219 S. Washington St., Easton, MD 21601, 410-822-1000 (12 miles)

NEARBY AIRPORT

Easton Airport: 29137 Newnam Road, Unit One, Easton, MD 21601 (16 miles)

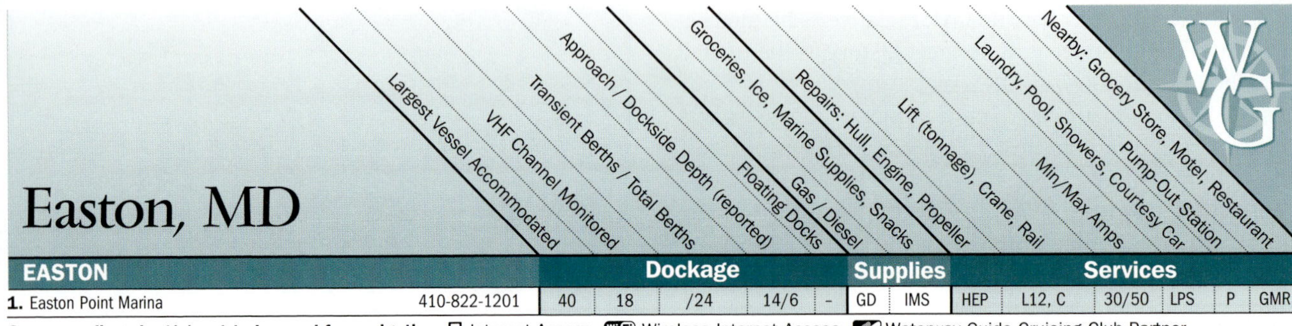

Easton, MD

EASTON		Largest Vessel Accommodated	VHF Channel Monitored	Transient Berths / Total Berths	Approach / Dockside Depth (reported)	Floating Docks	Gas / Diesel	Groceries, Ice, Marine Supplies, Snacks	Repairs: Hull, Engine, Propeller	Lift (tonnage), Crane, Rail	Min/Max Amps	Laundry, Pool, Showers, Courtesy Car	Pump-Out Station	Nearby: Grocery Store, Motel, Restaurant
		Dockage					Supplies		Services					
1. Easton Point Marina	410-822-1201	40	18	/24	14/6	-	GD	IMS	HEP	L12, C	30/50	LPS	P	GMR

Corresponding chart(s) not to be used for navigation. Internet Access Wireless Internet Access Waterway Guide Cruising Club Partner

See www.WaterwayGuide.com for current rates, fuel prices, web site addresses, and other up-to-the-minute information.

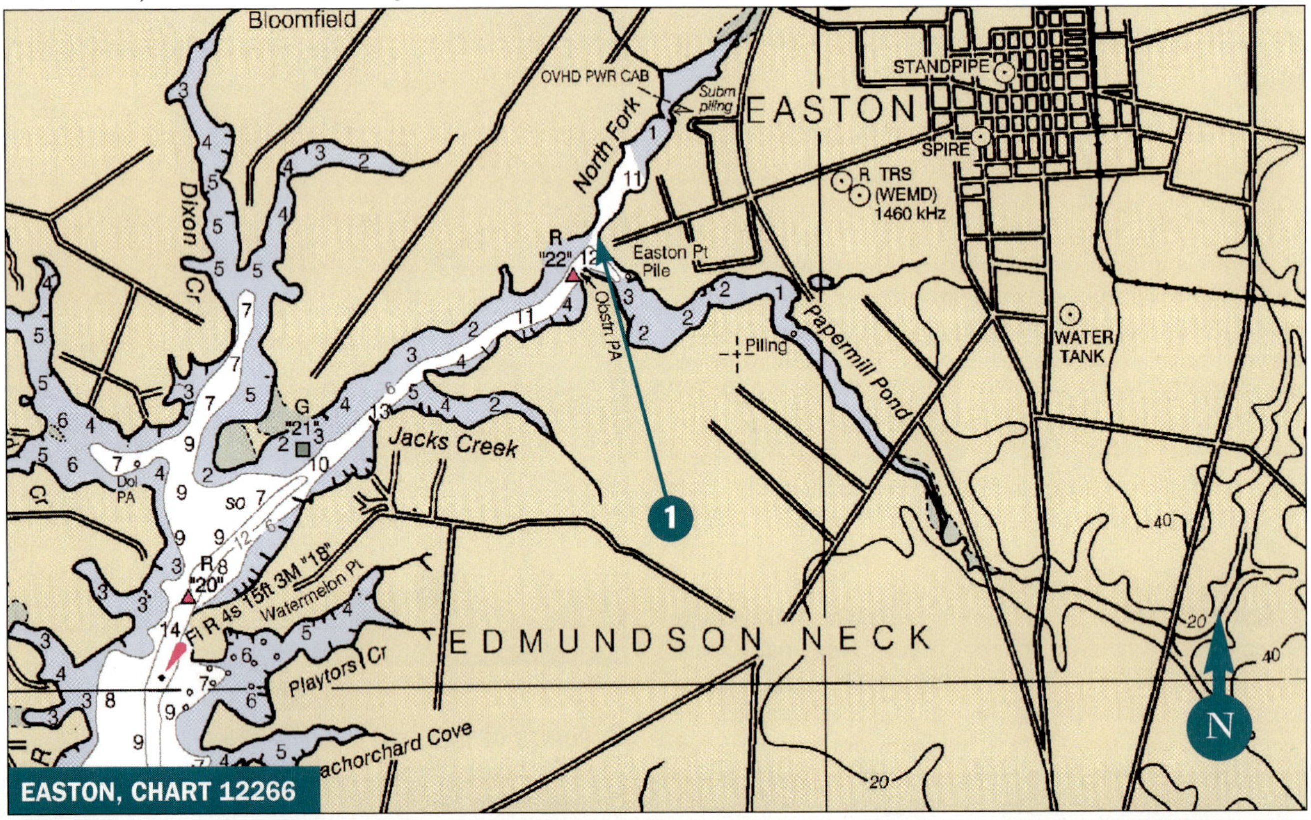

EASTON, CHART 12266

Looking southwest over Easton. (Not to be used for navigation.) Waterway Guide Photography.

Tred Avon River, Above Oxford

The seven miles from Oxford to Easton Point at the head of the Tred Avon River may be the most heavily cruised small waterway on the whole Eastern Shore, and for good reason: You can find an anchorage or explorable creek around almost every point.

Dockage: There is one marina in Easton: Easton Point Marina. Fortunately, they have gas and diesel, as well as a pump-out station and a pool.

Anchorage: Though anchorages and creeks abound, the place seems quiet, even in the peak of summer. These anchorages and creeks include Plaindealing Creek, just across the Tred Avon from Oxford; Goldsborough Creek; Trippe Creek and Peachblossom Creek, where the Eastern Shore's first peach trees grew in Colonial days. (Maryland was the country's largest peach producer until a devastating blight killed the trees.). Trippe Creek, the most open of these, is perfectly sheltered, so it is often the coolest on hot summer nights.

GOIN' ASHORE: **EASTON, MD**

Easton is sometimes called the New York City of the Eastern Shore. While that may be debatable (the highest-rise structure is probably a church spire) the town remains true to its roots as Talbot County's center of government and commerce. The arts and a great dining scene dominate the town's tourist offerings.

Points of Interest: Those interested in the area's history should stop by the Historical Society of Talbot County at 25 S. Washington St. (410-822-0773), not only to check out the exhibits, but to pick up a self-guided tour of Easton or sign up for a historic homes tour. A living example of the dawn of European civilization is here: the Third Haven Friends Meeting House at 405 S. Washington St., which dates to 1684. It is considered the nation's oldest wooden structure in continuous use for worship.

Easton has always been a haven for artists, including Art Deco sculptor Lee Lawrie and mid-century painter Clark Marshall. The Academy Art Museum (106 South St., 410-822-2787) dwells in a former 1820s schoolhouse and offers a permanent collection of works on paper that include major-league artists such as Jim Dine, Robert Rauschenberg, John Sloan, James Abbott McNeill Whistler and Grant Wood. Over at the restored art deco Avalon Theatre (40 East Dover St.), a notable variety of talent takes the stage, such as Taj Mahal or roots rockers Eilen Jewell, and Sarah Borges and the Broken Singles.

There are two nearby golf courses: The Easton Club (410-822-9800 or 800-277-9800), which is one mile away, and Hog Neck Golf Course (410-822-6079 or 800-280-1790), which is three miles away

Special Events: Visit the farmers' market, located on Harrison St., held every Saturday, April through early December. Plein Air Competition & Arts Festival, Easton, a competition for painters and the arts, unfolds over a week in July. Wildlife carvers, artists and collectors flock to the famous, annual Waterfowl Festival in mid-November, which sees approximately 18,000 people from around the country, including hunters and guides who compete in calling contests. Every month from 5:00 p.m. to 9:00 p.m., the First Friday Gallery Walk takes place in Easton's Town Center. The historic Avalon Theater, in the center of town, offers entertainment from the symphony to bluegrass, comedians to opera. Check out www.avalontheatre.com to see what's playing. In addition, the Avalon backs such community offerings as Friday outdoor movies in summer or outdoor concerts. Call for more information.

Shopping: Antiques and arts-lovers should have a field day here, as will those who enjoy a good boutique. Antiques options include: Janet K. Fanto Antiques and Rare Books at 13

Reference the marina listing tables to see all the marinas in the area.

INFORMATION
1 Historical Society of Talbot County

POINTS OF INTEREST
2 The Third Haven Friends Meeting House
3 Academy Art Museum
4 Avalon Theatre

SHOPPING
5 Janet K. Fanto Antiques and Rare Books
6 Foxwells
7 South Street Art Gallery
8 Troika Art Gallery
9 The News Center
10 Irish Traditions
11 Crackerjack Toys

DINING
12 Out of the Fire
13 Scossa Restaurant & Lounge
14 Mason's
15 General Tanuki's
16 CoffeeCat/NightCat
17 Hunters Tavern

LIBRARY
POST OFFICE
PHARMACY

Little Choptank River, MD

LITTLE CHOPTANK RIVER		Dockage					Supplies		Services					
		Largest Vessel Accommodated	VHF Channel Monitored	Transient Berths / Total Berths	Approach / Dockside Depth (reported)	Floating Docks	Gas / Diesel	Groceries, Ice, Marine Supplies, Snacks	Repairs: Hull, Engine, Propeller	Lift (tonnage), Crane, Rail	Min/Max Amps	Laundry, Pool, Showers, Courtesy Car	Pump-Out Station	Nearby: Grocery Store, Motel, Restaurant
1. Slaughter Creek Marina (formerly Taylor's Island Marina)	410-221-0050	80	16	20/105	6/6	-	GD	IMS	H	L25	30/50	LPS	P	MR
2. Madison Bay Marina & Campground (WiFi)	410-463-0325	55	-	5/45	6/6	-	-	IS	-	-	50/50	LS	P	GMR

Corresponding chart(s) not to be used for navigation. Internet Access (WiFi) Wireless Internet Access Waterway Guide Cruising Club Partner

See www.WaterwayGuide.com for current rates, fuel prices, web site addresses, and other up-to-the-minute information.

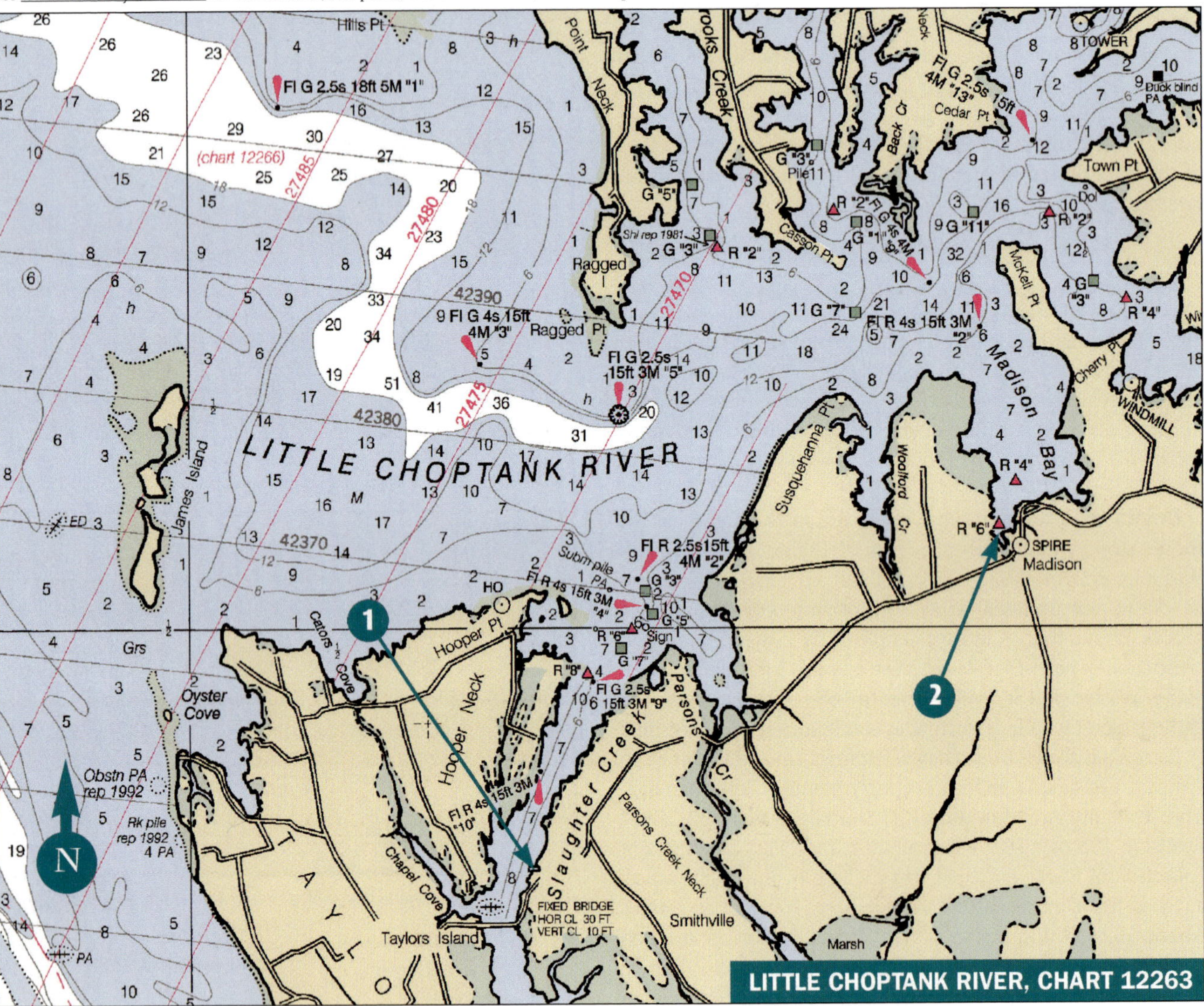

LITTLE CHOPTANK RIVER, CHART 12263

N. Harrison St. (410-763-9030) and Foxwell's, an antiques mall at 7793 Ocean Gateway (410-820-9705). A sampling of good galleries: South Street Art Gallery, 5 South St. (410-770-8350), and Troika Art Gallery, 9 South Harrison St. (410-770-9190). Everyone should be aware of The News Center at 218 N. Washington St. (in the Talbot Town Shopping Center), one of those stores that seems to always have that hard-to-find magazine (410-822-7212). One popular store, Irish Traditions at 35 North Harrison Street (410-819-3663), sells Irish and Scottish gifts, including kilts (which can be difficult to find on the Eastern Shore). For the younger ones, visit Crackerjack Toys at 7 South Washington Street (410-822-7716). This mom-and-pop store carries hard-to-find, good quality toys and collector items.

Dining: Good restaurants have become ubiquitous here, so consider this a tasting menu: Look for upscale Mediterranean fare and fancy pizza at Out of the Fire (22 Goldsborough St., 410-770-4777), while Scossa Restaurant and Lounge offers authentic Northern Italian food and great service (8 N. Washington St.,410-822-2202) and Osteria Alfredo (210 Marlboro Ave., 410-822-9088) has good pizza. Mason's (22 S. Harrison St., 410-822-3204) has been in town for eons and provides lovely meals and a gourmet deli. For sushi, check out General Tanuki's at 25 Goldsborough Street. They also offer "Hawaiian fusion" cuisine. CoffeeCat provides your java fix, as well as amazing (and huge) breakfast sandwiches. There is music in the evening next door at NightCat (1 Goldsborough St., 410-690-3662). And, to top it all off, an old-fashioned soda fountain still exists at Hill's Drug Store (30 E. Dover St., 410-822-2666). The ever-faithful and historic Tidewater Inn recently renovated its restaurant, Hunters' Tavern, which offers seafood and creative specials in an elegant atmosphere. The Tidewater Inn, with roots back to 1712, is a place where you're likely to see a Chesapeake Bay Retriever on the elevator with his hunter owner (101 East Dover St., 410-822-1300).

ADDITIONAL RESOURCES

- EASTON, MD: www.eastonmd.org
- TOUR TALBOT: www.tourtalbot.org
- THE TALBOT COUNTY VISITORS CENTER, 11 S. Harrison St., Easton, MD 21601, 410-770-8000

NEARBY MEDICAL FACILITIES
Easton Memorial Hospital (formally called The Memorial Hospital at Easton), 219 S. Washington St., Easton, MD 21601, 410-822-1000

NEARBY AIRPORT
Easton Airport: 29137 Newnam Road, Unit One, Easton, MD 21601 (1 mile)

TRANSPORTATION:
Bayrunner Shuttle provides daily transport to Baltimore-Washington International Airport, 410-912-6000

Bay Country Taxi, 410-770-9030

LITTLE CHOPTANK RIVER

About seven nautical miles below the mouth of the Choptank River, its cousin, the Little Choptank River, opens off to the east and leads to another tangle of creeks, coves and streams to explore. There are no towns on the Little Choptank; so much of it is natural and undeveloped, with only a few scattered clusters of houses.

Hudson and Brooks Creeks, off the Little Choptank

Anchorage: Hudson Creek opens on the north side, a couple of miles inside from the mouth of the Little Choptank River, with sheltered anchorage behind Casson Point, or in several coves farther up the creek (depths of 7 to 10 feet). The west side of the creek is only lightly developed, but these anchorages are popular with cruising clubs and likely to be crowded on weekends. The channel into Brooks Creek is narrow and ill-defined, with shoaling at the entrance. The only place to anchor is at the mouth before red daybeacon "2," and this spot is only good in winds from the northwest through northeast.

Slaughter Creek, off the Little Choptank

There are no marks in Slaughter Creek beyond the bridge (10-foot fixed vertical clearance) just past Chapel Cove, but you can take a fascinating dinghy trip through the marshes and woodlands all the way upstream, where the creek actually connects with the Chesapeake Bay at Punch Island Creek. It also eventually connects to the headwaters of the Honga River, via Great Marsh Creek. There is an amazing abundance and variety of wildlife along this stretch of Slaughter Creek, and the fishing and crabbing are good, too.

NAVIGATION: Use Chart 12266. Slaughter Creek is just around Hooper Point, on the south side of the Little Choptank. Shoaling to a depth of less than 3 feet MLW has been reported between Slaughter Creek light "4" and Slaughter Creek Daybeacon "6", extending across the channel. There is also shoaling across the channel between Slaughter Creek Daybeacon "6" and "7". Note: The Taylors Island Coast Guard Station, a mobile station, serves this area.

Dockage: Slaughter Creek Marina (formerly Taylors Island Marina), on the east side at the bridge (10-foot fixed vertical clearance), offers transient dockage, fuel, a bar and restaurant, boat and bike rentals, a pool, repairs and a ships store. Approach depth is 7 feet, with 6-foot depths dockside.

Fishing Creek, off the Little Choptank

A buoyed channel leads into Fishing Creek where the Little Choptank divides at Town Point. You will find a secluded anchorage, fronted by woods and a beach, south of red daybeacon "4" behind Cherry Point, however a charted shoal of 5 feet or less existed there in 2011. Generous depths continue up Fishing Creek, with stretches of woods between clusters of modest houses. This area features a mixture of summer cottages and watermen's homes.

Madison Bay

Madison Bay is 7 feet deep and is located between McKell Point and the unnavigable Woolford Creek. Madison Bay & Campground is here. Call ahead for depths and directions. It is located at the town of Madison.

Church Creek, off Fishing Creek

Church Creek is also more than 6 feet deep. Near the headwaters, the village that gave the creek its name has a number of old houses with gambrel roofs, small dormer windows and huge fireplaces. The village church probably dates back to before 1680, and its surroundings look just the way you would expect a country churchyard to look. Some of the old headstones mark the burial place of members of the illustrious Carroll family, which includes a former governor of Maryland and his daughter, Anna Ella Carroll, a close friend of Abraham Lincoln, who secretly advised him about strategy during the Civil War. ■

Oxford
Cambridge
Choptank River
MILE 71
Calvert Cliffs
Patuxent River
Solomons
MILE 86
Hooper Islands
Nanticoke River
Wicomico River
Salisbury
Page 178
50
13
9
St. Marys City
Bloodsworth Island
Southmarsh Island
Potomac River
Point Lookout
Page 185
Smith Island
Tangier Sound
Crisfield
Page 180
Page 190
Pocomoke City
113
Chincoteague Bay
MARYLAND
VIRGINIA
Smith Point
MILE 111
Reedville
Tangier Island
Page 188
Rappahannock River
17
Onancock
Page 192
Atlantic Ocean
Irvington
Urbanna
Deltaville
Piankatank River
Gwynns Island
MILE 134
N
13
York River
Mobjack Bay
Page 196
Cape Charles
Williamsburg
Yorktown
Gloucester Point
James River
64
Hampton
DOZIER'S WATERWAY GUIDE
THE CRUISING AUTHORITY
www.WaterwayGuide.com
Skipper's Handbook
GPS Waypoints 48
Tide Tables 50

Little Choptank to Cape Charles

CHARTS 12221, 12224, 12225, 12226, 12228, 12230, 12231, 12261, 12263

The broad expanses of water as you cruise along the lower Eastern Shore may appear desolate. The rivers, creeks and coves are often shallow, with wide marshes and flat shorelines. Planning a cruise in this area is somewhat akin to expedition cruising where you will at times be the only boat, save the occasional workboat. Wildlife abounds and the nights are dark here far from civilization. The stars seem so close you can almost reach out and touch them. Working the soil and water is still the way of life here, where there has been far less change over the years than on any other part of Chesapeake Bay. Change is coming, though, with retirees moving into towns like Onancock and Cape Charles, VA and increased traffic across the Chesapeake Bay Bridge-Tunnel at the mouth of the Bay.

Marinas that cater to recreational boats can be far apart in this area, so a skipper and crew must be more self-reliant than in more populated places. The terrain is low, and few landmarks rise above it, so it is common to be out of sight of land in all directions here. When summer thunderstorms roll in from the west, it can feel like a very lonely place. On the positive side, there are plenty of creeks and coves to explore, especially if your boat has a fairly shallow draft, and the people in this area are friendly and helpful to cruisers.

The watermen usually set out to tend their crabbing gear as early as 5:00 a.m., and few bother with engine mufflers. Depending on where you are anchored or tied off, you can sometimes expect to awaken early. Note the shoals and marshes, and arm yourself with swatters, repellents and screens to defend against the flies and mosquitoes that explore the air hereabouts. After years of cruising in this area we contend that the threat is often overstated, and we have very rarely been bothered with insects; however, forewarned is forearmed.

The lower Eastern Shore is approximately 90 miles long. It begins in Maryland, south of the Little Choptank River (roughly opposite the mouth of the Patuxent River on the Western Shore), crosses into Virginia opposite the Potomac River and runs down to Cape Charles at the mouth of the Chesapeake Bay. It includes Tangier Sound and Pocomoke Sound, several broad rivers and three remote, but interesting smaller islands: Deal, Smith, and Tangier.

HOOPER ISLAND, MD TO TANGIER SOUND

The 30-mile-long run south from the Little Choptank River, past Taylors Island and on to Hooper Strait, can seem like a long way, especially against a booming summer southerly wind. The only truly accessible shelter is across the Bay at Solomons Island on the Patuxent River, and many cruisers crisscross at this narrow section of the Bay to visit Solomons and then cross back to their intended cruising ground of the lower Eastern Shore.

Waterway Guide Photography.

HOOPER ISLAND
N 38°15.400'
W 076°15.000'

NAVIGATION: Use Chart 12264 and 12261. If the channel has been dredged recently, your vessel draws less than 4 feet and its masthead rises less than 24 feet above the water, you can use the channel into the Honga River at the north end of Upper Hooper Island. Picking up the entrance against the low, featureless shoreline can be a challenge, but once you have reached flashing red bell buoy "76" northwest of Barren Island on the main shipping channel, you should see flashing green "1." The well-marked route passes first through the marshes of Barren Island, then across Tar Bay and through Fishing Creek, dividing Upper Hooper Island from the mainland. It is narrow, shallow and subject to shoaling, and there is a fixed bridge (state Highway 335) at the eastern, or Honga River, end with a 24-foot fixed vertical clearance. At latest reports, there were some spots that were only 1-foot deep, and the most recent charts indicate 1-foot depths from the western entrance all the way to the bridge in the channel. Ask a local waterman or marina for the current depth, as dredging is intermittent.

HONGA RIVER, MD

The northern end of the Honga River is shallow. Passage through here is a challenge in a boat larger than a 25-foot outboard, unless you have good local knowledge. The lower Honga River is a well-buoyed channel that leads through deep water and lovely vistas as it meanders through rural

Nanticoke, Wicomico River, Salisbury, MD

	Phone	Largest Vessel Accommodated	VHF Channel Monitored	Transient Berths / Total Berths	Approach / Dockside Depth (reported)	Floating Docks	Gas / Diesel	Groceries, Ice, Marine Supplies, Snacks	Repairs: Hull, Engine, Propeller	Lift (tonnage), Crane, Rail	Min/Max Amps	Laundry, Pool, Showers, Courtesy Car	Pump-Out Station	Nearby: Grocery Store, Motel, Restaurant
		Dockage					Supplies		Services					
NANTICOKE RIVER														
1. Nanticoke River Marine Park (Internet Access) (Wireless Internet Access)	302-628-8600	64	16	30/87	8/8	F	GD	G	-	L30	30/50	LS	P	GMR
WICOMICO RIVER														
2. Wikander's Marine Services Inc.	410-749-9521	50	-	2/11	10/6	F	-	M	HEP	L25	30/30	LS	P	-
SALISBURY														
3. Port of Salisbury Marina (Internet Access) (Wireless Internet Access)	410-548-3176	100	16	10/86	14/6	-	GD	I	-	-	30/50	LS	P	GR

Corresponding chart(s) not to be used for navigation. Internet Access · Wireless Internet Access · Waterway Guide Cruising Club Partner

See www.WaterwayGuide.com for current rates, fuel prices, web site addresses, and other up-to-the-minute information.

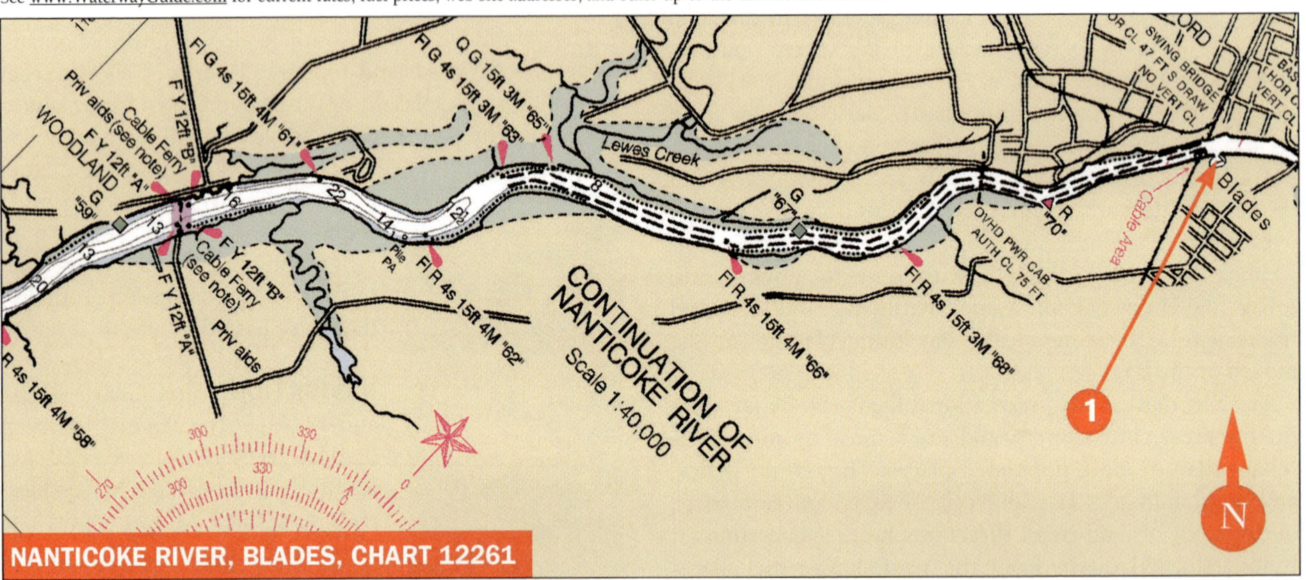

NANTICOKE RIVER, BLADES, CHART 12261

undeveloped low country between Wroten Island and Hooper Straight.

Anchorage: You can anchor off the main channel, south-southeast of red daybeacon "6" in Lakes Cove (4- to 7-foot depths, soft mud bottom), or southeast of flashing red "2" marking the channel into the village of Hoopersville (5- to 8-foot depths, mud bottom). The Hoopersville anchorage is exposed in northeast through southeast winds, and the Lakes Cove anchorage is open to the northwest and southwest. These are not particularly scenic places, but they are useful stopovers on the long passage between the Little Choptank River and Tangier Sound. While there are few obvious anchorages on the Honga, as with many rivers on the lower bay, cruisers often anchors along the side of the river where the openness ensures full benefit of the summer breezes. Any anchorage in this river that is deep enough for most cruising boats will be exposed to wind from some direction, so make sure to set the hook firmly.

HOOPER STRAIT

Hooper Strait is the 9-mile-long deepwater passage between Chesapeake Bay and Tangier Sound. It is well marked but a little circuitous at the eastern end.

Hooper Strait Light (41-foot-high skeleton tower with a black-and-white diamond dayboard; flashing white every 6 seconds) marks the western approach. Strong currents can impede or improve progress through Hooper Strait; the current floods east and ebbs west at about 1.5 knots.

Note that flashing red buoy "14" (on the eastern end of Hooper Strait and Sharkfin Shoal Channel) has been moved; keep an eye out for the new location, about one-third of a mile to the southeast. Give Sharkfin Shoal light a wide berth as the rip-rap extends farther out than you expect and is hidden at all but the lowest tides. Bloodsworth Island, on the south side of Hooper Strait, is a Navy bombing range, as evidenced by the bombed-out hulk of a target ship, and its marshes and beaches are full of unexploded bombs. Landing is strictly prohibited.

As you pass Bloodsworth Island and Holland Straights, you may catch a glimpse of Holland Island. Once a vibrant community with schools, churches and businesses, its last building washed into the Bay in 2010. Since being abandoned by man, Holland Island has become one of the largest breeding colonies for brown pelicans. This bird, which was nearly wiped out by DDT in the 1960s, has made a remarkable recovery. Brown pelicans can now be seen in this part of the bay from March through November.

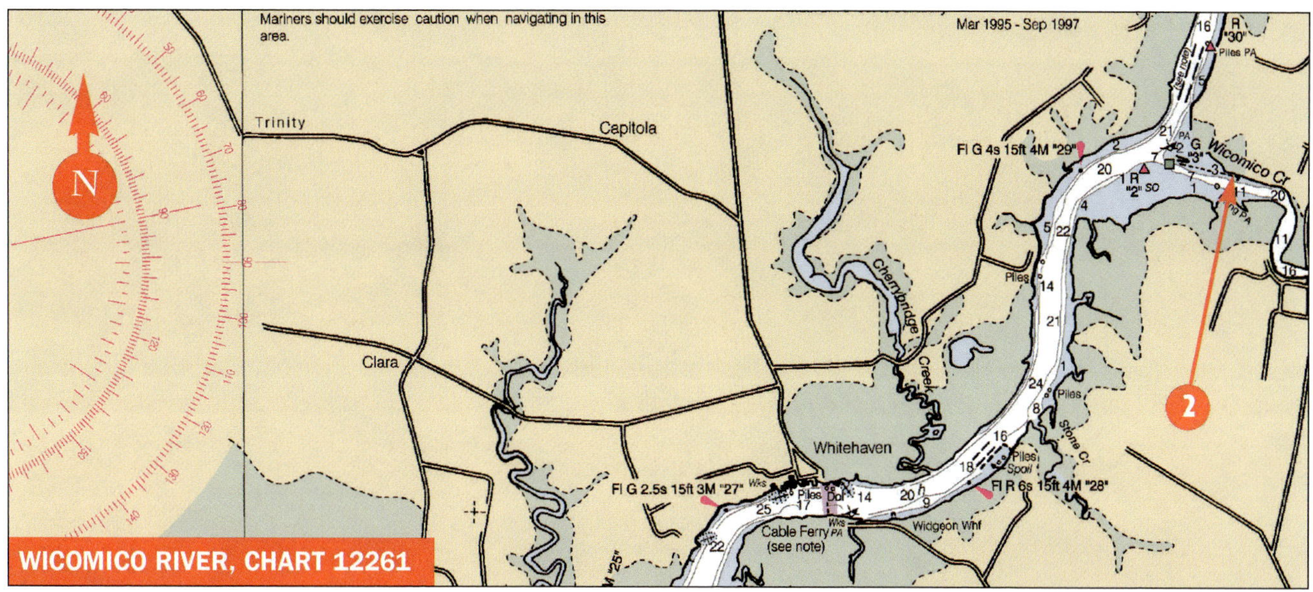

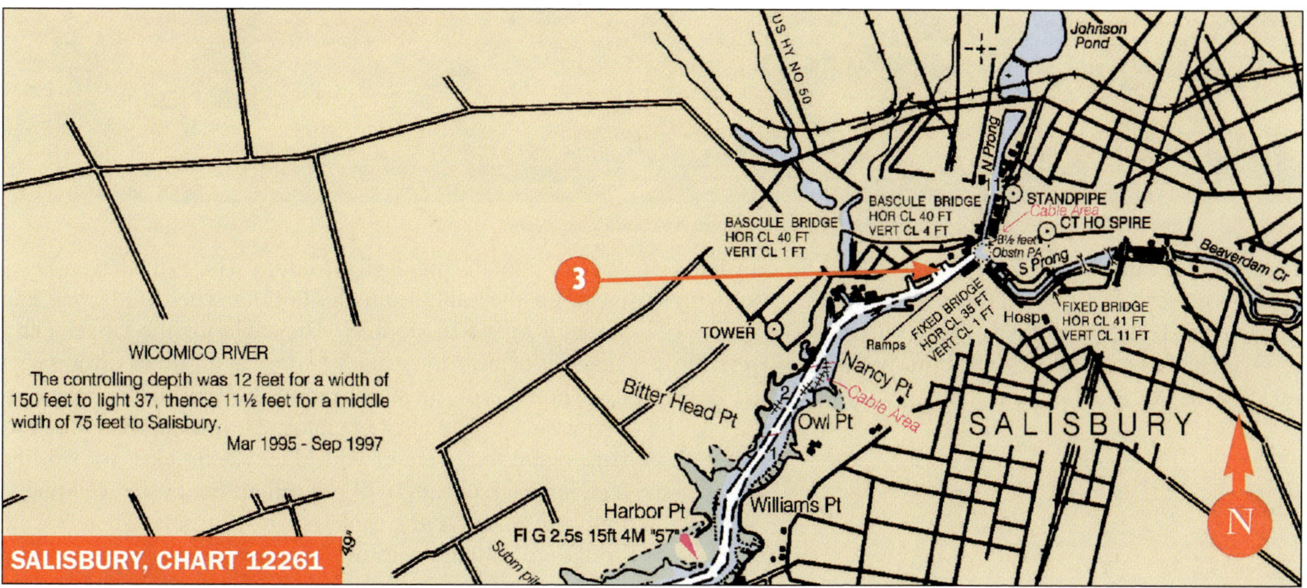

NANTICOKE RIVER, MD, DE

Commercial boats carrying 10-foot drafts frequently transit the 35-mile route on the Nanticoke River to Seaford, DE. The Nanticoke is a pretty, well marked, winding river lined with marshes that teem with wildlife, and it may remind you of the deep tributaries that branch off Delaware Bay or the sections of the Intracoastal Waterway (ICW) that meander through Georgia. As with other such waterways, the best times to visit are spring and fall, when the temperatures are moderate and bugs are in seasonal remission.

Two 50-foot fixed vertical clearance bridges cross the Nanticoke River, one at Vienna, MD and the second at Sharptown, MD.

The town of Vienna is one of Maryland's oldest settlements. The British attacked it in both the Revolutionary War and the War of 1812, when it was a thriving commercial center. Preserved and restored homes line its streets.

A charted cable ferry crosses the Nanticoke at Woodland, DE, about 31 miles up the river. When the ferry is moving, the cable is tight and hangs just below the water. Do not attempt to pass a moving cable ferry. Wait until the cable drops completely before proceeding.

Dockage: For years, there were no marinas on the Nanticoke, but the Nanticoke River Marine Park, which has gas and diesel and a fantastic barbecue restaurant next door, is across the river from Seaford in Blades, DE. Infrequently traveled by recreational boats, the river also has several anchorage possibilities off the channel for shallow-draft boats and creeks for dinghy exploration.

WICOMICO RIVER, MD

One of many rivers with the same name on the Chesapeake Bay, this Wicomico River has a common mouth with the Nanticoke but heads off more easterly towards Salisbury, MD.

NAVIGATION: Use Chart 12261. **Use Hampton Roads tide tables. For high tide at Whitehaven (Wicomico River), add 5 hours 28 minutes; for low tide, add 5 hours 42 minutes.** Despite its narrow nature, the river provides 11-foot depths

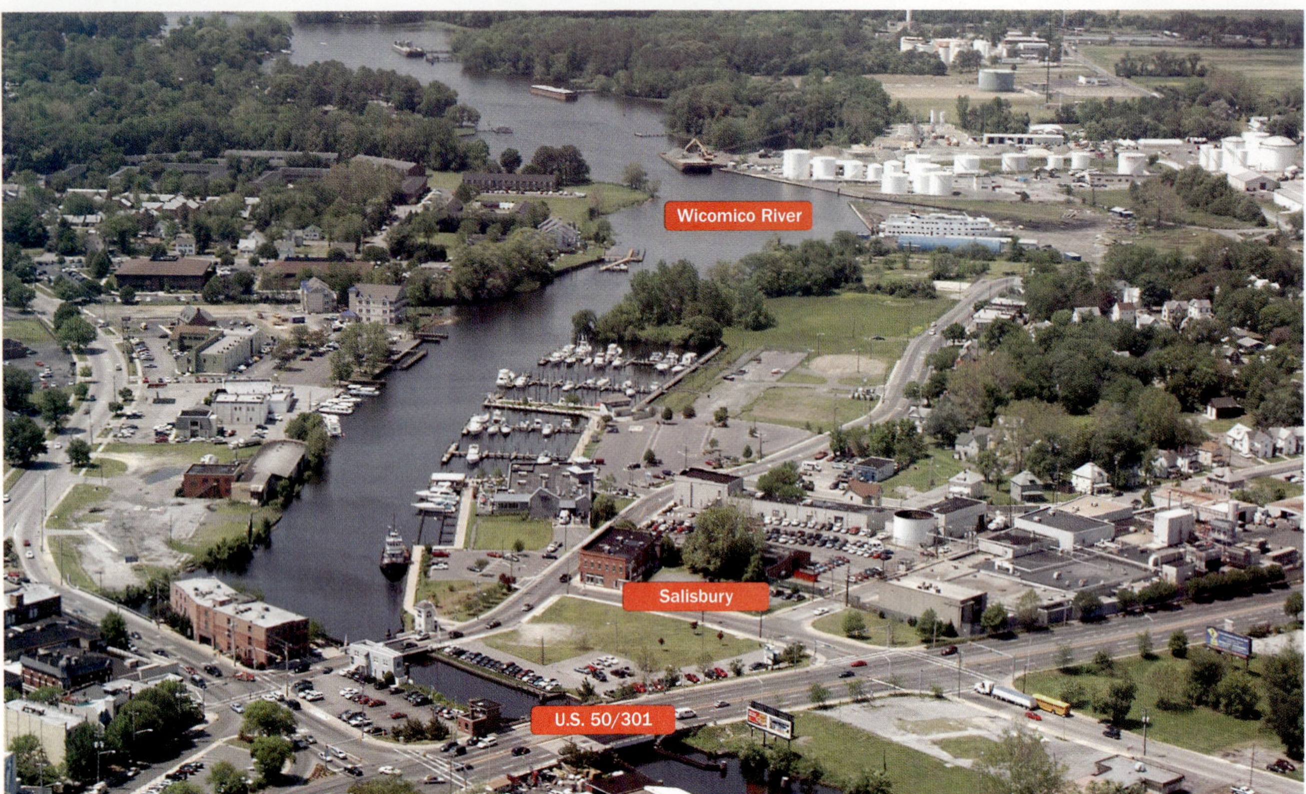

Looking southwest over Salisbury. (Not to be used for navigation.) Waterway Guide Photography.

for at least 20 miles to Salisbury, MD. Facilities for transients are at Webster Cove, about four miles above the mouth, on Wicomico Creek and at Upper Ferry.

Two charted cable ferries cross the Wicomico River, one at Whitehaven, MD and the other at Upper Ferry. Both operate only during daylight hours. The Whitehaven Ferry picks up the cable from the bottom when underway and slacks it off when stopped. The cable for the Upper Ferry hangs at or near the water's surface at all times during daylight hours. You must not cross the ferry's course without permission of the ferry operator. As you approach the ferries, signal the operator with one whistle blast (or call the ferry on VHF channel "13" or call on the posted cell phone number) to lower the cable before you pass. There are no bridges to contend with until you reach Salisbury.

Dockage: North of Whitehaven and south of Salisbury on the east side of the river is Wicomico Creek, which is the location of Wilkanders Marine Services, which has limited transient space. Port of Salisbury Marina, located in the heart of Salisbury, offers year-round transient dockage and gas and diesel fuel. Both facilities have pump-out service. Curiously, the tidal range is amplified by the long river and the range is over 3 feet in Salisbury.

QUICK FACT:
EMPEROR'S LANDING

In 2009 Vienna became a Chesapeake Bay Gateway Network site. The name of the Vienna Waterfront Park was changed to Emperor's Landing and was upgraded in a multi-year improvement program funded by the Maryland Department of Natural Resources. The town acquired the former industrial properties along the water; dilapidated structures were demolished and a new river walk, low profile stone revetment and marsh creation project were initiated. Extension of the river walk, floating docks, bulk heading and other substantial landscaping, including prototype signage for the John Smith Chesapeake National Historic Trail have been implemented in phases with funding help from NOAA, the Department of Natural Resources, and the Dorchester County Tourism Office. The renovation of the town-owned Coast Guard Station was completed in 2010. It now serves as a multi-purpose, visitor friendly facility. Construction of a nearby public picnic pavilion was completed in 2011. Other long-term development goals for the waterfront park include an expanded boardwalk with adjacent nature trails and additional walk ways and landscaping throughout the park.

GOIN' ASHORE: SALISBURY, MD

Salisbury is more urban than most Eastern Shore communities. It is, after all, the largest city on the Eastern Shore, serving as headquarters to poultry giant Perdue Farms and to Piedmont Airlines. As early as the 1800s, it was known as "The Hub of Delmarva." The Port of Salisbury Marina is within walking distance of downtown, but taxis can also get you into town. Once there, buses are another option for getting around. Salisbury University is located here.

History: Originally called Handy's Landing, Salisbury was founded in 1732 when the inhabitants petitioned the legislature to establish a town at the head of the Wicomico River.

The petition was granted, but the town struggled to establish itself. Forty-one years later, a group of residents again petitioned the assembly, this time asking that the original request be repealed and a new act passed "for the purpose of better promoting the advantages of the town." That request was denied. Eventually, Salisbury found its footing. The railroad came to town in 1860, and by 1888, several mills were operating in town. There were five churches, one opera house and no paved streets.

Points of Interest: Pemberton Hall (410-742-1741), a painstakingly restored 18th-century plantation house built by one of the city's founders, is located at Pemberton Historical Park, a 4.5-mile-long waterfront park. During an excavation at the park, a wharf made with 200-foot-long pine timbers in 1747 was uncovered and later reconstructed.

The Ward Museum of Wildfowl Art (909 S. Schumaker Dr., 410-742-4988), which boasts "the most comprehensive collection of wildfowl carving in the world," also features an extensive outdoor area. Stroll along the oyster shell walk bordering Schumaker Pond, where you are likely to spot bald eagles, red-tailed hawks and assorted waterfowl. The 13-acre Salisbury Zoo (755 S. Park Dr., 410-548-3188) is free but accepts donations.

Special Events: If you visit in April, you may want to pig out at the Pork in the Park BBQ Festival, which features food, arts and crafts, and blues at Winterplace Park. Also in early spring, the Salisbury Festival at Riverwalk Park offers carnival rides, jazz and food.

This being poultry country, there is an annual Delmarva Chicken Festival each June, with educational exhibits, games, a car show, mini grand prix, food and music. The Pemberton Colonial Fair takes place each September, with costumed re-enactors creating a Colonial market fair, featuring authentic food, craftsmen and dancing.

October brings the Wicomico County Autumn Wine Festival, held at Pemberton Historical Park.

Shopping: The Centre at Salisbury (2300 North Salisbury Blvd., 410-548-1694) is a large mall, but there are also boutiques and other shops, particularly antiques shops, at the pedestrian-friendly Downtown Plaza. The Country House, at 805 East Main Street, is the largest country store on the East Coast (410-749-1959). With 19 rooms, the offerings include gifts, furnishings and antique reproductions. Save-A-Lot grocery store at 220 Cypress Street (410-860-9399) is within walking distance of the marina.

Dining: Being an urban center, there are many chain restaurants in operation here, but the Local Owned Restaurant Association (LORA) prefers you eat with them. The association's website, www.lorarestaurants.com, offers information on alternatives; try the upscale Market Street Inn (130 W. Market St., 410-742-4145) and Escape Restaurant for breakfast, lunch and dinner (213 W. Main St., 443-859-8322).

ADDITIONAL RESOURCES

- CITY OF SALISBURY: www.ci.salisbury.md.us
- WICOMICO TOURISM: www.wicomicotourism.org

NEARBY MEDICAL FACILITIES
Peninsula Regional Medical Center: 100 E. Carroll St., Salisbury, MD 21801, 410-546-6400

NEARBY AIRPORT
Salisbury-Wicomico-Ocean City Airport:
5485 Airport Terminal Road, Salisbury, MD 21804, 410-548-4827, www.ifly.com/sby

TRANSPORTATION: Yellow Cab, 410-749-3500

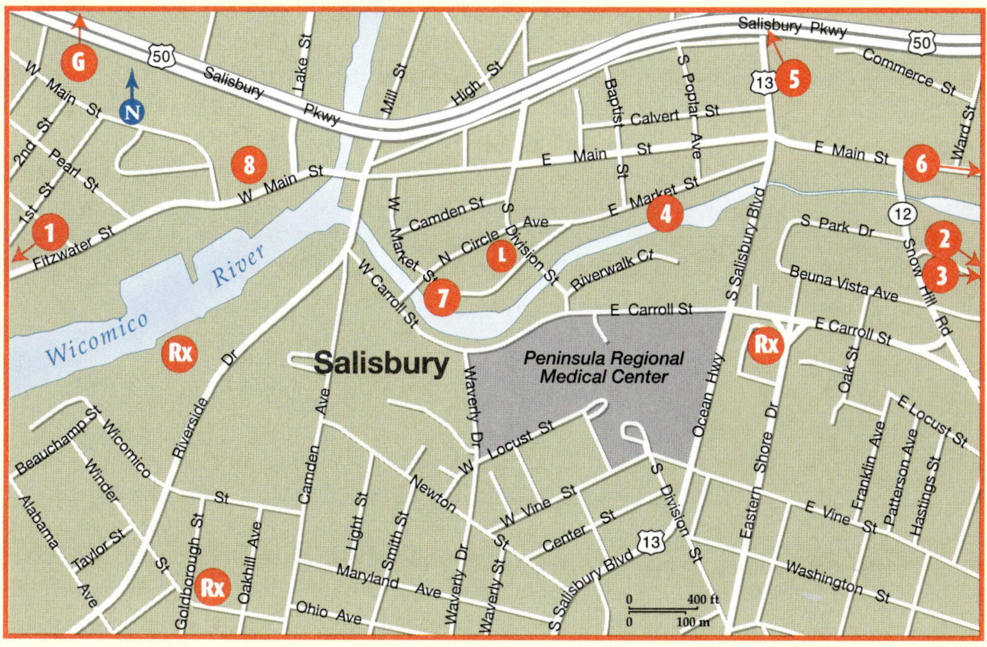

POINTS OF INTEREST
1 Pemberton Hall
2 The Ward Museum of Wildlife Art
3 Salisbury Zoo
4 Riverwalk Park

SHOPPING
5 The Centre at Salisbury
6 The Country House

DINING
7 Market Street Inn
8 Escape Restaurant

L LIBRARY
Rx PHARMACY
G GROCERIES

Reference the marina listing tables to see all the marinas in the area.

Little Annemessex R., Crisfield, MD

LITTLE ANNEMESSEX RIVER/CRISFIELD		Dockage					Supplies		Services					
		Largest Vessel Accommodated	VHF Channel Monitored	Transient Berths / Total Berths	Approach / Dockside Depth (reported)	Floating Docks	Gas / Diesel	Groceries, Ice, Marine Supplies, Snacks	Repairs: Hull, Engine, Propeller	Lift (tonnage), Crane, Rail	Min/Max Amps	Laundry, Pool, Showers, Courtesy Car	Pump-Out Station	Nearby: Grocery Store, Motel, Restaurant
1. Sea Mark Marine (Internet Access)	410-968-0800	60	-	2/29	5/5	-	-	M	HEP	L50	30/50	-	-	GMR
2. Somers Cove Marina (Wireless Internet Access)	410-968-0925	150	16/09	100/515	10/10	F	GD	IS	-	-	30/100	LPS	P	GMR

Corresponding chart(s) not to be used for navigation. Internet Access · Wireless Internet Access · Waterway Guide Cruising Club Partner

See www.WaterwayGuide.com for current rates, fuel prices, web site addresses, and other up-to-the-minute information.

DEAL ISLAND, MD

Even more than Smith and Tangier (described below), Deal Island is one of the last outposts of old-time Eastern Shore life. Although a bridge connects Deal to the mainland, the island receives less publicity than the other two and, subsequently, little tourist traffic. You can observe a few remaining working skipjacks here (the historic, sail-driven oyster boats that work the local waters), and the photographic possibilities are excellent. Labor Day weekend Deal Island hosts skipjack races. In the days leading up to the event, a number of these historic craft will make their way to the harbor. The Lion's Club hosts a festival as a fund raiser for their charitable programs. The highlight, of course, is the races themselves. For more information, visit www.webauthority.net/lions.htm.

This area has become a retreat for some talented artists and writers; you will have to inquire locally to find them, as they wouldn't be here if they craved attention.

Do not expect resort accommodations or extensive facilities of any kind. If you are interested in the working craft of the Chesapeake Bay watermen, Scott's Cove Marina services many of them, and it can be interesting to stroll through the boatyard. The closest place to provision or have a dinner out is Crisfield, MD, some 38 miles away by road, but only about 12 miles by boat. This is another example of the way Chesapeake towns developed—with their eyes toward the water—in the centuries before the advent of good roads.

NAVIGATION: Use Chart 12230. You reach the two settlements on Deal Island—Chance, at the northern end and Wenona, at the southern—through dredged channels from the northern end of Tangier Sound. The entrance channel to Chance shows more than 5 feet at low water. The western entrance to Wenona is charted at 3-foot depths at mean low water as of August 2009, with a mean tidal range of about 2 feet. Chance has only a few marine services at Scott's Cove Marina, and dockage at Wenona depends on the hospitality of the fishing fleet. Keep constant watch in the Tangier Sound channel near Chance, as crab pot buoys are everywhere.

QUICK FACT:

THE SKIPJACKS OF DEAL ISLAND

For the past 42 years, Deal Island has been host to a special sailboat race and festival each Labor Day weekend. The remaining working skipjacks (those that can manage to get repaired and repainted early enough before the oyster season, which begins November 1) gather here to determine who has the fastest boat or the best crew.

This little group of skipjacks is the last working sail fleet in America, relying entirely on wind power or their yawl boats—small launches with large automotive engines that can push them from astern. At work, they drag wire mesh bags called dredges across the bottom to scoop up the oysters as they move along.

State laws permit dredging with the aid of the yawl boat on a few days each week, a concession that helps these men make enough money to keep the vessels afloat. More than 10,000 people attend the event each year, which also features other types of sailboat races, regional foods and boat-docking contests.

The number of working skipjacks is dwindling as fast as the Bay's oyster population. Those who love the Bay and its heritage should try to support this and similar events before all the traditional skipjacks are gone. Many of these vessels supplement their oyster earnings by taking out paying passengers from popular tourist locations like Annapolis and Baltimore during the summer, and by taking charters for the races. For information about the races at Deal Island, call the Somerset County Tourism Office, 800-521-9189.

CRISFIELD, MD, LITTLE ANNEMESSEX RIVER

Crisfield, made famous by William Warner's Pulitzer Prize-winning book "Beautiful Swimmers," is home to one of the world's largest blue-crab fisheries. Over the years, spurred by the construction of a large state-owned marina, it became a destination for cruisers and, more recently, was the focus of real estate developers, as they bought up old seafood factories and retail storefronts and built condominiums.

NAVIGATION: Use Chart 12231. Use Hampton Roads tide tables. For high tide at Crisfield (Little Annemessex

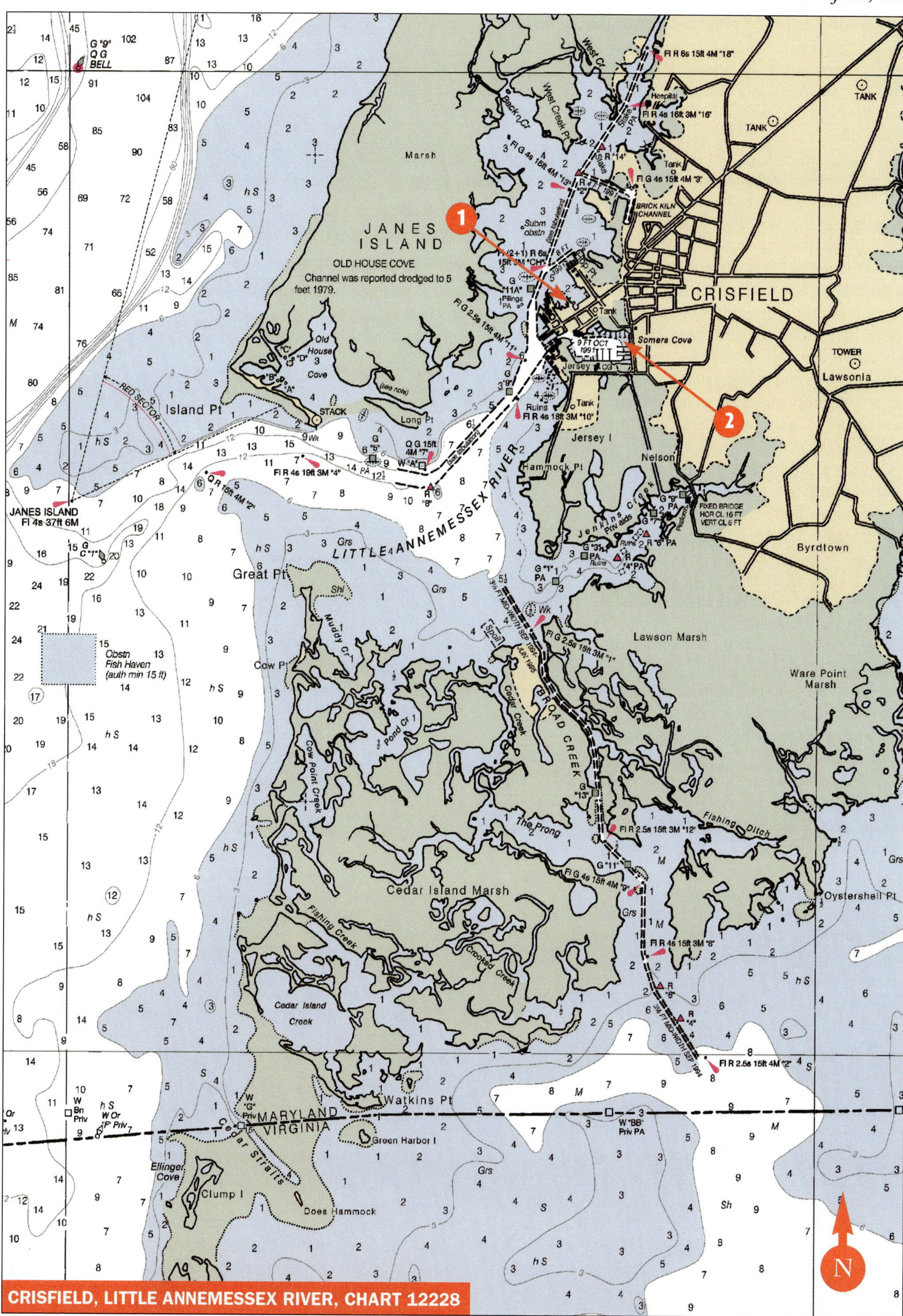

CRISFIELD, LITTLE ANNEMESSEX RIVER, CHART 12228

River), add 3 hours 51 minutes; for low tide, add 4 hours. The entrance to Crisfield via the Little Annemessex River begins at green can "1," southeast of Janes Island Light (37 feet high, flashing white every four seconds). If approaching from the north, do not cut flashing red buoy "8" or the Janes Island marker short, as there are 2- to 4-foot depths to the east. Once you have picked up green can buoy "1," follow the well-marked channel east to just past flashing green "11." At this point, make a slight turn to starboard and proceed into the unmarked channel toward the yacht basin, keeping the town dock to port. After another slight turn to starboard, you will enter the large harbor.

Dockage: The enclosed harbor at Crisfield once held 10-foot depths throughout and had ample space for anchoring. Today, the state-owned Somers Cove Marina on the north, east and south sides practically fills the harbor with its docks and pilings; a Coast Guard station adjoins it. There are plenty of transient slips available. The marina has gas and diesel fuel, a swimming pool and bicycles. Crisfield has several boat repair facilities, including Sea Mark Marine, which has a 50-ton lift.

Anchoring: Some anchoring space remains off the Coast Guard station on the south side of the cove, next to a busy boat-launching ramp.

Reference the marina listing tables to see all the marinas in the area.

GOIN' ASHORE: **CRISFIELD, MD**

Crisfield has long called itself "The Seafood Capital of the World," and there is still enough of the seafood industry at work to sneak a glimpse at a world that may be slipping away. As Tim Howard of the Crisfield Heritage Foundation put it, "Our maritime history is still here. There's the chance to see an old American lifestyle. It's not a re-creation."

The city is in transition. Land on the waterfront is relatively inexpensive, and the prices are considered a bargain. Over the last few years, 450 waterfront condominiums have been approved and are often purchased by weekend boaters. It seems the sands are shifting toward tourism, but there is no full-fledged tourist industry yet. The few shops and restaurants that cropped up are all clustered in the compact downtown, which retains some of the charm of yesteryear.

History: Not surprisingly, Crisfield is named for a man who envisioned the vast opportunities afforded by then-recently discovered oyster beds in nearby Tangier Sound. Before being renamed for John Crisfield, the town was known as Somers Cove, a name bestowed by boat captains who took cover in the cove during bad weather. After a survey identified oyster beds in the adjacent sound in 1854, John W. Crisfield extended the railroad down from Salisbury, allowing Chesapeake Bay goods to be sold throughout the northeast. Crisfield became the country's leading producer of oysters. With plentiful blue crabs and terrapins as well, it became known as the "Seafood Capital of the World." By 1904, it was the second largest city in Maryland, behind Baltimore.

Crisfield figures prominently in "Jacob Have I Loved," a Newbery Medal-winning novel for young adults. Well-known native sons include Harry Clifton (Curley) Byrd, the University of Maryland president known as "Father of the University of Maryland" and John Millard Tawes, Maryland governor from 1959 to 1967. The University of Maryland mascot, the Terrapin, was named by Curley Byrd after the Crisfield terrapin (a type of turtle) industry of the late 1800s and early 1900s.

Points of Interest: For an overview of the city's history, Stop by the Visitors Center/Heritage Foundation on West Main and then head over to the J. Millard Tawes Historical Museum (410-968-2501), which has a collection of model boats, depictions of seafood harvesting and processing and displays on Lem and Steve Ward, masters of decoy carving and

INFORMATION

1 Visitors Center/ Heritage Foundation

POINTS OF INTEREST

2 J. Millard Tawes Historical Museum
3 Ward Brothers Workshop
4 Governor Tawes Library
5 Chrisfield Heritage Foundation
6 Cedar Island Marsh Sanctuary
7 Janes Island State Park
8 Smith/Tangier Island Cruise Office

SHOPPING

2 J. Millard Tawes Historical Museum
9 The Sweet Shop
10 Debbi's Chocolate and Gift Shop
11 Goldsborough Marine
12 Gunter Hardware
13 Riggin's Grocery
14 The Crab Place

DINING

15 Gordon's Confectionery
16 The Watermen's Inn
17 Captain Tyler's Crab House
18 Circle Inn
19 Maho's Kitchen
20 Olde Crisfield Crab and Steak House
21 Blue Crab Garden Cafe
22 Linton's Crab House

L LIBRARY

PO POST OFFICE

Rx PHARMACY

Looking southwest over Crisfield. (Not to be used for navigation.) Waterway Guide Photography.

painting. The museum is located on the west side of Somers Cove Marina. More on the Ward brothers can be learned, by appointment, at the restored Ward Brothers Workshop, a series of three buildings where they carved and painted their prized decoys. From Memorial Day through Labor Day, a Port of Crisfield walking tour departs at 10:00 a.m. Mondays through Thursdays from the Tawes Historical Museum. It costs a few dollars and lasts about an hour. Depending on the season, the tour includes stops at at least one, and possibly all of the following: a soft shell crab processing plant, a hard-shell crab plant and an oyster processing facility.

Nearby is the Governor Tawes Library, located in the 1887 Victorian home where he was born at 25 Asbury Ave. Tawes, the state's 54th governor, banned discrimination in public accommodations and in state employment. All three museums are run by the Crisfield Heritage Foundation at 3 Ninth St. (410-968-2501).

If the outdoors beckon, there are several choices. Across the street from the Somers Cove Marina, the 330-acre Cedar Island Marsh Sanctuary is home to terrapins, hawks and waterfowl. Look out across Jenkins Creek, and you can see crab shanties and watermen toiling away. About three miles away is Janes Island State Park, which has a boat launch, canoe and kayak rental, and campsites. Most waterways here are protected, making them perfect spots for peaceful canoeing or kayaking. Also, the ferries for Smith and Tangier islands leave from Somers Cove. If you want to golf, call Great Hope Golf Course in nearby Westover (8380 Crisfield Hwy.) at 800-537-8009.

Special Events: Each May, Crisfield ushers in warmer climes with the Soft Shell Spring Fair at the City Dock. In June, grab a fishing pole for the annual Scorchy Tawes Pro-Am Fishing Tournament, with cash prizes in four categories and nightly entertainment. Fourth of July brings fireworks, while mid-July features the J. Millard Tawes Crab and Clam Bake, an all-you-can eat affair. The other end of summer (Labor Day Weekend) is bracketed with the annual (60-plus years) Hard Crab Derby and Fair at Somers Cove Marina. Highlights include crab-cooking and -picking contests, the famous crab race, workboat-docking contests, games, a carnival and more. More events information is available at www.crisfieldheritagefoundation.org.

Shopping: Authentic 10-layer Smith Island cakes, and that other kind of cake—crab cakes—are sold at The Sweet Shop at 341 W. Main St. (410-968-2200). Other shops include Debbi's Chocolate and Gift Shop (645 South Division St., 410-742-1571), and the gift shop at the Tawes Museum. For Marine supplies, Goldsborough Marine at 709 West Main St. (410-968-0852) specializes in outboards, and Gunter Hardware at 1000 West Main St. (410-968-0220). For reprovisioning, there is one grocery store nearby: Riggins Grocery (45 West Chesapeake Ave., 410-968-0484), but the Crab Place at 504 Maryland Ave. sells everything seafood and ships too! Call 877-328-2722 or visit www.crabplace.com.

Dining: Ever had a Scrapple sandwich? How about a chocolate zip? You can find them at Gordon's Confectionery. Located at 831 W. Main St., Gordon's (410-968-0566) opens around 4:00 a.m., in time to serve breakfast to the watermen. It is open until 8:00 p.m., serving up sandwiches, milkshakes, soda from a soda fountain and an authentic slice of old Crisfield. (Scrapple, by the way, is cornmeal mixed with something akin to sausage, while a chocolate zip is

Looking north over Smith Island and the towns of Tylerton, Rhodes Point and Ewell. (Not to be used for navigation.) Waterway Guide Photography.

milk, chocolate syrup and ice.) Other restaurants include The Watermen's Inn (901 W. Main Street, 410-968-2119), Circle Inn (4012 Crisfield Highway, 410-968-1969), Maho's Kitchen (712 Broadway, 410-968-2835), Olde Crisfield Crab and Steak House (204 S. 10th St., 410-968-2722), Blue Crab Garden Café (801 W. Main Street, 410-968-0444), Lintons Crab House/Deck (4500 Crisfield Highway, 410-968-0127 or 877-546-8667) and Captain Tyler's Crab House (410-968-1131) on the water at Somer's Cove .

ADDITIONAL RESOURCES

NEARBY MEDICAL FACILITIES

Edward McCready Memorial Hospital:
201 Hall Highway, Crisfield, MD 21817
410-968-1801

Janes Island, off the Little Annemessex River

Across the Little Annemessex River from Crisfield, Janes Island State Park (410-968-1565) makes a pleasant side trip. The Daugherty Creek Canal runs through the state park, which offers boat ramps, picnic areas, swimming and fishing.

NAVIGATION: Use Chart 12231. Boats with up to a 6.5-foot draft may be able to make the trip, but inquire locally first as the northern end of Canal is reported to have shoaled. At the southern end of the Daugherty Creek Canal, as you approach Crisfield, do as local watermen do, and use the brick chimney on the southern shore at Old House Cove—all that remains of an old fish factory—as a landmark to that anchorage on the south end of Jane's Island. You will have to look sharp, however, to see the channel entrance near Crisfield. The Daugherty Creek Canal goes northward from Crisfield to a branch channel at Flatcap Cove. Both Old House Cove and Flatcap Cove have protected anchorages for small boats, and Flatcap Cove has a T-pier with access to the white sand beaches on the Chesapeake Bay side of the island.

SMITH AND TANGIER ISLANDS

These two islands have grown in fame over the years, thanks to the countless newspaper and television features on their unique, isolated, blue-crab-driven cultures. Either island is worth a stopover if you are headed north or south on the Bay. Both offer grocery stores and friendly locals, not to mention amazing histories; the brogue spoken here is most distinctive.

Please note that both islands have trash disposal challenges. If possible, hold your trash for disposal on the mainland. Dockage is generally reserved for local fishing boats, but each island has marina slips for transient boaters. Be sure to call ahead if staying on the island is a deal-breaker when deciding whether to make the trip or not.

Smith Island, MD

NAVIGATION: Use Charts 12228 and 12231 for Smith Island. **Use Hampton Roads tide tables. For high tide at Smith Island, add 4 hours; for low tide, add 4 hours 26 minutes.**

It is best to approach Smith Island from the western (or Bay) side, where a well-buoyed channel carries 6-foot depths at mean low water to the harbor at Ewell, although the charted depths are less. This entrance was dredged in 2010. On the starboard side, after you pass flashing green "15," you will see a basin filled with fishing boats.

Dockage: Smith Island Marina has 6 slips with 30- and 50-amp electric, but you have to get water from a hose at the house. Watch out for the current as you maneuver. The Exxon fuel dock is just past the marina. Rukes General Store allows tie-ups after the tour boats depart at 2:00 p.m. Do not tie up at the Ewell fuel dock south of the main channel in the late afternoon (3:00 p.m. to 5:00 p.m.), as this is the time the local crabbing fleet usually fuels up for the next morning's work.

Farther on, you may find tie-up space at the dock in front of the Harbor Side Groceries & Deli, where the channel turns sharply to port and enters Big Thorofare. This is the route from the Bay to Tangier Sound; it is long and tortuous, with widely spaced markers and some spots considerably shallower than the reported 7-foot depths, although freight, passenger and mail boats from Crisfield make the run through it daily. Another marked channel branches off from Big Thorofare and leads to Rhodes Point, the second of Smith Island's three villages. A road connects Ewell and Rhodes Point, but only boats can reach Tylerton, the third village. Several marks were relocated in Big Thorofare in 2012. Keep a sharp watch while transiting the area, as only print-on-demand charts or electronic charts downloaded from the NOAA website will reflect these changes. Tylerton has space for transients at the town dock (no electric service). The channel is narrow but the ferries make it, so you can too, if you have nerves of steel. It is a lovely village and well worth a visit by dinghy.

GOIN' ASHORE:
SMITH ISLAND, MD

Maryland's last inhabited island supports three towns: Ewell, Rhodes Point and Tylerton, which is actually separated from the rest of the island by water. Like neighboring Tangier Island, a strong Methodism influences local life, and the island is dry (no alcohol). It also has no ATM. Local kids take the boat to Crisfield for school, and island businesses tend to open and close according to the ferry schedule.

History: Although visited by Capt. John Smith during his famous 1608 exploration of Chesapeake Bay, Smith Island is not his namesake. Rather, it takes its name from an early landowner, Henry Smith, according to a history on the island's Chesapeake Sunrise Inn website. The early settlers arrived in 1686 and apparently were the same English and Welsh whose dialect has been passed on to their descendants. Smith Island's distinctive accent is said to have been passed down from the Elizabethan era (i.e., "oysters" sounds like "arsters;" "room" is "reum;" and "house" comes out as "hayose").

A strict Methodism was introduced here about 1807, influenced by Joshua Thomas, "The Parson of the Islands," who held a camp meeting here. Historically, the locals fished and farmed. In the 1860s, they started taking oysters to Baltimore, home to 58 raw oyster packing houses and several steamed oyster canneries, according to "Maryland: A New Guide to the Old Line State," by Edward C. Papenfuse and others. As the 20th century progressed, crabbing became the economic mainstay. Now, the focus is preserving that way of life.

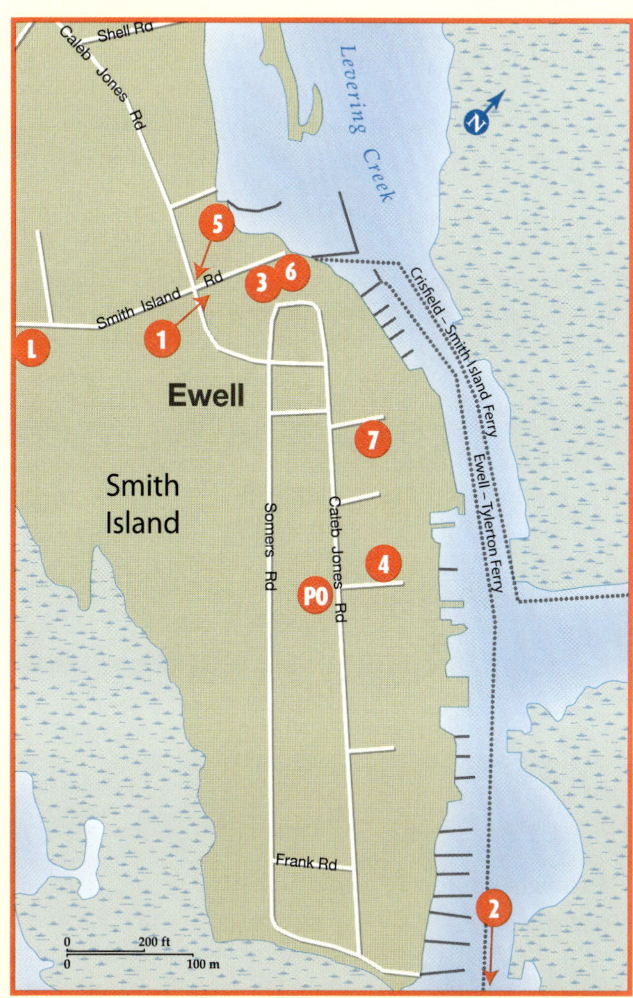

Reference the marina listing tables to see all the marinas in the area.

POINTS OF INTEREST
1. The Smith Island Center
2. Chesapeake Fishing Adventures

SHOPPING
3. Bayside Gifts
4. Smith Island Baking Co.

DINING
5. Rukes General Store and Seafood Deck
6. Bayside Inn
7. Harbor Side Groceries & Deli

L LIBRARY

PO POST OFFICE

Smith Island, MD Tangier Island, VA

SMITH ISLAND/TANGIER ISLAND		Largest Vessel Accommodated	VHF Channel Monitored	Transient Berths / Total Berths	Approach / Dockside Depth (reported)	Floating Docks	Gas / Diesel	Groceries, Ice, Marine Supplies, Snacks	Repairs: Hull, Engine, Propeller	Lift (tonnage), Crane, Rail	Min/Max Amps	Laundry, Pool, Showers, Courtesy Car	Pump-Out Station	Nearby: Grocery Store, Motel, Restaurant
		Dockage					Supplies		Services					
1. Smith Island Marina (Internet Access)	410-425-4220	60	78	6/6	4/7	-	-	-	-	-	30/50	LPS	P	GMR
2. Exxon Fuel Dock	410-425-2341	65	79	-	6/6	-	GD	GIMS	-	-	-	-	-	GMR
3. Parks Marina	757-891-2567	100	72	20/25	6/10	-	-	-	-	-	30/50	S	-	G

Corresponding chart(s) not to be used for navigation. Internet Access Wireless Internet Access Waterway Guide Cruising Club Partner

See www.WaterwayGuide.com for current rates, fuel prices, web site addresses, and other up-to-the-minute information.

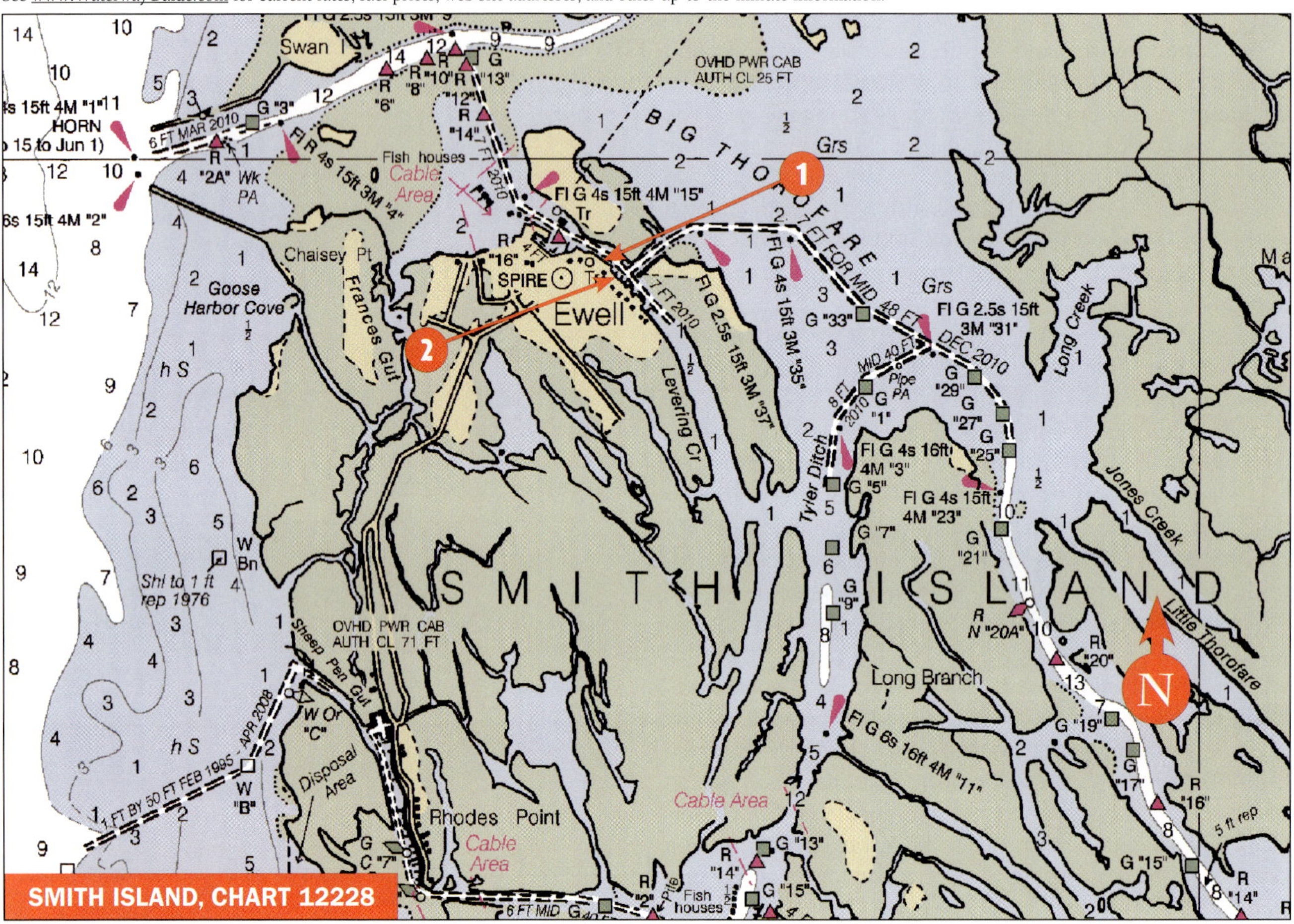

Points of Interest: The Smith Island Center greets visitors arriving ashore at Ewell, and it doubles as a museum and a visitors center. A 17-foot scale model of a scrape boat, used to harvest soft crabs, is on display. This is probably the place to find out where to rent a bicycle (open seasonally, 410-425-3351). Chesapeake Fishing Adventures guides anglers to some of the Bay's best fishing, where striped bass, flounder, bluefish and croaker await.

There are several water trails here; check www.visitsomerset.com for outfitters who may be able to arrange for a kayak or canoe.

Special Events: Smith Island Day in May celebrates the island life. Skiff-docking skills are demonstrated, as well as other water-related activities take place. For information, call 410-425-3351.

Shopping: The Smith Island Center has a gift shop, and there is one next door at Bayside Gifts. No visit to Smith Island is complete without sampling one of their famous 10-layer Smith Island cakes. The Smith Island Baking Company (410-425-CAKE) is home to these famous confectionaries, named by National Geographic as "One of America's Top Five Desserts." The recipe originated in the 1800s when the wives would send cakes out with their waterman husbands during oyster season. The multi-layered cakes with fudge frosting stayed fresher longer than traditional cakes, making them exceptional gifts. The bakery is located on Caleb Jones Road.

Dining: Barn-red Rukes Seafood Deck, a must for seafood and getting a feel for the locals who come and go, is located in Ewell (410-425-2311). Also, try Bayside Inn in Ewell (410-425-2771) or the Harborside Groceries and Deli on

Looking east across the passage through Tangier and Tangier Island. (Not to be used for navigation.) Waterway Guide Photography.

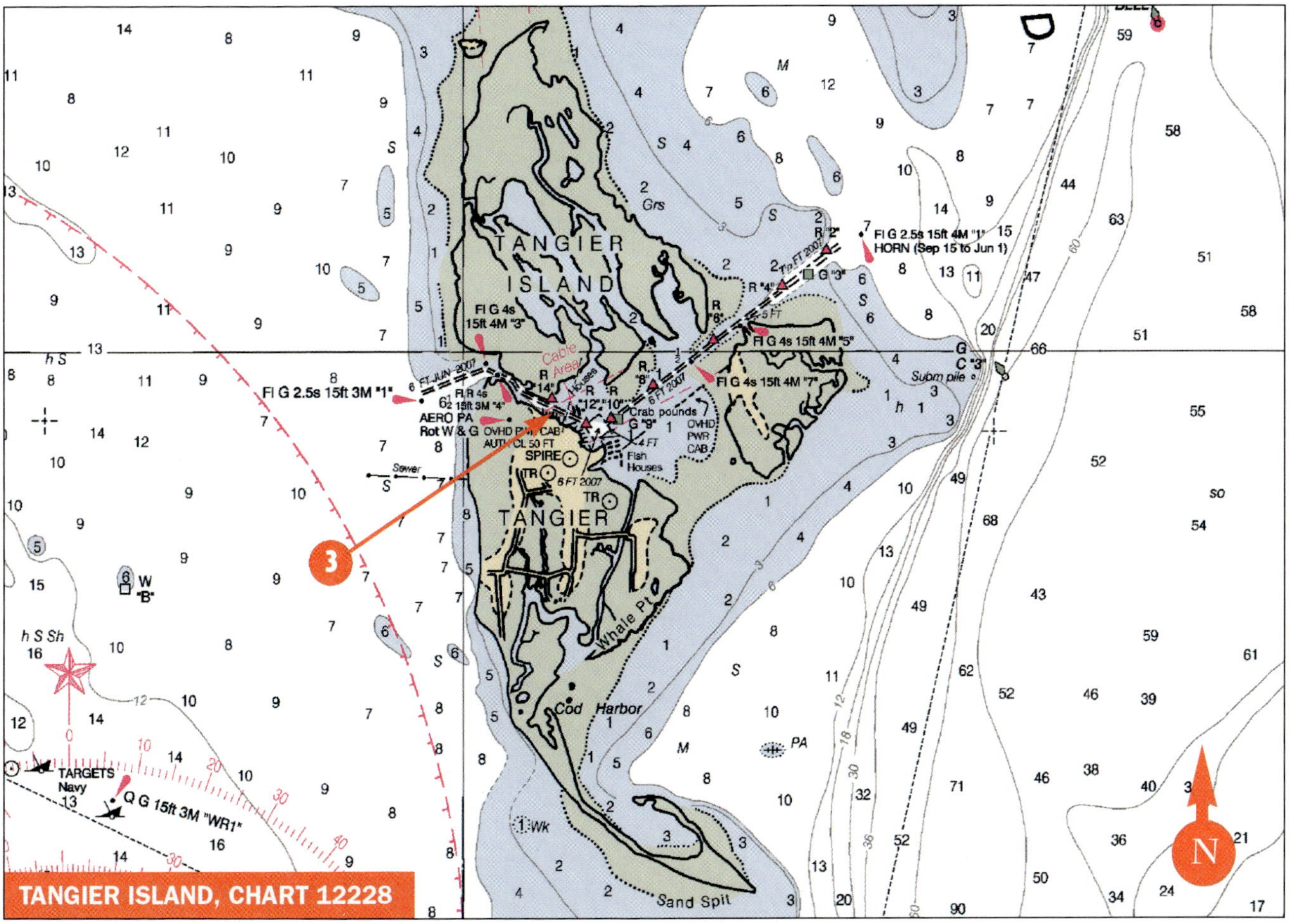

TANGIER ISLAND, CHART 12228

Whitelock Road (410-425-2525). Over in Tylerton, stop at the Drum Point Market (410-425-2108) for truly exceptional crab cakes. Don't just take our word on the crab cakes. This is where Tangier watermen go for a crab cake; you will find none better anywhere.

ADDITIONAL RESOURCES

■ SMITH ISLAND: www.smithisland.org

NEARBY MEDICAL FACILITIES
There are no physicians on the island.
Call 911 in case of emergency.

Tangier Island, VA

Lying just below the Virginia-Maryland State line, the main approach to Tangier Island is from the Bay (west) side, although the east channel from Tangier Sound is deeper (dredged spring of 2012), straighter, better marked and somewhat more reliable than the east channel at Smith Island. The channel from the Bay carries 6 foot depths at mean low water, while depths from Tangier Sound run about 7 feet. Tidal range is approximately 1.5 feet.

NAVIGATION: Use Charts 12225 and 12228 for Tangier Island. Most boaters will approach Tangier from the west. While local charts show a myriad of wrecks along the bay most of which are long gone, there are three that are significant hazards. Boaters approaching from the southwest have several particularly important marks to regard. These mark the remains of Navy targets sunk in 1921. The wrecks with exposed steel at low water, lie just below the water at high tide. All three wrecks shown on the western approach to Tangier Island deserve respect. They cannot be seen most of the time but they are there to capture the unwary.

Dockage: Parks Marina on Tangier Island on the main channel has 25 slips for visiting boats; inquire at the marina dock.

Anchorage: We advise you not to anchor in the basin at the center of the thoroughfare.

GOIN' ASHORE: TANGIER ISLAND, VA

Nosing through the channel leading to Tangier Island is a rare experience. There is no other way to put it. Contrasted against blue sky are small white crab shanties ,each with their own dock, lining the way on both sides like a welcoming committee for those arriving on Virginia's working waterman's island. As you proceed through the thoroughfare you will see a whole village of crab shanties standing on pilings out in the water. These are the peeler sheds where soft crabs are held until they molt, at which time they are packaged, refrigerated and taken to the mainland for distribution far and wide.

Pruitts, Parkses and Crocketts live on this one- by-three-mile island, with one school for all the kids, a doctor who visits (but everyone knows to call the physician's assistant at home if need be) and a fabled, lingering style of speech thought to be directly descended from early Elizabethan-era settlers. Folks drive golf carts, known around here as "golf buggies." Crab buggies are available to rent from Four Brothers Crab House in the heart of town. When dads head for work in the morning, they go down to their docks and their white sheds on the water, fire up their boats, and then head out for a day of crabbing.

Since everybody here knows one another, visitors are in the nice position of just asking anyone if there is something they need to find out.

History: Capt. John Smith stopped here during his landmark 1608 exploration of Chesapeake Bay, and John Crockett first settled the island in 1686. Note that his last name remains ubiquitous here, although answers a question that crosses many minds: A total of 53 last names dwell here among the 727 residents (according to the 2010 census).

Fabled Chesapeake preacher Joshua Thomas, a Tangier resident, preached to the British troops who occupied the island during the War of 1812 (telling them an attack on Fort McHenry would fail). Ft. McHenry is where Marylander Francis Scott Key wrote "The Star Spangled Banner." Methodism took root here in early in the 19th century and remains a strong influence.

Farming was the community's early work, but fishing, oystering and crabbing took on greater prominence during the 19th century. Land subsidence and erosion have eliminated all arable land. Early In the 20th century a shirt factory was built on the island. This offered financial income and a measure of independence for local women. It mysteriously burned to the ground, and all that remains is one section of the foundation. Today, the effort is underway to preserve the unique way of life found here. For example, some years ago, the locals famously rejected Paul Newman's "Message in a Bottle" (based on the Nicolas Sparks book of the same name) for its script, considered too racy for this conservative island's population. Apparently Newman traveled incognito to check out the place that said no to Hollywood. However, that way of life is in fact changing as the federal and state governments pump in millions of dollars for a new airport (there's an existing airstrip on the island), medical center, school, tourism promotions, and financial support to working watermen and their families.

Point of Interest: A "must-do" is to hop aboard one of the tour buggies driven by local women who will take you on an entertaining ramble around the island to point out the sights—such as the local gift shops and the Methodist Church. The buggies line up near the dock when the large tour boats pull in. Chesapeake House may be able to arrange a Waterman's Tour with a Tangier captain to see the island's soft shell crab farms. Call 757-891-2331 for more information.

The Tangier History Museum and Interpretive Cultural Center is located at 16215 Main Ridge. Learn about the island's history, local culture, watermen, the shrinking island and the impact of transportation on the island.

Free kayaks and canoes are available to folks who want to explore the island's water trails, bikes can be rented, and a spectacular 1.5-mile long white sand beach extends from the southern end of the island. Local birds include oyster catchers, pelicans, great blue herons, black skimmers and glossy ibis.

Shopping: The island's gift shops include Wanda's, Jim's Gift Shop, Sandy's Place and the The Crab Shack. You will have no trouble finding them.

Dining: Lorraine's Seafood & Sandwich Shop (757-891-2225) is open "late" and is the only year-round eatery. Other restaurants include the well-known Hilda Crockett's Chesapeake House (757-891-2331), launched in 1939 and serving home-cooked meals served family style (all you can eat) and includes crab cakes and clam fritters and butter pound cake. Last seating is at 5:00 p.m. Fisherman's Corner (757-891-2900) serves terrific seafood, as does The Waterfront Restaurant located at the ferry dock (757-891-2248). Despite its reputation as a crab capital, steamed crabs are not available in any of the local restaurants. There just is not enough tourist demand for them. Four Brothers Crab House opened in 2011 to serve 60 flavors of soft serve ice cream and crab pizza, as well as soft serve ice cream. Spanky's Ice Cream Parlor is also in town; be aware that Spanky goes to supper at 5:00 p.m. but reopens later.

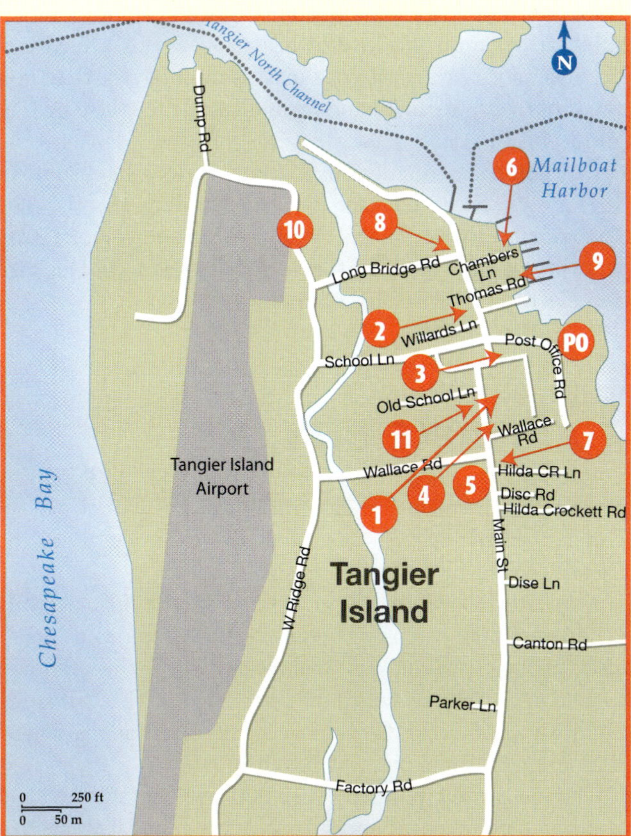

Reference the marina listing tables to see all the marinas in the area.

POINTS OF INTEREST
1 Tangier History Museum & Interpretive Cultural Center

SHOPPING
2 Wanda's
3 Jim's Gift Shop
4 Sandy's Place
5 The Crab Shack

DINING
6 Lorraine's Seafood & Sandwich Shop
7 Hilda Crockett's
8 Fisherman's Corner
9 Waterfront Restaurant
10 Four Brothers Crab House
11 Spanky's Ice Cream Parlor

PO POST OFFICE

ADDITIONAL RESOURCES

- TANGIER ISLAND, VA: www.tangierisland-va.com
- GO TANGIER ISLAND: www.tangierhistorymuseum.com

NEARBY MEDICAL FACILITIES
Tangier Community Health Center, 757-891-2412

NEARBY AIRPORT
Tangier Island Airport: 757-891-2496. During winter call the town office at 757-891-2438.

Watts Island

Only a few goats now inhabit Watts Island, four miles southeast of Tangier Island. Once an inhabited island with homes, farms and stores, the island is now used by the Chesapeake Bay Foundation as part of their ongoing educational programs for school children. Watts once served as a haven for British loyalists, and according to local legend, Tangiermen drove them out during the American Revolution. No one has lived on Watts Island for many years, and its ancient graveyard is falling into the water, stone by stone, as waves erode the shoreline. Other Eastern Shore islands are, unfortunately, suffering the same fate.

POCOMOKE RIVER, MD

Broad, relatively shallow Pocomoke Sound lies to the east, across Tangier Sound from Smith and Tangier islands. The entrance to the Pocomoke River is at the eastern end of the Sound, right on the Maryland/Virginia state line. Coming from Crisfield and the Little Annemessex River, you can take a shortcut south to Pocomoke Sound (if you draw 4 feet or less—preferably 3.5 feet) through Broad Creek, but pay close attention to the markers. The long way around adds some 26 nautical miles, as you will have to travel far south below Watts Island to reach the Pocomoke entrance channel, but a cruise through the wilderness of the Pocomoke is well worth the extra time. The Pocomoke River begins as a corkscrew river through extensive marshes. It has deep water and winds its way inland. The marshes offer a variety of colors with many shades of green and brightly colored flowering trees and bushes. Upstream, the marshes give way to cypress trees and soon you are wending your way through a cypress swamp. There is not a sound to be heard except the rumble of your engine. There is no sign of civilization for miles. You are seeing the river perhaps as Captain John Smith saw it 400 years ago.

Looking north over Pocomoke City, MD. (Not to be used for navigation.) Waterway Guide Photography.

Early colonists used the Pocomoke River as a commercial artery, and the impassable swamps have been havens for smugglers, bootleggers, runaway slaves and Civil War deserters. Today, the river provides a peaceful, scenic cruise. The river above Snow Hill is prime kayaking country, and outfitters in the town can rent you the necessary boats and gear.

NAVIGATION: Use Charts 12228 and 12230. **Use Hampton Roads tide tables. For high tide at Pocomoke City (Pocomoke River), add 5 hours 50 minutes; for low tide, add 6 hours 10 minutes.** The Pocomoke is a long, winding and deep river that cuts almost all the way across the Delaware/Maryland/Virginia (Delmarva) Peninsula. Navigable 26 miles upstream to Snow Hill, MD, it winds serenely through forests and cypress swamps. Making the approach from Pocomoke Sound calls for careful navigation going in the marked channel that cuts through The Muds, an area of shallow flats near the mouth of the river. The name tells you all you need to know. Heed the makeshift sticks placed by the commercial barges that regularly travel to the plywood mill at Pocomoke City, MD. If you are lucky, you can follow one of these barges through the passage. The channel shoals continuously, especially along the southern side. The current Coast Pilot lists 4.5 feet as the controlling depth, with a mean tidal range of 2.4 feet, but the most recent chart of the area (NOAA 12228 from October 2011) reports that the channel carries depths of at least 8 feet. Several markers have been moved or relocated. Only print-on-demand charts or NOAA electronic raster charts show these slight moves; keep an eye out for the new locations.

Navigation is easier once you get through the cut, and you can count on at least 7-foot depths to Pocomoke City and 5-foot depths to Snow Hill, with much more most of the time. It should be noted, however, that charts show an area with 5-foot depths inside the first horseshoe bend in the river just past Shelltown. The Pocomoke River is unmarked between the entrance and Shad Landing because it is deep to its banks; the markers resume at Shad Landing (about seven nautical miles above Pocomoke City). See the NOAA chart inset for the 10-mile stretch of river between Pocomoke City and Snow Hill. Along the upper river, saltwater gives way to freshwater, and the shoreline vegetation reflects this. The first bridge you will encounter as you approach Pocomoke City is a railroad swing bridge (narrow center span), with a 4-foot closed vertical clearance, that is normally left in the open position unless rail traffic is passing. Note the 57-foot-high power cable just below the railroad bridge. Next, a bascule bridge with a 3-foot closed vertical clearance crosses the river at the city park. The drawbridge operates on signal from 6:00 a.m. to 10:00 p.m. and is closed at all other times. A bit farther up from the drawbridge is a 35-foot fixed vertical clearance bridge. If your mast is too high for that, you can dinghy up to Shad Landing and catch the cruise boat to Snow Hill.

Dockage: Pocomoke River State Park (established in 1975) now offers dockage at Shad Landing Marina. The Pocomoke City Municipal Marina at the Pocomoke City Drawbridge has room for transient guests as well. Dockage and electricity are free for 48 hours.

GOIN' ASHORE:
POCOMOKE CITY, MD

Located on the Pocomoke River, this city bills itself as "The Friendliest Town on the Eastern Shore" but it is the deep, scenic river that beckons to visitors. Once they get there, the friendly, small-town feel is an extra.

Most attractions are within a block of the boat docking facilities and the extensive Cypress Park. A Nature and Exercise Trail begins at the park, and meanders into the swamp to a pond and back around to the river. The trail has a floating boardwalk, canoe/kayak launch, exercise stations, a pedestrian bridge, fishing pier and benches.

The town is surrounded by 12,000 acres of forest, which, along with swamps and marshland, offers abundant opportunities for bird watching.

History: After several name changes, Pocomoke City was incorporated under that name in 1878. Thanks to timber and shipbuilding industries along the Pocomoke River, the town became one of the largest in the area. Though it has just over 4,000 residents, it is still one of the larger Lower Eastern Shore communities today.

Many of the city's oldest buildings were lost in two fires, one in 1888 and one in 1922, but some historic homes and a one-room schoolhouse remain.

Pocomoke River, MD

POCOMOKE RIVER		Largest Vessel Accommodated	VHF Channel Monitored	Transient Berths / Total Berths	Approach / Dockside Depth (reported)	Floating Docks	Gas / Diesel	Groceries, Ice, Marine Supplies, Snacks	Repairs: Hull, Engine, Propeller	Lift (tonnage), Crane, Rail	Min/Max Amps	Laundry, Pool, Showers, Courtesy Car	Pump-Out Station	Nearby: Grocery Store, Motel, Restaurant
		Dockage					Supplies		Services					
1. Pocomoke City Municipal Marina	410-957-1333	75	–	35/50	7/10	–	–	GIS	E	–	30/30	LS	P	GR
2. Shad Landing Marina 🖳	410-632-3764	40	–	/25	14/7	–	G	GIS	–	–	30/100	LPS	P	–

Corresponding chart(s) not to be used for navigation. 🖳 Internet Access (WiFi) Wireless Internet Access Waterway Guide Cruising Club Partner

See www.WaterwayGuide.com for current rates, fuel prices, web site addresses, and other up-to-the-minute information.

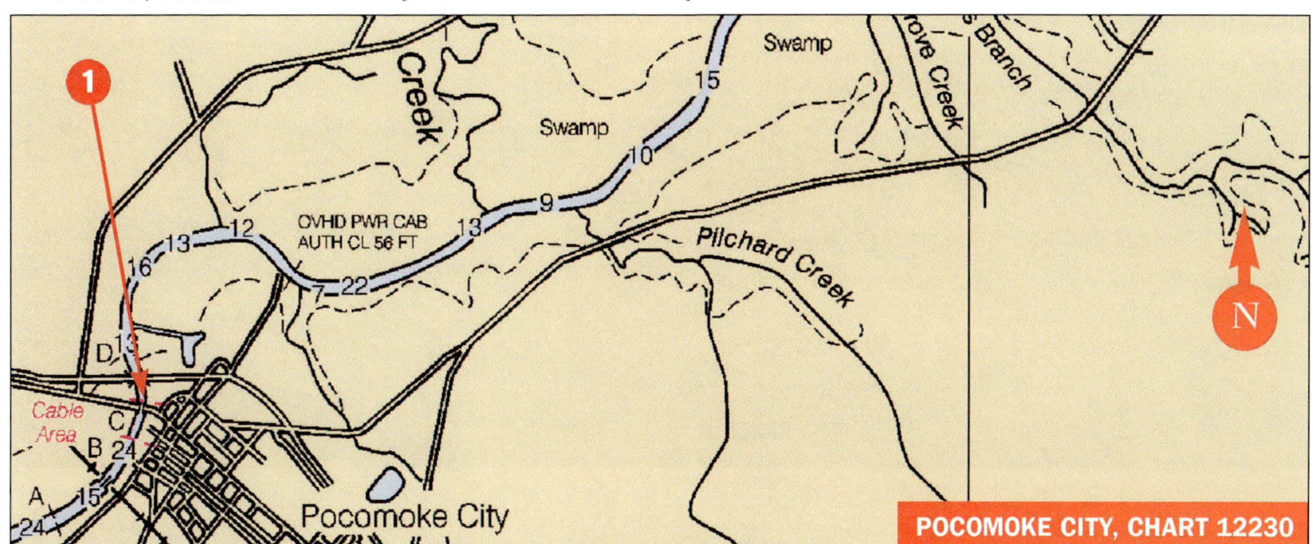

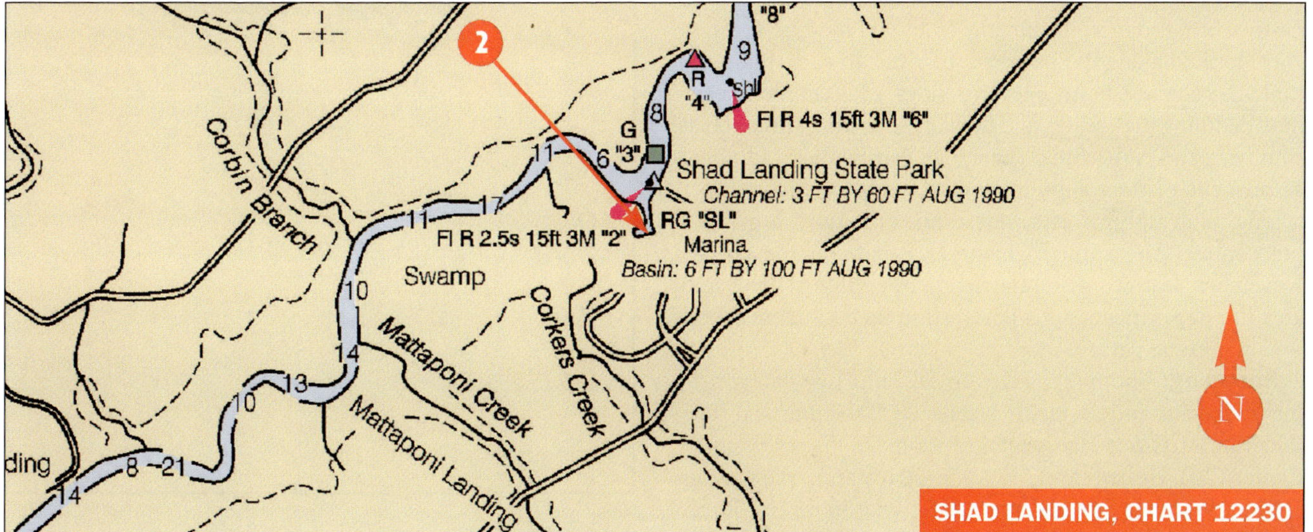

Points of Interest: The $1.1 million Delmarva Discovery Center at 2 Marker St. (410-957-9933, www.delmarvadiscoverycenter.org) aims to educate the public about the area's watershed heritage and life on the river over the past 300 years, including American Indians, shipbuilders and wildlife.

The Costen House Museum, the circa-1860 home of Dr. Isaac T. Costen, the city's first mayor, is open for tours, along with the surrounding gardens. The house is at 206 Market St. (410-957-3110). Nearby is the Sturgis One-Room School Museum, where African-American students in grades one through seven were taught until 1937, when the school closed. In 1996, the building was purchased for restoration and preservation purposes, and moved to Willow Street in the downtown area.

The Marva Theater, an Art Deco theater, was built in 1927. The theater has hosted vaudeville shows and performers like Roy Rogers. More recently, plays, ballets, concerts and movies have been presented. Architectural gems include original gold-embossed paneling and a draw drape. It is located at 103 Market St. (410-957-4230).

Pocomoke City, MD. Waterway Guide Photography.

Special Events: Each May, the annual American Indians Festival brings dance, drumming, crafts and foods to Cypress Park, located along the banks of the river. In early June, the three-day Cypress Festival features rides, entertainment, vendors peddling their wares and fireworks. The big attraction at summer's end is the Great Pocomoke Fair, with a traditional assortment of tractor pulls, livestock and equine competitions, blue ribbons pies, rides and, of course, a greased pig contest. The annual Christmas Parade, at the end of November, features marching bands from high schools and area fire departments, plus floats, all in their Christmas best for a nighttime parade.

Shopping: Shopping seems to fall into two categories: highly specific and decidedly practical. On the practical side, there is Harris Ace Hardware in Pocomoke Plaza Shopping Center (201 Hearne Ave., 410-957-2010) and, a few miles away, a Walmart Super Center (2132 Old Snow Hill Road, 410-947-9605).

Dining: Near the waterfront are The Lighthouse Café at 209 Clarke Ave. (410-957-2070) and Café Milano at 200 Market Street (410-957-4009).

ADDITIONAL RESOURCES

- **POCOMOKE CITY CHAMBER OF COMMERCE:** 6 Market St., 410-957-1919, www.pocomoke.com

NEARBY MEDICAL FACILITIES
Everest Medical Center: 1604 Market St., Pocomoke City, MD 21851, 410-957-9488

Peninsula Regional Medical Center: 100 East Carroll St., Salisbury, MD 21801 410-546-6400 (24 miles)

NEARBY AIRPORT
Salisbury-Ocean City-Wicomico Regional Airport: 5485 Airport Terminal Road, Salisbury, MD 21804, 410-548-4827 (25 miles)

ONANCOCK CREEK, VA

Onancock Creek lies almost 20 nautical miles southwest of the mouth of the Pocomoke River and about 5 nautical miles southeast of Watts Island. One of the most beautiful tributaries on Virginia's Eastern Shore, it is deep, well-marked and winds five miles from flashing green "1" at the creek's mouth east to the town of Onancock. The town center is a short walk up the hill through a residential area. Little in the way of provisioning is readily available, but

Onancock offers several good restaurants and interesting shops in a scenic town setting.

NAVIGATION: Use Chart 12228. **Use Hampton Roads tide tables. For high tide at Onancock, add 2 hours 56 minutes; for low tide, add 3 hours 14 minutes.** Start your approach by setting and following a course to flashing green "1," about 1 nautical mile west of Ware Point at the mouth of Onancock Creek. The approach channel from the Bay twists and turns, but if you move carefully from buoy to buoy, you should encounter no problems. Make sure that you do not wander outside of the markers—the numerous sand bars are bare at low tide. Shoaling has been reported near marker "2A". Dredging, commercial work boats and gravel barges keep the Onancock entry channel 8.5 feet deep to the town docks past green daybeacon "37." A large green storage tank is the most conspicuous landmark as you approach town. When you get closer, you will see Hopkins Brothers General Store to port.

Dockage: The Onancock Town Marina at Onancock Wharf, is to the right of Hopkins Brothers on Central Branch. Call the dockmaster on VHF Channel 16 (hail only, switch to working channel once contacted) for rates and availability. Reservations are strongly recommended, especially on weekends.

Anchorage: Do not anchor close to the marina (Onancock Wharf) or the commercial docks, where large tugs must maneuver barges at all hours. You will find several pleasant anchorages on Onancock Creek. A cove at the entrance to Cedar Creek, north of red daybeacon "26," and the eastern portion beyond the grassy points that enclose the mouth of the creek both have 5- to 8-foot depths if you sound your way in carefully. The little cove south of red daybeacon "34" has 5-foot depths, but enter around the east side of the marker and watch out for fish traps. Closest to the village, the anchorage between green daybeacon "37" and the neck of land between the middle branch and the south branch offers 6- to 8-foot depths just off the channel. This small anchorage is popular on summer weekends, but be sure to anchor outside the channel, as it is heavily used by gravel barges. A new town dinghy dock is located at the base of the bridge.

GOIN' ASHORE: ONANCOCK, VA

Wending your way up Onancock Creek, it is easy to imagine you are being led back in time. As you wander up the hill into town, you pass beautifully restored homes with manicured yards on immaculate streets. Hardly a building appears to have been erected post 1930, even on the town's outskirts, and none of them appears in need of fixing up. The frenzy of strip malls and fast-food shacks that have sprung up on the highway a scant mile away has so far not spread toward the old center, which remains peaceful and picturesque.

Despite its small size, Onancock has just about every business its residents might need on a daily basis. It also has a few more—art galleries, a gourmet shop and a vintage movie theater—to make it well worth a detour off the main thoroughfare, be that Route 13 or the Chesapeake Bay.

History: As its present-day name suggests, and the archeological record supports, Onancock was favored by American Indians long before Europeans discovered its bucolic serenity.

Industrious settlers harvested a bounty of tobacco from the flat, easily cultivated land of the Eastern Shore, and Onancock Creek provided rare deep-water access for extracting it for shipment to England. When, in 1680, the Virginia Assembly legislated for a port to be built in every county in the Colony, Onancock Creek was the natural choice of location to serve Accomack County.

Streets were surveyed and laid out in 1681, but little evidence remains of whatever structures may have been built on them, and even the town's original name, Port Scarborough, was lost in time. Most of the homes and buildings around the town square date from the early 19th century forward, from the period when regular visits by steamboats made Onancock once again a vital center for commerce.

Points of Interest: Onancock is its own main attraction, a compact town of essentially two streets and an abundance of tastefully restored and maintained buildings. One of the first sites when you come ashore is the "Liars Bench" at Onancock Wharf. It's where the "old salts" come to spin their fishing yarns—some true and some not so much.

Nearby, right on the Onancock Wharf, is the old Hopkins Bros. Store, built in about 1842 to serve the steamboat trade. The Association for the Preservation of Virginia Antiquities

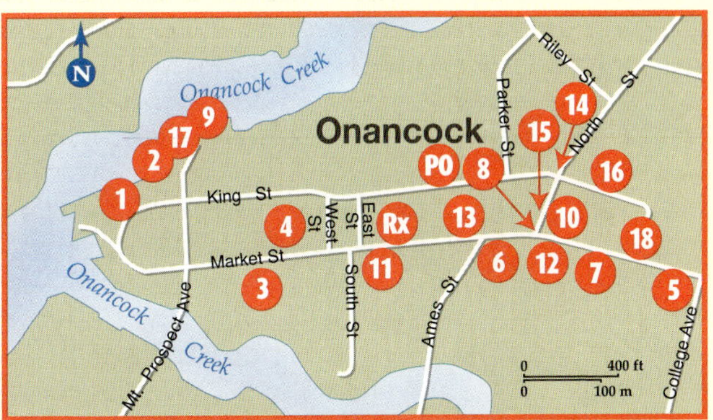

Reference the marina listing tables to see all the marinas in the area.

POINTS OF INTEREST
1 Liars Bench
2 Hopkins Bros. Store
3 Cokesbury Methodist Church
4 Town Square
5 Ker Place Museum
6 North Street Playhouse
7 Roseland Theater

SHOPPING
8 North Street Market
9 South East Expeditions
10 Purl's
11 Market Street Antiques

DINING
12 Corner Bakery
13 Bizotto's Gallery & Caffe
14 Onancock General Store
15 Charlotte Hotel & Restaurant
16 Blarney Stone Pub
17 Mallards at the Wharf
18 Scoops

Rx PHARMACY

PO POST OFFICE

Onancock Creek, VA

ONANCOCK CREEK		Largest Vessel Accommodated	VHF Channel Monitored	Transient Berths / Total Berths	Approach / Dockside Depth (reported)	Floating Docks	Gas / Diesel	Groceries, Ice, Marine Supplies, Snacks	Repairs: Hull, Engine, Propeller	Lift (tonnage), Crane, Rail	Min/Max Amps	Laundry, Pool, Showers, Courtesy Car	Pump-Out Station	Nearby: Grocery Store, Motel, Restaurant
		Dockage						Supplies		Services				
1. Onancock Town Marina (WiFi)	757-787-7911	100	16/09	14/17	10/9	F	GD	I	-	-	30/50	L	P	GMR

Corresponding chart(s) not to be used for navigation. Internet Access (WiFi) Wireless Internet Access Waterway Guide Cruising Club Partner
See www.WaterwayGuide.com for current rates, fuel prices, web site addresses, and other up-to-the-minute information.

ONANCOCK CREEK, CHART 12228

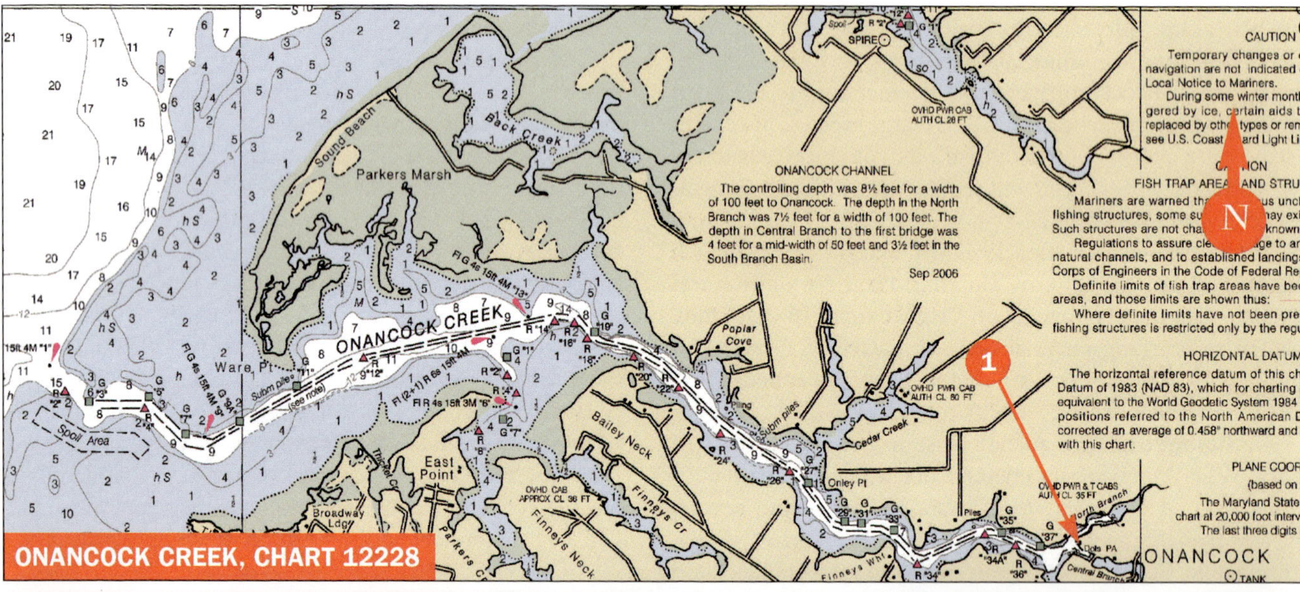

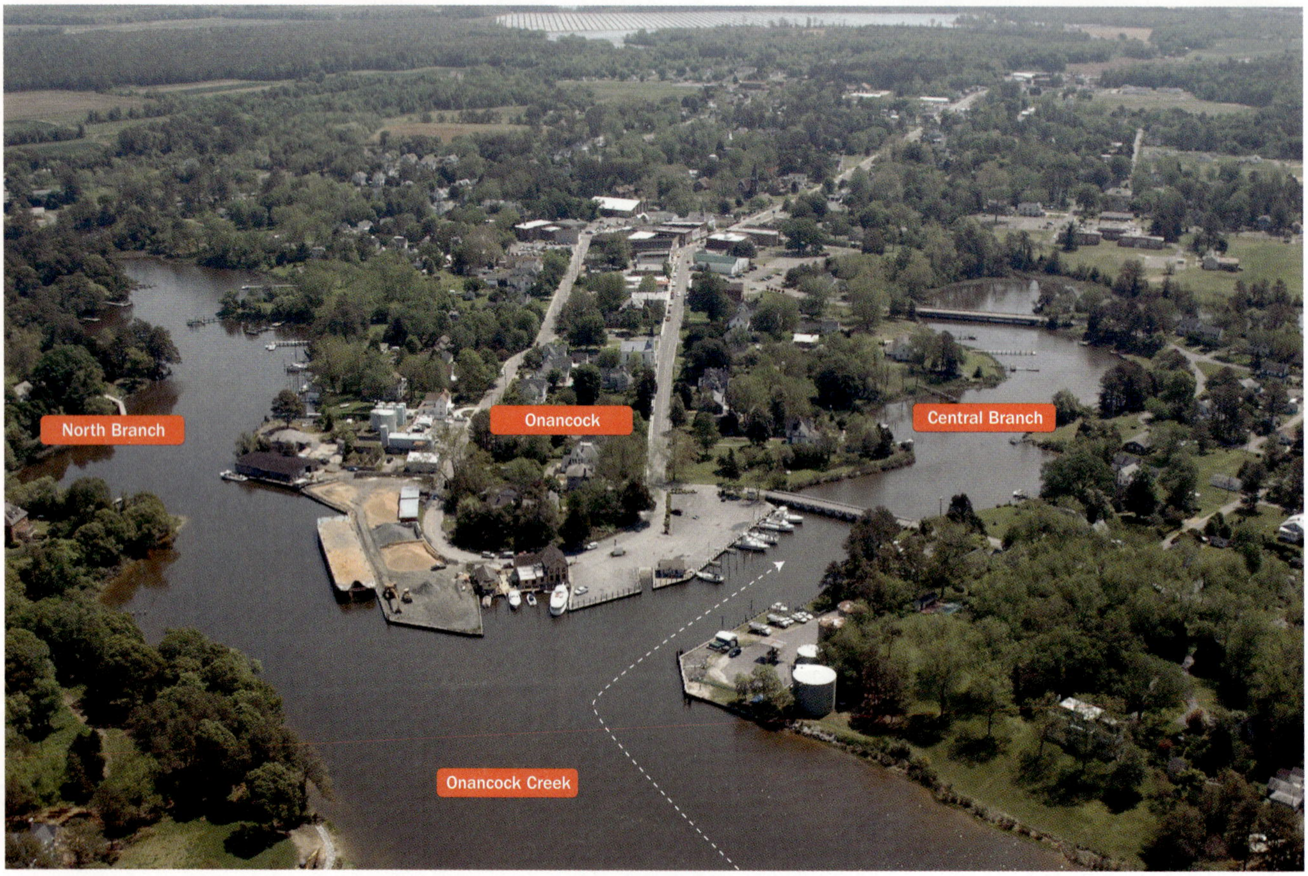

An eastern view of the town of Onancock and Onancock Creek. (Not to be used for navigation.) Waterway Guide Photography.

owns the historic building, but a private concession runs it as a restaurant. Just up Market Street, Cokesbury Methodist Church, built in 1854, is the oldest church still standing in the town. Its first congregation gathered in 1784, in the early days of the Methodist movement when circuit riders led meetings in members' homes.

All of the Colonial port towns had a town square, which would be used for public assemblies, as the market place and for drilling the militia. Onancock's has remained public property since 1681 and still fulfills its role as a meeting place. Memorials to war dead and individual heroes serve as quiet reminders of the town's contributions to its country.

Just east of the cluster of businesses that radiate on Market Street from its junction with North Street, Ker Place Museum commands attention with its setting and its exquisite proportions. One of the finest Federal-era brick houses on the Eastern Shore, it was built in 1802 by John Shepherd Ker and now appropriately houses the Eastern Shore of Virginia Historical Society (ESVHS; 757-787-8012, www.kerplace.org). (Note that many references use the spelling Kerr, but the ESVHS is reverting to the original Ker.)

The North Street Playhouse (34 Market St., 757-787-2050) coalesced as a drama group in 1986 and now occupies the former Dollar General storefront. It presents three separate theater series and more than 40 performances annually.

The Roseland Theater (48 Market St., 757-787-2010, roselandonancock.com) has had only two principal owners since 1950. It shows first-run movies on weekends and international films on the second Thursday each month.

Special Events: The Onancock Market is every Saturday from 8:00 a.m.-noon on the corner of Market and Ames Streets. Onancock celebrates a summer well spent with Harborfest, held in September on the weekend after Labor Day. Visit www.onancock.com for a listing of other annual events.

Shopping: In Onancock's eclectic mix, you will find art galleries, a pharmacy (located in the oldest bank building on the Eastern Shore) a deli and a bakery. The North Street Market at 5 North Street is an upscale gourmet food and kitchen store (for sale at press time in 2012.) SouthEast Expeditions at the Wharf (2 King Street, 757-354-4FUN) offers kayak tours, rentals and gear, as well as Eastern Shore wine, coffee, T-shirts, and Blue Crab Bay products. Purl's is a yarn shop at 6 North St. (757-787-2277) that offers classes and kits in addition to yarns and supplies. Market Street Antiques is now where the old hardware store used to be; you can spend an entire afternoon looking at all they have to offer (757-789-5199, www.antiquesmarketstreet.com). If your ship's stores are running low, call Star Transit (757-787-8322) for a pick-up to take you to the supermarket and other stores on Route 13. (The NAPA Auto Parts on Route 13 in Onley delivers, by the way, 757-787-8582.) Speaking of Onley, a side trip to Turner Sculpture to see the acclaimed bronze wildlife sculptures is worthwhile. Check it out at www.turnersculpture.com.

Dining: As one of the area's top retreats for city escapees, Onancock is where metro meets the Eastern Shore, and the grazing opportunities are as varied as the license plates.

The harbor at Kiptopeke Beach. (Not to be used for navigation.) Waterway Guide Photography.

Cape Charles, Virginia. Photo courtesy of Jani Parker.

Walk up an appetite for breakfast or pastries with a stroll to the Corner Bakery (36 Market St., 757-787-4520), a local focal point where the UPS driver makes the last, tasty pick-up of the day. For lunch, surround yourself with art in Bizzotto's Gallery-Cafe (41 Market St., 757-787-3103) or try the sandwiches at Onancock General Store at 49 King St. (757-787-9495).The Charlotte Hotel & Restaurant (7 North St., 757-787-7400), savor upscale bistro dining in a rejuvenated early 20th-century hotel hung throughout with the proprietor's art. Across the street, the Blarney Stone Pub (10 North St., 757-302-0300) offers a broad selection of on-tap ales to accompany "comfort food" in an Irish atmosphere. Close by the boats, Mallards at the Wharf (2 Market St., 757-787-8558) dishes up fine seafood, steaks and fusion in the Hopkins Bros. Store, its reception area walls still fitted out with period shelving. Scoops Ice Cream is a bit of a walk but worth it on a hot day (132 Market Street, 757-787-3230).

ADDITIONAL RESOURCES

- TOWN OF ONANCOCK:
- ONANCOCK BUSINESS & CIVIC ASSOCIATION: 757-302-0388

Shore Memorial Hospital: 9507 Hospital Avenue, Nassawadox, VA 23413, 757-414-8000

Eastern Shore, Onancock to Cape Charles

If you draw 5 feet or less, you can explore several scenic (but shallow) creeks between Onancock and Cape Charles, but the only marina facility along this rural 30-plus mile stretch of the Chesapeake's Eastern Shore is a small marine railway and Travelift at Davis Wharf, on the Occahannock River. The entrance approach to this beautiful undeveloped river is from the south. The markers are widely spaced, but the channel is relatively easy to navigate for several miles inland.

CAPE CHARLES, VA

The town of Cape Charles is not at the tip of the geographical Cape Charles; it is actually several miles to the north. This comely little town, an increasingly popular site for retirees and summer vacationers, is also growing in popularity as one of the Eastern Shore's destination ports. Cape Charles is the last stop southbound for good restaurants, shops and marine facilities before crossing the 14 mile wide mouth of the Chesapeake Bay toward Virginia Beach and Norfolk, VA.

NAVIGATION: Use Chart 12224. **Use Hampton Roads tide tables. For high tide at Cape Charles Harbor, subtract 11 minutes; for low tide, add 1 minute.** A well-marked, dredged channel from the south across Old Plantation Flats leads back north to Cape Charles Harbor. The channel entrance is just north of the Old Plantation Flats Light, which is 39 feet high on a pile with a black-and-white diamond-shaped daybeacon—flashing white every four seconds. Note that up to a 1.3-knot current runs along this coast, and adjust your course to allow for it. Look for the ranges in the channel and use them as guides. From flashing green buoy "1CC," proceed northeasterly to quick flashing red buoy "2." At quick flashing red buoy "2," turn to port, pass flashing red "4" to starboard, and then go between green can buoy "5" and red nun buoy "6." Continue on this course until you pass flashing red "8" to starboard. The jetty for Cape Charles Harbor will be just to the north of the harbor. If you are going to the harbor, turn to starboard before the jetty at flashing green "7" and then proceed into the basin.

If continuing to Kings Creek and Bay Creek Marina farther north, keep in mind that the channel markers have changed drastically in the last couple of years. From the south, first pass the Cape Charles jetty on your starboard side (250-foot) and proceed north-northeast on a course of about 032 degrees to flashing green "1CB," leaving it to port as you pass by. From flashing green "1CB," head north (020 degrees) for about one-half mile to pass between green marker "3" and red daybeacon "4." At this point, turn hard to starboard to 093 degrees (east) to follow the new channel to Kings Creek. Disregard red marker "2CI" to the northeast; it is an old marker still in place that marked the original Cherrystone Channel. Proceed east between green "5" and red daybeacon "6." A succession of lighted and unlighted markers will then lead you in toward the curving channel into Kings Creek and the marina. Latest on-site reports indicate 6-foot depths at mean low water from green "3" to the entrance to the creek, but hail the Bay Creek Marina on VHF Channel 16 for current conditions before entering, as the chart (April 2011 edition) still indicated only 5 feet.

Dockage: Adjacent to the town, a recent project expanded the Cape Charles Town Docks in the Harbor of Refuge. This marina now has 120 floating slips with extensive bulkheads, water and shore power and can accomodate vessels up to 170 feet. They have new air conditioned restrooms with showers and an on-site restaurant (Shanty, 508-284-3318). The marina also sells fuel.

Approximately 1 mile to the north, developers of the 1,700-acre Bay Creek community replaced the former Kings Creek Marina with a 224-slip state-of-the-art facility that accepts vessels up to 150 feet and sells fuel. Other facilities, including a ship's store, restaurant, a café and several attractive shops enhance Bay Creek's charm. Two golf courses are open, one designed by Arnold Palmer and the other by Jack Nicklaus. Golf carts can be rented to explore the town of Cape Charles.

Anchorage: You can anchor beyond flashing green "15" in 5- to 7-foot depths at Kings Creek, but note the charted 2-foot-deep lump in the middle of the creek. Do not anchor in the Cape Charles town dock basin. There is a town ordinance against anchoring in the harbor and outer area, where the tugs and barges maneuver and dock.

You can also anchor south of Cape Charles at Kiptopeke Beach State Park behind the sunken World War II concrete Liberty Ships. There are beautiful beaches, some of the clearest water in the Bay and rarely any jellyfish, making it a swimmer's dream. It can get uncomfortable, however, in the prevailing southeast sea breezes, when swells from the Atlantic Ocean wrap around Cape Charles, and downright rough in a southwesterly. The Liberty Ships form a breakwater at the site of the former Kiptopeke ferry terminal. The ships are dilapidated, and it is dangerous to approach them.

GOIN' ASHORE:
CAPE CHARLES, VA

Waterborne visitors to Cape Charles, VA can choose which face of the town they want to see first. Those who like to land in an upscale resort with shops, restaurants, two golf courses and a swimming pool can put into Bay Creek Marina

Reference the marina listing tables to see all the marinas in the area.

POINTS OF INTEREST

1 SouthEast Expeditions
2 Cape Charles Museum and Welcome Center
3 Palace Theater
4 Stage Door Gallery

SHOPPING

5 Breezes
6 Gallery 209
7 Bad Girlz Collective
8 Cape Charles Sea Glass
9 The Boardwalk
10 Watson Hardware Store Co.
11 Bailey's Bait & Tackle
12 Shore Treasures Market

DINING

13 Aqua
14 Coach House Tavern
15 Cape Charles Coffee House
16 Kelly's Gingernut Pub
17 Brown Dog Ice Cream
18 The Shanty
19 Bay Creek Railway

L LIBRARY

PO POST OFFICE

Rx PHARMACY

Cape Charles, VA

CAPE CHARLES		Largest Vessel Accommodated	VHF Channel Monitored	Transient Berths / Total Berths	Approach / Dockside Depth (reported)	Floating Docks	Gas / Diesel	Groceries, Ice, Marine Supplies, Snacks	Repairs: Hull, Engine, Propeller	Lift (tonnage), Crane, Rail	Min/Max Amps	Laundry, Pool, Showers, Courtesy Car	Pump-Out Station	Nearby: Grocery Store, Motel, Restaurant
		Dockage					Supplies		Services					
1. Cape Charles Town Harbor (Wireless Internet Access)	757-331-2357	170	16/06	30/120	18/18	F	GD	GIMS	E	-	30/100	S	P	GMR
2. Bay Creek Marina & Resort (Internet Access) (Wireless Internet Access)	757-331-8640	150	16/09	75/224	6.5/8	F	GD	GIMS	P	-	30/100	LPS	P	GMR

Corresponding chart(s) not to be used for navigation. Internet Access · Wireless Internet Access · Waterway Guide Cruising Club Partner

See www.WaterwayGuide.com for current rates, fuel prices, web site addresses, and other up-to-the-minute information.

on Kings Creek to the north of the town harbor. Surrounded by marshes and wetlands, the marina is at the center of a development that will eventually have 1,200 homes and condominiums.

If you prefer to mingle with watermen on a working waterfront, head for Cape Charles Town Harbor. Across the railroad tracks, you will find Mason Avenue, where the action is. As main streets go, it is a little disorienting, because there is only one side to it. The bank, the hardware store, the coffee shop, the restaurants and a host of art galleries and shops face a vista of railroad sidings, punctuated by a locomotive here and a flat car there. A couple of days a week, a barge unloads and loads rail cars, maintaining the link with Norfolk, VA, upon which the town was founded.

The harbor, Coast Guard station and a concrete plant make up the background. If it feels a bit like sitting in a theater from which the stage has been removed, it is because that is exactly what happened to Cape Charles.

History: For two and a half centuries, transportation in the Chesapeake Bay region was largely via water, and the Bay itself made a great and convenient thoroughfare. In the middle of the 19th century, railroads became the prime movers of commerce. To them, the Bay presented a barrier between the populous and industrial North and markets in the South. In 1884, the New York, Philadelphia and Norfolk Railroad (NYP&N) overcame that hurdle when it built a rail line to the lower Eastern Shore of Virginia and connected it to Norfolk, VA, with ferries for passengers and railcars.

Since no town existed in Northampton County to serve as the railroad's terminus and house its employees, the railroad company created one. In 1885, construction began on a planned community of 644 lots on a gridwork of streets laid out on a parcel of 136 acres. Most of the original structures still stand. This large, concentrated collection of Victorian, early 20th century homes and business buildings earned Cape Charles a listing on the National Register of Historic Places.

Looking north over Cape Charles. The entrance to Kings Creek is visible to the north. (Not to be used for navigation.) Waterway Guide Photography.

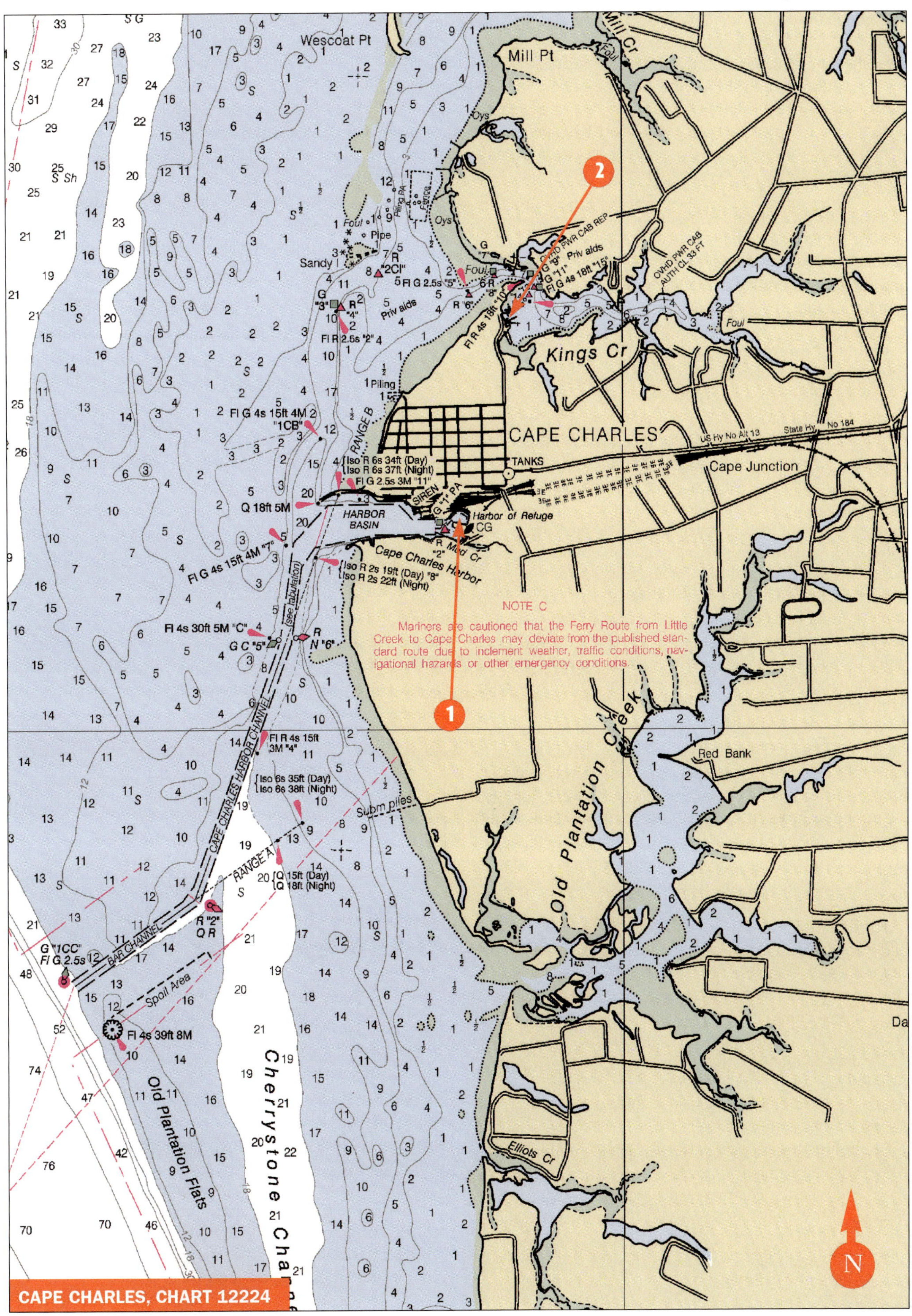

CAPE CHARLES, CHART 12224

Right up through World War II, when it was a key way station for troops on their way to Europe, Cape Charles boomed. After the war, truck transport made inroads into the railroad's business and when, in the 1950s, the vehicle ferry terminal was moved south to Kiptopeke, the town lost its economic anchor. The last passenger ferry sailed in 1958, and the terminal, which was the stage to the audience on Mason Avenue, is now gone.

Currently, Cape Charles is experiencing a renaissance. Attracted by its restored and restorable character homes, its small-town ambience and the largely unspoiled surrounding landscape of forest, field, bay and beach, boomers and retirees are homing in, bringing with them money, energy and a hunger for the artistic stimulation offered by communities in transition.

Points of Interest: At the Bay end of Mason Street, the one-mile-long town beach boasts a white, sandy beach (that is very wide when the tide is out) a fishing pier, gazebo and a summer concert program. You can rent a kayak or stand-up paddleboard from SouthEast Expeditions at 239 Mason Ave. (757-695-4001) to tour the surrounding area.

A walk of about a half a mile in the opposite direction will take you to the Cape Charles Museum and Welcome Center; just head for the water tower. The museum is in a generating station built in 1947, and its centerpiece is the Busch-Sulzer engine and Westinghouse generator that, until the 1980s, provided peak-hour power to the town. Other exhibits include models and photographs of ships, barges, sailing craft and the railroad ferries for which the town was built. Outside is a small collection of railroad buildings and rail cars. The museum is open for limited hours daily mid-April through November (757-331-1008).

Arts Enter Cape Charles is a vibrant performing arts association based in the Historic Palace Theatre, an Art Deco-style movie theater built in 1941 and listed in the National Register of Historic Places. As well as being a showcase for local talent, it also hosts such haute culture organizations as the Virginia Symphony (305 Mason Ave., 757-331-2787, www.artsentercapecharles.org). Arts Enter's visual arts division is headquartered in the Stage Door Gallery at 301 Mason St. (757-331-3669, www.stagedoorgallery.com).

The Eastern Shore is on the Atlantic Flyway, which makes it a prime destination for birders as well as birds. Several barrier islands off Cape Charles (the cape) and much adjacent land are under the protection of the Nature Conservancy and the National and State park systems. Kiptopeke State Park (757-331-2267) is the closest to Cape Charles (the town).

The Barrier Islands Center (757-678-5550, www.barrierislandscenter.com) in Machipongo, about 10 miles north of Route 13, depicts life on the Eastern Shore barrier islands in the early 19th century.

Shopping: Resort shopping is available at Bay Creek, while Mason Avenue downtown is home to a variety of art shops and galleries, gourmet food stores and even a Day Spa (Breezes, 321 Mason Ave., 757-331-3108). Among the shops are Gallery 209 (757-331-2433), Bad Girlz Collective (757-331-2293), Cape Charles Sea Glass (757-331-1095) and The Boardwalk (757-331-2424).

You may find boat supplies at Watson Hardware (757-331-3979) or Baileys Bait & Tackle at (757-331-1982), both on Mason Ave. The nearest grocery store is two miles away, at the highway, but Shore Treasures Market at the end of the Mason Ave. shopping district has limited groceries and a surprisingly good wine and beer selection, as well as hand-dipped ice cream at their deli counter (757-331-1546) .

Dining: Bay Creek has two restaurants (at opposite ends of town). Upscale Aqua (757-331-8660), looking out over the Bay, specializes in seafood and in-season local produce, while the Coach House Tavern (757-331-8631) offers a more pub-like atmosphere near the golf course.

In town, Cape Charles Coffee House (241 Mason Ave., 757-331-1880) serves breakfast and lunch daily, and dinner on special occasions, in the former Cape Charles Bank building. No railroad town would be whole without an Irish alehouse, and Kelly's Gingernut Pub (133 Mason Ave., 757-331-3222) fills that slot right down to the dart board. It, too, occupies a former bank, and the brick vault is still at its heart, opposite the long bar under a high tin ceiling. The menu has an Irish tilt, and the bar offers a good international selection of draft and bottled beers, ales and lagers. Brown Dog Ice Cream is popular, especially in the summer. At the Cape Charles harbor, the new (in 2012) The Shanty (508-284-3318) serves seafood inside or on a deck overlooking the water. There is a sandy "cornhole" court out back, next to the stage where live music is performed. Bay Creek Railway (757-331-8770) operates a dinner train in a restored 1913 self-propelled inter-urban dining car. The 2 1/2-hour excursion along the Bay Coast Railroad line takes diners through classic Eastern Shore countryside dotted with small towns, plantations and farmhouses.

ADDITIONAL RESOURCES

- TOWN OF CAPE CHARLES: www.capecharles.org

NEARBY MEDICAL FACILITIES
Shore Memorial Hospital: 9507 Hospital Ave., Nassawadox, VA 23413, 757-414-8000 (20 miles)

MOUTH OF THE CHESAPEAKE BAY

Between Cape Charles and Virginia Beach/Norfolk, nearly 25 miles to the south, conditions require a sharp lookout and attention to the weather.

Shipping channels carrying commercial and military vessels from the Atlantic to major ports, including Norfolk and Baltimore, crisscross the area. Stay well clear of all shipping both for security reasons and your own safety. Although large ships appear to be moving slowly because of the time it takes their long length to pass a given point, they are often moving in excess of 20 knots and can be upon you surprisingly fast.

Proximity to the open Atlantic Ocean can create wind and weather conditions very different than that found just a few miles farther inland. Pay close attention to offshore weather reports when transiting the area. ■

Maryland Western Shore

NORTH EAST RIVER TO MAGOTHY RIVER
SEVERN RIVER TO RHODE/WEST RIVERS
HERRING BAY TO PATUXENT RIVER
POTOMAC RIVER-MD (N.SHORE)/VA (S.SHORE)

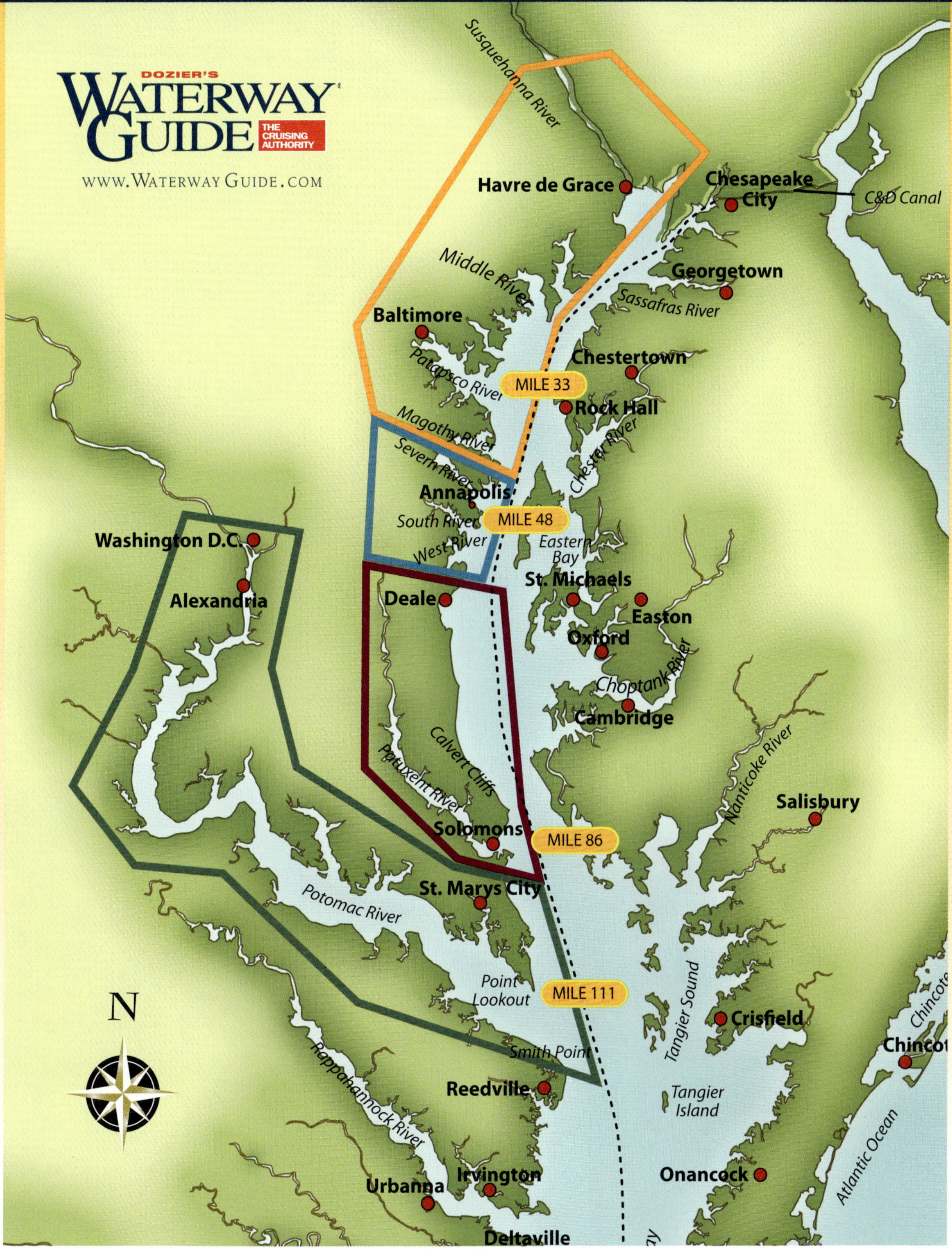

Skipper's Handbook

Introduction

Maryland's Western Shore

This stretch of the Chesapeake Bay truly offers just about anything a cruiser could want. You can anchor in a quiet cove off the North East River, and later, tie up in Baltimore—soaking in an Orioles Major League Baseball game at Camden Yards—before sundown.

The smaller ports of call are plentiful, too. Take Havre de Grace, near the mouth of the swift-flowing Susquehanna River. Established in the 18th century, Havre de Grace is an antique-lover's dream, offering not just regionally famous antiques stores, but terrific dining as well. Here you will also find shops displaying and producing duck decoys, known throughout the world for their elite level of craftsmanship.

Farther south, Baltimore, MD is just a short run up the Patapsco River. Once known more as a commercial shipping center than a recreational port, Baltimore is quickly becoming a requisite item on many cruisers' float-plans. And why not? Baltimore's waterfront neighborhoods like Fells Point and Canton now offer some of the finest yachting amenities on the Chesapeake. Tie up in either of these areas, and you can enjoy their 18th-century charm, including some excellent pubs and restaurants.

From Fells Point, you can catch one of Baltimore's convenient water taxis and head over to the renowned Inner Harbor, where Babe Ruth's birthplace, the Harborplace and Gallery shopping areas and Oriole Park at Camden Yards are located. The Inner Harbor is also the site of an ESPN Zone sports bar, an enormous Barnes & Noble bookstore and dozens of good restaurants. Baltimore's Little Italy, one of the most active and well-preserved ethnic neighborhoods on the East Coast, is just blocks away.

Continuing south past the cruising-friendly Magothy River, you come to Annapolis, known as the "Sailing Capital of the World," and also home of the U.S. Naval Academy. What else is there to say about this eye-popping little city, whose roots go back to the mid-1600s? Whether you take a mooring or berth on Spa Creek or find a good anchorage on Back Creek, all that Annapolis has to offer is within easy striking distance. It seems that the entire area—from its waterways to its picturesque shops and historic architecture—caters to the cruising boater.

The increasingly popular boating areas of South River (with the historic and often-photographed Thomas Point Light near its entrance) and the Rhode and West rivers are farther south. While the South River is a busy waterway with lots of amenities and nice anchorages, the Rhode and West rivers offer a more bucolic setting. Galesville, a historic little port town on West River, is definitely worth a visit for its traditional general store, museum, marine services and restaurants.

The Patuxent River is the next major tributary along Maryland's Western Shore. Solomons Island, a short passage up the Patuxent, has blossomed into a major recreational boating center, rivaling ports of call like Annapolis and St. Michaels. The Patuxent River itself is a sort of paradise for those who prefer a quiet anchorage, as is the Potomac River, a little farther down the Bay. Washington, D.C., the metaphorical pot of gold at the end of the Potomac, is where much of the nation's business unfolds—including the business of sitting in the cockpit and enjoying an ice-cold beverage. ■

Waterway Guide Photography.

North East River to Magothy River

CHARTS 12273, 12274, 12278, 12281, 12282

The northern part of Maryland's Western Shore represents one of the most remarkable cruising grounds on the Chesapeake. For starters, you have the mighty Susquehanna River, the Bay's mother tributary, and the pleasant town of Havre de Grace, with excellent boating facilities and transportation connections. As you go down the Bay, you pass miles of vacant waterfront land whose development is unlikely, thanks to frequent military explosions at Aberdeen Proving Ground.

Farther south is the major metropolitan harbor—and burgeoning yachting center—of Baltimore. Once known more for its shipping traffic than its yachting scene, Baltimore is making a bid to become a major stopover for cruisers looking for a taste of the big city amid the historic neighborhoods of Fells Point and Canton, to say nothing of the sightseeing and shopping available at the Inner Harbor.

Then, of course, you have Annapolis, MD, known as the "Sailing Capital of the World." Located on the Severn River, just off the Chesapeake proper, Annapolis is the epitome of the perfect cruising stopover, with its pubs, shops and historic sites all within an easy walk of the dinghy landing at City Dock.

If you are looking to break away from the action, check out the anchoring possibilities on tributaries like the Middle and Magothy rivers, with their plentiful anchorages and protected waters. Even though you will never be far from civilization here, most of the creeks are quiet on weekdays. It is entirely possible to spend years exploring this one section of the Bay; many local skippers do just that.

NORTH EAST RIVER

The North East River, at the head of Chesapeake Bay, is a busy boating center, with good yacht yards and numerous other marine amenities. These facilities serve not only Bay skippers but also those from Wilmington, DE and Philadelphia, PA, who keep their boats on the Chesapeake's protected waters.

The North East River has an advantage over the much larger Susquehanna in that its short length is relatively free of debris, even after heavy rains. The four-mile-long river, especially scenic as the leaves turn in early fall, is good for a spring layover while you wait for the nip to disappear from the air in New Jersey and New York. Between Turkey Point and the mouth of the North East River, Elk Neck State Park encompasses much of Elk Neck itself and provides beautiful scenery with sandy beaches and high, wooded bluffs.

Charlestown, overlooking the North East River's west shore about halfway up its length, began in 1742 as a shipping center for the area. You can anchor outside the town in a protected cove, but some report the holding is poor and recommend a slip for a worry-free night. The small historic district still contains good examples of 18th century buildings from the town's heyday in colonial and revolutionary times. The Wellwood (410-287-6666) offers fine dining inside or more casual fare on the patio, with live music on weekends, and dockage is available in their marina. Rivershack is located on the same property and is known for their crabs and fried seafood (open Thursday through Monday). In early September, the annual Riverfest offers a parade and fireworks, along with a number of other fun activities.

The town of North East, at the head of the river, is accessible by anchoring off the town park. Visitors will find a main street with friendly shops and restaurants. Marina facilities here are geared toward smaller dry-stored boats. The Upper Bay Museum is in the park. Open limited hours, the museum displays hunting, boating and fishing artifacts depicting the heritage and history of northern Chesapeake Bay. Call 410-287-2675 for more information. The Nauti Goose is a popular dock bar (200 Cherry Street, 410-287-7880) that also offers fine and casual dining on the waterfront. Woody's Crab House (29 South Main St, 410-287-3541) has an extensive seafood menu.

NAVIGATION: Use Chart 12274. Most of the North East River is quite wide, open and shallow. Chart 12274 shows that the progressively narrower channel, leading along the Susquehanna flats coming from the deeper waters of the Bay, is very near the high western shoreline of Elk Neck. The approach starts from Turkey Point, a high bluff at the mouth of the Elk River. Mind the 5-foot shoal making out 300 yards west of Turkey Point, marked by green and red can buoy "ER."

Flashing red buoy "6" lies five nautical miles north past the bluffs of Elk Neck and the state park, off Red Point at the mouth of the North East River. Follow the markers meticulously the rest of the way, and be sure to stay in the channel. Shoaling to 5 feet has been reported between green "7" and red "8", where the channel is quite narrow.

Dockage: Most of the significant area marinas for cruisers are in the triangle of deep water made by Hance

North East River, MD

NORTH EAST RIVER		Largest Vessel Accommodated	VHF Channel Monitored	Transient Berths / Total Berths	Approach / Dockside Depth (reported)	Floating Docks	Gas / Diesel	Groceries, Ice, Marine Supplies, Snacks	Repairs: Hull, Engine, Propeller	Lift (tonnage), Crane, Rail	Min/Max Amps	Laundry, Pool, Showers, Courtesy Car	Pump-Out Station	Nearby: Grocery Store, Motel, Restaurant
		Dockage					Supplies		Service					
1. Charlestown Marina (Internet Access) (Wireless Internet Access)	410-287-8125	65	16	20/265	6/6	-	G	IMS	HEP	L50	30/50	LS	P	GMR
2. Lee's Marina (Wireless Internet Access)	410-287-5100	40	-	3/68	3.5/3	F	-	IMS	HEP	L25	30/30	S	P	GR
3. McDaniel Yacht Basin Inc. (Internet Access) (Wireless Internet Access)	410-287-8121	65	16/09	6/200	6/6	-	GD	IMS	HEP	L50,C18,R55	30/50	LPS	P	GMR
4. North East River Yacht Club	410-287-6333	55	16	25/69	8/8	F	-	I	-	-	30/50	S	P	GMR
5. North East Yacht Harbour	410-287-6660	50	16	5/100	12/12	F	-	I	-	L40	30/30	-	-	-
6. Hance's Point Yacht Club	410-287-6090	35	-	1	4.5/4	F	-	IS	-	L7	-	PS	P	GR
7. Bay Boat Works Inc.	410-287-8113	50	-	10/136	6/6	F	GD	IMS	HEP	L50	30/50	S	P	-
8. Jackson Marine Sales/Shelter Cove Yacht Basin	410-287-9400	50	-	5/175	7/5	-	GD	IMS	HEP	L35	30/50	LS	P	-

Corresponding chart(s) not to be used for navigation. (Internet Access icon) Internet Access (Wireless Internet Access icon) Wireless Internet Access (Waterway Guide Cruising Club Partner icon) Waterway Guide Cruising Club Partner

See www.WaterwayGuide.com for current rates, fuel prices, web site addresses, and other up-to-the-minute information.

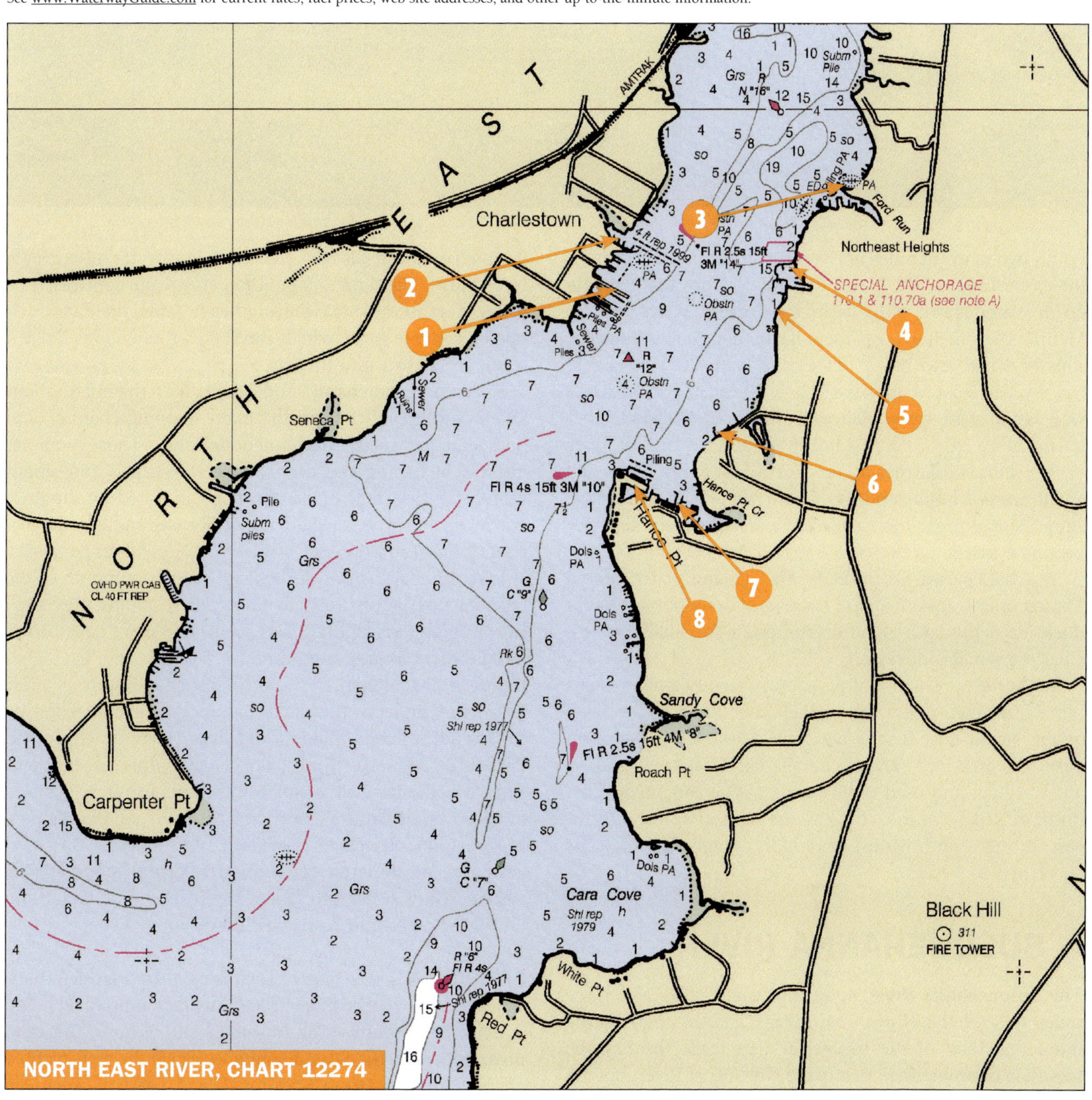

NORTH EAST RIVER, CHART 12274

Looking northwest over Havre de Grace and the Susquehanna River. (Not to be used for navigation.) Waterway Guide Photography.

Point, two nautical miles upriver (north) from Red Point on the eastern side of the North East River, Northeast Heights on the same shore and Charlestown on the west. Jackson Marine Sales/Shelter Cove Yacht Basin offers a few transient slips and fuel and has a full-service boatyard for repairs. Nearby Bay Boat Works Inc. has a 50-ton lift and fuel as well as transient space. Hance's Point Yacht Club is farther north, as are North East Yacht Harbor and North East River Yacht Club. Still farther up the North East River, McDaniel Yacht Basin is a full-service boatyard with an adjacent prop shop (M.R. Props) that sets aside a few transient slips for visiting cruisers.

At Charlestown, both Lee's Marina and Charlestown Marina offer transient space; however, Lees reports a 3-foot dockside depth so it is more appropriate for smaller boats. Charlestown also offers gas.

Anchorage: A high-and-dry storage facility and a restaurant create congestion in the anchorage basin at the head of the North East River's navigable portion, off the town park of North East. The anchorage basin's bottom is deep and irregular and used to be a quarry. You can anchor just north of Red Point in Cara Cove for protection from northeast through south winds; be careful, though, as the area is shoal, at 4 to 5 feet.

SUSQUEHANNA RIVER

The Susquehanna River flows into the Chesapeake three miles west of the North East River's mouth, contributing more than half of the freshwater that feeds the Bay. Its mouth is narrower than that of the North East River, but the Susquehanna reaches back more than 450 miles into upstate New York. The Conowingo Dam upstream controls flow of the river in this area. During heavy rains, the dam must open its release gates, which can send a tremendous burden of silt and debris into the Bay.

Both the Susquehanna and North East rivers are about seven nautical miles from the main shipping channel, and both can get rough and uncomfortable. Those with an interest in fishing can drop a line for striped and smallmouth bass (farther upstream to be explored by dinghy), but make sure you have a current license, and be aware of continuing restrictions on striped bass (rockfish) harvests.

Like the major cities of the East Coast, the mouth of the Susquehanna is on the Fall Line, where rapids prevented further water transport upstream in the early days of the nation. Richmond, Fredericksburg, Washington, D.C., Baltimore, Philadelphia, New York City and Boston all grew from this juxtaposition and became connected later by roads and railroads—and so did little Havre de Grace and Perryville. This quirk of history makes this an excellent spot to make transportation connections for crew changes or a visit home. Amtrak stops at Aberdeen, and the regional MARC train service to Baltimore, Washington, D.C. and Baltimore-Washington International Airport stops at Perryville. You will need to take a slip in Havre de Grace and take a short taxi ride to reach either station.

NAVIGATION: Use Chart 12274. **Use Baltimore tide tables. For high tide at Havre de Grace (Susquehanna River), add 3 hours 13 minutes; for low tide, add 3 hours 27 minutes.** Approach the Susquehanna River via the well-marked channel running from Spesutie Island (part of Aberdeen

Proving Ground) north to Havre de Grace. Opposite Fishing Battery Light, a 38-foot black skeleton tower with a white flashing light, stay mid-channel, and give a clear berth to the can and nun buoys leading into the islet's basin as you continue north. Be alert for commercial traffic here—mostly barge tows running to and from a huge gravel operation upriver. Also watch for crab trap markers in the channel.

Havre de Grace, on the Susquehanna

Everybody calls this pleasant little river town "have-er-dee-grayce," and you will get some funny looks if you try to impart any sort of French pronunciation to the name. Hurricane Isabel hit Havre de Grace's burgeoning waterfront hard in 2003, but the city has quickly rebuilt to position itself as an excellent cruising destination.

Dockage: The Havre de Grace City Yacht Basin has transient slips and fuel, with reported 6-foot approach depths. Nearby Penn's Beach Marina has transient slips on floating docks, as does Log Pond Marina. Tidewater Marina offers transient dockage, moorings, repair facilities and a sailing school. Havre de Grace Marina is north of the swing bridge (52-foot vertical clearance) and may have transient space. On the opposite side of the river in Perryville is Owens Marina.

Anchorage: It is possible to anchor just beyond Tidewater Marina, but it can be uncomfortable in southerly and easterly winds below the bridge. The holding here is only fair, and finding a place to tie up the dinghy can be a challenge. Locals frequently anchor for the day just west of the channel near Fishing Battery light to swim and fish in the fresh water.

Reference the marina listing tables to see all the marinas in the area.

POINTS OF INTEREST
1 Concord Point Lightkeeper's House
2 Havre de Grace Decoy Museum
3 Havre de Grace Maritime Museum
4 Susquehanna Museum
5 Stepping Stone Museum
6 Skipjack *Martha Lewis*

SHOPPING
7 Franklin Street Antiques & Gifts
8 Seneca Cannery Antique Mall
9 Courtyard Bookshop
10 Washington Street Books & Music
11 Vincenti Decoys
12 The Picture Show Custom Framing & Fine Art
13 River View Gallery

DINING
14 Tidewater Grille
15 Laurrapin Grille
16 Price's Seafood
17 MacGregor's Restaurant
18 Silks Restaurant
19 Bomboy's Candy & Bomboy's Ice Cream
20 Java by the Bay

INFORMATION
21 Office of Tourism

PO POST OFFICE
Rx PHARMACY
L LIBRARY

GOIN' ASHORE:
HAVRE DE GRACE, MD

In 1789, the nation was considering two towns for our permanent nation's capital: Washington and Havre de Grace. The House of Representatives vote ended in a tie, with the Speaker of the House casting the deciding vote in favor of Washington. With that, Havre de Grace turned to life as a "river city" along the mighty Susquehanna River.

Over recent years, the city has reinvented itself as a destination for tourists, but a place where the activity of everyday life is evident as well. You will pass a bustling local hospital aside Victorian homes en route to the more tourist-oriented waterfront. There, the wooden boardwalk, called The Promenade, stretches along three-quarters of a mile of Susquehanna riverfront, starting at the Decoy Museum. Next door stands a maritime museum, and, not far away, an old cannery has been converted to an antiques mall. Antiques (including the city's decoys) are tucked in among the old main street's other shops.

You will also note the fairly recent arrival of waterfront condominiums. One architectural element to look for throughout the city: Port Deposit granite, dug from the Susquehanna cliffs just upriver from the town of the same name.

History: Like many Chesapeake towns, Havre de Grace traces its roots to the Bay's 1608 exploration by Capt. John

Smith. He apparently encountered a group of Susquehannock Indians in this area. It took 174 more years before the Marquis de Lafayette, noting that a proposal had been floated to build a city here, suggested "Havre de Grace," or "Harbor of Mercy"—a nod to the French town of Le Havre. Like many Bay towns, Havre de Grace also saw the arrival of the British during the War of 1812.

A local militiaman by the name of John O'Neil was captured attempting to single-handedly save his hometown and was saved by his pleading daughter. Unfortunately, the city was burned. O'Neil went on to become the local lighthouse keeper, and today visitors can see the Concord Point Lighthouse.

The opening of the Susquehanna and Tidewater Canal and the railroad's arrival contributed to the city's 19th-century growth as it became an industrial town. Meantime, the Susquehanna Flats famously hosted huge flocks of ducks, as well numerous hunters—whether market hunters or sportsmen—making the city's decoys just as well known. Today, this Harford County town is just off Interstate 95, an hour from both Baltimore and Philadelphia.

Points of Interest: A great place to start when exploring Havre de Grace is the Office of Tourism at 450 Pennington Ave. (410-939-2100 or hdgtourism.com). The 1827 Concord Point Light & Keeper's House is not only the oldest continually operated lighthouse in Maryland, but workplace of keeper John O'Neil of War of 1812 fame. His keeper's house has been renovated. It is located at the foot of Lafayette Street (410-939-3213), not far from the Havre de Grace Decoy Museum. In back of this waterside museum you can see the actual workshop of local master carver R. Madison Mitchell, museum, which tells the tale of decoys here in the self-titled "Decoy Capital of the World." It is a good place to see decoys by many of the Chesapeake carving greats (215 Giles St., 410-939-3739).

The Havre de Grace Maritime Museum is home to the wooden boatbuilding school as well as an exhibit hall. Look for the permanent exhibit "Beyond Jamestown: Life 400 Years Ago" (100 Lafayette St., 410-939-4800). Check www.hdgmaritimemuseum.org for other (temporary) exhibits

A bit farther away near the north end of town, the Susquehanna Museum (also called "the lockhouse"), teaches about life along the Susquehanna and Tidewater Canal at the restored lockhouse that once marked the canal's southern terminus (817 Conesteo Street, 410-939-5780). On weekends, learn about Harford County's farm life at the Steppingstone Museum (461 Quaker Bottom Road, 410-939-2299).

And if you haven't yet taken a trip aboard a skipjack, see if the Martha Lewis is in port. The working oyster skipjack and sailing educational classroom docks at Tydings Park (www.skipjackmarthalewis.org).

If you prefer golf, visit Bulle Rock at 320 Blenheim Lane (410-939-8887).

Special Events: During the summer, there are regular free concerts in the Park on Fridays. The Decoy and Wildlife Art Festival takes place in early May, at the Havre de Grace Decoy Museum. There are auctions and a carving competition and decoys for sale. Havre de Grace Art & Craft Show (2011 marked the 48th outing) is held in mid-August and attracts more than 250 artists and crafters from around the country. Havre de Grace's annual Seafood Festival is in mid-August, in Millard E. Tydings Park and features artisans and crafters and, of course, "local and regional seafood delicacies."

Shopping: Keep an eye out for antiques, including decoys, as you hunt through the shops and galleries, including Franklin Street Antiques and Gifts (464 Franklin St., 410-939-4220); Seneca Cannery Antique Mall, a must-do in a huge former tomato cannery (201 Saint John St., 410-942-0701); Courtyard Bookshop (316 Saint John St., 410-939-5150); and Washington Street Books and Music with over 60,000 books and 100,000 comics (129-131 N. Washington St., 410-939-6215). Check out Vincenti Decoys at 353 Pennington Ave. (888-573-6301). Galleries include The Picture Show Custom Framing and Fine Art Gallery (301 St. John St.), and River View Gallery (224 N. Washington St., 410-939-6401). Island Jack features women's accessories, including Vera Bradley (114 N. Washington St, 410-939-4414). For something a little different, check out the Mount Felix Vinyard and Winery (410-939-0913) for tastings, but be sure to call about hours. Saturday mornings in the summer, the Farmer's Market offers produce, flowers and baked goods on Pennington Ave.

Restaurants: A large variety of restaurant choices are within easy walking distance of the town marinas. The renovated Tidewater Grille now sports an enclosed patio and a second deck, thereby expanding water views. Call for reservations at 410-939-3313 (300 Franklin St.). You might also want to try the Laurrapin Grille, named for an Appalachian word for "tasty" (209 N. Washington St., 410-939-4956), Price's Seafood for hardshell crabs (650 Water St., 410-939-2782), MacGregor's Restaurant for casual dining (331 Saint John St., 410-939-3003) or Silks Restaurant at Bulle Rock (320 Blenheim Lane, 410-939-8887). For treats, check out hometown Bomboy's Candy and Bomboy's Ice Cream (322 & 329 Market St., 410-939-2924). Get your coffee fix at Java by the Bay (118 N. Washington St., 410-939-0227).

ADDITIONAL RESOURCES

- HAVRE DE GRACE TOURISM: www.hdgtourism.com
- HARFORD COUNTY, MARYLAND TOURISM: www.harfordmd.com

NEARBY MEDICAL FACILITIES

Harford Memorial Hospital: 501 S. Union Ave., Havre de Grace, MD 21078, 443-843-5000

NEARBY AIRPORTS:

Harford County Airport: Churchville, MD 21028 410-836-2828

Baltimore-Washington International Thurgood Marshall Airport : www.bwiairport.com (38 miles)

Susquehanna River, Havre de Grace, MD

HAVRE DE GRACE		Largest Vessel Accommodated	VHF Channel Monitored	Transient Berths / Total Berths	Approach / Dockside Depth (reported)	Floating Docks	Gas / Diesel	Groceries, Ice, Marine Supplies, Snacks	Repairs: Hull, Engine, Propeller	Lift (tonnage), Crane, Rail	Min/Max Amps	Laundry, Pool, Showers, Courtesy Car	Pump-Out Station	Nearby: Grocery Store, Motel, Restaurant
		Dockage					Supplies		Service					
1. Havre de Grace City Yacht Basin	410-939-0015	35	16	24/240	6/5	-	GD	IS	-	-	30/50	S	P	GMR
2. Penn's Beach Marina (Internet Access)	410-939-4444	200	16	20/119	6/4	F	-	I	-	-	30/100	LPS	P	R
3. Log Pond Marina	410-939-2221	90	16/09	6/70	15/5	F	-	-	HEP	L15, C8	30/50	LS	P	GMR
4. Tidewater Marina (Internet Access) (Wireless Internet Access)	800-960-8433	60	16/09	10/160	14/8	-	GD	IMS	HEP	L35, C	30/50	LSC	P	GMR
5. Havre de Grace Marina	410-939-2161	30	-	3/40	16/6	F	-	IM	HEP	L15, C	30/30	S	-	GMR
6. Owens Marina	410-642-6646	40	-	6/180	50/4	F	-	IM	-	L	30/30	PS	P	GR

Corresponding chart(s) not to be used for navigation. Internet Access, Wireless Internet Access, Waterway Guide Cruising Club Partner

See www.WaterwayGuide.com for current rates, fuel prices, web site addresses, and other up-to-the-minute information.

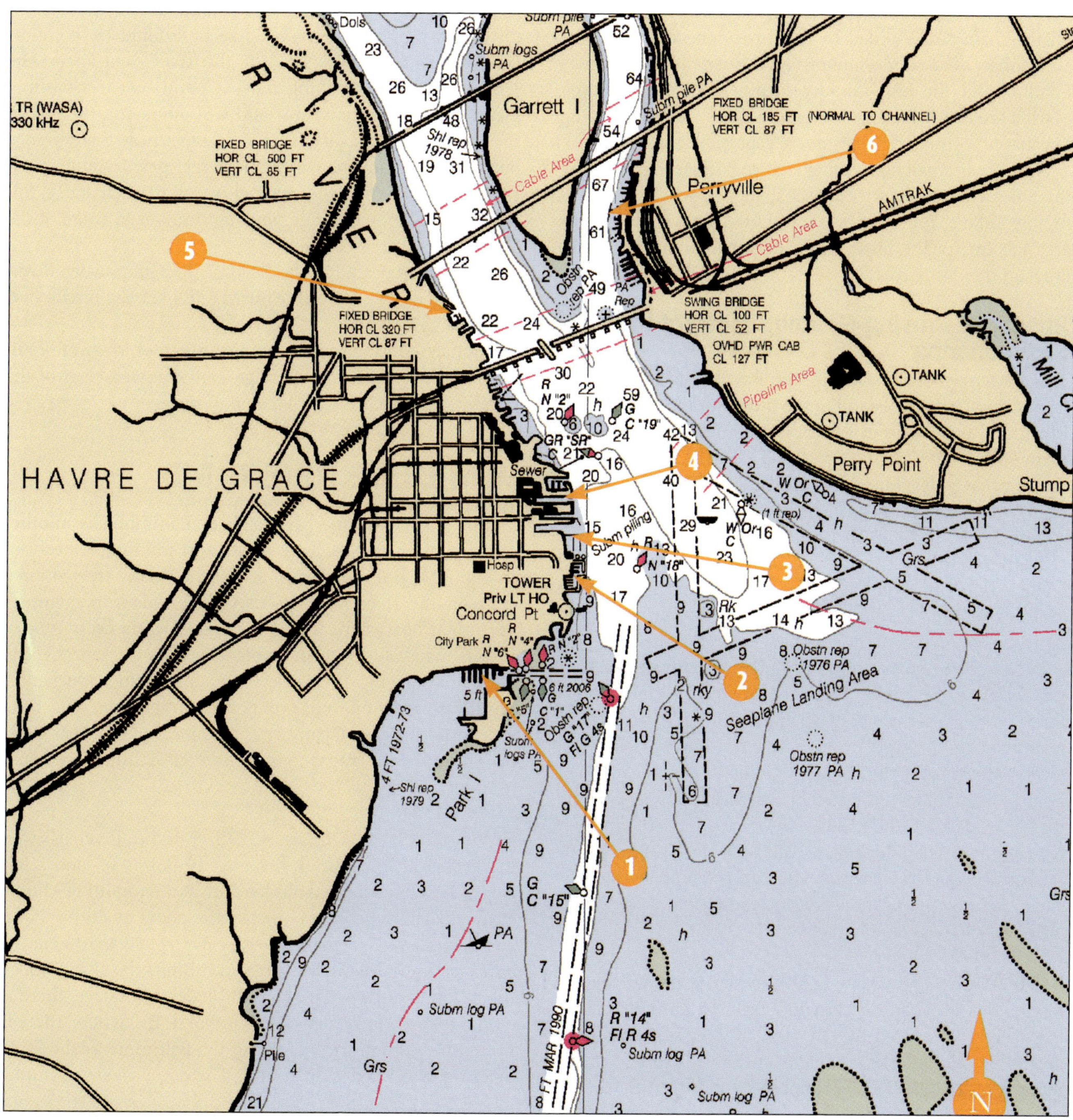

Perryville, MD

Perryville and Port Deposit, on the Susquehanna

The small town of Perryville is across the river from Havre de Grace. Perryville has two facilities: Owens Marina, which has transient slips in conjunction with a condominium development, and the friendly, low-key Perryville Yacht Club. The Rendezvous Restaurant is about a block from Owens Marina. Give 24-hours' notice if you cannot clear the 52-foot vertical clearance Amtrak Railroad Bridge at Perryville, so the tender can open it. The area is growing with considerable new development.

Port Deposit, a bit upriver from Perryville, is one of the most scenic little towns on the Bay, but the lack of transient dockage makes it hard to visit by boat. About four layers of houses hang onto the side of the cliff just off the waterfront. Recent restoration of the beautiful old Victorian row houses and stone buildings (literally carved from local rock) on the main street added to the town's cheerful and neat atmosphere. The condominiums on the waterfront at Tomes Landing and the high-and-dry facility at Tomes Landing Marina are the only signs of modern times. Tomes Landing Marina, unfortunately, does not accept transients.

Note: Only small boats can go above Port Deposit because the Susquehanna River becomes shallow, rocky and full of rapids. Take a guide unless you know the river well. This area has one of the most renowned smallmouth bass fisheries on the East Coast.

Aberdeen Proving Ground, South of the Susquehanna

The western shore of Chesapeake Bay, below the Susquehanna from Spesutie Island to the mouth of the Gunpowder River, and northwest of Pooles Island, lies within the U.S. Army's Aberdeen Proving Ground. This is the Army's testing area for newly developed weapons. Daily explosions during testing are audible more than 30 miles away. The lower sections of both the Bush River and the Gunpowder River also fall into this restricted area. Anchoring, swimming and going ashore are prohibited. The restricted navigation area is closed Monday through Friday from 7:00 a.m. until 5:00 p.m., except on federal holidays.

White patrol boats with an orange stripe warn straying vessels away from the restricted area. You can contact these patrol boats on VHF Channel 68 and 16 for information about passing through the restricted areas. Most local marinas carry the "Boater's Guide to Restricted Water Zones," a pamphlet published by Aberdeen Proving Ground that provides all the details (www.apgmwr.com/images/recreation/boatersguide.pdf or call 410-278-1150). Up the Bush and Gunpowder rivers, you can get supplies at a few small, friendly places that serve local craft.

Bush River

NAVIGATION: Use Chart 12274. When permitted by the restrictions of Aberdeen Proving Ground, entrance to the Bush River is marked by red nun "2" followed by lighted green "3" and a series of marks continue, keeping to the middle of the river as you proceed north with depths generally greater than 7 feet. About 6 miles above the river's mouth, a bascule bridge blocks further progress unless your vessel can fit under the 12 foot vertical clearance. The opening schedule for this bridge is extremely limited and set well in advance.

Anchorage: It is possible to anchor in Doves Cove, just north of Briery Point in 7 foot depths. Deeper in the cove the depths drop rapidly. Further up the river, just past quick green "WR7", an anchorage in the mouth of Lauderick Creek carries depths of about 5 feet.

Gunpowder River

NAVIGATION: Use Chart 12273. Keeping aware of the restrictions at Aberdeen Proving Ground, the well-marked entrance to the Gunpowder River is fairly easy to navigate. The river offers 5- to 7-foot depths throughout most of its length. Just south of Pooles Island, locate the 27-foot tower (flashing white every 2.5 seconds) and lay a course for flashing red buoy "2G" at the river's entrance. The remaining buoys (flashing reds "4" and "6" and flashing green "7") should be visible and will guide you the rest of the way in. Depths vary from 7 to 9 feet near the entrance but shallow to an average of 5 to 6 feet past flashing green "9" at Battery Point. The channel is well marked and, if followed carefully, will guide you well upriver to some of the Gunpowder's prettier reaches.

Dockage: Located at the head of the Gunpowder River, Gunpowder Cove Marina features a full-service repair yard and sells gas.

Anchorage: The broad cove just north of Maxwell Point is a popular weekend anchorage, but stay well clear of the point itself, which is restricted at all times.

MIDDLE RIVER, MD

Middle River, within easy reach of Baltimore, is another active boating area. A large number of marinas, waterfront restaurants and boatyards serve the many recreational craft on the river. Flotillas of Power Squadron members keep their boats here, and you can see nearly every type of vessel imaginable. You may also see old Chesapeake Bay log canoes racing in Hawk Cove on summer weekends. For information on local events and attractions, contact the Essex-Middle River Chamber of Commerce (443-317-8763) or The Marine Trades Association of Baltimore County (410-687-1002).

NAVIGATION: Use Chart 12278. Middle River is well marked clear to its head, but give all points of land a fair berth. Two fixed lighted markers are at the mouth of Middle River: Flashing green "5" marks the shoal at Booby Point and flashing red "6" marks Bowley Bar. A new marker at the entrance to Middle River lists speed limits; be sure to obey them. On Saturdays, Sundays and federal holidays, there is a 6-knot speed limit above Wilson Point. Elsewhere, there is no limit except in the vicinity of the Baltimore Yacht Club, where it is 6 knots year-round. There is a move to imple-

Gunpowder River, MD

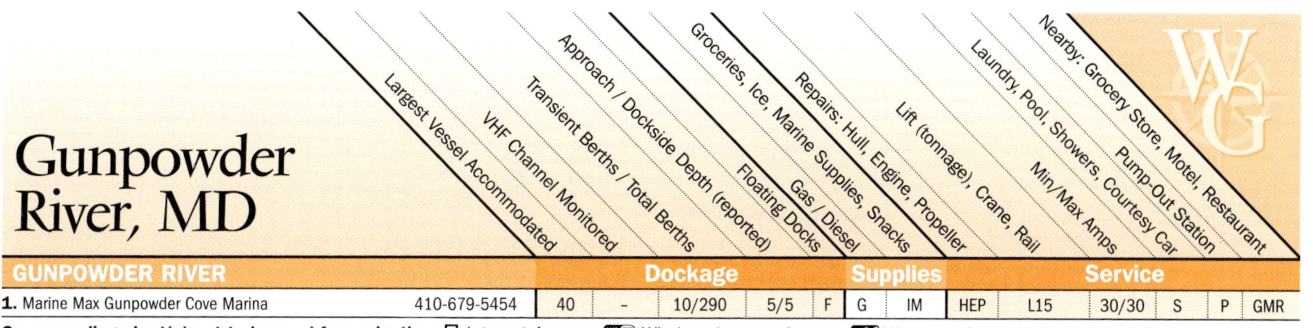

GUNPOWDER RIVER		Largest Vessel Accommodated	VHF Channel Monitored	Transient Berths / Total Berths	Approach / Dockside Depth (reported)	Floating Docks	Gas / Diesel	Groceries, Ice, Marine Supplies, Snacks	Repairs: Hull, Engine, Propeller	Lift (tonnage), Crane, Rail	Min/Max Amps	Laundry, Pool, Showers, Courtesy Car	Pump-Out Station	Nearby: Grocery Store, Motel, Restaurant
		Dockage					Supplies		Service					
1. Marine Max Gunpowder Cove Marina	410-679-5454	40	-	10/290	5/5	F	G	IM	HEP	L15	30/30	S	P	GMR

Corresponding chart(s) not to be used for navigation. Internet Access Wireless Internet Access Waterway Guide Cruising Club Partner

See www.WaterwayGuide.com for current rates, fuel prices, web site addresses, and other up-to-the-minute information.

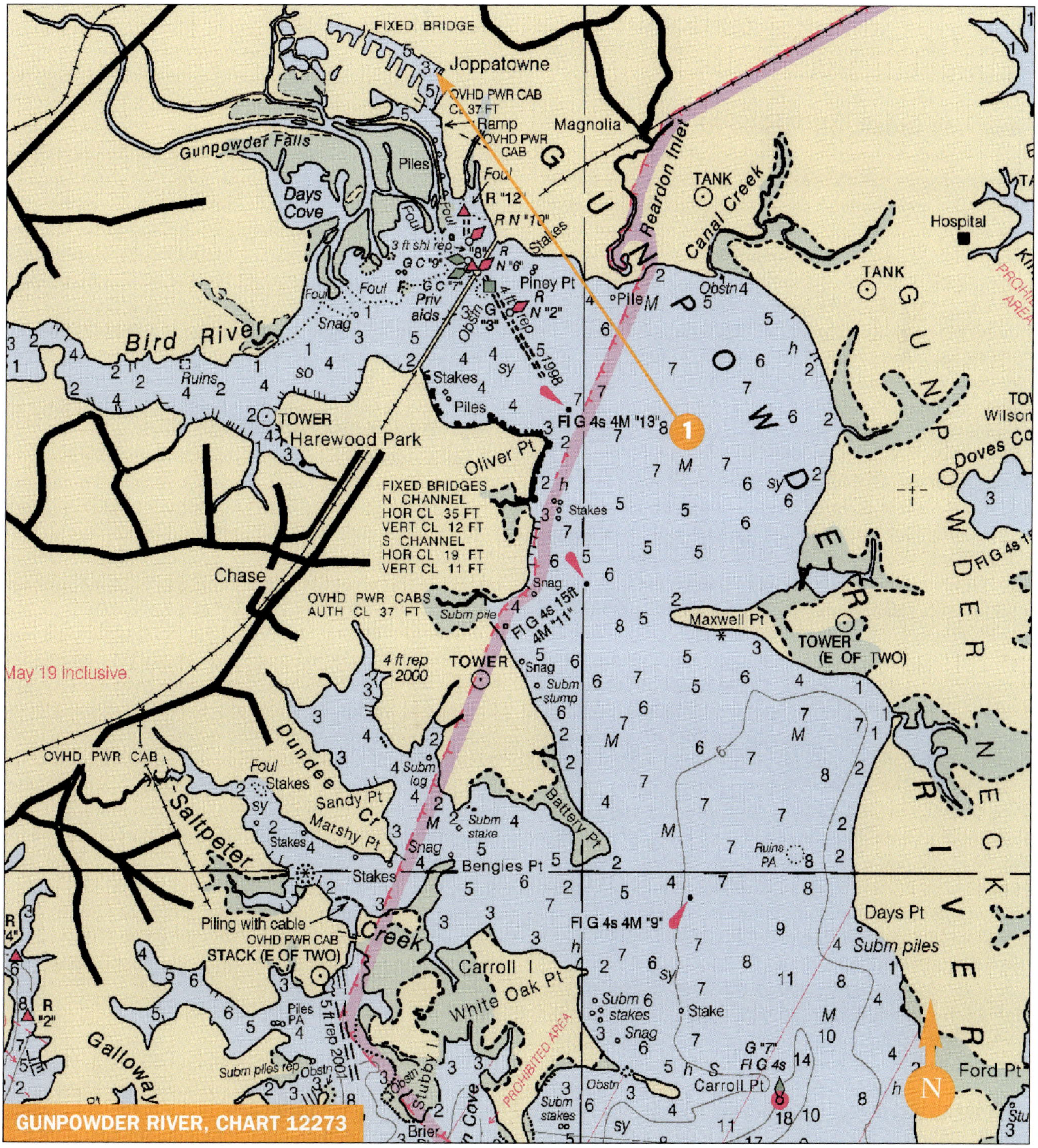

GUNPOWDER RIVER, CHART 12273

ment a 6- knot limit from the mouth of the river in the future, so watch carefully for the speed markers.

Dockage: Virtually every one of Middle River's creeks has yacht facilities. Not all can accommodate cruising craft, but several cater to those who want short-term dockage. Please refer to the marina locator chart and listings for details.

Anchorage: The northwest shore of Hart-Miller Island, southeast of Middle River's mouth, is a popular anchorage even though it is exposed to the north; a speed limit deters water skiers' wakes. All of Middle River is a concentrated boating area with lots of local traffic, but you will find especially pleasant overnight anchorages upstream at Frog Mortar Creek, Hopkins Creek and Sue Creek (at the river's mouth). Martin State Airport, near the head of Dark Head Creek, is active with air traffic and can be noisy.

Galloway Creek, off Middle River

This rounded, Y-shaped creek is immediately to starboard after entering the mouth of Middle River and clearing Bowley Bar and Bowley's Marina. It carries depths of 5 to 8 feet except near the shore. Holding ground is decent in firm to soft mud, with plenty of room to clock around with tide and wind. Galloway Creek is open to the south, however, and heavy boat traffic along Middle River tends to make the creek a better lunchtime anchorage than for overnight stays.

Dockage: One of the largest facilities on the Bay, 500-slip Bowley's Marina is located at the entrance to Galloway Creek northwest of quick flashing red "6," just west of charted Bowley Bar. Galloway Creek Marina is nearby.

Frog Mortar Creek, off Middle River

Frog Mortar Creek is the next creek to starboard as you continue up Middle River; turn to starboard on entry. The unique name of this creek is said to come from a corruption of a local family name, Throckmorton. Look for the flashing red (2+1) marker and a white-and-orange buoy off Wilson Point, marking the beginning of a speed-control area. This creek has plenty of deep water, many anchorages and a nature-lover's atmosphere, as well as several long-established commercial facilities for cruisers. The only stipulation offered here is the possible noise from nearby Martin State Airport, home of the Maryland Air National Guard.

Dockage: Chesapeake Yachting Center at the head of Frog Mortar can be useful for transiting cruisers, as there is a small shopping center within walking distance with hardware and liquor stores, along with a Wal-Mart. Edwards Boat Yard is nearby. Both sell fuel. Maryland Marina and Tradewinds Marina, Inc. are closer to the entrance of the creek, and Long Beach Marina is at Galloway Point, at the mouth of the creek. You can also dock at the Wild Duck Café (410-335-2121), located at Maryland Marina to starboard just past the airport runway and red "2". They offer complimentary dockage for patrons and a varied menu, along with entertainment on many weekend nights.

Stansbury Creek, off Middle River

The same white-and-orange buoy marks the entrance to peaceful Stansbury Creek, which offers good anchorages and nice swimming areas bordering Martin State Airport at Strawberry Point. This is the home of the Baltimore County Marine Police, the local Maryland Department of Natural Resources Police and the Maryland State Police Medevac helicopters. Noise can be an issue here, due to Martin State Airport's traffic.

Dark Head Creek

Back at Wilson Point and the flashing red (2+1) junction marker, continue up Middle River to reach Dark Head Creek. Leave green daybeacon "7" and green/red daybeacon "CP" to port as you head up the creek. At the head of the creek is the original home of the World War II-vintage Glenn L. Martin Company; a variety of seaplanes built at the plant were launched and tested here at Martin's Lagoon. Just beyond Carson's is Wilson Point Park. It features a children's playground, picnic pavilions and a boat ramp. From here, the Glenn L. Martin Maryland Aviation Museum at the airport (free admission) is a short walk.

Dockage: Stansbury Yacht Basin Inc. is located at the mouth of the creek. To starboard just before Martin Lagoon, Carson's Creekside Restaurant (410-238-0080) specializes in steaks and seafood (dine in or take out) and has slips available for patrons.

Anchorage: This secure anchorage is a popular place to waterski (some days have speed limits), and marine facilities are nearby.

Hopkins Creeks, off Middle River

To reach beautiful Hopkins Creek, go up the Middle River past the flashing red (2+1) marker at Wilson Point, until you reach the green and red "CP" junction marker off Clark Point, which you will leave to starboard as you turn to port into Hopkins Creek for a lovely, protected haven on either of its two branches. This is a busy thoroughfare, but the right-hand branch is less crowded and more scenic.

Dockage: Marli's Dockside Grill & Crabhouse (410-574-6275) serves casual lunch and dinner fare, offers slips for patrons and even provides dockside service. Riverwatch Restaurant, Marina & Nightclub is a popular local night spot with frequent entertainment and is well known for their beef and seafood, as well as the parties on weekends. This might not be the spot for a quiet night. Nearby is Markley's Marina, and farther up Hokins Creek is Deckleman's Boatyard and Essex Marina and Boat Sales, which may have transient space. Around the corner are Cutter Marine Inc. and Riley's Marina.

Deep water continues to the headwaters of Middle River, where there are still more marinas and businesses available. See the marina listings and locators in this section for details.

Hogpen and Norman Creeks, off Middle River

NAVIGATION: Use Chart 12278. Hogpen Creek and Norman Creek share an entrance to the southwest of Wilson Point. Hogpen Creek is the left-hand branch, and Norman Creek is marked by red daybeacon "2." Sunset Harbor Marina provides a limited amount of transient space at the head of

Looking north over the broad Middle River and its many marinas. (Not to be used for navigation.) Waterway Guide Photography.

Norman Creek. Both creeks are scenic with good anchorages and are favorite fishing spots among locals. Commercial facilities here mingle tastefully with private homes.

Sue Creek, off Middle River

NAVIGATION: Use Chart 12278. The entrance to Sue Creek, marked with 15-foot-high flashing green "1," is located to port after you enter Middle River past flashing green "5."

Dockage: It is home to the Baltimore Yacht Club (reciprocal privileges), as well as a few commercial facilities. Look for the Baltimore Boating Center if you need a tie-up for the evening; the marina has transient slips available.

Anchorage: Channel depths vary between 4 and 5 feet, and you can anchor here, just beyond the Yacht Club in pleasant residential surroundings.

Seneca Creek, North of Middle River

NAVIGATION: Use Chart 12278. Seneca Creek's entrance, marked by 18-foot-high flashing red "2S," is directly to the north of the mouth of Middle River. The channel is unmarked after this point but reportedly carries 5-foot depths all the way to the towering twin smokestacks of the Charles P. Crane power plant. Belonging to the Baltimore Gas and Electric Company, these stacks provide a reliable landmark both day and night in all kinds of weather. Beware of the charted obstructions and pilings, most of which are to port past flashing red "2S."

Dockage: A quiet community with several commercial facilities surrounds Seneca Creek; locals consider it a safe storm harbor. Porter's Seneca Marina has a small number of slips for transients and a fuel dock (gas only). Beacon Light Marina provides transient dockage during season (April 1 through November 30) and Goose Harbor Marina is here as well.

Hart-Miller Island, Hawk Cove— South of Middle River

Dredge spoil from Baltimore Harbor is gradually forming the 1,140-acre Hart-Miller Island, which forms the southern border of Hawk Cove. The southwestern shore of the island contains the 244 acre Hart-Miller Island State Park, with public restrooms, decks, a three- story observation tower and campsites. It includes a 3000-foot sandy beach. Use of the impoundment for dredge spoil stopped at the end of 2009 and the rest of the island is now being developed into protected wildlife habitat.

Anchorage: Hawk Cove is a fair-weather anchorage; avoid it if the wind is from the north or west. Note the long shoal, marked with red nun "2," extending south from Booby Point into Hawk Cove. The beach on the northwest side of the island is a popular weekend spot, complete with picnic tables, but you can only reach it by small boat or dinghy. The clean, sandy bottom shoals gradually here, and many people anchor out and wade ashore.

In 2011, the cut between Hart-Miller Island and the mainland Patapsco River Neck was dredged and offers minimum depths of 8 feet throughout. But boat traffic is heavy at times and the channel is quite narrow, so proceed carefully in deep draft boats.

BACK RIVER, MD

Back River is popular with sailors seeking in-water or boat-ramp marina services on the upper Western Shore. The Baltimore area is an alternative to Annapolis, where marina

Seneca Creek, Middle and Back River, MD

		Largest Vessel Accommodated	VHF Channel Monitored	Transient Berths / Total Berths	Approach / Dockside Depth (reported)	Floating Docks	Gas / Diesel	Groceries, Ice, Marine Supplies, Snacks	Repairs: Hull, Engine, Propeller	Lift (tonnage), Crane, Rail	Min/Max Amps	Laundry, Pool, Showers, Courtesy Car	Pump-Out Station	Nearby: Grocery Store, Motel, Restaurant
		Dockage					Supplies		Service					
SENECA CREEK														
1. Beacon Light Marina (Internet Access) (Wireless Internet Access)	410-335-6200	40	-	8/80	6/5	-	G	GIM	HEP	L15	30/30	S	P	GR
2. Porter's Seneca Marina	410-335-6563	50	16	5/5	6/3	F	G	IM	HEP	L30	30/50	PS	P	GMR
3. Goose Harbor Marina	410-335-7474	45	-	/200	6/5	-	G	IM	HEP	L	30/30	LPS	P	R
MIDDLE RIVER														
4. Bowleys Marina (Wireless Internet Access)	410-335-3553	55	09	10/500	8/6	-	GD	I	HE	L30	30/50	LPS	P	-
5. Galloway Creek Marina (Waterway Guide Cruising Club Partner)	410-335-3575	50	-	1/188	5/5	-	-	-	HEP	L15, C10	30/30	S	-	-
6. Baltimore Yacht Club	410-682-2310	74	-	RECIPROCAL PRIVILEGES		-	GD	IS	-	-	30/50	LPS	P	R
7. Baltimore Boating Center	410-687-2000	41	-	10/60	6/6	-	-	IM	HEP	L10	30/30	S	-	R
8. Long Beach Marina (Internet Access) (Wireless Internet Access)	410-335-8602	50	16	12/327	10/8	-	GD	IM	HEP	L35	30/50	LPS	P	GMR
9. Maryland Marina (Wireless Internet Access)	410-335-8722	55	-	10/360	9/6	-	-	IM	HP	L25	30/30	LS	P	GR
10. Edwards Boat Yard, LLC	410-335-2311	55	-	3/124	8/5	-	-	I	HEP	L50	30/30	S	-	GR
11. Tradewinds Marina Inc.	410-335-7000	45	-	5/78	6/6	F	-	IMS	HEP	L15	30/30	S	P	GR
12. Chesapeake Yachting Center (Wireless Internet Access)	410-335-4900	80	-	/200	6/8	-	GD	GIMS	HEP	L25	30/50	LPS	P	GMR
13. Stansbury Yacht Basin Inc. (Internet Access)	410-686-3909	45	-	/80	9/4	F	G	IM	HE	L8	30/30	S	P	R
14. Markley's Marina Inc.	410-687-5575	60	-	/53	9/6	F	-	M	HEP	L60, C	30/30	S	P	GR
15. Riverwatch Restaurant, Niteclub & Marina	410-687-1422	50	-	15/110	12/5	-	GD	IS	-	-	30/50	S	P	GR
16. Sunset Harbor Marina (Wireless Internet Access) (Waterway Guide Cruising Club Partner)	410-687-7290	50	-	2/35	4/4	-	-	I	HEP	L30	30/30	S	P	GMR
17. Deckelman's Boatyard Inc.	410-391-6482	50	16	10/10	6/6	-	-	M	HEP	L40, C	50/50	-	-	GR
18. Essex Marina & Boat Sales (Wireless Internet Access)	410-686-3435	50	16	10/70	8/7	-	-	IMS	HEP	L25, C	30/30	PS	P	-
19. Cutter Marine Inc. (Internet Access)	410-391-7245	60	-	/125	9/6	F	-	IMS	HEP	L25	30/50	PS	P	GMR
20. Riley's Marina	410-686-0771	40	-	10/95	6/5	-	-	M	HEP	L15	50/50	S	P	GMR
BACK RIVER														
21. West Shore Yacht Center (Internet Access) (Wireless Internet Access)	410-686-6998	50	-	15/85	8/4	F	G	IM	HEP	L10	30/30	LS	P	GR

Corresponding chart(s) not to be used for navigation. Internet Access — Wireless Internet Access — Waterway Guide Cruising Club Partner

See www.WaterwayGuide.com for current rates, fuel prices, web site addresses, and other up-to-the-minute information.

space can be scarce at times. The lack of development along Back River's wooded shoreline is a refreshing surprise so close to industrial Baltimore. This is a pleasant excursion, although the shallow water past red nun buoy "10" (4- to 7-foot depths) calls for a shoal-draft vessel. Although undeveloped, Back River does not have highly-protected anchorages since it is wide and exposed to the south and, to a lesser extent, the east.

NAVIGATION: Use Chart 12278. As you emerge from Middle River heading toward the Bay, turn southeast at flashing green "5" toward red nun buoy "2," making sure you give Booby Point a wide berth. From red nun buoy "2," proceed southwest down Hawk Cove toward flashing green "3" at Drum Point, and then wind carefully as you round Rocky Point (red nun buoy "6") toward the entrance to Back River. Check locally before using the small, marked channel between the mainland at Black Marsh and Pleasant Island (to the southwest of Hart-Miller) and proceed cautiously. Depths here may be less than 5 feet at mean low water and are only charted at 4.5 feet.

Dockage: West Shore Yacht Center is on the eastern shore of the Back Riverand has slips, gas and performs some boat repairs.

PATAPSCO RIVER TO BALTIMORE

Baltimore Harbor (Patapsco River) and its tributaries bustle with big-ship traffic. When visibility is poor, the ever-present tankers and barges can present navigational problems for small boats. Even on clear days, keep a sharp lookout astern, as these fast-moving giants can be right on your stern before you know it. There is generally room for cruising boats outside the main channels, and it is advisable to travel there whenever possible. The Coast Guard also advises that big ships can sometimes create 12-foot seas at Sevenfoot Knoll on the Craighill Entrance Channel. (NOAA Chart 12278 also warns of the same issue.)

A cruise up the Patapsco River offers a glimpse of the workings of industry and contrasts sharply with the renovated Baltimore Inner Harbor. However, two creeks on the lower south side—Bodkin Creek, at the mouth of the Patapsco, and Rock Creek, the next up the river—are major upper Western Shore boating centers. Stony Creek, just past Rock Creek, offers several good anchorages.

NAVIGATION: Use Chart 12278. Back north on the main Bay channel northwest of Fairlee Creek, use the auxiliary channel to save time to the Patapsco River and Baltimore.

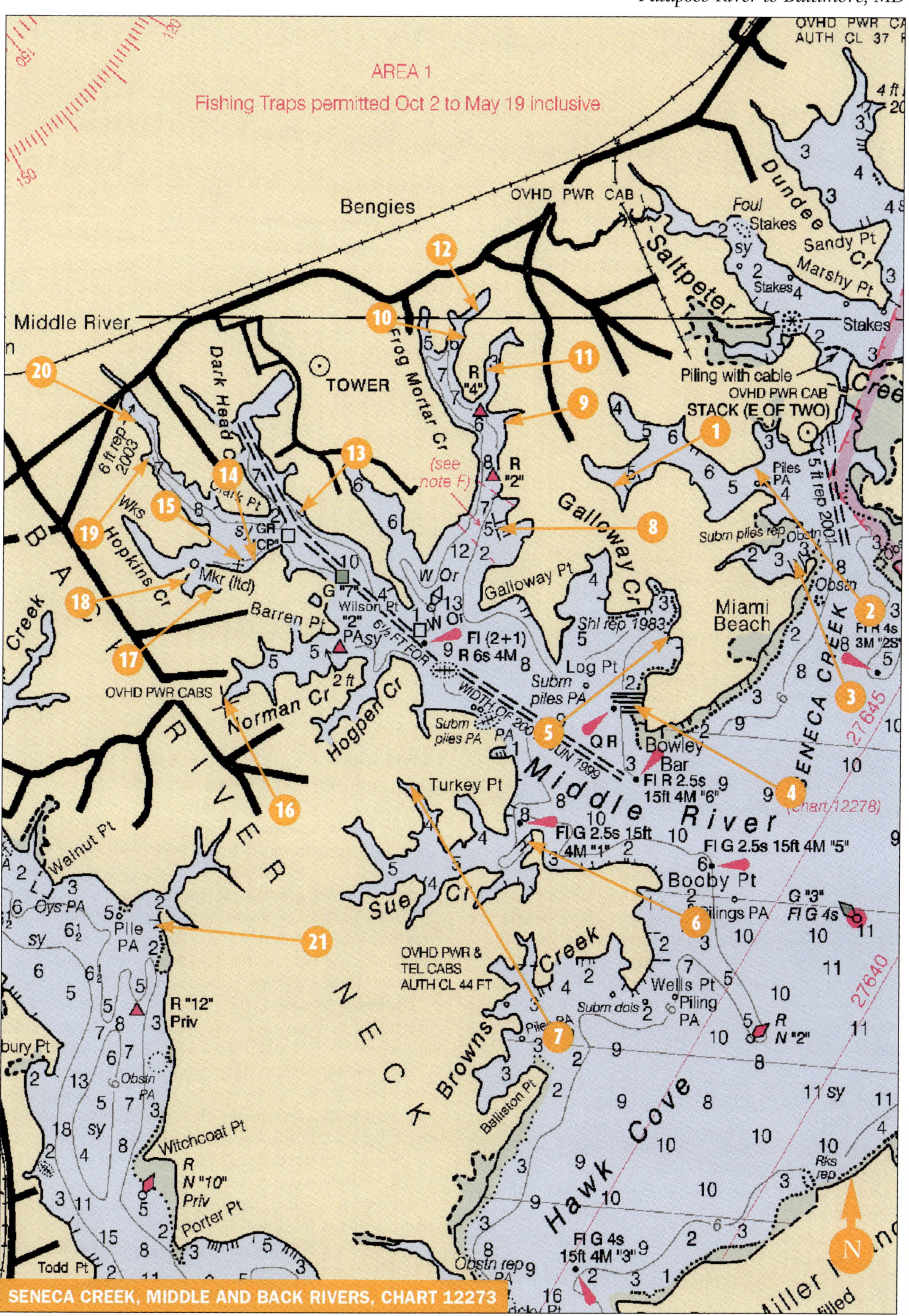

SENECA CREEK, MIDDLE AND BACK RIVERS, CHART 12273

Patapsco River, Baltimore, MD

PATAPSCO RIVER		Dockage					Supplies		Service					
		Largest Vessel Accommodated	VHF Channel Monitored	Transient Berths / Total Berths	Approach / Dockside Depth (reported)	Floating Docks	Gas / Diesel	Groceries, Ice, Marine Supplies, Snacks	Repairs: Hull, Engine, Propeller	Lift (tonnage), Crane, Rail	Min/Max Amps	Laundry, Pool, Showers, Courtesy Car	Pump-Out Station	Nearby: Grocery Store, Motel, Restaurant
1. Pleasure Cove Marina	**410-437-6600**	**200**	**69**	**20/60**	**7.5/7.5**	**-**	**GD**	**GIMS**	**HEP**	**L100**	**30/50**	**LPS**	**P**	**GR**
2. Atlantic Marina Resort	410-437-6926	37	-	/47	3/4	-	G	IMS	HE	L35	30/30	PS	P	R
3. Maryland Yacht Club	410-255-4444	75	09	/120	15/12	-	GD	I	-	-	30/50	LPS	P	R
4. Fairview Marina	410-437-3400	100	-	6/112	12/9	-	-	IM	HEP	L, C, R	30/50	LPS	P	GR
5. White Rocks Marina	410-255-3800	60	-	/375	14/10	-	-	I	HEP	L35	30/30	-	P	-
6. Oak Harbor Marina	410-255-4070	70	-	/95	15/8	-	-	M	HEP	L40, C15	30/30	LS	P	R
7. Anderson's Marine Service	410-255-1007	50	-	-	14/6	-	-	GIM	HEP	L	30/30	S	P	-
8. Pasadena Yacht Yard Inc.	410-255-1771	50	-	/55	12/8	-	GD	M	-	-	30/30	-	-	GMR
9. Maurgale Inn & Marina	410-437-0402	60	-	120/141	13/10	-	GD	-	HEP	L20, C, R	50/50	S	P	MR
10. Young's Boat Yard, Inc.	410-477-8607	40	-	4/100	6/6	-	-	-	-	L15	-	S	P	-
11. Anchor Bay East Marina	410-284-1044	150	16	20/75	12/9	F	GD	IMS	HEP	L75, C8.5	30/50	LS	P	GR
12. Sheltered Harbor Marina	410-288-4100	50	-	/172	8/10	F	-	-	HEP	L, C	30/30	LS	P	GR
BALTIMORE														
13. Baltimore Marine Center/Pier 7 (Boatel)	410-675-8888	100	16	/84	18/18	F	GD	IMS	HEP	L80	30/100	LPS	P	GMR
14. Baltimore Marine Center at Lighthouse Point	410-675-8888	300	16	100/500	20/16	F	GD	GIMS	HEP	L85	30/200+	LPS	P	GMR
15. Anchorage Marina	410-522-7200	150	16/67	100/565	15/15	F	-	IS	-	-	30/50	LPS	P	GMR
16. The Crescent Marina	**443-510-9341**	**60**	**16**	**/52**	**15/8**	**-**	**-**	**G**	**-**	**-**	**30/50**	**L**	**P**	**GR**
17. Henderson's Wharf Marina	410-732-1049	45	16/72	30/245	20/8	F	-	I	-	-	30/50	LS	-	GMR
18. Inner Harbor East Marina	410-625-1700	300	16	25/115	16/6	F	-	I	-	-	50/100	LPS	P	GMR
19. City of Baltimore Public Docks	410-396-3174	300	68	20/150	20/20	-	-	-	-	-	30/100	S	-	GMR
20. Baltimore Inner Harbor Marine Center	410-837-5339	300	16/69	100/135	40/15	F	GD	IM	-	-	50/200+	LS	P	GMR
21. HarborView Marina	410-752-1122	300	16	20/278	30/30	F	-	IS	-	-	30/100	LPS	P	GMR
22. Tidewater Yacht Service @ Port Covington Maritime Center	410-625-4992	300	16	10/28	30/30	F	-	IMS	HEP	L75, C18	30/100	SC	P	GMR

Corresponding chart(s) not to be used for navigation. Internet Access Wireless Internet Access Waterway Guide Cruising Club Partner

See www.WaterwayGuide.com for current rates, fuel prices, web site addresses, and other up-to-the-minute information.

Pick up this shortcut channel off Fairlee Creek, east of Pooles Island. The main channel buoy numbers are flashing green buoy "33" and flashing red buoy "34." Pick up the auxiliary channel marker, flashing green buoy "9," leaving it to starboard when southbound. Next, leave quick flashing red buoy "8" to port, and then go to flashing green buoy "7," just off the southern tip of Pooles Island. From there, follow a west-southwesterly course to the Brewerton Channel. It is not marked as a straight line until you get to the southern end of Pooles Island. A conspicuous marker (27 feet high) for Pooles Island is on course, just beyond flashing green buoy "7," which you should also leave to starboard. Be wary of crab trap floats in this "trap-free" channel. Depths are 10 feet or more.

Bodkin, Back and Main Creeks, off the Patapsco

Seven foot Knoll Light (58 feet high, flashing white every six seconds), a red skeleton tower on a platform with riprap around the base, serves as a useful marker for locating the entrance to Bodkin Creek. Dredging has deepened and widened the channel, but keep a lookout for freighters and other commercial vessels.

NAVIGATION: Use Chart 12278. From Seven foot Knoll Light, head southwest to intercept flashing green (2.5 second) "7" near the mouth of Bodkin Creek. From here, you can follow the creek in through its narrow, shoal-flanked mouth. Coming from the south, begin with flashing green (4-second) "3" northwest of the Craighill Angle. Shoaling is worst between green daybeacon "9A" and flashing green "7" in the entrance. Follow the markers, and go slowly; you will find good water inside as you go upstream. Even though the entrance to Bodkin Creek is a float-free channel, keep a lookout for the crab trap floats.

Dockage: Pleasure Cove Marina & Club is near the navigable head of Main Creek, the central and largest branch of Bodkin Creek, at the mouth of the Patapsco River. The creek's tributaries have steep, wooded banks and are generally deep inside. Pleasure Cove Marina offers large boat hauling, repairs, dry storage, and slips. You can golf next door, work out in the marina gym or play a few sets at the on-grounds tennis courts. Then, take a dip in the pool. The Cheshire Crab restaurant (410-360-2220) is on site, offering a full American menu, frequent specials and entertainment and docking is free for diners. The marina provides water taxi service on Bodkin Creek, making it easy to access the Cheshire Crab. Call them on VHF channel 69; they will be there until last call to return you to your boat.

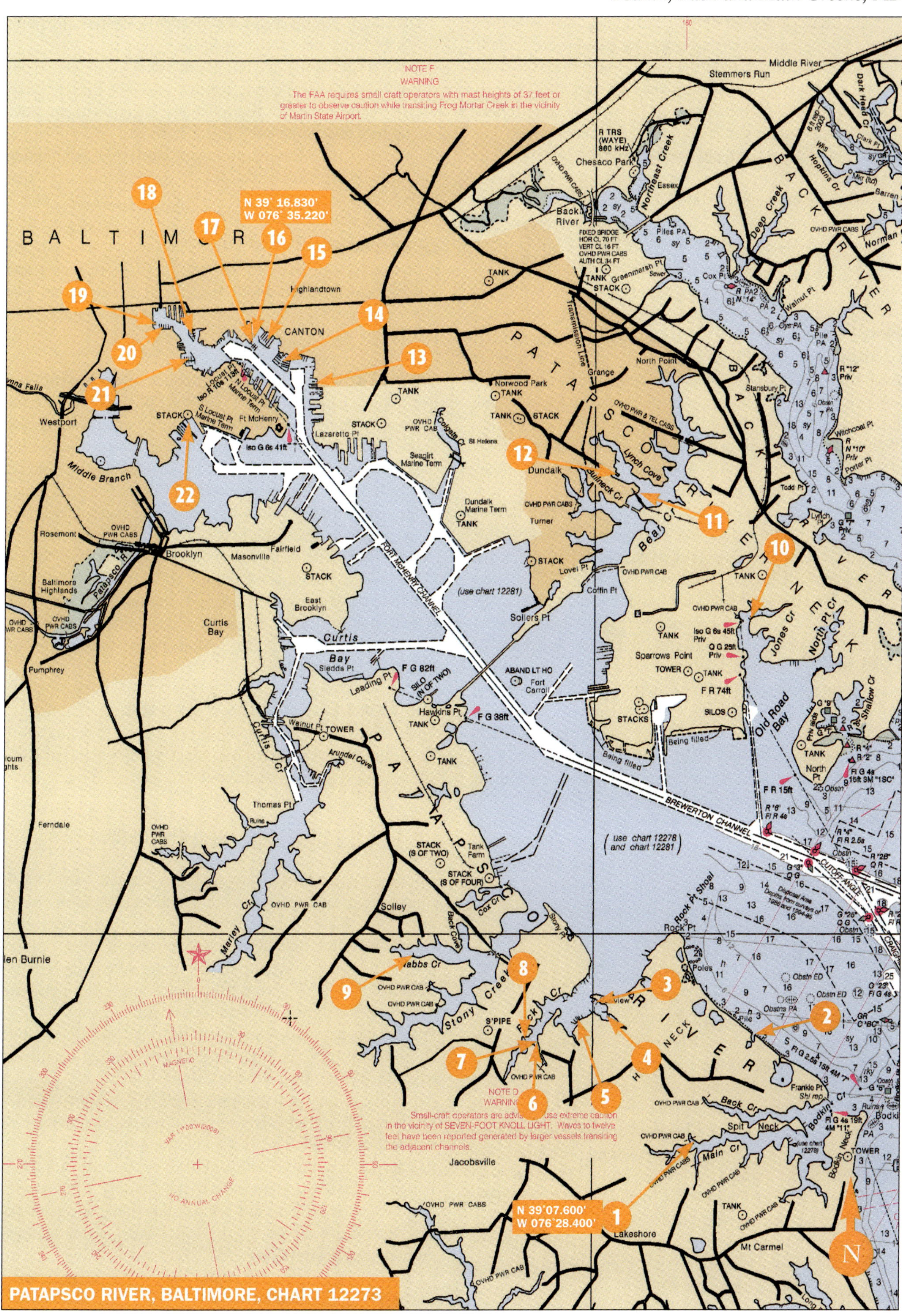
NOTE F
WARNING
The FAA requires small craft operators with mast heights of 37 feet or greater to observe caution while transiting Frog Mortar Creek in the vicinity of Martin State Airport.
N 39° 16.830'
W 076° 35.220'
BALTIMORE
CANTON
Highlandtown
PATAPSCO
BACK RIVER
Middle River
Stemmers Run
Chesaco Park
Northeast Creek
Essex
Deep Creek
Back River
North Point
Dundalk
Lynch Cove
Bullneck Cr
Bear Cr
Jones Cr
North Pt Cr
Old Road Bay
Shallow Cr
Sparrows Point
FORT McHENRY CHANNEL
BREWERTON CHANNEL
CUTOFF ANGLE
Ft McHenry
Lazaretto Pt
Seagirt Marine Term
Dundalk Marine Term
Middle Branch
Westport
Brooklyn
Masonville
Fairfield
East Brooklyn
Curtis Bay
Curtis Cr
Sledds Pt
Leading Pt
Hawkins Pt
Sollers Pt
Fort Carroll
Arundel Cove
Thomas Pt
Ferndale
Baltimore Highlands
Rosemont
Pumphrey
Marley Cr
Glen Burnie
Solley
Cox Cr
Rock Pt Shoal
Rock Pt
Stony Creek
Nabbs Cr
Back Cove
Rock Cr
Back Cr
Main Cr
Spit Neck
Bodkin Cr
Bodkin Neck
Lakeshore
Mt Carmel
Jacobsville
(use chart 12281)
(use chart 12278 and chart 12281)
NOTE D
WARNING
Small-craft operators are advised to use extreme caution in the vicinity of SEVEN-FOOT KNOLL LIGHT. Waves to twelve feet have been reported generated by larger vessels transiting the adjacent channels.
N 39°07.600'
W 076°28.400'
N
PATAPSCO RIVER, BALTIMORE, CHART 12273

Back Creek forks off to starboard, just inside Bodkin Creek. On its banks stands Hancock's Resolution; built in the mid-1600s, it is one of the oldest houses in Maryland. Several small yards and marinas are on Back Creek.

Anchorages: About half way up Main Creek and to port, Jubb Cove is a popular anchorage. Holding is good;, just stay to the south of the Main Creek channel. Almost directly across the creek from Jubb Cove is a small anchorage just to the east of the unnamed point there. Out closer to the creek entrance, south of red "12", is a large, open anchorage. This is fairly open to the north and can be choppy in any wind with a northerly component. This is also a popular area for water skiing.

Rock Creek, off the Patapsco

NAVIGATION: Use Chart 12278. You can easily identify Rock Creek, about four miles upriver, by the huge, partially submerged rocks off its entrance, marked with a white light, flashing 4 seconds. The formation, known (and charted) as "White Rocks," has been a navigational landmark since the time of Capt. John Smith. Beware of the shoal extending out from Rock Point. The channel into Rock Creek is straightforward.

Dockage: On the way to Rock Creek from Bodkin Creek, you will pass Atlantic Marina Resort, which has a reported 3-foot approach depth. Just inside, sheltered by Fairview Point, is the Maryland Yacht Club, a convenient place to get gas and diesel fuel. Just beyond the Yacht Club, Fairview Marina offers transient dockage, with a swimming pool and courtesy car, but no fuel. White Rocks Marina has a ship's store with a good selection of goods. Several other marinas are available farther up Rock Creek, including Oak Harbor Marina, Anderson's Marine Service and Pasadena Yacht Yard, although only a few offer berthing for transients. Most of these are boatyards specializing in repairs so call ahead before planning to spend the night.

Anchorage: The open cove between Maryland Yacht Club and White Rocks Marina is a popular anchorage in Rock Creek. Tar Cove, the second cove to port in Rock Creek, has 8- to 12-foot depths with good holding. Above Water Oak Point, you will find additional, very protected spots. Sound your way in, and choose a place with suitable depths. Note the 6-mph speed limit.

Stony Creek, off the Patapsco

NAVIGATION: Use Chart 12278. Well-marked Stony Creek is deep and easy to enter. The creek's entrance, recognizable by the red cliffs, merits some caution: Flashing red "4" is landward of the one-fathom line, so give it a wide berth. The entrance has at least 10-foot depths, and the creek's tributaries carry depths of 10 feet or more. The speed limit is 6 knots. You may contact the drawbridge (18-foot closed vertical clearance), which carries state Route 173 across Stony Creek, on VHF Channel 13 (or by phone: 410-255-6630). The bridge has various restrictions during morning and afternoon rush hours that change frequently, so call ahead to the bridge tender if you plan to navigate above the bridge.

Dockage: Maurgale Inn & Marina is located on Nabbs Creek and may have transient space.

Anchorage: Good anchorages in Stony Creek are Nabbs Creek, with 9- to 11-foot depths, and Big Burley Cove, off the main branch of Stony Creek, beyond the entrance to Nabbs Creek. Both are on the starboard side above the bridge and are pleasant and well protected, with good holding and wooded banks. Back Cove is a nice cove that branches off Nabbs Creek.

Bear Creek, off the Patapsco

Bear Creek, with facilities and repairs for both power and sail, is on the northern side of the Patapsco River, just above Sparrows Point and northeast of the Francis Scott Key Bridge.

NAVIGATION: Use Chart 12281. A buoy marks the entrance to the side channel south of Fort Carroll and leads into the creek, which has 10-foot depths in the center and holds good depths to the shoreline. There are three bridges: the Key Causeway Bridge with a 55-foot fixed vertical clearance, a bascule bridge that opens on signal (25-foot closed vertical clearance) and a railroad swing bridge that stays open except when a train is due (8-foot closed vertical clearance).

Dockage: Sheltered Harbor Marina is to port on Lynch Cove, and it has repair facilities and a lift. Just past the railroad bridge is Anchor Bay East Marina. They are a full-service boatyard with a 25-ton and an 80-ton travel lift, along with both gas and diesel. There is also a restaurant and bar on the premises.

Old Road Bay, off the Patapsco

Jones Creek and North Point Creek are off Old Road Bay. This is the location of Young's Boat Yard, which has transient slips on floating docks and sells gas and diesel.

BALTIMORE HARBOR

An expanding 21st-century skyline welcomes you to Baltimore. A great industrial center and busy seaport, many miles from the Atlantic, Baltimore is an attractive city with close-knit ethnic neighborhoods, interesting 18th-century architecture and a revitalized downtown where new condominiums seemingly sprout from the ground overnight. The Inner Harbor attracts thousands of mariners each year to its excellent restaurants, convenient marinas and imaginative shoreside attractions, including an outstanding aquarium, a science center, historic ship exhibits and Harborplace, an expansive dining and shopping area. Like Boston's Quincy Market, Harborplace offers every cuisine imaginable, as well as nautical supplies and elegant clothing stores.

There is an extra historical treat when you approach by water. Near the Francis Scott Key Bridge, a buoy with red and white stripes, and a blue star-spangled top marks the spot where the poet wrote the words to our national anthem. During the War of 1812, Key was a prisoner aboard a British barge and was looking for the flag above nearby Fort McHenry during the siege.

NAVIGATION: Use Charts 12278 and 12281. **Use Baltimore tide tables.** It is an easy run up the Patapsco to Baltimore, with a current that is not too strong, plenty of aids to navigation and well-disciplined commercial traffic. Note that Inner Harbor rules prohibit swimming, wakes, liveaboards and waterskiing. After passing Sparrows Point and the huge Bethlehem Steel plant (on the north shore of the Patapsco), proceed beneath the Francis Scott Key Bridge (185-foot vertical clearance at center). Once past the bridge, watch for the star-spangled buoy about 0.3 miles past the bridge in the summer months, June 1 to November 1.

Beyond the bridge to port is Curtis Bay, with a big Coast Guard station and repair yard, and many industrial plants. Curtis Creek is navigable about six nautical miles upriver, well past the bascule bridges off Walnut Point. The bridge carrying Interstate 695 has 60 feet of vertical clearance, but the bascule bridge carrying Pennington Avenue is only 40 feet. To request an opening of the Pennington Avenue Bridge, call 410-396-1154 at least an hour in advance and again on VHF Channel 13 or by phone when you arrive. Opening the I-695 Bridge during its restricted operating hours requires a call to the Key Bridge Police (410-537-7600) at least two hours in advance. You must coordinate the opening times and contact both operators if you need the I-695 Bridge opened, too. The railroad swing bridge near the Coast Guard station is normally open except when trains approach, but call 410-355-1439 for arrangements.

Across from Curtis Bay on the Patapsco is the Dundalk Marine Terminal, where containerships and other freighters load and unload cargo.

Note: Consult the *Local Notice to Mariners* online (www.navcen.uscg.gov) for the latest navigation restrictions around the Inner Harbor, as they change from time to time. Look under District 5.

Dockage: As you approach Fort McHenry, take the right-hand channel, charted as Northwest Harbor, to reach the Baltimore Inner Harbor, which has a strictly enforced 6-mph speed limit. You will find accommodations at the marinas and at the city docks, which are farther in. The public docks, straight ahead at the head of the Inner Harbor, do not accept reservations. You can use any unoccupied space except for the pier heads and the area used by the Clipper City (a large sailing vessel located on the southernmost pier). Call on VHF Channel 68 for information, or call the dockmaster at 410-396-3174.

Baltimore Marine Center at Lighthouse Point and Baltimore Marine Center at Pier 7 are the first large marinas on the starboard side as you enter the Northwest Harbor and Inner Harbor area. The Baltimore Marine Center at Pier 7 is primarily a boatel but does offer fuel and boat repairs. Anchorage Marina, also close by and easily recognizable by their bright blue awnings, offers transient dockage and has a floating pool and pump-out service. Baltimore Marine Center, Anchorage Marina, Cresent Marina and Henderson Wharf Marina are all convenient to the popular Fells Point and Canton neighborhoods. Baltimore Inner Harbor Marine Center, to port upon entering, has a restaurant on site and is a short walk to the aquarium, museums, Harborplace shops and restaurants. The marina also offers gas and diesel at their fuel dock. A white flashing light on a floating dock, past the fuel dock, marks the dockmaster's office; check via VHF before tying up. Inner Harbor East Marina is to starboard, a few hundred yards east of the National Aquarium. Tidewater Yacht Service Center's popular fuel docks remain at their current location (under the Domino Sugars sign), but their dockage has moved to the Port Covington Maritime Center, located on the south side of Locust Point in the Middle Branch of the Patapsco. HarborView Marina is located to port as you clear Locust Point at the base of a large white condominium and office building. They accept transients at their floating docks.

Anchorage: We advise anyone traveling in the Inner Harbor call ahead to the Harbor Dockmaster at 410-396-3174 before anchoring. You do not need to show an anchor light in the designated Inner Harbor anchorage area near the World Trade Center (between the submarine and the pier), which is marked by white buoys (not mooring buoys). The bottom here is very soupy, so dig in your anchor under power. Depths are around 20 feet, and the anchorage is fine in quiet weather, although the harbor is crowded with tourist-powered paddleboats, water taxis and visiting boats on weekends. A dinghy dock is located near the anchorage area, but be prepared to pay a fee. There is an anchoring opportunity between the Anchorage Marina and Baltimore Marine Center. You can anchor in 10 to 12 feet of water with mud, so dig your anchor in well. There is a public dinghy dock and easy access to markets and West Marine.

GOIN' ASHORE: **BALTIMORE, MD**

Baltimore is a city of neighborhoods, many of them benefiting from the winning mix of old-timers and newcomers. Then there is the added bonus of being on or near the water. The Baltimore Waterfront Promenade is a 7.5-mile walkway connecting people to the Inner Harbor and other points of interest. There is much to see along the way. Besides the waterfront and the neighborhoods—Little Italy, Mount Vernon, Federal Hill, Locust Point, Fells Point and Canton—there is a surprising array of museums. If walking isn't to your liking, hop on a water taxi.

The city's nickname, Charm City, came about in 1974, when an ad man came up with the idea of giving visitors a charm for a bracelet when they visited various landmarks. That idea never materialized, but the name stuck. It is easy to see why.

History: The name Baltimore is an Anglicized version of "Baile an Ti Mhoir," a Gaelic phrase meaning "Town of the Big House" and referring to the seat in County Cork of Lord Baltimore, for whom the city was named in 1729. One of the city's most historic events was not so much the defense of Fort McHenry during the Battle of Baltimore in 1814, as the fact that it inspired Francis Scott Key to write "The Star-Spangled Banner" here.

A February 19, 1861, clash between pro-South civilians and Union troops led to what is regarded as the first bloodshed of the Civil War. Later, Baltimore became an industrial

National Aquarium
Harborplace
Inner Harbor
Maryland Science Center

Looking north over Baltimore's Inner Harbor. (Not to be used for navigation.) Waterway Guide Photography.

center for chemicals, steel and textiles. A 1904 fire destroyed more than 1,500 buildings. The city slipped into decline in the 1970s, before urban renewal came to town, starting with the then-abandoned docks at the harbor, which are now called Harborplace—a bustling restaurant and shopping area.

Points of Interest: Check in at the Baltimore Visitor Center, 401 Light St. (www.baltimore.org), one of the most active on the East Coast. That way you're sure to pick up the latest happenings in the almost overwhelmingly active city.

The National Aquarium overlooking the Inner Harbor, includes dolphins, reptiles, an Australia exhibit, a 4D Immersion Theater and more. South of the Harbor is the Maryland Science Center, with a dinosaur wing, a planetarium and ever-changing exhibits. The Baltimore Museum of Industry, which pays homage to the city's industrial heritage, is located in the historic Platt Oyster Cannery Building in South Baltimore.

For sports fanatics, Oriole Park at Camden Yards and M&T Bank Stadium for the Ravens are about 3 blocks, or a 10-minute walk, from the harbor. Right next door, in an old railroad station, you will find Sports Legends at Camden Yards, with exhibits on the Baltimore Colts, the Orioles and others. Upstairs, there is an entirely different, yet similarly nostalgic, museum—Geppi's Entertainment Museum, which celebrates pop culture like comic books, cartoon characters, toys and more. The Babe Ruth Birthplace and Museum is a few blocks away. Near Camden Yards is the B&O Railroad Museum, housed in an original roundabout and featuring "Tom Thumb," the first American steam engine, along with preserved railway cars and equipment.

Baltimore, MD

Craving the unusual? You will find it at the American Visionary Art Museum, featuring amazing and sometimes loopy works by self-taught artists. For the more mainstream, there is the Baltimore Museum of Art, three miles north of the Inner Harbor or the Walter's Art Museum on North Charles. Also for something different, try the National Pinball Museum in the old chocolate Factory building on Water Street next to Power Plant Live! You can play the machines and also take a workshop on the electronics and art behind the machines.

History buffs will want to check out The Flag House Museum and Star-Spangled Banner Museum. The Flag House was the home of Mary Young Pickersgill, who made by hand the 30- by 42-foot flag that flew over Fort McHenry and inspired Francis Scott Key. The Star-Spangled Museum next door has a replica of the flag. The Fort McHenry National Monument and Historic Shrine is located at 2400 E. Fort Ave.

The Baltimore Area Convention and Visitors Association has a list of other tours on its web site, www.baltimore.org/

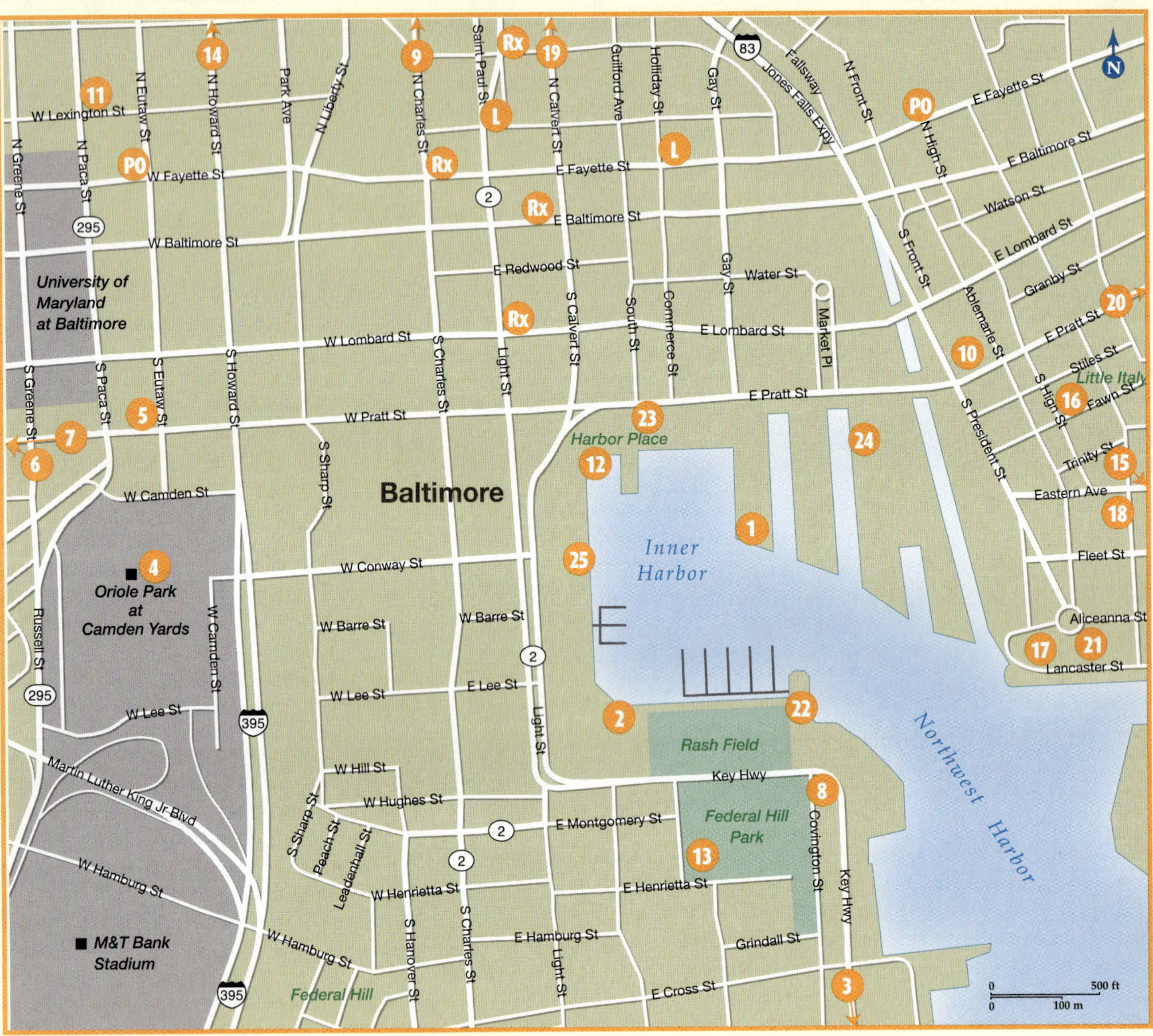

Reference the marina listing tables to see all the marinas in the area.

POINTS OF INTEREST

1 National Aquarium
2 Maryland Science Center
3 Baltimore Museum of Industry
4 Oriole Park at Camden Yards
5 Sports Legends/Geppi's Entertainment Museum
6 Babe Ruth Museum
7 B & O Railroad Museum
8 American Visionary Art Museum
9 Baltimore Museum of Art
10 Flag House/Star Spangled Museum

SHOPPING

11 Lexington Market
12 Harborplace
13 Federal Hill
14 Antique Row Stalls

DINING

15 Sabatino's
16 Chiapparelli's
17 Charleston Restaurant
18 Lemongrass
19 The Prime Rib
20 Obrycki's Crab House
21 Oceanaire Seafood Room
22 Rusty Scupper
23 Water Table
24 Power Plant

INFORMATION

25 Baltimore Visitors Center

L LIBRARY

PO POST OFFICE

Rx PHARMACY

Baltimore's Skyline. (Photo courtesy of Baltimore Area Convention and Visitors Association.)

visitors, while Walk Baltimore offers suggestions for self-guided tours at www.walkbaltimore.com. "Walk on the wildside" and see Baltimore on a Segway through Segs in the City (800-734-7393). If you prefer to walk while golfing, consider Mount Pleasant Golf Course at 6001 Hillen Road (410-254-5100).

Special events: In April, Federal Hill holds a Spring Block Party with music and food. In May, it is off to the races with The Preakness Derby Celebration, featuring events at Pimlico Park during the week leading up to the famed horse race. During the Preakness Crab Derby at Lexington Market, celebrities use spray bottles and long sticks with balls to coax crabs across the finish line, with the "purse" going to charity. June brings the Jazz and Blues Festival to Federal Hill. The Fourth of July is celebrated with fireworks, music, a parade and food vendors at the Inner Harbor. Artscape, the country's largest free public arts festival, features artists, craftspeople and fashion designers selling their goods over three days in mid-July (www.artscape.org). The Baltimore Book Festival, with author appearances and children's activities, typically occurs in late September at Mount Vernon Place. If you are still out cruising in October (a prime month on the Bay), you can satisfy your sweet tooth at the Chocolate Festival at Lexington Market. Maybe you can even enter—or win—the chocolate-eating contest.

Shopping: Harborplace—adjacent shopping pavilions at the water's edge—is where it all began, in terms of revitalizing the waterfront at the Inner Harbor. The buildings contain more than 100 shops, plus a plethora of eateries and restaurants. Harborplace is now home to more national chains than local stores and caters to families, although the famous Philip Seafood with its piano bar still reins. The second level is now a Ripley's Believe It or Not. From May to September, the water taxi starts here, hail them on VHF Channel 71 for a ride to shore (410-563-3900). Farther north off the water, Lexington Market, which first opened in 1782, has vendors selling produce, baked goods and, of course, seafood, including J.W. Faidley of crab cake fame.

The locals refer to 36th Street in Hampden as "The Avenue," where you will find boutiques, antiques stores, thrift shops. "Must sees" include Ma Petite Shoe, selling shoes and chocolate; Hometown Girl, for everything Baltimore; Atomic Books, selling alternative and underground publications; and Red Tree, for home furnishings and handmade goods.

Historically hip Federal Hill is home to unique shops such as the women's clothing store Holly G. Boutique, a gourmet dog bakery called Lucky Lucy's Canine Café, The Gilded Peach jewelry store and Patrick Sutton Home Antiques & Home Furnishings.

The fast-growing Harbor East neighborhood that came into being about a decade ago offers upscale shopping. Boutique and specialty shops dot Charles Street in the Mount Vernon neighborhood. Antique Row Stalls on North Howard Street has 10,000 square feet of antiques and art galleries.

Dining: It is just not possible to do justice to Baltimore's array of restaurants in so short a space. If you crave Italian cuisine, head to Little Italy. Some of the mainstays there are Sabatino's Italian Restaurant (410-727-2667) on Fawn Street, and Chiapparelli's (410-837-0309) open since 1940, on South High Street. You will find a concentration of restaurants at Harbor East, including Charleston Restaurant (410-332-7373) and Lemongrass (410-327-7835). For beef, head to The Prime Rib (410-539-1804) on North Calvert. Obrycki's Crab House (410-732-6399) on East Pratt Street is a local institution known for its steamed crabs. Oceanaire Seafood Room, with its Art Deco design, is an upscale seafood restaurant (801 Aliceanna St., 443-872-0000) convenient to the northwest harbor area. The Rusty Scupper has an unbeatable waterfront view at the Inner Harbor Marina (410-727-3678) and Harborplace now has a Bubba Gump Shrimp Co. and Johnny Rockets (www.harborplace.com). More waterview can be found at Watertable in the Renaissance Harborplace Hotel and the Power Plant is home to Houlihan's for burgers, and the Hard Rock Café on the waterfront.

ADDITIONAL RESOURCES

- **BALTIMORE VISITORS CENTER:** 401 Light St., Baltimore, MD 21202, 877-225-8466 www.baltimore.org

NEARBY MEDICAL FACILITIES

The Johns Hopkins Hospital: 600 N. Wolfe St., Baltimore, MD 21201, 410-955-5000

University of Maryland Hospital: 22 S. Greene St., Baltimore, MD 21201, 410-328-8667

Mercy Medical Center: 301 Saint Paul Place, Baltimore, MD 21202, 410-332-9000

Maryland General Hospital: 827 Linden Ave., Baltimore, MD 21201, 410-225-8000

NEARBY AIRPORT:

Baltimore-Washington International Thurgood Marshall Airport: 410-859-7100, www.bwiairport.com (7 miles)

TRANSPORTATION: City bus lines, taxis, water taxi and light rail are all readily available.

Looking northwest over the Patapsco River, Fells Point and Canton. (Not to be used for navigation.) Waterway Guide Photography.

GOIN' ASHORE: FELL'S POINT, MD

Fell's Point, just east of the Inner Harbor, is one of Baltimore's favorite and most spirited neighborhoods. With cobblestone sidewalks, a historic district and waterfront location, it is no wonder the area's row houses have been rediscovered and rehabbed. In fact, architecture is one of the main attractions in Fell's Point. From the Inner Harbor, you can get there by water taxi, or if you are in the mood for a meandering night, explore the Harbor East neighborhood, and then head into Fells Point.

History: Until the mid-19th century, Fell's Point was the second busiest port of entry for immigrants after Ellis Island, which helps account for a diversity of residents and restaurants even today. The original deep-water port in Baltimore, Fell's Point played a role in both the Revolution and the War of 1812. Several famous ships were built here, as were the first schooners that became known as "Baltimore clippers." The neighborhood was threatened by the expansion of Route 95 back in 1967, when locals banded together in opposition to the project.

Points of Interest: The Fell's Point Visitor Center at 1724 Thames St. is run by the Preservation Society, which also offers several tours relating to immigration, ghosts, the harbor and more. For more details, visit www.preservationsociety.com.

The Frederick Douglass Isaac Myers Maritime Park features exhibits on Douglass' life in Baltimore, from his childhood as a slave to his success as an abolitionist, on Myers, a free-born African-American who worked his way up in the shipyards to various positions of prominence and on Baltimore's black

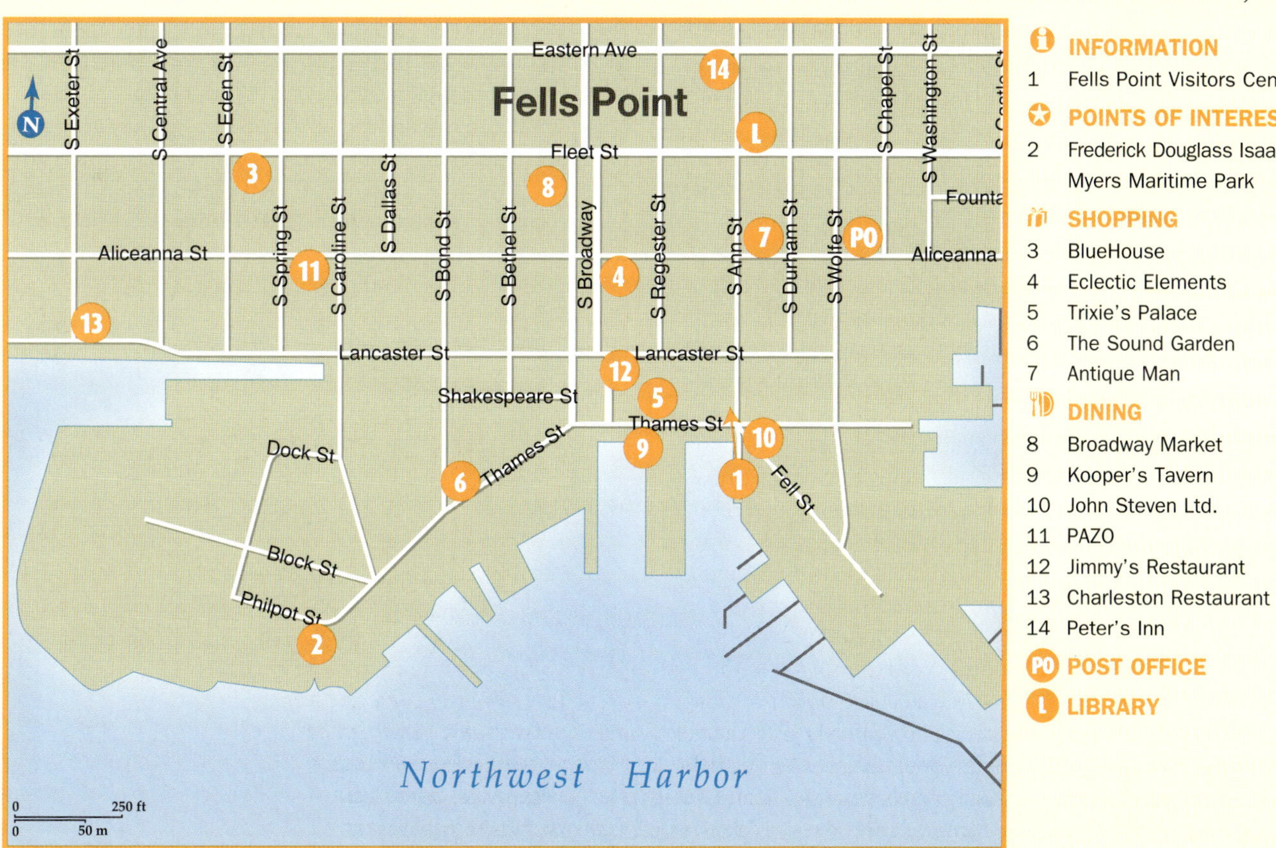

Reference the marina listing tables to see all the marinas in the area.

community in the 1800s. Reginald F. Lewis Museum of Maryland African American Culture features exhibits in three main areas: Maryland's black families and communities, black art and intellect, and the labor experiences of blacks. Lewis, a Baltimore native, was a Harvard graduate, a successful lawyer, entrepreneur and philanthropist.

Special events: In mid-April, the annual Fell's Point Privateer Day and Pirate Invasion celebrates the role of privateers in helping to defeat the British in the War of 1812. Events take place along the waterfront at Thames Street and Broadway, with period music, pirate storytelling, a mock sword battle and more. Visitors are encouraged to dress as wenches, merchants, pirates, sailors or privateers. On the first Friday of each month, you can check out new shows and other offerings at studios and galleries located along the Fells Point Art Loop, from 5:00 p.m. to 9:00 p.m. Some restaurants located along the loop walk offer specials.

Shopping: Shop for the home at BlueHouse on Fleet Street or Eclectic Elements on South Broadway. If you need to spice up your T-shirt selection with something at once retro and fashion forward, head to Trixie's Palace on Thames Street, then maybe amble to over to the independent record store, The Sound Garden. There are plenty of galleries and antique shops in the area, including The Antique Man, which occupies several storefronts on Fleet Street. Here you will find a ball of twine, more than 800 pounds that once made its home at the now-closed Haussner's Restaurant. The Fell's Point Farmers Market happens every Saturday during the summer on the Broadway Square.

Restaurants: Fell's Point is teeming with eateries. Kooper's Tavern (410-563-5423) serves great burgers and crab cakes on the Fell's Point waterfront. The old wood at John Steven Ltd. (410-327-5561) will make you feel as though you have stumbled into a treasured local haunt; the seafood and sushi will make you wish you could be one of the regulars. Two of Baltimore's best-known restaurateurs, Cindy Wolfe and Dan Foreman, run Pazo (410-534-7296), a tapas joint in an old warehouse in Fells Point. Their mainstay is Charleston Restaurant at Harbor East. Peter's Inn is the quintessential Baltimore restaurant on Ann Street. At the historic Broadway Market, you will find specialty shops, cafés and vendors selling fresh food and baked goods.

A Taste of Little Italy Tour, a two-hour walking tour followed by a progressive dinner, can be arranged by calling Concierge Plus at 401-580-0350.

GOIN' ASHORE: **CANTON, MD**

Baltimore is a city of distinct neighborhoods, and Canton, organized around a square named for its founder, sits on the water not far from Fell's Point. Once primarily a working-class area, Canton has seen the arrival of younger residents moving into its classic Baltimore row houses, along with some trendy restaurants. Plans by a busy community organization to plant trees and flowers in a local park were recently underway.

This is a neighborhood where you can both sit on the water and pick blue crabs, or hit up CakeLove, the Washington, D.C.-based bakery that recently arrived in Baltimore owned by former Washington, D.C., lawyer-turned baker

Warren Brown, host of Food Network's "Sugar Rush." The latter resides in The Can Company, the renovated retail-office complex that formerly housed The American Can Company, which operated from 1895 to 1987.

History: Irish sea captain John O'Donnell purchased a waterside plantation in 1785 and named it Canton. Purportedly, the plantation was named for the origin of the ship's cargo that paid for its purchase. That included tea, silk and satin from Canton, China. The well-located, 1,981-acre property later evolved into a real estate company that oversaw the arrival of major industries such as a cotton mill, shipyards and later, even small oil refineries. European immigrants, including those from Poland, Ireland, Germany and Wales arrived and made the neighborhood their own. Baltimore clippers anchored here, and a horse racing track once thrived here. Today, a new generation is discovering the neighborhood's old row houses and waterfront convenience.

It is said that the neighborhood's Lazaretto Lighthouse, demolished in 1926, may have inspired Baltimore resident Edgar Allan Poe's unfinished "The Lighthouse."

Points of Interest: Canton Waterfront Park and the Korean War Memorial are located here. Give Fido a break from the cruising life at the Canton Dog Park, located just north of Boston Street at the corner of South Bouldin and Toone streets. Canton's library is the first of Baltimore's famous Enoch Pratt Library branches in continual use since 1886.

Special Events: Howl-O-Ween, for the costumed canine in your life, is held in late October.

Shopping: Boutiques, spas and shops dot the neighborhood. For boat supplies, there's a West marine at 2700 Lighthouse Point E. (410-563-8905).

Dining: Take the water taxi to Bo Brooks Restaurant (2701 Boston St., 410-558-0202) for crabs, or Dockside (3301 Boston St., 410-276-8900). The water taxi takes a continuous route to set stops around the harbor. Check with your marina for the closest stop. The taxi does not pick up from moored boats.

Remember those candies called Pop Rocks? They are served in an appetizer with sashimi-grade tuna at the culinary creative Jack's Bistro (3123 Elliot St., 410-878-6542). Baltimore's fabled National Bohemian beer, better known as "Natty Bo," lives on at the casual Tex-Mex-style Nacho Mama's (2907 O'Donnell St., 410-675-0898).

Reference the marina listing tables to see all the marinas in the area.

POINTS OF INTEREST
1 Canton Waterfront Park
2 Korean War Memorial
3 Canton Dog Park

SHOPPING
4 West Marine

DINING
5 Bo Brooks Restaurant
6 Dockside
7 Jack's Bistro
8 Nacho Mamas

LIBRARY

ADDITIONAL RESOURCES

- CANTON COMMUNITY ASSOCIATION: www.cantoncommunity.org

MAGOTHY RIVER

Between Baltimore and Annapolis, the entrance to the Magothy River is about five miles south of Bodkin Point, along the Craighill Channel below the mouth of the Patapsco. All along its six beautiful miles, the river has creeks to explore and anchorages to enjoy, where you can choose either good protection from foul weather or a wide exposure for cooling summer breezes. Being part of the Baltimore-Washington corridor makes this river a heavily-used place on weekends and is a favorite for boats to raft and party. For a quieter time, choose an anchorage farther up the river. If the wind is howling on the Bay, you can spend two or three days exploring this pretty tributary's calm waters, staying in a different cove each night.

NAVIGATION: Use Chart 12282. Baltimore Light, with its red base and white house, is not far from the narrow entrance. The channel is supposed to be free of floats, but a few of the abundant crab pots along the edges inevitably drift in, and small fishing boats crowd the space. There is a speed limit of 6 mph in the narrow entrance to the Magothy River, but not inside.

Dockage: On your way into the Magothy River, you will pass the Podickory Point Yacht & Beach Club, on the west side of the river before the entrance to the Little Magothy. Several other marinas and boatyards welcome transients once inside the Magothy River.

Sillery Bay, off the Magothy

Sillery Bay, inside the Magothy to starboard, is one of the most popular anchorages in the upper Chesapeake. Water-skiers, jet skiers and high-powered speedboats keep the area churned up at times. You can find good protection behind Dobbins Island in depths of 10 to 12 feet, but the holding is marginal in some places, so set your anchor well. Sound your way toward the shore—the water is fairly deep up close to the island. The beach on the north side of Dobbins Island is pretty, but stay below the high-water mark since this is private property. Dobbins is popular and crowded with weekend partiers.

North of Dobbins Island, pass to the north around Little Island towards red "2" leading to Grays Creek. After an extremely narrow entrance, it opens up into a compact basin with anchorage for a few boats. Atlantic Marina on the Magothy is located here and has transient slips.

Waterway Guide Photography.

BALTIMORE LIGHT
N 39°03.500'
W 076°24.000'

Gibson Island, on the Magothy

NAVIGATION: Use Chart 12282. To reach the facilities at Gibson Island (if you are invited—the island is strictly private), run north up the center of Sillery Bay to pick up the pair of flashing lights (flashing green "3" and quick flashing red "4") that mark Magothy Narrows, between Holland and Long points. Stay approximately 25 feet off each light to keep in the channel, and follow the private markers slowly into the landlocked inner harbor. A private, non-commercial corporation of residents controls access to the island, either by boat or by car over the causeway from the mainland. Residents own all the moorings, and only sponsored visitors can use them, by advance arrangement.

Dockage: The Gibson Island Yacht Squadon is private but may have slips; call ahead.

Anchorage: You can anchor in the bight between Holland Point and Purdy Point. Not controlled by the Gibson Island Association, this spot has excellent protection.

Clean Marinas Initiative

Those who live near the Chesapeake take their Bay seriously. In response, both Maryland and Virginia have government programs to improve the water and shoreline quality near marinas, whose fuels, lubricants, solvents and runoff make them potentially messy places.

The Maryland Department of Natural Resources (DNR) runs the Maryland Clean Marina Initiative (www.dnr.state.md.us/boating/cleanmarina). To be certified, a facility must conduct a survey of itself (with assistance from the DNR, if needed), go through a checklist, correct any environmentally unsound conditions and be inspected by a representative from the DNR. When this process is complete, a Maryland Clean Marina may carry the certification emblem on its advertising and signs.

Virginia launched a similar marine initiative program (www.virginiacleanmarina.com) in response to strong interest by the marina industry and recreational boaters, which is run by the Virginia Marina Technical Advisory Program. Their guidebook for certification is available online at www.vims.edu/adv/vamarina. The process is similar to that in Maryland, with a self-assessment, confirmation visit and an annual report. You will see the Virginia Clean Marina emblem on the better marinas throughout the southern Chesapeake Bay.

With the popularity of Clean Marina programs increasing, other states are following suit. For more information on Clean Marina programs in your area, simply perform a Web search.

Magothy River, MD

MAGOTHY RIVER		Largest Vessel Accommodated	VHF Channel Monitored	Transient Berths / Total Berths	Approach / Dockside Depth (reported)	Floating Docks	Gas / Diesel	Groceries, Ice, Marine Supplies, Snacks	Repairs: Hull, Engine, Propeller	Lift (tonnage), Crane, Rail	Min/Max Amps	Laundry, Pool, Showers, Courtesy Car	Pump-Out Station	Nearby: Grocery Store, Motel, Restaurant
		Dockage					Supplies		Service					
1. ~~Gibson Island Yacht Squadron - PRIVATE~~	410-255-7632	90	78A	-	12/8	-	-	-	HE	L25	30/30	-	P	-
2. Atlantic Marina on the Magothy	410-360-2500	40	-	/35	8/6	-	GD	IMS	HEP	L15	30/30	S	P	GR
3. Cypress Marine (WiFi)	410-647-7940	105	16	5/40	10/8.5	-	-	-	HEP	L50,C15	30/50	LS	P	GR
4. Magothy Marina (WiFi)	410-647-2356	50	16/09	25/182	17/10	-	GD	IS	E	-	30/50	LPS	P	GR
5. Ferry Point Marina Yacht Yard (WiFi)	410-544-6368	50	-	/100	8/10	-	-	IMS	HEP	L25,C	30/30	LS	P	GR
6. Fairwinds Marina	410-974-0758	36	-	/100	7/6	-	G	IM	EP	L25	-	S	-	-
7. Podickory Point Yacht & Beach Club (WiFi)	410-757-8000	50	69	3/100	6/6	-	-	I	-	L	30/50	LPS	P	-

Corresponding chart(s) not to be used for navigation. Internet Access (WiFi) Wireless Internet Access Waterway Guide Cruising Club Partner
See www.WaterwayGuide.com for current rates, fuel prices, web site addresses, and other up-to-the-minute information.

Known locally as the "horse farm" because of the large farm directly across the water to the north, it attracts many boats on weekends, but generally has plenty of room. Just north of Holland Point is the entrance to Cornfield Creek. A convoluted entrance is well marked, but requires close attention. Once inside, stay in the middle for 7- foot depths in a quiet, residential neighborhood. "Eagles Nest" is the nick name for a great anchorage spot on the south side of the channel headed inbound for the Gibson Island Yacht Club. The small bay is south of the line between Holland Point and Purdy Point is quiet and family oriented.

Deep Creek, off the Magothy

South across the river from Sillery Bay is Deep Creek, one of an unknown number of Chesapeake Bay creeks with the same name. This one, like most other Magothy branches, has 7- to 8-foot depths beyond red daybeacon "4" and is well marked. You can find gas, slips and repair services in the creek at Fairwinds Marina.

Broad Creek, off the Magothy

This underdeveloped anchorage elbows its way off the north side of the Magothy, just west of Sillery Bay. Secure even when whitecaps are churning up the Magothy, Broad Creek makes a good hurricane hole, but its 360-degree protection makes it uncomfortable in hot weather.

Anchorage: Enter slowly and watch the depth sounder, keeping midway between green daybeacon "3" and red daybeacon "2." Mind the charted, but unmarked shoals until you reach the northeast corner and be sure to stay clear of the very shallow tongue that juts out from the north. Anchor in 8- to 11-foot depths. You can also anchor behind the entrance shoal at green daybeacon "3," which is continually growing westward. This anchorage is open to the south and with the heavy boat traffic on weekends, it can be a bit rolly.

Blackhole Creek, off the Magothy

Anchorage: This snug harbor has a partially-marked channel, private piers and boats on moorings. Thread the miniscule entrance carefully to find 7- to 10-foot depths with a soft mud bottom. The heavy concentration of moored boats leaves little room to anchor, however, and there are no services available.

Magothy River, Beyond Blackhole Creek

NAVIGATION: Use Charts 12278 and 12282. The Magothy continues north between the Blackhole Creek coves and green daybeacon "15," which marks the shoal off Focal Point. Both the cove between North Ferry and Pea Patch points and the cove between Pea Patch Point and flashing red "14" have good protection from the northeast. There is a moderate-sized area to the west, past red daybeacon "16," with 10- to 12-foot depths and high, protective banks. You will find enough depth to explore a good bit farther up the river.

Boats on moorings populate Cattail Creek and Cypress Creek. Dividing and Mill creeks have a common mouth above Stony Point. Be aware of unmarked shoals throughout this area. Forked Creek has a long, unmarked shoal off its northwest side. If confused by all the tributaries and you need a landmark, look for the tan townhouse development adjoining Mago Vista at green daybeacon "11," on the south side of the Magothy, just across from the entrance to Dividing and Mill creeks.

Dockage: The large docks of the Magothy Marina at Crystal Beach, between Cypress Creek and Dividing Creek, are conspicuous on the chart. Cypress Marina and Ferry Point Marina Yacht Yard are also located here.

Magothy River Pump-outs

Atlantic Marina on the Magothy	Magothy River/Grays Creek	410.360.2500
Ferry Point Marina & Yacht Yard	Magothy River/Mill Creek	410.544.6368
Hamilton Harbour Marina	Magothy River	410.647.0733
Magothy Marina	Magothy River	410.647.2356
Podickory Point Yacht & Beach Club	Chesapeake Bay	410.757.8000
Sandy Point State Park	Chesapeake Bay	410.974.2149
Struble's Marina	Magothy River/Cypress Creek	410.647.6191

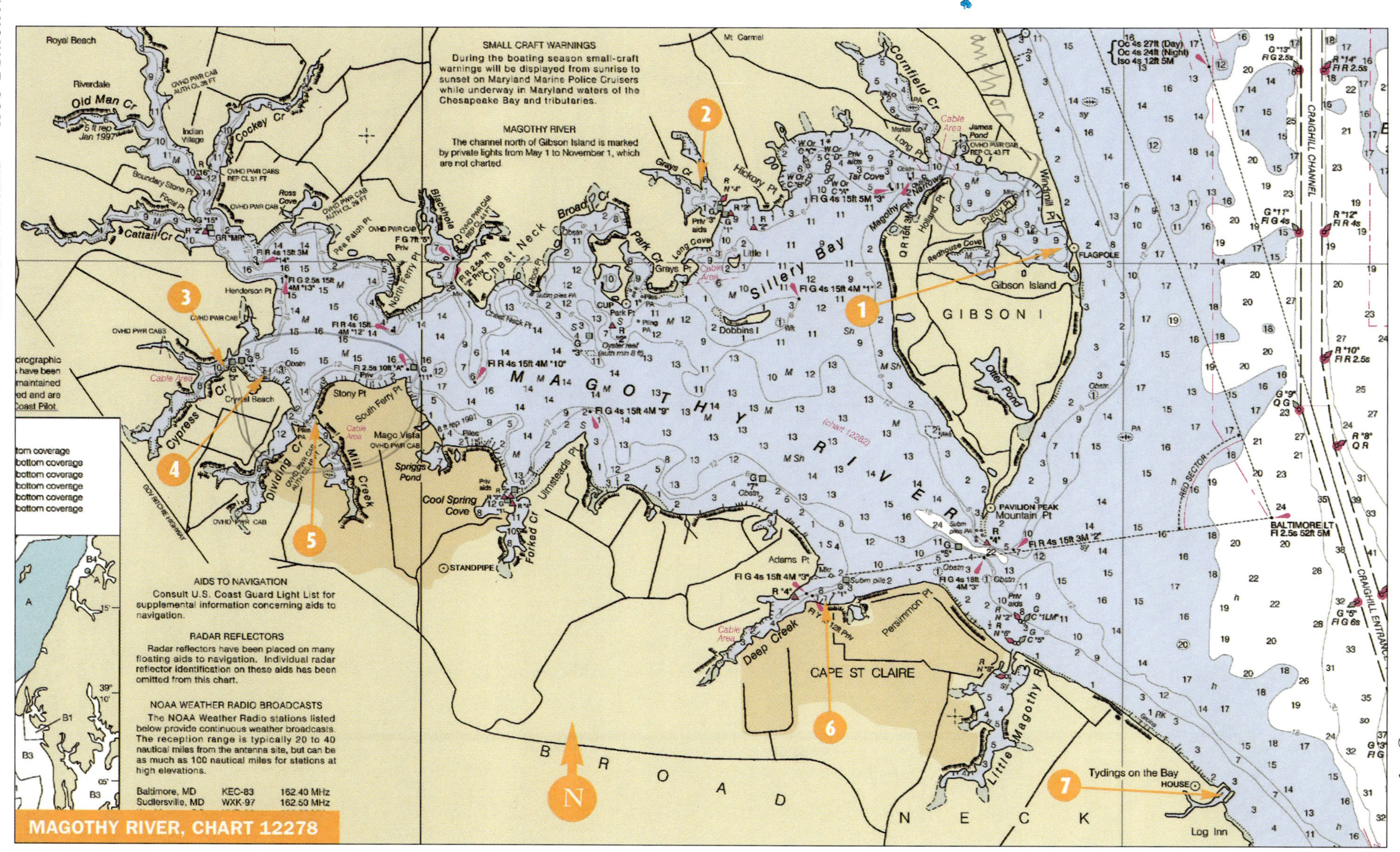
MAGOTHY RIVER, CHART 12278
SMALL CRAFT WARNINGS
During the boating season small-craft warnings will be displayed from sunrise to sunset on Maryland Marine Police Cruisers while underway in Maryland waters of the Chesapeake Bay and tributaries.
MAGOTHY RIVER
The channel north of Gibson Island is marked by private lights from May 1 to November 1, which are not charted.
AIDS TO NAVIGATION
Consult U.S. Coast Guard Light List for supplemental information concerning aids to navigation.
RADAR REFLECTORS
Radar reflectors have been placed on many floating aids to navigation. Individual radar reflector identification on these aids has been omitted from this chart.
NOAA WEATHER RADIO BROADCASTS
The NOAA Weather Radio stations listed below provide continuous weather broadcasts. The reception range is typically 20 to 40 nautical miles from the antenna site, but can be as much as 100 nautical miles for stations at high elevations.
Baltimore, MD KEC-83 162.40 MHz
Sudlersville, MD WXK-97 162.50 MHz
MAGOTHY RIVER
GIBSON I
Gibson Island
Sillery Bay
CAPE ST CLAIRE
BROAD NECK
CRAIGHILL CHANNEL
CRAIGHILL ENTRANCE
BALTIMORE LT
Tydings on the Bay
Log Inn
Cornfield Cr
Cockey Cr
Old Man Cr
Cattail Cr
Cypress Cr
Dividing Cr
Mill Creek
Forked Cr
Deep Creek
Little Magothy R
Cool Spring Cove
Stony Pt
South Ferry Pt
North Ferry Pt
Chest Neck
Broad Cr
Park Cr
Grays Cr
Hickory Pt
Windmill Pt
Mountain Pt
Persimmon Pt
Adams Pt
Dobbins I
Otter Pond
Royal Beach
Riverdale
Indian Village
Crystal Beach
Mago Vista
Mt Carmel

Baltimore
95
895
695
Patapsco River
MILE 33
Chesapeake Bay
10
97
32
Severna Park
Gibson Island
Magothy River
Severn River
3
301
Page 231
Whitehall Bay
Page 235
Annapolis
50
Chesapeake Bay Bridge
Page 248
South River
MILE 48
50
Page 256
Rhode River
Thomas Point Lighthouse
Page 256
West River
Galesville
Shady Side
Eastern Bay
Deale
Herring Bay
MILE 55

Skipper's Handbook

- GPS Waypoints 48
- Tide Tables 50

Severn River to Rhode/West Rivers

CHARTS 12263, 12270, 12282, 12283

This portion of Maryland's Western Shore is probably the busiest on the entire Chesapeake Bay. Besides Annapolis, there are cruising grounds like the high-banked Severn River, whose Round Bay area and assorted creeks enclose some of the finest anchorages anywhere. Not far south is the busy South River, a haven for both power boaters and sailors. There is also the serene splendor of the Rhode and West rivers and the pleasantly laid-back boating town of Galesville, the birthplace of one of the Bay's most famous indigenous racing sailboat, the Chesapeake 20.

Sandy Point, North of Annapolis

For the cruising mariner, Annapolis begins at the busy channel off of Sandy Point, south of the Magothy River and just north of the twin-span, high-level (186 ft. clearance) 4.3-mile-long Chesapeake Bay Bridge, referred to locally as the "Bay Bridge." This should not be confused with the 23-mile-long Chesapeake Bay Bridge-Tunnel, the only other Bay crossing, 120 miles to the south at the mouth of the Bay.

Waterway Guide Photography.

SANDY POINT
N 39°00.950'
W 076°23.067'

Dockage: You can dock at Sandy Point State Park during the day if you draw less than 8 feet, but the park prohibits overnight stays. The park has bait, gas, ice and other supplies. There is also a launching ramp for trailerable boats.

Whitehall Bay and Whitehall Creek, North of Annapolis

Whitehall Bay, with depths of 9 to 15 feet, lies between the Bay Bridge and the Severn River entrance to Annapolis.

NAVIGATION: Use Chart 12282. From the main Chesapeake Bay channel south of the Chesapeake Bay Bridge, first set a course to intercept green can buoy "1" south of Hackett Point, and then head northwest toward flashing red "2W," which marks the channel between North Shoal off Hackett Point and Whitehall Flats off Greenbury Point, both with depths of 3 to 4 feet. Keep a good distance from North Shoal, as it seems to be building farther south every year. From flashing red "2W," head north-northeast toward the flashing white light at Sharps Point (actually a shoreside private home modeled like the famous Thomas Point Lighthouse farther south) in Whitehall Bay. Continue toward Sharps Point until you are back in deeper water, and then bear to starboard to pick up red daybeacon "4" at the entrance to Whitehall Creek. Finally, follow the channel markers up Whitehall Creek, which has depths of at least 10 feet for a mile or so, and catch a glimpse of the attractive houses along the tree-lined banks.

Dockage: Whitehall Marina and Hinckley Yacht Services are both located here. Both offer some boat repair services in addition to transient space.

Anchorage: You can anchor in the northeast section of Whitehall Bay, but it can get rough in inclement weather, and the chop from the incessant boating activity can be bothersome. The anchorage fills up quickly on summer weekends. About a half-mile up Whitehall Creek to port is a finger of water where you can drop the hook in perfect security. Farther up, Ridout (pronounced "Ride-out") Creek (with 8-foot depths) is another favorite place for a quiet night.

Meredith Creek, off Whitehall Bay

Meredith Creek, east of Whitehall Creek and a favorite of boating writer Carleton Mitchell, has an entry channel intentionally obscured to keep the creek private. If you are adventurous and draw less than 4 feet, keep a lookout for the "secret" posts and markers (actually guides for the channel) on the shore when entering Meredith Creek and slowly feel your way in. The chart shows 1-foot depths at mean low water, but there is actually more, and those who make it past this point earn a serene, protected and almost wilderness-like experience in 9- to 10-foot depths. Be sure to bring your insect repellent.

Mill Creek, off Whitehall Bay

The entrance to Mill Creek is at the northwestern edge of Whitehall Bay. Follow the markers (beginning with flashing red "2M") to avoid the shoal off Possum Point. Despite its winding, sharp entrance, once inside, you will find that Mill Creek offers good depths and several nice anchorages. For some of the best steamed crabs in the area, visit the regionally famous Cantler's Riverside Inn, a seafood restaurant with dockage for diners on the west shore of Mill Creek about three-quarters of a nautical mile from the creek's entrance.

Dockage: Orchard Creek Marina is located here and may have transient space.

Whitehall Bay, Whitehall Creek, MD

WHITEHALL CREEK		Largest Vessel Accommodated	VHF Channel Monitored	Transient Berths / Total Berths	Approach / Dockside Depth (reported)	Floating Docks	Gas / Diesel	Groceries, Ice, Marine Supplies, Snacks	Repairs: Hull, Engine, Propeller	Lift (tonnage), Crane, Rail	Min/Max Amps	Laundry, Pool, Showers, Courtesy Car	Pump-Out Station	Nearby: Grocery Store, Motel, Restaurant
		Dockage					Supplies		Services					
1. Whitehall Marina	410-757-4819	50	-	/129	10/10	-	-	-	HEP	L25	30/30	-	-	R
2. Hinckley Yacht Services Annapolis (Internet Access) (Wireless Internet Access)	**410-349-2183**	**65**	**78**	**15/135**	**8/10**	**-**	**-**	**M**	**HEP**	**L25,C1**	**30/50**	**S**	**P**	**R**
3. Orchard Beach Marina	410-269-5182	80	-	17/17	13/11	F	-	-	-	-	30/30	S	-	R

Corresponding chart(s) not to be used for navigation. Internet Access Wireless Internet Access Waterway Guide Cruising Club Partner

See www.WaterwayGuide.com for current rates, fuel prices, web site addresses, and other up-to-the-minute information.

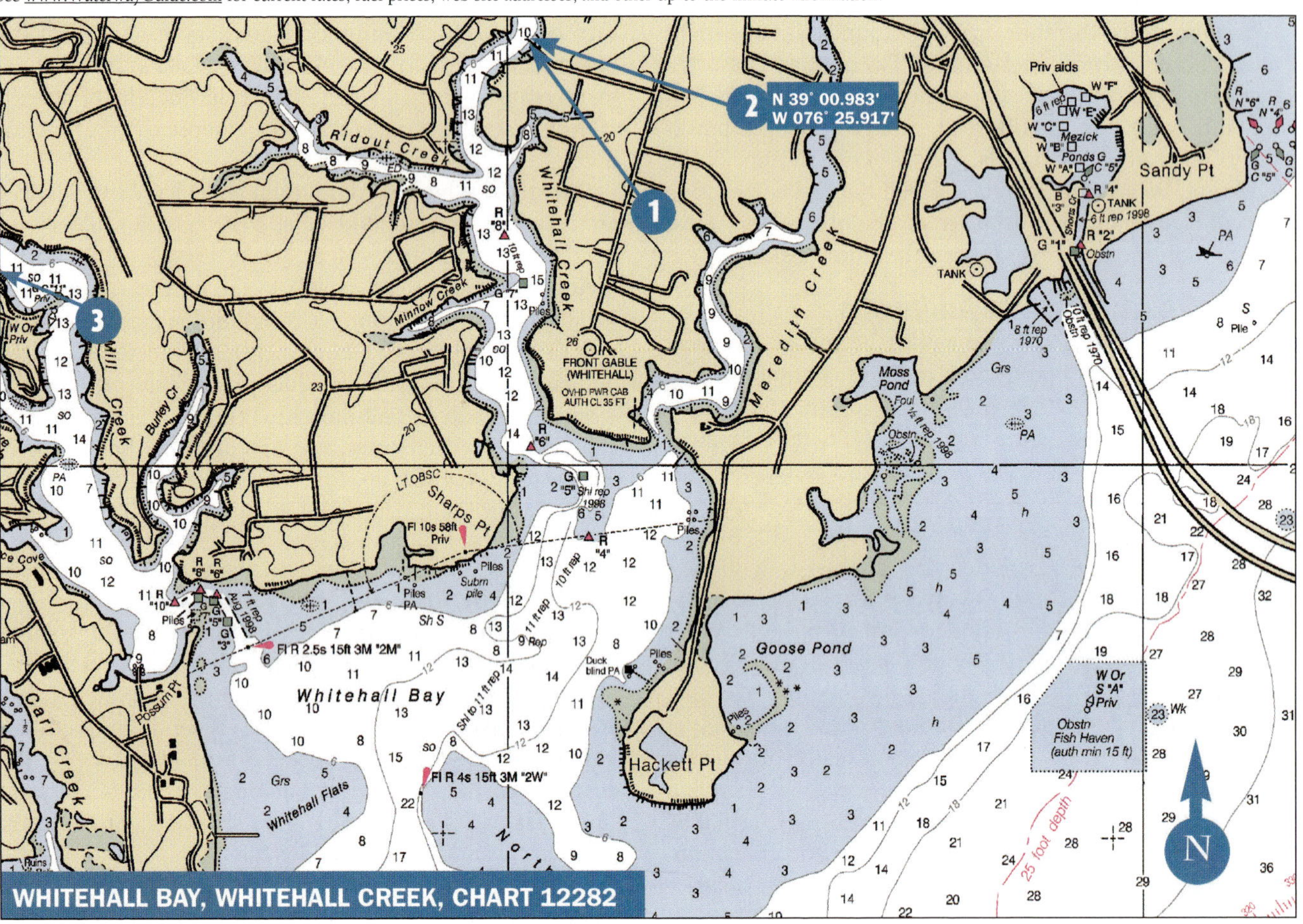

WHITEHALL BAY, WHITEHALL CREEK, CHART 12282

Lake Ogleton, off Severn River

If the creeks are crowded, try Lake Ogleton on the Annapolis side of the Severn River, due south of Greenbury Point. Proceed through the 5.5-foot-deep entrance channel at flashing green "1L," and you may be lucky enough to stake out one of the anchoring spots. It is a long and possibly rough dinghy ride to town from here, and it is not within walking distance to the town. Nevertheless, Lake Ogleton is a relatively quiet, residential anchorage, which is often overlooked.

Back Creek and Eastport, off Severn River

The land between Back Creek and Spa Creek is the peninsula of Eastport, with some marine stores, restaurants and waterfront apartments. Eastport is walking distance from downtown Annapolis.. All streets that dead-end at the water in Annapolis and Eastport are designated public landings for boaters and make excellent places to tie up the dinghy and go ashore for provisions or entertainment. Some of the landings have floating docks; others are just ladders to get up and over the bulkhead. Be sure to lock your dinghy securely during peak season. Eastport Shopping Center is about three-quarters of a mile from the marinas on the west (Eastport) side of Back Creek on Bay Ridge Avenue. Here, you will find a Rite-Aid pharmacy, with limited groceries and convenience items. About 1 mile farther up Bay Ridge Avenue are a West Marine, Fawcett's, a grocery store and drugstores. Fawcett's (919 Bay Ridge Road, 410-267-8681), a long-time chandlery favorite of sailors, continues to carry quality items for the serious cruiser. Although no longer conveniently located on the waterfront, it is worth the walk,

Looking northeast over marina-lined Back Creek off the Severn River. (Not to be used for navigation.) Waterway Guide Photography.

bike or cab ride to peruse their well-stocked shelves at their new location on Bay Ridge Ave. It is easier to reach this second group of stores from the marinas on the east side of Back Creek, although you may want to take a cab from either location. Reliable Cab Company (410-268-4714) serves Annapolis.

NAVIGATION: Use Chart 12282. **Use Baltimore tide tables. For high tide at Annapolis (Severn River), subtract 1 hour 30 minutes; for low tide subtract 1 hour 44 minutes.**

You will find good water as far as the head of Back Creek, but, as always, give points of land a fair berth, particularly here at the green markers. Entrance lights for Back Creek are now flashing green "1E" and flashing red "2E," but be sure to honor all the marks leading you into Back Creek, particularly green daybeacon "7," as a shoal there puts many unwary mariners aground every year.

Dockage: Some marinas are committed to local boats, but several cater to cruisers when possible. On the north shore of Back Creek (just south of Horn Point) is Horn Point Harbor Marina, which offers transient berthing inside its protected bulkhead. On the south shore (port upon entrance), is Annapolis Landing Marina. Not far beyond on the same shore is Port Annapolis Marina. On the north shore of Back Creek is Mears Marina, also the home of the Severn River Yacht Club. To either side of the yacht club are city streets that terminate at the water and are designated dinghy landings. Between the Mears Marina and Eastport Yacht Center (you will have to look closely between the maze of piers and pilings) is a small cove crowded with docks, at the head of which is a tiny city park with a dinghy dock. Across the street from the park is Davis' Pub (400 Chester Ave.), an intimate local watering hole with friendly service and good crab cakes. Farther upstream past the large Watergate apartment complex is Bert Jabin's Yacht Yard on the east side where, for a dinghy fee, you get access to the many marine repair businesses located there. Jabin's has transient dockage with all usual amenities and also boasts three 35-ton Travelifts, a 15-ton crane and is a certified Maryland Clean Marina. You can do the work yourself or utilize one of the many on-site service professionals contracted by the yard.

Anchorage: On the east shore of Back Creek near the water tower (marked "TANK" on the chart), a small, unmarked anchorage (8- to 10-foot depths) lies off Back Creek Nature Park. The park has a crabbing pier, picnic tables, barbecue pits, restrooms, water fountains and nature trails. This is a popular anchorage, even though the nearby water treatment plant can sometimes emanate less than pleasant smells. The city has installed five moorings in Back Creek near the nature park for boats up to 45 feet. Be careful not to block access to the marinas or the park when anchoring. One of the rules that is strictly enforced is "no anchoring within 75 feet of marinas or private docks."

GOIN' ASHORE: **EASTPORT, MD**

Eastport marches to the beat of its own drummer, despite having developed into a trendy Annapolis neighborhood in recent years. Long the city's maritime district, it has morphed into the "Maritime Republic of Eastport" after some local wags decreed that Eastport should secede from the city some years ago when the Spa Creek Bridge was closed for repairs. At the time, businesses were concerned about lost sales. Passports—better known as coupon books—were issued, Brussels sprouts were shot from muskets and much merriment ensued. And still does.

Downtown Eastport is within walking distance of Spa Creek and the marinas on Back Creek. Dinghy docking available at the end of each street welcomes boaters from the Annapolis harbor. With the exception of Annapolis City Marina and Petrini and Annapolis Harbor Boatyard, each located on Spa Creek, the marinas in Eastport are located on Back Creek; distances noted below are approximate and are based on traveling from these marinas.

History: Eastport didn't officially become part of Annapolis until 1951. According to the Eastport Civic Association Web site, the first European grant for the peninsula dubbed "Horne Point" came in 1665. The second husband of the woman married to the original grantee passed the property through his family.

During the Revolutionary War, a battery was built here, and Lafayette and his troops camped on the peninsula. (Look for the historical marker at the Eastport side of the Spa Creek Bridge.) Over time, the property was sold off or went about its business as a farm. In 1870 came the first bridge, subdivision of the property and establishment of the neighborhood as one for working folks. During World War II, sub-chasers and PT boats were built at the John Trumpy and Sons Yacht Yard, now the site of a Chart House restaurant.

Attractions: Not to be missed is the Annapolis Maritime Museum, which occupies the site of the old McNasby Oyster Packing Company plant on Back Creek. Located at 723 Second St., the museum is devoted to preserving the history of Eastport's maritime district and has a permanent exhibit which details the history of the local oyster industry. Call 410-295-0104 or check www.annapolismaritimemuseum.org for hours and upcoming events.

Special Events: The Maritime Museum also is the site of the first day of spring called "The Burning of the Socks." Traditionally, die-hard boaters are supposed to wear deck shoes without socks after this event, commemorating the end of winter and the beginning of boating season. In mid-June, the museum also hosts an all-day street party with live music, crafts and events for kids.

Sponsored by the Annapolis Yacht Club, Wednesday Night Races take place April through September, starting at 6:00 p.m. The best view is from your boat, tied up at a mooring or dock, but the folks at Boatyard Bar and Grill video tape the races so you can catch the replay at the restaurant afterwards.

The Annual Boatyard Bar and Grill Opening Day Fishing Tournament, a benefit for local organizations on the opening day of rockfish season (April), is catch and release. An after-party is held at the restaurant, which is located at the corner of Fourth Street and Severn Avenue.

An annual, light-hearted tug of war with a 1500 foot rope across the bridge to Spa Creek takes place in November. Called "A Slaughter Across the Water," the event highlights the mock rivalry between Eastport and downtown Annapolis.

Every year on the second Saturday in December, boats suddenly appear out of the cold winter night decorated in holiday lights on the rigging. Sponsored by the Eastport Yacht Club, the Lights Parade is a signature event for the harbor and is viewed by thousands from viewing spots along the waterfront

Shopping: There is limited shopping in Eastport. A small shopping center is located at 1031 Bay Ridge Ave., which has a liquor store and pharmacy. Further away is a Giant supermarket (948 Bay Ridge), a West Marine and Fawcett's (919 Bay Ridge). It will probably be necessary to take a cab to these locations.

Dining: An easy walk from the marinas, Severn Avenue has turned into an unbeatable restaurant row with Lewnes (401 Fourth St., 410-263-1617) and Ruth's Chris (301 Severn Ave., 410-990-0033) featuring the best steaks in town. O'Leary's Seafood Restaurant has been long popular, with an upscale, excellent seafood menu (310 Third St., 410-263-0884). Popular with local boaters, the casual Boatyard Bar and Grill donates one percent of its sales to environmental causes. (400 Fourth St., 410-216-6206). Across the street with the best water views in town, is Carrol's Creek with both an upscale but casual venue (410 Severn Ave., 410-263-8102). The Chart House has another excellent waterview and is unbeatable for watching the Wednesday night races (300 Second St., 410-268-7166). Davis' Pub is a dependable neighborhood pub, right in the heart of the maritime district (400 Chester Ave., 410-268-7432).

Reference the marina listing tables to see all the marinas in the area.

POINTS OF INTEREST

1 Annapolis Maritime Museum

SHOPPING

2 Eastport Shopping Center
3 Giant Supermarket
4 West Marine
5 Fawcett's
6 Maritime Solutions/ InflatableXperts

DINING

7 Lewnes' Steakhouse
8 Ruth's Chris
9 O'Leary's Seafood Restaurant
10 Boatyard Bar and Grill
11 Carrol's Creek Waterfront Restaurant
12 The Chart House
13 Davis' Pub

ADDITIONAL RESOURCES

- Annapolis Conference and Visitors Bureau: www.visit-annapolis.org
- Maritime Republic of Eastport: www.themre.org

NEARBY MEDICAL FACILITIES

Annapolis Urgent Care: 193 Green Street, Annapolis, MD 21401, 410-268-3627 (1 mile)

Anne Arundel Medical Center: 2001 Medical Parkway, Annapolis, MD 21401 443-481-4000 (4 miles)

Righttime Medical Care: 2114 Generals Highway, Annapolis, MD 21401, 410-224-6483 (5 miles)

NEARBY AIRPORT

Baltimore-Washington International Thurgood Marshall Airport: www.bwiairport.com (26 miles)

ANNAPOLIS HARBOR

Annapolis and the Naval Academy overlook the entrance to the Severn River. The river entrance itself is marked by three tall naval communication towers on the north shore. Annapolis Harbor has two main boating centers: Back Creek, to port as you enter from the Bay, and Spa Creek, in the heart of downtown Annapolis. The NOAA chart shows this configuration clearly.

NAVIGATION: Use Chart 12282. **Use Baltimore tide tables. For high tide at Annapolis (Severn River), subtract 1 hour 30 minutes; for low tide subtract 1 hour 44 minutes.** The entrance to Annapolis is straightforward and poses no problems other than heavy traffic. Obey the markers on both sides of the channel, do not take any shortcuts, and stay in the main channel at the tripod marker off Greenbury Point. The old 40-foot lighthouse base that locals called "The Spider" has been removed. Flashing red "4," west of the tripod, marks the Annapolis Harbor entrance. Here, you are almost abeam of the entrance to Back Creek, to port. The turning point to enter Annapolis Harbor is at flashing green buoy "9."

Be particularly careful not to shortcut the flashing 6-second white marker "HP" off Horn Point, which guards shoals that take their toll on even the local fleet. Ahead are the massive dormitory, field house and other buildings on the extensive grounds of the U.S. Naval Academy. At night, the lights on the waterfront playing fields can blind a mariner searching for navigational lights.

Keep alert as you navigate the waters around Annapolis, as freighters and large Navy vessels anchor near the junction of the main Bay channel and the Annapolis approach channel, and their tenders shuttle into town and back. Racing craft dash in every direction amid harbor tour boats and water taxis, Naval Academy training boats, student sailors, windsurfers, large powerboats, motor launches, and commercial and military craft are all here. The Marine Police request that you use extreme caution when you enter the harbor and recommend that sailboats proceed under power.

You may see a spectacular and beautiful exception if you are in town on Wednesday night, when the Annapolis Yacht Club sailboat races end in Spa Creek at the yacht club between the outer moorings and Spa Creek Bridge.

Speed Limits: The main stem of the Severn River has a speed limit of 35 knots during the day and 20 knots at night. Entering Back Creek and Spa Creek, it is 6 knots during the boating season west of a line of white speed limit buoys running from Triton Light (at the corner of the Naval Academy) to Horn Point Light to the first marker at the entrance to Back Creek "1E." Inside the harbor, on Spa Creek, on Back Creek and most of the creeks upstream, the strictly enforced speed limit is 6 knots. Keep an eye out for speed limit buoys along the entire Severn River entrance, as they seem to change location every year. The local Annapolis Marine Police and the Maryland Department of Natural Resources Police take the speed limits in this area very seriously and do not hesitate to hand out citations to violators. Many unknowing visitors blast the Severn River entrance only to be greeted with a flashing blue light.

Special Note on Registration: If you are using your dinghy to motor ashore from any of the mooring fields or anchorages, make sure your registration is current and that your registration numbers are visibly displayed. (Sail and rowing dinghies are exempt from this.) Local and state marine police officers stand by and write dozens of citations each day to dinghies that do not have registration numbers.

Annapolis, MD

SPA CREEK	Phone	Largest Vessel Accommodated	VHF Channel Monitored	Transient Berths / Total Berths	Approach / Dockside Depth (reported)	Floating Docks	Gas / Diesel	Groceries, Ice, Marine Supplies, Snacks	Repairs: Hull, Engine, Propeller	Lift (tonnage), Crane, Rail	Min/Max Amps	Laundry, Pool, Showers, Courtesy Car	Pump-Out Station	Nearby: Grocery Store, Motel, Restaurant
		Dockage					Supplies		Services					
1. Olde Towne Marina Ltd.	410-263-9277	85	-	5/14	14/14	-	-	-	-	-	30/30	S	-	GMR
2. Annapolis Yacht Club □ WiFi	410-263-9279	40	-	4/120	12/12	F	-	IS	-	C	50/50	LS	P	R
3. Yacht Basin Co. □ WiFi	410-263-3544	230	09	40/107	15/12	-	GD	I	-	-	30/100	LS	P	GMR
4. Annapolis Waterfront Marriott/Pusser's Landing WiFi	410-263-7837	80	16/09	-	15/8	-	-	-	-	-	30/30	S	-	MR
5. Annapolis City Docks □ WiFi	410-263-7973	125	09/17	22/22	15/10	F	-	GIMS	HEP	-	30/50	LS	P	GMR
6. Eastport Yacht Club	410-267-9549	30	08	/34	4.5/4.5	-	-	-	-	C	30/50	S	-	GMR
7. Annapolis Maryland Capital Yacht Club □ WiFi	410-269-5219	50	16	/81	9/9	-	-	I	HP	L7.5	50/50	PS	P	GMR
8. Annapolis Harbor Boat Yard [Cruising Club Partner]	410-268-0092	110	16	-	15/15	-	-	-	HEP	L30, C18	30/100	-	-	GMR
9. Annapolis City Marina, Ltd. WiFi	410-268-0660	65	09	19/85	15/12	-	GD	IMS	-	-	30/50	LS	P	GMR
10. Petrini Shipyard Inc. □ WiFi	410-263-4278	140	-	10/50	14/11	-	-	-	HEP	L150	30/50	LS	-	GMR
11. Sarles Boatyard & Marina □ WiFi	410-263-3661	56	-	4/46	8/8	-	-	I	HEP	L5, R	30/30	S	-	-
BACK CREEK														
12. Horn Point Harbor Marina	410-263-0550	120	-	5/54	9/12	-	-	-	-	-	30/100	S	P	GMR
13. Eastport Yacht Center □ WiFi	410-280-9988	60	-	20/106	9/7	F	-	GI	HEP	L35, C	30/50	LS	P	GMR
14. Mears Marina WiFi	410-268-8282	100	09	10/232	9/5	-	-	IS	-	-	50/50	LPS	P	GMR
15. Annapolis Landing Marina □ WiFi	410-263-0090	120	09/72	8/120	11/10	-	GD	GIMS	-	-	30/100	LPSC	P	GR
16. Port Annapolis Marina □	410-269-1990	70	16	20/290	9/8	-	-	IMS	HEP	L55, C30	30/50	LPS	P	R
17. Chesapeake Harbour Marina □ WiFi	**410-268-1969**	**120**	**16/73**	**20/200**	**8/8**	**-**	**-**	**GIM**	**-**	**-**	**30/100**	**LPS**	**P**	**GR**
18. Bert Jabin Yacht Yard □ WiFi	**410-268-9667**	**55**	**16**	**25/200**	**9.5/9**	**F**	**-**	**GIMS**	**HEP**	**L50, C30**	**30/50**	**LS**	**P**	**GMR**

Corresponding chart(s) not to be used for navigation. □ Internet Access WiFi Wireless Internet Access [Cruising Club Partner] Waterway Guide Cruising Club Partner

See www.WaterwayGuide.com for current rates, fuel prices, web site addresses, and other up-to-the-minute information.

If you have a motor on your dinghy, you need to have registration numbers displayed. Also, carry all required safety equipment and lights for nighttime use. (These regulations apply to both Maryland and Virginia waters on the Chesapeake and its tributaries.)

Dockage: Annapolis is perennially short of dock space for cruising boats. No matter how many new berths appear, local boats soon fill them to capacity, so this is one area where it is not only prudent but also essential to make reservations. Many overcrowded marinas simply cannot accommodate transient boats and will make that circumstance clear when necessary. As in Fort Lauderdale, many experienced cruising skippers stay tied up on weekends to avoid the crowds from nearby Washington and Baltimore. Remember to call ahead and be patient. Dockage for Back Creek and Spa Creek is discussed in the following sections on those creeks.

The enclosed basin of Chesapeake Harbour Marina, surrounded by a condominium development, is just two-thirds of a mile south of Back Creek, toward the Bay. This marina welcomes transients and offers dining at Sam's Waterfront Café.

There are also 18 slips and 315 feet of bulkhead in Ego Alley (a small canal-like section right in the heart of town), which are on a first-come, first-served basis, although there are a few spots on the Chandler Dock where Fawcett's used to be that take reservations. The Harbormaster can be reached on channel 17 or 9 although a city boat will come out to collect the fee.

Anchorage: You can drop the hook in the outer harbor along the Naval Academy seawall as long as you are well outside the channels. When the moorings are full, many large boats anchor in the outer harbor area, off the Naval Academy seawall, in the area where the chart shows "Naval Anchorage" and "South Anchorage." Make sure you are clear of the channel into Spa Creek. Holding is fair in dense mud. Unfortunately, the popularity of the place results in contemptuous wakes, varied scopes and less-than-cautious nighttime arrivals. An anchor watch is advisable, especially on busy weekends. This can be a very rough anchorage in any wind from the northeast through the south: It is open to a long fetch from these directions, and waves reflect off the seawall, reinforcing each other.

There are more restrictions on vessel traffic near the Naval Academy than in earlier years, so inquire before poking in too closely. Although it is technically illegal to anchor in the designated Naval Anchorage except with permission of the Superintendent of the Naval Academy, boaters commonly drop the hook here. The harbormaster warns that insurance companies might not honor their commitments if a boat incurs damage while anchored illegally. Boats on chain fare better than those on nylon rode here. If your anchor drags in an easterly blow, the rocky seawall is a real hazard. There are red-and-white danger buoys along the seawall to remind boaters to keep a safe distance off the jagged rocks. The legal anchorage is the south one, but most of it was dredged to 50-foot depths years ago, and the bottom is still quite hard.

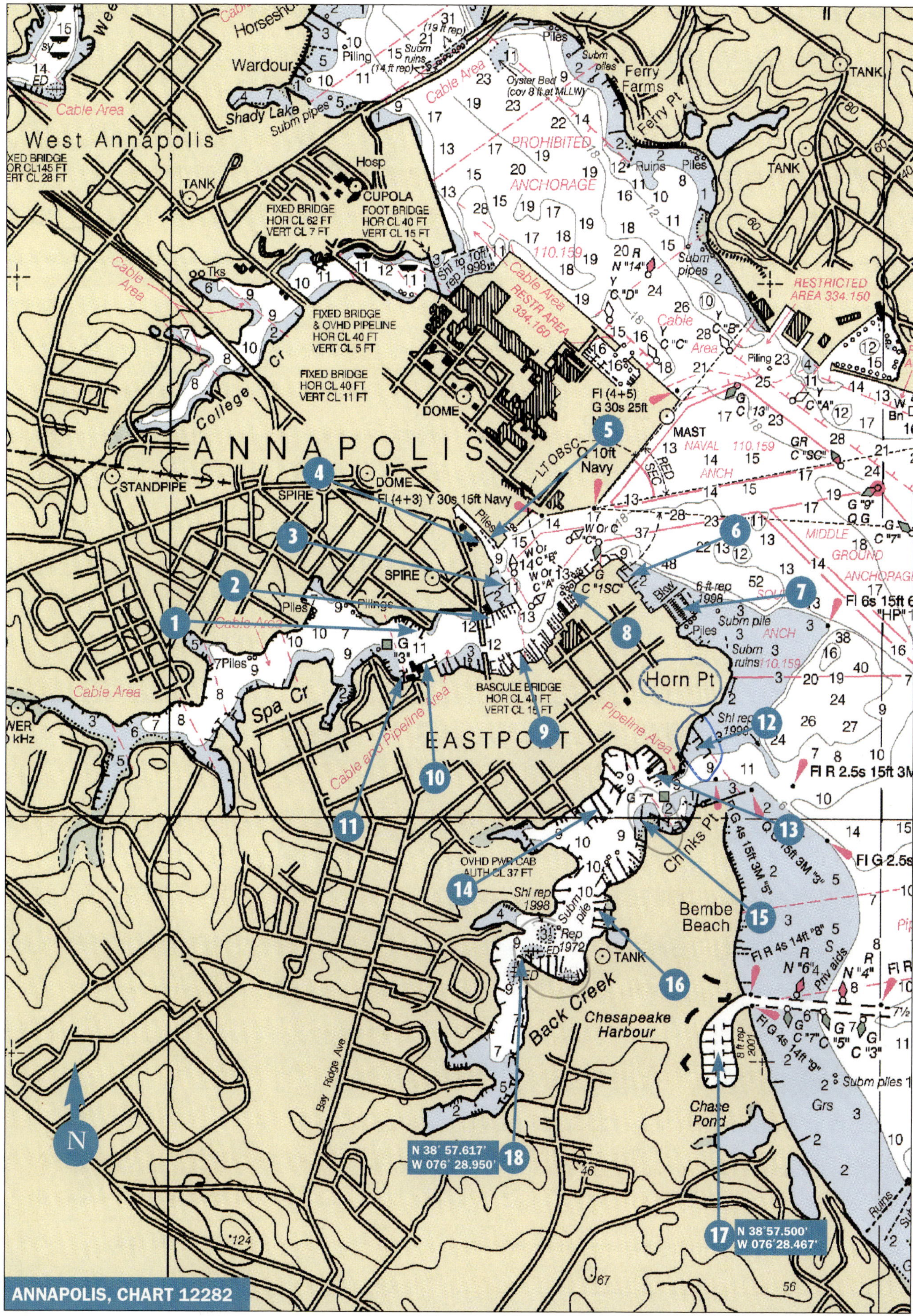
West Annapolis
ANNAPOLIS
EASTPORT
Horn Pt
Back Creek
Chesapeake Harbour
Bembe Beach
Spa Cr
College Cr
Ferry Farms
PROHIBITED ANCHORAGE
RESTRICTED AREA 334.150
MIDDLE GROUND ANCHORAGE
N 38' 57.617' W 076' 28.950'
N 38'57.500' W 076'28.467'
ANNAPOLIS, CHART 12282

Moorings: Below the Spa Creek Bridge, there are city-owned moorings for boats up to 35 feet. There are 73 400-pound mushrooms spaced about 100 feet apart that are checked annually. You must get the harbormaster's approval before rafting up. The city is planning future moorings for larger boats. All are on first come basis and check-out time is noon.

The dinghy dock is at the end of Ego Alley at the front of Main Street. Also, almost every street in Annapolis has a dinghy dock at the end of it. Make sure you secure your dinghy and vessel securely.

Pump-out Services: The Annapolis harbormaster operates a pump-out boat that will come to your vessel, whether docked in a marina or at anchor, and provides pump-out service for a minimal fee. The pump-out boat monitors VHF Channel 09 or 17 daily from 9:00 a.m. to 7:30 p.m.

GOIN' ASHORE: ANNAPOLIS, MD

America's Sailing Capital happens to host more 18th-century structures than any other town in the country. Don't even try to separate the city's past from its present; it simply can't be done. The Historic district (downtown) is full of shops and restaurants nestled along old streets running up the hill to either Church Circle or State Circle.

At the bottom of the hill stands City Dock, where a sculpted bronze salute to Alex Haley, the man who traced his roots at the nearby Maryland State Archives, is installed. "Ego Alley," also known as the Market Slip, is the thin slice of water where boaters come to parade their craft. It is considered good sport to steam up the narrow channel and then execute a U-turn before going back out to Spa Creek. Spa Creek is the busy body of water that separates the Historic District from the neighborhood of Eastport to the south.

Most of the shops, restaurants and attractions are within walking distance of City Dock. Watermark Cruises offers water taxi service throughout the harbor area (410-263-0033 or VHF 68). Rates range from $2 to $8 depending on destination. Also, almost every street in Annapolis has a dinghy dock at the end of it.

History: In 1695, Maryland's new governor decided to move Maryland's capital north from St. Mary's City to Annapolis, which was named for the heir to the British throne. Francis Nicholson laid out the Baroque-style city, with streets radiating from two circles. As the Colonial era wore on, Annapolis became known as a great social center and hosted a Golden Age, replete with a horseracing track.

When the Revolutionary War broke out, the city retained its standing, hosting important figures of the era such as George Washington. The Continental Congress met here from 1783 to 1784, accepting Washington's resignation from the Army and ratifying the Treaty of Paris. However, Baltimore's harbor soon eclipsed that of Annapolis. In 1845, the U.S. Naval Academy was established here.

Points of Interest: The Annapolis Visitors Center is located at 26 West Street (410-280-0445). The Maryland State House, 100 State Circle, is open to the public daily and is the nation's oldest statehouse in continuous use. Peek into the Old Senate Chamber, where the Continental Congress met when George Washington resigned his commission as commander-in-chief of the Army. That room has been undergoing archaeological examination.

The Banneker-Douglass Museum celebrates the state's African-American heritage, and its cornerstone structure is the Mount Moriah AME Church, built by freed slaves in the 1870s. Frederick Douglass himself—born a slave on the Eastern Shore—attended the dedication. The church is located at 84 Franklin St. off Church Circle in the Annapolis Historic District. Visit www.bdmuseum.com or call 410-216-6180 for more information.

For performing and fine arts, head to Maryland Hall for the Creative Arts, home to The Annapolis Chorale, Annapolis Opera, Annapolis Symphony Orchestra and Ballet Theatre of Maryland. The address is 801 Chase St. Visit www.marylandhall.org or call 410-263-5544 to check out current exhibits or activities.

Check out U.S. Naval Academy campus attractions such as its fabled chapel with John Paul Jones's crypt. To find out about tours and security requirements for visiting the Academy, check www.navyonline.com. For more information, the Armel-Leftwich Visitor Center is located at 52 King George St. Call 410-293-TOUR (8687). A photo ID is needed to enter the grounds.

The Mitchell Gallery at St. John's College is a hidden treasure on the campus of St. John's College, 60 College Avenue. The gallery's modern design won an award from the American

Institute of Architects and attracts over 10,000 visitors a year to its museum-quality exhibits, which have included the works of Rembrandt, Rodin, Motherwell and Johns, as well as photography of Aubrey Bodine and Marion Warren. The gallery is open Tuesday to Sunday, noon to 5 p.m. Call 410-626-2556, or go to www.stjohnscollege.edu).

Tour Annapolis with the Capital City Colonials, which sponsors culinary tours as well as walks through the historic district with guides dressed in colonial garb. Advance purchase of tickets is recommended, 800-979-3370 (www.capitalcitycolonials.com) You can even rent a Segway from one of two companies, but reservations need to be made by calling 410-280-1577 or 410-276-7347.

Watermark Cruises, 410-268-7601, operates Annapolis harbor cruises from the downtown dock several times a day, as well as walking tours. Visit www.watermarkcruises.com.

For golfers, there are three choices: the 9-hole Annapolis Golf Club (410-263-6771, www.annapolisgolfclub.net), which is three miles away; Bay Hills Golf Club, which is eight miles away in Arnold (410-974-0669, www.bayhillsgolf.com); or Eisenhower Golf Course (410-571-0973, www.eisenhowergolf.com), which is seven miles away in Crownsville.

Special Events: The annual croquet match between neighboring St. John's College and the U.S. Naval Academy takes place the last weekend in April and is a popular local happening. Check www.stjohnscollege.edu.

For a spectacle of mass gluttony, that is so big it is held at the Naval Academy Stadium, attend the annual Annapolis Rotary Club Crabfeast, held each August. Visit www.annapolisrotary.org for more information.

For more than 40 years, Annapolis has hosted the popular Sailboat and Powerboat shows at the city dock on consecutive weekends in early October. Visit www.usboat.com, or call 410-268-8828.

Shopping: There is plenty of shopping, mostly along Main Street, Maryland Avenue, State Circle and onto West Street. In addition, you can head over to Annapolis Street in West Annapolis, or venture over to the city's mall, Westfield Annapolis Shopping Center (still called Annapolis Mall by some) at the intersection of Bestgate Road and Route 178. Annapolis Town Center at Parole is the city's newest addition to the mall scene with a mixture of retail shops and restaurants. See www.visitatc.com.

As for shops, a few you might enjoy include Easy Street Gallery (8 Francis St., 410-263-5556), Plat du Jour (220 Main St., 410-269-1499) and A.L. Goodies, the old general store established in 1976 at 112 Main St. (410-269-0071). Dawson Gallery at 44 Maryland Ave. is an enchanting old art gallery

Reference the marina listing tables to see all the marinas in the area.

INFORMATION
1 Visitor Center

POINTS OF INTEREST
2 The Maryland State House
3 The Banneker-Douglass Museum
4 Maryland Hall for the Creative Arts
5 Armel-Leftwich Visitor Center
6 Mitchell Gallery, St. John's College
7 City Dock

SHOPPING
8 Easy Street Gallery
9 Plat du Jour
10 A.L. Goodies
11 Dawson Gallery
12 Mills Fine Wine & Spirits
13 Stevens Hardware

DINING
14 Joss Café and Sushi Bar
15 Café Normandy
16 Osteria
17 Pusser's
18 Chick and Ruth's
19 Harry Browne's
20 Galway Bay
21 Tsunami
22 Ram's Head
23 McGarvey's Saloon & Raw Bar
24 Dock Street Cafe & Coffee Shop
25 Cantler's Riverside Inn

LIBRARY

POST OFFICE

PHARMACY

Annapolis and the Naval Acadamy, looking north over the Severn River. (Not to be used for navigation.) Waterway Guide Photography.

Looking southwest into Annapolis Harbor and Spa Creek. (Not to be used for navigation.) Waterway Guide Photography.

(410-269-1299). Maryland Avenue has several antique shops and art galleries.

Mills Fine Wine & Spirits (87 Main St., 410-263-2888) has a wide selection of wines. Stevens Hardware is an old-fashioned hardware store that also sells items of interest to boaters (142 Dock St., 410-263-3390).

Dining: The Main Street Market has been going through troubled waters for years and may or may not be open when you get there. For sushi, try Joss Café and Sushi Bar, where a cry of "irasshai" goes up when you walk in the door (195 Main St., 410-263-4688). A comfy dining room and casual French fare (like crepes) are available at Café Normandy (185 Main St., 410-263-3382). The elegant Osteria features Italian coastal cuisine (177 Main St., 410-267-7700). Situated on "Ego Alley," Pusser's has one of the town's few waterfront views (80 Compromise St., 410-626-0004). For a breakfast to beat all breakfasts, check out Chick and Ruth's (165 Main St., 410-269-6737).

Up on State Circle, for 30 years, Harry Browne's has been a local institution known to serve "critically acclaimed" meals and is where you'll find many state legislators dining (66 State Circle, 410-263-4332). Around the corner at 63 Maryland Ave. stands Galway Bay Irish Pub (410-263-8333).

Over on West Street, Tsunami (51 West St., 410-990-9868), brought the Asian-fusion trend to town, while the nearby Rams Head Tavern has grown from a tiny beer pub years ago to a restaurant, microbrewery and entertainment venue (33 West St., 410-268-4545).

Several restaurants and coffee shops nestle around the city dock area including McGarveys Saloon and Raw Bar (8 Market Space, 410-263-5700) and Dock Street Café and Coffee Shop (18 Market Space, 410-269-0961). For the Chesapeake's famous hardshell crabs, Cantler's Riverside Inn, located outside of town, is the place to go. More accessible to boaters by water, it's up Mill Creek off Whitehall Bay (458 Forest Beach Road, 410-757-1311).

To get to some of Annapolis' restaurants, eCruisers (443-481-2422) can transport you to participating restaurants in eco-friendly electric cars with seating for five.

ADDITIONAL RESOURCES

- ANNAPOLIS VISITORS CENTER: www.visit-annapolis.org
- HISTORYQUEST, at 99 Main St., is the Historic Annapolis Foundation's central point for anyone interested in the city's numerous historical sites. 410-267-6656

NEARBY MEDICAL FACILITIES

Annapolis Urgent Care: 193 Green St., Annapolis, MD 21401, 410-268-3627 (1 mile)

Anne Arundel Medical Center, 2001 Medical Parkway, Annapolis, MD 21401, 443-481-4000 (4 miles)

Righttime Medical Care: 2114 Generals Highway, Annapolis, MD 21401, 410-224-6483 (5 miles)

NEARBY AIRPORT

Baltimore-Washington International Thurgood Marshall Airport: www.bwiairport.com (25 miles)

Annapolis Harbor alongside Dock Street. Photo courtesy of Wikimedia Commons.

Spa Creek, off the Severn

NAVIGATION: Use Chart 12282. Heading from the Severn River into Spa Creek, be sure not to bear to port too early, as there is a long shoal extending off of Horn Point. Flashing white "HP" marks the shoal with a white light (flashing every six seconds). Avoid it by nearing the Naval Academy seawall before turning to port and heading into Spa Creek proper, but keep an eye out for anchored vessels, as the increased number of city moorings is keeping more boats at anchor outside Spa Creek. The Spa Creek Bridge (15-foot vertical clearance) schedule is as follows: From May 1 to October 31 (Mon.-Fri.), the draw opens on the hour and half-hour except from 7:30 a.m. to 9:00 a.m. and from 4:30 p.m. to 7:30 p.m., when it will be closed. It will open at 6:00 p.m. and 7:00 p.m. for vessels waiting to pass. From November 1 to April 30 (Mon.-Fri.), it is the same except that the draw will open on signal from 9:00 a.m. to 4:30 p.m. and from 6:00 p.m. to 7:30 a.m. On Saturdays, Sundays and holidays year-round, the draw will open on the hour and half hour for vessels waiting to pass. (On the Fourth of July the bridge is closed from 8:30 to 11:00 p.m. for fireworks.) The bridge tender monitors VHF Channel 16.

The Spa Creek Bridge (15-foot vertical clearance) schedule is as follows: From May 1 to October 31 (Mon.-Fri.), the draw opens on the hour and half-hour except from 7:30 a.m. to 9:00 a.m. and from 4:30 p.m. to 7:30 p.m., when it will be closed. It will open at 6:00 p.m. and 7:00 p.m. for vessels waiting to pass. From November 1 to April 30 (Mon.-Fri.), it is the same except that the draw will open on signal from 9:00 a.m. to 4:30 p.m. and from 6:00 p.m. to 7:30 a.m. On Saturdays, Sundays and holidays year-round, the draw will open on the hour and half hour for vessels waiting to pass. (On the Fourth of July the bridge is closed from 8:30 to 11:00 p.m. for fireworks.) The bridge tender monitors VHF Channel 16.

Dockage: When rounding Horn Point, to port you will pass Annapolis Maryland Capital Yacht Club and Eastport Yacht Club. Both of these may have some transient space; call ahead. Upon entering Spa Creek, the first marina on the Eastport side of the creek is Annapolis Harbor Boat Yard (next to the Chart House restaurant), which provides haul-out service and repairs. Annapolis City Marina (near the east end of the Spa Creek Bridge) offers transient dockage, gas and diesel fuel and marine supplies. Above the Spa Creek Bridge is Petrini Shipyard offering transient berths, haul-outs and full repairs. Nearby is Sarles Boatyard & Marina, which has limited transient space and offers repairs.

On the Annapolis side, Olde Towne Marina above the Spa Creek Bridge may have space. Below the bridge, there are more choices: The members-only Annapolis Yacht Club is in the building at the west end of the Spa Creek bridge; Yacht Basin Co. is adjacent to the Marriott Hotel; and the popular Annapolis Waterfront Marriott/Pusser's Landing is here as well. The Annapolis City Docks are adjacent to Ego Alley, 315 feet of bulkhead on a first-come, first-served basis. The Annapolis City Docks are made up of 22 slips on fixed docks. The Harbormaster can be reached on channel 17 or 9 although a city boat will come out to collect the fee.

Severn River, MD

SEVERN RIVER		Largest Vessel Accommodated	VHF Channel Monitored	Transient Berths / Total Berths	Approach / Dockside Depth (reported)	Floating Docks	Gas / Diesel	Groceries, Ice, Marine Supplies, Snacks	Repairs: Hull, Engine, Propeller	Lift (tonnage), Crane, Rail	Min/Max Amps	Laundry, Pool, Showers, Courtesy Car	Pump-Out Station	Nearby: Grocery Store, Motel, Restaurant
		Dockage					Supplies		Services					
1. Absolute Marine Services	410-647-4450	60	-	/93	18/10	F	-	IM	HEP	L, R	30/30	-	-	-
2. Smith's Marina	410-923-3444	55	-	/65	8/6.5	-	GD	IMS	HEP	L35	30/30	S	P	GR

Corresponding chart(s) not to be used for navigation. Internet Access Wireless Internet Access Waterway Guide Cruising Club Partner

See www.WaterwayGuide.com for current rates, fuel prices, web site addresses, and other up-to-the-minute information.

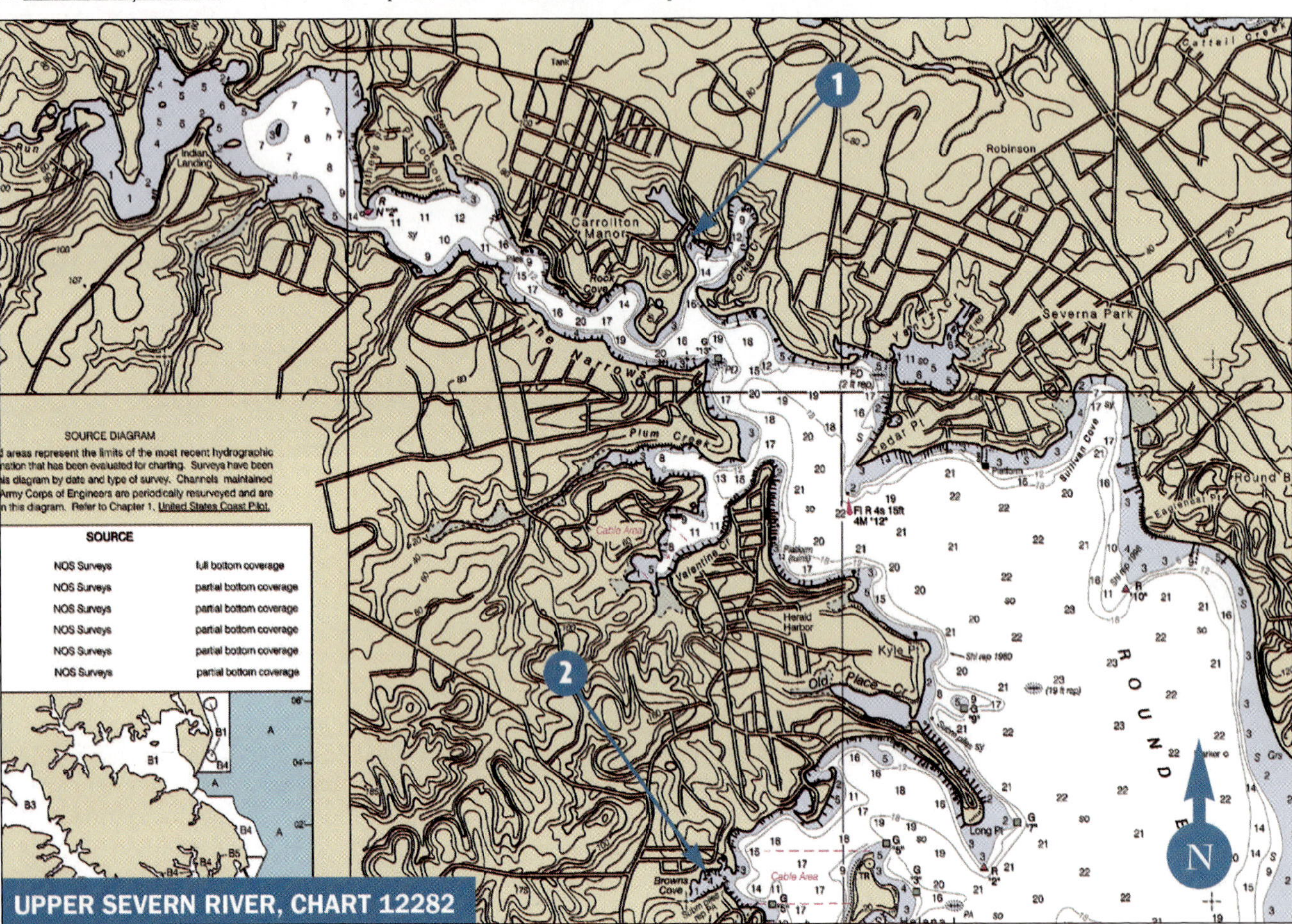

UPPER SEVERN RIVER, CHART 12282

Anchorage: The city prohibits anchoring in all mooring areas. There is no swing room in Spa Creek and it is not a recommended anchorage.

Moorings: Below the Spa Creek Bridge, there are city-owned moorings that rent for $35 per night for boats up to 35 feet. There are 73 400-pound mushrooms spaced about 100 feet apart that are checked annually. You must get the harbormaster's approval before rafting up. The best time to get a mooring is during the week. It is much more comfortable to take a mooring here instead of anchoring out, and it is easy to get ashore by water taxi or dinghy. Look out for racing sailboats that sometimes cut through the mooring area.

Spa Creek, Beyond the Bridge

Thomas Todd, one of the first settlers, built a shipyard on Spa Creek as early as 1650. The salty atmosphere and maritime flavor continue, whether you dock at a boatyard or marina or anchor out. Go ashore by dinghy at almost any street end on the north side of the creek, and you are in the midst of the residential Historic District, just a few blocks from the shops that line Main Street. Farther up the creek, there is a ramp and dock at Truxtun Park. Boaters frequently use the covered picnic pavilion here for potluck suppers or other gatherings.

NAVIGATION: Use Chart 12283. To get to the upper reaches of the ever-popular Spa Creek, go through the busy bascule bridge (closed vertical clearance 15 feet, horizontal clearance 40 feet). Contact the bridge tender on VHF Channel 13 (preferred) or at 410-974-3840.

Anchorage: You will find 10-foot depths well upstream in the main channel, snug anchorages in bights (if you can find a spot where it is permitted), and dockage and repair services on the south shore. All city streets that dead-end on the water are public dinghy landings. Some of the holding ground in Spa Creek is questionable, but you would need two anchors anyway, simply because it is so crowded, especially during the spring and fall migrations and during the boat shows in October. Private moorings in the coves add to the crowded conditions. Remember to always show an anchor light. Make sure you secure your dinghy and vessel securely, especially during the fall migration. Although it is nice to leave your vessel open to air out while you are ashore exploring for the day, we strongly advise against it.

SEVERN RIVER, ABOVE ANNAPOLIS

Above the Naval Academy's extensive waterfront installation, the Severn becomes an entirely different river. Some of its upper reaches bring to mind New York's Hudson River, while some of its creeks are reminiscent of Hamburg Cove on the Connecticut River. Some claim that a cruise to the head of the Severn is one of the prettiest on the Bay.

NAVIGATION: Use Chart 12282. You must negotiate two high-level fixed bridges as you proceed up the Severn. The first (the Naval Academy Bridge) has a 75-foot fixed vertical clearance. The second bridge is the U.S. Route 50/Route 301 Bridge (80-foot fixed vertical clearance), which carries the busy highway from the Annapolis side to the bluffs on the Winchester side.

Most of the Severn's creeks are quiet and secluded, with high, wooded shores and comparatively few houses. Characteristic of the upriver creeks is a long shoal extending into the mouth from the upstream side. Bear this in mind when entering. The speed limit on the Severn River is 35 mph in the daytime and 25 mph at night. In the narrows and in all of the tributary creeks, the speed limit is 6 mph, and water-skiing is prohibited on Saturdays, Sundays and holidays. The speed limit is being more strongly enforced by local law enforcement every year. Going upriver on the Severn, venturing past Annapolis, cruisers find the following creeks especially attractive.

Weems and Luce Creeks, off the Severn

Anchorage: When you enter Weems Creek, favor the south side. Mind the junction daybeacon "WC" (green over red) at the end of a bar making out from the starboard point.

An attractive anchorage is just inside, dotted with U.S. Navy mooring buoys that hold the Academy's small craft during hurricanes. The Navy moorings can be used by civilians as long as the Navy doesn't require them. They will ask you to vacate the mooring if there is the possibility of a major storm. Fourteen-foot depths continue for a half-mile through the swing bridge (8-foot closed vertical clearance) to a bridge with a 28-foot fixed vertical clearance. The swing bridge has a restricted opening schedule. From May 1 to September 30, the bridge opens on signal between sunrise and sunset. All other times are by appointment with 24-hours notice. To schedule an appointment, call 410-841-1009 Monday through Friday, between the hours of 7:30 a.m. and 4:00 p.m.

Back on the Severn, beyond the second fixed highway bridge, lovely Luce Creek has deep water (8 feet or more) inside with shoals on either side of the entry, so be sure that you keep to dead center as you enter. Luce also has Navy moorings which are a pleasant way to spend overnight.

Saltworks, Chase, Clements and Brewer Creeks, off the Severn

Anchorage: Pretty and deep (as much as 11 feet in mid-channel), Saltworks Creek is tricky to enter. The usual shoal projects southward halfway across the entrance, while a second shoal is building off the opposite point projecting northward. Favor the upper point. You will have no problem beyond it. Across the Severn, along its northeastern shore, is Chase Creek. Stay to starboard to avoid the long entry shoal, and, when Chase Creek forks, go midway between the points. Thirteen-foot depths continue up to the fork.

Clements and Brewer creeks are two small anchorages off the Severn's southern shore. They are exceptionally attractive, deep (16-foot depths carry well upstream) and easy to enter. Clements Creek has many moorings, both private and Navy-owned. The same rule applies in Clements Creek as in the other creeks pertaining to the Navy moorings.

QUICK FACT:

THOMAS POINT LIGHT TOURS

A National Historic Landmark and one of the most recognizable lighthouses on the Chesapeake, the Thomas Point Shoal Lighthouse is a sight to see.

The current Thomas Point Light, built in 1875, is the only screwpile light on the Bay still in its original location (the original shore light was built in 1825 and re-built in 1840) at the mouth of the South River. The one-and-a-half story wooden and cast iron hexagonal cottage is white with red roofing, a black lantern and stands 43 feet above water. Its flashing white 250-mm solar-powered lens, which replaced its previous fourth-order Fresnel lens, has an 11-mile range.

Thomas Point Shoal Lighthouse was placed on the National Register of Historic Places list in 1975 and reached National Historic Landmark status in 1999. The lighthouse is now owned by the city of Annapolis and is under the stewardship of the city, Anne Arundel County, the Annapolis Maritime Museum and the Chesapeake Chapter of the U.S. Lighthouse Society.

Visitors docking in Annapolis can sign up for a tour of Thomas Point Shoal Lighthouse at the Annapolis Maritime Museum's Barge House at 723 Second St., located across Spa Creek from Annapolis-proper on the Eastport peninsula. Tours include a 30-minute boat ride to the lighthouse, an on-board docent-led tour and a 30-minute return trip. Tours typically take place May through September. To learn more, call 800-690-5080.

South River, MD

SOUTH RIVER		Largest Vessel Accommodated	VHF Channel Monitored	Transient Berths / Total Berths	Approach / Dockside Depth (reported)	Floating Docks	Gas / Diesel	Groceries, Ice, Marine Supplies, Snacks	Repairs: Hull, Engine, Propeller	Lift (tonnage), Crane, Rail	Min/Max Amps	Laundry, Pool, Showers, Courtesy Car	Pump-Out Station	Nearby: Grocery Store, Motel, Restaurant
		Dockage					Supplies		Services					
1. Selby Bay Marina (WiFi)	**410-798-0232**	**60**	**16**	**3/93**	**10/6.5**	**-**	**GD**	**IMS**	**HEP**	**-**	**30/50**	**LS**	**P**	**G**
2. Holiday Point Marina (WiFi)	410-956-2208	50	16	/165	7/6	-	-	-	HEP	L35, C	30/30	S	P	GR
3. Anchor Yacht Basin	410-269-6674	60	-	/125	6/6	-	GD	IMS	HEP	L35	30/50	S	P	-
4. Burr Yacht Sales (Fleming Yachts Dealer)	410-798-5900	80	-	1/1	5/6	-	-	-	-	-	50/50	S	-	GR
5. South River Marina Inc.	410-798-1717	45	-	/156	6/6	-	-	IMS	HEP	L15	30/30	S	P	GR
6. Turkey Point Marina	410-798-1369	40	16	10/103	5/4	-	G	IMS	HEP	L12	30/50	S	P	GR
7. London Towne Marina	410-956-5077	60	-	/55	10/6	F	G	IS	HEP	L	30/30	S	P	R
8. Liberty Yacht Club (Internet) (WiFi)	410-266-5633	100	16	20/300	20/18	F	GD	GIMS	HEP	L25	30/50	PS	P	GMR
9. Oak Grove Marina (WiFi)	410-266-6696	63	-	/130	13/5	-	GD	IMS	HEP	L	30/50	S	P	R
10. Pier 7 Marina (Internet) (WiFi)	410-956-2288	100	09/72	20/200	20/15	-	-	I	EP	L	30/100	LS	P	GMR
11. Gingerville Yachting Center	410-573-1047	100	-	/60	12/	-	-	-	HEP	L80	30/50	-	-	R

Corresponding chart(s) not to be used for navigation. (Internet) Internet Access (WiFi) Wireless Internet Access Waterway Guide Cruising Club Partner

See www.WaterwayGuide.com for current rates, fuel prices, web site addresses, and other up-to-the-minute information.

Round Bay, off the Severn

About three miles above the U.S. Route 50 highway bridge, the Severn opens out to create Round Bay and, off to port, Little Round Bay. Points are generally well marked, and you can expect depths of 17 feet or more. The banks are high, wooded and residential.

Dockage: Smith's Marina is on Maynadier Creek and sells fuel.

Anchorage: A number of marshy creeks spoke out off Round Bay, and you will find protected, scenic anchorage anywhere inside St. Helena Island in Little Round Bay, or up Maynadier Creek, where depths range from 10 to 15 feet. This creek is often crowded on weekends. Many boats head for the hurricane holes in tributaries of Round Bay when severe weather threatens.

Beyond Round Bay, off the Severn

NAVIGATION: Use Chart 12282. Beyond Round Bay, the channel winds through The Narrows to Indian Landing, where water is deep, but the passage is slim and often busy with small motorboats during the day. The banks are just beyond your rail on either side in some places, but there are areas where you can pull out of the main channel and drop the hook overnight. Two narrow spots—the first just beyond Forked Creek, the second off Mathews Point—call for cautious navigation around long sandbars. For all practical purposes, Indian Landing is the head of navigation on the Severn, although you may be able to take a dinghy or canoe several miles up Severn Run. A small yacht club is located at Indian Landing. Two islets (privately owned) mark the entrance to the tiny harbor.

Dockage: A pretty creek off the north shore of the Severn, Forked Creek has a deep, narrow entrance that is difficult to find. Look for it after leaving Cedar Point and Yantz Creek to starboard. It has the usual shoaling at the entry, but depths of 11 to 13 feet once inside. Absolute Marine Services is located here with slips on floating docks. A shopping center with a supermarket and other stores is a half-mile above the head of Forked Creek.

Anchorage: Plum and Valentine creeks have a common entrance to sheltered water, both with 8- to 11-foot depths. Valentine Creek, crowded with private moorings, is to the southwest, while Plum Creek is rather quiet.

SOUTH RIVER

South River, the next significant tributary south of Annapolis and the Severn River, contains a recreational boating population second in size on the Bay only to Annapolis. On summer weekends, be cautious when threading your way through the cruisers and around the racing fleets. Weekdays are the best time to explore the many creeks along this stretch.

Up the South River are many deep creeks that are easy to enter. On the north side, they reach back into high, wooded banks with coves where you can anchor in surprising solitude during the week. Along the lower river, you will see ospreys nesting in almost every navigation marker.

Most creeks have a small boatyard or marina for local boats, but amenities for cruising visitors are in Selby Bay off the south side of the South River, about two miles up from the Bay. Another cluster of facilities is around the Route 2 Bridge, three miles farther up the South River. From here, it is not far to the commercial area that has grown up south and west of Annapolis. With a bicycle, you can (very carefully) go north on state Route 2 to the Parole area, with its large shopping malls, or south to the smaller strip shopping centers in Edgewater. Lee Airport, an active center for general aviation, is a short distance south of the bridge on state Route 2, but the only way to reach scheduled airline or rail transportation is via a long taxi ride to Baltimore-Washington International Airport (BWI).

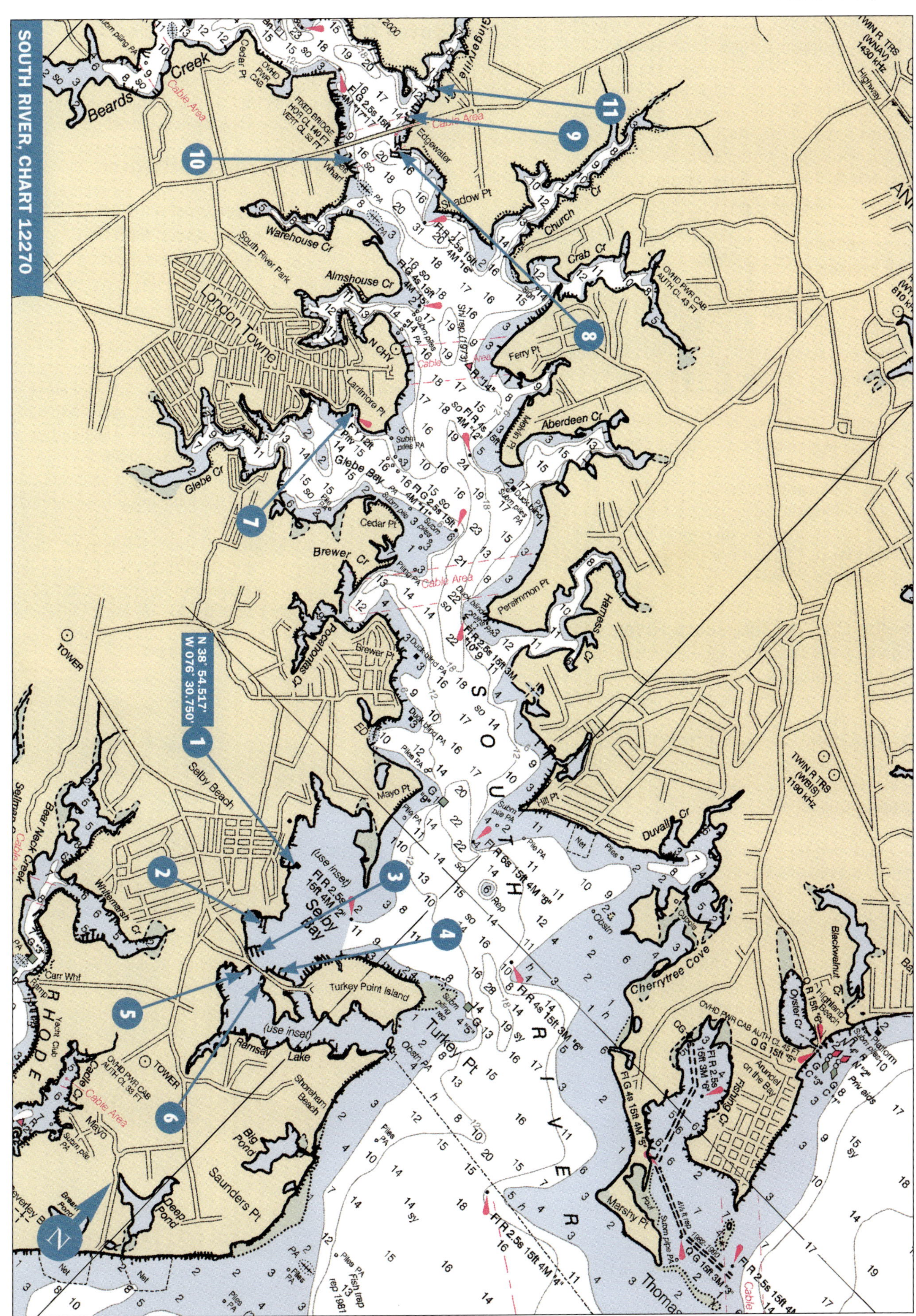
SOUTH RIVER, CHART 12270
N 38° 54.517'
W 076° 30.750'
SOUTH RIVER
Beards Creek
Warehouse Cr
Almshouse Cr
London Towne
South River Park
Glebe Cr
Glebe Bay
Larrimore Pt
Cedar Pt
Brewer Cr
Brewer Pt
Pocahontas Cr
Selby Beach
Selby Bay
Mayo Pt
Turkey Point Island
Turkey Pt
Ramsay Lake
Shoreham Beach
Big Pond
Deep Pond
Saunders Pt
Whitemarsh Cr
Bear Neck Creek
Carr Wht
RHODE
Edgewater
Shadow Pt
Church Cr
Crab Cr
Ferry Pt
Aberdeen Cr
Persimmon Pt
Harness Cr
Duvall Cr
Cherrytree Cove
Fishing Cr
Oyster Cr
Highland Beach
Blackwalnut Cr
Marshy Pt
Thomas
Cable Area
TOWER

NAVIGATION: Use Chart 12270. Round Thomas Point Light (a National Historic Landmark) to enter the South River. You may see local boats cutting inside the light, but do not follow their lead unless your vessel has a shoal draft. Crab pots (as well as dozens of fishing boats) often litter Thomas Point Shoal, which juts out almost to the light.

The speed limit in the lower South River is the same as the Severn River: 35 knots during the day and 25 knots at night. The creeks have a 6-knot speed limit on weekends and holidays, except for Broad Creek, which is the same as the main river. There is a waterski area on the upper South River. Otherwise, peaceful anchorages in the side creeks sometimes get blasts of noise from passing powerboats with marginal mufflers.

Waterway Guide Photography.

This well-marked river has a wide mouth, but it tends to shoal along the sides. The center is deep to the Route 2 Bridge five miles up and on beyond to a fixed 25-foot bridge at Riva Road. Keep an eye out for crab and eel pots that often line the channel.

Selby Bay, off the South River

This area is homeport to many boats, and they are always on the move. Both Selby Bay and Ramsay Lake have extensive dockage and services geared toward powerboats.

NAVIGATION: Use Chart 12270. There is a 14-foot fixed vertical clearance bridge separating Selby Bay from Ramsay Lake and a very shallow "local-knowledge exit" from Ramsay Lake to the Chesapeake. Transients can enter Selby Bay but not Ramsay Lake because of the bridge at one entrance and the shallow water at the other. Flashing red "2" marks the entrance to Selby Bay's popular harbor. There are occasional shoals inside, but you should not encounter any navigational problems if you stay in the well-marked channel.

Dockage: Selby Bay Marina and Anchor Yacht Basin both have gas and diesel. Holiday Point Marina, Anchor Yacht Basin, South River Marina, Turkey Point Marina and London Towne Marina all offer haul-out service. Turkey Point Marina and London Towne Marina also sell gas. Burr Yachts is the sales center for Fleming Yachts.

Anchorage: Mariners often overlook Selby Bay as an anchorage because of heavy traffic from its marinas and yacht clubs, but after you round Long Point, you will find a secluded anchorage, with depths of 7 to 11 feet, in the northwest corner of the bay. Deep water extends almost to its undeveloped shoreline. This anchorage is the closest on the South River to Chesapeake Bay.

Duvall Creek, off the South River

Of all the South River's many tributaries, Duvall Creek (the first noteworthy entrance on the north side) is too intricate for the stranger. It runs out of water quite suddenly, and only a native could follow the privately placed markers.

Harness Creek, off the South River

Harness Creek is a beauty, especially near sunset. You may have seen some of the magazine covers that were photographed here. Its eastern bank is Quiet Waters Park, which does not allow dinghy landings; obtain permission to tie up at the small-boat rental dock in advance (410-267-8742). The park holds a free outdoor concert series on Saturday nights in the summer (410-222-1777).

Anchorage: There is a wooded cove with two forks on the east side of Harness Creek just beyond the first sand spit; both are good for dinghy exploration or as anchorages for smaller boats. Note the shoal around Persimmon Point, to port upon entering. Bear to port after you enter and clear the narrow entrance into one of the most sheltered anchorages on the Bay. Powerboats and shoal-draft sailboats can come ashore on the sandy beaches here, to starboard around the hook just past the entrance.

Harness Creek itself carries 10-foot depths from shore to shore for about a half mile, and then 8-foot depths for another quarter mile. It is sheltered from the South River's surge and swells. Anchor near the kayak rental office and request permission to tie up to their dock. Walk 1 mile

Looking northeast over Selby Bay, the South River and Chesapeake Bay. (Not to be used for navigation.) Waterway Guide Photography.

through Quiet Waters Park, and you will find yourself near West Marine, McDonald's, Rita's and Fawcett Boat Supplies. A little farther down Bay Ridge Ave. is a Giant supermarket, liquor store, pizzeria and a Chinese restaurant.

Aberdeen Creek, off the South River

Anchorage: This deep creek (15-foot depths for a quarter mile) has an unmarked entrance. The usual bar makes out from the upstream shore. Little Aberdeen Creek, above Aberdeen, is easy to enter and carries 9-foot depths to a good anchorage sheltered from all directions but the south.

Crab and Church Creeks, off the South River

Dockage: Liberty Yacht Club is located at the foot of the state Route 2 high-level bridge. A large, full-service facility, Liberty Yacht Club accepts transients and can facilitate most types of repairs. Nearby is Oak Grove Marina, which may have transient space and sells fuel. Just off the South River is Gingerville Yachting Center with deep-water slips and some repair services.

Anchorage: Crab and Church creeks share a common mouth. Just inside Crab Creek, you must round a spit to starboard to get to the deep and well-protected water farther in.

To enter Church Creek, make for Crab Creek, and then turn sharply to port about 50 feet off the bulkhead-lined shoreline. The unmarked upstream point at the mouth extends out a long way. Church Creek is the local hurricane hole.

Brewer and Glebe Creeks, off the South River

Anchorage: On the South River's southern shore, outer Brewer Creek is wide open to northerlies, but the inner creek is protected. The narrow channel is subject to change, so check locally for information and sound your way in carefully. Glebe Creek, with a housing development on its banks, is less attractive, and its outer bay has a shoal middle ground. Favor the south side as you enter.

Almshouse and Warehouse Creeks, off the South River

Both Almshouse Creek and Warehouse Creek have good depths, and their shores are crowded with private docks. There are small boatyards, marinas, sheltered anchorages and outboard-powered boats buzzing around like mosquitoes on summer weekends.

An imposing brick mansion, once the county almshouse, stands at the mouth of Almshouse Creek. Known as the London Town Publik House in the 1700s, it is now a restored National Historic Landmark. Recent archaeological excavation is producing many artifacts related to late-17th-century life in this tobacco seaport town, which disappeared in the shadow of Annapolis.

A woodland garden featuring flowers and plants native to the region lies on the grounds. You are welcome at the dock, which holds 7 feet of water at its tip. This is a convenient stop if you need supplies, with a supermarket, a hardware store and a laundry all within a half-mile walk.

Rhode River, West River, MD

		Largest Vessel Accommodated	VHF Channel Monitored	Transient Berths / Total Berths	Approach / Dockside Depth (reported)	Floating Docks	Gas / Diesel	Groceries, Ice, Marine Supplies, Snacks	Repairs: Hull, Engine, Propeller	Lift (tonnage), Crane, Rail	Min/Max Amps	Laundry, Pool, Showers, Courtesy Car	Pump-Out Station	Nearby: Grocery Store, Motel, Restaurant
RHODE RIVER		**Dockage**						**Supplies**		**Services**				
1. Cadle Creek Marina	410-798-1915	35	-	/50	6/6	-	GD	IMS	HEP	-	30/30	S	P	GR
2. Casa Rio Marina Inc.	410-798-4731	40	16	3/39	5/5	-	-	IMS	HEP	L70	30/30	S	P	-
3. Blue Water Marina	410-798-6733	45	-	/63	12/10	-	-	-	HEP	R	-	-	P	-
4. Rhode River Marina Inc. WiFi	**410-798-1658**	**50**	**-**	**5/100**	**10/8**	**-**	**GD**	**GIMS**	**HEP**	**L25**	**30/50**	**LS**	**P**	**GR**
5. Holiday Hill Marina	443-871-3909	60	-	/145	7/7	-	-	I	HE	L6	30/30	LS	P	GR
WEST RIVER														
6. Clarks Landing–Shady Side	410-867-9550	55	16	-	5.5/4.5	-	-	-	HEP	L50	30/30	-	-	GR
7. Backyard Boats	410-867-4800	45	16	2/56	10/7	-	GD	IMS	HEP	L25, C	-	-	P	GR
8. Hartge Yacht Yard	410-867-2188	-	-	/20	-	-	-	M	HEP	L25	-	S	-	R
9. West River Yacht Harbor Condo Assoc. WiFi	410-867-4065	50	16	3/180	9/9	-	GD	GIMS	HEP	L40	30/50	PS	P	GMR
10. West River Fuel Dock	410-867-1444	135	16/09	10/185	8/9	-	GD	IMS	-	-	30/30	S	P	GMR
11. Pirate's Cove Internet WiFi	410-867-2300	62	-	/80	15/13	-	-	IS	-	-	30/30	LS	P	MR
12. Galesville Harbor Yacht Yard Inc. WiFi	410-867-7517	50	-	/186	9/7	-	GD	I	HEP	L30, C4	30/30	PS	P	MR
13. Hartge Yacht Harbor WiFi	**443-607-6306**	**70**	**09**	**/320**	**12/8**	**-**	**-**	**I**	**HE**	**L50, R70**	**30/50**	**S**	**P**	**R**

Corresponding chart(s) not to be used for navigation. Internet Access WiFi Wireless Internet Access Waterway Guide Cruising Club Partner

See www.WaterwayGuide.com for current rates, fuel prices, web site addresses, and other up-to-the-minute information.

A view to the north over Galesville and the West River. (Not to be used for navigation.) Waterway Guide Photography.

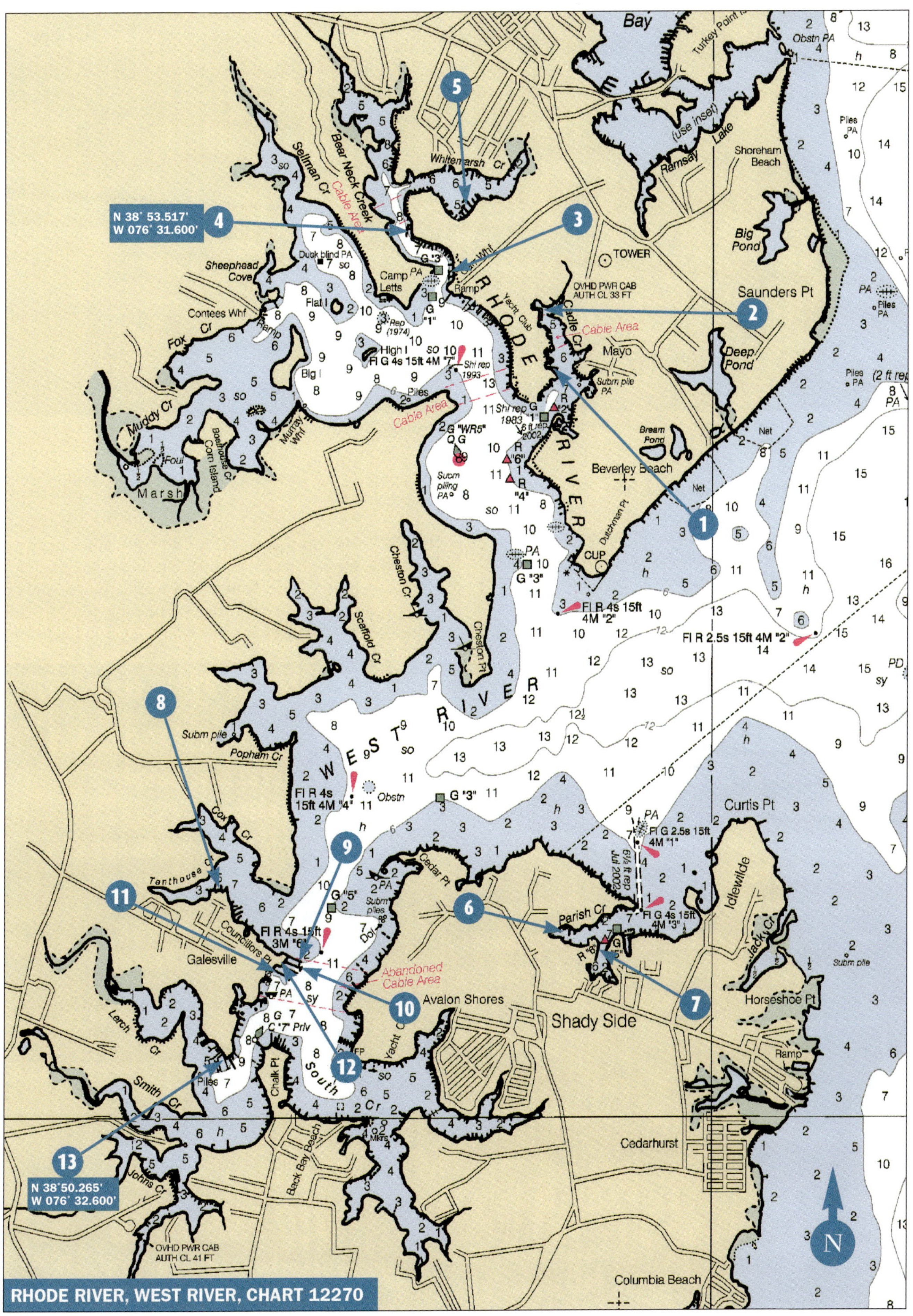

RHODE RIVER, WEST RIVER, CHART 12270

Looking south over Cadle Creek and the Rhode River. (Not to be used for navigation.) Waterway Guide Photography.

Looking northeast over Bear Neck Creek. (Not to be used for navigation.)

Edgewater, on the South River

This low-key, but fast-growing little community along the South River is rife with marine facilities and boatyards and serves as a suburb of Annapolis, Baltimore and Washington, D.C. Here you will find deep-water amenities, including restaurants with docks, sailboat rentals, repairs and full-service marinas. These facilities are above and below the bridge on both sides of the river and on adjacent Gingerville Creek, right next door.

NAVIGATION: Use Chart 12270. Be especially careful to mind the marked shoal making out from Poplar Point and the opposite shore. Note: Local marine police enforce the speed limit (6 knots) between flashing red "16" off Poplar Point (charted as Shadow Point on Chart 12270 and

unnamed on Chart 12263) and the first bridge with arrests and fines.

Take this warning seriously, as excessive speed on the river has caused severe, and even fatal, accidents here. On summer weekends, all manner of boats are in the channel.

Dockage: Pier 7 Marina, located at the south end of the Route 2 highway bridge on the Edgewater side, is only four miles up South River from the Bay. This pet-friendly marina welcomes transients as well as folks looking to lease a slip for the season. This marina also has an on-site restaurant, Coconut Joes, and its own beachfront picnic area. This is also a handy spot for provisioning. It's a half-mile walk to a CVS Pharmacy, a Giant supermarket, and various other stores.

Beards Creek, off the South River

The first entrance to port above the 53-foot vertical clearance Route 2 Bridge, Beards Creek has several developments along its western shore and a busy local airport on the eastern shore.

NAVIGATION: Use Chart 12270. Note the long shoal extending out from the right-hand shore at the entrance. As you head upstream, keep the green-and-red unnumbered daybeacon to starboard. Watch the depth sounder as you proceed about 50 to 100 feet past Cedar Point and then head upstream. The creek carries 10- to 14-foot depths for a mile and then shoals rapidly. Holding here is only fair, with many boats dragging during squalls.

Broad Creek, off the South River

Anchorage: To starboard immediately above the fixed Riva Road bridge (25-foot vertical clearance), Broad Creek carries 10-foot depths for half a mile and then shoals at its head. The shoreline is relatively undeveloped, and the creek is usually quiet. The upper creek narrows between its huge, wooded banks, and on summer weekends, water skiers are out in large numbers.

RHODE AND WEST RIVERS

These two rivers, next down the Bay from the South River, share a common entrance and are among the prettiest on the upper Western Shore. There is a lot of day-boating and cruising traffic here on weekends, and you may encounter a small-boat regatta almost any time, but these tributaries are wide enough that there is seldom a congestion problem. Thanks to the remoteness of this area by road, the Smithsonian's ownership of a large tract of land and the desire of locals to keep the environment rural, you will find a much calmer atmosphere here than on the rivers farther north.

With several highly regarded boatyards nearby, you will see some interesting vessels here. Keep an eye out for the Chesapeake 20 sloops, an indigenous design that

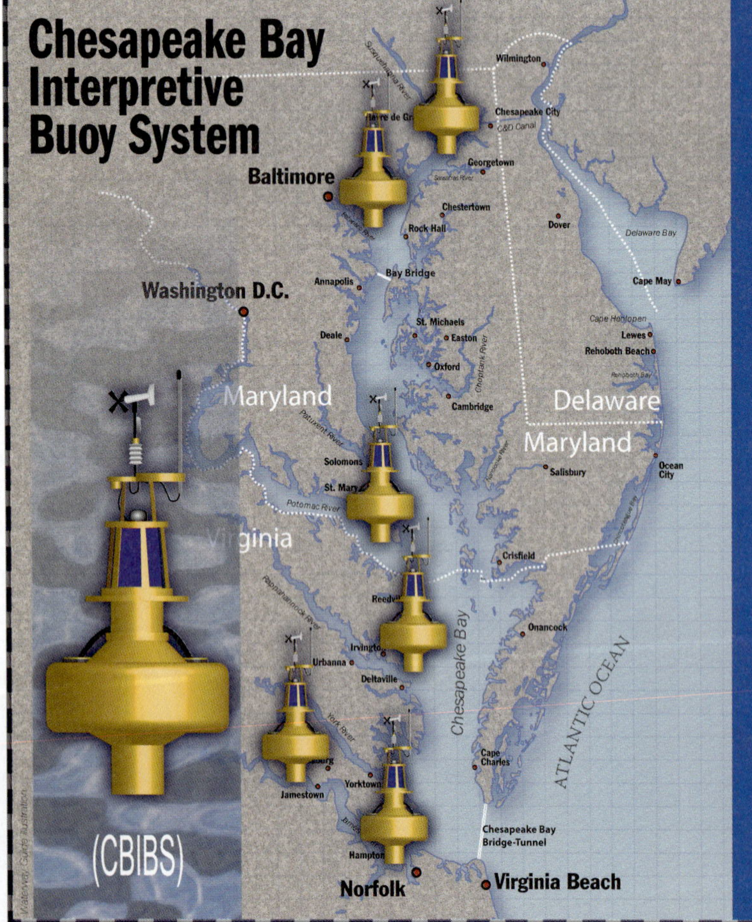

You set out from a small-boat launch or marina along the Chesapeake Bay—the same geography traveled by Captain John Smith some 400 years ago. As the first English settler to fully explore the Chesapeake Bay, Smith traveled more than 2,000 miles during 1607 and 1608 in an open "shallop" boat with no modern conveniences.

But your trip is quite different. You are equipped with a cell phone and maps of the Captain John Smith Chesapeake National Historic Trail—the National Park Service's first water-based national historic trail—giving you many advantages that the early explorers didn't have.

Today, you have access to the Chesapeake Bay Interpretive Buoy System (CBIBS), an observing system and trail guide managed by the National Oceanic and Atmospheric Administration (NOAA)'s Chesapeake Bay Office. CBIBS buoys mark points along the Trail and use wireless technology to transmit real-time observations on weather, water condition, and water quality. You can access all this information at toll-free 877-BUOY-BAY or at www.buoybay.org. Each buoy reports information important for your safety including wind speed, air and water temperature, and wave height.

Not only does CBIBS give you real-time wind and weather information, it can also tell you about John Smith's adventures during his voyages. The system features voice narration of natural and cultural history for the areas near each buoy.

—Text courtesy NOAA Chesapeake Bay Office

many consider the prettiest small sailboat ever created on the Bay.

NAVIGATION: Use Chart 12270. **Use Baltimore tide tables. For Galesville high tide, subtract 1 hour 48 minutes; for low tide subtract 1 hour 38 minutes.** Coming down from the north, lay your course from Thomas Point Light (abeam and just to the south of it) to flashing green buoy "1A," making sure to leave this buoy well to port on approach, and continue on the same course to flashing red "2." Leave flashing red "2" decidedly to starboard: It is on the edge of the shoal extending southeast from the beach between Saunders Point and Dutchman Point. You will encounter scattered trap markers on this course, so take some care to avoid their warps, particularly in poor light.

Beyond flashing red "2," however, alleged trap-free channels will make the going considerably easier. Although both channels are well marked, once you pass flashing red "2," you may want to set a compass course--particularly in poor visibility--to avoid difficulties with shoals that trace the shoreline well out from the land.

Coming up from the south, allow for the extensive shoals paralleling the shore from Herring Bay to Curtis Point. Head for flashing green buoy "1," just west of the shipping channel, well off the combined mouths of the West and Rhode rivers. Once abeam of flashing green buoy "1," you are safe to make the turn to port toward flashing green buoy "1A," avoiding the extensive shallows northeast of Curtis and Horseshoe points.

Rhode River

The Smithsonian owns most of the south side of the Rhode River. The river has buoys, stakes and structures marking scientific equipment above and below the surface. According to the Smithsonian Environmental Research Center (SERC), the equipment is fragile. If you want to visit SERC, call ahead (443-482-2200) and come by car. The pier is for the research fleet exclusively, and the banks prohibit trespassing because of research being done. You can anchor or explore by dinghy anywhere as long as you stay clear of the instruments. You may hear the morning bugle call at Camp Letts, which is marked on the chart.

NAVIGATION: Use Chart 12270. The approaches to the Rhode River from the north and south were covered in the previous navigation section under Rhode and West Rivers. Follow those instructions for entering the Rhode River.

Dockage: The north side of the Rhode River is well settled, and both of its main creeks have boatyards and marinas offering hauling and repairs, but transient slips are limited in number. In Cadle Creek, you will find Cadle Creek Marina, which sells fuel, and Casa Rio Marina (5-foot dockside depth), which has a 70-ton lift. Both have limited transient space. Farther north on the Rhode River at Carrs Wharf is Blue Water Marina, which may have transient space. Next is Rhode River Marina, up Bear Neck Creek, which offers gas and diesel, and some supplies and repairs in addition to slips. Finally, the 145-slip Holiday Hill Marina in White Marsh Creek sets aside a few slips for transients.

Anchorage: Immediately inside the entrance to the west, a big bight, part of SERC, provides a cool anchorage in hot weather, with depths of 8 feet. It is wide open to the southeast, and you may get some wake from the channel. For a snug spot, round Rhode River's flashing green "7," turn sharply to the west and, guided by your chart, drop the hook. Depths here are approximately 6 to 9 feet. The best spot is between High Island, now eroded to the point that it belies its name, and the south shore. It will probably be crowded with anchored boats. Shoals surround all three of the steadily diminishing islands in this pretty cove.

West River

NAVIGATION: Use Chart 12270. The structure of flashing red "4," which blends in with the shoreline, can be hard to pick up. Look for green daybeacon "3" to port. Run a compass course on your first time in. Approach the light closely, and then head for green daybeacon "5" and flashing red "6," which mark encroaching shoals. Expect a depth here of

Galesville, MD. (Photo Courtesy Ann DeMuth.)

about 10 feet. Give both markers a fair berth, steering carefully and keeping a good lookout.

Dockage: Galesville, on the West River, offers a surprising range of facilities for boating visitors. Immediately to starboard on approaching the Galesville waterfront, West River Yacht Harbor Condo Association has limited transient space and sells gas and diesel. West River Fuel Dock has transient slips as well as fuel, as does Galesville Harbor Yacht Yard. Pirates Cove may have space as well. Still farther along, the town dock (7-foot depths at dockside) is available to the public for up to 4 hours dockage (no overnight tie-ups allowed). Southward on the West River, just beyond Chalk Point, Hartge Yacht Harbor is a large, full-service, family-run marina at the mouth of Tenthouse Creek.

Anchorage: You will find a convenient anchorage in 7 to 8 feet of water in South Creek, off West River, but it is very open to northerlies. Deep-draft boats seeking protection from the north may have to go up the Rhode, while shallow-draft boats can anchor in South Creek off the Chesapeake Yacht Club, or farther. You will also find good holding and sufficient swinging room on West River past Chalk Point, beyond the Hartge Yacht Harbor mooring field. Boats drawing 5 feet or more may find the area significantly south of the mooring field uncomfortably shallow, particularly when low tide and a northerly blow combine.

Moorings: Hartge Yacht Harbor, just to the south, has 60 protected moorings which are heavily seasonal, but may have one available on short term..

GOIN' ASHORE: GALESVILLE, MD

Pretty little Galesville sits on the West River in southern Anne Arundel County and merits a five-star rating for its laid-back factor. Plan to stroll or bike this village with its handful of places to stop and explore. As Bob Platt, owner of the local landmark restaurant Inn at Pirate's Cove, said about the town: "It's the type of place where you sit on the bank of a river and take a nap with a fishing line."

History: Virginia Puritans John Brown and John Clark founded Galesville in 1652, arriving for religious freedom, then converting to Quakerism, which became a strong presence here—so strong, in fact, that Galesville is considered the birthplace of Quakerism in Maryland. The Quakers ended up leaving Galesville because the sizeable group of landowners opposed slavery.

The small village went through several names, starting out as Brownton, then West River Landing, then Galloways, then Galesville. This was designated a port of entry in 1684, then later a fishing and farming community as well as a steamship stop and a summer locale for tourists. Essentially isolated by water, Galesville's roads connecting it to other areas were not developed until well into the 1930s.

Points of Interest: The Quaker Burying Ground, located at the intersection of Routes 468 and 255, dates to 1672. Interestingly, the old Quaker graves are not marked because they did not believe in doing so, placing the emphasis instead upon good works when alive. However, numerous other locals are buried here. This may be the most obvious remnant of Galesville's Quaker past except, perhaps, Tenthouse Creek, so named due

Reference the marina listing tables to see all the marinas in the area.

POINTS OF INTEREST

1 Galesville Heritage Museum

2 The Hartge Nautical Museum

SHOPPING

3 The River Gallery

DINING

4 Inn at Pirate's Cove Restaurant & Marina

5 Thursday's Steak and Crabhouse

POST OFFICE

to the large gatherings of Quakers here along the creek. Among their number once was William Penn of Pennsylvania.

The Galesville Heritage Museum, 988 Main St., shows off photos of the steamship Emma Giles (as well as three of her deck chairs) and numerous other elements of local history. If you can't make its 1:00 p.m. to 4:00 p.m. hours each Sunday from April to November, either make arrangements by calling 410-867-9499, or check out the panels outside that depict Galesville's tale.

Another small museum that might be of interest is located at the Hartge Yacht Harbor. This well-known local family arrived in nearby Shady Side in the 1860s and established a boatbuilding yard at the site of the present-day yacht yard. The Hartge Nautical Museum, founded by Lawrence Hartge, holds memorabilia, including a piano built by an early family member before they moved on to boatbuilding, according to Emile Alexander Schlegel, namesake to one of the boatbuilders.

Shopping: The River Gallery (1000 Main S, 410-867-0954), shows a variety of work and is open Friday through Sunday, or by appointment.

Dining: The waterside Inn at Pirate's Cove Restaurant and Marina (4817 Riverside Dr., 410-867-2300) offers comfortable dining rooms and a deck, a wide-ranging menu and breakfast on Saturday and Sunday. Its Big Mary's Dock Bar is open May through September.

Thursday's Steak and Crabhouse, located on the old steamboat pier, serves hard-shell crabs (410-867-7200) and has a very active tiki bar with a fantastic view of the river. Thursday's has 27 boat slips for those who dock and dine.

ADDITIONAL RESOURCES

■ GALESVILLE HERITAGE SOCIETY: www.galesvilleheritagesociety.org

NEARBY MEDICAL FACILITIES

Anne Arundel Medical Center: 2001 Medical Pkwy., Annapolis, MD 21401. 443-481-4000

Calvert Memorial Hospital: 100 Hospital Road, Prince Frederick, MD 20678. 410-535-4000

Urgent care available at Dunkirk Medical Center: 10845 Town Center Blvd., Dunkirk, MD 20754 410-286-7911

NEARBY AIRPORT

Baltimore-Washington International Thurgood Marshall Airport: www.bwiairport.com

Parish Creek, off the West River

Even though it hasn't any room to anchor, Parish Creek is worth a visit. You can buy seafood here, and a full-service marina allows do-it-yourself repairs. The Johns Hopkins Chesapeake Bay Institute is on the southeastern corner.

NAVIGATION: Use Chart 12270. Parish Creek, on the south side of the Rhode/West River entrance, has a narrow entrance channel, but an uncharted range helps you line up the markers. If you draw more than 4.5 feet, enter at half tide or better, as the charted depths are only 3 feet.

Dockage: Both Clarks Landind-Shady Side and Backyard Boats are located in Parish Creek. Backyard Boats sells gas and diesel and both facilities offer boat repairs. (Note approach/dockside depths at Clarks Landing are reported at 5.5/4.5.) ■

Waterway Guide is always open to your observations from the helm. Email your comments on any navigation information in the Guide to: editor@waterwayguide.com.

Galesville
West River
Eastern Bay
MILE 55
St. Michaels
259
301
Page 266
Deale
4
Herring Bay
Page 267
Chesapeake Beach
N
Choptank River
MILE 71
Chesapeake Bay
2
Little Choptank River
231
235
St. Leonard
Page 267
Calvert Cliffs
Patuxent River
238
Page 271
Solomons
MILE 86
DOZIER'S WATERWAY GUIDE
THE CRUISING AUTHORITY
WWW.WATERWAYGUIDE.COM
Hooper Islands
Skipper's Handbook
GPS Waypoints 48
Tide Tables 50
St. Marys City
Potomac River

Herring Bay to Patuxent River

CHARTS 12263, 12264, 12266, 12270, 12284

An interesting vista of fossil-filled cliffs—tall, rugged and interrupted only by dredged basins—characterizes Maryland's Western Shore between the West River and the Patuxent River. Herring Bay, in fact, is the only natural harbor on this shore for some 35 miles before the Patuxent River below Cove Point. Eight miles south of West River, Herring Bay and Rockhold Creek provide good shelter and have a variety of marinas.

NAVIGATION: Use Charts 12270, 12266 and 12264. From Annapolis, head south from flashing green "1AH" (off Tolly Point at the junction of the Severn River and Chesapeake Bay), pass Thomas Point Light and then continue out into the main part of the Chesapeake Bay. Underway toward the Patuxent River, this direct course takes you so far out that you will be unable to clearly distinguish shoreline structures and activity. Engage the autopilot if you have one, but be on the lookout for other traffic, particularly ocean freighters and other commercial vessels, debris or crab trap markers that may drift all the way out to the big-ship channel. To avoid the ship traffic and to view the scenery, a course can be run closer to the western shore. Stay about two miles offshore to avoid shoals. This route will add less than two miles to the trip down the Bay.

As you proceed south from Annapolis, stay well off the broad, sandy shoal that bulges out from the contour of the eastern shoreline in the area of Sharps Island Light, near the mouth of the Choptank River. This shallow area has stranded more than one vessel when tides are lower than usual. Crab pots, oyster stakes and fishing nets clutter the area.

Heading south from flashing green "1AH" off Annapolis will take you to the easily identified natural gas pier off Cove Point, 32 miles away. This pier is a LNG (liquefied natural gas) unloading facility operated by Dominion Cove Point LNG. There is a restricted zone around the LNG facility that is clearly marked with white buoys. Do not enter this area. The pier has a security watch, and if you enter into the restricted zone, you will be directed to leave. If you do not promptly do so, they will call the Coast Guard. This has happened on several occasions, as the area is a popular fishing site, and boaters sometimes get too close to the facility.

HERRING BAY

From the water, the shore south of Herring Bay is very attractive. Houses stand high on hills with their lawns sweeping down to the beach, cluster together under cool shade trees along the steep hillsides or nestle in groups behind the sandy beaches. In addition to its beauty, Herring Bay is an important provisioning and repair center, for both power and sailboats.

NAVIGATION: Use Chart 12266. **Use Baltimore tide tables. For high tide at Fairhaven, subtract 2 hours 55 minutes; for low tide subtract 3 hours 1 minute.** Heading south from the West River or the Rhode River, work your way out to G"1" (which is the entrance to West River), turn to a course of 211 magnetic and proceed to green marker GC "83A." Alter your course and head for red marker "2" which is the entrance buoy for Herring Bay. Herring Bay is an open indentation in the shore, moderately protected by Long Bar, a two-mile-long shoal hanging down from the north. Unless yours is a very shoal-draft boat (Long Bar has 2- to 4-foot depths at its northern end), round flashing red "2" at the southern tip of the bar, then head back up to

QUICK FACT:

LNG TERMINAL

Just south of St. Leonard on the Chesapeake Bay in Cove Point, MD lies Dominion Cove Point LNG, one of country's largest liquefied natural gas (LNG) import facilities. The Cove Point facility began receiving shipments between 1978 and 1980, and was re-opened by Columbia Gas in 1995, when it was used to liquefy, store and distribute domestic natural gas for use in the mid-Atlantic. After several changes in ownership, Dominion received its first shipment at Cove Point in 2003.

The LNG facility sits on just over 1,000 acres, the majority of which is under protection; in addition to 800 acres under conservation management, 190 acres are freshwater marsh, and a country park accounts for another 80 acres of the property. Dominion says it is working with the environmental community to ensure the endangered plant and animal life, in and around the property, is researched and maintained. Dominion is also part of the Cove Point Natural Heritage Trust, a partnership with the Sierra Club and the Maryland Conservation Council.

LNG TERMINAL
N 38°24.181' W 076°23.069'

Waterway Guide Photography.

HERRINGTON HARBOUR NORTH MARINA

Looking southeast over Herring Bay. (Not to be used for navigation.) Photo courtesy of Herrington Harbor North Marina.

HERRINGTON HARBOUR SOUTH MARINA

Looking south over Herrington Harbour South. (Not to be used for navigation.) Waterway Guide Photography.

Deale and Herring Bay, MD

HERRING BAY		Largest Vessel Accommodated	VHF Channel Monitored	Transient Berths / Total Berths	Approach / Dockside Depth (reported)	Floating Docks	Gas / Diesel	Groceries, Ice, Marine Supplies, Snacks	Repairs: Hull, Engine, Propeller	Lift (tonnage), Crane, Rail	Min/Max Amps	Laundry, Pool, Showers, Courtesy Car	Pump-Out Station	Nearby: Grocery Store, Motel, Restaurant
		Dockage					Supplies		Services					
1. Herrington Harbour North	**800-297-1930**	**120**	**16/09**	**25/575**	**7/7**	**-**	**-**	**GIMS**	**HEP**	**L70, C15**	**30/50**	**LPS**	**P**	**GR**
2. Zimmerman Marine at Herrington Harbor	**410-867-4400**	**-**	**-**	**-**	**-**	**-**	**GD**	**MS**	**HEP**	**L50**	**-**	**LPS**	**P**	**-**
3. Shipwright Harbor Marina	410-867-7686	50	-	10/250	6/6	-	-	I	HEP	L15, C12	30/50	LPS	P	G
4. Bay Harbour Boatyard	410-867-2392	40	-	/15	5/5	-	-	-	HEP	L15	-	-	-	-
5. Rockhold Creek Marina & Yacht Repair	410-867-7919	40	-	3/47	8/6	-	-	I	HEP	L20,C7	30/50	S	P	GR
6. Harbour Cove Marina	410-867-1600	40	16	/80	5/5	F	G	IMS	HEP	L25	30/30	LPS	P	GR
7. Gates Marine	410-867-9666	40	-	/90	5/5	-	-	IM	HEP	L25	30/30	PS	P	GR
8. Sherman's Marina	301-261-5013	44	-	2/32	6/6	-	-	I	-	-	30/30	LS	P	GMR
9. Paradise Marina	443-964-8842	40	-	4/70	12/5	F	-	I	-	L	50/50	S	-	GR
10. Herrington Harbour South	**800-213-9438**	**90**	**16/09**	**40/600**	**7/7**	**-**	**GD**	**GIMS**	**HEP**	**L70, C**	**30/50**	**LPS**	**P**	**GMR**

Corresponding chart(s) not to be used for navigation. Internet Access · Wireless Internet Access · Waterway Guide Cruising Club Partner

See www.WaterwayGuide.com for current rates, fuel prices, web site addresses, and other up-to-the-minute information.

Rockhold Creek for the many marinas clustered around the fixed bridge (14-foot vertical clearance) at Deale. Depths were reported to be 7 feet in the channel into Rockhold Creek. Jetty improvements to reduce silting were completed in 2012.

Dockage: Collectively, the many Herring Bay marinas serve what is possibly the greatest aggregation of local powerboats on the entire Chesapeake Bay. These docks are convenient to the open Bay and comparatively close to the productive sportfishing grounds stretching along the opposite Eastern Shore.

Herrington Harbour Marina has two facilities: Herrington Harbour North, at the entrance to Rockhold and Tracys Creeks, and Herrington Harbour South, a man-made harbor inside Holland Point. These marinas have 575 and 600 slips, respectively, making them among the largest on the Bay. The north facility has a complete repair and service yard with multiple lifts and a very large area for haul-outs. On-site vendors provide all the services a boater requires. Several boat brokerage offices, fishing charters and a West Marine are also on site. The south marina features lodging, dining and resort amenities with a Caribbean motif. Pamper yourself in the hot tubs or spa, swim laps in the Olympic size pool or work out in the fitness center. Both the north and south marinas offer easy, direct access to the Chesapeake.

Rockhold Creek is lined with marinas, including (from north to south): Gates Marine, Harbour Cove Marina, Sherman's Marina, Rockhold Creek Marina & Yacht Repair, Bay Harbour Boatyard, Shipwright Harbor Marina and Paradise Marina. All of these have some transient space and several offer boat repair services; Harrington Harbour South (gas and diesel) and Harbor Cove Marina (gas only) are the only marinas here that sell fuels. Zimmerman Marine at Herrington Harbour (North) is a full-service boatyard (no transient slips).

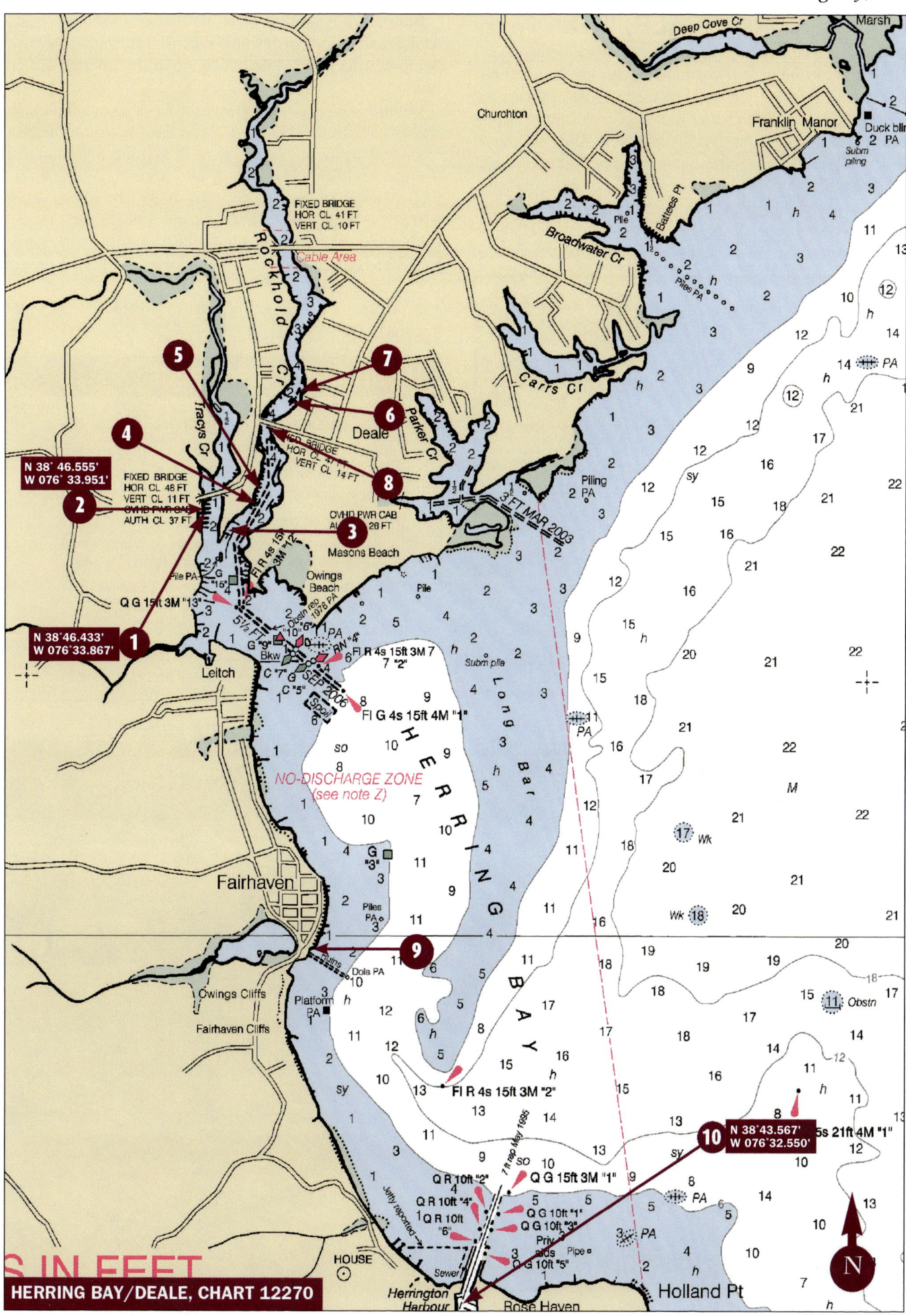

HERRING BAY/DEALE, CHART 12270
N 38° 46.555' W 076° 33.951'
N 38°46.433' W 076°33.867'
N 38°43.567' W 076°32.550'
FIXED BRIDGE HOR CL 41 FT VERT CL 10 FT
FIXED BRIDGE HOR CL 48 FT VERT CL 11 FT
OVHD PWR CAB AUTH CL 37 FT
Rockhold Cr
Tracys Cr
Parker Cr
Carrs Cr
Broadwater Cr
Deep Cove Cr
Churchton
Franklin Manor
Deale
Masons Beach
Owings Beach
Leitch
Fairhaven
Owings Cliffs
Fairhaven Cliffs
Herrington Harbour
Rose Haven
Holland Pt
HERRING BAY
Long Bar
NO-DISCHARGE ZONE (see note Z)
Cable Area
3 FT MAR 2003
FI G 4s 15ft 4M "1"
FI R 4s 15ft 3M "2"
Q G 15ft 3M "1"
Q G 15ft 3M "13"

GOIN' ASHORE: **DEALE, MD**

A small Chesapeake outpost close to Washington, D.C., Deale harbors numerous commuters who have figured out how to live the good life without spending all of their time on the road. A notable charter boat fleet docks at the Happy Harbor Restaurant along Rockhold Creek. And, of course, local restaurants know how to put their hands on very good (and tasty) hard-shell blue crabs. Deale did, after all, begin life as a waterman's community. Deale shops and restaurants are within a three-mile bike ride of Herrington Harbour North marina.

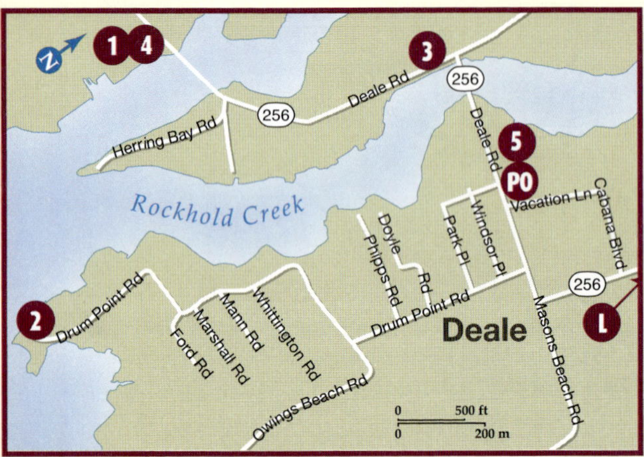

Reference the marina listing tables to see all the marinas in the area.

SHOPPING
1 West Marine

DINING
2 Skipper's Pier Restaurant
3 Happy Harbor Inn
4 Calypso Bay Restaurant
5 Umai Sushi House

PO POST OFFICE

L LIBRARY

Shopping: A grocery store, hardware store, library and bank are all located in downtown Deale. Herrington Harbour North Marina has a West Marine and other marine-related vendors.

Dining: Skipper's Pier, grown from life as an oyster packing facility back in the 1930s, '40s and '50s, is one of the best crab-cracking locales anywhere, with a deck and atrium that opens onto Rockhold Creek. It also has a mighty fine seafood menu and a seasonal dock bar (6158 Drum Point Road, 410-867-7110). They reserve slip space for diners. Happy Harbor Inn (533 Deale Road, 410-867-0949) is a local stalwart. Calypso Bay is a casual restaurant overlooking the water at Herrington Harbour North Marina. If you have a taste for Asian cuisine, be sure you try Umai Sushi House (651 Deale Road, 410-867-4433).

ADDITIONAL RESOURCES

■ **DEALE MERCHANTS ASSOCIATION:**
www.dealemerchants.com

Renditions Golf Course: 1380 W. Central Ave., Davidsonville, MD 21035, 888-451-4144 (16 miles)

NEARBY MEDICAL FACILITIES

Anne Arundel Medical Center: 2001 Medical Parkway, Annapolis, MD 21401, 443-481-4000 (18 miles)

Calvert Memorial Hospital: 100 Hospital Road, Prince Frederick, MD 20678, 410-535-4000 (17 miles)

Dunkirk Medical Center: 10845 Town Center Blvd., Dunkirk, MD 20754, 410-286-7911 (10 miles)

Boats at the ready on a summer day in Herring Bay. Photo courtesy of Tom Hale.

CALVERT CLIFFS TO SOLOMONS

From Chesapeake Beach to Drum Point, the Calvert Cliffs are a steep, almost unbroken 30-mile-long stretch of fossil-laden clay strata and beach. In some places, the land rises straight up as high as 100 feet. Scientists have found proof here that during Miocene times (10 to 25 million years ago) a considerable portion of this tidewater shoreline was submerged. The best fossil beds are near Chesapeake Beach, around Plum Point and at Governors Run. Call 410-394-1778 for details from the Calvert Cliffs State Park. If you cannot visit the cliffs, be sure to visit the Calvert Marine Museum at Solomons. It provides information about the cliffs and even lets you "dig." It has a dinghy dock and a convenient anchorage.

At the lower end of the Calvert Cliffs, old and new collide dramatically at the big nuclear power plant. Inquire locally if you would like to visit by land.

NAVIGATION: Use Charts 12264 and 12266. Take note of the restricted fish-trap area marked on your chart just south of Chesapeake Beach. Also, just north of Cove Point, an enforced security zone surrounds the nuclear plant at Calvert Cliffs and the LNG pier two miles farther south, and vessels must stay at least a quarter mile offshore. However, in other areas you can run fairly close inshore (with 7-foot depths or more) to see the cliffs, as long as you keep a sharp lookout for fish traps. This is especially true close to Cove Point. These unlit, low-lying hazards can cause serious underwater damage to your boat, as several cruisers have discovered. (Fish traps are large structures made of heavy wooden stakes connected by netting that traps fish for harvest. They often have a collection of assorted shore birds like cormorants and herons on top looking for a meal.)

Dockage: Several harbors in this area have substantial marinas catering largely to powerboats, especially sportfishing.

Chesapeake Beach has, as the chart shows, a man-made harbor off Fishing Creek. The creek's entrance jetties receive periodic rehabilitation, and project depths call for 7 feet; however, the latest NOAA chart 12266, Edition 30 shows 3 feet approach depths in the channel in May 2011. Make sure to call ahead for current local information.

Inside, the Chesapeake Beach Resort and Spa features the Rod 'n' Reel Dock marine complex, with a restaurant, and Rod 'n' Reel Marina West, a larger docking facility, above a bridge with a 10-foot fixed vertical clearance. Rod 'n' Reel Dock has 125 slips and provides transient or seasonal dockage. Both marinas sell gas and diesel. From either location you can walk to restaurants, grocery stores, laundry and a water park. You can also rent kayaks, canoes and bicycles. If fishing is your game, join one of the 25 charter fishing boats for a trip out on to the Bay. There is a small railroad museum here as a reminder of the days when this was a major tourist destination with hotels, gambling, an amusement park and passenger rail service.

Chesapeake Beach, Breezy Point, MD

		Largest Vessel Accommodated	VHF Channel Monitored	Transient Berths / Total Berths	Approach / Dockside Depth (reported)	Floating Docks	Gas / Diesel	Groceries, Ice, Marine Supplies, Snacks	Repairs: Hull, Engine, Propeller	Lift (tonnage), Crane, Rail	Min/Max Amps	Laundry, Pool, Showers, Courtesy Car	Pump-Out Station	Nearby: Grocery Store, Motel, Restaurant
CHESAPEAKE BEACH		**Dockage**					**Supplies**				**Services**			
1. Rod 'N' Reel Dock at Chesapeake Beach Resort & Spa	**800-233-2080**	**50**	**88**	**15/120**	**4.5/4.5**	**-**	**GD**	**IS**	**-**	**-**	**30/50**	**PS**	**P**	**GMR**
2. Rod 'N' Reel Marina West (Internet Access) (Wireless Internet Access)	**301-855-8450**	**45**	**16/10**	**40/225**	**6.5/4.5**	**-**	**GD**	**IMS**	**-**	**-**	**30/50**	**LPS**	**P**	**GMR**
BREEZY POINT														
3. Breezy Point Marina	301-758-9981	65	74	5/225	4.5/4.5	-	GD	GIMS	HEP	L20	30/50	S	P	GMR

Corresponding chart(s) not to be used for navigation. Internet Access · Wireless Internet Access · Waterway Guide Cruising Club Partner

See www.WaterwayGuide.com for current rates, fuel prices, web site addresses, and other up-to-the-minute information.

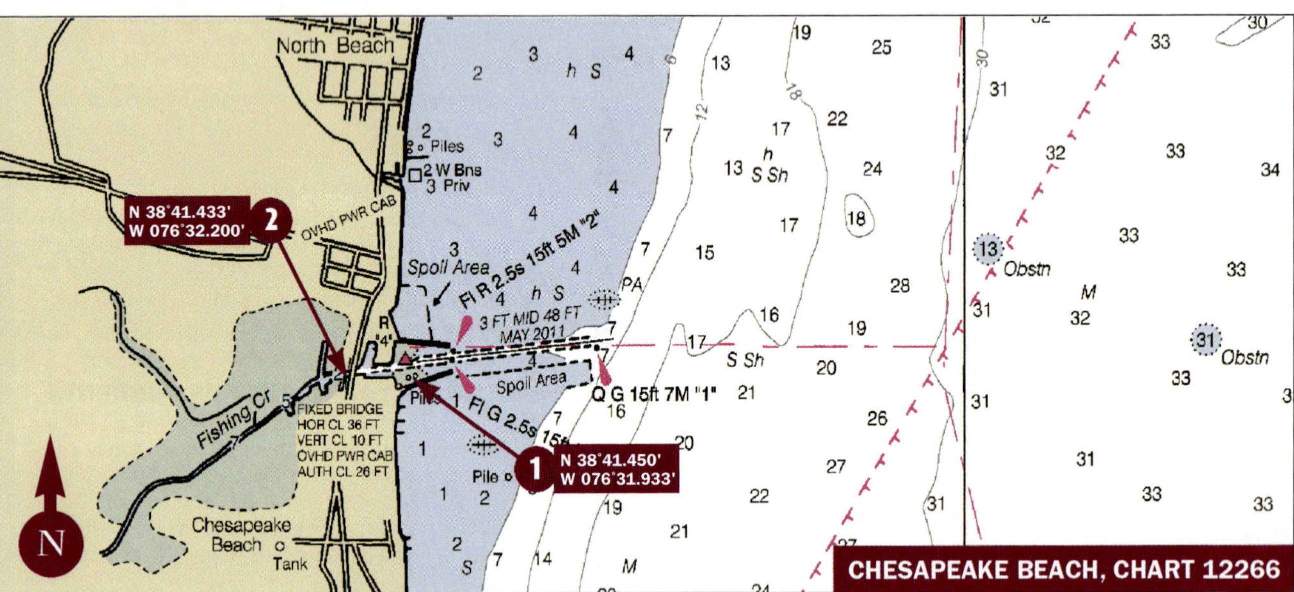

CHESAPEAKE BEACH, CHART 12266

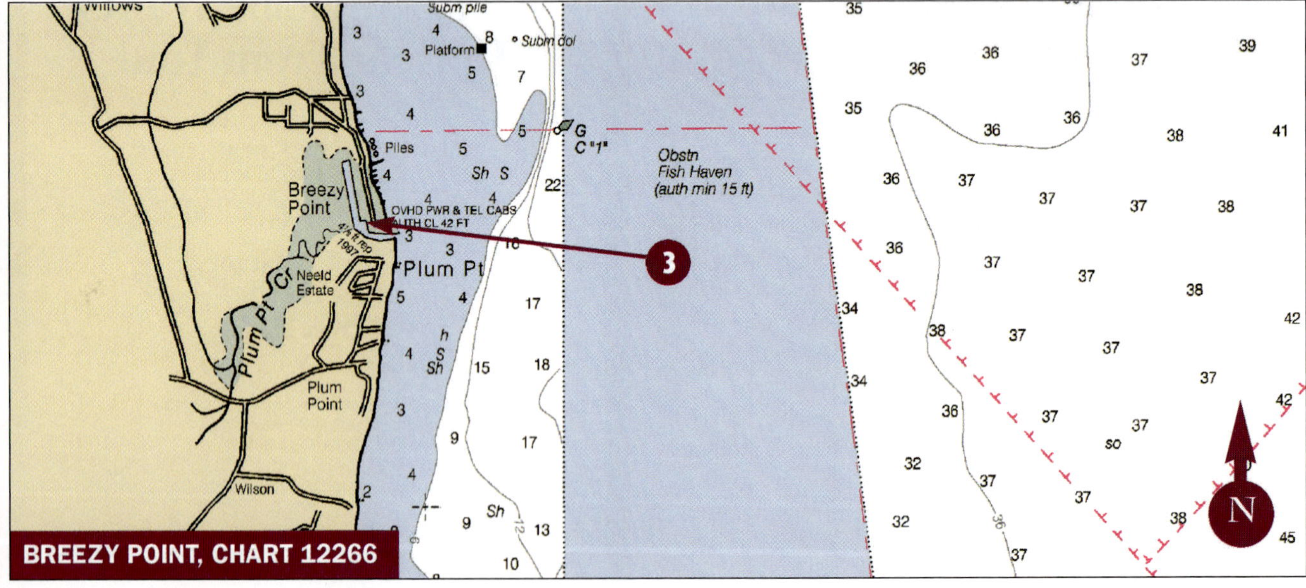

BREEZY POINT, CHART 12266

ANNUAL SLIPS • TRANSIENTS WELCOME

CHESAPEAKE BEACH

ROD N REEL Since 1946

CHARTER FISHING

CAPITAL of MARYLAND

TIMBER BREAKWATER

T-HEAD

A - DOCK

B - DOCK

MARINE LAYOUT ATTRACTIONS ARE COLOR CODED

PUMP OUT FUEL PIER Diesel & Gas

VALET PARKING

CHARTER BOAT ROW

OBSESSION
JODI LEE
BAY HUNTER II
CINDY MARIE
FLYING FEATHERS
SEMPER FIDELIS III
PLUMB CRAZY
HOOKER
MARY ELLEN
DAY DREAMER
PERSEVERANCE
REEL ATTITUDE
MISS LINDA
BEACHCOMBER
HOOKED UP II
BAY HOG II
MISS DEMEANOR
BAY HUNTER
KINGFISH
WORM
COMPENSATION
ROCK-N-ROBIN
MISS CHESAPEAKE BEACH

MEARS AVENUE

BAYSIDE ROAD - RT 261

EASY ACCESS TO THE BAY

Close by car, closer to the fish by boat, no other marinas in the Maryland or Washington, DC area have easier access to the Bay. Both Rod 'N' Reel Dock and Marina West offer annual and transient slip rentals at Chesapeake Beach Resort & Spa, the Charter Fishing Capital of Maryland, since 1946.

Ⓡ Ring Buoy | Ⓣ Trash
Ⓕ Fire Extinguisher |  Restroom

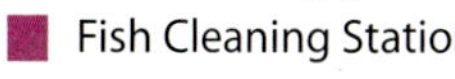

COMFORT & CONVENIENCES

- Over 120 boat slips, 25' to 50'
- More than 20 charter fishing boats
- Less than a 24 mile cruise from St. Michaels, Tilghman Island, Oxford & Annapolis
- Fueling dock, tackle shop, land storage, water & electric
- Walk to restaurants, grocery, laundry, water park and more
- Hotel Amenities, Indoor Pool, Showers, Laundry, Sauna & Fitness Center

PADDLE OR PEDAL

410-991-4268

Kayak, Canoe and Bicycle Rentals

MARINA WEST

1-800-233-2080

www.CBResortSpa.com

Flag Harbor, MD

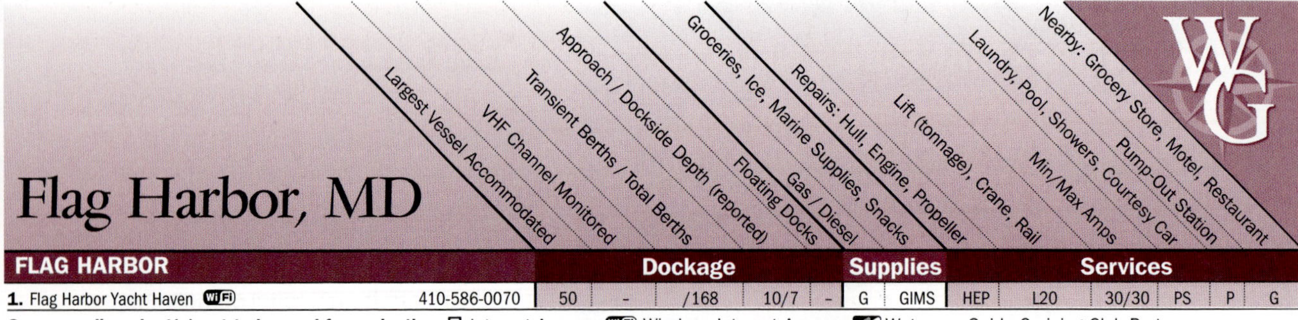

FLAG HARBOR		Largest Vessel Accommodated	VHF Channel Monitored	Transient Berths / Total Berths	Approach / Dockside Depth (reported)	Floating Docks	Gas / Diesel	Groceries, Ice, Marine Supplies, Snacks	Repairs: Hull, Engine, Propeller	Lift (tonnage), Crane, Rail	Min/Max Amps	Laundry, Pool, Showers, Courtesy Car	Pump-Out Station	Nearby: Grocery Store, Motel, Restaurant
		Dockage					Supplies		Services					
1. Flag Harbor Yacht Haven (WiFi)	410-586-0070	50	-	/168	10/7	-	G	GIMS	HEP	L20	30/30	PS	P	G

Corresponding chart(s) not to be used for navigation. Internet Access (WiFi) Wireless Internet Access Waterway Guide Cruising Club Partner
See www.WaterwayGuide.com for current rates, fuel prices, web site addresses, and other up-to-the-minute information.

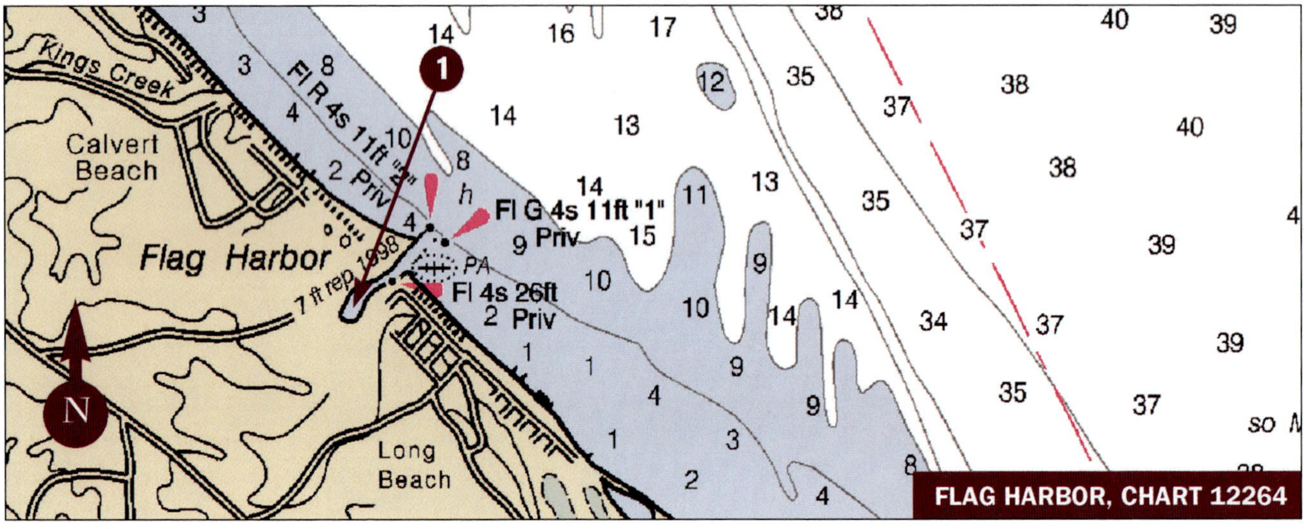

FLAG HARBOR, CHART 12264

Farther south, the channel into Breezy Point Marina at Plum Point has reported 4.5-foot approach and dockside depths; however, depths of 3 feet have been reported in the past. Call ahead for exact depths. Also note that a power cable, with a charted 42-foot vertical clearance, crosses the entrance to the harbor at Plum Point.

Even farther south again, Flag Harbor Yacht Haven is at Flag Harbor about six miles above Cove Point Light. It reports 10-foot approach depths and 7-foot dockside depths.

PATUXENT RIVER

Judged by cruising standards, the Patuxent River (110 miles long) is one of the Bay's outstanding rivers, with a freshwater trout stream in its upper reaches. The Patuxent is not only loaded with scenic and historic interest, but also has one of the Bay's most popular ports of call—Solomons Island—which is convenient to its broad entrance. The mouth of the Patuxent has been an easy harbor of refuge since John Smith mapped it in 1607. Whether cruising the Bay or hurrying along and looking for a stopover on the passage north or south, most boats transiting the Chesapeake stop at Solomons at some time.

If approaching the Patuxent River from the north, you will notice that the Bay's Western Shore arcs out into the big, projecting headland, Cove Point, marked by the Cove Point Lighthouse. Built in 1820, this is the oldest brick lighthouse on the Bay. The Calvert Marine Museum has taken over the Cove Point Lighthouse, and to tour the buildings and grounds, you must take the van from the museum. The Coast Guard continues to maintain the tower portion, which is not open to visitors.

NAVIGATION: Use Chart 12264. Heading toward the Patuxent from the upper Chesapeake Bay, note that the Bay becomes narrow and constricted at Cove Point between two very wide areas (like an hourglass). It is deep close to the western shore and therefore can kick up some mean waves and chop, especially when the wind and current (which is noticeable here) are in opposition. Below Cove Point, the shore falls away to the west, and the entrance to the Patuxent River is past the high bluffs of Little Cove Point and around Drum Point.

DRUM POINT
N 38°19.133'
W 076°25.250'
Waterway Guide Photography.

Coming down the Bay, it may be tempting to anchor overnight in the little cove just south of Cove Point Lighthouse, but it is not recommended. The holding ground is good, but the area gets surges from the large freighters transiting the main north-to-south Chesapeake Bay shipping channel. It is also infested with countless crab pots and wide open to the east and south. Be sure to hold well off Little Cove Point to avoid the 6-foot shoal that extends almost a half-mile offshore. Additionally, there is a large, charted fish trap area farther south.

The old familiar ruins of the Cedar Point Lighthouse, on the south bank of the Patuxent River at the mouth, are gone. The latest chart shows this area as "rip rap," instead of "abandoned lighthouse." Avoid it. Flashing green bell buoy "1PR" now marks the shoal.

SOLOMONS ISLAND

Solomons Island, just inside the mouth of the Patuxent River, has developed since the 1970s into one of the Chesapeake's top destinations for cruising boaters. Despite large fleets of local boats, Solomons' vast array of boatyards usually has no problem accommodating transient mariners. The operators of Solomons Marine Towing, a TowBoatU.S. affiliate (410-326-6801), act as unofficial harbormaster and will cheerfully answer requests for information about the Solomons area. Hail them on VHF Channel 16.

NAVIGATION: Use Charts 12264 and 12284. **Use Baltimore tide tables. For Solomons high tide, subtract 4 hours 38 minutes; for low tide, subtract 4 hours 46 minutes.** Note that the current edition of Chart 12284 was updated in April 2010, and there have been many changes to markers; consult the NOAA Web site (http://ocsdata.ncd.noaa.gov/nm) to update your older chart.

You can enter Solomons from the Patuxent River by either of two routes that encircle a patch of very shoal water (marked by flashing red "6" at its southern end). Both have adequate depths. The inner (northern) one, with 9- to 14-foot depths, is Swash Channel: Green daybeacons "1" and "3" and red daybeacons "2," "2A" and "4" mark the Drum Point shore inside the outlying shoal. If you take the southern route, give a fair berth to flashing red "6" off the shoal's southern tip. Then follow the markers running parallel to the spit on which the Chesapeake Biological Laboratory is located. Its long dock extends into the deep water.

Dockage: The majority of dockage at Solomons is on Back Creek, with the town's business district being located on the west side of the creek. Between the first marina (Harbor Island) and the small creek called the Narrows are several small docks, belonging to the Solomon's Island Yacht Club and the defunct Lighthouse Restaurant and Bowen's Inn.

Harbor Island Marina offers transient dockage, gas and diesel fuel, full repair services, showers and pump-out service. It is conveniently located just inside the harbor.

Solomons Yachting Center is to port, on the point of Back Creek on the opposite side of the Narrows. They offer floating docks with 40-foot finger piers. Let's Go Cruising charters has an office here.

The large full-service Calvert Marina complex is farther up Back Creek and to starboard, extending partially into Mill Creek. Its fuel dock is directly north of Molly's Leg, on the shortcut channel. Calvert Marina's docks extend for a considerable distance along the east side of Back Creek, up to its repair facilities at Washburn's Boat Yard.

Looking northwest over Solomons Island. Waterway Guide Photography.

Solomons, Patuxent River, MD

SOLOMONS		Largest Vessel Accommodated	VHF Channel Monitored	Transient Berths / Total Berths	Approach / Dockside Depth (reported)	Floating Docks	Gas / Diesel	Groceries, Ice, Marine Supplies, Snacks	Repairs: Hull, Engine, Propeller	Lift (tonnage), Crane, Rail	Min/Max Amps	Laundry, Pool, Showers, Courtesy Car	Pump-Out Station	Nearby: Grocery Store, Motel, Restaurant
		Dockage					Supplies		Services					
1. Harbor Island Marina	**410-326-3441**	**225**	**16/68**	**20/100**	**20/12**	**-**	**GD**	**GIM**	**HEP**	**L25, C**	**30/50**	**S**	**P**	**GMR**
2. Solomons Yachting Center	410-326-2401	170	16	12/110	12/	F	GD	IMS	HEP	L50	30/100	LPS	P	GMR
3. Back Creek Inn Bed & Breakfast	410-326-2022	44	-	2/2	8/8	-	-	-	-	-	30/30	S	-	GMR
4. Zahniser's Yachting Center	**410-326-2166**	**150**	**09/69**	**30/275**	**14/14**	**-**	**-**	**GIM**	**HEP**	**L75, C10**	**30/50**	**LPS**	**P**	**GMR**
5. Comfort Inn/Beacon Marina	410-326-6303	100	16	40/186	8/6	-	-	I	-	-	30/50	LPS	-	GMR
6. Spring Cove Marina	**410-326-2161**	**120**	**16/68**	**20/246**	**12/12**	**-**	**GD**	**GIMS**	**HEP**	**L50, C2**	**30/50**	**LPS**	**P**	**GMR**
7. Solomons Harbor Marina & Holiday Inn	**410-326-1052**	**100**	**16**	**20/80**	**12/8**	**-**	**-**	**I**	**-**	**-**	**30/50**	**LPS**	**P**	**GMR**
8. Washburn's Boat Yard Inc.	410-326-6701	140	16	-	12/12	-	-	M	HEP	L75, C	-	-	-	GMR
9. Calvert Marina	**410-326-4251**	**150**	**16/68**	**50/400**	**15/12**	**F**	**GD**	**IMS**	**HEP**	**L75**	**30/100**	**LPSC**	**P**	**GMR**
PATUXENT RIVER														
10. Blackstone Marina	301-373-2015	50	-	/65	15/12	-	-	I	HEP	L10, C	30/50	S	P	-

Corresponding chart(s) not to be used for navigation. Internet Access Wireless Internet Access Waterway Guide Cruising Club Partner

See www.WaterwayGuide.com for current rates, fuel prices, web site addresses, and other up-to-the-minute information.

On the west side of Back Creek is Back Creek Inn Bed & Breakfast, which has two slips. The extensive docks of Zahniser's Yachting Center, with its yard, repair facilities, brokerage, restaurant, marine store and pool, fill a large portion of the remaining west side of Back Creek. The sailboat masts are so thick here, you can hardly see through them.

There is a dinghy dock at the north end of the marina, and 8 moorings for transient boats up to 45 feet are available. The Comfort Inn/Beacon Marina is next, to port. The nicely wooded and landscaped Spring Cove Marina follows on the port side, with fuel, transient dockage, a pool, ship's store, and bike rentals. The last marina on Back Creek, also to port, is the Solomons Harbor Marina, with transient and long-term dockage. The Holiday Inn Solomons Conference Center is adjacent for guests who might not want to sleep aboard. The docks at the head of Back Creek off to starboard are part of the Harbour at Solomons condominiums (no transient slips).

Anchorage: The main harbor anchorage at Solomons, just inside the entrance of Back and Mill creeks to port (south and west of the breakwater-protected triangular island), is closest to the island's mile-long main street and its dozens of shops and restaurants. A free pump-out station and dinghy dock are a few hundred yards north of the harbor. Ordinarily, as many boats as possible squeeze into the main harbor and are sometimes too close for comfort, especially if the wind changes direction or increases in strength. On a calm night, the rather poor holding in the main harbor near Molly's Leg will probably suffice, but go farther up Back Creek or around to Mill Creek where less traffic and numerous protected branches provide for a more secure anchorage.

Mill Creek, the least commercial of the tributaries, provides the quietest places to stay at Solomons. Mill Creek shares a common entrance with Back Creek, north of Molly's Leg, and winds for several miles through residential and wooded lands. Mill Creek turns northeast at flashing red "2" off Ship Point with good holding ground beyond flashing green "3" on the west side of the channel. Private docks for the condominiums between Back and Mill Creeks occupy part of the area. Cruising groups sometimes form huge rafts of boats in this popular anchorage. Mill Creek, navigable

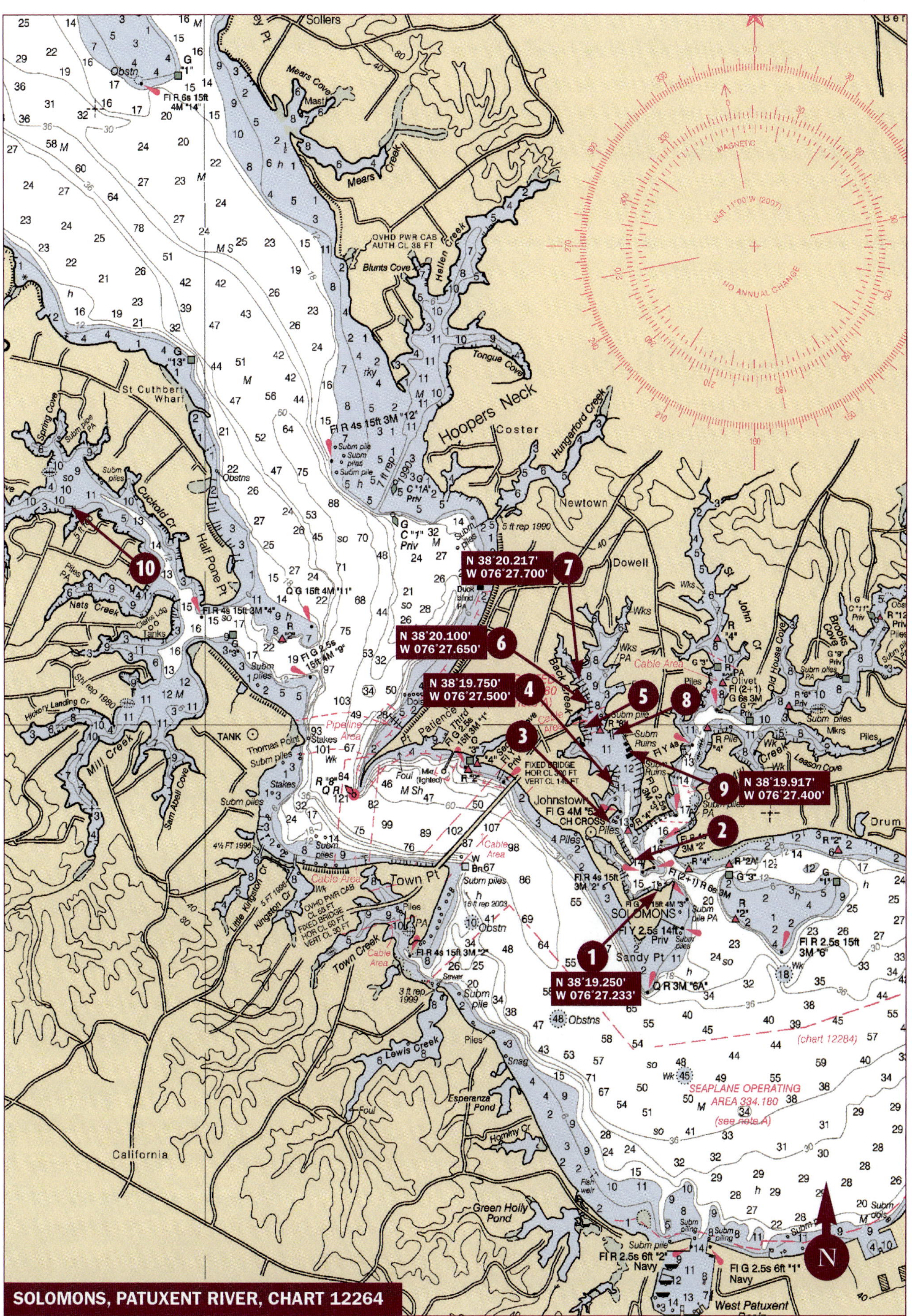

SOLOMONS, PATUXENT RIVER, CHART 12264

to its end, turns east (to starboard) at flashing green (2+1) "LP" at Lusby Point. St. John Creek goes straight ahead. This stretch offers many protected spots for anchoring. However, holding is poor up Mill Creek, in the area once known as a hurricane hole, past red daybeacon "8."

There is additional space for anchoring up the creek past Spring Cove and Solomons Harbor marinas. All anchorages around Solomons Island, but especially those near Harbor Island Marina, sometimes feel the roar of Navy aircraft taking off from and flying around the Patuxent Naval Air Station across the river. This is the Navy's active testing ground for new military aircraft.

GOIN' ASHORE:
SOLOMONS ISLAND, MD

Where the Patuxent River meets the Chesapeake Bay, you will find the compact little village of Solomons. You will see references to Solomons Island, too, which is part of the same town. Less than a mile long, the island is connected to the "mainland" by a car-length long, two-lane causeway. Many of the attractions, including shopping and restaurants, lie on the island itself, and are accessible from any of the marinas on the western side of Back Creek. Marinas farther north up the creek provide closer access to the newer commercial area with groceries, marine supplies and other necessities readily available.

Even though Solomons is small, there is a surprising amount to do—stroll the Riverwalk, visit the marine museum and its two lighthouses, or shop.

History: It was tobacco, not fishing, that brought the first settlers to this area. Several individuals owned the land until 1865, when Isaac Solomon, a Baltimore businessman, bought 80 acres known as "Sandy Island" and set up a cannery as well as housing for workers. He was taking advantage of the booming oyster industry after the Civil War.

With its accessibility, shipbuilding and the repair and provisioning of boats both thrived. By 1880, more than 500 locally built boats made up the Solomons fishing fleet. More Bugeyes—early sail-driven oyster workboats—were made in Solomons than anywhere else. Shipbuilding also hit a high point in the 1930s, when wooden yachts like the High Tide and the Manitou were made here.

Points of Interest: At the base of the high rise bridge over the Patuxent River, you will find the tourist information center. Just east of the center is the Calvert Marine Museum featuring a permanent exhibit telling the story of life along the Patuxent River, from tobacco farming to shipbuilding.The museum also has a boat basin with floating vessel exhibits, a marsh walk, two lighthouses and the 1932 J.C. Lore and Sons Oyster House (one-half mile away). The *Wm. B. Tennison*, a Bugeye that has been afloat since 1899, departs for hour-long cruises from the museum dock. The Drum Point Lighthouse, fully restored after being moved to museum property in 1975,

INFORMATION
1 Solomons Visitors Center

POINTS OF INTEREST
2 Calvert Marine Museum
3 The Drum Point Lighthouse Museum
4 Lore & Sons Oyster House
5 Annmarie Sculpture Garden
6 Patuxant Adventure Center

SHOPPING
7 Carmen's Gallery
8 Caren's Solomon Style
9 West Marine
10 Food Lion

DINING
11 CD Cafe
12 The Dry Dock Restaurant
13 The Back Creek Bistro
14 The Captain's Table
15 DiGiovanni's Dock of the Bay
16 Stoney's Kingfishers
17 Solomons Pier Restaurant

PO POST OFFICE

Reference the marina listing tables to see all the marinas in the area.

is one of just three remaining screwpile lighthouses of the original 45 on the Bay. The museum is located about two miles up the Patuxent River on Back Creek. The Cove Point Lighthouse, the oldest working lighthouse in Maryland, is still operated by the Coast Guard, but owned by the museum. It is located about 10 miles away, but there is no dock there. Visit www.calvertmarinemuseum.org or call 410-326-2042.

Annmarie Sculpture Garden is a 30-acre public sculpture park and garden on the east side of Back Creek. Visit www.annmariegarden.org or call 410-326-4640 for more information.

Solomons is the closest spot to arrange a fossil-hunting trip to Calvert Cliffs State Park. Inquire at the marine museum

Looking north over Solomons Island, Back Creek and the Patuxent River. (Not to be used for navigation.) Waterway Guide Photography.

and rent a car to drive up to the state park north of town. After a mile or two walk to the Bay, you will be able to pick up 10-million-year-old fossil shark teeth, scallop shells and other marine fossils right off the beach. It is the best Miocene deposit in North America.

Patuxent Adventure Center at 13860 C Solomons Island Road (410-394-2770, www.paxadventure.com) rents bikes, kayaks and stand-up paddleboards. If you prefer golf, Chesapeake Hills Golf Course is 5 miles away (410-326-4653, www.chesapeakehills.com).

Special Events: Each Fourth of July brings a fireworks display, with a rain day on the fifth. The third weekend in July features the Screwpile Lighthouse Challenge regatta (www.screwpile.net). On Columbus Day weekend, the Patuxent River Appreciation Days festival aims to raise awareness and appreciation of the river with exhibits, a craft fair, food and music. The popular Trawler Fest takes place in Solomons each fall, prior to the Annapolis boat shows. But many locals and visitors alike will tell you that the biggest event of the season is the opening of The Tiki Bar on the third Friday in April when the street closes for thousands of guests.

Shopping: Shops in the area include Carmen's Gallery, selling art, frames and unique gifts; Caren's Solomon Style, which sells women's clothing; and numerous boutique shops that offer nautical and gift items. A West Marine and a liquor store are just a few blocks north of the island itself. Patuxent Plaza is a few blocks farther north with more options. At the Solomons Towne Centre (a bike ride away), you will find a CVS Pharmacy, several fast food restaurants and a Food Lion grocery store. Also, a liquor store is in this same shopping center.

Everything in Solomons can be reached by walking and biking. Rental cars are located about eight miles away across the Patuxent River, but pick-up can be arranged by the marinas. The local bus system will take you across the river to more extensive shopping including a Wal-Mart and just about any of the other "big box" stores.

Dining: There are several restaurants to chose from here, including the C.D. Café (14350 Solomons Island Road, 410-326-3877), which offers a bit more than standard fare for both lunch and dinner, and the Dry Dock Restaurant (251 C St., 410-326-4817), operating more than 20 years at Zahniser's Yachting Center. There are several restaurants with dockage for diners on Back Bay, including The Back Creek Bistro at Calvert Marina (410-326-9900), The Captain's Table at Comfort Inn/Beacon's Marina, and DiGiovanni's Dock of the Bay (410-394-6400). On the river side are Stoney's Kingfishers Seafood House, known for its no-filler crabcakes the size of baseballs (410-394-0236); and Solomons Pier Restaurant (410-326-2424).

A southern view over the Solomons area. (Not to be used for navigation.) Waterway Guide Photography.

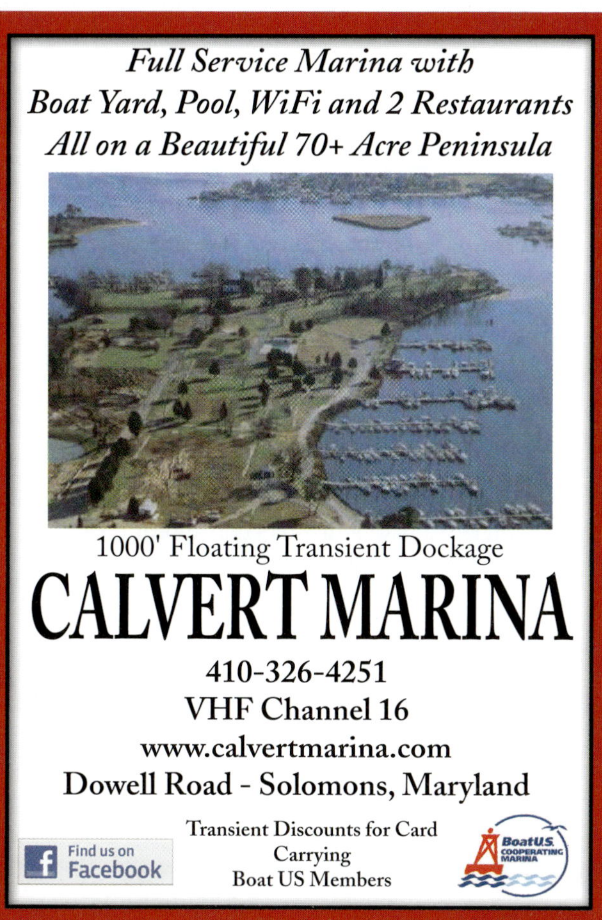

Full Service Marina with
Boat Yard, Pool, WiFi and 2 Restaurants
All on a Beautiful 70+ Acre Peninsula
1000' Floating Transient Dockage
CALVERT MARINA
410-326-4251
VHF Channel 16
www.calvertmarina.com
Dowell Road - Solomons, Maryland
Find us on Facebook
Transient Discounts for Card Carrying Boat US Members
BoatUS Cooperating Marina

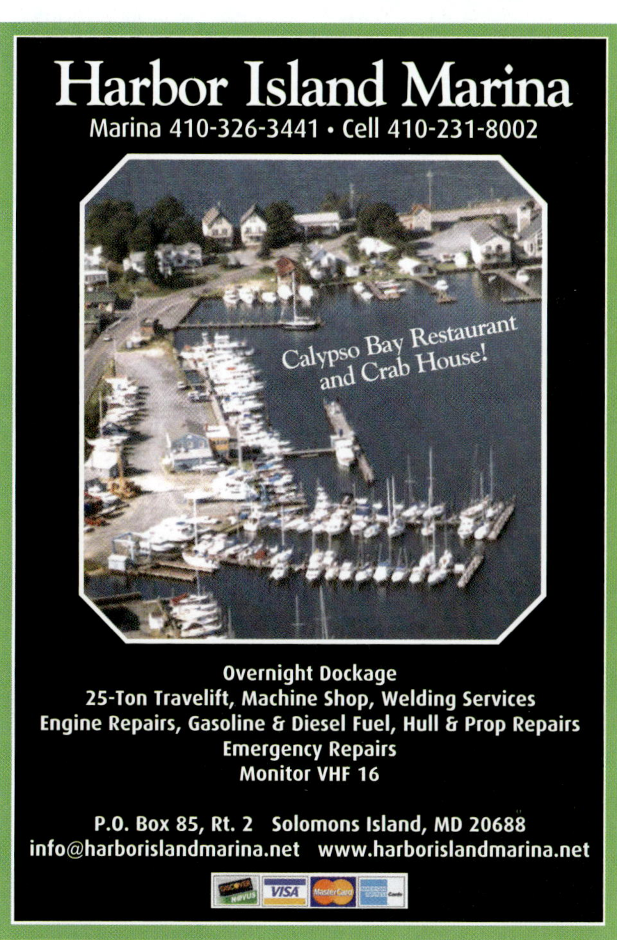

Harbor Island Marina
Marina 410-326-3441 • Cell 410-231-8002
Calypso Bay Restaurant and Crab House!
Overnight Dockage
25-Ton Travelift, Machine Shop, Welding Services
Engine Repairs, Gasoline & Diesel Fuel, Hull & Prop Repairs
Emergency Repairs
Monitor VHF 16
P.O. Box 85, Rt. 2 Solomons Island, MD 20688
info@harborislandmarina.net www.harborislandmarina.net
VISA

ADDITIONAL RESOURCES

- **SOLOMONS INFORMATION CENTER:** 14175 Solomons Island Road S., Solomons, MD 20688, 410-326-2042

NEARBY MEDICAL FACILITIES
Solomons Urgent Care Center: 14090 H.G. Trueman Road, Solomons, MD 20688, 410-394-2800 (1 mile)
Calvert Memorial Hospital: 100 Hospital Road, Prince Frederick, MD 20678, 410-535-4000 www.calverthospital.com (20 miles)

NEARBY AIRPORT
St. Mary's County Airport: 44200 Airport Road, California, MD 20619, 301-373-2101
The closest large airports are BWI in Baltimore (75 miles) and Reagan National in Washington, D.C. (65 miles)

Town Creek, off the Patuxent

Few cruising boats go past Solomons to the creeks farther up the Patuxent, where quiet and protected anchorages can break the monotony while waiting out bad weather. Continuing up the Patuxent from Solomons, the first sight is the Thomas Johnson Memorial Bridge (140-foot fixed vertical clearance) from Town Point on the St. Mary's County side to Johnstown, a mile north of Solomon's Sandy Point.

Some describe Town Creek, inside Town Point on the south side of the Patuxent, as Solomons on a reduced scale. The entrance is just as easy, the layout of the creeks is roughly similar, most of the side waters are quite deep and local boats, charter and private, are mainly used for fishing. Town Creek also has its share of marinas, but, unlike those in Solomons, most are preoccupied with local boats. Call ahead if visiting this area.

Mill and Cuckold Creeks, off the Patuxent

Above Town and Thomas points, inside Half Pone Point, several deep creeks offer good shelter and marinas. Both Mill Creek (not to be confused with the Mill Creek at Solomons) and Cuckold Creek provide excellent anchorage. Mind the shoal area off Clarks Landing, and favor the point. Mill Creek shares its entrance with pretty, but well-populated, Cuckold Creek, which has depths of 10 to 15 feet past the Blackstone Marina. Just behind the point at their shared entrance, to port (south), is a cove with 11- to 13-foot depths. Feel your way in with the depth sounder, and anchor with good holding in mud and protection from the north through the east to the south. Although some areas have a posted speed limit and restrictions on water-skiing, water skiers sometimes circle anchored boats in the unregulated areas. Blackstone Marina has transient space and offers some boat repairs.

St. Leonard Creek, off the Patuxent

Farther up on the north side of the river is St. Leonard Creek, another popular spot off the Patuxent River. St. Leonard Creek is wide and deep, with houses dotting the shoreline. The Jefferson Patterson Park is on St. Leonard Creek, overlooking the site of the largest naval battle in Maryland history, which took place in 1814. The 512-acre park offers a fascinating archaeology trail, special exhibits on Colonial and prehistoric sites, and a picnic area.

NAVIGATION: Use Chart 12264. Approaching St. Leonard Creek, you face a pair of markers that appear reversed. Note that flashing red "14" is for upstream Patuxent traffic and

QUICK FACT: PLANTATIONS ON THE PATUXENT

The entire Patuxent River shore is lined with attractive old houses: This was (and still is, in places) tobacco-plantation country. Several of the most interesting old houses are in the immediate area. Resurrection Manor, built on Cuckold Creek (mentioned below) in 1650, was one of the first manorial grants, and Sotterley Plantation, built in 1717, is on the south side of the river. Sotterley Plantation has limited its public access because it lacks the money for necessary structural repairs. If you are interested in stopping at the plantation's charted wharf, call ahead (301-373-2280) to check its status.

Patuxent River, MD

		Largest Vessel Accommodated	VHF Channel Monitored	Transient Berths / Total Berths	Approach / Dockside Depth (reported)	Floating Docks	Gas / Diesel	Groceries, Ice, Marine Supplies, Snacks	Repairs: Hull, Engine, Propeller	Lift (tonnage), Crane, Rail	Min/Max Amps	Laundry, Pool, Showers, Courtesy Car	Pump-Out Station	Nearby: Grocery Store, Motel, Restaurant
ST. LEONARD CREEK		Dockage					Supplies		Services					
1. Vera Beach Club Restaurant & Marina (WiFi)	410-586-1182	165	-	40/64	15/12	F	GD	G	-	L	30/50	LPS	P	GR
CAT CREEK														
2. Cape St. Mary's Marina	301-373-2001	-	-	10/	-	-	GD	I	HEP	L	30/30	S	P	R

Corresponding chart(s) not to be used for navigation. Internet Access (WiFi) Wireless Internet Access Waterway Guide Cruising Club Partner

See www.WaterwayGuide.com for current rates, fuel prices, web site addresses, and other up-to-the-minute information.

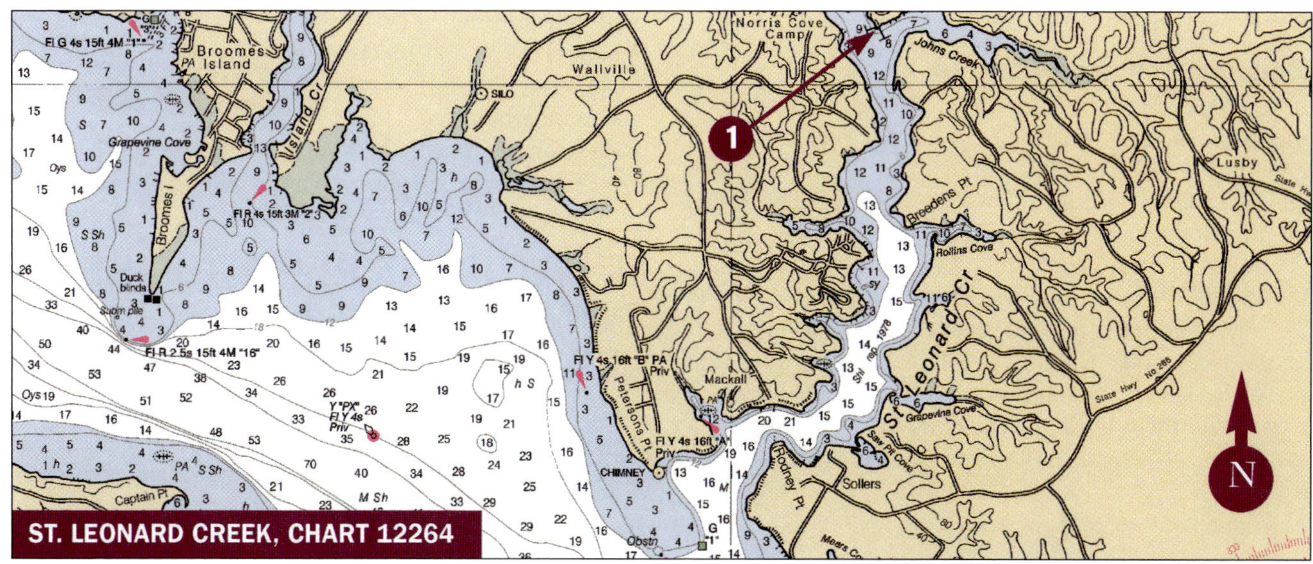

ST. LEONARD CREEK, CHART 12264

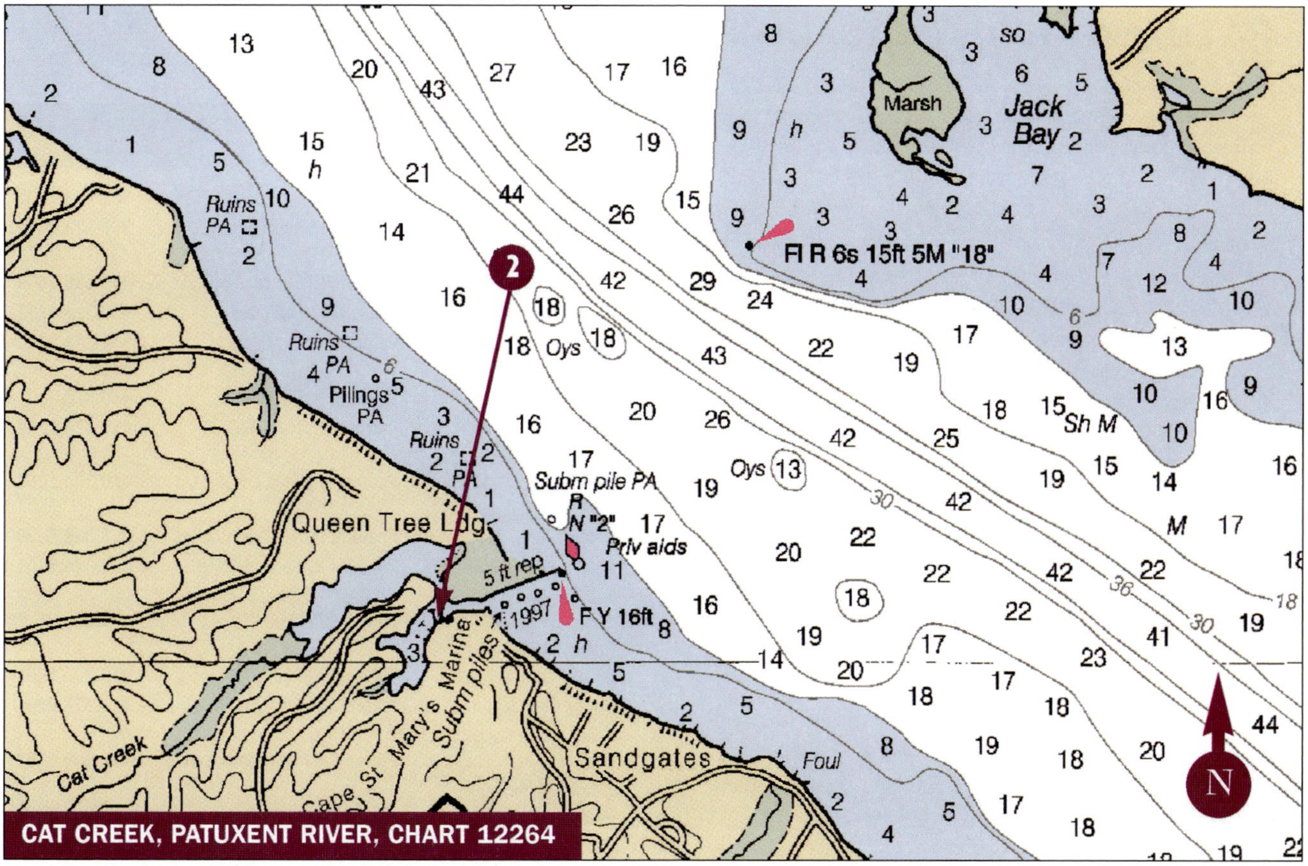

CAT CREEK, PATUXENT RIVER, CHART 12264

green daybeacon "1" for entering St. Leonard Creek, so enter the creek to the east of green daybeacon "1," leaving both flashing red "14" and green daybeacon "1" to port.

Dockage: There is transient dockage available for cruising boats at Vera's Beach Club Restaurant & Marina. Make sure to call ahead for reservations because it is the only marina on the creek, and this place gets really busy on weekends. The lively restaurant, Vera's White Sands, is only open from Wednesday through Sunday.

Anchorage: This creek abounds with good anchorages. There are many small coves and some small side creeks. Look for your preference of depths and set your hook securely. The depths range from 10 to 15 feet and there are a few shoals to watch out for, but all in all St. Leonard Creek is very pretty and won't disappoint you.

Benedict, on the Patuxent

If you have time and enjoy river cruising, go farther up the Patuxent River to Benedict. A historic river town 18.5 miles above the Patuxent's entrance, Benedict was named after the fourth Lord Baltimore. In August of 1814, when the British marched on Washington, D.C. and burned the White House and Capitol, they landed at Benedict, using the Patuxent as their highway. The Benedict Marina and Restaurant dock has gas and water. Turn to port just short of the red marker toward the white building with twin docks. Restaurant customers can tie up overnight without charge. On the way up the river you will pass Cat Creek on the west side. Cape St. Mary's Marina here offers slips and fuel.

Benedict is as far up the Patuxent as most cruising boats go, but the river continues deep and attractive for a considerable distance beyond. Even a boat with a 5-foot draft can cruise as far as Bristol Landing, 20 miles north. The swing bridge opens between 6:00 a.m. and 6:00 p.m., but only with advance notice (VHF Channel 13, 410-535-4634). Navigation through the numerous fish trap stakes can be difficult. Most of the Patuxent is a beautiful river for cruising, whether you are sailing or motoring.

Waterway Guide Photography.

POINT NO POINT
N 38°07.700'
W 076°17.400'

QUICK FACT:

PATUXENT RIVER NAVAL AIR STATION

The Patuxent River Naval Air Station Complex (NAS Patuxent River), or "Pax River" as it's known in the Navy and to locals, covers more than 6,000 acres at the mouth of the Patuxent River in St. Mary's County in southern Maryland. The facilities of the air station are visible to port as you enter the Patuxent River from the east.

In the years preceding World War II, the U.S. Navy's Bureau of Aeronautics elected to consolidate the number of scattered air testing facilities that had been established in the region; testing had been conducted at stations in Dahlgren and Norfolk, VA, the Washington Navy Yard, Naval Air Station Anacostia in Washington, D.C. and the Naval Aircraft Factory in Philadelphia, PA. The grounds selected for the new complex consisted three large farms, Mattapany, Susquehanna and Cedar Point, in southern Maryland. The location was chosen for its relative isolation and space. Facing the impending war, Pax River was established with a sense of urgency and formally commissioned in April 1943.

The complex supports naval aviation research, development, testing and evaluation and hosts the U.S. Naval Test Pilot School and Unmanned Aerial Vehicle operations.

PATUXENT RIVER TO THE POTOMAC RIVER

NAVIGATION: Use Charts 12230 and 12285. This is a straightforward and relatively short run on the Bay, but be aware of the electronic target range in the central Bay southwest of Hooper Island Light and about six miles south of Cedar Point. This is a prohibited area used by military aircraft. When it is active, a patrol boat will be in the area to contact you on channel 16 to make certain you stay well clear. As you move several miles further south through this section of the Bay, it is not unusual to see

Patuxent River Pumpouts

Benedict Marina	Patuxent R.	301.274.2882
Blackstone Marina	Patuxent R./Cuckhold	301.373.2015
Calvert Co. Comfort Station	Patuxent R./Back Creek	410.535.1600
Calvert Marina	Patuxent R./Back Creek	410.326.4251
Cape St. Mary's Marina	Patuxent R./Cat Creek	301.373.2001
Comfort Inn Beacon Marina	Patuxent R./Back Creek	410.326.3807
Harbor Island Marina	Patuxent R./Mill Creek	410.326.3441
Hospitality Harbor Marina	Patuxent R./Back Creek	410.326.1052
Mill Creek Boating Center	Patuxent R./Mill Creek	410.326.7089
Point Patience Marina	Patuxent R.(Second Cove)	410.326.5001
Solomons Landing Condo	Patuxent R./Back Creek	410.326.0527
Solomons Yachting Center	Patuxent R./Back Creek	410.326.2401
Spring Cove Marina	Patuxent R./Back Creek	410.326.2161
Vera's White Sands Corp.	Patuxent R./St. Leonards Creek	410.586.1182
Zahniser's Yachting Center	Patuxent R./Back Creek	410.326.2166

St. Jerome Creek, MD

ST. JEROME CREEK		Largest Vessel Accommodated	VHF Channel Monitored	Transient Berths / Total Berths	Approach / Dockside Depth (reported)	Floating Docks	Gas / Diesel	Groceries, Ice, Marine Supplies, Snacks	Repairs: Hull, Engine, Propeller	Lift (tonnage), Crane, Rail	Min/Max Amps	Laundry, Pool, Showers, Courtesy Car	Pump-Out Station	Nearby: Grocery Store, Motel, Restaurant
		Dockage					Supplies		Services					
1. Drury's Marina	301-872-4480	50	16	1/35	5/5	-	GD	I	-	-	30/30	S	P	G
2. Buzz's Marina	301-872-5887	40	-	/15	4/4	-	G	IMS	E	-	30/30	SC	P	GR

Corresponding chart(s) not to be used for navigation. Internet Access Wireless Internet Access Waterway Guide Cruising Club Partner

See www.WaterwayGuide.com for current rates, fuel prices, web site addresses, and other up-to-the-minute information.

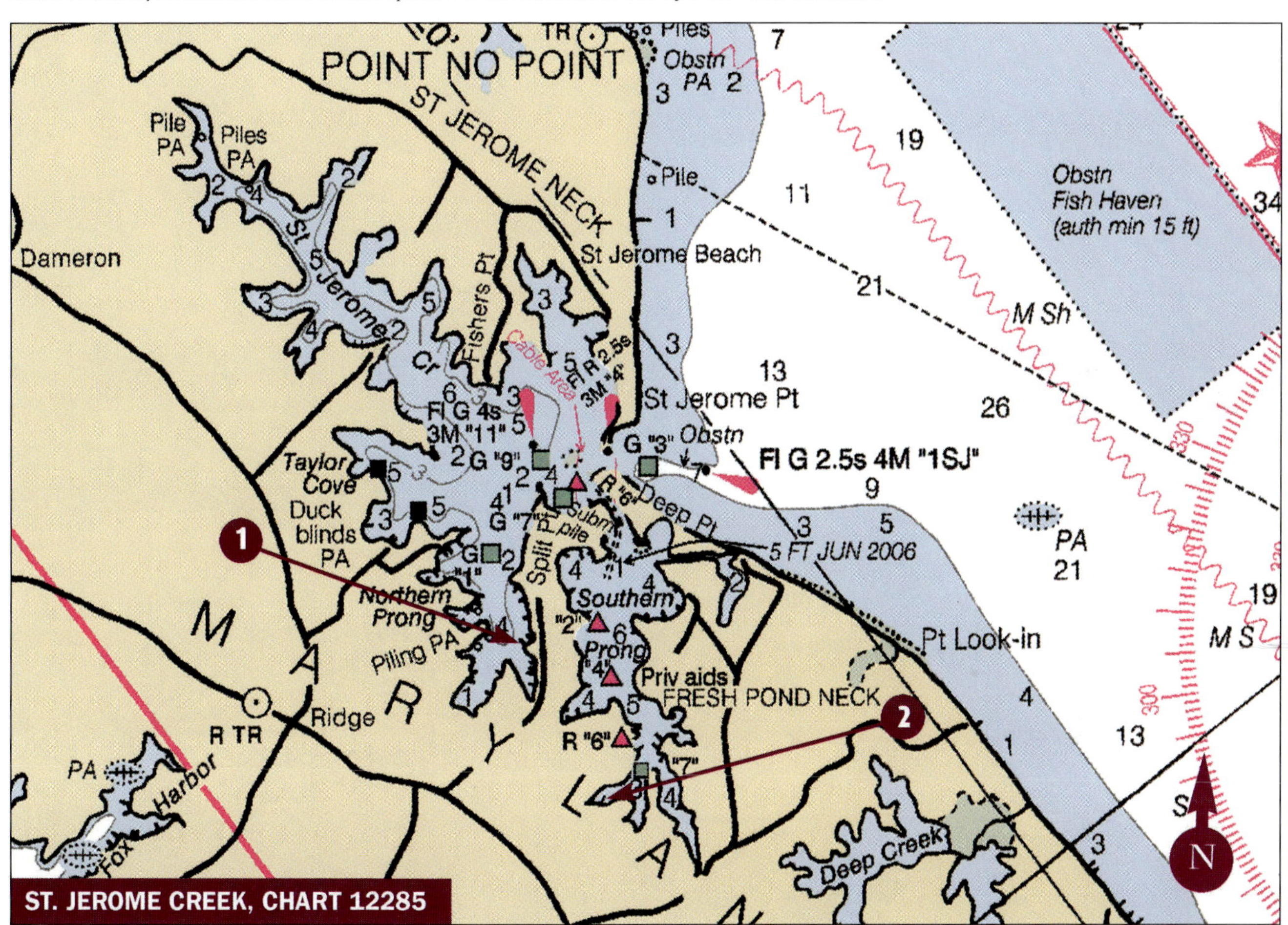

ST. JEROME CREEK, CHART 12285

Patuxent-based aircraft in "dogfights" or making simulated bombing runs on the grounded target ship visible to the east off Smith Island, MD.

St. Jerome Creek, South of the Patuxent

St. Jerome Creek breaks the length of the shoreline stretching from the Patuxent River to the Potomac's Point Lookout. Because it has a shallow, shifting entrance, this creek is only for shallow-draft vessels. The point shown on the most recent chart (NOAA chart 12285, Edition 40, April 2010) has washed away such that you cannot see the shoaling. Steer hard to port (closer to Deep Point) inside the private marker on the point. Two marinas upstream cater to powerboats: Drury's Marina and Buzz's Marina. Both have gas and Drury's has gas and diesel. ■

Waterway Guide advertising sponsors play a vital role in bringing you the most trusted and well-respected cruising guide in the country. Without our advertising sponsors, we simply couldn't produce the top-notch publication now resting in your hands. Next time you stop in for a peaceful night's rest, let them know where you found them—Waterway Guide, The Cruising Authority.

Waterway Guide is always open to your observations from the helm. Email your comments on any navigation information in the Guide to: editor@waterwayguide.com.

N
295
Magothy River
Severn River
Chester River
Stevensville
301
Annapolis
Grasonv
50
MILE 48
Chester
South River
West River
Eastern Bay
66
Page 312
Washington D.C.
Page 307
Alexandria
495
St. Michaels
Deale
Herring Bay
Page 302
Mount Vernon
5
Chesapeake Beach
Chesapeake Bay
Oxfo
Fort Belvoir
Choptank River
Indian Head
MILE 71
Page 299
Quantico
Little Choptank River
Calvert Cliffs
Nanjemoy Creek
Port Tobacco River
95
Patuxent River
301
Wicomico River
Page 293
Solomons
Dahlgren
MILE 86
Hooper Islands
Fredericksburg
Page 296
Leonardtown
Colonial Beach
Breton Bay
Page 290
St. Marys City
17
Potomac River
Page 286
Nomini Bay
St. Marys River
Page 288
Fort Ap Hill Millitary Reservation
Point Lookout
207
Yeocomico River
MILE 111
Smith Point
DOZIER'S WATERWAY GUIDE THE CRUISING AUTHORITY
Tappahannock
Reedville
WWW.WATERWAYGUIDE.COM
Rappahannock River

Skipper's Handbook

- GPS Waypoints 48
- Tide Tables 50

Irvington

Potomac River

CHARTS 12230, 12233, 12285, 12286, 12287, 12288, 12289

One of the nation's most historic rivers, and one of its most productive, the Potomac is second only to the Susquehanna in the amount of freshwater it contributes to the Chesapeake Bay. Even so, the Potomac—tidal for over 100 miles to the fall line at Washington, D.C.—remains undiscovered by most cruisers. Even in midsummer, cruisers are a rare sight on the Potomac; anchorages are deserted, marina slips are available. Legend has it that Capt. John Smith named the Potomac River from the Indian word meaning "where tribute is brought." By quirk of history, the entire river is within Maryland. Virginia begins at the high-tide line of the southern shore.

A Potomac cruise, which can take a few days to a few weeks, is well worth the effort. The river is very wide almost to Washington, D.C., and the channel alternately favors first one shore and then another as you head upstream. The lower Potomac's surroundings are broad and flat, while cliffs and houses line the shore upriver, offering breathtaking views. Most cruisers, especially those intent on reaching warmer climates during the autumn migration, are familiar only with the excellent, quiet anchorages near the mouth of the river. Waterfront facilities are only a few hours apart in a fast boat, but even if your boat is slow, you can reach anchorages and marinas in a full day's run. History unfolds all along the way, including George Washington's home at Mount Vernon and the fascinating old port town of Alexandria. You will also pass extensive military installations: Dahlgren Naval Surface Warfare Center, Quantico Marine Corps Base, Fort Belvoir, Bolling Air Base, Naval Support Facility Anacostia, Washington Navy Yard and Fort Myer. The reward at the end of the 90-plus-mile run is Washington, D.C., with its endless attractions.

NAVIGATION: Use Chart 12285. The Coast Guard has relocated many markers on the Potomac since Edition 38 40 was first last published in April 2010; only the latest Print On Demand or downloaded NOAA charts (http://chartmaker.ncd.noaa.gov) will show these changes.

The mouth of the Potomac can be rife with cross-currents, tidal rips and fish traps at times. Calculate the currents and study the weather for a comfortable crossing (a distance of nearly 12 nautical miles from Point Lookout in Maryland to Smith Point Lighthouse off the Virginia shore). The contours of the bottom combine with a southeastern exposure to produce some nasty conditions here when the prevailing summer southerly opposes an ebb current. After heavy rains, the outflow of the Potomac can create an almost washing machine-like swirl, especially when the tide is rising and the winds are out of the North or Northeast. Several world cruisers have said that this was the roughest place they have encountered in bad weather. Beware also of summer squalls that can pop up here, as this is not a place you would like to be when the weather worsens. Although you need to respect the entrance to this river in those conditions, you should not let this deter you from exploring the Potomac River.

Potomac tributaries, like the St. Marys River, Breton Bay, St. Clements Bay and, especially, the Wicomico River, are generally very wide and open. Choose anchorages in any of these areas with the wind direction in mind, as the long fetch can build up a chop when the breeze picks up.

As we discuss the Potomac, we will use approximate mile markers from Potomac River Red/White "A," located southwest of Point Lookout. (Keep in mind that entering the Potomac River from the south you will approach Potomac River G "1" near Smith Point Light House, some 11 miles before RW "A.") We will first identify the location, then give the distance from RW "A," whether the location is on the Maryland or Virginia side of the river and lastly, we will indicate the nearest navigational aid.

POTOMAC RIVER

Point Lookout's old lighthouse buildings are now part of Point Lookout State Park and are easy to identify from the water. The actual Point Lookout Light is a skeleton tower with a black and white diamond-shaped daybeacon with a flashing white light on a pile structure (watch for trap markers around it). If your boat has a deep draft, take care not to round Point Lookout too closely from the north—a fishhook-shaped shoal extends out in a southeasterly direction from the point itself.

POINT LOOKOUT
N 38°01.500'
W 076°19.400'

Waterway Guide Photography.

Point Lookout Creek, MD
(Mile 0, Maryland Side, at RW "A")

A mile and a half into the Potomac from Point Lookout, you will find Point Lookout Creek, a harbor of refuge with a jetty-lined entrance. Be sure to observe all the markers and do not cut corners. The dredged channel is 100 feet wide and splits the jetties down the middle. Inside depths are 6 feet near the channel and 2 to 4 feet elsewhere.

Dockage: There is a Boating Facility/Camp Store at Point Lookout State Park with reported 6-foot approach and dockside depths. Call ahead about dockage. This public

Point Lookout, Smith Creek, MD

SMITH CREEK		Largest Vessel Accommodated	VHF Channel Monitored	Transient Berths / Total Berths	Approach / Dockside Depth (reported)	Floating Docks	Gas / Diesel	Groceries, Ice, Marine Supplies, Snacks	Repairs: Hull, Engine, Propeller	Lift (tonnage), Crane, Rail	Min/Max Amps	Laundry, Pool, Showers, Courtesy Car	Pump-Out Station	Nearby: Grocery Store, Motel, Restaurant
		Dockage					Supplies		Services					
1. Point Lookout Marina	**301-872-5000**	**250**	**16/68**	**40/160**	**14/9**	**-**	**GD**	**GIMS**	**HEP**	**L35,C,R80**	**30/50**	**LPSC**	**P**	**GR**
2. Corinthian Yacht Club-Potomac	301-872-5187	50	-	8/	14/	-	-	IS	-	-	30/50	LPS	-	MR
3. BluHaven Piers	301-872-5838	50	16	/50	10/10	-	-	IMS	HEP	-	30/50	S	P	-

Corresponding chart(s) not to be used for navigation. Internet Access Wireless Internet Access Waterway Guide Cruising Club Partner

See www.WaterwayGuide.com for current rates, fuel prices, web site addresses, and other up-to-the-minute information.

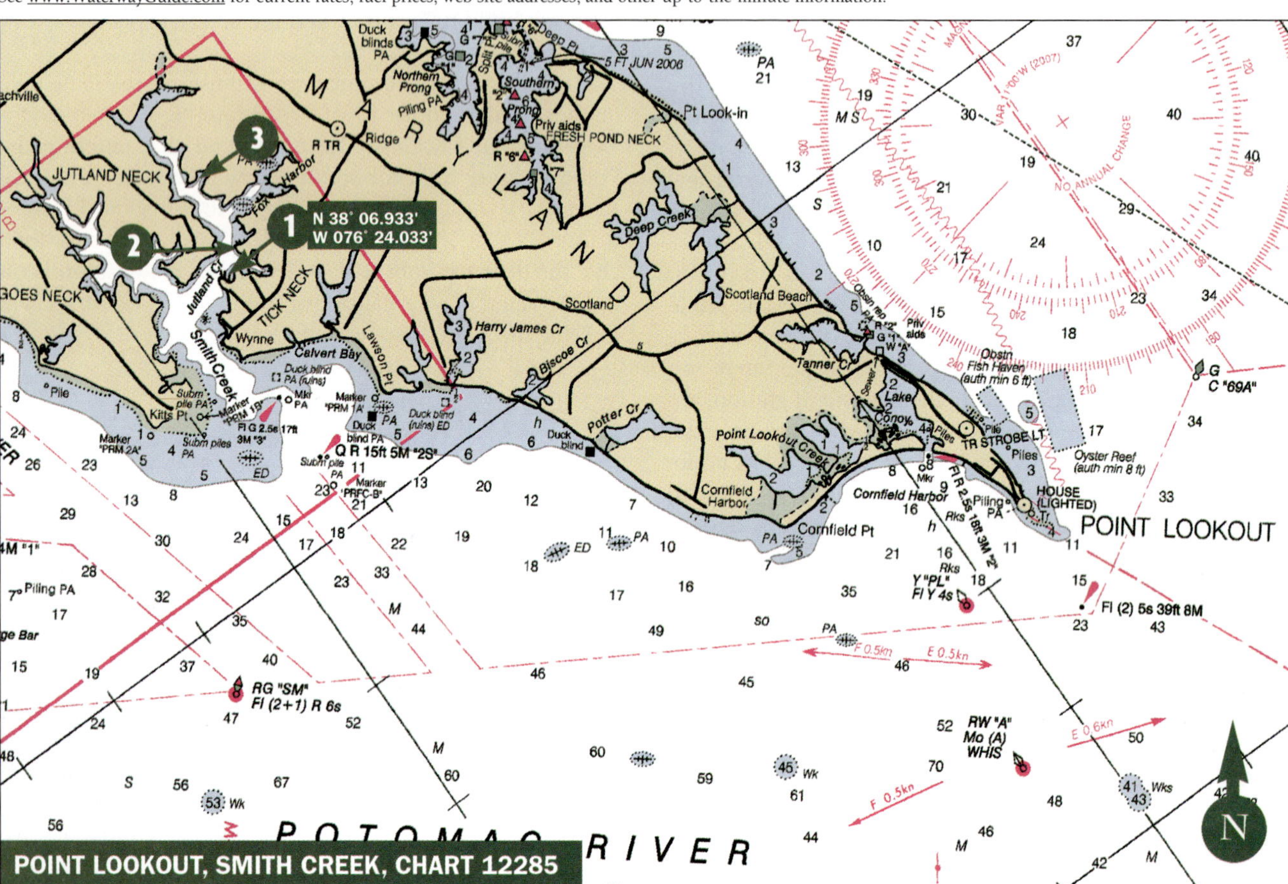

POINT LOOKOUT, SMITH CREEK, CHART 12285

park includes an old lighthouse and Civil War-era prison camp, picnic grounds, a launching ramp and a beach.

Anchorage: A mile and a half into the Potomac from Point Lookout, you will find Point Lookout Creek, a harbor of refuge with a jetty-lined entrance. Be sure to observe all the markers and do not cut corners. The dredged channel is 100 feet wide and splits the jetties down the middle. Inside depths are 6 feet near the channel and 2 to 4 feet elsewhere. Lake Conoy, part of Point Lookout State Park, is simply a spot for shoal-draft boats to drop anchor in the daytime. This public park includes an old lighthouse and Civil War-era prison camp, picnic grounds, a launching ramp and a beach.

Smith Creek, MD

(Mile 4, Maryland Side, after G "7")

NAVIGATION: Use Chart 12285. Smith Creek is a protected, attractive backwater, with a deep, narrow and well-marked zigzag entrance channel. At the entrance, locate the narrow band of deep water between quick flashing red "2S" and 17-foot-tall flashing green "3." Give a wider berth to the points within Smith and Jutland creeks than the chart indicates.

Good depths continue to the head of the creek, and there is a good choice of deep, attractive anchorages here and in the local hurricane hole. The creek abounds with wildlife. Canada geese feed here in the winter, eagles nest in pine trees along the shore, osprey and great blue herons rest in the fish stakes off Kitts Point at the creek entrance, and Chesapeake Bay blue crabs fill the waters.

Dockage: Wynne, a small settlement on the east side of the entrance, has a few commercial docks. Farther east is the full-service Point Lookout Marina, offering fuel, pump-out, a restaurant, pool and a haulout. It is an easy seven-mile bicycle ride on one of the marina's courtesy bikes to Point Lookout State Park, and just three miles to the town of Ridge, which has a grocery store, an ATM and a post office.

Also near Ridge on Smith Creek are Scheible's Fishing Center and Restaurant and Courtney's Restaurant & Seafood. Both offer complimentary tie-up while dining. Call ahead for approach depths.

Jutland Creek, off Smith Creek

Jutland Creek branches off Smith Creek, almost within sight of its clearly defined entrance channel.

Dockage: The friendly Corinthian Yacht Club is set on 14 acres and has laundry, a pool, grills and a large clubhouse. They also have cottages available for visiting friends and family. Bluhaven Piers, at the head of the creek, is a 50-slip marina with showers and pump-out service. They also have Hobie rentals, if you want to downsize for the day!

Anchorage: In the St. Marys region, almost any cove in the Smith/Jutland creeks area will be sheltered, deep and quiet.

Coan River, VA, The Glebe and Kingscote Creek (Mile 3, Virginia Side, at G "7")

The Coan River and its sister tributaries, the Glebe and Kingscote Creek, all garner high praise among cruising skippers for their easy, unobstructed entrances, deep water and marinas for cruising boats. The Coan River area is one of the last undeveloped rural cruising grounds on Virginia's Northern Neck.

NAVIGATION: Use Chart 12285. The Coan River, the Glebe and Kingscote Creek share a common entrance channel. The approach channel starts in the Potomac River at flashing green bell buoy "7" and then leads south past a series of red nun buoys to flashing green "5," where the channel starts a dogleg turn. Bear to port at flashing green "5," and then be sure to mind flashing red "6" at the point off the mouth of Kingsote Creek.

Farther inside you can leave red daybeacon "8" to port and enter The Glebe or Kingscote Creeks. Although the entrance to Kingscoat Creek is not marked, if you proceed with caution there is a deep if narrow channel. Once past the entrance, the creek opens up and you will feel less constrained. If you anchor near the head of the creek where it forks, you will find a special anchorage with views out over the marshes and across Judith Sound to the Potomac. About a half-mile west of the Coan River, The Glebe carries depths of 9 to 13 feet to the fork a mile and a half up. Watch for the shoal extending from the point on the south side about a half-mile above the entrance. There is a lovely protected anchorage with good summer breezes in the small bay just beyond the shoal point.

You can leave daybeacon "8" to starboard and continue up the Coan River, but be aware, as trap markers and stakes can clutter the entrance. They are difficult to sort out in good weather and downright impossible to see when it is rough. As you head south towards the Coan you may see several large fields of trap floats. These are the cages for an

Looking west over Smith Creek. (Not to be used for navigation.) Waterway Guide Photography.

oyster aquaculture farm. They tend to be placed in shallow water and should not affect your navigation. Red daybeacon "14" looks frighteningly close to Walnut Point, but don't worry; the water is at least 10 feet deep here. Beyond, the river is deep to the once-busy wharves at Coan and Bundick. Boats usually anchor in the wide lower river between Walnut Point and red daybeacon "20." Note the long shoal marked by green daybeacon "19."

Dockage: The Coan River's main marina (Coan River Marina) is just inside the entrance to starboard near red nun buoy "2" at Stevens Point and offers limited transient dockage and gas and diesel fuel.

Another marina that may have transient space (Lewisetta Marina) is inside the entrance to Kingscote Creek at an unnamed point, to the north at Lewisetta. Shoals on both sides make the entrance narrow, but the creek carries 8- to 10-foot depths for most of its one-mile length.

■ ST. MARYS RIVER, MD

(Mile 8, Maryland Side, at Red/Green "SM")

St. Mary's River is considered by most cruisers to be one of the most wonderful anchorages on the bay. It is a wide, deep and beautiful river with high banks and mature forests. The cove at Horseshoe Bend is a very popular anchorage. With historic St. Mary's City, the Dove, and St. Mary's College of Maryland nearby to visit, you'll want to spend a full day exploring. Go around Kitts Point to enter the historic St. Marys River. Each August, St. Marys College hosts 300 to 400 boats from the Governor's Cup Race (and the famous party afterwards), the largest sailing race on the East Coast. The overnight race begins in Annapolis and culminates in a whole day of festivities at St. Marys City.

NAVIGATION: Use Baltimore tide tables. For St. Marys City high tide, subtract 6 hours 21 minutes; for low tide, subtract 7 hours 2 minutes.

Dockage: St. Marys College maintains a 275-foot-long dock at the Teddy Turner Waterfront that can accommodate a few boats. Cruising boats may tie up at the dock for two hours or less during daylight hours. You must check in at the dockmaster's office, which is located in the River Center Building (open 8:30 a.m.-5:00 p.m.).

Anchorage: Charted Horseshoe Bend at St. Marys City provides a good deepwater anchorage (16- to 17-foot depths) with beaches for dinghy landings.

St. George Creek, off the St. Marys River

A marked channel branches off to port into St. George Creek at the mouth of the St. Marys River. Note that flashing red "2" at the entrance is not at the tip of the sandbar it marks, and that the channel is quite narrow there. The Seafarers International Union trains merchant seamen at the Harry Lundeberg School of Seamanship at Piney Point.

Anchorage: St. George Creek has an open area between flashing green "3" and flashing red "4" close to St. George Island. You can anchor on the south side of the channel off flashing red "4" in 8-foot depths. You can tie up for dinner

Coan River, VA

COAN RIVER		Largest Vessel Accommodated	VHF Channel Monitored	Transient Berths / Total Berths	Approach / Dockside Depth (reported)	Floating Docks	Gas / Diesel	Groceries, Ice, Marine Supplies, Snacks	Repairs: Hull, Engine, Propeller	Lift (tonnage), Crane, Rail	Min/Max Amps	Laundry, Pool, Showers, Courtesy Car	Pump-Out Station	Nearby: Grocery Store, Motel, Restaurant
		Dockage					Supplies		Services					
1. Coan River Marina 🖳 WiFi	804-529-6767	60	01	5/55	12/7	F	GD	IMS	HEP	L25, C	30/50	LS	P	-
2. Lewisetta Marina, Inc.	804-529-7299	50	-	1/19	-	-	GD	GIMS	HEP	L25	30/50	S	P	G

Corresponding chart(s) not to be used for navigation. 🖳 Internet Access WiFi Wireless Internet Access Waterway Guide Cruising Club Partner

See www.WaterwayGuide.com for current rates, fuel prices, web site addresses, and other up-to-the-minute information.

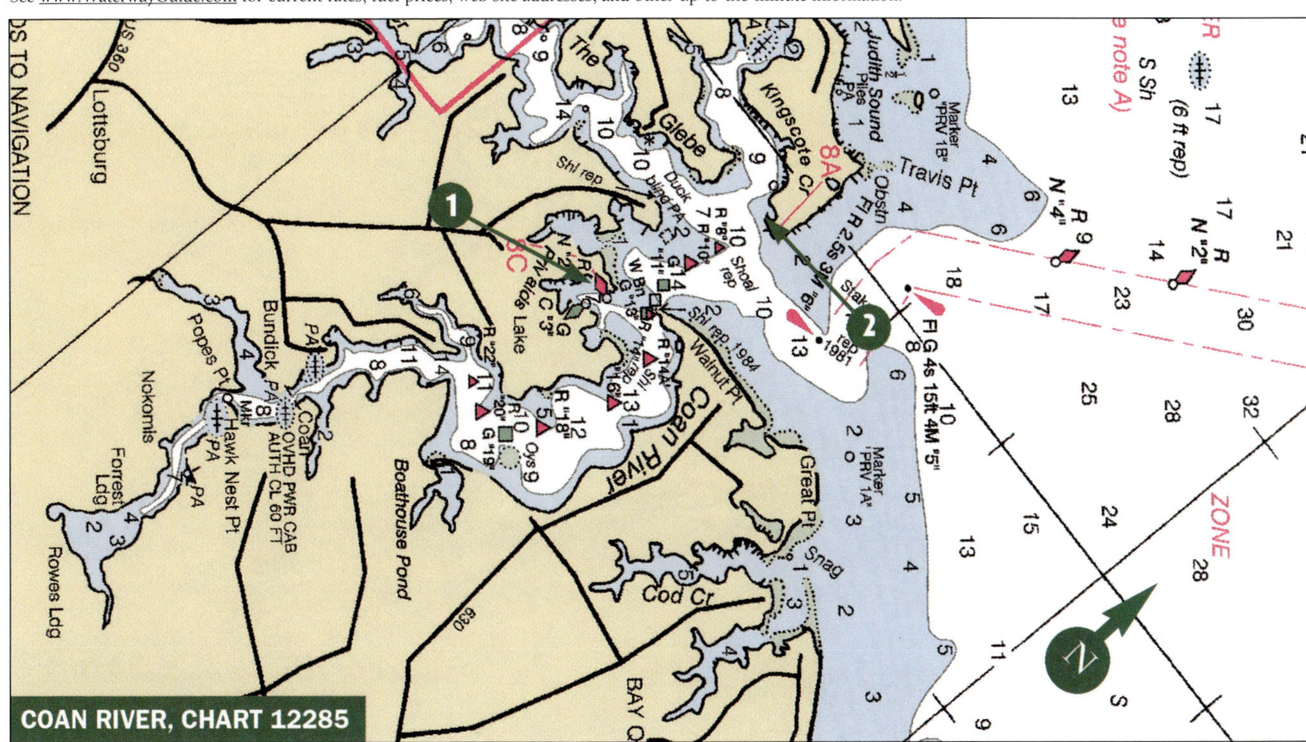

COAN RIVER, CHART 12285

at Evans Seafood Restaurant (301-994-9944). You can also anchor in the protection of tall trees and ample swinging space well beyond the town of Piney Point, particularly if your boat draws 5 feet or less.

Piney Point and Herring Creek, MD

(Mile 17, Maryland Side, past Ragged Point Light)

Piney Point on the Potomac (not the one on St. George Creek) is easy to identify by its prominent fuel terminal pier, which often has a tanker alongside. Herring Creek's jetty-lined entrance is about three miles northwest of Piney Point and almost nine miles west of the St. Marys River entrance.

Dockage: Piney Point Lighthouse Museum and Park has 6-foot approach and dockside depths but few amenities. Call ahead for overnight availability. The Museum features exhibits depicting the construction and operation of the Lighthouse and the role of the United States Coast Guard. Also on exhibit is information about the German submarine, U-1105, which was sunk off the coast of Piney Point. (Located at Mile 14, past RW "B" and seasonally marked with a Blue/White mooring).

While the full-service marinas in Herring Creek, such as Tall Timbers Marina and Cedar Cove Marina, usually fill with local boats, they can sometimes accommodate transients. Both of these facilities offer some marine supplies and boat repairs and sell gas; Tall Timbers also sells diesel and has a restaurant, The Reluctant Navigator (301-994-1508).

Carthegena Creek, off the St. Marys River

This narrow, deep, well-marked creek on the west side of the St. Marys River has charted depths of at least 9 feet at mean low water all the way to Dennis Point Marina. Pick up green daybeacons "1" and "3" in the wide mouth of the creek, and leave them to port.

Dockage: This narrow, deep, well-marked creek on the west side of the St. Marys River has charted depths of at least 9 feet at mean low water all the way to Dennis Point Marina & Campground, which offers transient dockage, a 75-ton lift and repair yard, and a pool and restaurant. They also sell gas and diesel and can accommodate boats up to 120 feet. Pick up green daybeacons "1" and "3" in the wide mouth of the creek, and leave them to port.

St. Marys River and Environs, MD

ST. MARYS RIVER, ST. GEORGE CREEK		Largest Vessel Accommodated	VHF Channel Monitored	Transient Berths / Total Berths	Approach / Dockside Depth (reported)	Floating Docks	Gas / Diesel	Groceries, Ice, Marine Supplies, Snacks	Repairs: Hull, Engine, Propeller	Lift (tonnage), Crane, Rail	Min/Max Amps	Laundry, Pool, Showers, Courtesy Car	Pump-Out Station	Nearby: Grocery Store, Motel, Restaurant
		Dockage					Supplies		Services					
1. Dennis Point Marina & Campground (Internet Access)	**301-994-2288**	**120**	**16/68**	**12/100**	**10/10**	**F**	**GD**	**GIMS**	**HEP**	**L75**	**30/50**	**LPS**	**P**	**GR**
2. Tall Timbers Marina (Wireless Internet Access)	301-994-1508	65	16	20/130	8/6	-	GD	IMS	HEP	L25	30/50	S	-	GMR
3. Cedar Cove Marina	301-994-1155	55	16	5/66	10/5	-	G	IM	HE	L25	30/30	LS	P	GMR

Corresponding chart(s) not to be used for navigation. Internet Access · Wireless Internet Access · Waterway Guide Cruising Club Partner

See www.WaterwayGuide.com for current rates, fuel prices, web site addresses, and other up-to-the-minute information.

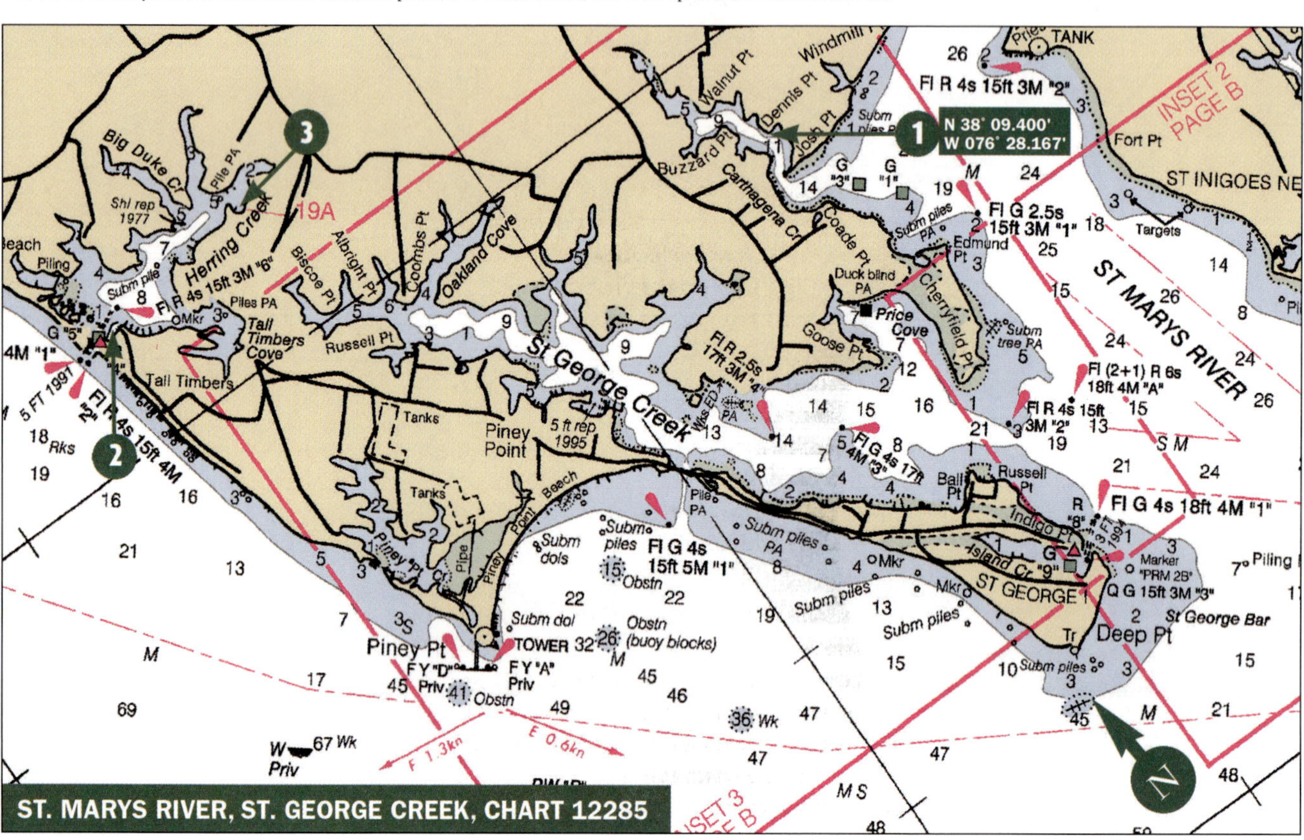

Anchorage: Carthegena Creek can shelter a few boats near the marina beyond Josh Point.

St. Inigoes Creek, off the St. Marys River

Give a wide berth to Priests Point (marked with flashing red "2") to enter attractive St. Inigoes Creek. Also be sure to give the point at Lucas Cove a wide berth after you enter.

Anchorage: Give a wide berth to Priests Point (marked with flashing red "2") to enter attractive St. Inigoes Creek. Also be sure to give the point at Lucas Cove a wide berth after you enter. Favor the west side past the charted wreck (not visible) and choose a spot to drop the hook in the wide creek between Milburn Creek and Church Cove in 13 to 16 feet. The St. Inigoes Coast Guard Station is in Molls Cove, to starboard upon entering.

Yeocomico River (Mile 9, Virginia Side, at G "9")

The Yeocomico is an attractive river with three forks. Shannon Branch extends to starboard as you enter; West Yeocomico River forms the middle fork almost dead ahead; and South Yeocomico River goes to the south (port) and branches to Mill and Lodge creeks.

NAVIGATION: Use Chart 12285. The Yeocomico River makes an even better harbor of refuge than the Coan when crosscurrents and northerly winds on the Chesapeake Bay demand it. The Yeocomico River is just a few miles farther up the Potomac than the Coan, with more to offer. It is easy to enter and has well-protected coves and good marinas.

The network of tributaries around the Yeocomico River may look complex, but everything is well marked and easy to navigate. Sixteen-foot-high flashing red "2," which is just outside the mouth, looks like a cupcake with a tilted top and a single erect candle (known locally as "The Birthday Cake") and leads you into the Yeocomico. The next marker, flashing green "3," lies off Barn Point, about two miles upriver from the Yeocomico River's mouth on the south side.

Proceed southwest past red daybeacon "2," marking a long shoal off Horn Point, toward Kinsale on the West Yeocomico—or head south into the South Yeocomico toward Harryhogan Point and Lodge Creek.

The West Yeocomico divides into two branches. The right branch has the town of Kinsale, a wharf, a grain elevator, stores, a post office and a marina before an 8-foot fixed vertical clearance bridge. Along the left, beautiful homes are perched on a high bluff. Kinsale is one of the oldest Potomac settlements and is also a War of 1812 battlefield site.

Dockage: Just inside White Point on Shannon Branch is White Point Marina, offering dockage, fuel and a courtesy car. Port Kinsale Marina is on the West Yeocomico between Horn Point and Allen Point as is Kinsale Harbour Yacht Club. Kinsale is one of the oldest Potomac settlements and is also a War of 1812 battlefield site. Past Harryhogan Point on Lodge Creek you will find the 199-slip Olverson's Lodge Creek Marina. They sell fuel and reserve some space for transients.

Anchorage: A pretty cove with high banks is on the north side of the West Yeocomico River between Seldom and Sloop points. Fittingly called Long Cove, it carries 8-foot depths, provides good holding and is within dinghy distance of Kinsale. Avoid the shoal with 2-foot depths off Sloop Point. It may have private markers to assist you.

You can also anchor off Great House Point where the river branches. The area is attractive and well protected from all angles, and you will have at least 9- to 10-foot depths here with good holding in mud.

The South Yeocomico River has many creeks and coves, but trap markers litter some. Drum Cove off Mill Creek (South Yeocomico River) is a well-protected spot for one or two boats, depending on their size. Do not cut the east point too closely. The depths here are around 7 to 8 feet. Just past red daybeacon "6," there are protected anchorages to port in Dungan Cove or to starboard behind Harryhogan Point with depths of 7 to 10 feet.

Black Panther Historic Shipwreck Preserve (Mile 14, past RW "B" and seasonally marked with a Blue/White mooring)

The U-1105, a modified Type VII-C German submarine, now serves as a historic dive site. The British turned it over to the U.S. Navy. After some preliminary testing the Navy sunk it in 1949. An exhibit with more information is located at the Piney Point Lighthouse Museum.

Coles Neck, VA (Mile 17, Virginia Side, at the Ragged Point Light)

Ragged Point is one of Blackbeard the Pirate's reported landing sites. One local saltwater pond is named Blackbeard's Pond while another, on what was once a part of King Carter's great plantation, is appropriately named Long Pond. Both are part of Coles Point Plantation, and you can explore them by dinghy.

Dockage: Just before Ragged Point you will discover Coles Point Plantation Marina immediately off the Potomac. This is a full-service facility with a pool and an on-site restaurant.

Herring Creek, MD (Mile 17, Maryland Side, past Ragged Point Light)

Piney Point on the Potomac (not the one on St. George Creek) is easy to identify by its prominent fuel terminal pier, which often has a tanker alongside. Herring Creek's jetty-lined entrance is about three miles northwest of Piney Point and almost nine miles west of the St. Marys River entrance.

Dockage: While the full-service marinas in Herring Creek, such as Tall Timbers Marina, usually fill with local boats, they can sometimes accommodate transients.

Lower Machodoc Creek (Mile 19, Virginia Side, at G "11")

Lower Machodoc Creek is one of the Potomac's busiest oyster-packing centers. It carries at least 8-foot depths up to the turn at red daybeacon "2," although the channel gets quite narrow at Plumb Point.

Nomini Bay (Mile 25, Virginia Side, before G "13")

Continue past Lower Machodoc Creek west up the Potomac to Nomini (accent on the first syllable) Bay, where deep and well-marked Nomini Creek leads off to the south, and

Yeocomico River, VA

YEOCOMICO RIVER		Largest Vessel Accommodated	VHF Channel Monitored	Transient Berths / Total Berths	Approach / Dockside Depth (reported)	Floating Docks	Gas / Diesel	Groceries, Ice, Marine Supplies, Snacks	Repairs: Hull, Engine, Propeller	Lift (tonnage), Crane, Rail	Min/Max Amps	Laundry, Pool, Showers, Courtesy Car	Pump-Out Station	Nearby: Grocery Store, Motel, Restaurant
		Dockage					Supplies		Services					
1. White Point Marina (Wireless Internet Access) (Waterway Guide Cruising Club Partner)	**804-472-2977**	**110**	**16/68**	**15/50**	**10/8**	**-**	**GD**	**GIMS**	**HEP**	**R50**	**30/50**	**LPSC**	**P**	**MR**
2. Port Kinsale Marina & Resort (Internet Access) (Wireless Internet Access)	804-472-2044	90	16	32/112	12/10	-	GD	GIMS	HEP	L30, C	30/50	LPS	P	GMR
3. Kinsale Harbour Yacht Club	804-472-2514	50	16/68	20/99	10/8	-	-	IS	-	L	30/30	LPS	P	GR
4. Olverson's Lodge Creek Marina, Inc. (Internet Access) (Wireless Internet Access)	800-529-5071	100	16	10/200	10/10	-	GD	IS	-	-	30/50	LPSC	P	-

Corresponding chart(s) not to be used for navigation. ☐ Internet Access (WiFi) Wireless Internet Access Waterway Guide Cruising Club Partner

See www.WaterwayGuide.com for current rates, fuel prices, web site addresses, and other up-to-the-minute information.

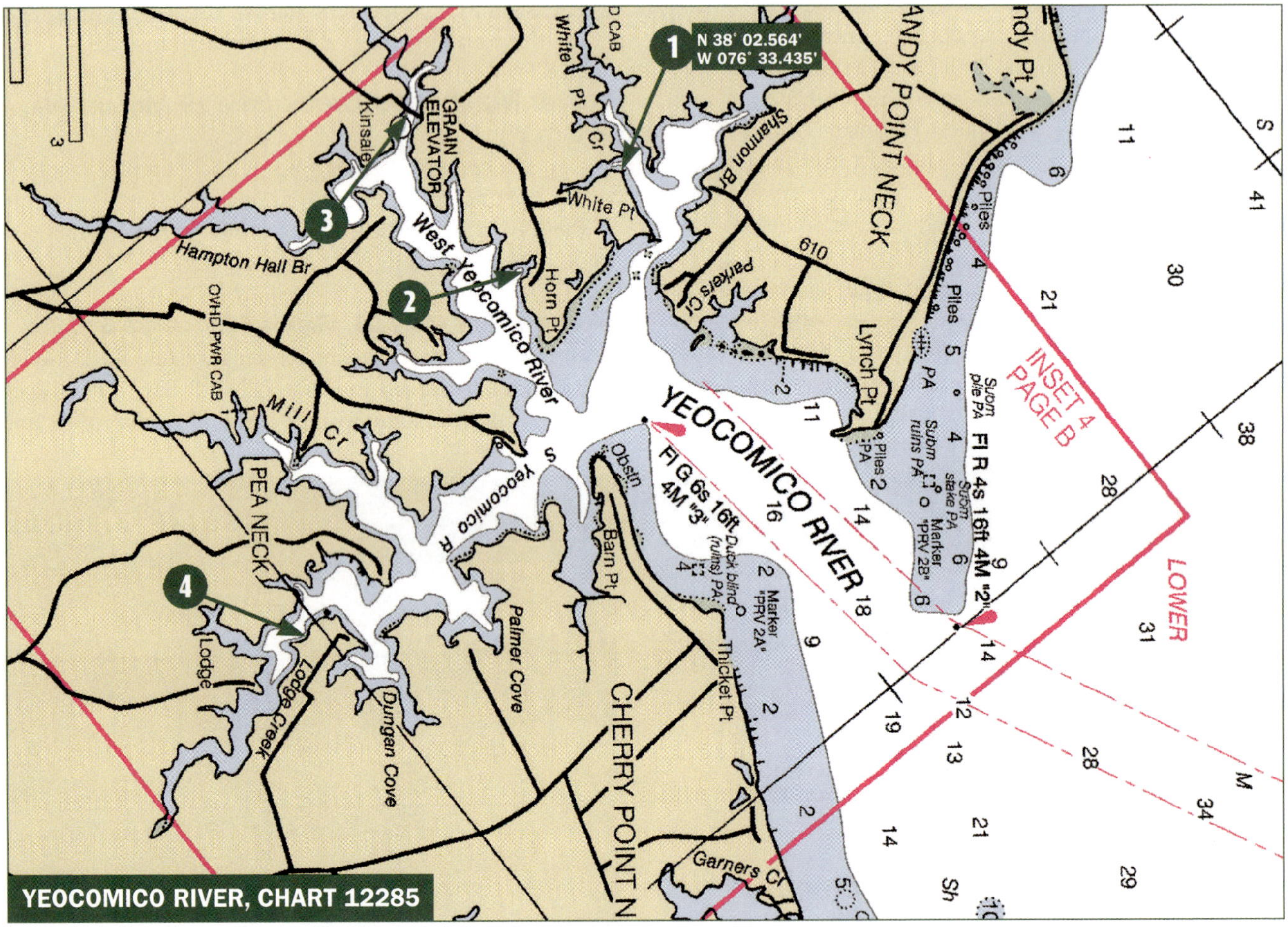

YEOCOMICO RIVER, CHART 12285

Currioman Bay extends to the west. Currioman Bay has depths of 8 to 10 feet in the middle, but the entrance is only suited for those carrying less than 4 feet of draft. Seek local knowledge before trying this passage. Also, be aware that Hollis Marsh (as known as Shark Tooth Island) at the entrance to the creek is privately owned, although cruising boats are often anchored there and dinghies can be seen lined up on the beach.

Breton Bay and Leonardtown, MD (Mile 25, Maryland Side, after R12 at R/G "HI")

Breton Bay carries markers for five nautical miles up to Leonardtown, an important shipping point. The town, atop a low hill, has a grocery store, drugstore, laundry

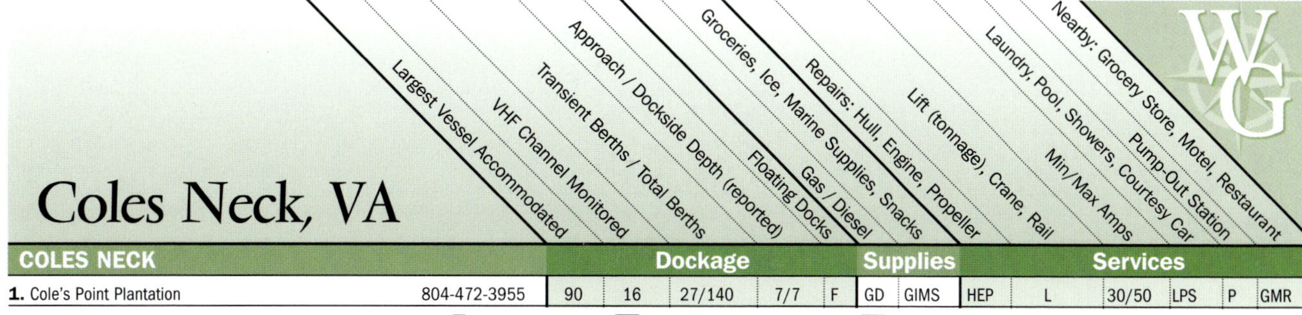

Coles Neck, VA

COLES NECK		Largest Vessel Accommodated	VHF Channel Monitored	Transient Berths / Total Berths	Approach / Dockside Depth (reported)	Floating Docks	Gas / Diesel	Groceries, Ice, Marine Supplies, Snacks	Repairs: Hull, Engine, Propeller	Lift (tonnage), Crane, Rail	Min/Max Amps	Laundry, Pool, Showers, Courtesy Car	Pump-Out Station	Nearby: Grocery Store, Motel, Restaurant
		Dockage					Supplies		Services					
1. Cole's Point Plantation	804-472-3955	90	16	27/140	7/7	F	GD	GIMS	HEP	L	30/50	LPS	P	GMR

Corresponding chart(s) not to be used for navigation. Internet Access Wireless Internet Access Waterway Guide Cruising Club Partner

See www.WaterwayGuide.com for current rates, fuel prices, web site addresses, and other up-to-the-minute information.

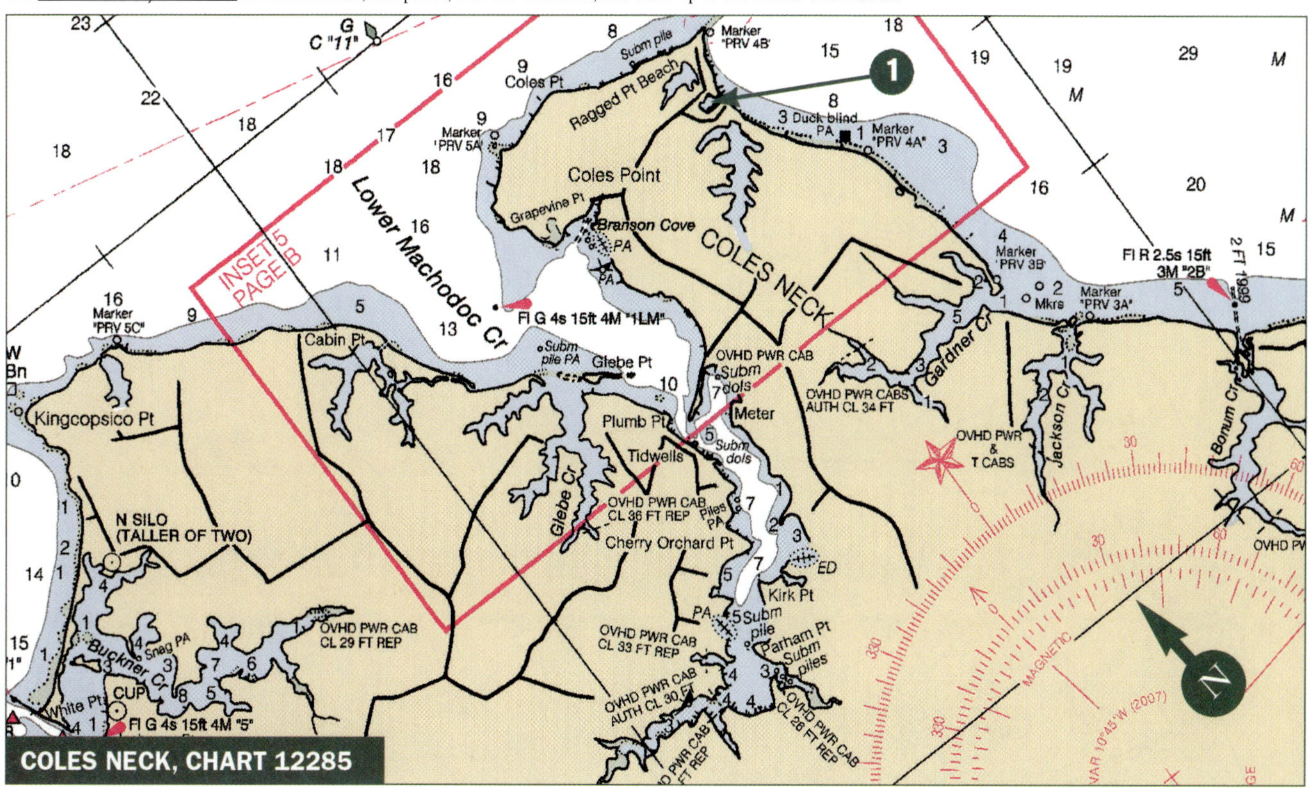

COLES NECK, CHART 12285

and restaurant all within walking distance of shore. Leonardtown has many historic buildings, including an old jail that houses a small museum. Leonardtown Wharf, the waterfront town park, is a worthy stopover. Stretch your legs along the walkways that span the waterway and traverse the wetland. While there is no dockage along the promenade wall, there is a kayak ramp you could use if you choose to dinghy to shore. Call the town office at 301-475-9791 for more information.

NAVIGATION: Use Chart 12285. Breton Bay narrows and becomes more pastoral as you wind north. Pay strict attention to navigational aids, and give points of land plenty of room. The course turns west past flashing green "11" at Buzzard Point. Give the point a wide berth, and feel your way slowly from here to Leonardtown, where you can anchor in 8- to 10-foot depths.

Dockage: The Combs Creek Marina, on the northwestern shore of Breton Bay, has limited transient space and sells some supplies.

Anchorage: You can anchor off Leonardtown in 8- to 10-foot depths and take advantage of the town park or in any of the coves past Lovers Point.

St. Clements Bay, MD (Mile 25, Maryland side, after R "12" at R/G "HI")

Heading west from Breton Bay's mouth, round Newtown Neck to reach St. Clements Bay. Note the shoal starting at Kaywood Point off the end of Long Point; an unnumbered white daybeacon marks the longest shoal area. Great blue herons, egrets, cormorants and ospreys congregate on the staked fishnets, waiting patiently to steal the fisherman's catch. Heron Island Bar and St. Clements Island protect the mouth of St. Clements Bay. Once inside, you have good shelter in a typical lower-Potomac estuary. St. Clements Island, site of the first landing of colonists in Maryland, eroded badly over past centuries, but an intense state effort has now stabilized it.

A charted, white 40-foot-high commemorative cross, marking the location where religious tolerance in America had its foundation, as well as being the colonist landing

Breton Bay to St. Clements Bay, MD

BRETON BAY TO ST. CLEMENTS BAY		Largest Vessel Accommodated	VHF Channel Monitored	Transient Berths / Total Berths	Approach / Dockside Depth (reported)	Floating Docks	Gas / Diesel	Groceries, Ice, Marine Supplies, Snacks	Repairs: Hull, Engine, Propeller	Lift (tonnage), Crane, Rail	Min/Max Amps	Laundry, Pool, Showers, Courtesy Car	Pump-Out Station	Nearby: Grocery Store, Motel, Restaurant
		Dockage					Supplies				Services			
1. Combs Creek Marina LLC	301-475-2017	42	–	2/38	6/6	–	–	I	–	–	30/50	S	P	R
2. Cather Marine Inc.	301-769-3335	45	16	2/70	6/6	–	G	GIMS	EP	L30		SC	P	G
3. Coltons Point Marina 🖳 WiFi	301-769-3121	65	16	8/100	5/5	–	GD	IMS	HEP	L30	30/50	LS	P	G

Corresponding chart(s) not to be used for navigation. 🖳 Internet Access WiFi Wireless Internet Access Waterway Guide Cruising Club Partner

See www.WaterwayGuide.com for current rates, fuel prices, web site addresses, and other up-to-the-minute information.

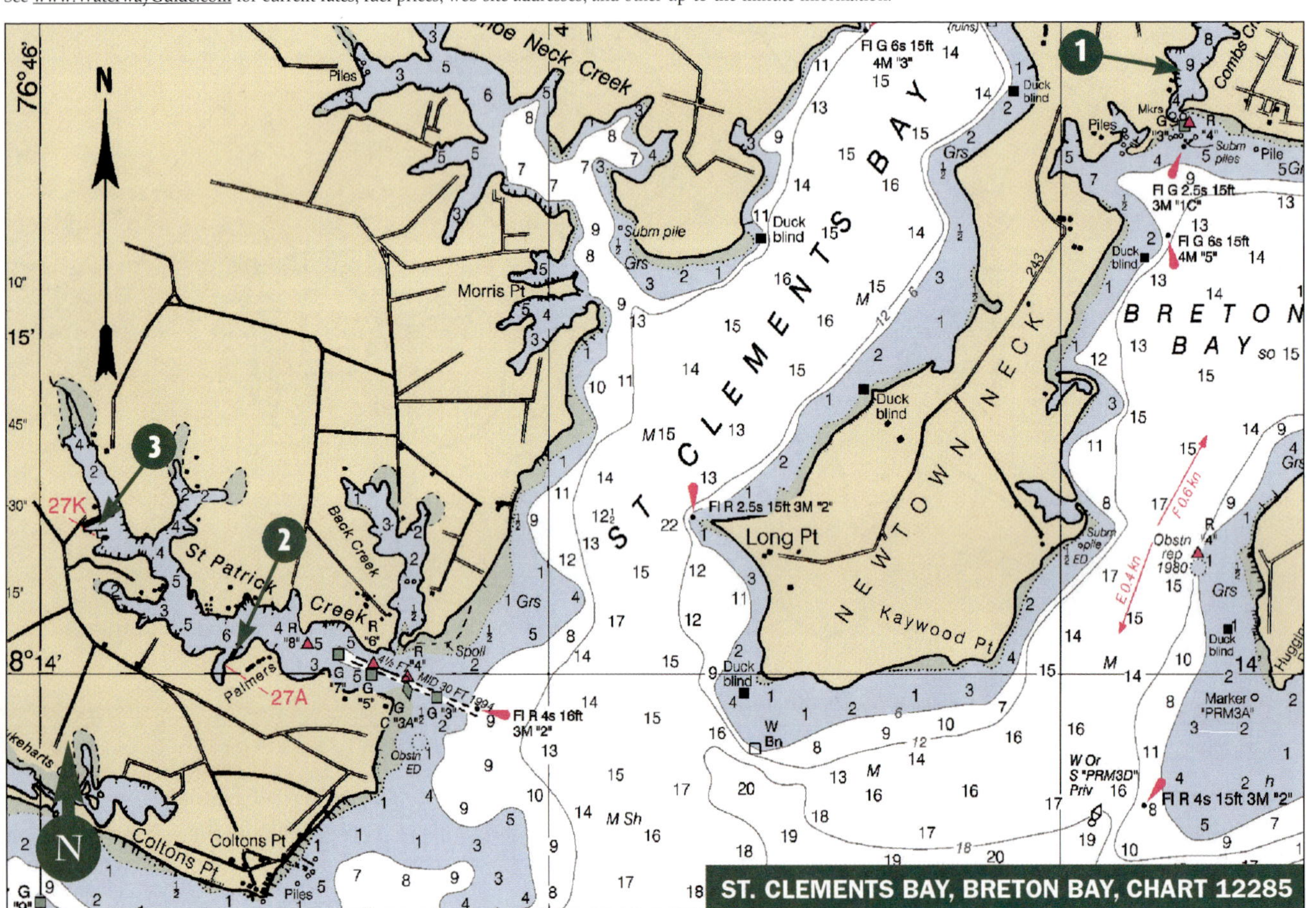

ST. CLEMENTS BAY, BRETON BAY, CHART 12285

site for The Ark and The Dove, faces the Potomac River. Both the cross and a replica of the Blackistone Lighthouse are visible to passing boats. Boat tours to the island run on a regular schedule from Coltons Point, across Dukeharts Channel from St. Clements Island. The St. Clements Island-Potomac River Museum is also at Coltons Point. This is a great place to beachcomb for shells and fossils or just to enjoy the quiet of this placid island park. An osprey pair has been nesting on the aforementioned cross for years. If you are lucky, you may be able to spot one catching its morning meal just offshore.

NAVIGATION: Use Chart 12285. We recommend that you not take the shortcut through the Dukeharts Channel behind St. Clements Island without local knowledge of the depths. We instead recommend entering St. Clements Bay through Heron Island channel. St. Patrick Creek, on the west side of the Bay, has dockage.

Dockage: A public dock at St. Clement's Island Potomac River Museum at Coltons Point has 6-foot depths, and groceries are nearby. Call ahead for availability. A public dock (short-term tie-up) is on the inside of St. Clements Island, but be aware of the shoal water surrounding the island before approaching. A marked channel north of Coltons Point leads to St. Patrick Creek where Cather Marine and Coltons Point Marina have limited transient space. Both sell gas and Coltons Point sells diesel. Coltons Point reports 5-foot approach and dockside depths; call ahead for actual depths.

Canoe Neck Creek, off St. Clements Bay

Anchorage: Canoe Neck Creek, about a one mile journey up St. Clements Bay to port, is a protected anchorage. Enter from St. Clements Bay, favoring the port side until you reach the first cove to starboard, while keeping an eye out for the numerous trap markers. Give the shoal off the unnamed south point a wide berth, and then anchor in 7- to 9-foot depths with good holding. Pretty farms surround the cove, and blue herons populate the lower point. You can tie up for dinner at Morris Point Restaurant (301-769-2500). Another anchorage is below Shipping Point with 10- to 13-foot depths and good holding. This quiet, attractive spot provides good protection from the northwest.

MIDDLE DANGER ZONE, MD (Mile 27 to Mile 43, R "14" to R "32")

Caution: Be sure to monitor VHF Channel 16 in this area to hear about any firing exercises from the Naval Surface Weapons Center in Dahlgren, VA, just upriver from Colonial Beach. Labels and dashed magenta lines indicate the three zones on Chart 12285.

The uppermost zone, for long range and aerial machine gun firings, and the lowest zone, for aerial bombing and strafing, are generally unused.

The middle zone is important, as it is normally active daily from 8:00 a.m. to 4:000 p.m., except on weekends and national holidays. The middle firing range begins approximately on a line between St. Clements Island and Currioman Bay at Mile 26.7 and extends to the Harry Nice Bridge (U.S. Route 301) at Mile 43.5. Before entering this area, call Dahlgren Range Patrol on VHF Channel 16, give the name of your boat and ask if you may proceed. You will receive notification that the range is "hot" (active) or "cold" (inactive). When the range is active, the Range Patrol usually instructs small craft to proceed outside the boundary line along the Maryland shore. Delays are rare.

Note the white beacon marking the long shoal extending southward from Swan Point on the Maryland shore. Stay tuned to VHF Channel 16 when in the area; this is a place where you will appreciate having a remote station for your VHF or a handheld unit in the cockpit. The range boats are usually at their stations and will contact you if you go into the territory.

Wicomico River, MD (Mile 30, Maryland Side, after R "14A" at RG "WR")

West of St. Clements Island is the mouth of the Wicomico River, one of four with the same name on the Chesapeake Bay. The state pier and launching ramp at Bushwood Wharf, on the east side of the river, are popular with locals.

NAVIGATION: Use Chart 12285. Be sure to avoid the long shoal west of St. Margaret Island. Red daybeacon "2W" is located far out into the Wicomico River; leave it to starboard when going into the river. The marked channel behind St. Catherine Island and St. Margaret Island may look tempting, but do not attempt it without local knowledge and a shallow-draft boat.

Anchorage: You can anchor in the curve of the river off Bushwood Wharf (about three miles up the Wicomico River on the east side) in 7- to 12-foot depths with good

Cobb Island, MD

COBB ISLAND		Largest Vessel Accommodated	VHF Channel Monitored	Transient Berths / Total Berths	Approach / Dockside Depth (reported)	Floating Docks	Gas / Diesel	Groceries, Ice, Marine Supplies, Snacks	Repairs: Hull, Engine, Propeller	Lift (tonnage), Crane, Rail	Min/Max Amps	Laundry, Pool, Showers, Courtesy Car	Pump-Out Station	Nearby: Grocery Store, Motel, Restaurant
		Dockage					Supplies				Services			
1. Shymansky's Restaurant & Marina	301-259-2221	100	16/68	10/110	8/6	-	GD	GIMS	HEP	L	30/50	S	P	GR
2. Captain John's Crabhouse & Marina (WiFi)	301-259-2315	50	-	10/40	10/6	-	G	GIMS	-	-	30/30	-	P	GR
3. Pirate's Den Marina (WiFi)	301-259-2879	44	16	8/88	15/5	-	G	GI	-	L14	30/50	S	P	G

Corresponding chart(s) not to be used for navigation. Internet Access (WiFi) Wireless Internet Access Waterway Guide Cruising Club Partner

See www.WaterwayGuide.com for current rates, fuel prices, web site addresses, and other up-to-the-minute information.

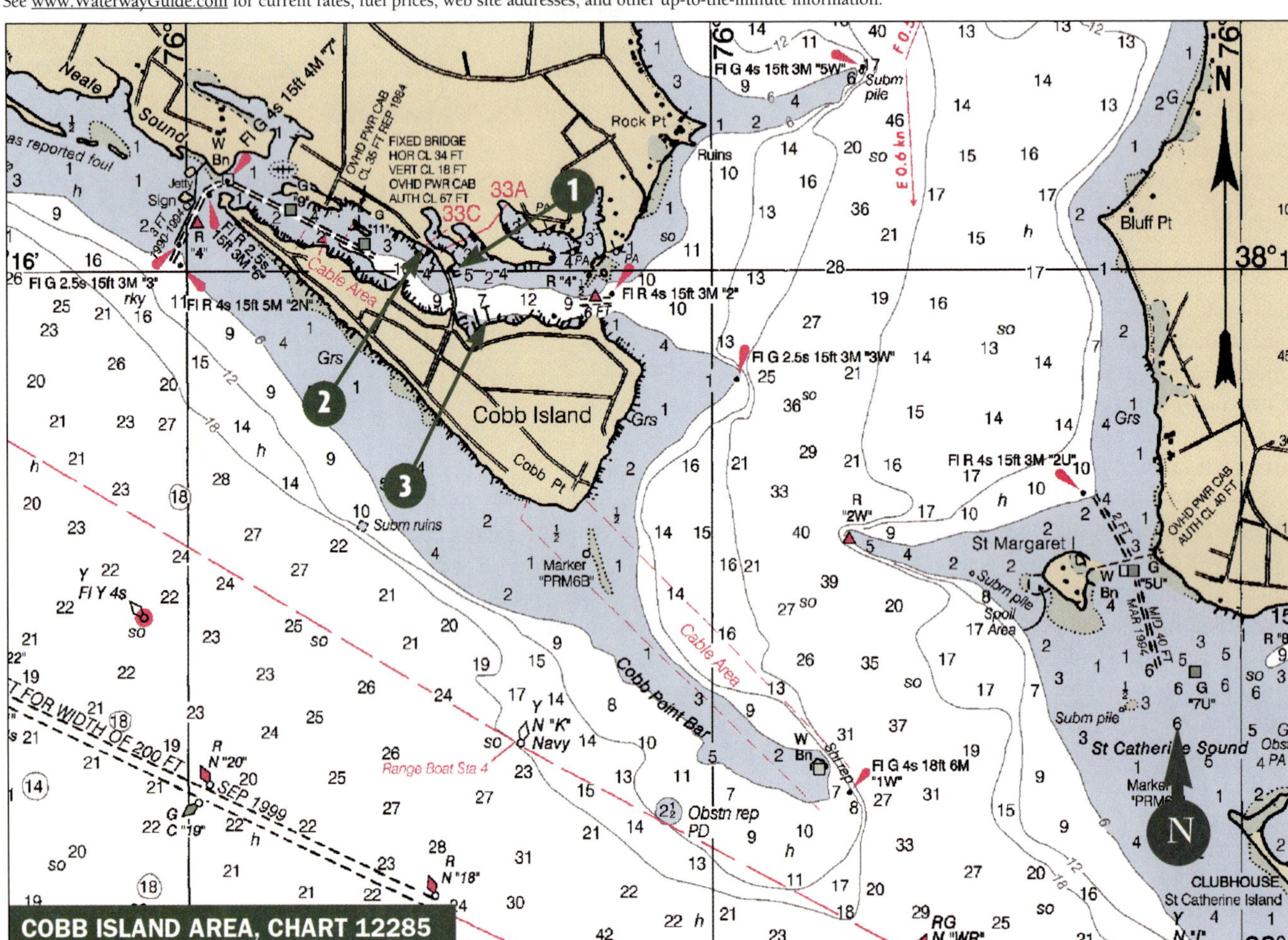

holding but watch for trap markers. The wakes from local watermen's boats may jostle you a bit. Also, if the wind is strong from the west through the south, seas can make you uncomfortable and even put you on a lee shore if your anchor drags.

The same friendly family has run the Quades Store (301-769-3903) near Bushwood Wharf on the Wicomico's northeast shore for more than 50 years. Usually open from 7:00 a.m. to 6:00 p.m., it stocks all the essential supplies and also serves breakfast and lunch. To get there, beach the dinghy nearby, or climb up the local bulkhead (there is no ladder). Impressive Chickahominy Mansion, a private home built in 1907, is to the left of the grocery store, and just up the hill. Private owners are restoring the 17th-century Mansion House as a home.

Cobb Island, off the Wicomico

Cobb Island is a tiny hamlet with several popular restaurants, a good grocery store and a post office. More and more sailors who enjoy the good winds, clean water and the broad five-mile width of the Potomac at this point are calling the island their home port.

NAVIGATION: Use Chart 12285. Cobb Island, on the west side of the mouth of the Wicomico River, provides a good harbor in the marked passage between it and the mainland, although the Wicomico River entrance to Cobb Creek is sometimes thick with trap markers. You can enter either from the Wicomico River or through a shallower channel from the Potomac River at the west end of the island. Latest

Colonial Beach, Dahlgren, VA

COLONIAL BEACH, DAHLGREN, VA		Largest Vessel Accommodated	VHF Channel Monitored	Transient Berths / Total Berths	Approach / Dockside Depth (reported)	Floating Docks	Gas / Diesel	Groceries, Ice, Marine Supplies, Snacks	Repairs: Hull, Engine, Propeller	Lift (tonnage), Crane, Rail	Min/Max Amps	Laundry, Pool, Showers, Courtesy Car	Pump-Out Station	Nearby: Grocery Store, Motel, Restaurant
		Dockage					Supplies		Services					
1. Colonial Beach Yacht Center (Internet Access)	804-224-7230	100	16	30/150	8/8	F	GD	IMS	HEP	L30	30/30	S	P	MR
2. Stanford's Marine Railway	804-224-7644	55	-	1/30	4/7	-	-	M	HE	L, R	30/30	S	-	R
3. Winkie Doodle Point Marina	804-224-9560	50	-	5/65	6/5	-	-	-	-	-	30/30	-	P	GMR
4. Nightingale Motel & Marina	804-224-7956	40	-	10/36	5/5	-	-	IS	-	-	30/30	S	-	GMR
5. Bayside Marina and Restaurant (Wireless Internet Access)	804-224-7570	50	16	/40	4/6	-	-	GIS	-	-	30/30	PS	-	GMR
6. Stepp's Harbor View Marina	804-224-9265	60	16	/144	7/7	-	G	GIMS	HEP	L40	30/50	PS	P	G
7. Machodoc Creek Marina (formerly Dahlgren Marine Center)	540-663-2741	60	16/68	6/64	7/6	-	GD	IMS	E	L	30/30	S	P	GMR

Corresponding chart(s) not to be used for navigation. Internet Access · Wireless Internet Access · Waterway Guide Cruising Club Partner

See www.WaterwayGuide.com for current rates, fuel prices, web site addresses, and other up-to-the-minute information.

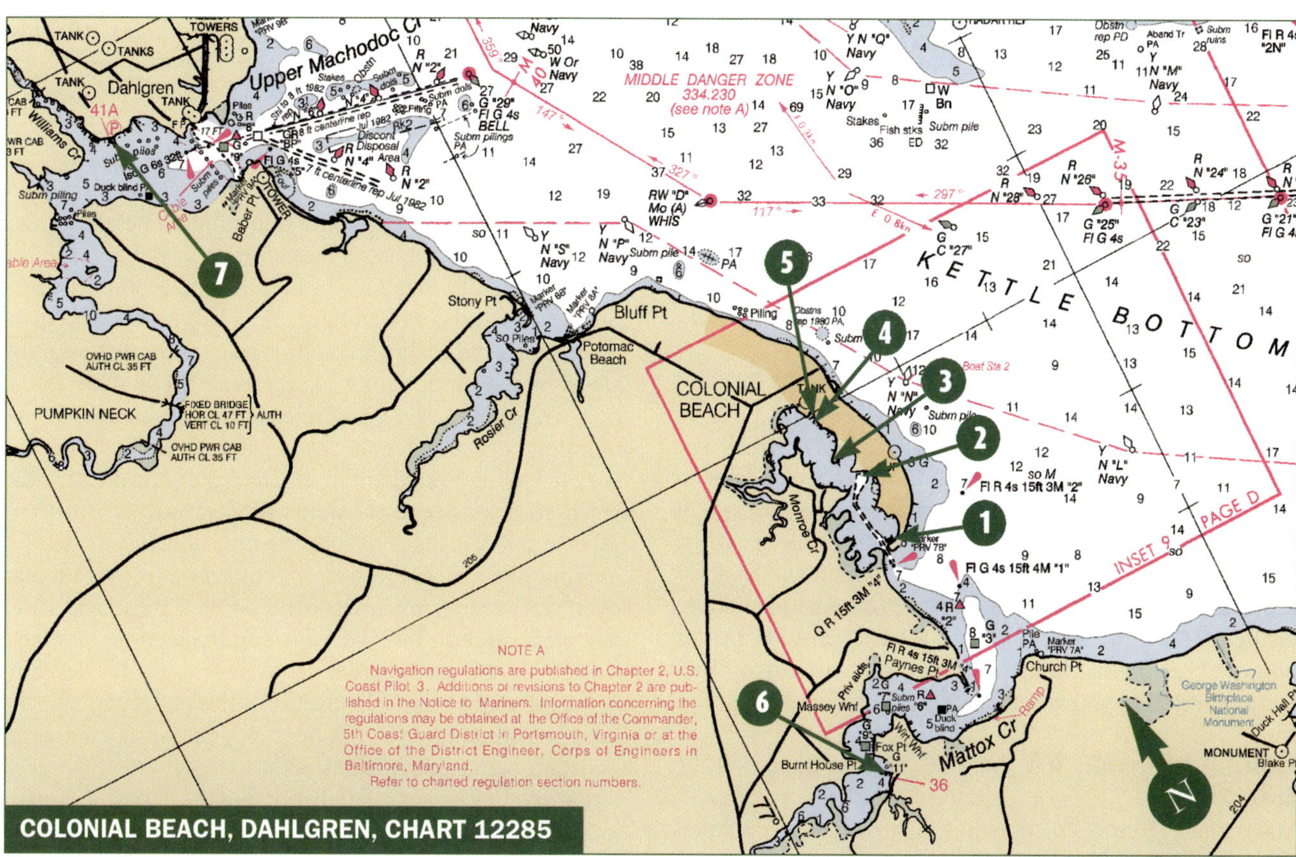

COLONIAL BEACH, DAHLGREN, CHART 12285

reports show the lowest depth in the east entrance as 6 feet near red daybeacon "4." The channel from the Wicomico River is very narrow. Two boats can scarcely slip through together, so do not try the passage when you see another vessel coming out nor attempt to cut between flashing red "2" and red daybeacon "4." Also, do not try crossing directly from the island marina to the mainland marinas because the area is shoaling.

The Cobb Creek (Neale Sound) entrance from the Potomac (west) was charted at 5 feet in 2009. With its narrow channel and sharp turn at green daybeacon "7," the Neale Sound channel is not recommended without local knowledge.

A fixed bridge (18-foot vertical clearance) and an overhead power cable (67-foot vertical clearance) divide the passage. Once inside, you will find several marinas that welcome cruising boats.

Dockage: Captain John's Crabhouse and Marina offers transient dockage (free for diners), gas and a popular dockside restaurant (301-259-2315). To the east, Shymansky's Marina has gas and diesel fuel. You can go ashore at the paved road beside the marina, but this is private property, so go into the bar or restaurant and ask permission first. Pirates Den Marina (east of the bridge) has gas and an onsite restaurant (Scuttlebutts, 240-687-3113). It operates seasonally. Another dining option is Draft Away Bar & Grill

(301-259-4900), which hosts area bands. For art with your coffee, try Cobb Island Gallery (301-259-4900). The Cobb Island Market has some supplies for reprovisioning.

Stratford Hall Plantation (Mile 30, Virginia Side, after R "14A")

This area of the Potomac River has a cliff-based shoreline and no access to shore by boat. Stratford Hall is best visited by car from Colonial Beach. Stratford Hall, the 1738 ancestral home of the Lee family of Virginia, is several miles inland from Currioman Bay. This distinguished family includes two signers of the Declaration of Independence and Gen. Robert E. Lee, commander of the Confederate Army during the Civil War, who was born here. The 1,600-acre Stratford Plantation extends to the Potomac, but, even though Thomas Lee maintained a "wharff" there to load tobacco, there is no landing now.

Interpreters in period dress conduct tours; the walking trails pass through extensive gardens. The Stratford Hall Plantation museum display in the visitor center describes the Lee family's contributions to American history. The plantation is open every day from 9:30 a.m. to 4:00 p.m., and the dining room is open Tuesdays through Sundays for lunch, from 11:00 a.m. to 3:00 p.m., during season. For more information, call 804-493-8038 or visit www .stratfordhall.org. Colonial Beach, farther up the Potomac, is the most convenient stop to visit Stratford Hall and Wakefield.

Popes Creek, VA (Mile 32, Virginia Side, at G "19")

Farther upstream from Currioman Bay is Wakefield, the birthplace of George Washington, on Popes Creek (not to be confused with the other, non-navigable Popes Creek—off the Potomac's Maryland shore—about three miles past the U.S. Route 301 Bridge). Now a national monument (look for it on the chart), it includes a working Colonial plantation, picnic grounds, a monument and a Georgian-style manor house. (The original house burned.) You can dinghy into Popes Creek, but you will find no landing on the river.

Colonial Beach, VA (Mile 35, Virginia Side, at G "25")

Mattox and Monroe creeks, which almost share a common entrance beyond the high cliff shoreline, are the access points for Colonial Beach. Colonial Beach, at approximately the halfway point to Washington, D.C., is a supply point and the last diesel-fuel stop for boats heading up the Potomac that draw more than 5.5 feet. It is a logical overnight stop on the run to or from Washington, D.C., as well as a good base for exploring the nearby historic houses and sites. Several restaurants, gift shops and supply stores are here.

NAVIGATION: Use Chart 12285. Depths fluctuate around here, according to the direction and force of the wind, and the state of the tide. Tidal currents as strong as 2 or 3 knots are a factor in negotiating the narrow entrance to Monroe Creek and the marina immediately inside the entrance. Cruisers reported shoaling off the east side of the entrance in recent years. We advise you to favor the west side of the channel.

Dockage: Mattox Creek is home to Stepp's Harbor View Marina, which may have transient space and sells gas and has a grocery nearby. On Monroe Creek is the Colonial Beach Yacht Center, with dockage, fuel, repairs, a beach and a restaurant. Stanford's Marine Railway is nearby for boat repairs. Winkie Doodle Point Marina is next, and then Nightingale Motel & Marina. Farther north in the harbor, closer to town, is the Bayside Marina and Restaurant. They provide some groceries and marine supplies and have an on-site restaurant. Call ahead for approach depths. Downtown is one block away.

GOIN' ASHORE: COLONIAL BEACH, VA

While it is well off the regular snowbird route, Colonial Beach, the only port of call on the Virginia shore of the Potomac River that even resembles a town, is boat-friendly. Its decided individuality is one more reason to explore the river that meanders through America's past, all the way up to Washington, D.C.

Colonial Beach is a rare commodity in the Chesapeake Bay region in that it combines a beachfront atmosphere with the infrastructure of a small town. Located about 30 miles from Interstate 95 and about an hour and a half from both Washington, D.C. and Richmond, VA, it offers an escape from the city without exclusion from society. Building on these assets, the town has launched a redevelopment program to improve its appeal both to potential new residents and to visitors. To date, it has renovated the municipal pier and boardwalk, which, in deference to the devastation caused by Hurricane Isabel in 2003, is made of concrete instead of wood.

Irving Avenue, where seafront cottages face the Potomac River, is regaining its gentility. The varied vintages and styles of homes reflect the town's fortunes and fashions as they have evolved over the past century or so. New residential developments are underway to landward of the old town, and the business community is working to upgrade vacation accommodations and eating establishments.

History: Once the dust of the Civil War had settled, Americans discovered the recreational and therapeutic possibilities offered by sojourns at the seashore. America's love affair with the beach began. One of its early trysting partners was a two-mile stretch of beach on the Virginia shore of the Potomac River, about 65 miles downstream from Washington. Thanks to the perfection of the steamboat during the war, it was only hours away. To serve this new leisure-time activity, a settlement of summer cottages, hotels and attendant entertainments sprang up on the spit of land between the Potomac River and Monroe Bay. The destination had already been popular for 25 years when, in 1892, it was incorporated as the Town of Colonial Beach.

Fortunes faltered in the mid-1930s when the steamboats disappeared, but construction of the Harry W. Nice Bridge to carry U.S. 301 across the Potomac in 1941 reconnected Colonial Beach to its clientele in Washington, D.C. and extended its reach to Baltimore, MD. With the motor car came the weekend visitor and day tripper, and a new phenomenon, the motor court, to accommodate them.

In the 1950s, Colonial Beach saw its popularity rise again when it became the only point in Virginia with access to legalized gambling. Under the Colonial-era land grants that created Virginia and Maryland, the border between them lies at the high-tide mark on the Virginia side of the Potomac. Soon after gambling was approved in Charles County, MD, entrepreneurs established casinos on piers extending into Maryland waters from Colonial Beach, bringing slot machines within arm's reach of Virginia patrons. That respite ended in 1958 when Charles County lost its license for gambling. Overnight, the casinos lost their customers. Fires subsequently consumed several of the structures.

Today, a single betting parlor exists in Colonial Beach. The recently refurbished Riverboat on the Potomac offers off-track betting on horse racing and sells both Maryland and Virginia lottery tickets.

Points of Interest: Of the vestiges of Colonial Beach's Victorian heyday that remain, the Bell House, at 821 Irving Ave., facing the river, is perhaps the grandest. Built in 1883 by Col. J.O.P. Burnside, the son of the Civil War General Ambrose Burnside, it was subsequently owned by Alexander Graham Bell's father and then by Bell himself. It is listed on the National Register of Historic Places and is also a Virginia Historic Landmark. It operates as a bed and breakfast.

In the heart of town, the Riverview Inn at 24 Hawthorn St., a motor court built in 1949 in retro Art Deco style, is a colorful reminder of the town's post-World War II identity.

The Museum at Colonial Beach (128 Hawthorn St., 804-224-3379), open daily from mid-April to mid-December, provides insights into the town's historical development.

Colonial Beach is a "golf cart town." Holders of a valid driver's license can save their legs while taking in the sights and flavors. Rentals are available at Metro Golf Carts and Scooters (116 Washington Ave., 804-224-2278). A trolley circulates around the town on summer weekends.

Special Events: To recreate the town's festive past, the cultural and business associations of Colonial Beach hold activities throughout the year. The vibrant and growing arts community, represented by the Colonial Beach Artists' Guild, presents the Second Friday Art Walks from April through December. Other events include Bluegrass on the Potomac, the Potomac River Festival and a number of fishing tournaments.

Dining: A variety of restaurants are all within a walk or a golf-cart drive of the marinas and the Monroe Bay anchorage. At the Dockside Restaurant and Blue Heron Pub (804-224-8726), located at the Colonial Beach Yacht Center, offers your choice between formal dining room, pub seating or screened-in and open porches. Choose between white tablecloth or cozy English Pub settings. High Tides on the Potomac (205 Taylor St., 804-224-1211) is central on the boardwalk, and offers American fare and seafood served inside or out on the deck looking over the Potomac. Dine at Riverboat on the Potomac (301 Beach Terrace, 804-224-7055) in either the casual, smoky atmosphere of a betting

Reference the marina listing tables to see all the marinas in the area.

POINTS OF INTEREST

1 The Bell House
2 Riverview Inn
3 Colonial Beach Historical Society Museum

DINING

4 Dockside Restaurant & Blue Heron Pub
5 High Tides on the Potomac
6 Riverboat on the Potomac
7 The Lighthouse Restaurant & Lounge
8 Espresso Station
9 Tattle Tale Coffee Shop

LIBRARY

ADDITIONAL RESOURCES

- COLONIAL BEACH CHAMBER OF COMMERCE: www.colonialbeach.org
- COLONIAL BEACH: www.colonialbeachva.net

Popes Creek, Port Tobacco River, MD

301 BRIDGE TO PORT TOBACCO RIVER		Largest Vessel Accommodated	VHF Channel Monitored	Transient Berths / Total Berths	Approach / Dockside Depth (reported)	Floating Docks	Gas / Diesel	Groceries, Ice, Marine Supplies, Snacks	Repairs: Hull, Engine, Propeller	Lift (tonnage), Crane, Rail	Min/Max Amps	Laundry, Pool, Showers, Courtesy Car	Pump-Out Station	Nearby: Grocery Store, Motel, Restaurant
		Dockage					Supplies		Services					
1. Goose Bay Marina Inc.	301-932-0885	45	16	20/250	5/4	-	GD	GIMS	E	L10	30/30	PS	P	G
2. Port Tobacco Marina and Restaurant	301-870-3133	42	16	3/80	3/3	-	G	GIMS	HEP	L15, C	30/30	S	P	GR

Corresponding chart(s) not to be used for navigation. Internet Access Wireless Internet Access Waterway Guide Cruising Club Partner

See www.WaterwayGuide.com for current rates, fuel prices, web site addresses, and other up-to-the-minute information.

parlor or in a white tablecloth setting perched over the water. The upscale Lighthouse Restaurant & Lounge is next to Bayside Marina on Monroe Bay (11 Monroe Bay Ave., 804-224-7580) and offers "sunset views from every seat in the house." Seafood and steaks are their specialties. For fine authentic Thai and French cuisine, try Seaside Restaurant at 201 Wilder Avenue (804-224-2410). At Tattle Tale Espresso Station Coffee Shop (215 Washington St., 804-224-0045), take in the local meeting place at the center of everything.

Upper Machodoc Creek, VA (Mile 41, Virginia Side, at G "29")

Dahlgren and the Naval Surface Weapons Center are at Upper Machodoc Creek, some four miles upriver from Colonial Beach on the Virginia shore.

QUICK FACT:

HARRY W. NICE BRIDGE

The Governor Harry W. Nice Memorial Bridge, spanning the Potomac River between Newburg in Charles County, MD and Dahlgren, VA, is located north of green can buoy "35" and has a 135-foot fixed vertical clearance.

Once Route 301, a north-south alternative to bypass the Baltimore/Washington area, was completed, a bridge was needed to transit the Potomac River. President Franklin D. Roosevelt presided over the opening of the Potomac River Toll Bridge in 1940. The bridge, the first south of the District of Columbia linking Maryland and Virginia, was re-named in 1967 for Harry W. Nice, Governor of Maryland from 1935-1939.

The narrow bridge has one 11-foot lane in each direction, which can prove slow and frustrating during rush hour, weekends and holidays. The bridge is 1.7 miles in length and cost $5 million to construct. Its 1986 rehabilitation cost more than $17 million, but was funded entirely by tolls. The Maryland Transportation Authority initiated the Harry W. Nice Memorial Bridge Improvement Project in June 2006 to explore alternatives to the main span, which is responsible for bottlenecking. In November 2008, the more than 5 million dollar project began, and at press time in 2012, it was not completed.

NAVIGATION: Use Chart 12285. Two marked channels lead into Upper Machodoc Creek, past some dangerous shoals near the Navy base at Dahlgren. From there, depths are 6 feet or less along the approach to the civilian marine facilities. Machodoc Creek Marina (formerly Dahlgreen Marine Center) with transient space and fuel is located here.

Cuckhold Creek, MD (Mile 41, Maryland Side, at G "29")

NAVIGATION: Use Chart 12285. Cuckold Creek, the next harbor above Cobb Island on the Potomac, is shallow, and 30-foot-high overhead cables cross its upper reaches. Keep a sharp eye aloft and on the depth sounder if you take a chance on this creek.

U.S. Route 301 Harry W. Nice Bridge (Mile 44)

The Potomac River narrows above Dahlgren on the Virginia shore and the power station at Morgantown on the Maryland shore. Here, the Harry W. Nice Bridge (fixed vertical clearance 135 feet) carries U.S. Route 301 across the river while allowing oceangoing ships to reach Alexandria, VA and Washington, D.C. The Nice Bridge marks where channel buoys begin their count with Upper Potomac River green can buoy "1." This area of the Potomac River is generally regarded as area where salt water fishing ends and fresh water fishing begins. This is the approximate midpoint between Washington, D.C. and the mouth of the Potomac River.

In this area, you enter the uppermost part of the danger zone for the Naval Weapons Center range. This seldom-used area extends only as far as the mouth of the Port Tobacco River (on the Maryland side).

Popes Creek, MD (Mile 46, Maryland Side, before R "2")

Dockage: Conveniently located on the Maryland side of the Potomac River at Popes Creek, two miles above the Harry Nice/Route 301 Bridge, Gilligan's Pier (301-259-4514) and Captain Billy's Crabhouse (301-932-4323) are great places to stop for lunch as you head upriver on the Potomac. Slips are available for dining guests, and Captain Billy's may be able to offer overnight dockage with minimal electric service. The locally popular restaurants feature full seafood menus. Boats drawing more than 4 feet should ask for water

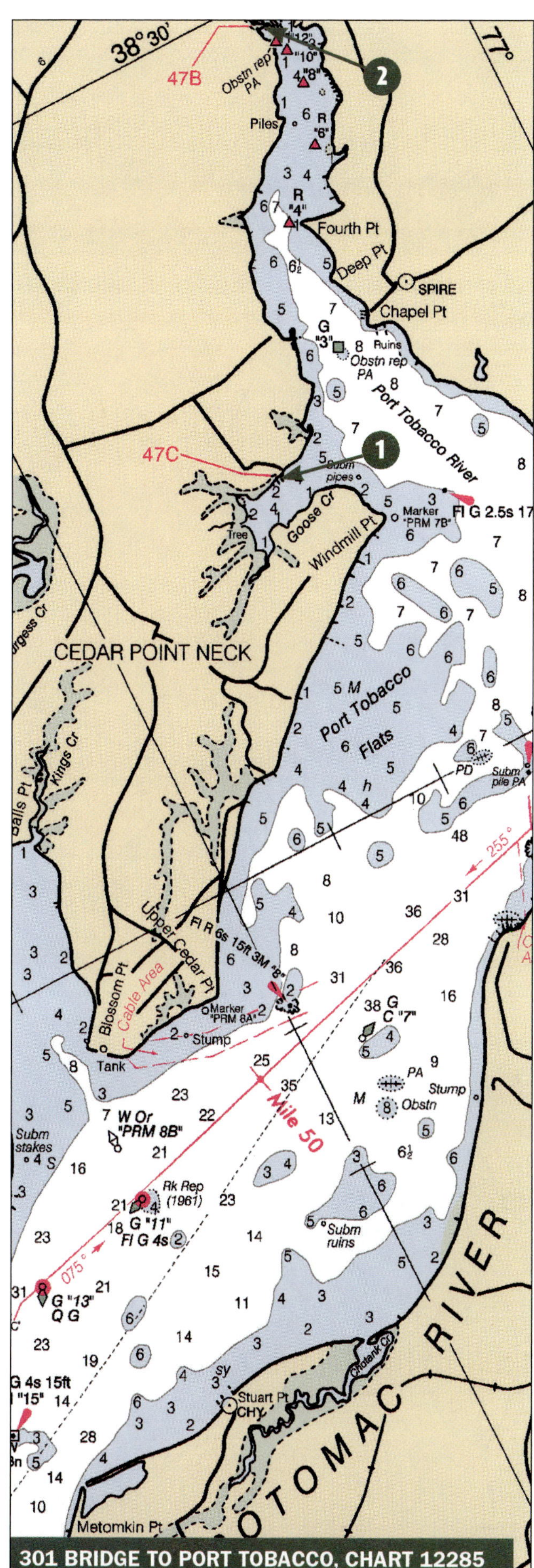

301 BRIDGE TO PORT TOBACCO, CHART 12285

depth information at the docks. In season, Gilligan's runs a water taxi to anchored boats.

Port Tobacco River, MD (Mile 48, Maryland Side, between R "4" and R "6")

You can enter the Port Tobacco River from the south by leaving Potomac River flashing red buoy "2" to port—or from the west by leaving flashing red "6" to port. At both points, the depth drops suddenly from as much as 100 feet to as little as 7 or 8 feet, and numerous trap markers crowd the waters.

Dockage: Although too shallow for most boats (3-foot approach depths), about three miles up the Port Tobacco River is the Port Tobacco Marina and Restaurant with transient berths (3-foot dockside/approach depths). There is a Tiki-style restaurant on site. Also on the Port Tobacco River is Goose Bay Marina. They have 250 slips and offer fuel, some boat repairs and a pump-out station. They have a reported 5-foot approach depth and 4-foot dockside depth.

Anchorage: Inside the river on the east side, you may anchor near Chapel Point (part of a Maryland state park) in 7- to 8-foot depths, where holding is good in mud. Past Deep Point there is plenty enough water to anchor nearly to daymarker "4. You can also anchor across the river in Goose Bay in 4 to 5 feet of water.

Nanjemoy Creek, MD (Mile 51, Maryland Side, at G "11")

Guarded by Blossom and Benny Gray points, Nanjemoy Creek is too shallow for all but the shallowest draft boats. Depths range from 5 to 8 feet at the mouth, but quickly shallow to 3 to 4 feet mid-channel between Tanners and Balls points. This is a beautiful creek to explore, but we recommend doing so by dinghy.

Potomac Creek, VA (Mile 58, Virginia Side, between G "21" and R "22")

NAVIGATION: Use Chart 12285. Approximately four miles from the Harry W. Nice Bridge, the Potomac makes a wide turn to port around Mathias Point, which is marked by flashing green light "5." For the next eight miles, favor the Maryland shore until the river makes another wide turn to starboard at Maryland Point Light. Potomac Creek is a well marked but shallow creek guarded by Marlboro Point and Bull Bluff. Only those carrying 4 feet of draft or less should enter.

Dockage: Waugh Point Marina is located to the south of green can "5" in Potomac Creek. The marina has 4-foot approach/dockside depths and may have some transient space.

Anchorage: Some four miles above the big mid-river light marking the bend at Maryland Point, Potomac Creek is a pleasant anchorage for shoal-draft boats. Charted depths hold at about 4 feet up Potomac Creek to green daybeacon "7." You will pass Fairview Beach before entering Potomac Creek where, on a summer weekend, you will likely find several boats anchored enjoying the sand bottom and water taxi service to the

Potomac Creek, VA

POTOMAC CREEK		Largest Vessel Accommodated	VHF Channel Monitored	Transient Berths / Total Berths	Approach / Dockside Depth (reported)	Floating Docks	Gas / Diesel	Groceries, Ice, Marine Supplies, Snacks	Repairs: Hull, Engine, Propeller	Lift (tonnage), Crane, Rail	Min/Max Amps	Laundry, Pool, Showers, Courtesy Car	Pump-Out Station	Nearby: Grocery Store, Motel, Restaurant
		Dockage					Supplies		Services					
1. Waugh Point Marina Inc.	540-775-7121	40	16/09	/80	4/4	-	-	M	HEP	L7	30/50	S	P	-
2. Aquia Bay Marina	540-720-7437	44	-	/135	8/3.5	F	GD	IMS	HEP	L35	30/50	LS	P	-
3. Hope Springs Marina (Internet Access) (Wireless Internet Access)	540-659-1128	60	-	10/180	6/6	-	GD	GIMS	HEP	L11	30/30	LS	P	R

Corresponding chart(s) not to be used for navigation. Internet Access · Wireless Internet Access · Waterway Guide Cruising Club Partner

See www.WaterwayGuide.com for current rates, fuel prices, web site addresses, and other up-to-the-minute information.

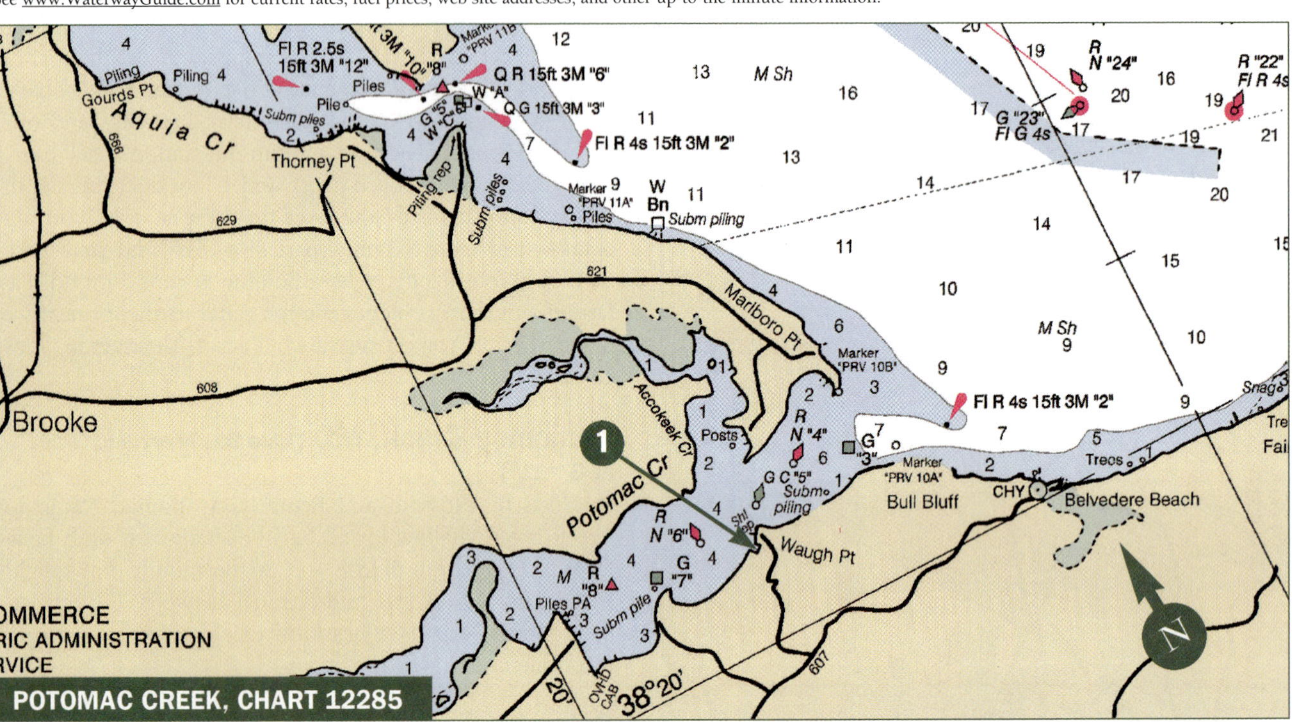

POTOMAC CREEK, CHART 12285

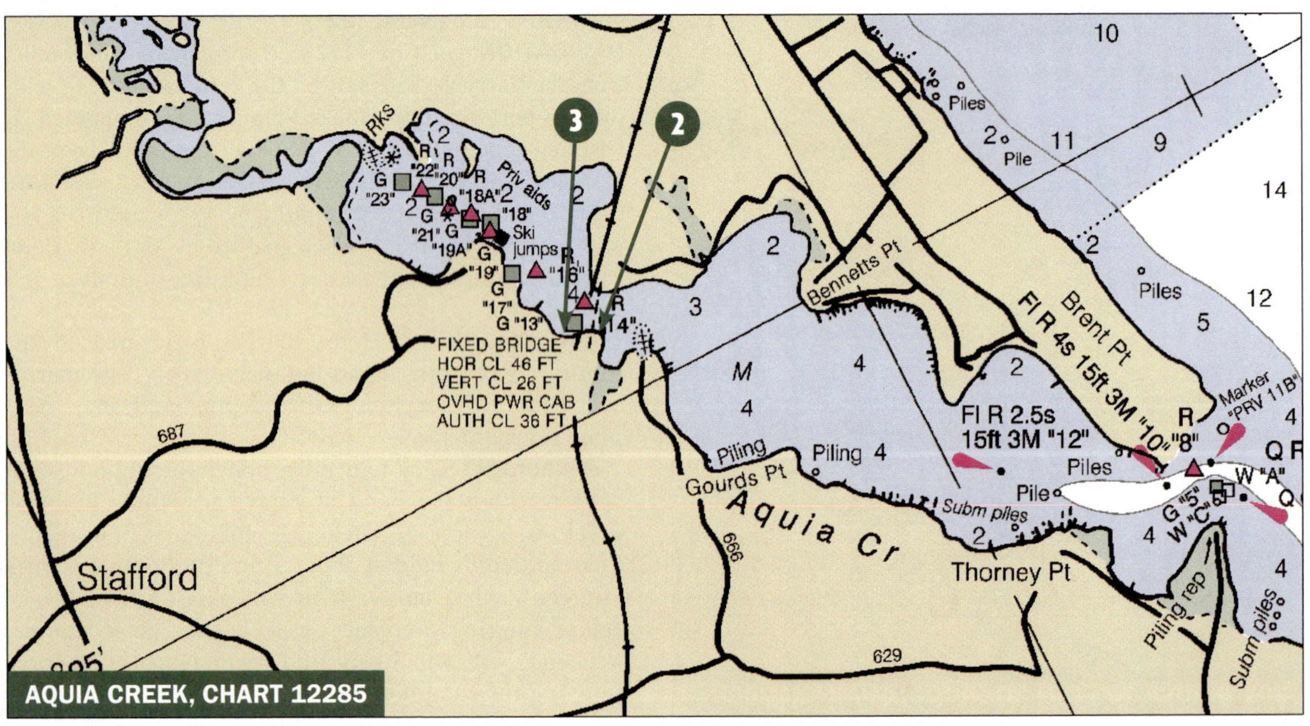

AQUIA CREEK, CHART 12285

beach front restaurant (Tim's II Restaurant & Crab House, 540-775-7500).

Aquia Creek, VA (Mile 60, Virginia Side, after R "26")

The deep, recently dredged, well-marked entrance to Aquia Creek is just north of Potomac Creek. Stay well to port of flashing red "2" marking the shoal jutting out southeasterly from Brent Point. The deep channel is well marked the rest of the way.

Dockage: Hope Springs Marina (180 slips) is a full-service marina located just after the fixed railroad bridge. Aquia Bay Marina also sells fuel and does some boat repairs. Call ahead for depths.

Anchorage: Inside, 4-foot depths continue several miles up to the fixed railroad bridge (26-foot vertical clearance). Although the creek is well-marked and easy to enter, do not go beyond the last lighted marker (flashing red "12") without local knowledge. The south bank rises high over the undeveloped creek; there are no services.

Wades Bay, MD (Mile 63, Maryland Side, after R "30" and Smith Point)

Wades Bay, between red nun "32" and "34" is too open to the west to be an anchorage except in very settled weather. However, you can anchor securely in 5 to 10 feet of water and go ashore to walk the beaches here. It is a lovely spot to lunch and look for fossilized shells and sharks teeth. An exposed bed of dark clay is full of ancient life forms.

Mallows Bay, MD (Mile 65, Maryland Side, after R "40")

Although there are no services, nor is there an anchorage, Mallows Bay is home of the Ghost Fleet of Mallows Bay, the largest shipwreck fleet in the Western Hemisphere, if not the world. In World War I, there was a need for mass transportation to support the war in Germany. Not wanting to affect the naval shipyards, a plan was created to build a 1,000-ship fleet of wooden transport ships. The war ended before they could be useful, therefore 285 ships eventually had to be salvaged. The intent was to salvage the metal and burn the wooden hulls. The ships were brought into Mallows Bay, the bay was dammed to evacuate the water, then the steel was recovered and the hulls burned until all ships had been salvaged. Today, there are 88 hulls that have been identified of the 110 ships believed to have been in Mallows Bay. As you look to starboard heading up river, you will likely see the remains of other ships that have been scuttled, but are not part of the Ghost Fleet. A look at Mallows Bay from Google Earth is worth the effort. You can also read Donald G. Shomette's "Ghost Fleet of Mallows Bay: And Other Tales of the Lost Chesapeake."

Quantico Marine Corps Base, VA (Mile 67, Virginia Side, after G "43")

Quantico Marine Corps Base is a training base for new Marine Corps enlisted and officer personnel. It is also home base for Marine Helicopter Squadron One, the much coveted organization responsible for all helicopter flights for the President of the United States. A small marina in the town of Quantico serves only Department of Defense entitled personnel but will help others in an emergency. Call on VHF Channel 09.

Mattawoman Creek, MD (Mile 71, Maryland Side, at R "46")

Just beyond Quantico, you will pass under the high-level power cables (authorized vertical clearance of 70 feet, but 170 feet over the main channel) at Moss Point. Keep a watch for trap markers in this area.

Dockage: Smallwood State Park is about one mile up from the mouth around the first point of land on the south side of the creek. They have a marina (Sweden Point Marina) with slips, restrooms, showers and laundry facilities.

Anchorage: Just beyond the cables, to starboard, is Mattawoman Creek, with a popular anchorage carrying 6-foot depths opposite Deep Point. Be sure to stay out of the channel and the cable area when anchoring and always use an anchor light. Cruisers report shoaling off the tip of Cornwallis Neck, so watch your depth sounder. For more sheltered anchorage, follow the markers into Mattawoman Creek, where you can anchor off Grinders Wharf in 6-foot depths. A large-scale chart shows an unmarked channel farther up Mattawoman Creek to a more secluded anchorage. The state park by Sweden Point has a ramp, ice and food, but no diesel. You will find 4- to 8-foot depths here. Dense Hydrilla growth, that may clog sea strainers, has been reported beyond green daybeacon "3."

Neabsco Creek, VA (Mile 72, Virginia Side, at G "47")

Dockage: Just past Freestone Point is the marked channel into Neabsco Creek which has two three full-service marinas:, the E-Z Cruz Marina, Pilot House Marina & Boat Sales and Hampton's Landing Marina, where Potomac Marine is located. All sell gas and Hampton's Landing also has diesel. The depths into Neabsco Creek are said to be 6 feet, but have been reported to barely be 4 feet in some places at low tide, so be aware prior to attempting entry.

Occoquan Bay and Belmont Bay, VA (Mile 73, Virginia Side, at G "51")

Occoquan Bay's wide open waters offers 5- to 7-foot depths outside of the marked channel; however, the channel provides 7- to 10-foot depths and serves commercial tugs as well as a number of recreational boat slips. The picturesque town of Occoquan, at the headwaters of the Occoquan River, is perched on a hillside upriver beyond Belmont Bay. It retains its small town charm while being only minutes

Occoquan River, VA

OCCOQUAN RIVER		Largest Vessel Accommodated	VHF Channel Monitored	Transient Berths / Total Berths	Approach / Dockside Depth (reported)	Floating Docks	Gas / Diesel	Groceries, Ice, Marine Supplies, Snacks	Repairs: Hull, Engine, Propeller	Lift (tonnage), Crane, Rail	Min/Max Amps	Laundry, Pool, Showers, Courtesy Car	Pump-Out Station	Nearby: Grocery Store, Motel, Restaurant
		Dockage					Supplies		Services					
1. E-Z Cruz Marina	703-670-8115	41	16	3/200	8/5	-	G	IMS	HEP	L25, C	30/50	LS	-	G
2. Pilot House Marina & Boat Sales	703-670-6900	40	-	/250	4/6	-	G	IMS	HEP	L	30/30	S	P	-
3. Hampton's Landing Marina (Internet Access) (Wi-Fi)	703-221-4915	53	16/06	5/140	5/5	-	GD	IMS	HEP	L25	30/50	S	P	-
4. Tyme 'n Tyde Marina Inc.	703-491-5116	31	-	/12	4/5	F	G	IMS	HEP	-	30/30	S	P	G
5. Belmont Bay Harbor (Wi-Fi)	**703-490-5088**	**50**	**16/68**	**3/155**	**7/6**	**F**	**GD**	**IM**	**-**	**-**	**30/50**	**LS**	**P**	**GMR**
6. Occoquan Harbor Marina (Wi-Fi)	703-494-3600	65	16	/219	8/8	F	GD	GIS	HEP	L25	30/50	S	P	GR
7. Hoffmaster's Marina (Wi-Fi)	703-494-7161	45	-	4/135	20/5	-	G	IMS	HEP	L30	30/50	S	P	GMR
8. Prince William Marina (Internet Access) (Wi-Fi)	703-494-6611	60	16	-	7/7	F	GD	IMS	HEP	L50, C10	30/50	LPS	P	GMR
9. Sweden Point Marina	301-743-7613	36	-	/50	6/6	-	G	IS	-	-	30/30	LS	P	R

Corresponding chart(s) not to be used for navigation. Internet Access · Wireless Internet Access · Waterway Guide Cruising Club Partner

See www.WaterwayGuide.com for current rates, fuel prices, web site addresses, and other up-to-the-minute information.

from the nation's capitol. Its historic atmosphere is shared by the many shops and restaurants conducting events throughout the year such as the semiannual arts and craft festivals. It is also home to the Occoquan Boat Club, which hosts competitive skulling (rowing) regattas and training camps from spring through early November. The waterfront Belmont Bay Town Center has retail shops and restaurants as well as a marina, golf course and trails. You can take the Virginia Railway Express (VRE) into Union Station in D.C. from here as well.

Dockage: In Occoquan Bay, Tyme & Tyde Marina may have transient space on their floating docks. They also sell gas and have groceries nearby. Belmont Bay Harbor sells gas and diesel and has limited transient space and a restaurant within walking distance. There is a city dock of approximately 100 feet available to transients in Occoquan. Beyond the first set of bridges with 44-foot vertical clearance, you will find the 219-slip Occoquan Harbour Marina with fuel, pump-out and an on-site restaurant. Prince William Marina and Hoffmaster's Marina are located farther upstream beyond the 44-foot bridges and have repair facilities and sell some marine supplies.

Mount Vernon, VA (Mile 83, Virginia Side, at G "71")

Use Baltimore tide tables. For high tide at Mount Vernon, subtract 17 minutes; for low tide, subtract 42 minutes. Upriver from Occoquan Bay and just west of little

QUICK FACT:

AMERICAN BALD EAGLE HABITAT

From here to the Wilson Bridge, you will likely see a Bald Eagle. It is not unusual to see them fishing, perched on a tree or buoy or just flying through the sky. We have seen a lot of ospreys in the area, so keep an eye out for them. When you see the white head and tail feathers, with brown everywhere else, you have spotted one. The area between the Occoquan River and Mount Vernon has the highest concentration of eagles in the area.

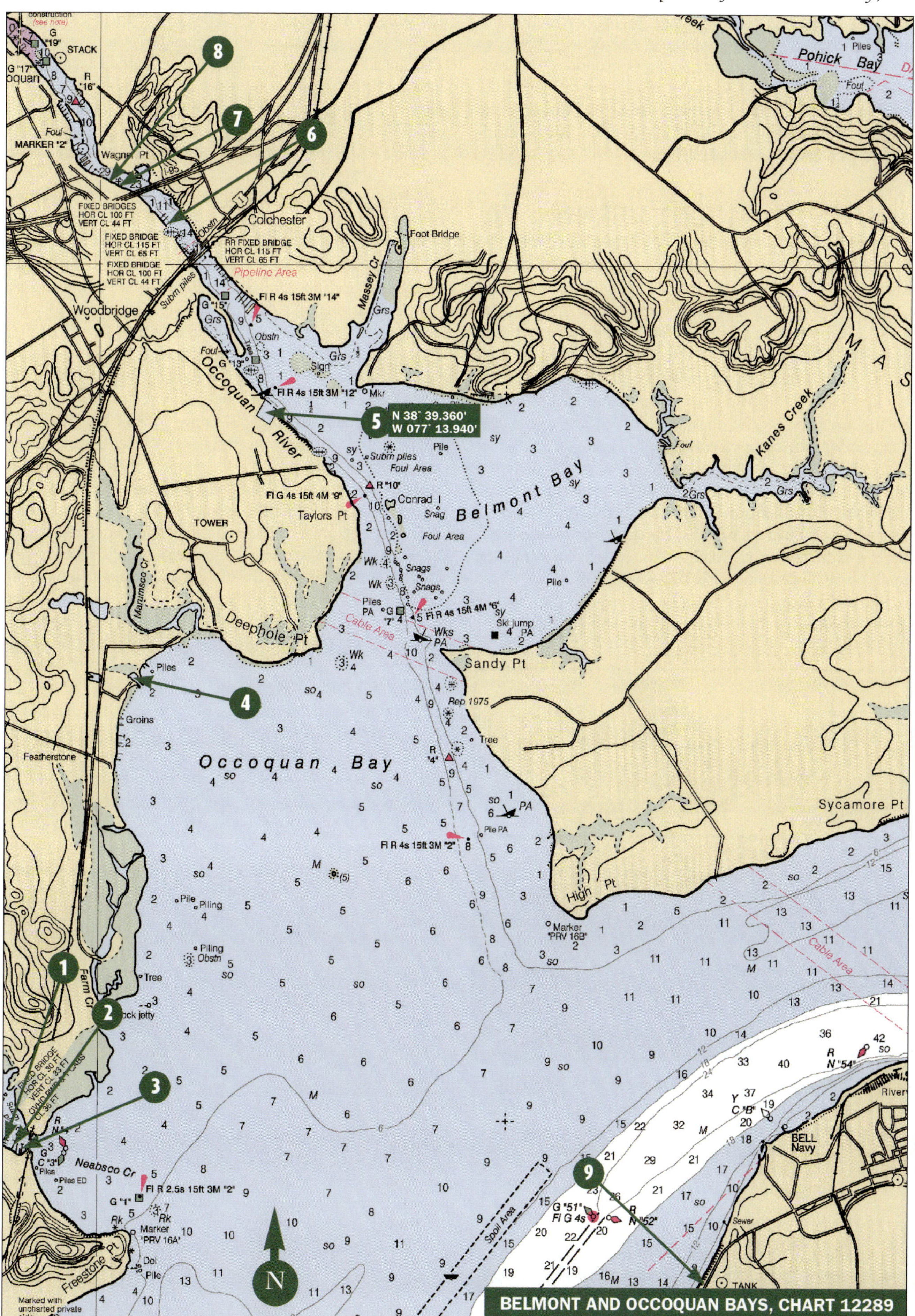

Occoquan River
Belmont Bay
Occoquan Bay
Pohick Bay
Kanes Creek
Massey Cr
Marumsco Cr
Farm Cr
Neabsco Cr
Woodbridge
Colchester
Featherstone
Taylors Pt
Deephole Pt
Sandy Pt
Sycamore Pt
High Pt
Freestone Pt
Wagner Pt
Conrad I
TOWER
STACK
MARKER "2"
FIXED BRIDGES HOR CL 100 FT VERT CL 44 FT
FIXED BRIDGE HOR CL 115 FT VERT CL 65 FT
FIXED BRIDGE HOR CL 100 FT VERT CL 44 FT
RR FIXED BRIDGE HOR CL 115 FT VERT CL 65 FT
Foot Bridge
Pipeline Area
Cable Area
Spoil Area
Fl R 4s 15ft 3M "14"
Fl R 4s 15ft 3M "12"
Fl G 4s 15ft 4M "9"
Fl R 4s 15ft 4M "6"
Fl R 4s 15ft 3M "2"
Fl R 2.5s 15ft 3M "2"
Rep 1975
Ski jump
Marker "PRV 16B"
Marker "PRV 16A"
N 38° 39.360'
W 077° 13.940'
BELL Navy
TANK
Marked with uncharted private aids
N
BELMONT AND OCCOQUAN BAYS, CHART 12289

Hunting Creek is Mount Vernon, George Washington's estate. Although dockage is limited, one or two boats can dock while visiting the mansion and grounds. You may also anchor directly off from the residence and out of the channel. For those not wanting to stop, you can take the tourist cruises or bus trips to Mount Vernon from Alexandria, Washington, or National Harbor.

GOIN' ASHORE: MOUNT VERNON, VA

George Washington is probably the most revered of the Founding Fathers, so it is hardly surprising that his home, Mount Vernon, receives more visitors than any other historic estate in America. Most come by land, but it is possible to bring a boat here. Call ahead (703-799-6856) or e-mail (wharf@mountvernon.org) to reserve a space.

On a busy weekend, you might have to anchor in the river but keep clear of the main channel. You can land your dinghy on the beach below the dock. According to a custom that dates back to the night of Washington's death, on December 14, 1799, mariners passing by Mount Vernon on the Potomac River toll the ship's bell in his honor. Do that, then double back, follow the marked channel to the pier, and find a slot where you will be clear of the tour boats. The depth alongside is about 6 feet at mean low water. To tie up, you have to pay admission to the estate, but overnight docking isn't permitted.

History: Construction began on the present-day house in 1741 on property that had been in the Washington family since 1674. George Washington first lived there in 1735 when his father, Augustine, took up residence. After Augustine's death in 1743, George's much older half-brother, Lawrence, inherited the property and renamed it Mount Vernon. He died in 1753, leaving his wife a "life's interest," which, George purchased from her in 1757, giving him sole possession.

Many of the improvements—such as enlarging the house twice—and agricultural experiments George Washington carried out at Mount Vernon he did in the 18 years that preceded the outbreak of the Revolutionary War. From the time he was appointed commander-in-chief of the Continental forces in 1775 to the end of his term as President in 1797, duties prevented him from spending much time at all at Mount Vernon.

After Washington's death, even though occupied by his descendants, the estate began to deteriorate. Then, in 1853, Ann Pamela Cunningham and a band of patriotic women founded the Mount Vernon Ladies Association for the purpose of preserving Mount Vernon for posterity. The group purchased the estate in 1858, only to have the Civil War interrupt the work of restoring the house and grounds just as it was getting underway. During the war, soldiers of both armies visited the estate to pay their respects to the United States of America's first President, but they were required to lay down their arms before entering the property. The Mount Vernon Ladies Association, a private, non-profit organization, owns Mount Vernon to this day, maintaining it in trust for the people of the United States. In the process, the Ladies (as they are referred to by staff) have created a formidable, self-sustaining enterprise that accepts no public funds from any source.

Points of Interest: Mount Vernon is open 365 days a year. Of the 500 acres that have been preserved of the estate's original 8,000 acres, 50 are devoted to gardens restored to how they might have appeared in 1799. Twenty structures on the grounds, including slave quarters, stables and Washington's famous 16-sided barn, date from the same period.

When you arrive by boat at The Wharf, which is probably how many visitors did in the 18th century, you will approach the house as they did, through the grounds. You can bypass the shops and the orientation center flanking the main entrance, but you might want to pay them a visit to pick up a guidebook and see the movie on the life of George Washington. One path leads from The Wharf to the George Washington Pioneer Farmer Site, which demonstrates the innovations Washington brought to farming.

Other paths lead to the Fruit and Garden Nursery, Washington's Tomb and the Slave Memorial. The Mount Vernon Shops cater to a range of tastes and carry everything from souvenirs to scholarly texts. In 2007, Mount Vernon opened a reconstruction of Washington's distillery (it is on the original site, about three miles from the estate), and special legislation passed by the Virginia General Assembly allows it each year to produce 5,000 gallons of whiskey, which can only be sold through the Mount Vernon gift shop.

Dining: Refreshments—burgers, sandwiches, pizza, ice cream—are available in the Food Court, adjacent to the shops. For a quieter, white-tablecloth experience, go next door to the Mount Vernon Inn.

Ft. Washington, Piscataway Creek, MD

FT. WASHINGTON AND PISCATAWAY CREEK		Largest Vessel Accommodated	VHF Channel Monitored	Transient Berths / Total Berths	Approach / Dockside Depth (reported)	Floating Docks	Gas / Diesel	Groceries, Ice, Marine Supplies, Snacks	Repairs: Hull, Engine, Propeller	Lift (tonnage), Crane, Rail	Min/Max Amps	Laundry, Pool, Showers, Courtesy Car	Pump-Out Station	Nearby: Grocery Store, Motel, Restaurant
		Dockage					Supplies		Services					
1. Fort Washington Marina	**301-292-7700**	**60**	**16**	**40/300**	**6/5**	**F**	**GD**	**IMS**	**HEP**	**L35**	**30/50**	**LS**	**P**	**R**
2. Tantallon Marina	301-651-7016	80	-	-	-	F	-	-	-	-	30/100	LS	P	GR

Corresponding chart(s) not to be used for navigation. Internet Access Wireless Internet Access Waterway Guide Cruising Club Partner

See www.WaterwayGuide.com for current rates, fuel prices, web site addresses, and other up-to-the-minute information.

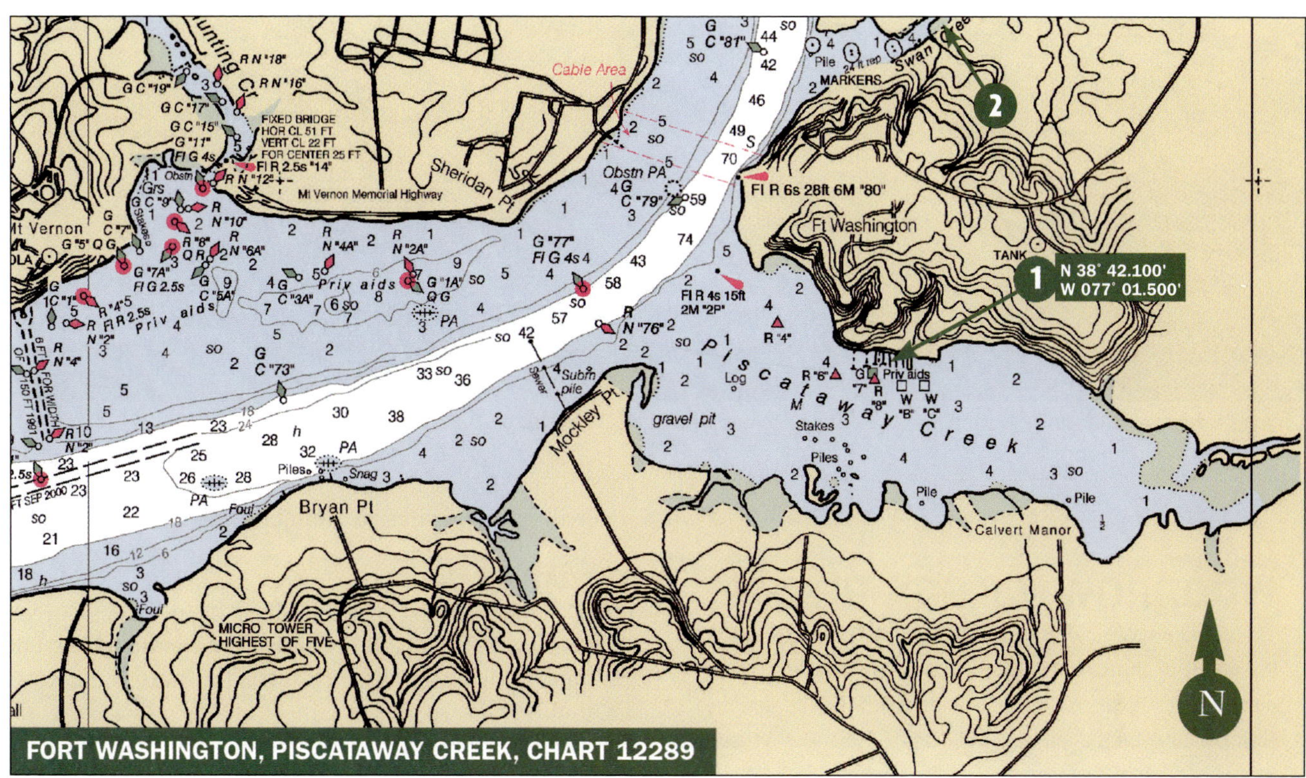

FORT WASHINGTON, PISCATAWAY CREEK, CHART 12289

Piscataway Creek, MD (Mile 85, Maryland Side, at G "79")

Be careful as you enter well-marked Piscataway Creek, just past the ruins of historic Marshall Hall Amusement Park on the Maryland shore. The channel is narrow and is charted to be 4 feet at mean low water. To port as you enter the creek is Fort Washington, with its miniature lighthouse on shore, and as you round the curve, you will get a glimpse of the U.S. Capitol dome.

Dockage: The 300-slip Fort Washington Marina is located on the north shore of Piscataway Creek. This full service marina has fuel, an on-site restaurant and a 35-ton lift—one of the few on the northern Potomac. South of Piscataway Creek is Swan Creek, home of Tantallon Marina.

National Harbor, MD (Mile 90, Maryland Side, at R "90")

Dockage: Just before the Wilson Bridge is the newest waterfront complex in the area. National Harbor, with the Gaylord Hotel and Convention Center as its anchor, has hotels, upscale shops, restaurants and a full-service marina capable of supporting yachts to 250 feet. Water taxi service is available to Alexandria. Navigation aids clearly mark the channel that should be entered just before flashing red buoy "90." The channel into Smoots Cove is marked with red daybeacon "2" before green daybeacon "1"; however, this should not affect your ability to see this channel with 12-foot depths.

Anchorage: Although once a good anchorage, it is no longer recommended. The channel going into National Harbor occupies most of the deeper water. Also, due to boat and water taxi traffic, anchoring could be uncomfortable.

Woodrow Wilson Bridge, Over the Potomac (Mile 91)

You are entering Washington, D.C. waters. The buoy numbering restarts at "1," and anyone operating a boat is required to have proof of approved boating safety training

Looking west over downtown Alexandria, VA on the Potomac River near Washington D.C. (©IstockPhoto/mikadx)

QUICK FACT:
WOODROW WILSON BRIDGE

The Woodrow Wilson Memorial Bridge, named for the 28th President of the United States, spans the Potomac River connecting Alexandria, VA and Oxon Hill, MD. The double-leaf bascule bridge carries I-95 and I-495. The Wilson Bridge's original span opened in December 1961. While the original six-lane, 5,900-foot-long bridge was designed to handle 75,000 vehicles per day, it was estimated that nearly 200,000 vehicles were crossing the structure daily in the 1970s and '80s, due to rapid growth in Washington, D.C. After a complete re-decking in 1983, plans were announced to double the bridge's capacity and increase the draw's height to minimize openings, and construction on replacement facilities and approaches began in 1999.

A new outer loop span opened in June 2006, and the new inner loop span opened in May 2008. The new spans, 20 feet higher than the originals, allow most boats to pass underneath without requiring a bridge opening. The Federal Highway Administration projected that openings would be reduced from approximately 260 a year to 65.

In addition to the completion of the highway project and the upgraded Telegraph Road interchange (by 2013), the new bridge features a pedestrian and bicycle trail which opened in May 2009. The entire construction project was estimated to cost a total of $2.5 billion.

(with some reciprocity from other state programs). In most, if not all cases, firearms are prohibited here.

NAVIGATION: Use Charts 12285 and 12289. Note that many of the channel markers above Mattawoman Creek were relocated in late 2007. **Use Baltimore tide tables. For Alexandria high tide, add 8 minutes; for low tide, subtract 17 minutes.**

The Woodrow Wilson Memorial Bridge, carrying busy Interstate 495 around Washington, is at Jones Point just below Alexandria, VA. Automobile traffic is dense and tense as commuters cross the bridge between their jobs in Washington and their homes in the suburbs and travelers move between Maine and Florida. A multi-billion dollar project to replace the old 50-foot high bridge is complete and the old span was demolished with explosives. The Metropolitan Marine Police report the clearance as 75 feet over the Federal Channel. (It is charted as 76 feet on NOAA chart 12285, edition 40. This information is not on the most current chart from April 2010.)

Most recreational vessels will have no trouble passing under the new span, but in case your boat is too tall, you can arrange a transit time or pass through with commercial vessels that have scheduled an opening. The Wilson Bridge cannot be opened Monday through Friday, from 5:00 a.m. to 12 midnight; Saturday, Sunday and Federal holidays, 7:00 a.m. to 12 midnight, except the bridge may open beginning at 10:00 p.m. on Saturday, Sunday or a Federal holiday for the passage of a recreational vessel if the owner or operator of the vessel notifies the

Alexandria, VA, National Harbor, MD

NATIONAL HARBOR, ALEXANDRIA		Largest Vessel Accommodated	VHF Channel Monitored	Transient Berths / Total Berths	Approach / Dockside Depth (reported)	Floating Docks	Gas / Diesel	Groceries, Ice, Marine Supplies, Snacks	Repairs: Hull, Engine, Propeller	Lift (tonnage), Crane, Rail	Min/Max Amps	Laundry, Pool, Showers, Courtesy Car	Pump-Out Station	Nearby: Grocery Store, Motel, Restaurant
		Dockage					Supplies		Services					
1. Alexandria City Marina	703-838-4265	200	16	22/40	20/20	-	-	-	-	-	30/30	S	P	G
2. National Harbor Marina (Wireless Internet Access)	**301-749-1582**	**250**	**16**	**20/80**	**9/9**	**F**	**GD**	**GIMS**	**-**	**-**	**30/100**	**LS**	**P**	**GMR**

Corresponding chart(s) not to be used for navigation. Internet Access Wireless Internet Access Waterway Guide Cruising Club Partner

See www.WaterwayGuide.com for current rates, fuel prices, web site addresses, and other up-to-the-minute information.

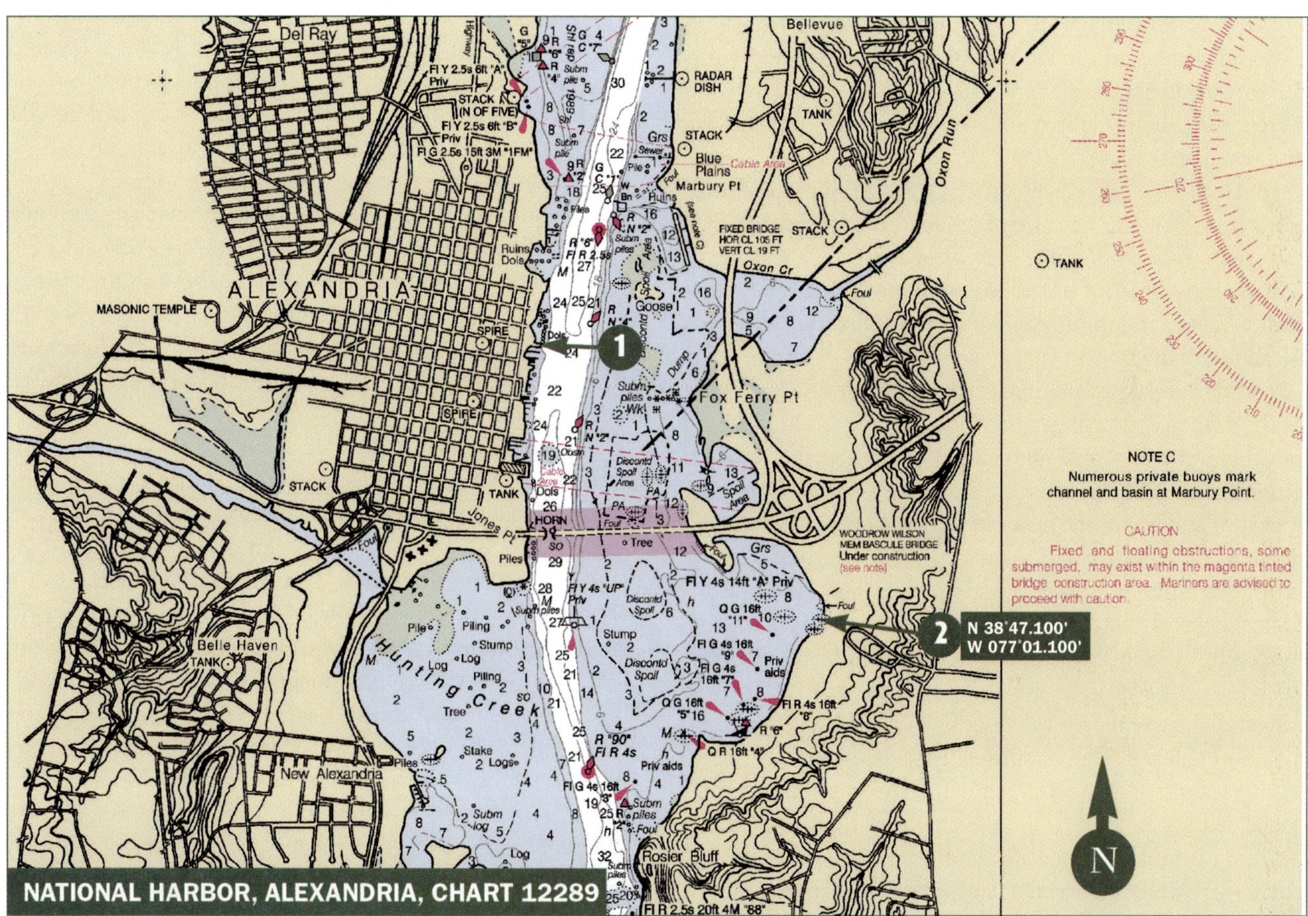

Bridge Tender of the time of that passage by not later than 12 hours before that time. A vessel's captain must contact the operator's tower 12 hours in advance with an estimated time and then 4 hours in advance of the actual time. Call 703-836-2396 or check www.wilsonbridge.com for current information. The web site also indicates that the bridge is not always manned, but try them on VHF Channels 13 and 16. If you do go through late at night, you will find yourself in a busy area where lights from the city and the approach path from Reagan Washington National Airport are easy to mistake for lights along the channel.

There is a poorly marked No-Wake Zone from the Woodrow Wilson Bridge to beyond the Alexandria Wharves.

Alexandria, VA (Mile 92, Virginia Side, near R "4")

Dockage: In Alexandria, just above the Woodrow Wilson Bridge on the Virginia shore, transient berths are available at the Alexandria City Marina adjacent to the attractions and shopping at historic Old Town Alexandria. Alexandria is a great destination but has limited transient dockage at the Alexandria City Docks. If you can stop here going or coming from D.C., it will be worthwhile. You can also access Alexandria by water taxi from National Harbor.

Up-to-date navigation and cruising news are always available at www.waterwayguide.com.

GOIN' ASHORE: ALEXANDRIA, VA

Old port cities where the public waterfront has long been the center of commerce often present a friendly aspect to modern-day visitors who come by boat. In this respect, Alexandria, VA sets a fine example. Right off the boat, you step onto Waterfront Walk, which runs the length of Alexandria's Old Town frontage on the Potomac River. What is most impressive about Alexandria is the extent of its Old Town. Luckily, it was spared the raze and replace method of urban renewal post-World War II.

The City Marina doesn't have a great number of berths for transients, but it is right in the heart of Old Town, and many of the important architectural and cultural sights are within easy walking distance. Two blocks away, you will find yourself on streets lined with 200-year-old homes and converted warehouses, many of them now with businesses at street level and residences above.

History: Tobacco was literally a "cash" crop in the British Colony of Virginia: Because of an acute shortage of coin of the realm, tobacco became the currency. And so it came to pass in 1669, that for "six thousand pounds of Tobacco and Cask," Scotsman John Alexander acquired the tract on which Alexandria now stands.

As the number of plantations grew, the need for a port in the upper Potomac became clear, and in 1749, tobacco growers, shippers and merchants petitioned the Virginia General Assembly to establish one. They named the town Alexandria to honor the descendents of John Alexander, who donated much of the land where it was to be built. Young George Washington made the survey. He later took up residence at nearby Mount Vernon and, for much of his life, looked on Alexandria as his hometown. He might not have been too pleased had he lived to see the War of 1812, when Alexandria surrendered to the British in 1814 without firing a shot in defense. That act probably saved from destruction a busy seaport and an internationally renowned cultural and social center.

Union troops occupied Alexandria from the outset of the Civil War, when it served as an important supply base for the Union Army, and again, although many buildings were commandeered by the military, damage to them was largely superficial.

After the war, while the port continued to thrive, it began to feel competition from the railroads and from Georgetown, which was better located to serve the nation's growing capital city of Washington. In the end, it was the burgeoning federal government that gave Alexandria its next, and current, lease on life. Offices in the new commercial center, in Arlington County, filled with companies that do business with the government. Many of their employees chose to make their homes amid Alexandria's dowdy antiquity. This injected a new sense of urban pride that is plainly manifested throughout Old Town, where historic preservation began to get underway in the 1960s.

Points of Interest: As soon as you step onto Waterfront Walk, you are facing the Torpedo Factory, where nearly 200 artists have their studios. You can watch painters, potters and sculptors at work and, if your timing is right, catch one or two in an inspiration break to talk about their creations.

Two blocks up King Street, stop in at the visitors center in Ramsay House (703-838-5005), where you will find detailed information on more activities than you can fit into a summer.

Around the corner, at 121 N. Fairfax St., is Carlyle House (703-549-2997), built in 1752 by John Carlyle, one of Alexandria's founders. A block west, at 134 N. Royal St., Gadsby's Tavern (703-838-4242) has been restored so that even George Washington, for whom it was a favored watering hole, would recognize it. It is now a museum.

A little farther away, but still within Old Town at 902 Wythe St., the Alexandria Black History Museum (703-838-4356) occupies the once segregated library.

The Northern Virginia Fine Arts Association makes its home in the Athenaeum, (201 Prince St.,703-548-0035), a Greek Revival building built in 1851, which is now an art gallery. Little Theatre of Alexandria (600 Wolfe St., 703-683-0496, www.thelittletheatre.com) is the area's oldest continuously operating theater. It puts on a year-round program of musicals, comedies and dramas.

The energetic can take bicycles on the 18.5-mile Mount Vernon Bike Trail, which extends from Mount Vernon to the south to Theodore Roosevelt Island to the north. Bikes can be rented at Wheel Nuts (302 Montgomery St., 703-548-5116). If you prefer a walk with golf clubs, your best bets are Greendale Golf Course (5 miles; 703-971-3788) or Top Golf Kingstowne (8 miles; 703-924-2600).

The city's DASH bus connects points of interest with local transit hubs and a free weekend shuttle along King Street (703-370-3274, www.dashbus.com). Metrobus connects Alexandria with outlying areas, and the free King Street Trolley will transport you from the Potomac River waterfront to the King Street Metro. The Metro will take you under the river to Washington.

The Potomac Riverboat Company (703-684-0580) operates a water taxi between Old Town Alexandria and the National Harbor development across the Potomac on Smoots Cove, just south of the Woodrow Wilson Bridge. Tours are also available to Mount Vernon, Georgetown and the Washington Nationals baseball stadium.

Shopping: Since its beginnings as a colonial village, the people of Alexandria have brought home exotic bounty to share and sell. That shopping experience continues today with chic boutiques, unique antiques and many other gifts and specialty stores. The shopping atmosphere combines the latest fashion with a charming historical setting. Visit www.visitalexandriava.com for a complete list.

Dining: Alexandria has scores of eateries dotted among its ancient streets. Drop in to the Chart House on Waterfront Walk (703-684-5080) for steak and seafood served

INFORMATION

1 Ramsey House Visitors Center

POINTS OF INTEREST

2 Waterfront Walk
3 Torpedo Factory
4 Carlyle House
5 Gadsby's Tavern Museum
6 Alexandria Black History Museum
7 Athenaeum
8 Little Theatre of Alexandria
9 Wheel Nuts Bicycle Shop
10 Potomac River Boat Company

DINING

5 Gadsby's Tavern Restaurant
11 Chart House
12 Murphy's Irish Pub
13 Bilbo Baggins Restaurant
14 The Wharf

LIBRARY

PHARMACY

Reference the marina listing tables to see all the marinas in the area.

with an incredible view. Bilbo Baggins is a global wine café and restaurant with an amazing microbrew beer selection (208 Queen St., 703-683-0300). Similarly, Murphy's Irish Pub serves robust Irish-American meals and has live music nightly at 713 King St. (703-548-1717). Torpedo Factory artists are loyal to The Wharf (119 King St., 703-836-2836), which opened in 1971, in the early days of the Old Town renaissance. If your urge is to channel George Washington, try Gadsby's Tavern Restaurant (138 N. Royal St., 703-548-1288).

ADDITIONAL RESOURCES

- CITY OF ALEXANDRIA: http://alexandriava.gov
- VISIT ALEXANDRIA: www.visitalexandriava.com
- ALEXANDRIA CONVENTION AND VISITORS BUREAU: www.funside.com

NEARBY MEDICAL FACILITIES

Inova Alexandria Hospital: 4320 Seminary Road, 703-504-3000, www.inova.org (3 miles)

National Harbor, MD

GOIN' ASHORE: NATIONAL HARBOR

Located on 300 acres along the scenic Potomac River, National Harbor is a new waterfront community that offers views of downtown Washington, D.C. and Old Town Alexandria with all the amenities of a large town. In addition to being the home of National Harbor Marina, one of the premiere marinas in the region, National Harbor features five hotels, condominiums, townhouses, promenades with scores of shops and offices. As the property continues to grow, many more attractions and interesting amenities will be added in the near future.

Points of Interest: Shops, restaurants and hotels gather around the main plaza and marina where a variety of recreational activities can be found. Families can rent paddle-boats, kayaks and canoes, and weekends bring live music, fireworks, a farmer's market and outdoor movies shown on a big screen. There is a rope course featuring two zip lines and three-story pirate ship for the young at heart, and a children's museum is scheduled to open in 2013. You can also embark here for various sightseeing cruises and charters or rent a Segway for touring the sculptures and murals dotted throughout the community.

Special Events: National Harbor hosts Das Best Oktoberfest in September, and is the end point for the Woodrow Wilson Bridge Half Marathon in October. There is also a Food and Wine Festival (May); Beer, Bourbon & Barbecue Festival (July); car show (August); Chesapeake Crab & Beer Festival (August); Abbey Road on the River concert (September); Restaurant Week (October); and Capital Bacon & Beer Bash (November). Check the web site at www.nationalharbor.com for a complete listing of events.

Shopping: Fashion boutiques, art galleries and gourmet shops are found here alongside a bakery, a pet supply store, and a hat store. There are over 35 specialty stores to choose from in National Harbor. For boating supplies, a West Marine is located across the river in Alexandria (601 South Patrick St., 703-549-7020), and for provisioning, there is Potomac Gourmet (180 American Way, 301-839-2870) and Capital Teas (145 Waterfront St., 301-567-8327), plus a Safeway grocery store in Alexandria (500 Royal St., 703-836-0380). There is also a farmer's market every Saturday morning between Memorial Day and Labor Day.

Dining: With over 30 restaurants, from Italian to Mexican to Thai, there is something here to suit all tastes. After lunch or dinner, there are options for ice cream, gelato or cupcakes. Or, opt for a lunch or dinner cruise on the Potomac aboard the Odyssey (866-306-2469) or Spirit of Washington (866-302-2469), both departing from Commercial Pier.

POINTS OF INTEREST
1 Artcraft
2 Swarovski
3 Water Taxi
4 Calleva Ropes Course
5 The sculpture "Awakening"

DINING
6 Bond 45
7 McLoone's Pier House
8 Rosa Mexicano
9 Grace's Mandarin

SHOPPING
10 Potomac Gourmet Market
11 Peeps & Company
12 Farmer's Market

INFORMATION/MARINA OFFICE

PHARMACY

Reference the marina listing tables to see all the marinas in the area.

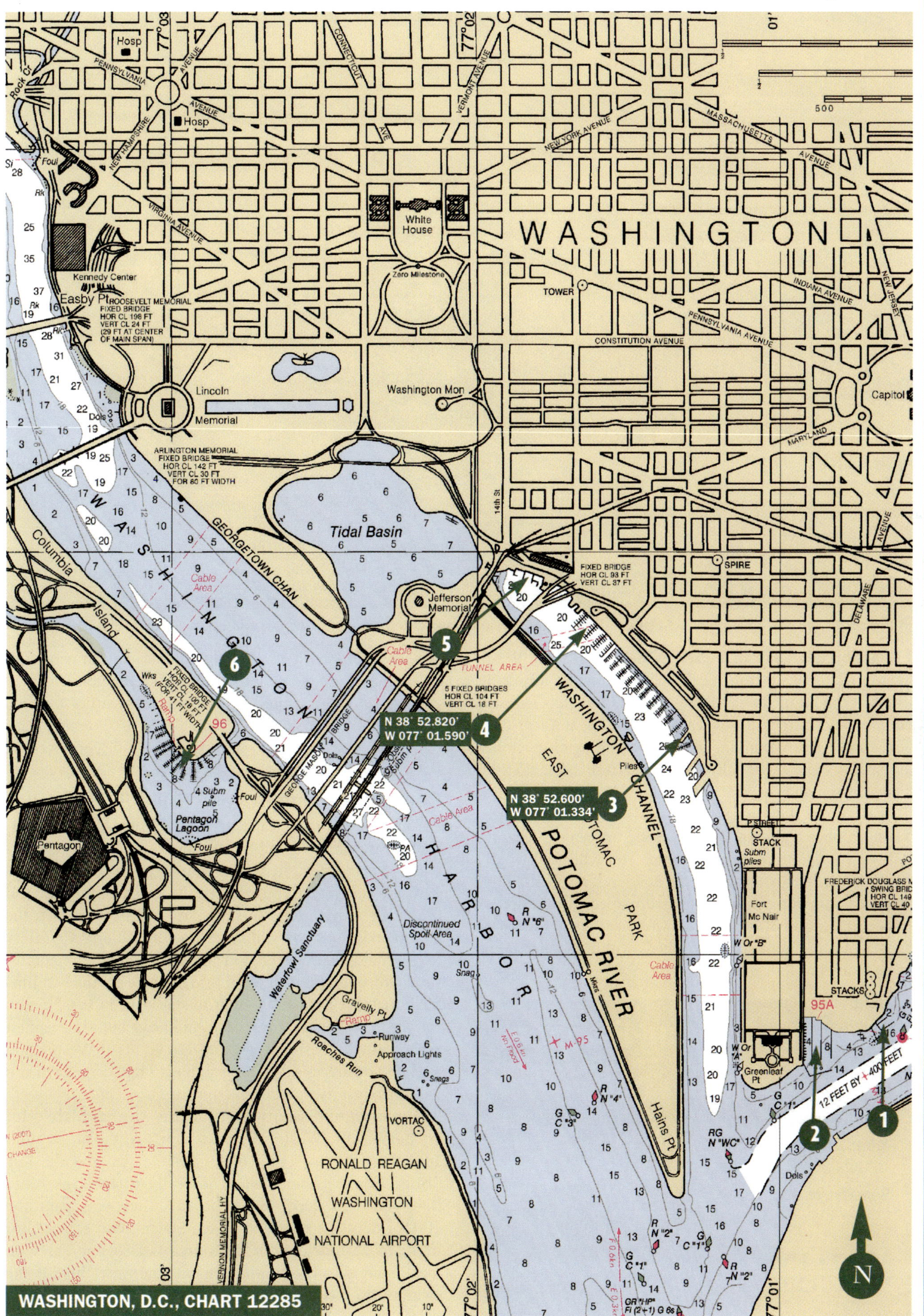
WASHINGTON
White House
Zero Milestone
Kennedy Center
Easby Pt
ROOSEVELT MEMORIAL FIXED BRIDGE HOR CL 198 FT VERT CL 24 FT (29 FT AT CENTER OF MAIN SPAN)
Lincoln Memorial
ARLINGTON MEMORIAL FIXED BRIDGE HOR CL 142 FT VERT CL 30 FT FOR 80 FT WIDTH
Washington Mon
Tidal Basin
Jefferson Memorial
GEORGETOWN CHAN
TOWER
CONSTITUTION AVENUE
Capitol
FIXED BRIDGE HOR CL 93 FT VERT CL 37 FT
SPIRE
TUNNEL AREA
5 FIXED BRIDGES HOR CL 104 FT VERT CL 18 FT
N 38˚ 52.820' W 077˚ 01.590'
N 38˚ 52.600' W 077˚ 01.334'
WASHINGTON CHANNEL
EAST POTOMAC PARK
POTOMAC RIVER
WASHINGTON HARBOR
Columbia Island
Pentagon
Pentagon Lagoon
Waterfowl Sanctuary
Discontinued Spoil Area
Gravelly Pt
Roaches Run
Runway
Approach Lights
VORTAC
RONALD REAGAN WASHINGTON NATIONAL AIRPORT
Hains Pt
Fort Mc Nair
Greenleaf Pt
STACK
STACKS
FREDERICK DOUGLASS SWING BRIDGE
12 FEET BY 400 FEET
Cable Area
95A
96
1
2
3
4
5
6
N
WASHINGTON, D.C., CHART 12285

A northern view over the Potomac River and Washington Channel toward the Mall. (Not to be used for navigation.) Waterway Guide Photography.

Anchorage: You can anchor in the center of the Washington Channel, in front of the Capital Yacht Club docks (north of the tunnel area) in 16- to 20-foot depths with fair holding and purchase privileges to the Capital Yacht Club for a small fee. When anchoring in Washington Channel, be sure to leave enough room for cruise boats to pass between you and the Case Bridge. The Metropolitan Marine Police control the area. Notify them—either at the Marine Harbor Police Station at 202-727-4582 or on VHF Channel 17—as soon as you have anchored. You will need to give boat name, length, owner's name, address and telephone number, number of people aboard, expected duration of visit and location of anchorage. Two weeks is the maximum length of stay in one location. Check with the police if you wish to anchor longer.

There is proposed development in the area that may jeopardize the future of anchoring in the Washington Channel. New marina piers would extend 200 feet further into the basin, and 50 moorings would line the East Potomac Park bulkhead. Check with www.waterwayguide.com for the latest updates.

Georgetown and Beyond (Mile 99)

For vessels that can clear the railroad bridge's 18-foot vertical clearance, you will get a view of Washington, D.C. that is spectacular. Just after you clear the railroad and 14th Street bridges, you will see the Pentagon to port and the Jefferson Memorial to starboard. Before you reach the Memorial Bridge, you will see Arlington National Cemetery to port and the Washington and Lincoln Monuments to starboard. After the Memorial Bridge, there are the Iwo Jima Memorial and Kennedy Center to starboard in Washington Harbor. You can tie up to the bulkhead here but cannot stay overnight. Besides the great restaurants at Washington Harbor, you are an easy couple of blocks to Georgetown and its shops, history and dining.

Anchorage: Twenty-foot depths are available for anchoring in Washington Harbor. A more popular anchorage is past Three Sisters Island, beyond the Key Bridge. Three Sisters Island is really three large rocks that you will keep to starboard. After you pass the 70-foot depths parallel to Three Sisters, you can anchor in 12 to 25-foot depths. This area is also popular with local boaters in the summertime as the water here is the cleanest on the northern Potomac.

U.S. Capitol Building in Washington, D.C.
(©IstockPhoto/Olga Bogatyrenk)

GOIN' ASHORE: WASHINGTON, D.C.

On your approach to Washington Channel, you will be greeted by the imposing structures of the National War College at Fort McNair on Greenleaf Point. Once moored, you are well placed for a walking tour, though locals recommend restricting that activity to daylight hours.

Even though it is well-endowed with waterfront, Washington, D.C. presents itself with a severe face. Modern concrete and glass buildings overlook the marinas along Water Street and, although they are not tall, they seem somewhat aloof from walkers and joggers taking advantage of the public promenade that runs along the river. The docks at Gangplank Marina and the Capital Yacht Club are behind a tall security fence.

You are, though, in the heart of the nation's capital, and the Washington Monument, clearly visible from the marinas, stands as a beacon to guide you toward the city's cultural and historical heritage.

History: After successfully cutting loose from Britain in the Revolutionary War, the newly independent United States of America needed a capital city and all the trimmings attendant to the governing of a democratic republic. For its location, Congress homed in on the upper reaches of the tidal Potomac River as being both close to the geographical center of the new country and also accessible to oceangoing ships.

George Washington himself picked the exact site. The 10-square-mile capital region included the ports of Georgetown, MD, at the fall line of the Potomac, and Alexandria, VA, as well as two smaller settlements on the Maryland bank. (Alexandria unraveled itself from the arrangement in 1847.) In 1790, Congress approved the site. In 1791, Washington appointed Pierre Charles L'Enfant as the city's planner and, in 1792, construction began on government buildings. During the War of 1812, on August 24, 1814, the British exacted revenge of a sort by sailing up the Potomac and burning many federal buildings, including The White House.

Already encompassing two busy ports, the "Territory of Columbia," as the Federal District was initially named, gained in population as the government grew and its suburbs filled with workers, but despite its strategic importance and the proximity of secessionist Virginia, Washington saw little fighting during the Civil War.

Points of Interest: Washington has an infinitely long must-see list. Anyone who goes there should have a plan, whether it is to see the government buildings along The National Mall and Pennsylvania Avenue, to view one small corner of the extensive Smithsonian, to take in a play at Kennedy Center or to pay respects at the Vietnam Veterans Memorial.

If you just showed up on a whim and want to take your chances, you can do worse than head north from the marina, which will take you to The National Mall. That is a fair enough starting point to begin your immersion in the nation's capital.

Dining: There is public Washington and there is neighborhood Washington, both of which are served by eateries too numerous to count. If you choose to stay close to the boat, several restaurants overlook the marinas. The specialty at Phillips Flagship (900 Water St. SW, 202-488-8515) is an all-you-can-eat seafood buffet. They also have dockage available for their diners. Pier 7, at the Channel Inn (650 Water St. SW, 202-554-2500), presents fine dining in a refined atmosphere. The Cantina Marina (600 Water St. SW, 202-554-8396) is on a pier over the water at the Gangplank Marina. Sample Tex-Mex and Cajun seafood while watching the Washington Monument change color in the setting sun.

To experience an old D.C. tradition, walk up the promenade toward the Washington Monument. Just past the Capital Yacht Club, you will find Fish Wharf, where vendors offer every kind of seafood imaginable.

Getting Around: If you have come to Washington with a plan, you will already be equipped with route maps for Metrobus and the Metro (www.wmata.com). If not, marina staff will be able to give you the lowdown on the best ways to get where you want to go. If you are at a Water Street marina, buses and taxis are available close by, and the Waterfront-SEU Metro station is about three blocks away on M Street SW.

D.C. Streets: Streets are lettered and numbered starting from the Capitol. Numbered streets run north and south, lettered streets run east and west, and they are further identified by quadrants of the compass. If you are on 6th St. SW at G St. SW, you are southwest of the Capitol. If you walk along G and come to a higher number street, you are going west. If you walk along 6th and come to H, you are going south. It is a simple arrangement until you encounter an avenue. Named for the states, these radiate diagonally from the Capitol, from the White House. ■

ADDITIONAL RESOURCES

- WASHINGTON TOURISM: www.washington.org
- VISIT WASHINGTON, D.C.: www.thedistrict.com
- D.C. ONLINE: www.visitwashingtondconline.com
- METRO: www.wmata.com

NEARBY MEDICAL FACILITIES
George Washington University Hospital:
900 23rd St. NW, 202-715-4000

NEARBY AIRPORT
Reagan National Airport:
www.metwashairports.com/national

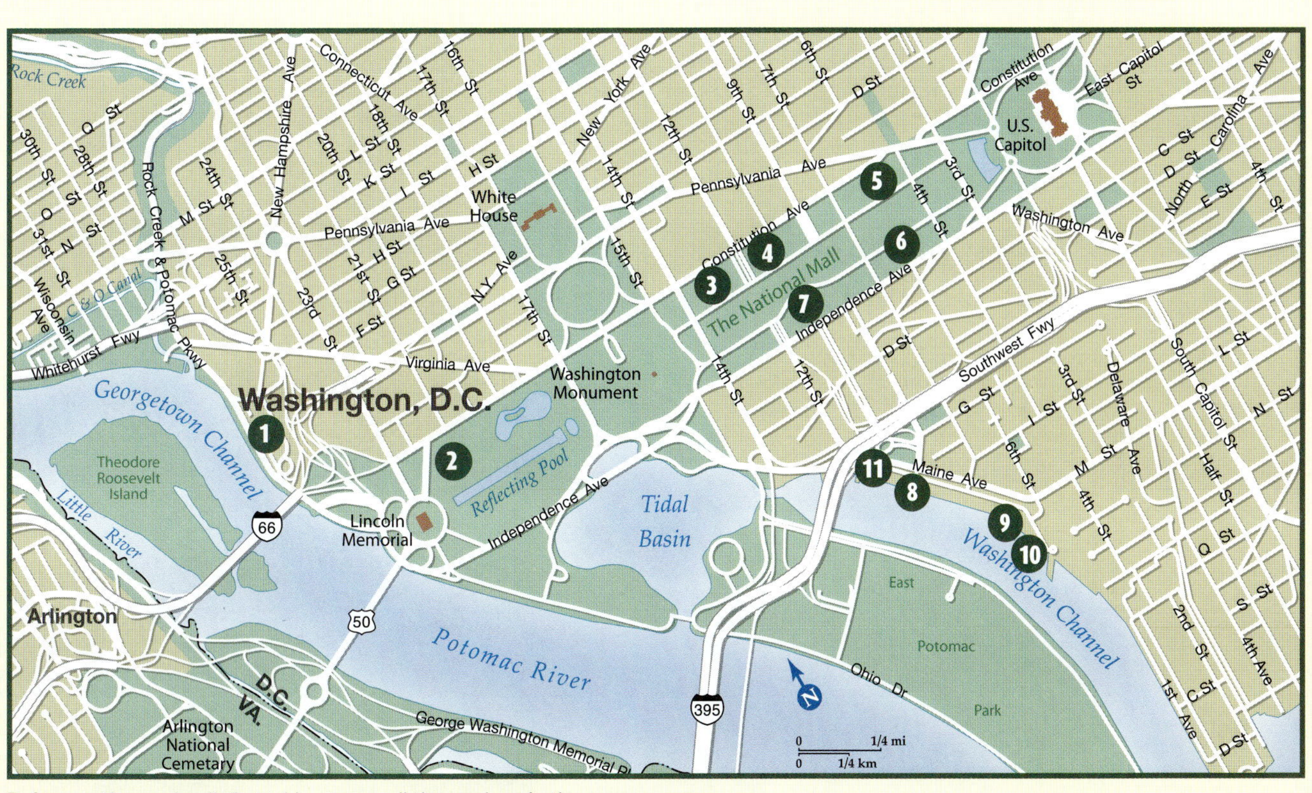

Reference the marina listing tables to see all the marinas in the area.

POINTS OF INTEREST

1 Kennedy Center
2 Vietnam Veterans Memorial
3 National Museum of American History
4 National Museum of Natural History
5 National Gallery of Art
6 National Air and Space Museum
7 Smithsonian Institution Building

DINING

8 Phillips Flagship
9 Pier 7, at the Channel Inn
10 The Cantina Marina
11 Fish Wharf

marinalife®
ENHANCING YOUR YACHTING LIFESTYLE

ml

Virginia Western Shore

SMITH POINT, VA TO DELTAVILLE, VA
DELTAVILLE TO HAMPTON ROADS
HAMPTON ROADS, JAMES RIVER, CAPE HENRY
NORFOLK, ELIZABETH RIVER
DELMARVA COAST

Photos Courtesy of Mike Kucera and Waterway Guide.

Virginia Western Shore

- SMITH POINT, VA TO DELTAVILLE, VA
- DELTAVILLE TO HAMPTON ROADS
- HAMPTON ROADS, JAMES RIVER, CAPE HENRY
- NORFOLK, ELIZABETH RIVER
- DELMARVA COAST

Introduction

Virginia's Western Shore

Virginia's Western Shore of the Chesapeake kicks off with the Great Wicomico River. The Great Wicomico (just south of the Potomac River) meanders in a westerly direction, and its deep waters and intriguing little tributaries make excellent playgrounds for boaters. Likewise, the historic fishing town of Reedville—on Cockrell Creek, which is off the Great Wicomico—is a must-visit port for cruisers in this area. Known for its major menhaden fishery, it also happens to be an excellent place if you are looking for good seafood and friendly locals. Reedville is also home to the Reedville Fisherman's Museum, which opens a window to the town's colorful past.

To the south of the Great Wicomico, you will find gunkholes galore, like those off Dividing Creek and the tributaries of Fleets Bay. Next comes the historic Rappahannock River, which—along with the Potomac to the north—sets the boundaries for Virginia's Northern Neck. Between the Rappahannock River and the York River to the south lies Virginia's Middle peninsula.

The Rappahannock River is rimmed by perfect tributaries for cruisers, such as the Corrotoman River, along with convenient ports of call, like Irvington and Urbanna.

The Rappahannock River on the north and the Piankatank River to the south provide access to the major recreational boating center of Deltaville. Deltaville is laid-back, but stylishly southern, with a plethora of docking space and several nice dining options, marine provisioning stores and some attractive bed and breakfast homes. Farther up the Piankatank River are first-rate anchorages like Wilton Creek and Berkley Island.

The next major cruising ground off Virginia's Western Shore is Mobjack Bay, with its many tranquil tributaries, including the North and East rivers. Other rivers in the region south of Mobjack Bay include the York—which is steeped in Colonial history—and the James, where the first permanent English colonists landed more than 400 years ago, beginning the British Colonial Empire as well as modern America.

Tidewater Virginia encompasses the southern extremes of Chesapeake Bay and ports like Hampton, Newport News and Norfolk. Alongside the Hampton River, this city appears practically designed for walking, with its downtown area confined to a handful of blocks and dotted with points of interest that include the Virginia Air and Space Center and the Hampton Roads History Center.

The primary big-city destination on this part of the Bay is Norfolk. Like Baltimore, Norfolk was traditionally known as a major shipping port, but cruisers' options here have increased greatly over the past decade. Today, Norfolk features attractions like The Waterside and MacArthur Center shopping and dining complexes, the battleship *USS Wisconsin* and Nauticus, which holds some of the world's most advanced interactive maritime exhibits. Norfolk is an important spot for another reason, too: The Elizabeth River, which flows along Norfolk's waterfront, marks the beginning of the Atlantic Intracoastal Waterway. ■

Photo courtesy of Mike Kucera.

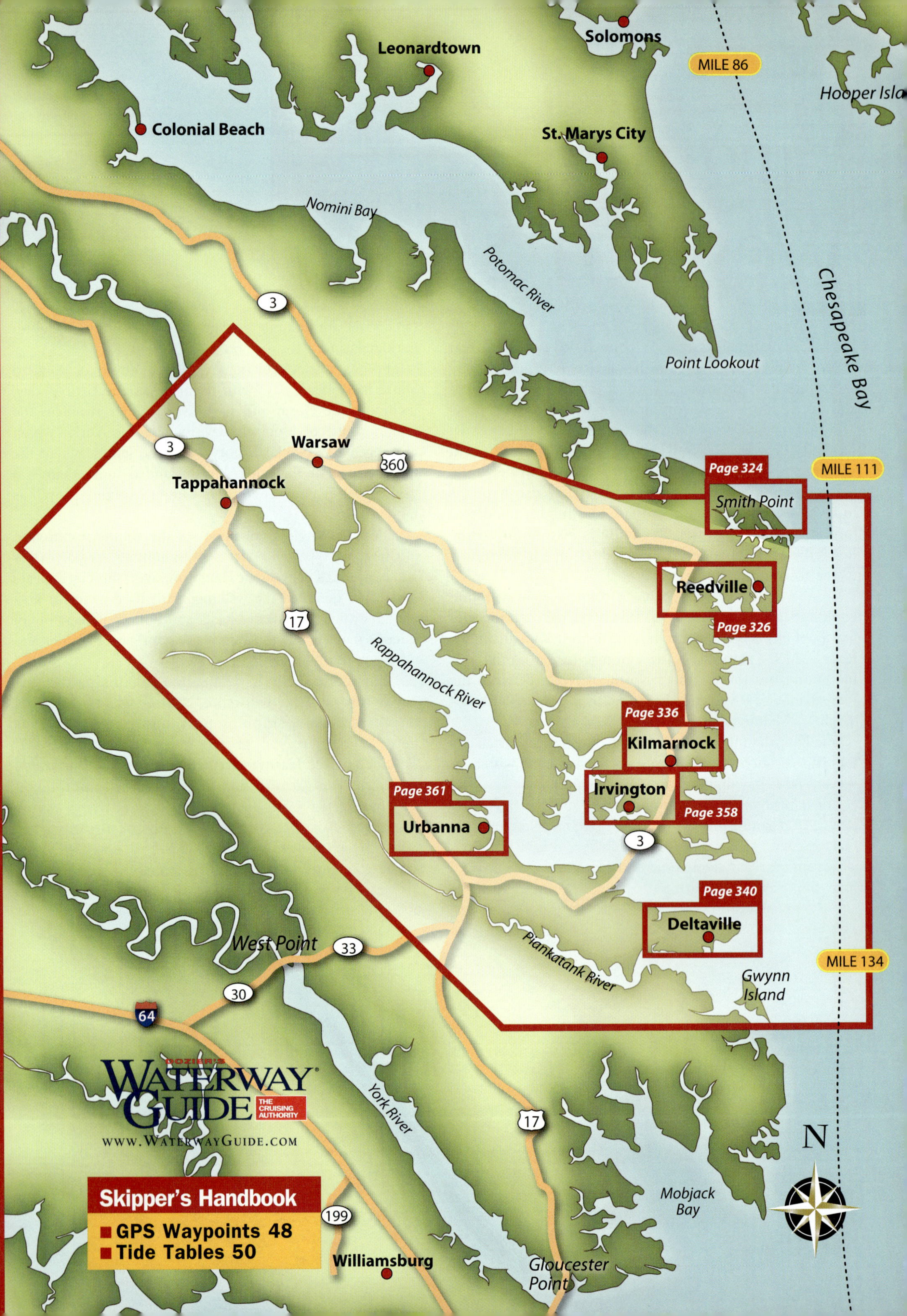

Skipper's Handbook

- GPS Waypoints 48
- Tide Tables 50

Lancaster County

in Virginia's Northern Neck

Hospice Turkey Shoot Regatta on the Rappahannock River.

WHAT IS VIRGINIA'S NORTHERN NECK?

This history-laden peninsula between the Potomac and Rappahannock Rivers has impact. Impact because of the Washington and Lee families who settled here, built homes, farmed tobacco, and raised families who grew up to chart the course of our nation's development. Impact that predates John Smith's 1608 explorations when the Virginia Indians encountered Smith's shallop, or sailing barge, in the Northern Neck's numerous navigable creeks and along the rivers. Early impact that started about 35 million years ago when the Chesapeake Impact Crater was formed by a hit from a mountain-sized meteorite off the coast of Virginia to create the Chesapeake Bay. English settlers kept the Indians' names of their villages and rivers. The dense quiet woods that provided the resource for the early log homes later propelled the timber industry, when sawmills dotted the area. The mill ponds remain, which bear the names of old families whose descendants live here today, and appear unexpectedly around curves on scenic drives through the Northern Neck and provide mirror-like reflections of the surrounding forests.

Visit Good Luck Cellars or The Dog and Oyster vineyard.

You'll find scenic views and quiet stops in all four counties of the Northern Neck-Westmoreland and Northumberland on the Potomac River with Lancaster and Richmond Counties off the Rappahannock. Stop by for a day or a lifetime.

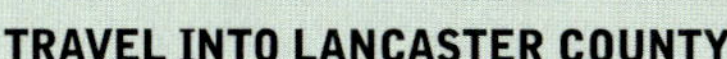

TRAVEL INTO LANCASTER COUNTY

Filled with great small towns and rich history, Lancaster County is bounded by the Chesapeake Bay and Rappahannock River. Stop in our small towns and marinas and experience the laid back lifestyle and hospitality of the region. Three hundred miles of shoreline invite you to stay and explore just like Capt. John Smith did.

Sail into Indian Creek to stop in Kilmarnock or start at Windmill Point on the Chesapeake then follow the Rappahannock River around to Irvington and cruise into Carter's Creek, home of the world famous Tides Inn and Irvington Steamboat Era Museum. Go farther upriver to the Corrotoman River, an Indian name from the Cuttawoman tribe of the Powhatan nation. Yankee Point Marina is the home of the annual Turkey Shoot Regatta benefiting the National Hospice Alliance.

Continue up the Rappahannock past Belle Isle State Park, with fabulous programs for all ages, to Morattico, a quaint former steamboat landing. Learn about the life of the Chesapeake Bay waterman and the canning industry of the Northern Neck at the Morattico Waterfront Museum, housed in a 1901 general store.

Lancaster County features great fishing tournaments, regattas and nearly a year 'round boating climate. Plus some of the finest local crabs and oysters around the Bay. Our communities offer Americana at its best with outdoor recreation, performing arts, historic sites plus great antiqueing, shopping and dining.

Stop in, restock and get to know us. You just might want to stay awhile.

Smith Point to Deltaville

CHARTS 12221, 12224, 12225, 12226, 12228, 12231, 12235, 12237, 12238, 12241, 12243, 12285

Scenic Tidewater Virginia occupies Chesapeake Bay's lower Western Shore. These bustling Virginia rivers are busy with recreational craft, along with traditional commercial fishing boats. The area has undergone considerable development over the years, so the many once-rural and bucolic creeks and rivers now have been "discovered."

In this part of the world, you can spend a quiet night in a scenic anchorage, or tie up at a plush marina/resort and enjoy the shoreside amenities. You can visit many of the places whose names are consecrated in American history—Jamestown, Yorktown, Williamsburg. Some of the towns you will see here have entered the 21st century, but retain pieces of their antique cultures. Go ashore in these areas and you will hear much of the folklore of the Chesapeake, handed down through generations and still fresh in the minds of many. After all, oyster wars were fought zealously here as recently as 65 years ago.

Three separate peninsulas comprise much of Virginia's Western Shore—the Northern Neck, Middle Peninsula and Peninsula—created by the Potomac, Rappahannock, York and James rivers. Cruise this part of the Bay, and savor all three; each has its own nuances and is enticing in its own way. You will need to run a mile or more offshore to avoid the clearly charted shoal waters as you cruise among them. The Northern Neck runs from Smith Point to the Rappahannock River and includes the Great Wicomico River, Dividing Creek and Fleets Bay tributaries. The Middle Peninsula starts south of the Rappahannock and includes the Piankatank River, Gwynn Island and Mobjack Bay, ending at the York River. The highlight of the Peninsula, bounded by the York and James rivers, is the Historic Triangle, which includes Jamestown, Williamsburg and Yorktown.

Many experienced cruisers consider this the best cruising ground on the Chesapeake. It is much less crowded than the upper- and mid-Bay, but more populated than the lower Eastern Shore. A recent influx of well-to-do retirees has brought facilities like supermarkets and a modern hospital to the Northern Neck. Recognition of recreational boat traffic on the Bay prompted growth in marinas and boat suppliers on parts of the Middle Peninsula, while Mobjack Bay remains a truly unspoiled area within a day's sail of Norfolk and Hampton Roads. The Lower Peninsula's tourist attractions offer a complete change of pace for the cruiser, especially if children aboard are getting bored and restless.

SMITH POINT, VA

Smith Point, at the southern side of the Potomac River's mouth, is the halfway point between Annapolis and Norfolk. The Potomac and Little Wicomico rivers meet the Bay here.

Smith Point and Little Wicomico River

Smith Point marks the Virginia side of the river's mouth. The Little Wicomico River itself is in a strategic location at the tip of Smith Point, and also one of the prettiest rivers leading off the Potomac.

The Little Wicomico is often overlooked as a cruising destination because the entrance channel had been a bit be tricky and prone to shoaling; the entrance was dredged in 2010 but has already shoaled significantly since. A visit is well worth the effort if you draw less than 4.5 feet, but local knowledge is recommended. Sand is encroaching and topping the north jetty. Once inside, you will find several miles of sheltered cruising in pretty, rural surroundings. We don't recommend attempting this inlet with a rough sea.

NAVIGATION: Use Charts 12235, 12225. While waters at the mouth of the Potomac often live up to their rough reputation, particularly when a strong southerly wind blows against ebb current, they can also be glassy smooth on a calm day. Northbound, even if your boat has a deep draft, you can find shelter in the Great Wicomico River, six miles south of the Little Wicomico River, before attempting to round Smith Point. Watch for fish pound nets and crab pots if you are traveling on this course.

Waterway Guide Photography.

SMITH POINT
N 37°52.783'
W 076°11.017'

The huge caisson of the Smith Point Lighthouse stands in the Bay some 2.5 miles offshore. The light is unmanned and automatic and was sold into private hands in 2005 and was recently renovated as a 4-bedroom home.

The Little Wicomico River is normally approached from the southeast, especially by deeper draft boats. When you arrive about half a mile south east of "2LW" head 310 degrees and approach the mark leaving it very close to starboard, then head for quick flashing red "4" at the end of the north jetty. Stay to the north side of the channel upon entering the jetties, then, once in, angle towards the south side of the channel where the deeper water will be the rest of the way. You will cross a shallow bar (5 feet reported) as you angle over. The entrance is often filled with small fishing

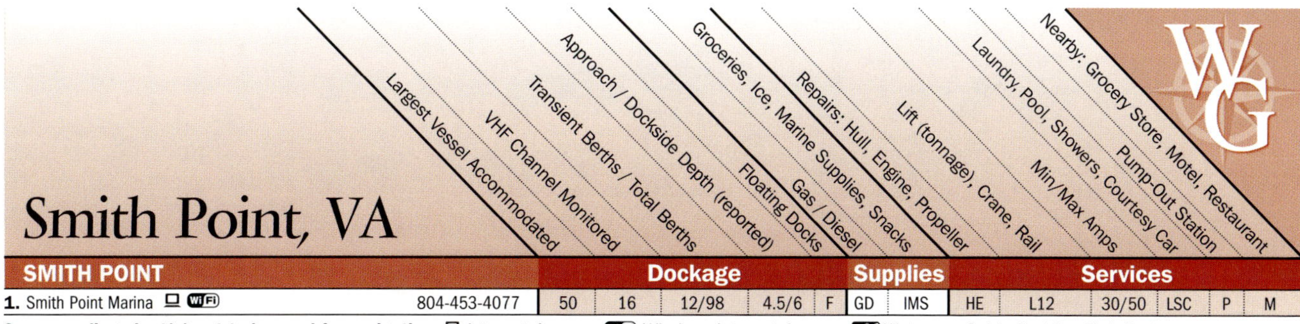

SMITH POINT		Largest Vessel Accommodated	VHF Channel Monitored	Transient Berths / Total Berths	Approach / Dockside Depth (reported)	Floating Docks	Gas / Diesel	Groceries, Ice, Marine Supplies, Snacks	Repairs: Hull, Engine, Propeller	Lift (tonnage), Crane, Rail	Min/Max Amps	Laundry, Pool, Showers, Courtesy Car	Pump-Out Station	Nearby: Grocery Store, Motel, Restaurant
		Dockage					Supplies		Services					
1. Smith Point Marina	804-453-4077	50	16	12/98	4.5/6	F	GD	IMS	HE	L12	30/50	LSC	P	M

Corresponding chart(s) not to be used for navigation. Internet Access · Wireless Internet Access · Waterway Guide Cruising Club Partner

See www.WaterwayGuide.com for current rates, fuel prices, web site addresses, and other up-to-the-minute information.

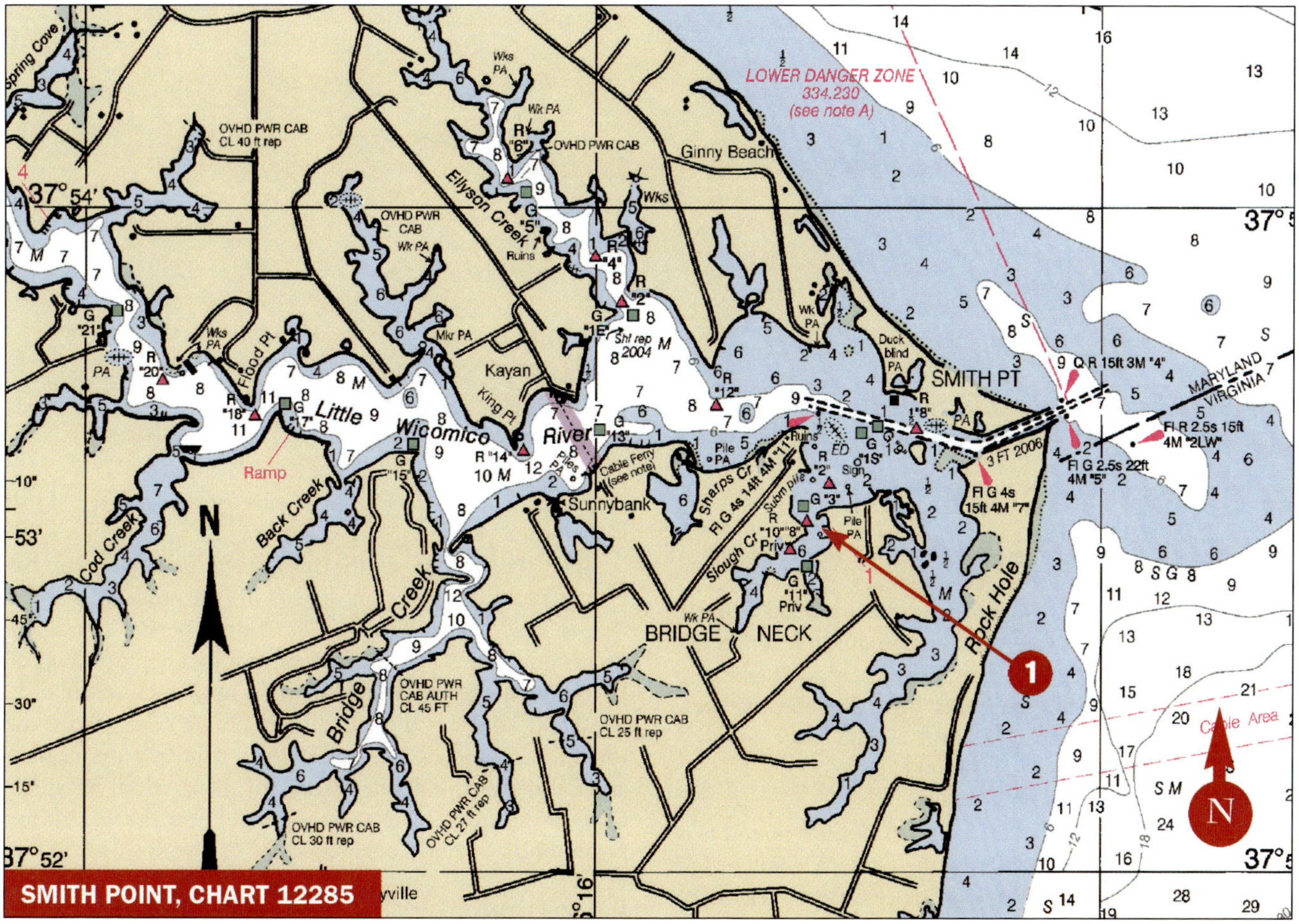

SMITH POINT, CHART 12285

boats, so keep a sharp lookout for them. Expect the shoaling to increase over time as sand continues to top the jetty. To get the latest on channel conditions, call Smith Point Marina (804-453-4077) or Smith Point Sea Rescue on VHF Channel 16. The Northumberland County Sheriff's office can relay a message to Smith Point Sea Rescue if needed (804-580-5221), or call 911 if you need emergency assistance.

Smith Point Sea Rescue started in 1972, and today is a thriving organization of about 49 members. It handles distress calls from Point Lookout, at the mouth of the Potomac, to Windmill Point, at the mouth of the Rappahannock. Sea Rescue also covers the Lower Potomac River from Coles Point on the Virginia side and Tall Timbers on the Maryland shore to Point Lookout. Much like a volunteer fire department, the Sea Rescue is on call seven days a week, 24 hours a day and will help boats that are grounded or out of fuel as well as in emergency situations.

Note: A mile and a half above the entrance to the Little Wicomico, a charted cable ferry crosses the river at the town of Sunnybank. When the ferry is underway, the cable lurks just below the surface. Do not cross its path until the ferry has stopped completely; the cable should have dropped by this point.

Dockage: Smith Point Marina, three quarters of a mile inside to port welcomes transient boats and offers fuel, pump-out and a lift for haul-outs.

Anchorage: Nearly landlocked, the Little Wicomico provides lake-like conditions even when it is howling out on the Bay. The shoreline is lightly populated with traditional houses, and local watermen ply their trades here. Nothing much happens in these parts, but that is a big part of its charm.

Smith Point as viewed from the west. (Not to be used for navigation.) Cloud 9 Photography Deagle/Kucera

GREAT WICOMICO RIVER IN VIRGINIA

The Great Wicomico is a complete cruising ground in itself, with a pleasant town, waterfront restaurants, a few marinas and plenty of quiet anchorages. This is a good place to run and hide when the Bay kicks up a fuss and the crew threatens mutiny if you don't find a calm place to stroll ashore or anchor for a swim.

NAVIGATION: Use Chart 12235. Be alert for fish pound nets and crab pot floats when entering the Great Wicomico. The mark for the Great Wicomico's entrance is Great Wicomico River Light—a spidery, skeletal structure that is 42 feet high and easily identifiable (flashing white light every six seconds). To enter Cockrell Creek and go to Reedville, head toward red nun buoy "4" from Great Wicomico Light, leave it to starboard, and then make a northward turn toward the creek past red quick flashing red buoy "6," making sure to avoid the shoal making out from Fleeton Point as you head for 15-foot flashing green "1."

Cockrell Creek, Reedville, VA, off the Great Wicomico

Reedville, on Cockrell Creek, is a quiet little town with a lot to offer, including several small marinas, waterside seafood vendors, restaurants and a friendly bunch of locals. Reedville is also home to the famous fleet of menhaden fishing ships and their attendant onshore processing plant. Reedville remains a major fish landing port, and by many accounts is second only to Dutch Harbor Alaska for the tonnage of fish landed each year.

Since the decline of the menhaden fishery, there has been a rapid decline from dozens of fish processing factories, to one: Omega Protein. The former persistent odor of processing plants is less of a deterrent to a trip up Cockrell Creek thanks to the installation of a new stack scrubber in 2010. No longer is there a tell tale plume rising above the town. The branches and coves of this tributary are pleasant and calm and the upper reaches of the creek at Reedville are quite attractive. Since stores are not near the waterfront, provisioning requires a trip by car.

NAVIGATION: Use Chart 12235. **Use Hampton Roads tide tables. For Reedville high tide, add 2 hours 59 minutes; for low tide add 3 hours 6 minutes.** The marked channel to Reedville up Cockrell Creek has 8- to 14-foot depths. There are few markers past flashing green "1" at the mouth to Cockrell Creek, but good depths prevail in the middle. Past Tim Point (about one nautical mile up from the entrance), a series of daybeacons guide you along farther upstream toward Reedville-proper. Follow the arc of the channel as you loop around the newly restored brick smoke stack, a monument to the menhaden fishing industry, that is often illuminated in the evening during special events.

Dockage: Before the smokestack on the west side of Cockrell Creek are Jennings Boatyard and Fairport Marina, both with transient space. Fairport Marina also has a new restaurant, Leadbelly's. Reedville Marina and Crazy Crab Restaurant, located at the foot of the town of Reedville, has 14-foot dockside depths and offers transient slips and dining. Buzzard's Point Marina, past Tim Point and up the marked channel of Cockrell Creek, has good shelter in depths of 8 feet. During warm months, and as long as the good weather lasts in fall, a 150-passenger excursion boat makes daily runs to Tangier Island from Buzzard's Point Marina (call 804-453-3545 for information). Buzzard's Point Marina provides free dockage for your boat while you take the cruise to Tangier Island, a voyage of a few hours. See Chapter 3, "Little Choptank to Cape Charles," for more information about Tangier Island.

Anchorage: You will find anchorages in several branches of Cockrell Creek. Use your charts and depth sounder carefully. There are no markers in most of them, and the bottom can shoal dramatically in these side waters. One good anchorage is in the east fork past the tank and boatyard, where holding is good in 8-foot depths, but check the depths all around your swinging circle. Visiting boaters often tie up their dinghies at the boatyard or Tommy's Restaurant. The seafood deli (you can't miss the bright red Crabs sign) is open daily in season and sells ice. Watch for the commercial crabbers unloading their catch in the mornings.

GOIN' ASHORE: **REEDVILLE, VA**

Rusted steel sheds and crumbling brick chimneys, reminders of a once vigorous menhaden industry, line the approach to Reedville along Cockrell Creek. For many cruisers, their first visit to Reedville was their last, thanks to an often overwhelming odor emanating from the menhaden processing plant. However, in 2010 a new exhaust system with a high-tech scrubber was installed, significantly reducing and sometimes eliminating the previously ever-present odor.

Up to the mid-1930s, when most commerce was conducted by steamboat, Reedville was a small town full of bustle. A stroll along Main Street in the shade of majestic magnolias and sculpted crape myrtles gives you the sense that time stopped the moment the highway arrived. You would be convinced of that on the weekend of the museum's Antique and Classic Boat Show in early September, when the boats grace the docks behind the houses and antique cars line the driveways.

History: Reedville was built upon the menhaden fishing industry. In 1874, Elijah Reed brought his menhaden business south from Brooklin, ME to the Great Wicomico River, where the seemingly limitless bounty of the Chesapeake Bay has supported it ever since. The sole remaining factory, owned by Omega Protein, processes 100,000 metric tons per year of the inedible fish into a range of products that appear in everything from fertilizer to vitamin pills. This is a quantity that makes Reedville the second largest fishing port in the U.S. in terms of fish landed!

Conservationists, environmental activists and sportfishers object to the sheer size of the catch, but the plant and the boats that supply it are the mainstay of Reedville, whose residents are not eager to give it up. The dispute hangs over the town, as does, in a southerly breeze, the characteristic odor of the process that, in its heyday, made its Main Street among the richest on the continent.

Points of Interest: The history of both town and fishery, inextricably linked, are described in the permanent exhibit at the Reedville Fishermen's Museum at 504 Main St (804-453-6529). Also on display are several locally built boats; a working buy boat, Elva C; and a restored skipjack, Claude W. Somers. In the boat shop, museum members and volunteers engage in an active boatbuilding program, a highlight of which is a family weekend in the summer. In 2006, the volunteers built a replica of the vessel in which John Smith explored Chesapeake Bay and its tributaries in 1607 and 1608. Spirit of 2008 is usually on show when it is not supporting Colony-founding commemorations around the region. Check the museum's Web site (www.rfmuseum.org) or call for details of

Looking south over Reedville, VA. (Not to be used for navigation.) Cloud 9 Photography Deagle/Kucera

the numerous activities the museum sponsors over the course of the year.

In the 1920s, a railway was proposed to link Reedville and the Northern Neck with Fredericksburg. It never came to be, but you can see what might have been in the Model Shop attached to the Reedville Fishermen's Museum.

The real Main Street is on the National Register of Historic Places and presents a catalog of the architecture of the American home from the late 19th century to the present day. Several of the Victorian examples have been converted into bed and breakfasts, including the town's most stunning and celebrated house, The Gables, built by a menhaden captain and laid out on the cardinal points of the compass.

Apart from a couple of crab docks at the foot of the street, little business activity remains in Reedville. The Omega plant and docks are across Cockrell Creek in Fleeton. A colonnaded, single-story bank building attempts to match the grandeur of The Gables at the business end of the one-street town, and the post office has been exiled to the other, where Route 360, the sole road, ends.

Halfway up Main Street, though, at the Reedville Marine Railway, George Butler continues his family's 100-year tradition of building wooden boats. Those who hanker for the perfume of cedar and oak shavings will find it here, and perhaps witness a deadrise boat being built or repaired.

Special Events: Reedville's community of professional watermen and recreational boaters is tight-knit, a relationship that led in 1974 to the creation of Smith Point Sea Rescue, a non-profit organization supported entirely by private subscription and donations. A number of events each year help support it, the principal one being the annual Reedville Bluefish Derby. Based at Buzzard's Point Marina, the derby, held the second weekend in June, reels in contestants from far and wide (www.smithpointsearescue.com).

The annual Blessing of the Fleet takes place the first weekend in May, and Reedville holds a Good Old-Fashioned Fourth to celebrate Independence Day.

Shopping: SF Barnes grocery store is located at 910 Fleeton Road, about one mile away. Jett's Hardware also offers marine supplies (18425 Northumberland Highway) and is about three miles away.

Dining: Perched above the Reedville Marina, the Crazy Crab (902 Main St., 804-453-6789) offers Chesapeake waterfront fare and a panoramic view of Cockrell Creek. Tommy's (729 Main St., 804-453-4666) serves a substantial American fare and attracts many local gentry, with its non-gentrified prices.

Across at Cockrell's Creek Seafood Deli (567 Seaboard Road, 804-453-6326), you can lunch at outside tables overlooking the creek and take fresh fish, crabs and other marine delicacies back to the boat. Temporary tie-ups are available. For a very special crab picking evening, order a couple dozen steamed crabs for pick up at closing time, 5:00 p.m. The restaurant closes and the grounds are deserted, but you can pick your crabs at the tables under the shade of the trees while enjoying the view across Cockrell Creek.

Reedville, Great Wicomico River, VA

		Largest Vessel Accommodated	VHF Channel Monitored	Transient Berths / Total Berths	Approach / Dockside Depth (reported)	Floating Docks	Gas / Diesel	Groceries, Ice, Marine Supplies, Snacks	Repairs: Hull, Engine, Propeller	Lift (tonnage), Crane, Rail	Min/Max Amps	Laundry, Pool, Showers, Courtesy Car	Pump-Out Station	Nearby: Grocery Store, Motel, Restaurant
REEDVILLE		Dockage					Supplies		Services					
1. Jennings Boatyard Inc.	804-453-7181	45	-	3/28	15/9	-	-	M	HP	L35, C35	30/30	S	P	-
2. Fairport Marina (WiFi)	804-453-5002	100	16	16/48	15/8	-	GD	IS	-	-	30/50	S	P	R
3. Buzzard's Point Marina (Internet) (WiFi)	804-453-3545	75	16	4/40	8/8	F	GD	IM	HEP	L10	50/50	S	P	MR
4. Reedville Marina and Crazy Crab Restaurant	804-453-6789	200	16	7/19	15/14	-	GD	IS	-	-	50/50	S	P	GMR
GREAT WICOMICO RIVER														
5. Ingram Bay Marina (Internet) (WiFi)	804-580-7292	65	16/06	10/55	12/6	-	GD	GIMS	E	-	30/50	LSC	P	M
6. Tiffany Yachts Inc. (Internet) (WiFi)	**804-453-3464**	**80**	**-**	**5/21**	**12/10**	**-**	**GD**	**IM**	**HEP**	**L88, R**	**30/50**	**S**	**P**	**-**
7. Great Wicomico River Marina	804-453-3351	45	-	-	10/7	-	G	I	-	-	30/30	LS	P	R

Corresponding chart(s) not to be used for navigation. Internet Access · WiFi Wireless Internet Access · Waterway Guide Cruising Club Partner
See www.WaterwayGuide.com for current rates, fuel prices, web site addresses, and other up-to-the-minute information.

No afternoon or after-dinner stroll would be complete without a pause at Chitterchats Ice Cream Parlor (846 Main St., 804-453-3335), where coconut is but one of the parlor's many exquisite ice cream flavors.

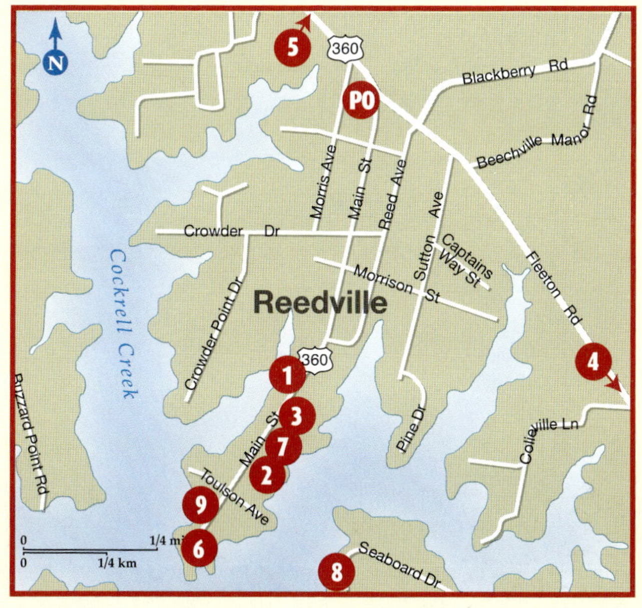

Reference the marina listing tables to see all the marinas in the area.

POINTS OF INTEREST

1 Reedville Fishermen's Museum
2 The Gables
3 Reedville Marine Railway

SHOPPING

4 SF Barnes
5 Jett's Hardware

DINING

6 The Crazy Crab
7 Tommy's
8 Cockrells Creek Seafood & Deli
9 Chitterchats

POST OFFICE

ADDITIONAL RESOURCES

■ **REEDVILLE FISHERMANS MUSEUM:** www.rfmuseum.org

NEARBY MEDICAL FACILITIES
Rappahannock General Hospital, 101 Harris Road, Kilmarnock, VA 22842, 804-435-8000, 800-296-8009
www.rgh-hospital.com (20 miles)

Great Wicomico, Beyond Reedville and Cockrell Creek

Upriver on the Great Wicomico, past Cockrell Creek and Reedville, the Great Wicomico winds past rural vistas with the occasional home or small waterfront enterprise peeking through the lush green foliage. Several creeks worth exploring open through the forested banks that line the river.

NAVIGATION: Use Chart 12235. Flashing lights "8," "9," "10" and "11" were relocated in late 2007, so be careful as you pass the points of land they indicate. Between "10" and "11" don't let green daymarkers "ICW" fool you into leaving it to port. It marks the entrance to Warehouse Creek on the north side of the river. The bridge at Glebe Point, a fixed span with a 55-foot vertical clearance five miles up the river, is as far as most cruisers go. There is a set of overhead power cables just beyond the bridge with 54-foot vertical clearances. Adventurous sailors can press on upriver to explore a few more miles and several more anchorages but without navigational aids. Follow your charts carefully.

Dockage: Tiffany Yachts builds large custom sportfishing powerboats, specifically designed for the productive but rough waters off the Bay's entrance, at its yard just

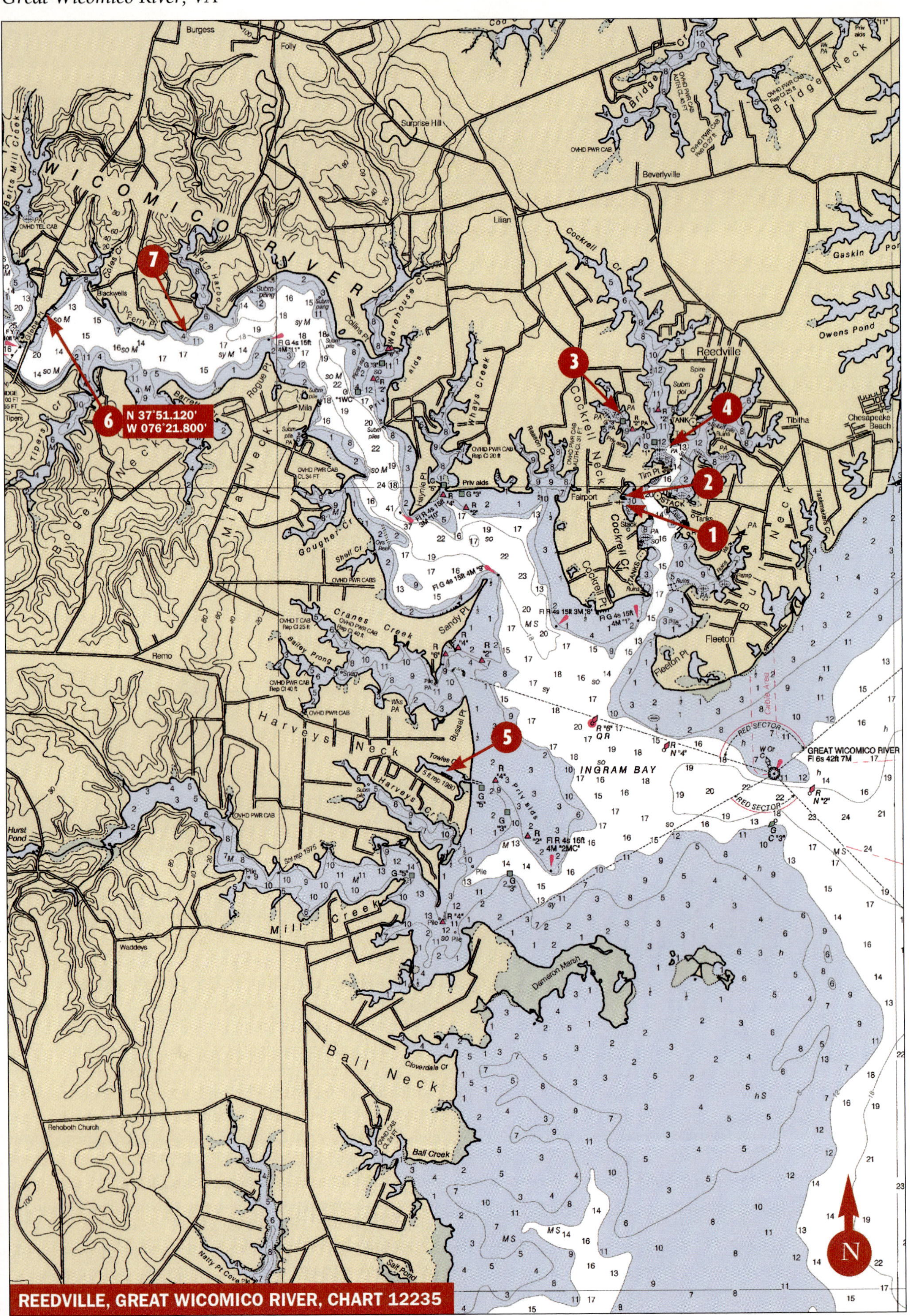

REEDVILLE, GREAT WICOMICO RIVER, CHART 12235
N 37°51.120'
W 076°21.800'
WICOMICO RIVER
Reedville
Cockrell Neck
Fairport
Harveys Neck
Mila Neck
Ball Neck
INGRAM BAY
GREAT WICOMICO RIVER
Fl 6s 42ft 7M
Dameron Marsh
Fleeton
Burgess
Folly
Surprise Hill
Beverlyville
Lilian
Tibitha
Chesapeake Beach
Owens Pond
Gaskin Pond
Cranes Creek
Mill Creek
Ball Creek
Rehoboth Church
Remo
Waddeys
Hurst Pond

inside Glebe Point, below the bridge. Tiffany Yachts has two marine railways and a 60-ton lift, and offers complete repair, interior design and customized services for sail or powerboats. There are a few slips available for transients as well as fuel.

Anchorage: You can trust the chart when choosing an anchorage on the Great Wicomico. Good coves are on both sides below and above the Glebe Point Bridge, so sound your way in, and select the one that affords the best protection. When winds are from the east and south, the bight behind Sandy Point, approximately two miles from the river's entrance, is the anchorage most skippers choose for a quick stop on the route south between Solomons Island, MD and Deltaville, VA. Be sure to back down on your anchor to make sure it is set.

Horn Harbor, off the Great Wicomico

Anchorage: Up the Great Wicomico River on the north side about a mile east of the Glebe Point Bridge, Horn Harbor is a small, protected hurricane hole that will allow boats with 5-foot drafts or less to pass over the entrance bar. To enter, watch the fish stakes and run parallel to the shore. Find the entrance by turning westerly when crossing the bar, and then turn abruptly north again as you enter. In daylight, this procedure is self-evident, but do not try it at night. Once inside, you will find a delightful, scenic anchorage with good holding.

Barrett Creek, off the Great Wicomico

Anchorage: You can anchor in Barrett Creek, off the southern shore of the Great Wicomico, and enjoy views of lovely houses dotting the bluffs on the shore. You will need to feel your way into the entrance; shoals border the channel. Depths here are in the 9- to 10-foot range.

Balls Creek, off the Great Wicomico

Anchorage: If you can fit under the 55-foot bridge at Glebe Point, you can anchor in Balls Creek, off the southern shore immediately past the bridge. Avoid the oyster bed stakes at the entrance. Giving the points of land a wide berth, you'll find 10-foot depths gently tapering to 5- to 6-foot depths where the creek splits a mile upstream. This anchorage is quiet and well protected with high treed bluffs on both sides.

Towles Creek, South of the Great Wicomico

NAVIGATION: Use Chart 12235 Leave day beacon "2MC" to starboard and head towards the north west. Follow the channel and you will see nothing less than 7 feet at mean low water.

Dockage: Family owned, built and managed, Ingram Bay Marina has transient berths for vessels up to 65 feet. Billy and Mary Pipkin will go out of their way to accommodate you. Billy is a very experienced Chesapeake Bay Fishing guide. You might want to lay-over for a day and learn a few fishing tips on a day charter with Captain Billy.

Mill Creek, South of the Great Wicomico

Mill Creek is south of Ingram Bay (at the mouth of the Great Wicomico River), almost opposite Cockrell Creek. One reason to visit Mill Creek is the Jaycey Vineyard at 619 Train Lane in Wicomico Church (804-580-4053). The winary and restaurant can be accessed by dinghy from the north side of Mill Creek.

Anchorage: This secluded creek is a fine anchorage in any weather, with wooded shores and 9- to 12-foot depths. Make the entrance from the Great Wicomico River Light using a course of 254 degrees magnetic to flashing red "2MC." After rounding this marker, proceed to green daybeacon "3," and, once past it, turn to port. As you approach green daybeacon "3," do not confuse the markers off to starboard, which are marking Towles Creek. After turning at green daybeacon "3," proceed southwest toward red daybeacon "4," making sure to give it a wide berth to avoid shoaling. At this point, turn to starboard, and proceed past green daybeacon "5" into several anchorages. It is easy to become confused when approaching this creek from the river. Sort it all out beforehand, especially if you are relying on radar, and follow the chart and depth sounder carefully on the approach. The markers may be difficult to see in choppy conditions. Inside, Mill Creek will take you back to the way most of the Bay once was.

Dividing Creek, South of the Great Wicomico

Anchorage: Shoals from both the Great Wicomico River and Fleets Bay separate this creek in the middle of the Northern Neck. Give all points and shoals a particularly wide berth here. Dividing Creek is a very nice, easy to enter and well-marked body of water, with 12-foot minimum depths at its entrance and many anchorages throughout its length. The cove to the north off the town of Ditchley has 8-foot depths almost to the shore. It is open to the southeast, but a shoal at the point does help to limit chop. Shoals above the last daybeacon (red daybeacon "10") are unmarked, so use the depth sounder to feel your way upstream. The beautiful sandy shoreline along Hughlett Point at the entrance to the creek (north side) is part of a 200-acre nature preserve. You can dinghy over to swim or picnic, but fires and fishing are prohibited.

FLEETS BAY, ABOVE THE RAPPAHANNOCK

For southbound vessels, Fleets Bay is the entrance to the last four creeks on the Northern Neck: Indian (the most popular, prettiest and easiest to enter), Dymer, Tabbs and Antipoison. All but Tabbs have depths of at least 10 feet at their entrances and beyond.

Indian Creek, off Fleets Bay

NAVIGATION: Use Chart 12235. Indian Creek is easy to enter, with depths of 12 to 18 feet, and many consider it the

Looking southeast over Indian Creek. (Not to be used for navigation.) Photo courtesy of Kucera/Deagle.

Fleets Bay, Windmill Point, VA

	Phone	Largest Vessel Accommodated	VHF Channel Monitored	Transient Berths / Total Berths	Approach / Dockside Depth (reported)	Floating Docks	Gas / Diesel	Groceries, Ice, Marine Supplies, Snacks	Repairs: Hull, Engine, Propeller	Lift (tonnage), Crane, Rail	Min/Max Amps	Laundry, Pool, Showers, Courtesy Car	Pump-Out Station	Nearby: Grocery Store, Motel, Restaurant
		Dockage					Supplies		Services					
FLEETS BAY														
1. Chesapeake Boat Basin (Internet Access) (Wireless Internet Access)	804-435-3110	60	16/09	20/70	12/10	F	GD	GIMS	HEP	L10	30/50	PSC	P	GMR
WINDMILL POINT														
2. Windmill Point Marina (Internet Access) (Wireless Internet Access)	804-436-1818	100	16/72	40/96	5.5/6	F	GD	GIMS	-	-	30/50	LPS	P	GR

Corresponding chart(s) not to be used for navigation. Internet Access Wireless Internet Access Waterway Guide Cruising Club Partner

See www.WaterwayGuide.com for current rates, fuel prices, web site addresses, and other up-to-the-minute information.

prettiest creek on the Northern Neck. Watch for stakes and pot floats in the channel.

Dockage: Indian Creek Yacht Club, located on a cove on the north shore, is a private member club. Chesapeake Boat Basin at Kilmarnock Wharf upstream welcomes cruising boaters and has a well-stocked ship's store that also sells charts. They also have new floating docks and a pool. It is only a mile and a half up the road to the town of Kilmarnock, a popular retirement community with a grocery store, laundry facilities, post office, banking, a liquor store and several nice restaurants.

Anchorage: By following the chart carefully, you can find several good anchorages on Indian Creek. On the north side near the entrance, Henrys Creek offers good protection in all but southeasterly winds. Farther upstream on the south shore, Pitmans Cove has 9- to 14-foot depths, although pot floats may be across the channel entrance and along the banks. The very soft mud and accumulations of slowly decaying leaves can make holding in Pitmans Cove poor. Back down on your anchor to ensure that you get a good set. This cove, scenic and quiet, is slowly losing some of its charm as a result of development.

Kilmarnock, VA. Photo courtesy of Mike Kucera.

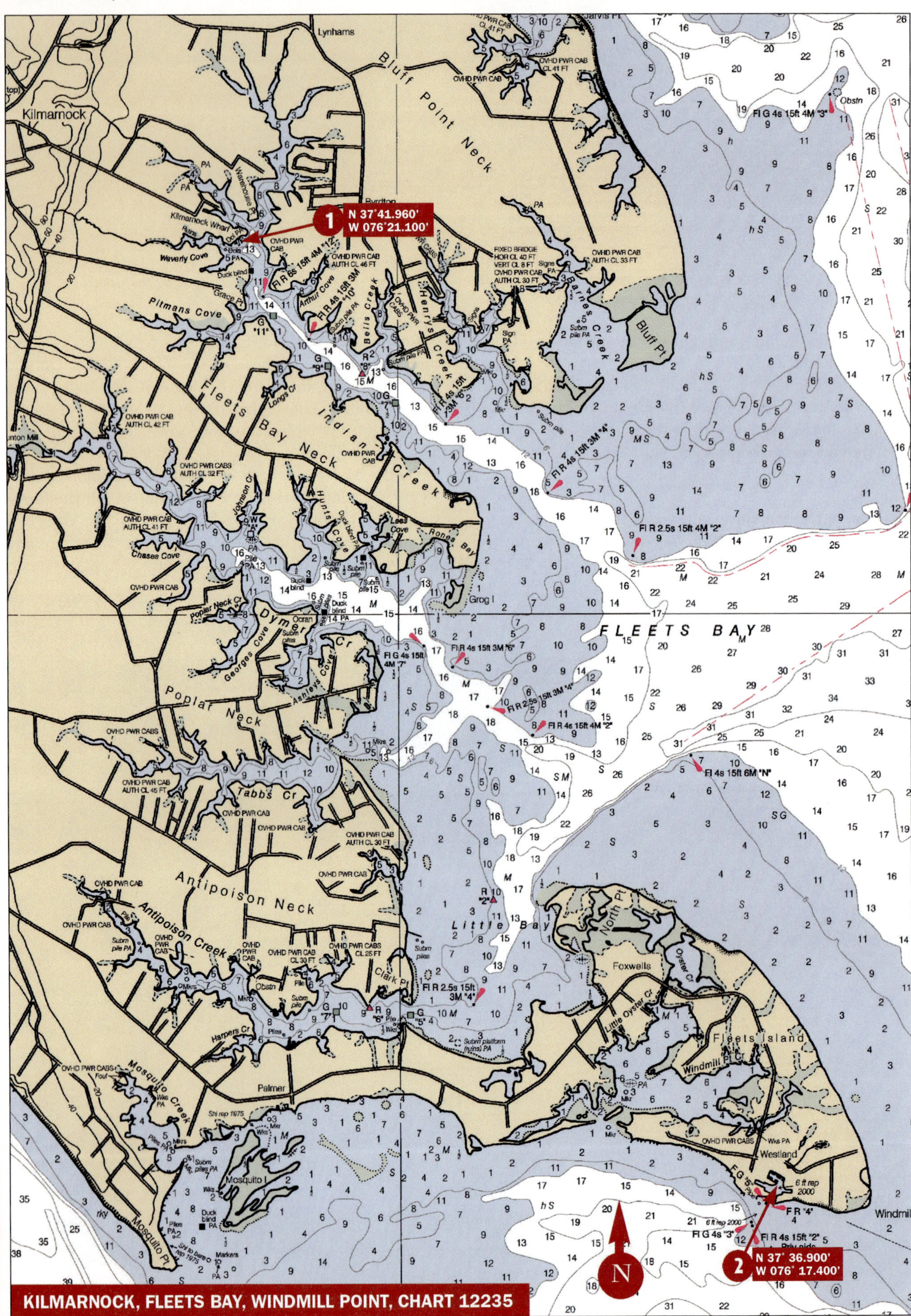

KILMARNOCK, FLEETS BAY, WINDMILL POINT, CHART 12235

Chesapeake Bay
Windmill Point Marina
Rappahannock River
Windmill Point

Looking southeast over Indian Creek. (Not to be used for navigation.) Cloud 9 Photography Deagle/Kucera

GOIN' ASHORE: **KILMARNOCK, VA**

Kilmarnock is a small town where you'll find big things going on! From dining to shopping to just enjoying a walk down Main Street you'll be transported to a relaxing place and time.

First, you'll dock at what locals call the "Kilmarnock Wharf" at the Chesapeake Boat Basin, where steamboats landed in the 19th and early 20th centuries when they were the mode of transportation for humans and commerce alike. There is still a grain elevator that collects corn, wheat and soybeans from the area's farmers. Arrive during one of these harvests and you'll see trucks of all sizes lined up to weigh in their bounty. Walk, hop a bike or catch a lift on Chesapeake Boat Basin's courtesy van the short 1 and ½ miles into charming Kilmarnock. Or, on Fridays and Saturdays from May to October, grab the Triangle Trolley and head into town for dining, shopping or just strolling the quaint small town. The trolley runs a one-hour round trip through Kilmarnock and on to the towns of Irvington and White Stone. It's an easy way to stock up on provisions too with large retailers, grocery stores, pharmacies and hardware along the way.

Often called the "New York of the Northern Neck" during the early 20th century, Kilmarnock remains the commercial hub of the lower Northern Neck. Where better to restock, refuel and relax?

History: First settled in the mid 1600s, Kilmarnock was originally known as "The Crossroads". The town probably had its beginnings at the intersection of Indian paths, which later became the locations of Main Street and East Church Street. It was here in the early 1700's that William Steptoe began to operate a storehouse and ordinary so that the crossroads came to be called "Steptoe's Ordinary". There's a restaurant at this location today. In 1764, Robert Gilmour, an agent for a mercantile firm based in Glasgow, Scotland, is thought to have been involved in giving the name of "Kilmarnock" to the crossroads location using the name of Kilmarnock, Scotland, where he apparently also owned land. The earliest known record referenced to "Kilmarnock, Virginia," can be found in a deed recorded in 1778. It was incorporated as the "Town of Kilmarnock" by an act of the Virginia General Assembly in 1930.

Kilmarnock has weathered three major fires—in 1909, 1912 and 1952— that could have devastated a lesser community. In 1909, the first fire started in the kitchen of the town's Eubank Hotel, spread to the livery stable and then onto a store on Main Street. It eventually burned an area north of Waverly Avenue and Church Street. The hotel, store and stable were rebuilt from brick instead of wood. Today's Palmer Building on E. Church Street is the rebuilt Eubank Hotel. On July 6, 1915, the second major fire started in a bowling alley on Main Street on the northern edge of town, burning both sides of the street until it reached brick buildings at E. Church Street. Upon rebuilding, merchants used fire-retardant materials with brick and concrete block construction; however, they had common attics with no firewall between them. This would prove costly on March 17, 1952, when the St. Patrick's Day fire began in a large, four-story building. High winds prevailed and fire swept Main Street. After each fire, the buildings were rebuilt and life continued on.

Points of Interest: The Kilmarnock Museum (76 N. Main St., 804-436-9100) houses a collection of artifacts from the town's history, including items from the 1952 fire, along with memorabilia from Kilmarnock's sister city, Kilmarnock, Scotland. Stop by for a glimpse of Kilmarnock then and now. Want to explore a little further afield? Visit Historic Christ Church (804-438-6855, www.christchurch1735.org) or the Irvington Steamboat Era Museum (804-438-6888, www.steamboateramuseum.org) aboard the Triangle Trolley. If Fido is on board stop at Scottie Yard, Kilmarnock's dog park, so everyone can stretch their sea legs. The park has separate fenced areas for small and large dogs. It is also on the trolley route and is located across from the post office.

Special Events: Come in June for the annual Wine Festival (see www.lancasterva.com) featuring wineries from the Chesapeake Bay Wine Trail (www.chesapeakebaywinetrail.com). The Kilmarnock Volunteer Fire Department's annual carnival starts the last Thursday of July and runs through the first week of August. You pass the carnival grounds as you proceed up Waverly Avenue towards Kilmarnock. The carnival has been the department's major fundraiser since 1935 and is a family tradition for nine nights every summer.

Shopping: Just a mile and a half from the Kilmarnock Wharf is everything you'll need! Main Street is pedestrian friendly with wide sidewalks, open storefronts and something charming for everyone. You can visit art galleries, clothing stores, jewelers, and antiques and home decorating centers. There is even an ATM if you need more cash for shopping! From wine and spirits stores to general groceries, you can get your pantry filled. There is a Food Lion (804-435-1163) on Main Street (Lancaster Square Shopping Center) and a Tri-Star Grocery store (804-435-3800), located at 81 Irvington Road. Northern Neck Ace Hardware is also in Kilmarnock (96 School St., 804-435-1519), as is a Wal-Mart and two large drugstores.

For those who are more interested in arts and antiques, there are three "must dos" in the downtown area: the Rappahannock Art League Studio, the Kilmarnock Antique Gallery and Rappahannock Hang-Ups Gallery.

Restaurants: Over 20 restaurants have something for every palate. There are take out and eat-in options from gourmet to down home cooking. A few examples: Town Bistro (62 Irvington Road, 804-435-0070) offers the quintessential bistro experience, while the Thai Pot (36 N. Main St., 804-435-8424) has authentic thai cuisine. Savannah Joe's BBQ (55 Irvington Road, 804-435-6000) offers hickory-smoked barbecue and a variety of sauces to suit all tastes. They also have live entertainment every Friday on the deck from spring through fall. A specialty and gourmet store with foods "to be eaten in or carried away," Carried Away Cuisine, is located at 10 North Main Street (804-435-9191). Be sure to ask about their signature "Boat Bag" filled with gourmet packaged goods. If you are lucky, you will be in town when Specials Wine Sellers (804-436-WINE) at 52 South Main St. hosts one of their popular wine tastings.

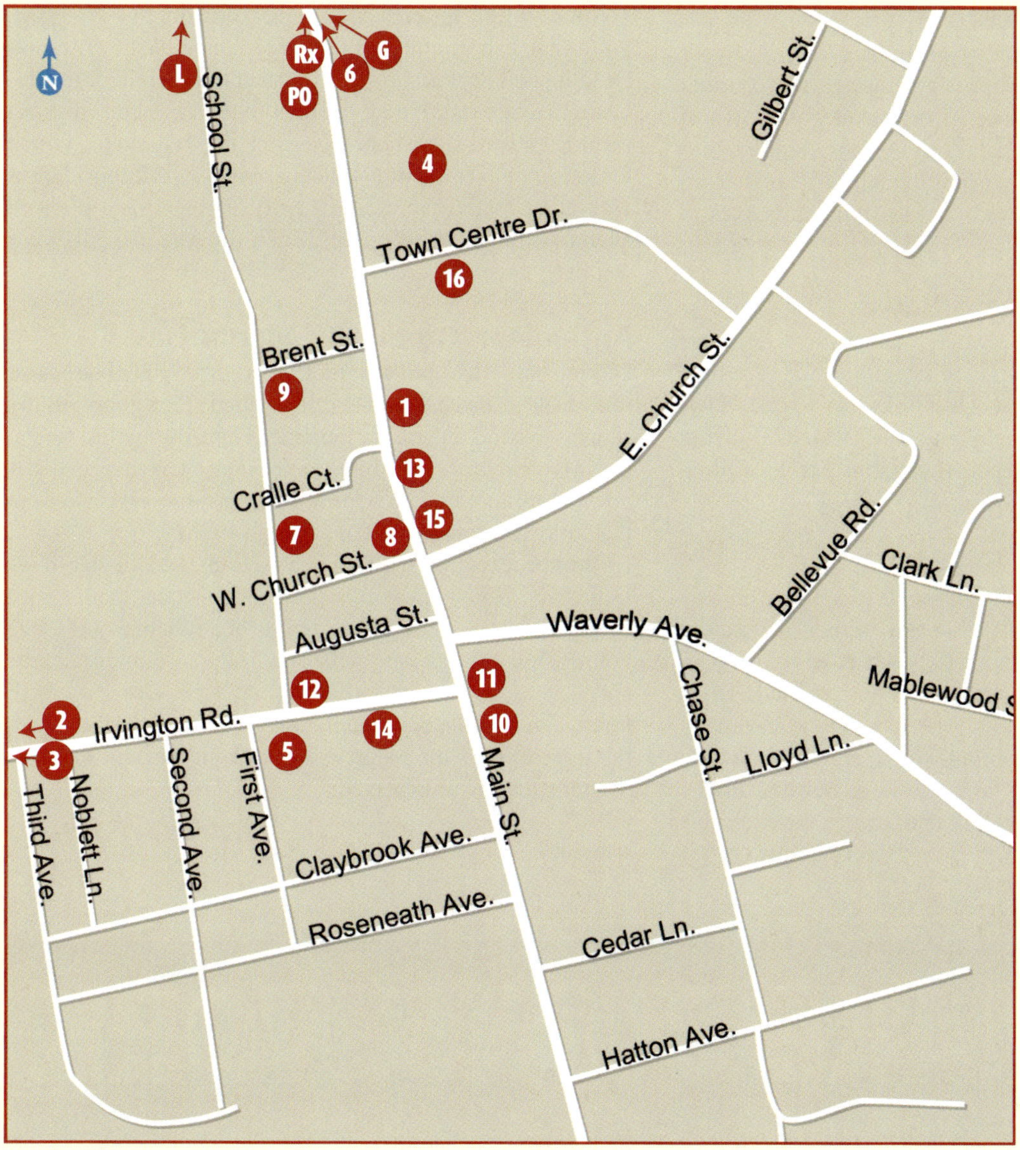

POINTS OF INTEREST

1 Kilmarnock Museum
2 Historic Christ Church
3 Steamboat Era Museum
4 Scottie Yard

SHOPPING

5 Tri-Star Supermarket
6 Wal-Mart
7 Northern Neck Hardware
8 Rappahannock Art League Studio
9 Kilmarnock Antique Gallery
10 Rappahannock Hang-Ups Gallery
11 Specials

DINING

11 Specials Wine Seller
12 Town Bistro
13 Thai Pot
14 Savannah Joe's Bar-B-Que
15 Carried Away Cuisine
16 River Lanes & Grill (Bowling)

L LIBRARY

PO POST OFFICE

Rx PHARMACY

G GROCERY

Reference the marina listing tables to see all the marinas in the area.

Dymer Creek, off Fleets Bay

Anchorage: Every bit as pretty as Indian Creek, Dymer Creek has good depths far upriver, although the channel is unmarked past the entrance. Grog Island, just north of flashing green "7," once sizable, has almost eroded into the creek and bay, with only marsh remaining. Further up the creek there are many lovely homes and cozy coves to duck into.

Tabbs Creek, off Fleets Bay

Anchorage: Uncharted, privately maintained entrance markers lead into Tabbs Creek, a beautiful hurricane hole with 9- to 10-foot depths just south of Dymer Creek. However, the entrance bar is tricky and blocks boats drawing more than 2 feet. Cruisers report that Tabbs Creek is filling in again, despite regular dredging.

Little Bay, off Fleets Bay

Little Bay is a stunning anchorage and, except on holiday weekends, is largely deserted. While day trippers do use the beach on weekends in season, the beach is yours early in the morning and in the evening and spring and fall. There is lovely beach here with shark's teeth to be found. A dinghy ride around to the north side brings you to more white sandy beaches, deserted except on rare occasions. Further dinghy explorations into the marshes will take you to the back side of the lovely beach on the north face of Fleet's Island.

Anchorage: Enter passing day beacon "N" to port. Watch for fish pounds on the eastern side of the entrance. Head for red daybeacon "2" in Little Bay, keeping it to starboard. Private stakes mark a shoal to the east. You can start turning toward the anchorage after the last stake. Watch for crab pots! You can anchor in about 7 to 9 foot depths with good holding in close to North Point. It is a pleasant anchorage on summer nights when the forecast calls for a southerly breeze and clear skies.

Antipoison Creek, off Fleets Bay

Legend says that Indians took mud from the bottom of this creek to make a poultice that cured Capt. John Smith's stingray wound suffered at Stingray Point during his Chesapeake Bay exploration in 1608. Homes and a few small fisheries now dot Antipoison Creek, only a stone's throw overland from the northern shore of the Rappahannock River.

Anchorage: Enter through a well-marked dogleg from Little Bay. You can anchor in about 9-foot depths with good holding in a cove three-tenths of a mile beyond Clark Point, while other spots farther up carry 7- to 8-foot depths and have good protection. Little Bay itself, close to North Point, can be a pleasant anchorage on summer nights when the forecast calls for a steady breeze from the south and no thunderstorms are expected.

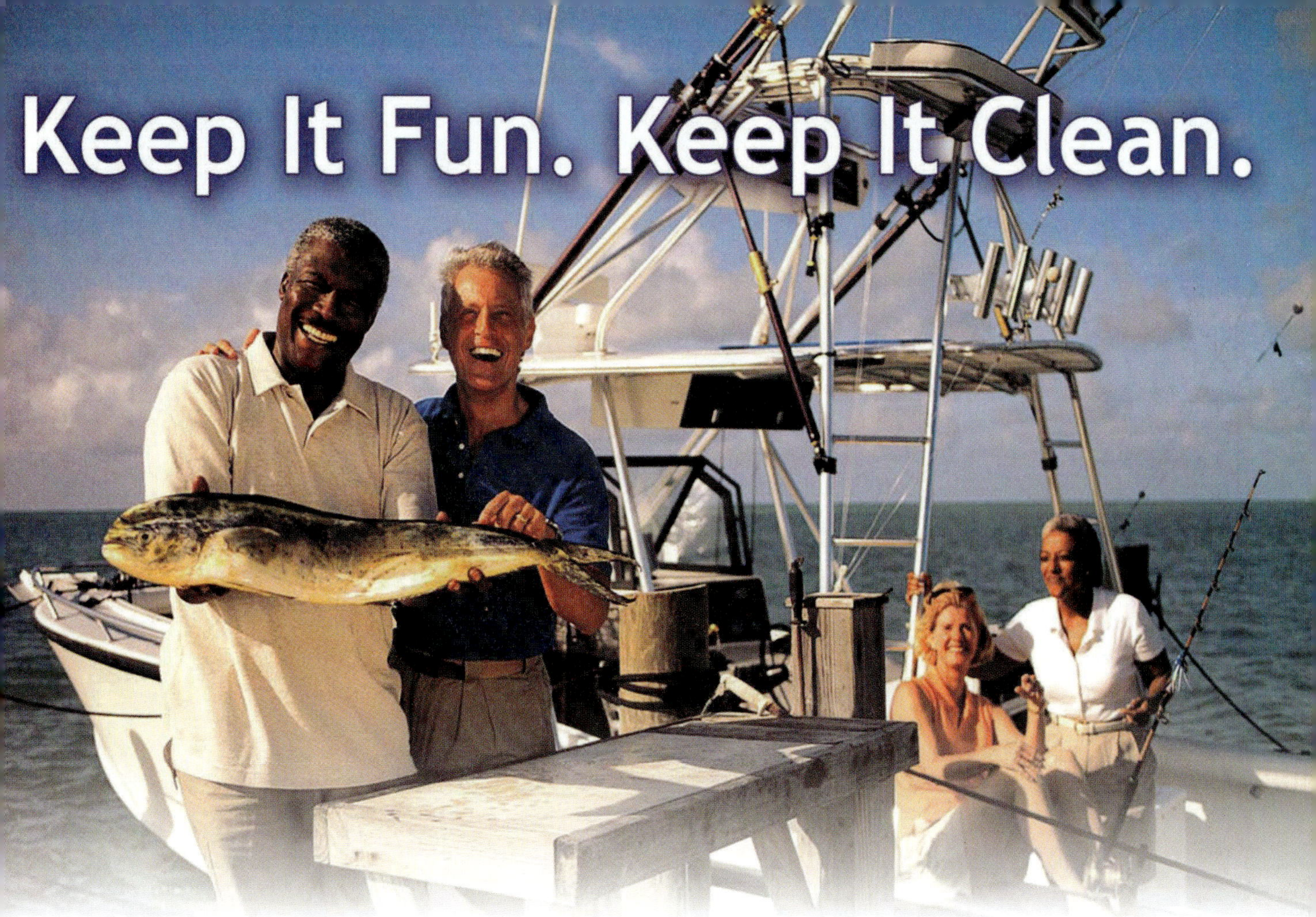

Keep It Fun. Keep It Clean.

Raw and improperly treated vessel sewage discharged into our waterways poses a potential threat to public health and the environment. Prevent the discharge of sewage into our waters – use pump-out and dump station facilities.

For a list of marine sewage pump-out stations in Virginia please visit the Virginia Department of Health Marina Program website at:
www.vdh.virginia.gov/EnvironmentalHealth/ONSITE/MARINA/CVA.htm

To report improperly working sewage pump-out stations or for information on Boating Infrastructure Grant facilities in Virginia, please call **(804) 864-7468.**

Protecting You and Your Environment
www.vdh.virginia.gov

Virginia Department of Health
109 Governor Street, Fifth Floor Richmond, Virginia 23219

KEEP OUR WATER CLEAN– USE PUMPOUTS

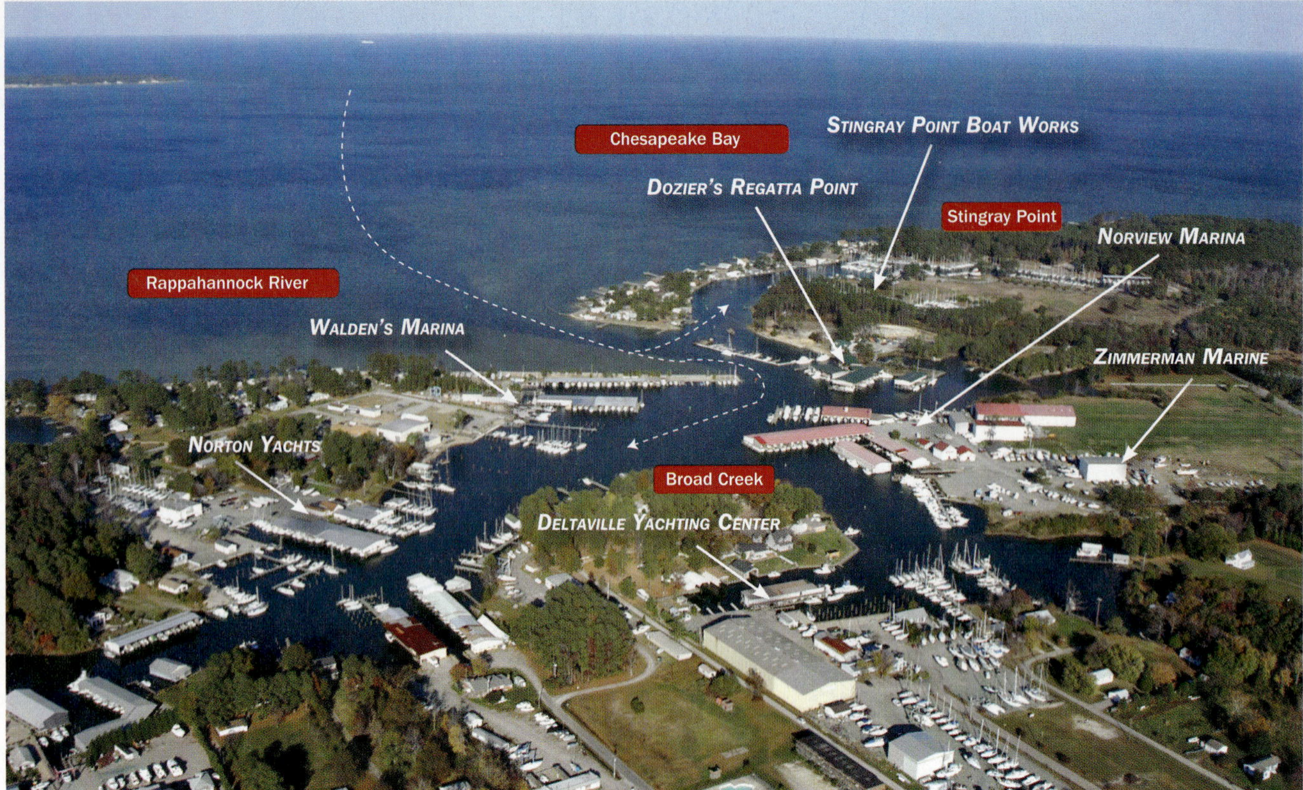

Looking east-northeast over Deltaville's marina-lined Broad Creek. (Not to be used for navigation.) Waterway Guide Photography.

RAPPAHANNOCK RIVER

The Rappahannock River, more than three miles wide at the mouth, is one of Chesapeake Bay's great historic rivers. Many experienced cruisers say that the Rappahannock has the best cruising on the Bay, and it is certainly easy to spend a full week exploring the area.

NAVIGATION: Use Charts 12235 and 12237. If your vessel draws less than 5 feet, you can shortcut behind Windmill Point Light to the Rappahannock River as you go south down the Bay, although this involves some amount of risk. If you yield to this temptation, be careful, and watch for numerous crab pot floats. No one should shortcut this point when seas have built up because heavy waves on the shoal can bottom out even shallow-draft boats.

The Rappahannock is deep and wide in its lower 16 miles to Urbanna, VA, pleasant for 40 miles to Tappahannock and navigable about 93 miles up to Fredericksburg. The Robert O. Norris Bridge (110-foot vertical clearance) crosses the Rappahannock between Deltaville and Urbanna. It carries State Route 3 and is known locally as the White Stone Bridge or Rappahannock River Bridge. A fixed bridge with a 50-foot vertical clearance crosses the river at Tappahannock. Commercial tows regularly make the journey all the way to Fredericksburg.

Windmill Point, off the Rappahannock River

Dockage: The marked channel into the basin of Windmill Point Marina is a half-mile west of the geographical Windmill Point. There are 96 slips, a pool, (Charlie's Tiki Bar has closed but a new tiki bar and restaurant was slated to open at press time in 2012) and a newly dredged entrance channel with 5.5-foot depths.

DELTAVILLE, VA

A day's run midway between Solomons, MD and Norfolk, VA, Deltaville, close by the ICW route, is a convenient stopover for boats heading north or south and a popular base from which to explore the lower Bay. Deltaville has blossomed into a major dockage, service and yacht sales destination for Bay cruisers. It is a little village, but it is all about boats here. You can find any supply or service your craft may require among the 17 marinas and marine-related businesses in town. Bicycles will be very useful here for running errands or exploring the side roads for fun. Boats outnumber residents by nearly four to one (800 residents to 3,000 boats), and transient boats from around the world swell the number even more.

Broad Creek, the North Entrance to Deltaville on the South Shore of the Rappahannock River

NAVIGATION: Use Chart 12235. **Use Hampton Roads tide tables. For Broad Creek high tide, add 1 hour 31 minutes; for low tide add 1 hour 59 minutes.** In 2010, the Broad Creek channel into Deltaville was dredged to depths of 8-foot-plus with a width of over 100 feet. The water in this area is usually clear and the bottom easy to see. Just one-half mile up the Rappahannock from Stingray Point, the marked entrance channel from flashing green "1" to green

DELTAVILLE
MARITIME MUSEUM
THE BOATING CAPITAL OF THE CHESAPEAKE
Deltaville, Va.
37° 33' 17" N / 76° 20' 13" W
Discover the simple life that Deltaville, Virginia has to offer. Experience quaint shops, tasty restaurants, and living Americana. Deltaville is all about seafood, art festivals, parades, crab races, and old-timer baseball games. Deltaville offers cruisers a choice of excellent marinas and nationally recognized boatyards.
Add Deltaville to your cruising plans and visit a place where life is still simple and traffic lights don't exist.
Chesapeake Bay
Visit these fine marinas and boat yards
Deltaville Boatyard
deltavilleboatyard.com
Norton Yachts
nortonyachts.com
Norview Marina
norviewmarina.com
Regatta Point
doziermarine.com
Zimmerman Marine
zimmermanmarine.com

daybeacon "5" is straight in from the Rappahannock, with red daybeacons marking the western edge. At flashing red buoy "6," the channel turns a bit to port towards the first of many marinas and service facilities.

Inside, you share the water with both sail and power yachts, including weekend cruisers from throughout Virginia and veteran cruisers from around the country. You are also likely to see foreign-flagged vessels in this popular port. (You can also reach Deltaville from the south side of the Deltaville peninsula, via the Piankatank River to Jackson Creek or Fishing Bay.)

Dockage: Broad Creek, on the Rappahannock River side of Deltaville, is lined with marinas with all manner of services. This single creek has 12 marinas including 7 service yards with haul-out services.

Stingray Point Marina and Stingray Point Boat Works are first to port past White Point. Turn at nun red "6A" to port and follow the markers back. Neither of these offer transient slips, but Stingray Point Boat Works is a full-service yard with a 25-ton lift for boats up to 50 feet. Next to port is Dozier's Regatta Point Yachting Center, a family-run facility at the mouth of the creek that has concrete floating transient docks, fixed covered dockage, a pool and courtesy cars and bikes. You can relax on the Southern-style front porch of the clubhouse with vistas of the Rappahannock. Drinking water is provided by a reverse osmosis system for guests. Regatta Point is the home of Dozier Media Group/*Waterway Guide* and *Skipper Bob* Publications corporate office. (Production and editorial offices are based in town.) The other Dozier marina, Port Urbanna, is 14 miles upriver in Urbanna.

Immediately past Regatta Point, Norview Marina offers fuel and has transient slips. Norview has both fixed covered dockage and floating transient slip, and can handle vessels up to 80 feet. Norview Marina also has a pool, a recreational area and a covered picnic area. Zimmerman Marine, builder of the Zimmerman 36, 38, and 46 operates the hauling (80-ton lift) and service operation at Norview. In addition to hauling, Zimmermans can provide fiberglass and engine service, as well as marine painting, and commissioning and layup of vessels. Their original yard remains on Mobjack Bay.

Deltaville Yachting Center has 75 covered and open slips with 6- to 8-foot depths alongside, a fully enclosed Hi-Dri Boatel and a large gravel boatyard, a private pool and clean restrooms, all within one mile of the Bay. Deltaville Yachting Center's a full-service repair yard is known for high customer service ratings and quality service. It is within easy walking distance to shopping and restaurants, and they will even supply town maps.

Welcome to Deltaville, Virginia

Country Charm • City Convenience

The Boating Capital of the Chesapeake Bay lies halfway between Norfolk and Solomons Island.
Visit us online at DeltavilleVA.com

Coastal Marine, J&M Marina and Chesapeake Cove Marina have limited transient dockage on a first-come, first-served basis.

Back at the mouth of the creek, across from Regatta Point, is Walden's Marina. In addition to transient dockage, fuel and a full-service boatyard, Walden's boast a huge parts inventory. If they don't have a part in stock, they can usually get it the next day.

Third generation family-run Norton Yacht Sales, on the western branch of Broad Creek, offers a full-service yard, power and sailboat sales and charters and some transient space. Norton's has been in operation since 1945 and are known for their prompt and friendly service. It is only a short walk from here to downtown Deltaville. Rivertime Marina & Boatyard is under new management and is located just past Norton's. They have some transient space and offer boat repairs.

Anchorage: There is limited anchorage space in Broad Creek, but there is space to anchor in Jackson Creek, Deltaville's southern approach.

GOIN' ASHORE: **DELTAVILLE, VA**

Be warned: Deltaville is the kind of place where people arrive by boat and suddenly find they have no good reason to leave. Over the years, it has evolved from a working waterman's town into a recognized yachting center, yet it still retains its down-to-earth feel. It has a great deal to offer those who join the community and, indeed, volunteers from every walk of life join together to support activities and operations in the unincorporated town. Young and not-so-young, rich and not-so-rich all blend together in this unique and congenial community.

The numerous creeks that give this peninsula between the Rappahannock and Piankatank rivers its delta-like topography provide havens for boats far greater in number than the year-round population. Boatyards and marinas abound, and it would be a fussy skipper indeed who couldn't find exactly the right place to keep, maintain or live aboard a boat.

The town itself, with no well-defined downtown, consists of an eclectic collection of structures strung out along either side of General Puller Highway (state Route 33) for a distance of less than two miles, just before it fades out at Stingray Point—named for Colonial explorer Capt. John Smith's near-death encounter. Signs on a large proportion of those buildings advertise businesses related to boating. Many shops and restaurants are a mile or two from the marinas, but accessible with either the bicycles or courtesy cars that several marinas offer.

Dockage and service prices in Deltaville are reasonable, and you will find most everything that is available in Annapolis and Solomons is also here in a friendly, small-town atmosphere. Most marine dealers can provide overnight delivery for parts not on their shelves, and many local businesses provide

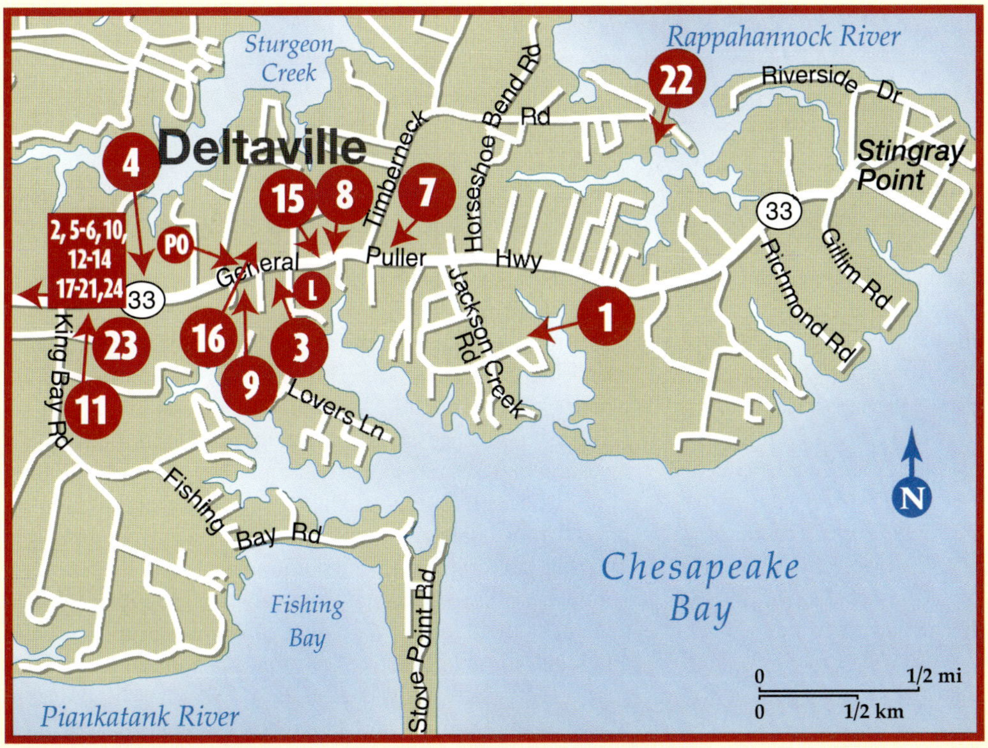

Reference the marina listing tables to see all the marinas in the area.

POINTS OF INTEREST

1 Deltaville Maritime Museum
2 Waterway Guide

SHOPPING

3 Hurd's True Value Hardware Store
4 West Marine
5 Deltaville Auto & Marine
6 Fish On Bait & Tackle
7 The Ship's Tailor
8 Ullman Sail Loft
9 Coastal Comfort
10 Nauti Nell's/Kaptain Krunch Lettering
11 Latitude's
12 Crabby Couple
13 Gone Coastal
14 Deltaville Market

DINING

15 Cafe by the Bay
16 Taylor's Restaurant
17 Doghouse Deli
18 Stan Strings
19 The Galley
20 Sunset Grill
21 J&W Seafood Market
22 Cocomos
23 Toby's

SERVICES

24 Olive For Yoga

PO POST OFFICE

L LIBRARY

Deltaville, Rappahannock River, VA

BROAD CREEK		Dockage					Supplies		Services					
		Largest Vessel Accommodated	VHF Channel Monitored	Transient Berths / Total Berths	Approach / Dockside Depth (reported)	Floating Docks	Gas / Diesel	Groceries, Ice, Marine Supplies, Snacks	Repairs: Hull, Engine, Propeller	Lift (tonnage), Crane, Rail	Min/Max Amps	Laundry, Pool, Showers, Courtesy Car	Pump-Out Station	Nearby: Grocery Store, Motel, Restaurant
1. Dozier's Regatta Point Yachting Center	**804-776-6711**	**120**	**16/72**	**30/110**	**8/7**	**F**	**-**	**IS**	**E**	**-**	**30/100**	**LPSC**	**P**	**GMR**
2. Walden's Marina	**804-776-9440**	**65**	**16**	**4/73**	**8/8**	**-**	**GD**	**IMS**	**HEP**	**L35**	**30/50**	**S**	**P**	**R**
3. Norton Yachts	**804-776-9211**	**55**	**16/68**	**8/65**	**6/6**	**-**	**GD**	**GIM**	**HE**	**L35, C**	**30/50**	**LSC**	**P**	**GMR**
4. Rivertime Marina & Boat Yard	804-776-7574	60	16/22	1/12	6/6	-	-	-	HEP	L30	30/30	S	-	GMR
5. Chesapeake Cove Marina	804-776-6855	55	16/68	3/40	5/5	-	GD	IM	HEP	L30, C10	30/50	LSC	P	MR
6. J & M Marina	804-776-9860	60	-	/63	6/6	-	-	IMS	HEP	L40, C, R	30/50	S	-	R
7. Coastal Marine	804-776-6585	-	-	-	6/	-	-	M	HEP	L50	-	-	-	GMR
8. Deltaville Yachting Center	**804-776-9898**	**50**	**16/72**	**4/75**	**8/6**	**-**	**G**	**IMS**	**HEP**	**L50**	**30/50**	**PS**	**P**	**MR**
9. Zimmerman Marine in Deltaville	**804-776-0367**	**110**	**68**	**4/6**	**8/6**	**F**	**GD**	**M**	**HEP**	**L80**	**30/50**	**LS**	**P**	**MR**
10. Norview Marina	**804-776-6463**	**80**	**16/72**	**15/100**	**8/6.5**	**F**	**GD**	**GIMS**	**HEP**	**L80**	**30/100**	**LPS**	**P**	**MR**
11. Stingray Point Boat Works	**804-776-7070**	**50**	**-**	**-**	**6/6**	**-**	**GD**	**M**	**HEP**	**L25, C5**	**30/30**	**-**	**-**	**GMR**
12. Stingray Point Marina	804-776-7272	50	-	/235	7/7	F	-	I	HEP	L25, C5	30/30	LPS	P	GMR
FISHING BAY, JACKSON CREEK														
13. Deltaville Marina	**804-776-9812**	**110**	**16/69**	**10/80**	**9/10**	**-**	**GD**	**GIMS**	**HEP**	**L75, C15**	**30/50**	**LPSC**	**P**	**GMR**
14. Deltaville Boatyard	**804-776-8900**	**-**	**16/69**	**-**	**9/10**	**-**	**GD**	**GIMS**	**HEP**	**L75, C15**	**30/50**	**LPS**	**P**	**GMR**
15. Fishing Bay Yacht Club	804-776-9636	50	-	3/99	8/8	-	-	IS	-	-	30/30	PS	-	R
16. Ruark Marinas Inc.	804-776-9776	45	-	1/50	20/16	-	-	I	-	-	30/30	S	-	GR
17. Fishing Bay Harbor Marina	804-776-6800	200	16	10/130	18/18	F	GD	IMS	-	-	30/100	LPS	P	GMR
18. Chesapeake Boat Works	**804-776-8833**	**150**	**16**	**8/15**	**26/16**	**-**	**-**	**M**	**HEP**	**L50,C5,R300**	**30/50**	**LS**	**-**	**GMR**
19. Porpoise Cove Marina	804-854-8227	40	-	/21	6/5	-	-	I	-	-	30/30	LS	P	GR

Corresponding chart(s) not to be used for navigation. Internet Access Wireless Internet Access Waterway Guide Cruising Club Partner

See www.WaterwayGuide.com for current rates, fuel prices, web site addresses, and other up-to-the-minute information.

mechanical, refrigeration, electrical, sail, rigging, fiberglass and wood repair services. Locals will often go out of their way to provide quick turnaround service.

History: The John Smith incident aside, Deltaville has avoided mention in the history books, perhaps because it was known as Union, Unionville and finally Sandy Bottom until the early 1900s. That is when it formally changed its name to Delta, only to be notified by the U.S. Postal Service that that name was already taken by a town in the Virginia mountains, thus the addition of "ville." It has, in the past, laid claim to the title of Boatbuilding Capital of the Chesapeake, and indeed for over a century supplied watermen with wooden workboats of all types and sizes. As recently as the late 1970s, there were about 20 boatbuilders in the town, but sadly, it is now almost a lost art.

While little actual boatbuilding goes on today, the importance of boats to the local economy is evident. Some are owned and lived on by a mix of from-heres and come-heres (the ones who forgot to leave), but the vast majority belong to residents of the inland population belt connected by major highways. Even in summer, when the human population balloons, the place never seem crowded and retains the atmosphere of a well-kept secret.

Points of Interest: Perhaps because it has been centered around boats for so long, the community in Deltaville is tightly knit. It hosts a couple of baseball teams, a ballpark and a community center wherein its denizens gather to teach, learn, perform or just hobnob.

A product of all that socializing has become Deltaville's most absorbing attraction. The Deltaville Maritime Museum, which opened in 2001, presents the history of the region and its dependence on boatbuilding. Among its exhibits is a revealing exposé of the deadrise construction technique once used extensively in this part of the world for building workboats. Unfortunately, in July 2012 a devastating fire destroyed the main building and several outdoor exhibits of the museum. Some artifacts were salvaged and others were being replaced as soon as the day after the fire. A fund was set up to rebuild and hundreds of people pledged monetary and physical (labor) support. It was Family Boatbuilding Week at the museum when the fire occurred and all the boats were lost.

Luckily, the boat shop was not damaged, nor the boats at the dock, including the F.D. Crockett, a nine-log-bottom, 60-foot-long Chesapeake Bay "Buy Boat" built in the 1930s. In 2007, museum members constructed a replica of the sail/rowing boat that was brought over in pieces by the Jamestown settlers in 1607, the boat that Capt. John Smith was exploring the bay in when he received a near-fatal stingray wound at nearby Stingray Point. The boat makes appearances around the Bay and is used in an annual summer play at Stingray Point to commemorate Smith's encounter with the stingray. It survived the fire as well.

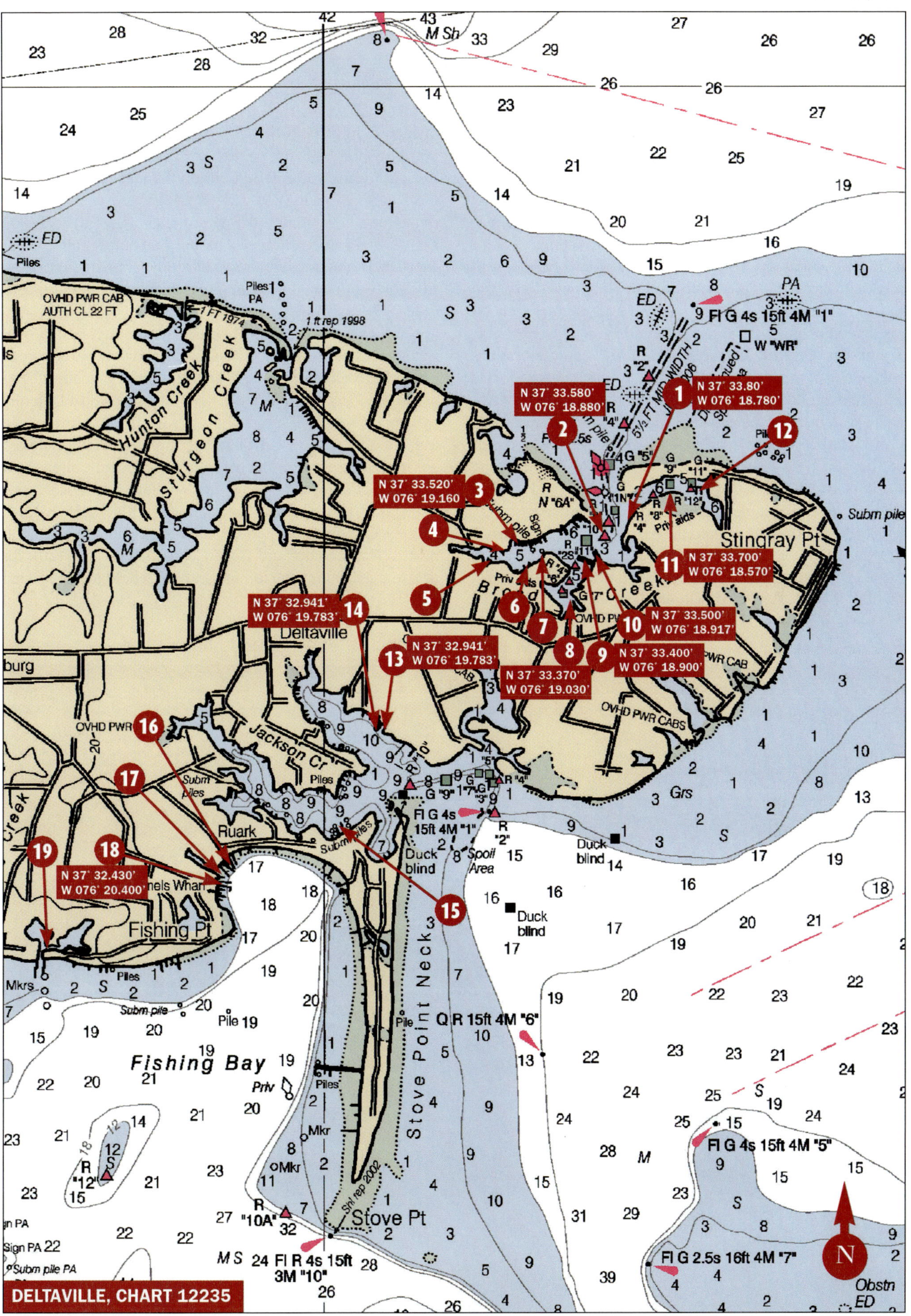
1
N 37° 33.80'
W 076° 18.780'
2
N 37° 33.580'
W 076° 18.880'
3
N 37° 33.520'
W 076° 19.160'
4
5
6
7
8
N 37° 33.370'
W 076° 19.030'
9
N 37° 33.400'
W 076° 18.900'
10
N 37° 33.500'
W 076° 18.917'
11
N 37° 33.700'
W 076° 18.570'
12
13
N 37° 32.941'
W 076° 19.783'
14
N 37° 32.941'
W 076° 19.783'
15
16
17
18
N 37° 32.430'
W 076° 20.400'
19
Hunton Creek
Sturgeon Creek
Deltaville
Jackson Cr
Broad Creek
Stingray Pt
Ruark
Fishing Pt
Fishing Bay
Stove Point Neck
Stove Pt
Fl G 4s 15ft 4M "1"
Q R 15ft 4M "6"
Fl G 4s 15ft 4M "5"
Fl G 2.5s 16ft 4M "7"
Fl R 4s 15ft 3M "10"
N
DELTAVILLE, CHART 12235

The Maritime Museum is surrounded by Holly Point Nature Park, featuring an educational nature walk, complete with bronze wildlife statues. The museum is a half-mile from Deltaville Marina on Jackson Creek Road, and just a bit farther from the marinas on Broad Creek. Opening hours and activity schedules for both museum and park are posted on the community Web site (www.deltavilleva.com), or you can call 804-776-7200.

For golfers, the closest golf course is Piankatank River Golf Club (804-776-6516), which is 9 miles from the marinas in Hartfield. See www.virginiagolf.com/piankatank.html for details. If you are more into yoga, Olive for Yoga is convenient (in the shopping center next to Doghouse Deli) and welcomes "drop ins." Call 804-832-0079 or visit on Facebook for schedules and other information.

Special Events: Deltaville's Heritage Day celebrations coincide with the July 4 weekend and feature parades for pets and children, crab races, live music, craft vendors, hometown parade and fireworks. Area bed and breakfasts and a small motel provide lodging. Other special events are held on the grounds of the Maritime Museum, including Family Boatbuilding week, held in July or August; the Holly Point Art and Seafood Festival, held in October; and the popular "haunted woods," which debuts the weeks preceding Halloween. "Grooving at the Museum" lawn concerts are held regularly throughout the summer. Bring a lawn chair or blanket, dinner and a cooler. A monthly farmers market is held on the museum grounds the fourth Saturday of each month.

Shopping: Hurd's True Value hardware and merchandise store (804-776-9241) is the closest thing to a "downtown" that Deltaville has. (Locals are fond of saying, "If Hurd's doesn't have it, you don't need it"). A short distance west of that is the new 15,000-square foot West Marine, which opened in July 2012 (804-776-7890). (There were two West Marines, one-half mile apart, for several years.) Deltaville Auto & Marine (804-776-9020) on the main road, and Fish On Bait and Tackle (804-776-0820), located behind Sunset Grill, may have some boating supplies as well. There are also several canvas shops, including The Ship's Tailor (804-776-7044) and an Ullman sail loft (804-776-6151). Coastal Comfort Mattress and Bedding sells boat mattresses and bedding (804-776-9099).

Nauti Nell's (804-776-9811) sells marine supplies on consignment as well as nautical books, gifts and jewelry. Be sure to go out the back door and discover the lot full of "goodies." You may score a wetsuit, dinghy oars or a boat stove! Boat Lettering by Kaptain Krunch is located here as well; he can provide gold leaf, hand lettering or vinyl lettering and on-site application.

There are several other gift and consignment shops and a couple of antiques stores. Shops include Latitude's (804-776-0272), described as "colorful with a touch of whimsy"; Crabby Couple (804-776-0075), a crab-themed gift shop next to Nauti Nell's; and Gone Coastal (804-763-9420), for new and consignment clothing and household items, located just past Sunset Grill.

DOZIER'S
REGATTA POINT
YACHTING CENTER
Deltaville, Virginia
All New Marina and Clubhouse
Waterway Guide Corporate Office
30 Transient Slips to 110'
7' Water Depth
Floating Docks
Courtesy Cars
First Marina on Broad Creek
Pool & Deck w/ Gazebo
Lounge w/ Satellite TV
Private Bathrooms
Meeting Facilities
Filtered Water System
Full Service Available
Free Wi-Fi at All Slips
Dozier Yacht Sales
We love pets – pets love us!
137 Neptune Lane
P.O. Box 1188
Deltaville, VA 23043
Phone: 804-776-8400
800-REGATTA
Fax: 804-776-0672
Email: info@DozierMarine.com
www.DozierMarine.com
Baltimore
Annapolis
Washington, D.C.
Maryland
Delaware
Maryland
Solomons
Virginia
Chesapeake Bay
Richmond
REGATTA POINT
Norfolk
Regatta Point is the favored choice for knowledgeable boaters & cruisers for rendezvous & meetings–MTOA, AGLCA, Monk 36, Nordic Tug, Power Squadron, Coast Guard Auxiliary, Yachts Clubs, Cruising Associations.
Chesapeake Bay's Port of Distinction

"Superb staff and facilities - value rates."

BoatU.S. Cooperating Marina

Virginia Clean Marina

Cruising Club Partner

DOZIER
YACHTING CENTERS
Visit Our Other Marina – Port Urbanna – in the Historic Town of Urbanna

Chesapeake Bay
Piankatank River
Deltaville Marina & Boatyard
Fishing Bay
Jackson Creek
Deltaville

Looking southeast over Jackson Creek and Deltaville. (Not to be used for navigation.) Cloud 9 Photography Deagle/Kucera

Looking east over Fishing Bay. (Not to be used for navigation.) Waterway Guide Photography.

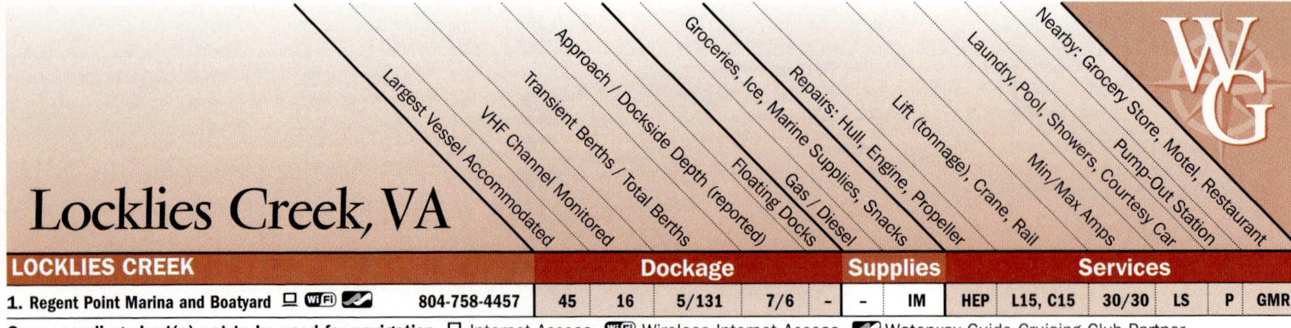

Locklies Creek, VA

LOCKLIES CREEK		Largest Vessel Accommodated	VHF Channel Monitored	Transient Berths / Total Berths	Approach / Dockside Depth (reported)	Floating Docks	Gas / Diesel	Groceries, Ice, Marine Supplies, Snacks	Repairs: Hull, Engine, Propeller	Lift (tonnage), Crane, Rail	Min/Max Amps	Laundry, Pool, Showers, Courtesy Car	Pump-Out Station	Nearby: Grocery Store, Motel, Restaurant
		Dockage					Supplies		Services					
1. Regent Point Marina and Boatyard ☐ WiFi ⛵	804-758-4457	45	16	5/131	7/6	-	-	IM	HEP	L15, C15	30/30	LS	P	GMR

Corresponding chart(s) not to be used for navigation. ☐ Internet Access WiFi Wireless Internet Access ⛵ Waterway Guide Cruising Club Partner

See www.WaterwayGuide.com for current rates, fuel prices, web site addresses, and other up-to-the-minute information.

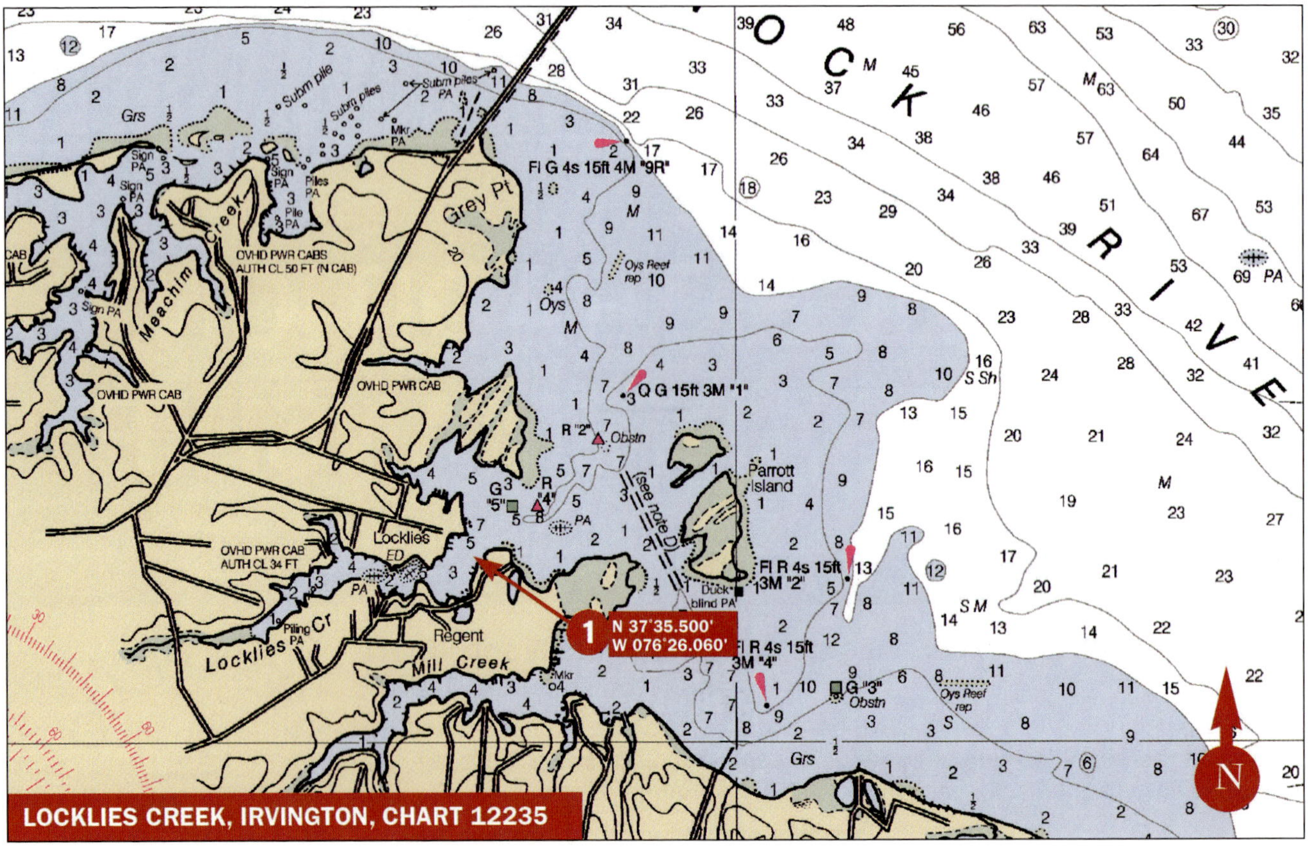

1 N 37°35.500' W 076°26.060'

LOCKLIES CREEK, IRVINGTON, CHART 12235

For reprovisioning and other supplies, Deltaville Market is biking distance from the marinas (three miles), as is a shopping center with a liquor store, an EVB (bank), pet store, and the *Waterway Guide* production office (804-776-8999). (Please feel free to stop by and say "hello"!)

Dining: A handful of eateries can be found on General Puller Highway. Most are within a mile or two of the marinas, which are, on the whole, helpful in providing transportation. Working west from the marinas, Café by the Bay (804-776-0303) is open for breakfast and lunch and prepares imaginative sandwiches and also retails sundry gourmet products and coffee. Taylor's Restaurant (804-776-9611), the town's original home-style restaurant, offers a full menu of seafood and favorite standbys for lunch and dinner. Doghouse Deli (804-776-7021) offers deli sandwiches and ice cream, and across the street, StanStrings (new in 2012) offers pizza, sandwiches and the like (804-776-7095). The Galley (16236 General Puller Highway, 804-776-6040) is a town gathering and eating spot. (Try the black and blue tuna steak sandwich.) Across the street is The Sunset Grill, a restaurant/bar (804-776-8803) with bands on weekends. For those who prefer to cook their own food, J & W Seafood (804-776-

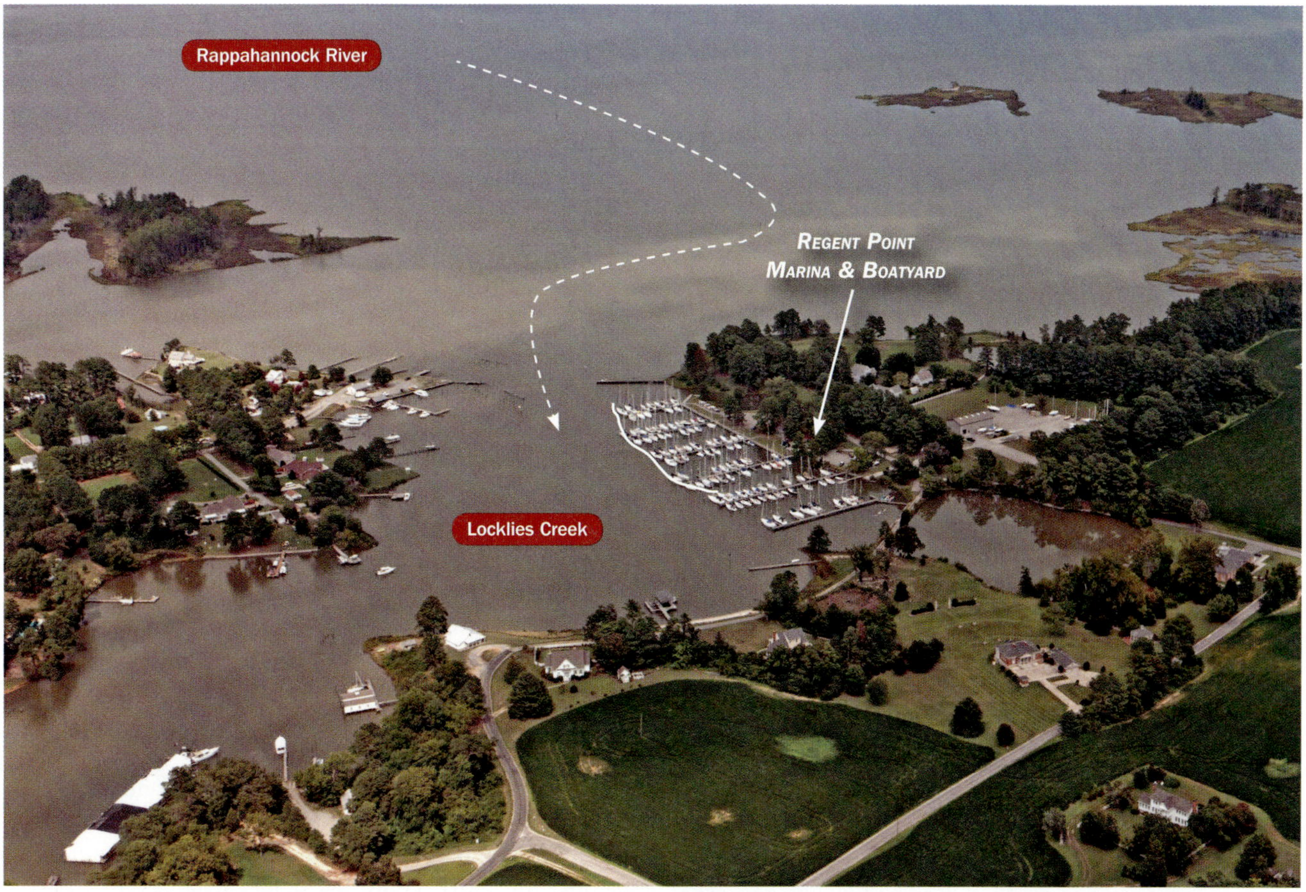

Looking northeast over Locklies Creek and the Rappahannock River. (Not to be used for navigation.) Cloud 9 Photography Deagle/Kucera

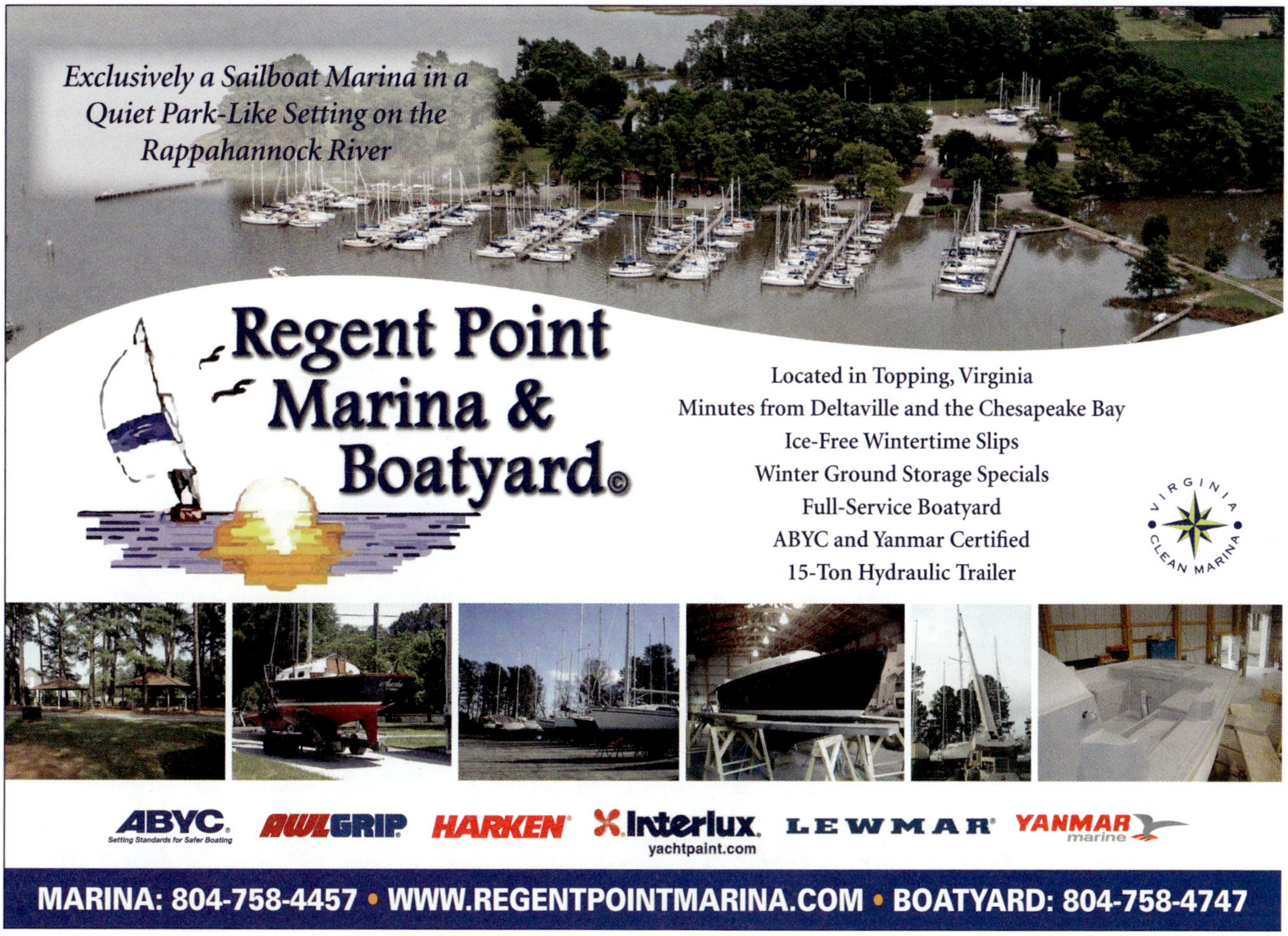

9740) sells a broad range of fresh seafood as well as fishing tackle and is located back up the street a bit.

Other restauarants in town include Cocomo's (1134 Timberneck Road, 804-776-9311), which presents a rather more hip dinner atmosphere on the shore of Broad Creek, and Toby's, at 220 Jack's Place, which offers several fine seafood and specialty selections (804-776-6913) and is frequented by the boating crowd.

ADDITIONAL RESOURCES

- **DELTAVILLE COMMUNITY ASSOCIATION:** www.deltavilleva.com

NEARBY MEDICAL FACILITIES

Riverside Fishing Bay Family Practice: 16681 General Puller Highway, Deltaville, VA 23043 804-776-8000 (1 mile)

Rappahannock General Hospital: 101 Harris Road, Kilmarnock, VA 22842, 804-435-8000, 800-296-8009 www.rgh-hospital.com (23 miles north)

Riverside Walter Reed Hospital: 7519 Hospital Drive, Gloucester, VA 23061, 804-693-8800 (23 miles south)

Jackson Creek, the South Entrance to Deltaville, on the North Shore of the Piankatank River

Jackson Creek is one of the southern entrances to Deltaville on the Piankatank River's north shore. You can also reach Deltaville from Fishing Bay, west around Stove Point Neck. The northern entrance to Deltaville is Broad Creek, leading in from the Rappahannock River.

NAVIGATION: Use Chart 12235. Mind the markers carefully as you approach Jackson Creek's entrance. The channel was dredged to 7 feet and widened significantly in late 2010. While well marked, it runs frighteningly close to shore before making a sharp turn to port. From there, follow the newly marked channel around to the west. Once you are inside, the creek carries depths of 8 feet, but stay off the points. Be careful of the charted shoal dividing the two main branches, which head off to the northwest and southwest of the point.

Dockage: Of Jackson Creek's two deep branches, only the northern one has a commercial marina that welcomes cruising boats. Deltaville Marina is to starboard and has complete transient amenities and courtesy bikes to ride into Deltaville for groceries. At the same location, Deltaville Boatyard offers full repair services, haul-out facilities and storage. The private Fishing Bay Yacht Club on the southern branch offers limited dockage for members of reciprocating yacht clubs.

Anchorage: There are many excellent, protected anchorages in Jackson Creek, but some are vulnerable to a southeasterly storm or gale. The bottom provides good holding in sandy mud. A favorite of our editor's is just off Deltaville Marina in 9- to 10-foot depths.

Fishing Bay, at Deltaville

Deltaville is a long walk or a pleasant bike ride away from the marinas of Fishing Bay, but you may be able to get a lift. If you are tempted to take a walk along the quiet and picturesque Stove Point Neck, please be aware that the neighbors are friendly, but all the land there, including the road, is private.

NAVIGATION: Use Chart 12235. To get to Fishing Bay from the mouth of the Piankatank River, make a three-mile dogleg around Stove Point Neck. Go around flashing red "8" and red nun buoy "8A," and then give a wide berth to flashing red "10," marking the hard sand shoal at the tip of Stove Point. Then, head approximately west and then north, well past red daybeacon "10A," but before red daybeacon "12." Up in the bight of Fishing Bay, you will find boatyards

Looking southeast over Irvington, Carter Creek and Eastern Branch. (Not to be used for navigation.) Cloud 9 Photography Deagle/Kucera

and marinas. Note that Fishing Bay Yacht Club regularly runs small-boat races in this protected bay.

Dockage: Chesapeake Boat Works (formerly Chesapeake Marine Railway), on the western side of Fishing Bay, is one of the oldest yards in the area and is well known for large wood boat repair and restoration. In addition to two large marine railways, they have a mobile lift, storage yard and full maintenance services. Fishing Bay Harbor Marina is located next to it on the northwest shore of Fishing Bay. Next door to that is Ruark Marina, which has limited transient space. Porpoise Cove Marina is in a protected basin to the west of Fishing Bay. The channel has not been dredged recently and shoals often. Call ahead for depths.

Anchorage: Fishing Bay is a favorite anchorage for boats heading up or down the Bay. However the anchorage is deep by Chesapeake standards with 18 feet of water in many areas. The anchorage is well protected from winds from west through north to east directions, and winds from southeast through southwest funnel in, producing comfortable conditions in hot weather. Back down on the anchor firmly, and maintain an anchor watch in strong shifting winds.

Coverage of the Piankatank River continues in the next chapter.

Sturgeon Creek, Three Miles up the Rappahannock River on the South Shore

A long 5-foot shoal extending north into the river off of Sturgeon Creek is marked by a flashing marker. A 2- to 3-foot deep bar across the mouth of the creek prevents entry into this otherwise deep and scenic creek.

Locklies Creek, Seven Miles up the Rappahannock River on the South Shore

Just below the Rappahannock River bridge, Locklies Creek is entered from the northwest side of Parrot Island. Regent Point Marina, a popular sailboat marina and service yard, is located inside. Regent is clean and friendly and situated in a wooded, park-like setting. They offer all amenities and do some boat repairs.

Carter Creek, Nine Miles up the Rappahannock River on the North Shore

Named for Robert King Carter, a 17th-century planter and one of the largest landowners in the Virginia colony, Carter Creek—off the Rappahannock's northern shore, one mile above the 110-foot Route 3 (Robert Norris) high rise bridge—is the home for several marinas and one of the most prestigious yachting amenities in the Mid-Atlantic region.

Irvington, VA

IRVINGTON		Largest Vessel Accommodated	VHF Channel Monitored	Transient Berths / Total Berths	Approach / Dockside Depth (reported)	Floating Docks	Gas / Diesel	Groceries, Ice, Marine Supplies, Snacks	Repairs: Hull, Engine, Propeller	Lift (tonnage), Crane, Rail	Min/Max Amps	Laundry, Pool, Showers, Courtesy Car	Pump-Out Station	Nearby: Grocery Store, Motel, Restaurant
		Dockage					Supplies		Services					
1. Carter's Cove Marina (WiFi) (Cruising Club Partner)	804-438-5273	90	-	/36	8/8	-	-	I	-	-	30/50	LS	P	-
2. Ampro Shipyard & Diesel	804-438-6050	200	-	-	15/10	-	-	-	HEP	R	50/50	-	-	-
3. The Tides Inn and Marina (Internet) (WiFi) (Cruising Club Partner)	804-438-5000	125	16	60/60	9/9	-	GD	IS	-	-	30/100	LPS	P	R
4. Rappahannock Yachts	804-438-5353	60	16	4/40	12/10	-	-	M	HEP	L30	30/50	S	P	R
5. Custom Yacht Service	804-438-5563	70	16	-	12/9	-	-	M	HEP	L50	30/50	-	-	MR

Corresponding chart(s) not to be used for navigation. Internet Access WiFi Wireless Internet Access Waterway Guide Cruising Club Partner

See www.WaterwayGuide.com for current rates, fuel prices, web site addresses, and other up-to-the-minute information.

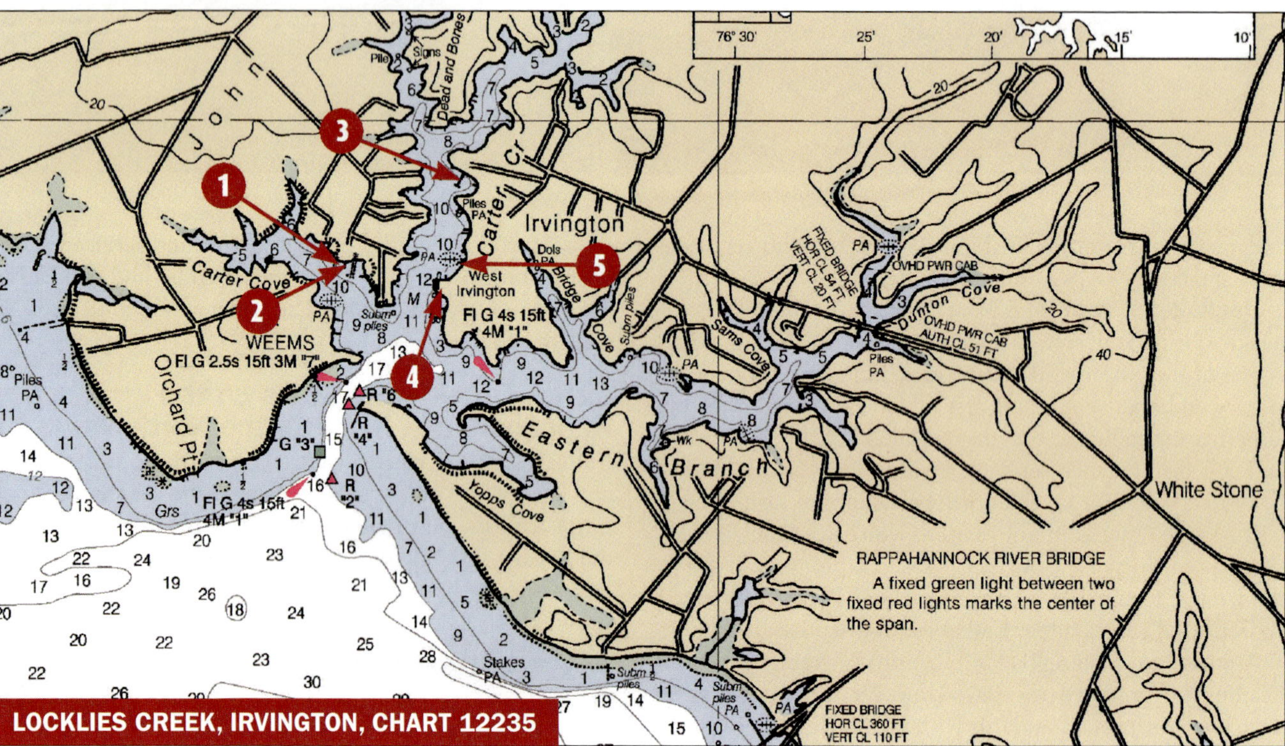

The entrance to Carter Creek is deep and straightforward. From the small village of Irvington, you can make side trips to the historical area and interesting old buildings such as Christ Church, circa 1735, an outstanding example of a Colonial church.

Dockage: Use Hampton Roads tide tables. For high tide at Orchard Point (Rappahannock River), add 2 hours 29 minutes; for low tide, add 2 hours 46 minutes. Several marinas and boatyards are located on the North and Eastern branches of Carter Creek that offer service and repairs. The Tides Marina, farther up on Carter Creek, is part of the large and well-known resort complex, called The Tides Inn. Tides Inn is a more formal lodge and resort destination, especially for golfers. Rappahannock Yachts and Custom Yacht Service are nearby as well with limited transient space.

On the Weems (west) side of Carter Creek are several oyster- and crab-packing houses, a commercial oyster hatchery and a large railway, as well as Carter's Cove Marina and Ampro Shipyard & Diesel, which may have transient space.

Anchorage: Many cruising boats use Carter Creek's Eastern Branch; there is good holding in 9-to13-foot depths here. Yopps Cove offers a nice spot away from traffic. Continuing up the main (north) branch past The Tides, follow Carter Creek beyond a private marker, also to starboard, to anchor in 7- to 8-foot depths in Dead and Bones Cove. Be sure to show an anchor light. Another great anchorage is Carter Cove to the west of the creek entrance. Here you will find good holding ground in an anchorage open to the summer southerly winds. This anchorage is a good spot when the weather is warm.

GOIN' ASHORE: IRVINGTON, VA

Once a bustling community centered around a steamboat wharf, Irvington is today the quintessential sleepy Northern Neck town graced with handsome Victorian homes set among stately trees. It is better kept than most of its neighbors; few abandoned buildings, so common in this part of the world, mar the face it presents to visitors coming by water or by land.

When the steamboats stopped coming, Irvington turned its gaze inland. The town is not visible from the water except to those who venture up the Eastern Branch of Carter Creek. You will want a bicycle (available for free if you stay at the Tides Inn Marina) to get to the shops and the local restaurant.

History: From the mid-17th century, the plantations in this part of the Northern Neck, long dominated by the Carter family, played a key role in Colonial-era trade with England. Carter Creek, with its fingers of deep water reaching far back into the land, allowed easy transfer of agricultural products to the ports from which they would be shipped abroad.

Although it does not appear to have been blessed with a name until 1891 (and was only incorporated in 1955), it rapidly became a social and commercial center and even boasted an opera house. In 1917, the Great Fire of Irvington destroyed many of the principal structures, and while the town struggled to rebuild, the age of highways arrived. The last steamboat departed Irvington in 1937, taking with it much of the town's reason for existing. Even today, the community initially appears as little more than a bend in the road marked by a gas station.

Irvington's reprieve came in 1947 with the establishment of the Tides Inn, a world-class, full-service resort. Bounded by Carter Creek and furnished with its own golf course and

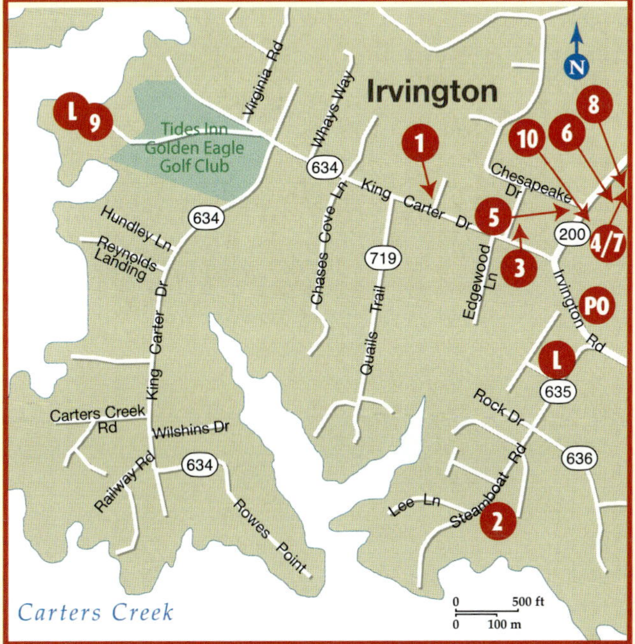

Reference the marina listing tables to see all the marinas in the area.

POINTS OF INTEREST
1 Steamboat Era Museum
2 The Old Post Office Art Gallery & Antiques
3 Hope and Glory Inn
4 Christ Church

SHOPPING
5 The Dandelion
6 Jimmy & Sook
7 Dog and Oyster Vineyard

DINING
3 Hope and Glory Inn
8 The Local
9 The Tides Inn
10 Nate's Trick Dog Cafe

L LIBRARY

PO POST OFFICE

a marina, the Tides Inn has treated thousands of visitors to a taste of the Northern Neck's bucolic ambience.

Points of Interest: Part of the last steamboat to leave the wharf has returned to revive the town's interest in its origins. The Potomac's deckhouse rests on the grounds of the Steamboat Era Museum, which opened in 2004 and traces the region's history through the development and ultimate decline of its once crucial network of waterborne communications. Located on King Carter Drive, the museum is a short walk from the Tides Inn and only a little farther from the other marinas. Check the Web site, or call for hours and information on current exhibitions that periodically supplement the permanent displays (www.steamboateramuseum.org, 804-438-6888).

A couple of hundred yards south of King Carter Drive is Steamboat Road, where many of the handsome buildings that remain from the steamboat era have been converted to modern uses—post office to art gallery, for example. Another example, is the Hope and Glory Inn (65 Tavern Road, 1-800-497-8228), a boutique hotel that began as a small school in 1890, which has 6 rooms and 10 cottages.

In the 1730s, a wealthy gentleman by the name of Robert "King" Carter, commissioned the building of Christ Church. The church is a National Historic landmark and is open every daily from 9:00 a.m. to 4:30 p.m., except for the Thanksgiving, Christmas and New Year's holidays. The Carter Reception Center museum is open April through September.

There are three nearby golf clubs: Tides Inn (804-438-5000, www.tidesinn.com), King Carter (804-435-7842, www.kingcartergolfclub.com) and Tartan (804-438-6005, www.tartangolfclub.com).

Shopping: Where King Carter Drive meets Irvington Road (Route 3), a small cluster of stores provides an eclectic shopping diversion. Dandelion (4372 Irvington Road, 804-438-5194) has sophisticated sportswear and accessories as well as elegant evening wear and gifts. Jimmy and Sook is located at 4345 Irvington Road (804-438-6010) and offers their original polo shirt in multiple colors as well as other sportswear for jimmys (male crabs) and sooks (female crabs). A little more walking brings you to the Dog and Oyster Vineyard where you can taste and purchase wines made on the premises. The Dog and Oyster tasting room is open from 11:00 a.m. to 6:00 p.m. during summer months. (See www.hopeandglory.com/thevineyard/winery.html, 804-438-5559). The Dog and Oyster is part of the Chesapeake Bay Wine Trail, which includes 13 Virginia wineries, many of which are located on or near waterways of the Bay. Visit chesapeakebaywinetrail.com for more information.

Dining: The Local (4337 Irvington Road, 804-438-9356) is a coffee shop and deli in Irvington that serves breakfast and lunch. The upscale Tides Inn (480 King Carter Drive, 804-438-5000) has three restaurants in the main buildings and another in the clubhouse on the golf course. Nate's Trick Dog Café (4357 Irvington Road, 804-438-6363) serves sumptuous meals with an elegant presentation. The Hope and Glory Inn (detailed above) also offers fine dining.

Corrotoman River, VA

CORROTOMAN RIVER		Largest Vessel Accommodated	VHF Channel Monitored	Transient Berths / Total Berths	Approach / Dockside Depth (reported)	Floating Docks	Gas / Diesel	Groceries, Ice, Marine Supplies, Snacks	Repairs: Hull, Engine, Propeller	Lift (tonnage), Crane, Rail	Min/Max Amps	Laundry, Pool, Showers, Courtesy Car	Pump-Out Station	Nearby: Grocery Store, Motel, Restaurant
		Dockage					Supplies		Services					
1. Yankee Point Marina (Internet Access, Wireless Internet Access)	804-462-7018	100	16/68	10/103	9/9	F	GD	IMS	HEP	L40	30/50	LPS	P	MR

Corresponding chart(s) not to be used for navigation. Internet Access, Wireless Internet Access

See www.WaterwayGuide.com for current rates, fuel prices, web site addresses, and other up-to-the-minute information.

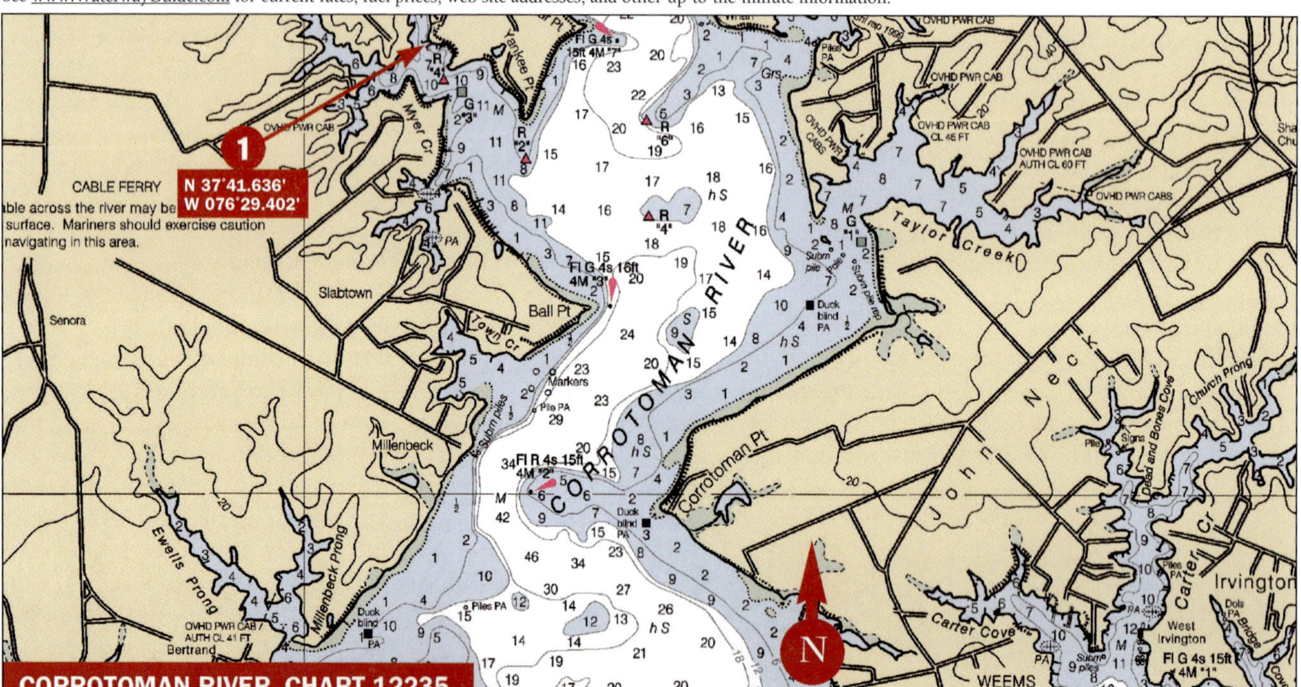

Looking southeast over the Corrotoman and Rappahannock rivers. (Not to be used for navigation.) Waterway Guide Photography.

ADDITIONAL RESOURCES

- TOWN OF IRVINGTON: www.townofirvington.com
- NEARBY MEDICAL FACILITIES
  Rappahannock General Hospital, 101 Harris Road, Kilmarnock, VA 22842, 804-435-8000, 800-296-8009
  www.rgh-hospital.com (5 miles)

Corrotoman River, Eleven Miles up the Rappahannock River on the North Shore

The Corrotoman is a river of many creeks off the Rappahannock's northern shore about 11 miles in from the Rappahannock mouth. It is well marked, easy to navigate (watch for the long points), has many attractive anchorages on both sides and both branches. Widely spaced and beautiful residences dot the shoreline, making it one of the most beautiful tributaries on the entire Chesapeake Bay.

NAVIGATION: Use Chart 12235. The main entrance divides into two major branches, the Eastern and Western; both are navigable a long way upstream and contain many fine anchorages. Heading up the Eastern Branch, avoid the shoal creeping northwestward off of Moran Wharf. Up the Western Branch, one of the last remaining free ferries in Virginia still carries cars between Merry Point and Ottoman Wharf. Do not approach the ferry when it is operating; the ferry's cables lie just below the surface, and you could foul them (and yourself). The ferry area is clearly marked on the chart.

Dockage: Yankee Point Marina, in Myer Creek just beyond Ball Point, has transient slips, supplies and services, and while it primarily caters to sailboats, power boaters are always welcome. It is the only marina on the Corrotoman River.

Anchorage: You can anchor in the cove in front of Yankee Point Marina. A very popular summer anchorage is in the cove at West Point, where you will be sure to catch the summer evening breezes. Or head into the Eastern Branch where a very lovely anchorage exists north of the sandy point about a mile past Moran Wharf. There is a sandy beach here with deep water right up to the shore. Additional anchorage space is available in Hills Creek or Bells Creek off of the Eastern Branch with depths of 7 to 10 feet and good holding in mud. Both points are tipped with duck blinds. The banks are high, with fine houses secluded in the trees. Additional excellent anchorage spots can be found in the numerous coves along both branches of the Corrotoman River.

Urbanna Creek, Fourteen Miles up the Rappahannock River on the South Shore

Urbanna is a favorite walking town for boaters because of its location beside the water and the compactness of the town. This is one of only a handful of bayside towns with a grocery store within walking distance of the harbor. The easily entered harbor has 9-foot depths, and several marinas

Urbanna, VA

URBANNA		Largest Vessel Accommodated	VHF Channel Monitored	Transient Berths / Total Berths	Approach / Dockside Depth (reported)	Floating Docks	Gas / Diesel	Groceries, Ice, Marine Supplies, Snacks	Repairs: Hull, Engine, Propeller	Lift (tonnage), Crane, Rail	Min/Max Amps	Laundry, Pool, Showers, Courtesy Car	Pump-Out Station	Nearby: Grocery Store, Motel, Restaurant
		Dockage					Supplies		Services					
1. Urbanna Town Marina at Upton's Point	804-758-5440	65	16	14/32	10/5	-	-	IS	-	-	50/50	LS	P	GMR
2. Dozier's Port Urbanna Marine Center	**804-758-0000**	**100**	**16/72**	**3/50**	**10/10**	**-**	**-**	**I**	**HEP**	**L30**	**30/100**	**S**	**P**	**GMR**
3. Schroeder Yacht Systems	804-758-2331	-	-	-	-	-	-	IM	HE	L40	-	S	-	GMR
4. Urbanna Yachting Center	804-758-2342	80	16	5/87	10/10	-	GD	IM	HE	L20	30/50	S	P	GMR
5. Remlik Marina/Mike's Marine Services	804-758-5450	65	16	30/135	6/6	-	G	GIMS	HEP	L30, C	30/50	PS	P	G

Corresponding chart(s) not to be used for navigation. Internet Access · Wireless Internet Access · Waterway Guide Cruising Club Partner

See www.WaterwayGuide.com for current rates, fuel prices, web site addresses, and other up-to-the-minute information.

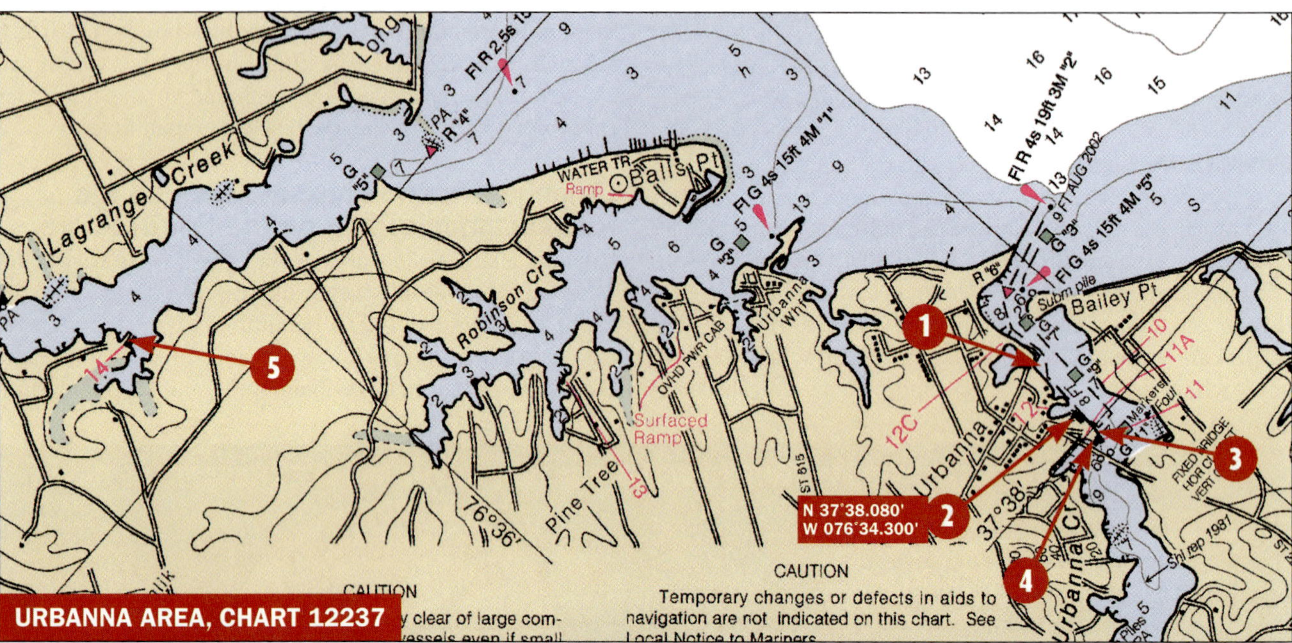

URBANNA AREA, CHART 12237

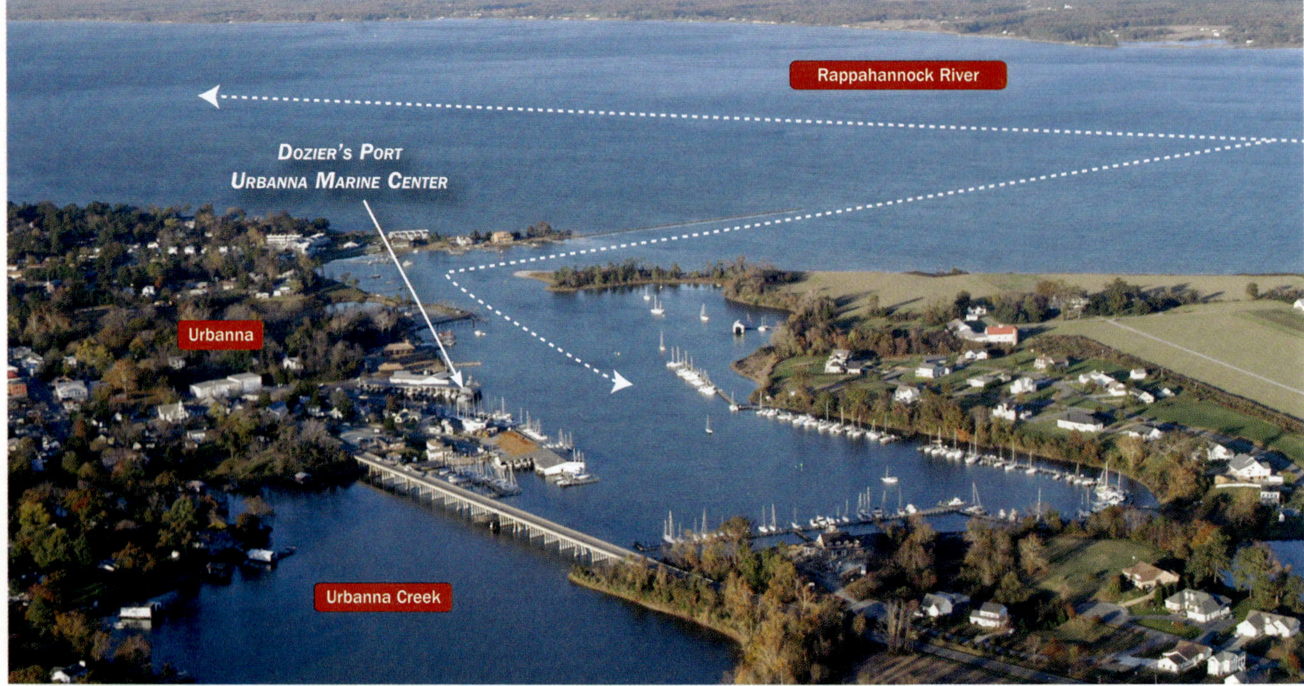

Looking north over Urbanna Creek, Urbanna and the Rappahannock River. (Not to be used for navigation.) Waterway Guide Photography.

are located on the creek, including a qualified boatyard offering marine supplies and mechanical assistance. There is also space to anchor in the protected harbor opposite the town or above the bridge for boats that can clear the 21-foot fixed structure.

Perched high on a hill, the friendly river town of Urbanna has a number of historic buildings. Rosegill Farm, built in 1650 across the creek from Urbanna, was once the residence of a colonial governor.

NAVIGATION: Use Chart 12237. Green daybeacons "3," "7," "9" and "11" in Urbanna Creek were relocated in 2008. **Use Hampton Roads tide tables. For high tide at Urbanna (Rappahannock River), add 2 hours 45 minutes; for low tide, add 3 hours 4 minutes.**

Dockage: Three marinas catering to transients line the town (right) side of the harbor. Urbanna Town Marina at Upton's Point (the first marina on the right when entering the creek) has transient dockage within easy walking distance of local attractions. Dozier's Port Urbanna Marine Center, in the middle of Urbanna, is a marine complex with a full-service yard and a waterfront restaurant. Services include professional painting, fiberglass repair, metalworking and engine repair, as well as rebuilding and refurbishing services for all types of vessels performed by Schroeders Yacht Systems. It has 50 covered permanent slips, plus uncovered space for transients and long term dry storage.

Farther up the creek, Urbanna Yachting Center also has dockage and fuel. Across the creek at Rosegill, Urbanna Harbor is a private marina.

Anchorage: You can anchor behind Bailey Point near the white boathouse, or farther south in 8- to 10-foot depths. Holding is fair in soupy mud. For an easy walk to town, you can tie up your dinghy by the ramp at the town marina; just keep it out of the way.

GOIN' ASHORE: **URBANNA, VA**

Tucked up a creek off the Rappahannock River, Urbanna, VA, settled in 1680, still retains its historic atmosphere mixed with a blend of modern life. Recent grants have enabled the town to redevelop its waterfront and enhance its streets with landscaping and gas-style lights. Within the town center, and only a block or two from the water, are several restaurants, a grocery store, liquor store, drugstore, unique clothing, gift and antiques shops and churches.

A short walk from any of the marinas brings you to the heart of a compact town that, for its small size, hosts a wide variety of retail businesses and historic buildings. In Urbanna, you can replenish your stores while refreshing your memories of what an old-fashioned small town used to be.

History: Early settlers were often drawn to locations that Native Americans had already been using for centuries, and usually for the same reasons: They provided access to the water and were defendable. The Nimquits occupied present-day Urbanna until Ralph Wormeley in 1649 patented 3,200 acres and chased them off it so he could build a plantation and grow tobacco.

Like many of his kind, Wormeley preferred to ship his products directly to England rather than deal with officialdom. The Virginia House of Burgesses took a dim view of this practice and in 1680, passed legislation establishing locations for 20 official port towns through which all business of the Colony would be conducted. The port Wormeley had built to serve his plantation, Rosegill, was one of them, and in due course, a town of 50 acres was platted out around it. In 1705, the port had achieved sufficient standing in services to The Crown that it was named Urbanna, in honor of Queen Anne.

Largely unscathed despite being bombarded in the Revolution, the War of 1812 and the Civil War, the town prospered quietly until the steamboats ceased their regular runs up and down Chesapeake Bay in the 1930s, when Saluda, inland on Route 17, became the commercial and judicial center for the region. Urbanna, like many steamboat ports on the Bay, went into a sort of hibernation, supported largely by the crab and oyster fisheries.

In recent years, Urbanna has seen something of a resurgence. Retirees and Richmond-area commuters, attracted to this small town surrounded by water, forest and farmland, are bringing to it new blood and fresh civic energy. Several bed and breakfasts are available in town, including The Chesapeake Inn Virginia Street, a boutique inn in which each room is decorated in a different eclectic nautical motif.

Points of Interest: A short walk into town from the waterfront takes you up the old Prettyman's Rolling Road (now Virginia Street), along which hogsheads of tobacco were rolled to and from the harbor. On your left is the Old Tobacco Warehouse, built in 1766 and recently restored to house the visitors center. It is one of four buildings in the historic district listed on the National Register of Historic Places. A couple of hundred yards ahead, on Virginia Street, is another, the Urbanna Courthouse, which was built in 1748 and is one of only 11 court houses of the Colonial era still standing in Virginia. Across the street is Lansdowne, a Georgian-style home once owned by one of Virginia's ubiquitous Lee families.

Colonial plantations, Rosegill and Hewick, both on the National Register of Historic Places and both privately owned, still stand, one on each side of town. A stir arose around Rosegill recently when its 800-acre estate was rezoned for a development of 700 homes.

Special Events: Despite the paucity of the harvest in recent years, oysters hold Urbanna's place on the map and in the consciousness of Virginians today. The Urbanna Oyster Festival (www.urbannaoysterfestival.com), held the first weekend in November of each year, attracts as many as 75,000 visitors to its two-day, town-wide festival (no small undertaking for a town of 800). Highlights include almost continuous live music, two parades, numerous food and craft vendors, educational exhibits and the famed oyster shucking contest, where state champions complete for the right to attend the national championship in Maryland. And, of course, there is the crowning of the Oyster Festival Queen and her Little Miss Spat (baby oyster).

A juried outdoor art show, Art on the Half Shell, kicks off the summer activities in May, followed by the Fourth of July

Boat Parade and Fireworks, and Family Fun Day on Labor Day weekend. Every second Saturday of the month, from May through October, the Farmer's Market attracts vendors of wares of all sorts. Check the town web site for dates and details (www.urbanna.com).

Shopping: On Cross and Virginia streets, several small stores tempt the shopper with antiques, art and clothing. At their junction, Bristow's (804-758-2210) occupies the 19th-century general store that formerly sold goods brought in from Baltimore, MD and elsewhere by steamboat. In Marshall's Drug Store (50 Cross St., 804-758-5344), you can get a milk shake at a 1950s-style soda fountain. Urbanna Market (335 Virginia St., 804-758-2250) is a full-service supermarket a half-mile walk from the water. Pick up crabmeat at Payne's Crab House (804-758-5301), on the water at 10 Virginia St., a legendary, traditional seafood operation run untraditionally by women (sisters Catherine Via and Beatrice Taylor).

Dining: All Fired Up Smokehouse & Grill (804-286-9016) is located in Dozier's Port Urbanna Marina. Just up the hill are Cross Street Coffee Shop (804-758-1002) and nearby Virginia Street Café (804-758-3798), which serves breakfast, lunch and dinner at the corner of Virginia and Cross streets. At 230 Virginia St., Café Mojo (804-758-4141) caters to the more daring palate. Urbanna Oyster House (804-758-2059) is also on Virginia Street. It is very convenient to the marinas and serves a wide variety of seafood and American specialties. At the foot of the bridge, Colonial Pizza (804-758-4079) serves local and Italian dishes.

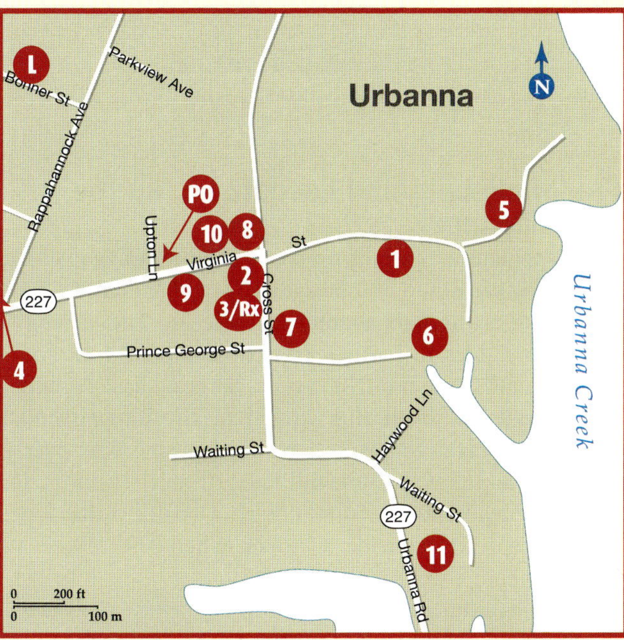

Reference the marina listing tables to see all the marinas in the area.

POINTS OF INTEREST
1 Old Tobacco Warehouse/ Visitors Center

SHOPPING
2 Bristow's
3 Marshall's Drug Store

GROCERIES
4 Urbanna Market
5 Payne's Crab House

DINING
6 All Fired Up Smokehouse
7 Cross Street Café
8 Virginia Street Café
9 Café Mojo
10 Urbanna Oyster House
11 Colonial Pizza

L LIBRARY

Rx PHARMACY

PO POST OFFICE

ADDITIONAL RESOURCES

- TOWN OF URBANNA: www.urbanna.com
- URBANNA OYSTER FESTIVAL: www.urbannaoysterfestival.com

NEARBY MEDICAL FACILITIES

Urbanna Family Practice:
5399 Old Virginia St. 804-758-2110 (.75 mile)

Rappahannock General Hospital, 101 Harris Road, Kilmarnock, VA 22842, 804-435-8000, 800-296-8009
www.rgh-hospital.com

Riverside Walter Reed Hospital, 7519 Hospital Drive Gloucester, VA 23061, 804-693-8800

Rappahannock River, Above Urbanna

Cruising up the wide, well-marked Rappahannock River is pleasant. High red bluffs, wooded banks, farms, villages and beautifully maintained old houses line the shores. Traffic is sparse, consisting mostly of local watermen and fishermen in open runabouts.

NAVIGATION: Use Chart 12237. The current (27th) edition is dated 2003, and a number of Rappahannock River markers from "22" to "78" have been changed or relocated; be sure your chart has been updated from the NOAA web site (http://chartmaker.ncd.noaa.gov), as it contains the additions. Keep a careful watch for fish-pound stakes that edge the narrow channel. Some of the old stakes are broken off, and few are clearly marked. A shoal draft makes the trip easier, but keep your eye on the depth sounder. The first marina north of Urbanna is Remlick Marina/Mike's Marina on Lagrange Creek.

Greenvale Creek, Bowlers Wharf and Totuskey Creek, off the Rappahannock

Greenvale Creek is 17 miles above the mouth of the Rappahannock, just above Urbanna on the north side of the river. The entrance here is shallow but was dredged to 7 feet in 2009; there are depths of 5 feet inside. The small Greenvale Creek Marina has dockage and Conrad's Upper Deck Restaurant, a popular local dining spot, is also here.

Twenty-nine miles above the entrance to the Rappahannock River on the south shore is Bowlers Wharf, with a marina (Garrett's Marina) that welcomes visitors. Boats drawing less than 4.5 feet will have no trouble entering this

"The Suzanne" rests at anchor on Mill Creek. Owners John and Suzanne are long-time WATERWAY GUIDE enthusiasts.
Waterway Guide Photography.

quiet cove. Just upstream, on the north shore, deep and well-marked Totuskey Creek provides sheltered anchorage for several miles along its length if you can get through its entrance depths (shown as about 4 to 5 feet). Many markers on this creek have been changed or relocated; be sure your chart was printed since then.

Hoskins Creek, off the Rappahannock

The highlight of Hoskins Creek is the lovely little hamlet of Tappahannock. A pretty, historic town, Tappahannock has an interesting waterfront with both new and old houses and the campus of St. Margaret's Episcopal School for Girls. There are two beaches: one is part of the campus, but the other is public. Groceries, gasoline, a Wal-Mart Superstore, a restaurant and a post office are nearby. You can pick up walking-tour information at the town office.

NAVIGATION: Use Chart 12237. Protected Hoskins Creek, 25 miles upstream from Urbanna, has range lights, markers and two tall white structures, which are part of the local granary, to guide you in. In late 2008, the creek entrance was charted at 6 feet at mean low water, but feel your way in carefully with your depth sounder. The regular movement of grain barges helps keep the creek depths stable. The creek has a 5-mph, No Wake ordinance. Explore the narrow creek by dinghy; there is neither dock space nor a place to anchor here. You can anchor in the Rappahannock clear of the creek entrance—the current is strong, so set your hook securely. Dinghy to the public beach or to the boat ramp opposite the granary, but remember to lock your dinghy to some structure ashore.

Fredericksburg and Leedstown, up the Rappahannock

The Rappahannock winds on past the 50-foot fixed vertical clearance U.S. Route 360 Bridge at Tappahannock to Fredericksburg at the Rappahannock's Mile 93. The closing of some companies in Fredericksburg—companies that once required supplies brought in by barges—has decreased commercial traffic on this stretch of the Rappahannock River, but gravel barges still make the run. The river is navigable all the way to the fall line at Fredericksburg, and it offers breathtaking vistas along its sparsely developed shores, especially during October when the leaves are changing color.

Fifty-three miles upriver you pass Leedstown, where the Potomac River is only about 10 miles away across the Northern Neck. Colonial Potomac River planters like the Lees, Washingtons, Turbevilles and Carters received their furniture and luxuries from England on this shore rather than having their goods landed on the exposed shoals of the Potomac. On the north shore near Leedstown is a dock providing access to Ingleside Plantation Winery where tours are available. Do not block access to the tour boat that arrives daily from Tappahannock. ■

Kilmarnock

Irvington

Urbanna

Rappahannock River

Deltaville

Page 383

West Point 33

30

Piankatank River

Page 372

Gwynns Island

MILE 134

17

Page 376

North River

Ware River

Page 374

East River

Horn Harbor

Page 374

Mobjack Bay

Chesapeake Bay

Severn River

Page 376

York River

199

Williamsburg

Gloucester Point

64

Yorktown

Page 379

MILE 156

Poquoson River

Poquoson

Back River

N

Fort Eustis

James River

Hampton

MILE 168

Smithfield

Newport News

664

MILE 178

564

258

Norfolk

Portsmouth

DOZIER'S WATERWAY GUIDE THE CRUISING AUTHORITY

WWW.WATERWAYGUIDE.COM

Skipper's Handbook

- GPS Waypoints 48
- Tide Tables 50

Deltaville to Hampton Roads

CHARTS 12221, 12225, 12235, 12238, 12243, 12244, 12245

This stretch of Tidewater Virginia is brimming with attractive anchorages and ports of call, particularly for cruisers with a serious bent toward the historical. You can go up the York River to Yorktown and Yorktown Battlefield, where Gen. George Washington and his French allies soundly defeated their imperial counterpart, Gen. Charles Lord Cornwallis, establishing the former colonies as an independent country on October 19, 1781. You can tour the extant battlements and an excellent museum on the premises.

Going back farther into history—and a little farther upriver between the York and James Rivers—you can take transportation to visit Williamsburg, VA, an immaculately preserved Colonial-era city between the York and James rivers. The Historic Williamsburg Foundation maintains Williamsburg and ensures that the 18th-century architecture remains true to its original form. The same pubs frequented by the likes of George Washington, Ben Franklin and Patrick Henry are still open and serving finer grogs than ever, and we haven't even gotten to the first-rate anchorages you will find on rivers like the Piankatank and the tributaries of Mobjack Bay.

PIANKATANK RIVER, ON THE SOUTH SIDE OF DELTAVILLE

The serpentine Piankatank River, though not as large as some Virginia rivers, offers extensive cruising possibilities, beautiful anchorages, foul weather protection and an abundance of boating amenities. Just south of the far larger Rappahannock, the Piankatank is well worth exploring.

You will have most of it to yourself, as most boats do not go beyond the Jackson Creek or Fishing Bay entrances to Deltaville. There are many cruising choices in this little river, from the intricate passages of Milford Haven and the remoteness of Gwynn's Island on the south shore, to the intimate surroundings of the tiny creeks farther upstream.

NAVIGATION: Use Chart 12235. Use caution and sort out the curvy Piankatank River entrance if you have not been there before. In December 2007, the previous spider light structure marking Stingray Point between the Rappahannock and Piankatank rivers was replaced with a cylindrical structure rising 10 feet above the water with a 20-foot-tall steel skeleton tower, moved about 50 feet west, and its range was increased. The rocks protecting the previous lighthouse are still in place so use caution and give them and the shoal extending approximately one quarter mile east of the new light adequate leeway. From Stingray Point Light, run a compass course to flashing green lights "5" and "7," both now fixed markers, abeam of Cherry Point on the south side of the river's entrance. Be careful of the crab pot floats that are sometimes in the channel near quick flashing red "6." At these markers, there is a three-way junction of waterways—you have Jackson Creek to the northwest, Milford Haven to the south and Fishing Bay upriver. (For coverage of the Deltaville tributaries of Jackson Creek and Fishing Bay, see the previous chapter, "Smith Point to Deltaville.") The long shoals extending northwest from Cherry Point and southeast from Stove Point carry clear marks, but make sure you spot the markers in advance and do not cut any corners. South of fixed flashing red marker "8" off Stove Point, an additional red nun buoy "8A," is relocated as needed to mark the shoal that continues to build to the south.

STINGRAY POINT LIGHT
N 37°33.700' W 076°16.383'

Waterway Guide Photography

Queens Creek, off the South Side of the Piankatank

At the mouth of the Piankatank, on the south side, almost directly across from Stove Point, is Hill's Bay. This open bay, which is shallow near the shore, provides access to two other waterways: Queens Creek to the southwest and Milford Haven (discussed below) to the southeast. For Queen's Creek, follow the marked channel at flashing red "2" into the narrow creek. It was last dredged in 2009 and has shoaled a bit so proceed carefully. A good anchorage is on the south side of Queen's Creek, just inside the entrance and, for shallow draft boats, further in, behind the shoal across from Miller Cove. (Queens Creek Marina may have transient space if you can reach it but no amenities.) Back out at the mouth of Queen's Creek is a lovely beach for swimming and lunching.

Milford Haven, off the South Side of the Piankatank

Milford Haven is the body of water that separates Gwynn's Island from the mainland at the mouth of the Piankatank on the south shore (off Hill's Bay). Although referred to on the chart as "Gwynn" Island, the Island is actually "Gwynn's" and the onshore community is "Gwynn."

Milford Haven, VA

MILFORD HAVEN		Largest Vessel Accommodated	VHF Channel Monitored	Transient Berths / Total Berths	Approach / Dockside Depth (reported)	Floating Docks	Gas / Diesel	Groceries, Ice, Marine Supplies, Snacks	Repairs: Hull, Engine, Propeller	Lift (tonnage), Crane, Rail	Min/Max Amps	Laundry, Pool, Showers, Courtesy Car	Pump-Out Station	Nearby: Grocery Store, Motel, Restaurant
		Dockage					Supplies		Services					
1. Narrows Marina	804-725-2151	60	-	5/100	10/6	-	D	-	-	-	-	S	-	M
2. Morningstar Marinas - Gwynns Island	804-384-9698	32	-	-	5/6	-	G	IS	HEP	-	30/30	S	P	MR
3. Mathews Yacht Club	804-725-3165	75	-	3/53	7/6	-	G	GIM	-	-	30/50	S	-	GMR

Corresponding chart(s) not to be used for navigation. Internet Access Wireless Internet Access Waterway Guide Cruising Club Partner

See www.WaterwayGuide.com for current rates, fuel prices, web site addresses, and other up-to-the-minute information.

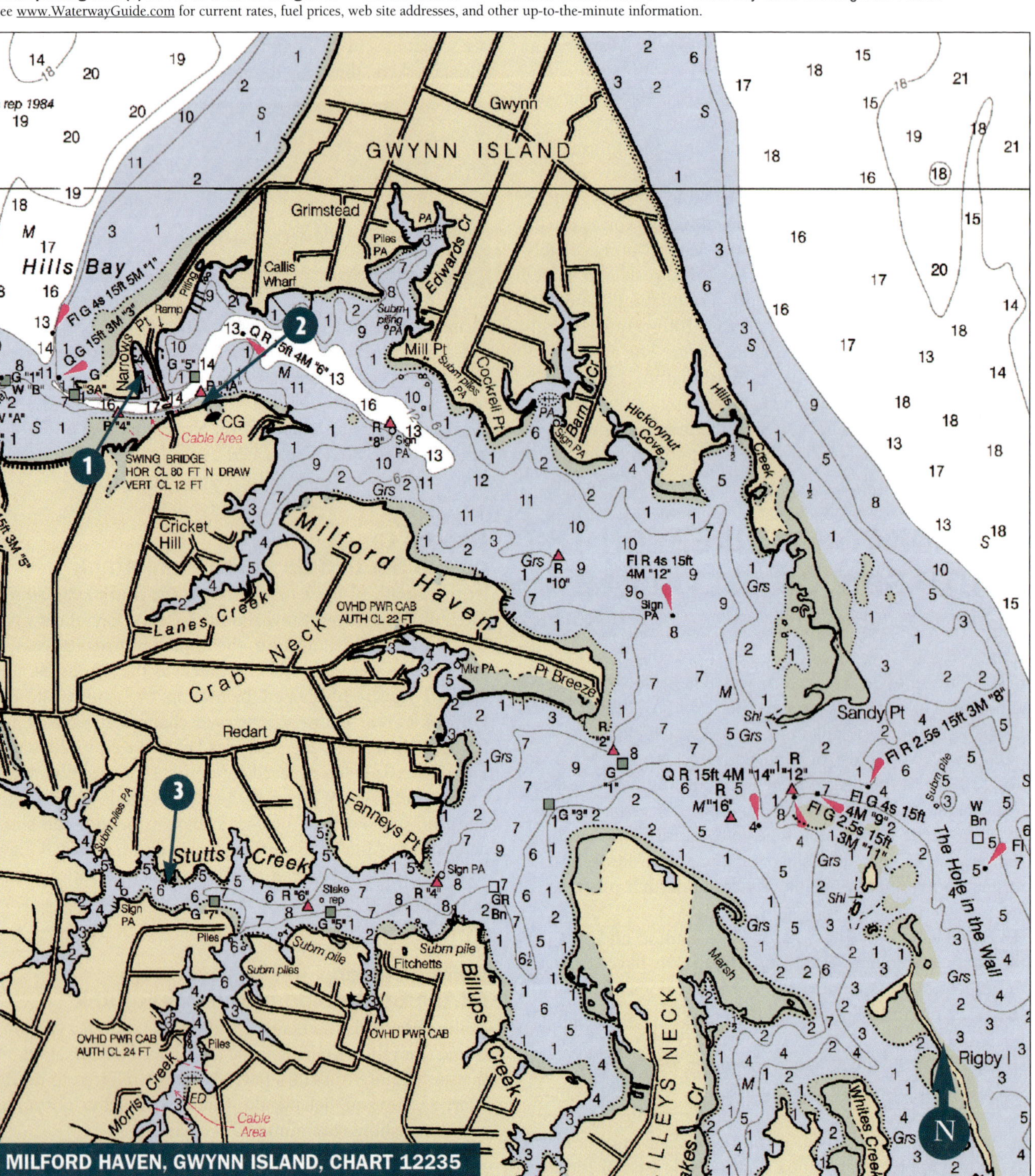

A southeast view over Milford Haven. (Not to be used for navigation.) Waterway Guide Photography

NAVIGATION: Use Chart 12235. **Use Hampton Roads tide tables. For high tide at Yorktown (York River), add 11 minutes; for low tide, add 6 minutes.** Milford Haven's main entrance from the Piankatank is deep and well marked. A Coast Guard search and rescue station is on the mainland side, just east of a swing bridge, which has a 12-foot closed vertical clearance. Red daybeacon "4," just west of the bridge, is right at the edge of a sharp shoal. Avoid another trouble spot about 100 yards west of red daybeacon "4" by staying close to the docks at the marina when passing.

The eastern entrance to Milford Haven, from the Chesapeake proper, is the aptly named The Hole in the Wall, a break in a low bar that shoal-draft boats can cross with care. The Hole in the Wall channel has shoaled to around 4 feet in places. Do not attempt the passage unless your vessel has a shoal draft and obtain local knowledge prior to running the channel.

The Gwynn's Island Bridge (swing, 12-foot closed vertical clearance) monitors VHF Channel 13 and opens on signal. This drawbridge has the most openings of any moveable bridge in Virginia and opens on signal 24 hours daily. All boat traffic entering or leaving Milford Haven should use the northern side of the swing bridge. The area between the bridge and Morningstar Marinas—next to the Coast Guard station, east of the bridge on the mainland side—can be very congested with boat traffic during summer weekends.

Dockage: Morningstar Marina has fuel (gas and diesel), boat repair facilities and a pump-out station. The Narrows Marina just west of the swing bridge offers little in cruising amenities. Few repairs have been made since extensive damage from Hurricane Isabel in 2003. The Islander Motel and Restaurant remain closed. The Mathews Yacht Club, on Stutts Creek, is private but may maintain a few transient slips. Seabreeze Restaurant on the Gwynn Island side has some transient space for diners as well as a boat ramp. Call ahead for depths.

Anchorage: Many protected anchorages are between the Gwynn Island Bridge and Hole in the Wall, the shallow southern entrance to Milford Haven. You can drop the hook in Milford Haven between green daybeacon "5" and quick flashing red "6", out of the channel on the north side, across from the Coast Guard station in 9 to 10 feet of water. For a quieter spot, Edwards Creek provides an excellent protected anchorage. Unmarked Lanes Creek has long shoals on both sides of its entrance. Honor red daybeacon "8" and look for stakes marking the shoals; be sure to proceed slowly and keep an eye on the depth sounder. Stutts Creek near the south end of Milford Haven is marked for approximately one mile with water depths of 7 to 9 feet. It is best to stay near the mouth; there's not much swing room inside the creek. The more shallow Billups Creek is a less developed anchorage with lovely vistas of undeveloped marshes and forests. But the true gem is the anchorage just inside of the barrier Islands at the eastern end of Milford Haven. Here you can anchor in 7 feet of water about 300 yards from a barrier beach that is seldom visited except on holiday weekends. You are likely to have the beach all to yourself most of the time. This, of course, is only recommended in fair weather, as there is little protection from storms from all directions except north.

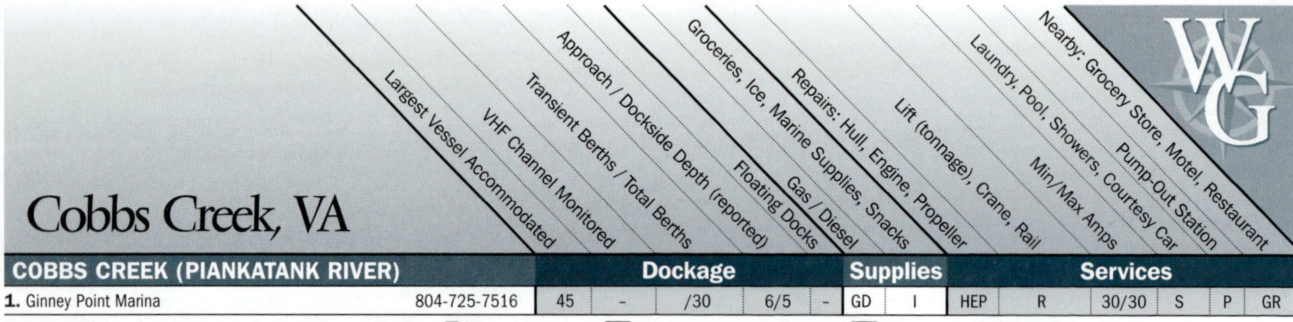

Cobbs Creek, VA

COBBS CREEK (PIANKATANK RIVER)		Dockage					Supplies		Services					
		Largest Vessel Accommodated	VHF Channel Monitored	Transient Berths / Total Berths	Approach / Dockside Depth (reported)	Floating Docks	Gas / Diesel	Groceries, Ice, Marine Supplies, Snacks	Repairs: Hull, Engine, Propeller	Lift (tonnage), Crane, Rail	Min/Max Amps	Laundry, Pool, Showers, Courtesy Car	Pump-Out Station	Nearby: Grocery Store, Motel, Restaurant
1. Ginney Point Marina	804-725-7516	45	-	/30	6/5	-	GD	I	HEP	R	30/30	S	P	GR

Corresponding chart(s) not to be used for navigation. Internet Access Wireless Internet Access Waterway Guide Cruising Club Partner

See www.WaterwayGuide.com for current rates, fuel prices, web site addresses, and other up-to-the-minute information.

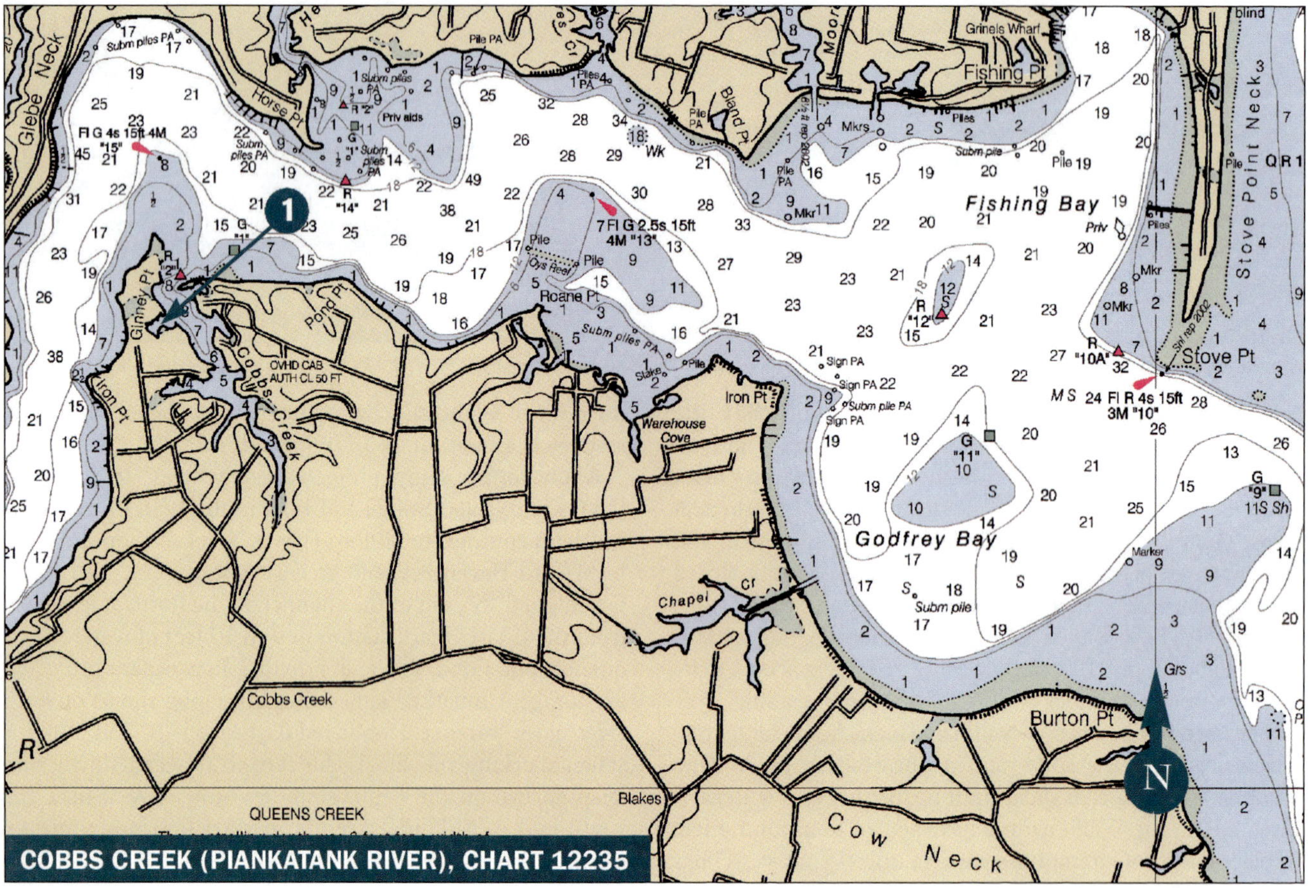

COBBS CREEK (PIANKATANK RIVER), CHART 12235

GOIN' ASHORE:
GWYNN ISLAND, VA

Connected to the rest of Mathews County by a drawbridge, Gwynn's Island encloses Milford Haven, an expansive, sheltered bay that has provided a livelihood for generations of watermen. Not much else goes on here, other than construction of a growing number of waterfront homes for the well-to-do. That makes it a good place to sit back and contemplate the comings and goings of a traditional Chesapeake Bay working waterfront.

Nothing sums up the Gwynn Island approach to yachting more succinctly than the sign for the "Budget Yacht Club." You won't find a trophy room or a bar to serve you a martini here, but you might catch one of the club's founding members around the docks working on a deadrise crab skiff or a classic wooden sailing yacht.

The Islander Motel has been closed since 2003, when Hurricane Isabel wrought considerable havoc in these parts, but some of the marina slips are in commission, although they may be without services. The boatyard and marina still look a little worn, but the number of pilings still green with pressure-treatment chemicals indicates a recovery is in the works.

History: Remains of Native American settlements dating back 10,000 years have been found on Gwynn Island, and native people certainly inhabited it when the Virginia Colony was in its infancy.

According to legend, Hugh Gwynn, while exploring the Chesapeake Bay in 1611, rescued an Indian maiden from drowning. The girl turned out to be a princess—Pocahontas—and she thanked Gwynn by giving him the island. The official record suggests he acquired his patch through a more conventional land grab. In 1635, Hugh Gwynn applied to King Charles of England for a land patent and in 1640 was granted 1,700 acres on the island. Milford Haven, named for a harbor in southern Wales, reflects the Gwynn family's Welsh origins.

In an otherwise uneventful history, one episode has merited a state historic marker. In 1776, a growing revolutionary movement drove Lord Dunmore, the Colonial Governor of Virginia, out of Norfolk. Taking several ships and about 500 men, he holed up on Gwynn Island. Some months later, General Andrew Lewis set up a battery on Cricket Hill, on the mainland, and bombarded Dunmore's fleet, inflicting enough damage for Dunmore to flee north to Maryland, where he was sent packing, eventually to return to England.

The community maintained its island status, connected to the rest of Mathews County by ferries, until the Gwynn Island Bridge opened in 1939.

Points of Interest: Gwynn Island's contributions to history are recorded and displayed in the Gwynn's Island Museum (804-725-7949). Established in 1991 as a community project, it is housed in a 100-year-old building that was built as the Odd Fellows Lodge and was later used for the community's first public school. From May to October, it is open Fridays, Saturdays and Sundays.From the museum, a short stroll will take you around the heart of the village, which is centered around the Baptist Church and the Cultural Center.

Shopping: There is no place to shop on the island, and it is not recommended that you cross the drawbridge on foot due to sometimes heavy traffic and the lack of a footpath along the roadside. If you have transportation, the community of Hudgins is less than two miles away. There you will find a convenience store, post office, hair salon and barber, antiques shop and auto parts store. This is also the home of the family-owned and operated Donk's Theater (Virginia's Lil' Ole Opry) where you can enjoy live country music shows in an old movie theater (a Virginia historical landmark). Donk's is open twice a month (every other week) on Saturdays from February through the Christmas show in December. For show times and information, call 804-725-7760 or visit www.donkstheater.com.

Dining: The only spot on Gywnn's Island is Seabreeze (804-725-4000), across Old Ferry Road from the marina and overlooking Milford Haven beside a public boat ramp where there is space to tie up a dinghy. It is open all day except Mondays for American fare and fresh seafood. They have slips for diners. At Island Seafood (Hwy 656, 804-725-4962), you can buy fresh seafood plus homemade tuna salad and deviled crabs.

ADDITIONAL RESOURCES

- **GWYNNS ISLAND MUSEUM:** www.gwynnislandmuseum.org
- **MATHEWS COUNTY:** www.visitmathews.com

NEARBY MEDICAL FACILITIES
Riverside Walter Reed Hospital: 7519 Hospital Drive, Gloucester, VA 23061, 804-693-8800 (16 miles)

Upriver on the Piankatank

The number of boats docked on the Piankatank River's upriver section is anyone's guess. You will see all sorts of vessels at the marinas and yards of Deltaville, at small marinas in such upriver tributaries as Cobbs Creek, and at private docks up the numerous side creeks and coves.

NAVIGATION: Use Chart 12235. The banks are high for the five miles up to the fixed bridge at Wilton Point (43-foot vertical clearance) and several miles beyond. Handsome old houses and interesting modern homes peek out from behind the trees along the shoreline. The Piankatank is deep, but study the chart carefully. Note the shoal extending toward the channel from Roane Point at flashing green "13" and the double shoal on the north at red daybeacon "14" off Horse Point.

Moore Creek, located just east of Fishing Bay, has 7 and 8 foot depths inside but is shoal at the entrance (marked as 1 foot on the chart), making it navigable only by dinghy or extremely shoal draft boats.

Cobbs Creek, off the Piankatank

Anchorage: The Piankatank River has a wide choice of sheltered and attractive anchorages. One of the best is Cobbs Creek, which has a marked entrance channel on the Piankatank's south side, just before Ginney Point. Just follow the markers to enter Cobbs Creek (green daybeacon "1" marks the entrance), and then watch the depth sounder after passing red daybeacon "2." When inside, leave the private mooring buoy to port, then proceed slowly. You will find Ginney Point Marina, with fuel, to starboard and good anchorage in 8 feet of water in the cove just beyond the marina. Note the overhead cable (clearance 50 feet) about halfway up the creek.

Wilton Creek, off the Piankatank

Anchorage: Wilton Creek, off the Piankatank's north shore just before Wilton Point and the 43-foot fixed bridge, has high, protective banks and is a great hurricane hole. This creek does not have aids to guide you in, but there is plenty of water if you simply stay in the middle. This narrow, high-banked creek has 8-foot depths through the first cove to starboard and carries 5- to 6-foot depths for nearly a mile upstream from the entrance.

THE PIANKATANK UPRIVER BEYOND THE BRIDGE

For vessels able to clear the 43-foot Route 3 Bridge, a trip upriver has much to offer. Homes are scattered along both shores, and there is an excellent anchorage behind Berkley Island off the north shore just above the bridge. (Note that Berkley Island itself is privately owned by and part of a conference center and is used by the center in the summer months.). At the headwaters, about 5 miles above the bridge, you can anchor at Freeport at the mouth of Harper Creek, beyond this the river becomes a wide but shallow bay. Further on the river narrows marking the beginning of Dragon Run, a stream bordered by swamps and wildlife that twists and turns another 35 miles westward. The first few miles can be explored by dinghy, but the westward sections are explored by canoes that can be portered over fallen trees. The Dragon Run is known for being one of the most pristine waterways in Virginia.

HORN HARBOR AND WINTER HARBOR

Heading south on the Chesapeake Bay takes you past 52-foot-high Wolf Trap Light, a large, easily identified caisson structure. Shoals extend from shore behind the light, and strong currents in this area can produce a nasty chop when flowing against an opposing wind. Horn Harbor, a haven for boats with up to 5.5-foot drafts, is six miles south of Hole in the Wall (Gwynn Island) and 4.5 miles west-southwest of Wolf Trap Lighthouse.

WOLF TRAP
N 37°23.400'
W 076°11.400'

Waterway Guide Photography

NAVIGATION: Use Chart 12238. Horn Harbor and Winter Harbor, the only ones close to the channel for the 30 miles between the Piankatank River and Back River (near Hampton Roads), are almost side-by-side, but their marked entrances are nearly two miles apart. Only very small boats can enter Winter Harbor, which is located just to the north of Horn Harbor. Deeper-draft vessels must go south to Mobjack Bay for shelter. If you decide to enter Winter Harbor, note that many markers have been relocated, and the chart indicates only 2- to 3-foot depths near white daybeacons "C" and "D."

Dockage: Horn Harbor Marina is a pleasant two-mile cruise from the entrance and is in a hurricane-safe and tranquil setting. They can accommodate boats with up to 6-foot draft and in addition to transient dockage, they offer gas and diesel fuel. There are many sheltered anchorages in Horn Harbor. There is shopping in the area but transportation will be necessary. Approximately 5 miles away (in Mathews, VA), there is a Food Lion market, a liquor store, a pharmacy and a hardware store, along with other shops and dining choices.

MOBJACK BAY

Four rivers—the East, North, Ware and Severn—feed the 10-mile-long expanse of Mobjack Bay. This cruising ground has its own particular charm—and its own particular chop when wind and tide are in opposition. This wide tributary is distinctly salty, with pelicans wheeling overhead and dolphins chasing mullet into airborne flashes of silver. Its creeks are remote by land, so all is quiet and rural. If you need marinas and nightlife, go elsewhere, but if you seek sheltered anchorages and honking geese instead of honking cars, this is the place to be.

NAVIGATION: Use Chart 12238. Look for the tall white shaft of the unmanned New Point Comfort Lighthouse (labeled "Aband Lt Ho" on the chart) at the entrance to Mobjack Bay as you approach from the north. A direct course from 52-foot-high Wolf Trap Light will set you on the shoals off New Point Comfort Light; do not approach the light directly.

NEW PT. COMFORT
N 37°18.063'
W 076°16.683'

Waterway Guide Photography

Two less visible lights mark the shoal. The 20-foot-high easternmost one is 2.5-second flashing red "2," which looks like an ordinary red Intracoastal Waterway marker and can be hard to see. The other light, 15-foot-high, 4-second flashing red "4," is on a platform to the west. Note the shoal water just north of the two markers, and do not drift off course when traveling from one to the other. The whole area is a maze of fish stakes and trap markers. After passing flashing red "4," make sure you spot red daybeacon "6MB" as you turn northwest into Mobjack Bay. At one time, you could dinghy to the sandy beach behind the New Point Comfort Lighthouse, on the Mobjack side, for beachcombing or picnicking; however, this area has now eroded and shoaled so badly that going ashore is not recommended.

Davis Creek, a small creek just inside Mobjack Bay from New Point Comfort, has shoaled in badly; the current chart indicates only 1 foot of water. Do not try Pepper Creek, which branches off from Mobjack Bay before the East River. Pepper Creek looks like a possible anchorage at first, but the creek is very open, shallow and marked only at the entrance. The water depths here are questionable, despite the soundings indicated on the current chart.

East River, off Mobjack Bay

The East River is the first major tributary to the north as you approach from New Point Comfort. It is well marked and navigable for a considerable distance, and many cruisers call it the prettiest of the Mobjack Bay tributaries. Be on the lookout for crab trap markers; some of them manage to find their way into the main channel. The entrance is straightforward and, as you proceed upstream, you will pass many lovely private homes along the shores. The public Williams Wharf is home of the Mobjack Rowing Association, which holds camps throughout the summer, and the Mathews High School rowing team.

About two miles up the East River on the starboard side, across from green daybeacon "11," is an interesting old wooden tide mill with a paddle wheel. This mill sits on property that is also occupied by a large white house that was once owned by John Lennon and Yoko Ono, prior to Lennon's death. Unsubstantiated rumors claim that they were going to turn it into a studio. The old mill was in good repair until Hurricane Isabel damaged it severely in 2003.

NAVIGATION: Use flashing green light "1" and red daybeacon "2" as your initial entry marks.

Horn Harbor, East River, North River, VA

		Largest Vessel Accommodated	VHF Channel Monitored	Transient Berths / Total Berths	Approach / Dockside Depth (reported)	Floating Docks	Gas / Diesel	Groceries, Ice, Marine Supplies, Snacks	Repairs: Hull, Engine, Propeller	Lift (tonnage), Crane, Rail	Min/Max Amps	Laundry, Pool, Showers, Courtesy Car	Pump-Out Station	Nearby: Grocery Store, Motel, Restaurant
HORN HARBOR		Dockage					Supplies		Services					
1. Horn Harbor Marina & Boatyard	804-725-3223	80	16	8/60	6/6	F	GD	IM	HEP	L25, R	50/50	PS	P	-
EAST RIVER (MOBJACK BAY)														
2. Zimmerman Marine Inc. 🖳 WiFi	**804-725-3440**	**75**	**68**	**-**	**7/7**	**-**	**-**	**-**	**HEP**	**L40**	**30/50**	**C**	**P**	**-**
3. Compass Marina 🖳 WiFi	804-725-7999	50	68	3/17	8/8	F	-	-	-	-	30/100	LS	P	-
NORTH RIVER (MOBJACK BAY)														
4. Mobjack Bay Marina	804-725-7245	50	-	/90	10/4	-	GD	-	-	-	-	S	-	-

Corresponding chart(s) not to be used for navigation. 🖳 Internet Access WiFi Wireless Internet Access Waterway Guide Cruising Club Partner

See www.WaterwayGuide.com for current rates, fuel prices, web site addresses, and other up-to-the-minute information.

Dockage: Compass Marina, located near flashing green "9", may have transient space on their floating docks. (Call ahead to confirm.) The original yard of Zimmerman Marine, respected for its high-quality boatbuilding and restoration work, is just across the river from Williams Wharf. (Their second location is in Deltaville at Norview Marina on Broad Creek.) This is a working boat yard and does not offer transient slips.

Anchorage: Wakes may be troublesome, but there are many anchorages along the East River, including a deep spot just south of Williams Wharf (in the area of green daybeacon "13"); several below Long Point, on either side of the channel south of Williams Wharf; and several others above Long Point. The area below Long Point can accommodate a small cruising group off the private docks there. Another good spot is above Long Point, with depths of about 10 feet, good holding in mud and only a few trap markers. Anchor in the bight between green daybeacons "15" and "17."

Many boats anchor in 10- to 11-foot depths in the mouth of Put in Creek, off the East River, but there are often bush stakes and trap markers. At high tide you can take a dinghy up Put in Creek to the small town of Mathews, the only place off the East River to get any supplies, including groceries. There is not an actual dinghy dock but a muddy landing that will put you steps from the heart of downtown Mathews, where you will find exceptionally good restaurants and specialty shops. A park is under construction at the head of the creek.

North River, off Mobjack Bay

The North River is next as you travel counterclockwise around Mobjack Bay. Both banks of the deep tree-lined North River boast beautiful homes, both old and new, and above Elmington Creek, you will see Elmington, a mansion resembling Thomas Jefferson's Monticello estate. Keep a sharp eye out for markers that have been relocated.

Dockage: Mobjack Bay Marina in Greenmansion Cove off the North River may have space for transients.

Anchorage: Across from the Elmington Mansion on the upper North River is a nice place to anchor in 6- to 10-foot depths. There are no navigational aids beyond Elmington (green daybeacon "7" at Back Creek is the last). You can also anchor in Blackwater Creek, branching to the north off the North River, with 8- to 10-foot depths.

Ware River off Mobjack Bay

The Ware River, which might get the award for having the greatest number of fish stakes on the Chesapeake (weir is a set of stakes set to trap fish, hence the name "Ware"), looks like a picket fence in some spots. Ware River empties into Mobjack Bay at Ware Neck Point. This river is also lined with beautiful estates.

NAVIGATION: Use Chart 12238. Be aware of the shoal extending southward from Ware Neck Point. The channel mark for this shoal is red daybeacon "2." A short dogleg leads around Windmill Point to port, and another to starboard at Jarvis Point, with an island behind it, marked by quick flashing red "6." Note the long shoal off the islet. Do not attempt to pass between the islet and the mainland, as it is bare at low water.

Anchorage: Wilson Creek, off the south side of the Ware River past Windmill Point, is a good anchorage. Follow the creek's private markers closely, as these unnumbered markers are barely visible just above the waterline. The only way to distinguish them is by shape, if you can see them at all. Use the depth sounder and feel your way in to a suitable depth. Another anchorage is in the shallow cove behind Windmill Point. This spot is well-protected from the east and south. (There are numerous "Windmill Points" on the Bay; make sure you know which one you are headed for.)

Severn River, off Mobjack Bay

The Severn River is more remote and marshy than the other three rivers of Mobjack Bay, particularly at its lower end. Very unlike its Annapolis, MD counterpart in appearance, the river splits off into the Northwest and Southwest branches at Stump Point, both fairly well marked, with good depths.

Dockage: The full-service Severn River Marina is on the northern shore of the Southwest Branch of the Severn River past red daybeacon "4" and offers transient vessels 6-foot depths alongside fixed and floating docks and has a 75- ton lift. Holiday Marina, across the river from Severn River Marina, is a working (waterman's) marina.

Anchorage: In the Northwestern Branch the most popular anchorage is in the cove opposite green daybeacon "5" in Bryant Bay. Another popular spot is a quiet place near the mouth of Free School Creek, in depths of 4 to 10 feet. The holding is good in mud, and you will find little development and few crab trap markers here. Cruisers consider the Southwestern Branch less attractive than the Northwestern, and the Southwestern Branch entrance, although easy to enter, can be confusing from a distance—leave both lighted flashing green "3" and then green daybeacon "1" to port. The area by red daybeacon "2" off Stump Point was shoaling to 7-foot depths in recent years. The creeks to port are all shoal except for Rowes Creek, which has a marked channel for a short distance.

■ YORK RIVER

There are three ways to approach the York River from the north: the Swash Channel, the marked channel between York Spit Light and quick flashing red gong buoy "14" in the York River Entrance Channel, and east of York Spit Light. If you are entering the York River from the (south) Poquoson River in a shallow-draft boat, you can use the Goodwin Islands Thorofare, which has maximum 3-foot depths.

NAVIGATION: Use Chart 12238. Use **Hampton Roads tide tables. For high tide at Yorktown (York River), add 11 minutes; for low tide, add 6 minutes.** You can use the Swash Channel to enter the York when coming down from Mobjack Bay. This marked channel cuts through the shallowest part of the York Spit shoal, between the Guinea Marshes

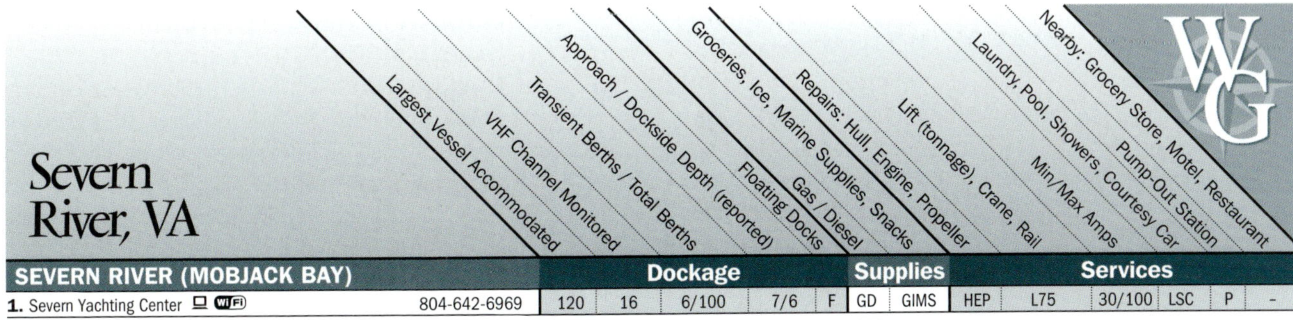

Severn River, VA

SEVERN RIVER (MOBJACK BAY)		Largest Vessel Accommodated	VHF Channel Monitored	Transient Berths / Total Berths	Approach / Dockside Depth (reported)	Floating Docks	Gas / Diesel	Groceries, Ice, Marine Supplies, Snacks	Repairs: Hull, Engine, Propeller	Lift (tonnage), Crane, Rail	Min/Max Amps	Laundry, Pool, Showers, Courtesy Car	Pump-Out Station	Nearby: Grocery Store, Motel, Restaurant
		Dockage					Supplies		Services					
1. Severn Yachting Center 🖳 WiFi	804-642-6969	120	16	6/100	7/6	F	GD	GIMS	HEP	L75	30/100	LSC	P	-

Corresponding chart(s) not to be used for navigation. 🖳 Internet Access WiFi Wireless Internet Access Waterway Guide Cruising Club Partner

See www.WaterwayGuide.com for current rates, fuel prices, web site addresses, and other up-to-the-minute information.

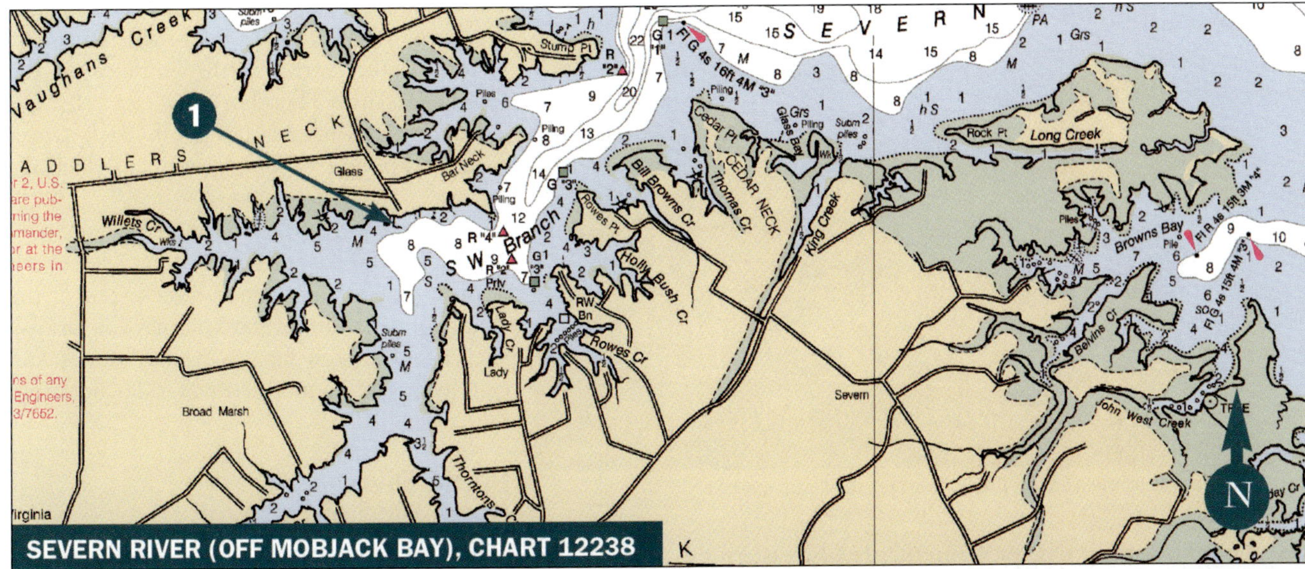

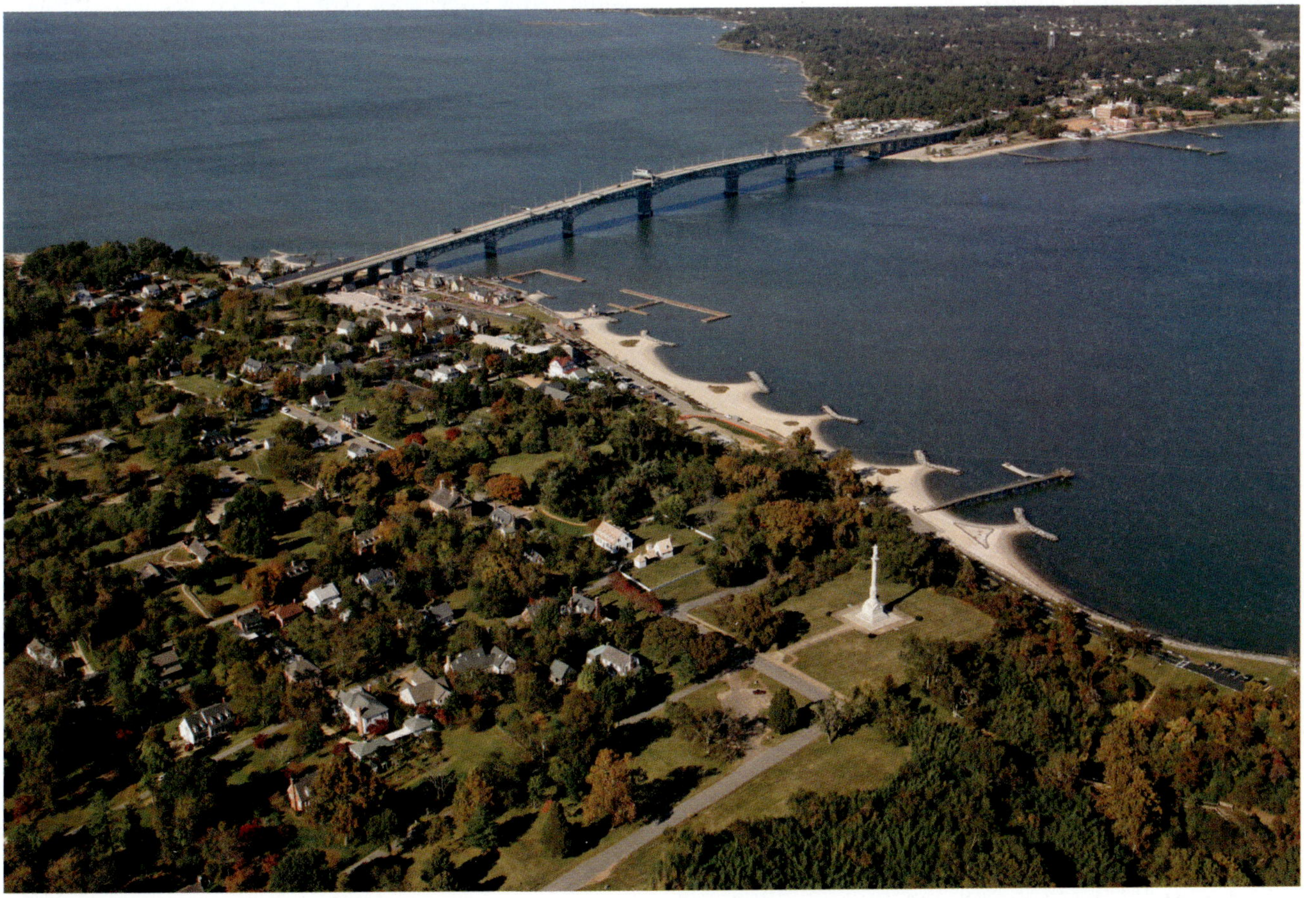

Looking northwest over the York River. (Not to be used for navigation.) Waterway Guide Photography

Looking southwest over Sarah Creek. (Not to be used for navigation.)
Waterway Guide Photography

and the white "shoal" daybeacon on the shallow eastern tip of the bar. The only lighted marker is flashing green "3," at the middle of the shoal, which is followed by unlighted red daybeacon "2" when headed south. This channel is used regularly by local boats, but use this approach cautiously and you will find 7 feet through the channel. Depths here are charted at 7 to 9 feet.

Farther east, the second route begins with red nun "2" and green can "1NP" about four miles east of New Point Comfort Light at the mouth of Mobjack Bay. Next, the route heads southwest between red nun "4" and green can "3," and then daybeacons "6" and "5." Finally, the route enters the York River between York Spit Light and quick flashing red gong buoy "14" in the York River Entrance Channel. This route is supposed to be trap-free; if you get out of the channel, you will have to go around many fish pound nets.

The third route is east of York Spit Light at green can "1MB" and red nun "2MB." From there, travel west to the York River Entrance Channel between flashing green buoy "9" and flashing red buoy "10," and then flashing green "11" and flashing red buoy "12." It is safe to go inside York Spit Light as long as you pass east of quick flashing red gong buoy "14" to avoid the end of the shallowest part of the York Spit Sandbar and the pound nets.

Goodwin Islands Thorofare, South Side of the York River

NAVIGATION: Use Chart 12238. When coming north from the Poquoson River to the York River, unless you know these waters, do not use the Thorofare between Goodwin Islands and Goodwin Neck, even at high tide. This passage at the mouth of the York to Back Creek has shoaled badly in recent years. If the 2-foot tidal range here permits your boat to get through to the York River side from the entrance south of Tue Marshes Point, note that navigational aids run from the Bay side. "Red-right-returning" is toward the York (north) entrance to the Goodwin Islands Thorofare.

Dockage: Mills Marina is on Back Creek with 60 slips and 7-foot approach and dockside depths.

Anchorage: The area between green daybeacon "7" and flashing green "1" in Back Creek in Seaford, just off Claxton Creek (out of the channel) and south of the Thorofare, is an easy anchorage not too far off the Bay. Enter and exit from the Poquoson River side, not from the York.

Perrin River, North Side of the York River

The first tributary off the north side of the York is the Perrin River, lined with a series of commercial-fishing docks and repair yards catering largely to the fishermen of Guinea Neck.

NAVIGATION: Use Chart 12238. Follow the channel carefully, especially if you draw more than 5 feet. Be sure to keep flashing red "8" close to starboard on entering.

Dockage: Crown Pointe Marina and B.R. Marine Service and Railway are located on the Perrin River. Crown Pointe Marina offers fuel, haul-out (50-ton lift) and transient berths. B.R. Marine Service and Railway offers transient slips but no facilities (laundry, shower, etc.).

Wormley Creek, South Side of the York River

Above the oil refinery and power plant on the south shore, the dredged channel leading in to Wormley Creek is straightforward but narrow and carries 6-foot depths. The Yorktown Coast Guard Training Center is located on the peninsula to the west. Just inside the entrance on the east shore is Wormley Creek Marina with a full-service yard and reported 6-foot approach and dockside depths.

Sarah Creek, on the North Shore of the York

Sarah Creek, the area's major yachting center, is six miles up the York River on the north side, just below the high-rise Coleman Bridge between Yorktown and Gloucester Point.

NAVIGATION: Use Chart 12238. **Use Hampton Roads tide tables. For high tide at Yorktown (York River), add 11 minutes; for low tide, add 6 minutes.** Entering Sarah Creek, a mild zigzag channel takes you close to shore from red daybeacon "6" to flashing red "8," and then between two sand spits at green daybeacon "9." If you are in the mood for some dinghy exploration and want to do a little shopping, you can follow the northwest branch of Sarah Creek all the way to its end. The last 100 yards are through a drainage canal lined with marsh grass. There, you can go ashore into the back parking lot of York Crossing Shopping Center in Gloucester, which has a Food Lion and a movie theater, among other things.

Dockage: York River Yacht Haven welcomes transients and has a large, well-stocked ship's store, pool, on-site restaurant and courtesy car. Jordan Marina, up the northwest branch, has a railway and lift and is mainly a "working yard." They are difficult to get in touch with because they do not monitor the radio, so a phone call is necessary.

Anchorage: Sarah Creek, across from York River Yacht Haven, is a popular spot with 8-foot depths and good holding in mud. Do not go shoreward of the trap markers. At low water, the entrance channel is 7 feet deep. Clumps of stakes, some with flags, mark critical spots. You may use the showers at the York River Yacht Haven for a fee, but the pool is for marina guests only. Tie up your dinghy on the floating dock adjacent to the ship's store.

A bit farther up the York River above the entrance to Sarah Creek, the Virginia Institute of Marine Science, a division of William and Mary College, is in the red brick buildings just below Gloucester Point at the Route 17 Coleman Memorial Bridge (dual swing, 60-foot closed vertical clearance). One building features exhibits and a large marine library.

Yorktown, on the South Shore of the York River

A tall monument to the Battle of Yorktown, the penultimate land battle of the American Revolution, where Cornwallis surrendered to George Washington on Oct. 19, 1781, stands on the southern shore of the York River below the Coleman Memorial Bridge at Yorktown. Many of the original redoubts are intact, and the battlefield and victory center nearby are well worth a visit.

NAVIGATION: Use Chart 12243. The Coleman Memorial Bridge (twin-span swing) at Yorktown has a closed vertical clearance of 60 feet.

Dockage: Riverwalk Landing Marina, a public York County dock, lies at the foot of the Coleman Memorial Bridge on the York River's south shore with ample transient dockage. Be careful when docking here, as the tidal river current can be strong through this constricted area. Even a light wind opposing the current can cause swells to develop, a factor that should be considered when choosing an overnight berth. Electric, water, showers and pump-out are available.

Anchorage: The area between Riverwalk Landing Marina and Point of Rocks is a popular anchorage, particularly during the Yorktown Fourth of July celebration and fireworks. The water is deep here (30 to 40 feet) and the current runs at 1.5 knots. Unless you have 300- to 400-feet of anchor rode (for 10:1 scope), you will have to set your hook on the narrow shelf on the south side of the river. There is, however, another option. There are a number of white mooring balls along the Yorktown shore. If you can pass a pennant through the eye on the top of the ball, you can tie securely to these moorings. These mooring balls are reportedly placed by the US Park Service and managed by the Riverwalk Landing Marina.

QUICK FACT:

VIRGINIA INSTITUTE OF MARINE SCIENCE

Half of humanity and more than two-thirds of all Americans live within 50 miles of the sea. The Chesapeake Bay watershed now holds 16 million people and will likely hold 18 million by 2020. As human pressures on the coastal zone increase, so too does the need for scientific research to guide the wise management of marine resources for current and future generations.

The Virginia Institute of Marine Science (VIMS) is uniquely positioned to provide the knowledge-based guidance that research brings. Located on a 40-acre campus on the shores of Chesapeake Bay in Gloucester Point, Virginia, VIMS has a 70-year history of providing knowledge and solutions to address the many challenges facing the coastal ocean. VIMS research helps sustain fish and shellfish stocks, improve water quality, keep our beaches clean, develop new energy sources, and better understand the intricate web that supports ocean life. Chartered in 1940, VIMS is one of the leading marine research and education centers in the U.S. Research at VIMS extends from inland watersheds to the open ocean, with a primary emphasis on the coastal zone. VIMS has a three-part mission to conduct research, educate students and citizens, and provide advisory service to policy makers, industry, and the public. VIMS provides these services to Virginia, the nation, and the world. The School of Marine Science at VIMS is the graduate school in marine science for the College of William & Mary. VIMS alumni serve leading roles in academia, government, and industry.

GOIN' ASHORE: **YORKTOWN, VA**

Yorktown and its battlefields, of both the Revolutionary and Civil wars, are part of Virginia's Historic Triangle and are linked to Colonial Williamsburg and Jamestown Settlement by the Colonial Parkway. Those, along with the historical homes and buildings sitting on the hill overlooking the river, are well worth a visit.

History: Yorktown had, from 1634, been the seat of local government when an act passed in 1691 by the Virginia House of Burgesses established it as one of the official ports through which trade goods could enter or leave the Virginia Colony. The town was laid out on a 50-acre parcel of land on the York River and quickly grew in importance serving Williamsburg, where the capital of Virginia had been moved after the rebel Nathaniel Bacon burned Jamestown in 1698.

In the mid-1700s, Yorktown's significance as a port declined as tobacco planters, having exhausted the soil in the region, moved westward in search of more fertile lands. In 1781, it suddenly drew less welcome attention when Lord Cornwallis, hoping to keep a grip on the southern colonies, chose it as the site for a navy base. When, on September 5 of that year, Admiral de Grasse cut off his supply lines by defeating the British fleet in the Battle of the Capes, Cornwallis dug in. The allied American and French armies dug in around him, and the ensuing Siege of Yorktown ended on Oct. 19, 1781, when Cornwallis surrendered his army to Gen. Washington, effectively bringing the Revolutionary War to a conclusion. (A small sand stone cave on Water Street was supposedly used as the headquarters for Cornwallis when he realized defeat was imminent.)

After the war, Yorktown recovered slowly but suffered further setbacks. In 1814, a fire razed buildings on the waterfront, and in 1863, a couple of Union Army powder magazines exploded, destroying a large area of the town.

To this day, the seat of York County, Yorktown has remained small and the creation around it of the Colonial National Historical Park has protected it from the strip-mall development seen elsewhere along U.S. Route 17.

Points of Interest: There is one compelling reason to visit Yorktown, and that is to visit the Yorktown National Battlefield. If you have the endurance, walk through the refreshingly unspoiled village to get there—it is about half a mile from the town dock to the visitor center. There is a footpath that takes you by the Victory Monument, dedicated to the victory of the battle of Yorktown, on the way to the visitor center and adjacent battlefields. During summer months, a trolley runs between the visitor center and the Yorktown Victory Center, about a half-mile in the opposite direction, with several stops around the town and along the riverfront.

If you plan on taking in the Historic Triangle, a free shuttle bus runs from late April to October 19 between the

Yorktown Victory Monument. Credit: National Park Service

York River, VA

YORK RIVER		Largest Vessel Accommodated	VHF Channel Monitored	Transient Berths / Total Berths	Approach / Dockside Depth (reported)	Floating Docks	Gas / Diesel	Groceries, Ice, Marine Supplies, Snacks	Repairs: Hull, Engine, Propeller	Lift (tonnage), Crane, Rail	Min/Max Amps	Laundry, Pool, Showers, Courtesy Car	Pump-Out Station	Nearby: Grocery Store, Motel, Restaurant
		Dockage					Supplies		Services					
1. Crown Pointe Marina (Internet Access) (Wireless Internet Access)	804-642-6177	50	16	20/225	7/6	-	GD	IMS	HEP	L20	30/50	LPS	P	-
2. York River Yacht Haven (Internet Access) (Wireless Internet Access)	804-642-2156	160	16/09	20/288	8/14	F	GD	IMS	HE	L60, C	30/100	LPSC	P	GMR
3. Jordan Marine Service	804-642-4360	70	-	10/24	7/7	-	-	MS	HEP	L60, R	50/50	S	P	-
4. Riverwalk Landing Marina	**757-890-3370**	**375**	**16/68**	**30/30**	**50/20**	**F**	**-**	**I**	**-**	**-**	**30/100**	**S**	**P**	**MR**
5. Wormley Creek Marina	757-898-5060	70	16	4/90	6/6	-	-	IMS	HEP	L35, C	50/50	S	P	R
6. Mills Marina, Inc. (Internet Access) (Wireless Internet Access)	757-898-4411	75	-	10/60	7/7	-	-	I	-	-	30/50	S		-

Corresponding chart(s) not to be used for navigation. Internet Access Wireless Internet Access Waterway Guide Cruising Club Partner
See www.WaterwayGuide.com for current rates, fuel prices, web site addresses, and other up-to-the-minute information.

battlefield, Colonial Williamsburg and Jamestown Settlement (757-898-2410).

York County Historical Museum (757-890-3508), on Main Street, traces Yorktown and the surrounding region from its origins. Grace Church, which dates to 1697, is one of the few authentic colonial churches that remain in Virginia. The Watermen's Museum (309 Water St., 757-887-2641), just west of the Coleman Bridge, examines the lives and livelihoods of the men, accorded the title "waterman" only on Chesapeake Bay and England's River Thames, who have contributed so much to the economy of the region from the time of the first European settlers.

Shopping: In a move that would have astounded Cornwallis, Riverwalk Landing shopping plaza (www.riverwalklanding.com) opened in 2005 on the site where British forces surrendered 224 years earlier to the Confederacy. To their credit, York County and its principal partner in the development, the National Parks Service, exercised rigid architectural control and the brick and clapboard structures imitate, in their proportions and style, the genuine Colonial-era buildings that remain today in the village on the bluff above. One of the original shops is Yorktown Shoppe (308 Main St., 757-898-2984), which is a venue for colonial era recreations and replicas, and there are several antique shops as well. The new Riverwalk businesses include an ice cream shop, a coffee café, and a wine store. There is also a patriotic-themed store, Stars & Stripes Forever (757-898-0288); a home and garden store, the Yorktown Onion (319 Water St., 757-872-8232); and hooked rug creations from Claire Murray (757-877-3353), among other specialty shops. Patriot Tours & provisions (321 Water St., 757-969-5400) offers Segway tours, bike rentals, beach supplies and more.

Dining: For lunch daily and dinner on summer weekends, Carrot Tree (411 Main St., 757-988-1999) in the Cole Diggs House on Main Street, the oldest home in the town, hints at the atmosphere of 1720, even serving "High Tea" on Tuesday and Wednesday afternoons. A couple of spots on Water Street east of Riverwalk Landing offer a bit more color. Beach Delly (524 Water St., 757-886-5890) provides family fare, and next door, the Yorktown Pub (540 Water St., 757-886-9964)

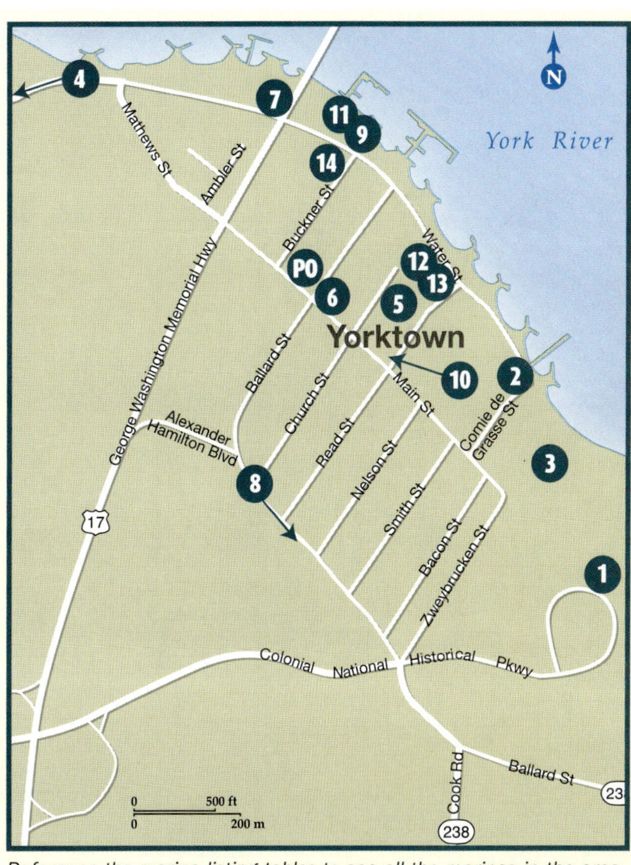

Reference the marina listing tables to see all the marinas in the area.

POINTS OF INTEREST
1 Yorktown Battlefield Visitor Center
2 Cornwalls Cave
3 Yorktown Victory Monument
4 Yorktown Victory Center
5 York County Historical Museum
6 Grace Eiscopal Church
7 Waterman's Museum

SHOPPING
8 Historic District
9 Riverwalk Landing

DINING
10 Carrot Tree in the Cole Diggs House
11 Riverwalk Restaurant/High Tide Bar & Grill
12 Beach Delly
13 Yorktown Pub
14 Ben & Jerry's Ice Cream

PO POST OFFICE

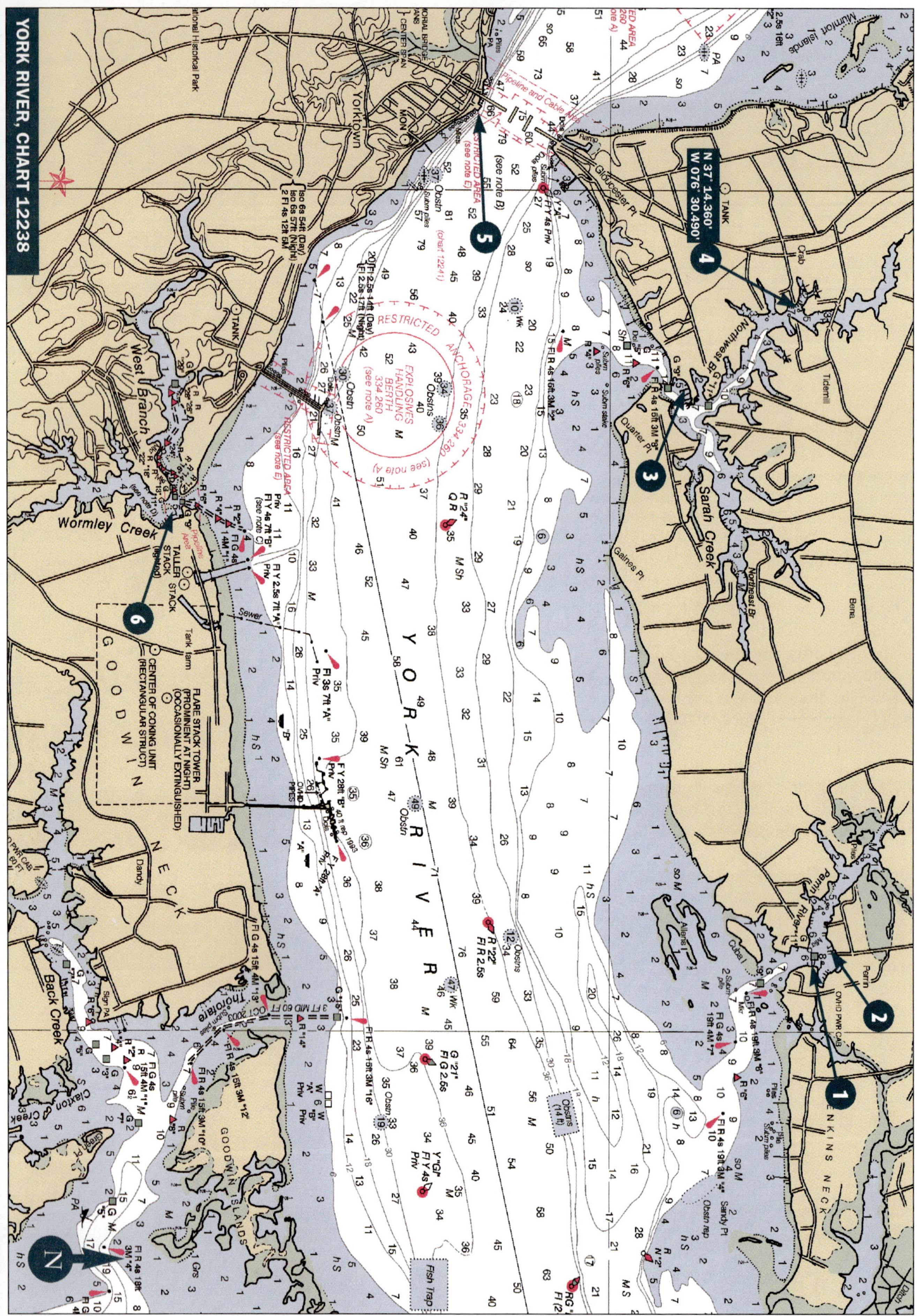
YORK RIVER, CHART 12238
N 37° 14.360'
W 076° 30.490'
Yorktown
Gloucester Pt
Sarah Creek
Northeast Br
Northwest Br
Quarter Pt
Gaines Pt
Perrin River
Crab
Tidemill
JENKINS NECK
Sandy Pt
Allens I
Cuba I
Mumfort Islands
RESTRICTED ANCHORAGE
EXPLOSIVES HANDLING BERTH
RESTRICTED AREA
Y O R K R I V E R
West Branch
Wormley Creek
GOODWIN NECK
GOODWIN ISLANDS
Back Creek
Claxton Creek
Thorofare
FLARE STACK TOWER (PROMINENT AT NIGHT) (OCCASIONALLY EXTINGUISHED)
CENTER OF COKING UNIT (RECTANGULAR STRUCT)
TALLER STACK
Tank farm
Fish Trap
Dandy
National Historical Park

caters more to an adult clientele, with live music on weekends. There are also two restaurants in the same location at Riverwalk Landing: The Riverwalk Restaurant and High Tide Bar & Grill (323 Water St., 757-875-1522). If you are craving something sweet and refreshing, there is a Ben & Jerry's Ice Cream at 332 Water St.

ADDITIONAL RESOURCES

- YORK COUNTY: 757-890-3300, www.yorkcounty.gov
- COLONIAL NATIONAL HISTORICAL PARK: 757-898-3400, www.nps.gov/colo
- YORKTOWN BATTLEFIELD: 757-898-2410, www.nps.gov/york

NEARBY MEDICAL FACILITIES
Riverside Regional Medical Center:
500 J. Clyde Morris Blvd., Newport News, VA 23601
757-594-2000, www.riversideonline.com (8 miles)

NEARBY AIRPORTS
Newport News/Williamsburg International Airport (PHF), 757-877-0221 (10 miles)

Upriver on the York

The north shore of the river is Gloucester County, birthplace of Dr. Walter Reed, discoverer of the cause of yellow fever, and where a private mint fashioned the first coin ever made in America, the Gloucester token, in 1714. Many old and beautiful houses, some dating back hundreds of years, line the riverbank between the Coleman Memorial Bridge and West Point.

Thirty miles up from its mouth, the York River brings you to the junction of the Mattaponi and Pamunkey rivers at West Point. There are no protected anchorages on the York River above the bridge before West Point, and there is no transient dockage above the bridge at Gloucester Point. Observe the restricted government areas on the south shore between the Coleman Bridge at Yorktown and Queen Creek, several miles upriver.

West Point, on the York

If you have a sense of adventure, the cruise up the York to West Point is rewarding. The upper river is beautiful with high wooded banks, occasional marshy areas and red cliffs. On hazy days, the York River shores are too far away for a good view, and even on clear days, you may need binoculars to see the farms and large white plantation homes with their wide, well-tended lawns.

From the water, West Point looks like a miniature Charleston, and residents are restoring many of the old houses. A new town dock and marina are also planned for the future, but currently there is no dockage. A small beach at the southern tip of the town's peninsula is public and provides a spot for landing a dinghy, and a public launch ramp is just above the bridge on the Mattaponi River. Currents are strong in the area and the bottom is mud.

Cruiser enjoying the sunny day. (Photo Courtesy of Reesa Kugler)

Poquoson River, VA

POQUOSON RIVER		Largest Vessel Accommodated	VHF Channel Monitored	Transient Berths / Total Berths	Approach / Dockside Depth (reported)	Floating Docks	Gas / Diesel	Groceries, Ice, Marine Supplies, Snacks	Repairs: Hull, Engine, Propeller	Lift (tonnage), Crane, Rail	Min/Max Amps	Laundry, Pool, Showers, Courtesy Car	Pump-Out Station	Nearby: Grocery Store, Motel, Restaurant
		Dockage					Supplies		Services					
1. Dare Marina	757-898-3000	65	16/18	3/175	8/5	F	GD	IMS	HEP	L10	30/50	S	P	G
2. York Haven Marina	757-868-4532	65	-	2/70	15/6.5	-	-	-	HEP	L50	30/30	S	P	GR
3. Whitehouse Cove Marina (Wireless Internet Access) (Waterway Guide Cruising Club Partner)	757-508-2602	100	-	21/165	10/10	-	-	IMS	EP	-	50/50	LS	P	GMR

Corresponding chart(s) not to be used for navigation. Internet Access Wireless Internet Access Waterway Guide Cruising Club Partner

See www.WaterwayGuide.com for current rates, fuel prices, web site addresses, and other up-to-the-minute information.

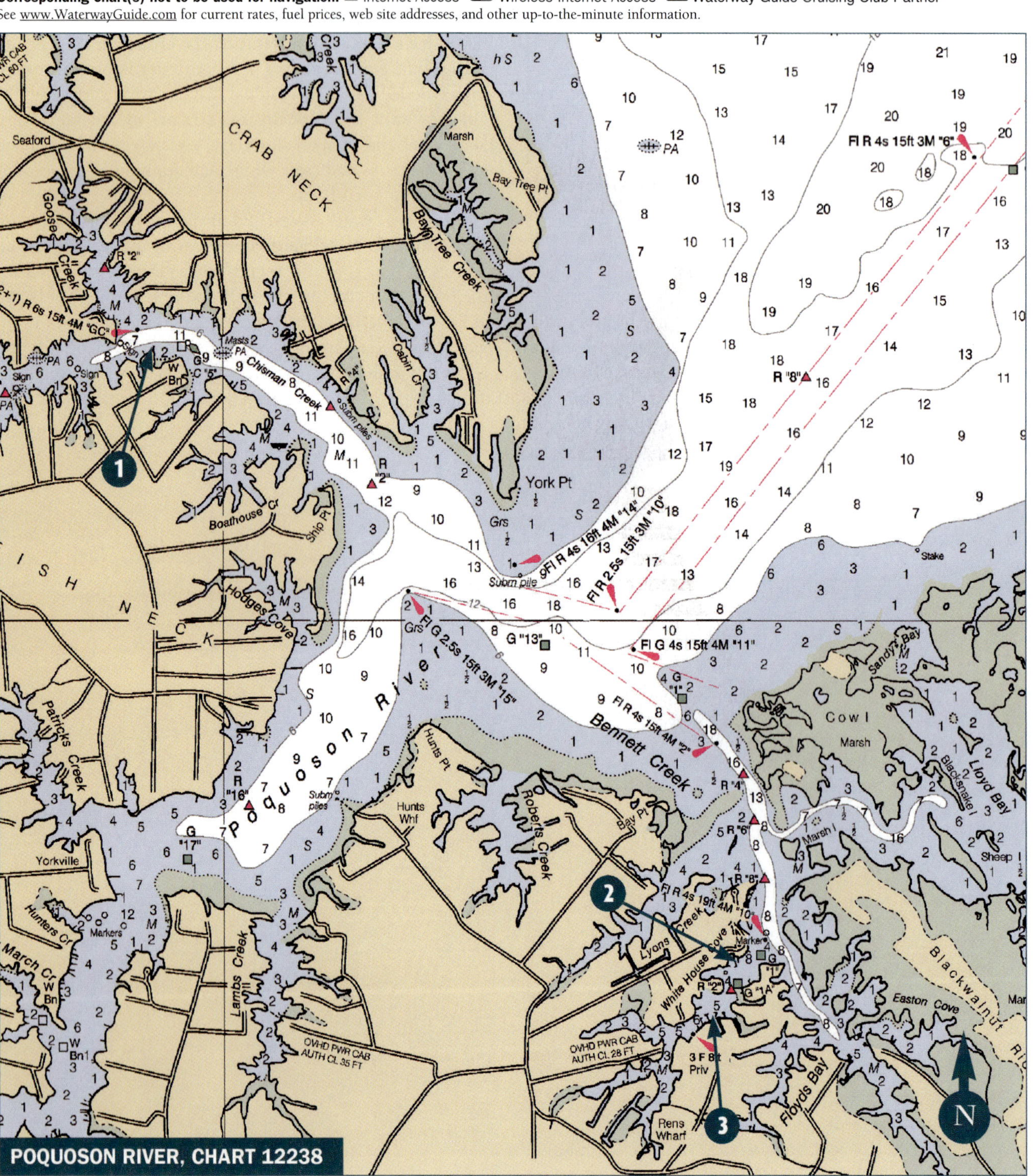

POQUOSON RIVER, CHART 12238

NAVIGATION: Use Chart 12243. The channel up the York is well marked and easy to follow, but the fish stakes and nets upriver are amazingly dense in places. You will encounter little commercial traffic except for tugs with barges headed for the paper mill at West Point.

Mattaponi and Pamunkey Rivers, top of the York River

Both rivers are beautiful, deep and marshy, and the Pamunkey is noticeably undeveloped except for numerous large farms and old estates. Both rivers offer few good anchorages because of depths and swift currents. Both rivers are navigable past the American Indian reservations on their shores, where members of the Mattaponi and Pamunkey tribes live.

NAVIGATION: Use Chart 12243, 12244. An overhead power cable with authorized vertical clearance of 60 feet is above the Pamunkey River Bridge. It droops in the middle, but you can get more clearance by passing close to shore on the northeast side of the channel. A 62-foot-high cable crosses the river above the Mattaponi Bridge. There are two high-level bridges: the Lord Delaware Bridge over the Mattaponi and the Eltham Bridge over the Pamunkey. The Lord Delaware Bridge is fixed with 55-foot vertical clearance. The Eltham Bridge opens with advance notice: 757-424-9903 (VDOT) and has 56-foot closed vertical clearance.

Anchorage: With caution, you can anchor on the Pamunkey River side of West Point in 15- to 20-foot depths, below the bridge. Watch for rotted pilings on the outside of the Pamunkey River channel on both sides of the river below the bridge.

■ POQUOSON RIVER OFF THE CHESAPEAKE BAY SOUTH OF THE YORK RIVER

South of the York River, the Poquoson River is now almost completely populated by people who work in nearby Newport News, Hampton or at Langley Air Force Base.

NAVIGATION: Use Chart 12238. The Poquoson River's entrance from the northeast has clear markings. Be sure to avoid the Poquoson Flats to the south. Inside the entrance, the river shoals near its banks. Watch for fish stakes.

Dockage: Dare Marina on Chisman Creek has transient accommodations and repair services. York Haven Marina and White House Cove Marina are located in White House Cove off of Bennett Creek to the south of the Poquoson River proper and may have transient space.

Anchorage: Chisman Creek, off the north side of the Poquoson, has a good anchorage on its southwest side between red daybeacon "4" and green can buoy "5" in 7- to 10-foot depths. Bennett Creek (to the south) and the creeks and coves that branch off from it are not popular for

QUICK FACT:

DR. WALTER REED (1851-1902)

Lemuel Sutton Reed and Pharaba White Reed welcomed young Walter into the family on September 13, 1851; he was the youngest of their five children. Reed attended two year-long sessions at the University of Virginia, the second devoted entirely to the medical curriculum, and he completed an M.D. degree on July 1, 1869, the youngest graduate to date in the history of the medical school.

Reed interned at a number of hospitals in the New York metropolitan area, including the Infants' Hospital on Randall's Island and the Brooklyn City Hospital. The large and diverse population of New York, with its many immigrant communities and dense, tenement housing, provided countless medical cases to treat and study; these served to expose Reed to the vital importance of public health and developed in him a lifelong interest in the field. Reed consequently resolved to join the Army Medical Corps, both for the professional opportunities it offered immediately and for the modest financial security it could provide to a young man without independent means.

Reed remained in the Medical Corps for the rest of his life, spending many years of the '70s, '80s and early '90s at difficult postings in the American West.

When he returned from his last western appointment in 1893, Reed joined the faculty of the Army Medical School in Washington, D.C., where he held the professorship of Bacteriology and Clinical Microscopy.

In 1896, a research trip to investigate an outbreak of smallpox took him to Key West, and there he developed a close friendship with Jefferson Randolph Kean, a fellow Virginian and colleague in the Medical Corps ten years his junior. When Reed traveled to Cuba in 1899 to study typhoid in the army encampments of the U.S. forces, Kean was already there, and Kean was still in Cuba when Reed returned as the head of the Army board charged by Surgeon General George Miller Sternberg to examine tropical diseases including yellow fever. Kean served as quartermaster for the famous series of experiments at Camp Lazear. After the dramatic and conclusive success of those experiments, Kean actively—though unsuccessfully—promoted Reed's candidacy for Surgeon General.

In November 1902, Reed developed what had been for him recurring gastro-intestinal trouble. This time, however, his appendix ruptured, and surgery came too late to save him from the peritonitis which developed. He died on November 23, 1902, almost two years to the day from the opening of Camp Lazear and the stunning experimental victory there.

Courtesy of Historical Collections & Services, Claude Moore Health Sciences Library, University of Virginia. (http://yellowfever.lib.virginia.edu/) The full article can be found at http://yellowfever.lib.virginia.edu/reed/reed.html.

Back River, Bloxoms Corner, VA

		Largest Vessel Accommodated	VHF Channel Monitored	Transient Berths / Total Berths	Approach / Dockside Depth (reported)	Floating Docks	Gas / Diesel	Groceries, Ice, Marine Supplies, Snacks	Repairs: Hull, Engine, Propeller	Lift (tonnage), Crane, Rail	Min/Max Amps	Laundry, Pool, Showers, Courtesy Car	Pump-Out Station	Nearby: Grocery Store, Motel, Restaurant
BACK RIVER		Dockage					Supplies		Services					
1. Marina Cove Boat Basin	757-851-0511	55	-	1/	14/7	-	GD	GIM	HEP	L	30/100	S	P	R
2. Dandy Haven Marina	757-851-1573	45	-	/75	6/5	F	-	M	HEP	L25	30/50	-	P	-
3. Bell Isle Marina (WiFi)	757-850-0466	50	16/13	10/75	7/7	F	GD	GIMS	HEP	L13	30/50	S	P	GMR
BLOXOMS CORNER														
4. Southall Landings Marina	757-850-9929	60	16	30/200	8/8	-	-	IS	-	-	30/50	LPS	P	R
5. Salt Ponds Marina (Internet)	757-850-4300	110	16/09	10/280	8/8	F	GD	I	-	-	30/50	LPS	P	MR

Corresponding chart(s) not to be used for navigation. Internet Access (WiFi) Wireless Internet Access Waterway Guide Cruising Club Partner

See www.WaterwayGuide.com for current rates, fuel prices, web site addresses, and other up-to-the-minute information.

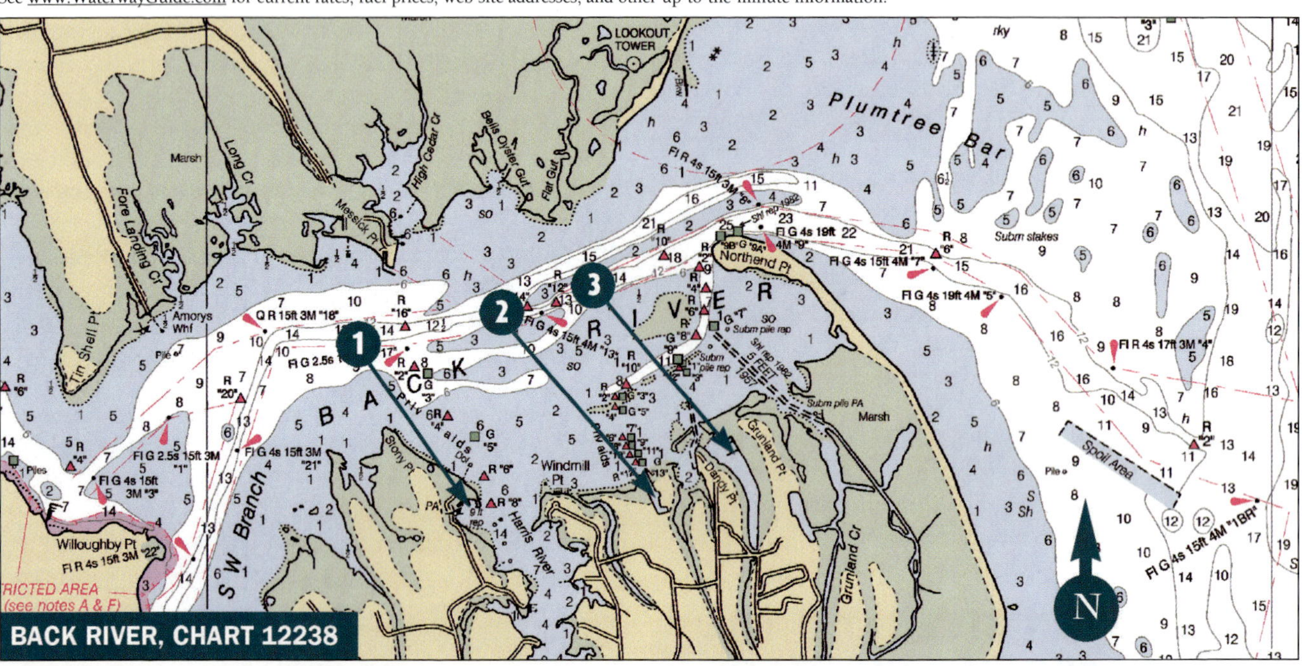

BACK RIVER, CHART 12238

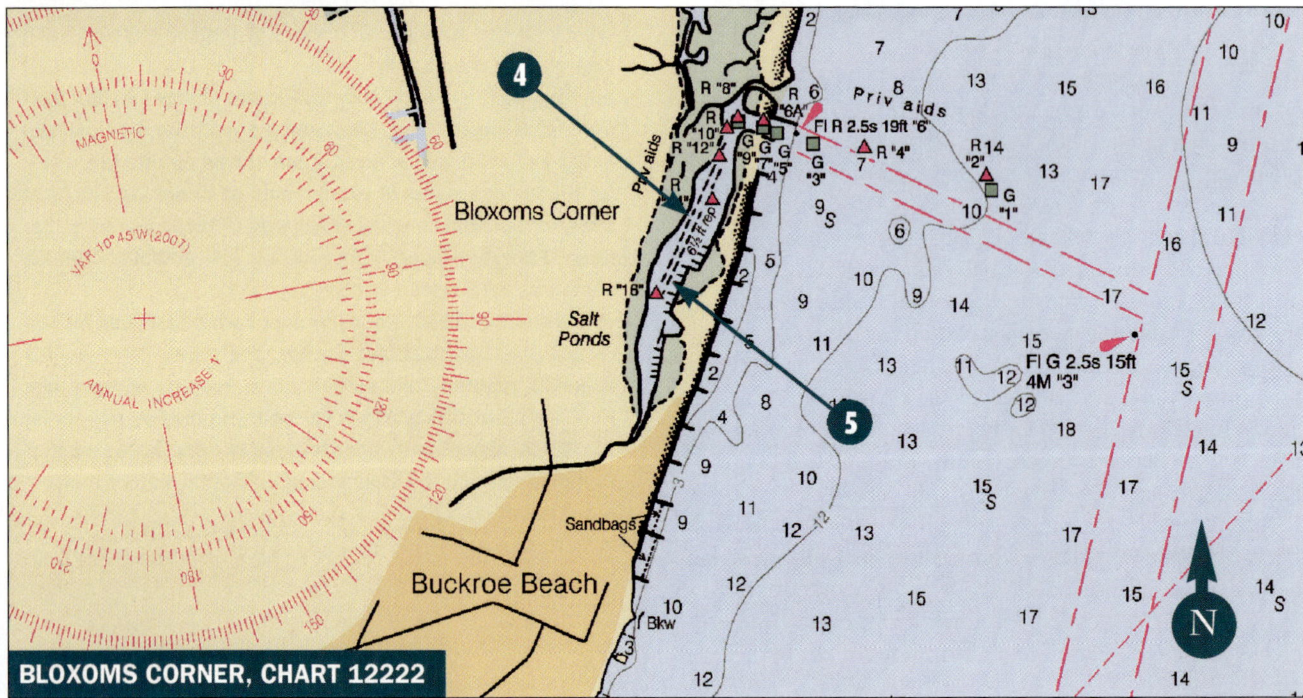

BLOXOMS CORNER, CHART 12222

Looking south over Back River and Salt Ponds. (Not to be used for navigation.) Photo Courtesy of Mike Kucera

anchoring; most of the side waters here are shoal, and the main channel is narrow.

Back River and Salt Ponds

Skippers of shoal-draft cruising boats should know about Back River, on the south side of Poquoson Flats, even though it is not regularly frequented. Once inside, it is easy to reach the boating facilities or to find anchorages away from the main channel.

Directly off the Bay, tiny Salt Ponds Harbor at Bloxoms Corner is halfway between Back River and Old Point Comfort (the entrance to Hampton Roads Harbor). The entrance is prone to shoaling but is otherwise easy to enter. Maintenance dredging was completed in April 2009.

NAVIGATION: Use Chart 12238 and Chart 12222. The Poquoson Flats Channel, marked by daybeacons, begins at York River Channel between flashing green lights "11" and "9," and leads across Horseshoe and Thimble shoals to Old Point Comfort. From this channel, you will find the markers leading to Back River and to Salt Ponds.

Dockage: Bell Isle Marina, off of Back River, can be accessed via the well-marked channel that begins at Northend Point's sandy beach. The marina offers slips as well as a full-service and do-it-yourself yard. Nearby are Marina Cove Boat Basin and Dandy Haven Marina (5-foot dockside depth) Major shopping and attractions of Hampton, VA are only 15 minutes away by car.

Back River Outfitters (28 Dandy Point Road, 757-851-9732) sells custom saltwater tackle, live and frozen bait, boating supplies, apparel and kayaks. They are just a short walk or bike ride from Bell Isle and the marina will even give boaters a ride up the street when possible. Back River's pristine creeks and marshlands lie in stark contrast to the hustle and bustle of Hampton Roads just minutes away.

Salt Ponds Marina on Salt Ponds has transient dockage on floating docks, fuel, a pool and a restaurant. Southall Landings Marina is across the channel and offers gated piers, a pool and tennis courts.

Anchorage: Salt Ponds Harbor has limited room to anchor but good protection in 6.5 to 8 feet of water. Attractive residences line the shore.

HAMPTON ROADS

This huge harbor is home to vessels of all kinds: commercial, military, foreign and recreational. Not for the faint of heart, this nautical freeway can become a free-for-all, so pay attention, and monitor both VHF Channels 13 and 16. ■

N
Deltaville
Piankatank River
West Point
MILE 134
64
Richmond
17
Mobjack Bay
York River
Williamsburg
Gloucester Point
Yorktown
Cape Charles
MILE 156
Chesapeake Bay
13
Jamestown
Page 403
Atlantic Ocean
James River
64
Page 390
Hampton
Page 401
Smithfield
Page 396
Newport News
258
MILE 168
Chesapeake Bay Bridge-Tunnel
Wakefield
MILE 178
564
Page 406
Little Creek
Page 408
Cape Henry
Lynnhaven Bay
460
Norfolk
Page 410
Rudee Inlet
Portsmouth
664
Windsor
264
464
Virginia Beach
Chesapeake
58
168
DOZIER'S WATERWAY GUIDE
THE CRUISING AUTHORITY
WWW.WATERWAYGUIDE.COM
Skipper's Handbook
GPS Waypoints 48
Tide Tables 50

Hampton Roads, James River and Cape Henry, VA

CHARTS 12207, 12221, 12222, 12245, 12254, 12255, 12256

HAMPTON ROADS, VA

This huge harbor is home to vessels of all kinds: commercial, military, foreign and recreational. Not for the faint of heart, this nautical freeway can become a free-for-all, so pay attention and monitor both VHF Channels 13 and 16. Hampton Roads Harbor begins at the line between Old Point Comfort on the north shore and Willoughby Spit to the south.

Hampton Roads, James River and Cape Henry, VA

Hampton Roads harbor, site of the famous Monitor and Merrimac naval battle of 1862, continues today as one of the world's greatest natural harbors. Hampton Roads is also home to the world's largest naval base, a major shipbuilder and several great commercial ports. The busy port cities of Norfolk, Hampton, Newport News, Virginia Beach and Portsmouth set the tone for cruising Hampton Roads and the lower Chesapeake Bay. They create a saltwater economic zone reaching from the mouth of the James River, out the Chesapeake to Rudee Inlet, six miles down the Atlantic coast.

The waters of Hampton Roads teem with major shipping of all kinds. Commercial fishermen work the ocean waters; a menhaden fleet plies the lower Bay; tugs push barges to loading terminals; naval craft of all sorts make their way out of the base at Norfolk; and an enormous fleet of freighters waits for dockage at shoreside terminals. Mariners must carefully find their way among all these vessels and aids to navigation in this great nautical crossroads. Stay tuned to VHF Channel 16 and, if your radio scans, also to Channel 13, the channel on which commercial traffic will be communicating.

The twin, three-mile-long Hampton Roads Bridge-Tunnels joins the north and south sides of Hampton Roads (from Hampton to Norfolk) between Old Point Comfort and Willoughby Spit. The 20-mile-long Chesapeake Bay Bridge-Tunnel crosses the entrance to the Chesapeake Bay farther to the east. Another bridge-tunnel complex, the Monitor-Marrimac, crosses the James River from Newport News to Portsmouth. Channels over the tunnels are well marked, but they also serve as bottlenecks through which all of the big-ship traffic must pass.

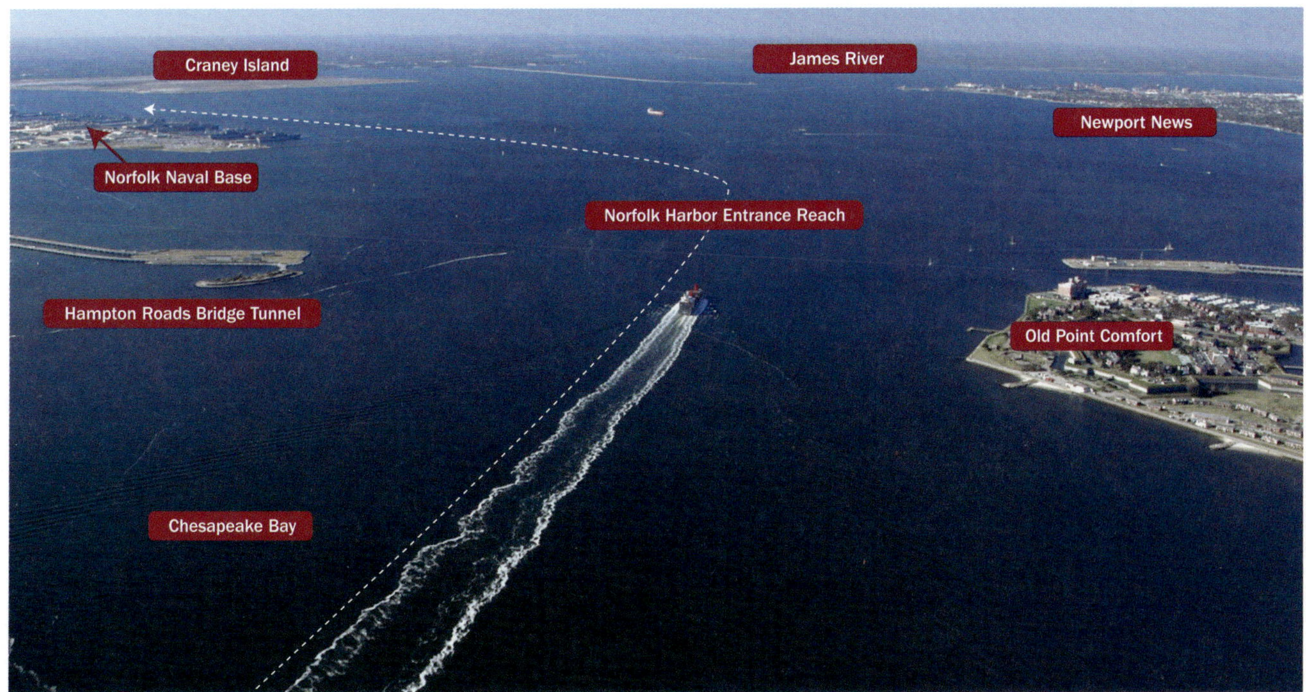

Looking west over the entrance to Norfolk Harbor. (Not to be used for navigation.) Waterway Guide Photography.

Hampton River, VA

HAMPTON RIVER		Largest Vessel Accommodated	VHF Channel Monitored	Transient Berths / Total Berths	Approach / Dockside Depth (reported)	Floating Docks	Gas / Diesel	Groceries, Ice, Marine Supplies, Snacks	Repairs: Hull, Engine, Propeller	Lift (tonnage), Crane, Rail	Min/Max Amps	Laundry, Pool, Showers, Courtesy Car	Pump-Out Station	Nearby: Grocery Store, Motel, Restaurant
		Dockage					Supplies		Services					
1. Bluewater Yachting Center (Internet Access) (Wi-Fi)	**757-723-6774**	**200**	**16**	**60/200**	**12/12**	**F**	**GD**	**IMS**	**HEP**	**L100**	**30/100**	**LPS**	**P**	**GR**
2. Bluewater Yacht Yards (Internet Access) (Wi-Fi)	**757-723-0793**	**80**	**16**	**6/36**	**12/8**	**F**	**-**	**M**	**HEP**	**L100**	**30/50**	**-**	**P**	**GR**
3. Sunset Boating Center (Internet Access) (Wi-Fi)	757-722-3325	44	16	10/38	10/8	F	GD	GIS	HEP	L	30/30	LS	P	GR
4. Hampton Yacht Club (Wi-Fi)	757-722-0711	100	-	/192	10/8	F	-	MS	-	-	30/50	S	P	GMR
5. North Sails Hampton Inc.	757-722-4000	70	-	-	12/12	-	-	-	-	-	-	S	-	GMR
6. Downtown Hampton Public Piers (Internet Access) (Wi-Fi) (Cruising Club Partner)	757-727-1276	130	16/68	27/27	12/11	F	-	I	-	-	30/100	LPS	P	GMR
7. Joys Marina (Wi-Fi)	757-723-1022	50	-	3/70	12/6	-	-	-	-	-	30/50	S	P	GMR
8. Old Point Comfort Marina (Wi-Fi)	757-788-4308	50	16/68	/352	19/14	F	GD	GIMS	EP	L6	30/50	LS	P	GR

Corresponding chart(s) not to be used for navigation. Internet Access, Wireless Internet Access, Waterway Guide Cruising Club Partner

See www.WaterwayGuide.com for current rates, fuel prices, web site addresses, and other up-to-the-minute information.

Looking northwest over the Norfolk entrance with Old Point Comfort and Hampton beyond. (Not to be used for navigation.) Waterway Guide Photography.

HAMPTON AND NEWPORT NEWS, VA

Almost the entire northern side of Hampton Roads is occupied by two cities—Hampton, at the mouth of the harbor, and Newport News, farther in on the James River. At Old Point Comfort, the conspicuous historical brick landmark, the Chamberlin Hotel, is visible from the Bay and marks the north side of the entrance to Hampton Roads Harbor. Fort Monroe and Hampton University are on the eastern side of Hampton Harbor. Hampton, just west of Old Point Comfort, is located on both sides of the short, busy Hampton River.

Founded in 1610, Hampton is the oldest English-speaking city in America and is now Virginia's main seafood-packing center. Upriver on the James, the manufacturing city of Newport News appears just west of the Hampton River. It is home to the largest shipyard in the world, Newport News Shipbuilding, where the cruise liner United States was built; this is the only shipyard capable of building the giant super-carriers. In fact, they are the nation's sole designer, builder, and refueler of nuclear-powered aircraft carriers. They are currently building the next generation of carriers—the Gerald R. Ford class. Both the Gerald R. Ford (CVN 78) and the John F. Kennedy (CVN 79) are currently under construction.

NAVIGATION: Use Chart 12222. **Use Hampton Roads tide tables. For high tide at Newport News, add 24 minutes; for low tide, add 23 minutes.** A marked channel into the Phoebus neighborhood of Hampton is located between Old Point Comfort and the Hampton Roads Bridge-Tunnel. Flashing green light "1" marks the entrance. Stay in the channel until well past green daybeacon "3," and then anchor between the channel and the bridge-tunnel. Holding is good, but the area

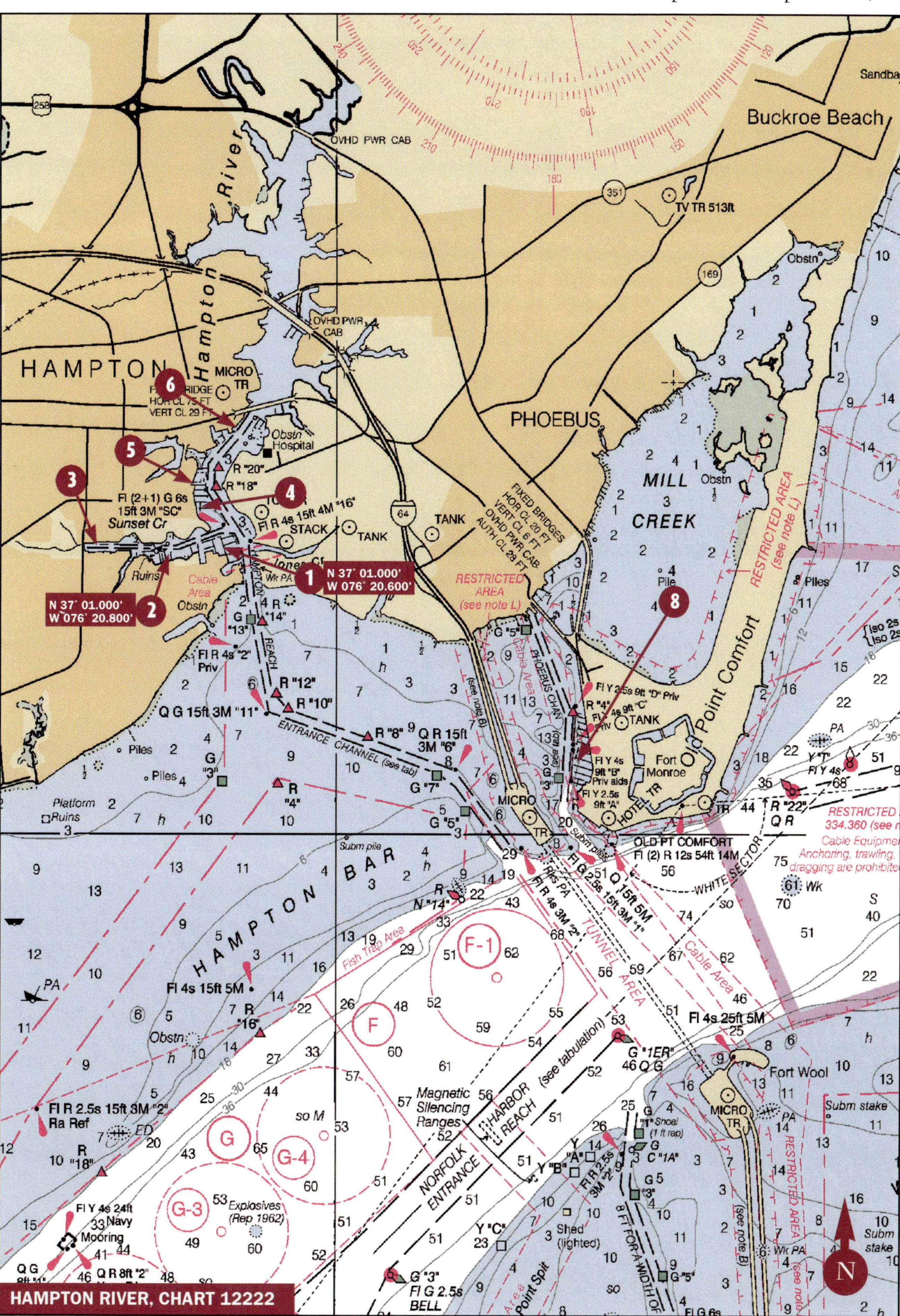

Buckroe Beach
HAMPTON
Hampton River
PHOEBUS
MILL CREEK
Old Point Comfort
Fort Monroe
HAMPTON BAR
Fort Wool
N 37° 01.000' W 076° 20.600'
N 37° 01.000' W 076° 20.800'
Sunset Cr
Jones Cr
ENTRANCE CHANNEL (see tab)
PHOEBUS CHAN
RESTRICTED AREA (see note L)
FIXED BRIDGES HOR CL 20 FT VERT CL 6 FT OVHD PWR CAB AUTH CL 28 FT
OLD PT COMFORT Fl (2) R 12s 54ft 14M
TUNNEL AREA
NORFOLK HARBOR ENTRANCE REACH (see tabulation)
Magnetic Silencing Ranges
Explosives (Rep 1962)
Fish Trap Area
Cable Area
HAMPTON RIVER, CHART 12222

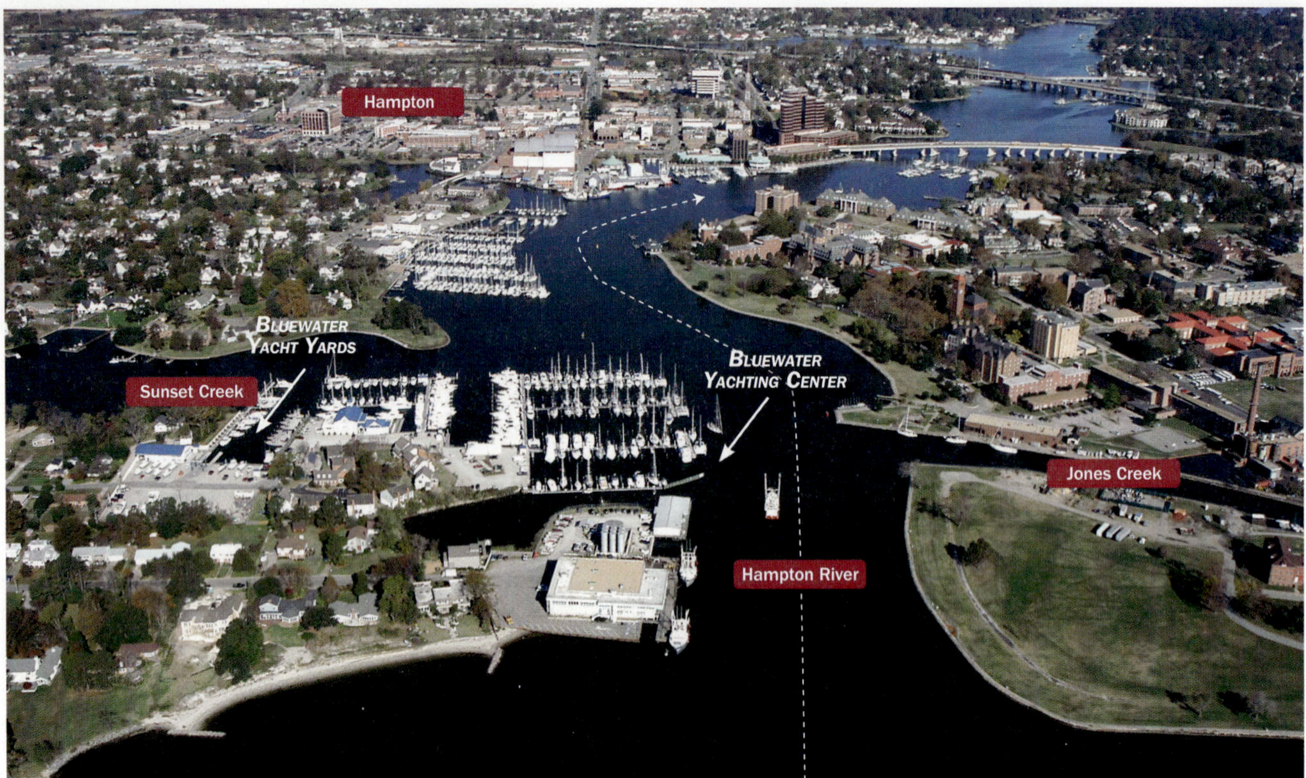

Looking northwest over the Hampton River. (Not to be used for navigation.) Waterway Guide Photography.

can be uncomfortable in winds west through southeast. Old Point Comfort Marina, which used to be a military marina, opened to the public as of August 2011.

After you cross the twin tunnels of the Hampton Roads Bridge-Tunnel, pick up flashing red "2" marking the start of the dogleg channel into the Hampton River. Take care not to cut the riprap too close at the tunnel's entrance islands; some of the rocks extend out farther than one might expect. The channel into the Hampton River makes a turn to port at quick flashing red light "6" and green daybeacon "7" and then to starboard at quick flashing green "11" and red daybeacon "12." Despite the curviness, the channel is deep and easy to follow. Both commercial and recreational boats frequently use the channel.

Dockage: Old Point Comfort Marina at Fort Monroe is located before you arrive in Hampton. It is now open to the public with good facilities and nearby shopping. There is also a restaurant on the premises. Hampton's marinas are all to port, either up the Hampton River or on Sunset Creek, which leads off to the west from the main Hampton River channel. Bluewater Yachting Center is the first marina to port as you turn into Sunset Creek, along with the Surfrider Restaurant, a yacht sales offices and a complimentary water shuttle service to downtown. Next door is Bluewater Yacht Yard; both have transient space. Sunset Boating Center is also on Sunset Creek. Heading north past Sunset Creek, you will come to the Hampton Yacht Club, which holds a few spots for transients who are members of reciprocating yacht clubs. Nearby is North Sails Hampton Inc. with limited transient space.

Below the bridge, the Downtown Hampton Public Piers, and a few other facilities, maintain slips for cruising boats at floating piers just upriver of the Maritime Center. The docks have finger piers and enough room for 26 boats docked stern- or bow-to. The tour boat to Fort Wool uses the slip next to the Maritime Center. Farther upstream, at the far end of the docks, is the dinghy docking area. Short-term dockage is available for four hours. Stay longer, and you will be charged for a full day, based on the length of your boat. (Note: The Crowne Plaza hotel on the waterfront features a formal restaurant, a sports lounge, a waterside raw bar, a pool and a fitness center, which are all available to boaters.) Joys Marina is opposite the public piers (on the east side of the river) and has limited transient space with 6-foot dockside depths.

Anchorage: You can anchor on the Hampton River above red daybeacon "20," opposite the Downtown Hampton Public Piers, on the Hampton University side out of the channel. A Coast Guard-designated anchorage, marked by three yellow buoys, is located across from the Hampton Public Piers. Boats may anchor anywhere past red daybeacon "20" on the red-marker side of the channel. Depths are 6 to 15 feet; use your depth sounder. Do not block traffic or interfere with the private marina or with the city dock. Boats that can get under the 29-foot fixed vertical clearance of the highway bridge at the end of the channel can find good anchorage upstream; again, exercise caution in shoal areas. The holding is good with 6 to 10 feet of water and a mud bottom. There are some new markers starting at the first bridge, marking a channel through all the bridges, but there is still plenty of room for anchoring.

GOIN' ASHORE: **HAMPTON, VA**

Overlooking the confluence of Chesapeake Bay and the James and Elizabeth Rivers, Hampton is as strategically convenient to traveling boaters in the 21st century as it was to Colonial-era maritime traffic in the 17th century, but entering the Hampton River, you would never know you were approaching what claims to be the longest continuously settled town of English Colonial origin.

To starboard is Hampton University and its collection of registered landmark buildings dating from after the Civil War, and dead ahead are the curved roofs of the Virginia Air & Space Museum, which swoop skyward above a moored fleet of fishing trawlers. After an introduction like that, nobody should be surprised at the random juxtapositions they will encounter when making forays ashore.

Centered around the Hampton River, the recently restored and revitalized town center provides a variety of recreational outlets for crews looking to stretch their legs ashore. A well-appointed, deep-water haven accommodates both power and sailing boats.

Hampton is also a good choice for skippers looking to combine a maintenance stop with excursions into Virginia's Lower Peninsula, where modern America was born and still struggles to define its identity. The harbor is well supplied with support and repair services, just one of the reasons the 75-strong Caribbean 1500 Rally sailboat fleet assembles here every fall to prepare for its cruising rally to the British Virgin Islands.

History: In April 1607, the Virginia colonists landed at nearby Point Comfort before sailing upriver to establish their settlement at Jamestown. They were apparently impressed by the commanding view and field of fire the peninsula gave over the approaches from the ocean because in 1609, they returned to construct Fort Algernourne, the first of a progression of defenses built on the site, which is today part of Fort Monroe.

In 1610, Sir Thomas Gates, then the Governor of Virginia, drove the Indians out of their village of Kecoughtan. In its place, he established a town that he named Hampton to honor the Earl of Southampton, an important benefactor of the Virginia Colony.

The open roadstead upriver of Point Comfort, named Hampton Roads after the same investor, provided a secure and accessible anchorage. This made it so popular with the captains of the sailing ships ferrying goods into and out of the colony that Hampton was designated the site for the Royal Customs House, through which all goods imported into the Virginia Colonies were processed.

As the gateway to Virginia's Lower Peninsula, Hampton saw intense action in both the Revolutionary and Civil wars, and the town was burned in both. In the latter war, it was the Confederate General Magruder who set the torch, to deny the Union Army its shelter.

Hampton has a special place in African-American history. The Union Army occupied Fort Monroe throughout the Civil War, and this isolated outpost surrounded by the Confederacy became a haven for freed and runaway slaves, whom the Union considered "contraband of war" and therefore under its protection. Over the course of the war, thousands took refuge here, many of them in the Grand Contraband Camp, which they built from material scavenged from the scorched ruins of Hampton.

In 1861, Mrs. Mary Smith Peake began teaching their children, an enterprise that contributed to the foundation in 1868 of the Hampton Normal and Agricultural Institute, now Hampton University, dedicated initially to the education of emancipated slaves. Coincidence or irony, it was in Hampton that, in 1619, the first group of Africans to be brought to a British colony had landed.

Through its long history with coastal defenses, Hampton is an Army town, and close ties with that service led to the establishment of Langley Field, first as a center for aeronautical research and later as a major air base; between the two World Wars it was the center of gravity of both the Army Air Corps and the Army Air Service. The National Advisory Committee for Aeronautics (NACA) commenced operations at

Reference the marina listing tables to see all the marinas in the area.

POINTS OF INTEREST

1 Town Dock
2 1920s Carousel
3 Virginia Air and Space Center
4 St. Johns Church
5 Hampton History Museum/ Visitors Center

SHOPPING

6 7-11 Convenience Store

DINING

7 Brent's Fine Food
8 Taphouse on Queens Way
9 Goody's Deli & Pub
10 La Bogeda Deli
11 Musasi Japanese Restaurant
12 Marker 20 Restaurant

LIBRARY

POST

PHARMACY

GROCERIES

Langley in 1917. In 1958, NACA became NASA, and Langley remains a NASA research Center to this day.

In 1952, Hampton, the adjacent town of Phoebus and Elizabeth City County merged to form the independent City of Hampton.

Points of Interest: The Downtown Hampton Public Piers provide a handy base for a walking tour of the carefully regentrified old city center. Public transportation brings more distant attractions within reach.

Next door, take a spin in the restored 1920s vintage carousel, and then step across the street to the gull wing-roofed Virginia Air and Space Center (757-727-0900). In the main hall, real aircraft from biplanes to F-16s hang in mid-air, some looking as though they just flew in, with grease on the landing gear and paint chipped off the bolt heads. The museum IMAX Theater offers several films daily.

Once you successfully cross four-lane Settlers Landing Road, you will find Hampton's old section, attractively laid out with brick sidewalks and cobbled streets. Restaurants, antique shops and boutiques blend appealingly into the varied architecture and the old-world proportions of the buildings. A certain randomness seems to pervade the town.: Your first view of St. Johns Church, one of six buildings whose walls still stood after General Magruder's retreating army burned the town in 1861, might be through the razor wire atop the wall surrounding the jail. Close by is the Hampton History Museum (120 Old Hampton Lane, 757-727-1610), which traces the town's history from the Kecoughtan Indian settlement forward to the 20th century. The town's visitor center is conveniently located in the lobby.

Greater Hampton has a full quota of attractions for tourists. Langley Speedway hosts NASCAR (757-867-RACE or www.langley-speedway.com), Air Power Park offers yet more air- and spacecraft displays (413 West Mercury Blvd., 757-727-1163), Busch Gardens near Williamsburg gratifies thrill seekers (800-343-7946 or www.buschgardens.com), and the Casemate Museum at Fort Monroe provides a very solid insight into the region's conflicted history (757-788-3391).

A special draw for Hampton is that it can serve as a base from which to explore Virginia's origins and its enduring contribution to American history. The Jamestown Settlement, Colonial Williamsburg and the battlefields of Yorktown are a short drive away, and you can rent a car in Hampton.

Across the Hampton River, the Hampton University campus has several National Historic Landmark buildings (and a National Historic Landmark tree, the Emancipation Oak) including the Hampton University Museum (757-727-5308), the oldest African-American museum in the country.

In Phoebus, the American Theatre, a restored 1908 vaudeville theater, houses a center for the performing arts that caters to a broad range of clientele (125 E. Mellon St., 757-722-2787, www.hamptonarts.net).

If you prefer to spend your time on a golf course, there are two choices here: The Woodlands Golf Course, which is .5 mile away (757-727-1195, www.hampton.va.us/thewoodlands), and The Hamptons Golf Course, which is 6 miles away (757-766-9148, www.hampton.va.us/thehamptons).

Shopping: There is a 7-11 convenience store (at the corner of Settlers Landing Rd. and Armistead Ave.); Walgreens Pharmacy (500 Settlers Landing Rd., 757-723-7614); if you dinghy to the far end of Sunset Creek and tie up to the last dock on the right, you can walk about a quarter of a mile (over the bridge) to a Food Lion market (3855 Kecoughtan Rd.). On Fridays and Saturdays, there is a free shuttle (BID Bus) which will take you to more extensive shopping beyond the downtown area. Bus schedules are available at the Welcome Center. There is a North Sails dealer here as well (757-722-4000).

Dining: A variety of dining options can be found in the old town along pedestrian-friendly East and West Queens Way. Brent's Fine Food (9 E. Queens Way, 757-722-1185) offers a taste of the South; Taphouse on Queens Way (17 E. Queens Way, 757-224-5829) serves those with a palate for craft beers and tavern fare; Goody's Deli and Pub (11 E. Queens Way, 757-722-3662) dishes up sandwiches and beverages all day and well into the night; Marker "20" (21 E. Queens Way, 757-726-9410) is open for breakfast, lunch and dinner; if you have a yen for Sushi and Japanese fare, try Musasi (49 W. Queens Way, 757-728-0298); for a wide selection of wine, cheese, beer and deli food, try the La Bodega Hampton (22 Wine St. 757-722-8466).

ADDITIONAL RESOURCES

- **HAMPTON VISITOR CENTER: 757-727-1102**
  www.visithampton.com
- **HAMPTON CONVENTION & VISITOR BUREAU:**
  757-722-1222, www.hamptoncvb.com

NEARBY MEDICAL FACILITIES
Sentara CarePlex Hospital: 3000 Coliseum Drive, Hampton, VA 23666, 757-736-1000 (3 miles)

NEARBY AIRPORT
Newport News/Williamsburg International Airport, Jefferson Avenue at Interstate 64, Newport News VA 23602, www.nnwairport.com (12 miles)

Norfolk International Airport: 2200 Norview Ave., Norfolk, VA 23518, www.norfolkairport.com (17 miles)

WILLOUGHBY BAY

A less crowded and less protected layover than Hampton is available at Willoughby Bay on the opposite (south) side of Hampton Roads, behind Willoughby Spit (where the Hampton Roads Bridge-Tunnel ends).

NAVIGATION: Use Chart 12222. Two marked channels take you into Willoughby Bay between Willoughby Spit and Sewells Point. The Navy-maintained south channel by Sewells Point is in a restricted area near the carrier docks, so we recommend using the North Channel near the bridge tunnel into Willoughby Bay. Be prepared for strong currents at the entrance by Fort Wool. The northern Willoughby Channel depth is 10 feet with a width of 200 feet, as of a May 2009 survey. When entering the North Channel, stay clear of green daybeacon "1," and use flashing red "2" as the entrance point. Give the green markers a wide berth, especially green daybeacon "3."

Dockage: Willoughby Harbor Marina is located on the north side of Willoughby Bay on Willoughby Spit. The large marina offers numerous transient slips at floating docks, a laundry, restrooms and showers. The marina is convenient to the large Norfolk Naval Base nearby and provides convenient access to the Bay. Rebel Marina has a few slips on floating docks reserved for transients. There is a 7-11 convenience store located one mile from the marinas (on Ocean View Ave.); however, if you need to do more extensive provisioning or other shopping, there is a Farm Fresh supermarket approximately 3 miles away.

Anchorage: Anchor holding in Willoughby Spit past the marina complex (just past the entry on the north side of the bay) is good in approximately 10 feet of water, but watch for submerged, marked pilings and crab markers in the area. In addition to reported debris on the bottom, an unmarked telephone cable crosses this area. Note: The highly active Norfolk Naval Air Station airport on the southern shore of Willoughby Bay can be noisy but interesting. In addition to the runway near the water, helicopters conduct practice exercises over the water and Hovercraft are very active and extremely noisy. There is also a significant amount of boat traffic here.

QUICK FACT:
LANGLEY AIR FORCE BASE

Langley Air Force Base is three miles north of Hampton, VA, between the northwest and southwest branches of the Back River. The first military base built in the United States specifically for air power, Langley is home to the United States Air Force's 1st Fighter Wing and the 480th Intelligence Wing.

The 1st Tactical Fighter Wing was active during both Operations Desert Shield and Desert Storm, flying more than 6,200 sorties and logging 25,000 flying hours. The Wing also flew hundreds of training and combat sorties in support of Operation Iraqi Freedom. The 480th Intelligence Wing is the Air Force lead wing for geospatial intelligence, Distributed Common Ground System (DCGS) operations and intelligence products for combat mission planning and execution.

Langley covers approximately 2,900 acres and is home to more than 8,800 military and approximately 2,800 civilian employees.

JAMES RIVER

In 1607, a band of English colonists followed the James upriver to found Jamestown, the New World's first permanent English settlement. Ever since then, the James River has served commercial craft. Now joining the freighters that take cargo up to Richmond, more and more recreational boats are plying its waters. The lower river is busy with sail and powerboats, and more boats are exploring upstream, venturing into the south and north shores' tributaries. Some travel up to the Chickahominy and Appomattox rivers to view the historic sites of some of America's most important events.

The 78-mile trip up the James to Richmond is beautiful and fascinating but is not for the inexperienced or for those unaccustomed to being almost entirely on their own. Few marinas serve the area above the Chickahominy, and little dockage is available.

Newport News, on the James

At Newport News, most of the James River's shoreline is dominated by the Newport News Shipbuilding facility. There is a Coast Guard-enforced security zone in the waters off the facility. Do not approach within 500 yards.

Dockage: At the north end of the James River Bridge, Leeward Municipal Marina offers slips, gas and diesel and pump-out. The only nearby restaurant is the Crabshack on the James (7601 River Rd., 757-245-2722), which sits directly over the water and has great views of the river. The Papco Oil Company, at 407 Jefferson Ave. in the Newport News city commercial basin, next to Davis Boat Works, pumps high volumes of fuel to the largest recreational vessels that pass through the area. Davis Boat Works does all kinds of boat repairs and offers limited transient dockage.

GOIN' ASHORE: NEWPORT NEWS, VA

Viewed from the James River, Newport News is impressive. Miles of wharves, cranes and dry docks line the shore, evidence of the shipbuilding that is still the core of the city's economy. Since its founding in 1886, the Newport News Shipbuilding has built countless vessels for the U.S. Navy, including all of its massive nuclear-powered aircraft carriers and many of its nuclear submarines.

The town of the 20th century was built around the convergence of railroads, the sea and shipbuilding, and has seen all the booms and lapses of fortune typical of East Coast industrial cities. Large areas still exhibit varying degrees of urban blight, and it is not the kind of place to wander around if you don't know where you are going.

Willoughby Bay, VA

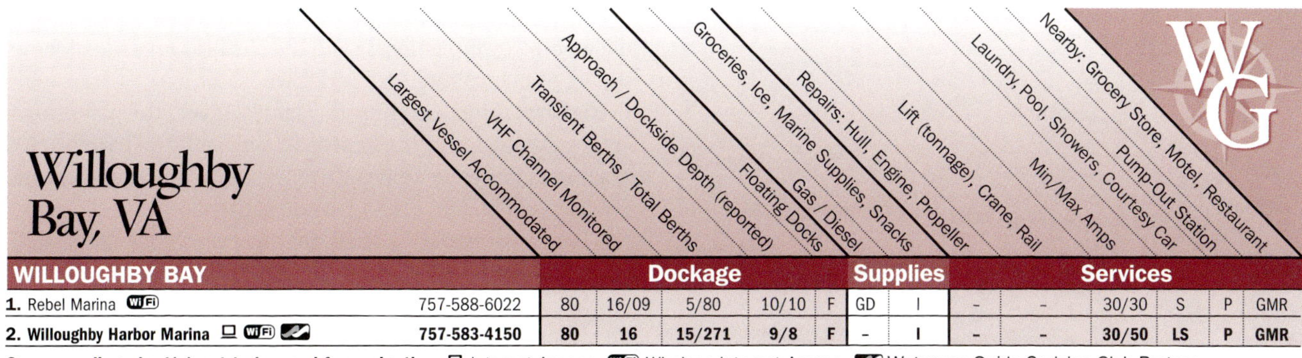

WILLOUGHBY BAY		Largest Vessel Accommodated	VHF Channel Monitored	Transient Berths / Total Berths	Approach / Dockside Depth (reported)	Floating Docks	Gas / Diesel	Groceries, Ice, Marine Supplies, Snacks	Repairs: Hull, Engine, Propeller	Lift (tonnage), Crane, Rail	Min/Max Amps	Laundry, Pool, Showers, Courtesy Car	Pump-Out Station	Nearby: Grocery Store, Motel, Restaurant
		Dockage					Supplies		Services					
1. Rebel Marina (Wireless Internet Access)	757-588-6022	80	16/09	5/80	10/10	F	GD	I	-	-	30/30	S	P	GMR
2. Willoughby Harbor Marina (Internet Access, Wireless Internet Access, Waterway Guide Cruising Club Partner)	**757-583-4150**	**80**	**16**	**15/271**	**9/8**	**F**	**-**	**I**	**-**	**-**	**30/50**	**LS**	**P**	**GMR**

Corresponding chart(s) not to be used for navigation. Internet Access · Wireless Internet Access · Waterway Guide Cruising Club Partner

See www.WaterwayGuide.com for current rates, fuel prices, web site addresses, and other up-to-the-minute information.

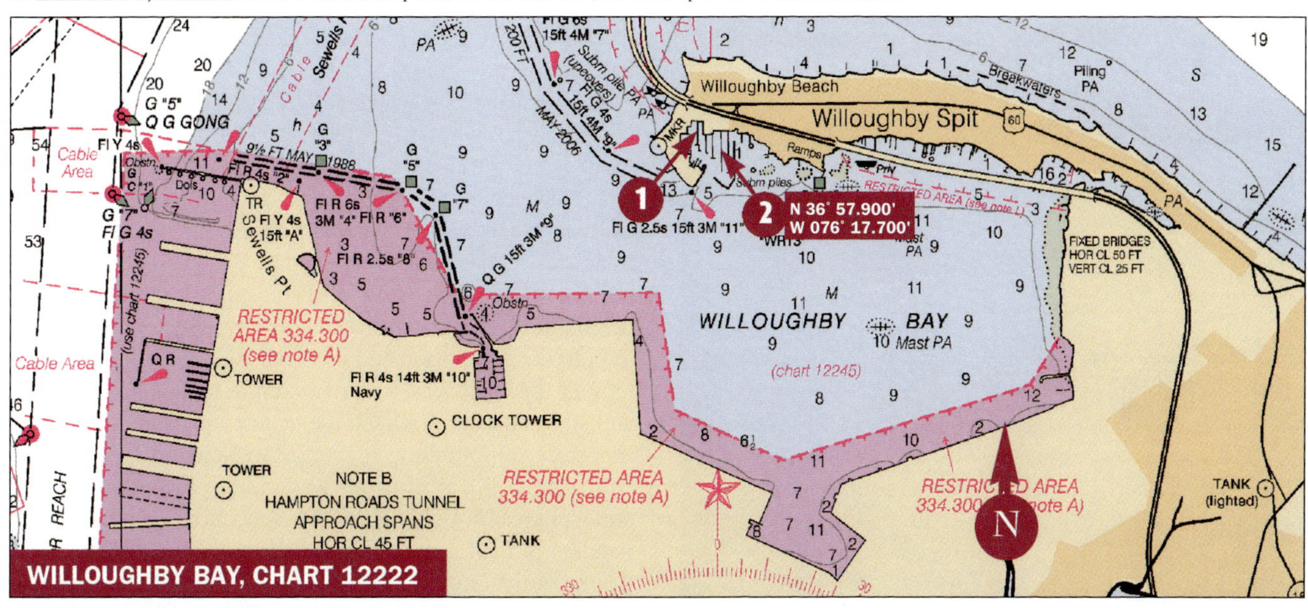

WILLOUGHBY BAY, CHART 12222

Willoughby Harbor Marina

A view over Willoughby Harbor and the Hampton Roads Bridge Tunnel. (Not to be used for navigation.) Waterway Guide Photography.

A good bet is to rent a car to explore the area, along with the whole Lower Peninsula and the Historic Triangle of Jamestown, Williamsburg and Yorktown.

History: After entering the James River, the Jamestown colonists sailed past the exposed river bank (that would 300 years later prove so amenable to industry) and chose to land 20 miles upstream, on an island that while readily fortified, was barely habitable. In 1610, the emaciated, sick and disillusioned survivors of what was by then a failed enterprise were on their way back down the river, bound home for England on a ship commanded by Christopher Newport, when they encountered three vessels bringing men and supplies from England. According to one version of history, Newport News was so named because it was where Newport learned this good news.

It might also have taken its name from an Irish family named Neuce who settled here. Whichever version is closer to the truth, the area was settled by 1621, and the name Newport News emerged from several different spellings. In the Colonial era, it built its wealth on tobacco, but few plantation buildings of that time survive today. Because of the strategic importance of Virginia's Lower Peninsula, Newport News and neighboring communities were plundered by foraging armies in both the Revolution and the Civil War.

After the Civil War, the arrival of the railroads, coal, steam and steel, and the new technology to employ them in industrial-scale shipbuilding, converged in Newport News. By the end of the 19th century, it was rapidly losing its pastoral atmosphere. In 1896, Newport News became a city, independent of the County of Warwick.

One of the city's more notable contributions to the American experience is Hilton Village. The rapid expansion of shipbuilding that followed the entry of the United States into World War I created a shortage of housing for workers. In response, the government entered the housing business. Hilton Village, the first federally subsidized planned community in the United States, was dedicated in 1918. Today, it appears as the nucleus around which Newport News is rebuilding its civic pride and self-awareness. The edgy boutiques, art galleries and restaurants that often accompany neighborhoods in transition have taken root in its business district on Warwick Boulevard.

Points of Interest: The Mariners Museum (757-596-2222 or www.marinersmuseum.org) is widely recognized as one of the finest such institutions in the world, which makes it all the more frustrating that you can't get anywhere close to it by water. Nevertheless, it is a must-see for anyone the least bit interested in maritime matters.

Several large galleries hold permanent exhibits on topics from the Age of Exploration to the Age of Steam. The International Small Craft Center holds a collection of vessels from all over the world, stunning in their variety both in shape and

Newport News, Pagan River, VA

NEWPORT NEWS		Largest Vessel Accommodated	VHF Channel Monitored	Transient Berths / Total Berths	Approach / Dockside Depth (reported)	Floating Docks	Gas / Diesel	Groceries, Ice, Marine Supplies, Snacks	Repairs: Hull, Engine, Propeller	Lift (tonnage), Crane, Rail	Min/Max Amps	Laundry, Pool, Showers, Courtesy Car	Pump-Out Station	Nearby: Grocery Store, Motel, Restaurant
		Dockage					Supplies		Services					
1. Davis Boat Works Inc. (Internet Access)	757-247-0101	135	-	5/5	12/12	-	GD	M	HEP	L250	30/100	S	P	GR
2. Leeward Municipal Marina	757-247-2359	43	16	40/200	7/8	F	GD	I	-	-	30/50	LS	P	R
PAGAN RIVER														
3. Smithfield Station (Wireless Internet Access) (Waterway Guide Cruising Club Partner)	757-357-7700	130	16	35/100	8/6	F	-	IMS	-	-	30/50	LPSC	P	GMR

Corresponding chart(s) not to be used for navigation. Internet Access · Wireless Internet Access · Waterway Guide Cruising Club Partner

See www.WaterwayGuide.com for current rates, fuel prices, web site addresses, and other up-to-the-minute information.

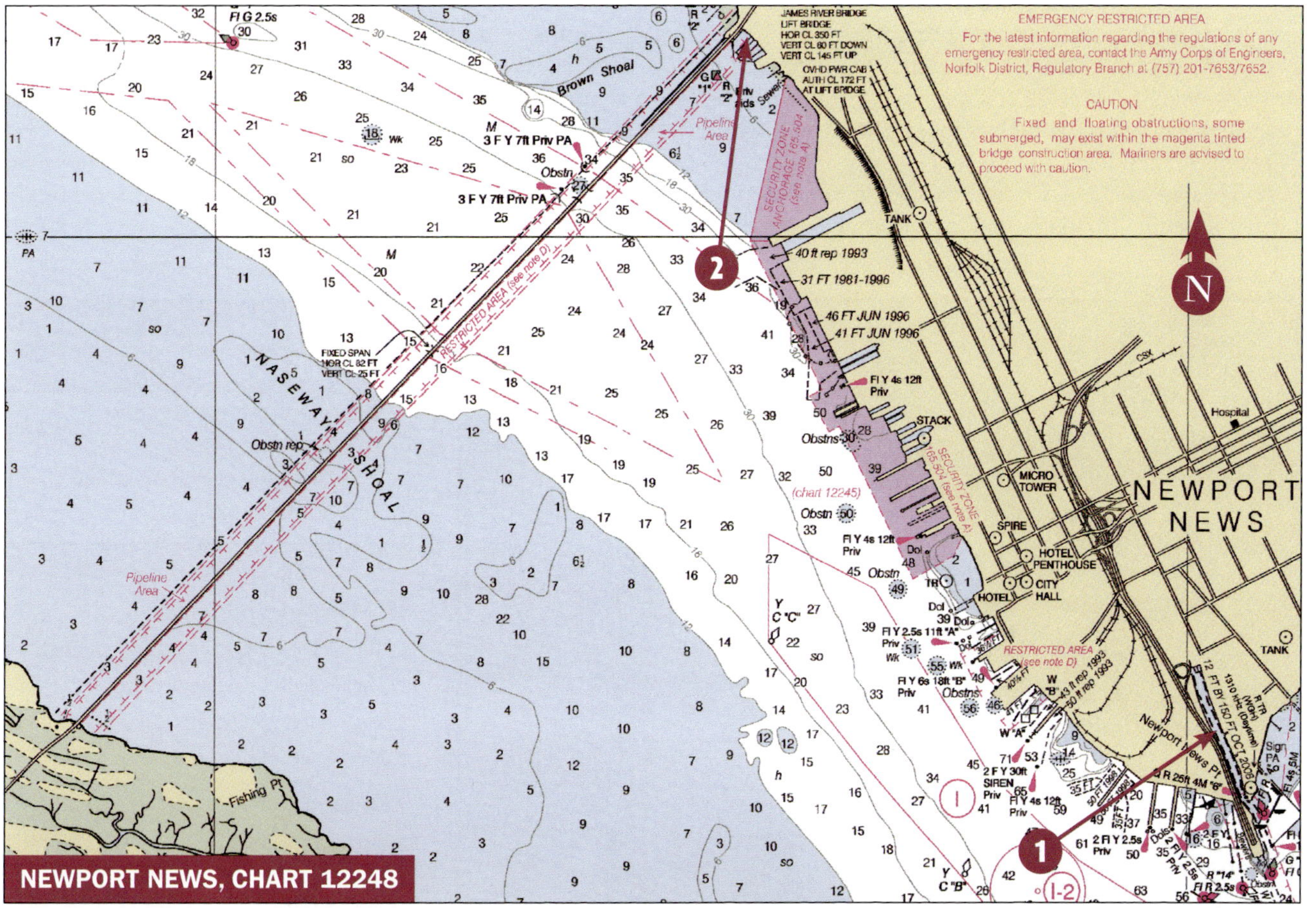

NEWPORT NEWS, CHART 12248

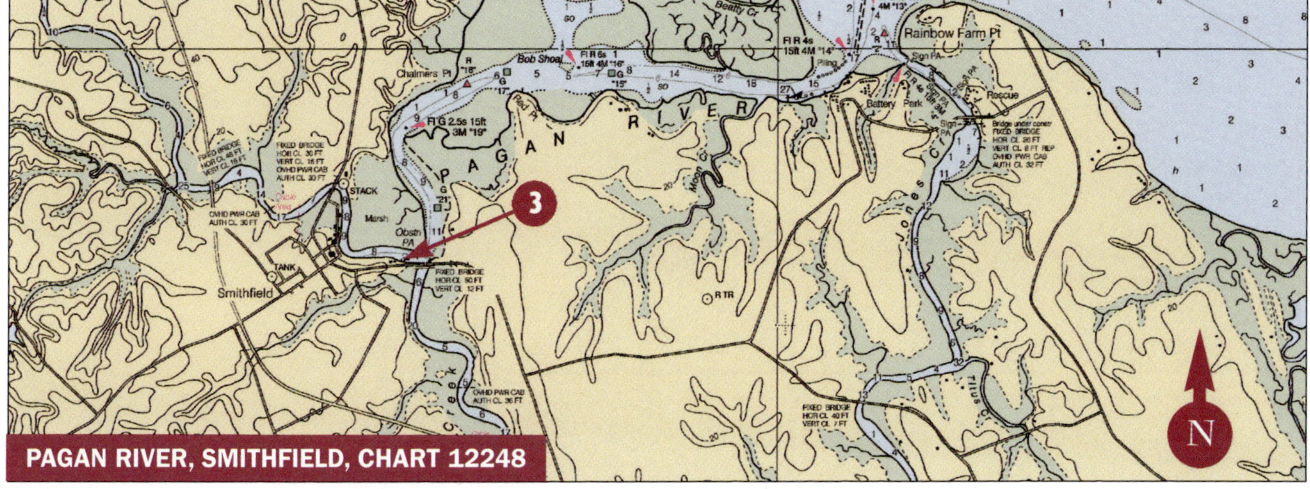

PAGAN RIVER, SMITHFIELD, CHART 12248

purpose, and the extensive library is a valuable resource for students, researchers or those simply besotted with the sea. It holds the archives of Chris Craft and other small and large boat and shipbuilders.

The most recent addition to the museum is the USS Monitor Center, which tells the story of the development and demise of the ironclads, Virginia and Monitor. Mock-ups of the ironclad's major components (the real ones, raised from the Monitor's wreck off Cape Hatteras, can be seen pickling in preservative-filled tanks) are arranged in a glass-walled hall that looks out onto a full-scale replica of the vessel's hull and deck.

The museum was started in 1932 by Archer Milton Huntington, the son of Collis Huntington who founded Newport News Shipbuilding, and his wife, sculptor Anna Hyatt Huntington. It is surrounded by a park laced with walking trails and graced with an outdoor sculpture garden.

Next door to the Mariners Museum is the Peninsula Fine Arts Center (757-596-8175 or www.pfac-va.org), which hosts permanent and transient exhibitions and holds interactive art programs for children.

A mile away, at 524 J. Clyde Morris Boulevard, the Virginia Living Museum (757-595-1900) provides a close-up look at natural history as it can be touched and seen in Virginia. You can view fish in the aquarium, study the night sky in the planetarium or watch wildlife from elevated walkways that take you through wetlands and other habitats.

The Virginia War Museum, in Huntington Park at the foot of the James River Bridge (9285 Warwick Boulevard, 757-926-8000), depicts the history of the U.S. military from the eve of the Revolution to the present day. Visit www.war museum.org for operational hours and exhibit information.

Hilton Village is listed in the National Register of Historic Places. It was built to imitate the styles, though not quite the small scale, of the mixed dwellings found in an English village of the early 20th century. An area of colorful speciality shops marks the stretch of Warwick Boulevard that runs by the development.

Dining: Check out Hilton Village, then take dinner at 99 Main Restaurant (99 Main St., 757-599-9885), named as one of the top restaurants by Hampton Roads Magazine or try Circa1918 Restaurant (10367 Warwick Blvd., 757-599-1918). There are numerous restaurants and shopping opportunites in this area, but transportation is definitely necessary.

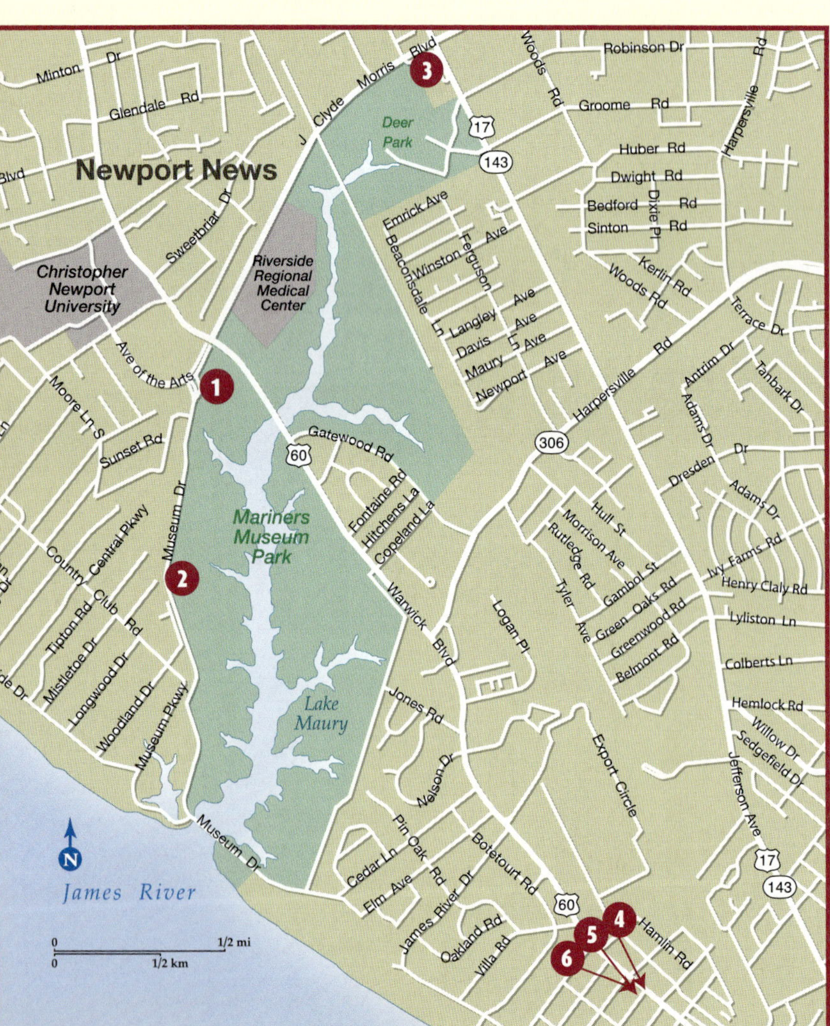

Reference the marina listing tables to see all the marinas in the area.

ADDITIONAL RESOURCES

■ NEWPORT NEWS TOURISM DEVELOPMENT OFFICE:
757-926-1400 or 888-493-7386
www.newport-news.org

ATTRACTIONS

1 The Mariners Museum
2 Peninsula Fine Arts Center
3 Virginia Living Museum
4 The Virginia War Museum

DINING

5 99 Main Restaurant
6 Circa 1918

Nansemond and Pagan Rivers, off the James

NAVIGATION: Use Chart 12248. **Use Hampton Roads tide tables. For high tide at Smithfield (Pagan and James Rivers), add 1 hour 29 minutes; for low tide, add 1 hour 23 minutes.** The Nansemond River, southwest across the James River from Newport News, is navigable well upstream to Suffolk, although a 35-foot fixed vertical clearance bridge crosses it just downstream of the city. The Pagan River, three miles up from the James River Bridge (60-foot closed vertical clearance lift bridge, requires advance notice to open), carries good depths to Smithfield. The Pagan was recently dredged by the Army Corp of Engineers, and the channel is now maintained to minimum depth of 10 feet.

A fixed bridge with a 12-foot closed vertical clearance limits exploration of Cypress Creek off of the Pagan River before Smithfield. A 15-foot fixed vertical clearance bridge is just upstream of the Cypress Creek junction on the Pagan River proper at Smithfield. Both the Nansemond and Pagan rivers carry commercial traffic to their upriver cities. Be careful when anchoring; the tidal current in these waters can be substantial.

Dockage: There is ample depth for vessels with 6-foot drafts to get up to Smithfield Station Waterfront Inn, Restaurant and Marina. The marina has an on-site restaurant, outdoor pool, wireless Internet and floating docks that can accommodate vessels up to 120 feet. Reservations are recommended from May through September.

Anchorage: Anchorage is available past the Smithfield Station Marina. The creek continues farther and there is good depth. You can anchor in front of the large complex of brick buildings and use the long dock for your dinghy. It's a short walk to the quaint town of Smithfield.

GOIN' ASHORE: SMITHFIELD, VA

Historic Smithfield on the Pagan River, famous for its peanut-fed hams, is a pretty, specialized little hamlet. The name Smithfield has been synonymous with pork, hogs and hams for more than 200 years. At the turn of the 20th century, several companies had processing and packing houses in the town. Today, there is one: Smithfield Foods, a relative latecomer founded in 1936, has effectively absorbed all the others, and as you follow the meandering Pagan River up to Smithfield, it is hard to ignore its presence. The company's massive plant and corporate headquarters for this Fortune 500 Company loom over the town, much like baronial castles did over medieval English villages.

Once you get off the boat at Smithfield Station to walk up South Church Street, the gray factory quickly becomes obscured behind a skyline of dormers, gables and turrets of homes that embody every style of architecture from late Colonial to late Victorian. These are but an overture to a remarkable collection of more than 70 architecturally important buildings that testify to Smithfield's former stature as a port.

History: About 25 miles downstream of Jamestown and opposite Newport News, the Pagan River emerges from the south bank of the James River. It had long been home to Warascoyak Indians when the first Europeans began to move into the region.

In 1637, Arthur Smith patented 1,450 acres on a neck of land between the Pagan River and Cypress Creek. With its deep-water access, the Smith property became a center for commerce, and in 1750, Arthur Smith IV laid out a grid of four streets on the family's fields to create a formal town. Many of its 72 lots were purchased by merchants and ships' captains, and many of the houses they built still stand.

Local lore places Smithfield hams on the tables of European monarchs as far back as the late 17th century, but, according to the Smithfield Foods Web site, the first official record of their exportation as a commodity appears in 1779, when Captain Mallory Todd delivered a shipment to St. Eustatius, in the West Indies. He later built a packing house that was home to the Todd Ham Company for 120 years.

The growth in international trade that followed the American Revolution is measured by the number of buildings of this period that survive in Smithfield today. Another growth spurt occurred after the Civil War when peanuts joined the list of commodities flowing through the port. This ended in 1921, when a fire destroyed the peanut warehouses, and peanut growers transferred their allegiance to the railroad in nearby Suffolk.

Despite a healthy meat-packing industry, Smithfield went into a period of decline after World War II. Businesses and property owners tried to revive it, but it wasn't until 1988, when Joseph W. Luter, III, President of Smithfield Foods, Inc., stepped in with a challenge grant that a rehab program gained the needed funds to give it traction. Today, the town of Smithfield features a beautifully restored and vibrant Historic Downtown District. The next phase of the effort will be focused on South Church Street between Smithfield Station and Main Street.

Points of Interest: Pick up a walking tour brochure at Smithfield Station (415 South Church St., 877-703-7701) to see where to go and what you will see along the way. The brochure conveniently includes the locations of historic homes and attractions, restaurants, shops and galleries so as you continue your tour, you can pace your exertions between pauses for coffee, lunch and ice cream.

Located right in the heart of the three-block downtown district are several interesting and free attractions. The Isle of Wight County Museum (103 Main St., 757-356-1223) offers an overview of local history and its most notable artifact–the world's oldest, edible cured ham. Just across the street is the Old Courthouse of 1750, modeled after the Capital Building in Williamsburg. Farther down, at 516 Main Street, is the Schoolhouse Museum (757-365-4789), an African-American History Museum of Public Education. Originally built in 1932, it was lovingly restored and moved to its present location in 2007.

The new Windsor Castle Park, located right in the heart of the downtown district, features walking trails, picnic areas, a dog park and a small non-motorized boat ramp/launch and kayak rentals.

Smithfield is quickly making a name for itself as an arts destination.The Smithfield & Isle of Wight Visitor Center is located at 319 Main Street, where it shares space with the Arts Center @ 319. This unique space offers everything a visitor to the area needs, as well as a gift shop, gallery and the chance to chat with the resident artists who work at the Center. In addition, Smithfield boasts five art galleries in its three-block downtown district.

If golfing is more your style, Cypress Creek Golfers Club is nearby (757-365-4774, www.cypresscreekgolfersclub.com).

Special Events: The Smithfield Little Theatre (210 N. Church St., 757-357-2501, www.smithfieldlittletheatre.org), one of the finest community theater groups in the region, produces three plays annually, as well as a Christmas special and "One Act Play Festival" in the summer. The town hosts several special events throughout the year including Aiken & Friends Music Fest in October, the "Pork & Fork" Barbecue Cook-Off, Smithfield Olden Days Festival held each June, and the Friday Night Summer Concert Series, free seasonal concerts held each week at the Times Gazebo on Main Street.

Shopping: A boutique, sweet shop, book store and nautical gift shop have opened in the new Boardwalk Shops at Smithfield Station. On Main Street, along with the Arts Center, you will find a variety of additional art galleries and specialty shops (international tea shop, gourmet bakery and old-fashioned ice cream parlor). The Genuine Smithfield Ham Shoppe (224 Main Street) is a showcase for Smithfield Foods gourmet products and other Virginia foodstuffs. And don't miss the little gift shop at the Isle of Wight County Museum. Approximately 2 miles from Smithfield Station Marina, you can find a Food Lion market, an ABC liquor store, a hardware store plus various other shopping and eateries.

Dining: Smithfield Station (757-357-7700) has a restaurant for fine dining, with many menu items based on ham, seafood and steaks, solo or in combination. The Station also features the IBX Lounge with an ala carte menu and live music every Wednesday night. On Sundays they have a great brunch at reasonable prices.

The Smithfield Inn (112 Main St., 757-357-1752) opened as a tavern in 1759 in a building that dates from 1752. It is now owned by Smithfield Foods and Joseph Luter III, whose father and grandfather founded Smithfield Foods and whose mother's family owned the building when it operated as Sykes Inn. The menu features dishes with a southern influence. If it's a hot and humid day, you will probably want to visit Smithfield Ice Cream Parlor (208 Main St., 757-357-6166). And be sure to try Smithfield Gourmet Bakery and Café (218 Main St., 757-357-0045).

Reference the marina listing tables to see all the marinas in the area.

POINTS OF INTEREST
1 Isle of Wight County Museum
2 Old Courthouse of 1750
3 School House Museum
4 Windsor Castle Park

SHOPPING
5 Arts Center @ 319
6 Smithfield Little Theatre
7 Boardwalk Shops
8 Genuine Smithfield Ham Shoppe
9 Smithfield Station
10 Wharf Hill Antique

DINING
9 Smithfield Station Restaurant
11 The Smithfield Inn
12 Smithfield Ice Cream Parlor
13 Smithfield Gourmet Bakery/ Deli

INFORMATION
14 Visitors Center

POST OFFICE

PHARMACY

LIBRARY

ADDITIONAL RESOURCES

- CHAMBER OF COMMERCE: www.theisle.org
- ISLE OF WIGHT COUNTY: www.co.isle-of-wight.va.us
- TOWN OF SMITHFIELD: www.smithfieldva.gov
- SMITHFIELD AND ISLE OF WIGHT CONVENTION & VISITORS BUREAU: 757-357-5182, www.visitsmithfieldisleofwight.com
- SMITHFIELD HAM TIMELINE: www.smithfieldfoods.com/Consumers/cooking.aspx

NEARBY MEDICAL FACILITIES

Sentara Urgent Care at Sentara St. Luke's, 20209 Sentara Way, Carrollton, VA 23314, 757-542-1100 (4 miles)

Riverside Regional Medical Center: 500 J. Clyde Morris Blvd., Newport News, VA 23601, 757-594-2000 (11 miles)

Sentara Obici Hospital: 2800 Godwin Blvd., Suffolk, VA 23434, 757-934-4000 (10 miles)

Smithfield on the Pagan River. (Not to be used for navigation.) Waterway Guide Photography.

Deep Creek and Warwick River, off the James

NAVIGATION: Use Chart 12248. Across the James from the Pagan River, Deep Creek—with a marked entrance and marinas—and Warwick River almost share a common mouth. Shoaling has been reported in the Deep Creek entrance channel, and charts now show 4 feet controlling depth as of July 2010. Additionally, the channel entrance has narrowed to approximately 100 feet (60 feet at the mouth of the harbor), and only 4.5-foot depths in the turning basin. If you are doubtful, favor the green-marker side of the channel. The narrow, upper creek carries day markers for about .3 miles beyond the basin. The Warwick River has an active sailing club and holds frequent regattas and local races off the river's entrance. There are two marinas inside the creek: Deep Creek Landing and James River Marina. Each has some transient space reserved.

Skiffes Creek, off the James

A little farther up the James, where it begins to curve around Hog Island, you pass the marked channel to Skiffes Creek and Tidewater Virginia's Army-transportation post, Fort Eustis. Here you will pass the James River Reserve Fleet, row after row of precisely aligned military vessels in mothball storage. The so-called "mothball fleet" is rapidly shrinking as older ships are scrapped. The white-hulled Savannah, the only nuclear-powered freighter in the world, has been moved from here to a berth along the Elizabeth River in Norfolk. Note the charted restricted area around Fort Eustis, east of Deep Water Shoals Light. The marked secondary channel around Hog Island (with depths of more than 10 feet) is a mile shorter than the main channel.

Jamestown, on the James

About 26 miles up the James River on the north side is Jamestown, with its main dock right on the river (replicas of the Godspeed, Susan Constant and Discovery, the ships of the Jamestown Expedition, are moored at this dock). Jamestown Settlement, a living history museum operated by the Commonwealth of Virginia, is a remarkable tribute to the original Jamestown, which was established on May 14, 1607, the first permanent English settlement in America. Call 888-593-4682 or visit www.historyisfun.org for more information.

NAVIGATION: Use Charts 12248 and 12251. **Use Hampton Roads tide tables. For high tide at Jamestown Island (James River), add 2 hours 58 minutes; for low tide, add 3 hours 31 minutes.** Do not attempt the secondary back entrance behind James Island (on a tributary fittingly named Back River). The main river is, of course, well marked.

Anchorage: In settled weather only, cruisers can anchor in the James River, upriver from the ferry dock, and come by dinghy into the dock where the Jamestown vessels are located. If all else fails, you might anchor below the ferry slip on the Scotland side, and take the ferry across the river to Glass Point, but attempt this only in settled weather. Note the ruins of an old wharf. A strong current runs through here, and you may pitch and roll if the wind and current are opposed. There is little wake, though.

Kingsmill, Deep Creek, VA

Kingsmill, Deep Creek, VA		Largest Vessel Accommodated	VHF Channel Monitored	Transient Berths / Total Berths	Approach / Dockside Depth (reported)	Floating Docks	Gas / Diesel	Groceries, Ice, Marine Supplies, Snacks	Repairs: Hull, Engine, Propeller	Lift (tonnage), Crane, Rail	Min/Max Amps	Laundry, Pool, Showers, Courtesy Car	Pump-Out Station	Nearby: Grocery Store, Motel, Restaurant
		Dockage					Supplies		Services					
DEEP CREEK (JAMES RIVER)														
1. Deep Creek Landing	757-877-9555	50	16	7/80	6/4	F	GD	IS	HEP	L12	30/30	LS	P	GR
2. James River Marina	757-930-1909	54	-	5/28	13/8	F	G	IMS	HEP	L6.5	30/50	S	-	R
KINGSMILL (JAMES RIVER)														
3. Kingsmill Resort Marina	757-253-3919	100	16	15/72	8/7	F	GD	IMS	-	-	30/50	PS	P	MR

Corresponding chart(s) not to be used for navigation. Internet Access · Wireless Internet Access · Waterway Guide Cruising Club Partner

See www.WaterwayGuide.com for current rates, fuel prices, web site addresses, and other up-to-the-minute information.

Kingsmill, on the James

Dockage: Transient slips on concrete floating docks are available for boats up to 100 feet at Kingsmill Marina (part of the Kingsmill Resort and Spa) directly on the James River. There is a wooden breakwater for moderate protection and transportation is provided to Colonial Williamsburg, Busch Gardens and Water Country U.S.A. Make your dockage reservations early for holiday weekends or during golf tournaments.

Chickahominy River, off the James

NAVIGATION: Use Chart 12251. Be sure to get a recent printing or an electronic version from the NOAA Web site (http://chartmaker.ncd.noaa.gov), as this edition is old, and many markers on the rivers have been relocated. Flowing into the James from the north, four miles above Jamestown, the Chickahominy River has several winding, narrow, deep creeks for gunkholing.

Note that the old swing bridge (officially the Barrets Ferry Highway Bridge) near the entrance has been replaced with a fixed high level (52-foot vertical clearance) bridge.

Boats can anchor below the bridge on the west side in 10 feet of water or anywhere above the bridge out of the channel, but you would be wise to buoy the anchor. You may encounter the wake of water skiers or outboard-powered fishing boats in this area. The channel is marked for 12 miles and navigable for 18 miles to Walker Dam Lock, but a 44-foot-high cable crosses 8 miles up. Nine miles upriver is lovely Brickyard Landing, with little development. Visitors may enjoy the little public park with a marina for small boats just beyond. Along this freshwater stretch, submerged stumps may be hidden in the silt-laden waters. Be cautious when entering any of the James River creeks.

Dockage: In an easily entered protected harbor where the James and Chickahominy Rivers meet, Two Rivers Yacht Club and Country Club has slips and gas and diesel. Dockage includes use of the club facilities. Farther north on the river is Rivers Rest Marina & Resort, which may have transient dockage and sells gas.

Up-to-date navigation and cruising news are always available at www.waterwayguide.com.

James River, beyond the Chickahominy to Richmond

NAVIGATION: Use Charts 12251 and 12252. Above Dancing Point, the James River narrows considerably, and the shores are lined with cypresses and plantation houses. The lift bridge at Jordan Point, officially known as the Benjamin Harrison Lift Bridge, has a closed vertical clearance of 50 feet, according to the latest charts. No tide boards are posted. The bridge is closed from 8:00 p.m. until 6:00 a.m.

At Hopewell, the James joins the Appomattox River, which serves historic Petersburg, 10 miles upstream. A dual bridge with 40-foot fixed vertical clearance crosses the Appomattox a mile above the entrance.

Along its upper reaches, the James narrows and, for the 14-mile stretch upstream from Hopewell, takes a winding course known as The Corkscrew. The river's bends themselves are called Curles of the River, and the U.S. Army Corps of Engineers has eliminated three of them by digging canals.

At Richmond Deepwater Terminal, five miles below Richmond itself, big-ship traffic ends. Arrange for another means of transportation if you want to continue on to Richmond to visit its museums and monuments, or stay at RockettsLanding Marina and visit from there.

For those who make the trek up the James River to Richmond, you will be richly rewarded with all that Richmond has to offer. It has made the top 10 lists for "Best Neighborhoods for Shopping," "Best Old House Neighborhoods" and "Best Places to Start Over." Richmond boasts a symphony orchestra, ballet, theater and opera companies, and art galleries. Innumerable restaurants, including Millie's Diner (804-643-5512) on East Main, Bottoms Up Pizza (804-644-4400) on Dock Street and Strawberry Street Café (804-353-6860), will satisfy your appetite. Legend Brewing Company (321 W. 7th St., 804-616-3061) is a great place for a beer and a burger.

Parks abound near the waterfront including Great Shiplock, Libby Hill, Chimborazo and Gillie Creek. Visit the Edgar Allan Poe Museum (1914 East Main St., 804-648-5523) to learn more about this favorite American author. The Valentine Richmond History Museum (1015 E. Clay St., 804-649-0711) houses permanent exhibits including the Wickham House, the "Settlement to Streetcar Suburbs" and "Creating History" exhibits, and the Edward Valentine

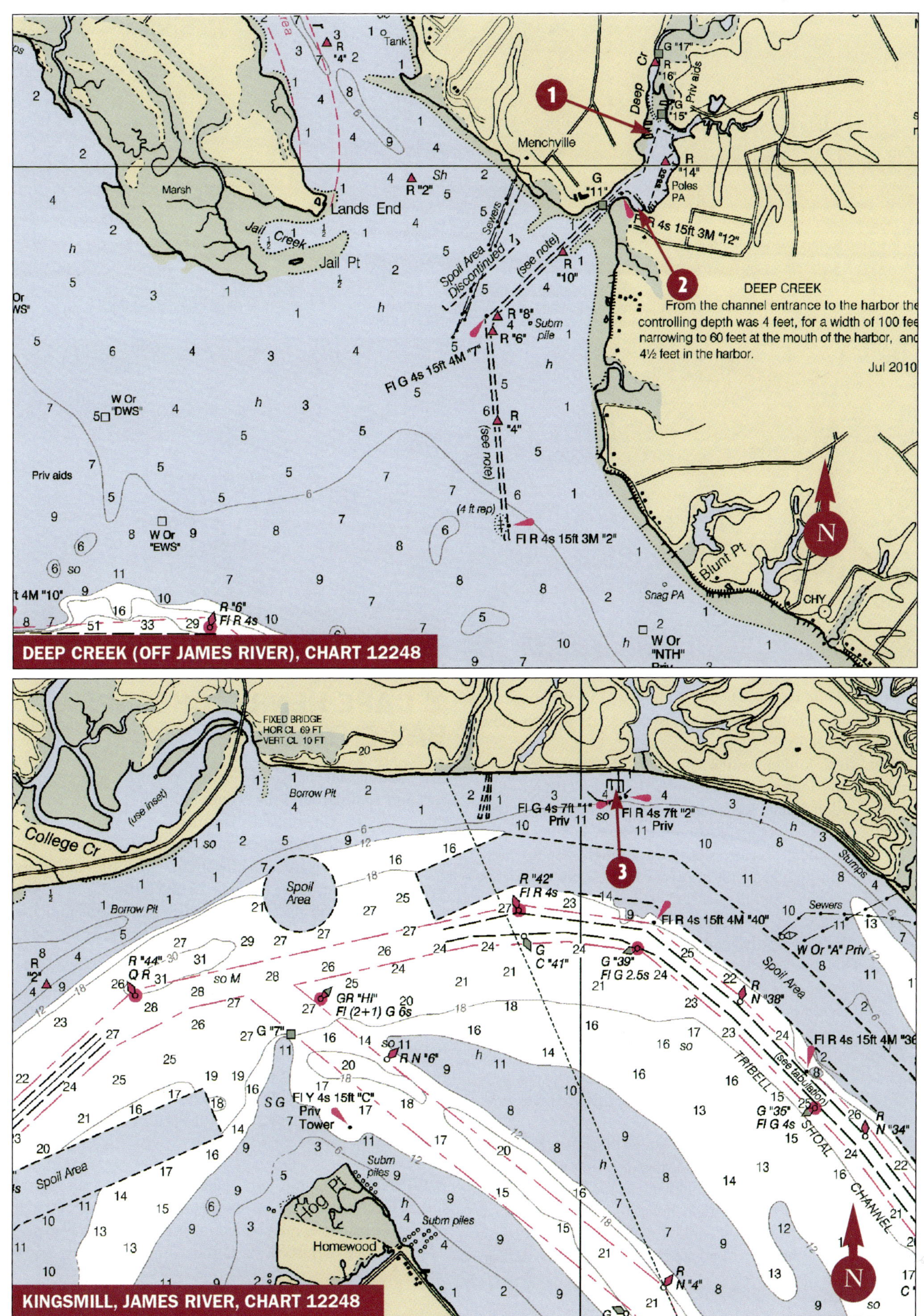

DEEP CREEK (OFF JAMES RIVER), CHART 12248

KINGSMILL, JAMES RIVER, CHART 12248

Chickahominy, Jordan Point, VA

		Largest Vessel Accommodated	VHF Channel Monitored	Transient Berths / Total Berths	Approach / Dockside Depth (reported)	Floating Docks	Gas / Diesel	Groceries, Ice, Marine Supplies, Snacks	Repairs: Hull, Engine, Propeller	Lift (tonnage), Crane, Rail	Min/Max Amps	Laundry, Pool, Showers, Courtesy Car	Pump-Out Station	Nearby: Grocery Store, Motel, Restaurant
CHICKAHOMINY RIVER (JAMES RIVER)		Dockage					Supplies		Services					
1. Two Rivers Marina & Yacht Club (Wireless Internet Access)	757-258-4863	50	16	10/78	8/8	F	GD	I	-	-	30/50	LPS	P	R
2. River's Rest Marina & Resort (Internet Access) (Wireless Internet Access) (Waterway Guide Cruising Club Partner)	804-829-2753	100	16/69	30/60	15/15	F	G	GIMS	-	-	30/100	LPS	P	MR
JORDAN POINT (JAMES RIVER)														
3. Jordan Point Yacht Haven	804-458-3398	42	16/68	2/95	4/4	F	GD	GIMS	HEP	L25	30/50	PS	P	R

Corresponding chart(s) not to be used for navigation. Internet Access · Wireless Internet Access · Waterway Guide Cruising Club Partner

See www.WaterwayGuide.com for current rates, fuel prices, web site addresses, and other up-to-the-minute information.

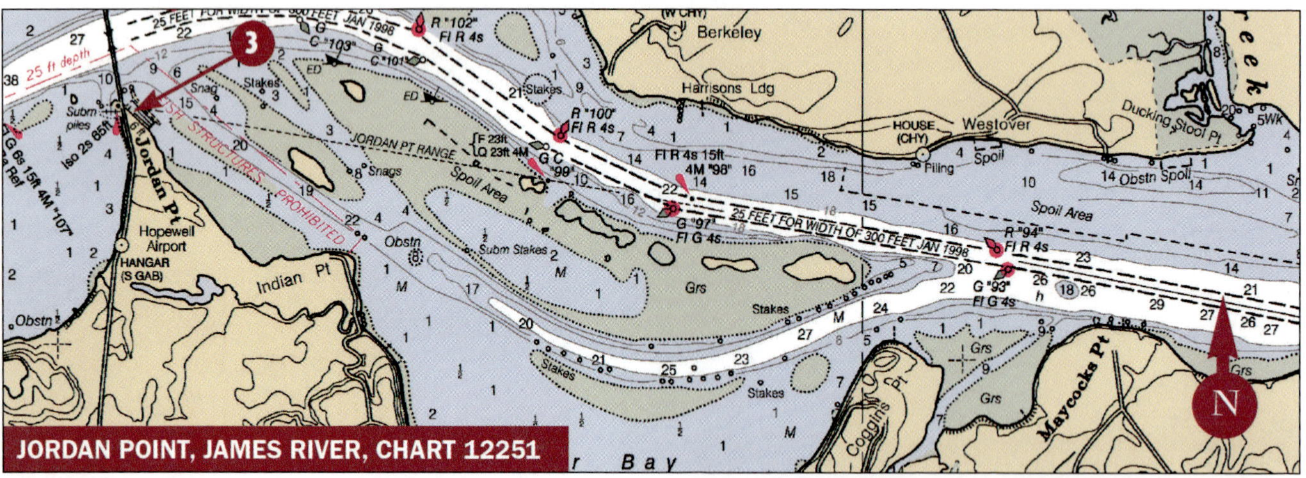

JORDAN POINT, JAMES RIVER, CHART 12251

Sculpture Studio. The History Center within the museum also provides changing exhibitions for variety and to show off their collection.

Dockage: Jordan Point Yacht Haven has some transient space at the foot of the Benjamin Harris Lift Bridge, just below Jordon Point. Rocketts Landing is the only marina on the James River in Richmond. Their floating docks will accommodate boats to 60 feet. Residents of Rocketts Landing will be given first priority for slips, but transients should be able to find dockage. Call ahead to be sure.

Anchorage: At the lower end of the Turkey Island Cutoff, 61 miles up the James, a cable ferry crosses to the Presquile National Wildlife Refuge. Do not attempt to pass the ferry when it is crossing. You can also take the original river route and go around Turkey Island Bend. Enter at the lower end, favoring the northwest (port) shore. Anchor anywhere the depth is satisfactory, but before you reach the sand and gravel works, and allow for a 3-foot spring tidal range. The area is quiet and pretty, with little traffic except on weekends.

At Jones Neck, 64 miles up the James River, you can drop anchor in the old river bend. Be sure to sound your way in to avoid shoals off the gravel pit near the lower bank and off the point to port (west). Favor the east side once you have passed the piles along its bank. Anchor in 10- to 12-foot depths in good holding opposite the inactive pit located on the port side.

CAPE HENRY, CHESAPEAKE BAY ENTRANCE

An exciting side trip from Hampton Roads will lead you east and south around the corner of Cape Henry, where the mouth of the Chesapeake Bay meets the Atlantic Ocean. Along this southernmost stretch of the Chesapeake, you will encounter the sportfishing frenzy of Little Creek and Lynnhaven Inlet, pass through or over the 17 mile long Chesapeake Bay Bridge Tunnel, and arrive at Rudee Inlet on the ocean at the southern end of Virginia Beach, VA, seven miles below Cape Henry.

Little Creek off the Chesapeake

The home of a naval amphibious base, Little Creek has a deep and well-maintained entrance. Its proximity to the Atlantic Ocean and to the urban areas of Norfolk and Virginia Beach are attractive to those seeking the best of both worlds. The abundance of marinas attests to its strategic location.

NAVIGATION: Use Chart 12254. For deep-draft or tall boats, this harbor is closest to the ocean. The wide, straight entrance channel is maintained to accommodate naval craft. The entrance is just west of the Chesapeake Bay Bridge Tunnel.

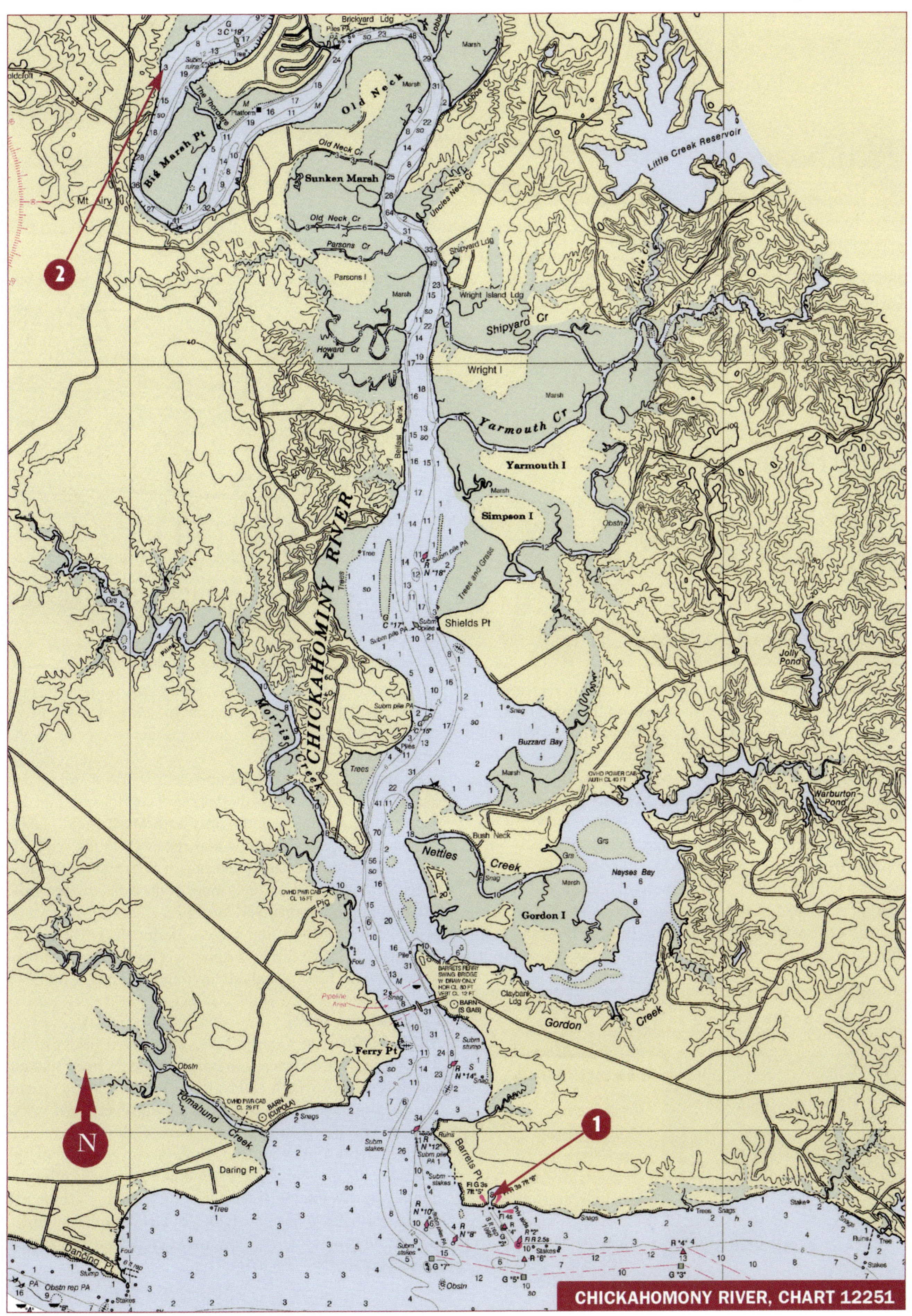
Big Marsh Pt
Old Neck
Sunken Marsh
Old Neck Cr
Parsons Cr
Parsons I
Howard Cr
Little Creek Reservoir
Shipyard Cr
Wright Island Ldg
Wright I
Yarmouth Cr
Yarmouth I
Simpson I
CHICKAHOMINY RIVER
Shields Pt
Jolly Pond
Buzzard Bay
Warburton Pond
Morris Creek
Bush Neck
Nettles Creek
Gordon I
Nayses Bay
Pig Pt
Claybank Ldg
Gordon Creek
Ferry Pt
Tomahund Creek
Daring Pt
Barrets Pt
Dancing Pt
N
1
2
CHICKAHOMONY RIVER, CHART 12251

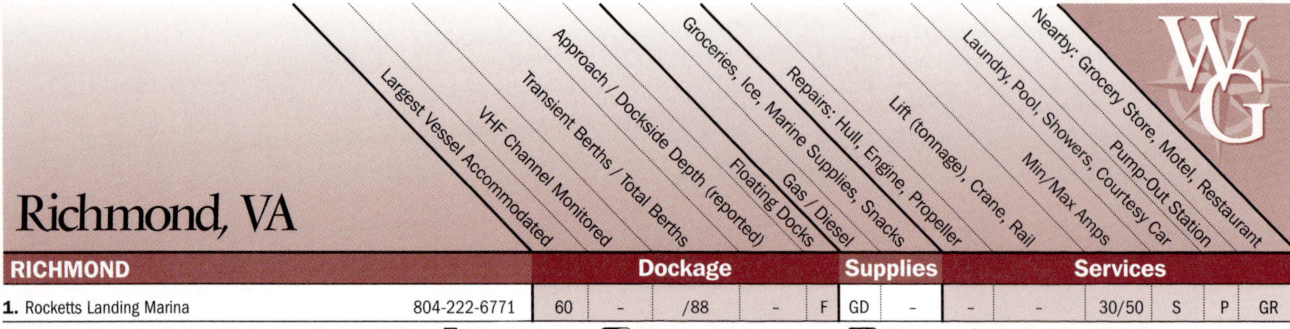

Richmond, VA

RICHMOND		Largest Vessel Accommodated	VHF Channel Monitored	Transient Berths / Total Berths	Approach / Dockside Depth (reported)	Floating Docks	Gas / Diesel	Groceries, Ice, Marine Supplies, Snacks	Repairs: Hull, Engine, Propeller	Lift (tonnage), Crane, Rail	Min/Max Amps	Laundry, Pool, Showers, Courtesy Car	Pump-Out Station	Nearby: Grocery Store, Motel, Restaurant
		Dockage						Supplies		Services				
1. Rocketts Landing Marina	804-222-6771	60	-	/88	-	F	GD	-	-	-	30/50	S	P	GR

Corresponding chart(s) not to be used for navigation. Internet Access Wireless Internet Access Waterway Guide Cruising Club Partner

See www.WaterwayGuide.com for current rates, fuel prices, web site addresses, and other up-to-the-minute information.

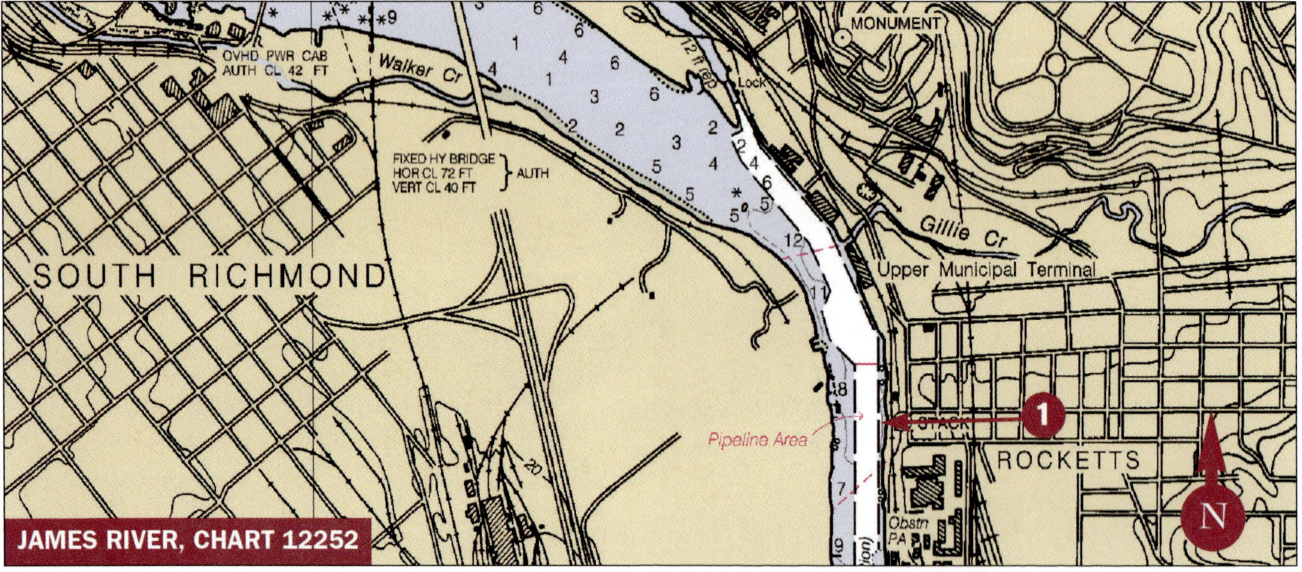

JAMES RIVER, CHART 12252

Dockage: Numerous marinas catering to recreational boats are located in Fishermans Cove, on the first branch of water to starboard (to the west) after entering Little Creek. Just inside Fishermans Cove to starboard on entry is Bay Point Marina, which offers transient dockage at floating slips and The Lagoon restaurant. Next, as you work your way upstream, is Little Creek Marina, which also pumps gas and diesel fuels. Next on the north shore are Cutty Sark Marina with a small bar and café and East Beach Marina, featuring The Blue Crab Restaurant. Vinings Landing Marina is situated near the bridge on the south side of Fishermans Cove with transient slips on floating docks and gas and diesel fuel. The Surf Rider Restaurant is here as well.

Cobb's Marina and boat yard is on the south side of Fisherman's Cove and offers boat repairs in addition to transient slips. There is also a large military marina connected to the Little Creek Naval Base.

Shopping: Little Creek abounds with marinas and several repair facilities. (Refer to the listing of marinas within this section of the Guide.) Both Cutty Sark Marina and Cobb's Marina have extensive yards and repair facilities. There is a Food Lion market at the corner of Shore Dr. and Little Creek Rd., a short (one-half mile) walk from the marinas. Other shopping is relatively nearby; i.e., a hardware store, pharmacies, fast-food, and a West Marine. Salty Dog (9557 Shore Dr., 757-362-3311) is a compact marine consignment store that will have just about anything you might need.

Lynnhaven Inlet

NAVIGATION: Use Chart 12254. Twin fixed bridges with 35-foot vertical clearances prevent sail boats from making use of this inlet, which is the closest to the Atlantic Ocean. The well-marked entry is dredged about every two years, and the entrance markers are moved to allow for shifting channel depths. It would be advisable to call one of the towing companies on your VHF radio for current information about this inlet as it is constantly changing. There is a large sportfishing fleet operating out of Lynnhaven Inlet, and traffic can be heavy. Note that Lynnhaven Bay and its tributaries are No-Discharge Zones.

Little Creek, VA

LITTLE CREEK		Largest Vessel Accommodated	VHF Channel Monitored	Transient Berths / Total Berths	Approach / Dockside Depth (reported)	Floating Docks	Gas / Diesel	Groceries, Ice, Marine Supplies, Snacks	Repairs: Hull, Engine, Propeller	Lift (tonnage), Crane, Rail	Min/Max Amps	Laundry, Pool, Showers, Courtesy Car	Pump-Out Station	Nearby: Grocery Store, Motel, Restaurant
		Dockage					Supplies		Services					
1. Bay Point Marina	**757-362-8432**	**120**	**16/78**	**15/314**	**6/7**	**F**	**GD**	**GIS**	**HEP**	**-**	**30/50**	**LPS**	**P**	**GR**
2. Little Creek Marina	**757-362-3600**	**120**	**16**	**15/130**	**15/8**	**F**	**GD**	**IMS**	**HEP**	**-**	**30/50**	**LPS**	**P**	**GR**
3. Cutty Sark Marina	757-362-2942	125	-	2/96	12/12	-	-	IMS	HEP	L50	30/50	S	P	GMR
4. East Beach Marina	757-362-5000	90	-	/120	8/10	F	-	IS	-	L	30/100	LPS	-	GMR
5. Vinings Landing Marine Center	**757-587-8000**	**65**	**16/09**	**20/220**	**10/8**	**F**	**GD**	**GIMS**	**-**	**-**	**30/50**	**LPSC**	**P**	**G**
6. Cobb's Marina Inc.	**757-588-5401**	**100**	**16/68**	**5/95**	**16/8**	**-**	**-**	**IMS**	**HEP**	**L75, C**	**30/50**	**S**	**P**	**R**

Corresponding chart(s) not to be used for navigation. Internet Access, Wireless Internet Access, Waterway Guide Cruising Club Partner. See www.WaterwayGuide.com for current rates, fuel prices, web site addresses, and other up-to-the-minute information.

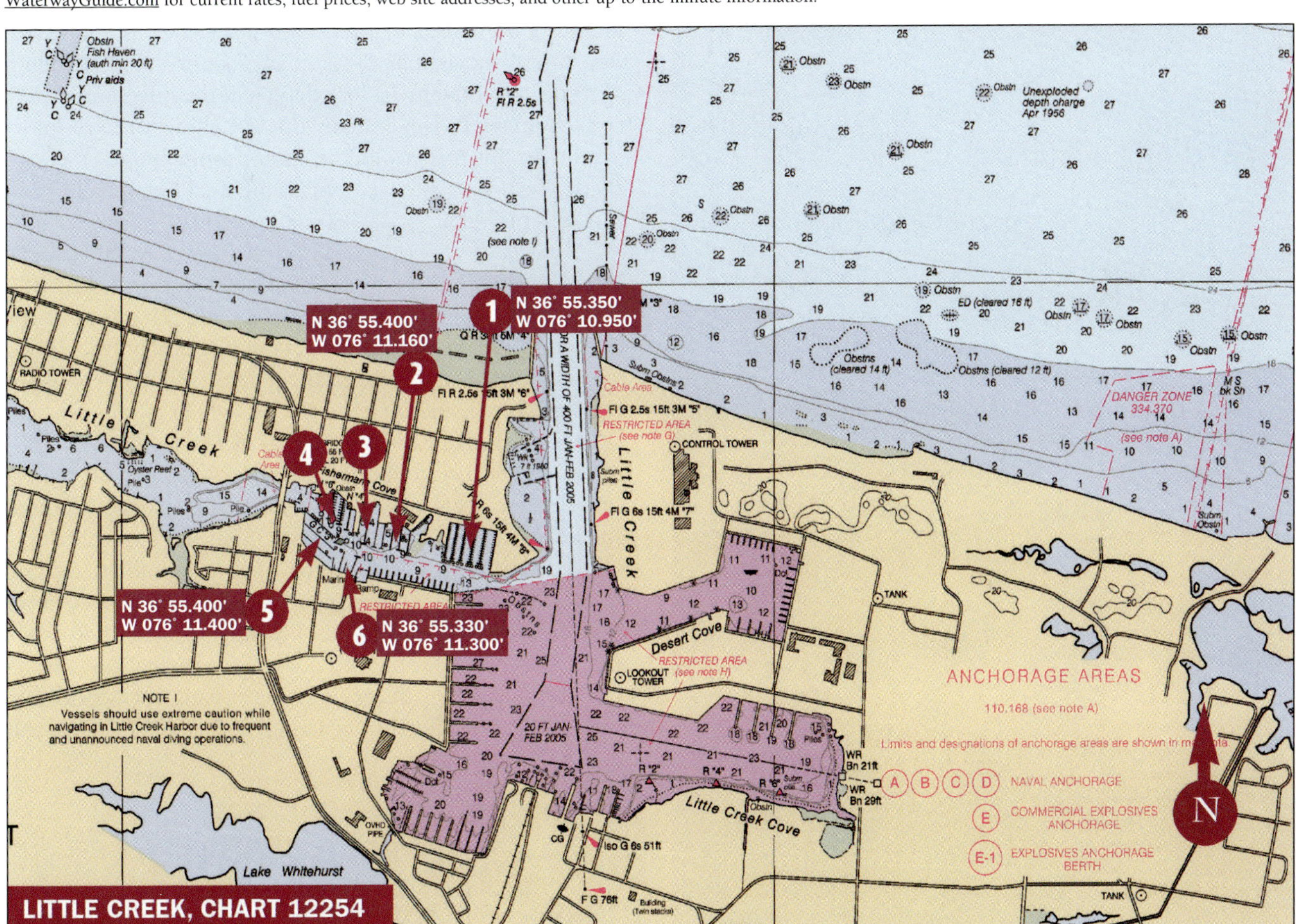

LITTLE CREEK, CHART 12254

Dockage: Marinas and other establishments here cater to sportfishermen, and you will find repairs and services located on Lynnhaven Bay and Long Creek. Docks and restaurants line the north shore (to port) after passing underneath the twin fixed bridges. Long Bay Pointe Boating Resort is here, as is Marina Shores Marina, which offers all fuels and transient dockage. Most importantly, from here, you will have access to all of the wonderful activities that Virginia Beach, VA has to offer by land and water. Nearby Capps Boatworks Inc. specializes in full-service repairs and haul-outs with their 70-ton lift.

A large West Marine store (on N. Great Neck Rd.) is just a short walk away from the two marinas mentioned above. About one mile from the marinas, you will find a Food Lion market (2817 Shore Dr.), Rite Aid pharmacy, Hot Tuna Bar and Grille along with some other shops and salons.

Broad and Linkhorn Bays

The entrance to Broad Bay, which is crossed by Great Neck Road Bridge (35-foot fixed vertical clearance), must be negotiated by a slow turn to the east through a dredged cut in a marsh area. This channel tends to shoal to about 5 feet deep and has a width of 90 feet. Beyond Broad Bay, the

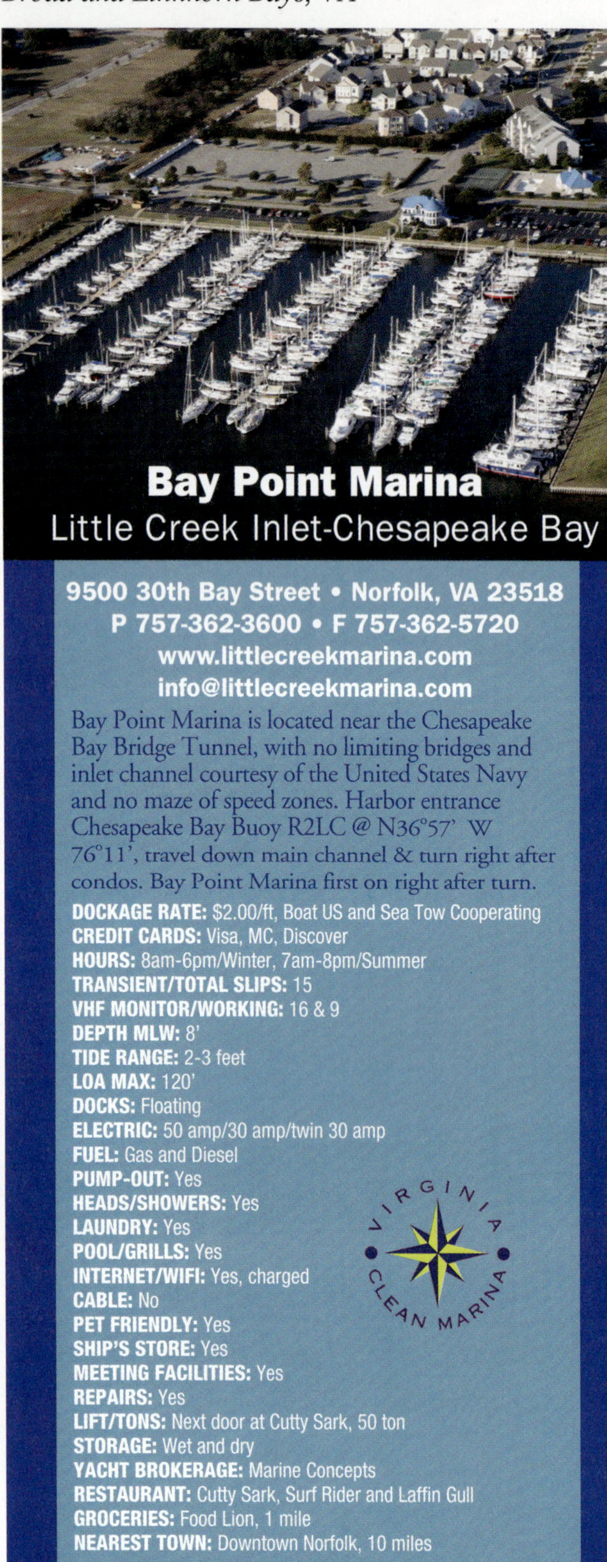

route then continues through The Narrows (6-foot depths) south into Linkhorn Bay. Broad Bay and Linkhorn Bay have 8-foot depths, good anchorages and some of the most picturesque waters on the Chesapeake. Visitors are advised to observe the No-Wake markers, as police boats and helicopters actively patrol this area. The private Cavalier Yacht Club is located to the east at the fork on Linkhorn Bay, and additional dockage is at the end of the eastern branch, near the oceanfront.

Rudee Inlet, on the Atlantic South of Cape Henry

Six miles south of Cape Henry is Rudee Inlet, at the southern end of the famous Virginia Beach boardwalk. Near-constant dredging is part of a beach-replenishment program, which, in turn, keeps the channel deep enough for the lake's numerous marina-based boats. This is a dynamic area where shoals may develop after storms. The dredging attempts to maintain 10-foot depths in the inlet, and it may be as much as 14 feet at many times. Calling for local information on this inlet would be wise. It is the home of a large charter boat fleet, so it is well maintained but shoaling is a constant problem.

NAVIGATION: Use Chart 12205. **Use Hampton Roads tide tables. For high tide at Cape Henry add 31 minutes; for low tide, add 36 minutes.** Start at the sea buoy "RI" to follow your passage through the jettied entrance.

Dockage: Inside on Lake Rudee, which is crossed by a twin fixed bridge (28-foot vertical clearance at high tide), are several marinas and restaurants. Outside the bridge is a marina for boats needing unrestricted clearance (the Virginia Beach Fishing Center Annex), but the passage to it is subject to shoaling; get local information before attempting it. Marinas inside Rudee Inlet provide easy access to all oceanfront activities. Virginia Beach Fishing Center, Fisherman's Wharf Marina and Rudee's Inlet Station Marina are within walking distance of the oceanfront boardwalk, which includes landscaping and an attractive bike path. All

of these facilities offer fuel, transient dockage and pump-out stations. Around the corner from Rudee's Inlet Station Marina is Virginia Beach Marlin Club Marina, which mostly caters to large fishing boats, as does Virginia Beach Fishing Center Annex at Lake Wesley.

The Cape Henry LightHouse

In 1607, a cross was planted near the current home of the Cape Henry Lighthouse to give thanks for a safe passage across the Atlantic. Now, the 164-foot structure guides mariners into the Bay for destinations such as Norfolk and Baltimore. In many other locations, lighthouses have been refurbished, moved or replaced. However, with the Cape Henry Lighthouse, or should we say lighthouses, an additional lighthouse was built after the elder lighthouse began to show wear and tear.

Construction began on the "old" Cape Henry Lighthouse, the first lighthouse to be approved by the then fledgling U.S. government, in 1792. It stood alone proudly, 90 feet tall with its "octangular truncated pyramid" shape, for the next 100 years. In 1881, construction was completed on the "new" Cape Henry Lighthouse, a mere 350 feet from the original structure. No longer manned after 1983, it is now fully automated and is still in use.

The Association for the Preservation of Virginia Antiquities bought the original lighthouse in 1930, and it is now renovated and visited by many tourists every year. It is a National Historic Landmark as well as a National Historic Civil Engineering Landmark. Both lighthouses have had supporting roles in "Hearts of Atlantis," a 2001 movie. They are located within the city limits of Virginia Beach on the Fort Story Army Base.

GOIN' ASHORE:
VIRGINIA BEACH, VA

Boating activities in Virginia Beach are centered on two areas: Rudee Inlet and Lynnhaven Inlet and its tributaries. Virginia Beach is renowned as a base for fishing. Head boats, private sportfishing craft and commercial vessels fill the marinas, rigged for whatever is running up or down the Atlantic coast according to the season. The reason many people come to Virginia Beach is the three-mile-long boardwalk and the adjacent amenities found at a beach resort.

Finding great outdoor fun and adventure here is easy; deciding among all the options is the challenge! The waters of the Atlantic Ocean and Chesapeake Bay are obvious draws, but swimming and beach time is just the beginning. There is a significant surfing community in Virginia Beach, and the oceanfront hosts the annual East Coast Surfing Championships, North America's longest-running surf competition.

Vinings Landing
Norfolk
8166 Shore Drive • Norfolk, VA 23518
P 757-587-8000
www.viningslanding.com
A great place to spend the night. Three miles west of the Chesapeake Bay Bridge Tunnel in very safe Little Creek Basin. Water depth averages 8' to 9' at mean low tide. Floating Docks. Transient Slips Always Available.
DOCKAGE RATE: $2/ft. Boat US and Sea Tow Cooperating
CREDIT CARDS: AMEX/MC/Visa
HOURS: Winter, 8am-5pm; Summer, 7am-8pm
TRANSIENT/TOTAL SLIPS: 10 (220 wet, 448 dry)
VHF MONITOR/WORKING: 16/09
DEPTH MLW: 8'
TIDE RANGE: 2'-3'
LOA MAX: 60'
DOCKS: Floating
ELECTRIC: 50 amp/30amp
FUEL: Diesel/Gas
PUMP-OUT: Yes
HEADS/SHOWERS: Yes
LAUNDRY: Yes
POOL/GRILLS: Yes
INTERNET/WIFI: Yes-charged
CABLE: No
PET FRIENDLY: Yes
SHIP'S STORE: Yes
MEETING FACILITIES: Yes
REPAIRS: Yes
LIFT/TONS: 6 tons
STORAGE: Wet/Dry
YACHT BROKERAGE: Marine Concepts
RESTAURANT: SurfRider and Captain's Galley
GROCERIES: Food Lion, walking distance
NEAREST TOWN: Downtown Norfolk, 10 miles
VIRGINIA CLEAN MARINA
VALVTECT
MARINE FUEL
Vinings Landing boasts a New 448 storage capacity boatel, easy access to fishing w/3 stations for cleaning, and a country club atmosphere with all the best amenities. Come visit us and see why Vinings Landing Marine Center is the marina for fishermen, sailors, and families!
VMG
VININGS MARINE GROUP

Whale-watching and dolphin-watching are also popular activities. Virginia Beach boasts the Mid-Atlantic's largest population of Bottleneck Dolphins, which migrate off the Virginia Beach coast during the summer. Sailing, boating and fishing are nearly year-round activities here – the waters have been called "the Striped Bass Capital of the World" – while

Looking northeast over Little Creek. (Not to be used for navigation.) Waterway Guide Photography.

kayaking or paddle-boarding the ocean or remote lakes, rivers and marshes is another outdoor-lover's opportunity.

On land, there are more than a dozen top-rated golf courses designed by such world famous course architects as Fred Couples, Arnold Palmer and the legendary Pete Dye. These courses, highlighted by Virginia Beach National, are sure to intrigue beginners and challenge the pros.

There are more than 19 miles of biking and hiking paths in the 2,888-acre First Landing State Park where you will also find boating, swimming and picnicking. The 4,321-acre False Cape State Park has six miles of unspoiled beaches and nine miles of hiking/biking trails. The park features primitive camping and an extensive environmental education program in one of the last undisturbed coastal environments on the East Coast. The Back Bay Refuge contains 9,000 acres with a wide assortment of wildlife, including threatened and endangered species such as loggerhead sea turtles, piping plovers, peregrine falcons, and bald eagles.

Few American cities offer the combination of powerful business environment and wonderful lifestyle that you will find in Virginia Beach. This is a city that lets you enjoy the benefits of both worlds. Because, after all, all work and no play is just about impossible here.

History: Christopher Newport and other leaders of the Virginia Company's pioneer group of settlers landed near Cape Henry, about six miles north of present-day Virginia Beach, on April 26, 1607. On opening their sealed orders, they set up a cross to commemorate their visit.

Within 30 years, settlers from England had established themselves in the Virginia Beach area. Prominent among them was Adam Thoroughgood, who proceeded to name places in the region after his home in Kings Lynn in the county of Norfolk, England. His house, part of which dates to 1636, still stands, and is today a museum.

As the Virginia Colony expanded, it was divided for legislative purposes into counties. The area around Thoroughgood's properties was named Princess Anne. It remained largely rural until the end of the 19th century, when the railway arrived to connect a small resort on Virginia's longest beach to the populous Navy town of Norfolk. Automobiles soon followed, and many of the people who moved to the area for the jobs in the military installations around Hampton Roads elected to live at the beach and commute to work.

Virginia Beach grew geometrically. Its population, barely 20,000 in 1940, doubled every decade through the 1970s and has only slightly tapered off since. In 1952, it became an independent city, but so dominated Princess Anne County that in 1963, the two entities merged to form the present City of Virginia Beach. With close to 450,000 residents, it is the most populous city in Virginia.

While one Virginia Beach was growing to cater to vacationers, another was expanding to accommodate the military; within the city's boundaries today are Little Creek Amphibious Base, Fort Story, Camp Pendleton and Oceana Naval Air Station.

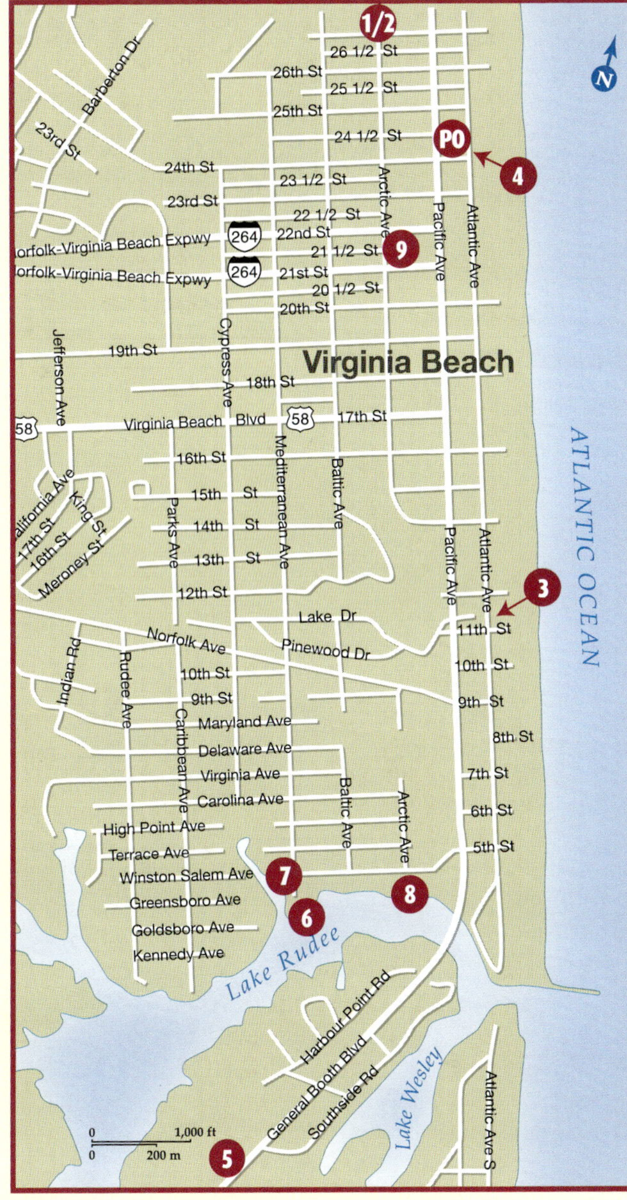

Reference the marina listing tables to see all the marinas in the area.

POINTS OF INTEREST

1 Naval Aviation Monument Park
2 Neptune Sculpture
3 Atlantic Wildfowl Heritage Museum
4 Old Coast Guard Station
5 Virginia Aquarium & Marine Science Center

DINING

6 Rudee's Restaurant and Raw Bar
7 Rockafeller's Restaurant
8 Big Sam's Inlet Café

INFORMATION

9 Visitor Information Center

PO POST OFFICE

You will likely be lucky enough to witness the maneuvers of the F/A-18 Hornet fighter jets. Their speed and agility is unforgettable.

Points of Interest: The Virginia Beach Department of Museums is extensively involved in the conservation of the natural environment and the preservation of historic resources. In addition, residents and visitors can visit a variety of historic attractions, including the Adam Thoroughgood House, Francis Land House and the Cape Henry Lighthouses.

Lynnhaven Bay, VA

LYNNHAVEN BAY		Largest Vessel Accommodated	VHF Channel Monitored	Transient Berths / Total Berths	Approach / Dockside Depth (reported)	Floating Docks	Gas / Diesel	Groceries, Ice, Marine Supplies, Snacks	Repairs: Hull, Engine, Propeller	Lift (tonnage), Crane, Rail	Min/Max Amps	Laundry, Pool, Showers, Courtesy Car	Pump-Out Station	Nearby: Grocery Store, Motel, Restaurant
		Dockage					Supplies		Services					
1. Marina Shores Marina	757-496-7000	45	16	20/155	8/5	F	GD	IS	HEP	L5	30/50	LPS	P	GMR
2. Capps Boatworks Inc.	757-496-0311	75	-	4/27	8/8	F	-	-	HEP	L70	30/30	-	-	GMR
3. Long Bay Pointe Boating Resort	757-321-4550	200	16	14/215	10/6	F	GD	GIMS	HEP	-	30/50	S	P	GMR

Corresponding chart(s) not to be used for navigation. Internet Access · Wireless Internet Access · Waterway Guide Cruising Club Partner

See www.WaterwayGuide.com for current rates, fuel prices, web site addresses, and other up-to-the-minute information.

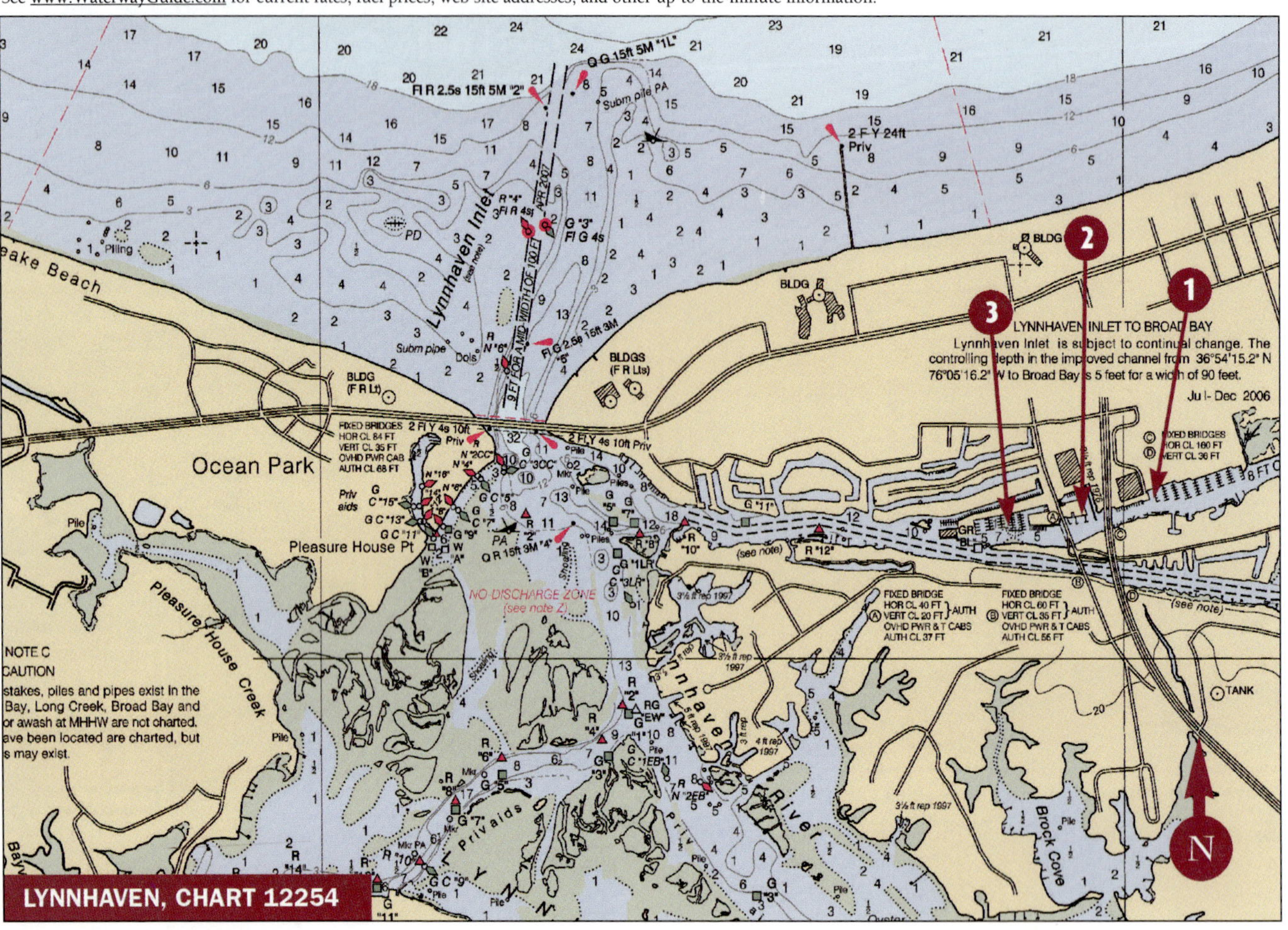

LYNNHAVEN, CHART 12254

There are information kiosks located on the Boardwalk at 17th Street and on Atlantic Ave. at 24th Street describing the local attractions. Among them are the Naval Aviation Monument Park, dedicated to the long association between Virginia Beach and naval aviators. King Neptune, 24 feet tall and 12 tons of bronze and stone, holds court with his retinue of sea creatures at 31st Street.

The southern end of the Boardwalk brings you to one of the famed surfers' beaches (a popular break occurs just off the north jetty of Rudee Inlet). From here, the Boardwalk extends three miles northward through a welter of resort attractions, ranging from art shows to outdoor concerts to the 1,000-foot-long fishing pier. The Atlantic Wildfowl Heritage Museum on the corner of 12th and Atlantic (757-437-8432, www.awhm.org) displays art and artifacts related to migratory wildfowl indigenous to eastern Virginia. The Old Coast Guard Station, at 24th Street, was built in 1903 and now houses a museum of shipwreck memorabilia, and lifesaving equipment and techniques (757-422-1587, www.oldcoastguardstation.com).

South of Rudee Inlet, is the Virginia Aquarium and Marine Science Center (717 General Booth Blvd., 757-385-7777) on the shore of Lake Rudee. For an up-close look at the amazing world of underwater life off our shores, the Virginia Aquarium is 700,000 gallons of mystery and entertainment. The touch tanks, exhibits and live animal habitats make it one of the top ten visited museums in the country. Exhibits in two pavilions connected by a nature trail examine Chesapeake Bay wildlife of

A northwest view of Lynnhaven Inlet, the Lynnhaven River and Long Creek. (Not to be used for navigation.) Cloud 9 Photography© (Deagle/Kucera)

QUICK FACT:

THE CAPE HENRY LIGHTHOUSE

In 1607, a cross was planted near the current home of the Cape Henry Lighthouse to give thanks for a safe passage across the Atlantic. Now, the 164-foot structure guides mariners into the Bay for destinations such as Norfolk and Baltimore. In many other locations, lighthouses have been refurbished, moved or replaced. However, with the Cape Henry Lighthouse, or should we say lighthouses, an additional lighthouse was built after the elder lighthouse began to show wear and tear.

Construction began on the "old" Cape Henry Lighthouse, the first lighthouse to be approved by the then fledgling U.S. government, in 1792. It stood alone proudly, 90 feet tall with its "octangular truncated pyramid" shape, for the next 100 years. In 1881, construction was completed on the "new" Cape Henry Lighthouse, a mere 350 feet from the original structure. No longer manned after 1983, it is now fully automated and is still in use.

The Association for the Preservation of Virginia Antiquities bought the original lighthouse in 1930, and it is now renovated and visited by many tourists every year. It is a National Historic Landmark as well as a National Historic Civil Engineering Landmark. Both lighthouses have had supporting roles in "Hearts of Atlantis," a 2001 movie. They are located within the city limits of Virginia Beach on the Fort Story Army Base.

Photo courtesy of Wikipedia.

Looking west over Rudee Inlet. (Not to be used for navigation.) Waterway Guide Photography.

land, sea and air. Walk through a half-acre aviary, or take in a movie at the IMAX Theater. www.virginiaaquarium.com).

Farther afield (transportation required), there is shopping, dining and museums galore, including a Military Aviation Museum (1341 Princess Anne Rd., 757-721-7767). More entertainment can be had at The Contemporary Art Center of Virginia (2200 Parks Ave., 757-425-0000), the 1,200-seat Sandler Center for the Performing Arts (201 Market St., 757-385-2787) and the The Virginia Beach Amphitheater, a 20,000-seat outdoor concert venue featuring national acts. In your prefer golf, Red Wing Lake Golf Course is nearby (757-437-2037, www.redwinglakegolf.com).

Special Events: Beach Street USA is a summer-long concert along the boardwalk, while all across the city, especially along the famous boardwalk, you can enjoy relaxing outdoor dining and fresh-caught seafood.

Dining: Right on the waterfront, Rudee's on the Inlet (227 Mediterranean Ave., 757-425-1777) has been a popular spot with both the fishing community and visitors for 25 years. The building is a copy of the original Seatack Lifesaving Station on the beach, which is now the Old Coast Guard Station museum.

Rockafeller's Restaurant (308 Mediterranean Ave., 757-422-5654), across the street, is another establishment of long standing serving a reliable American menu with emphasis on seafood.

For a little more "character," Big Sam's Inlet Café and Raw Bar (300 Winston Salem Ave., 757-428-4858) has more of a sports bar atmosphere.

Down on the beach strip, anything and everything goes, from pizza on the run to white linen and a 10th-floor view over the Atlantic. ■

ADDITIONAL RESOURCES

- **VIRGINIA BEACH VISITOR CENTER:** 2100 Parks Ave., Virginia Beach, VA 23451 800-822-3224 or 757-437-4919, www.vbfun.com
- Information kiosks are located on the Boardwalk at 17th Street and on Atlantic Avenue at 24th Street.

NEARBY MEDICAL FACILITIES

Sentara Virginia Beach General Hospital: 1060 First Colonial Road, Virginia Beach, VA 23454 757-395-8000.

Sentara Bayside Hospital: 800 Independence Blvd., Virginia Beach, VA 23455, 757-363-6100

NEARBY AIRPORT

Norfolk International Airport: 2200 Norview Ave., Norfolk, VA 23518, www.norfolkairport.com

Rudee Inlet, VA

RUDEE INLET		Largest Vessel Accommodated	VHF Channel Monitored	Transient Berths / Total Berths	Approach / Dockside Depth (reported)	Floating Docks	Gas / Diesel	Groceries, Ice, Marine Supplies, Snacks	Repairs: Hull, Engine, Propeller	Lift (tonnage), Crane, Rail	Min/Max Amps	Laundry, Pool, Showers, Courtesy Car	Pump-Out Station	Nearby: Grocery Store, Motel, Restaurant
		Dockage					Supplies		Services					
1. Virginia Beach Fishing Center	757-491-8000	100	16/68	25/60	10/7	F	GD	GIMS	-	-	30/200+	S	P	G
2. Fisherman's Wharf Marina (Internet Access, Wireless Internet Access)	757-428-2111	100	16/68	20/90	10/8	F	D	I	E	-	30/50	S	P	M
3. Rudee's Inlet Station Marina (Internet Access, Wireless Internet Access)	757-422-2999	100	16/68	12/60	8/8	F	GD	I	E	-	30/100	LS	P	GMR
4. Virginia Beach Marlin Club Marina	757-422-2999	80	16/68	6/25	7/7	-	GD	I	E	-	100/100	LS	P	GMR
5. Virginia Beach Fishing Center Annex	757-491-8000	120	16/68	10/15	15/10	-	D	GIS	-	-	30/100	S	-	GMR

Corresponding chart(s) not to be used for navigation. Internet Access · Wireless Internet Access · Waterway Guide Cruising Club Partner

See www.WaterwayGuide.com for current rates, fuel prices, web site addresses, and other up-to-the-minute information.

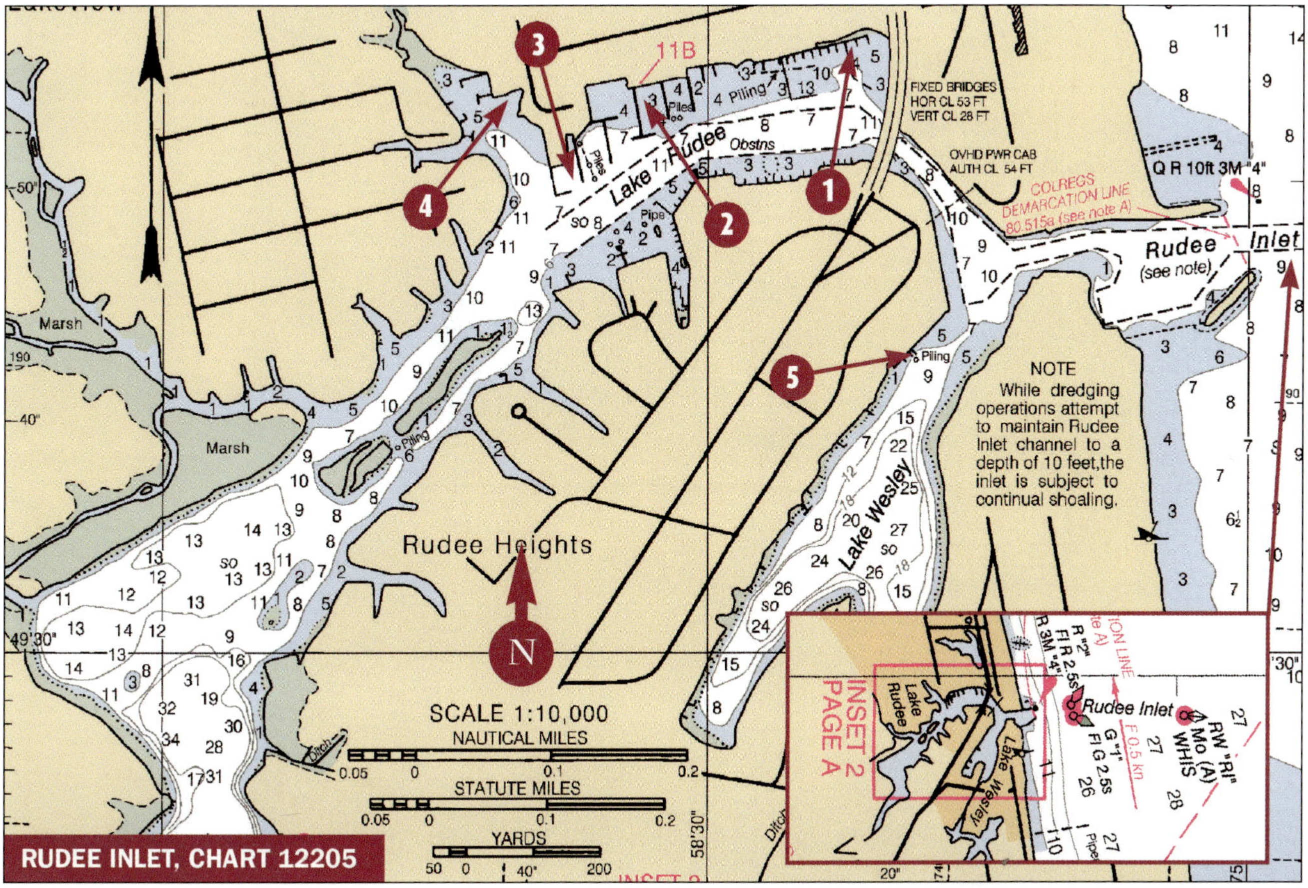

NOTE
While dredging operations attempt to maintain Rudee Inlet channel to a depth of 10 feet, the inlet is subject to continual shoaling.

SCALE 1:10,000

RUDEE INLET, CHART 12205

Waterway Guide advertising sponsors play a vital role in bringing you the most trusted and well-respected cruising guide in the country. Without our advertising sponsors, we simply couldn't produce the top-notch publication now resting in your hands. Next time you stop in for a peaceful night's rest, let them know where you found them—Waterway Guide, The Cruising Authority.

Waterway Guide is always open to your observations from the helm. Email your comments on any navigation information in the Guide to: editor@waterwayguide.com.

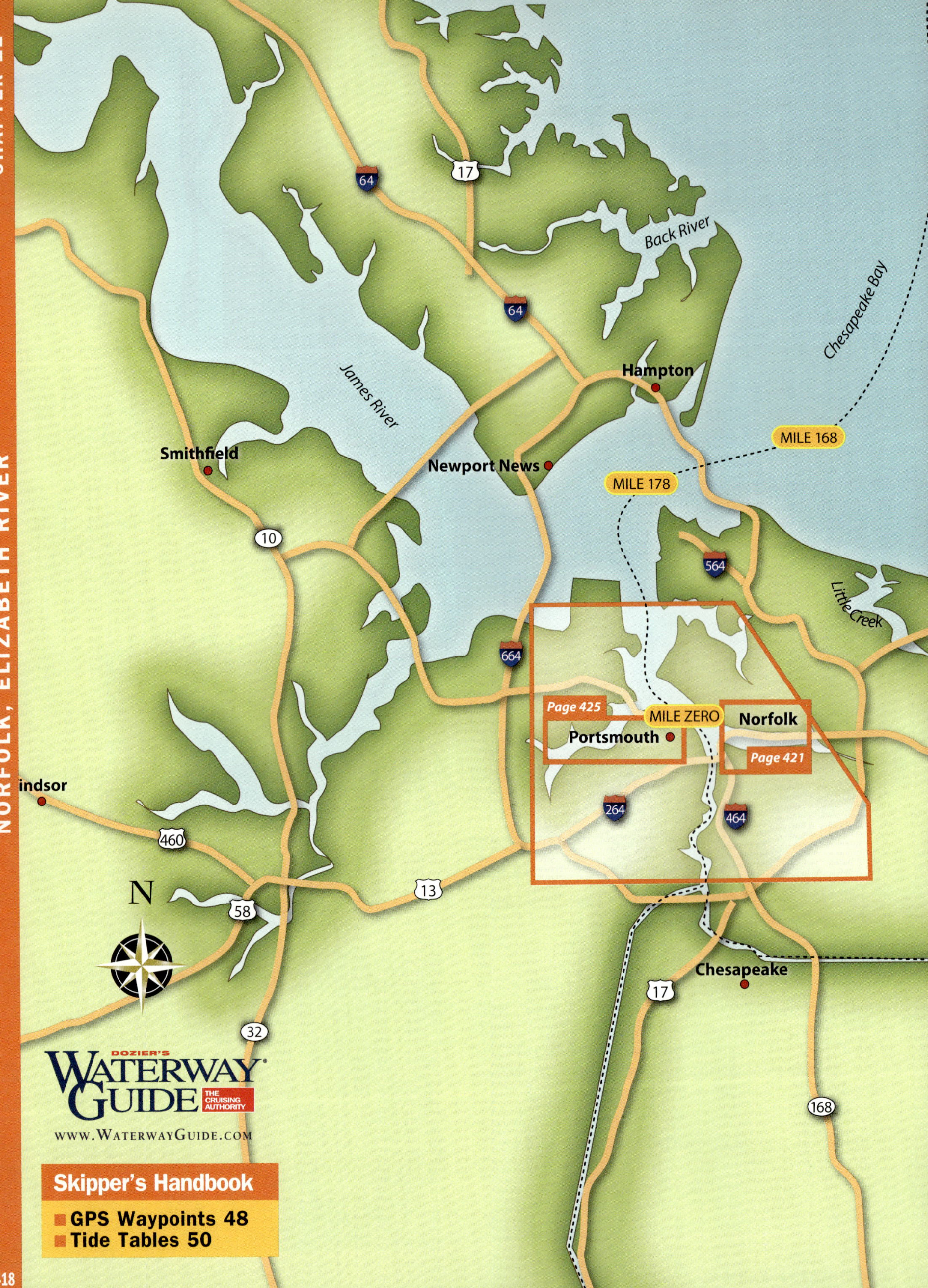

Skipper's Handbook

- GPS Waypoints 48
- Tide Tables 50

Norfolk, Elizabeth River

ICW Mile Zero–Mile 7

VHF Virginia Bridges: Channel 13

CHARTS 12206, 12207, 12221, 12222, 12245, 12253

Strategically situated at Mile Zero, the "official" beginning of the Atlantic Intracoastal Waterway (ICW), Norfolk and Portsmouth, VA, offer nearly every kind of marine service and equipment and are especially good fitting-out places in preparation for a cruise south or north. Norfolk and Portsmouth are also exciting places to visit, with rejuvenated waterfronts filled with shops, restaurants, hotels, museums and historic sites.

The world's merchant fleet loads and unloads cargo at the Hampton Roads and Elizabeth River piers. Colliers fill their holds here with 100,000 tons of coal at a time. The Norfolk Naval Station, the largest naval installation in the world, is homeport for aircraft carriers, cruisers, destroyers, frigates, nuclear submarines and admiral's barges.

There are mutiple daily bus tours of the naval base in summer months. The 45-minute tour departs from the Naval Tour and Information Center located at 9079 Hampton Blvd, next to Gate 5. Bus tours conducted by Navy personnel ride past aircraft carriers, destroyers, frigates, amphibious assault ships and the busy airfield. The tour also drives by historic homes from the 1907 Jamestown Exposition. There is a charge for the tour. A picture ID is required for all adults. Tour schedules are subject to change, so call the tour office at 757-444-7955 before going .

The Confederate ironclad *Merrimac*, which famously dueled with the Union's *Monitor* in 1861, was built in the Norfolk Naval Shipyard, which is actually across the river in Portsmouth. Many of today's huge ships are still built at a private shipbuilding and dry-dock company in nearby Newport News; this shipyard also builds giant supercarriers.

Warning: When transiting this area, keep your boat at least 500 yards from Navy ships. Vessels passing within 500 yards must do so at slow speed. No vessel may approach closer than 100 yards of any U.S. Navy vessel. Patrol boats are in abundance around the berthed vessels at the Norfolk Naval Station, Norshipco and the Norfolk Naval Shipyard. This perimeter is strictly enforced. Also, delays can occur as Coast Guard vessels escort ships in and out of the harbor. Commercial ships, especially containerships, are often escorted in and out of the harbor. Rules state that you cannot pass these vessels from behind but are free to go by them from the opposite direction. Be sure to stand by the VHF radio and maintain the largest possible distance between you and large ships. When in doubt, hail the ship on VHF Channel 13. See the "Port Security" section of our Skipper's Handbook in the front of this Guide for details on dealing with security zones and perimeters.

The Norfolk-Portsmouth area is a good centralized spot for sightseeing in the surrounding countryside, for picking up or dropping off guests and for flying in to rejoin a boat. Limousine service to and from Norfolk's airport is easy to arrange.

NAVIGATION: Use Chart 12222. **Use the Hampton Roads Tide Table. For high tide, add 18 minutes; for low tide, add 15 minutes.** Even with all its commercial and military activity, navigating through Norfolk Harbor is relatively easy during daylight hours. If southbound from Hampton Roads, pick up the marked channel past Sewells Point at the western end of Willoughby Bay and continue on into the Elizabeth River. Southbound past Sewells Point, you will see a great array of Naval vessels to port, from aircraft carriers to submarines. The harbor itself begins at Craney Island, where you can switch to Small-Craft Chart 12206. At night, navigation can be a bit more difficult with all the illumination ashore, making aids to navigation more difficult to detect.

As in New York Harbor, you can run outside the marked channel if ship traffic is heavy. Depths alongside the channel are good. The main hazard is flotsam, which can be in the form of wooden planks or piles the size of telephone poles. If you choose to run outside the channel, use the western side until you are past the Norfolk Naval Base and port operations to the east. Patrol boats and security barriers line the Restricted Area (shown as a purple shaded area on your chart) on the eastern side of the channel. From Craney Island southward, remain inside the channel to avoid shallows and military or port facilities.

The current can be strong here and can produce a marked delay in arrival time. Expect less current as you proceed from ICW Mile Zero southward. Heavy commercial traffic, bridge schedules and lock openings can also sometimes cause marked delay in arrival time, so planning ahead is a good idea before proceeding southward. There are frequent construction and diving operations to the north in Hampton Roads. Be alert for these and give a slow pass.

Anchorage: An anchorage up the Lafayette River is directly across from the yacht club and just outside the channel at the red marker. Several boats are here on permanent moorings. Depths are 8 to 9 feet just off the channel, shoaling gradually farther in. Although the club is private

Looking north over the Elizabeth River. (Not to be used for navigation.) Waterway Guide Photography.

and the anchorage exposed to the west, you will find a suburban setting with little traffic. For boats that can clear a 24-foot fixed vertical bridge, there is a lot of additional anchorage farther up the river in 8 to 9 feet of water with ample swing room and protection. The spot is good for a layover if you are not planning to stop in Norfolk or Portsmouth.

Western Branch, Elizabeth River

NAVIGATION: Use Chart 12253. South around the main channel's bend at Lamberts Point, the Western Branch of the Elizabeth River leads off to starboard. Note the magenta restricted area on the chart east of Lovett Point on your approach to Western Branch. A 45-foot fixed vertical clearance bridge just west of Lovett Point makes it impossible for some sailboats to pass farther upstream. Those who can clear the fixed bridge will find depths of 15 to 20 feet all the way to the Churchland Bridge (38-foot fixed vertical clearance) farther on.

NORFOLK BRIDGES
Mile 2.5-5.8

Waterway Guide Photography.

Dockage: Virginia Boat and Yacht Service, located on the north side of Western Branch before the 45-foot bridge, has 62 slips with some transient space. They also have a 35-ton boat lift.

Engines 1, a division of Western Branch Diesel Inc., also conveniently located on the north side before the bridge, offers installation, service and parts for vessels of all sizes and a 35-ton boat lift, in addition to transient space.

MILE ZERO

NAVIGATION: Use Chart 12253 or 12206. NOAA's Office of Coast Survey released an updated Chart 12253, which provides a new inset of Norfolk Harbor and the Elizabeth River at 1:10,000 scale. This inset provides updated depth and more details based on recent surveys. Be sure to update your charts or access print on demand, as there are over 600 600 updates and new bathymetry along the entire Norfolk waterfront. Elizabeth River quick flashing red buoy "36,"just east of Hospital Point, marks Mile 0 and the beginning of the 1,243-mile-long ICW. All mileage on the Norfolk-to-Florida segment of the ICW is measured in statute rather than nautical miles. Appropriately named, Hospital Point—located on the western side of the main Elizabeth River channel, south of the Western Branch junction—is home to a huge and recently enlarged Naval hospital, which is the nation's oldest.

Anchorage: Late arrivals and those who prefer to anchor out normally use the harbor's small-boat anchorage, south and west of the channel at flashing red buoy "36,"between the large brick Naval hospital and Tidewater Yacht Marina. Unfortunately, it gets shaken up by endless passing traffic, including giant commercial vessels and is relatively exposed to high winds that can tunnel down the river, particularly during summer thunderstorms. The anchorage is popular and quite often has numerous boats. The bottom is good here as well as the holding. In this area the bottom is mud so set your anchor well. A chain rode will always help.

You can take the dinghy (you will need an outboard motor) and, for a small fee, make fast inside the Waterside Marina on the Norfolk waterfront across the river. Dinghy dockage and use of some facilities is available at the Tidewater Yacht Marina adjacent to the Portsmouth side of the river, also for a fee. There is no dinghy dockage available at Tidewater Yacht Marina or Waterside Marina during special events such as Harborfest in early June. Water taxi service is available on weekend evenings and for some special events.

Norfolk—Elizabeth River (East Shore)

Dockage: The city of Norfolk has constructed a wave screen directly in front of the Festival Marketplace at the 60-slip Waterside Marina to provide a protected area for vessels moored there. Transient space is available at modern floating slips with access to restrooms, showers, laundry facilities and an athletic club. The dockmaster will arrange for discount fuel and transportation for reprovisioning for overnight slipholders on request. The city of Norfolk has recently opened a new smaller marine facility (15 slips) for overflow from Waterside close by at Nauticus. Call Waterside Marina for information and reservations for the Nauticus Marina.

GOIN' ASHORE: NORFOLK, VA

For two centuries, Norfolk has been a Navy town, and to this day, it is flanked on north and south by ships in gray livery. Before the Navy came into existence, merchant ships and sailors called Norfolk home, and cargo vessels of all types still call to load, to discharge or to undergo repairs.

A large city and several dormitory communities have grown up around all this maritime activity, flourishing with its booms and languishing with its busts. For several post-WWII decades, America's focus was on its highway systems, and maritime hubs received scant resources with which to maintain their infrastructures, both social and physical. In the 1980s, that tide changed, and Norfolk has ridden it to a new high water mark of civic pride and urban dynamism.

Anyone arriving in Norfolk by boat from either direction, whether from the isolated small towns of the Chesapeake Bay or from the cypress-bound sounds of North Carolina, is in for re-entry shock. It begins with the visual stimulation of the sheer volume of water traffic and intense industrial activity on both banks of the Elizabeth River and culminates with immersion into the din and clamor of a vibrant city. Enjoy it, because when you leave, in either direction, you will go a long way before encountering anything like it again.

History: Norfolk, home of the world's largest naval base, has roots that begin at the waterfront and are entwined with it throughout history. Long before the arrival of English Colonists in the Chesapeake Bay, the Chesapean Indians had a settlement here, on the right bank of the Elizabeth River. By the time the Jamestown group arrived, Chief Powhatan—with whom the colonists, too, would have their own skirmishes—had wiped them out.

One of the earliest English settlers in the area was Nicholas Wise, who, in 1622, purchased 200 acres of the land on which Norfolk now stands. He was a shipwright, and the surrounding vast forests of cypress, pine and oak laced with deep rivers must have provided bounty of proportions unimaginable in his homeland.

In 1682, in response to a 1680 decree from the Virginia House of Burgesses, Norfolk Towne was established on 50 acres purchased from the trustees of the Wise tract. Strategically located near the entrance to the Chesapeake Bay, and well served with sheltered deep water, Norfolk expanded rapidly to become one of the largest ports in Virginia. At the outbreak of the Revolutionary War, its importance was duly noted by the English, who sent a fleet of ships to bombard it. What they left of the town, Colonial troops razed to prevent the English from occupying it.

Reconstruction of the town began in 1783, and in 1801 the Continental Navy established its first Navy Yard. During the Civil War, Norfolk's strategic location again made it the focus of the attention of both sides, which took turns destroying much of it again—until, shortly after the spectacular but inconclusive battle between the ironclads *Virginia* and *Monitor* in 1862, the city surrendered to the Union Army. The occupation ended when Virginia was re-admitted into the Union in 1870; thereafter, Norfolk grew apace once more. Connected to the north by the Chesapeake Bay, to the west by railroads and to the south by the Albemarle and Chesapeake Canal (which had opened in 1859), it soon became, according to the city's official history, the world's largest seaport.

By itself, Norfolk, with a population approaching 250,000, is the second largest city in Virginia. The urban sprawl it forms with the surrounding towns and cities—Virginia Beach, Chesapeake, Suffolk and Portsmouth—is the largest in the state. It is not surprising that Norfolk supports many of the cultural and recreational outlets associated with bigger cities. It has a symphony orchestra, several museums, professional sports teams and a downtown shopping mall full of high-end retail stores.

At its heart, Norfolk is still a seaport and a Naval base, and the rejuvenation of its city center has been an arduous fight against the grittiness that adheres to port cities everywhere. It has been largely successful in the downtown area of Town Point, where Norfolk's waterfront basks in light reflected off high-rise office buildings and hotels. It is here that visiting boaters will tie up, either at Waterside or at the Nauticus Marina, within walking distance of many of Norfolk's must-sees. An early stop should be the visitors center at the entrance of Nauticus to pick up information on current events and a map.

Getting Around: Hampton Roads Transit connects with destinations beyond downtown and with all the cities in the Hampton Roads area via bus, light rail and ferry. Call 757-222-6100 or visit www.gohrt.com for details.

The pedestrian ferry ($1.50 adults and children ñ seniors and disabled $0.75) connects Waterside to downtown Portsmouth across the Elizabeth River, so whichever side you moor your boat, you will have access to the amenities of both. And because you are in a city, taxicabs and rental cars are available to take you farther afield. Norfolk International Airport is a mere five miles from downtown.

Norfolk's light-rail transit system, The Tide, opened in spring 2011 and connects the city center with points west and east, including the waterfront baseball field at Harbor Park. It operates in connection with the bus system so you can switch back and forth. Fares for both are $1.50 for adults, $1.00 for youth and $0.75 for seniors.

Norfolk Electric Transit (NET) is a free electric bus service that operates in the downtown area only. The weekend route differs from the weekday route, so pick up a map at the visitors center (757-664-6222, www.norfolk.gov/parking).

Points of Interest: Nauticus is a fusion of science museum, game arcade and theme park, centered around humankind's historic engagement with the ocean and its denizens. Here, you can touch a shark, design a battleship or see how the earth's atmosphere and oceans interact to create and influence climate and weather. In the same building, the Hampton Roads Naval Museum showcases the U.S. Navy's 200-year association with the Hampton Roads region. Berthed alongside is the *USS Wisconsin*, veteran of three wars and the last battleship built for the U.S. Navy. Tours by bus or boat provide a close-up view of active-service ships at Naval Station Norfolk. Call 757-664-1000 for operating hours and information.

A city whose lifeblood is the military must necessarily cope with death, and several memorials remind visitors of the ultimate price our warriors pay. The MacArthur Memorial, where General Douglas MacArthur and his wife are laid to rest, is both a celebration of his life and achievements, and a tribute to the millions of men and women who served in America's wars, from the Spanish-American War to Korea. More evocative at a personal level, the Armed Forces Memorial in Town Point Park tells its story through examples of letters written home by servicemen and women who subsequently died in action. A good time to visit is in late afternoon, when warm light and long shadows highlight the messages, each one borne on cast bronze sheets and displayed as though strewn across the plaza by the wind.

Energetic walkers can follow the marked Cannonball Trail, which loops through the downtown area, taking in many city sights including Town Point, the Freemason Historic District, St. Paul's Church and the MacArthur Memorial. Those who care to make a morning or afternoon of it will find abundant opportunities for refreshment along the way. If you prefer golf, Ocean View Golf Course is at 9610 Norfolk Ave. (757-480-2094, or www.oceanviewgc.com).

Norfolk has museums big and small with focuses broad and narrow. A sampling:

Chrysler Museum of Art: 245 W. Olney Road (757-664-6200, www.chrysler.org).

The Norfolk History Museum at the Willoughby-Baylor House: 601 E. Freemason St. (757-333-6283, www.chrysler.org).

Hermitage Foundation Museum: 7637 N. Shore Road (757-423-2052, www.hermitagefoundation.org).

Hunter House Victorian Museum: 240 W. Freemason St. (757-623-9814, www.hunterhousemuseum.org).

Norfolk Town Point/Tall Ships. Photo courtesy of Norfolk Convention & Visitors Bureau.

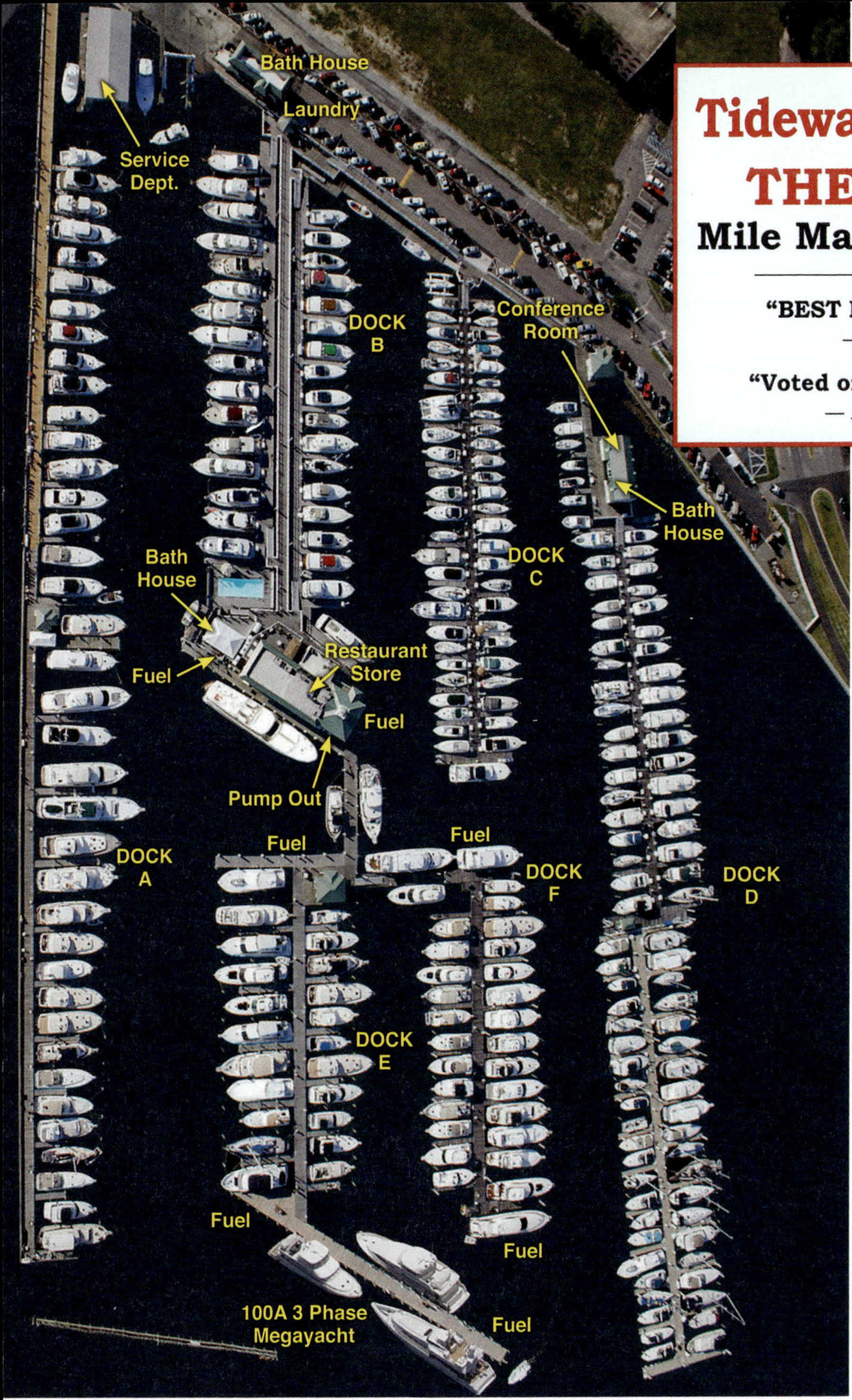

A little farther afield, the Norfolk Botanical Gardens (757-441-5830) and the Virginia Zoo (757-441-2374) provide windows on nature contained, for those intimidated by the wildness of the Great Dismal Swamp.

Entertainment: Norfolk is home to a symphony orchestra, an opera company, a professional theater and several venues for concerts and other cultural expositions.

The Virginia Stage Company is based in the Wells Theater, 254 Granby St., a restored Beaux Arts landmark that opened in 1913 as a vaudeville theater (757-627-1234, www.vastage.com).

The Attucks Theatre (1010 Church St.), was built in 1919 in what was then the heart of the minority district. After being idle and neglected for decades, it has been refurbished and reopened in 2008 to once again stage performances with an African-American influence (757-662-4763, www.attuckstheatre.org).

In the course of its 42-week season, which runs from September through June, Virginia Symphony plays at several venues in the Hampton Roads area (757-892-6366, www.virginiasymphony.org).

Virginia Opera performs at the Harrison Opera House, located on the corner of Virginia Beach Boulevard and Llewellyn Avenue, about a mile and a half from Waterside (866-763-7282, www.vaopera.org).

Special Events: Norfolk is home to a professional ice hockey team, the Admirals, who play at the Norfolk Scope Arena and a baseball team, the Tides, who play at the waterfront Harbor Park. Town Point Park hosts cultural and musical festivals throughout the summer. The annual Harborfest has its origins in Operation Sail, the tall ship tour that was part of the America's Bicentennial celebrations in 1976.

Dining: Restaurants in downtown Norfolk serve every gastronomic taste from meatballs to highballs. At Waterside Festival Marketplace, you will find Mama Mia Pizzeria, Joe's Crab Shack, an Outback Steakhouse and Hooters, plus the usual food-court offerings are available at the MacArthur Center.

For a more adventurous dining experience, forage along Granby Street and its neighbors in an area studded with restaurants. Try Granby Bistro & Deli (225 Granby St., 757-622-7003), Jack Quinn's Restaurant & Irish Pub (241 Granby St., 757-623-2233)or Thai cuisine at Rama Garden (441 Granby St., 757-616-0533). Every continent is represented here, and the restaurants are numerous, but just as Norfolk is to some degree still finding itself, so too are some of these establishments. Take your lead from the visitor's guide, but don't be surprised if you find changes. Norfolk has an active nightlife, so the action at some restaurants doesn't get heavy until late in the evening.

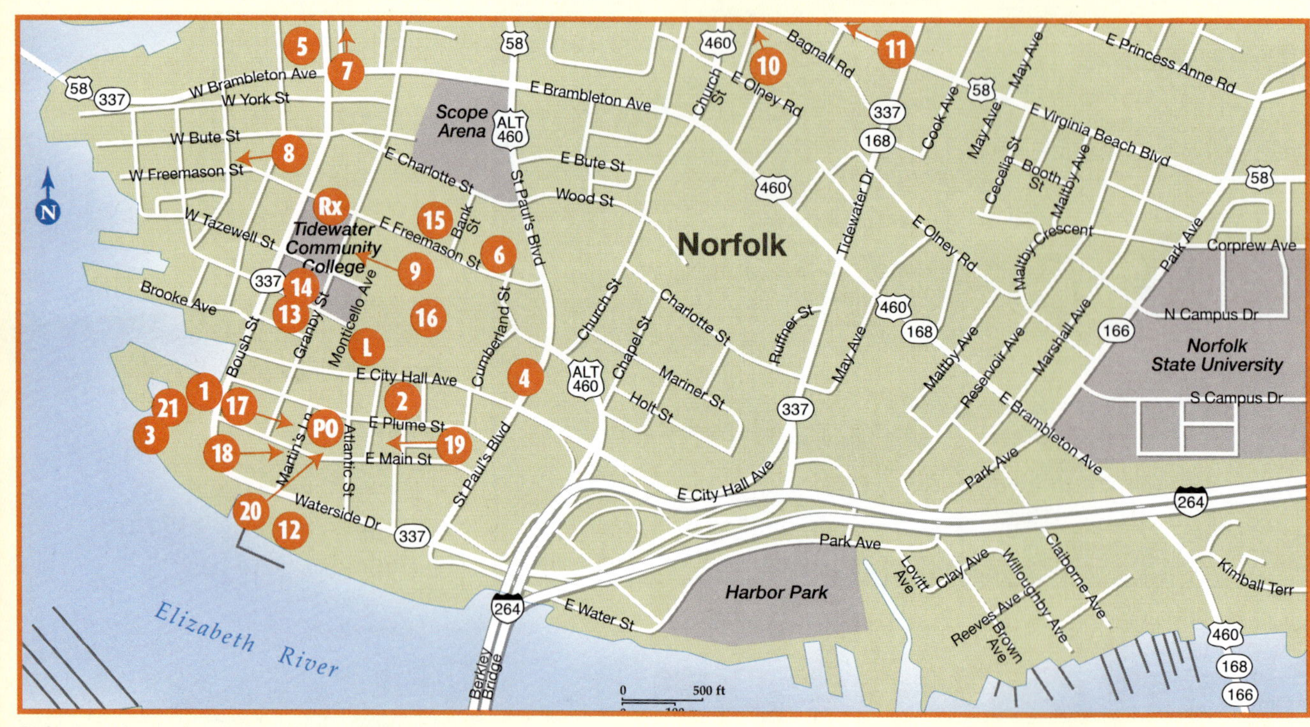

Reference the marina listing tables to see all the marina in the area.

POINTS OF INTEREST
1 Nauticus/Hampton Roads Naval Museum
2 The MacArthur Memorial
3 Armed Forces Memorial
4 St. Paul's Church
5 Crysler Museum of Art
6 Norfolk History Museum
7 Hermitage Foundation Museum
8 Hunter House Victorian Museum
9 Wells Theater
10 Attucks Theater
11 Harrison Opera House

DINING
12 Waterside Festival Marketplace
13 Granby Bistro & Deli
14 Jack Quinn's Restaurant & Irish Pub
15 Rama Garden

SHOPPING
16 MacArthur Center
17 Selden Archade
18 Prince Books & Lizard Cafe
19 W.T. Brownley Co.

INFORMATION
20, 21 Convention & Visitors Bureaus

LIBRARY
POST OFFICE
PHARMACY

Shopping: Shopaholics can head for the Waterside Festival Marketplace, where the fare is touristy, or to the MacArthur Center, with its full quota of mid- and upscale mall stores anchored by Dillard's and Nordstrom. A variety of emporia line the streets in between, and the Selden Arcade houses art workshops and galleries. At Prince Books, 109 E. Main St. (757-622-9223), the discriminating bibliophile can browse a broad and eclectic selection of books and partake of a restorative coffee and a muffin in the on-site Lizard Café.

If the onboard navigation system or library need updating, or the compass needs adjusting, a visit to W.T. Brownley Co. (established 1932) is a couple of miles from the waterfront at 523 W. 24th St.(757-622-7589). You will need some form of transportation to get there.

ADDITIONAL RESOURCES

- **CONVENTION & VISITORS BUREAU:** Satellite offices at 232 E. Main St. and One Waterside Drive, 757-441-1852, 800-368-3097 www.norfolkcvb.com

- **NEARBY MEDICAL FACILITIES** Sentara Norfolk General Hospital: 600 Gresham Drive Norfolk, VA 23507; 757-388-3000, www.sentara.com (3 miles)

Portsmouth—Elizabeth River (West Shore)

Directly on the ICW's first mile, this is a convenient location to regroup for the journey south or to recoup from the rigors of "The Ditch"when heading north. **Use Hampton Roads Tide Table. For high tide, add 9 minutes; for low tide, add 10 minutes.**

The Portsmouth Renaissance Hotel and Conference Center is on the waterfront at the entrance to the Elizabeth River's Southern Branch. The first basin, located just above the hotel, is North Harbor Landing (formerly known as Portside Ferry Landing), which offers ferry service and short-term dockage (no overnights, but dinghies are welcome). Private vessels may make fast for up to two hours, but must stay clear of the ferry.

Free public docking, but no overnight dockage, is also available in High Street Landing, a small basin with an entrance below the hotel. The Olde Towne Portsmouth historic shopping and entertainment district is adjacent to High Street Landing, with numerous shops and restaurants and the restored Art Deco-style Commodore Theatre.

Dockage: Dockage on the Portsmouth side of the Elizabeth River is available on Scotts Creek at the full-service Scott's Creek Marina and at Portsmouth Boating Center, known for its high-speed diesel pumps and reasonable fuel prices (as well as a 70-ton boat lift).

Directly opposite Town Point, on the Portsmouth (west) side of the Elizabeth River, the full-service Tidewater Yacht Marina has 100 deep-water slips available for transients, as

Norfolk, Portsmouth, VA

NORFOLK, PORTSMOUTH		Largest Vessel Accommodated	VHF Channel Monitored	Transient Berths / Total Berths	Approach / Dockside Depth (reported)	Floating Docks	Gas / Diesel	Groceries, Ice, Marine Supplies, Snacks	Repairs: Hull, Engine, Propeller	Lift (tonnage), Crane, Rail	Min/Max Amps	Laundry, Pool, Showers, Courtesy Car	Pump-Out Station	Nearby: Grocery Store, Motel, Restaurant
		Dockage						Supplies		Services				
1. Engines 1 a Div Western Branch Diesel, Inc.	**757-673-7200**	**200**	**-**	**4/62**	**12/7**	**-**	**-**	**M**	**HE_**	**L35**	**30/50**	**LS**	**-**	**R**
2. Virginia Boat & Yacht	757-673-7167	150	-	5/62	12/8	-	-	-	HEP	L35	30/50	LS	-	GMR
3. Scott's Creek Marina 🖳 WiFi	757-399-BOAT	65	16/68	8/135	14/12	-	-	GIMS	-	-	30/50	LPS	P	GMR
4. Portsmouth Boating Center 🖳 WiFi	757-397-2092	80	16	10/40	8/10	-	GD	IMS	HEP	L70	30/50	LS	P	GMR
5. Nauticus Marina 🖳 WiFi	**757-625-3625**	**60**	**16**	**15/15**	**45/20**	**F**	**-**	**GIS**	**-**	**-**	**30/100**	**LS**	**P**	**GMR**
6. Waterside Marina 🖳 WiFi	**757-625-3625**	**400**	**16/68**	**60/60**	**45/20**	**F**	**-**	**GIS**	**EP**	**-**	**30/100**	**LS**	**P**	**GMR**
7. Tidewater Yacht Marina 🖳 WiFi	**757-393-2525**	**300**	**16/68**	**100/300**	**12/11**	**F**	**GD**	**GIMS**	**HEP**	**L60**	**30/200+**	**LPS**	**P**	**GMR**
8. Ocean Marine Yacht Center 🖳 WiFi	757-399-2920	350	16/09	25/122	45/30	F	GD	GIMS	HEP	L125	30/100	LS	P	GMR

Corresponding chart(s) not to be used for navigation. 🖳 Internet Access WiFi Wireless Internet Access Waterway Guide Cruising Club Partner

See www.WaterwayGuide.com for current rates, fuel prices, web site addresses, and other up-to-the-minute information.

well as diesel and gas fueling stations, substantial lift and repair facilities and a well-stocked ship's store with charts, clothing and groceries. The marina offers a floating swimming pool, a laundry, multiple bathhouses and conference facilities. The Deck Restaurant, situated above the marina store and office, has a commanding view of the harbor.

Ocean Marine Yacht Center is easily accessible one-half mile south with floating slips and one of the largest yacht service yards in the Mid-Atlantic region.

Portsmouth's waterfront and the adjacent streets offer a wide venue of entertainment features, restaurants, shops and museums and are all within walking distance of both Tidewater Yacht Marina and Ocean Marine Yacht Center. Reprovisioning in downtown Portsmouth is possible at a Food Lion grocery about two miles from the marinas. You will still need a taxi (757-235-5099, Portside Taxi) or a marina courtesy car. Mile Marker "0", which is conveniently located at One High Street (at Water Street), offers marine supplies as well as transportation for the boating community and other such services. You can go to the supermarket, West Marine and other stores from here.

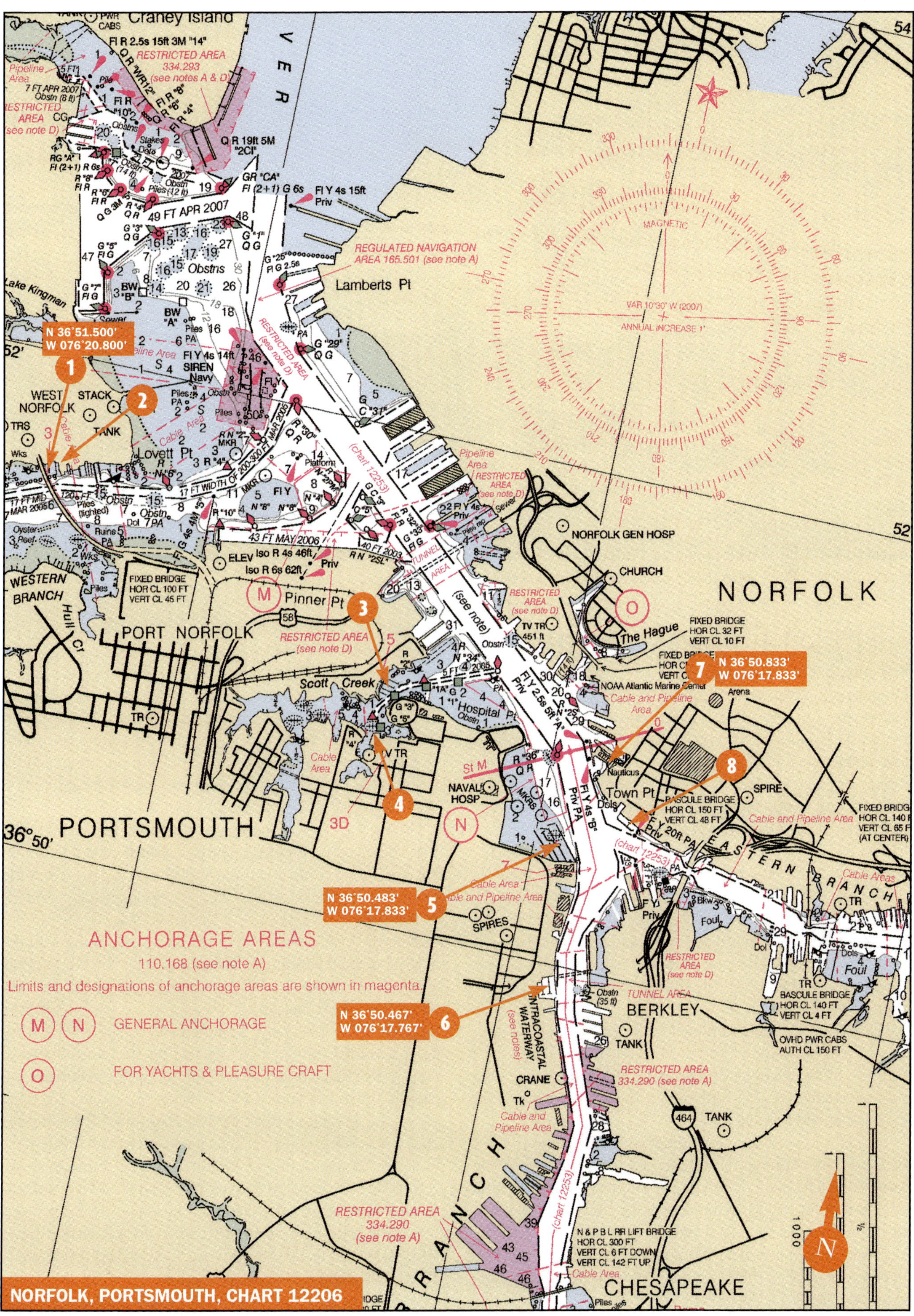

N 36°51.500'
W 076°20.800'
N 36°50.833'
W 076°17.833'
N 36°50.483'
W 076°17.833'
N 36°50.467'
W 076°17.767'
NORFOLK
PORTSMOUTH
PORT NORFOLK
WEST NORFOLK
BERKLEY
CHESAPEAKE
Craney Island
Lamberts Pt
Pinner Pt
Town Pt
Hospital Pt
Scott Creek
The Hague
WESTERN BRANCH
EASTERN BRANCH
NORFOLK GEN HOSP
NOAA Atlantic Marine Center
Nauticus
ANCHORAGE AREAS
110.168 (see note A)
Limits and designations of anchorage areas are shown in magenta.
GENERAL ANCHORAGE
FOR YACHTS & PLEASURE CRAFT
RESTRICTED AREA
334.293
REGULATED NAVIGATION AREA 165.501 (see note A)
FIXED BRIDGE HOR CL 100 FT VERT CL 45 FT
FIXED BRIDGE HOR CL 32 FT VERT CL 10 FT
BASCULE BRIDGE HOR CL 150 FT VERT CL 48 FT
BASCULE BRIDGE HOR CL 140 FT VERT CL 4 FT
OVHD PWR CABS AUTH CL 150 FT
RESTRICTED AREA 334.290 (see note A)
N & P B L RR LIFT BRIDGE HOR CL 300 FT VERT CL 6 FT DOWN VERT CL 142 FT UP
INTRACOASTAL WATERWAY
NORFOLK, PORTSMOUTH, CHART 12206

Portsmouth skyline. Photo courtesy of the Portsmouth Convention & Visitors Bureau.

GOIN' ASHORE: **PORTSMOUTH, VA**

Portsmouth has long served as a key point at the beginning or end of a passage through the ICW. For many years before the city began construction on the new face it now presents to the Elizabeth River, it was a place to hit only to take aboard fuel and provisions before running for the less threatening open spaces of the Bay or the ICW. Today, it is a destination worth exploring for its own sake.

Directly across from Portsmouth, a couple of America's largest warships, berthed in gargantuan floating dry docks, are undergoing refits. Upstream, shipyards stretch as far as you can see. Downstream, towers of glass and concrete in Norfolk's business district loom above the Waterside Festival Marketplace, Town Point Park and Nauticus. The river itself teems with traffic. Threading its way among it all is the pedestrian ferry on which you can take passage to Norfolk to see what is offered over there.

History: Although complimented in 1607 by Capt. John Smith on its beauty and blessed with similar natural resources to those of its neighbor across the Elizabeth River, the area that eventually became Portsmouth developed much more slowly than did Norfolk.

In 1620, John Wood, a shipbuilder, obviously impressed by the wealth of timber the region possessed, petitioned King James for a land grant. It appears he was unsuccessful, as little evidence of his enterprise remains in the record. Plantations in the region did flourish, pouring agricultural and timber products into the trade with England, but it was Norfolk that got the nod in 1680 to build one of the 20 official ports through which the Virginia House of Burgesses decreed that all of the Colony's business was to be conducted.

Despite that setback, the settlement steadily grew in size and importance. In 1752, it was established as a town by the Virginia General Assembly. Its founder, Col. William Crawford, named it Portsmouth, after his home town and England's preeminent Naval port, and laid out an area of 65 acres with a grid of streets and squares after the fashion then popular in England.

During the Revolutionary War, squabbles between groups with differing loyalties led to parts of the town being burned, but the defeat of Lord Dunmore at Great Bridge spared the town from the utter destruction the English had wrought on Norfolk.

After the war, the town continued to grow, along with the new nation's expanding international trade and in support of the Navy charged with protecting it. In 1827, the U.S. Navy chose Fort Nelson for the site of the first naval hospital. In 1833, the Navy expanded the Gosport Navy Yard in Portsmouth but named the facility the Norfolk Naval Shipyard so that it wouldn't be confused with the Portsmouth Naval Shipyard in Kittery, Maine that is named after the town across the Piscataqua River in New Hampshire (proving that the Navy is consistent even in its inconsistencies). At the same time, the Portsmouth and Weldon Railroad came to town, connecting the canal system of the Roanoke River with the port facilities adjacent to Hampton Roads.

Two World Wars brought further growth in the naval and maritime facilities, and the scaling back of activity after each triggered economic setbacks, too. In 1952, the first highway under the Elizabeth River opened, and ferry

Looking north over the busy Intracoastal Waterway heading south from Norfolk. (Not to be used for navigation.) Waterway Guide Photography.

services, which had driven commercial, cultural and social interaction between Portsmouth and Norfolk for three centuries, shut down, depriving both waterfronts of the foot traffic upon which downtown businesses once flourished. Portsmouth, long dependent on shipbuilding, suffered further when that industry moved to the Far East, and by the 1970s, in common with many American port cities, it was in serious decline.

Dismayed at the town's condition, loyal residents formed civic groups to rescue its historic buildings and its spirit. In the 1980s, Portsmouth began to bounce back. Despite being hampered by its limited tax base, almost half of the town's area is occupied by the U.S. Navy and other tax-exempt organizations. The city, with support from the Olde Towne Business Association and other civic groups, has reinvented itself, beginning with downtown. The waterfront area has been largely rebuilt, High Street is vibrant with commerce once again, and several museums and cultural centers provide distractions enough to fill a visit of several days.

Points of Interest: A significant number of Portsmouth's attractions, whether culinary, cultural or recreational, are within easy walking distance of both downtown marinas.

In the Olde Towne Historic District, one block from the waterfront, scores of historically and architecturally important structures line leafy streets that still follow the original grid pattern laid out in 1752. Because of the damage inflicted by all sides during both the Revolutionary and Civil wars, few Colonial-era buildings survived, but the private homes, churches and public buildings so far restored reflect every architectural style, from Federal and Queen Anne to Victorian and Art Deco. Stop in at the Visitor Center at 6 Crawford Parkway, pick up the Olde Towne walking tour brochure, and immerse yourself in a fascinating world of art, invention and extemporization, as manifested in two centuries of urban architecture.

Some buildings are as interesting for their social significance as for their age. Emanuel AME Church, at 637 North St., was built in 1857 to replace one on Glasgow Street that burned down in 1856. It is not only the second oldest church building in the town, it was also built by Portsmouth's oldest black congregation, which itself dates to the 1730s.

Resurgent and pre-resurgent neighborhoods everywhere are usually initially recolonized by the arts fringe drawn to the creative opportunities presented by antique buildings at low rents. Portsmouth's Olde Towne is no exception and has been a magnet for artists in all media. Their works are on display and on sale in a number of cooperative galleries and work spaces, as well as in businesses that welcome the color and cachet they add to the neighborhood.

More formal exhibits appear in regular sequence in the Courthouse Galleries, housed in the architecturally impressive and historically significant 1846 Courthouse on the corner of High and Court streets (757-393-8543, www.courthousegalleries.com for hours and calendar).

On the waterfront at the foot of High Street are the Naval Shipyard Museum and the Lightship Museum, the latter housed in a refurbished, but now landlocked, lightship (757-393-8591, www.portsnavalmuseums.com). Two blocks away at 221 High St. is The Children's Museum of Virginia (757-393-5258, www.childrensmuseumva.com). A Key Pass is available that gives access to all three museums and the Courthouse Galleries.

The Virginia Sports Hall of Fame & Museum, at 206 High St., celebrates Virginians who have made important contributions to the world of sports (757-393-8031, www.vshfm.com). Multimedia and interactive exhibits include soccer, baseball, basketball, golf, and auto racing. If you want to play golf on an actual course, the closest one is about five miles from downtown at Bide-A-Wee Golf Course (757-393-8600, bideaweegolf.com).

Special Events: Both the town and its various civic and cultural organizations put on events year-round, most of them centered on Olde Towne and the waterfront. An annual Memorial Day Parade gets summer off to a spirited start, fireworks off the seafront punctuate the sky on Independence Day, and a fleet of schooners arrives in mid-October at the finish of the annual Great Chesapeake Bay Schooner Race. Various art and musical festivals and gatherings fill in the gaps between.

Live concerts by recognized musicians in many genres draw crowds all summer long to the Harbor Center nTelos Pavilion on the waterfront at 901 Crawford St. (757-393-8181, www.pavilionconcerts.com for schedules and advance tickets).

Dining: A stroll along High Street will take you past a variety of eateries with offerings from the ordinary to the exotic and from the Mediterranean to the Pacific for breakfast, lunch, cocktails and dinner, as well as baked goods or ice cream for the in-betweens.

Perhaps the most unusual is the Commodore Theatre at 421 High St. A fully-appointed dining room occupies the main auditorium of this restored movie theater built in 1945 in Art Deco style and listed on both the National Register of Historic Places and the Virginia Landmarks Register. Dine while watching first-run movies screened in all their digital and Dolby glory, but be sure to call ahead for schedules and reservations (757-393-6962, www.commodoretheatre.com).

Sports fans and pool players will enjoy the big screens and billiard room at Roger Brown's Restaurant and Sports Bar at 316 High St. (757-399-5377). Thumpers Olde Towne Bar & Grille, at (600 Court St., 757-399-1001), offers a broad range of fare with a Cajun flavor, from burgers and sandwiches to steaks and seafood, and also features a raw bar.

At the Bier Garden (438 High St., 757-393-6022), you can wash down home-cooked German cuisine with your choice from a menu of 250 beers from around the world. If you have a craving for seafood, stop by Blue Water Seafood Grill (467 Dinwiddie Street, 757-398-0888).

To get a java fix and a vibe on the Olde Towne social scene in an artsy atmosphere, try The Coffee Shoppe (300 High St., 757-399-0497). If you need local information with your cup of coffee, try Starboards Coffee Kiosk at the foot of High Street by the ferry landing.

Shopping: Shopping, whether for needs or knickknacks, centers on the first seven blocks of High Street, and its tributaries. You will find art, antiques, a pharmacy and sundry specialty stores all within a comfortable walk in attractive and well-maintained surroundings. SkipJack Nautical Wares (One High Street, Portsmouth, 757-399-5012) has a fantastic inventory of nautical gifts and artwork and is very happy to assist boaters. Right next door is Mile Marker "0"Marine Supplies,

Reference the marina listing tables to see all the marinas in the area.

POINTS OF INTEREST
1 Emanuel AME Church
2 Courthouse Galleries
3 Naval Shipyard Museum and Lightship Museum
4 The Children's Museum of Virginia
5 The Virginia Sports Hall of Fame
6 Commodore Theatre
7 High Street Elizabeth River Ferry Landing
8 Harbor Center nTelos Pavilion

DINING
9 Roger Brown's Restaurant & Sports Bar
10 Thumpers Olde Towne Bar & Grille
11 Bier Garden
12 Blue Water Seafood Grill
13 The Coffee Shoppe

SHOPPING
14 SkipJack Nautical Wares
15 Mile Marker "0" Marine Supplies
16 Dollar General

INFORMATION
17 Visitors Center
18 Starboards Kiosk

L LIBRARY
PO POST OFFICE
G GROCERIES
Rx PHARMACY

which has propane, batteries, brass and stainless hardware, and cleaning and maintenance supplies. You can also use this store as a mail-drop. They are also providing transportation to and from the supermarket, West Marine and other stores. This is a really great service and this cruising editor hopes that the boating community supports his efforts by frequenting the store. There is also a Dollar General nearby.

For provisioning, there is a Food Lion supermarket and all the usual associated stores, about two miles out (a cab ride) on London Boulevard. Also at that end of town, there is a Kroger supermarket or Harris Teeter Market.

ADDITIONAL RESOURCES

- PORTSMOUTH VISITOR CENTER: 6 Crawford Parkway Portsmouth City Hall, 801 Crawford St.; Portsmouth, VA 23704, 757-393-8000, www.portsmouthva.gov
- OLDE TOWNE BUSINESS ASSOCIATION (publishes the Visitors Guide): 757-405-3500 www.oldetowneportsmouth.com

NEARBY MEDICAL FACILITIES
Bon Secours Maryview Medical Center:
3636 High St., Portsmouth, VA 23704, 757-398-2200 **(3 miles)**

Eastern Branch, Elizabeth River

Do not mistake this for the ICW route, which follows the Southern Branch. Beyond Mile Zero, Town Point on the Norfolk side marks the mouth of the Elizabeth River's Eastern Branch. Commercial traffic is extremely heavy in this area, with tugs passing through and large commercial vessels maneuvering into and out of the docks. It is a good idea to monitor VHF Channel 13 and to call any tug or other vessel whose intentions are unclear. Sometimes, though, listening is enough. Always yield to commercial traffic in this area.

NAVIGATION: Use Chart 12253. Before reaching Town Point, study your chart. The Eastern Branch of the Elizabeth River curves around Norfolk's Waterside development to port, and the Southern Branch (ICW) bears to starboard around Portsmouth. There are no aids to navigation in this area, and none are needed, as the water is deep to the shoreline. Many mariners mistakenly continue along the Eastern Branch thinking it is the ICW, only to turn around two miles later at its end.

Southern Branch, Elizabeth River (ICW)

Norshipco is the yard on the Norfolk side with the huge dry docks that mark the intersection of the Southern Branch. Leave this facility to port heading south to enter the Southern Branch. Large Naval and cruise ships can normally be seen in the dry docks. The Norfolk Naval Shipyard is farther up the Southern Branch of the Elizabeth River (heading south), on the Portsmouth (west) side. As many signs warn, no landings are permitted. Navy and Coast Guard patrol boats guard the naval vessels docked along both sides of the river.

NAVIGATION: Use Chart 12206. Proceeding southward on the Southern Branch of the Elizabeth River, you will encounter a seven-mile-long congested stretch with a six-mph speed limit (enforced) and six bridges. Be sure to monitor VHF Channel 13, where all commercial vessels communicate and bridge traffic is handled. Most bridges open promptly, except during

The Portsmouth Lightship Museum. Waterway Guide Photography.

restricted hours. (See bridge tables in the Skipper's Handbook section in the front of this Guide for opening schedules and restrictions.) Northbound vessels leaving the lock at Great Bridge at the same time are usually required to bunch together for openings of all the bridges in Norfolk, whether the vessels are fast or slow, power or sail.

The Jordan Lift Bridge (state Route 337) at Mile 2.8 was dismantled in 2009 and the center lift span was removed, eliminating one bottleneck in this section of the ICW. The Gilmerton Bridge (11-foot closed vertical clearance) at Mile 5.8 opens on signal, except during restricted hours. The new schedule dictates no openings Monday to Friday from 6:30 a.m. to 9:30 a.m., and 3:30 p.m. to 6:30 p.m., except during an emergency. To avoid a delay of up to three hours while idling in river currents, plan departures and arrivals carefully. The bridge will open hourly on the half hour during non-restricted time periods. The two railroad lift bridges on either side of the Jordan Bridge (the Belt Line Railroad Bridge at Mile 2.6 and the Norfolk and Western Railroad Bridge at Mile 3.6) are usually open, but closures do occur and are announced in advance on VHF Channel 13. Boaters should always monitor VHF Channel 13 while transiting this area.

The Gilmerton Bridge (U.S. 13) at Mile 5.8 (bascule, 11-foot closed vertical clearance) is followed immediately by the Norfolk and Western Railroad Bridge (7-foot closed vertical clearance, normally open). The railroad bridge's openings are announced on VHF Channel 13, and it is operated remotely with light, horn and audio signals when opening and closing. (This is not to be confused with the Norfolk and Western Railroad Bridge, located on the Eastern Branch; when a train passes through, both bridges usually close, one after the other.)

Situated on a bend in the river, these bridges are hard to see until you are nearly upon them. Be sure both are open completely before you start through. The highway bridge will not open unless the railroad bridge is open. You can call the Gilmerton bridgetender on VHF Channel 13, but the railroad bridge is unmanned and does not respond to VHF calls. The railroad spans can get tied up when long trains pass. Of the three railroad bridges in this stretch, the Norfolk and Western is the most frequently closed. Caution: Do not mistake St. Julian Creek, Mile 4.9, for the ICW. (This is easier to do northbound than southbound, just north of the Gilmerton Bridge.) A 45-foot-high overhead power cable crosses this creek. Beacons warning of the power cable were placed at the mouth of St. Julian Creek in late 2007 after two dismastings during the spring and summer.

Anchorage: Boats often anchor south of the Gilmerton Bridge and just north of the ICW behind the floating red "24,"where there is 9 to 13 feet of water. Boats anchor here to wait out railroad bridge closures (and sometimes stay all night), where they are safely out of the waterway.

Cruising Options—Two Routes

Those traveling south from Norfolk on the ICW must now choose between two routes into North Carolina: either Dismal Swamp or Virginia Cut. Each has its advantages, but careful consideration must be given to this decision. Read the chapter immediately following this one, "Virginia Cut, Dismal Swamp,"for complete details. ■

Waterway Guide advertising sponsors play a vital role in bringing you the most trusted and well-respected cruising guide in the country. Without our advertising sponsors, we simply couldn't produce the top-notch publication now resting in your hands. Next time you stop in for a peaceful night's rest, let them know where you found them—Waterway Guide, The Cruising Authority.

Waterway Guide is always open to your observations from the helm. Email your comments on any navigation information in the Guide to: editor@waterwayguide.com.

Starting Down The ICW

For southbound boats, the first 200-mile-stretch of the Atlantic Intracoastal Waterway (ICW) presents a diverse array of navigational challenges. The route passes through locks, canals, land cuts and open water sounds along the way. Some of the open water offers the challenges associated with long fetches and shallow depths—namely, choppy wave action when the wind kicks up. Still, the run to Morehead City, NC is full of fascinating sights, side trips and ports of call.

Once you have begun the journey south from Norfolk, VA, the trip just gets more interesting as you enter the major Carolina waters of the Albemarle and Pamlico sounds. From the sounds, side trips to waterside villages, such as Edenton, NC, Washington, NC and New Bern, NC, offer diversion from the ICW proper. Meanwhile, to the east of the ICW, you will find the famous wilds of North Carolina's Outer Banks, with shipwreck-strewn beaches, massive dunes and excellent bird-watching opportunities.

On Croatan Sound, which connects the two aforementioned sounds, boaters can put in to the little port town of Manteo, NC, located on Roanoke Island, where one of the earliest American settlements was established—and from which the same settlement mysteriously vanished.

All of these areas are covered in our Atlantic ICW 2012 Edition of the Waterway Guide, which provides coverage south to Fernandina Beach, FL.

Note: Paper small-craft charts have each five-statute-mile increments marked along the "magenta line" of the ICW, and these "Mile Markers" on the charts are commonly used to identify the locations of bridges, businesses, marinas, aids to navigation, anchorage locations, etc. In much, but not all of North Carolina (and sporadically in other ICW states), the Corps of Engineers has placed signs just outside the channel marking each five-mile increment along the route. But the numbers on these signs do not necessarily correspond to the "Mile Markers" on the charts. Some are the same, some are different by 100 yards or so, some by as much as a mile. If you are using the actual signs to determine your location in relation to a timed bridge or marina location, you may find yourself a lot closer or farther away than you thought. Use the paper charts for this information. Also note that the magenta line may have been removed from recent charts in locations that are frequently dredged, where there are shifting shoals or where markers may be moved frequently. In some cases, the magenta line may be drawn on the wrong side of a few markers; if you observe this to be the case, seek local knowledge, but keep in mind that the markers are in place for a reason. ■

Bridges/Distances (Approximate Statute Miles from Mile Zero, Norfolk)

NORFOLK

Location	Mile	Clearance
Norfolk; Mile Zero (ICW flashing red buoy "36")	0	
N&P Beltline Railroad Lift Bridge (Normally open)*	2.6	6'
Norfolk & Western RR Lift Bridge (Norm.open)*	3.6	10'
Gilmerton Bascule Bridge	**5.8**	**11'**
Norfolk & Western Railroad Bridge	5.8	7'
Highway Bridge (Interstate 64)	7.1	65'

VIRGINIA CUT ROUTE

Location	Mile	Clearance
Dominion Boulevard Bridge (aka "Steel Bridge")	**8.8**	**12'**
Great Bridge Lock	**11.3**	
Great Bridge Bascule Bridge (Rte. 168)	**12.0**	**8'**
Highway Bypass Bridge (SR 168 Bypass)		
Albemarle & Chesapeake Railroad Bridge (Normally open)*	13.9	7'
Centerville Tpk. Swing Bridge (SR 170)	**15.2**	**4'**
North Landing Swing Bridge (SR 165)	**20.2**	**6'**
Pungo Ferry Bridge (SR 726)	28.3	65'
North Landing River Marker Q Fl G "87"	39.3	
Coinjock Bridge	49.9	65'
North River Entrance Marker Fl R 4 sec "170"	65.3	
Alligator River Entrance Marker FL G "1AR"	79.0	

DISMAL SWAMP ROUTE

Location	Mile	Clearance
Dismal Swamp Entrance Marker Fl R "30"	7.3	
Deep Creek Lock	**10.5**	
Deep Creek Bridge (U.S. 17)*	**11.1**	**4'**
Visitor Center Foot Bridge	28.0	0'
Highway Bridge	31.5	65'
South Mills Bridge*	**32.6**	**4'**
South Mills Lock	32.7	65'
Pasquotank River Junction	37	
Norfolk Southern Railroad Swing Bridge (Normally open)*	47.7	3'
Highway Bridges (U.S. 158)	**50.7**	**2'**

ICW ROUTES REJOIN

Location	Mile	Clearance
Alligator River Swing Bridge (U.S. 64)	84.2	14'
Alligator/Pungo Canal Entrance Q Fl "54"	105.0	
Fairfield Bridge (SR 94)	113.9	65'
Walter B. Jones Bridge (U.S. 264)	125.9	64'
Durante Point, Belhaven Q Fl R "10"	135.4	
Wades Point Marker Fl (2+1) R 6s "PR"	145.9	
Hobucken Bridge (SR 33/304)	157.2	65'
Neuse River Junction Fl (2+1) R 6s	166.5	
Garbacon Shoal Fl 4 sec "7"	180.6	
Core Creek Bridge (SR 101)	195.8	65'
Beaufort Channel Hwy. Bridge (U.S. 70)	203.8	65'
Beaufort Channel Railroad Bridge	203.8	4'
Beaufort Bridge	**Off ICW**	**13'**

Call 757-201-7500 opt. 3 (Army Engineers Dept. of Waterway Maintenance) for conditions in the Dismal Swamp route. Clearance is vertical, closed, in feet. *Not radio-equipped. Bridges and locks in bold type have restricted openings.

Lewes
Page 443
Rehoboth Beach
Page 446
Indian River Bay
Bethany Beach
Page 436
Ocean City
Oxford
Choptank River
Cambridge
Nanticoke River
Salisbury
DELAWARE
Solomons
St. Marys City
Point Lookout
Potomac River
Smith Point
Reedville
Tangier Sound
Crisfield
Pocomoke Sound
Tangier Island
MARYLAND
VIRGINIA
Page 450
Chincoteague
Chincoteague Bay
Tom's Cove
Atlantic Ocean
Onancock
Irvington
Rappahannock River
Deltaville
Wachapreague
Page 451
Chesapeake Bay
Hog Island Bay
Outlet Bay
South Bay
Cape Charles
Gloucester Point
Hampton
N
DOZIER'S WATERWAY GUIDE
THE CRUISING AUTHORITY
www.WaterwayGuide.com
Skipper's Handbook
GPS Waypoints 48
Tide Tables 50

Delmarva Coast

An Alternative to the Chesapeake Run

CHARTS 12210, 12211, 12214, 12216, 12221, 12224

Cruising the Delmarva (Delaware, Maryland, Virginia) coast presents an alternative if you choose to run offshore or behind the Atlantic barrier islands, rather than transiting the Chesapeake Bay.

Of course, prudence dictates that you must have a thorough understanding of yourself, your boat, your charts and your crew's abilities before running offshore.

In this section, WATERWAY GUIDE covers the Atlantic Ocean offshore passage—the outside run from Cape May to Cape Charles—and then doubles back to cover the inside run behind the barrier islands, including the Virginia Inside Passage route from Chincoteague to Cape Charles.

Cruising Conditions: In spring and summer, winds along this stretch of the Atlantic coast are generally out of the south-southeast to southwest, though passing weather systems create temporary westerlies and northeasterlies in summer. As on the Chesapeake Bay, expect thunderstorms more frequently May through September, sometimes with strong, gusty winds and driving rain. In the fall, winds out of the east and northwest become more frequent, while hurricanes and tropical depressions tend to brush the Atlantic coast more frequently than they do the Bay. Sea fog can occur in late spring and fall, and occasional summer haze reduces visibility.

This coastline is hot in summer and cold in winter, but sea breezes temper the weather in all seasons. In summer, inshore you will need plenty of sun block and insect screens to keep the bugs out; in winter, you will need a heater. Although ice can close inland waters from November to March, inlets usually remain open, and the Coast Guard tends them for off-season travelers.

Running Outside: After you cross the 12-mile-wide mouth of Delaware Bay from Cape May, NJ to Lewes, DE, you will make several outside "hops" between safe inlets. The first is 17 nautical miles, from Delaware's Indian River Inlet to Ocean City, MD. The second is 20 nautical miles, from Chincoteague Inlet to Wachapreague Inlet. From there, the last run takes you 32 miles to Cape Charles and the mouth of Chesapeake Bay.

Running Inside: The waterways behind the Atlantic barrier islands are wild and lovely. Much of the southern part is virtually unpopulated, and the shallow inside route snakes and weaves its way through a gorgeous, primitive landscape of marshland. In the fall, flocks of migrating ducks and geese rise off the water with choreographed precision. In spring, nesting shore birds crowd the relatively inaccessible islands and the waters of Assateague Island National Seashore.

Weather Reports: Weather, of course, must be a key consideration in any offshore passage, and so it is here. Be careful in choosing what weather reports to heed. Though broadcasts from Baltimore and Annapolis stations reach easily across the Delmarva Peninsula, their forecasts seldom apply here because they are oriented to the Chesapeake Bay area and its milder weather conditions. Instead, rely upon weather reports from Ocean City NOAA. VHF-FM makes continuous weather broadcasts on WX-3 from Salisbury, MD; the signal extends halfway down the peninsula. A continuous VHF-FM forecast on WX-1 from Norfolk, VA covers the southern sector. The Coast Guard broadcasts marine information on schedule: Cape May, VHF Channel 22A, at 6:03 a.m. and 6:03 p.m.; Chincoteague, VHF Channel 22A, at 6:45 a.m. and 9:00 p.m.; and Hampton Roads, VHF Channel 22A, at 6:20 a.m. and 9:30 p.m.

Tidal Range: Tidal range along the Atlantic Coast of the Delmarva Peninsula averages about 4 feet, but wind will affect depths as much as tide. A long easterly blow will increase it up to 3 feet, and a westerly will decrease it a like amount. Currents can be considerable throughout, particularly in and near inlets, where they commonly run at velocities up to 3 knots. (Note: Residents report that the tide times on the Ocean City weather broadcast may be an hour or two off for certain areas, so inquire locally.)

THE OUTSIDE (OCEAN) RUN

NAVIGATION: Use Charts 12304 and 12214. Heading down the Atlantic coast from Cape May to Ocean City (about 40 nautical miles), lay your course to pass east and south of the Hen and Chickens Shoal off Cape Henlopen. The shoal can be extremely nasty, with rough seas that break in heavy weather. From here, follow the beach (stay a couple of miles offshore to clear obstructions and shoal areas) past the Indian River Inlet sea buoy and through a well-marked, but defunct, firing range off Fenwick Island.

Hurricane Holes: The first storm havens are Breakwater Harbor, behind Cape Henlopen (12 miles from Cape May), along with Lewes (inside Roosevelt Inlet). Although it looks very open, Breakwater Harbor is secure enough in moderate weather for an overnight stay, but move into a more sheltered spot if a serious storm is expected. See the section on Lewes later in this chapter. Indian River Inlet, a 10 mile offshore run below Cape Henlopen, is crossed by a fixed bridge with a 35-foot vertical clearance.

Indian River and Ocean City Inlets

NAVIGATION: Use Charts 12214 and 12211. Like all other inlets on this coast, you should approach Indian River and Ocean City inlets from their respective sea buoys. Breaking shoals extend seaward a mile or more from the south jetty of each. Use caution and good seamanship when using an inlet, especially from seaward. Onshore winds against an ebbing tide can cause significant (and sometimes hazardous) wave action.

Indian River Inlet: In spring 2012, a new, higher (45-foot fixed vertical clearance) suspension bridge with two 240-foot towers was opened beside the old (35-foot vertical clearance) bridge. The old bridge was being demolished at press time (summer 2012). Inside the inlet, currents run at breakneck speeds through the bridge, and things can get dangerous when wind and wave are opposed. Low-powered vessels should use caution here. Normally, passage to Indian River Bay is easy, but the channel shifts, and the remains of old beacons and other structures destroyed by winter ice are a hazard in spring. The convenient Delaware Seashore State Park marina with fuel and amenities is just past the bridge on the north shore. Use Chart 12216 for navigation behind the barrier islands here.

Ocean City Inlet: Ocean City Inlet is the most-used inlet on the Delmarva coast. Nonetheless, approach it with a little caution, and note that deeper water offshore is to the north of the inlet, with a shoal to the south. Seas sometimes break on shoals south of the inlet, and spring tides or strong easterlies may submerge the outer leg of the south jetty. The north jetty seldom submerges, but make sure that you know its location. The inlet channel normally holds at 10 feet deep, and the U.S. Army Corps of Engineers says that jetty rehabilitation will curtail the shoaling here. Be sure to observe the charted location of the jetty and prepare for strong currents in the inlet.

Pass between flashing red "4" (at the offshore end of the north jetty) and flashing green "5" to the south. A 28-foot lighted horn midway along the north jetty marks the beginning of the channel buoys. At this point, the channel jogs southerly to leave flashing red "8" to starboard and the partially submerged jetty to port.

To go north to Ocean City's marinas, once you have entered from the Atlantic, round easily to the north after passing the flashing red buoy "10" south of the Coast Guard station. You must guard against strong flood currents pushing through the inlet, which can set you onto the submerged pilings of an old bridge on the western side of the channel. A dolphin-mounted white flashing light and a daybeacon mark the piles.

■ OCEAN CITY, MD

Ocean City, MD, the Delmarva Coast's biggest resort, is eight nautical miles below Fenwick Light and the Delaware-Maryland line. The city stands on the south end of Fenwick Island, the barrier of land running southward from Rehoboth Beach, DE, between the Atlantic Ocean and the Assawoman and Isle of Wight bays.

Ocean City is full of high-rises, condominiums and summer homes, and its harbor bustles with sport and commercial fishermen. The most serious fishing enthusiasts head for the ocean in search of marlin, tuna and wahoo. Others try the 700-foot fishing pier, shallow Sinepuxent Bay or local surfcasting. Ocean City's main attraction is the long ocean beach and boardwalk lined with shops, hotels, restaurants and, at the inlet end of the boardwalk, an amusement park with rides, arcades and a fun house. This strip of town and beach plays host to more than 18 million visitors a year.

NAVIGATION: Use Chart 12211. The harbor at Ocean City Inlet is a No Wake Zone, with a 6-mph speed limit that is strictly enforced. The Coast Guard reports that stone piers placed at the base of the U.S. Route 50 Bridge (18-foot closed vertical clearance) have created hazardous currents under the bridge, particularly under the west span, so use caution. From May 25 to September 15, from 9:00 a.m. to 10:00 p.m., the bridge opens at 25 and 55 minutes past the hour, for a maximum of five minutes. From October 1 to April 30, from 6:00 p.m. to 6:00 a.m., three hour's notice is required and on Saturdays, from 1:00 p.m. to 5:00 p.m., opens on the hour and remains open until all vessels pass. Otherwise, it opens on demand. The bridge tender's phone is 410-289-7126. Give right-of-way to vessels traveling with the current.

Dockage: Large boats can put in at one of several marinas at Ocean City—all have gas and diesel—located mostly to the north of the Ocean City Inlet. The 170-slip Ocean City Fishing Center, located just northwest of the inlet, without the inconvenience of the drawbridge, has fuel, a swimming pool, a laundry facility and a bar and restaurant. There is also a bait, tackle and nautical store on the property. Across the channel, on the Ocean City (east) side, you will find White Marlin Marina, Old Town Marina and Talbot Street Pier; all have gas and diesel as well as transient space. Farther north are Harbour Island Marina and Bahia Marina, both with fuels and cruiser amenities.

Anchorage: Cruising boats can anchor south of the bridge just west of the channel in 9- to 11-foot depths. Mind the very strong current here and consider setting two hooks

TWO MARINAS

FIRST CLASS, EXCEPTIONAL SERVICES

ocean city fishing center

SUNSET MARINA
OCEAN CITY MARYLAND

2011 Marina of the Year
Marina Dock Age

FISHING CENTER AMENITIES: 1/8 Mile from Ocean City Inlet, Over 170 Slips, Full Service Fuel Dock, Dockside Dining, Tackle Shop, Vessels up to 65 Feet, Home of the Ocean City Tuna and Shark Tournaments, Coin Operated Laundry, Nautical Shoppe (Apparel & Gifts), Heated Swimming Pool, Climate Controlled Bath Houses, Largest Fishing Charter Fleet in Ocean City, Transients Welcome.

www.OcFishing.com | Channel 16 / 71

SUNSET MARINA AMENITIES: 1/8 Mile from Ocean City Inlet, Full Working Yard, 8- Ton Travel lift, Sunset Grille (Dockside Dining), Teasers Dockside Bar, 204 Surge Free Slips, Climate Controlled Bath Houses, Vessels up to 110 feet, Heated Swimming Pool, Diesel & Gas Sales, Spacious 90 Foot Fairways, Sunset Provisions (Beer, Bait, Marine Supplies), Transients & Groups Welcome.

www.OcSunsetMarina.com | Channel 16 / 74

Ocean City, MD

OCEAN CITY		Largest Vessel Accommodated	VHF Channel Monitored	Transient Berths / Total Berths	Approach / Dockside Depth (reported)	Floating Docks	Gas / Diesel	Groceries, Ice, Marine Supplies, Snacks	Repairs: Hull, Engine, Propeller	Lift (tonnage), Crane, Rail	Min/Max Amps	Laundry, Pool, Showers, Courtesy Car	Pump-Out Station	Nearby: Grocery Store, Motel, Restaurant
		Dockage					Supplies		Services					
1. White Marlin Marina (Internet Access) (Wireless Internet Access)	410-289-6470	130	16/68	50/50	12/12	-	GD	IS	-	-	30/50	PS	-	MR
2. Old Town Marina	410-289-6720	50	16/68	15/15	12/6	-	GD	IS	-	-	30/30	S	-	GMR
3. Talbot Street Pier (Wireless Internet Access)	410-289-9125	70	16/68	8/8	12/6	-	GD	IS	-	-	50/50	-	-	MR
4. Harbour Island Marina	410-289-3511	70	16/68	10/30	/8	-	GD	IS	-	-	30/50	PS	P	GMR
5. Bahia Marina	410-289-7438	75	68	2/75	6/5	-	GD	GIMS	HEP	-	30/50	S	-	GMR
6. Ocean City Fishing Center (Wireless Internet Access)	**410-213-1121**	**65**	**71/71**	**12/170**	**7/7**	**-**	**GD**	**GIS**	**HEP**	**L35**	**30/50**	**LPS**	**P**	**GMR**
7. Ocean City Fisherman's Marina (Internet Access)	410-213-2478	100	16/11	15/50	10/8	-	GD	IS	EP	-	30/50	LS	-	GMR
8. Sunset Marina (Internet Access) (Wireless Internet Access)	**410-213-9600**	**110**	**16/74**	**50/204**	**9/9**	**-**	**GD**	**GIMS**	**-**	**L8**	**30/100**	**LPS**	**P**	**GMR**

Corresponding chart(s) not to be used for navigation. Internet Access | Wireless Internet Access | Waterway Guide Cruising Club Partner

See www.WaterwayGuide.com for current rates, fuel prices, web site addresses, and other up-to-the-minute information.

if staying for any length of time. Another favorite anchorage is just south of Ocean City, behind Assateague Island, in the vicinity of green daybeacon "3" in 8 to 10 feet of water. Hail the water-taxi service on VHF Channel 16 or 68.

GOIN' ASHORE: **OCEAN CITY, MD**

The first thing there is to mention about Ocean City is the boardwalk. No matter your age, you will have fun on the boardwalk. The three-mile long walkway, which is actually made of wooden boards, will take you back to a magical childhood world of amusement rides, arcades and salt water taffy. And, as Maryland's only ocean resort, there is, of course, a big, beautiful beach.

Dockage in and around the town is within walking distance to some attractions, but there is also a bus that runs the full 10-mile length of the beach 24 hours a day, 7 days a week, and you can ride all day, getting on and off as often as you like, for just $2. Other transportation options include bikes, a boardwalk tram and taxis.

History: While many Eastern Shore towns boast a lively history extending back to Colonial times, the story of Ocean City is more recent. Until the mid-1800s, the only visitors were fishermen arriving by rowboat. But things changed once a hotel opened on the barrier island. In fact, the July 4, 1875 opening of the Atlantic Hotel is regarded as Ocean City's founding date. A new railroad bridge, built over the bay the following year, increased the number of visitors, and just after the turn of the century, the Trimper family opened an amusement park that still operates today.

The fishing industry grew, and the fishermen's wives started operating inns and hotels for visitors seeking refuge from city life at the beach. There was just one problem: Vacationers found it hard trudging through the sand. And so, in 1902, hotel owners laid out sections of wood—the boardwalk—that had to be stored on their porches at high tide. Sportfishing came to town after a 1933 hurricane created an inlet that linked the ocean and the bay. Soon after, the first white marlin was caught off the coast, leading to Ocean City's moniker "White Marlin Capital of the World."

Points of Interest: After the beach, the Boardwalk is the main attraction. You will find several souvenir shops and fast food offerings, plus Trimper's Amusement Park with its beautifully restored 1902 carousel and vintage 1950s kiddie rides and Marty's Playland Arcade at the southern end. The Ocean City Life-Saving Station Museum, in a restored life-saving station for the agency that was the precursor to the Coast Guard, includes a wide assortment of entertaining exhibits, including fans from around the world, vintage bathing suits, mermaid-themed items and shipwreck artifacts. Each morning in the summer, the museum offers free educational exhibits outside on the boardwalk. Call 410-289-4991 or visit www.ocmuseum.org for more information.

Special Events: Each May, big top tents are set up at the Inlet Parking Lot and beach for Springfest, featuring food—some of it gourmet—entertainment, and unique arts and crafts. This four-day festival celebrates the arrival of Spring. In June, upwards of 100 artists come to town for Art's Alive at Northside Park.

On summer evenings, the town sponsors free beach concerts on Wednesdays, bonfires on the beach on Thursdays, concerts at Sunset Park on Mondays, and Sundaes in the Park, when, for a small fee, you can make your own ice cream sundae and listen to music on Sundays (naturally) at Northside Park. July 4th features two fireworks displays and patriotic music on the beach, plus games, arts, food and music at Northside Park.

Summer's End is celebrated, and perhaps mourned, with Sunfest in mid-September. The four-day festival includes hayrides, a treasure hunt on the beach and shows featuring well-known performers.

Shopping: Much of the shopping along the boardwalk is typical tourist fare, but do stop in at Dolle's Candyland, an old-time candy store that sells homemade saltwater taffy, caramel popcorn, chocolates and more. Tucked off the boardwalk, you will find Inlet Village, a small collection of shops modeled after an old fishing village.

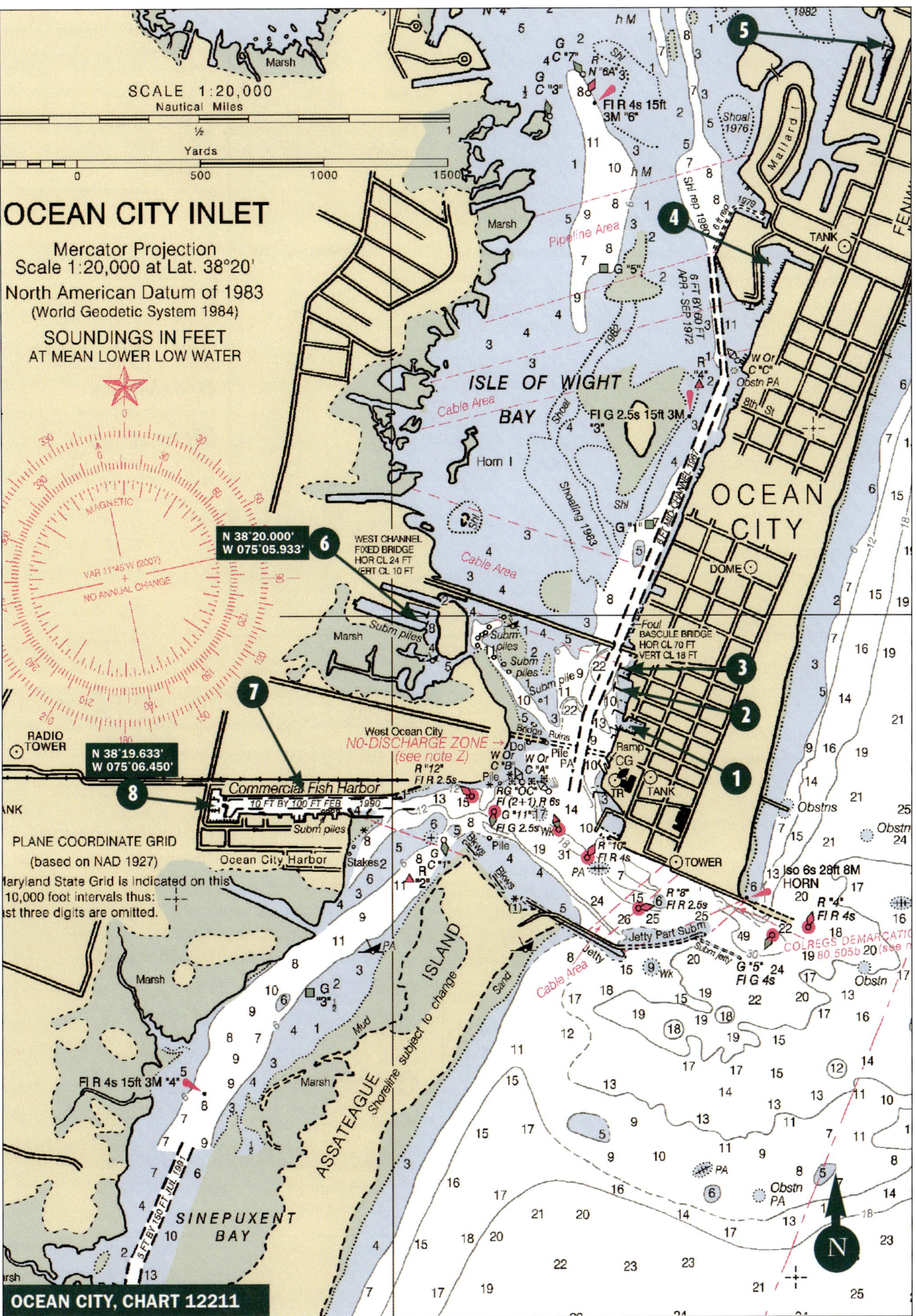
SCALE 1:20,000
Nautical Miles
Yards
OCEAN CITY INLET
Mercator Projection
Scale 1:20,000 at Lat. 38°20'
North American Datum of 1983
(World Geodetic System 1984)
SOUNDINGS IN FEET
AT MEAN LOWER LOW WATER
ISLE OF WIGHT
BAY
OCEAN
CITY
Horn I
Marsh
Cable Area
Pipeline Area
N 38°20.000'
W 075°05.933'
WEST CHANNEL
FIXED BRIDGE
HOR CL 24 FT
VERT CL 10 FT
BASCULE BRIDGE
HOR CL 70 FT
VERT CL 18 FT
RADIO TOWER
N 38°19.633'
W 075°06.450'
West Ocean City
NO-DISCHARGE ZONE
(see note Z)
Commercial Fish Harbor
Ocean City Harbor
PLANE COORDINATE GRID
(based on NAD 1927)
Maryland State Grid is indicated on this
10,000 foot intervals thus:
last three digits are omitted.
ASSATEAGUE
ISLAND
Shoreline subject to change
SINEPUXENT
BAY
Jetty
Iso 6s 28ft 8M
HORN
COLREGS DEMARCATION
TANK
DOME
TOWER
Mallard I
OCEAN CITY, CHART 12211

POINTS OF INTEREST

1 Boardwalk
2 Trimper Rides & Amusements
3 Life-Saving Station Museum

SHOPPING

4 Inlet Village Shops

DINING

5 Shenanigan's Irish Pub and Grille
6 Bahama Mama
7 Harrison's Harborwatch
8 Marina Deck
9 Hooper's Crab House
10 The Shark on the Harbor
11 Sunset Grille
12 Harborside Bar & Grill

INFORMATION

13 Information Center

POST OFFICE

Reference the marina listing tables to see all the marinas in the area.

Dining: Harrison's Harbor Watch (806 South Atlantic Ave., 410-289-5121) serves up a view of the inlet with its raw bar. Marina Deck on the waterfront at 306 Dorchester Street (410-289-4411) offers an array of seafood specialties, as does Bahama Mamas Crab House at 221 Wicomico St. (410-289-0291). We love an Irish Pub and waterfront dining, so we have to include Shananigans Irish Pub & Grille 309 North Atlantic Ave. (410-289-7181).

In West Ocean City (across the bridge), Hooper's Crab House offers a lively atmosphere and over 100 craft beers to go with your appetizer or entrée (12913 Ocean Gateway, 410-213-1771). Other popular restaurants include The Shark on the Harbor (12924 Sunset Ave., 410-213-0924) and nearby Sunset Grille (12933 Sunset Ave., 410-213-8110). Harborside Bar & Grill (12841 South Harbor Rd., 410-213-1846), home of the "Orange Crush," serves lite fare as well as a full dinner menu with Happy Hour Monday through Friday and weekly specials. They have some slips reserved for diners.

Note: Please note that pets are only allowed on the beach and boardwalk between October 1 and April 30. There is a dog playground available year-round at 94th Street and Bayside. Call 410-250-0125 for more information.

ADDITIONAL RESOURCES

- **THE OCEAN CITY DEPARTMENT OF TOURISM:**
  4001 Coastal Highway; 800-626-2326
  http://ococean.com

- **THE GREATER OCEAN CITY CHAMBER OF COMMERCE:**
  12320 Ocean Gateway; 410-213-0552
  www.oceancity.org

NEARBY MEDICAL FACILITIES

Atlantic General Hospital: 9733 Healthway Drive, Berlin, MD 21811, 410-641-1100 (6 miles)
www.atlanticgeneral.org

75th St. Medical: 7408 Coastal Highway, Ocean City, MD 21842, 410-524-0075

NEARBY AIRPORTS

Ocean City Municipal Airport: 12724 Airport Road, Berlin, MD 21811, 410-213-2471

Salisbury-Ocean City-Wicomico Regional Airport: 5485 Terminal Road, Salisbury, MD 21804 410-548-4827

Looking southeast over the Ocean City Inlet and the busy fishing fleet. (Not to be used for navigation.) Waterway Guide Photography.

Ocean City Commercial Fish Harbor and Sinepuxent Bay

NAVIGATION: Use Chart 12211. If you are going on to the charted Commercial Fish Harbor or south into Sinepuxent Bay for the start of the inland route, cross the northbound channel, and you will come to a group of buoys and fixed flashing lights. The entrance to Commercial Fish Harbor is dredged to a depth of 12 feet (the chart indicates 10 feet), but the shoaling is constant around here; work your way in carefully.

Dockage: Sunset Marina is in a huge dredged basin with an entrance channel to the west of the Ocean City Inlet, just before the Commercial Fish Harbor. This state-of-the-art marina is capable of accommodating up to 130-foot boats at 204 surge-free slips. Fuel, a swimming pool, a laundry, a convenience store, a bar and grill, water-taxi service and an 88-ton lift are on the premises. Ocean City Fisherman's Marina, at the head of the Commercial Fish Harbor, can accommodate boats up to 100 feet. Harborside Bar & Grill has slips for diners.

Chincoteague, Wachapreague and Great Machipongo Inlets

A long but straightforward run down the coast from Ocean City Inlet in Maryland eventually delivers you to Cape Charles, Virginia, at the north side of the entrance to Chesapeake Bay. In between, Chincoteague and Wachapreague inlets lead to safe harbor. Most of the coast along this entire stretch is remote and undeveloped with large areas of National Seashore and State conservation areas.

NAVIGATION: Use Charts 12211 and 12210. Watch for wrecks (charted) on the southwest sides of Winter Quarter Shoal and Blackfish Bank. These ocean shoals are located to the northeast and east, respectively, of Chincoteague Inlet. Attempt the ocean run only in settled weather. It's 20-nautical-miles to Chincoteague Inlet, then 17 miles to Wachapreague Inlet, then 14 miles to Great Machipongo Inlet and a final 20 miles to Cape Charles; all these inlets can be fairly nasty in moderate wind conditions. All three inlets have breakers a mile or more offshore on either side of the marked channel that you can see from some distance. There are no buoys between the Chincoteague sea buoy and the Wachapreague sea buoy, so stay several miles off the coast and run a compass course.

Chincoteague Inlet: Many commercial fishermen and some recreational craft use Chincoteague Inlet, 30 miles south of Ocean City, but you should only attempt this inlet in calm weather. The marked (although not charted as such) channel through the inlet changes frequently, breakers are on both sides of the channel, and the tidal current runs quite swiftly. There are several marked, 6-foot-deep shoals near the entrance, with deeper water inside. The Corps of Engineers charted the controlling depth of the inlet at 12 feet in 2011. Below Chincoteague, run the ship buoys to clear the shoals of Great Machipongo and Sand Shoal inlets (neither is usable). Lay your course from red nun "2" below

Chincoteague Shoals, past the mooring buoy on Porpoise Banks, to the ship buoy marking Parramore Banks, 17 nautical miles away.

Wachapreague Inlet: Boats with 6-foot drafts or less can enter Wachapreague Inlet, but you should try to follow a local charter or sportfishing boat. Note that Chart 12210 was updated in May 2008; use only a current Print On Demand chart or download the latest one from the NOAA Web site (http://chartmaker.ncd.noaa.gov/). In fine weather, you can follow the buoys and anchor in the fairway south of the now-closed Parramore Beach Coast Guard Station. The inlet breaks along a bar extending a considerable distance offshore. The 232 residents of Wachapreague (from 2010 census) cater to the fishing trade.

Great Machipongo Inlet: One of the deeper inlets along this section, it is used by local commercial fishing boats and local recreational fishermen. Great Machipongo Channel leads northwest through marshes to the tiny village of Willis Wharf.

Great Machipongo Inlet to Chesapeake Bay

Once you pass Great Machipongo, heading south along the Atlantic coast, your next decision will be whether to enter Chesapeake Bay.

NAVIGATION: Use Charts 12210 and 12221. From Parramore Banks to Smith Island Shoal (27 nautical miles), run from red ship buoy to red ship buoy in order to clear inshore shoals. From Smith Island Shoal to Cape Henry (20 nautical miles across the mouth of Chesapeake Bay), you will pass unmanned Cape Charles Lighthouse, cross heavy shipping and naval traffic (including submarines), and adjust endlessly for tidal currents. Watch for charted shoals near the Cape Charles Lighthouse.

Chesapeake Bay Entrance: To enter the Chesapeake Bay, you can go under a fixed bridge (75-foot vertical clearance) near the Fishermans Island (north) end of the Chesapeake Bay Bridge-Tunnel (watch out for Nautilus Shoal, two miles southeast of Fishermans Island). You can also pass over the highway tunnels beneath the northern Chesapeake Channel or southern Thimble Shoals Channel. These entrances to Hampton Roads and the Chesapeake are busy with commercial shipping of all kinds, as well as naval vessels headed for the base at Norfolk. Offshore-ready boats can cross the Bay's mouth for Rudee Inlet at Virginia Beach or find full marine services at Little Creek just inside the south end of the Chesapeake Bay Bridge Tunnel.

(See Virginia Inside Passage below for more options.)

■ THE INSIDE ROUTE SOUTH FROM DELAWARE

This route, which passes through some of the last unspoiled scenery on the East Coast, is tough to navigate except in boats with the shallowest drafts. Channels wind through marshy guts, the markers are confusing and often missing, the tidal range is great and the bugs are infuriating. The channel ahead may be open or closed, depending on the phase of the moon or the influence of a northwest wind, which can blow all the water away. Still, if draft and time permit, this inside passage can provide an adventure to remember. Most who make it consider it time well spent.

The controlling depth through Maryland waters is 6 feet. Two fixed bridges (35- and 38-foot vertical clearances, respectively) north and south of Ocean City limit passage even where shoals permit.

Roosevelt Inlet, at Lewes

Roosevelt Inlet, just west of Cape Henlopen, DE, is the beginning of the Delmarva inside route.

NAVIGATION: Use Chart 12216. From the Cohansey River down Delaware Bay, or from the Cape May Canal across Delaware Bay, head for the Cape Henlopen Harbor of Refuge, adjust your course for tidal current and keep watch for the Cape May-Lewes ferryboat. The Roosevelt Inlet jetties are roughly three miles west of Cape Henlopen. The outer arms of the jetties are submerged, but range lights will help you through the all-weather entrance.

Just inside Roosevelt Inlet is a basin for the University of Delaware, along with a yacht club and a Coast Guard substation, which opens for service around May 1 each year. If you need assistance during the winter months, call the Cape May Coast Guard on VHF Channel 16. If the boatyards and marinas at Lewes are full, or if weather forces you in, inquire about tying off at the University of Delaware's docks.

Playing in the surf, Ocean City, MD. (Ocean City Convention & Visitors Bureau)

Lewes, DE

LEWES BEACH		Largest Vessel Accommodated	VHF Channel Monitored	Transient Berths / Total Berths	Approach / Dockside Depth (reported)	Floating Docks	Gas / Diesel	Groceries, Ice, Marine Supplies, Snacks	Repairs: Hull, Engine, Propeller	Lift (tonnage), Crane, Rail	Min/Max Amps	Laundry, Pool, Showers, Courtesy Car	Pump-Out Station	Nearby: Grocery Store, Motel, Restaurant
		Dockage					Supplies		Services					
1. Lewes Yacht Club	302-645-8525	32	71	/66	5/4	F	G	IMS	-	-	-	PS	-	MR
2. Pilottown Marina	302-645-5355	40	-	/76	10/7	-	-	I	-	-	30/30	S	P	GMR
3. Lewes Harbor Marina	302-645-6227	60	71	/30	10/6	-	GD	IMS	-	L75	30/30	S	P	GMR
4. City of Lewes	302-644-1869	55	-	10/19	12/6	F	-	GI	-	-	30/100	LS	P	GMR

Corresponding chart(s) not to be used for navigation. Internet Access Wireless Internet Access Waterway Guide Cruising Club Partner

See www.WaterwayGuide.com for current rates, fuel prices, web site addresses, and other up-to-the-minute information.

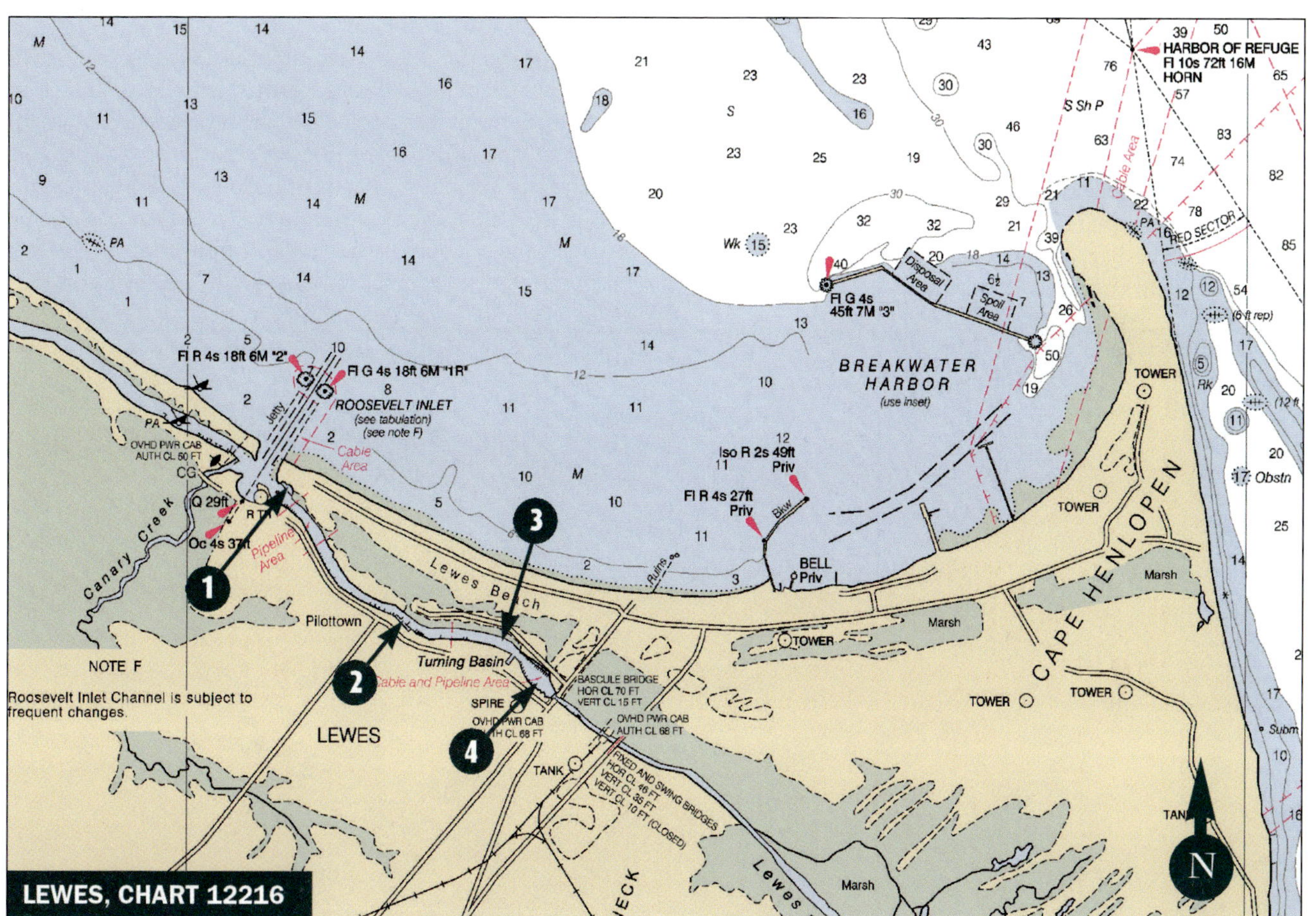

Lewes and the Lewes and Rehoboth Canal

Inshore about a mile and a half, on the Lewes and Rehoboth Canal, is the village of Lewes, home to many Delaware Bay pilots. Among the village's attractions is the Zwaanendael Museum, commemorating the first settlement of Delaware by the Dutch in 1631, a house hit by a British cannonball during the War of 1812 and the retired lightship Overfalls.

NAVIGATION: Use Chart 12216. The Lewes and Rehoboth Canal is straight and easy to follow. There are generally 6.6-foot depths in the canal as far in as the turning basin at Lewes. (Cruisers have reported shoaling inside Roosevelt Inlet where the canal meets the Broadkill River.) Beyond the turning basin at Lewes, shoals around the railroad bridge and a shifting sandbar below the fixed bridge leave about 4 feet at high water. Depths improve for a short way, but the canal narrows, with fallen trees along its edges and banks washing in toward the channel.

A fixed span at Lewes sets vertical clearance on the canal at 35 feet. The bascule bridge at Rehoboth Beach (16-foot closed vertical clearance) opens on signal between 7:00 a.m. and 8:00 p.m., April 1 to October 31; otherwise, it requires 24 hours advance notice to open. Dewey Beach Bridge, with a fixed vertical clearance of 35 feet, is a half-mile south of the Rehoboth Beach Drawbridge.

Dockage: Several marinas at Lewes can accommodate visiting boats. Lewes Yacht Club is first (to port) on the canal after Roosevelt Inlet. Next is Pilottown Marina (to starboard), followed by Lewes Harbor Marina (to port). The town dock, the last marina before the bridge (to starboard) offers slips on floating docks plus the usual amenities; pay at City Hall. Here you are only a block from restaurants, motels and stores.

GOIN' ASHORE: **LEWES, DE**

Walk the streets of this seafaring town (pronounced "Lewis") along the banks of the Rehoboth and Lewes Canal and find yourself immersed in historic and nautical activities, all while breathing the fresh sea air of the Atlantic Ocean. Nearby beaches provide swimming, fishing, boating and many other watersports to choose from. From the time you step ashore in the harbor of Lewes, you will feel that this town has it all and truly reflects its location at the intersection of the Atlantic Ocean and the Delaware Bay.

From historic walks through Shipcarpenter Square to sunbathing on local beaches, Lewes leaves the visiting yachtsman with a renewed spirit to continue a voyage east, south or west up the Delaware Bay. This is a stop not to be missed where one can stock up on some of the famous local produce at open markets, wander the pristine beaches of Cape Henlopen, or simply hang out on board and get lost in the beautiful sunsets while enjoying the fresh catch of the day.

History: First settled by the Dutch in 1631 as a whaling station, 22 years after it was discovered by Henry Hudson, Lewes settlers were destroyed by a group of local inhabitants. The town was visited by Captain Kidd and other pirates in the late 1600s. Through its hectic history, Lewes remained a seafaring town with its excellent harbor and remains an East Coast port of call. Today, it is the home to a large fleet of charter fishing boats stationed on the canal along Pilottown Road.

Lewes is also the base of the Delaware Bay and River Pilots Association, and the southern terminus of the Cape May-Lewes Ferry.

Points of Interest: Historic attractions maintained by the Lewes Historical Society (110 Shipcarpenter St., 302-645-7670) provide numerous sites worth a visit on a walking tour of Lewes. Some of the sites include the Zwaanendael Museum (102 Road 268, 302-645-1148) with permanent and changing displays and exhibits; Fisher-Martin House (120 Road 268), a gambrel-roofed house moved from the country at Coal Spring as part of the celebration of the 350th anniversary of the first European settlement on Delaware; and the nearby Ryves Holt

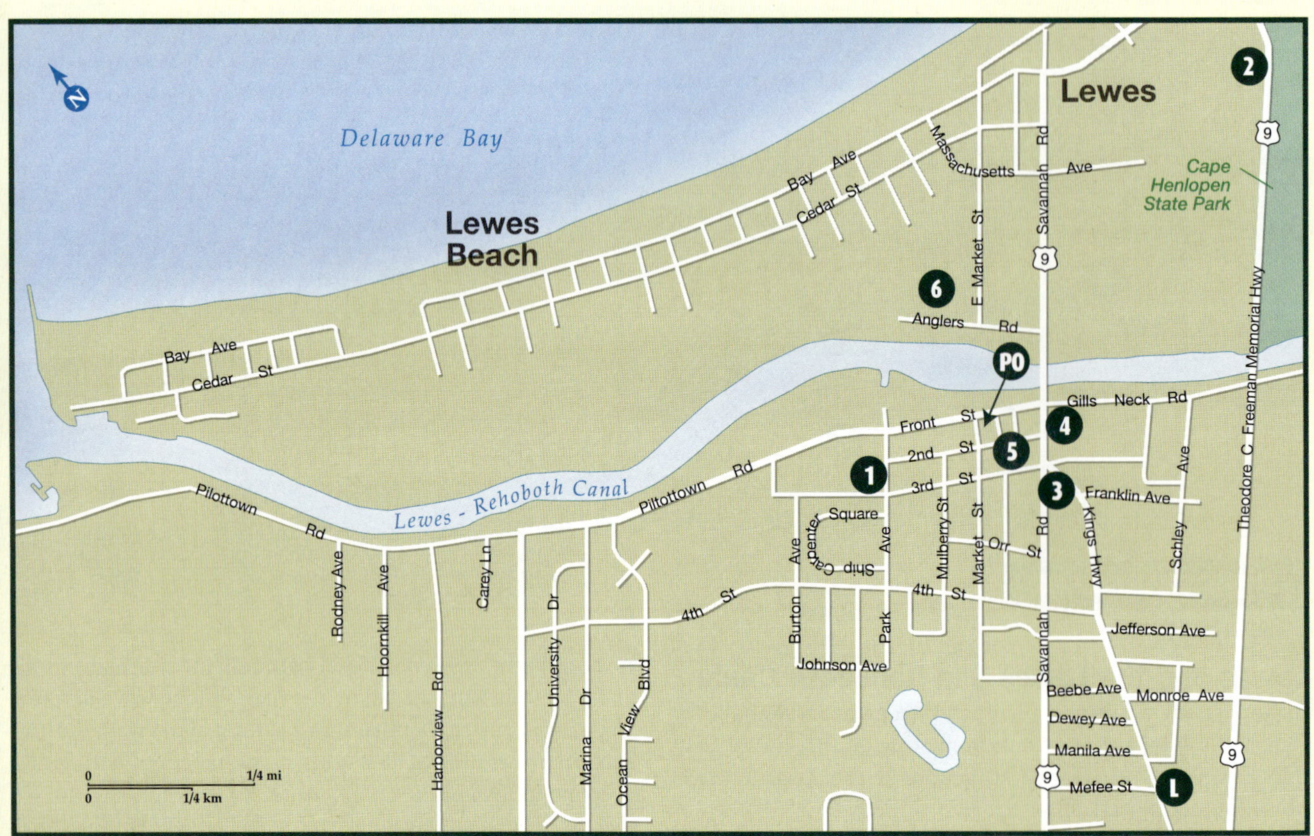

Reference the marina listing tables to see all the marinas in the area.

POINTS OF INTEREST
1 Lewes Historical Society
2 Cape May Lewes Ferry
3 Zwaanendael Museum

DINING
4 Striper Bites
5 The Buttery
6 Irish Eyes Pub & Restaurant

L LIBRARY
PO POST OFFICE

House, believed to be the oldest house in the state. Visit www.historiclewes.org for more information.

Another attraction in Lewes is the Cape May-Lewes Ferry that runs often between Cape May, NJ and Lewes, DE. The ride is an exciting way to see the Delaware Bay and perhaps some of the bird life for which it is famous. It is also an opportunity to visit Cape May. The ferry terminus is located at 43 Cape Henlopen Drive; call 302-644-6033 for schedules.

Bike riding and fishing boat charters are also popular attractions in Lewes. Cape Henlopen State Park is approximately one mile from town and easily accessed by bike, car or an energetic walk. The park features ocean beaches, picnic areas, showers, a nature center, hiking and bike trails.

Tours in Lewes include the Nassau Valley Vineyards, Delaware's only winery with wine tasting and wine-making (302-645-9463). If you prefer golf, visit the Heritage Inn and Golf Club (302-644-0600).

Shopping: The Historic District in Lewes features charming shops, restaurants, bed and breakfasts and other accommodations. Additional shops can be found along the canal and throughout Lewes. Don't miss the Historic Lewes Farmers Market, every Saturday from 8:00 a.m. to 12:00 p.m., June 7 through September 13 at the Lewes Historical Society at 110 Shipcarpenter Street, where local produce is abundant.

Dining: Many restaurants to please every taste and budget abound throughout Lewes. Striper Bites, at the end of Savannah Road overlooking the canal, is very hospitable and has served good seafood for some time (107 Savannah Rd., 302-645-4657). Another favorite is the Buttery, offering brunch, lunch and dinner seven days a week (102 Second St., 302-645-7750). You will find Irish Eyes Pub on the waterfront, canal-side (213 Anglers Rd., 302-645-6888). They reserve slips for diners. For more local restaurants, see www.delawarebeachguides.com/dining.

ADDITIONAL RESOURCES

- ADDITIONAL HISTORY: **www.lewes.com** or **www.historiclewes.org**
- LEWES CHAMBER OF COMMERCE: **www.leweschamber.com**
- **NEARBY MEDICAL FACILITIES**
  Beebe Medical Center: 424 Savannah Road, Lewes, DE 19958, 302-645-3300
  www.beebemed.org

Ferryboat Lewes, DE to Cape May, NJ crossing. ©IstockPhoto/nano

Rehoboth Bay, off the Lewes and Rehoboth Canal

The resort town of Rehoboth Beach, a favorite with Washingtonians, is near the end of the Lewes and Rehoboth Canal. At the northeast end of its broad, pretty expanse, Rehoboth Bay has marinas, marine supplies, boat rentals, fishing stations and restaurants.

This area of the Delaware coast is changing with the expansion of Delaware Seashore State Park. The state owns much land north of Indian River Inlet, including Burton Island.

NAVIGATION: Use Chart 12216. Controlling depth through the channel is about 4 feet at mean low water. Rehoboth Bay is dredged periodically, but it shoals at its southern end, and there is a sandbar just before you go into Massey Ditch (a cut that takes you through the marshes to Indian River Bay). There is also another bar at the lower end of Massey Ditch. Many markers in Rehoboth Bay have been relocated; be sure to apply the updates to Chart 12216, which was updated to the 29th edition in June 2012.

Dockage: One area marina, Rehoboth Bay Marina, has a total of 190 slips and 5-foot approach and dockside depths. North on Rehoboth Canal is Henlopen Acres Marina, which may have transient space. Call ahead for availability. The Indian River Marina at Delaware State Park, east of Barton Island, is very friendly and helpful, and offers transient dockage, gas and pump-out service.

GOIN' ASHORE: REHOBOTH BEACH, DE

You don't have to be a beach bum to appreciate the beauty and serenity of miles of sandy beach and the endless blue ocean. If your vessel draws less than 4 feet, you can enter Rehoboth Bay through the Lewes Rehoboth Canal and enjoy the beautiful passage through one of the most picturesque areas on the East Coast. There are several anchorages throughout the Rehoboth and Indian River Bays, one block from the ocean, where beautiful sunsets are frequent, and numerous restaurants and cafes are nearby.

If you draw more than 4 feet, leave your boat in Lewes, and walk or ride over the Rehoboth and Dewey beaches. The walk is about six miles, but it is a local and visitor favorite. And don't forget to take advantage of the shopping at the Tangier Outlet Center.

History: Legend has it that pirates raided the town in 1690 and 1698, after which a law was passed requiring all citizens to own a musket and ammunition for protection from future raids. Captain Kidd supposedly buried a chest of gold in the Cape Henlopen sand dunes during a visit in 1700 on his trip to the West Indies.

In 1873, Rehoboth Beach Camp Meeting Association founded a site for Methodist camp meetings similar to spots on the Jersey Shore like Ocean Grove. The association was disbanded in 1881, and in 1891, the location was incorporated by the Delaware General Assembly and named Henlopen City, shortly after which it was renamed Rehoboth Beach. In the early life of Delaware, the town produced six of the state's governors in the 19th century. Today, Rehoboth

Rehoboth Beach, DE at sunset. ©IstockPhoto/ElisaRose

Beach is a favorite summer resort for Washington legislators and visitors.

Point of Interest: There are so many attractions in Rehoboth Beach that it is impossible to mention them all, and there is no reason, rain or shine, not to find something exciting to do here. In addition to the mile-long boardwalk, lined with shops for food, clothing and more, this is also a popular spot for deep-sea and freshwater fishing, sailing, swimming, biking, kayaking, camping, walking, shopping and dining. Delaware Seashore State Park (302-227-2800) has a popular campground and Indian River Marina (302-227-3071), part of the park, is located just next to the inlet.

Great family activities abound in Rehoboth Beach, including nature cruises, dolphin and whale watching; ferry rides on the Cape May-Lewes Ferry; and shuttle tours on the Jolly Trolley of Rehoboth Beach. There are more than 100 antique stores throughout Sussex County. Various maps and brochures can be picked up at the Rehoboth Beach-Dewey Beach Chamber of Commerce Visitors Center, located at 501 Rehoboth Ave. (800-441-1329), in downtown Rehoboth Beach. If you prefer to golf rather than antiquing, the Heritage Inn and Golf Club is nearby (302-644-0600), as is Old Landing Golf Course (302-227-3131).

The Rehoboth Art League is located at 12 Dodds Lane (302-227-8408) in picturesque Henlopen Acres. The facility hosts year round exhibitions, lecture series, concerts and workshops for adults and children in many diverse fields. The Rehoboth Beach Historical Society also has a Walking Tour that begins with the Anna Hazzard Museum located at 17 Christian St. in Rehoboth Beach. (Call 302-227-7310 for more information.) There are numerous museums throughout town as well.

Special Events: The Rehoboth Farmers Market at Grove Park is open for business every Tuesday from 3:00 p.m. to 6:30 p.m., June through October. Concerts and other musical events are held during the summer season at the Bandstand on Rehoboth Avenue. Band concerts begin at 8:00 p.m. (Call 302-644-2288 for a schedule or visit www.rehobothbandstand.com.)

Delaware Open Bluefish Tournament, Indian River Inlet happens in May; the Rehoboth Summer Children's Theatre is June through August; July 4 fireworks are on the beachfront that day; Cottage Tour is during the second week in July; the Outdoor Art Show is the second and third weekends in August; the Coastal Music and Arts Festival is in September; the Rehoboth Beach Jazz Festival, is in October; and the Seawitch Halloween and Fiddlers Festival is in October. The Qajaq USA (kayak USA) annual retreat on Rehoboth and Indian River bays takes place during the first week in October.

Shopping: Delaware's lack of sales tax is an incentive to shop. Visit the Tanger Outlets in Rehoboth (www.tangeroutlet.com/rehoboth), and enjoy the Tanger Trolley (302-226-9223), which provides transportation between the three outlet shopping centers. There is also great shopping to be found in the many upscale boutiques along the boardwalk and Rehoboth Avenue.

Dining: For patio dining on the beach, it is hard to beat Victoria's (2 Olive Ave., 302-227-0615), which offers a menu to please every taste. Obies by the Sea has kid-friendly oceanfront seafood dining (1 Olive Ave., 302-227-6261), and Back

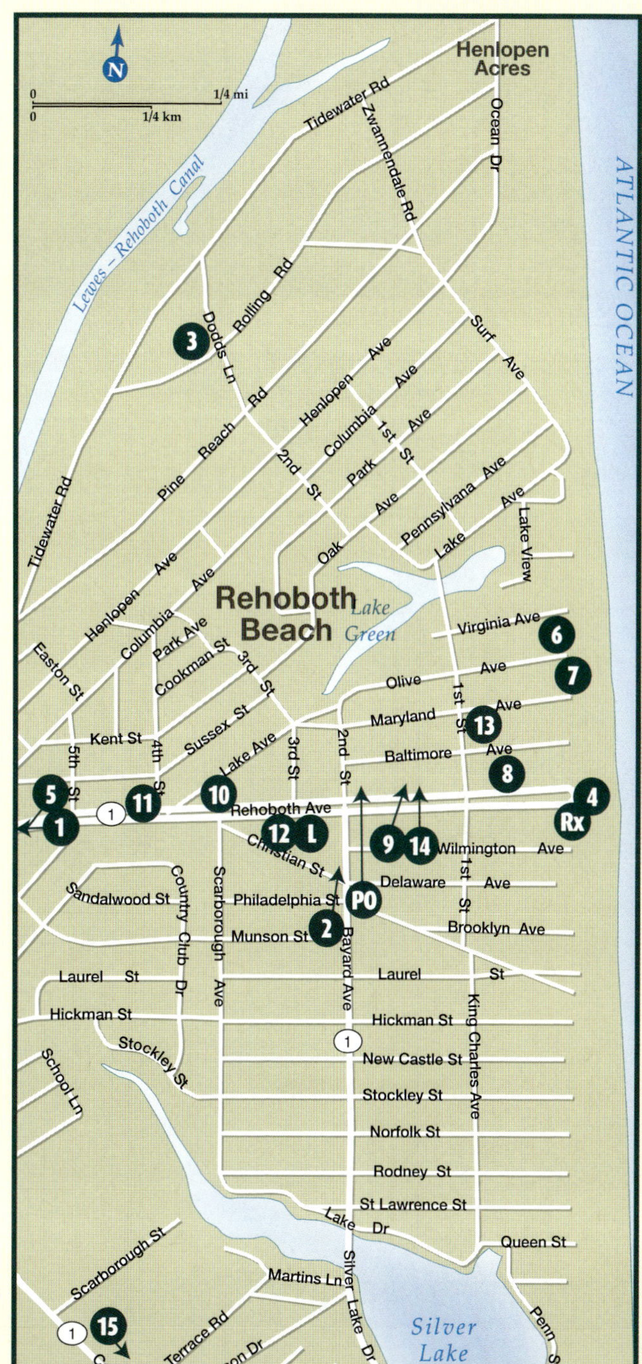

Reference the marina listing tables to see all the marinas in the area.

POINTS OF INTEREST

1 Chamber of Commerce Visitors Center
2 Anna Hazzard Museum
3 Rehoboth Art League
4 Bandstand

SHOPPING

5 Tanger Outlets

DINING

6 Victoria's
7 Obie's by the Sea
8 Back Porch Cafe
9 Blue Moon
10 Catchers Restaurant
11 Dogfish Head Brewings & Eats
12 Cloud 9
13 Jake's Seafood
14 Planet X
15 Rusty Rudder

L LIBRARY

Rx PHARMACY

PO POST OFFICE

Rehoboth Beach, DE

REHOBOTH BEACH		Largest Vessel Accommodated	VHF Channel Monitored	Transient Berths / Total Berths	Approach / Dockside Depth (reported)	Floating Docks	Gas / Diesel	Groceries, Ice, Marine Supplies, Snacks	Repairs: Hull, Engine, Propeller	Lift (tonnage), Crane, Rail	Min/Max Amps	Laundry, Pool, Showers, Courtesy Car	Pump-Out Station	Nearby: Grocery Store, Motel, Restaurant
		Dockage					Supplies		Services					
1. Henlopen Acres Marina	302-227-9950	35	-	/63	4/4	-	-	-	-	-	30/30	LS	P	GMR
2. Rehoboth Bay Marina 🖳	302-226-2012	45	16	25/190	5/5	-	G	IMS	-	-	30/30	LS	P	GMR

Corresponding chart(s) not to be used for navigation. 🖳 Internet Access WiFi Wireless Internet Access Waterway Guide Cruising Club Partner

See www.WaterwayGuide.com for current rates, fuel prices, web site addresses, and other up-to-the-minute information.

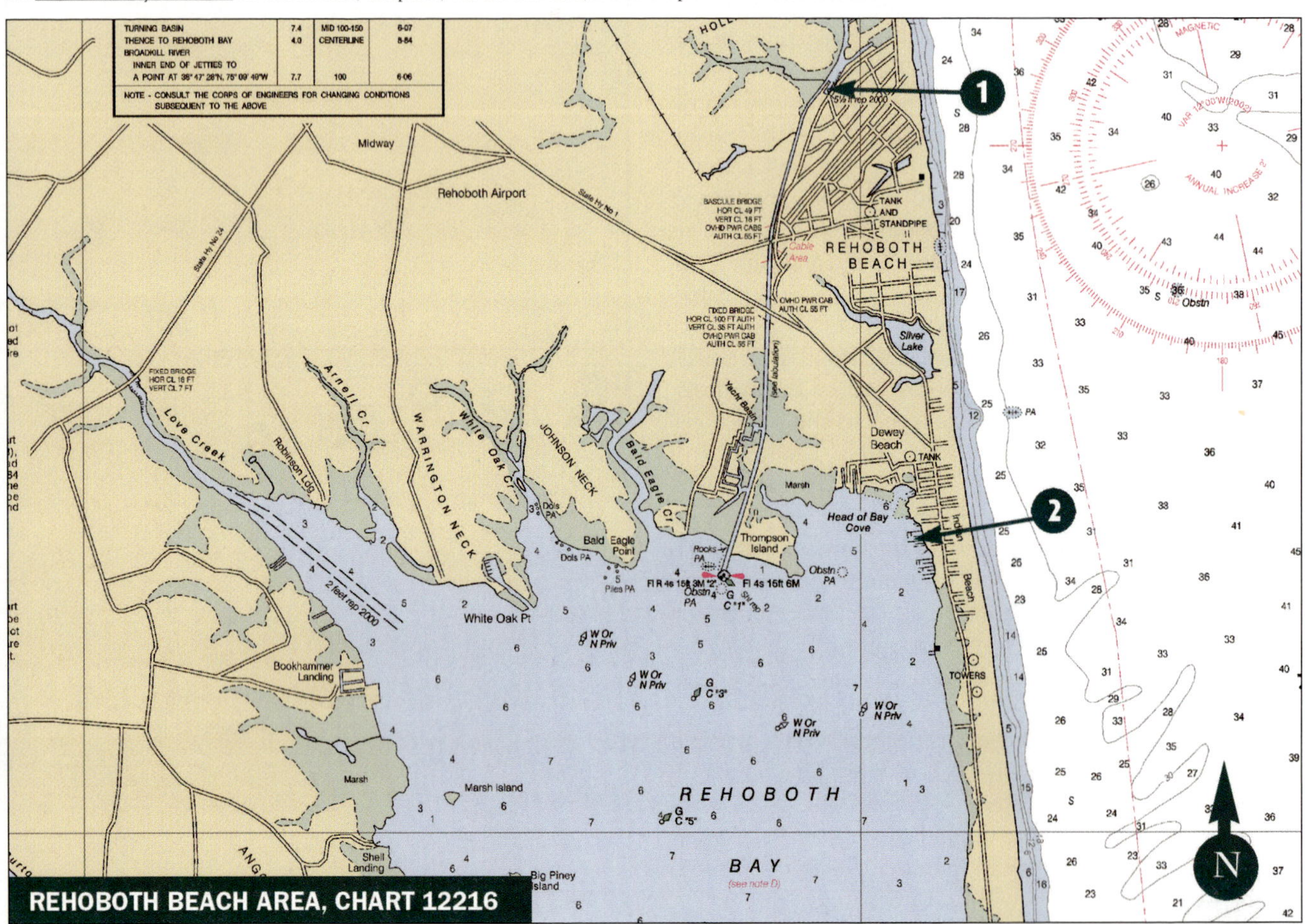

REHOBOTH BEACH AREA, CHART 12216

Porch Café has a more innovative menu (59 Rehoboth Ave., 302-227-3674). Blue Moon (35 Baltimore Ave., 302-227-6515), also has upscale dining, as well as nightly entertainment in a relaxed atmosphere. Catchers Restaurant (249 Rehoboth Ave., 302-227-1818) has seafood, and Dogfish Head Brewings & Eats at 320 Rehoboth Ave. (302-226-2739) is a great place for lunch or dinner. (It gets crowded later.) Try Cloud 9 (234 Rehoboth Ave., 302-226-1999) for more elegant dining. For a more family-friendly atmosphere, try Jake's seafood, located at 29 Baltimore Ave. (302-227-6237); be sure to ask about the award-winning crab cakes.For a change of pace, Planet X, features free range, local and organic ingredients at their funky and eclectic location at 35 Wilmington Ave. (302-226-1928). The Rusty Rudder has slip space for diners (302-227-3888).

ADDITIONAL RESOURCES

- REHOBOTH BEACH, DE: **www.rehoboth.com** or **www.beach-fun.com**
- DELAWAREBEACHGUIDES: **www.delawarebeachguides.com**
- REHOBOTH BEACH MAIN STREET: **www.rehomain.com**
- GREATER DELMAR CHAMBER OF COMMERCE: **www.delmar-chamberofcommerce.com**

NEARBY MEDICAL FACILITIES
Beebe Medical Center: 424 Savannah Road, Lewes, DE 19958, 302-645-3300, **www.beebemed.org**

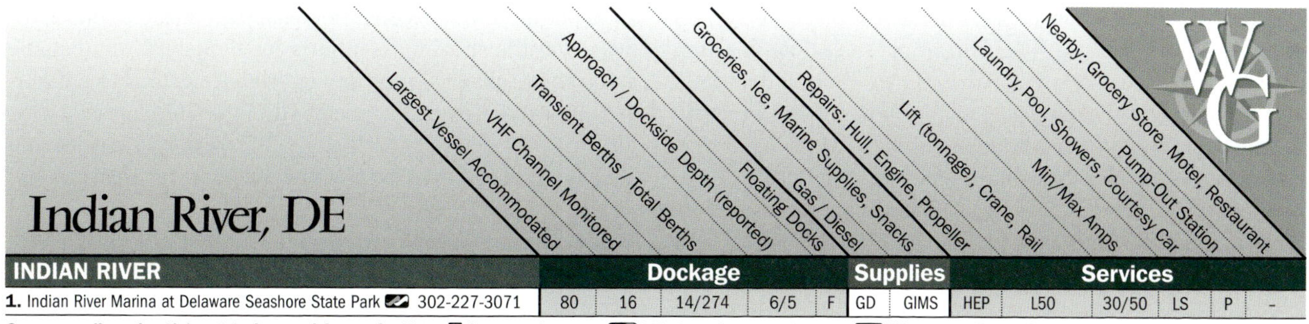

Indian River, DE

INDIAN RIVER	Largest Vessel Accommodated	VHF Channel Monitored	Transient Berths / Total Berths	Approach / Dockside Depth (reported)	Floating Docks	Gas / Diesel	Groceries, Ice, Marine Supplies, Snacks	Repairs: Hull, Engine, Propeller	Lift (tonnage), Crane, Rail	Min/Max Amps	Laundry, Pool, Showers, Courtesy Car	Pump-Out Station	Nearby: Grocery Store, Motel, Restaurant
	Dockage					Supplies		Services					
1. Indian River Marina at Delaware Seashore State Park 302-227-3071	80	16	14/274	6/5	F	GD	GIMS	HEP	L50	30/50	LS	P	-

Corresponding chart(s) not to be used for navigation. Internet Access · Wireless Internet Access · Waterway Guide Cruising Club Partner

See www.WaterwayGuide.com for current rates, fuel prices, web site addresses, and other up-to-the-minute information.

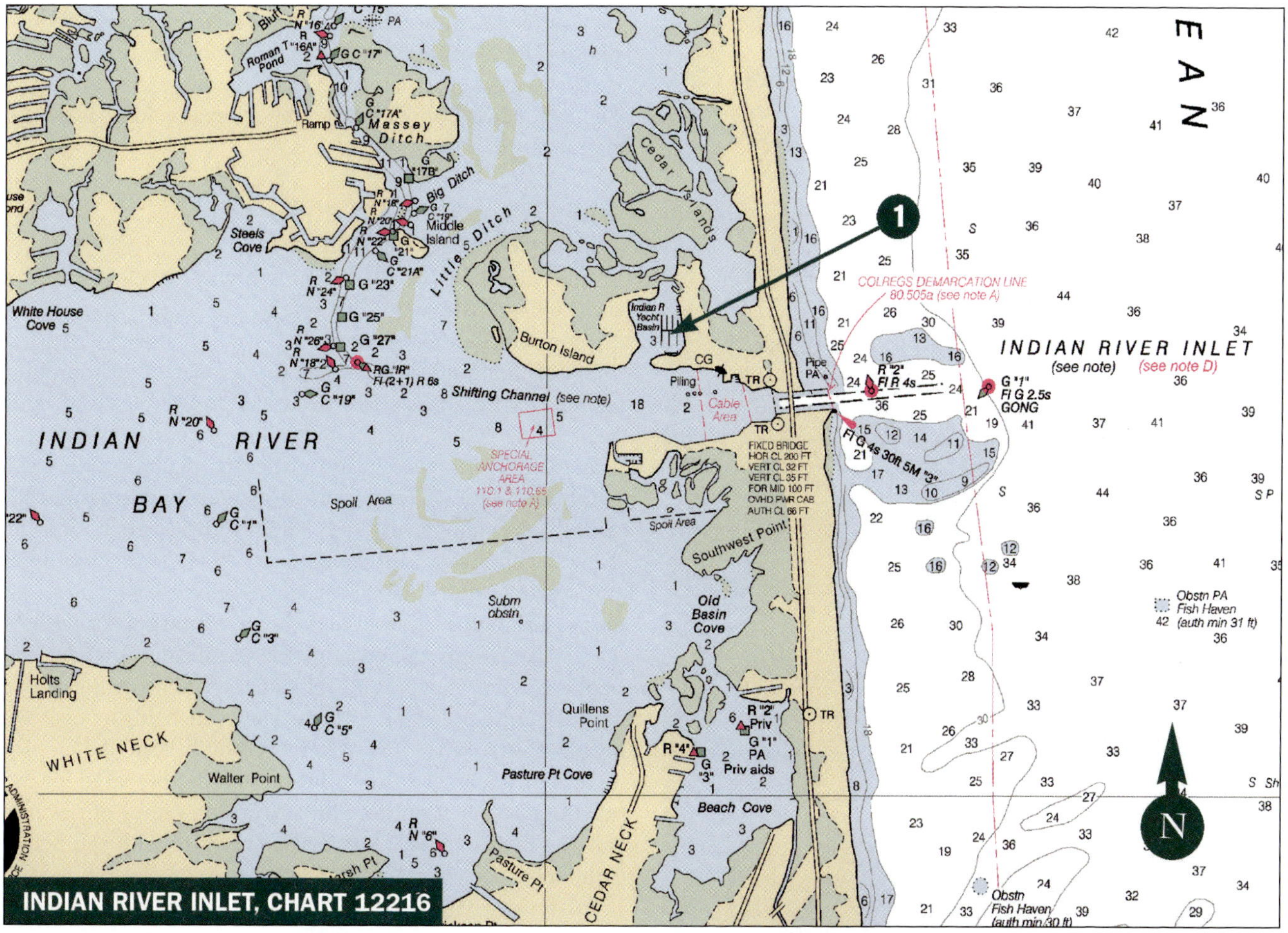

INDIAN RIVER INLET, CHART 12216

Indian River Inlet, White Creek and Assawoman Canal

Indian River Inlet is a popular passage for charter and head boats on their way to prolific ocean fishing grounds. Dockage, fuel, repairs and supplies for cruisers and fishermen are near the inlet and on White Creek, south of the inlet, off of Indian River Bay. Indian River Inlet is often carpeted with all sorts of craft with fishermen aboard vying for a chance at a trophy striped bass, flounder or bluefish. Indian River Marina at Delaware Seashore State Park is located here with fuel and some supplies.

NAVIGATION: Use Chart 12216. Strong currents along Indian River Inlet and the waters inside pull buoys under occasionally, but the pilings shown on even the most current version of Chart 12216 in front of the Coast Guard station are gone now. A new bridge (with 45-ft. vertical clearance) adjacent to the old inlet span (35-ft. clearance) is nearing completion, so keep an eye out for construction traffic.

Assawoman Canal

Assawoman Canal from White Creek south to Little Assawoman Bay is open only to skiffs because of low fixed bridges (10-foot vertical clearances) and shallow, 1- to 3-foot depths. To go south to Ocean City, you must go outside for a 17-nautical-mile run to Ocean City Inlet.

Sinepuxent and Chincoteague Bays, south of Ocean City

Sinepuxent Bay leads from Ocean City to Chincoteague Inlet. Below Ocean City, civilization begins to disappear.

NAVIGATION: Use Chart 12211. Make sure you are using the most recent (February 2011) chart or consider downloading the latest corrected one from the NOAA Web site (http://chartmaker.ncd.noaa.gov/) if you plan on making the trip through this area. A fixed bridge (35-foot vertical clearance) crosses the route south down Sinepuxent Bay, which leads through Chincoteague Bay to Chincoteague Inlet. These bays, one narrow and one wide, separate Assateague Island, famous for its resident wild ponies, from the mainland. Both have dredged, marked channels, which vary from 4 to 6 feet in depth, but both become very shallow outside of the channels, and the shoaling continues indefinitely. Note that the buoy colors change sides from red-right-returning to red-left-leaving as you exit Sinepuxent Bay into Chincoteague Bay. Be sure to leave flashing green "39" to port upon leaving Sinepuxent Bay's dredged channel. Keep the next daybeacon, green "29," southeast of Robins Marsh Island, to starboard when heading south toward Chincoteague. Be careful not to confuse the white and orange nun buoys ("A," "B," "C," "D," "E," "F," F1" and "G") marking the Maryland-Virginia border with the beacons marking the channel.

Just after sunrise, a wild pony grazes in the marsh within the Assateague Island National Seashore. ©IstockPhoto/HKPNC

Tides run an average of two hours behind those for the Atlantic coast. Although the average tidal fluctuation is only about a foot, winds blowing from the northeast or southwest can raise or lower water levels, exposing sandy shoals. Shallow depths and crab-pot buoys make for hazardous night cruising conditions.

Chincoteague Inlet and Chincoteague Island, VA

Unlike Ocean City, which has a highly developed resort atmosphere, Chincoteague retains the flavor of a rustic fishing village. Generations of watermen have tended the world-famous oyster beds in the waters surrounding Chincoteague Island. The beds are privately owned, and trespassing is forbidden. The bivalves harvested from these waters are world-renowned for their particularly sweet, yet salty taste. Trucks leave Chincoteague daily during the "R" months (September through April) with oysters bound for New York, Europe and Japan.

Chincoteague is famed for its wild ponies, which can be seen running on the beaches. Miles of unspoiled beaches and nature trails, along with the Assateague Lighthouse, make up the Chicoteague National Wildlife Refuge. The annual Pony Swim & Auction has been held for over 80 years. Every July, "salt water cowboys" herd the ponies across the channel at low tide and they are prepared for the auction. The auction not only provides a source of revenue for the fire company, but it also serves to trim the herd's numbers. To retain the permit to graze on the refuge, the herd must not exceed 150 horses. Visit www.assateague island.com or call 757-336-3696 for more information.

NAVIGATION: Use Chart 12211. The northerly approach into Chincoteague from Chincoteague Bay follows a well-marked dogleg channel. The depths outside the channel are quite shoal, so keep alert and follow the markers. Be aware that at low tide, a 3.5-foot draft vessel might touch bottom between red daybeacons "6" and "4" just before entering Chincoteague, even though the chart shows 5-foot depths in the channel. The town is connected to the mainland by a swing bridge (15-foot closed vertical clearance) that can sometimes be difficult to contact by radio. The bridge tender maintains a watch on VHF Channel 13. You will see quite a few big fishing boats north of the bridge in the commercial harbor.

The Corps of Engineers calls Chincoteague Inlet a "very dynamic" area. The Corps tries to maintain a 12-foot controlling depth; however, it is best to play it safe here. Enter with caution, stick to the centerline, and keep an eye on the depth sounder. The Chincoteague Coast Guard Station can provide the latest conditions.

Dockage: The town has completed an improved commercial dock and a new harbor of refuge, which has depths of 10 feet. Pay the posted fee across the street at the fire station/town hall or at the police station. Beyond the town dock is a seafood restaurant, The Chincoteague Inn (757-336-6415), with good food, but limited dock space.

Anchorage: The best Chincoteague anchorage is in Black Narrows, across from the Coast Guard station, just south of the town swing bridge. Charted depths vary from 8 to 20 feet. Any dredging of the main channel is apt to change the bottom contour at the entrance to Black Narrows. Local boats swing wide around the marshy island; deeper-draft vessels should carefully sound their way in. Check the chart and pick your spot. A very strong current runs through here.

VIRGINIA INSIDE PASSAGE

The Virginia Inside Passage (locals call it "the Waterway on the coast of Virginia") winds through marshland southward from Chincoteague for 68 nautical miles to Cape Charles. Periodic dredging is done on this section in an attempt to keep channel depths at 4 feet. Extensive shoaling, however, has occurred near Chincoteague Point and also by green cans "55," "55A" and "57" farther south. You will want to do your homework before committing to transiting the area.

The controlling vertical clearance along the Virginia Inside Passage is 40 feet, set by fixed bridges at Wallops Island, near the beginning of the passage, and the Chesapeake Bay Bridge-Tunnel at the end. Call the Norfolk office of the Corps of Engineers (COE) at 757-201-7500 to check on conditions.

NAVIGATION: Use Charts 12210 and 12221. Many of the markers around the Chincoteague Inlet area and farther down the coast have been changed in recent years. Be sure to update a current chart with the latest *Local Notice to Mariners* (from the NOAA Web site) before setting out south from Chincoteague. The northern end of the Virginia Inside Passage begins at white daybeacon "AA" on Hammond Point at the western end of Chincoteague Point. As you go south, leave white daybeacon "AA" to port. Be sure to honor flashing red "2" and white daybeacon "A" as you head southeast past Chincoteague Point, and then swing wide to go back west at white daybeacon "B" toward flashing green "3."

Just below Chincoteague is the Mid-Atlantic Regional Spaceport (MARS) located at NASA's Wallops Flight Facility, where NASA has its oldest missile station. If boats are lined up waiting in the channel, a missile launch is imminent. (The launch schedule is available at marsspaceport.com.) During the summer, you can tour the station. Call 757-824-1344 or visit www.nasa.gov/wallops for information. Science on a Sphere Theater at the Visitors Center (757-824-2298) features a 6-foot globe with visual effects signifying scientific events. (There is no public dock on Wallops Island, so you must tie up in nearby Chincoteague.) Government agencies occasionally engage in activities that may be hazardous to mariners. The Coast Guard broadcasts information about these activities on VHF Channel 22A. Coast Guard Sector Eastern Shore makes advisories on rocket firings at 10:00 p.m. Sundays and 7:00 a.m. Mondays. Coast Guard Sector Hampton Roads broadcasts advisories of firing exercises and helicopter minesweeping at 10:30 p.m. on Sundays and 7:20 a.m. Mondays.

Island Hole Narrows to Burtons Bay

NAVIGATION: Use Charts 12210 and 12221. This stretch of the Virginia Inside Passage winds through marshland, first through Island Hole Narrows, then past Bogues Bay and south to Kegotank Bay. The Corps of Engineers sometimes dredges the inlet shoaling at Kegotank Bay, but keeping ahead of Mother Nature is a continuous challenge in these thin waters. The channel continues south past Gargathy Inlet and Gargathy Bay through Wire Passage, which leads into Metompkin Bay. In 2010, parts of this channel were charted at 2 feet. It then cuts through marshland on the west side of Burtons Bay, where depths were only 1.5 feet in June 2009, before arriving at Wachapreague.

Wachapreague

Twenty-five nautical miles south of Chincoteague and six nautical miles south of Metompkin Bay, Wachapreague is

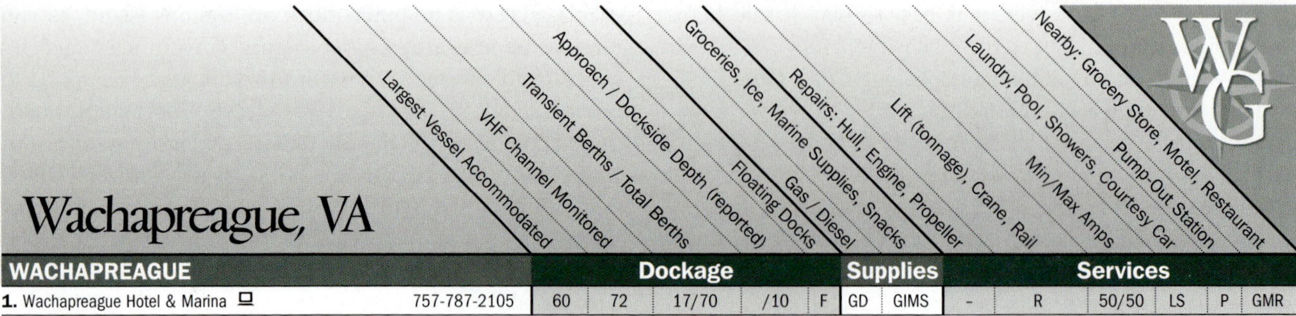

Largest Vessel Accommodated
VHF Channel Monitored
Transient Berths / Total Berths
Approach / Dockside Depth (reported)
Floating Docks
Gas / Diesel
Groceries, Ice, Marine Supplies, Snacks
Repairs: Hull, Engine, Propeller
Lift (tonnage), Crane, Rail
Min/Max Amps
Laundry, Pool, Showers, Courtesy Car
Pump-Out Station
Nearby: Grocery Store, Motel, Restaurant

Wachapreague, VA

WACHAPREAGUE		Dockage					Supplies		Services					
1. Wachapreague Hotel & Marina □	757-787-2105	60	72	17/70	/10	F	GD	GIMS	-	R	50/50	LS	P	GMR

Corresponding chart(s) not to be used for navigation. □ Internet Access WIFI Wireless Internet Access Waterway Guide Cruising Club Partner

See www.WaterwayGuide.com for current rates, fuel prices, web site addresses, and other up-to-the-minute information.

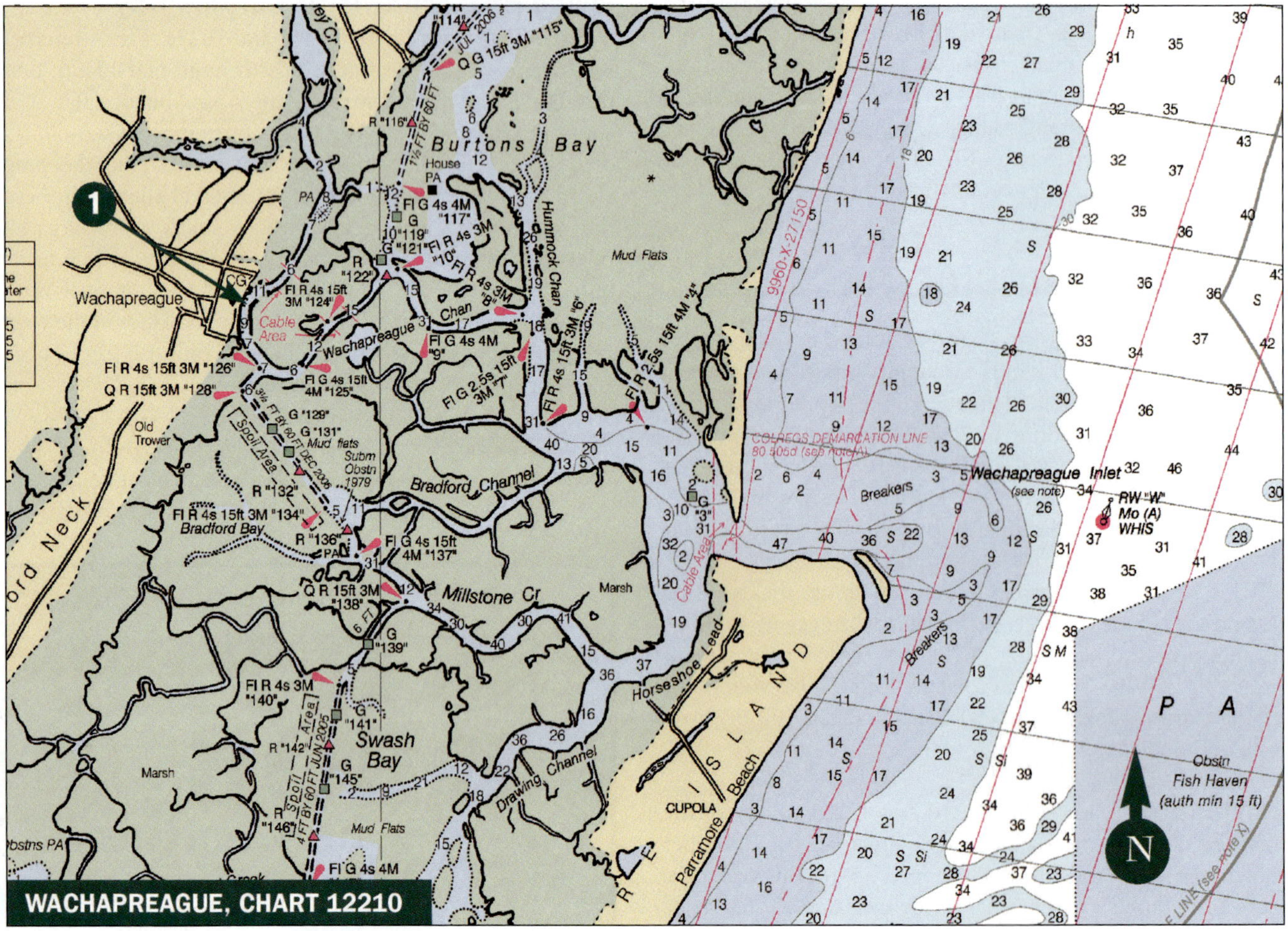

WACHAPREAGUE, CHART 12210

popular with cruisers as well as the sportfishing set. The town has a marina (Wachapreague Hotel and Marina) with both gas and diesel fuel, and groceries are nearby. If you anchor off the channel near Wachapreague, show an anchor light, and be ready for wakes, because the sportfishing fleet leaves early (before dawn) and travels fast (planing). A small boat Coast Guard Station is located in Wachapreague.

Wachapreague to Mockhorn Channel, Along the Virginia Inside Passage

NAVIGATION: Use Charts 12210 and 12221. Caution: This area has experienced severe shoaling in recent years. The Virginia Inside Passage continues on past Wachapreague, winding among more marshlands through a land cut that leads to Bradford Bay. This land cut has a chronic shoaling problem, and the depth legend on the chart was changed to reflect 4-foot depths in 2008. Beyond Bradford Bay, charted depths increase dramatically when you get to Millstone Creek (although shoaling in such narrow channels is a constant problem). The channel turns sharply to starboard shortly after you enter Millstone Creek. It goes through the Swash Bay cut before abruptly doglegging west at Little Sloop Channel and Sloop Channel farther south. Swash Bay Channel (south of flashing green "147") and Sloop Channel may be entirely impassable at publication time. A 2006 chart change reflected 2-foot depths in Swash Bay Channel and in 2008, showed one foot in Sloop Channel. You should inquire locally at Wachapreague about the conditions here before departing. Sloop Channel becomes Cunjer Channel, just before the Virginia Inside Passage jags west through the North Channel, which had shoaled to 1 foot in 2010. At the North Channel's terminus, the passage connects to the Great Machipongo Channel, which is quite deep. Note that the inside passage no longer proceeds through Gull

Looking north over Wachapreague, VA. Photo courtesy of Mike Kucera.

Marsh Channel (near the Great Machipongo Inlet). Instead, it heads westerly through The Deeps, where it enters The Ramshorn, which leads to Ramshorn Channel (maintained by the Corps of Engineers) and the little town of Oyster. The passage then enters Mockhorn Channel, which leads to the head of Magothy Bay.

Quinby, Oyster, Magothy Bay and Cape Charles

NAVIGATION: Use Chart 12221. The 14-nautical-mile passage from Oyster to Beach Channel buoy off Wise Point on the Chesapeake Bay side of Cape Charles was dredged in January 2009, but was charted in April 2010 at 4.5 feet in the channel from Magothy Bay to the Chesapeake Bay. You can anchor out of the way of traffic on the west side of The Thoroughfare, below Mockhorn Channel. Cross Magothy Bay by day if possible, but, in any case, do not head for Cape Charles Light, on the southernmost side of the Smith Islands, as it will lead you to impassable Smith Island Inlet with its accompanying breakers. The route across the tip of the mainland, past Cape Charles itself, is subject to crosscurrents that make it difficult to keep to the narrow channel. It leads under a fixed bridge portion (40-foot vertical clearance) of the Chesapeake Bay Bridge-Tunnel, and then doglegs into Chesapeake Bay to the Wise Point buoy.

Cruising Options

To reach Lynnhaven Inlet, almost due south, go under the 75-foot fixed vertical clearance bridge used by menhaden boats just west of Fishermans Island, and pick your way across the shipping traffic of Chesapeake and Thimble Shoals channels. To get to Little Creek, west of the Chesapeake Bay Bridge-Tunnel, skirt around the breaking seas on Inner Middle Ground Shoal, and then head southwesterly. To get to Willoughby Bay, Norfolk, the Elizabeth River and the start of the Atlantic Intracoastal Waterway to Florida, head more westerly for Fort Wool and the crossing of the Hampton Roads Bridge-Tunnel. Keep an eye out for the many large and fast naval and commercial vessels maneuvering in this area, and give them plenty of room.

For those traveling north along the New Jersey coast and farther into New England, coverage now picks up with our Waterway Guide Northern edition. The trip south on the Intracoastal Waterway to Florida is covered in detail in our Waterway Guide Atlantic ICW edition.

To get your copies of Waterway Guide, visit your local marine store, order online at www.waterwayguide.com or call us at 800-233-3359. ■

Waterway Guide is always open to your observations from the helm. Email your comments on any navigation information in the Guide to: editor@waterwayguide.com.

Extended Cruising

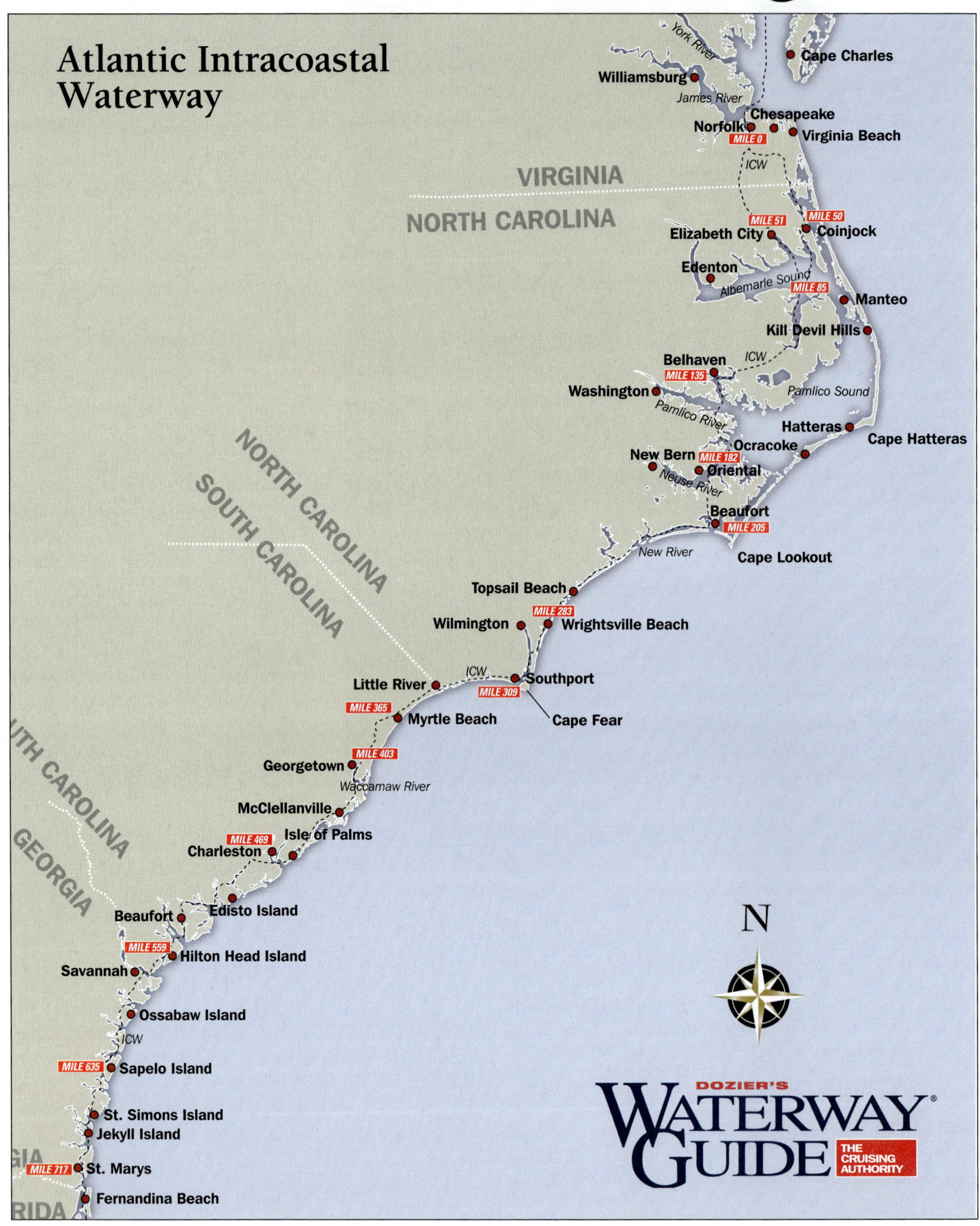

For detailed navigational information, charts, and extensive marina coverage see Waterway Guide, Atlantic ICW Edition. Purchase online: www.waterwayguide.com or call 800-233-3359.

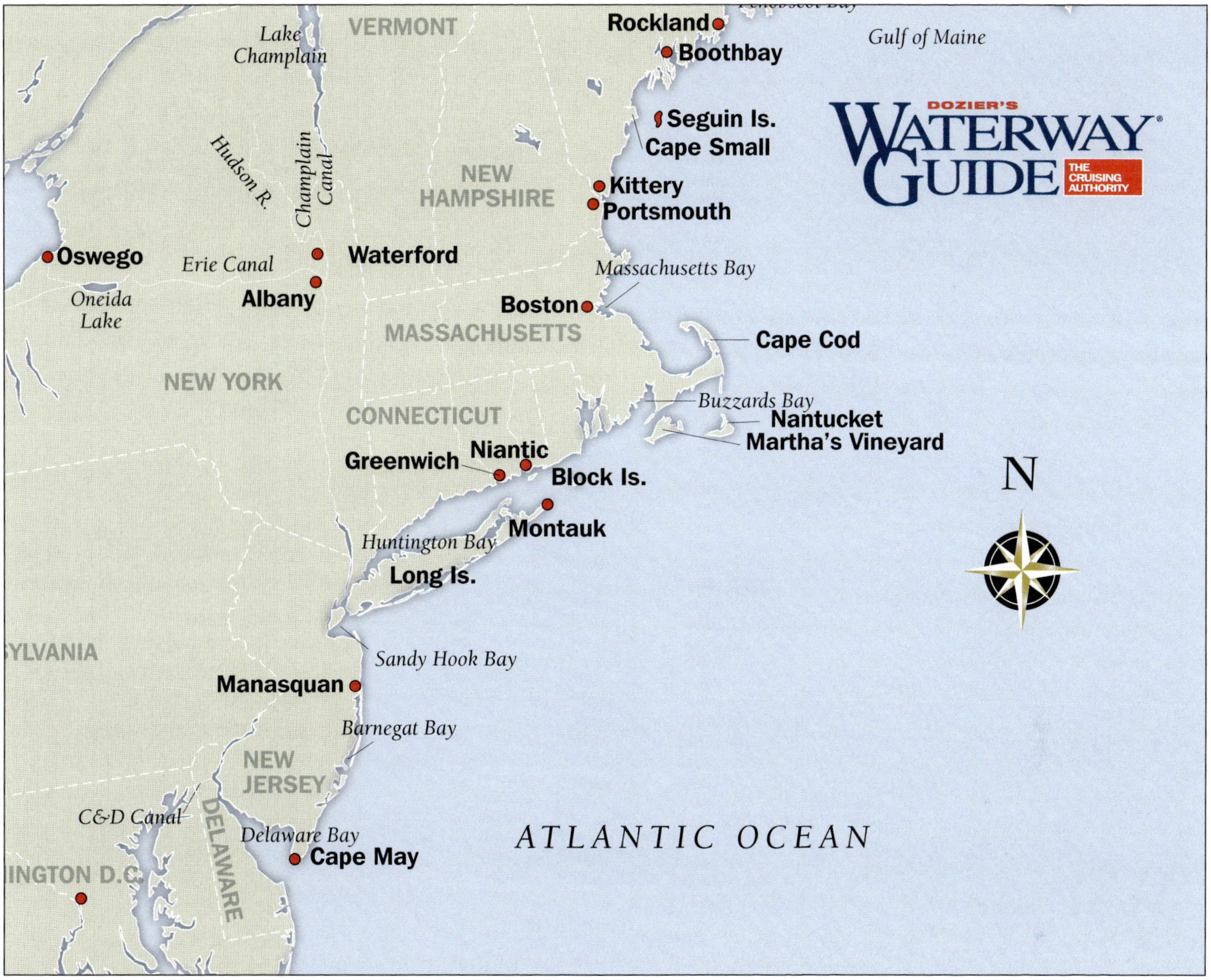

For detailed navigational information, charts, and extensive marina coverage see WATERWAY GUIDE, Northern Edition. Purchase online: www.waterwayguide.com or call 800-233-3359.

Kent Narrows, MD. (Courtesy of Terry Grant)

For detailed navigational information, charts, and extensive marina coverage see WATERWAY GUIDE, Southern Edition. Purchase online: www.waterwayguide.com or call 800-233-3359.

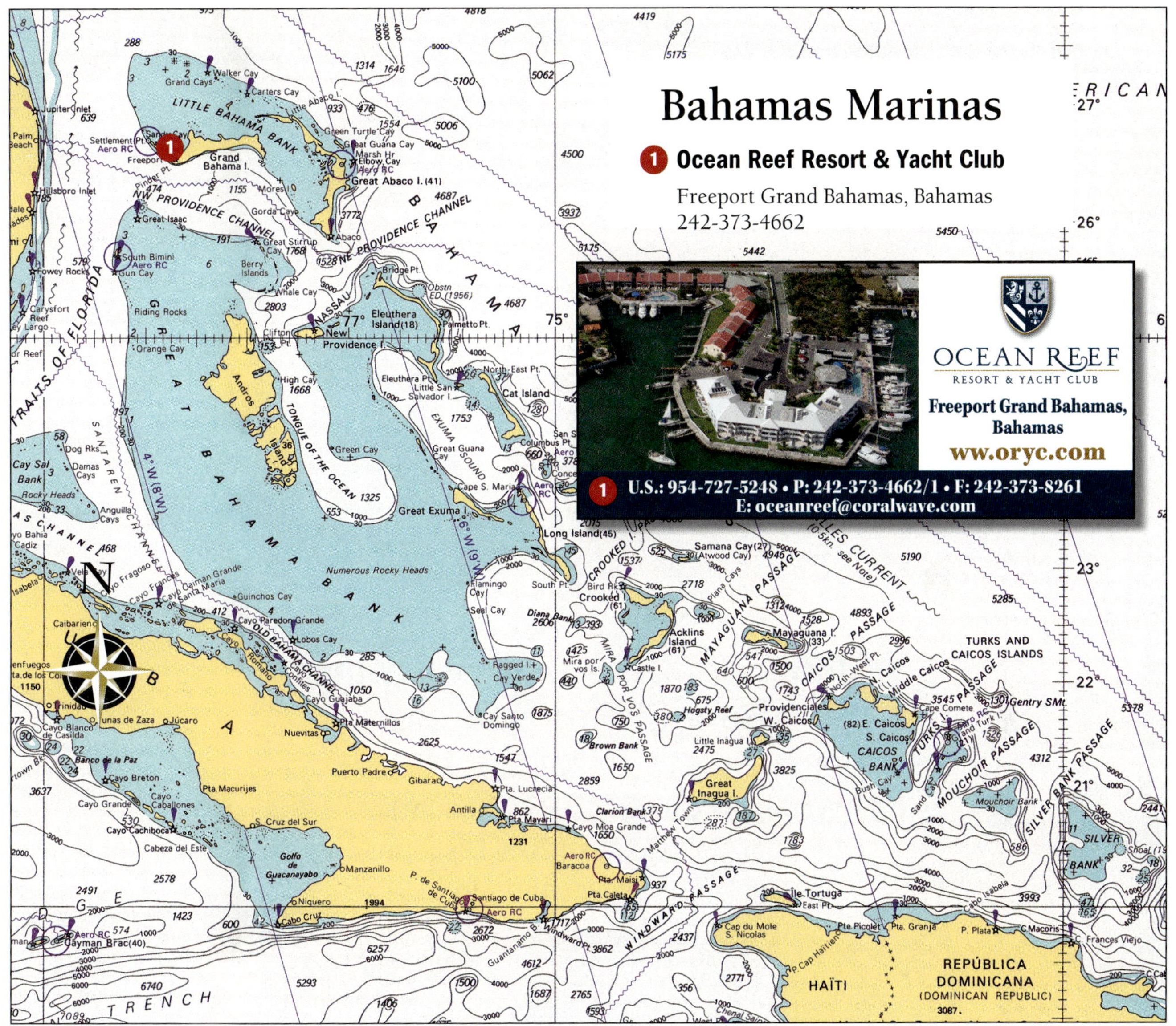

For detailed navigational information, charts, and extensive marina coverage see Waterway Guide, Bahamas Edition. Purchase online: www.waterwayguide.com or call 800-233-3359.

Skipper's Notes

Waterway Guide Cruising Club Partners

Simply show your Cruising Club membership card at these participating businesses to start saving money on fuel, dockage, supplies and more. Also receive discounts on *Waterway Guide* and *Skipper Bob* products online at www.waterwayguide.com.

To sign up for your **FREE** membership call 800-233-3359 or go to www.waterwayguide.com.

List current as of 8/15/12

ALABAMA

The Wharf Marina
251-224-1900
www.thewharfmarina.com

Turner Marine
877-265-5863
www.turnermarine.com

BAHAMAS

Abaco Inn
800-468-8799
www.abacoinn.com

Bimini Big Game Club Resort & Marina
800-867-4764
www.biggameclubbimini.com

Brendals Dive Center
242-365-4411
www.brendal.com

Green Turtle Cay Club
242-365-4271
www.greenturtleclub.com

Leeward Yacht Club & Marina
242-365-4191
www.leewardyachtclub.com

Marina at Emerald Bay
242-336-6102
www.marinaatemeraldbay.com

Master Harbour Marina
242-345-5116
www.turnquestinvestments.com

Port Lucaya Marina
242-373-9090
www.portlucaya.com

Sail and Dive
242-577-0867
www.sailanddive.net

Sunrise Resort and Marina
800-932-4959
www.sunriseresortandmarina.com

CONNECTICUT

Landfall Navigation
203-487-0775
www.landfallnavigation.com

North Cove Yacht Club
860-388-9132
www.northcoveyc.com

Seaview House Marina
203-219-4693
www.seaviewhousemarina.com

Saybrook Point Marina
860-395-3080
www.saybrookpointmarina.com

West Cove Marina
203-933-3000

WASHINGTON, DC

Capital Yacht Club
202-488-8110
www.capitalyachtclub.com

FLORIDA

Adventure Yacht Harbor
386-756-2180
www.adventureyachtharbor.com

All American Covered Boat Storage
941-697-9900
www.aaboatstorage.com

Always for Sail
904-625-7936
www.alwaysforsail.com

Amelia Island Yacht Basin
904-277-4615
www.aiyb.net

Anclote Isles Marina
727-939-0100
www.ancloteisles-marina.com

Austral International Marina
305-325-0177
www.australinternational.net

Belle Harbour Marina
727-943-8489
www.belleharbourmarina.com

Camachee Cove Yacht Harbor
904-829-5676
www.camacheeisland.com

Cape Haze Marina
941-698-1110

Captains License Class
888-937-2458
www.captainslicensclass.com

City of Fort Myers Yacht Basin
239-321-7080
www.cityftmyers.com

Delray Harbor Club Marina
561-276-0376
www.delrayharborclub.com

Dolphin Marina and Cottages
305-797-0878
www.dolphinmarina.net

Everglades National Park Boat Tours

Fernandina Harbor Marina
904-491-2089
www.fhmarina.com

Fishermens Village Yacht Basin
941-575-3000
www.fishville.com

Florida Marina's Clubs
239-489-2969

Fort Pierce City Marina
772-464-1245
www.fortpiercecitymarina.com

Glades Boat Storage, Inc.
863-983-3040
www.gladesboatstorage.com

Gulf Harbour Marina
239-437-0881
www.gulfharbormarina.net

Harbour Isle Marina
772-461-9049
www.harbourisleflorida.com

Hopkins-Carter Marine Supply
305-635-7377
www.hopkins-carter.com

Kennedy Point Yacht Club & Marina
321-383-0280
www.kennedypointyachtclub.com

Laishley Park Municipal Marina
941-575-0142
www.laishleymarina.com

Loblolly Marina
772-546-3136
www.loblollymarinainfo.com

Loggerhead Club and Marina
561-625-9443
www.loggerheadjupiter.com

Marathon Marina & Boat Yard
305-743-6575
www.marathonmarinaandresort.com

Marina at Naples Bay Resort
239-530-5134
www.naplesbayresort.com

Marina Bay Marina Resort
954-791-7600
www.marinabay-fl.com

Mariner Cay Marina
772-287-2900
www.marincaymarina.org

Marker 1 Marina
727-487-3903
www.marker1marina.com

Metropolitan Park Marina
904-630-0839
www.coj.com

Nettles Island Marina
772-229-2811
www.nettlesislandmarina.com

Night Swan Intracostal B&B
386-423-4940
www.nightswan.com

Palafox Pier & Yacht Harbor
850-432-9620
www.marinamgmt.com

Palm Bay Club Marina
305-751-3700
www.palmbaymiami.com

Palm Cove Marina
904-223-4757
www.palmcovemarina.com

Pirates Cove Resort & Marina
772-223-9216
www.piratescoveresort.com

Regatta Pointe Marina
941-729-6021
www.regattapointemarina.com

Rivers Edge Marina
904-827-0520
29riveredgemarina.com

Sailfish Marina of Stuart
772-283-1122
www.sailfishmarinastuart.com

Sandy Beach Catamaran Sailing Charters
954-218-0042
www.catamaransailcharter.com

Seaside Sailing
800-569-7245
www.seasidesailing.com

Sombrero Marina Condo. Assc.
305-743-0000
www.sombreromarina.com

The Jacksonville Landing
904-353-1188
www.jacksonvillelanding.com

Turnberry Isle Marina Yacht Club
305-933-6934
www.turnberryislemarina.com

Twin Dolphin Marina
941-747-8300
www.twindolphinmarina.com

Water Street Hotel and Marina
850-653-8801
www.waterstreethotel.com

Yacht Management
954-993-9368
www.YMISF.com

GEORGIA

Hidden Harbor Yacht Club
912-261-1049
www.hiddenharboryachtclub.com

Hinckley Yacht Services
912-629-2400
www.hinckleyyachts.com

Hyatt Regency Savannah
912-721-4654
www.hyattdockssavannah.com

Isle of Hope Marina
912-354-8187
www.iohmarina.com

Morning Star Marinas at Golden Isles
912-634-1128
www.morningstarmarinas.com

River Supply Inc.
912-354-7777
www.riversupply.com

Sunbury Crab Co. Restaurant & Marina
912-884-8640
www.sunburycrabco.com

Thunderbolt Marina
912-210-0363
www.thunderboltmarine.us

ILLINOIS

31st Street Harbor (A Westrec Marina)
312-742-8515
www.chicagoharbors.info

LOUISIANA

Lake Pontchartrain Harbor Marina
985-626-1517

Retif Oil and Fuel
504-349-9113
www.retif.com

Ship To Shore Co.
337-474-0730
www.shiptoshoreco.com

MASSACHUSETTS

Pickering Wharf Marina
978-740-6990
www.pickeringwharf.com

Seaport Inn and Marina
508-997-1281
www.seaportinnandmarina.com

Vineyard Haven Marina
508-693-0720
www.mvhm.com

MARYLAND

Annapolis Harbor Boatyard
410-268-0092
www.annapolisharbor.net

Back Creek Inn B&B
410-326-2022
www.backcreekinnbnb.com

Campbell's Bachelor Pt. Yacht Co.
410-226-5592
www.campbellsboatyards.com

Campbell's Boatyard @ Jack's Pt.
410-226-5105
www.campbellsboatyards.com

Campbell's Town Creek Boatyard
410-226-0213
www.campbellsboatyards.com

Galloway Creek Marina
410-335-3575
www.dredgeanddock.com

Paradise Marina
301-832-6578
www.Paradise-Marina.com

Point Lookout Marina
301-872-5000
www.pointlookoutmarina.com

Rock Hall Landing Marina
410-639-2224
www.rockhalllanding.com

Sunset Harbor Marina
410-687-7290
www.sunsetharbor.com

MAINE

Edwards Harborside Inn
207-363-2222
www.EdwardsHarborside.com

Landings Restaurant & Marina
207-594-4899

MICHIGAN

Belle Maer Harbor
586-465-4534
www.bellemaer.com

Crosswinds Marine Service
231-894-4549
www.crosswindsmarineservice.com

Detroit Yacht Club
313-824-1200
www.dyc.com

Jacobson Marina Resort, Inc.
231-620-0474 (winter)
www.jacobsonmarinaresort.com

Onekama Marine Inc.
231-889-5000
www.onekamamarine.com

Terry's Marina
586-709-9559
www.terrysmarina.com

Toledo Beach Marina
734-243-3800
www.toledobeachmarina.com

MISSISSIPPI

Isle Casino Biloxi
916-834-4112
www.biloxi.isleofcapricasinos.com

NORTH CAROLINA

Anchors Away Boatyard
910-270-4741
www.anchorsawayboatyard.com

Bennett Brothers Yachts
910-772-9277
www.bbyachts.com

Cape Fear Marina
910-772-9277
www.bbyachts.com

Joyner Marina
910-458-5053
www.JOYNERMARINA.com

Morehead City Yacht Basin
252-726-6862
www.mcyachtbasin.com

Page After Page Bookstore
252-335-7243
www.pageafterpagebook.com

Portside Marina
252-726-7678
www.portsidemarina.com

South Harbour Village Marina
910-799-3111
www.southharboursales.com/marina.html

Whittaker Pointe Marina
252-249-1750
www.whittakerpointe.com

Wilmington Marine Center
910-395-5055
www.wilmingtonmarine.com

NEW JERSEY

Captains License Class
888-937-2458
www.captainslicensclass.com

Green Cove Marina
732-840-9090
www.greencovemarina.com

Hinkley Yacht Services
732-477-6700
www.hinckleyyachts.com

Miss Chris Marina
609-884-3351
www.misschrismarina.com

Seaside Sailing
800-569-7245
www.seasidesailing.com

NEW YORK

Ess-Kay Yards
315-676-7064
www.ess-kayyards.com

Glen Cove Marina
516-759-3129
www.glencovemarina.com

Half Moon Bay Marina
914-271-5400
www.halfmoonbaymarina.com

Harbor's End Marina
315-938-5425
www.harborsendmarina.com

Hudson River Maritime Museum
845-338-0071 x12
www.hrmm.org

Hyde Park Marina
845-473-8283
www.hydeparkmarina.com

Minneford Marina
718-885-2000
www.minnefordmarina.com

Patsy's Bay Marine
845-786-5270
www.patsysbaymarina.com

Riverside Marine Services Inc.
518-943-5311
www.riverviewmarineservices.com

Sunset Harbour Marina
631-289-3800
ILoveMyMarina.com

Triangle Sea Sales
631-477-1773
www.triangleseasales.com

ONTARIO, CANADA

Boblo Island Marina
519-736-1111
www.boblomarina.com

General Wolfe Marina
613-385-2611
www.generalwolfehotel.com

White Sea Resort
705-283-1483
www.whitesearesort.ca

RHODE ISLAND

Apponaug Harbor Marina
401-739-5005
www.apponaugmarina.com

Newport Yachting Center Marina
800-653-3625
www.newportyachtingcenter.com

SOUTH CAROLINA

Bohicket Marina & Market
843-768-1280
www.bohicket.com

Bucksport Marina & RV Resort
843-397-5566
www.bucksportplantation.com

Harborwalk Books
843-546-8212
www.harborwalkbooks.com

Harbourgate Marina
843-249-8888
www.Harbourgatemarina.com

Heritage Plantation Marina
843-237-3650
www.heritageplantation.com

Lady's Island Marina
843-522-0430

Osprey Marina
843-215-5353
www.ospreymarina.com

Pierside Boatworks
843-554-7775
www.piersideboatworks.com

Port Royal Landing Marina, Inc.
843-525-6664
www.portroyallandingmarina.net

UK-Halsey Charleston Sailmakers
843-722-0823
www.ukhalseycharleston.com

TEXAS

Freeport Municipal Marina
979-236-1221
www.myfreeportmarina.com

VIRGINIA

Bay Point Marina
757-362-3600
www.littlecreekmarina.com

Carter's Cove Marina
804-438-5273
www.carterscovemarina.com

Chesapeake Boat Works
804-776-8833
www.chesapeakeboatworks.com

Cobb's Marina
757-588-5401
cobbsmarina.com

Deltaville Yachting Center
804-776-9898
www.dycboat.com

Downtown Hampton Public Piers
757-727-1276
www.downtownhampton.com

Dozier's Port Urbanna Marine Center
804-758-0000
www.doziermarine.com

Dozier's Regatta Point Yachting Center
804-776-6711
www.doziermarine.com

Harborside Yacht Center
414-273-0711
www.harborsideyachtcenter.com

Little Creek Marina
757-971-8411
www.littlecreekmarina.com

Ocean Marine Yacht Center
757-321-7432
www.oceanmarinellc.com

Regent Point Marina
804-758-4457
www.regent-point.com

River's Rest Marina and Resort
804-829-2753
www.riversrest.com

Scott's Creek Marina
757-399-BOAT

Smithfield Station
757-357-7700
www.smithfieldstation.com

Stingray Point Boat Works
804-776-7500
www.stingraypointboatworks.com

The Tides Inn & Marina
804-438-4465
www.tidesinn.com

Top Rack Marina
757-227-3041
www.toprackmarina.com

Urbanna Town Marina at Upton's Point
804-758-5440

Vinings Landing Marine Center
757-587-8000
www.viningslanding.com

Whitehouse Cove Marina
757-508-2602
www.whitehousecovemarina.com

White Point Marina
804-472-2977
www.whitepointmarina.com

Willoughby Harbor Marina
757-583-4150
www.viningsmarine.com

Yankee Point Marina
804-462-7018
www.yankeepointmarina.com

Marina Index

Sponsors are listed in **BOLD**.

A

B

C

D

MARINA INDEX

E

F

G

H

I

J

K

L

M

Skipper's Notes

Subject Index

Most relevant pages are listed in **BOLD**.

D

E

F

SUBJECT INDEX

Q

R

S

T

SUBJECT INDEX

Goin' Ashore Index

Skipper's Notes

Skipper's Notes